"I've always looked at the sea
as a laboratory in the making
of a new world order."

ELISABETH MANN BORGESE
1918–2002

OCEAN YEARBOOK 18

OCEAN YEARBOOK 18

Pacem in Maribus

Sponsored by the International Ocean Institute

Edited by
Aldo Chircop and
Moira McConnell

Assistant Editor: Scott Coffen-Smout

Supported by the Marine and Environmental Law Programme of Dalhousie Law School

The University of Chicago Press

Chicago and London

The University of Chicago Press, Chicago 60637
The University of Chicago Press, Ltd., London

Printed 2004 in the United States of America

International Standard Book Number: 0-226-10449-4
Library of Congress Catalog Card Number: 79:642855
International Standard Serial Number 0191-8575

The paper used in this publication meets the minimum requirements of American National Standard for Information Sciences—Permanence of Paper for Printed Library Materials. ANSI Z39.48-1984.♾

Contents

Living Resources

Non-Living Resources

Maritime Transport

Maritime Security

Regional Developments

Education and Training

Appendices

Editors' Foreword

Volume 18 is a unique issue. It is the first volume produced without the founding editor, the late Elisabeth Mann Borgese. It is most appropriate that the first issue produced without the founding editor not only be a message of continuity, but also be a work dedicated to her memory. Covering three generations, the authors to this volume were invited to contribute on the basis of a connection with Elisabeth. All were influenced by Elisabeth in some way as inspiration, mentor, *provocateur,* or friend. Each author considers an important and contemporary ocean governance or law of the sea issue. The eclectic collection that results surely reflects Elisabeth's breadth of interest and enjoyment of creative mixes and sparks. A consideration of such diverse issues is also appropriate as the 10th anniversary of the coming into force of UNCLOS (November 2004) is on the horizon and with it the prospect of a review conference.

The volume begins with the voice of Elisabeth in a lecture given about 3 years before her death as she reflects on her life and the factors that shaped it. It provides a vibrant and moving counterpoint to the three remarkable tributes that follow. Sunil Shastri, a scholar, whose life was changed in so many ways by his contact with Elisabeth, recounts her many public successes and the international importance of her beloved legacy—the IOI. This is followed by a deeply personal insight into the *persona* of Elisabeth Mann Borgese, a woman whose life was fundamentally shaped by the intellectual and political public concerns that prevailed at the time of her birth and by the two men whose names she carried. Peter Serracino Inglott, in a scholarly exegesis of the literary works of both Thomas Mann and Elisabeth, combined with his personal knowledge and experience of Elisabeth, provides us with a deeper understanding of Elisabeth and her driving passion for the ocean and a different, more just world order. In a third tribute, Agustín Blanco-Bazán reflects on Elisabeth's deep concern for *Pacem in Maribus.*

The balance of this volume is devoted to exploring contemporary ocean issues and challenges from a variety of perspectives. Although they appear diverse in their concerns, a common theme is that all, in one way or another, exemplify the growing perception that there is need for focused attention to a system and institutions for ocean governance, not simply as a default or by-product of international governance, particularly in areas outside national jurisdiction. Alan Beesley speaks of Grotius and the new law of the sea in exploring the challenges that still remain after UNCLOS: The Third United Nations Conference on the Law of the Sea. Moritaka Hayashi, a longtime friend of Elisabeth's and law of the sea expert, writes of gaps in the law of the sea as it relates to foreign commercial vessels in port. Rob Huebert also writes of another, largely unaddressed, issue in UNCLOS—the Arctic waters. Gunnar Kullenberg and Hiroshi Terashima provide two insightful articles on the important role of education in promoting ocean governance.

Salvino Busuttil examines the impact of globalization and the sea, while François Bailet presents us with work that he and Elisabeth conducted together shortly before her death: human security as an element of ocean governance. Abul Kalam Azad outlines the opportunities and constraints for cooperation on regional security matters in South Asia. Adalberto Vallega speaks to modernity, knowledge and the law of the sea. Annick de Marffy examines in detail the very concrete problems of ocean governance and effective management. Christopher Pinto, from a differing perspective, also speaks to issues of governance in his examination of participation and compliance in international law. Klaus Töpfer and Amy Hindman consider questions relating to integration, coordination, and implementation of marine governance as they came to the fore in discussions about sustainable development at the World Summit.

Joeli Veitayaki, Nathan Evans and Robin South examine the emerging governance model found in the Pacific Island Regional Oceans Policy. Francisco Orrego Vicuña considers the problem of high seas fisheries and the need for principles to address these problems. On a related topic, Patricia Birnie, Sidney Holt and John Van Dyke, Emily Gardner and Joseph Morgan combine forces in three articles to give a breadth of vision and commentary on problems relating to the protection of cetaceans, an issue that raises a broad range of socioeconomic and ecological concerns. Awni Behnam speaks of the problem that long preoccupied Elisabeth—the issue of flags of convenience and their impact on workers and the protection of the ocean. With respect to the fundamental goal of international equity, Orio Giarini and Ikechi Mgbeoji, in differing ways, reflect on this point when considering the tremendous wealth of the seabed and common heritage. Aldo Chircop also considers the role of the Authority and the implications of the revenue sharing formula under UNCLOS for coastal States wishing to exploit resources on continental shelves beyond 200 nautical miles. Alexander Yankov writes on the experiences and future challenges that international commitments pose for the protection and sustainable development of the marine environment.

The contributors and contributions to this volume attest to Elisabeth's legacy. She cultivated an extensive personal network of colleagues and friends that she mobilized to speak for the oceans. In turn, this network has had and continues to have a significant multiplier effect, as its members further speak for the oceans and influence the next generation to do so. This fitting tribute provides a sense of how remarkable Elisabeth was and how influential her contributions to the law of the sea and marine affairs were over the last three decades of her life.

The International Ocean Institute

Pacem in Maribus

The International Ocean Institute (IOI) was created to promote education, capacity building, and research as a means to enhance the peaceful and sustainable use and management of ocean and coastal spaces and their resources, as well as the protection and conservation of the marine environment, guided by the principle of the Common Heritage of Mankind. Professor Elisabeth Mann Borgese founded the IOI in 1972 as an independent, non-profit, non-governmental organisation headquartered at the University of Malta.

For 30 years the IOI has stood at the forefront of organisations in addressing these issues with the concern of future generations through an interdisciplinary and comprehensive approach. The IOI has also prepared working papers for the Third United Nations Conference on the Law of the Sea (UNCLOS III: 1973–1982), the Preparatory Commission for the International Seabed Authority, and for the International Tribunal for the Law of the Sea (1982–1994), as well as for various governments. It has provided consultants to UNEP, the World Bank, the United Nations Industrial Development Organisation (UNIDO), and the Asian-African Legal Consultative Committee (AALCC). It contributed to the formulation of recommendations of the World Summits in Rio de Janeiro (1992) and Johannesburg (2002) and of the World Water Forum in Japan (2003) on oceans, coasts and islands, as well as to the review of the developments in ocean affairs through the United Nations open-ended informal consultative process.

The goals of the IOI are to:

- Enhance the ability of developing countries to develop and manage their own resources sustainably for their own benefit, to establish self-reliant development, and help with education and eradication of poverty from community to national levels;
- Enhance abilities for self-reliant development at the community level, taking into account the diversity in developing as well as developed countries, including control and protection of natural resources for future generations; the eradication of poverty in coastal areas; and mitigation of and adaptation to natural hazards;

- Enhance participation of people, in particular women, in development projects that take into account environmental issues;
- Establish sustainable mechanisms able to tackle interrelated social, environmental and economic issues in an integrated fashion.

The approach by which the IOI gradually achieves its goals include:

- Strengthening of institutions through capacity building, sharing and dissemination of information, and generating incentives and contact between local and national authorities;
- Establishing partnerships and networks with the IOI Operational Centres, other NGOs, donors and between authorities and communities;
- Increasing awareness and understanding of the sensitivity and the importance of the coastal zone and the marine environment of sustainable development, through demonstrations, training, provision of educational material and information to local NGOs, schools and authorities;
- Encouraging self-reliant development of sustainable livelihoods by means of aquaculture, farming, value added processing of resources, protection of water resources and application of traditional and new technology;
- Emphasising decentralised decision making to local authorities and communities, and implementation of agreements, regulations, and development projects with the involvement of the private sector; and
- Increasing the abilities at local and national levels to transfer and apply scientific (social and natural sciences) knowledge and information, from generators to users, through hands-on training, case studies, and demonstration sites; and providing incentives through linkages to other sites, and to international agreements and commitments.

The IOI's activities include training projects, information dissemination, conferences, research and publications:

- Training of hundreds of decision-makers and professionals, mainly from developing countries, through short and long duration interdisciplinary courses in ocean and coastal management;
- Ocean governance advocacy within the United Nations system through participation in and contribution to intergovernmental meetings and conferences;
- Development work among coastal communities with the objective of

improving their livelihood while restoring and preserving coastal ecology;
- Information dissemination to international organizations and national institutions through the global IOI Network and the IOI web site;
- Organisation of the annual *Pacem in Maribus* Conference and other seminars and workshops;
- Research on a variety of ocean-related areas such as international and regional agreement and policies on oceans and the coastal zone; on regional and sub-regional co-operation and on scientific and technological approaches to sustainable management of living and nonliving marine resources;
- Education and awareness-creation about ocean resources, marine and coastal environments, and the need to care for them;
- Publication of the *Ocean Yearbook* in collaboration with the Dalhousie University Law School, Canada; IOI's web site (www.ioinst.org). Regional operational centres also publish their own newsletters, research papers and reports; and
- Services include advice, consultancy, and information regarding ocean and coastal environments.

The IOI gained a worldwide respect and reputation through its contribution to the codification and implementation of the Law of the Sea Convention, and to the subsequent development of the concept of sustainable development as it applies to the ocean. Furthermore, through the launching of such projects as the coastal and eco-villages projects, dedicated women and youth programmes, training in ocean governance, risk assessment and others, the IOI has contributed positively to the implementation of ocean governance, with a particular focus on developing nations. The IOI is now developing an international ocean governance education programme that will consist of a network of education, training and research centres with expertise in ocean, coastal and marine-related affairs and governance. The Centres will be joined together in a partnership so as to provide for an interdisciplinary and comprehensive coverage of the subject areas. The overall objective will be to enhance the abilities of developing countries to develop and govern their own marine and coastal resources and environment sustainably.

The IOI scope and presence is truly international with 23 Operational Centres around the globe and with several new Centres and affiliates in the development stage. The IOI network provides a flexible mechanism with a governing and co-ordinating structure that generates synergism and strategic planning of the network of semiautonomous nodes. This cohesive and comprehensive mechanism is capable of co-operating equally well with other intergovernmental systems and the private sector. The current centres and their host institutions are:

> IOI–Canada, Dalhousie University; IOI–China, National Marine Data and Information Service, State Oceanic Administration, China; IOI–Costa Rica, Universidad Nacional, Costa Rica; IOI–India, Indian Institute of Technology, Madras, India; IOI–Japan, Yokohama City University, Japan; IOI–Malta, University of Malta, Malta; IOI–Black Sea, National Institute for Marine Research and Development 'Grigore Antipa', Romania; IOI–Senegal, Centre de Recherches Oceanographiques de Dakar–Thiaroye, Senegal; IOI–Southern Africa, University of Western Cape, South Africa; IOI–Eastern Africa, Kenya Marine and Fisheries Research Institute, Mombasa, Kenya; IOI–Ukraine, Institute of Biology of the Southern Seas, Sevastopol, Ukraine; IOI–Russia, State Institute of Oceanography; IOI–Western Africa, Nigerian Institute for Oceanography and Marine Research, Lagos, Nigeria; IOI–Thailand, Office of Thai Marine Policy and Restoration Committee, Bangkok, Thailand; IOI–Caspian Sea, Astrakhan State Technical University, Astrakhan, Russia; IOI–Volga River Basin, Nizhny Novgorod State University of Architecture and Civil Engineering, Russia; IOI–Indonesia, Centre for Marine Studies, University of Indonesia; IOI–Western South Atlantic, Centre for Marine Studies, Foundation of the Federal University of Panama, Brazil; IOI–Germany, Centre for Tropical Marine Ecology, Germany; IOI–South American Cove, Catholic University of Valparaiso, Chile; IOI–Regional Centre for Australia and the Western Pacific, International Marine Project Activities Centre, Australia; IOI–Baltic, University of Kalmar, Sweden; IOI–Islamic Republic of Iran, Iranian National Centre for Oceanography (INCO), Tehran, Iran; IOI–Slovenia, Marine Biology Station at the Institute of Biology, Piran, Slovenia.

Each Operational Centre is autonomous, identifying its own priorities for research, capacity building and development within the broad mission of the IOI, while benefiting from the support of the overall IOI Network. Regional approaches to research and capacity building enable the Institute to draw upon the different strengths of the Operational Centres to cater to the needs identified within each region. A director, generally supported by a small staff with a large number of experts and volunteers on call, runs each Centre. Fifteen directors are members of the IOI Committee of Directors, which meets annually. The IOI is governed by a Board that takes decisions on policy, programme and budget matters.

Growing steadily and responding to global changes, the IOI Network is now aiming at a multiplier effect to its spectrum of activities. It plans to move from direct training to training-the-trainers; from direct implementation of projects to offering advisory and consultative services; from a network of centres to a network of regional clusters and affiliates.

Marine and Environmental Law Programme Dalhousie Law School

Established in 1883, Dalhousie Law School is the oldest common law school in Canada. As a leading law school, Dalhousie has traditionally played a critical role in the development of national legal education in Canada, in servicing the needs of the Atlantic region and as a focal point for graduate level education globally. The Law School offers the full breadth of undergraduate and graduate level education and is home to the Marine and Environmental Law Programme (MELP), the Indigenous Blacks and Mi'kmaq Programme, the Health Law Institute, the Commonwealth Judicial Institute and the Law and Technology Institute.

Dalhousie Law School is pleased and honored to support and provide a home for the *Ocean Yearbook* through the Marine and Environmental Law Programme. In 1974, MELP was established as a center of excellence for students wishing to pursue research, practice, and teaching in the marine and environmental law fields. The core Programme faculty teach courses and conduct research on business and environmental law, coastal zone management, environmental law, international environmental law, land-use planning, law of marine environmental protection, law of the sea, maritime law and practice, maritime law and policy (carriage of goods by sea), ocean law and policy (international fisheries), and oil and gas law. The Programme has attracted students from numerous countries from all regions. Its principal offerings include a Certification in Marine or Environmental Law for Bachelor of Laws (LL.B.) students and thesis and research opportunities in these fields at the Master of Laws (LL.M.) and Doctorate in the Science of Law (J.S.D.) levels.

MELP is further supported by the Sir James Dunn Law Library, which houses one of the largest collections in marine and environmental law and policy in North America. In 1980, the law librarian initiated the *Marine Affairs Bibliography*. The MELP faculty and students have had a prolific research and publication record in most major periodicals in these fields. Further, faculty are active in legal and policy development projects and networks involving governments and international NGOs in Canada, Europe, in various developing regions and countries, including the South Pacific, Asia, South Asia, Latin America and the Caribbean. The Halifax metropolitan area boasts one of the largest concentrations of expertise in coasts and oceans in the world. The city is home to the Bedford Institute of Oceanography, six universities, various federal and provincial government agencies with coastal and ocean management capabilities, and a strong private sector base in marine science, technology, and consulting. This wealth of expertise has enabled Dalhousie to identify ocean studies as an area of focus in its mission statement. As a result, most faculties and departments have developed unique strengths in coastal and ocean studies, contributing in turn to a rich multi- and interdisciplinary environment. MELP interacts with a wide variety of departments and programs dealing with ocean studies at Dalhousie. In particular, the Marine Affairs Program, the School for Resource and Environmental Studies, the Department of Biology, the Department of Sociology, and the Department of Oceanography have strength in various aspects of ocean studies.

Acknowledgments

The editors are grateful for the contributions by the authors in this special issue of the *Ocean Yearbook* dedicated to the memory of the late Elisabeth Mann Borgese, all of whom were invited. We are grateful for the ongoing administrative and substantive support provided by the Marine and Environmental Law Programme and the Sir James Dunn Law Library at Dalhousie University Law School. The assistance of the International Ocean Institute is also recognized. The Editors wish to particularly acknowledge the continuing key role played by the Assistant Editor, Scott Coffen-Smout. We extend thanks to Jacqui Shaw and Tricia Warrender for their research and editing assistance, and to Susan Rolston for compiling the volume index and for revising the directory of oceans-related organizations. As in past issues, warm thanks also go to members of the Board of Editors for continuing support and to the University of Chicago Press for its editorial and infrastructural support. Special thanks are extended to Teresa Mullen and Rick Bell at the University of Chicago Press.

THE EDITORS

The Years of My Life

Elisabeth Mann Borgese

I cannot thank the organizers enough for the honour they have bestowed on me by inviting me to deliver this Nexus lecture.[1] Rob Riemen has been kind enough to give me quite a bit of information about this Institute, its genesis, and the people who have delivered this lecture before me, and, indeed it is an honour to step into this series, and I feel particularly privileged to see Her Majesty the Queen in this distinguished audience.

At the same time, I am struck by a heavy feeling of responsibility. I have of course recently reread my father's famous lecture of the same title, Meine Zeit, The Years of My Life, and, quite apart from the fact that he was my father, I am terror-struck by the mere idea that anybody could compare my inadequate efforts with that masterpiece of literature, history, and philosophy! Never, never would I even dream of stepping into my father's shoes! His shoe size is by several numbers too big for me!

Well, but let us get on with the theme I have been assigned.

I was born in 1918, and my memory goes back to 1919, when I was one year old. At that time my great-grandmother, Hedwig Dohm, Social Democrat, a writer and fighter for women's freedom, died. I remember when the news came, through a telephone call from Berlin. I was sitting on my father's lap and he was feeding me a raw beaten egg with sugar, as he often did because I was a bit pale and anaemic. I could not talk yet, but understood some of what the big people said. And this is the idea of death I made myself at that time, and it remained for ever in my memory: An old rag doll, moving, like the pendulum of a clock, from one side to the other and back again, and then dropping on the floor.

I found it fascinating, retrospectively, that a one-year-old, incapable of speech, could conceive an image of death. Could we deduce some notion of how animals—speechless as I was—might think about death? These problems, as to how animals think, communicate among themselves and with us, have become important problems of "my time," and important insights have been gained. These may well contribute to a change in our attitudes towards

[1]Editors' Note.—The Nexus Lecture was presented on 12 May 1999 at the Nexus Institute, Tilburg, The Netherlands. The lecture was previously published in Dutch in *Nexus* 24, (1999): 5–37, and is published with the permission of the Nexus Institute.

Ocean Yearbook 18: 1–21

nature and our place in it, which is so urgently needed now, if we want the human race to survive at all.

My next memory goes back to the time I was three years old. I see myself riding on the old little ramshackle wooden rocking horse, a dapple-gray, its white and grayish paint somewhat crumbling—it must have served my older brothers and sisters long before me: There was not much money around, those days, to buy new toys—and it had a short handle-bar through its neck on which the rider could hold herself as it went up and down, up and down. Each time it went up in front, I would sing, "the dollar rises," and as it went down, "the dollar falls."

It was the time of the insane post-World War I inflation in Germany, when my mother would bicycle to the market to do the food shopping for the family. She would stop at her usual vegetable stand, where the spinach that day would cost one hundred thousand Mark a pound. Let me look a bit around, she would say; perhaps she could find a dealer who would sell it for less. After ten minutes she would come back to her stand, but the women behind the table informed her that prices had just gone up, and her spinach now cost one million Mark!

"The dollar falls," "the dollar rises" was something we heard every day when my parents read the papers or phoned the bank! And this is how I envisaged it.

My older siblings, Erika and Klaus, gave another twist to my little song. This is what they sang, in the Berlin of the "roaring twenties":

> The dollar rises
> Let us fall!
> Why should we be more stable than our currency!

For my father, in fact, this inflation signified the end of bourgeois society and morality. And today, trying to think ahead, I could imagine that the historians of economics of the next century or the century after that might consider that episode of financial insanity as the beginning of the disintegration of the glorious Western economic system that appears to be in course today, in "my time" and will force us to rather radical reconceptualizations, transcending both the centrally planned and the free-market systems, hostile brothers, both born in Europe at the time of the first industrial revolution, and no longer adequate today.

Another major issue of "my time" impressed itself on me when I was five years old. That ties up, again, with the death of my great-grandmother, but nothing did I know, when I was one year old, about the problems of being a woman in our Western culture, from the days of Lysistrata to those of my great-grandmother. That dawned on me about four years later, when my parents were entertaining some guests for tea, M. Romain Rolland and Madame. The Kinderfraeulein was instructed to dress us, my four-year-old brother and myself, in our "Russenkittel"—both identical—and we were introduced to the illustrious guests. "Which one is the boy, and which one is the girl," my mother asked teasingly. Madame did not hesitate with her answer. "That one is the boy," she said, pointing to my little brother, "he looks more serious." That stung my five-year-old mind. From then on, not only did I put on a fierce and funereal mien any time I was introduced to somebody or saw a camera lurking somewhere; I devoted about 30 years of my life to study all aspects of the problem. My concerns were heightened by statements such as my mother's: "Don't try to be a musician: women don't make good musicians"; or my father's: "Women are good second class."

I must confess it: Both my parents were unabashed male chauvinists, but I say this without any rancour, I say it with filial affection, and even with some amusement. Actually I think they were amused by it themselves. Deep down they knew better.

I finally rid myself of the problem—one of the serious problems of "My Time"—with the publication, in 1964, of a book I called *The Ascent of Woman,* which was a pun on *The Descent of Man.* In that book I developed the theory that the problem was overwhelmingly cultural, not natural: that in more community-oriented societies women fared better than in individualistic societies; that, in fact there was some sort of affinity between what was "feminine" and what was "collective" and that this affinity could be traced not only in sociology, but in the arts, in mythology and religions, as well as in linguistics, where, it appears, the plural form and the feminine form evolved together. It can be traced even in the "cultures of nature," i.e., in the animal kingdom, where collectivistic societies, such as the social insects, are ruled by females. Gender determination, among many so-called "lower animals," is not genetically fixed but socially determined, and this includes the possibility of gender change if and when changes in the social environment demand it! The woman problem really is not a woman problem but a social problem and we cannot solve it until we change the social environment, starting with the structure of the household. If we get a better balance between the collective and the common good and the individual and its interests, or, better, if we understand that there is no conflict between the two: they are one and the same: the two sides of the same coin—and this, I think is one of the fundamental problems of "my time" then we will also get a better balance between women and men.

The role of women in our societies and the role of women in development certainly is one of the major and unresolved problems of our time, and we have to grapple with it in one way or another before we really can do much else.

I was twelve years old when the founder of Paneuropa, Richard Count Coudenhove-Kalergi, came for dinner with his wife and his Hungarian sheepdog named Baer. The Count was half of Austrian-aristocratic, half of Japanese origin. I had never seen a Japanese before and was immensely impressed by what I was told were his fine oriental features which somewhat charmingly contrasted with his Austrian accent. He was elegant, soft-spoken, but sure of himself and most convincing. As a matter of fact, I don't know what impressed me more: the Count or his shaggy dog, or the fact that he brought his dog for dinner. In any case, before taking leave, he gave me a Paneuropa pin; and encouraged me to join the Paneuropean Youth group in Munich—which I did, and I have been a European Federalist ever since. The problems we started to discuss at that time are still actual.

At school we learned that European Federalism was starry-eyed utopianism and that the "hereditary enemies," Germany and France could never live under the same political roof. The lesson I drew from that, retrospectively, was: "the utopians of today are the realists of tomorrow; the realists of today are dead tomorrow."

Alas, another kind of "Paneuropa" took over not long after that: I was not yet fifteen when Hitler came to power and established his supposedly "thousand-year" Reich which, eventually was to engulf most of Europe. With it came exile, in France, in Switzerland, in the United States. The horrors of Nazism and Fascism; the question: How could they ever have happened in civilized countries in the 20th century; the growing feeling that only armed intervention, a world war could bring them down; all this now filled our conversations and determined our lives. It also brought together exiles not only from Germany, but from Italy and Spain and, later from Gaullist France. That broadened the horizon and brought new insights. One of the leading Italian exiles, G.A. Borgese, had written a book, *Goliath, the March of Fascism*, explaining the phenomenon of fascist totalitarianism in the broader context of Roman/Italian culture and history and, in particular, of the absolutism of the Roman Catholic Church. The David who was to bring down the giant was to be international democracy: political and economic democracy. Not only swords were needed, but ploughshares as well, and we had to have a clear vision of the world that was to be after the fall of Fascism and Nazism. A return to the status quo ante would not be the end of Fascism; for if you release an ex-criminal into the same environment which made him a criminal in the first place, he will become a criminal again.

I devoured Borgese's work when I was eighteen years old and decided that was my man. We met in Princeton in 1938, during antifascism's darkest days, when Neville Chamberlain had sacrificed Benesch's Czechoslovakia in the Munich agreement and proclaimed "peace in our time"—an event, which Einstein, our neighbour in Princeton, described as the darkest day in his life. Borgese and I got married in 1939 and began to cooperate in the writing of a collective little book, involving a number of exiles including my father and antifascist Americans such as Lewis Mumford. The book was both a call to arms but, more than that, a manifesto for the world order that should emerge from the ruins of the war. Borgese, who was 36 years older than myself, became not only my husband and the father of my children, but my teacher, whose influence on the development of my thinking matched that of my parents. There were some parallels and convergences between my father's and my husband's intellectual peregrinations: both started from somewhere on the "right," as nationalists and romantics; both ended as socialist humanists or humanist socialists. The peroration, at the end and culmination of my father's lecture, "Meine Zeit," calling for a World Government, is clearly inspired by Borgese.

Was the war a war against fascism or was it a power struggle against Germany and the Germans and, incidentally, against the Italians, or was it both?

The end of the war was ambiguous. The great democracies were both victorious and vanquished. The nuclear destruction of Hiroshima and Nagasaki, crimes against humanity, undoubtedly, marred their ethical credibility. Fear and hatred of Communism distorted their policy. And as they had, before the war, secretly, or even openly, supported Nazism and Fascism as a bulwark against Communism, so did they now continue to support criminal little dictatorships in many places rather than enhancing the forces of democratic socialism, deemed less useful in the fight against Communism.

Was Communism really the danger it was made out to be? Did the Cold War really have any substance? Were there not more common interests between the United States and the Soviet Union than they cared to admit? During the years of exile and war and Cold War, many comparisons were made between Fascism/Nazism on the one hand, and Russian Communism on the other. There were those who equalized them: Evils, both, that had to be eradicated. Prominent among these were the ex-Communists, many of whom had changed a (+) sign into a (−) sign, but the value, the content of their message remained the same. The ex-Communist was as absolutist as the Communist. Many of them, incidentally, were paid by the Central Intelligence Agency of the United States (CIA), whether wittingly, unwittingly, or not wanting to know.

My mentors, my parents and husband clearly differentiated between the two evils. Nazism/Fascism was evil, inhuman, antihumanistic in its theory and goals as well as in its practice. Communism, after all, was humanistic in theory; social and economic justice; the equalization of incomes; the eradication of poverty, the right to free education and health care, the right to work, the protection of the underdog, these were goals we all shared, but the Communist regimes perverted the means: Violence, oppression, executions and contempt for human life, and absolutism were as bad as under Nazism. Such means cannot be conducive to humanistic ends.

Today the goals and ideals of what used to be called socialism are shared even more broadly than ever, in the context of "sustainable development"; but, alas, today, too, there is a discrepancy between ends and means, albeit less stark, less cruel. But over-reliance on the "market" and market-driven globalization, privatization and deregulation are enhancing competition rather than cooperation, individual power struggle rather than commitment to the community, short-term profit rather than long-term durability. The humanistic goal of "sustainable development," based on the eradication of poverty and the conservation of our biosphere, remains unattainable through these means. The gap between the rich and the poor is growing, whether between countries or within countries, and many of the achievements of social democracy and the welfare state during this century are lost. George Soros, the capitalist, went as far as to say that the "market" today constitutes a threat to democracy far greater than "Communism."

Another chasm between ends and means seems to me to lie at the heart of the Kosovo tragedy. Is it possible to protect human rights by destroying human lives? To enhance the rule of international law by blatantly violating it? To pursue humanitarian goals with barbarous and atavistic means?

A great part of the work on the nuclear bomb was done in the Stag Field of the University of Chicago, whose genius President, Robert M. Hutchins, one of the truly great Americans, had been gathering quite a number of exiles from a number of countries, including a number of great physicists like the Italian Enrico Fermi—I remember his enigmatic smile which seemed to come from another world—the Hungarians Leo Szilard and Edward Teller—Szilard was one of those geniuses who entered the revolving door behind you and came out in front of you! Teller did whatever he did with an intensity that was a bit scary in daily life. Then there was the German James Franck, with the endearingly soft eyes that often characterize the eyes of people who are hard of hearing—and others. A profound feeling of guilt gripped Chicago as the mushroom clouds rose over Hiroshima and Nagasaki. The guilt-ridden physicists founded their Bulletin of the Atomic Scientists at the University just about at the same time when Borgese launched the slogan that the University that had contributed so much to splitting the atom, now had the moral responsibility of uniting the world. Encouraged by Hutchins, and in cooperation with a number of faculty members and scholars from other universities, we founded the Committee to Frame a World Constitution at the University and its journal, *Common Cause* (1948–53). It was an immensely stimulating and creative time. The fear of nuclear holocaust was as pervasive as the fear of environmental disaster is today.

Both fears are wholly justified. It is, however, somewhat disconcerting to note how the obsession with a particular form of doomsday changes periodically, about every five-to-ten years.

People simply get used to living with a particular threat, and, without resolving it, and after talking and writing about it until it gets boring, they turn their minds to something new.

The nuclear scientists did a great job, but their perspective was perhaps a bit narrow. Americans, who until 1945 felt invulnerable and secure behind their oceans, now, for the first time, felt that they, too, could be victims of a nuclear attack. That made a difference. Other people, accustomed to the ravages of war throughout history, cared less. Whether they were killed by "conventional" weapons or by nuclear weapons did not make much difference to them.

Driven by guilt and atomic fear, the physicists, in cooperation with some great American statesmen, Bernard Baruch and David Lilienthal, came up with a plan with some great insights which were way ahead of their time. Their proposal, in 1946, for the establishment of an international atomic energy authority, was based on the awareness that it was impossible to prevent the production of atomic weapons if one did not control the peaceful uses of atomic energy; that peaceful and military uses of atomic energy were inextricably linked; and that, to control both, the Authority would have to be the owner and manager of uranium resources anywhere in the world. Uranium could not be "owned" by any State, but was to be, in a way, a "Common Heritage of Mankind."

Jean Monnet, another one of the great geniuses of "my time," based his proposal, the Monnet-Schuman plan for the Coal and Steel Community of 1950, on the same principle: If you want to prevent the military uses of the German coal and steel industries, you had to internationalize their peaceful uses. This, of course, was the beginning of the European Union.

At the same time, a vibrant vigorous World Federalist movement came into being: strongest in the United States where it was led by a young war veteran, Cord Meyer Jr., who had lost his twin brother and one of his eyes in the war. In Europe, the world federalist movement had to compete with the stronger European federalists and the debate, whether world federalism was realistic before European federalism was realized; or whether you could realize European federalism without a global federalist framework, or whether you had to have both at the same time, reached sometimes somewhat Byzantine dimensions. It also was a naive expression of Eurocentrism.

Globally, world federalism was supported by the best minds everywhere, from Einstein and Bertrand Russell to Sartre, the Abbé Pierre and Cames to Gandhi and Nehru, to name only a few.

When I saw Nehru the last time, in April 1964, just weeks before his death, I asked him, "Do you feel that we have made any progress at all, that we are nearer to the establishment of a world government than we were in the fifties, when you were an ardent advocate of world federalism?" "Yes, in a way," he said, with a deeply melancholy smile, "for, come it will eventually: and thus, with every year that passes, we are coming closer. But how much misery and suffering will the world have to go through before it comes!"

The movement covered a wide range of attitudes. There was the rather inchoate fringe of World Citizens, followers of the young Garry Davis who had torn up his American passport on the steps of UNESCO in 1950 and issued World Citizens passports to anybody who wanted one. I remember visiting him in his barracks where he was working with a French Colonel, who had served with the French army I think in Vietnam, and a staff of volunteers, absolutely overwhelmed by the thousands of passport applications that were pouring in every day from all over the world.

Another part of the world government movement was led by a British MP, Henry Usborne, who generated a lot of enthusiasm with his initiative for the calling of a People's World Convention in 1950 to draft and adopt a world constitution and establish the world State. Delegates to this People's Convention were to be elected in every country of the world. Curiously enough, in the whole wide world, it was only in the State of Tennessee, that Henry Usborne met with full success. In 1949, the Government of Tennessee held State elections to elect a Delegate to the Peoples World Convention in 1950. A lawyer, Fyke Farmer, was duly elected. A token People's World Convention had to be organized in haste, to receive him. Nobody paid much attention to it.

There were scholarly contributions to the movement, above all Grenville Clark's and Louis Sohn's monumental work on a federal constitution for the world, *World Peace through World Law.* Its lasting merit, perhaps was the detailed attention devoted to the establishment of a system for the peaceful settlement of disputes, and it should be noted that one of the two authors, Louis Sohn, was later one of the main authors of the comprehensive, flexible and binding system for the settlement of disputes in the Law of the Sea Convention, one of the proudest achievements of that Convention. *World Peace through World Law,* however, was based on the premise that enforceable world law is to be limited to the prevention of war, total disarmament, under the control of a world police force. "The powers of the organization should be restricted to matters directly related to the maintenance of peace. All other powers should be reserved to the nations and their peoples."

This represented the so-called "minimalist" position, vigorously opposed by the Committee to Frame a World Constitution. We spearheaded the "maximalist" position of the movement. While Clark and Sohn considered it "wise for this generation to limit itself to the single task of preventing international violence or the threat of it," the University of Chicago—already in the forties!—sought to transcend the "sectoral" approach and to think of government or governance in an interdisciplinary and holistic mode, much closer to today's thinking. The Chicago draft of a world constitution is based on the conviction that the arms race is a symptom not a cause, and to eliminate it, one had to eliminate its root causes, and these were social and economic inequity. Peace and justice stand and fall together: Pax opus justitiae, and without social and economic justice, national and international, there could not be peace, which is more than the absence of war.

While fully aware that our Constitution was not "realistic" in the sense that the international community could adopt it in the immediate tomorrow, we intended it to be a blueprint pointing in the direction of a desirable, or probably, ineluctable future. We went as far as to suggest that, on the basis of the present economic system and its Roman Law concept of ownership, economic justice was unattainable. Borrowing from the Dean of Canterbury, the Reverend Hewlett Johnson, our Constitution declares that the four elements of life—earth, water, air, and energy—are the common property of the human race. The management and use of such portions thereof as a vested in or assigned to particular ownership, private or corporate or national or regional, of definite or indefinite tenure, of individualist or collectivist economy, shall be subordinated in each and all cases to the interest of the common good. "Earth" included not only the surface real estate but the mineral resources of the subsoil as well. "Water" meant both the oceans and freshwater resources; "air" meant the atmosphere, as a traffic highway and a resource, and a part of our biosphere of vital importance for human survival; and "energy" includes all form of energy, nonrenewable or renewable.

Utopian as that might have appeared to be in the forties, one part of it has found its topos. The United Nations Convention on the Law of the Sea of 1982 declares the seabed and ocean floor, beyond the limits of national jurisdiction, to be the Common Heritage of Mankind, which cannot be appropriated by any State, company, or individual but must be managed, under the aegis of the International Sea-bed Authority, for the benefit of humankind as a whole, with particular consideration for the poor. It also is reserved for exclusively peaceful purposes and must be managed with due consideration for the conservation of the marine environment so that also future generations can share its benefits.

The Chicago Constitution also guaranteed "the right of everyone everywhere to claim and maintain for himself and his fellow men release from the bondage of poverty and from the servitude and exploitation of labour, with rewards and security according to merit and needs"—anticipating today's generally accepted emphasis on the "eradication of poverty" as a condition for sustainable development.

This, as some have pointed out, makes it in fact a document of "socialist humanism," or "humanist socialism."

There are several kinds of "utopianism." There is "escapist" utopianism, sometimes indulged in by those who "fiddle while Rome is burning"; "blasphemous utopianism," envisaging earthlings with powers that only God can wield, would be a subspecies of this kind of utopianism; and, on the other hand, there is "constructive" utopianism. The Chicago Constitution belongs to the latter, as a forerunner of the Law of the Sea and the sustainable development efforts of today.

When one critic, the famous theologian Reinhold Niebuhr accused us of the sin of blasphemous utopianism, my father, in his introduction to the German edition of the World Constitution, made this extraordinary statement, still so actual today:

> Is it sure that these men have the right idea of sin? Sin, in my opinion, is to live against the spirit and against truth: to live as if we did not live the present hour but an hour passed long since. Sin is to cling with stupid tenacity to what has been surpassed by time, to what is inadequate, clearly repudiated; sin is to turn a deaf ear to the will of God. The abyss that is gaping between that which still dares to call itself reality and, on the other side, the truth—that is, the goals reached long since by the spirit—this abyss is simply a religious scandal: a blasphemy screaming for deluge, fire and brimstone. And fire and brimstone will not fail to come. No one is more aware of this than the authors of the project for a universal, renovating law, which is at the same time fully realistic inasmuch as it adheres to the facts given by reality. The authors know full well that their ordering proposals may be taken into consideration only after the cataclysm—if anything will have remained to be ordered. They have done their duty, at any rate, and prepared a plan: May its time arrive. The readiness is all.

I could give many more details about the continuity between the utopian, academic efforts of the Chicago Committee to Frame a World Constitution and, twenty years later, the global, political effort to frame what was to be called "a Constitution for the Ocean," that was to absorb the international community for fourteen years, and continues to absorb it. But that would fill a book, not a lecture.

We had to deal with the issue of sovereignty in an interdependent world; with "governance," from the local to the national to the regional to the global level; with "virtual" regions, based on communality of cultures; with new, emerging forms of democracy and the role of "civil society"—all issues alive and kicking today!

The world constitution, dedicated to Gandhi, was translated into about 50 languages and distributed all over the world in millions of copies. It was certainly the most successful world constitution, and, it may be surprising to you, literally hundreds of world constitutions were produced at that time, by escapist, blasphemous, and constructive utopians! We collected them, and analysed dozens of them in our journal, *Common Cause.*

That was half a century ago.

Then, in the fifties, the intellectual skies darkened. In the USA, McCarthyism reared its ugly head, and "good Americans" behaved pretty much the same way "good Germans" had behaved under Hitler: They betrayed and denounced one another; and witch hunting was the order of the day. "Peace" became a dirty word. Anyone who dared to speak out for peace, was branded as a Communist, condemned to silence and fired from his job. My father's lectures at the Library of Congress were cancelled. So were my husband's broadcasts in Chicago. After a brave struggle to protect his professors from the witch hunt, Robert Hutchins left the University, and many of the exiles, among them my family, left the United States and returned to Europe.

Robert Hutchins re-emerged, after a few years, and founded the Center for the Study of Democratic Institutions, first conceived as an arm against McCarthyism; but McCarthies come and go, while the issues of democratic institutions are much broader, and, as Hutchins soon recognized, are not self-contained within any country no matter how big; they are inextricably linked to global issues. In 1964, Hutchins invited me to join the Center and to resume the work on our world constitution. I did. It still looked to me like a very great piece of work. It did not need improving. It was the world that needed improving!

At that time, the ocean issue began to move into the foreground. President Truman of the United States issued a Declaration in 1945 claiming sovereign rights over its continental shelf to a depth of 200 metres, far exceeding the traditional limit of 3 miles of the territorial sea. This was followed by a slew of claims by states in Latin America and Africa expanding their territorial seas from 3 to 12 to 50 up to 200 miles. The maritime powers, especially the United States and the Soviet Union, were increasingly concerned about the threat to the freedom of movement of their navies and fleets, At the same time, fish stocks were endangered by overfishing, pollution and loss of breeding grounds and habitat due to increasing population pressure on coastal areas, to industrialization, urbanization, and technological development. Two United Nations Conferences on the Law of the Sea, in 1958 and 1960, tried to grapple with these problems, but were not able to solve them.

It was in this situation that the great ambassador of a small State, Arvid Pardo of Malta, delivered his epoch-making ocean address to the United Nations. That was November 1, 1967.

Malta had gained its independence from England and joined the United Nations as a sovereign State in 1964. It was the second-smallest Member State, and had not yet developed a large diplomatic staff. Arvid Pardo thus was appointed Ambassador to the United Nations, to the United States, and the Soviet Union, and High Commissioner to Canada, the Caribbean countries, all at the same time. That kept him pretty busy! At age 85 he now lives in complete retirement somewhere in Texas.[2] Although little known to the world, he is one of the great men of the twentieth century who has contributed decisively to shaping the world of the twenty-first. Pardo has an encyclopaedic mind and complex temperament, phlegmatic and intensely productive at the same time, committed and detached; idealistic and realistic; revolutionary and conservative; religious and cynical. His influence on my thinking and on my life is commensurate only to that of my parents and my husband.

In his 1967 marathon speech, that kept the General Assembly spellbound for four hours, Arvid Pardo stressed the enormous importance of

[2] Editors' Note.—Ambassador Arvid Pardo died on 19 June 1999.

the world ocean to the wealth and welfare of the human race, throughout history and for the future. How the development of science and technology had intensified and diversified ocean uses and led to conflicts between uses as well as between users. The traditional law of the sea, based on the freedom of the high seas with national jurisdiction restricted to a narrow belt of coastal water, called the territorial sea, had become obsolete and dysfunctional. Neither sovereignty nor freedom could resolve these problems and cope with the mounting perils of pollution, the extinction of living resources and armed conflict. A new principle was needed as a basis for a new Law of the Sea. This principle was to be that of the Common Heritage of Mankind which transcended both sovereignty and freedom.

The Center for the Study of Democratic Institutions, at that time focussing its energies on world order and peace, organized a series of international conferences, under a name borrowed from Pope John XXIII great Encyclical Pacem in Terris. That Encyclical stated:

> The public authority of the world community must tackle and solve problems of an economic, social, political or cultural character which are posed by the universal common good. For, because of the vastness, complexity and urgency of those problems, the public authorities of the individual states are not in a position to tackle them with any hope of resolving them satisfactorily.

That became the Center's leitmotiv.

In 1967 I suggested to President Hutchins that it was not likely that rapid progress could be made with our world constitution; that the Cold War could end and peaceful change towards this kind of new world order could be implemented; that there was, however, a huge part of our planet, the ocean, where matters were in flux—apologizing for the pun—where new and revolutionary concepts could be introduced; where our utopian ideals and ideas of world governance could be brought down and tested in the arena of real politics. The ocean, I said, could be our great laboratory for the making of a new world order.

Hutchins gave me carte blanche to organize, at the Center, a three-year project leading up to a Conference in 1970 which, paraphrasing the Pope's Pacem in Terris, "Peace on Earth," I called Pacem in Maribus, "Peace on the oceans." We joined forces with Ambassador Pardo and decided to have the Conference in Malta, his home base. Malta, a small country without big vested interests, in the middle of the Mediterranean Sea, at the confluence of European, African and Asian cultures, and with the historic merit of having triggered the whole contemporary Law of the Sea development, was an ideal place for a global project on ocean governance. Pacem in Maribus was extremely successful and became the starting point of a long series of now 26 Conferences. For the conduct of these conferences to enhance a broad, interdisciplinary dialogue on ocean law and development, we established the International Ocean Institute in Malta. It became one of the "think tanks" for the evolving process of the Third United Nations Conference on the Law of the Sea, which was in preparation since 1968 and concluded its work in 1982 with the adoption of the United Nations Convention on the Law of the Sea. We followed UNCLOS III very closely, analysed its emerging results, and proposed new approaches and solutions. All the major actors in UNCLOS III participated in Pacem in Maribus conferences, and the President of UNCLOS III was also the President of the Governing Board of the International Ocean Institute.

The International Ocean Institute today is a network of 10 Operational Centres all over the world, conducting policy research, training, courses and organizing conferences and publications. It still has its headquarters in Malta.

The adoption of the United Nations Convention on the Law of the Sea has been praised, by the Secretary General of the United Nations, as the most important event in international relations since the adoption of the United Nations Convention itself. The President of UNCLOS III called it "A Constitution for the Oceans."

The Convention marks a point of breakthrough in the history of international law and relations. It is the beginning of a process, continued and developed through the United Nations Conference on Environment and Development (Rio, 1992) and its many follow-up conferences, conventions, agreements and programmes, and pointing towards the new political, social, and economic world of the twenty-first century.

Let me just indicate quite briefly why this document is of such importance.

The Convention introduces a novel principle into our legal and economic world order: the principle of the Common Heritage of Mankind. The Convention restricts the application of this revolutionary principle to the area and the resources of the deep seabed beyond the limits of national jurisdiction; but the second great concept, introduced by this Convention that "the problems of ocean space are closely interrelated and must be considered as a whole," in a way belies this restriction. If there is a systems change in one part of ocean space, it will necessarily affect the whole ocean system. The Common Heritage principle is of fundamental importance, not only for the oceans, but as a basis for sustainable development in general. "Sustainable development" either is nothing, a tautology, because development that is not sustainable is no development; or it is the new name, the new form of "humanistic socialism" or "socialist humanism" that we need for the next century.

The Convention deals with the concept of "sovereignty" as creatively as it deals with the concept of "ownership." It limits, transforms, and transcends the concept of "sovereignty" in an interdependent world.

With the introduction of the Exclusive Economic Zone, the Archipelagic Waters, the Regime for Islands, and the new definition of the Continental Shelf, the Convention achieved the most extensive peaceful redistribution of ocean space in history. This is not to say that this redistribution did not create as many problems as it solved; or that it will stay for ever: It may be transitional, leading up to intensified development of regional cooperation and organization. But, to start with, it has replaced a system of laissez-faire in the ocean with a framework for management. That, I think, is its main conceptual merit.

The Convention has created what still today is the only existing comprehensive, binding international environmental law, covering all kinds of pollution from all sources, whether oceanic, land-based or atmospheric, and on a global basis: a framework which can and must be filled by more specific, geographically or functionally limited agreements and conventions, of which there are already several hundreds; but without this framework, the subsequent effort of the Earth Summit in Rio in 1992 would have remained ineffective, or it would not even have taken place.

The Convention creates a new regime for marine scientific research, which will be of tremendous theoretical and practical importance—the new discoveries being made almost continuously are mind-boggling and are changing the vision of our planet, our biosphere and the role of humans in it. The Convention gives to marine scientific research the importance it deserves, devoting almost 100 of its 320 articles to it, based on a concept of science that is interdisciplinary, cooperative and reserving it for peaceful purposes.

The Convention creates what is today the best available framework for cooperative technology development, especially for developing countries.

Finally, the Convention creates the most comprehensive, binding yet flexible system for the peaceful settlement of disputes ever accepted by the international community.

This is not to say that this Convention is perfect. Nothing human ever is perfect; and this Convention is riddled by political compromises, concessions to greed and power and vested interests, the struggle between the old and the new. So much so that Arvid Pardo, really the father of this new Law of the Sea as Grotius was the father of the old Law of the Sea, was bitterly disappointed by what he thought was a dilution, even a betrayal of his ideas. I, on the contrary, was surprised to see how much of his original design had survived the wrangling of the political arena from which no concept can emerge in its virginal purity!

Arvid Pardo said, the glass is half empty.

I said, the glass is half full.

There was, I think much on which we could build further, especially in the sphere of institution-building which was left badly behind by the Convention so that there is a serious gap between legal agreements and provisions on the one side, and the institutions available for their realization and implementation—if the broader historical context will allow us to build further. That context, however, is not something given, predestined and fixed, but may be modified by what we build in our great laboratory, the ocean.

The twentieth century, My Time, ends with an International Year of the Ocean, 1998, and UNCLOS +5, 1999, the year in which the United Nations is undertaking a comprehensive review of ocean affairs, five years after the Law of the Sea Convention entered into force.

At the International Ocean Institute, we have quite an agenda, to follow that review and to help bridge that institutional gap for the next century.

I want to start at the local level, the people's level. The sustainable development literature—which must be read together with the Law of the Sea literature—is consistent and unanimous in stressing the importance of the local coastal community for implementation.

Community-based management, integrating, horizontally, all users into planning and decision-making, and, vertically, providing a forum for cooperation between local and national authorities, is also called "co-management." It may constitute a much-needed countervailing force against the ill effects of "globalization." Furthermore, it inserts itself organically into the contemporary process of "reshuffling" of the socio-political map. For this is what is going on in "my time": a reshuffling of the socio-political map we had inherited from the time of Grotius, from the time of the Westphalian peace treaty ending the Thirty Years War. States which we thought were to be there for ever in their present form, tend to devolve more power and more responsibility to smaller, local entities—if they do not altogether break up under cultural, religious, or linguistic or ethnic pressures. At the same time they tend to yield some powers to wider, supranational unions such as the EU, in response to economic, environmental, and technological imperatives. The local component, however, can succeed only if, in this process, it can establish proper linkages with the national and the supranational, in particular, regional level. This can be advanced in several ways: There can be direct cooperation among local communities across state boundaries; and this is already happening in many places: e.g., through associations of port cities or cooperation for the protection of the environment as between the Canadian Provinces and the US States in the Gulf of Maine, independent of their Federal Governments; or the cooperation of the municipalities around the Sea of Japan. In Europe, there exists a European Outline Convention on Transfrontier Cooperation between Territorial Communities or Authorities (Madrid, 1980).

Another, most important way is through the direct participation of local communities in intergovernmental organisations. This has already been realized in the Mediterranean Commission on Sustainable Development (MCSD) within the Barcelona Treaty system. This Commission consists of States, socio-economic actors, NGOs and local communities. All members have the same rights, including the right to vote. The importance of this innovative approach has not been given sufficient attention in the literature. To my mind, it is a real breakthrough and should be taken up by all other regional organisations. The direct participation of "civil society," and, in particular, local communities, will contribute to the democratization of international relations and organisation.

Which takes me to the final observation on community-based co-management: At a time when everything is changing, it is not likely that democracy alone will remain unchanged. It, too, will evolve and change. Democracy means the empowerment of people: their right to choose their own form of government and to participate in decision making. The European-born, political-party based model of democracy is not the only way through which this can be achieved. The "Westminster model" had its historic justification in Europe and has reached splendid results. Its exportation all over the world was a part of the global triumph of Western culture. Today, perhaps, it is a last vestige of colonialism. In the "North," in many places, the political party system shows signs of "commercialisation" and corruption. Perhaps it was not suitable for the "South" to start with. Perhaps, outside the European cultures, democracy should have been rooted in local cultures and traditions rather than in the Western political party system. Quite conceivably, community-based co-management fits more organically into non-European cultures. Quite conceivably, community-based co-management may be the form of democracy in the next century, which will no longer be culturally dominated by Europe.

If the movement towards community-based co-management advances; if the influence of "civil society" increases; if the understanding of the interdisciplinary, trans-sectoral and "systemic" character of contemporary issues matures, changes corresponding to those at the "grassroots level" will take place at the level of national governments as well. In fact, they are already in course. Interministerial Councils, Parliamentary Committees on the oceans, national round-tables or other forms of consultation with "civil society," including local communities, are inevitable, and they are coming. In the Netherlands you have an excellent system for the management of your North Sea sector, comprising all the ministries involved, Parliament, as well as the major users. I often refer to this Dutch model as an example of how this can be done.

At the regional level, I can see three innovations which would benefit regional cooperation and organisation in all parts of the world, responding to the changes at the local and national level.

The first is the establishment of regional Commissions on Sustainable Development, studying and adapting the Mediterranean model. This model brings another important innovation, besides those I have already mentioned. It transcends the sectoral approach that still limits the horizons of most institutions even though they may pay lip service to interdisciplinarity. The United Nations Commission on Sustainable Development, for instance, has a Ministerial Segment, but it is attended exclusively by the Ministers for the Environment. The Mediterranean Commission, the first regional commission on sustainable development, has broken this mould. It includes Ministers from any department involved one way or another in sustainable development—and almost every department is involved.

This flexibility, then, could provide the basis on which to build the second innovation, that is a mechanism to enhance cooperation in research and development, South-South and North-South, in environmentally and socially sustainable technology at the regional level, interacting with local communities. Ten years ago, the International Ocean Institute proposed a very simple model, following the precedent established by institutions like EUREKA and others in Europe, which generated billions of dollars of investment in R&D in high technologies through the synergism of public and private investment at the international (European) level. This could be adapted, opened to the full and equal participation of developing countries, and implemented under the aegis of the Ministers of Science and Technology composing the Ministerial Segment of the regional CSD. In Europe, EUROMAR, the marine sector of EUREKA is presently in a process of reorganization, aiming, in particular, at the inclusion of the developing Mediterranean countries. This now could be achieved, building on what is already there. Placing the project under the aegis of the MCSD would guarantee that the technologies selected are environmentally and socially sustainable.

There is another reason which makes the creation of such a system, at the regional level, particularly urgent now. The Law of the Sea Convention was the first to mandate the establishment of "regional centres" for the enhancement of technology development and transfer. This mandate has not been implemented. Subsequently, each one of the conventions, agreements, and programmes adopted within the UNCED process has its own elaborate provisions to facilitate this cooperation. But this multiplicity of arrangements is obviously ineffective, considering that the technologies needed to facilitate the implementation of the different conventions are mostly the same. What is needed today is one single system of technology cooperation at the regional level, serving the needs of all the conventions, agreements, and programmes. The Mediterranean may provide the best pilot application of this concept, but the system can be generalized and, with the necessary adaptations, it can be introduced in all regional seas.

The third innovation would impact on the whole system of global governance in a rather profound way. It concerns the maintenance of security. There is today universal agreement that "security" is not what it was half a century ago when the United Nations came into existence. Then it was primarily inter-state; today it is primarily intra-state; then it was military; today it has economic and environmental dimensions; then it was primarily global; today it is primarily regional; then it was the security of the State; today it is human security: Human security at the regional level. The devastating effects of the violation of human security at the regional level are tragically demonstrated by the Kosovo war, with its inherent threat of escalation into an international civil war—which, I think, is the form World War III will assume.

These changes in the nature of security, obviously must have institutional implications. We do need an institutional framework to deal with human security at the regional level. This is required also by the United Nations' *Agenda for Peace.*

This institutional framework is now emerging. It is already so near the surface that it is almost breaking through!

Sustainable development also has a security dimension, besides its economic, environmental and equity dimensions. Without peace and security, most certainly there can be neither economic development nor protection of the environment, in all its aspects. If sustainable development has a security dimension, this too, must have its institutional implication. Where is the institutional framework to deal with sustainable development including its security dimension? It is already there: all we have to do is to use it. The framework is given in the flexible regional Commission on Sustainable Development, including in its Ministerial Segment any minister from any department involved in sustainable development. And are not the Ministers of Defence or the Secretaries of the Navies involved? Indeed they are. In case of armed conflict, they could meet in the Ministerial Segment as a "virtual regional security council." In the absence of armed conflict they could deal with cooperation in the peaceful uses of navies, from regional common oceanographic research (underwater acoustics; hydrographic measurements, etc.) as well as with humanitarian assistance—search and rescue; disaster mitigation; and joint surveillance and enforcement of compliance with environmental agreements and the conservation of living resources. A pilot experiment could well be undertaken in the Mediterranean—without any changes in the Barcelona Convention or the Mediterranean Action Plan—with the MCSD already in place and functioning flexibly and in a genuinely interdisciplinary way.

These three innovations at the regional level—establishing regional commissions on sustainable development; generating a system for technology cooperation and "transfer" that would meet the needs of all UNCLOS/UNCED conventions, agreements and programmes; and a system integrating sustainable development and regional human security—would considerably strengthen regional organisation and cooperation, and this is essential for the implementation of the Law of the Sea Convention as well as for the implementation of all UNCED conventions, agreements and programmes. They all rely and call on regional organisations.

Moving now to the level of the United Nations, there are a number of proposals that ought to go forward. I will deal with only one—because of its simplicity and immediate feasibility. This proposal deals with the establishment of a sort of Ocean Assembly, where all States and competent non-State actors could consider the closely interrelated problems of ocean space as a whole—and respond to the ongoing changes at the regional and local levels. Everybody today agrees that such a body is needed. There is also general agreement that it is only the General Assembly, with its universal membership and comprehensive, trans-sectoral mandate, that could do the job. But we all know that the General Assembly, with an agenda that is already overburdened, simply does not have the time to deal effectively with these issues and generate a global, integrated ocean policy. The agenda for an "effective, comprehensive, integrated and multisectoral review of ocean issues" is enormous and of a bewildering complexity, as indicated by the ever more comprehensive Reports of the Secretary-General—the current one consisting of 493 paragraphs! Serious consideration of this volume of information, coupled with the challenge to take a more active part in anticipating areas of concern and devising strategies to address them effectively" would about double the already heavy work-load of the General Assembly. There are possible solutions, however. The best appears to be that the General Assembly should establish a Committee of the Whole, that is, open to the participation of all States—one could call it a Standing Committee, or a Seventh Committee of the General Assembly, or simply "Working Group". Whatever its name, it should meet at regular intervals, long enough to examine the Secretary-General's Report and give policy guidelines.

We have put forward this proposal at the International Ocean Institute, we also had it included among the recommendations of the Independent World Commission on the Ocean, which was established on the initiative of the International Ocean Institute. The general idea was intensively discussed by the Seventh Session of the Commission on Sustainable Development—CSD7—and in a somewhat watered-down form it has been included in the recommendations of the Commission. While admitting that there was no unanimity on the proposal, the Commission recommends the establishment of an "open-ended working group" which should meet annually, for the week preceding the opening of the General Assembly, to give more time to the serious consideration of ocean issues. The Chairman of the Commission called this a "breakthrough" in the development of ocean governance, and I agree with him: although much work will still be needed to develop it into the sort of "Ocean Assembly" that is needed. The General Assembly should act on it later this year.

Thus a procedure is now in place to determine the shape of "ocean governance" for the next century.

The development of ocean affairs and the Law of the Sea, during these past thirty years, has been difficult and tortuous. Breakthrough events, like the Maltese Ambassador's historic address on November 1, 1967, or the adoption of the Convention in 1982, and the record number of 119 signatures it obtained at that time; its entry into force in 1994 and its merger with the stream of ocean-related parts of the UNCED conventions, agreements, and programmes, were always counteracted by the forces of inertia. Contemporary obsessions with the "market," with privatisation, deregulation and downsizing conflict with the principle of the Common Heritage of Mankind and slow down progress towards sustainable development, including both the eradication of poverty and the conservation of the environment. Opportunities have been missed. Mistakes have been committed; international law has been violated; human tragedy has reached new dimensions. Sometimes it seemed that the law of the sea kept progressing in spite of itself, led by some inscrutable necessity.

In spite of all difficulties, and looking back over three decades, progress has been enormous, almost unbelievable. People think differently today from the ways they thought thirty years ago. The International Year of the Ocean has contributed to accelerating these changes in thinking.

The emerging system of ocean governance, both structure and process, reaching from the local to the national to the regional subsystem to the global system, comprehensive, consistent, participatory and non-hierarchical, in what Gandhi called "the majesty of the oceanic circle" will, I believe, respond to the requirements of the new Law of the Sea in conjunction with the new environmental international law as developed by UNCED; it will respond to the needs of the post-industrial age, including the information revolution, while countervailing the ill effects of "globalization" and reflecting the pattern of all cultural evolutions, not just the European, and it is bound to enhance nonviolence, peace and security, and a new phase in the evolution of democracy, local and global.

There has been a lot of dramatic change in "my time"; but also a lot of continuity. There has been a lot of tragedy, but also a lot of hope. In some ways it has been a time of "breakthrough."

On a historical time scale, it marks the end of what has been called the Westphalian age of the nation state, the end of State-centrism, and the end of Eurocentrism. The new socio-political map starts with the local community, and expands, through concentric circles, to the United Nations. This may mean the emergence of a new form of democracy and a new, community-based economic order. I believe that the new emphasis on community and on cooperation, coupled with technological developments, will also enhance a new gender balance.

On an evolutionary scale, one might say that humankind has experienced a "mutation." A species that can fly is not the same species as one that cannot. A species that can overcome gravity and move among the planets is not the same as a species that is earth-bound. A species whose members can undergo sex change is not the same as a species that cannot! Whether these "mutations" have been effected by "nature" or by "culture" is not really relevant, as culture is a part of nature in any case. And that, again is one of the great changes in "my time" we have seen taking place on a historical time scale: our attitude towards "nature" and our place in it: our attitude towards our fellow living creatures on this planet, has drastically changed in "my time," and has come closer to the way we felt when we were children.

This is not to say that I believe that the changes in "my time" are unique. Everybody's time has had its incredible changes and breakthroughs. When the first railroad was built in Sicily, during my husband's childhood, people felt pretty much the same way our generation felt when the first astronaut took off. The Sicilians in the 19th century, so my husband told me, did not believe the human body could withstand the inhuman speed of fifty or even sixty kilometres per hour these new iron horses achieved! It was against human nature. It was against nature in general!

As T.S. Eliot put it:

> Time present and time past
> Are both perhaps present in time future.
> And time future contained in time past.

The feminist-socialist ideals of my great-grandmother's time; the socialist humanism or humanist socialism of my father's and my husband's time are still with us. The democratic ideals, the ideal of universal peace are still with us, time present and time past, in time future. But time present, My Time, has transformed them, as future generations will transform what we have tried to build.

Elisabeth Mann Borgese: Metaphysician by Birth

Peter Serracino Inglott
International Ocean Institute Operational Centre, Malta

> Once upon a time, long, long ago, there was a wise and powerful king. He was, in fact, the wisest and most powerful king on earth. But his power was based on a secret: . . . he understood the calls of the dolphins; and even the fish, which we think to be dumb, would vocalise and reveal ocean's secrets to him.[1]

The opening words of Elisabeth Mann Borgese's third published book, *The White Snake*, like its title, allude to a myth. But its content is mostly made up of performed experiments, narrated blow by blow, with prosaic precision. The title of the American edition, demythicized, became: *The Language Barrier: Beasts and Man.*[2] When those opening words about dolphins and fish were written, it was still before all the piebald representatives of Otherness had assembled in Elisabeth's mind and been incorporated into the singular figure of Ocean. In other words, simpler and more superficial, it was before the full concentration of her interests on the law of the sea had occurred. However, it is already notable that, right at the beginning, she associates the problem of human-animal communication with, on the one hand, political power and good governance in a global perspective ("on earth") and on the other hand, with "ocean" (without the article, quasi-personified, although not capitalised).

In her later years, the public had become accustomed to Professor Borgese's tackling the often abstruse political problems of ocean space paradoxically in a very down-to-earth manner. She had the reputation of being an idealist but she was ready to compromise on most issues (unlike her mentor on law of the sea matters, Arvid Pardo) as if she were a born kitchen cabinet wheeler-dealer. It was the same accommodating spirit that she displayed (again unlike Pardo) in those rare and brief encounters with local political figures that she had to accept as inevitable during her short or long visits to Malta. But occasionally she would let it transpire, as if in a glass darkly, that her deeper interests were still, as always, in what one might call the

1. E. Mann Borgese, *The White Snake* (London: Macgibbon and Kee, 1966).
2. E. Mann Borgese, *The Language Barrier: Beasts and Man* (New York: Holt, Rinehart and Winston, 1968).

Ocean Yearbook 18: 22–74

symbolic, metaphysical, transcendent dimensions of the sea: the sea as the space where the eschatological future of mankind was even now being dimly adumbrated.

Obviously, the "First Lady of the Ocean"[3] deserves a full-scale study that would bring out the dialectic between the personal and the political dimensions of her life, in detail.[4] Here I will only attempt to discern a pattern although with somewhat fuzzy outlines in the multifariousness of her concerns. There are indeed, I think, unifying threads running through the apparently disconnected topics of her writings, as she moves from musicology to surrealist fiction to experiments with animal communication to an odd manifesto of idiosyncratic feminism to the economics of self-management in productive organisations and, finally, to the endless circuitry of the law of the sea.

This convoluted, literary itinerary will be much less likely to fox a reader if he or she is aware of the genesis of its motivation in the 35 years of silent gestation that preceded EMB's first autonomous publication, especially in her relationship to two men. The first was inevitably her father, under the brilliance of whose shadow she lived until she was over 20. The second was her husband, Giuseppe Antonio Borgese, with whom she lived for 13 years and who was in reality, another father figure; his rich personality and self-critical creativity, if not reputation, were equal or comparable to those of Thomas Mann himself, both as a writer of fiction and as a political thinker.

Then, in conclusion, it should be possible, having looked at the roots and branches of her writing, to identify the personal, core contribution that she made to the development of the concept of the Common Heritage of Mankind, as it came to be introduced and established in international law. She built here on the bare foundations laid by the Maltese diplomat Arvid Pardo, whom she herself described as the "third man" to have decisively influenced her life-work.

FAMILIAR WATERS

Remaining a Mann: Baltic Moorings

In the book that must now be regarded as her testament, *The Oceanic Circle*, she wrote:

3. *Elisabeth Mann Borgese Die Meer-Frau*; Gespräch mit Amadou Seitz in der Reihe "Zeugen des Jahrhunderts"; herausgegeben von Ingo Hermann; Redaktion, Jürgen Voigt, (Göttingen: Lamuv Verlag GmbH, 1993).

4. Meanwhile, cf. K. Holzer, *Elisabeth Mann Borgese Ein Lebensportrait* (Berlin: Kindler Verlag GmbH, 2001).

> We find music and the sea intimately linked in the writings of my father, Thomas Mann. . . . Although I was not conscious of it until much later, my father's love affair with the ocean must have influenced me powerfully. Rereading his works in my mature years, when I have become myself so deeply involved with the oceans, I find his analysis of the human relationship to nature, and specially the sea, the most profound I have come across.[5]

This declaration of indebtedness to her father surprised many. I myself have often heard it said that EMB always insisted that she be treated as herself, rather than as her father's daughter. Her fervour for autonomy is beyond doubt. Nevertheless, at least in her later years, I never found her reluctant to talk about her father (including his complex sexuality, which also influenced his "love-affair" with the sea) even before the publication of his *Diaries*,[6] or her family. She often acknowledged the importance in her formation of her cosmopolitan descent (Jewish grandfather, Brazilian grandmother). Above all, she always showed awareness of the fact that her father had actually hailed her birth in a unique poem as the morning star of a new, troubled age, and some years later, in an undisguised manner in a short story, her childhood as the disturbance of the sort of (family) life he had established by what he intuited to be "the call of the deep." Of course, at first blush she had rejected / not grasped her father's oracle-like reading of her destiny, but that rejection had not prevented her from unconsciously following the foreseen path. The life-goal she pursued was, in more than one sense, precisely the reconciliation of what Family and Ocean stood for in her father's mind and in reality.

On Saturday, November 2nd, 1918, barely more than 6 months after EMB's birth, Thomas Mann inscribed in his *Diaries* the following brief sentence: "In the morning began writing a prose draft of the poem 'To My Youngest Child'." Then, where one would have expected an outline of the content of the poem, the entry continues: "In Vienna the revolution is threatening to pass over into anarchy and Bolshevism. The 'Red Guard' being led by a Galician Jew who was once mentally ill . . . Word has it that Scheidemann considers revolution unavoidable here (in Munich) as well." The *Diaries* make it clear: revolution, in its heart and essence, was the meaning, according to Thomas Mann, of this special baby daughter, for him and for the world.

The entry for Thursday, November 7th begins "Worked on the draft in the morning, Got down two hexameters." He then apparently changes tack:

5. E. Mann Borgese, *The Oceanic Circle: Governing the Seas as a Global Resource* (Tokyo: United Nations University Press, 1998), pp. 54–55.

6. T. Mann, *Diaries 1918–1939*, Selection and Foreword by H. Desten, trans. from German by R. and C. Whinston, (London: Robin Clark, 1984), pp. 16–17.

"At three o'clock there was a large demonstration . . . All stores closed . . . Red flags . . . Cries: 'Down with the dynasty!' 'Republic!'" The word 'dynasty' pinpoints Family-based power as the symbol of what the Revolution is overturning. The Ocean so far is only dimly prefigured in the obscure tonality of the prose as the symbol of the transcendent Assailant poorly represented by the wretched Red Guard and flags.

Thomas Mann keeps noting his progress on the sort of mock-epic that he was composing to celebrate EMB's advent into his world while at the same time noting also how "the little one" was doing in her initiation into the Mann-family style of life: "Her ear is being treated with hydrogen peroxide – itself half-a-hexameter for my poem: 'its dull muffled roar numbs her hearing' – so that she rolls her eyes and appears to fall asleep. Carried her about for some time and entertained her with the pot-bellied roly-poly doll, which I set dancing on the table. Her cold is greatly hampering her, but still, she made several attempts at talking: 'Dada' and 'Gaga'." Thomas Mann does not only alternate self-mocking hints of his struggles to produce another family epic like *Buddenbrooks* in hexameter verse with glum echoes of the historic, violent revolution brewing outside. He also interlards, with apparent bathos but deep intent, micro-observations of the incipient struggle for survival of Little-Girl with insights into the barbaric birth pangs of the post-First-World-War world.

Most commentators have read the poem as saying that the child was not for her father merely the romantic fulfillment of his fairy-tale love for her mother Katia Pringsheim, his "princess bride," but also a sort of sacrament of the New Times. Henceforth what he had previously dreamt of as private—his family-life—was to be ineluctably fused with the political and indeed the cosmic.

Like Isaiah or Jeremiah or one of the prophets, but visibly tongue in cheek, Thomas Mann addresses EMB as follows:

> Last-born and yet for me in truth
> First-born! – for important years
> Had passed since I, maturing as a man,
> Last became a father . . .
> . . . All the reality which surrounded me,
> Did it not stem more from dream than from life?. . .[7]

Indeed, 8 years had passed since the birth of Monika, the sister who was the latest comer before Elisabeth. The period in Thomas Mann's life from the turn of the century (when he was just over 25 years old and when he enjoyed the extraordinary literary success of *Buddenbrooks*) right until the outbreak

7. Translation from N. Hamilton, *The Brothers Mann* (New Haven: Yale University Press, 1979), p. 197.

of the first world war had been exhilarating for him. But the outlook had darkened drastically with the war. *Après le Deluge,* Mann expresses disillusionment. But, with his unfailing irony, he manages to give the poem an ambivalent turn, through binding up the feared opening of the floodgates of change with fervour at the birth of baby Elisabeth. The particular interest displayed by the great writer in this particular baby daughter contrasts with his habitual distance-keeping, bordering on aloofness, towards all his other intimates, of which there are indices throughout the *Diaries.* Its motivation is, however, readily comprehensible. The exceptional interest is clearly intertwined with the assistance the child provided towards his execution of such artistic endeavours as the poem. Portraying the child was the only artistic means he could find by which the radiant hope he still felt in his heart could be fleshed into the general picture of a sombre and darkening world that as an artist he had to depict.

The period between the world wars indeed coincided with the first 20 years of EMB's life and determined the auspices under which her sails were to be hoisted; but I do not think that such considerations plausibly made by many literary critics really pinpoint the reason why Thomas Mann greeted his fifth child as if she had been the first. The deepest reason for his strange feeling seems to have been that before the birth of the fifth child, he had not realized that the essence of paternity was the capacity to help mould a child in an analogous way to that in which a novelist fashions his characters; they become, as they develop, largely his own creations and only a little bit God's. He had learnt this lesson mainly from Freud's theories on intra-family relationships that he had been carefully reading in those years of crisis.[8] It is true that incidentally, then, intergenerational relations, the crucial mode of transmission of the past to the future, would also appear as the key to understanding history and even the evolutionary cosmos. But the determining reason why Thomas Mann indubitably decided that he would seek to play a more deliberately involved paternal role in the moulding of Elisabeth's life than the detachment adopted towards her elders does not appear to have been that the historical crisis demanded it (because Family stability was being threatened by Oceanic invasion). It was rather that his conception of patterning one's life like a work of art implied to some degree treating one's children in certain ways like characters are in a novel by the author: granting them autonomy, but setting them a vocation.[9]

The *Diaries* enable the reader to see how Thomas Mann shifts key as he moves from the near-farcical feigned seriousness of the poem to the almost deadly serious, feigned lightheartedness of the prophetic short story,

8. T. Mann, "Mon Rapport à la Psychanalyse, 1926," in *Être Écrivain Allemand à notre Époque* (Gallimard: Arcades, 1996), pp. 187–88.

9. The subtitle of H. Kurzke's biography of Thomas Mann is "Life As a Work of Art!," English Translation (London: Penguin, 2002).

Disorder and Early Sorrow. Indeed I do not think it is too far-fetched to read this *novelle* as almost a rite of artistic consecration by which EMB is ordained future priestess of Ocean. Freud was later (1929) to discuss Romain Rolland's idea that "a sensation of 'eternity,' a feeling as of something limitless, unbounded – as it were 'oceanic' is the source of all religious energy."[10] Freud rejects this view in favour of his own theory relating the birth of religious feeling to the child's intra-family experience and indeed infantile sexuality. Thomas Mann's short story, a real happening narrated in fictional dress, centres on the early epiphany of innocent sexuality. This tragi-comic flash-out in turn serves as the manifestation of the supremacy of the Unconscious whenever Collectivity wins over the Individual. (The poetic name of the Unconscious in Mann-ic idiom is Ocean).

Thus *Die Zauberer,* the Magician, took upon his lap the child whom he had begotten at the age of 42 and with his singular consummate art and irony, forged her into an icon. She incorporated, in her unknowing innocence, both the lovable aspect, possibly redemptive, of the emerging future, and also those features of it that appeared to be menacing: the sexual revolution, oriented towards the Leonardesque ideal of androgyny, and the socialist political order.

In *The Oceanic Circle,* EMB quotes her father saying that "the sea, its rhythm, its musical transcendence, somehow is present everywhere throughout my books – even, often enough, when it is not mentioned explicitly."[11] What constituted the Ocean, in Thomas Mann's perspective? Its first essential feature was its Otherness with respect to humanity, its alien character to land-dwelling animals, its incomprehensibility to the limited power of understanding of such "rational" beings as we are. EMB says that: "The ocean provided religious inspiration" for her august father. "The sea was Infinity." It represented "a metaphysical dream (of) extra human magnificence . . . beyond articulation and measure." The two factors of Infinity ("beyond measure" and "beyond articulation"), which constitute the "extra human magnificence" of the Ocean, make it ambivalent. In Thomas Mann's perspective the two attributes could be either divine or diabolical or both at once.

The second central feature of the meaning of the Ocean in her father's work is not explicitly adverted to in his daughter's succinct account that is mainly about the music-ocean correlation. EMB herself refers the reader of *The Oceanic Circle* to "a recent, more complete analysis of Thomas Mann's relationship to the ocean" in a magazine article.[12] But there is hardly any critic of standing who has totally ignored Thomas Mann's marine imagery. Often they have related it to sexual themes; for instance, Andrew J. Webber

10. S. Freud, *Civilization, Society and Religion* (London: Penguin, 1991), p. 251.

11. Borgese (n. 5 above), p. 54.

12. E. Goebel, "Thomas Mann und das Meer," in *Mare,* I. 1, (Hamburg: Dreivierel Verlag, April 1997).

says that Mann's "favoured scene for the leit-motif of illicit desire is the sea . . . The seaside . . . makes a spectacle of the body's exposure for anybody willing to view. It is, in other words, a sort of carnival space, its irregular freedoms available only as a regulated counterpart to social order . . . The rushing noise of the sea recurrently intoxicates Mann's protagonists when they become subject to its ambiguous propulsion . . . A rhythmic displacement over which the intoxicated subject has no control becomes, in the language of dreams, a representation of the ambivalent lure of homosexual desire."[13] Thomas Mann himself wrote in his *Diaries* that the sea had "an aphrodisiacal effect" on him.

The third feature of Thomas Mann's Ocean is its "wildness." There is a beastliness, a brutality about it which is antithetical to domesticated and civilized humanity. Moreover, this savagery is replete with intimations of the death-instinct, *Thanatos,* that Freud associated with aggressivity. The most essential characteristic of the sea for Thomas Mann is its rhythmic repetition. Its ceaseless, undular movement seemed to him the *eschaton* towards which history tended when events repeated themselves cyclically and uncreatively in a negative version of Nietzsche's Eternal Return.

A peculiar evocation of this theme—repetition as incitement to death—occurs on the occasion when the birth of Elisabeth, which had given her father such a sense of firstness, novelty, and originality, was soon afterwards to be repeated by the birth of another child. This theme of similar siblings born in succession, or even worse, of twins, was to haunt EMB, the writer of fiction, no less than it would later haunt Iris Murdoch's novels.[14]

On Saturday, September 28th, 1918 Thomas Mann slipped in an entry into his diary, in which he speaks of EMB in a manner that acted like a delayed action bomb. Its explosive effect was evidently only felt with the publication of the *Diaries* in 1977. Thomas Mann wrote: "A sixth child? There is no great difference between five and six . . . Aside from Katia's health, I really have no objection except that it will subtract something from the experience of 'Lisa' (in a certain sense, my *first* child)."

The person here spoken of as just having been conceived but whose continued existence was being put into question, was eventually called

13. A. J. Webber, "Mann's Man's World: Gender and Sexuality," in *The Cambridge Companion to Thomas Mann,* ed. R. Robertson (Cambridge: Cambridge University Press, 2002), pp. 68–75.

14. Iris Murdoch, an only child, spoke of the frequent and often sinister depiction of twins in her novels as of "a harmless obsession" in a BBC interview with A. S. Byatt on 8.02.68, but, in another interview in 1978 with J. L. Chevalier of the University of Caen, she related the proliferation of twins in her and Sartre's novels to the search for imaginary brothers and sisters, "the lost, the other person one is looking for," in other words to the sense of a partially lost identity, due to deprivation of a complete family, or of the feeling of fully belonging to it and total security within it.

Michael and nicknamed 'Bibi' by his nurse. Michael, when grown up, started upon a musical career but abandoned it in order to become a professor of German Studies at Berkeley. Until 1975, he refused to undertake any business that had anything to do with his father's works. Finally, he agreed to edit a selection from the *Diaries* for the centenary of his father's birth. He felt it was his duty once Erika his elder sister was no longer able to do it.

Inter alia, he read: "Monday September 30th 1918: After supper, telephone conversation with Dr. Faltin on the pregnancy question. Given Katia's moral scruples, he seemed very reluctant to undertake an abortion and reinforced our resolve to let the matter take its course."

Michael on the 14th October 1975 wrote in *his* diary "Here am I an embryo whose abortion had been programmed . . . There was only one reason or almost (why the father contemplated it), that was that another 'little child' would restrict the joy which he relished as a poet in the presence of the little child 'Lisa' (Medi)."[15]

Michael, whose mental condition was already troubled, fell into a deep depression. Even before he read the *Diaries*, which happened only after he had reached the age of 40, he must have had an intimate inkling of the circumstances of his coming into existence. He must have sensed that his mother who, as is clearly indicated in *Disorder and Early Sorrow* and elsewhere, had sought to compensate for the extra tenderness shown by the father to Little-Girl by doing the same to the little boy.

Another more questionable part of the maternal strategy with the same purpose was to fuse the two children together, so that they would appear to be a single human unit: "Two souls with but a single thought, who have all their adventures in common."[16] In *Disorder and Early Sorrow*, the "Little-Girl" actually has a boy counterpart who is exactly like her in appearance, merely of a different sex. It is difficult not to be reminded by this boy-and-girl conjunction of the opening passage of the Epilogue to EMB's *The Ascent of Woman*: "I still remember it as if it had happened yesterday; forty years have passed in the meantime. My little brother (Michael) was two years old, and I was three. We were dressed alike: a sort of Russian blouse, belted, over shorts. We had the same hair-do; bangs, in page fashion: my mother was proud of us. How cute, the guests said. Are they twins? No, one year apart . . . Two little boys? No, a boy and a girl. I still hear the voices ringing in my ear."[17] Also, in a short story, EMB has the mother of twins write in her diary: "Doctor Edgecomb says to separate them: they would grow better he says . . . Yoshi says, they want to be two, but the dasus prevent it (sic) . . . If

15. M. Mann, *Fragmente eines Lebens*, Lebensbericht und Auswahl seiner Schriften von F. C. und S. P. Tubach (München Verlag, Heinrich Ellermann, 1983), p. 121.

16. T. Mann, *Collected Stories* (London: Everyman's Library, 2001), p. 579.

17. E. Mann Borgese, *The Ascent of Woman* (London: Macgibbon and Kee, 1963), p. 211.

they cannot be two, they'll bring on the earthquake . . . Help them be two."[18] EMB obviously felt that her mother's strategy had not resulted quite in the balance restoring that had been its good intention.

There is a moving literary snapshot of EMB and Michael in an article in *Vogue* by Erika. In it she describes that when their father set up house in Stockton Street, Princeton, Michael used to play the violin accompanied by EMB on the new piano that had been bought for her. Erika reports that Thomas Mann applauded their performance and was particularly pleased at the reciprocal understanding that was evident in their joint playing. He thought the private performance could have fittingly been given in public. The text is all the more moving in that although Erika was fully aware of the real foundations of *Disorder and Early Sorrow*,[19] she could not have known the content of the diaries or guessed its secret.

Michael Mann died on the 31st December 1976. That night, he had consumed both alcohol and barbiturates. For Elisabeth, it was a bitter coincidence, rather similar to occurrences in the grotesque short stories she had herself written some 20 years before. Life often imitated fiction, rather than the other way about, as Leonardo Sciascia, the foremost Sicilian admirer of her late husband, has notoriously maintained in famous writings at just about the same time in the mid-seventies.

The intimations of mortality signified by the Ocean's essential repetitiveness were not exclusively conveyed by the fatal similarity of siblings, but also in other ways. For instance, Thomas Mann's special cherishing of his youngest daughter as if she were an epoch-symbolizing work of art implied that she had to undergo an unintended process of isolation and even alienation from the others in the family, a sort of death.[20] This painful experience was not just the inevitable result of receiving a fateful, personal call, but also of the nature of the call: that of confrontation with Otherness, *alias* the far-off Ocean.

There is no mistaking Mann's deep Freudian indebtedness here. The Other, whatever form it takes, is always related to the Unconscious (Sex and Death) in Mann's vision. He associates the Ocean with Nirvana as with Sleep (on which he has written a famous essay) as both approximating to formlessness. The fluidity of the sea implied the relaxation not only of rigid boundaries, but also of individuation.

The "Original" sea for Thomas Mann was the Bay of Luebeck, the city of his childhood. He also had been deeply impressed by the Baltic Sea washing the small town of Travemuende where he spent his childhood summers.

18. E. Mann Borgese, *To Whom It May Concern* (London: Macgibbon and Kee, 1960), pp. 107–08. The American edition was published by Braziller, New York, 1959.

19. E. Mann, *Mein Vater, der Zauberer* (Reinbek: Rowohlt Taschenbuch Verlag, 1999), p. 23.

20. Cf. *Die Meer Frau*, p. 21 and elsewhere where EMB herself gives many other reasons for her "isolation" *en bloc* with Michael from the other, older siblings.

He wrote that if his colours have been found opaque, it may be because of the pale grey hues of the sea in that Northern corner of the world. He also wrote: "The sea is not landscape. It is the experience of . . . nothingness and death."[21]

Hence, in the face of the Ocean, human beings rightly felt "fear and alienation"; if they overcame these feelings, then they would become in its regard the perpetrators of "illicit . . . adventure." Even just by going to the sea in ships, human beings turned it, in Thomas Mann's eyes as in those of the Ancient Classical and Biblical writers, "into the role of road, of highway for travellers"; from "spiritual perspective on eternity," it becomes utilitarian "environment."

The situation at EMB's birth was pictured by Thomas Mann in a manner such that had he been using the biblical-mythical technique that he developed in *Joseph and His Brothers,* it would have fallen naturally into a version of the story of Noah. In fact the drama that he narrated in the story prosaically called *Disorder and Early Sorrow* is a tale of the Family whose domain is flooded by an irrational Ocean.[22]

It was in this satirical short story, rather than in the *Poem* or the *Diaries,* that Thomas Mann made maximum literary use of his then 7-year-old youngest daughter. In the story, as in real life, the disorder of the post-war world invades the citadel of privacy that the distinguished German intellectual's household had been until then. The invasion is double. The inflationary state of the economy (magnified in the newspapers) forces itself inside in the shape of financial constraints. The children of the intellectual magnate likewise bring their friends inside the parents' normally staid home to celebrate a jazz party just as Thomas Mann's elder children, Klaus and Erika, did at the time.

The jazz is described by the narrator in the gently ironic language of a basically unappreciative listener, trying hard however to sympathize with the young enthusiasts of the alien music, even to achieve a degree of empathy with them, to the extent that he is tempted for an instant to dance to it. It appears to have been an Europeanized, white-man's dilution of the Afro-American, hot soul outpourings just then coming, literally, from across the Ocean. Metaphorically, the music seemed to Mann rather to have come *out of* the Ocean, in as much as the Ocean stood for Alterity in itself or for Freud's Unconscious or indeed for anything of analogous uncategorizability.

Most important of all in Mann's outlook, the casting of ocean-sourced and ocean-scale tempestuousness into music becomes, as in Shakespeare's

21. Borgese (n. 5 above), pp. 54–56.

22. "On my fiftieth birthday, the *Neue Rundschau* issued a special number for which a contribution by me was solicited. It was *Disorder and Early Sorrow* . . . which I am inclined to rank among the best of what I have written," quoted from Mann (n. 8 above), p. 59.

Twelfth Night, the "food of love" or rather of sexual turbulence. The main symptom of existential crisis turns out to be not so much the double invasion, the "disorder," as rather "the early sorrow" to which the title of the story alludes. This "early sorrow" is that of the youngest daughter—5 years old—of the great intellectual: she fell in helpless love with a teenager student who "danced" with her at the party! Thus Little-Girl had turned herself into the logo that her father had been looking for after 1918. She enables political disorder to be absorbed within sexual topsy-turvydom. The *Medi* of the story clearly stands as heroine-victim of the transformation of age/gender roles that typifies the more general social, egalitarian revolution at an agonisingly critical juncture in history. Jazz, as the antithesis of classical music, has acted as the diabolic agent of Ocean. Little-Girl's "sorrow" is the natural reaction to the brutishness and inarticulateness of the Other.

On the battlefield that is the Little-Girl's soul, the antagonists are not Freud's titans. It is rather more of a David-Goliath confrontation. The forces grouped under the Family sign appear pigmy-sized in comparison with Ocean. They are the cherishing of privacy and intimacy, the sadness of anticipating the departure of loved ones from home which used always to be felt as that of a minor mode of death, nostalgia for a past that was wishfully thought of as timeless—a poor and paltry army to face the savage, crashing and crushing, elementary power of Ocean.

What was EMB's reaction to the literary creation by her father of the image of herself as battlefield between Family and Ocean? The reference to her father that has been quoted from *The Oceanic Circle* is entirely positive. Some recent writers have accepted such purely eulogistic expressions of filial devotion to her father without question.

The usually well-informed Hans Wisskirchen has written: "After the death of Golo Mann, she carried out the role of representative and spokesman of the Mann *family* more and more often, which led her repeatedly and publicly to protest against the very widespread cliché, according to which Thomas Mann had been a great artist, but a bad *paterfamilias.*"[23] However, it always seemed to me that EMB's account of her response to her father's paraded icon of herself was never simple. Even more, a careful reading of the public statements in defence of the Mann family by EMB, reveals that they ran on the lines that she herself somewhat facetiously parodied in what is probably her most poignant short story. In it, a wretchedly unfulfilled poet pens a verse eulogy of poetic justice in the form of an apologia of the wife who had killed his presumed twin brother, as follows . . . "Extrapolate the facts and intrapolate the systems and differentiate and integrate . . . which is not enough . . . to get the whole, complex infiniplex truth to the

23. H. Wisskirchen, *Thomas Mann et les Siens,* trans. Ph. Legionnet Bartillat, Paris, 2002, p. 173, originally published in German by Rowohlt Taschenbuch Verlag GmbH, 1999 (my translation from the French).

n^{th} power. Somehow no value can be assigned to Guilt in these equations. It whittles down, infinitesimal."[24]

The precise implications of such apologias are not easy to fathom, yet unraveling some of the knots in EMB's relation with her father is a necessary precondition for understanding her basic philosophy and especially the depth of her approach to law of the sea matters.

In *The Ascent of Woman,* EMB herself recalls a traumatic point in her girlhood: she "fell in love, a romantic, unreachable love, and was sent to a psychiatrist." When EMB told this declaredly autobiographical episode in *The Ascent of Woman,* she does not seem to have forgotten that her father had narrated something similar and prototypical in *Disorder and Early Sorrow,* but it seems rather that she wished to balance her father's artistically transfigured account with her own point of view, placing the experienced conflict between institutionalized personal relations and the inner drive to transcend them in a wholly real rather than partly mythified context.

EMB was obviously, at least in retrospect, as deeply shaken by her fully lived inner struggle as her father had been, in however different a way, by its archaic prefiguration. She claims that it took her "about twenty years; a marriage and its end; the raising of daughters, who now are young women;" in order to attain a more peaceful state of mind. Nevertheless her father's picture of herself as the unsuspected importer of deconstructive Chaos into the family stronghold never ceased to haunt her memory. Her instinctive behaviour as a child had been turned by her father's magical art into a paradigm of simultaneous political and sexual revolution. It was as if in her father's eyes she was a sort of miniature version of the grown-up figure of the actor Heizel: a disturbed and disturbing melange of "melancholy" and "make-up," dangerous as a mixture of alcohol and barbiturates. She had been portrayed by her father, at a time when she could not yet read what he wrote, as the herald of the Otherness that was displacing the old world. She was bearer of the apocalyptic image derived by her father from both the Bible and personal experience: Ocean overrunning Earth.

EMB, as late as 1963, could still proclaim: "I believe in rebellion."[25] She stresses that, even as a child, she rejected stereotypes. She certainly did not deliberately set out to become in real life what she was projected as in the icon fabricated by her father. In any case that was evidently no stereotype, if anything a neotype; and if the Magician's strange prophecy turned out to be, as I suspect, largely self-fulfilling, yet she managed to give it a quite original, autonomous, and more constructive turn.

Her writings up to the direct confrontation with the sea beginning roughly in 1968 can be seen as preliminary skirmishes with the three features of the ocean that her father had identified. Alterity was the topic tackled in

24. Borgese (n. 18 above), p. 135.
25. Borgese (n. 17 above), p. 213.

its Protean forms in *To Whom It May Concern*, the "erotic" dimension is explored in *The Ascent of Woman*, the inarticulateness in *The White Snake*. Only thereafter the Child of the Flood who had never ceased to heed her father's warning never to seek to denature Ocean succeeds in going beyond him towards a conversation and conviviality between the polar opposites without sacrifice of authenticity on either side. The vocation she actually accepted was this extraordinary brokerage.

There are striking verbal echoes of Thomas Mann's very words in the typical presentation of Elisabeth's own ideas that I heard her deliver in the first activity that she organised together with me.[26] "The oceans in a way are the most sublime expression on earth of what is extra human, superhuman, indomitable . . . Ivan the Terrible called the ocean 'God's Road'." (The full irony and force of her father's reference to the sea being lowered into the role of a "human road" is likely to be missed if one does not recall Ivan the Terrible's dictum that lies behind it.)

In *The Oceanic Circle*, EMB follows up the quotations from her father by asking whether the apparently utilitarian ideal to which she had dedicated herself, which was precisely establishing a system of management over the ocean even beyond those narrow areas over which human nations had hitherto claimed jurisdiction, would not have seemed abhorrent to her father. She is convinced that it would not. On the contrary, the new law of the sea was intended to curb pollution; to prevent the industrial revolution from ravaging (because it was unthinkable to prevent it from reaching) the ocean depths; to cast a rational order over not the enormity and wildness of the sea, which is impossible, but over the human encroachments and profanation of its profundity and Nirvana-like nature.

That is what one might call "the EMB paradox": the commitment to political activism and the acknowledgement of its limits; the half-sceptical aspiration to a happy synthesis between technology and mysticism; the urge to explore scientifically and exploit economically the resources of the ocean for the prosperity and good governance of all living creatures but always in awe and respect of it as the sign and sacrament of what Wittgenstein called the Enigma. Throughout her contributions to the Ocean governance debate, the most important of its resources remained in her estimation the psychological and the metaphysical.

It is striking that the several erudite writers who have written explicitly about the Mann *family* have had very little to say about her. Their high-priest, Reich-Ranicki, in his prickly critical studies of *Thomas Mann and His Family* only refers to her twice: the first time to report that even when she was still living at her father's home, he often forgot her birthday; the second time, to list her last, apparently in some pecking order of literary distinction, after

26. Malta Summer School, on "Hydrospace and its development for mankind," 28 July–10 August 1969.

Erika, Klaus, Golo, Michael, and Monika, as "the journalist Elisabeth Mann."[27] Hans Wisskirchen is much more generous. He gives a one-page potted biography of her at the end of his book, but none of her books are included in the bibliography, which includes those of her brothers and sisters.[28] The reason for this neglect may well be the difficulty to perceive the relation (which I intend to keep highlighting) between the literary brilliance in the expression of metaphysical insights that appears to be the genius of the Mann family and the pursuit of a New Law of the Sea amid the bureaucratic boredom and sub-Kafkaesque petty politicking of the United Nations.

The family biographers all seem to completely disregard Thomas Mann's pre-portrait of the figure that he supposed EMB was destined to become. With regard to his dramatic picturing of her in a situation of liminality, on the threshold between Family and outer Otherness, they are just iconoclasts. They do not therefore think of enquiring whether she rejected her father's collocation of her on the family mission plan or whether operating within the profile delineated by the Magician was the proper affirmation of her Mann-hood.

Even more mind-boggling is the fact that she does not get much deeper coverage from practically anyone of the members of her family, although almost all of them have written some kind of book, or even a series of books, related to the clan. Of course, practically all of them refer to the infant "Medi" as a sort of marvel, mainly because of her effect on *Die Zauberer.* They are all intrigued by her success in attracting their awesome parent's attention as no other product of his flesh-and-blood or of his personal relations had ever been able to do.

Apart from this tour-de-force that was more her father's doing than her own, she is also spoken of, in tandem with her younger brother Michael, in the hectic days of the move in 1933 from Munich to 'exile' in Switzerland. Golo narrates with his professional historian's literary skill and mannerisms how he accompanied the two young brats and enabled them to change soil.[29] Elder sister Erika narrates mainly in reports to her father how she ensured that Elisabeth continued her schooling, first in the basic humanistic studies

27. M. Reich-Ranicki, *Thomas Mann and His Family,* originally published in German by Deutsche Verlags-Anstalt GmbH, Stuttgart, 1987, English trans. first published by Collins, 1989, edition used here Fontana, 1990, p. 196.

28. Wisskirchen (n. 23 above); Cf. also M. Kruell, *Im Netz der Zauberer, Eine andere Geschichte der Familie Mann,* (Berlin: S. Fischer, 1997).

29. G. Mann, *Erinnerungen und Gedanken: Eine Jugend in Deutschland* (Frankfurt am Main: Fischer, 2001). EMB normally presented herself as cosmopolitan rather than German, but of course occasionally her German origins would emerge declaredly; for instance, she attributed the near-illegibility of her neat-looking but spidery handwriting to having been taught in her childhood to write in Gothic script. Probably, despite her choice to write in English rather than German, there are subtle traces of her origins in her style, as well as in her calligraphy; but I lack the competence to set them out.

and then in music at advanced level, while their father was engrossed in the writing of *Joseph and His Brothers.*

But what a contrast there is between Golo's and Erika's accounts and those I heard viva voce from Elisabeth herself as we walked by the waters of Lake Leman after the Third United Nations Conference on the Law of the Sea (UNCLOS) meetings in Geneva. Then Elisabeth often alluded to her Swiss girlhood, squeezed in between childhood in Munich and access to adulthood in America. At the time I happened to be in semi-exile from Malta, because of the Mintoff government's anti-University (and anti-IOI) policy. She used to smile sympathetically, but enigmatically. She would say that ever since she had undergone the throes of uprooting as a little girl, she knew that on earth there were only different forms of exile to be experienced. She would add with a wicked twinkle in her eye that perhaps there was no home to be found on dry land for living beings; zoologically speaking, we were all immigrants from the sea. Nevertheless, in her brother's and in her sister's rapid allusions to Elisabeth's girlhood ordeals, it is palpable that she was at the time held to be supremely important to the family in some mysterious way.

Then a brusque change occurs. Especially after her marriage, although her image in parental and sibling eyes remains perpetually that of 'Medi', she becomes marginal in the context of the family. No one of her kin seems to have grasped the deep connections between the great themes and concerns that were the common heritage of the Mann Family and her commitment to the concept that the seabed beyond the limits of national jurisdiction was the common heritage of mankind. The only significant exception to this rule was, somehow, her mother Katia who kept following and helping her daughter in those quixotic Ocean endeavours right up to her death in Kilchberg, in 1980, aged 97.[30]

It is impressive that EMB herself says that after her marriage to the elderly Professor Borgese, Erika "became nasty and difficult." This seems to have happened not so much after the suicide of Klaus, which had greatly distressed her, as much as after her unsuccessful attempt to establish a permanent liaison with the conductor Bruno Walter, 30 years her senior. However EMB, always peace-loving in family as in political matters, was extremely joyful when, years later, the broken-down Erika, now miserable and housebound in the family home after her globe-trotting life, was ready to receive again tokens of her younger sister's abiding Mann-clan solidarity. Elisabeth wrote amusing letters to Erika that she sometimes signed 'Dulala' and in which she mocked herself in the style of her sister (addressed affectionately as 'Erimouse'). For instance, on the occasion of the first Hydrospace conference I have just referred to, Elisabeth sent Erika the following limerick:

30. *Meine ungeschriebenen Memoiren,* ed. E. Plessen and M. Mann (Frankfurt: S. Fischer, 1974).

There once was a lady in Malta
Who feared that her forces might falter
She bunzeled a lot
But nowhere she got
't was a fate that no one could alter.[31]

EMB was here accurately reflecting her understanding of the prevailing misunderstanding of the real significance of her "bunzling" (which I take to be a word of the Edward Lear or Lewis Carroll style of vintage). Likewise EMB's letters to Erika from Italy about her "school for dogs" and from India about elephantine as compared to canine scholastic achievements hardly show a trace of the seriousness of her engagement with Self-Other (or Family-Ocean) bridge building, that is of her response to the challenge leveled at her by their Father and unacknowledged by the rest of the Family.

Some critics have noted that parts of the story of the Mann family almost recall the patterns of Greek Tragedy. It may be that the tragic dimension of this family experience—for instance, the marked suicide-proneness—may itself have suggested the basic image of the kinship structure being overrun by a fatally manipulated Ocean or perverse divinity, as the Atreids were. EMB of course refused to be a merely unconscious actor in such a drama, but looked to the Ancient Greek world itself for suggestions of a way out. In Classical Antiquity, indeed the ideal seems to have been to transcend the collective family destiny through the institution of a non-tribal, that is, non-family, *polis* or citizen-based democratic power structure. It seems that EMB actually sought to resort to the marriage mechanism to become part of a more professional involvement in politics as a move towards the same kind of liberation that the Ancient Greeks sought to achieve from family Fate. Eventually she came to the conclusion that establishing literally a truly democratic ocean regime was paradoxically the least slippery stepping stone to the universal good governance that she saw as the only possible salvation from the thralls of flesh-and-blood in its negative aspects.

Becoming a Borgese: Mediterranean Cruising

EMB, without ceasing to be a Mann, became a Borgese. She has written that, after her father, the man who most influenced her thinking was her husband, Giuseppe Antonio. He was a Sicilian self-exiled in Chicago whom she married in 1939, when he was 57 and she 21, and who died suddenly in 1952. When she moved into her husband's "princely" embrace, the young Mrs. Borgese in the interest of marital understanding, had now to learn to

31. Quoted from Holzer (n. 4 above), p. 187.

see the world with eyes peering in the twilight of life, under the declining suns of the Romantic Self and of the Nation-State.

She was almost forced to perceive a very differently coloured sea than she had been accustomed to. Her father, inspite of the Baltic nature that had always remained for him the essential characteristic of Seaness, had certainly also sought to describe the "other" sea, the Mediterranean. It stood to the Baltic as South to North. The Mediterranean is depicted not only obviously as part of the background to such masterpieces as *Death in Venice,* but also as the subject of *ex professo* autobiographical essays, such as 10 pages of "travel notes" that appeared for the first time in a magazine in 1925 and are now reprinted in the 1983 Fischer edition of *Ueber mich sellst.* Here Thomas Mann speaks, for instance of the "sober and clean Hamburg atmosphere" that prevailed on board the trim cruise-liner, "a veritable godsend after the exotic extravaganzas (of the Mediterranean spaces) into which it had borne you."[32] The Mediterranean is a sophisticated and overnavigated fringe, untypical of the Ocean in itself. A somewhat different picture of it naturally lived in the mind of EMB's Sicilian husband, partly analogous and partly antithetical.

Notably enough, G. A. Borgese too had written realist-mythic novels and short stories. One of the most celebrated of the short stories is called "The Sea." It speaks of an employee in a bureaucratic job who dreams and actually plans to take a holiday by the sea instead of in the mountains, as usual with the Milanese. In fact, the Sea is a much more eloquent emblem of Alterity than the Mountain. He spent months picturing himself swimming as though it were a ritual of re-birth and a symbolic retrieval of his childhood past. He also spent time contemplating his return from the experience by the sea rejuvenated and ready to face the future with the optimism of the twice-born.

He daydreamed that the firm that employed him was a fisherman's net, and he a fish caught in it, seeking to find a vent through which to escape.

> O Great God of the sea and liberty! . . . Trembling all over, suddenly, I realise that my whole body from snout to tail, is immersed, submerged in the water. Stupendous depths, rocks covered with curly manes, silken algae on which I could voluptuously sidle for an instant on my shiny and white belly, intermediate zones where the afternoon light has the delicacy of dawn! And what an aroma of salt and procreative activity invades my lungs and nostrils, makes me open wide my eyes, sharpens my scales and polishes them one by one! There is a deep silence, but this odour has the force of thunder, of a powerful, confused and incessant sound, capable of stunning you. But how can human beings be complacent about and not disgusted with their earthy, unctuous and

32. T. Mann (n. 8 above), p. 82.

> revolting smells? What is more insipid and disheartening than the perfume of a rose? More cadaveric than the stink of earth after rain, the stink of a can of worms.[33]

He went to the theatre, drawn by the poster for a play the name of which was: "The Lady of the Sea." The leading lady uttered the following words: "I believe that if human beings live at sea, or perhaps in the sea – we would be more fulfilled. Not only better, but also happier." The hero of the tale could not help yelling out, in the silence, "You're right!", but he was shush-shushed by the fans of the great actress who was playing the Lady of the Sea. (Would Borgese have believed a gypsy if she had told him that a book about his future wife would have just that title?)

On the day of departure, however, the hero of Borgese's story cannot find the key to the house he had rented by the sea. After a great flurry of searches and fruitless enquiry, he ends up spending his vacation in his Milanese flat. Nevertheless, he feels that his imaginary experience of the sea had proved to be more beautiful than the actual experience could possibly have been!

G. A. Borgese's masterpiece is, however, undoubtedly the full-length novel, *Rubé* (1921). Filippo Rubé, the protagonist of the novel, is a young Sicilian who looks upon war at its outbreak in 1914 as some sort of drug that would release all the frustrated ambitious young men like him from the claustrophobia generated in them by the closed society of early 20th century South Europe. Rubé, however, is soon rejected by the war machine and retires, wounded in more senses than one, to a bureaucratic job in industrialised Milan. The plot becomes very complex but it only serves to exhibit the Romantic Self reduced to wreckage. The novel evolves more in terms of images that act in the novel rather like the leit-motifs in Wagner's music. One of the major recurrent images is that of the Sea. It stands most often for, more simply than in Mann, Alterity as destiny. The most decisive event in Rubé's life is when he takes a girlfriend out on a boat and, by a unfortunate set of circumstances, she drowns. The Sea features as the gigantic grave into which the Romantic Self topples. Rubé, in a last desperate search to find himself, returns to his Sicilian native village; the result is the opposite: he undergoes a psychological regression away from individuality. In his own words, he drowns in the "wetness of life" back in the Great Mother's womb.

Another leit-motif is that of music itself, particularly if played on the violoncello. As in Schopenhauer, music in Borgese's novel appears as the image of the will peacefully resigned to the alienating Destiny of which the sea appears as the embodiment. Through these images, the psychological analysis is integrated with a political vision. Filippo, in his delirium, proclaims himself a victim of society, a martyr, and dreams up a project of

33. G. A. Borgese, *La Città Sconosciuta* (Milano: Mondadori, 1924), pp. 200–01.

universal governance to be drawn up by "failures" of his own ilk. It happened, of course, that Borgese in his American self-exile, at the time when he formed his partnership with Elisabeth Mann, was working on the "Preliminary Draft of a World Constitution" (1948), which he regarded as his masterpiece and EMB as the foundation and permanent framework of her own political thought. There can be no doubt that she welcomed Pardo's dimly delineated concept of the Common Heritage of Mankind with such enthusiasm only incidentally because of its initial application to the sea, but essentially because it seemed to be a possible realistic first step to the system of world governance passionately excogitated by Giuseppe Antonio Borgese, together with some others.

Only a few years ago, when we met at a UNESCO meeting in Agrigento, (*Multaqa Mediterranéen,* 17–18 September, 1998), Elisabeth told me how deeply she had been impressed by her husband's self-identification with a fish caught in a net and at the astonishing empathy with which he described the sensations of the fish escaping back into the Ocean. It was not insignificant that her father maintained that you could only see the essential sea from a viewpoint on shore, not from a ship; and was not an islander's a necessarily rather similar viewpoint to that from a ship? A viewpoint that did not allow a decent, perspectival distance. A viewpoint that arose from within the oceanic ambit itself and hence induced an excess of subjective involvement.

In *The Oceanic Circle,* EMB quotes from her father's curious reflections on this score in *Crossing the Atlantic with Don Quixote.* (Cervantes was chosen by Thomas Mann as the just-in-time reading at the moment of self-exile. The outmagicked Magician is here carrying out the same journey as accomplished by Jazz in *Disorder and Early Sorrow,* but in the reverse direction.)[34] Golo confirms his father's exclusively shore-based "love" of the sea, in a blasé description of his father's discomfort when a breeze ruffled the surface of the lake on the very exceptional day on which he had taken Medi with him for a boat-ride.[35] G. A. Borgese's image of the Sea was much more thoroughly Romantic, especially in his manner of picturing its engulfing, tomb-like embrace in *Rubè.* Like Thomas Mann (and probably influenced by reading him), his Sicilian admirer associates the Sea intimately with *thanatos,* but not so much because of any abstract perception of repetitious undularity as much as because of familiarity with the sudden rise of wind and storm in the Mediterranean, and its implacable moods.

Borgese, born in 1882 near Palermo, began his university career with a thesis on the history of romantic criticism that already illustrates his deep grasp of the Romantic Self and its dissolution. (EMB always spoke of her relation to her husband as "deeply romantic.") He then was for most of his

34. Cf. T. Mann, *Meerfahrt mit Don Quixote* (Berlin: S. Fischer, 1934). E. Mann Borgese (n. 5 above), p. 55.

35. G. Mann (n. 29 above), p. 513.

life a professor of German literature, first in Italy, then in the United States. One of his major critical interests was Thomas Mann. The innate affinity between the two is as clear as the temperamental contrast. One of Borgese's earliest studies is entitled *Mefistofele* (1911); it explores the Faustus theme long before it was taken up by Thomas Mann.

Borgese was a firm antifascist, as indeed all violence was alien to him and, finding himself on a lecture tour in the United States in 1931 when an oath of loyalty was required from all university professors by the Fascist government, he refused to take it and decided to stay in the United States. He taught in California from 1932 to 1936 and in Chicago afterwards.

It has been frequently noted that Thomas Mann speaks respectfully of G. A. Borgese in his *Diaries* at first, but after a certain point he ends up almost calling him names (e.g., "chauvinist Italian"). EMB replied to this kind of comment saying that there never were profound intellectual differences between the two men, but only petty tensions rooted in such personality differences as emerged in their contrasting performances before the ladies in the intellectual salons of California and Chicago. EMB gives several curious instances of Mann-Borgese discord, (for example, that her father "flirted aesthetically" with the Catholic Church, while her husband did it with freemasonry), but brings up neither the marriage circumstances nor any later crisis in her married life. EMB found that Mediterranean-type, sudden squalls often disturbed the domestic Borgese waters and even created a turbulent atmosphere somewhat suffocating in comparison with the cool, Baltic originated airs in which she had grown up. For instance, EMB said that it was only very rarely that she spoke with her father about serious matters. She could only recall one occasion in her lifetime when she had a real conversation with him. It was on his 70th birthday, when she had turned up at the celebratory party after having already had a few drinks. On that unique day, she recalled having argued brilliantly with him. On all other occasions, she had just enjoyed listening. It was obviously not the same with her husband, an extrovert and indefatigable talker, who expected answers to his provocations and their formulation with rhetorical skills of quite unMannian type.

Her mother seems to have played the decisive role in finding a solution: it consisted of the Borgeses leaving America (where McCarthyism still flourished and the Korean and the Vietnam wars were brewing) and starting a new life in Italy centered more on culture and music than politics.

After 1946, with Elisabeth and their two daughters, Borgese although teaching in Milan, lived mostly in his beloved Tuscany. (Elisabeth has written a splendid article describing their setting up a summer house closer to the sea than Florence in Forte dei Marmi; the house—the first of any she had lived in that was to her own tastes—was praised in Italian architectural journals as a minor masterpiece).

Yet there is no doubt that Borgese's deepest interest (shared in an impressive way by EMB) was in *Sicilitudine*, that is, the defining features of being

Sicilian. This was, of course, before the great debate between Giuseppe Tommasi di Lampedusa's interpretations of the decadence of Sicily as due to the sheer anachronism of the nobility and Sciascia's holding that it was due to the ordinary Sicilian's gut-feeling that the identity of their island was that of the Valley of Death. Borgese's stance seems to anticipate Sciascia rather more than *Il Gattopardo.* In one of EMB's short stories, there occurs this snippet of conversation between two Americans: "That Sicilian woman who came in to clean up . . . she was tiny and black and her eyes stung. I still hear the click of her clogs and she kept hissing at me *ammazzalo,* you should kill him." "Sicilians are quick at that." EMB is satirizing American cliché mongering, but also recognising the centrality of death in Sicilian culture. For Borgese, Sicily was lapped by the waters of death. A style of life had developed there that was as anti-natural as, for Mann, to live perpetually on a ship.

Naturally because we, in Malta, are the Sicilians' closest neighbours, and we define ourselves largely through distinction from them, I always listened with ears pricked and extended to donkey length when Elisabeth conveyed her impressions of Sicily. She visited Palermo many times, usually in connection with commemorative celebrations in honour of her husband. She took immense interest (purely academic, of course) in the political methodologies of a (Sicilian) *mafioso* type as opposed to the (Florentine) Machiavellian type. I always assumed, very stupidly, that Elisabeth used to relay to me and others slightly transmogrified versions of her husband's understanding of *Sicilitudine.* I now realise that what she gave me were always her own personal interpretations of history: the problem with Sicily in her view was that it had lost its "island" status (sea-determined national *habitus*) and been "integrated" unnaturally with the continental landmass, with its corresponding regime, inappropriate to Sicily.[36] She always added that we Maltese should take it as a warning. Like Rubé's and Borgese's, EMB's central concern always transcends *Sicilitudine*: it is the question of man's immanence or transcendence with respect to nature. She wanted to bring some Baltic shade and shadow into an excessively solar heated sphere.

Borgese's literary style may well have been his most profound influence on his wife's writings. It is characterized by a very sharply clear architecture, which, because of its classical delineation, allows the writer to indulge in all sorts and any amount of internal meanderings without danger of the reader getting lost or losing sight of the wood for the trees.

36. It may be noted here that in 1961 EMB edited a volume of *Testimonianze Americane sull' Italia del Risorgimento,* and she had a thorough knowledge of what the unification of Sicily to mainland Italy had truly meant to Sicily from the point of view of prosperity (although Sicily had been subject to exploitative foreign domination of one kind or another for centuries). A confessed or unconfessed desire for the independence of the island had played a part both in the rise of the phenomenon of banditry and in some related Mafia developments. EMB devotes also 11 pages of analysis of the Italian situation in *The Ascent of Woman.* She spoke Italian fluently and remained fascinated until the end by the culture of the whole peninsula, so closely bound to the surrounding sea, as well as by its adjacent islands.

Elisabeth's husband was obviously not only a scholar who had an extraordinarily empathic understanding of her father's work and became his collaborator in such team-productions as *The City of Man*,[37] but also in some ways served as a substitute for him. In his *Diaries*, Thomas Mann first notes that he heard of Elisabeth's "relationship" with "Borgese, who wishes to marry her," not directly from her, but only from his wife Katia on their quasi-ritual daily walk together. Some 2 months later, he noted that he had received a letter from his elder daughter, Erika, "concerning her visit to Borgese and the marriage idea." His comments are typically terse: "Poignant and strange."[38]

Strange? Surely he must have remembered the episode of Elisabeth taken "out of her brother's arms" and danced with (by the absolutely charming-looking) Herr Hergesell . . . "It looks very comic."[39] And later of her "trying to hold" him "by his coat" when he goes dancing with (another) Fräulein with her father trying "to catch up his little sweetheart as she passes and draw her to him", but E. eluding him, "almost peevishly to follow her fancy"[40]; of her "suffering . . . without understanding and so also without restraint"; and then of Herr Hergesell (now turned, in Papa's eyes, into his true semblance of undergraduate gnome) appearing in Elisabeth's bedroom, "obviously quite pleased with his role of swan knight and fairy prince." Is it not strange that the master novelist used to describe the same pattern of events repeating itself in people's lives without any discernible causal framework determining the recurrence, and yet found it strange that a young girl who once fell in love with a man who in age could have been her father, would do it again? Had he not himself made Herr Hergesell tell Elisabeth "You're all right! Just as you are . . . You've only got to grow up."[41]

Poignant? Not the usual adjective to be applied to the sound of wedding bells! Most people would tend to find it more appropriate to something like the plaintive wail of wave breaking after wave on a rocky coast. Perhaps the virtual bell ringing on this occasion imbued the mind of the "Ironic German" with the always somewhat eerie feeling of the *dejà entendu*. The depth of the poignancy came from perhaps the endlessly spinning, humming waters in a whirlpool, the oceanic clamour of recurrent waves, the perennial echo of *La Ronde*.

According to Erika, Elisabeth told her that she regretted having to choose one man as a husband, since she was also attracted, although much less "romantically" than by Borgese, to the Austrian writer Hermann Broch (1886–1951). He was soon to become the author of the celebrated political-musicological novel *The Death of Virgil*, a masterpiece with some analogies to Thomas Mann's *Doctor Faustus*. Broch was at the time aged 53, again a

37. F. Aydelotte, G. A. Borgese and W. A. Neilson (Committee of Fifteen), *The City of Man* (New York: Viking Press, 1940).
38. Mann (n. 6 above), p. 326.
39. Mann (n. 16 above), pp. 587–88.
40. Ibid., p. 594.
41. Ibid., p. 600.

sort of father figure/substitute. Can one say that, in these years, EMB was confronting Alterity in the form of elderliness? In her youthfulness, she was surely learning a lot about the apparent importance of the time-factor in human lives by contrast with the apparent timelessness of the Sea. And yet already now, as much as later, her dominant urge is to bridge the gap.

Perhaps the most surprising and illuminating reflection on the matter comes obliquely from EMB herself. Her *Ascent of Woman* has an Epilogue, entitled "My Own Utopia." In this very personal Utopia, children are born sexless. Then "between the ages of eighteen and twenty, when their primary education is completed, they will *all* grow to be *women.*" As women they will spend 4 years doing conscripted work. Afterwards "the women will also be ready to found families." Where will the men come from?, Elisabeth herself asks on the reader's behalf. The answer is: "When the children in a family have all grown into young women, . . . then, of course comes the moment for a woman to grow and mature into *manhood.* The transition will be smooth and spontaneous. The woman, who is now about forty five years old . . . will grow into the position of a man; she will become a man."[42]

In order to render this surrealist Utopia less implausible in appearance, Elisabeth quotes instances of animals, such as snails of the genus *Crepidula,* who after an asexual beginning, become first male and finally female. She also mentions that change of sex is common among "a good many kinds of fish–our closest relatives." Moreover she quotes Nietzsche, in *Human All too Human* suggesting that every man in his twenties should marry an older experienced woman and only in his late thirties a young girl, as well as St. Augustine speculating on whether women will not resurrect as men. She quotes many other writers who in different ways prospect the transcendence of sexual differences (although oddly enough she does not quote the most famous and brilliant upholder of the view she discusses, namely Leonardo Da Vinci).

If this Utopia seems to throw light on why Thomas Mann felt that his favourite daughter's marriage proposal in 1939 was "poignant and strange," the most bizarre element in EMB's account of her Utopia is that it explicitly derives its main inspiration from the example of "a good many kinds of fish – our close relatives." Here once more, well before EMB's concentration of her energies on the law of the sea (beginning roughly at the age of 50), she keeps uncannily thinking of the Ocean as the scene where the anticipation of the eschatological future of humanity was being enacted "in a glass darkly."

Attuning Elisabeth Veronica: Only One Ocean

Her official name was Elisabeth Veronica. The name of the daughter of a novelist who treats her almost like one of his own characters is a kind of

42. Mann Borgese (n. 17 above), pp. 219–21.

dedication. "Elisabeth" was quickly shortened into "Lisa," but this affectionate abbreviation was soon eclipsed by the nickname "Medi": the word in the Bavarian dialect for "Little-Girl." Henceforth the second name "Veronica" is never used except for very official purposes but Elisabeth is transformed into "a true icon." She is treated almost as if she were an allegorical figure, a type rather than an individual, almost an abstraction, just the pretty personification of "Little-Girlhood."

Her acidly-tongued, cabaret-star elder sister Erika occasionally appended a cadenza to the Little-Girl sobriquet: Medi became "Medulala"[43] or even disappeared into an expanded and exalted form of the cadenza on its own: "Princess Dulala."[44] This elevation of Elisabeth to the ranks of Ubuesque royalty occurs in a letter by Erika to her father 3 days after the 21-year-old Elisabeth married G. A. Borgese: it is a sort of prize awarded to Little-Girl for stubbornness. The title seems to combine the sound of the budding Little-Girl musician tiresomely practising *solfeggio* with a romantic echo of dark Africa. Partly to keep up in my own mind the memory of this nominal reduction of a person into a cipher, I decided to refer to her as EMB, unless there was some special reason for doing otherwise and although at the Headquarters of the International Ocean Institute in Malta, everybody, including of course myself, practically always called her Elisabeth.

It was only after the death of her husband that EMB began to publish her own literary works. But during the long period of public silence (until she was past 30), she had kept drinking at the bittersweet wellsprings of music. This deep immersion in the world of sound as organised by the master composers of the Baroque and Romantic ages may have been as important a factor, in EMB's unconscious apprenticeship in preparation for her future act as the "Ocean-Lady," as her father and her husband had certainly been.

In silence, she harkened. She heard the angels sing, the demons moan and yelp. She heard the patriarchal Bach creating harmony out of contrasting melodies, the infant prodigy Mozart burying the cries of agony beneath the brilliance of waves dancing on the surface and manic-depressive Schumann extracting a questing mysticism out of his mental illness. This trio of composers were to be equally important points of reference when EMB came to face the choice between alternate worlds and sought to do it with as much autonomy and social responsibility as humanly possible.

The music she learnt to most appreciate was that in which individual voices or instruments could still produce a deeply consonant harmonic effect, even if they seemed to move superficially at cross-purposes. The composers she admired most were those who presented visions of "another" world than that of possessive individualism, a world in which a sense of community was realised through the harmonisation of a plurality of independent motives.

43. E. Mann (n. 19 above), p. 155.
44. Ibid., p. 141.

In *The Ascent of Woman*, she wrote "I wanted to be a musician. I was full of music and I worked hard."[45] She often repeated, especially after she was appointed a Professor of Political Science at a very distinguished Canadian university in 1980, that the only academic training she had ever received was in music. She regarded this training in music as having laid in her an excellent disposition for her life-work in ocean politics.

I have already quoted part of her commentary on her father's confession in an occasional essay that "the sea and music (had) entered a sentimental union" in his heart. No such simple fusion was possible in the heart of EMB. The relationship between Music and Ocean was much too complex to allow it. The attention she devoted to Schenker's theory of musical analysis in the course of translating it had resulted in her conviction of the rightness of his assault against antiharmonic contemporary music. At the time her father had not, of course, conceived his Faustus book, which was written after EMB had already left him to Erika's dedicated secretarial assistance, and EMB was independently clarifying her own feelings.

Full awareness of the deep music-ocean rapport is shown in *The Oceanic Circle.* An enthusiastic eulogy of Debussy's *La Mer* is the culmination of a two-page disquisition on the history of music's conciliatory approach to the otherness of the Ocean.[46] In these dense pages, she examines briefly those musical compositions that mimic the sound of the sea as the objective correlative of the tempestuous passions that surge in the human heart as well as of their irregular alternations with rarer moments of calm or indifference. But she leaves the question open in her reader's mind: was just that the whole aim of the Romantic composers and, more notably, of Wagner in *The Flying Dutchman*? (Surprisingly, she does not note that Wagner had borrowed the figure of pairs of undulating pitches in his famous overture from Mozart's *Così fan tutte*, Act I, the trio *Soave sìa il Vento.*)

In reality, as her father had observed, it is not the ability of music to echo the sound of the sea as an analogue to psychological experience that is the deepest reason for their affinity. It is rhythm. Essentially both the sea and music are made of waves. Sound is physically just undulating energy; holistically, it is the way in which a part of our body which evolution has specialized for the task, the ear, captures and transfers undular movements from outside to within ourselves. Conversely, the sea is the most visible expression available to our eye of movement in waves.

In Thomas Mann's first great novel, *Buddenbrooks*, as A. J. Webber says, the sea is seen not as "endless protean variety, but as brazenly copying itself . . . The narrative (itself) simulates the work of mimesis, actually reproducing verbatim the earlier reproductions of its own copybook. The sea is described as a shiny and metallic surface . . . This prepares it for reflection and repro-

45. Mann Borgese (n. 17 above), p. 212.
46. Mann Borgese (n. 5 above), pp. 52–54.

ducibility . . . The leit-motif of the sea is thus established as a framework for human scenarios of repetition" that takes Mann back to the sea.[47]

Repetition is not just an element needed for the construction of rhythm and hence for the forging of the most intimate bond between sea and music, but also, as Kierkegaard emphasized, repetition is the essence of sin. (Adam's original sin was the desire to be not just like God, but His exact replica.) In Thomas Mann if, as EMB says, the sea was "beyond articulation" (*ungegliederter Raum*), in Webber's words, it "represents both the morally unspeakable and the radical poetic resistance to articulate discourse." It has already been indicated that Thomas Mann regularly associates this inarticulateness with the impression of intoxication that is often induced in the sea-borne. Notably in his *Gesang vom Kindchen*, the poem that he wrote for Elisabeth, Mann alludes to a drunken sailor song when discussing *Death in Venice*.

Elisabeth knowing of my interest in the subject used frequently to send me notes about sea-music and its place in her father's philosophy. From these notes it was clear that their joint understanding went well beyond the significance given to it by the Romantics and also beyond that implied by Debussy, namely that the good life, as was first hinted at by Heraclitus, is life in tune with the rhythms of nature. The sea is also, I understood Elisabeth to be saying, in echo of her father, a reminder that no human endeavour can be undertaken without a background of noise, that there is a chaotic rumble that is a perennial foil to our auditory perception of the world, that there is a voracious bog, which is at the same time a creative spring, at the dark deep bottom of the well of language, that there is a never-lifting fog hanging out tirelessly on the outskirts of our conversation; and that is where the sources of light and poetry are usually concealed and occasionally revealed. But thirdly, and here one could hear Elisabeth's most individual accent, or rather the voice of the Elisabethan sea: not the silence of death, nor the noise of Chaos, but the music of reconciliation and liberation.

SEAS OF ALTERITY

EMB's first three books present three forms of "the Other": totally irreconcilable, totally reconcilable, and limitedly reconcilable.

Amid the Shoals of the Antihuman

EMB first tried her hand at creative work, apart from musical performance, with a collection of nine short stories, written a few years after she became

47. Webber (n. 13 above), p. 69.

a widow (1952). The shortest of them is only six pages long and the longest, 32. The first impression is, therefore, one of great disparity. A hint that this impression might be fake is given by the division of the book into three parts indicated by the Roman numerals I (4 stories), II (3 stories), III (2 stories). The parts are not given any subtitles. I make bold to suggest some, in order to highlight the fact that, throughout the book, EMB is exploring Otherness, when it is of human making.

Part I *Divinely Ambitious Humanity*. Practically all the stories in the book turn out to be about counterproductive attempts at producing heaven on earth. The first set of four seems to conjure up one aspect after another of *collectivist* Utopias. The first is about human beings trying to re-mould animal nature to get more out of the animals. The second is about the ominous prospect for humanity of the humanization of machines. The third concerns programmed immortality or cheating death of its empire through imitating frozen fish. The fourth is about moulding one's eternal self in a laboratory that is a sort of antiheaven, a cosmetic parlour in which humans seek to receive individual fixed identities by stereotyped methods. It begins to appear at this stage that the stories that initially appeared to be totally disconnected are rather more like the chapters in a sequential book.

Part II might, I suggest, have been called *The Repetitious Universe.* It conjures up an aspect per story of the self-reversals of individualistic society, or a variation on William Golding's "Satan is Entropy" theme. Part III could be called: *Graal Quests in Hallucinated Landscapes.* The two very complementary episodes illustrate the illusoriness of Utopias.

EMB was to name the calculatedly happy sounding epilogue of *The Ascent of Woman* "My Own Utopia." Before writing it, in *To Whom it May Concern* EMB had taken Utopian, Antiutopian, or Distopian thinking through the crucible of her critical imagination.

The title *To Whom It May Concern* (from now on: *TWIMC*) is in fact that of the second (which happens to be also the shortest) story. The bureaucratic formula is used as such in the heading of the story but acquires an ironic dimension, rhetorically implying that it is *all* who should be concerned, when transposed and elevated to the heading of the whole volume. It is perhaps an interesting irony that, in order to avoid using the phrase "Common Heritage of Mankind," as originally proposed by Malta, the United Nations General Assembly decided to refer to climate change as a matter of "common concern."

Indeed the tone of all EMB's stories is calculated to raise concern in all human beings. They reflect the climate of the time when they were published between 1955 and 1958. Fear of a nuclear holocaust was at its apocalyptic height. Despite the defeat of Nazism, Thomas Mann's "fear that evil may become universal, with no way out or refuge for the human mind" (22.5.1940) was still unexorcized.

Splurges of Chaos

The first story of part I of *TWIMC* is called *The Rehearsal* (suggesting a trial run for a happening put in Hitchcockian suspense). Its beginning recalls the book of *Genesis*. There, Adam names all the animals, which in Biblical parlance means determines their essence. In EMB's story, human beings are seen trying to redefine the nature of the ape. Human beings have always when trying philosophically to define their own nature taken animals as the Other that enabled them to solve their identity problem at least negatively, by showing distinctly what the nonhuman was. In EMB's story, human beings are seen trying almost to abolish the distinction between themselves and the Other by inducing an ape to conduct an orchestra of human players.[48] The obvious risk in this enterprise is that of themselves becoming the Other, instead of vice-versa.

This attempt at redoing Adam's initial and perhaps not altogether successful naming exercise in turn recalls the eschatological vision of the Prophet Isaiah: "The wolf will share a dwelling place with the lamb and the leopard lie down with the kid of a goat, the ox and the lion cub will graze together and the young boy will herd them" (Chap. II, V.6). Here the Otherness between animals and humans, especially the young, is almost obliterated; they merge into one community as the different families of musical instruments join in producing a single harmonious sound. In EMB's story, the place of Isaiah's young boy as leader is taken by the ape quite naturally because the herd is composed of humans. Unfortunately it all ends with the members of the orchestra mutilating themselves and each other and the ape trainer firing pistol shots under a cloud of tear gas. The moral of the story seems to be that Earth and Ocean cannot be reconciled except in chaos, if not on the day prophesied by Isaiah.

The ape normally extracts a collectively superb performance from the orchestra until a mistake is made. Then the ape reverts to brutishness, not having acquired understanding of such graces as forgiveness or redemption. The picture of the ape given here shows human anticipation of inordinately greater perfectibility than EMB remotely envisaged in her later personal endeavours at teaching a chimpanzee to type or a dog to play the piano, but there is also much less—although quite a lot—of Franciscan brotherly feeling for the beast on the narrator's part.

How surreal are the imagined events? Obviously, realistic details abound. There is disagreement among animal trainers as to whether chimpanzees are naturally musical and in particular as to whether they have a sense of rhythm. L. Heck in 1985, tentatively suggested that: "It is not impossible that the natives (of the Kamerun received) the first impulse to their

48. In *The White Snake* (n. 1 above), EMB reports "that in Marineland, Florida, a chorus of dolphins sings, in a siren-like fashion, to the waving of a baton." p. 12.

method of drumming . . . from the drumming and stamping practised by chimpanzees."[49] More confidently, R. M. Yerkes of Yale University, perhaps the greatest expert on apes in history, wrote in 1929 that "Fondness for music or at least for rhythm was exhibited . . . chimpanzees would dance about, keeping time to music and showing appreciation of rhythmic sounds." This ability is denied however, by others, such as Leonard Williams, who has been both a professional musician and a keeper of monkeys at the zoo.

However, verisimilitude is not the issue in EMB's story. The ape is a sort of minor Neptune. The brute has the ability to acquire the mastery of the kind of eternal repetitiousness that Thomas Mann had evoked as negative "oceanic feeling," but the same incapacity as the sea to tolerate the 'illicit' adventures of human beings in its regard.

Incidentally after the ape's second fiasco we are told that it "was sent back to Yerkes Laboratory" from where it had come. The composition that the orchestra was performing was unsurprisingly enough, given that the musical *forte* of apes is supposed to be rhythm: Ravel's *Bolero*, obviously because of its obsessive reiterations. For the same reason, it is perhaps the piece of music that is most evocative of the repetitious aspect of the sea that Thomas Mann had been particularly struck by. As a rendering of this abstract figure out of the rich repertoire of features that make up the sea's complex identity, it is inevitably much more effective than Debussy's comprehensive attempt, perhaps the most successful in the history of music, at giving a holistic image of the sea. Less significantly but equally impressively, EMB's account of the reaction to the ape's missing the entry of the second violinist sounds very like accounts of the sort of reaction that took place historically at the first performance of Stravinsky's *Rites of Spring.* "Human emotions and sensations became small in the face of his (the ape's) passion. There was the jungle and there was the universe . . ."[50]

The story is told (as is the greater part of the book, which despite the apparent discontinuities, is given in this way a certain stylistic unity) as if by an omniscient but rather humble and quiet-voiced narrator. He reports in an unflurried and unhurried mode the introspective musings and then the doings of a violinist in the orchestra who is called Willem de Foe. This character slowly emerges as the undefeated enemy of human attempts to monkey about with the course of evolution and as a living negation of the increasingly culturally dominant self-portrait of man as the naked ape. He is almost a glorified form of Winston at the end of Orwell's *1984.* The twin perspective in which the perception of the indifferent, quietly passive narrator and that of the character who is quietly active in opposition to the invasive alternate world, enables EMB to give the reader the feeling both that the narrative

49. This and the subsequent quotation are taken from L. Williams, *The Dancing Chimpanzee* (London: Allison and Busby, 1980), pp. 54–55.

50. Mann Borgese (n. 18 above), p. 20.

is objective and that he is also being given at least one subjective moral evaluation. The technique is typically Mannian.

If the animal kingdom is given as the Other to Humanity on the same basis that the Ocean is the Earth's Other, it is a different sort of Otherness with which machines confront man—and woman, especially sign processors, because the machines unlike the animals are man-made with in-built man-made definitions. As among animals the closest to humans is the ape, so among machines the robot is closest to its human maker. Human fear of rebellion and deposition from the throne of power has been mostly directed towards robots or so called automata. But although she was writing in the fifties, EMB realized that it is the machines most directly involved in the semiotic process (precisely because of their key role in linguistic exchanges) that are the most likely to be felt by human beings to be threatening in the postindustrial information age.

The second story in *TWIMC* is just a letter written by a machine on its own behalf requesting employment from a firm of humans. The promissory content of the letter sounds, of course, more than a bit like Mephisto asking for the honour of serving humans; he is sure that the service given to them will serve him as a stepping stone towards achieving lordship over his entrapped lords, in a kind of Hegelian Master-Slave dialectic blocked in one step.

The image of the literate typewriter that itself authors the letters typed by it seems to be an imaginary ancestor *both* of the computers quite plausibly supposed really capable of tomorrow becoming generators of other computers *and* of the peculiarly individualized typewriter uniquely produced by Olivetti for EMB's dog, Arli, (short for Arlecchino, Harlequin, because of his patched fleece). The machine is illustrated photographically in *The White Snake* and looks indeed like some monstrous insect worthy of being a protagonist in some Ambrose Bierce or Edgar Allan Poe literary concoction.[51]

On the face of it, EMB's anthropomorphically self-operating Typewriter would appear to be an extreme example of Henri Bergson's idea of the essence of laughter—provocation—the miscegenation of organic and mechanical. Of course, whether one laughs or not, depends on how distant or close to reality one considers the Ascent of the Machine to be today, taking into account the succession of the mechanical by the electronic age already recorded in the annals of history (with joint human and computer efforts). In EMB's stories, the products of apprentice sorcerers have always an in-built tendency to self-destruction.

In parallel with the identification of the human being as essentially a naked ape,[52] by a common acquaintance in Malta of both Elisabeth and my-

51. Cf. W. V. O'Connor, *The Grotesqe: an American Genre* (Carbondale, Ill: S. Ill. Univ. Press, 1962); or W. Kaysen, *The Grotesque in Art and Literature* (New York: McGraw, 1966).

52. D. Morris, *The Naked Ape* (London: Jonathan Cape, 1967), written in Malta where Morris resided at the time.

self, Desmond Morris, to which allusion has already been made, here the human being is somewhat more provocatively and also hopefully, identified as an "immortal fish." Fish for the obvious reason that life, in evolutionary history, emerged from the sea, and that as individuals we begin life in the watery womb in very fishlike shape. Immortal, because this exercise in yet another kind of nonrealist fiction is the first of a spectrum of variations in the book on the Freudian quandary as to which of Thanatos and Eros is primary. It has as its starting point a scientist's attempt at circumventing mortality. Its end is death's always accidental necessity. (A logically valid answer to the question: "Why do we all die?" can only be given in the form of a myth.)[53]

The body of the story is an uproarious parody of a court-room scene in which absurd answers to questions of bioethical responsibility are sophistically spun out, as if such issues could reasonably be resolved by complex juridical argumentation, instead of by just the simple intuition, available to all of us, of what it is to be human.[54]

Had there been no intent of parody, but of realism "frozen fish" would have been the title instead of "immortal." A scientist who feared that his discoveries would take much time before giving fruit ordered his subaltern to freeze him alive in order that he could then be de-frozen at the right moment to enjoy the glory owed to him for his scientific bravura. (Incidentally one of his prophecies was that scientists could make "the oceans . . . yield food for all.") When the scientist was eventually brought back to life, he did not lose much time before he got himself accidentally knocked over in traffic and killed. It asserts the impossibility of re-incarnation as the same person.

The title of the fourth story of Part I *The True Self,* immediately makes known that the question is once again that of the identity of the human being. This time, the quasi-eschatological setting is a beauty parlour—reminiscent of the funeral parlours in Evelyn Waugh's *The Loved One*—that turns out to be an epiphany of a neuropathic picture of paradise. The cosmetician's ambition is to be a superior cosmologist, a more efficient God than the gross blunderer of Genesis. It results in the living/dead contradiction of a stereotyped or assembly line type of process aimed at personalizing looks. Pseudoseraphs and (male) angels fix the icon of your (female) identity in this salon suite; in effect, it is an anti-heaven of entropic sameness, permeated by a tangible feel of refrigerated sexuality.

Waves of Repetition

In the second group of three stories that constitute part II of *TWIMC,* repetition works towards its entropic end. First Statistics take the place of Fate for humans fearful of free decision taking. Secondly an accidental killer has his victim apparently reincarnated as his own son. Thirdly the psychic insepara-

53. Cf. P. Serracino Inglott, *Beginning Philosophy* (Malta: Media Centre, 1987).

54. Cf. Th. Nagel, *Mortal Questions* (New York: Cambridge University Press, 1979).

bility and rivalry unto death of twin brothers emerges as the converse of the Esau-Jacob biblical paradigm.

Stories involving statistics and chance in the working out of human lives and history were to make Thomas Pynchon, among others very celebrated years after *TWIMC.* Such stories have acquired an immensely greater topicality since the flourishing of the Theory of Chaos and the discovery of the patterning of events outside the operation of deterministic causal systems. An excellent example of the genre is precisely *Delphi Revisited.*

The reference to Delphi in the title of the story is clearly not only because people nowadays go to the offices of statistics in the hope of getting hints about the future as the ancient Greeks went to the priestesses at Delphi, but also of course because Delphi is linked to the Socratic maxim: Know Thyself. The issue of identity is bound to crop up, at least implicitly woven into that of Fate. EMB herself has written that *Delphi Revisited* is about Fate having "been replaced by statistics, in post-individual society."[55]

What occurs in the story is repetition that goes beyond all probability. In the town where a certain Howard lives, the citizens mail almost exactly 802 postcards each year without stamping them. Howard puts in an extraordinary effort to get hundreds more posted without stamps in a year, but he fails to bring about a different result than the usual 802. He is told when he points out what he had done to the department of statistics—'don't you know that every year there is a crack-pot who tries to upset the statistics?' Howard becomes a Buddhist monk.

The interest is evidently in the recurrence of the same event like the breaking of wave after wave on the seashore. No conspiracy seems able to stop the repetitive turns of the wheel of history any more than Canute could call a halt to the rolling in and rolling out of the waves.

The title of the second story in part II, *Again,* is quite openly the keyword or better still, the crucial word. The story is that of a quite ordinary person who in total innocence kills a boy in a car accident. He then begets a son who is the exact image of the boy he ran over and bears no resemblance whatsoever to any one of his parents. Here the protagonist is pursued by the past literally in impersonated form. The Delphic inscription is, in this case internalized by the ceaselessly self-questioning protagonist like the daemon of Socrates. The image obsessing his consciousness and his conscience is literally incarnated and embodied in flesh of his own flesh and blood of his own blood. This story is a strong provocation to meditate seriously on Kiekegaard's *Repetition.*

Twin's Wail is once more a landlubber's story, but the protagonists are surnamed Sailor, and there are enough in the family, including in-laws, to make up a crew of sorts. Clearly, the surname comes replete with forebodings, like Coleridge's *Ancient Mariner.* Every occurrence of the word "sea"

55. Mann Borgese (n. 17 above), p. 57.

generates iterations and traces that keep multiplying echoes in paragraph after paragraph, page after page.

This is the story in which shifts in the mode of narration occur most frequently. It begins with a single paragraph attributed to a third person, omniscient narrator who, however, writes in a manner that is, on the face of it, far from reader-friendly. He begins by referring to a "he" whom of course we have no means of identifying at this stage; but this is perhaps for us to think of "him" as Everyman or Adam or our own selves.

"He" talks of "Martha's Fault" but then goes on to speak of "any Martha" and to add, "I too had a Martha like that." That suggests that Martha is not simply a proper name that could have been Mary or Magdalene or any other biblical or nonbiblical name. Curiously enough, Camus also named Martha the woman who killed in order to "buy" "a future happiness by the sea" in *Le Malentendu.*[56] Perhaps Martha means Everywoman or daughter of Eve, at least in the intention of the still anonymous "he" with whom EMB's narrator has brought us into contact without properly introducing him.

Amends will be made for this discourtesy in a little while, although not by the narrator himself; he, right after the puzzling kick-off, disappears completely from the scene and story, having thoroughly achieved the whole point of his/her existence by summarily creating for us a nightmarish atmosphere. There remain, however, in the air (thanks to the rapidly disappearing act of our trickster narrator) omens of guilt, presumptions of madness ("people simply thought he was crazy"), reversals of such hasty judgements and an inexplicable licence for life to go on. In brief, the opening notes of *Twin's Wail* are a riddle. Eventually we learn that we have not been plunged, Vergilian Style, in medias res, but in the finale, so that the intermediary sections are a series of flashbacks, and at the end we will have turned full circle and returned to the starting point.

The place of the narrator, immediately following his vanishing act, is taken up by the writer of a diary. (Mrs. Sailor's log!) Despite the inducement inherent in the diary form, EMB steadfastly resists adopting the techniques of fragmentation and nonsequiturs that have become commonplace among writers wishing to suggest that the world is a madhouse. Her narrative structure continues throughout to reflect the world-view of someone who stoically believes that beneath the most chaotic appearances, there lie hidden quasi-mathematical order and predestination.

The contents of the diary turn out to be dialogue (or rather an alternation of voices that express non-criss-crossing views) between a Hindu maid and her Christian mistress. Embedded in a mish-mash of chit-chat, hints of forthcoming sinister events rear their muffled heads, somewhat as in the *Diaries* of Thomas Mann himself (which of course EMB could not at the time have read, not even with the exercise of maximum slyness). The entries

56. B. Stoltzfus, *Lacan and Literature* (New York: SUNY Press, 1996), p. 107.

are dated "Christmas," "Halloween," "Palm Sunday," and so on. The diarist is the wife of a missionary in India, whose Christ, however, appears to bring about a sense of inescapable terror, rather than redemption and salvation.

She is the mother of twins, baptised Willy (for Willoughby) and Philly (for Theophil). The names appropriately stress the voluntaristic character of the one and the loving (besides philosophical) nature of the other. The twins, although EMB does not say or imply it, are somewhat reminiscent of the most famous biblical twins: Esau, who came out first from Rebecca's womb, and Jacob, who followed Esau, firmly grasping his brother's ankle (and weak point) with his hand. Despite the various attempts at severance, the lives of Esau and Jacob remain entangled until the end. The mother persists in holding that "these two children . . . are really only one. And you don't know where one ends and the other begins." In 1921, an earthquake results in her death and that of Willy. (Elisabeth was of the same age.)

Picking the thread up from here, Phil takes up the story 30 years later. He recalls being taken by his father back to Chicago, but disbelieving his father's statement that his mother and twin brother were in Heaven. One day, we are told, Phil looked in the mirror and (as if to spite Lacan before the hour) "overjoyed," says: "There is my Will." The 30 years pass. Then Phil's attention is drawn to a news item according to which Will Sailor, an Anglo-Italian author of travel and adventure books, had been killed by his wife in Rome, the Eternal City. Phil's companions point out that the victim whose picture was shown in the papers, looked exactly like him. Phil rushes to Rome and the next nine pages of the story consist of another, longer dialogue, this time between himself and reputed Killer Martha. Its texture, unlike that of the first dialogue, is antiphonic, that is, the male/female voices now constantly intersect and interlock in contrast with the parallel structure of the two-woman Western-Eastern failed encounter of 30 or more years before. Phil succeeds in persuading Martha that, by converse analogy with his own matrimonial experience, she is not guilty. He then solemnly presents a Memorandum, written in studied but atrocious verse, to a lawyer. It is the "Twin's Wail" of the title. The last lines sound like an epitaph in a stoic graveyard:

> Our wills are tied throughout the ages across the spaces . . .
> It always was like that between us and was all written down.

Meanwhile he has slept with the woman and she informs him that she is pregnant with twins. End of story.

In this story the potential resemblance of human beings to the waves of the sea is pushed to extreme limits. The twins resemble each other as wave resembles wave. The continuity between them is like that of wave succeeding wave. Determining the identity of each is as problematic as that of determining the identity of a wave. Over the whole story, the figure of inexorable Fate looms, as dominant as the Ocean over a few, paltry detached rocks, near a shore-line.

Circular Undercurrents

An alternative title for Part III of *TWIMC* instead of that suggested earlier, could have been "Descents of Hell." The two stories are both essays in circularity and closure. Both iterate the hellishness of going around in circles. The first is a comic elegy on the devotees of the speedy automobile. The second illustrates the frustration of a lost soul that attempts to cross the Ocean with death in its luggage and overtones of the myth of Wagner's *Flying Dutchman* in the air. Superficially, the narrative style in both appears to be quite naturalistic, but a little scratching below the surface suffices to make an almost medieval, allegorical potentiality come into the open. The narration proceeds at a tortoise-slow pace and gives the reader ample time to delve beneath the upper layer of meaning. Anybody who could boast of a Jesuit schooling would moreover naturally read these stories as Ignatian-style meditations on the Last Things.

The title-word *Flowers* immediately evokes the vegetal kingdom—the biosphere—and its contrary, the Kingdom of the Dead. The couple in whose company the reader is going to remain for the whole length of the story have just left a night club called *Paradiso.* The word is, of course, a transcription of a Greek word for garden, and here, of course, it alludes to the pre-lapsarian Garden in which the mortality of Man had been decreed. Soon on their road, the couple will meet the flower arrangements in wreaths and the flower scatterings over coffins that are conventional at both Christian and pagan funerals. They are driving in a car capable of diddling the most bloodthirsty curves, a death-defying machine. He is obviously more in love with the machine than with his professionally voluptuous passenger. She tries as hard as she can but not very successfully to eke sweet nothings out of his heart and mind. It is not at all easy in the context to distinguish with certainty between the animate and the inanimate.

Almost inevitably the Ocean almost in breach of the biblical claim that insuperable limits had been set to its domain, begins to seep into our couple's stream of consciousness. Their car keeps finding itself in the midst of crowds "billowing around it: a motor-boat against the heavier waters of a deader sea." Later on: "What do you like better," he said, "travelling by train or by boat, flying or going by car?" "Boats, I guess," she said, ". . . the rest . . . are all so boring." The man is called "Dr Shapiro, dentist of New York, New York . . . He looked . . . a Monday morning sailor, scrubbing amidships." He recalls that: "when I was a boy, I had a gala sailor suit . . . All the boys had Sunday suits like that." ". . . And then?" "From Sunday-sailor on parade to Monday-sailor scrubbing amidships. That's a career."

The woman is called 'Unesco'! She had been singing a song about death in Italian (left untranslated) and death's paradoxical combination of characteristics: necessity and accidentality. As the story proceeds, it is increasingly difficult not to see them as embodiments of Freud's *Thanatos* and *Eros.*

The fulcrum of the story is a sort of Damascus-road experience undergone by Dr Shapiro. At a certain point, he sees "flowers as far as the eyes could reach along both sides on the down-sloping fields." He drives on, but soon begins to question whether the sight had not been a hallucination. All the time Shapiro pursues a silent, thanatos-driven dialogue with himself, very rarely, briefly and spasmodically interrupted by spoken, eros-driven pseudo-dialogue with Unesco. He decides to drive back to check on the reality or delusiveness of the flower vision ("the perfect beauty of the vision seemed lifeless, the perfection of death") but ends up, through some error, at the starting point: the night club called *Paradiso.*

A circle can only be perfectly drawn by means of an instrument, such as a compass; it is an abstraction with the uncanny force of a bad dream. Clearly circularity is hellishness and going round in circles the symptom of the sort of diabolically dominated form of life that EMB's father was to write about in *Dr Faustus* and her brother Klaus had done before him in *Mephisto.* They had recorded that form of life as an aberrant historical happening in the recent past. Her own short stories seem to constitute a sustained attempt to forestall possible future variants and developments of the diabolic tendencies inherent in the human condition. They tell us what it will be like if the wheels of world history keep turning like a windmill caught in a hurricane. It will be radically worse than the diabolic happenings of the recent past.

The final story has *Straits* as its title. The word is a sea-related geographical term with, of course, strong metaphorical connotations made even stronger for readers of Paul Celan throughout his splendid poem on the subject. The sea, especially if distant and deep (in other words if it falls within the domain of the Common Heritage) has been often chosen as the site for the imagining of alternate words, fantastic or horrendous or both together (So have ships, of course, as with our by now old acquaintance, Wagner's *Flying Dutchman*). The sea is not, however, the location chosen by EMB for her original and laterally conceived thought experiments in narrative form about human, animal, and vegetal life on earth, present and future, its actual dry and solid state and its potential dissolution and destruction by the waters of the Ocean. Despite the interpretation of the rainbow shared by Jews, Christians, and Muslims alike, the obsession of universal death by water given powerful expression by Eliott in his early 20th century *Wasteland* continues to haunt mankind.

In *Straits,* the sea comes finally into view in the very last few of the 167 pages of *TWIMC.* The main character is a Lost Soul (Professor Meier by name) who forgot the name of the straits that were his destination, the setting out point or port for a crossing of the Ocean. An occasional lapsus such as saying instead of "Hotel Alba, Lido" "Hotel Alba, Limbo," the words of a German hymn that Meier recalls his pupils singing, certain similes like that of the children who kept away from his black violin case "fearfully, as from an open coffin," are symptoms betraying a world with hidden dimensions like the depths of the Ocean. Above all, when Meier reaches the point of departure, an atmosphere is conjured up as ominous as that in Benjamin Britten's *Peter Grimes.* The last revelation of the book is a detail that proclaims that Evil cannot be as successful at self-concealment as Satan has been alleged to be by Christian authors from Augustine to C. S. Lewis: Meier's fifth bag contains his dead child.

What did EMB achieve in *TWIMC*? I suppose that she started mainly with preoccupation about the extent to which human life was determined by predestination/coincidences. Then, as she proceeded, hardly knowing clearly what she was doing, she began hitting upon the various, component parts of the Otherness archetype. In building up, story upon story, *TWIMC,* the born metaphysician that EMB was, whose breeding by the Magician had been compounded by his Sicilian proxy, ended up constructing the identikit of a wanted (top priority) X, suspected of being called (for want, as yet, of better identification): Ocean.

EMB very occasionally wrote stories of a similar kind to those in *TWIMC* later in life.[57] It is clear that she had not lost all faith in the validity of the literary form, but she had shifted the focus of her interest elsewhere, although still in the domain of the exploration of "The Other."

In the same period as *TWIMC* was written, EMB is said to have also written three short plays. I am familiar just with one: *Only the Pyre.* The text was included with the gramophone record of the music composed for it by the distinguished Sicilian composer and conductor Franco Mannino; it was issued in 1987 after the performance of the opera at the Pirandello Festival, in Agrigento, Sicily, in October of that year.

In the play, a certain Mrs. Richie Calder (whom a niece calls Aunt Witchie) demands her own destruction as punishment for her habitual criminal activity consisting in somehow procuring the crashing of airliners.[58] The judge to whom she resorts in the first place refuses to exterminate her because he holds that responsibility for terrorist evil-doing is shared by everybody.

The priest, to whom she resorts in the second place, apparently in the confessional, also refuses to condemn her of murder on the ground that she is a mere agent of Satan; moreover, he fails in his attempts at exorcising her, apparently because of his lukewarm faith.

In the third instance, the woman on a psychiatrist's couch is told that all wickedness is madness, and therefore she is exempt from punishment.

57. Such as: *Wie Gottlieb Hauptmann die Todesstrafe abschaffe* (no city quoted: Erzählungen, 2001). In *Die Meer-Frau* (n. 3 above), EMB expressed the intention of collecting several stories of the kind scattered in magazines, p. 108.

58. *Only the Pyre,* subtitled *Tragic Farce,* is listed as published in Milan by Bompiani, in 1961, and a second play is listed as: *Eat your Fishballs, Tarquin* (Santa Barbara: 1965), in *Die Meer-Frau* (n. 3 above), p. 124.

In order to show her that she was deluded in believing herself guilty, the psychiatrist accompanies her on a flight that of course ends in a crash.

Can Evil be defeated, if responsibility for it or its very existence is denied? That question is the result if Evil is projected solely on Otherness. Probably EMB was thinking at the time of responsibility for escalating nuclear armament, possibly even implanting nuclear weapons on the seabed, as the acme of evil.

The music is mostly recitatif. Mannino, it seems, wished his music to be a mere emphasizing of the words, somewhat like medieval plain chant, in keeping with the allusions to witchcraft and evil on a supernatural scale that permeate the text. Mannino had as far back as 1956 written the music for a choreographed version of Thomas Mann's *novella Mario and the Magician*, produced for the *Scala* in Milan (and later Hamburg) by Luchino Visconti (later director of *Death in Venice*, a film which EMB very much liked).[59] In it, Mannino showed that he could write sparkling music if he so wished, but "the little-soul music similar in manner to Cechovian understatement" (such as he is said to have written for Luchino Visconti's film *L'Innocente*, somewhat related in theme to EMB's play, as the title suggests) is more characteristic of Mannino's spirit.

Despite his venerable age, Mannino was commissioned by EMB to compose a symphony for a *Pacem in Maribus* convocation in 1992. In it Mannino undoubtedly sought to render EMB's uncanny concept of the Ocean, yet EMB never cited the symphony, to my knowledge, when speaking as she often did of the deep music-ocean relationship, despite the admired Mannino's unheimlich capacity to express states approaching Nirvana in sound.

Out of the Straits of Gender

Three years after publishing the English edition of *TWIMC*, EMB published *The Ascent of Woman* (1963). Her demarche calls to my mind that of another writer. Albert Camus, after spending years contemplating death in essays, novels, and plays (such as *Sisyphus*, the *Plague*, and *Caligula*), took a turning and announced: "I know I shall never come close to the world (unless I go) naked, then dive into the sea, still scented with the perfumes of the earth, and wash the latter in the former, consummating on my flesh the embrace for which sun and sea, mouth to mouth, have for so long been sighing."[60]

59. According to Daniel Johnson in the introduction to *Thomas Mann Collected Stories*, "Mario and the Magician" is, after "Death in Venice," Mann's first and most famous work of shorter fiction. In it, once more, Elisabeth and Michael are the obvious models of the two children who play an incidental part in the short story, but they are not individually characterized, unlike the Little-Girl in *Disorder and Early Sorrow*.

60. "Noces," in *Essais*, vol. 2, Gallimard (Paris: Pleiade, 1965), p. 76.

There is a similar redolence of sexuality in these sea-thoughts of Camus as there was in Thomas Mann's.

A Camus critic noted: "The sea, especially in French through homonymic association (*mer/mère*) is a conventional symbol for the mother."[61] For EMB, as for Martha, in *Le Malentendu* by Camus, "the day when at last we will have reached the sea" will also be the day when "she will bask in the warmth of a lost maternal presence."[62] The association of the Ocean with the feminine is indeed ancient. It looms large in all EMB's works. Moreover, as in her father's work, the link between Ocean and Woman is collectivity.

On the last page of *Male and Female: An Approach to Thomas Mann's Dialectic*, Inta Miske Ezergailis[63] sums up the main conclusion of her study: "The Ocean is an image of the relaxation of individuation. In this, it is related to the female principle . . ."

I personally heard Elisabeth link Ocean and Woman on many occasions. In 1987, with the change of Government in Malta from one which did little to help the cause of the new Law of the Sea for which EMB stood, to one constituted by the same party that had appointed Arvid Pardo ambassador of Malta to the United Nations and promoted the concept of the common heritage of mankind, I was appointed rector of the University of Malta and invited EMB to give a course of lectures to all the students. I suggested that she could take *The Ascent of Woman* as one of her themes. EMB demurred. She said that she was no longer up-to-date with feminist issues. However, she began her lectures on the Law of the Sea by referring to Botticelli's so-called *Birth of Venus* that represents Aphrodite or the Goddess of Love emerging out of her seashell.

Botticelli painted the image in 1485 after a long period during which the myth had not been represented in art. EMB pointed out that Botticelli's wedding of Woman and Ocean heralded the start of a new civilization in which classical mythology and biblical revelation would exert a healthy influence upon each other. Woman arising out of the Ocean was pictured by the Florentine artist 7 years before Colombus caught sight of the marine outskirts of the American continent, named after one of Botticelli's greatest friends from Florence, Amerigo Vespucci. Woman is not extracted by any kind of surgical or butcher's operation from the flesh and bones of Man but out of the realm of the sea. She is born out of the surf (*aphros*) like a watery phoenix that the waves of the Ocean resuscitate more beautifully than the ashes of the earth. As Jacques Darras was to put it, the Florentine painters of the quattrocento went further in their imaginary journeys than Vasco Da Gama or Magellan. By positing the figure of woman without reference

61. V. Mistacco, "Nomadic Meanings" in *Albert Camus, L'Exil et le Royaume: The Third Decade*, ed. A. Rizzuto (Toronto: Paratexte, 1988), p. 77.

62. Stoltzfus (n. 56 above), p. 107.

63. I. M. Ezergailis, *Male and Female: An Approach to Thomas Mann's Dialectic* (The Hague: Nijhoff, 1975), p. 188.

to any male source of origin but referring her to the Ocean they issued a manifesto the full implications of which have yet to be realized.[64]

Similar considerations surface in a chapter of *The Ascent of Woman* that EMB called the Feminine Revolution. She began the book with a dialogue between *Credo*, who states the principles of gender equality, and *Vedo* who states how matters stand. But soon, the principal thesis that EMB presents viz. the association of the feminine with the collective, takes over complete possession of the text. The second chapter is entitled Women and Crowds; the fifth, Women and the Face of the Crowd. The Crowd is everywhere. The return of women to equality with men is seen as an aspect of the recovery of the sense of community and the decline of extreme individualism as an ideal in politics. EMB wrote: "The affinity between the feminine and the collective seems to have penetrated man's unconscious and to reflect itself in language and art, in myth and faith."[65] This is not the place to carry out an assessment of the way in which EMB seeks to establish this thesis. Reference has already been made to some of the boldest of her other ideas such as the ideal of sex change. The main point that deserves highlighting in the present context is that EMB explores femininity perceived as a major form of otherness by the typical individualist man and woman of our times. Women had begun to displace animals as man's main means to negative self-definition. However, at the same time as Darwin's apes seemed to be fudging the distinctness of the boundary line between human being and beast, then also some women began to call into question the existence of any sharp distinction in nature between man and woman.

In writing *The Ascent of Woman* EMB was, I believe, still reacting as she had been in writing *TWIMC*, to the basic polarity between the formless Ocean and the articulated Family that is perhaps the most fundamental of all the several antitheses with which her father's work is famously riddled. *The Ascent of Woman,* however, constitutes her first sustained attempt to sketch out a possible rapprochement between the two opposites. In discussing Thomas Mann's image of the sea, I sought to bring out its relevance to sexuality, to which EMB herself had not drawn explicit attention. It was, however, upon the need for a sexual revolution even more far-reaching than anything her father had conceived when he chose her as its incidental emblem, that EMB focussed her attention very soon after she began speaking with her own voice. In so doing, she surpassed her father's great expectations by a long stretch.

Towards a Coastal Zone Landing

Three years after *The Ascent of Woman*, EMB published *The White Snake* (1966). This book might have been called The Ascent of Animal. It was

64. J. Darras, *La Mer Hors d'Elle-même* (Paris: Hatier, 1991), pp. 142–43.
65. Mann Borgese (n. 17 above), p. 53.

intended to be, in EMB's own concluding words, a "contribution to the understanding of linguistic behaviour and learning in animals and to the possibility of communicating with them."[66] It is also mainly, like *TWIMC*, a collection of stories. However, these stories are perfectly true, although they too are in their way extraordinary. They are written in a style that parodies that of academic research reports to the point where it becomes hard to distinguish the imitation from the original. They are not accounts of fearful anticipations of the plight of the human family overrun by oceanic devilry, but accounts of minor, liminary preparations for reconciliatory manoeuvres between the Opposites. They are exploratory exercises on the shore where the dreaded forces of Otherness wash the thresholds of human habitations: a more appropriate landing place for Noah's Ark than Mount Ararat.

There is an almost inevitable prelude to the triad of EMB autobiographical stories. It is a brief history of the most intelligent horses of whom there are records. Between man and horse there has now been a plurimillennial relationship of mastery and complicity. Horse riding has been one of the phenomena that has most accelerated human civilization and been a decisive factor in many aspects of human history. Consequently, the horse does not feature among the emblems of Alterity that EMB chose to experiment with. But she could not altogether exclude him from consideration among the heroic denizens of a Platonic Coastal Zone between the human and the nonhuman.

At a *Pacem in Maribus* meeting in Vienna, Elisabeth, who knew of my love of the circus, led me and other kindred spirits to take time off from our concentration at the time on how to derive peaceful benefits from the military uses of the sea, to watch a training session at the famous Spanish Riding School. On the way, Elisabeth told me about her youthful passion for horses and her exploits in riding them Cosack style. She loved animals in the wild, but even more when they were happily integrated with human life and civilization.

The exercises at the Riding School were the remnant in the form of solemn spectacle of the ancient chivalrous paradigm of the man-horse military alliance. This noble wartime phenomenon had already given rise in the 18th century to the comic popular spectacle then called "equestrian theatre," a term that has been revived in recent years. Then there occurred the distortion of the square patterns of cavalry manoeuvres into the recurring circles of the circus, within which human acrobats and clowns and exotic animals and inanimate objects play the game of pretending equality of status. The "theatre of the world" of the Baroque age had turned into the "circus of the world" in the following centuries. It was what Shakespeare's Ariel would call "a sea-change." The circus, it is said, was born on horseback. It is not surprising that EMB begins her book on breaking the barrier in communication between animal and human with a discussion of horse-sense.

66. Mann Borgese (n. 1 above), p. 149.

Soon we were watching the horses with their haunches shining under the electric light and their hooves glinting on the ground. The naturally heavy beasts had obviously become weightier by their training. They seemed to be the ideal medium for keeping their human riders earthbound. The high degree of understanding through conventional signs between man and beast was manifest in the way a horse would subtly moderate the elan of its gallop according to the minute indications received through bit and bridle and its other trappings. But soon the flesh of both horse and rider were oozing sweat in the clearest possible exhibition of their common animality and in the starkest contrast with the glamour of rider's uniform and horse's trappings. In one of the Homeric hymns, Poseidon, god of the sea, is also called "tamer of wild horses," but there was little that spoke of the Ocean in the superbly harmonious movements of these horses, except perhaps for the occasional glimpse we could catch of a crazy-looking eye, wide open and steady in lateral observation. Horse and rider had become too Centaur-like in a totally nonmonstrous way, for horses to be of any real challenge to a would-be promoter of human-animal communication, such as EMB. The optimum level of relationship had already been reached.

Dog Adrift into Concrete Poetry

The first story, after the equestrian introduction, is about a dog, Arli, whom EMB teaches to type—even without dictation, producing his own "rhythmic prose," in EMB's words. When Arli had reached this stage of achievement, EMB stopped teaching him, because he was no longer happy learning, despite rewards. The characteristic of EMB's approach to animals is that while striving hard to break the barrier that makes animals Other than human beings, she never presses towards an impossible total assimilation.

It may be recalled that in 1918, the year of EMB's birth, Thomas Mann had written the text called "A Man and his Dog." This 70-page stretch of idyllic prose is usually included among his short stories, although it hardly lives up to that description. The shaggy dog who is the author's companion in country walks provided him with a pretext for an essay on man's relationship with nature in general and canine nature in particular. Daniel Johnson says, "this pot-boiler . . . is, by some distance, the worst thing that Mann ever wrote," but it has remained until today one of his most popular works.

The reason for this popularity may be that the man-in-the-street has an unconscious appreciation of the mythical dimension of Mann's most apparently naturalistic writing greater than that of the literary critic. Just as *Disorder and Early Sorrow* stirs deeply embedded memories of the myth of the Fall, so too is "A Man and his Dog" deeply evocative of Adam's relationship to the animals, which is one of the principal themes of the book of *Genesis.*

Thomas Mann's attitude to his dog may be said to differ from that of his daughter in the same way as their approaches to the sea differ. The elder Mann does not seek to alter the nature of man-dog relationships. (Incidentally, he contrasts the human attitude to the sea in general and his own in particular with that of the Dog: "I would even say that only in contemplation of it do I achieve true self forgetfulness and feel my own limited individuality merge into the universal . . . I am lost to time." On the contrary, the dog acts as if the only justification of the existence of water was so that, just on those days when it is very hot, he can cool his underbelly with it, although "never of his own free will wetting the upperparts"). EMB, on the other hand, strives to add new dimensions to human-animal communication.

It is true that Thomas Mann begins the account of his relationship with his dog as follows: "I give a whistle in two notes, tonic and lower fourth, like the beginning of the second phrase of Schubert's *Unfinished Symphony*" and he receives a quick response in the form of the tinkling of "a metal licence-tag . . . against the trimmings of a leather collar." However, this sort of musical collaboration is not really comparable to that which I personally witnessed between Elisabeth and her dog in Canada. There, in Elisabeth's house in Halifax, which was only the second (after the Tuscan first) to which she was attached of the many in which she had dwelt, again within earshot of the sea, I heard Elisabeth play together with one of her dogs a few pathetic notes from Schumann. (Actually they were notes that to me personally had always sounded almost like the shattering premonition of his impending madness.) Elisabeth ceremoniously placed the score on its proper place on the piano and opened it. She played the right hand part of the melody, the dog pressed the left hand notes on the enlarged keys of the specially constructed piano with his nose. He seemed to enjoy playing the piano much more than Arli had done typing concrete poetry of his own making. The language of the emotions was clearly easier for dogs to share with humans than the language of thought. Certainly, there was no shade of resemblance between the dog-pianist and the ape-maestro of *The Rehearsal*. The dog had no ambition to be a conductor. There was nothing robot-like about his playing. He pricked his ears and listened to Elisabeth's right hand hitting the keys and took his cues instantly. I was enormously pleased to see that the dog had such a sense of rhythm. I was a trifle less pleased, although having read the story of Arli in *The White Snake* not surprised, to observe that the dog rose to the almost incredible height of his performance because of the incentive of a portion of minced meat instead of the usual vegetarian diet he shared with his mistress.

Elephants Splashing in Labour Pool

The second story is about elephants. EMB observes their instruction in South India as they are prepared for working life, starting not before they are eighteen. The idea of a working animal is no less paradoxical than that of a talking animal. Work has usually been considered to be as much a human prerogative as speech. Both work and speech are significant activities. Elephants are presented not only as working, but also as working in a team.

Indeed, EMB's account of what she saw almost invites the question: will elephants ever form a trade union? Probably the answer to the facetious question is that elephants practice participative and not adversarial democracy.

EMB reports on the controversy between those who affirm and those who deny the elephant's natural intelligence. She relates stories from her own experience to show that elephants tend to be more or less of the same ability as dogs and horses. They are capable of associating sound with sign and, EMB supposes, of learning to type at least as well as Arli had done, with their trunk of course. The picture of the Elephant that emerges from EMB's essay is the animal image that most resembles her final picture of the Ocean.

On the other hand, the elephant is a much more powerful symbol of the Other than any dog can be, since the dog has become a wholly accepted part of human life, while the elephant because of size and strength continues to inspire awe, to some extent like the Ocean. Moreover, most Westerners still carry in their cultural baggage ancient images of Hannibal crossing the Alps with his elephants embodying an alien threat to our Roman-rooted civilisation. We vaguely know that then the elephant disappeared from the European scene for about a thousand years, until a lone elephant was brought to Europe by Charlemagne, a rare reminder of the existence of other worlds beyond Christiandom.

In recent centuries, zoos and circuses and later the media have demythified the pachyderm and despoiled him of much of his previous Otherness. Moreover even in days when fables were important and in continents where the elephant is a majestic presence and manifestly stronger than either lion or bear, he has never been considered by human beings as a candidate for the kingship of beasts, precisely because of the friendliness of his relationship with human beings. Unalterably awesome, but potentially amicable, the elephant is a perfect forecast of EMB's futuristic vision of the Ocean.

Chimp Stranded on the Shores of Humour

The third story is about Bob, a real chimpanzee from Sierra Leone, who ended up like the fictional Maestro of *The Rehearsal* at the Yerkes Laboratory for Primate Biology, in Atlanta, Georgia. However, there is a very striking difference between EMB's attitude to the one and to the other. The Maestro's musical abilities were alien to those of human beings; he dominated the orchestra with a forceful direction that can only be truly called brute. The result is not any form of dialogue across the barrier. That possibility requires reciprocal respect of the different identity of the other.

The difference between EMB's images of Ape/Chimp in *The Rehearsal* and *The White Snake* corresponds, it seems to me, to that between the attitudes to the Sea of such Hebrew Bible writers as the author of *Psalm* 107 on the one hand and of Jesus according to the Synoptic Gospels, on the other hand. Elisabeth had publicly expressed her appreciation of this difference after I had pointed it out in a paper, read at Yokohama, on *The Sea in the Bible.* In the Hebrew Bible, the Sea is always addressed as a chaotic force, hostile to God, usually in sarcastic tones. In the Gospels, Jesus addresses it as though, in spite of its present negativity, it could be "exorcised" and turned into a partner in a constructive dialogue![67]

This kind of dialogic relationship is precisely that which EMB eventually adopts towards the sea; it is the attitude that she first adopts towards Bob, the Chimpanzee, in stark contrast with the Ape-Maestro of *The Rehearsal.* EMB bought Bob, then taught him in parallel and sometimes together with the dog Arli. The chimp has the obvious advantage of hands that are to some degree capable of grasping and doing much more than animals who need to use them for locomotion. The chimp naturally typed with his fingers yet despite his closeness to human beings, he had to be kept in a cage and not exposed to making many mistakes, (in this he is quite like the Maestro), as that would lead him to become uncooperative. Communication would break down. On the whole the chimp like the dog is not as awe inspiring as the elephant. Nevertheless the sense of Otherness continues to prevail strongly between himself and human beings.

In conclusion, the experiments with animal-human communication seemed to have prepared EMB for her later work with regard to human-ocean relations in two ways. First she learnt that such phenomena as pre-language and pre-religion prove that the barrier between Humanity (land-lubber) and Brutishness (oceanically inarticulate) is not absolute. As regards language EMB thinks that, starting from a common basic communicative use of sound, humans and animals then moved in different directions, but the common root is sufficiently strong to offer possibilities of greater understanding than there exists at present. As regards religion, EMB points out that onomatopoeic effects such as imitations of thunder or the wailing of the sea are often used by human beings when casting magical spells and may "represent a survival of a proto-language which we have in common with the animals."[68] Of course the practice of ritual by animals is very well known.

The maximum degree of human-animal communication has probably been achieved, since *The White Snake,* with dolphins. However, paradoxically perhaps as EMB was to show in her book *Sea Farm,* the most notable advance in the integration of human and animal relations occurred when humans learnt to breed fish instead of hunting them. Aquaculture, which came so long after agriculture, is not only of the greatest economic and practical importance in terms of food supply but also a major evolutionary step in the long and difficult process of the reconciliation of man and nature. The prospect was left hanging in nostalgic suspense in the picture of "A Man

67. *Mark,* 4, 34–41. Cf. also C. Reynier, *La Bible el la Mer* (Paris: Cerf, 2003).
68. Mann Borgese (n. 1 above), p. 147.

and his Dog" painted by Thomas Mann, writing in obvious self-consolatory vein in the last year of the First World War among human beings. His daughter, born in that very same, grim year, promoted (and herself took practical steps towards) admittedly partial realisations of the desideratum.

Secondly, EMB was convinced that one should never press the overcoming of basic barriers beyond certain limits. Hence, human beings should, for instance, strive to achieve not only a measure of familiarity but also of domiciliarization within the depths of the Ocean, but without denying that the nature of man is to be a land animal. In many of the *Pacem in Maribus* convocations, notably that held in 1973 at Malta, the prospect of underwater habitation was discussed in non-science-fiction mode, as well as both stationary (anchored) and mobile out-at-sea architecture. The German environmental artist Jürgen Claus said: "We are entering the age of the genesis of floating civilisations. The immense task for the marine architect and artist is to give shape to the rising civilisations of the sea." EMB especially applauded Claus's conclusion that "What is called the innerspace of the planet Earth corresponds in its development to the inner space of man: to his imagination, to his creative mind."

However, before plunging into the great, cosmic-scale brokerage between family-ensconced and Ocean-open Spirits, encouraged by her successful experiments aimed at building communication bridges between human beings and different species of animals, without even nourishing any illusion about the little that could be achieved, EMB still wanted to devote some effort to bring together groups of human beings divided among each other not by natural but by cultural barriers such as nationality, class or religion, not to speak of gender. Social peace is the first of three steps, to be followed by cosmic and inner peace.

AT LAST, THE DEEP

Adopting the Corsair Model of Mutiny Preemption

In 1968, EMB returned to the United States of America. She had reached the shore where she was now close enough to the sea to begin to tackle the prospects of a new form of life. The spheres of private and public were to interlock directly. Her base of operations was the Center for the Study of Democratic Institutions in Santa Barbara, California. In that context, she came to the conclusion that "The parliamentary democracy we have inherited from the eighteenth and nineteenth centuries is at the end of its tether even at the level of the nation-State."[69] Hobbes, like others among his

69. E. Mann Borgese, "Towards an International Ocean Regime" (paper presented at the Malta Summer School on "Hydrospace and its Development for Mankind," Malta, 28 July–10 August 1969), p. 20.

predecessors and successors who wrote political philosophy with a biblical background, chose Leviathan, the monster from the depths of the ocean, as the symbol of the State. Fusing the image of the State with that of an animal, however mythical, serves to make the State feel almost as Other as the Ocean. The choice of the symbol has come to be particularly associated with Hobbes because it was in his age that the otherness of State and individual became sharp in philosophic awareness if not yet in the general consciousness.

After having established the maximum of the limited means of communication with elephants, apes and their likes from the kingdom of beasts, EMB now felt ready for an intellectual confrontation with Leviathan. EMB does not share the reverential attitude of Hobbes towards the State. She is rather more concerned with the fact that the stigma of Otherness often came to be imposed not so much upon the State but rather upon a class of people such as the working class or the "barbarians" of whom people like the Ancient Greeks or her father (at least for a time) were even more afraid than of the Ocean or the Unconscious.

The main problem was that decisive issues were being worked out at levels either below that of the nation State, such as the family and the business corporation or at levels above it, regional or global. New political systems needed to be created to take account of both the greater space being clamoured for by every individual (or microgroup) and of the exigencies arising out of the realization that our world is just one very small planet in a corner of the cosmos.

EMB wrote that a "new form of democracy is already recognizable: we call it participational democracy. The most interesting experiments in this direction have been attempted in Yugoslavia with the 1963 constitution . . . The theory of participational democracy is quite simple, really. It is based on the recognition that modern government has not only a political dimension, but an economic, a social, a cultural dimension as well. It presupposes that you cannot represent men only on the basis of 'numbers or heads' but that you must consider them also as workers or students, members of a church, a co-operative, a corporation . . . Enterprises, Universities, corporations and co-operatives . . . must participate in the decision-making processes of government . . . Participation, responsibility and initiative are more important incentives than profits . . . Co-operation today is more productive than competition . . . Consensus is more important than coercion."[70] Her major concern was to "decrease the number of human robots in the planet."[71] Her

70. Ibid. EMB says that participatory democracy is a system which creates a communicative network between infranational, national and supranational levels of action.

71. E. Mann Borgese, *Self-Management: New Dimensions to Democracy*, ed. I. Adizes and E. Mann Borgese (Santa Barbara, California: American Bibliographical Center, 1975).

inspiration was Lewis Mumford, with whom both her father and her husband had collaborated. Technological progress was requiring intelligent workers. EMB quotes Mumford's vision of the "stimulation of invention and initiative within the industrial process . . . and the transformation . . . of the social opportunities of factory production into effective forms of political action."[72]

Despite her undoubtedly somewhat naive enthusiasm for Yugoslavia (which, at the time, was setting itself up as a mediating interface between the first and the second worlds locked in the Cold War), EMB quotes Ichak Adsizes saying that the State ownership of productive enterprises in Yugoslavia was actually "a barrier to the future development of self-management" and concludes that "self-management is a process that moves on a different plane from that of ownership."

Evidently EMB at this stage is finding herself in great difficulty having to separate myth from reality. Yugoslavia, for instance, had really made a breach in the great dividing wall of the Cold War, but the "participatory democracy" inscribed in its 1963 constitution remained essentially a paper achievement. Like her father, who had found out that after 1945, he could not easily turn from Anti-Nazi to Cold Warrior overnight, so EMB hankered after a third way between Soviet Collectivism and American Individualism. Such wishful thinking led her to invent mythical synthesizers between thesis and antithesis.

Her vision of factory workers derobotized and operating with intelligence and cool responsibility in policy making and decision taking at the level of the enterprise is expounded in the book she edited in 1975: *Self Management: New Dimensions to Democracy*. Despite the tragic collapse of Yugoslavia, the prospect of participatory democracy has become much more realistic with the electronic revolution and in expectation of the knowledge society.

Navigating on a Raft from Ogygia

EMB met the person whom she eventually came to regard as the third greatest influence on her thinking, Arvid Pardo, in 1967 after he made his proposal to the United Nations on behalf of Malta that the Ocean beyond national jurisdiction should be declared Common Heritage of Mankind.[73] According to the Maltese proposal as EMB read it, the marine sphere that had been set up in separation from land, the domain of man, was to be networked with its terrestrial opposite, but its Otherness was not being negated, since the concepts of

72. Ibid.

73. Malta, in particular the islet called Gozo, has been identified by many Homeric scholars as Ogygia, the island from where Calypso was ordered to free Ulysses, help him build a raft and instruct him on how to navigate towards his goal Book V of the *Odyssey*.

property and sovereignty, considered to be keystones of humanity's dwelling on earth, were being declared inapplicable to ocean space.

Pardo has declared several times that he had never thought of his proposal in this quasi-metaphysical way. He had only intended it to be an ad hoc solution to the immediate tangles in the application of the Law of the Sea that had arisen as a result of contingent developments, such as the realization that the supply of fish was not inexhaustible and that technology was making it increasingly possible, although neither easy nor cheap, to get down to the deep sea bed to extract precious metals and minerals from it.

EMB, however, had had her attention drawn to Pardo's proposal by some unknown gentleman who pointed out its relevance to the ideals of the Center for the Study of Democratic Institutions which Robert Hutchins had founded in Santa Barbara, California, after he had ceased to be President of the University of Chicago. EMB had returned to America in 1968 as a Fellow of the Center to pick up work on the World Constitution to which her late husband had made the most important contribution.

In this connection, the Center was greatly impressed by Pope John XXIII's encyclical *Pacem in Terris.* The 81-year-old former Vatican diplomat, head of the Catholic Church since only 4 years before, had issued the encyclical a few months before his death as almost his spiritual testament to the world. It was the first document of its sort to be formally presented to the United Nations. It had been highly praised by both President Kennedy and Comrade Kruschev, even though the bitingly bitter climate of the Cold War still prevailed. The encyclical had two great themes.

The first was that philosophers had often spoken of the "common good" as the goal of political activity, but they did so in terms of the common good of the city-state or the nation-state according to the epoch. Now it was time to think in terms of the common good of humanity as a whole. To achieve the shift, the Pope urged the United Nations to take concrete steps towards the establishment of Federal World government on the basis of a new consideration of human rights.

The second great theme of the encyclical was that dialogue in this direction was possible notwithstanding the ideological rift dividing the world into hostile camps. The Center for the Study of Democratic Institutions funded an international symposium inaugurated at the Headquarters of the United Nations with Secretary General U. Thant, who had felt directly challenged to act by the Pope, as host. The Symposium continued then at the New York Hilton.

EMB was actively present. Typical of her back room contributions was her seminal meeting with Pietro Nenni, the official delegate of the Italian Government. He has published an intriguing reference to this conversation of his "with the widow Borgese, daughter of Thomas Mann."[74] To understand

74. P. Nenni, *Gli Anni del Centro Sinistra, Diari 1957–1966* (Milano: Sugar Co. Edizioni, 1982), pp. 447–51.

its significance, one needs to recall that the presence of John XXIII as Bishop of Rome had opened the way to the controversial formation of the first Centre-Left government in Italy much to the displeasure of the United States of America. The Italian government had decided to send the Socialist Leader and former ally of the Communist Party, Nenni, now largely unoccupied as minister without portfolio, to New York for the symposium on *Pacem in Terris* with the express agreement of the Pope. John XXIII had not seen the "opening to the left" of the Italian Government as valuable so much within the framework of domestic Italian policy as much as because it was a clear indicator of an international movement in the direction of peace, despite the ideological differences between East and West, as these terms were then understood. EMB's meeting with Nenni had served to whet the Italian leader's appetite to look at the Ocean as the sphere in which a system of world governance could be projected and in which the United States of America-USSR polarity could be transcended. Nenni's intervention,[75] one of the very few at the Symposium which truly focus on the central ideas of *Pacem in Terris* rather than serve as space for the speaker to gallop away on his hobby-horse, has as its keystone the theme of participatory democracy, dear to Elisabeth, and transferred from the industrial-national sphere where it had been first deployed by Pope John in his encyclical *Mater et Magistra,* now to the international sphere, in *Pacem in Terris.*

The grafting of Pardo's law of the sea ideas on to the framework of John XXIII's *Pacem in Terris* led directly to the idea of *Pacem in Maribus* convocations being summoned annually in November, in Malta. The Center for the Study of Democratic Institutions was put in charge of organizing the first convention on behalf of the Government of Malta. (The ungrammatical "Pacem," in the accusative, was retained deliberately in order not to blur the allusion to the Pope's Encyclical). Until then, declaring the ocean bed (emblematically, in terms of the world governance perspective) "common heritage of mankind" had emerged as the only concrete proposal whereby the great idea of the Pope, the "common good of mankind," could begin to be really adopted as the goal of the United Nations and a principle of international politics. This fact enabled me to raise support and enthusiasm in Malta for Pardo's idea, in both popular and political circles, which otherwise were blind to sea bottom potentiality. Hutchins, in his announcement of *Pacem in Maribus* to be held under Maltese auspices, combined together both the Pardo and the Borgese perspectives, although each is held distinct from the other: "*Pacem in Maribus* is an international and interdisciplinary effort aimed at promoting the clarification of all the issues raised by the use of ocean space and resources. *Pacem in Maribus* considers the emerging law of the sea as a model for the framing in the future of international law and organisation."[76]

75. Published in *To Live as Men: An Anatomy of Peace* (Santa Barbara: Center for the Study of Democratic Institutions, 1965).

76. This quote is from the circular announcing the Pacem in Maribus conference.

Pardo (then in the Department of Political Science, University of Southern California) collaborated with EMB in the production of the book *The New International Order and the Law of the Sea: A Projection.*[77] Pardo's contribution was to propose adaptations and additions to the "Single Negotiating Text", then serving as the basis for the ongoing UN Conference on the Law of the Sea: that of EMB was to marry it indissolubly to the principles and objectives of the New International Economic Order that had emerged at the time as a Third World bandwagon. (The Maltese proposal about the Law of the Sea had already contributed to galvanize and, for a time, make coalesce the so-called Group of 77). However, Pardo was never really happy about the way in which the New International Economic Order was being promoted and realistically feared that it might draw the Common Heritage concept into shipwreck with it through the pursuit of over-ambitious aims. To EMB, on the other hand, the greater picture had always to be kept in sight.

Thus, at the same time (1968) that she produced *The Ocean Regime,* she also produced *The World Communities.* In the series of books in which she was basically concerned with raising awareness of the varied potentialities of the Ocean, she always canvassed the symbolic and even the mythical dimensions of the practical issues or material resources in question. Both literal and metaphoric elements tend to occur in the very titles of her books: *Tides of Change* (1975), on environmentally friendly, peaceful uses; *Sea Farm* (1980) on fisheries and aquaculture; *The Mines of Neptune* (1985) on mineral extraction from the seafloor; *Ocean Frontiers* (1992), on scientific research and institutes. The same kind of presentation of the realities of ocean space in a manner that resonates with their metaphysical and quasi-mystical meanings for humankind is made in books written in a more popular vein, such as *The Drama of the Oceans* (1975) and even in a zanily illustrated book for children, *Chairworm and Supershark* (1992). The most holistic approach, integrative of also the cultural, literary, musical, and spiritual aspects of the Ocean, is of course the last book, with its Gandhian-inspired title: *The Oceanic Circle* (1998).

Attaining the Still Harbour of the Heart

Among other honours received, EMB was awarded the Francis of Assisi environment prize. She was particularly pleased because, although she was allergic to most of the institutional manifestations of the Catholic Church, she loved St. Francis very sincerely. I myself, when Rector of the University of Malta wished that we had a suitable doctorate that we could offer her Honoris Causa, as

77. Published as *IOI Occasional Papers,* Number 4, by the University of Malta in cooperation with RIO (Reviewing the International Order) and the Center for the Study of Democratic Institutions.

would have been for instance a Doctorate in Generosity. Unfortunately, our University offers such doctorates no more than any other does. It is widely known that the *Pacem in Maribus* conferences usually ended in the red, but the deficit was always made up by "an anonymous donor." Sometimes Elisabeth let me see that she had pangs of conscience over whether her disbursements in aid of the Ocean's cause were fair to her daughters, but she also never failed to take measures that restored her peace of mind on this account.

There were of course others besides the editor of *Die Meer-Frau* who referred to her as the "Lady of the Sea"; some even referred to her as the Queen of the Oceans, and it would have been an appropriate title if queenship had retained the spiritual sense which it had for, say, Louis X at Sainte Chapelle, but the role has been too charlatanized. I remember on one occasion somebody singing the finale of the British opera *King Alfred* (1740) which is the famous *Rule, Brittania Rule the Waves* but substituting Elisabeth for Brittania. EMB laughed heartily. I wonder whether she remembered Erika teasingly referring to her as the Princess that she had been in her father's eyes at least, with fairytales in mind, not real seas. But the two worlds have much in common.

Always EMB seemed to live in a magnetic field that had as its two poles the Family and the Ocean. Family and Ocean might in fact be seen as the summation of all the antitheses that the anti-structuralists have sought to deconstruct. The middle term between Family and Ocean for EMB was politics. Although the occasions that called for her to stand up and be counted in political party disputes were quite rare, when they arose EMB usually declared herself a Socialist, but it was participatory democracy that was her ideal. I suspect that she accepted the Socialist label partly out of dislike of its right-wing adversaries, notably Italian Christian Democrats. She was keen on meeting Nenni in New York also for this reason.[78] Her smile was, if one were to resort (as almost naturally one is driven) to angelology, not so much fervidly seraphic, as impishly cherubic.

Many times over more than 3 decades, while on conferences or teaching in courses all over the world, I accompanied Elisabeth for a swim at break of dawn. The contact that she sought with the Ocean was, I felt, mystical as well as physical. It never became routinized into ritual, never became a formal convention, but always remained an act of concrete commitment to the Transcendent. The break of the waves sounded like the echo of the repetitive cock-crow that signaled my patron saint's experience of betrayal on the night of Christ's passion. The Ocean as we have seen was not God. Some degree of badness if not outright malevolence was in-built into the sea.

I remember many a time walking with Elisabeth in the streets of Valletta. The sea, visible from practically every street corner, seemed, because of his-

78. Of course, the whole arena of Italian politics was, in her view, already as polluted as at the time the Mediterranean Sea seemed likely soon to become.

torical association, to grin masochistically: century after century, it had facilitated the arrival on our shores of marauders and armadas bent on ransacking and ravaging the place and its people. Elisabeth almost always in this context asked me about my family, obviously recalling that Malta had the reputation of being not only a buttress against invaders from the Ocean but also a stronghold of the family. The antithesis was not between individualism and totalitarianism or similar political oppositions but simply that of microcosm and macrocosm. I realized that EMB had attempted a deeper reconciliation of great myth and petty reality than that achieved in *Joseph and his Brothers.* The tetralogy had been her father's major preoccupation at the time when she was growing up from the child whose destiny had been prefigured in her father's mind to a closely observant but rationally detached young adult. Her own life work could be truly said to have been familiarization of the Ocean. Of the grand life project dreamt up for her by her Father-magician, she had realized a deeply qualified version, a simultaneously theoretical and practical reconciliation between Man and the Other, without negating the identity of either.

There were times during UNCLOS when I walked in the evening with Elisabeth in the streets of Geneva. The hours on such occasions were slow to pass. Progress at the conference was generally so laborious as to appear interminable. The sky above was invariably a mass of grey cloud, without a patch of blue sky. Yet she would never moan. After long silences, she would speak a few words, and they would be like a soft breeze that yet had the power to sweep away loads of debris—the tons of dirt that had collected in corners for days and months, the gigantic puffs of smoke that had given thick and dark service as screens behind which the truth could be hidden, the dead leaves and left-over straw—and also to set free bees out of bonnets and birds out of cages, for them to soar to the highest heavens.

At times EMB described herself as some kind of Buddhist. But I doubt if she meant anything more by this than that her ideal in life was the easing of the tension between the pulls of Family and Ocean: peace at heart.

Tributes

Elisabeth Mann Borgese: A Life Dedicated to Pacem in Maribus

Sunil M. Shastri
University of Hull, Scarborough Campus, United Kingdom

It was my good fortune, high honour, and proud privilege that Elisabeth Mann Borgese was my friend, philosopher, and guide for almost 20 years. This is my personal tribute to her. Most of what follows was written with a 'noble' purpose. It was also meant to coincide with the 20th anniversary of the opening for signature of the United Nations Convention on the Law of the Sea,[1] something for which EMB devoted her life for over 35 years, first to the making, then to the interpretation, implementation, and development of the Convention.

EMB and I met in April 1983 in Germany. We met frequently since and, more importantly, wrote to each other ever so regularly, but in November 1990 a letter arrived that would have a series of poignant memories for me. EMB had just written a book for children during a flight from Jamaica to Halifax and she had enclosed the manuscript, complete with her own concepts and ideas for sketches and drawings. *Chairworm and Supershark*[2] (for children from 8 to 80) was the book! In December 1995, she presented a copy to my son with the inscription, "Dear Sumedh, Please take care of the oceans! With love from your Aunt Elisabeth." My parents used to visit me every summer for a few months, and in the summer of 2001 my father read some of Elisabeth's writings including *Chairworm and Supershark*. He was keen to translate/transliterate the same into Marathi (our mother tongue) and perhaps into Hindi (our national language). EMB readily gave him her consent to do so. Unfortunately, just as the translation/transliteration was complete, both EMB and my father died, suddenly as they did, within days of each other. Through this book, I feel, three generations of my family have been touched by EMB.

The last few occasions EMB and I met were memorable, each in their own way. In Genoa in May 1998 at the aquarium, I saw her looking at the sharks in childlike amazement reminiscent of the famous picture of Einstein

1. United Nations, *United Nations Convention on the Law of the Sea,* UN Doc. A/CONF.62/122 (New York: United Nations, 1982).
2. E. M. Borgese, *Chairworm and Supershark* (Kingston, Jamaica: The Mill Press, 1992).

Ocean Yearbook 18: 75–87

watching the self-inverting top. She was also equally keen looking at the children's art on display at the Palazzo Ducale and surprised the organisers when she asked for a self-drive car to go to Milan. In April 2000, she was honoured with the Caird Medal in a ceremony at the National Maritime Museum in London and I took her to see the Greenwich Observatory and the Millennium Dome. In October 2000, I had an early birthday present when she took me with her to Buckingham Palace where she presented the Duke of Edinburgh with a copy of *The Oceanic Circle*[3] followed by a celebratory meal at the Athenaeum Club. In November/December 2000, the great and the good of the International Ocean Institute (IOI) gathered together in Hamburg at the splendid Vierjareszeiten for the 28th *Pacem in Maribus* conference, held in the brand new premises of the International Tribunal for the Law of the Sea. My last meeting with EMB was during the Paris Conference in December 2001. We shared what would be our last few double measures of single malt whiskey (I had recently converted her from her favourite Chivas Regal). In due course, the last Niederegger Lubeck Marzipan would arrive in time for the New Year with the message "Have a good year, despite all!" I did not get a reply to my e-mail of 6 February 2002.

As I have indicated, this piece was prepared with a 'noble' purpose in mind and it is now my tribute to Elisabeth Mann Borgese. EMB and her work, including the work of the organization she founded, the IOI, are inextricably linked. IOI, the life's work of EMB, during the 3 decades of its existence, has established itself as the most important and significant global network of 24 Operational Centres in all parts of the world. The cause of Peace in the Oceans (*Pacem in Maribus*) is served through policy research, training and education, publications, conferences, and leadership seminars.

IOI activities rest on the conviction that the United Nations Convention on the Law of the Sea, which entered into force in November 1994, together with the conventions and agreements emanating from the United Nations Conference on Environment and Development 1992, provide a comprehensive international framework for ocean governance. This framework was conceived in the spirit of Principle 25 of the Rio Declaration (1992).[4] It upholds that "Peace, development and environmental protection are interdependent and indivisible"; that peace and human security must be founded on sustainable development; that sustainable development must be founded on peace and human security; and that both human security and sustainable development must be based on equity. IOI has always been in the forefront of exploring the ethical, economic, institutional, and peace-building implications of this principle and its practical implementation at local, national, regional, and global levels.

3. E. M. Borgese, *The Oceanic Circle: Governing the Seas as a Global Resource* (Tokyo: United Nations University Press, 1998).

4. United Nations, *Conference on Environment and Development*, UN Doc. A/CONF.151/26 (New York: United Nations, 1992).

I have also said that the piece was also meant to coincide with the 20th anniversary of the opening for signature of the United Nations Convention on the Law of the Sea, which has been hailed as the "Constitution for the Oceans." EMB dedicated her whole life first to create it and then to profess and propagate it through her own work and that of the IOI.

> An international regime for the peaceful uses of the ocean space shall provide a pattern for the future framework of international organisation.[5]

Elisabeth Veronica Mann was born in Munich, Germany on 24 April 1918, the fifth of six children of Katia Pringsheim and Thomas Mann (1875–1955, Nobel Literature Laureate 1929). Her teens saw the beginnings of the horrors of Nazism and Fascism and the inevitable exile in France, then Switzerland and the United States. Her psyche was moulded and shaped by the writings of Giuseppe Antonio Borgese (1882–1952), whom she considered to be one of the most important and significant influences on her life and work. They married in 1939.

Her lifelong preoccupation was the search for peace and justice for all. She recognised the problems of "being a woman" from her early days and in the tradition of her great grandmother Hedwig Dohm resolved the issue, at least for herself, through her book *Ascent of Woman.*[6] Indeed, this book delves into the affinity between the "feminine" and the "collective," a theme that would develop into the ideas of community management or co-management that she explored in her more recent book, *The Oceanic Circle.*[7]

At the heart of her life and work was her position, following from both her parents and her husband, of a "socialist humanist" or "humanist socialist," a position that found its beginnings in her early collaborative work on world government at the University of Chicago, the place she thought of as "my school; that is where I learned." The goals and ideals of that philosophy are shared more broadly than ever in present-day ideas such as sustainable development. EMB always professed that we have to learn to change our attitude towards nature and our place in it.

The University of Chicago, which had contributed so much to the splitting of the atom, must take the moral responsibility to unite the world, she thought. This led her to contribute to the founding of the Committee to Frame a World Constitution and its journal, *Common Cause* (1948–53). Indeed, there is much similarity between the threat of nuclear holocaust then and that of an environmental disaster today. She readily recognised that just

5. E. M. Borgese, *The Ocean Regime* (Santa Barbara: Center for the Study of Democratic Institutions, 1968).
6. E. M. Borgese, *Ascent of Woman* (New York: G. Braziller, 1963).
7. Borgese (n. 2 above).

as the peaceful and military uses of atomic energy were inextricably linked and required an international agency to govern them, the same applied equally in the area of environmental protection and ocean governance, and just as a combination of guilt and fear led to the concept of an international atomic energy authority, there was a need to create an authority to look after the environment in general and the oceans in particular.

In other areas too, including the coal and steel industry, it was realised that the only way to ensure the prevention of their military use was to vigorously ensure the internationalisation of their peaceful uses. Taking on from the principle that led to the European Union, globalisation was seen by many as the way forward. But for EMB, the means were just as important as the end because she was equally concerned about the consequences of the "evils" of the market. According to her, the market forces may constitute a great potential threat to peace, goodwill, and indeed to democracy.

Way back in the 1940s, the Chicago Draft of a World Constitution[8] was based on the conviction that peace was not merely the absence of war and that the arms race was a symptom rather than a cause, while the root causes were social and economic inequity and only their elimination would lead to the elimination of strife. The constitution proclaimed that earth, water, air, and energy, the four elements of life, were the common property of the human race. Indeed, this was the beginning of the principle of the Common Heritage of Mankind. The concept of the Common Heritage of Mankind germinated as a result of internal discussions in Malta, then a newly independent developing state, in its search for a foreign policy. The concept was later propounded and developed by Maltese Ambassador Arvid Pardo in his famous United Nations General Assembly speech of 1967.[9] EMB, in close cooperation with Arvid Pardo, "the father of the new Law of the Sea," was later instrumental in developing the principle as the basis of a Constitution for the Oceans.

Despite the obvious criticism that this sounded like Utopianism, EMB clung to her ideals of socialist humanism or humanist socialism and often said, "the Utopians of today are the realists of tomorrow; the realists of today are dead tomorrow." "Constructive Utopianism" has been the forerunner of the new law of the sea and sustainable development efforts of our times. There is thus a clear link between the Utopian academic efforts of the Chicago Committee to Frame a World Constitution and the global political efforts to frame what would be called "A Constitution for the Oceans." There is little doubt that EMB was the intellectual link, with her unstinting endeavours over the last 4 decades.

8. R. M. Hutchins, *Preliminary Draft of a World Constitution* (Chicago: University of Chicago Press, 1948).

9. The Statement of Ambassador Pardo was presented on 1 November 1967 to the First Committee of the General Assembly.

Some of the issues that EMB grappled with in the World Constitution are appropriately dedicated to Mahatma Gandhi, that greatest apostle of peace in our times, and are equally relevant even today: sovereignty in an interdependent world; governance from the local to the national to the regional to the global; virtual regions, based on community of cultures; new emerging forms of democracy and the role of "civil society." Just as the eradication of poverty was proclaimed to be the prerequisite for peace, it is now the precondition for sustainable development, thereby inextricably linking eradication of poverty, peace, and sustainable development.

It was in the 1960s at the Center for the Study of Democratic Institutions in Santa Barbara, California that EMB came into her own. The activities of the Center were focused on world order and peace, and on a series of conferences titled *Pacem in Terris*, a phrase borrowed from the Pope John XXIII's encyclical.[10] In 1967, EMB determined that it was in the oceans, where new and revolutionary concepts could be introduced, where the Utopian ideals and ideas for world governance could be tried and tested, and be subsequently implemented in the area of realpolitik.

This was to be the beginning of a 3-year project that was to culminate in what is now a 3-decade-old "System." A series of six preliminary workshops, to which the best national and international experts were invited, was organised by EMB at the Center in Santa Barbara, at the United Nations Institute for Training and Research (UNITAR) in New York and in Rhode Island. The workshops resulted in six volumes delving into all aspects of ocean governance and the realisation that the problems of ocean space are interrelated and need to be considered as a whole: a concept close to the *problematique* of the Club of Rome of which EMB was the only woman founding member.

"The oceans," she said, "are our great laboratory for the making of a new world order." This indeed became the cornerstone of all her work. She paraphrased the Pope and called her first conference in Malta in 1970 *Pacem in Maribus* (PIM). The conference attracted some of the best minds from across the oceans who would subsequently become leaders at the United Nations Conference on the Law of the Sea III (UNCLOS III). Indeed, one of them would even be the President of the Conference, as well as the first President of the IOI. The PIM has since evolved into a highly successful series of annual conferences. The 30th such conference was held in Kiev, Ukraine in October 2003.

The first PIM, in 1970, spawned a Continuing Committee comprising a group of extraordinary people from the east and west, the north and south. This was the cue for EMB the institution builder. Some of the early projects

10. Pope John XXII, "Pacem in Terris," 11 April 1963, http://www.vatican.va/holy_father/john_xxiii/encyclicals/ (accessed on 28 November 2003).

EMB developed contributed to the Barcelona Convention[11] and the Mediterranean Action Plan, a fact generously and frequently credited to the IOI by the United Nations Environment Programme (UNEP). With the funding from those early projects and support from the United Nations Development Programme (UNDP), EMB formally established the IOI as an international nongovernmental organisation at the University of Malta in 1972.

Thereafter, project followed successful project during much of the 1970s: disarmament in the oceans remained a prime commitment, involving personalities such as the Nobel Laureate Alva Myrdal. Other projects investigated the physical, social, economic, legal, and institutional linkages of oceans in governance issues. IOI projects contributed greatly to the work of the New International Economic Order (NIEO) and the Reshaping of International Order (RIO), led by another Nobel Laureate, Jan Tinbergen.

In 1976, EMB published *The Drama of the Oceans*,[12] which was selected by the American Book of the Month Club and netted her royalties of over US$300,000. She spent these on *Pacem in Maribus* in Okinawa, a major event at which the Chairmen of all the Working Committees of UNCLOS III participated, and which exercised a major impact on its work. All this gave IOI an immense intellectual credibility, which in turn was augmented by the continued success of the PIMs. EMB had to look beyond ideas: practical outcomes resulting from great ideas must be demonstrated.

Training programmes provided that breakthrough. EMB recognised the need to train a large number of highly competent personnel to represent their own countries, particularly in developing countries. She was able to enlist the support of the Swedish International Development Agency (SIDA) and, albeit after some initial hesitation, the Canadian International Development Agency (CIDA), which went on to become one of the most important sources of funding for IOI over the last 3 decades. Support came from other quarters, including the Commonwealth Secretariat and the Organisation for Petroleum Exporting Countries (OPEC) Fund, with the ongoing success of existing programmes and as more innovative programmes were established.

The IOI training programmes were indeed the first to apply a genuinely interdisciplinary approach, based on the awareness that the problems of ocean space are closely interrelated and need to be considered as a whole. They advocated social and economic, intragenerational and intergenerational equity, based on the principle of the Common Heritage of Mankind. More than merely providing information and teaching skills, these programmes carried a message: that peace, development, and environmental protection are interdependent and indivisible; that peace and human security must be founded on sustainable development; that sustainable develop-

11. Convention for the Protection of the Mediterranean Sea Against Pollution (Barcelona), http://www.unepmap.org/ (accessed 28 November 2003).

12. E. M. Borgese, *The Drama of the Oceans* (New York: H. N. Abrams, 1975).

ment must be founded on peace and human security; and finally that both human security and sustainable development must be based on equity.

Since the first training programme in 1979, the Class A Programmes on Sea-Bed Mining, the Class B Programmes on Exclusive Economic Zone (EEZ) Management and the Class C Programmes on Regional Issues have become annual events. In the Regional Programmes, EMB saw another potential and opportunity. These programmes were, to borrow a phrase, "of the region, by the region, for the region." EMB embarked on the process of setting up regional "Operational Centres." A major grant from the Global Environment Facility (GEF) jointly administered by the World Bank, UNDP and UNEP would start the evolution of IOI from an Institute to the System that it is today.

Starting with Malta in 1972, and Canada in 1979, four centres in Costa Rica, Fiji, India, and Senegal were established. These were followed by 11 new centres in China, Japan, Kenya, Romania, South Africa, Thailand, Ukraine, Australia, Nigeria, Brazil, and in Chile. It is a testimony to EMB's foresight that they are all well and active on their own initiative and their own means. The agreement for the establishment of an Operational Centre in Germany, at the University of Bremen, was signed on the occasion of the award of the Commander's Cross of Merit by the Government of Germany to EMB. There are more Centres in the offing in Italy, Taiwan, and Russia, and yet more are anticipated in the not too distant future.

The *Ocean Yearbook*, a flagship IOI publication, is another EMB brainchild. Seventeen volumes edited by her have been published, supported by the University of Chicago Press, the East-West Center at the University of Hawaii and the Marine and Environmental Law Programme at Dalhousie University Law School. This, the 18th, is a tribute to her. The *Ocean Yearbook* has become a highly regarded universal source book for students, researchers, scholars, professionals, and writers. The publications of IOI include, inter alia, the PIM proceedings, occasional papers, reports on commissioned projects, reports to and for organisations.

EMB was a visionary; She recognised that all institutions serve their useful purpose in about 20–25 years and then they must look for newer horizons. She realised that the IOI system must also now gear itself for the challenges of the new century, indeed the new millennium.

This would entail both innovative approaches and new collaborations. IOI concluded Memoranda of Understanding (MOUs) with existing host institutions where the Centres are based. MOUs were also signed with the United Nations University (Japan), the Intergovernmental Oceanographic Commission (UNESCO), the University of Rhode Island (USA), the International Centre for the Promotion of Enterprises (Slovenia) as well as the M. S. Swaminathan Foundation and the Murugappa Chettiar Centre (both in India). The TRAIN-SEA-COAST network of the UNDP provided the opportunity for IOI to expand its network to Fundacao Universidade de Rio

Grande (Brazil), the University of Wales (U.K.), the Prince Songkla University (Thailand), ICLARM (The Philippines) and the University of Delaware (U.S.A.).

IOI has established contacts with the United Nations Economic Commission for Africa (UNECA), the United Nations Economic and Social Commission for Asia and the Pacific (UNESCAP), the East Asian Seas Programme, the South Pacific Regional Environment Programme (SPREP), the South Pacific Forum, the West African Regional Seas Programme, the Mediterranean Action Plan, the United Nations Programme on Ocean and Coastal Areas (UNEP/OCA), among others, to integrate their research and training programmes with those of IOI. All these had a profound impact on the governance of the IOI system itself. EMB believed and worked true to the words of the Mahatma, "Be the change you are trying to create."

EMB next took the initiative in 1995 to bring like-minded people together to establish the Independent World Commission on the Oceans (IWCO). She entrusted the presidency of this Commission to Mario Soares, then President of Portugal, in the hope that he would continue the tradition of international social democracy in the spirit of Willy Brandt, Olaf Palme, and Gro Harlem Brundtland. She remained as vice-president and provided much of the initial input, until her resignation, prompted by fundamental disagreements with the Portuguese administration. I know, however, that she was equally keen to reconcile, and I think there was some evidence of this at the Paris meeting, the last time I had the honour and privilege of spending substantive quality time with her. IOI Operational Centres in Canada, China, Fiji, India, Japan, Senegal, and South Africa conducted regional hearings for the Commission. These focused on the North-South divide; the links between the Law of the Sea, Agenda 21, the Biodiversity Convention, the Climate Change Convention, and other recent developments; coastal management issues; and the conferences on habitat, population, straddling stocks, highly migratory species, and small island developing states. The agenda set by IOI was thus all embracing and comprehensive.

Although theoretical work on "integrated coastal management" was quite advanced, it tended to concentrate on physical phenomena such as pollution, erosion, silting, and living resources. The one element that appeared to be missing in most studies was people. This inspired EMB to follow the precedent given by M. S. Swaminathan's work on "eco-villages." She suggested that this experience should be transferred from agricultural villages to poor coastal villages, whose quality of life had to be improved and whose inhabitants had to be integrated into "integrated coastal management," if this term was to have any meaning.

Thus an Eco-Village Project, that now includes 40 villages, was established in the State of Tamilnadu in India, where environmentally and socially sustainable technologies were introduced. These included rainwater harvesting and *spirulina* culture, among others. From India, the project has been transferred to other Operational Centres. Seaweed mariculture operations have been initiated in St. Helena Bay in South Africa, and similar community initiatives were started in Costa Rica, Senegal, and the South Pacific. Funding for these activities has come from the German Foundation for Technical Cooperation (GTZ), a private Swiss donor, the Japan Fund for Global Environment, and the UNDP, among others.

IOI's system-wide activities are focused on action-oriented policy research that encompasses, inter alia, cooperation and transfer of fishing and fish farming technology; risk management as a part of community-based integrated coastal management; the youth programme and the women and the sea programme; contributions to the implementation of the Global Programme of Action for the Protection of the Marine Environment from Land-Based Activities (GPA); the revitalisation of the UNEP's Regional Seas Programme; and finally and most significantly, major contributions to the establishment of an institutional framework capable of implementing and enforcing the rich juridical heritage of the past half century. Thus the IOI played a crucial role in the establishment of the United Nations Informal Consultative Process on Oceans and Law of the Sea (UNICPOLOS) and remains actively involved in its work.

IOI's most recent project, vigorously advanced by EMB, was the establishment of the IOI Virtual University (IOIVU). This will be another breakthrough in the work of the IOI. It is the most ambitious, challenging and innovative project the IOI has undertaken. IOIVU will accept qualified students globally and award an internationally recognised interdisciplinary master's degree in ocean affairs and the law of the sea. This will be an institutional arrangement without precedent, integrating and upgrading the work of the entire IOI network of Operational Centres and their host institutions and blending new educational technology with traditional classroom and internship methodology. The project is envisaged to be co-sponsored by the United Nations University, UNESCO/IOC, and the World Maritime University. Cooperation has also been established with the United Nations Peace University in Costa Rica.

In the last 3 decades, the IOI and the PIM became virtual "think-tanks" in all matters related to oceans and the marine environment. The training programmes established IOI as an undisputed leader in that area. The *Ocean Yearbook* has further strengthened the intellectual and scholarly image of IOI. And EMB, the institution builder, became an institution in her own right. EMB was a fund raiser *par excellence* and a vivacious speaker with a passion that can only come from the courage of conviction of an indefatigable worker: in her own words, "I am too lazy to give up!"

As the IOI goes from strength to strength, the activities of this organisation which is EMB's life's work have grown to encompass every conceivable ocean-related issue, and are providing new ideas and fresh approaches to solving some of the most burning problems of our planet in this new century.

EMB was the brightest star in the firmament of the galaxy of those who have dedicated their lives to the cause of global peace through equity and justice. Indeed, she was called the "Mother of the Oceans" and was instrumental in encouraging world leaders to rethink our relationship with the oceans and our management of marine resources and relate it to global issues.

EMB and her work have come full circle. Her quest for a constitution for the oceans was rooted in her quest for a constitution for the world. The oceans were where the action was going to be, where dreams could become politics and policies, where grand ideas could be tied down to practical activities and realities.

> The oceans are our great laboratory for the making of a new international order, based on new forms of international co-operation and organisation, on a new economic theory, on a new philosophy.[13]

How very true! Her quote then of 1968 at the beginning of this document is nothing short of prophetic.

In two of her most recent books, *Ocean Governance and the United Nations*[14] and *The Oceanic Circle*,[15] she attempted to develop a comprehensive, consistent, transsectoral and participatory system of ocean governance, reaching from the local community to the level of the United Nations. This grand design follows Mahatma Gandhi's vision of a new social world order endowed with "the majesty of the oceanic circle," and is based on the principle of the Common Heritage of Mankind.

In her last days, more work on the Economics of the Common Heritage was in progress. This included development of projects on the economics of peace, taking up a theme dear to Jan Tinbergen in his last years. Another project initiated by her, integrating sustainable development and regional security within the framework of the UN's Agenda for Peace and UNEP's Regional Seas Programme, will be carried out through a series of IOI regional leadership seminars.

Professor Elisabeth Mann Borgese contributed greatly to create and enhance public awareness of the immense importance of the world oceans as a crucial part of our life-support system. The oceans are a major and increasingly important component of the global environmental and economic systems, and the frontier of new thinking on fundamental concepts such as sovereignty, security, and peace. I am honoured that the editors of *Ocean*

13. E. M. Borgese, *The Future of the Oceans: A Report to the Club of Rome* (Montreal: Harvest House, 1986).

14. E. M. Borgese, *Ocean Governance and the United Nations*, 2d rev. ed. (Halifax, N.S.: Centre for Foreign Policy Studies, Dalhousie University, 1996).

15. Borgese (n. 2 above).

Yearbook have given me the opportunity to pay my humble tribute to this great human being, to her splendid work, and to the legacy she has left behind.

ELISABETH MANN BORGESE

Curriculum Vitae

Born in Munich, Germany, 1918. Parents: Thomas Mann and Katia Pringsheim. Emigrated with her parents to United States in 1938. Married Giuseppe Antonio Borgese in 1939. Two daughters: Angelica and Dominica; 1 foster son: Marcel Deschamps; 5 grandchildren; 2 great-grandchildren.

Education

- BA, Classical studies, Freies Gymnasium Zurich; Switzerland, 1935
- Diploma, Conservatory of Music, Zurich, Switzerland, 1937

Career

- Research Associate, University of Chicago, 1946–52
- Editor, *Common Cause*, University of Chicago Press, 1948–52
- Editor, Intercultural Publications, 1952–62
- Senior Fellow, Center for the Study of Democratic Institutions, 1964–78; where she initiated the ocean project; organised the first *Pacem in Maribus* Conference, Malta, 1970; published many papers on peace, disarmament, human rights and development, and the Law of the Sea in the Centre Magazine and other journals
- Killam Senior Fellow, 1979 Dalhousie University
- Professor of Political Science, 1980–2002 Dalhousie University, where she taught regular courses on the Law of the Sea and ocean affairs as well as a 10-week training programme for mid-career civil servants from developing countries
- Adjunct Professor of Law, 1996–2002 Dalhousie University
- Member of Austrian Delegation to the Third United Nations Conference on the Law of the Sea and to the Preparatory Commission for the International Sea-bed Authority and for the International Tribunal for the Law of the Sea, 1974–1987
- Consultant to World Bank, UNIDO, and UNESCO
- Chairperson, International Centre for Ocean Development 1987–92
- Founder and Honorary Chairperson for Life, International Ocean Institute
- Founding Member, Club of Rome
- Member, World Academy of Arts and Sciences

- Associate Member, Third World Academy
- Member, Pugwash Conference

Books

- *To Whom it May Concern*, 1962
- *Ascent of Woman*, 1964
- *The Language Barrier*, 1967
- *The Ocean Regime*, 1968
- *The Drama of the Oceans*, 1976
- *Seafarm: The Story of Aquaculture*, 1982
- *The Mines of Neptune*, 1986
- *The Future of the Oceans: A Report to the Club of Rome*, 1987
- *Chairworm and Supershark* (for children from 8 to 80), 1994
- *Ocean Governance and the United Nations*, 1995
- *Der unsterbliche Fisch* (short stories), 1998
- *The Oceanic Circle: A Report to the Club of Rome*, 1998
- *The International Sea-bed Authority: New Tasks*, 1999
- *Wie Gottlieb Hauptmann die Todesstrafe abschaffte* (short stories), 2001

Books edited

- *Pacem in Maribus*, 1971–1995
- *The Tides of Change*, 1974
- *Ocean Yearbook*, 1978–2002
- *Ocean Frontiers*, 1994

Translations

- Heinrich Schenker, Harmony, 1954
- Max Weber, Philosophy of Law (with Max Rheinstein)

Many reports, articles and short stories in *New Directions*, *The Nation*, *Atlantic Monthly*, *The Vogue*, Law Journals, United Nations/UNESCO Journals, UNCLOS III.

Honours

- Hohes Verdienstkreuz, Government of Austria
- Order of Canada, Government of Canada
- United Nations Sasakawa Prize for the Environment
- Francis of Assisi Environment Prize
- Friendship Prize, Government of China
- Order of Colombia, Government of Colombia

- Lifetime Achievement Award, Nuclear Age Peace Foundation
- Gold Medal "Muenchen Leuchtet," City of Munich, Germany
- Caird Medal, United Kingdom
- Member of Honour, IUCN—The World Conservation Union
- Grosses Bundesverdienstkreuz, Government of Germany

Doctorates honoris causa

- Mount St Vincent University, Halifax, Canada
- Concordia University, Montreal, Canada
- Dalhousie University, Halifax, Canada
- Yokohama City University, Japan
- Costanta "Ovidius" University, Romania

Peace and the Law of the Sea

Agustín Blanco-Bazán*
Legal Office, International Maritime Organization, London

The full commitment of Elisabeth Mann Borgese to the oceans has been insistently characterized as her second life, after years as a writer, journalist, musician, and political activist. True, but only up to a certain point, because that sea which was to become her main occupation during her last years was a persistent leitmotiv of her life since childhood. Hence, her holistic, transcendental view of the oceans as a space representing much more than subject matter to be legally regulated for the sake of passing economic and political interests. The economy and the law of the oceans were for her the expression of a deeply rich and comprehensive cultural and philosophical approach to life. Peace was the ultimate ethical value at the core of her disquisitions on subjects such as the preservation of marine resources, sustainable development of coastal areas, or development of the international law of the sea.

The following reflections address the sources, features, and ultimate meaning of the law of the sea, as an expression of universal peace.

FIRST ENCOUNTER

What triggered Elisabeth's commitment to the seas in the first place? Was it law, economy, or politics? None of these. It was poetry. In the German edition of *The Oceanic Circle*,[1] her 1998 Report to the Club of Rome, she provides an answer to her existential question of. . .

> why the sea? Now it is clear to me. Two streams flow together inside me. One of them has its origin in my early childhood. We were at the beach. I can still see myself. I trembled partly because it was cold and partly because of excitement. I, five years old, held the hand of my fa-

*Editors' Note—The opinions reflected in this article are those of the author and do not reflect the views of the International Maritime Organization or the United Nations.

1. E. Mann Borgese, *The Oceanic Circle: Governing the Seas as a Global Resource* (Tokyo: United Nations University Press, 1998).

Ocean Yearbook 18: 88–97

> ther and of my brother Michael . . . We both looked at the sea for the first time in our lives. My father was proud to show us the sea. He was always very proud at HIS sea, the east sea in Travemünde . . . What mostly impressed me was the horizon. 'This is the horizon' explained my father. 'And what is after the horizon?' I asked. 'The horizon . . . and after, . . . again the horizon'. The more you advance the more the horizon retreats. In this way you always see the horizon until at last land comes to your sight; then the horizon disappears! But you can find it again if you turn back . . . In such a way the horizon of the universe expands itself again and again, and finitude becomes infinitude . . . Soon became very clear to me that my father needed the sea to live. It was part of his life and his work and this has surely influenced me. Today I live and work by the sea. In Nova Scotia you can promenade during hours without meeting anyone, no car, not even a telephone post. Only the beach, rocks, woods and, naturally, the sea. My deep love towards the sea has surely played a role in the choice of the purpose of my life. It is a love upon which the emotional and aesthetic foundations of my life are built.[2]

THE SECOND STREAM

It was not without reason that Thomas Mann was nicknamed "The Magician" by members of his own family. His image of the horizon was a successful trick to awake his daughter's fascination with the infinitude of the oceans. The second stream pushing Elisabeth towards her full oceanographic vocation was the result of her political awareness, as a 30-year-old German refugee in post-war, pre-McCarthyist United States. The devastation of Planet Earth represented by the destruction of Hiroshima, Nagasaki and the German cities, made Elisabeth a convinced believer in global solutions as the only means of counteracting further catastrophes. Not surprisingly, her attitude toward the then recently established United Nations was critical:

> . . . World peace could not be established on the basis of a status quo. The first condition for World Peace was, already then, international social justice: *pax justitiae.* The United Nations was not in a position to promote this goal. It represented nothing else but the powers victorious in the Second World War who had made up their minds that their task was to avoid a new war. . .[3]

2. E. Mann Borgese, *Mit den Meeren Leben* (Cologne: Kiepenhauer & Witsch, 1999), pp. 17–19.
3. Ibid., p. 19.

Peace was not possible unless this defensive tactical attitude was reverted in favour of a proactive plan of action toward the achievement of international social justice:

> Peace and justice stand and fall together: *Pax opus justitiae* and without social and economic justice, national or international, there could be no peace, which is more than the absence of war.[4]

Inspired by this conviction, Elisabeth and her husband, Giuseppe Antonio Borgese, together with a distinguished group of academics at the University of Chicago immediately went into action. They established the Committee to Frame a World Constitution, and already in 1948, millions of copies of the Chicago World Constitution were circulating in 50 different languages.

Elisabeth said, continuously (dare I say every day?), that "the utopians of today are the realists of tomorrow," and the two following paragraphs of her 1999 Nexus address explain how the utopia of the World Constitution somehow became a reality in the United Nations Convention on the Law of the Sea:[5]

> While fully aware that our Constitution was not "realistic" in the sense that the international community could adopt it in the immediate tomorrow, we intended it to be a blueprint pointing in the direction of a desirable, or probably, ineluctable future. We went as far as to suggest that, on the basis of the present economic system and its Roman Law concept of ownership, economic justice was unattainable. Borrowing from the Dean of Canterbury, the Reverend Hewlett Johnson, our Constitution declares that the four elements of life—earth, water, air, energy—are the common property of the human race. The management and use of such portions thereof, as vested in or assigned to particular ownership, private or corporate or national or regional, of definite or indefinite tenure, of individualist or collectivist economy, shall be subordinated in each and all cases to the interest of the common good. "Earth" included not only the surface real estate but the mineral resources of the subsoil as well. "Water" meant both the oceans and freshwater resources; "air" meant the atmosphere, as a traffic highway and a resource, and a part of our biosphere of vital importance for human survival; and "energy" includes all forms of energy, non-renewable or renewable.

4. E. Mann Borgese, "The Years of My Life" (The Nexus Lecture, Tilburg, The Netherlands, 12 May 1999).

5. United Nations Convention on the Law of the Sea, 1982. Adopted 10 December 1982, entered into force, 14 November 1994.

> Utopian as that might have appeared to be in the Forties, one part of it has found its topos. The United Nations Convention on the Law of the Sea of 1982 declares the sea-bed and ocean floor beyond the limits of national jurisdiction, to be the Common Heritage of Mankind, which cannot be appropriated by any State, company, or individual but must be managed, under the aegis of the International Sea-Bed Authority, for the benefit of humankind as a whole, with particular consideration for the poor. It also is reserved for exclusively peaceful purposes and must be managed with due consideration for the conservation of the marine environment so that also future generations can share its benefits.[6]

After the exile imposed by the McCarthyist era, Elisabeth was summoned again by Robert Hutchins to continue with their quest for the implementation of the Constitution of the World, this time at his Center for the Study of Democratic Institutions in Santa Barbara, California. She noted that the Constitution did not need improving, "It was the world that needed improvement!"[7] But she was ready to settle by starting to change the world beyond the coastlines. This time, Arvid Pardo, Ambassador of Malta to the United Nations, replaced Thomas Mann as the magician in charge of releasing the second and final stream leading her to the oceans. In line with Pardo's famous United Nations ocean address on 1 November 1967, Elisabeth suggested to Hutchins that if the Cold War made the operation of the World Constitution unlikely, the United Nations seemed more receptive to accept a World Constitution . . . at least for the seas. "The oceans, I said, could be a great laboratory for the making of a new world order."[8] The Center organized a 3-year project leading to a Conference that paraphrased Pope John XXIII's encyclical letter *Pacem in Terris*[9] to explain a relatively more modest but by all means no less ambitious project, *Pacem in Maribus.*

FROM RES COMMUNIS TO COMMON HERITAGE

Elisabeth's approach to the UNCLOS concept of the Area[10] as the Common Heritage of Mankind was basically a derivative of the philosophy of the Constitution of the World, albeit with an important difference: the Constitution

6. Borgese (n. 4 above).
7. Borgese (n. 4 above).
8. Borgese (n. 4 above).
9. Pope John XXII, "Pacem in Terris," in Encyclical on *Establishing Universal Peace in Truth, Justice, Charity, and Liberty,* 11 April 1963, http://www.vatican.va/holy_father/john_xxiii/encyclicals/.
10. See Articles 136 and 137, UNCLOS (n. 5 above).

proclaimed the concept of common property (not heritage) of the seas in general. The UNCLOS notion of common heritage applies only to the area defined as "the seabed and ocean floor and subsoil thereof, beyond the limits of national jurisdiction"[11] and its resources. This unwanted limitation was noted by both Elisabeth and Arvid Pardo and explains the latter one's reflection that UNCLOS was a half-empty glass. With characteristic optimism, Elisabeth counterclaimed that the glass was half-full and added an important observation: the limitations to the principle of common heritage are belied by the operation of a wider, more comprehensive UNCLOS principle according to which the problems of ocean space are closely interrelated and must be considered as a whole. "If there is a systems change in one part of ocean space, it will necessarily affect the whole ocean system."[12] It is through this reasoning that the holistic nature of the concept of sustainable development can be recognized:

> The Common Heritage principle is of fundamental importance not only for the oceans but as a basis for sustainable development in general. 'Sustainable development' either is nothing, a tautology, because development that is not sustainable is not development; or it is the new name, the new form of 'humanistic socialism' or 'socialist humanism' that we need for the next [21st] century.[13]

The lack of extension of the concept of common heritage to other oceanic spaces was considered by Elisabeth as a necessary compromise between the old and the new. The old is represented by the shortcomings of the misguided Western political thinking according to which the concept of territorial sovereignty of Roman Law should also apply to the oceans. By definition, the vision of the infinitude of the oceans that Thomas Mann imprinted on his daughter's mind means a lack of frontiers. While appropriation of land through conquest is at the core of the establishment of any Western nation, the sea cannot be conquered according to the same principles. It is on the basis of this distinction that Hugo Grotius, after explaining how sovereignty on land operates as the basic tool of domination by States over their subjects, elaborates on the concept of freedom of the seas as the absence of State sovereignty over ocean space.

Grotius's approach to the freedom of the seas is essentially based upon the conceptualisation of the sea as res communis and accordingly not subject to territorial appropriation. Although the expression res communis implies common property, the concept is essentially a negative one. Res communis is in fact res nullius. To say that something belongs to everybody in the same

11. Article 1 (1) UNCLOS (n. 5 above).
12. Borgese (n. 4 above).
13. Borgese (n. 4 above).

way means exactly the same as saying that it belongs to nobody. At the time of Grotius the doctrine was peacefully accepted because the sea in itself was not seen as a source of economic wealth. Freedom of the sea could not mean freedom to exploit the sea's resources, in particular the seabed, because this was by definition an impossible task. Accordingly, freedom at sea in Grotius's times could only mean freedom of navigation. The principle of nonappropriation of the seas only meant that coastal States were not entitled to intercept foreign ships on the basis that they were entering their territory. The obvious consequence of this notion is that the law at sea was only the law of the flag State on board ships. There was not, there could not be any law governing ocean space as such.

The only activity of exploitation of sea resources known at Grotius's time, namely fishing, was never understood as an exploitation implying appropriation of territory. By its very nature, fishing was an activity exclusively to be exerted by fishermen of coastal States. The notion of foreign vessels coming from far away to fish on sea areas historically exploited by coastal fishermen was unthinkable until a few decades ago. Neither the technology nor the economic rationale existed to justify a fleet crossing overseas distances to appropriate fish stocks traditionally serving as the source of nourishment and economic activities that only made sense for local fishermen.

This status quo did not change until well into the 20th century, when scientific research and technological progress demonstrated the extent to which marine resources were a source of economic wealth. It particularly irritated Elisabeth Mann Borgese that the response to these discoveries was the recycling of the Roman Law concept of territorial appropriation to conquer the seas. She nevertheless accepts that UNCLOS

> deals with the concept of 'sovereignty' as creatively as it deals with the concept of 'ownership.' It limits, transforms, and transcends the concept of 'sovereignty' in an interdependent world. . . With the introduction of the Exclusive Economic Zone, the Archipelagic Waters, the Regime for the Islands, and the new definition of the Continental Shelf, the Convention achieved the most extensive peaceful distribution of ocean space in history. This is not to say that this redistribution did not create as many problems as it solved; or that it will stay forever. It may be transitional, leading up to intensified development of regional cooperation and organization. But, to start with, it has replaced a system of laissez-faire in the ocean with a framework for management.[14]

Of particular importance to understand the trading between old and new legal principles represented by UNCLOS are Mikis Manolis's views quoted

14. Borgese (n. 4 above).

by Elisabeth Mann Borgese in *The Oceanic Circle* on the Exclusive Economic Zone (EEZ):

> In terms of unbundling or disaggregation of the traditional package of sovereign territorial rights, it would seem that the EEZ involves a partial negation of mutually exclusive territoriality in that inclusive rights of use, with respect to such activities as navigation and overflight, are incorporated in the same geographical area in which the adjacent coastal state enjoys exclusive rights with respect to certain resources and economic activities, such as the exploitation of living and nonliving resources.[15]

Indeed, one of the most important tasks to enhance the implementation of the philosophy of cooperation at the core of UNCLOS is the further disaggregation of sovereign territorial rights for the sake of a better management of natural resources on the basis of the consideration not only of the interests of the coastal State but also global and regional interests.

The importance of these concepts is obvious. They reflect an in-depth understanding of the radical change in the main features of the relationship between humans and the oceans and the consequential need to change basic notions of international law and the law of the sea. From space for commercial navigation, the sea had progressed to become a space for economic exploitation. It was no more possible to avoid regulating at a global level the activities implied in this exploitation. The Western response to the discovery through scientific research of the economic value of ocean resources and the availability of technology to exploit them was simply to try to apply old-fashioned legal concepts of sovereignty and appropriation as the legal basis for exploitation of the oceans. Elisabeth's alternative proposal is clear: The sea should not be appropriated to be exploited. Resources could be legitimately used without being owned.

USERS, NOT OWNERS

Elisabeth's understanding of the concept of users is developed in her report to the Club of Rome: "It is a concept of non-ownership under which natural or legal persons have *user rights* and management prerogatives, but not ownership rights in the Roman Law sense."[16] The reference to a negative concept (nonownership) to introduce a positive one (users), although not hermeneutically felicitous, nevertheless demonstrates the philosophical dilemma implied in the transition of Grotius's philosophy regarding a space in

15. Borgese (n. 1 above), p. 119.
16. Borgese (n. 1 above), p. 59.

which the res communis in fact meant res nullius to the misguided approach according to which the sea would have to be appropriated to be exploited. The negative concept of users as non-owners can only be transcended through a positive element if a valid legal title is to be established to regulate the concept of use of the seas through proper management. In Elisabeth's version, this title is necessarily of an ethical kind:

> The Common Heritage principle has a fundamental ethical component: for both user rights and management prerogatives must be exercised with due consideration of the common good, which includes the rights of the poor countries and poor people (intra-generational equity) as well as the rights of future generations with which it must be shared and for which it must be conserved (inter-generational equity). It has an economic development dimension, it has an environmental dimension, and it has a peace-building dimension: for, in the definition given by the Law of the Sea Convention, the Common Heritage of Mankind must be reserved for exclusively peaceful purposes.[17]

COASTAL COMMUNITY MANAGEMENT

Hardly ever do we see articles today on the law of the sea and maritime law occupied with the consideration of the comprehensive ethical questions that lie at the core of the very concept of any legal discipline. One of the unwanted results of this fundamental shortcoming is the analysis of oceanic legal questions in isolation, without establishing their correlation with other branches of law. Elisabeth Mann Borgese's approach firmly reasserts ethics as the coordinating factor of the law of the sea with international law and basic human rights of the individual. It should not be forgotten that the expression "oceanic circle" reproduces thoughts on integration of the human race inspired by the thinking of Mahatma Gandhi, quoted in Elisabeth's report to the Club of Rome:

> In this structure, composed of innumerable villages,
> there will be ever-widening, never ascending circles.
> Life will not be a pyramid
> with the apex sustained by the bottom.
> But it will be an oceanic circle
> whose centre will be the individual,
> always ready to perish for the villages,
> the latter ready to perish for the circle of villages,
> till at last the whole becomes one life

17. Borgese (n. 1 above), p. 59–60.

> composed of individuals,
> never aggressive in their arrogance,
> but ever humble,
> sharing the majesty of the oceanic circle
> of which they are integral units.[18]

In Elisabeth's view, the primacy of the individual is not understood as the upholding of the individual's right to assert his or her rights through competitive economic activities at the cost of the community.

> The individual, however, is not conceived as an ego whose interest or whose growth is limited or in conflict with the interests of the community (the dualistic view) but as part of the whole . . . This concept of the individual and his/her relationship to the whole contains within itself the two fundamental principles on which the Law of the Sea is founded: the principle of the Common Heritage of Mankind, and the principle of the close interrelationship of all problems of ocean space, which need to be considered as a whole. It also accords with the guidelines for institution-building laid down in *Our Common Future* and *Agenda 21*.[19]

Through these assertions, Elisabeth manages to complete her cycle: After starting with a proposal for a Constitution for the World and transacting with something less ambitious, namely a constitution for the oceans, she uses the fundamental ethical principles of the latter to build up a proposal for coastal State integration, based on cooperation which by definition transcends frontiers. In the Nexus lecture she unashamedly proclaims the goal at the core of the Constitution of the World, namely that of abolishing the Westphalian concept of nation States:

> For this is what is going on in 'my time': a reshuffling of the socio-economical map we had inherited from the time of Grotius, for me the time of the Westphalian peace treaty ending the Thirty Years War. States which we thought were to be there forever in their present form, tend to devolve more power and more responsibility to smaller, local entities . . . The local component, however, can succeed only if, in this process, it can establish proper linkages with the national and the supranational, in particular, regional level.[20]

Always aware of the need to avoid proclaiming ideals without relating them to already given realities, she then mentions concrete cases of direct cooper-

18. Borgese (n. 1 above), p. 1.
19. Borgese (n. 1 above), p. 133.
20. Borgese (n. 4 above).

ation among local communities across State boundaries, such as the associations of port cities, cooperation for the protection of the environment between the Canadian Provinces and the U.S. States in the Gulf of Maine, and the cooperation of municipalities around the Sea of Japan. She even reminded us of the existence of the frequently neglected 1980 European Outline Convention on Transfrontier Cooperation between Territorial Communities or Authorities.[21] As an example of the direct participation of local communities in intergovernmental organizations, she mentions the Mediterranean Commission on Sustainable Development within the treaty system established by the Barcelona Convention.[22]

The originality of Elisabeth's thinking in this regard can be noted in particular through two main features. She did not appraise these examples of supranational integration as separate regional initiatives, but as steps to a global coordination of community-based ocean management. Furthermore, she conceives local coastal communities as units where all individuals become users of the oceans. And she reminds us that, as in any other branch of public law, the law of the sea finds its ultimate justification as an instrument of peace and justice if it becomes a tool to serve the needs of poor coastal villages, poor countries, and poor regions. The process of increasing welfare through appropriate coastal management does not stop at coastal areas. Their prosperity is a first step to create further prosperity in inland areas. Peace at sea meant for Elisabeth only a first step to achieve peace on earth: through *Pacem in Maribus* to *Pacem in Terris* by operation of international law and the law of the sea.

21. European Outline Convention on Transfrontier Cooperation between Territorial Communities or Authorities, 21 May 1980, http://conventions.coe.int/treaty/en/Treaties/Html/106.htm.

22. Convention for the Protection of the Marine Environment and the Coastal Region of the Mediterranean (Barcelona Convention), adopted 16 February 1976, entered into force 12 February 1978, amended 10 June 1995 (not yet in force), http://www.unepmap.org/.

Grotius and the New Law*

J. Alan Beesley, O.C., Q.C.
Head of Canadian Delegation, Ambassador to the Law of the Sea Conference and Chair of Conference Drafting Committee (1967–1983)

Elisabeth and I were friends and colleagues for 35 years. From the early days of the United Nations Law of the Sea Conference and later during a series of Pacem in Maribus Conferences, Elisabeth played a unique role blending idealism, perseverance, and commitment, reflected in a continuum of concrete proposals and related negotiations. No one who came to know Elisabeth was unaffected by her. I also had the good fortune to go skiing with her in Switzerland and recall the occasion as one characterized as much by laughter and good fellowship as athletic skill. I will miss Elisabeth and her approach to life, both professionally and personally.

INTRODUCTION

We have been privileged to hear three stimulating speeches, any one of which is a tough act to follow, especially in the presence of Ambassador Satya Nandan, a friend and colleague for many years. Who would envy me, speaking after Minister Brian Tobin and Premier Clyde Wells, two of Canada's foremost orators? Fortunately, my role is a modest one, which is simply to set the stage for our discussions of the law of the sea. In so doing, I shall try to be mindful of the inscription on a plaque given to me by Leonard Legault when he thought I was retiring, which reads: "Old lawyers never die; they simply lose their appeal."

The Thesis

It is my thesis that, firstly, the international community has entered a transitional period in the history of the law of the sea. We are witnessing the close

*Editors' Note.—This paper was presented at the Memorial University of Newfoundland Colloquium on the Oceans on the occasion of the 50th Anniversary of the United Nations, 17 November 1995, St John's, Newfoundland, Canada.

Ocean Yearbook 18: 98–116

of a major law-making process, and the beginning of one of consolidation, implementation, and enforcement. How we act, and when we act, will most certainly determine the fate of the world's oceans and their living resources. Second, we seem finally to have reached a turning point, and must now decide whether we shall continue to pursue a competitive rights-based approach, or whether we move beyond these primitive concepts and begin to accept the responsibilities that go hand-in-hand with rights in any viable system of law. One wearies of hearing that we must fill real or imagined lacunae in the law. While the law-making process is continuous, what we need most is not more law, but more respect for the law. Unenforced law undermines the Rule of Law itself. Third, we must further develop the scientific and institutional basis for an Ecosystem Assessment and Management regime that is vital to sustainable fisheries. That process, already begun, must be maintained and accelerated.[1] Such basic shifts in thinking are difficult to achieve, but they can be encouraged and developed on such occasions as this very Colloquium.

Questions For Consideration

Thus the first question I would like to pose is, has the system of international law of the sea failed us, or have we failed the system? Has the law been inadequate, or have we, in the way we have applied it?

I propose to illustrate the relevance of these questions by referring to a very recent document, comprising a checklist of action required by States pursuant to the Fisheries and Environmental provisions of the 1982 United Nations Convention of the Law of the Sea. It is presented in the form of an annotated Chart, entitled "Conservation and Management of the Marine Environment" and was prepared by Professors Douglas M. Johnston and Phillip M. Saunders, under the auspices of the World Conservation Union (IUCN).[2] I had the honour of distributing this document at the Ceremonies in Kingston, Jamaica, celebrating the coming into force of the Convention, on 16 November 1994. It was received with great interest, and clearly made an impact on the participants.[3]

1. L. A. Kimball and D. M. Johnston, *The Law of the Sea: Priorities and Responsibilities in Implementing the Convention* (Gland, Switzerland: IUCN, 1995), Part I.

2. Official Records to the Third United Nations Conference on the Law of the Sea. Vol. XVII, UN Document A/CONF.62/122. New York: United Nations, 1984. D. M. Johnston and P. M. Saunders, *Conservation and Management of the Marine Environment: Required Initiatives and Responsibilities under the 1982 U.N. Convention on the Law of the Sea,* (Gland, Switzerland: The World Conservation Union and Commission on Environmental Law, 1995).

3. EDITORS' NOTE.—The following text needs to take into consideration that: (1) Canada's Oceans Act was enacted in 1996 and came into force in 1997; and (2)

I wonder how many of us here today would raise our hands if we were asked which of us has analysed that document and compared it to Canada's existing and proposed legislation, including the new Canada Oceans Act?[4] Has anyone proposed that the checklist be updated so as to embody the requirements of the August 3, 1995 Draft Agreement for the implementation of the provisions of the 1982 UN Convention relating to straddling and highly migratory fish stocks?[5] Is legislation already being drafted by Canadian officials to implement the 1995 Agreement? If so, are we all in accord as to which of the provisions of the 1995 Agreement are directed towards the more effective implementation and enforcement of the 1982 Convention and which ones embody new law? Is everyone agreed on whether non-parties to the 1982 Convention are entitled to ratify or accede to the 1995 Agreement? Are both treaties included within the "The New International Law of Fisheries" which is to be the focus of our discussions? Can we seriously discuss the new law without addressing these issues? I hope these questions will be addressed and discussed seriously.

To facilitate our deliberations, I must revisit the past briefly, and propose to divide my comments as follows:

(i) Grotius as the High Priest: 1608–1967
(ii) Grotius Defrocked: 1967–1982
(iii) Grotius, Selden, and the Ecology: 1982–1994
(iv) Grotius and the Pirates: 1994–1995

GROTIUS AS THE HIGH PRIEST: 1608–1967

Presumably, everyone knows that Hugo Grotius is commonly regarded as the father of international law. Every law student and every old sea dog is aware of the victory by Grotius over Selden in their classic dispute over the basic concepts on which the law of the sea should be founded. Selden argued persuasively for extended coastal jurisdiction in his treatise *Mare Clausum*,[6] and Grotius argued more persuasively in his *Mare Liberum* for freedom of

that Canada became a party to the United Nations Fish Stocks Agreement in 1999, and the Agreement came into force in December 2001.

4. Oceans Act, S.C. 1996, c. 31, assented to on 18 December 1996, in force 31 January 1997 pursuant to section 109 and as fixed by the Governor in Council.

5. Agreement for the Implementation of the Provisions of the United Nations Convention on the Law of the Sea of 10 December 1982 Relating to the Conservation and Management of Straddling Fish Stocks and Highly Migratory Fish Stocks, A/CONF.164/37 (8 September 1995), entered into force 11 December 2001, http://www.un.org/depts/los/.

6. J. Selden, *Of the Dominion; or, Ownership of the Sea* (New York: Arno, 1972). Translation of *Mare Clausum*, Reprint of the 1652 ed.

the high seas, except for a narrow territorial sea.[7] Grotius was so successful that his teachings went unchallenged for over 350 years; that is to say, from 1608, the date of *Mare Clausum*, to 1958, the date of the first UN Law of the Sea Conference.

As pointed out by Jan Schneider in her provocative article in the *Virginia Journal of International Law*, "Grotius' views were the commonly accepted theory and practice for hundreds of years, even as late as the First and Second U.N. Conferences on the Law of the Sea in 1958 and 1960."[8] She points out that: "As far as the maritime waters and their resources were concerned, Grotius continued to reign supreme at UNCLOS I on the Convention on the High Seas, the Convention on the Territorial Sea and the Contiguous Zone, and the Convention on Fishing and Conservation of the Living Resources of the High Seas."[9] It is for these very reasons, of course, as I can attest personally, that Canada has never ratified these Conventions. Somewhat unkindly, Jan Schneider goes on to comment: "Although UNCLOS II dealt solely and explicitly with the question of the limits of territorial waters, its participants were unable to reach an agreement on even a small extension, the majority refusing to accept anything wider than the traditional three-mile territorial sea and twelve-mile contiguous zone."[10]

Jan Schneider does concede that: "Selden's ideas, nevertheless, made some inroads on history in the Convention on the Continental Shelf, which did allow coastal State assertion of sovereignty to a depth of 200 metres or, beyond that limit, to where the depth of the superjacent waters admits of the exploitation of the natural resources of the said areas."[11] Once again, I can attest personally that it was precisely because of such considerations, of particular interest to the area where this Conference is being held, that Canada ratified the 1958 Geneva Continental Shelf Convention, on 6 February 1970, at a time when such extensive coastal claims were already being strongly opposed by the champions of the common heritage of mankind. It should be added, in a spirit of objectivity, that certain provisions from the 1958 Conventions were later incorporated, on a highly selective basis, into the 1982 UN Law of the Sea Convention, in those cases where the disciples of Grotius had won over the followers of Selden.

7. H. Grotius, *Mare Liberum: sive, De iure quod Batavis competit ad Indicana commercia dissertatio* (New York: Carnegie Endowment for International Peace, 1952).

8. J. Schneider, "Something old, something new: some thoughts on Grotius and the marine environment," *Virginia Journal of International Law* 18, no. 1 (1977–78): 147–64, 149–50.

9. Ibid., p. 150.; For 1958 Geneva Conventions, see *Official Records of the United Nations Conference on the Law of the Sea*, vols. I to VII. United Nations publication, Sales No.: 58. V.4, vols. I to VII.

10. Schneider (n. 8 above), p. 150.

11. Ibid.

Questions For Consideration

If we are to draw any lessons from this brief revisiting of the past, the first, I suggest, is the incredible continuity of thinking concerning the basic concepts and the fundamental choices reflected in the history of the law of the sea. It is clearly a history of competing rights. Should we follow Grotius, or Selden, or chart a new course, drawing on the lessons of each? A secondary but very concrete point is that Canada must eventually decide between the 1958 UN Convention on the Continental Shelf and the 1982 UN Convention on the Law of the Sea, Part VI of which spells out in precise, albeit complex, terms the extensive claims accorded to countries such as Canada. An underlying question being asked, which takes us from the past not only to the present but the future is should Canada continue to assert the rights accorded to coastal States under the 1982 Convention, while not becoming a party to the Convention? I hope there will be some discussion on these points, and I would encourage a little creative tension.

Pressures For Change

It is necessary to turn now from the modest attempts to modify the Law of the Sea in 1960 to the radical, almost revolutionary restructuring of the law reflected in the eventual 1982 UN Convention. How did we get from there to here—and beyond? It didn't just happen. The developments of which I speak reflected deeply divergent views of what the law should be, and even of what the law already was. It was clear to some of us, even in the mid-1960s, that the traditional concept of the freedom of the seas according to Grotius was no longer viable. Neither, however, was the wholly opposite approach argued by Selden of unchecked coastal jurisdiction. Accommodations between the two competing doctrines seemed to be essential. However, the system still in place at that time was that of Grotius. It was necessary, if we were to change the law, to unfrock Grotius, a shocking act to which I plead guilty. The doctrine of Grotius reflected a functional approach, valid for its time, and it was a very long time. Clearly, however, it no longer sufficed. Serious and widespread pressures for change began to develop. The commentary by Lee A. Kimball contained in the 1995 IUCN publication, "The Law of the Sea: Priorities and Responsibilities in Implementing the Convention" provides an objective analysis of the pressures for changes in the law, written from the point of view of disinterested NGOs.[12]

It is not difficult to summarize the state of the law of the sea by 1967, when the first steps were taken which led to the launch of the Third Law of the Sea Conference. Put simply, the law was in a state of chaos due to

12. Kimball (n. 1 above).

the inability of the 1958 and 1960 Law of the Sea Conferences to adjust to the demands for change in the traditional law of the sea.

It is not necessary to recount the series of claims and counter claims that arose between the Second and Third Law of the Sea Conferences. Fisheries and boundaries disputes broke out between developed States, and newly independent countries began to challenge the strictures of the past, which they had had no hand in developing. The advent of new technology, particularly factory trawlers and supertankers, began to drive this process. The law of the sea was approaching anarchy, and it was ripe for change. If we recall the long-winded joke about which profession is truly the oldest, it will be noted that the engineer indignantly defended his profession's claim by saying, "Before the creation of the world, clearly an engineering feat, there was only chaos," whereupon the lawyer allegedly replied, "And who do you think created the chaos?"

It is not widely known that in the early 1960s, Canada and the United Kingdom tried together to develop a Law of the Sea Convention, outside the United Nations, based on the failed proposals of the second conference, nor that their efforts were abandoned only when the United States of America refused to support the initiative, after giving lengthy consideration to the results of their joint representations to many countries.[13]

The New Law of the Sea

It is more widely known that in 1967 two new and seemingly unrelated diplomatic initiatives were launched, each of which was supported by the United States. The first and most well-known initiative was the famous 3-hour speech in the United Nations by Ambassador Arvid Pardo of Malta, in November 1967, in which he proclaimed the concept of the common heritage of mankind to be applicable to the seabed and ocean floor beyond national jurisdiction.[14] Ever afterwards, all continental shelf claims, indeed, all coastal claims to jurisdiction beyond the territorial sea, including fishing zones, were regarded, or at least portrayed, as examples of unbridled greed, encroaching upon the common heritage. It was during this same period that the United States and the USSR jointly proposed, outside the United Nations, in a series of coordinated demarches a regime for a territorial sea extending to a maximum of 12 M, coupled with freedom of navigation

13. Author's personal confidential experience. No documentation.

14. Arvid Pardo, "Examination of the Question of the Reservation Exclusively for Peaceful Purposes of the Seabed and the Ocean Floor, and the Subsoil thereof, underlying the High Sea Beyond the Limits of Present National Jurisdiction, and the Use of their Resources in the Interest of Mankind," (Agenda item presented to the First Committee of the 22nd United Nations General Assembly, 1 November 1967).

through a high seas corridor in international straits. A third element proposed to the two superpowers by Canada and some other States demanded preferential coastal fishing rights in the adjacent high seas. The joint two-power proposal was later amended to include a fourth element, binding adjudication of disputes on fisheries, a first for the USSR.

These parallel initiatives eventually met and coalesced, on 17 December 1970, in a UN Resolution convening the Third United Nations Law of the Sea Conference.[15] By then it was clear, in the UN Sea-Bed Committee, created in 1967, that the two initiatives had one element in common—resistance to extensions of jurisdiction by coastal States. The disciples of Grotius were at it again. Because this approach did not reflect Canada's interests, the Canadian delegation played an extremely active role in the negotiations leading to the decision to convene a Third UN Law of the Sea Conference. I had the privilege of chairing those negotiations and subsequently introducing into the United Nations the draft resolution emerging from them, on which the decision to hold the Third Conference was based.[16] This decision reflected the Canadian view that a conference limited to the three issues of the territorial sea, passage through straits, and coastal fishing rights, the so-called "manageable package," favoured by the superpowers, would never succeed, and that the agenda must be comprehensive and deal with the whole range of issues left unresolved or resolved imperfectly by the past two UN Conferences. Thus Resolution 2750 (XXV) decided on an agenda including the regime and international machinery for the seabed resources beyond national jurisdiction; a definition of the international area; the regime of the high seas; the continental shelf; fishing and conservation of the living resources of the high seas, including the preferential rights of coastal States; the preservation of the marine environment, and the prevention of pollution; and the regime for scientific research as well as the three issues proposed by the superpowers.[17]

Shortly after the introduction of the resolution proposing the convening of the Third Law of the Sea Conference, I had the privilege of introducing into the General Assembly, on behalf of all the sponsors of the resolution, a series of procedural "understandings," including the "package deal" on which the Conference negotiations thereafter were based.[18]

15. UN Resolution 2750 (XXV), 17 December 1970. Reservation exclusively for peaceful purposes of the sea-bed and the ocean floor, and the subsoil thereof, underlying the high seas beyond the limits of present national jurisdiction and use of their resources in the interests of mankind, and convening of a conference on the law of the sea. D. J. Djonovich, ed., *United Nations Resolutions: Series 1, General Assembly* v. XIII 1970–71 (New York: Oceana Publications, 1975), p. 241–43.

16. Ibid.

17. Ibid.

18. UN Resolution 2749 (XXV), 17 December 1970. Declaration of Principles Governing the Sea-Bed and the Ocean Floor, and the Subsoil Thereof, beyond the Limits of National Jurisdiction. D. J. Djonovich, ed., *United Nations Resolutions: Series*

GROTIUS DEFROCKED: 1967–1982

Positions diverged sharply on every issue. It had to be demonstrated why the law of the sea required a radical restructuring—a basic law reform process, rather than a tinkering with the law, as in 1958 and 1960. We set out to debunk the mystique surrounding the two absolutist concepts on which the law of the sea had been founded—the sovereignty of States and the freedom of the high seas.

I am accused of defrocking Grotius, because I was the first to quote in the United Nations the following excerpt from his famous 1608 treatise *Mare Liberum*.

> Most things become exhausted with promiscuous use. This is not the case with the sea. It can be exhausted neither by fishing nor by navigation, that is to say in the two ways in which it can be used.[19]

Yes, I did say it, and was the first to do so. However, I defended Grotius for not having been able to foresee the days of factory trawlers and supertankers, nor that the freedom of the high seas would be transformed into the right to overfish and a license to pollute. I characterized the traditional concept of the freedom of the high seas as a doctrine tailored to the needs of sailing ships and global empires, but increasingly irrelevant to the needs of the 20th century. I deliberately attacked sacred cows, and was occasionally gored. Nonetheless, I described flag State jurisdiction as roving sovereignty, and derided as ludicrous a system of law that entitled a State to sink a polluting ship but not to direct it into safe shipping lanes.

We described the *Torrey Canyon* incident as marking the turning point from "Britannia Rules the Waves" to "Britannia Waives the Rules." We defended Canada's unilateral action on fishing zones, the 12 M territorial sea, and the Arctic Waters Pollution Prevention Act as legitimate examples of action directed towards developing customary international law by State practice, just as the territorial sea itself and the straight baseline system from which it may be measured had been created.[20] We cited the Truman Proclamation[21] and the Aleutian Exclusion Zone for nuclear testing as precedents. I personally returned protest notes from allies presenting identical

---

1, Resolutions Adopted by the General Assembly, vol. XIII 1970–1971 (New York: Oceana Publications, 1975), p. 240.

19. Grotius (n. 7 above).

20. Arctic Waters Pollution Prevention Act. R.S. 1985, c. A-12, http://laws.justice.gc.ca/en/A-12/text.html.

21. Policy of the United States with Respect to Coastal Fisheries in Certain Areas of the High Seas, Truman Proclamation on Conservation, Presidential Proclamation No. 2668 (28 September 1945), http://www.oceanlaw.net/texts/truman2.htm.

notes. It was a very wearing period, stressful, risky, but stimulating, and creative, as the law began to change. At times it was fun, but never a laughing matter. The Latin American States expressed gratification that we were characterizing them as pioneers rather than outlaws. We questioned why flag State jurisdiction mysteriously disappeared as an oil tanker sank, leaving only an oil slick devoid of any flag State responsibility for the damage. We cited this as a classic example of the need for rights and responsibilities to go hand-in-hand. For the first time, recently independent countries from Asia, Africa and the Pacific began calling into question the legal rules they had no part in developing. Questions were asked about the morality as well as the legality of such rules.

In the midst of this controversy, I was elected to the Chairmanship of the Drafting Committee of the Conference, and thus became a member of the Collegium, the Conference decision-making group. The job also entailed the arduous task of overseeing the processing and acceptance of over 7000 drafting changes to the Convention, aimed at transforming political, economic and legal principles into legal rules.

This rather unusual diplomacy was not merely confrontational; it was coupled with serious negotiations seeking functional accommodations. It was part of a deliberate policy, combining unilateral, bilateral and multilateral negotiations directed towards the attainment of clear policy objectives. As part of that process, there was a very active public programme of speaking engagements, participation in seminars, articles in learned journals, appearances on TV and radio programmes, liaison with academics and parliamentarians, and even visits to Washington to meet with U.S. Congressmen. There was also active collaboration in the development of two films, the CBC documentary "Who Owns the Sea," and the Newfoundland government film "Norma and Gladys." This demanding and complex process was consciously aimed at changing people's thinking. It was recognized that individual decision makers, not abstract entities called States, had to be persuaded that the principles they had learned in school and university had become outmoded. This was a very difficult task, for whole generations of statesmen, diplomats, scholars, jurists, bureaucrats, and even news people had teethed and grown up with the conviction that freedom of the high seas was tantamount to being the 11th Commandment. Rightly or wrongly, shock treatment was chosen as the means of forcing people to rethink their instinctive attitudes. I recall vividly a conference at Ditchley House, one of the stately homes of England available for special meetings, which the then Minister for Northern Affairs, Jean Chrétien, and I attended together, to discuss Canada's Arctic Waters Pollution Prevention Act. We expected to be given a chilly reception, and we were. The Arctic was warm by comparison. Nevertheless, we survived and gave as good as we got.

We never attacked traditional concepts without proposing "functional" accommodations of interests. We called for acceptance of the notion of "custodianship" or "stewardship." We suggested the legal device of "delegation of powers" to coastal States, to make clear that they were not God-given. One British wit wrote a poem, reading in part: "Our rights are too measly, according to Beesley; through delegation of powers, it all will be ours." I found that unkind.

GROTIUS, SELDEN AND THE ECOLOGY: 1982–1994

It will be noted that if Noah was the first to be concerned with biological diversity, and Jonah the first real marine biologist with insider information, then Grotius might at least be regarded as the first ecologist for his doctrine linking uses of the sea to sustainability. It would be wrong, however, to discount Selden as a mere exponent of overfishing and pollution. Selden at least attempted to take into account as relevant the nature of the resources the law could claim in asserting "there remains not either in the nature of the sea itself, nor in the Law of either Divine, Natural, or of Nations, any thing which may so oppose private Dominion thereof, that it cannot be admitted by every kind of law."[22] On the other side of the debate, Grotius conceded that in the case of fish in small, enclosed water, "the question is by no means settled how long these may be said to belong to no one."[23] Neither of these great legal gurus was quite as arbitrary as his followers, as is often the case.

It was clear to those of us charged with the negotiations that there were no doctrinal guidelines or traditional approaches on which we could rely. So we developed new legal concepts, such as the exclusive economic zone, going well beyond the territorial sea but stopping well short of sovereignty, limiting coastal jurisdiction to resources, marine pollution, and scientific research. Equally novel legal regimes and mechanisms were devised to reflect the concept of the common heritage. One whole part of the Convention (Part XII) consists of an "Umbrella Treaty" on the Protection and Preservation of the Marine Environment.[24] Even the regime devised for passage through international straits owed more to Grotius than Selden. (The term "transit passage" is actually attributed to a member of the Canadian delegation.)

During the lengthy period of the law of the sea negotiations, there were strongly divergent views amongst States, ranging from claims to a 200-M territorial sea to a flat rejection of any claims beyond 3 M. There was, at least, general acceptance of the need to develop the law, and not merely codify

22. Selden (n. 6 above), p. 4, author's Preface.

23. H. Grotius, *The Law of War and Peace* (Indianapolis: Bobbs-Merrill, c. 1925), p. 296.

24. See Part XII, UNCLOS (n. 2 above), Articles 192–237.

it, as it became apparent that the attempts to contain coastal claims were not succeeding.

It is not inappropriate to be critical of the results of the Conference. It is foolish, however, to ignore the realities of the negotiations. On every issue, and Canada was necessarily involved in most, there was an often lengthy and always arduous negotiation between competing interest groups. Canada had much to do with the creation of some key interest groups, such as the coastal group, the marine pollution group, the continental shelf "margineers" group, the "equidistance" boundaries group, the nickel production ceiling group, et cetera, always formed through informal working luncheons, later carried on with shirt sleeves and sandwiches. Such groups were needed to draw the lines of disagreement and launch negotiations to resolve them.

There was fierce resistance by powerful maritime States to the 12-M territorial sea because of its potential impact on international straits, and even broader opposition to the 200-M economic zone; the continental shelf claims of Canada and its allies beyond 200 M were rejected by the land-locked States and even coastal States supporters of the 200-M economic zone who had no physical shelf beyond that limit; important high seas fishing States flatly rejected new fisheries rules relating to straddling stocks and anadromous species, and some also opposed the 200-M fishing zones. Coastal States clashed over boundary delimitation rules.

It is sometimes forgotten today that the Conference had agreed to reach all decisions by consensus, and that all issues were to be treated as interrelated. Accommodations had to be hammered out—and were—on each of these issues, within various formal or informal groups established for the particular purposes, and the results had to be woven together into an integrated whole, in accordance with the "package deal" concept. Then the results had to be processed through the Drafting Committee, to translate them into legally binding language. It should not be forgotten, either, that it was the very State which had most vigorously insisted on decisions by consensus which demanded a vote in the closing hours of the Conference, a development which shocked delegations from around the world. Ironically, the issue chosen by President Reagan to bury the Convention, unsuccessfully as it turned out, was the mining system proposed for the deep ocean seabed by Dr. Kissinger, which had been accepted by the Conference and included in the Convention after many months of painful negotiations.

What is the relevance of these references to the 1982 Convention? It is, I suggest, that there is in existence a vast body of law comprising a comprehensive Constitution of the Oceans, which has not yet been implemented.[25]

25. Editors' Note.—Specific provisions of UNCLOS may be said to have been implemented in Canada via, inter alia, the Oceans Act (n. 4 above) and the ocean disposal provisions of the Canadian Environmental Protection Act, C-15.31 (1999).

The Convention only came into force on 16 November 1994. The question might well be asked whether the fisheries disputes of the past decade would have dragged on if the Convention had been in force, and the binding dispute settlement mechanisms had been utilized. It is not an easy question to answer. To ask this question is not to disparage the achievements reflected in the Agreement on the Implementation of the Provisions of the 1982 Convention Relating to Straddling and Highly Migratory Fish Stocks. Indeed, I chaired the first international gathering of experts, intended as a preparatory meeting leading to a UN Conference. That meeting of experts was held here in St. John's at the Marine Institute in September 1990. Ambassador Nandan was present at that meeting. There was no disagreement as to our common objective. It was just such an Agreement as was achieved this summer in New York under the skilful guidance of Ambassador Nandan, although only the most optimistic amongst us would have predicted the measure of success achieved.

Before considering the 1995 Agreement, it is worthwhile to examine the legal regime established by the 1982 Convention, if only to ensure that we don't throw out the baby with the bath water. There are two other important reasons for considering the legal regime on fisheries established by the Convention. Firstly, it represents existing law, and may for some time to come, pending entry into force of the 1995 Agreement. Second, it provides the only legal basis for judging the legality of the actions by Spain, the European Union, and Canada.

The Fisheries Regime of the 1982 UN Convention

Let us begin by considering how that Convention is regarded by knowledgeable experts, as follows, from *Our Common Future, World Commission on Environment and Development*:

> The United Nations Convention on the Law of the Sea was the most ambitious attempt ever to provide an internationally agreed regime for the management of the oceans. The resulting Convention represents a major step towards an integrated management regime for the oceans. Indeed, the most significant initial action that nations can take in the interests of the oceans' threatened life support system is to ratify the Law of the Sea Convention.[26]

Let us think about that statement, not merely in terms of what the international community ought to have done, but in terms of the consequences of

26. G. R. Brundtland, World Commission on Environment and Development, *Our Common Future* (Oxford: Oxford University Press, 1987).

not having taken such action. Let us be more up-to-date, which requires that we cite the results of the Rio Conference from Agenda 21, Chapter 17:

> International law, as reflected in the provisions of the UN Convention of the Law of the Sea, referred to in this chapter of Agenda 21, sets forth rights and obligations of states and provides the international basis upon which to pursue the protection and sustainable development of the marine and coastal environment and its resources. This requires new approaches to marine and coastal management and development, at the national, subregional, regional and global levels, approaches that are integrated in content, and are precautionary and anticipatory in ambit.[27]

Surely that conclusion gives us guidance for our discussions.

A more recent appraisal of the nature and significance of the Convention was provided by the UN Secretary General at the Kingston ceremonies as "one of the greatest achievements of this century," because it comprises a comprehensive constitution of the oceans; established rights and duties going hand-in-hand under the rule of law, the themes stressed by the Canadian delegation throughout the Conference; made a major contribution toward prevention and resolution of conflict; and, of special relevance to this Colloquium, promoted peace, security, and sustainable development. Others described it as a "high-water mark" in the progressive development and codification of international law.

If we have such a remarkable legal basis for oceans management, why are we meeting here? A part of the answer can be drawn from the fourth and fifth Preambles to the 1995 UN Agreement on Straddling and Highly Migratory Fish Stocks, which read as follows:

> Calling for more effective enforcement by flag states, port states and coastal states of conservation and management measures adopted for such stocks; Seeking to address in particular the problems identified in Agenda 21, Chapter 17, Programme 6, adopted by the United Nations Conference on Environment and Development, namely that the management of high seas fisheries is inadequate in many areas and that some resources are over-utilized; noting that there are problems of unregulated fishing, over-capitalization, excessive fleet size, vessel reflagging to escape controls, insufficiently selective cooperation between states.[28]

27. Chapter 17 of Agenda 21. "Protection of the oceans, all kinds of seas, including enclosed and semi-enclosed seas, and coastal areas and the protection, rational use and development of their living resources," http://www.un.org/esa/sustdev/agenda21chapter17.htm.

28. United Nations Fish Stocks Agreement (n. 5 above), Preamble.

There we have quite a catalogue of problems. Some appear to be in the process of resolution, some not. There is much to sink our teeth into in the hours ahead. Let us consider each of these issues, some of which are very controversial, during our panel discussions.

THE "DUTY TO COOPERATE" MYTHOLOGY

If one were to sum up the fisheries conservation law that emerged from the Conference, it would be impossible to attribute the results to Grotius or Selden, or, indeed, anyone but the negotiators. What were the results? Well, contrary to various recent statements, the 1982 Law of the Sea Convention did not merely impose "a general duty to cooperate". . . far from it. Article 63(2) on straddling stocks imposes a legal obligation on States in providing that States "*shall* seek, either directly or through appropriate subregional or regional organizations, to agree upon the measures necessary for the conservation of these stocks." This same language is retained in Article 7(1)(a) of the 1995 UN Agreement.[29] Article 300 of the 1982 Convention imposes the legal obligation that "States *shall* fulfil in good faith the obligations assumed under this Convention," not ought to fulfil, or have a mere duty of best efforts to fulfil.[30] Exactly the same language is found in Article 34 of the 1995 Agreement.[31] Article 300 of the 1982 Convention also stipulates as a legal obligation that "states shall exercise the *rights*, jurisdiction and *freedoms* recognized in this Convention in a manner which would not constitute *an abuse of right.*"[32] The same language is used in Article 7(1)(a) of the 1995 Agreement, except for the deletion of the words "jurisdiction" and "freedoms."[33] Nowhere does either instrument suggest that merely to join the appropriate regional organization is to discharge these significant legal obligations.

Where then does one find this mere "duty to cooperate"? Article 118 of the 1982 Convention clearly—not vaguely, or ambiguously—imposes the legal obligation that "States shall cooperate with each other in the conservation and management of living resources of the high seas."[34] This is not hortatory language. It lays down a legally binding obligation. Article 118 goes on to provide that

> States whose nationals exploit identical living resources in the same area, *shall* enter into negotiations with a view to taking the measures

29. United Nations Fish Stocks Agreement (n. 5 above).
30. UNCLOS (n. 2 above), Article 300.
31. United Nations Fish Stocks Agreement (n. 5 above).
32. UNCLOS (n. 2 above), Article 300.
33. United Nations Fish Stocks Agreement (n. 5 above), Article7(1)(a).
34. UNCLOS (n. 2 above), Article 118.

> necessary for the conservation of living resources concerned. They *shall*, as appropriate, cooperate to establish subregional or regional fisheries *to this end.* (Emphasis added)[35]

These are clear legal obligations, going well beyond a mere duty to cooperate. As in the case of Article 63(2) of the 1982 Convention, it is impossible to argue that a State fulfills in good faith the obligations assumed under the Convention merely by joining a regional organization. The purpose of the obligation to enter into negotiations is clear cut, namely, "with a view to *taking the measures* necessary for the conservation of the living resources concerned."[36] This obligation cannot be met by negotiating to avoid or *undermine* such measures. And finally, the establishment of regional organizations is not proposed as an end in itself, but is explicitly stated to be "to this end"; that is to say, the taking of conservation measures.

Even Article 116 of the 1982 Convention makes clear that "all States have the right for their nationals to engage in fishing on the high seas *subject to*: (b) the rights and duties as well as the interests of coastal States provided for inter alia, in Article 63 paragraph 2" et cetera.[37] This is clear and unambiguous language, imposing legal conditions. Even Article 87, elaborating the Freedom of the High Seas, including freedom of fishing, explicitly provides that "Freedom of the High Seas is exercised under the conditions laid down by this Convention."[38] Thus the freedom of the high seas is clearly not an unfettered right to overfish at will, but is a right subject to the obligations cited earlier.

There is, of course, if one searches for it, a duty to cooperate embodied in Article 117 of the Law of the Sea Convention, which provides that

> All States have the duty to take, or to cooperate with other States in taking, such measures for their nationals as may be necessary for the conservation of the living resources of the high seas.[39]

Clearly, there is a duty imposed on all States, severally and collectively, to take such conservation measures. This language is not vague or ambiguous. It does not leave a gap wide enough to permit a coach and four to be driven through. Presumably this duty could not be interpreted as including a right to overfish quotas imposed unilaterally after unilateral rejection of the quota accepted by all others in a multilateral forum. The article also, of course, imposes the infamous "duty to cooperate," characterized negatively so often.

35. Ibid., Article 118
36. Ibid., Article 63(2).
37. Ibid., Article 116.
38. Ibid., Article 87.
39. Ibid., Article 117.

Even with respect to this mere "duty to cooperate," however, it would require very flexible interpretation to conclude that merely to join a regional fisheries organization constitute fulfillment of the duty. Surely the duty to cooperate applies to the conservation measures recommended, for example, by the Scientific Council of NAFO. It is not stretching the rules of interpretation unduly to say that the duty to cooperate might even extend to the decision-making process of the regional organization in question. Quite frankly, I have no doubt that a duty to cooperate that evaporates once the decision-making process begins is no duty at all, but a mere facade. Of course we are not left with Article 117, which, standing alone, might not comprise a legal regime. On the contrary, the duties imposed by Article 117 are strongly reinforced by the legal obligations imposed in Article 63, 116, 118, and 300, which are repeated in the 1995 UN Agreement. Let us hope, therefore, that these provisions are not meaningless.

Interestingly, the phrase "duty to cooperate" recurs in the 1995 UN Agreement[40] in Article 5 (in the chapeau); in Article 7(2)(a), where a duty to cooperate for the purpose of achieving compatible measures is imposed; in Article 7(3), referring again to the duty to cooperate to agree on compatible measures; Article 8(1) provides that States *shall* pursue cooperation in relation to straddling fish stocks; this goes beyond a mere duty to cooperate; but Article 8(3) refers again to "their duty to cooperate," without citing the source of this duty. Article 8(5), however, clearly stipulates that States "*shall* cooperate" to establish organizations or arrangements.

Having discussed the Law of Nations, as Grotius would have characterized it, one finds it is now time to determine—or at least consider—whether there have been recent breaches of the law, and even, perhaps, who committed them. Unfortunately, we do not seem to have budgeted for the creation of an ad hoc tribunal to consider this question, so you must make do with me.

In sum, there were times when we considered that Grotius was atrocious, and times when we thought that what is Selden is wonderful.

GROTIUS AND THE PIRATES: 1994–1995

It is said that Grotius was fascinated by pirates. In any event, he wrote of them more than once, as all of us present undoubtedly recall. Some of his writings are better known than others. During my term on the International Law Commission—yes, that was me—I had occasion to turn to Grotius yet again on the subject of environmental crimes. Sure enough, he didn't fail me. I was pleased to be able to quote to the Commission and, thus, for posterity, the following dictum: Today's pirate may be tomorrow's Head of

40. United Nations Fish Stocks Agreement (n. 5 above).

State.[41] Now, I would ask that this statement not be taken literally. I do not necessarily, for example, refer to the present Spanish Presidency of the European Union . . . not necessarily. Indeed, in many places, except, of course, in St. John's, the problem is to determine who is the pirate. I shall forego asking, "Will the real pirate please stand up?" It is no secret that Spain, the EU and even Brittan of Britain has accused Canada of piracy, and named Minister Tobin as the Pirate Chief.

Perhaps enough salt water has flowed under the bridge to render it unnecessary to ask if the use of the NAFO Objections Procedure 53 times in 10 years constituted an abuse of right, or whether the repeated rejection of quotas based on unanimous scientific advice constitutes negotiating in good faith.[42] Perhaps, and perhaps not . . . only time will tell. But just in case, let us not disparage or denigrate the existing legal regime on high seas fisheries until we are sure a better one is in place, one which, we might hope, would eliminate the Jolly Roger from the high seas, whether by means of the recent FAO Code of Conduct for Responsible Fishing,[43] the September NAFO enforcement decisions, the 1995 UN Agreement, or all of these. I would also add Canada's recent unilateral action as a part of the New Law of Fisheries, or, if you prefer, the Right of Self Protection, as exemplified by the *Torrey Canyon* and *Estai* incidents.

The 1995 UN Agreement on Straddling and Highly Migratory Stocks

I have drawn attention to some provisions of the 1995 Agreement that some might characterize as weaknesses. I most emphatically disassociate myself from any such position. The Agreement incorporates a whole range of legal rules, procedures, and decision-making processes that make a major contribution to the "New Fisheries Law." This Colloquium provides us with a timely opportunity to consider them, shortly before the Agreement is presented for signature in the General Assembly, on 4 December 1995. I look forward to hearing and even participating in the deliberations of the multidisciplinary panels that will certainly be addressing the important innovative provis-

41. This is an interpretation of Grotius's quote, "Nevertheless a transformation may take place, not merely in the case of individuals, as when Jephtes, Arsaces, and Viriathus instead of *being leaders of brigands became lawful chiefs*, but also in the case of groups, so that those who have only been robbers embracing another mode of life became a state." [Emphasis added]. Various translation and interpretation questions arise with the many quotations from Grotius. See H. Grotius, *De Jure Belli Ac Pacis Libri Tres,* translation by F. W. Kelsey, reprinted in *The Classics of International Law,* vol. 2, ed. J. B. Scott (Oxford Press, 1925), pp. 632–33.

42. NAFO objection counts recorded by the author over a 10-year period ending November 1995.

43. FAO Code of Conduct for Responsible Fisheries, 1 November 1995, http://www.fao.org/fi/agreem/codecond/ficonde.asp.

ions of the 1995 Agreement. Some of the positive features of the Agreement that should be discussed are as follows:

1. Its binding nature, itself a major achievement;
2. Its data collection system, a concrete and constructive feature;
3. Its emphasis on the precautionary approach, one of the most positive features of the Agreement;
4. Its data sharing system, important and constructive;
5. Its focus on subsistence fishing, a new approach;
6. Its strengthening of regional organizations, an important and long overdue development;
7. Its transparency provisions, of great potential;
8. Its dispute settlement provisions, which may help make the system workable;
9. Its provisional entry into force, coupled with entry into force after only 30 ratifications or accessions, a preferable approach to the requirements for 60 ratifications of the Law of the Sea Convention, which has delayed its entry into force for so long;
10. Its enforcement provisions, the most important of all its features.

It is highly desirable, I suggest, that we organize our discussions so that time is given to consider each of these features, with particular reference to their future application, implementation, and enforcement, including the changes necessary to existing Canadian legislation, as well as the ratification issue.

An important characteristic of the Agreement is that it comprises a three-pronged, multidisciplinary approach. Not surprisingly, it focuses on enforcement, perhaps its most important legal feature, and the related institutional mechanisms. It also emphasizes the long-standing need for compatibility of measures in the high seas with those in the economic zone, representing a blend of legal and ecological approaches. Finally, it stresses the scientific basis for the precautionary principle, with concrete requirements for data collection and sharing. The Agreement thus adapts a multidisciplinary approach, which is the key precondition to Ecosystem Assessment and Management, on which the New Law of Fisheries must be based. The validity of this approach is demonstrated convincingly in Lee Kimball's Commentary to the 1995 IUCN document, "Priorities and Responsibilities," already cited.[44]

THE ENVIRONMENTAL DIMENSION

Before concluding, I should like to note that I have deliberately omitted any analysis or commentary on that aspect of the new fisheries law that interests

44. Kimball (n. 1 above), p. 8.

me most—the environmental dimension. That is the one area of law that, I suggest, is most in need of continuing development. No one needs to be reminded of the success achieved by Canada at the Stockholm Conference on the Environment in obtaining agreement by consensus on legal principles based on the Trail Smelter case,[45] and in later translating these principles into binding obligations in the 1982 UN Law of the Sea Convention, particularly the "Canadian provision" Article 192 contained in Part XII.

It is indicative that Stockholm Principle 21 was adopted and reaffirmed 20 years later at the Rio Conference.[46] Time constraints preclude even cataloguing the wide range of environmental law instruments concluded over the past 2 decades that are explicitly or implicitly based on the Trail Smelter case, exemplified in Stockholm Principle 21. This environmental lawmaking process must not only be maintained, but also accelerated. I have been much involved personally in recent years in the elaboration of two recent and potentially far-reaching nongovernmental environmental proposals, the 1995 IUCN Global Covenant on Environment and Development[47] and the 1995 Cuixmala Model Draft Treaty on the Protection of the North American Environment.[48] I hope that each will make some impact into the thinking of governments. We NGOs try to make a difference.

I hope that our discussions will focus on these issues. In so saying, may I acknowledge our collective debt and gratitude to Ambassador Satya Nandan, who has once again demonstrated his exceptional courage, patience, determination, negotiating skill, and wisdom in exercising the leadership needed once again to bring about the 1995 UN Agreement, as he has done so often in the past. I express my thanks and my congratulations to Ambassador Nandan, and my appreciation to the organizers of this Colloquium for having included me in such a timely and useful exercise.

45. Convention for Settlement of Difficulties Arising From Operation of Smelter at Trail, British Columbia, U.S. Treaty Series No. 893 (Signed at Ottawa, 15 April 1935; ratifications exchanged 3 August 1935).

46. Stockholm Declaration of the United Nations Conference on the Human Environment, adopted 16 June 1972; Rio Declaration on Environment and Development. *Report of the United Nations Conference on Environment and Development.* A/CONF.151/26 (Vol. I). (Rio de Janeiro: 3–14 June 1992).

47. *Draft International Covenant on Environment and Development.* IUCN Environmental Policy and Law Paper No. 31, 2nd ed. 2000, http://www.iucn.org/themes/law/pdfdocuments/EPLP31ENsecond.pdf.

48. A. Székely, J. A. Beesley and A. E. Utton, "Cuixmala Model Draft Treaty for the Protection of the Environment and the Natural Resources of North America," *Natural Resources Journal* 36, no. 3(2)(1996): 591–633.

Globalisation and the Sea

Salvino Busuttil
Ambassador of Malta to France and Portugal
Professor Emeritus, University of Malta
Former Coordinator, UN Mediterranean Action Plan

INTRODUCTION

As a repository of common goods, the ocean is a primary subject, and at the same time, object of the globalisation process. Marine resources are of themselves global in their essence and destination, and their very nature thus exposes them to the process. Considered as a menace to a predetermined order of res naturae, globalisation can mark the sea and its resources as unwilling prey in the acquisitive hunt to bag as much as possible of humanity's patrimony into a world market-oriented system.

Conceived as an opportunity, the global nature of marine resources offers an excellent paradigm of common governance affirming common heritage. This contribution examines the ways in which menace and opportunity interrelate with reference to the sea in the globalisation process, attempting answers to queries concerning the relative merits of regionalisation and globalisation in the ocean context.

That the sea, with its mineral and fish resources, with its climatic effects, with its potential for communications and tourism, is par excellence as a conduit of internationality, is an essential element of humankind's story and of our own evolution in the flow of history. It is to the universal ocean that we have clamoured physically and symbolically, in our search either for enrichment or transcendence, to build empires or deeply to seek our identity. Prophetic and mythological lore make Jonah and Ulysses creatures of the ocean for all time. The sea, teasing the boundaries of the human spirit, goads us to search that infinity that the ocean itself has seemingly always yearned to embrace, while implicitly acknowledging that the human species, physically puny in relation to the sea's prowess, nonetheless enjoys a superiority born of technology, potentially lording it over that very ocean.

It is in this paradox between imagined potency and actual force that the sea and humans, so juxtaposed, have provided, in a globalizing age, a setting now threatening, now importuning, where the dramatis personae are the sea, as living and quasi unchanging scenario, while we are almost as

Ocean Yearbook 18: 117–122

transient actors, whose entrances and exits are scripted by a destiny that often eludes our selective memory.

GLOBAL OCEAN AND GLOBAL HUMAN

Is the former just the stage and the latter the comedien? Is globalisation meant, or intended, to offer the oceans on a silver platter to the political and economic overlords of this only one earth so that 71 percent of the planet becomes de facto *their* only one sea? Are not global fisheries, for example, already availing themselves of globalisation so that, inter alia, tunas and sardines are produced, processed, and profited by through an oligarchic Mafia whose devotion to sustainable development is labial rather than cardial. Is not surface transport, whether for pleasure (cruise liners) or for business (cargo and oil) not already the domain of multinational carriers? Is not maritime industrial technology, whose advances would, in the pious thought of my compatriot and friend Arvid Pardo, have made accessible seabed riches (albeit beyond national jurisdiction) to all humankind without appropriation, largely the province of those who can afford to develop and/or profit by it?

Provider of food, largely edible fish, shellfish, and fishfarm products, and of water, primarily through desalination, the ocean has an economic value and potential that we are only now beginning to appreciate. As a source of energy, through, inter alia, tidal power generation and ocean thermal energy conversion (OTEC), the sea offers enormous prospects for alternative energy, it being calculated, for example, that the heat generated daily by the absorption of solar radiation in tropical seas is equivalent to that of about 170 billion barrels of oil.

Oil is, of course, another major product of the ocean. Offshore drilling (subject to close environmental monitoring), not just on continental shelves but also in deeper waters, now contributes significantly to international petroleum production. Minerals, whether within the seawater itself or lying on subseafloor consolidated rocks or in sediments on the deep seabed, are the newly revalued riches of the ocean, some, such as phosphate deposits and manganese modules being relatively recent discoveries.[1]

It was, indeed, the prospect of deep-sea mining and offshore oil drilling beyond the territorial limits that fired the debate on ownership and appropriation and eventually led to the 1982 United Nations Convention on the Law of the Sea (UNCLOS).[2] And it was the realization of the impact of the oceans on climate change and global warming that convinced the United Nations that climatic matters were the "common concern" of all.

1. Polymetallic sulphide deposits near the Galapagos were identified in 1978.
2. United Nations Convention on the Law of the Sea (1982), http://www.un.org/depts/los/.

Following the same philosophy, the United Nations, which had already identified the environmental importance of the oceans in 1972 (when the first United Nations Conference on the Environment convened in Stockholm), sought to control those human activities deemed detrimental to marine ecology, whether through oil spills and plant and sewage effluent or through herbicide and pesticide pollution (sometimes carried by winds and rivers). It was in this setting that the United Nations Environment Programme (UNEP), and especially the Regional Seas Programmes entrusted to it, embarked on its mission. The "common heritage" was thus the springboard of that literal sea change in international law.

What is the Relationship between Ocean Globalisation and the Common Heritage?

For the votaries of globalisation, as a religion, the doctrine of the common heritage may present a facile argument. Tantalisingly, they may posit that the common heritage of itself implies or denotes globalisation which, thus considered as "good," acquires thereby respectability and potentially universal acceptance.

Such a line of thinking belies no small hypocrisy. For if the common heritage, (applied not just, as in the original tenet, to seabed resources, but to all common goods which of themselves should not be appropriated) were reduced to that moral least common denominator where all that is economically "good" (i.e., "feasible," "profitable," "having due return on capital") is then universally valid, then that "heritage" would itself be subject to the laws of Mammon rather than to the ethos of distributive social justice.

Thus bereft of its essential commonality in the service of all the species, the common heritage would mean, in such an ocean context, that that new international order in which global ocean governance would be exercised for the well being of the species, now and for the future, would be forever jeopardised.

In such a setting it would be difficult to envisage that the original intent of the common heritage doctrine as an instrument of peace, and of global ocean governance as a first step towards the attainment of that peace, would be fulfilled. Globalisation as now practised can hardly be deemed to foster peace. It may, on the contrary, widen income gaps between and within nations. Fomenting, in consequence, social pressures, it could strengthen discord. Rather than forging scythes for peaceful pasture, it may well model swords for profitable belligerence.

Equating the common heritage and globalisation threatens the whole notion of peace for and through the oceans. While the common heritage stresses no ownership, the philosophy of globalisation de facto subscribes to an ethics of a "new" international order where maximum profit, at any cost, is the absolute; and hence, it is essentially amoral in its basic negative of the "common good."

"When we speak of a philosophy of the common heritage," Elisabeth Mann Borgese wrote, "we do not mean the concept of the common heritage. We are referring instead to the ideological and philosophical setting required for the application of that concept. The notions of peace and development and the protection of man and nature do not reside in a legal and institutional framework or in an economic theory, as necessary as these may be. In the final analysis, they reside in the minds of men."[3] In her perspective, a pragmatic course of action would be designated zones of peace, on the theorem that one should think globally and act regionally.

Indeed, one increasingly notices that one major answer to the debate over globalisation and the common heritage may well lie in that regional approach that has wrought valuable results in the UNEP Regional Seas Programme, especially now that an evolution of that Programme has led to the creation of regional Commissions for Sustainable Development.[4]

One cannot doubt that the United Nations-led plans of action for Regional Seas have enhanced ocean conservation and exploitation more than ocean activities conducted "globally," even as we laud the scientific achievements of important organs such as the Intergovernmental Oceanographic Commission (IOC).

One may object that while the regional approach may reduce the more negative aspects of globalisation, it may however, also dilute the common heritage philosophy. Academic though such a debate may be, yet the application of that philosophy, pragmatically evaluated, to regionality, and particularly, to regional environment initiatives such as the Regional Seas exercise, commands considerable merit. Rather than negating the philosophy, the regional dimension de facto strengthens it.

Indeed, to the extent, for example, that Exclusive Economic Zones (EEZs) may be regionally designated (because unlike territorial seas, which are de jure sovereign, the EEZ is a functional, shared economic sovereignty) through regional accords, the shared resources (which, in the spirit of Article 88 of UNCLOS, should be reserved, like the high seas, for peaceful purposes) would take the concept of Zones of Peace one step closer to realization.[5]

3. E. Mann Borgese, *The Future of the Oceans* (Harvest House: Montreal, 1986), p. 124.

4. When the author directed the UNEP Mediterranean Action Plan (1991–93), Elisabeth Mann Borgese discussed with him a draft proposal on the setting up of a Mediterranean Commission for Sustainable Development. After the original initiative embarked on by Malta, this proposal led, with Tunisian cooperation, to the establishment of the Commission in 1995 through an additional instrument to the 1975 Barcelona Convention on the Conservation and Protection of the Mediterranean Sea.

5. See also Article 137 (n. 2 above), "No state should claim or exercise sovereignty or sovereign rights over any part of the Area or its resources, nor shall any

Such Zones of Peace can, in my view, only materialize within a solid economic framework, one that to use "parallel thinking" parlance, would demonstrate that the holistic advantages of working within such a framework are economically greater than if any one nation unilaterally exploited its EEZ rights. While not necessarily arguing that a Zone of Peace must be a regional EEZ, yet there is political and not just economic merit in pursuing the idea in appropriate circumstances.

One such possibility, already mooted 20 years ago or so, concerns the central Mediterranean where it would make economic sense to pool off-shore oil drilling activities, (thus avoiding the Median Line disputes that have plagued Maltese-Libyan-Tunisian oil exploration). The rationale for such an approach would be to seek (through the Five plus Five Process involving Spain, Portugal, France, Italy, and Malta, together with Libya, Tunisia, Algeria, Morocco, and Mauritania) an understanding that (i) an EEZ be declared by and for the participating countries; and (ii), in consequence, that the EEZ evolve, that is "behave," as a Zone of Peace under mutually agreed conditions within a regional structure.

Because the Five plus Five Process shows promising signs of resurgence, one may propose that an ad hoc meeting of the member states be convened at an early date. In so doing, the European Member States would de facto ensure the presence of the European Union, while the Organization of African Unity would participate through the Northwest African States.

An agreement so based could be fleshed out to include related projects such as the proposed Mediterranean Centre for Research and Development in Marine Industrial Technology which, known as MEDITECH, has been under discussion since 1980. As set out initially by Elisabeth Mann Borgese herself, such a Centre would:

- promote regional cooperation in the peaceful uses of the Mediterranean Sea;
- promote the implementation of Articles 276 and 277 of the 1982 United Nations Convention on the Law of the Sea which prescribes the establishment of regional centres for marine scientific and technological research, to stimulate and advance the conduct of marine scientific research by developing States and foster the transfer of marine technology; and
- encourage new forms of scientific-industrial cooperation between the developed and the developing countries in the Mediterranean region.[6]

---

state or natural or judicial person appropriate any part thereof. No such claim or exercise of sovereignty or sovereign rights nor such appropriation shall be recognised." See also, in this respect, Article 89.

6. See Annex 2, in S. Busuttil and P. Catalano, *Euro-Mediterranean Technological Co-operation, with Special Reference to Marine Technology,* (Foundation for International Studies/ISPROM, Malta, 1993). The proposal was first made in Mann Borgese's

This exercise of itself raises the question of governance, although normally related to the political denouement not just of the central and western Mediterranean, where the Five plus Five Process operates, but of the Eastern Mediterranean and of the Middle East as well, the governance issue may also offer possibilities towards the East. If the Five plus Five Process can inject a measure of solidarity through commonly perceived national advantages for the participating States, it may well prepare the ground for wider initiatives, in the same way whereby, mutatis mutandis, the 1975 Barcelona Convention on the Mediterranean Sea made possible a Mediterranean Action Plan (MAP) which, through subsequent protocols, extended the brief of agreed common projects well beyond the narrow confines of a conservatively defined approach to marine conservation. That MAP which now acts also on land-based projects (e.g., species conservation, historic sites and monuments, maritime cities) demonstrates that the confluence of common interest, properly identified and defined through appropriate institutional instruments and arrangements and empowered with functional mechanisms not just of governance (e.g., Conference of the Contracting Parties) nor just of compliance (e.g., the Coordinating Unit of MAP) but also of prospective activities (e.g., MEDITECH), holds reasonable promise.

It is, therefore, regionally rather than globally, that governance of the seas shows signs of realistic achievement. Subsidiarity is, in this respect, a vital principle guiding regional tools of governance.[7]

Should We Forego Global Governance to Profit Regional Governance of the Oceans?

There is, in my view, no antithesis in these considerations. Rather than serving political expedience, the regional stance is realistic and serves equitable social justice. To the extent that that justice is honestly served, we will have rendered a good account of ourselves to those future generations whose heritage shall be as "common" to them as it is to us, in the pledge that, as Elisabeth Mann Borgese has so deeply inspired us, we bequeath to them not what is commonly inferior, but what is supremely common for it is theirs, by us responsibly legated, for all time.

---

article in *The Mediterranean in the New Law of the Sea,* (Valletta: Foundation for International Studies, 1987), pp. 95–104.

7. See in this connection, S. Busuttil, "The Governance of the Mediterranean," in Busuttil and Catalono (n. 6 above).

Issues and Prospects

The Riches of the Ocean for Humankind: Rethinking Value in Economics and Development

Orio Giarini
The Risk Institute and The Geneva Association, Geneva

INTRODUCTION

I had the privilege of knowing Elisabeth Mann Borgese for over 20 years. I first met her on the occasion of the conferences of the Club of Rome. She was clearly one of those persons who provides you with an example of how human beings, from time to time and thanks to exceptional individuals, are capable of creating a better standard for the civilized part of our human history.

I am still so grateful to her for having been interested in my efforts to better understand "in the present world" the search for the wealth of nations that is really going on. Over 50 years of experience in the chemical industry, industrial and technological research, the financial sector studying the management of risks and uncertainties, teaching my subject (service economics) at university, and having even some political experience within the European Federalist Movement, have been the references to build up some hypotheses and ideas. I have also drawn on the views expressed in relevant economic and social literature. But it is clear that my views have grown somewhat diverted from those of the economic establishment.

Elisabeth was in fact looking for a better answer to the question "What is the value of the oceans?" Value in conventional economics—as it was borne of a consequence of the development of the Industrial Revolution—is linked to the basic notion of scarcity of resources and to their pricing in the market system. Resources that are not scarce and are not exchanged have in principle no theoretical value. But what about those resources that are not scarce in the beginning, but which become scarce when over-exploited or polluted?

Adam Smith wrote the fundamental starting text of economics over 2 centuries ago, *The Wealth of Nations*. What about the economic price-value of goods and services that have become scarce after having been available at no cost?

Furthermore, at the macroeconomic level, the average educated person is not conscious that a measure of the gross national product is a measure of

Ocean Yearbook 18: 123–136

the flow, whereas talking, for instance, of the value of the oceans and of any other resource on earth is a matter of evaluating a stock. That is, a stock that can become scarcer and therefore more and more costly and "valuable" and where sometimes technology and advancement in research are capable of creating a situation of such abundance that the products of services become almost free, as could be the case in the telecommunications sector. All this is linked to what I have tried to describe in a few books as the passage from the industrial economy, which is the basis for modern economics, to a service-based economy where the notion of stock, performance, and uncertainty in time replaces day-by-day equilibrium-based traditional economic theory.

I am a sea and ocean lover, but I am not an ocean expert. Nevertheless, the question of identifying the economic and social value of the oceans has inevitably to do with the identification and measurement of a stock (i.e., in terms of price and indicators), whatever its nature.

I was always very thankful to Elisabeth for having grasped the essence of my attempts to enter and develop this debate. As a consequence, she made reference to my writings in many of her books and articles.[1] In one of her last writings,[2] she even went on to the issues of risk and uncertainty that are inevitably linked to the new service economy and to the identification and discussion of any policy that has to do with the performance and sustainability of any stock—and even more so the oceans—in the future. In the following paragraphs, I insist on two key issues: the economics of common heritage and the notion and strategy of sustainable development.

THE ECONOMICS OF COMMON HERITAGE

The Concepts of Common Heritage of Mankind and Dowry and Patrimony: In Quest of an Adequate Notion of Economic Value

The concept of Common Heritage of Mankind as developed by its principal author, Arvid Pardo, Ambassador of Malta to the United Nations in the 1960s, is characterized by the following:

- the nonappropriability of the common heritage;
- a system of management in which all users share;
- an active sharing of the profit and benefits derived from shared management and transfer of technologies;

1. E. Mann Borgese, "Integrating Development and Environment Concerns: New Economic Theories," Chapter 4, in *Ocean Governance and the United Nations* (Halifax: Centre for Foreign Policy Studies, Dalhousie University, 1995), p. 246; E. Mann Borgese, "The Economics of Common Heritage," *Ocean and Coastal Management* 43 (2000): 763–779.

2. Borgese, 2000 (n. 1 above).

- the reservation of ocean space for peaceful purposes; and
- its reservation for future generations.

As Elisabeth Mann Borgese stated in her report to the Club of Rome, *The Future of the Oceans*,[3] there are some startling similarities between the concepts of Common Heritage and Dowry and Patrimony (D&P) developed in the report to the Club of Rome.[4] In fact, a lot of work has been done in the last few decades by private research centers, as well as by international organizations, to define the value of so-called noneconomic goods.[5] Although I respect and take into account all these efforts, I feel the necessity to become more provocative and to say that conventional economic wisdom does not fundamentally provide instrument measures that are adequate to evaluate the real economic value of oceans as common heritage.

This article therefore will be very risky for its author. Firstly it will try to prove that conventional economics does not provide the necessary tools for what is needed. Secondly, it has to explain why the fundamentals of conventional economics have been developed in quite another context and with other objectives for measurement that are now out of context. Thirdly, this short article has to open some avenues to find other plausible and useful references.

The reader will admit that such tasks are almost equivalent to intellectual suicide. I have a little excuse in the fact that these ideas are based on more than 40 years of research and practical testing in economic activities, both in industry and services. Perhaps the most demanding element of this article is to try to explain how and why a conventional economic theory functions as it does today, and why it is theoretically inadequate.

Measuring Value in the Industrial Revolution: The Monetarized Flow

It is essential to understand that the measurement of value in economics refers to the measurement of a flow. This can best be explained as a bathtub with two taps, as shown in fig. 1. The bathtub contains a certain amount of water *W*, representing a stock of wealth that we use for our needs and pleasure. This stock of water *W* is fed by two taps:

3. E. Mann Borgese, *The Future of the Oceans: A Report to the Club of Rome* (Montreal: Harvest House, 1986), p. 144.

4. O. Giarini, *Dialogue on Wealth and Welfare–An Alternative View of World Capital Formation* (Oxford: Pergamon Press, 1980).

5. Many of the research centers and international organizations are listed in Annex 14 of the paper "The Contribution of Oceans and Ocean Development to Wealth and Welfare," by O. Giarini and M. Börlin (presented to the International Centre for Ocean Development [ICOD] in Halifax, Nova Scotia, Canada, 2 December 1988).

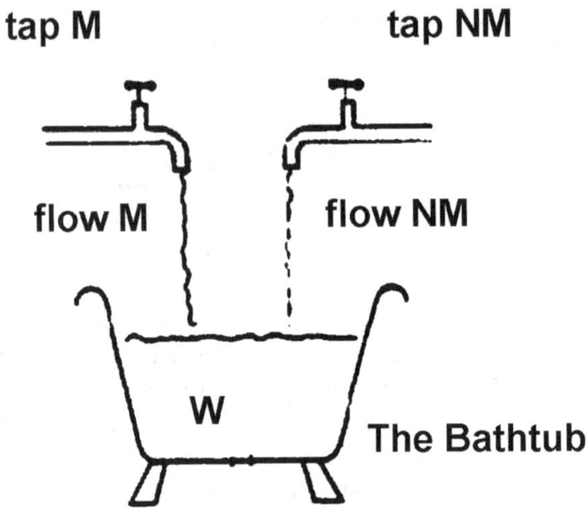

FIG. 1.—The Bathtub of Economic Wealth

Flow M	The flow of monetarized goods and services including money itself.
Flow NM	Flow of goods and services that also increase wealth but the production of which is nonmonetarized: unpaid human contributions, or free goods such as air.
W	The stock of wealth that we use for our needs and pleasure; the utilization value of this stock depends on the quality and quantity available.

- the tap *M* represents the flow of monetarized production, which pours additional wealth into our stock *W*;
- the tap *NM* symbolizes the flow of goods and services that also increase our wealth, but the production of which is nonmonetarized. It refers for instance to free, unpaid human contributions, or free goods like air.

When reading about economic indicators, many problems arise in our mind from the lack of distinction between what relates to our stock of wealth *W* (monetarized or not) and what refers to the flow *F* (monetarized or nonmonetarized). The value added in economics is essentially a measurement of the *monetarized flow.*[6] It measures how much monetarized production is passing through tap *M* to increase the stock of wealth *W*. The underlying assumption rooted in the Industrial Revolution is that any additional flow represents an equivalent increase of the stock *W* (i.e., a value added).

6. Monetarized refers to any goods or services exchanged, monetarized or not. Nonmonetarized refers to goods or services with no relation to exchange.

The first reason for choosing the monetarized flow *FM* instead of the stock of wealth *W* as the measurement reference is that the statistical measurement of the flow is easier to do. The measurement of the stock, in contrast, appears much more complex because all sorts of nonmonetarized production that inevitably intervenes may not be noticed and because, in the case of the sale of a part of our stock, a definite reference value to refer to the loss in stock or wealth may not be available. However, the fundamental assumption of this reasoning still is that the production of the monetarized flow *FM* is equivalent to an increase in wealth *W*!

Over the last 20 years, we have perceived the emergence of a new type of problem linked to environmental and ecological constraints, which strongly suggests that the monetarized flow is not always an addition to wealth; the monetarized flow contains a nonnegligible part of pollution that does not add to, but destroys wealth.[7] Part of the "added value" is then in fact a "deducted value." The measurement of growth as expressed in the gross national product is precisely and only the measurement of such a monetarized flow at the macroeconomic, national level. It excludes the standard accounting practice used by all industrial companies and individuals: an accounting of total assets or stock available, and total liabilities incurred (the balance sheet), of which the analysis of the flow of activity performed during a given period of time (the statement of income and expenses) is an integral part. At the microeconomic level, it is a matter of common knowledge and common sense that the differential in total value of assets (e.g., stock) does not necessarily coincide with the volume of activity performed over a given period of time. The accounting of assets is a process that determines the accumulation of an activity during a longer period of time, rather than simply measuring if the monetarized flow during this same period of time has increased or decreased, but remaining always by definition bigger than 0!

During the classical Industrial Revolution, it could be assumed that the amount of monetarized flow largely corresponded to increases in the stock of wealth. In the modern economy,[8] this is no longer true; the real level of wealth (i.e., the stock) depends also on nonmonetarized contributions and deducted values. In the first phase of the industrial revolution, value added coincided largely with the real utilization value and as such became the primary indicator of the growing wealth. The notion of utilization value itself refers to the assets (stock) and the way it is used in time, in

7. See the notion of "deducted values" in Giarini (n. 4 above), p. 121.

8. The modern economy which in fact we call the "service economy" for reasons described by O. Giarini and W. R. Stahel, "The Limits to Certainty–Facing Risks in the New Service Economy," in *International Studies in the Service Economy Series,* vol. 4, ed. Kluwer Academic Publishers (Dordrecht: Kluwer Academic Publishers, 1993), p. 294.

contrast to the notion of added value referring to the flow of monetarized production.

The measurement of such stock can of course only be approximate and will be partly subjective: this means that the decision of what has value partly becomes a matter for political consensus. The future choice may well be between a system of flow measurement that is quantitatively precise but is increasingly losing its significance, and systems of asset measurements that might be less precise but will be more relevant to the real world. The quantification of nonmonetarized wealth elements can be achieved by adequate indicators. This is a crucial topic, as any method of asset accounting would also enable a better definition of riches and poverty, and this avoids the perpetuation of a system accounting a misleading level of wealth, as the nonmonetarized contributions to the wealth of one country may be higher than the one of another country.[9]

Old and New Shortcomings: Wealth and Riches

Classical economists, and in particular, Ricardo, were well aware that the accounting of economic wealth that they were elaborating was not really comprehensive of the real level of wealth of an individual or a country. A clear distinction was made between the notion of riches, on the one side, and of wealth, on the other.[10] There was even an implicit admission that an increase in wealth could eventually correspond to an increase in riches.

However, these considerations remained secondary because the main problem during the Industrial Revolution was to identify the most dynamic system of increasing the wealth of nations, that is, the industrialization process, and to concentrate on its development. Inconveniences and discrepancies between wealth and riches were considered of minor importance. The writings in classical economics and some of the later commentators[11] were a consequence of the fact that the first formalization of economic theory was a description of the industrialization process; the priority was to measure a flow of goods and the value added.

In the modern economy,[12] when the industrialization process, although important per se, is no longer identified as the prime mover to increase the wealth of nations, the problem is quite different and the contradiction between wealth and riches becomes much more important. The divergence

9. See A. Tevoedjre, *La Pauvreté, Richesse des Peuples* (Paris: Les Éditions Ouvrières, 1977).

10. See W. A. Weisskopf, *The Psychology of Economics* (Chicago: University of Chicago Press, and London: Rougledge & Kegan Paul, 1955, also University of Chicago Press, Midway Reprint, 1975), p. 52, ff.

11. See Weisskopf (n. 10 above), pp. 11 ff., 33 ff., 166 ff.

12. See Giarini and Stahel (n. 8 above).

of the notion of riches versus the notion of wealth corresponds to what can be called the development of deducted values in the modern economy. The increase of these deducted values stems from the increasingly higher allocation of economic resources to activities that do not add to the real level of wealth or of riches, but which are in fact absorbed by the rising costs of the functioning of the economic system (e.g., the costs for waste management).

The Global Stock of Our Riches: The Dowry and Patrimony

The stock of riches, which provides all the resources and the environment for our life on Earth, can be summarized in the following table. We call this stock Dowry and Patrimony (D&P) and we would like to underline the fact that it is the ultimate source of economic value. Within these different types of riches, there is one, the monetarized patrimony, which represents the contribution of the Industrial Revolution to the overall accumulation of wealth.

Obviously the oceans, as any other Earth resource, are a combination, in terms of riches, of the various types of D&P mentioned in fig. 2.

Assessing Riches, Wealth and Welfare

In the previous paragraphs we have already tried to point out two key elements that make conventional economics an inadequate tool to evaluate the economic value of common heritage and of the oceans in particular. The first concerns the very notion of value, which relates to a flow of monetarized (or implicitly monetarized) goods and services. This flow is always supposed to be positive, but in fact it is also negative in terms of wealth accumulation. Secondly, it is a measurement that is very partial with regards to both the nonmonetarized flows and the results of all flows on the level of riches or D&P. All this intellectual construction of classical economics rests upon the assumption that the flows of added values are adding to wealth, at least as a priority tool, and as such remain the major reference for economic policy.

We contend that although the management and stimulation of value added in this sense is still very important, it tends to be of secondary importance, at least in the terms conceived during the Industrial Revolution, in an economy where one has to evaluate the final results on the level of the riches on the one side, and where the very process of the production of added value depends more and more on service activities.[13] The real problem we have to face at this stage is to reformulate a definition of value so that we can elaborate a system of indicators more appropriate to evaluate,

13. Ibid.

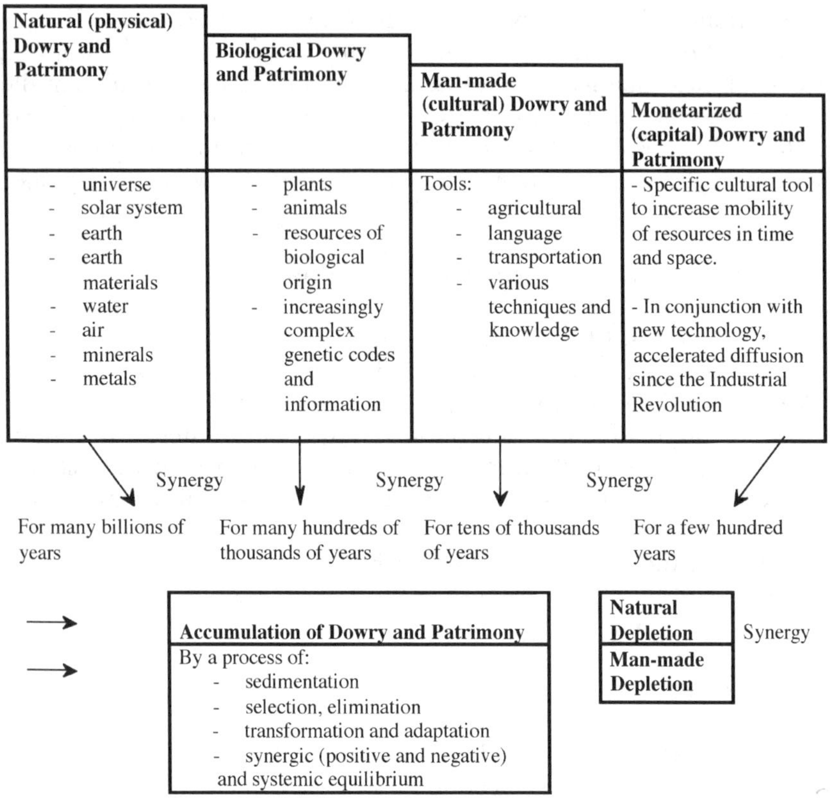

FIG. 2.—Dowry and Patrimony (D&P): The Accumulation Process of Resources[14]

monitor, and establish economic policies, and to complement the single indicator of the monetarized value added.

At this stage we have to go back to consider all the indicators that have been provided for the last decades to measure various aspects of economic activities. Many indicators have been proposed and used in both a socioeconomic context ("social accounting"), in an institutional company context ("social audit"), or even in an individual context ("satisfaction indices"). The World Bank has made in the last few years consistent steps in our direction by publishing reports integrating various welfare indices. The problems and criticism against such indices vary.

The first criticism, coming from economists, is that social indicators are sociological tools that do not directly concern economics. This criticism de-

14. Ibid

rives once more from the identification of economics with the monetarized economy. In fact, it should be recognized that these indicators are related to the definition of and search for wealth and welfare, and that their existence and even proliferation are a sign of the growing dissatisfaction with the traditional tools of economic measurement, precisely in view of economic goals (i.e., developing the wealth of nations) and research objectives.

The second criticism is that the indicators are very often too qualitative and difficult to quantify. This is obvious; however, there are also clearly many cases in which quantification is, in reality, a meaningless process. For example, because value added entails certain deducted values, it can no longer be considered a reliable indication of wealth and welfare even though it can be measured relatively easily. The first requirement is to be sure that the measurement in question has the expected significance. To select factors in a system on the basis of their direct measurability and not in terms of the behaviour of the system in itself and its goals clearly leads to aberrations.

The third criticism relates to the multiplicity and variety of these indicators. The "indicators" movement may seem to be the outcome of different situations; it leads to very different types of motivation. Two types of answers can be discussed. The first is that wealth and welfare can be differently defined in different places and cultures, as well as in different moments in time. It is the very inflexibility of the traditional concept of value in economics that may constitute an unacceptable factor, because it presupposes a world in which living conditions, constraints, and appreciations are uniform. The diversity which, in fact, exists should not be taken as evidence of any lack of consistency and logic of the "indicator" movement. On the other hand, the earlier-mentioned lack of any adequate theory of wealth and welfare has probably impeded a more successful use of such indicators.

A more comprehensive theory of wealth and welfare of the kind proposed here tries to provide a basis for a more consistent approach and actually encourage utilization of the indicators. In fact, the whole target of this article can be defined in the following way:

a. first define a new theory of value (utilization value);
b. then devise the most appropriate methods and possibilities of measurement and the judgment (selection of indicators);
c. in this way open the possibility of defining new operational economic policies, for instance, in the fiscal and monetary field as well as in the preservation and development of nonmonetarized resources.

We will therefore bring together the various ideas on D&P, utilization value, and deducted and added value in an attempt to set out a systematic reference framework for assessing wealth and welfare on the basis of fig. 3. Figure 3 proposes a logical sequence of D&P formation and use in time and space, a prerequisite for any research on its general structure.

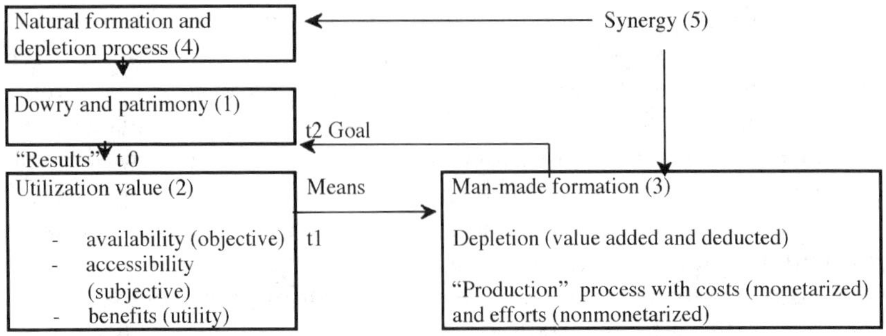

FIG. 3.—The Dynamics of Dowry and Patrimony and the Classification of Indicators.

Central to the notion of wealth and welfare is the concept of Dowry and Patrimony (D&P, box 1), including every available resource and asset, material and nonmaterial, monetarized or nonmonetarized. Economists have taken a timid partial step in this direction when they talk of human capital, including qualitative indicators. D&P, as we have already indicated has a *utilization value* (box 2), which represents the (objective) availability of D&P (e.g., apples on a tree, the music of Beethoven, a bank account) and the (subjective) accessibility to it (i.e., both material and cultural: I appreciate Beethoven, I am in a position to use my bank account and to get the apples from the tree). It represents, to use a keyword much in favour with economists, the notion of utility in its widest sense.

Utilization value allows humankind to live and therefore to produce (i.e., positive and negative yields, and added and deducted values in their monetary and nonmonetary sense). Box 3 relates to *man-made formation and depletion* of D&P, and box 4 indicates the *natural D&P formation and depletion* process, which influences directly the total D&P, but which develops in *synergy* (point 5) with the man-made process. Boxes 3 and 4, in their synergy (point 5) determine the level of total D&P. Utilization value is then the reference for identifying the economic value of a stock, which in fact in our case would also refer to common heritage and the oceans.

If we take the notion of utilization value from another angle, we can identify this notion with the contemporary "service economy," which we have tried to identify in another context.[15] We are here, in fact, confronted with another fundamental crossroad: the manufacturing industry, the producer *par excellence* of value added, has become in a modern economy more and more based on service functions (70 percent to 80 percent of their total "production" costs). Within the industrial system, this is transforming the

15. For more details, see Chapter 3 of Giarini (n. 4 above).

notion of value from a reference related to the instant encountering of supply and demand in a given moment in time, to a notion of value incorporating performance of systems in future time. Whereas, uncertainty becomes a key issue for management and the idea of equilibrium in economics is replaced by the notion of dynamic disequilibrium. In other words, the reality and the evolution itself of modern industry on the one side, constraints of the environment on the other side, are converging in a way to put in evidence what are the key concepts for the economics of common heritage:

a. acknowledgment of the value of a stock;
b. the identification of its economic value in terms of performance or utilization in time (i.e., in a probabilistic setting).

In a theoretical sense, what it is at stake here is in fact the development of a general new economic theory that will provide the basic groundwork to mobilize researchers on issues related to indicators. This is to have a consistent frame of reference that can be used and managed for the purpose of efficiently managing our common heritage, our stock of riches, and the use of resources of all sorts in a new context. Many fundamental questions and some of the answers of traditional economics are still valid, but the frame of reference for their application has changed too much today to be used as such simple adaptations. If you are used to driving a car, you do not simply fly an airplane applying the same rules as those used for driving.

Our final pledge would then be that to establish the economics of common heritage, it is essential today to stimulate fundamental research in economics on which depends the development of adequate measurement tools for applicable economic policies.

SUSTAINABLE DEVELOPMENT: AT THE CROSSROADS BETWEEN ECONOMICS AND ECOLOGY

The Basic Problem for Development

The basic problem that development has to tackle is one of scarce resources. Such resources are of a material, human, technological, and cultural nature. It is on the very notion of scarcity that economic science has been founded more than 200 years ago. It was then that Adam Smith wrote his book on the wealth of nations as a strategy to overcome the limitations to development due to scarce resources.

The Industrial Revolution successfully concentrated for over 2 centuries on the possibilities of increasing the manufacturing sectors to reduce scarcity of products. The key issue has been the mobilization and improvement of all available resources to make them more abundant and apt to produce wealth. One cannot deny the great overall successes of the Industrial Revolution, thanks to which life expectancy of human beings has increased at an unprecedented pace, mainly in the industrialized countries, but also, very largely, in the less industrialized ones.

The Political Aspect of the Industrial Revolution: A New Basis for Legitimacy, Credibility, and Governability

For the last 2 centuries, the legitimacy and the credibility of governments have centred around the methods and ideas proposed concerning the building and development of the "wealth of nations" through the development of the manufacturing systems, that is, the political management of the industrial revolution. The process of industrialization has been the key reference for building political consensus. The long-lasting competition between a liberal and a Marxist system has finally come to an end by the failure of Marxist methods to efficiently control and stimulate this process. Such a failure has resulted in a total loss of the political consensus and has therefore given way to political disaggregation. Even if the liberal system has shown many shortcomings and has experienced very great crises during the last 2 centuries, both political and economic, it has finally proved to be the least imperfect of the systems and the most efficient one, in the era of the Industrial Revolution.

The Ecological Movement and the Crisis in the Traditional Notion of the Wealth of Nations: In Quest of Sustainable Development

The Industrial Revolution, after its great successes in developing the wealth of nations, has come to a point at which there is a growing doubt in its capability of pursuing the goal of developing the wealth of nations without some very strong and in-depth adaptations. The ecological and environmental movements in the world are critical of the point that the industrialization process is in fact the right way to improve welfare and well being of humanity in present conditions. Hence, the efforts of all those involved in promoting economic activity to integrate as far as possible the ecological and environmental requirements not only as an economic opportunity, but above all to reintegrate the very reference upon which the political consensus has been built in the past.

The notion of "sustainable development" refers precisely to the major problem of development that was at the very core of preoccupations of the pioneers of industrialization: the mobilization and development of scarce resources. The word "sustainable" refers essentially to the fact that the industrialization process, in certain cases, instead of increasing wealth tends to produce scarcity of resources. This happens in particular when those resources that were once available in an unlimited quantity (e.g., air, water, land) are themselves submitted to a process of progressive increase of scarcity. In this case, the entry of resources into the market-priced system that were once not taken into account because they were available in an unlimited quantity, is indicative of a growing level of scarcity and therefore of poverty.

The question of "sustainable development" has to do finally with the necessity to cope with the danger of producing scarcity, making resources more and more rare. A particular connotation of this phenomenon is its tendency to be of medium, long, and very long term. This contrasts in particular with an industrial economic process that is strongly conditioned by the market operations in the short term. Sustainability means in the end that resource development has to be mastered simultaneously in the short and long term, and this implies also concentrating on the issue of uncertainty.

Acting for Sustainable Development

We acknowledge the inadequacy of the ancient model to develop the wealth of nations and the recognition that both economics and ecology are about the best possible way of managing world and human resources to achieve a better wealth of nations. The rebuilding of economics and of a credible strategy for increasing the wealth and well being of nations is today at the center of the problem of providing a sound basis for the legitimacy and credibility of public institutions and governments. If the dichotomy between traditional economic goals and new ecological and environmental requirements for sustainable development will not credibly combine, the political consensus and the legitimacy of governments at the local, national, and international levels will have a tendency to produce on the new liberalizing world disaggregation effects that could be as extensive as those witnessed in former Marxist countries.

Hence, the strategic priority consists of reviewing the meaning of the wealth of nations today and in finding the best economic methods to promote it in a credible and adequate way, with a vision aimed at strengthening the credibility and the legitimacy of the democratic economic systems. In terms of sustainable development, it means to find a reasonable compromise between the short and the long term to reduce scarcity now and in the future, avoiding the undermining of the patrimony composed by earth resources.

The Way of Sustainability

We recognize the fact that a modern industrial economy is essentially a service-based one and that the notion of value has shifted from the production of goods to the production of performances. Service activities of all sorts have today become dominant in every "manufacturing" sector. Services are about performances measured by results expressed in terms of level of health, wealth, well being, happiness, and pleasure, et cetera. These levels of well being do not depend only on the quantities of goods available, but on the way in which they are used and they affect the quality of life of human beings in time. This is what is meant by "performance," which also must integrate the cost of depleting resources and the management of waste (a service activity) in the long term. From this point of view, the integration of wisdom from 2 centuries of economic thinking and the legitimate requirements of the ecological and environmental needs and demands should naturally find their synthesis in a new notion of value. This is a notion of value where the basis for both economy and ecology are recognized as being the same; the best possible utilization and maintenance of human and natural resources for the well being and for the wealth of nations. A clear strategy for sustainable development depends largely on the vision generated by the combination of economic and ecological views attacking together the problems of scarcity.

Modern, Late Modern, and Postmodern Ocean: The Challenge to Knowledge

Adalberto Vallega*
University of Genoa, Italy

INTRODUCTION

This article aims to contribute to the discussion of the "crisis of knowledge" referred to by Elisabeth Mann Borgese in her article in *Ocean Yearbook 15*.[1] The approach is based on a "triangle of ocean knowledge building," whose vertices represent, respectively, i) the ontological dimension (i.e., ocean reality, consisting of the ocean natural milieu, together with human presence and resource use); ii) the semiotic dimension (i.e., the representation of ocean reality); and iii) the hermeneutic and epistemological dimension (i.e., explanations, theories, and narratives induced by representation). In this framework, modern knowledge building, triggered by rationalism and carried out especially by positivism (analysis of the natural ocean features), and structuralism (analysis of economic and social conditions) led to assuming the meta-narrative of progress as the cardinal vision of the societal evolution, and the narrative of economic development as the pathway where progress solidifies. This knowledge system persisted unrefuted till the 1980s, namely up to the conceptual atmosphere, which marked the preparation of the United Nations Conference on Environment and Development (UNCED) in 1992. As a result of the conceptual triggering role of that event, two options have arisen concerning the ocean episteme building. The former option consists of the late modern approach, according to which the rationalism-based knowledge building is thought of as still epistemologically valid and useful for praxis. It should only be reoriented and implemented to deal with an ocean reality that has become increasingly complicated, essentially because of the associated inputs from climate change and globalisation. The latter option consists of the postmodern approach, according to which the

*Editors' Note.—The drawings in this article were prepared by Paola Salmona, International Centre for Coastal and Ocean Policy Studies (ICCOPS), Genoa, Italy.

1. E. Mann Borgese, "The Crisis of Knowledge," in *Ocean Yearbook 15*, ed. E. Mann Borgese, A. Chircop and M. McConnell (Chicago: Chicago University Press, 2001), pp. 1–6.

Ocean Yearbook 18: 137–161

rationalism-based knowledge building should be abandoned in favour of, or at least integrated by, a more humanistic approach, which would focus on cultural aspects, consider places and their cultural identity instead of spaces, take into account the hyper-real places built up by imagination and creation, and, more importantly, replace the rationalist hard rhetoric with a humanistic soft rhetoric. This option makes the present time as one of the most intriguing after the rise of rationalism and the enlightenment atmosphere.

A CRISIS OF KNOWLEDGE

> Recent decades have witnessed a radical shift in the philosophy of science, a 'paradigm change.' Since the age of enlightenment, scientists thought that they knew much and were learning more and more so that in the future they would have enough data to be able to model, and make linear projections of, processes and developments. Today, we have recognized that the more we know, the better we know how little we know; that our knowledge will remain forever incomplete; that the systems with which we are dealing are exceedingly complex; that the behaviour of complex systems is non-linear and unpredictable; and that uncertainty is the name of the game. Additional data on additional factors, making systems more complex, will induce chaos rather than enhance predictability.[2]

This statement by Elisabeth Mann Borgese has posed the question of "knowledge building," which is more or less linked with the question of "policy building," a subject discussed by Mann Borgese in the past. For example, the knowledge-building question was in the background of her well-known writings.[3] Nevertheless, her latest article has much more relevance to the subject than do the previous ones, at least because, first, the question of knowledge building is explicitly assumed as cardinal vis-à-vis the effectiveness of ocean policy, hence the interaction between the ocean episteme and ocean action is called to the fore, and secondly, because the root of the issue is placed on the enlightenment, hence the role of modernity in building up both science and policy is assumed as fundamental for discussing the present epistemological and political conditions.

Mann Borgese's discussion moves from the consideration of how science has become weak in explaining increasingly complicated ocean pro-

2. See Borgese (n. 1 above), p. 1.

3. E. Mann Borgese, *The Future of the Oceans* (Montreal: Harvest House, 1986); E. Mann Borgese, "The Oceanic Circle," in *Ocean Yearbook 14,* ed. E. Mann Borgese, A. Chircop, M. McConnell and J. R. Morgan (Chicago: The University of Chicago Press, 2000), pp. 1–15.

cesses and in predicting their evolution, particularly of those processes that follow nonlinear trajectories, hence the weakness of science in designing action patterns. It is self-evident that the question is, What kind of ocean knowledge has been built up?, and subsequently, What kind of episteme for action has been designed by modern society? To contribute to this discussion, which has acquired a background role in the atmosphere of the 2002 World Summit of Sustainable Development (WSSD),[4] I will deal with the question from a perspective different from, but complementary to, the one adopted by Mann Borgese. It will be discussed how knowledge, in our case ocean knowledge, has been built up in the framework of modern society and modernity, and whether it should undergo a refutation process. This perspective is justified by two ascertainments that are respectively concerned with the epistemological context and with the interaction between episteme and praxis and which merit some mise-au-point.

The Modern Epistemological Context

The rise of modernity, which was essentially due to the Kant and Descartes speculative constructions, led to the rationalist knowledge building, which first supported positivism and then structuralism, two speculative settings having deeply influenced the modern approach to the ocean. The rationalist thought was built up by moving from a very limited assessment of natural and social processes, namely from a small amount of data, particularly if compared with the huge amount of data marking our times. In spite of these constraining conditions, modern thinkers were able to build up such an energetic knowledge system as to support more than 2 centuries of science evolution and implementation. As a result, the weakness of the basic assessment vis-à-vis speculative strength was a characteristic of modernity. Differently, at the present time the opposite occurs: the information and assessment basis has become unexpectedly wide, but up till now, speculation has failed in building up a postmodern episteme, replacing the rationalist one, and in so doing, designing a better conceptual approach and a more effective linkage between science and policy. As a result, the width of assessment vis-à-vis the weakness of thought is a characteristic of our times.

The Interaction between the Modern Episteme and Praxis

During the 20th century, the evolution of modern society was sustained by the concept of economic development. This concept was first the result of

4. See *Report of the World Summit on Sustainable Development, Johannesburg, South Africa, 26 August–4 September 2002.* United Nations. A/CONF.199/20. New York: 2002. http://www.johannesburg.org/ (accessed 12 September 2003).

intense discussions in the scientific arena, particularly by the masters of economic theory, and then it was applied in political approaches, moving from North America to many other regions of the world. Therefore, the input moved from science towards policy, and it was successful. In the 1990s, as a result of the UNCED Summit, the narrative of development was replaced by that of sustainable development. The input moved in the opposite direction, since the sustainability concept was first sketched in the 1980s within the political framework—the World Commission on Environment and Development[5] had a leading role—and then the scientific community had to speculate on trying to make it rational and tailor it to the need to carry out interdisciplinary approaches, embracing natural and social sciences. Hence, the input moved from policy to science, asking scientists to build up knowledge about a principle that, just at the time of its enunciation, appeared so ambiguous as to justify an ample range of actions conceptually differing from, and even conflicting with, each other. Moreover, it appeared conceptually weak because it was not supported by solid economic and social theory that had supported the concept of development. Bearing this framework in mind, the modern and postmodern approaches to the ocean may be compared by focusing on the interaction between science and policy, knowledge and action. This basis consists of a three-dimensional discussion pattern that may be represented by a triangle whose vertices host (Fig. 1):

- *ocean reality,* which involves the ontological dimension of knowledge. It encompasses those parts of the ocean that are regarded as objects of knowledge, and consequently, as arenas for action;
- *ocean representation,* which involves the semiotic dimension of knowledge. It consists of any kind of descriptions, including models and maps, that may be considered as signs leading to knowledge;
- *ocean episteme,* which involves the hermeneutical and epistemological dimensions of knowledge: the hermeneutical one, in that it consists of the interpretation of signs, and the epistemological one, in that it leads to signifieds—meant in a semiotic sense, namely consisting of theories, values, assumptions—justified by signs.

As a matter of fact, in the framework of modern society, the modern episteme was conceived as a hierarchical structure of signifieds including, *at the upper level,* the meta-narrative of progress that was thought of in the enlightenment atmosphere and was kept unrefuted up to the present time; *at the intermediate level,* the narrative of development that had a leading role during most of the 20th century and, as a result of UNCED, it should be replaced by the narrative of sustainable development; *at the lower level,* the individual

5. World Commission on Environment and Development (WCED), *Our Common Future* (Oxford: Oxford University Press, 1987).

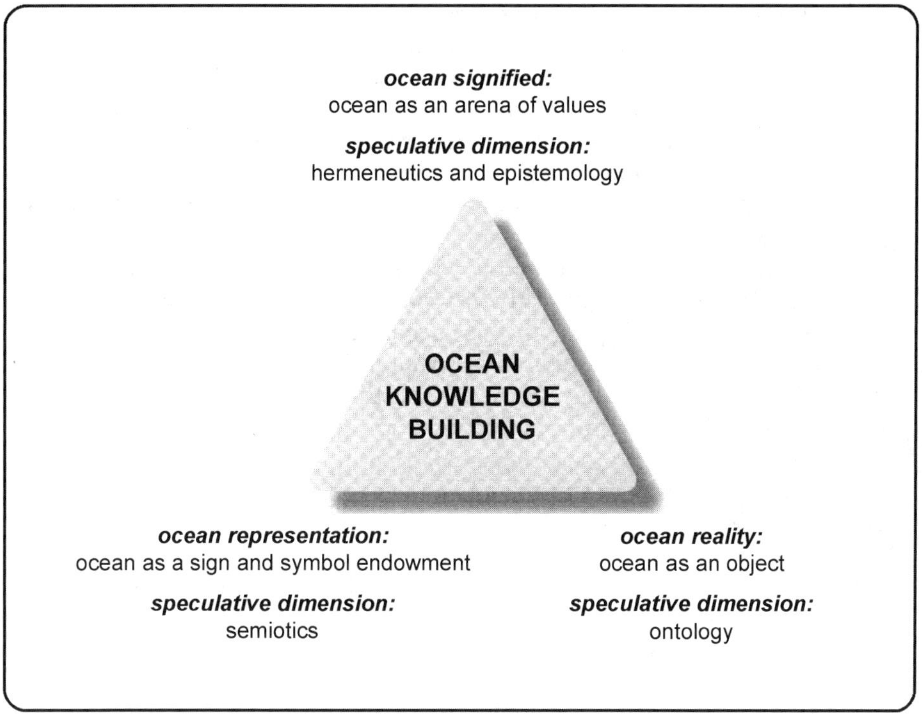

FIG. 1.—Ocean knowledge building

scenarios and action designs that, moving from the earlier-mentioned narratives, are built up on the national and local scales.

This background brings forth two implications, both useful for discussion. First, the relationship between the sign (semiotic dimension) and reality (ontological dimension) may be usefully assumed as having a metaphorical role. The sign is a metaphor of the object, namely something that stands for something other.[6] Representation, essentially consisting of modelling ocean processes, is a metaphorical history of the object, in our case of the ocean, coastal, and island contexts, and it replaces reality in giving shape

6. "A sign . . . [in the form of a *representamen*] is something that stands to somebody for something in some respect or capacity. It addresses somebody, that is, creates in the mind of that person an equivalent sign, or perhaps a more developed sign. That sign that it creates I call the *interpretant* of the first sign. The sign stands for something, its *object*. It stands for that object, not in all respects, but in reference to a sort of idea, which I have sometimes called the *ground* of the representamen." Ch. Sanders Peirce, *Collected Writings*, 8 vols., ed. Ch. Hartshorne, P. Weiss and A. W. Burks (Cambridge: Harvard University Press, 1931–1958), par. 2.228.

to signifieds. The relationship between the sign and signified—this is the second implication—may be univocal (mono-semiotic) or plurivocal (pluri-semiotic). In the former case, a deterministic relationship arises, since the sign leads to one, and only one, signified. This is a key feature of the rationalist thought, which has been used as a basis for the building up of positivist and structuralist approaches to the ocean: it is the realm of reason and objectivism. In the latter case, an individual sign leads to a range of signifieds, giving shape to a nondeterministic relationship with the signified. This kind of relationship is incompatible with the rationalist one—for example, the cause-effect explanation of the interaction between biomass use and climate change, or the design of coastal urbanisation as a linear process—and needs for transcending positivist and structuralist approaches: it is the realm of emotion and imagination, and of subjectivism. The discussion triangle, the conceptual background of which is inspired by Olsson,[7] leads to designing our representation of the ocean as metaphors of ocean reality because, as the representation is designed, it becomes something that replaces reality, and in so doing it becomes the only basis on which signifieds are built up. For example, where the ocean is designed as a complex system interacting with climate change and globalisation, this vision replaces ocean reality and becomes the basis on which our theories, values, scenarios, and narratives of the ocean sustainable development are settled.

Where this triangle-referred approach is applied to discuss how ocean knowledge has evolved as a result of modernity, it may be assumed that modern society was born as the combined inputs from the industrial revolution, which brought about a new societal organisation and enlightenment, which brought about a new vision of society, marking the 19th and most of the 20th century. The modern vision of the world, based on faith in progress and the compression of time on space, provoked by technological and economic improvements, started being implicitly confuted as a result of the 1972 United Nations Conference on the Human Environment. The cardinal reason of such a turning moment was essentially due to the fact that the environmental component of reality was included in the political designs. A second, more influential turning moment occurred 20 years after, when UNCED led to replacing the concept of development with the principle of sustainable development. As is well known, these changes brought about extended and profound effects in the ocean arena: in 1974, international cooperation on ocean environmental protection was launched with the adoption of the Regional Seas Programme by the United Nations Environment Programme (UNEP), while in 1992, integration was assumed as the key concept to operate coastal and ocean management coherently with the sustainable development principle.

As a result of the UNCED discussions and materials, two new avenues have emerged with the aim of overcoming the modern approach. The for-

7. G. Olsson, "Heretic cartography," *Fennia,* no. 2 (1994): 115–30.

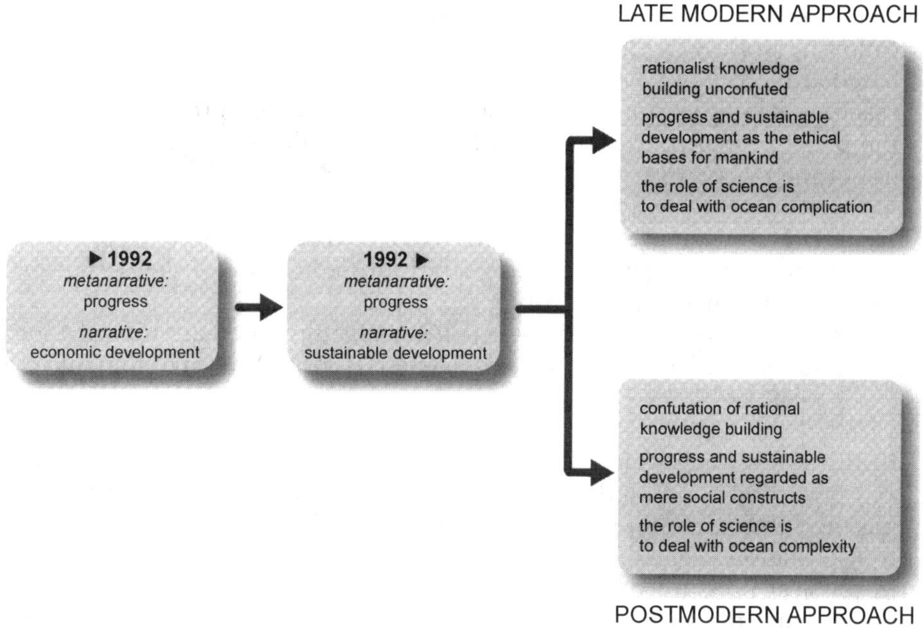

FIG. 2.—Modern, late modern and postmodern approach to the ocean

mer avenue was that of the enunciation of the principle of sustainable development, regarding it as an implementation of the concept of development to respond to the rise of new human needs. As a result, a narrative was replaced to refresh the sense of the meta-narrative of progress. The prospects designed by this change may be regarded as the "late modern avenue." The latter avenue has arisen as a result of a double refutation: the refutation of the meta-narrative or progress, meant as an avoidable outcome of rationalist attitudes, which implies rejecting either the principles of development and that of sustainable development; the refutation of the rationalist way of knowledge building. This approach may be regarded as characterising the "postmodern avenue" (Fig. 2).

An arena to discuss the interaction among the three above-mentioned avenues to ocean knowledge building will be sketched in the following sections.

THE MODERN AVENUE

The increase of ocean uses was the main characteristic of the ocean reality during 2 centuries, that is, from the late 18th century to the 1980s.

Transportation, biomass exploitation, oil and gas extraction, and communication networks were the cardinal uses on which the role of the ocean was based at the eve of UNCED, when the modern approach to the ocean was reaching its momentous manifestations. To give a comprehensive view of the pressure that transportation, which traditionally is the most important use of the ocean, exerted on the ocean, two indicators may be used:[8]

- the tonnage pressure indicator (TPI), expresses how many gross registered tons (grt), on average, sail through 1 km^2 of the ocean (grt: sq km) at any moment in a year; and
- the cargo pressure indicator (CPI), expresses how many tons of goods are carried on 1 km^2 of ocean water (t:sq km) at any moment in a year.

In the 1990s, each square kilometre of the ocean was bearing 1.4 grt and 26 t of carried goods, indicating a pressure nine times the one exerted during the 1950s when an unprecedented growth of merchant navigation and transportation began. This process has brought about not only an increase in physical pressure on the ocean ecosystem, but also an increase in the dependence of national and regional economic systems and social life-styles upon merchant sea transportation and, consequently, on the strategies operated by maritime powers. The increase in degree and the spatial extent of this dependence may be estimated using two indicators, proposed by Vigarié,[9] and presented here with some adaptation:

- the gross-tonnage dependence indicator (GDI, originally called *index d'équipement maritime*), expresses how many gross registered tons (grt), on average, are in operation for each of the world inhabitants (grt: p) at any moment of a year:

$$GDI = grt/p$$

and

- the transport dependence indicator (TDI, originally called *index de dépendance maritime*), expresses how many tons of goods, on average, are carried to each of the world inhabitants (t:p) at any moment in a year:

$$TDI = t/p$$

8. A. Vallega, "The Role of Ocean Resources," in *Ocean Governance. A Geographical Perspective* (London: Routledge-Taylor, 2001), Chapter 5.

9. A. Vigarié, *La Circulation Maritime* (Paris: Génin, 1968), pp. 115–18; A. Vigarié, "L'Espace-coût et la Nouvelle Géographie Océanique du Monde," in *Marine Marchande 1973* (Paris: Journal de la Marine Marchande, 1974), pp. 33–44.

During the second half of the 20th century the tonnage dependence indicator increased from 3.4 to 8.6 grt per person, while the transport dependence indicator increased from 42 to 165. This indicates how intense was the use of the ocean as a medium for the movement of raw materials and finished goods during the roaring decades following World War II. Moreover, as regards the finished goods, since the late 1950s the use of containerised transportation has been increasing, thereby triggering a spatial process that, while approaching the end of the century, was acquiring a leading role to implement globalisation.

That process was associated with a parallel process involving biomass use. Between the mid-1940s and the early 1960s, world fish catches increased from 18 to 30 million tons. In the course of the 1960s, this figure almost doubled, and by the early 1970s the world population was consuming 60 million tons a year. "During the 1970s fisheries growth declined, reaching only 68 million tons by 1982," but afterwards their "growth again accelerated, matching 86 million tons in 1989, a value close to the world potential estimated by FAO at about 100 million tons."[10] A rapid increase in the rate of exploitation of ocean biomass has characterised the last part of the 20th century: 83 million tons of production (inclusive of aquaculture) was reached at the time of UNCED, while the need to apply the rationale of sustainable use of living resources to both national and international waters is perceived as cardinal.[11]

During the 1960s, as a result of intense technological advances, the take-off of the offshore oil and gas exploitation solidified. The process was given fresh impetus in the 1970s as a consequence of the 1973–1974 oil market crisis resulting from the policy of the Organization of the Petroleum Exporting Countries (OPEC). In addition, industrialised countries tried to widen the geographical scope for buying oil and gas by encouraging offshore production with the final aim of reducing their dependence on Arab producers. As a result of concurrent processes and strategies, at the time of UNCED, many parts of the ocean were involved in exploitation: the North Sea was the main spatial focus of the newly adopted strategy by the Western world, but the Mediterranean Sea, and marginal and archipelagic seas of the Southeast Asia and other parts of the ocean world, including the Arctic Ocean were also involved to some extent, whilst output from the Gulf of Mexico was steadily increasing.[12] In the mid-1990s, offshore oil and gas

10. S. M. Garcia, "Ocean Fisheries Management: The FAO Programme," in *Ocean Management in Global Change,* ed. P. Fabbri (London: Elsevier Applied Science, 1992), pp. 381–418.

11. D. Squires, "Sources of growth in marine fishing industries," *Marine Policy,* no. 1 (1994): 5–18; Independent World Commission on the Oceans, *The Ocean, Our Future* (Cambridge: Cambridge University Press, 1998), pp. 97–9.

12. B. G. S. Taylor, "Offshore oil and gas," *Ocean and Shoreline Management,* no. 3-4 (1991): 259–73; Vallega (n. 8 above), pp. 104–7.

represented some 30 percent and 20 percent, respectively, of total world production.[13] Meanwhile, during the 1950s the ocean network of telephone cables arose but only to decline again 20 years later because of the debut of satellite-based communication systems. Nevertheless, while UNCED was being celebrated, fiberoptic cables were successfully diffusing, therefore designing a rebirth of the ocean as a communication arena. [14]

Moving from the ontological dimension to the semiotic dimension of the modern discourse on the ocean, an ample range of representations of this reality may be found, where the whole scientific improvement and the background political approaches, which have marked the 19th, and more intensively the 20th century, are mirrored. The most attractive representation is that of the ocean as a trivial machine, consisting of a tectonic structure that has evolved during geological times, and in so doing it has brought about the background processes that characterise the Earth's crust and provide the arena for the use of natural resources by human communities. The production of crust in the ocean ridge, the displacement of crust from the centre to the periphery of the ocean beds, the consumption of crust along the colliding lines of plates, and other dynamic features give a comprehensive vision of the ocean very sensitive to the paradigm of the rational mechanic, according to which reality consists of structures generating functions. Meanwhile, this vision demonstrates that the ocean hosts the mechanisms that shape the entire Earth's surface, including continental areas that have produced immense mineral riches, essentially polymetallic nodules. The ocean as the fulcrum of the planet's evolution has consequently been designed. During the 1980s, this representation, concerned with the tectonic signs, is flanked by another one according to which the ocean is that part of the Earth that most deeply interacts with the atmosphere and, in so doing, is profoundly involved in climatic change. At the time of UNCED there was not a clear idea of how the ocean-atmosphere interaction works, but there was the feeling that it should have been influential.

A couple of these physical visions are complemented by a couple of visions concerned with the interaction between this "trivial planetary machine" and humankind. The ocean as a vast Earth space where global networks have been designed and operated by the technological and organisational improvement of modern society, has triggered the former representation. The routes along which raw materials move from the developing countries and from the Arab world to the developed countries—essentially the Western world—transferring oil and gas, coal, iron, bauxite, and others, the containerised routes along which the finished products are transferred from the Western countries

13. Independent World Commission on the Oceans (n. 11 above), p. 101.

14. E. Wagner, "Submarine cables and protection provided by the law of the sea," *Marine Policy,* no. 2 (1996): 127–36; Vallega (n. 8 above), pp. 101–4.

to the rest of the world, and finally the communication cables laid on the sea bottom, were the key elements of this vision, which may be regarded as the geoeconomic representation of the ocean. The latter representation shows the ocean as a space divided by the range of maritime boundaries regulated by the United Nations Conferences on the Law of the Sea, essentially by the 1958 Conference, which initiated this process, and by the 1973–1982 Conference, which gave shape to an articulated and comprehensive line design delimiting the territorial waters and contiguous sea, the continental shelf and the exclusive economic zone, the archipelagic waters, high seas and the deep seabed. This was the geopolitical representation of the ocean.

The whole signs arising from the earlier-mentioned four representations, which marked the UNCED approach to the ocean, led to a couple of narratives that were considered as the result of the meta-narrative of progress mirrored into the ocean. The ocean was considered as an essential resource reservoir for sustaining economic development, provided that its physical and chemical processes were kept under control to mitigate the environmental degradation and to prevent the damaging consequences of forcing climatic change. Secondly, the ocean was considered as a space where, through the establishment of jurisdictional maritime zones, coastal and island states were able to remarkably expand the prospect of harvesting resources and of implementing their economies (Fig. 3).

To sum up, four representations and two signifieds marked the modern vision of the ocean in the minds of the scientific community and policy makers when UNCED posed the question of the ethical legitimacy of that approach and, therefore, opened the way to trace new visions. At that point, the late modern and postmodern avenues arose endowed with different approaches to the question of knowledge building.

THE LATE MODERN AVENUE

The need to change the approach to the ocean, which justifies discussing the "crisis of knowledge" that Mann Borgese focused on,[15] mirrored a general need, which has progressively involved the whole scientific arena and which was in the background of crucial events such as the 1999 World Conference on Science (WCS) in Budapest. This need is double-faced; that is, the need for new kinds of assessment and approaches as a result of the adoption of the sustainable development principle, and the gap of knowledge vis-à-vis the representation and predictability of global processes. Apparently this issue has only a scientific nature because, since its rise, huge political implications appeared self-evident. After, and as a result of inputs from UNCED, two options have arisen to overcome the epistemological crisis:

15. See Borgese (n. 1 above).

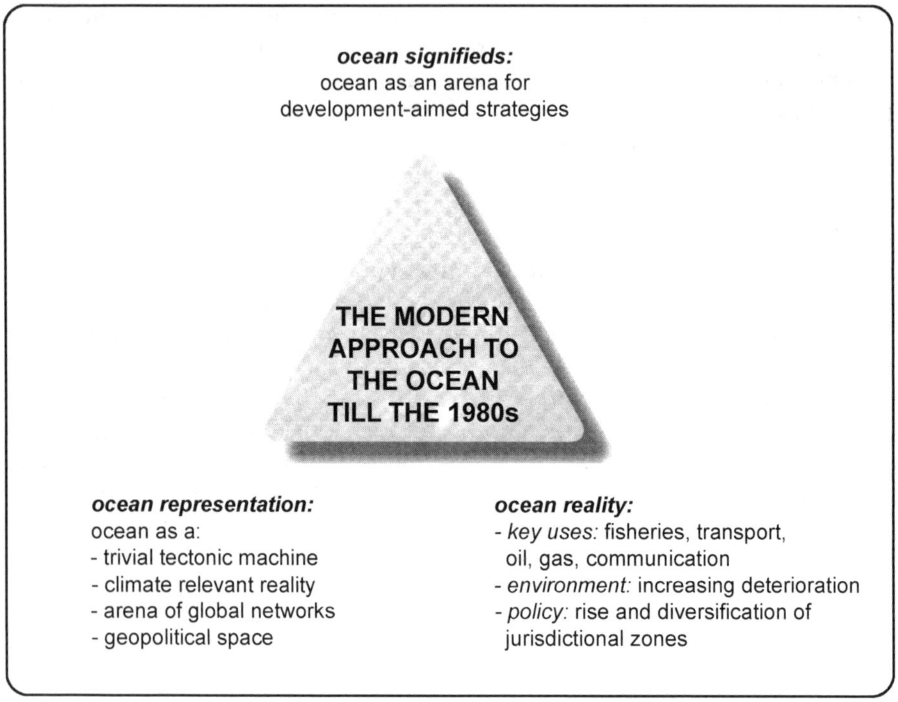

FIG. 3.—The modern approach to the ocean till the 1980s

the former one, that may be called the "late modern option," consists of implementing knowledge without changing the modern mechanisms of knowledge building, namely without facing the epistemological foundations; the latter one, that may be called the "postmodern option," implies the change of the epistemological basis.

The late modern approach moves from the consideration that the need for knowledge has widened so much and has become so complicated to the point of jeopardising the capability of science to pursue two basic objectives: i) to provide an adequate explanation of ocean processes (cognitive issue); ii) to design reliable projections and scenarios (predictability issue). In this framework, it is presupposed that rationalist approaches, on which the modern knowledge building is based, are still adequate to deal with these arising needs, provided that methodologies improve, especially along two directions: the design of models able to frame an increasing number of variables; and to join variables of natural and social processes in model building. Bearing this in mind, the nature of complication, involving the ontological dimension of the ocean discourse, and the basic representations of the ocean, involving the semiotic dimension, may be considered.

As regards the ontological dimension, it is not the case to provide a comprehensive view of how ocean uses have grown and expanded since the UNCED Summit, and of how much they have increased human pressure either in coastal and in deep-ocean areas. The increase in biomass consumption that has exacerbated the crisis in fisheries and has brought about such a huge expansion of sea farming to provoke conflicts with other coastal uses, the expected seaward expansion of oil and gas exploitation, the expected debut of deep-sea mining, and the expansion of coastal and island international tourism associated with increasing urbanisation have given shape to a web of factors that, being linked to those of climate change, have triggered much more worrying conditions than those that were assumed at the basis of the UNCED approach. Leaving aside the consideration of the individual uses, three issues that more or less have involved ocean uses may be considered as foci of the conditions in which nature and society have been jointly involved.

The Ocean and Atmosphere

According to the 2001 reports by the Intergovernmental Panel on Climate Change (IPCC),[16] the intertropical latitudes at which developing populations are concentrated are expected to be mostly involved because of at least three processes: i) the changes in the El Niño Southern Oscillation atmosphere-ocean system, which are expected to affect vast parts of oceans and seas; ii) the expansion and strengthening of extreme events, particularly coastal flooding; and iii) changes in the whole water cycle, involving fresh water and its interaction with coastal waters. This is likely the arena where the predictability problem is unexpectedly demanding.

Food Security

This subject has been marked by a double complication. On the one hand, the earlier-mentioned expansion of biomass uses has occurred, calling for strong implementation of research. In this respect, till the UNCED Summit the physical and chemical branches of ocean science had been implemented much more than the biological ones, to the point of giving shape to a

16. See particularly: Intergovernmental Panel on Climate Change (IPCC), *Climate Change 2001: The Scientific Basis* (Cambridge: Cambridge University Press, 2002); Intergovernmental Panel on Climate Change (IPCC), *Climate Change 2001: Synthesis Report* (Cambridge: Cambridge University Press, 2002).

strong imbalance between the assessment of the abiotic and biotic components of the ocean ecosystem. As a result of the UNCED materials, particularly the 1992 Convention on Biological Diversity,[17] the scientific community has been encouraged to fill this gap, particularly monitoring the productivity, biodiversity, and resilience of the oceans' trophic webs. Nevertheless, since the beginning of this new course it was self-evident that good outcomes would not be achieved in a short time, therefore management programmes and actions are still diffusely unbalanced.

Globalisation

Two circumstances are worth being compared. The former circumstance is concerned with the setting up of transportation and communication networks and the human pressure. As is well known, through containerisation and undersea fiberoptic cables, the ocean was an important arena where the global transportation and communication networks, which were the hard background for globalisation, have arisen and expanded. According to the French terminology, they have given shape to the so-called *mundialisation*.[18] Moreover, since more than half of the world population is concentrated on coastal and island regions, the ocean domain has also become a part of the world very sensitive to the consequences of the globalisation-aimed strategies undertaken by multinational actors. The latter circumstance is concerned with the scientific approach: apart from a few specific aspects, the scientific community has not been able to focus on the coastal and island dimensions of these strategies. This gap between spatial processes and their perception from the scientific community representation—between the ontological and semiotic dimensions of the discourse of ocean globalisation—is expected to influence the management patterns, planning and actions in many parts of the world, particularly in developing coastal regions where the population is concentrated and the consequences of globalisation processes are widespread.

Consequences of Representation

At this point a question comes to the fore, namely, What needs for the representation of the ocean would arise as a result of the earlier-mentioned cardinal changes in ocean reality? As a preliminary approach, it could be shared that the need for four background representations has arisen, con-

17. Convention on Biological Diversity, 1992. Adopted 5 June 1992. http://www.biodiv.org/ (accessed 5 January 2001).

18. P. Claval, *La Géographie Culturelle* (Paris: Nathan, 1995), pp. 344–7.

sisting partly of the implementation of conventional, modern representations, and partly of new kinds of representation.

Representing Global Change

In the late modern approach, the representation of the ocean as a trivial machine, which was the result of the plate tectonic theory and marked the modern visions of the ocean, has been progressively perceived as worthy of encompassing also the biotic components and processes. The Convention on Biological Diversity 1992 states that the ecosystem is a holos, including biotic and abiotic elements, therefore science should optimise efforts to design holistic views of this system. Unfortunately, no progress has been achieved yet along this direction: the holistic view embracing physical, chemical, and biological aspects has not yet been provided by science, and the approach to the ocean from UN organisations and programmes is still based on the distinction, even on the separation, of these two components. This lack has profound roots and epistemological consequences, because it hides the challenge to integrate the sciences of matter with those of life. As a matter of fact, the inclusion of the biotic components in the representations of the ocean requires the positivist approach, which has sustained physical sciences, to be integrated with the approach from life sciences, which in its turn is not so consistent with positivism. Hence this lack of knowledge, which Mann Borgese draws our attention to, mirrors a lack of epistemological discourse.

Representing Globalisation

Late modern science has dealt with the challenge to represent the ocean in the framework of globalisation. Modern science was successful in investigating and representing the individual ocean uses, however, it has faced remarkable difficulty in representing the whole use structure and, at the present time is incapable of giving shape to holistic visions of globalisation processes and of their impacts on the deep-ocean, coastal and island world. Hence, a sort of decline may be found in representing the ocean according to the economic and social elements that it has been marked by, and particularly in representing the interaction between local systems and globalisation. This decline could depend on the circumstance that this new representation is conceptually different from the modern one, since it would require to integrate the consideration of global strategies with that of the local systems, with the final aim of understanding how coastal and island communities could optimise the advantages, and minimise the disadvantages, from global processes. The two recent decades were marked by efforts to design visions of climate change and of its consequences, while ongoing efforts are expected to focus on globalisation, and on the linkage between its consequences and the impacts from climate change. In this respect, another much more demanding challenge arises, namely, the integration between the natural and social sciences. It was augured by the WCS in 1999, but it is still to be achieved.

Representing Spatial Strategies

Geopolitical and geostrategic features and processes have not yet been included in the representations of the ocean. The scientific community has been too inclined to focus on the "objective" issues of the ocean, namely on the environmental and economic dimensions, to nourish interest in investigating the political dimensions. The only aspect of this perspective, on which literature has attributed consideration, is that of the ocean boundaries born as a result of the evolution of the international law of the sea, namely the boundaries determined by the establishment of territorial seas, contiguous seas, exclusive economic zones, and other jurisdictional zones. Nevertheless, these sea lines[19] have been considered from topically limited aspects, particularly as regards conflicts between states upon oil and gas exploitation, and on biomass consumption. Moving from this basis, the more the actual and potential conflicts between states solidify, the more the representation encompassing holistic views of the geopolitical aspects in the ocean visions and scenarios acquires relevance to ocean sustainable development.

Urbanisation and Human Pressure

Since the UNCED Summit, urbanisation has been perceived as the fulcrum of the increasing human pressure on coastal areas. The scientific community has shared the estimates indicating that more than a half of the world population lives within 60 miles of the coastal fringe, and has intensified efforts to represent the evolution trends of cities. In this respect, representations are inclined to focus on a double aspect, namely the spatial patterns that coastal urbanisation is going to be marked by, and the interaction between climate change, together with the subsequent acceleration in coastal erosion and sea-level rise, and urban growth. As regards the former subject, namely the spatial patterns, the concept of megacity, regarded as an urban structure of no less than eight million people, was adopted, and the representation of the geographical distribution showed that most megacities will be located in coastal belts, therefore exacerbating the implications of human pressure.[20] Although useful, this approach is not sufficient to make the view of the cardinal features of the issue: that is, representations are expected to embrace human conditions of urbanised coastal and island areas, and to focus on their cultural heritage.

19. G. Francalanci and T. Scovazzi, *Lines in the Sea* (Dordrecht: Martinus Nijhoff, 1994).

20. R. J. Nicholls, "Coastal megacities and climate change," *GeoJournal,* no. 3 (1996): 369–79; A. Vallega, "Urban waterfront facing integrated coastal management," *Ocean and Coastal Management,* no. 5-6 (2001): 379–410.

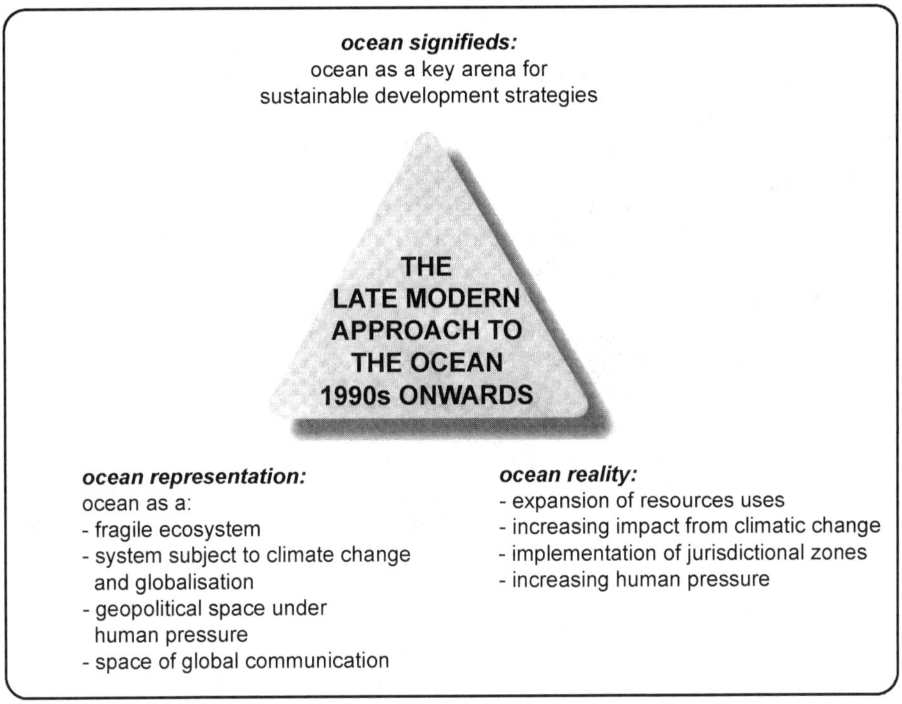

FIG. 4.—The late modern approach to the ocean 1990s onwards

To sum up, since the UNCED Summit the ocean has been represented as a fragile ecosystem, a resource reservoir, and a space of global communication. This approach is clearly too weak vis-à-vis changes in ocean reality, particularly the associated and interlinked changes triggered by climate change and globalisation. As a result, it should be expected that the late modern approach to the ocean will be characterised by huge efforts to produce more effective representations that at least would embrace i) the whole ecological nature of the ocean; ii) the interacting effects of climate change and globalisation; iii) the changing geopolitical conditions; and iv) the impacts from human pressure (Fig. 4).

At this point a background question comes to the fore. It could be wondered whether the earlier-mentioned implementation of ocean representations, which is expected to mark the late modern avenue, is only a matter of widening the information basis, or differently, it implies also dealing with an epistemological issue. To be explicit, it should be explored whether this avenue may be followed by continuing to use the rationalist approach, which has supported the modern approach to the ocean, or a different, nonrationalist background should be looked for. Bearing in mind that, as a result of the Global Ocean Observing System (GOOS) and subsequent data management, the information basis has expanded without precedent, it could be reasonably stated that a question of information does not exist, and that the late modern knowledge building requires some changes, namely that the issue is essentially concerned with epistemology. If this is shared, it may be deduced that the Cartesian principles, presented in Table 1 become, or are going to become, inadequate. Such an inadequacy would depend on the lack of sense of two principles, namely the reduction and causalism ones, vis-à-vis the need to provide holistic views of the coastal and island systems involved in climate change and globalisation. As a result, a duo including the ontological and the semiotic-epistemological dimensions arises: that is, complication in ocean reality (ontological dimension) is associated with complexity in building up representations (semiotic dimension) and the subsequent ocean episteme. To meet the need for approaches effectively consistent with the holistic design and with the pursuit of ocean sustainable development, some principles, alternative to those from rationalism and tailored to meet complication and complexity, need to be enunciated and operated. Table 1 shows the relevant changes in approaches. As a matter of fact, this challenge does not exclusively relate to the ocean knowledge building, but mirrors a wider challenge concerned with knowledge building per se. Therefore, the ocean may be regarded as a cardinal arena for the epistemological struggle marking our times.

THE POSTMODERN AVENUE

This breakdown shows how the late modern approach could be implemented from the epistemological perspective. An alternative avenue to the late modern could consist of the postmodern approach. As is well known, except for some pilot writings such as that by Steinberg,[21] the postmodern approach to the ocean has not yet been applied. As a result, it could only be imagined what features and outcomes it could be marked with and where it would be operated.

The background characteristic of postmodernism may be found in the discussion of the relationship between the ontological dimension and the semiotic and epistemological ones. While the late modern approach is based on the assumption that, at the present time, the scientific community has to deal with an ontological issue, namely the complication in ocean reality, and therefore there is no need to confute the rationalist way of knowledge building, the postmodern avenue adopts the opposite approach of stating

21. P. E. Steinberg, *The Social Construction of the Ocean* (Cambridge: Cambridge University Press, 2001).

that, first of all, the issue does not regard reality but rather the way of representing it, and of building the subsequent episteme. This conflict may be perceived looking at the triangle presented in Figure 1, which designs knowledge building as an itinerary moving from (ocean) reality to the representation of reality, and finally to the episteme, namely to the design of values, theories, and narratives. According to the modern and late modern approaches, the representation of reality consists in building up models of reality based on the discovery of cause-effect relationship. This leads to believing that the elements under consideration being understood, only one representation is possible and, more importantly, that this representation must replace reality to build up the episteme. For the same reason, *only* one episteme is possible moving from this representation, because a cause-effect relationship must occur between the signs that reality is represented with and the deductions that may be drawn from. Differently, the postmodern thought, which is very sensitive to the criticism developed in the framework of post-structuralism, designs an opposite approach.

First, it refuses any possibility of tracing a rationalist design of reality and, as a consequence, postulates that, moving from the same object, for example, a coastal system, a number of signs meant as mere metaphors may be conceived, and that all of these are valid and acceptable in themselves (Fig. 5). The key consequence consists of confuting the possibility of achieving objectivist knowledge, because a plurality of signs is postulated to move from the same object. The subject replaces the object in the core of knowledge building, therefore from the objectivist episteme, characteristic of the modern and late modern approaches, one moves towards a subjectivist episteme. This step is followed by another consequent step, which refers to the relationship between the sign (representation) and signified (explanation). The rationalist thought, which has supported any positivist and structuralist knowledge building and has exerted huge influence on ocean research, is refused because the existence of a cause-effect relationship between the representation and the signified is not accepted: an individual sign is postulated to lead to a plurality of signifieds. This step completes the design of the subjectivist episteme building. As a matter of fact, according to the postmodern approach, the episteme is a mere social construct,[22] namely it is a tool through which, in a given historical moment, a given society designs a priori signifieds and proclaims them as true and then asks science to justify it. In this there is no objectivism, but only a presumption of truth. As a result, the meta-narrative of progress, on which the modern society has been based, together with any subsequent narrative—from that of development (modern society) to that of global change and sustainable development (late modern society)—is regarded as a mere product of the social context, and the building of knowledge is regarded as something used to justify this construct.

22. Ibid.

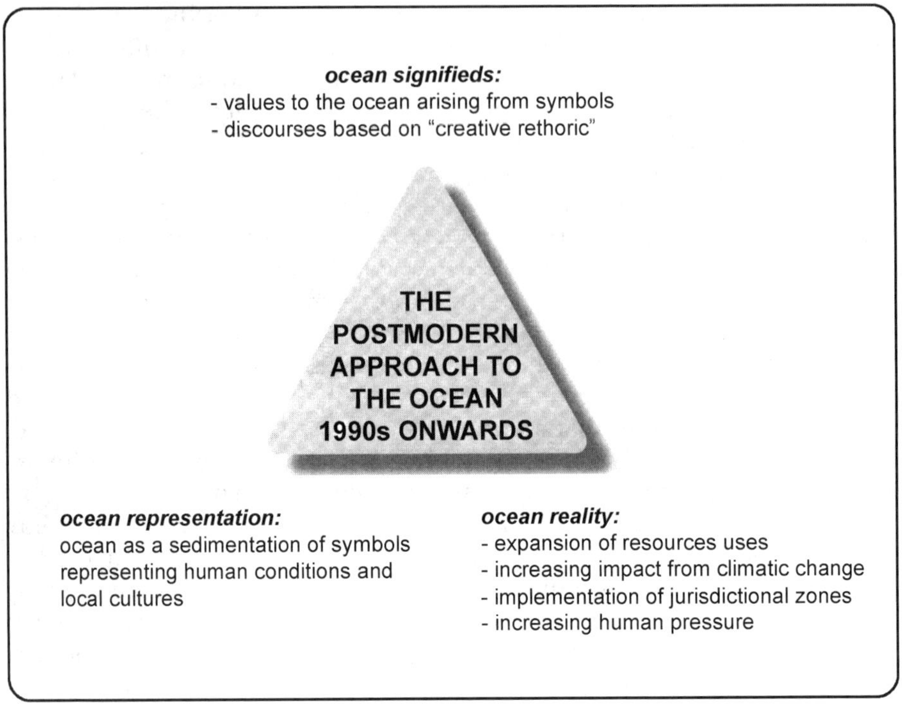

FIG. 5.—The postmodern approach to the ocean 1990s onwards

Truth in itself does not exist, the meta-narrative and narratives cannot be justified by science, but only in themselves. It follows that knowledge building is functional to the achievement of a priori-defined result.

Putting the subject at the centre of knowledge building, and therefore at the centre of the ocean episteme building, and refusing the cause-effect principle as making the episteme true: these may be the cardinal bases of a postmodern discourse about the ocean. At this point, a self-evident deduction may be drawn: the modern and late modern approaches may be rooted on a well-designed and widely experienced epistemological background supported by the four Cartesian principles (Table 1); by contrast, the postmodern approach does not provide any alternative basis to replace the rationalist one. Hence, it seems to exert only a confuting role because it has not yet been able to follow up the design of another way to design any episteme. Nevertheless, the question may not be shrunk into such a simple term because it is worthy of arguing what kind of elements would be included in a postmodern episteme, if it could be designed, and what kind of consequences would arise in representing ocean realities.

TABLE 1.—RATIONALIST VERSUS COMPLEXITY-SENSITIVE KNOWLEDGE BUILDING

Rationalist knowledge building	*Complexity-referred knowledge building*
Principles	
Evidence	*Pertinence*
Describing only those elements of the ocean reality which are clear.	Describing those elements of the ocean reality which are perceived as essential to management.
Reduction	*Holism*
Desegregating the components of the ocean reality, then describing the individual elements, separately.	Describing the ocean reality as a unique system interacting with its external environment.
Causality	*Teleology*
Moving from the simplest elements of the ocean towards the most complicated ones.	Leaving out the existence of a cause effect relationship between the elements of the ocean.
Supposing that the role of the elements is regulated by cause-effect relationship.	Considering the evolution of the ocean system with reference to its *project,* that is, the goals which are pursued through its organisation.
Exhaustiveness	*Aggregativeness*
Assessing all the elements of the ocean in detail, and ensuring that nothing has been left out.	Selecting those elements which pertain to ocean management, that is, the goals and projects of the ocean system, and leaving out the rest.
Postulating that, only where these conditions are met, the subsequent knowledge is objective.	Being aware that knowledge is relativist and partisan per se.

A basic change in the representations and visions of the ocean, which could be achieved by adopting a postmodern epistemological approach, could be found in the rise of a humanistic approach, namely an approach much more sensitive to human conditions and local cultures than the modern and late modern have been so far. As a matter of fact, as a result of UNCED inputs, the late modern approach has designed the ocean and coastal areas according to two basic perspectives. On the one hand, from the perspective of the impacts from climate change, and of the subsequent changing interaction between human communities and nature; and on the

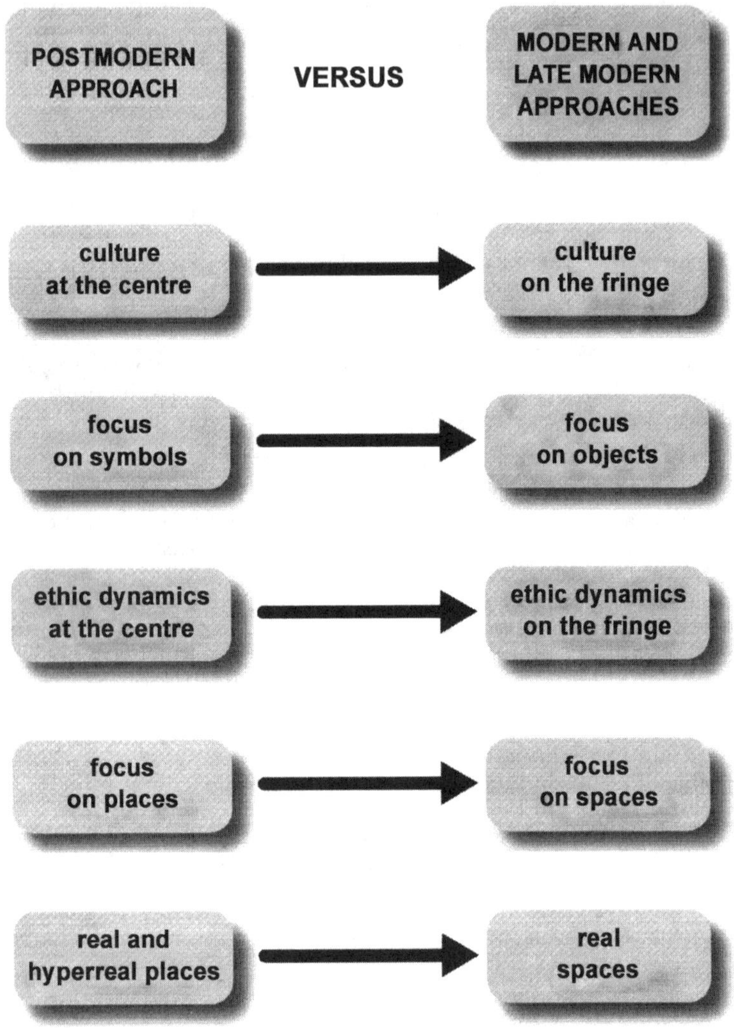

FIG. 6.—Postmodern subject areas vis-à-vis the modern and late modern approaches

other hand, from the economic perspective, according to which the ocean is regarded as a galaxy of local economic systems interacting with natural resources. According to the postmodern representation, the focus shifts to the role that the ocean has acquired in the framework of the existential conditions of local communities. This shifting leads to at least four consequences (Fig. 6).

First, the cultural roots of local communities, which are left out by the rationalist modern and late modern approaches, are included in representations. As a result, attention is focused on the interaction between the rise and diffusion of modern conditions—essentially consisting of standardised patterns of production and consumption, in homogeneous social patterns and in rationalist planning of urban and rural areas—and the local cultural roots, which form the foundation of traditional lifestyles. The approach to the ocean, coastal areas and islands from Agenda 21, Chapter 17,[23] presupposed that the cultural issue—except for some consideration of small islands and small islands states—would have not been included in management patterns and, as a result, it presupposed that the efficiency of (integrated) management patterns would only depend on how much they would be rationalist. This approach is implicitly confuted by the postmodern vision, which differently presupposes that efficiency would depend on the consideration of the role of local cultures *vis-à-vis* the diffusion of the modern, globalisation-based patterns.

This leads to the second consequence. Focusing on local culture would imply considering the symbols that, with history, local communities have attributed to the coastal areas and islands where they live, and the values and narratives that these symbols lead to. Therefore, the interaction between local cultures and globalisation processes would not only be considered in terms of economic and social changes, but also as an interaction between symbols and values. Where coastal areas have become the destination of immigrant flows—circumstances that have increasingly characterised the boreal temperate latitudes—the interaction between local symbols and values, on the one hand, and those imported by the external milieus, on the other, should be regarded as a key factor of human development.

The third consequence of the adoption of a postmodern approach would consist of focusing on the diffusion of multiethnic features in coastal and island communities considering the cultural changes and complications that these spatial processes provoke. The modern and late modern vision of the ocean focuses on *spaces,* namely on more or less spatial extents, considering them as abstract as to be useful for designing rationalist management patterns. Differently, the postmodern approach—this is the fourth consequence of this changing perspective—is inclined to focus on *places* in such a way as to consider the human and cultural conditions marking the individual local communities, and therefore focusing on cultural diversity. The latest consequence merits some specification. The ocean, coastal, and

23. Chapter 17, Agenda 21, "Protection of the Oceans, All Kinds of Seas, Including Enclosed and Semi-Enclosed Seas, and Coastal Areas and the Protection, Rational Use and Development of Their Living Resources." http://www.un.org/esa/sustdev/agenda21chapter17.htm (accessed 15 October 2001).

island spaces are considered by the modern and late modern approaches as real and homogeneous spaces. Considering only material spaces, namely only physical and human milieus, is an essential geographical way to apply positivist (as regards nature) and structuralist (as regards society) criteria, and meanwhile imagining the ocean space as a homogeneous reality is essential to build up rationalist programmes and plans. The postmodern approach differs from both sides. First, space is considered as a culturally heterogeneous reality because the individual areas and places are endowed with the cultures of indigenous peoples, which differ from each other, and in many cases they interact with those of the immigrants. Secondly, the postmodern approach gives room for the consideration of hyper-real spaces, meant as immaterial spaces that are the product of the imagination of local communities. Imagined spaces are a realm hosting the values and narratives of the individuals and groups reacting to local realities, such as the landscape, and to the external inputs, such as globalisation.

OPTIONS AND UNCERTAINTY

The latest consideration merits some mise-au-point. Because they arise from emotion instead of from reason, the hyper-real spaces are under-evaluated by the rationalist episteme building, which has inspired the modern and late modern approach to the ocean. In modern and late modern approaches, only causalism-inspired representations of reality are admitted and therefore knowledge building has been characterised by a reduction of reality, and this characteristic has been widely appreciated by policy. Nevertheless, in recent times speculative movements to rehabilitate emotion as a knowledge source have catalysed increasing consensus to the point of justifying some attempts to take into account the products of emotion, which consist of hyper-real ocean spaces hosting values and social expectation. If these attempts are successful, some new ocean episteme could arise, where the reasons of the reason are flanked by the reasons of emotion. This widening of the knowledge building should be regarded as one of the most profound characteristics of the postmodern approach. Following this discussion pathway, it is worthy of consideration that the modern and late modern approaches to the ocean consist of producing a hard rhetoric, because the cause-effect principle justifies believing the epistemes as objectivist. According to Berdoulay,[24] it is a matter of "prison-rhetoric," because signs and symbols in which representations consist lead to impose a given signified (theory, value, etc.). For example, the sustainable development principle was a typical product of a "prison-rhetoric." Differently, where emotion is

24. V. Berdoulay, "Discours et Creativité," in *Des Mots et des Lieux: La Dinamique du Discours Géographique* (Paris: CNRS, 1988), Chapter 1.

TABLE 2.—THE POSTMODERN VIS-À-VIS THE MODERN AND LATE MODERN APPROACHES

Postmodern approach	*Modern and late-modern approach*
Emotion	Reason
Symbol	Sign
No trivial machine	Trivial machine
Cultural diversity	Biological diversity
Comprehension	Explanation
Discourse	Theory
Soft rhetoric	Hard rhetoric
Holism	Causalism
Existence	Essence
Aesthetics	Ethics
Culture	Nature

included in the factors leading to knowledge, a soft rhetoric arises since a nondeterministic relationship is postulated between the sign and symbol and the signified. According to Berdoulay, one could speak of "creative rhetoric." Objectivism is left out but humanism is embraced, and it joins a group of other conflicting attitudes (Table 2).

To sum up, the issue of ocean knowledge building to which Mann Borgese draws attention, mirrors a wider and more profound issue, namely that of the justification of knowledge building on which modern society and modernity—the former meant as economic and social organisation, the latter as the culture triggered by enlightenment and rationalism—have been based. Where this issue is regarded as due to the increasing complication in reality, there is no doubt that the rationalist thought, of which positivism and structuralism are the key expressions, is kept unrefuted, and that there is only a need of updating and improving our modelling of reality. Differently, where this issue is regarded as epistemological, particularly as a result of the rising lack of justification of rationalism, the search for alternative representations of the ocean arises, and the postmodern arena may be useful for discussing, and possibly for improving the knowledge building up.

Ocean Governance: A Process in the Right Direction for the Effective Management of the Oceans

Annick de Marffy*
Division for Ocean Affairs and the Law of the Sea, Office of Legal Affairs, United Nations, New York

INTRODUCTION

The theme of ocean governance was certainly the driving force behind the continued enthusiasm and energy displayed by Elisabeth Mann Borgese in her fight for the efficient management of the oceans. Her strong belief and mature vision of this concept is the result of 4 decades of her life devoted to the study and promotion of the oceans. She recognized that only an holistic and inclusive approach could lead to good ocean governance and attain the philosophical goal that she had championed: The establishment of "an oceanic circle whose centre will be the individual . . ."[1]

This rather new concept of ocean governance has acquired only recently a more meaningful content. Although still a process in need of further progress on the road leading to its effective implementation, it has certainly moved a step forward.

The first thinking about the necessity of establishing an efficient governance of the oceans, taking into account all the synergies existing between activities in the oceans, started during the meeting of *Pacem in Maribus* XIX in 1991.[2] No definition of the concept has been offered so far. However, based on the principles of holistic and inclusive approach set out in the Convention, which states in its preamble that "the problems of ocean space are closely interrelated and need to be considered as a whole," four main pillars could be seen as constituting the foundation to effective governance.

*Editors' Note.—The opinions expressed in this article are those of the author and do not necessarily represent the views of the United Nations.

1. Quotation extracted from M. K. Gandhi, "India of My Dreams," in E. Mann Borgese, *The Oceanic Circle: Governing the Seas as a Global Resource* (Tokyo: United Nations University Press, 1998), p. 1.

2. See P. B. Payoyo, ed., *Ocean Governance: Sustainable Development in the Seas* (Tokyo: United Nations University Press, 1994), p. 369.

Ocean Yearbook 18: 162–192

These four pillars are as follows:

1. The legal pillar, which sets up the legal framework under which all activities in the oceans must be carried out;
2. The political pillar, which deals with actions taken by intergovernmental bodies;
3. The institutional pillar, which represents the administrative mechanism needed to ensure the integrated approach, in particular in enhancing coordination and cooperation between all international actors having a role to play in the management of the oceans; and finally,
4. The capacity-building pillar, including the financial component, which constitutes the necessary tool to achieve effective ocean governance.

The present study will focus only on the international aspect of ocean governance, on the understanding that it is essential that those four pillars also be implemented mutatis mutandis at the national level.

THE LEGAL PILLAR: BINDING OR NONBINDING INSTRUMENTS

The establishment of a coherent and comprehensive legal regime is at the center of any ocean governance. The legal process started with the adoption of UNCLOS, which set up the indispensable stage.

The international community has witnessed extraordinary legal developments during the last 30 years with respect to the oceans and seas, in particular in the field of marine environment to which Elisabeth Mann Borgese devoted her skill, time, and energy, ranging from basic awareness, especially the link between economic development and preservation of the environment to proactive initiatives through the adoption of legal and political tools to meet environmental challenges.

Three important dates have been especially crucial for the development of a comprehensive marine environmental law: 1972, 1982, and 1992.

In 1972, the United Nations Conference on the Human Environment was the first international meeting to address the issue of the environment.[3] The principles contained in the Stockholm Declaration, such as the duty of States to prevent marine pollution and their responsibility to ensure that

3. United Nations, *Report of the United Nations Conference on the Human Environment, 5 to 16 June 1972.* A/CONF.48/14/Rev.1 New York: 1973, p. 77.

their activities do not cause damage to the marine environment outside their jurisdiction, served as the basis for the drafting of the general framework for the provisions on the protection and preservation of the marine environment in the United Nations Convention on the Law of the Sea (the 1982 Convention).[4]

The 1982 Convention represents the most important legal milestone. Never before had a set of global rules containing important and far-reaching obligations been drafted. Part XII of the Convention, which deals specifically with the protection and preservation of the marine environment, sets forth the only comprehensive, binding, and directly enforceable rules on the ocean environment. Although this Part of the 1982 Convention covers different sources of marine pollution linked to human activities at sea or affecting the sea, as a general framework, it calls for the development of more detailed rules covering either specific sectors or geographic regions.

Ten years later, in 1992, the United Nations Conference on Environment and Development (UNCED) adopted a very ambitious programme of action. It was designed to ensure the sustainable development of the resources of the planet. The outcome of the Conference was a comprehensive blueprint for action to be taken not only by governments and United Nations organizations but also by nongovernmental organizations, independent sectors and groups in every area in which human activities have an impact on the environment. This blueprint known as Agenda 21[5] devotes its entire Chapter 17 to the oceans and seas. The introductory paragraphs of Chapter 17 confirm that the 1982 Convention sets forth rights and obligations for States and provides the international basis upon which to pursue the protection and sustainable development of the marine environment and its resources.

"Between 1972 (Stockholm) and 1992 (Rio) global awareness moved from a sectoral to a comprehensive approach, from the protection of the environment to sustainable development."[6]

From the UNCED process have emerged many new conventions, agreements, programmes of action and guidelines developed to respond to the call for action contained in Agenda 21 and also to fill gaps wherever needed.

Thirty years have now elapsed since this process began. The World Summit on Sustainable Development, which took place in Johannesburg in 2002

4. *United Nations Convention on the Law of the Sea, 1982.* Adopted 10 December 1982, entered into force 14 November 1994. http://www.un.org/depts/los/ (accessed September 4, 2003).

5. The text of Agenda 21 is available online at the web site maintained by the United Nations Division for Sustainable Development. http://www.un.org/esa/sustdev/agenda21text.htm (accessed September 4, 2003).

6. E. Mann Borgese, "Sustainable development in the oceans," *Environmental Policy and Law* 27/3 (1997): 206.

was convened to assess the progress achieved and look at the challenges ahead, particularly in considering how the 1982 Convention and its related Agreements have been implemented, as well as the goal contained in Chapter 17 of Agenda 21 in response to the environmental problems still facing the oceans and seas. The commitments agreed in the Plan of Implementation[7] reflect a shift since Agenda 21 from the development of new instruments to the implementation of those that exist. Target dates have been recommended to ensure that key commitments, such as to achieve sustainable fisheries or to advance the implementation of the GPA, will be implemented.

As the main thrust of Chapter 17 is constituted by the protection of the marine environment and the conservation of living marine resources, they will be both reviewed in light of the instruments adopted since 1992.

The Protection of the Marine Environment

The obligations and principles contained in the 1982 Convention, essentially in Part XII, have set the pace for the development of a comprehensive framework of international environmental law drafted in response to the deterioration of and threats to the marine environment. The 1982 Convention was designed to operate as an umbrella for further global, regional, and national action. In addition to its norm-setting function, Part XII expressly recognizes and mandates regional approaches. It is also important to reiterate that provisions regulating the marine environment are found outside Part XII, which reflects the close relationship among the different parts of the 1982 Convention. The question of the marine environment affects or is affected by almost every other issue of ocean use dealt with in the 1982 Convention. The 1982 Convention as a whole has struck an important balance between the protection of the marine environment and the use of the oceans and its resources.[8]

The 1982 Convention has three important features that have contributed to shape the development of marine environmental law:

- The Convention calls for international rules, standards, and recommended practices and procedures to be further developed at the global and regional levels, as long as the specific obligations assumed

7. See United Nations. "Plan of Implementation." *Report of the World Summit on Sustainable Development, Johannesburg, South Africa, 26 August–4 September 2002.* United Nations. A/CONF.199/20. New York: 2002. http://www.johannesburgsummit.org/ (accessed September 4, 2003).

8. See *Report of Secretary-General of the United Nations on Protection and Preservation of the Marine Environment.* A/44/461. 1989. http://www.un.org/depts/los/ (accessed September 4, 2003).

by States under special conventions are carried out in a manner consistent with the general principles and objectives of the 1982 Convention (Article 237);

- The Convention as a dynamic instrument requires that rules established through competent international organizations or diplomatic conferences be reexamined from time to time as necessary; and
- The Convention has permitted the development of nonbinding instruments (soft law), such as recommended practices, guidelines, and criteria, that establish benchmarks for the development of national laws and policies.

Besides rules that apply to sources of pollution originating from activities on land and at sea, a number of principles have been developed, that contributed to strengthen the body of international environmental rules. Some emanated from the Stockholm Conference, such as the duty not to transfer damage or hazards or transform one type of pollution into another, which was incorporated in the 1982 Convention (Article 195). Some other principles emanated from UNCED, in particular, the now widely recognized principle of the precautionary approach, stated in the Rio Declaration (Principle 15), which constitutes the backbone of the Agreement for the Implementation of the Provisions of the United Nations Convention on the Law of the Sea of 10 December 1982 relating to the Conservation and Management of Straddling Fish Stocks and Highly Migratory Fish Stocks (1995 United Nations Fish Stocks Agreement),[9] and the principle that polluters should bear the cost of pollution.

Chapter 17 of Agenda 21 considers two different types of activities for which action needs to be taken: land-based activities and sea-based activities.

Land-based Activities

Land-based sources of pollution are responsible for most of the contamination of the oceans and affect the most productive areas of the marine environment. The 1982 Convention sets out specific provisions for the prevention, control, and reduction of pollution from land-based sources. However, the 1982 Convention gives States a certain degree of discretion with respect to the implementation of international rules in deference to the sovereignty that a State exercises over the territory where such land-based pollution may arise.

9. See *Agreement for the Implementation of the Provisions of the United Nations Convention on the Law of the Sea of 10 December 1982 Relating to the Conservation and Management of Straddling Fish Stocks and Highly Migratory Fish Stocks*. UN Doc. A/CONF.164/37. 8 September 1995. http://www.un.org/depts/los/ (accessed September 4, 2003).

Under Article 207 of the 1982 Convention, States shall adopt laws and regulations to prevent, reduce and control pollution from land-based sources, taking into account internationally agreed rules, standards, and recommended practices and procedures, and shall endeavor to establish such rules, standards, and recommended practices and procedures at the global and regional levels, acting especially through competent international organizations and diplomatic conferences. However, in such endeavors, the economic capacity of developing States and their need for economic development shall be taken into account. In addition, States are required to enforce such laws and regulations and to implement applicable international rules and standards in keeping with Article 213 of the 1982 Convention.

At the time of the adoption of the 1982 Convention, only regional rules were in existence, for instance the Paris Convention on Land-based Sources adopted in 1974. There were no global rules or standards in place. The Governing Council of the United Nations Environment Programme (UNEP) identified in 1982 the question of the land-based sources of pollution as one of the three priorities for the development of environmental law.

Action at the Global Level

Chapter 17 of Agenda 21, on the basis of the Montreal Guidelines adopted in 1985, made a major contribution in advancing the issue of land-based sources of pollution with the emphasis placed on an integrated approach. The UNEP Governing Council recommended a set of management related activities, in particular, to "consider updating, strengthening and extending the Montreal Guidelines." UNEP convened an intergovernmental meeting on the protection of the marine environment from land-based sources. UNCED helped to reformulate the concept to encompass the broader implications of marine and coastal degradation. Thus came about the reference to "land-based activities."

In November 1995, in an effort to implement the recommendations of UNCED, two international documents were adopted by an intergovernmental conference: the Washington Declaration on the Protection of the Marine Environment from Land-based Activities and the Global Programme of Action for the Protection of the Marine Environment from Land-based Activities (GPA).[10]

The General Assembly of the United Nations, at its 51st session, adopted the institutional arrangements for the implementation of the GPA and designated UNEP as the lead agency in the implementation of the GPA.

The GPA addresses the impacts of land-based activities on the marine

10. Texts of the Declaration and the GPA are available online at the web site maintained by the United Nations Environment Programme, http://www.gpa.unep.org/documents/about-GPA-docs.htm (accessed September 4, 2003).

and coastal environment, including contaminants, physical alteration, point and nonpoint sources of pollution, and such areas of concern as critical habitats, habitats of endangered species and protection of ecosystem components, such as breeding and feeding grounds. The GPA was designed to be a source of conceptual and practical guidance to assist States in addressing land-based sources of pollution.[11] From a strictly legal perspective, both the Washington Declaration and the GPA have no binding force and are considered to be "soft law." However, they have both obtained an enormous amount of support from States and intergovernmental and nongovernmental organizations that view the GPA as an essential instrument for combating marine environmental degradation from land-based sources of pollution. Such an endorsement was certainly reinforced when the United Nations Open-ended Informal Consultative Process on Oceans and the Law of the Sea (the Consultative Process), the new body of the General Assembly established under resolution 54/33, chose the question of land-based activities and the GPA as one of the main issues in need of further review and implementation. Resolution 55/7 of the General Assembly had incorporated the recommendations on this subject emanating from the Consultative Process.[12] The Conference held in Montreal in November 2001 to review the GPA to make it more efficient made a call to link the implementation of the GPA with the regional seas programme and to take advantage of their revitalization.

Another important development at the global level, in conjunction with the protection of the marine environment from land-based activities, recommended by the Commission on Sustainable Development (CSD) at its seventh session (CSD 7) in paragraph 31 of its decision 7/1, was the adoption in May 2001 of the Stockholm Convention on Persistent Organic Pollutants (POPs).[13] Those organic pollutants are chemicals that are persistent, bioaccumulate in fatty tissues, biomagnify through the food chain, and adversely affect human health and the environment. The Convention represents a major achievement in the control of intentional production or unintentional production or use, as well as releases from stockpiles and wastes of 10 of the most dangerous chemical substances released in the marine environment.

11. See *Report on the Work of the United Nations Open-ended Informal Consultative Process on Oceans and the Law of the Sea at its First Meeting, Held at United Nations Headquarters from 30 May to 2 June 2000.* A/55/274, p. 1, par. 84.

12. See the Resolution by the General Assembly, *Oceans and the Law of the Sea.* A/RES/55/7, paras. 27, 28 and 29 at the website maintained by the Division for Ocean Affairs and Law of the Sea/Office of Legal Affairs—United Nations, http://www.un.org/depts/los/ (accessed September 4, 2003).

13. See Convention, UNEP/POPS/CONF/4, at the website maintained by the United Nations Environment Programme, http://www.chem.unep.ch/pops/ (accessed September 4, 2003).

The soft law, which has mainly developed at the global level during the last 20 years in relation to land-based activities, coexists at the regional level with binding instruments in the form of protocols that have been adopted to complement regional environmental agreements.

Action at the Regional Level

Several regional conventions of a general nature were adopted under the regional seas programme of UNEP, established in the 1970s,[14] and seen as the most comprehensive institutional framework for regional cooperation in the oceans.[15]

Currently five Regional Seas Conventions have protocols that deal with land-based sources of pollution:

1. Protocol for the Protection of the Mediterranean Sea against Pollution from Land-based Sources (LBS Protocol), adopted in 1980, in force on 17 June 1983, amended in 1996 as the Protocol for the Protection of the Mediterranean Sea against Pollution from Land-based Sources and Activities, following the revision of the Barcelona Convention in 1995. The concepts that were being promoted at UNCED in the context of sustainable development, such as the precautionary principle and the polluter pays principle, were incorporated in the preamble of the Protocol;
2. Protocol on Protection of the Black Sea Marine Environment Against Pollution from Land-based Sources adopted in 1992, in force in 1994;
3. Protocol Concerning Marine Pollution from Land-based Sources and Activities (Wider Caribbean), adopted in 1999, not yet in force. It provides for the adoption by the Parties of guidelines concerning environmental impact assessments and review where a planned land-based activity on a territory is likely to cause substantial pollution of, or significant and harmful changes to, the convention area;
4. Protocol for the Protection of the Marine Environment against Pollution from Land-based Sources, adopted in 1990, (Kuwait Region) in force in 1993. This Protocol also provides for environmental impact assessment; and,
5. Protocol for the Protection of the South-East Pacific against Pollution from Land-based Sources, adopted in 1983 and in force in 1986.

14. For the list of conventions and protocols see Report by the Secretary General. *Oceans and the Law of the Sea.* A/56/58. The texts of those conventions and protocols can be found in the UNEP regional seas web site, maintained by the United Nations Environment Programme, http://www.unep.ch/seas/main/hconlist.html (accessed September 4, 2003).

15. Borgese (n. 1 above), p. 145.

Although international rules and programmes at the global and regional levels have been developed in combating marine and coastal degradation, progress still needs to be made particularly at the national level in terms of capacity building and mobilizing funds in furthering their implementation.

The other sources of pollution of the marine environment dealt with by the 1982 Convention are regrouped as sea-based activities.

Sea-based Activities

These sea-based activities as addressed in Agenda 21 relate to the prevention, reduction, and control of degradation of the marine environment, in particular from shipping and dumping. The 1982 Convention provides once more the general framework and can only be implemented through the adoption of relevant international rules and standards developed by or through the "competent international organization or organizations."[16] In this context, States are obliged to adopt international rules and standards as minimum standards in national law. At the same time, any State may enact standards more stringent than the global minimum, with the exception of those affecting international navigation, that is, standards for vessel construction, design, manning and equipment.

The 1982 Convention calls on relevant international organizations to formulate and keep under review detailed international rules, regulations, and procedures and recommended practices in a number of areas. The International Maritime Organization (IMO) is the main "competent international organization" in the UN system responsible for developing the global rules and standards relating to maritime safety, prevention of marine pollution from vessels and dumping.

Pollution from Shipping

States are required by Article 211 of the 1982 Convention to establish international rules and standards to prevent, reduce, and control pollution of the marine environment from vessels and to promote the adoption, in the same manner, wherever appropriate, of routing systems designed to minimize the threat of accidents. The rules and standards are to be established acting through the competent international organization or general diplomatic conferences and reexamined from time to time as necessary. For a flag State such global rules and standards constitute the minimum standard, which it must adopt for vessels flying its flag and enforce in accordance with Article 217 of the 1982 Convention. Article 94, which sets out in general terms the duties of the flag State, is also relevant in this context.

16. On the question of "competent international organizations," see *Law of the Sea Bulletin*, no. 31 (1996), pp. 79–95, published by the Division for Ocean Affairs and the Law of the Sea, Office of Legal Affairs, United Nations.

A major IMO instrument regulating pollution from ships, which States are required by the 1982 Convention to implement and enforce, is the International Convention for the Prevention of Pollution from Ships, 1973, as modified by the Protocol of 1978 relating thereto (MARPOL 73/78). Routing measures are provided for in the International Convention for the Safety of Life at Sea (SOLAS), the International Regulations for Preventing Collisions at Sea and the IMO General Provisions on Ships' Routing. In addition to these instruments there are also a number of other IMO safety-related conventions, the implementation of which is critical for the safety of navigation and thus the protection and preservation of the marine environment, for example, instruments addressing the human element are crucial for preventing accidents at sea, given the fact that human error is the cause of most accidents.

To effectively respond to a pollution incident, States are required by Article 199 of the 1982 Convention to jointly develop and promote contingency plans. A major IMO instrument in this regard is the 1990 International Convention on Oil Pollution Preparedness, Response and Cooperation.

Article 235 of the 1982 Convention requires States to cooperate in the implementation of existing international law and the further development of international law relating to responsibility and liability for the assessment of and compensation for damage caused by pollution of the marine environment, and the settlement of related disputes as well as, where appropriate, development of criteria and procedures for the payment of adequate compensation. In this regard, most of the liability conventions currently in force provide compensation in the event of an oil spill.

During the last decade, significant progress has been made in further developing the global rules and standards referred to in the 1982 Convention and in implementing the commitments in Chapter 17 of Agenda 21, and those agreed to at various sessions of the CSD relating to the prevention, reduction, and control of degradation of the marine environment from shipping. A number of instruments, binding or of a voluntary nature, have been adopted following requirements made in paragraphs 30, 32, 36, and 37 of Chapter 17. There was a call in both Chapter 17 and CSD decisions 4/15 and 7/1 for supporting wider ratification and implementation of shipping conventions and protocols. The two most important treaty instruments relating to maritime safety and the prevention of marine pollution, that is, SOLAS and MARPOL 73/78, have both been widely ratified.

Other measures adopted by IMO to improve effective implementation of international rules and standards include the adoption in 1994 of the International Safety Management (ISM) Code, which focuses on the shipowner's management responsibilities as well as the adoption in 1999 of the Flag State Self-Assessment Form, which establishes a uniform set of internal and external criteria that can be used by flag States on a voluntary basis to obtain a clear picture of how well their administrations are functioning and to make their own assessment of their performance as flag States.

In 2001, MARPOL 73/78 was amended to provide for a new global timetable for accelerating the phase-out of single-hull oil tankers above 5,000 tonnes.

In October 2001, IMO adopted the International Convention on the Control of Harmful Anti-fouling Systems on Ships. It will ban as from 2003 the application of organotin compounds, which act as biocides in antifouling systems on ships' hulls, and the presence of such compounds on ships' hulls or external parts or surfaces will be banned beginning in 2008.

A significant achievement was the entry into force in 1995 of the 1990 International Convention on Oil Pollution Preparedness, Response and Co-operation (OPRC Convention) and the adoption in 2000 of a Protocol to the OPRC Convention to cover hazardous and noxious substances. Developments at the regional level include the adoption or entry into force of new requirements for the Eastern African region, the Black Sea region, the Baltic Sea, the North-east Atlantic and Antarctica.

IMO adopted in 1996 the International Convention on Liability and Compensation for Damage in Connection with the Carriage of Hazardous and Noxious Substances by Sea (HNS Convention). As of 30 November 2003, only four States had ratified the HNS Convention. A Correspondence Group has been established with the aim of helping to resolve any practical difficulties in setting up the new regime and assisting potential claimants and contributors to the HNS Fund and relevant industry parties.

Among the voluntary instruments adopted by the IMO Assembly in 1997 were the Guidelines for the Control and Management of Ships' Ballast Waters to minimize the transfer of harmful aquatic organisms and pathogens. The measures adopted by IMO are in line with the implementation of Article 196 of the 1982 Convention dealing with the introduction into the marine environment of new or alien species that may cause significant and harmful changes thereto.

New revised guidelines for the designation of special areas under MARPOL 73/78 and guidelines for the identification and designation of particularly sensitive sea areas (PSSAs) have been adopted by the IMO Assembly in November 2001. The new guidelines replace the 1991 IMO Guidelines, which were amended by the Assembly in 1999. Three PSSAs have been so far established by IMO: the Great Barrier Reef of Australia in 1990, the Sabana-Camagüey Archipelago of Cuba in 1997, and IMO has recently designated (November 2002) the marine areas around the Florida Keys of the United States as PSSAs.

To date, no coastal State has asked IMO to approve, pursuant to Article 211(6) of the 1982 Convention, the adoption of more stringent measures than the applicable global rules and standards for a clearly defined area of its exclusive economic zone, which, because of its oceanographic and ecological conditions, as well as its utilization or the protection of its resources and the particular character of its traffic, is in need of such measures.

The 1982 Convention also imposes a duty to enforce the laws and regulations adopted in compliance with international rules and standards. Port State control, the concept of which has been developed in Article 218 of the Convention, means generally the rights of a State to exercise jurisdiction over vessels entering its port voluntarily to ensure compliance with the requirements of international maritime conventions dealing with vessel source pollution, adopted through the competent international organization or diplomatic conferences. This concept has been widely developed by IMO as a means of compensating for the weakness or the unwillingness of the flag State, with which rests the primary responsibility for the enforcement of rules and standards, to fulfill its obligation vis-à-vis vessels flying its flag. IMO has encouraged States to initiate regional cooperation for the development of port State control through the adoption of memoranda of understanding (MOU). MOUs have been developed in Europe, Asia and Pacific, Latin America and the Caribbean, the Mediterranean, the Indian Ocean Region, and West Africa. MOUs play an important role in the elimination of substandard ships, very often the origin of grave maritime incidents causing pollution as illustrated once more by the sinking of the tanker *Prestige*, a substandard ship off the coast of Galicia, Spain.

However, IMO has not concluded its consideration of the invitation in CSD decision 7/1, paragraph 35(a), to ensure that ships of all flag States meet international rules and standards so as to give full and complete effect to the 1982 Convention, especially Article 91, as well as provisions of other relevant conventions. In this context, it is to be noted that the lack of effective flag State control of fishing vessels has been identified as a key factor in the problem of illegal, unreported, and unregulated fishing.

Pollution by Dumping

States are required by Articles 210 and 216 of the 1982 Convention to adopt and enforce national laws, regulations, and measures that must be no less effective in preventing, reducing, and controlling pollution by dumping than the global rules and standards to be established by States acting through competent international organizations or diplomatic conferences. The global rules and standards referred to in the 1982 Convention are contained in the Convention on the Prevention of Marine Pollution by Dumping of Wastes and Other Matter, 1972 (London Convention). Chapter 17, paragraph 17.30(b) and CSD decision 7/1, paragraph 35(b) have recommended further action to control this source of pollution.

In 1996, following a detailed article-by-article review of the London Convention, a Special Meeting of the Contracting Parties adopted a Protocol to the London Convention, which will eventually replace the Convention. The Protocol represents a major change of approach to dumping from the

1972 Convention. It enhances the application of the precautionary approach and of the polluter pays principle. The Protocol prohibits the dumping of any waste except those listed in the treaty. This is a reversal of the system used by the parent Convention, which forbids the dumping of some substances but allows dumping in principle subject to certain conditions.

In September 2000, the Contracting Parties to the London Convention adopted guidelines for the respective assessment of each of the eight wastes permitted to be dumped under the 1996 Protocol.

Other developments since UNCED in the area of waste management, mainly relevant for the fulfillment of the commitments in chapters 20 (hazardous wastes) and 22 (radioactive wastes) of Agenda 21, include the adoption of a Protocol on Liability to the Basel Convention; the entry into force of amendments to the Basel Convention, providing for the prohibition of all transboundary movements of hazardous wastes destined for recycling or recovery operations from OECD to non-OECD countries; and the adoption and entry into force of the Joint Convention on the Safety of Spent Fuel Management and on the Safety of Radioactive Waste Management.

Progress in this area requires also wider ratification and more effective implementation. In this regard, the CSD, in decision 7/1, paragraph 35(b) recommended that States be encouraged to become parties to and implement the 1996 Protocol to the 1972 Convention. The UN General Assembly at its 54th, 55th, and 56th sessions also called upon States to become Parties to and to implement the 1996 Protocol.

At the regional level, three Regional Seas Conventions have also adopted Protocols dealing with dumping:

1. The Protocol for the Prevention and Elimination of Pollution of the Mediterranean Sea by Dumping from Ships and Aircraft (Dumping Protocol), adopted in 1976, in force in 1978, revised in 1995 as the Protocol for the Prevention and Elimination of Pollution of the Mediterranean Sea by Dumping from Ships and Aircraft or Incineration at Sea;
2. The Protocol on the Protection of the Black Sea Marine Environment Against Pollution by Dumping, adopted in 1992, in force in 1994. These two Protocols are very similar in that they both employ a mechanism that prohibits the dumping of certain named substances and materials and at the same time seeks to regulate and control dumping of other scientifically less harmful substances based on a permit system;
3. The Protocol for the Prevention of Pollution of the South Pacific Region by Dumping was concluded in 1986 and entered into force in 1990.

The other key commitments contained in Agenda 21 relate to the sustainable development of the resources of the planet and in particular the conservation of marine living resources.

CONSERVATION OF MARINE LIVING RESOURCES

While the 1982 Convention recognizes, inter alia, the sovereign rights of the coastal State over marine living resources within the 200-M exclusive economic zone (EEZ), the high seas beyond the EEZ are left to an open access regime ruled by the freedom of fishing. With respect to straddling fish stocks and highly migratory fish stocks that "straddle" and move in and out of lines of jurisdiction, as referred to in Articles 63(2) and 64 of the 1982 Convention, respectively, many States, especially coastal States, believe that the Convention did not adequately settle the issue of their conservation and management. They are of the view that unregulated exploitation of the resources on the high seas adjacent to the EEZ has affected the viability of the resources within the EEZ, since straddling fish stocks and highly migratory fish stocks may be available simultaneously within and beyond the EEZ or they may be found mainly outside at one time and inside at another. Notwithstanding the provisions of the Convention, however, States are required to cooperate for the conservation and management of these stocks beyond the EEZ. The lack of an enforcement regime for high seas fisheries has left the obligation ignored, making therefore the establishment of a fisheries cooperative scheme for adjacent high seas in respect of straddling fish stocks and highly migratory fish stocks a matter of urgency.

Concerned about this situation, the United Nations Conference on Environment and Development (UNCED) requested the United Nations to convene a Conference on Straddling Fish Stocks and Highly Migratory Fish Stocks (the Conference),[17] in view, inter alia, of the inadequacy of the management of high seas fisheries and for the purposes of promoting the effective implementation of the provisions of the 1982 Convention on straddling fish stocks and highly migratory fish stocks. After 3 years of negotiations, the Conference adopted in 1995, without a vote, the UN Fish Stocks Agreement that entered into force on 11 December 2001.

17. Paragraph 17.50 of Chapter 17 of Agenda 21, "Protection of the oceans, all kinds of seas, including enclosed and semi-enclosed seas, and coastal areas and the protection, rational use and development of their living resources," adopted in Rio de Janeiro at the United Nations Conference on Environment and Development, 3–16 June 1992, available online at the web site maintained by the United Nations Division for Sustainable Development, http://www.un.org/esa/sustdev/documents/agenda21/english/agenda21chapter17.htm (accessed September 4, 2003).

Besides the adoption of this Agreement, other developments have taken place in relation to the conservation and management of living resources either through the adoption of binding agreements or instruments of a voluntary nature.

Binding Agreements

The 1995 United Nations Fish Stocks Agreement[18]

The Agreement covers all aspects of fisheries conservation and management. It also includes a comprehensive system of dispute settlement that incorporates the procedures for the peaceful settlement of disputes provided in Part XV of the 1982 Convention.

The Agreement includes, in addition to the principles already provided in the 1982 Convention, such as the need to promote the objective of optimum utilization and the requirement of the best scientific evidence in the conservation and management of marine living resources (i) principles aimed at strengthening or facilitating the implementation of the general provisions of the Convention; and (ii) principles presenting a significant development vis-à-vis those provided in the Convention.

> *(i) Principles aimed at strengthening the provisions of the 1982 Convention*
> These provisions in the Agreement introduce action-oriented measures that reinforce and give concrete meaning to the general principles provided in the Convention. These concern the need for States to minimize pollution and prevent overfishing; cooperate in various aspects of fisheries conservation and management; reinforce the role of fisheries bodies; strengthen the responsibilities of the flag State; and stress the importance of the dispute settlement procedures provided in the 1982 Convention.
>
> *(ii) Principles and concepts not specifically provided for in the 1982 Convention*
> A number of provisions of the 1995 UN Fish Stocks Agreement develop principles introducing new norms and rules not specifically provided in the 1982 Convention. The most significant among them are those dealing with the precautionary approach, the compatibility of conservation and management measures, the regional cooperation in enforcement and port State enforcement.

18. See A. Tahindro, "Conservation and management of transboundary fish stocks: Comments in the light of the adoption of the 1995 Agreement for the Conservation and Management of Straddling Fish Stocks and Highly Migratory Fish Stocks," *Ocean Development and International Law* 28, no. 1 (1997): 1–59.

Some other agreements were adopted to give effect to the relevant provisions of the Rio Declaration and to ensure a better management of the fisheries. The Agreement to Promote Compliance with International Conservation and Management Measures by Fishing Vessels on the High Seas[19] was adopted in 1993 under the auspices of FAO for the purpose of strengthening flag State responsibility in respect of fishing vessels entitled to fly its flag and operating on the high seas, including the authorization by the flag State of such operations, and with a view to fostering international cooperation in the conservation and management of high seas fisheries, as provided for in the 1982 Convention.

A number of instruments of a voluntary nature were also concluded.

Instruments of a Voluntary Nature

The General Assembly played an important role as well as FAO, which negotiated instruments to direct the actions of States in areas not covered by binding treaties.

Resolutions of the General Assembly

In view of implementing the relevant provisions of Chapter 17 of Agenda 21, which requests States to take effective action to ensure that marine living resources are managed in accordance with the 1982 Convention, the General Assembly of the United Nations has adopted since 1992 decisions aimed at enhancing the sustainable use and conservation of marine living resources both on the high seas and in areas under national jurisdiction.

In response to the request in Chapter 17 of Agenda 21[20] that States should fully implement resolution 46/215 on large-scale pelagic driftnet fishing, the General Assembly adopted in 1994 resolution 49/436 that expressed serious concern over reports of continuing conduct of driftnet fishing despite the establishment of a global moratorium, and urged member States to take greater enforcement responsibility, including appropriate sanctions to ensure full compliance with resolution 46/215.

In 1994, the General Assembly also adopted resolution 49/116, which called upon States to take the responsibility, consistent with their obligations under international law as reflected in the 1982 Convention, to ensure that no fishing vessels entitled to fly their flag fish in zones under the national jurisdiction of other States unless duly authorized by the competent authori-

19. Agreement to Promote Compliance with International Conservation and Management Measures by Fishing Vessels on the High Seas, (1993), online at the web site maintained by the Food and Agriculture Organization of the United Nations, http://www.fao.org/legal/treaties/012t-e.htm (accessed September 4, 2003).

20. Agenda 21, Chapter 17 (n. 17 above), par. 17.54.

ties of the States concerned. The Assembly further pointed out that such authorized fishing operations should be carried out in accordance with the conditions set out in the authorization.

In addition, pursuant to Chapter 17 of Agenda 21, which requested States to ensure that fishing activities by vessels flying their flags on the high seas take place in a manner as to minimize incidental catches,[21] the UN General Assembly adopted resolution 49/118 (1994), which, inter alia, stressed that the issue of by-catch and discards in fishing operations warranted serious attention by the international community and needed to be addressed effectively to ensure the long-term and sustainable development of fisheries. To this end, the General Assembly invited, on the one hand, FAO to formulate fisheries by-catch provisions in its Code of Conduct for Responsible Fisheries, and on the other hand, the then United Nations Conference on Straddling Fish Stocks and Highly Migratory Fish Stocks to elaborate fisheries by-catch and discard provisions in the draft Agreement. Moreover, the General Assembly requested relevant subregional and regional fisheries management organizations and arrangements and the FAO, within their respective areas of competence, to review the impact of the issue on the sustainable use of marine living resources.

To facilitate a holistic approach to fisheries issues, the General Assembly started in 1995 to consolidate in one single resolution its review of the implementation of the global moratorium on large-scale pelagic driftnet fishing, the monitoring of unauthorized fishing, and the minimization of fisheries by-catch and discards in fishing activities.

In 2002, the Assembly decided to consolidate under one item and in one single resolution all fisheries issues.[22] That will take place at the 58th session. The sub-item will be entitled: "Sustainable fisheries, including through the straddling fish stocks and highly migratory fish stocks Agreements, and related instruments."

Instruments Adopted under the Auspices of FAO

In 1995, FAO adopted a Code of Conduct for Responsible Fisheries,[23] which is based on relevant rules of international law, including those reflected in the 1982 Convention, and which establishes principles for responsible fish-

21. Agenda 21, Chapter 17, (n. 17 above), paras. 17.46 (c) and 17.51.

22. See General Assembly draft resolution A/57/L.49, online at the web site maintained by the Division for Ocean Affairs and Law of the Sea/Office of Legal Affairs—United Nations, http://www.un.org/depts/los/ (accessed September 4, 2003).

23. See "Code of Conduct for Responsible Fisheries" 1 November 1995, in FAO, *International Fisheries,* (New York: 1998), online at the web site maintained by the Food and Agriculture Organization of the United Nations, http://www.fao.org/fi/agreem/codecond/ficonde.asp (accessed September 4, 2003).

ing and fisheries activities, taking into account, inter alia, all its relevant biological, technological, economic, social, environmental, and commercial aspects.

In addition, FAO adopted in 1999 three International Plans of Action for the Management of Fishing Capacity, for Reducing Incidental Catch of Seabirds in Long-line Fisheries, and for the Conservation and Management of Sharks, respectively.[24]

Another International Plan of Action (IPOA) to Prevent, Deter and Eliminate Illegal, Unreported and Unregulated Fishing (IUU fishing)[25] was adopted by the FAO in February 2001. The prevalence of IUU fishing on the high seas, in contravention of conservation and management measures adopted by subregional and regional fisheries management organizations and arrangements, is considered to be one of the most severe problems currently affecting world fisheries. The IPOA on IUU fishing adopted for the purpose of complementing the existing international instruments is a further milestone in the battle against IUU fishing. IPOA is aimed at addressing the legal and economic dimensions of IUU fishing in an integrated manner, whereby flag States, port States, and coastal States are invited to take measures at the national, regional or global level to combat illegal fishing activities.

However, progress is being hindered by, inter alia, the failure by States to accept and implement relevant international instruments, the lack of willingness by those States to delegate sufficient responsibility to regional bodies and the lack of the effective enforcement of management measures at both national and regional levels. Inadequate financial resources, ineffective decision-making procedures, and IUU fishing by vessels flying flags of convenience also adversely affect the performance of many regional fisheries management organizations.

The rapid development of international environmental rules has generated many difficulties for a great number of States in dealing with a plethora of instruments[26] and more importantly to implement them. While contributing to international norm setting, the multiplicity of norms has made implementation at the national level more and more difficult. In addition, the proliferation of autonomous institutional arrangements established by environmental treaties complicates even further the task of efficiency and coor-

24. For the texts, see the web site maintained by the Food and Agriculture Organization of the United Nations, http://www.fao.org/fi/ipa/ipae.asp (accessed September 4, 2003).

25. Ibid.

26. See Division for Ocean Affairs and the Law of the Sea. *The Law of the Sea, Multilateral Treaties, A Reference Guide to Multilateral Treaties and Other International Instruments Related to the United Nations Convention on the Law of the Sea.* UN publication, Sales No. E.97.V.9. New York: 1997.

dination.[27] The most needed synergy among such instruments is complicated and cumbersome. Very few States are able to navigate through this maze of environmental agreements and programmes of action, which hinders the taking of decisions at the national level. Some efforts have been made at the international level to ensure that the necessary political actions have been taken to promote the legal rules and ensure their efficient implementation in an integrated manner.

THE POLITICAL PILLAR: ACTIONS BY INTERGOVERNMENTAL BODIES

The necessity to establish a number of structures that could prevent a sectoral approach to oceans issues detrimental to their efficient management and promote concerted actions at all levels was raised at the 6th Meeting of States Parties to the 1982 Convention. However, some delegations rejected the idea to use the Meeting of States Parties to that effect, arguing that the Convention attributes to the meeting only administrative functions. For them the General Assembly was to remain the only forum to debate ocean issues. The seventh meeting of the CSD convened to review the implementation of Chapter 17 on Oceans and Seas became the forum chosen to discuss any possible solutions that could lead to a better management of the oceans.[28]

One of the main focuses of CSD 7 mandated to review the implementation of Chapter 17 was the question of cooperation and coordination, which has been viewed by UNCED and reflected in Agenda 21 as an area in need of serious attention.

Decision 7/1 of the CSD reiterated in paragraph 38 its conviction that "a more integrated approach is required to all legal, economic, social and environmental aspects of the oceans and seas."

The CSD concentrated a great deal of its effort on this matter. It urges relevant institutions, whether national, regional, or global, to enhance collaboration with each other, taking into account their respective mandates with a view to providing coordinated approaches, avoiding duplication of effort, enhancing effective functioning of existing organizations, and ensuring better access to and broadening the dissemination of information.[29] On

27. R. R. Churchill and G. Ulfstein, "Autonomous institutional arrangements in multilateral environmental agreements: A little-noticed phenomenon in international law," *American Journal of International Law* 94, no. 4 (October 2000): 623–59.

28. A. de Marffy, "La Gouvernance des Mers," in *Annuaire du Droit de la Mer* (Paris: Pédone, 1998), pp. 71–86.

29. Commission on Sustainable Development, Decision 7/1, par. 37. See online at the web site maintained by the United Nations Division for Sustainable Development, http://www.un.org/esa/sustdev/csd1999.htm (accessed September 4, 2003).

this basis, three requests were made to the UN Secretary-General: 1) to undertake measures aimed at ensuring more effective collaboration, 2) to complement his annual reports to the General Assembly with suggestions and initiatives, and 3) to improve the effectiveness of the Subcommittee on Oceans and Coastal Areas of the Administrative Committee on Coordination (SOCA). At the same time, the General Assembly was invited to consider ways and means to enhance the effectiveness of the annual debate on oceans and the law of the sea.

In this context, the Commission recommended to establish an open-ended informal consultative process with the sole function of facilitating the effective and constructive consideration of matters, within the General Assembly mandate of resolution 49/28 of 1994 adopted following the entry into force of the 1982 Convention.

In 1999, resolution 54/33 established the Consultative Process, which was designed according to the principles and practicalities set forth in the recommendations of the CSD 7.[30] It has been a little easier to describe the Process than it was to give it a clear title. The preoccupation with its title was hint of the caution of States, and perhaps their natural sensitivity about its implications. Through the 3 years of experience it has shown its value and lifted up the fear that some delegations had that the issues chosen and the discussion on them could endanger the balance achieved in the Convention. The title "Open-ended Informal Consultative Process on Oceans and the Law of the Sea" that describes best the process has finally been agreed during the negotiation of the draft resolution (A/57/L.48) under the General Assembly item "Oceans and the Law of the Sea," to be adopted in December 2002.

The Consultative Process, consistent with the legal framework provided by the 1982 Convention and the goals of Chapter 17 of Agenda 21, was established to respond to the need for an integrated approach for the oceans, which requires a transectoral review taking into account all aspects legal, economic, political, and environmental. The work of the Consultative Process is to discuss the annual report of the Secretary-General on oceans and the law of the sea and suggest particular issues to be considered by the General Assembly, with an emphasis on identifying areas where coordination and cooperation at the intergovernmental and interagency levels should be enhanced. Moreover, the Consultative Process is intended to study overall developments in ocean affairs.

The originality of the Process is based on different parameters required by the resolution. For example, the participation in the process is to be as wide as possible. The meetings are open not only to Member States but also to members of specialized agencies, States Parties to the Convention,

30. See A. de Marffy, "Une nouvelle tentative pour mieux gérer les océans: le processus consultatif officieux," *Annuaire du Droit de la Mer*, tome V (2000): 55–70.

international organizations competent in marine affairs, and observers to the General Assembly. The meetings are also open to the participation of nongovernmental organizations representing the major groups identified in Agenda 21. Another original feature required by the resolution is that two chairpersons preside over its work. This is intended to take into account the need for representation from developed and developing countries, as well as from legal and nonlegal backgrounds. For the first meeting held in May 2000, the president of the General Assembly appointed, after consultations of Member States, Ambassador Tuiloma Neroni Slade (Samoa) and Mr. Alan Simcock (United Kingdom), in accordance with paragraph 3 (e) of General Assembly resolution 54/33. Both Chairmen were reappointed for the second and third meeting, which took place in May 2001 and 2002.

Another important element of the Process is that the discussions focus only on specific issues that needed to be addressed urgently or requiring concrete action, after an overview of overall developments relating to ocean affairs and the law of the sea. The areas of focus discussed during the three meetings were (a) responsible fisheries and illegal, unreported, and unregulated fisheries: moving from principles to implementation; (b) economic and social impacts of marine pollution and degradation, especially in coastal areas; (c) marine science and the development and transfer of marine technology as mutually agreed, including capacity building; (d) coordination and cooperation in combating piracy and armed robbery at sea; (e) protection and preservation of the marine environment; and (f) capacity building, regional cooperation and coordination, and integrated ocean management, as important cross-cutting issues to address ocean affairs, such as marine science and the transfer of technology, sustainable fisheries, the degradation of the marine environment, and the safety of navigation.[31]

On the basis of consultations and deliberations with delegations, the cochairpersons proposed to the first meeting of the Consultative Process a draft format for discussions and an annotated provisional agenda. The format provided, among other things, the opportunity to receive input from major groups, as identified in Agenda 21, especially nongovernmental organizations. The Process has received indeed invaluable input from the major groups, especially from nongovernmental and intergovernmental organizations. The process worked through plenary sessions and discussion panels.

Discussions at meetings started with plenary sessions to discuss the reports of the Secretary-General on oceans and the law of the sea,[32] as well as

31. See UNICPOLOS Reports A/55/274, A/56/121 and A/57/80 for 2000, 2001 and 2002, respectively. These documents can be viewed at the web site maintained by the Division for Ocean Affairs and Law of the Sea/Office of Legal Affairs—United Nations, http://www.un.org/depts/los/ (accessed September 4, 2003).

32. See Reports of the Secretary-General on Oceans and the Law of the Sea, A/55/61, A/56/58 and A/57/57 for 2000, 2001 and 2002, respectively. These doc-

other documents, including written submissions by States and international organizations.

The reports of the Consultative Process adopted by consensus at each of the meetings[33] were composed of three parts: (a) issues to be suggested and elements to be proposed to the General Assembly; (b) cochairpersons' summary of discussions; and (c) issues for consideration for possible inclusion in the agendas of future meetings.

Many of the recommendations contained in the reports of the Consultative Process have been incorporated in the General Assembly resolutions.

It is important to note in this context the increased role of General Assembly resolutions in relation to oceans matters, particularly in the last 3 years. They first can be seen as annual plans of action incorporating all issues of importance dealing with oceans affairs, such as maritime space, settlement of disputes, the Area, the continental shelf, the functioning of the institutions established by the 1982 Convention, the marine environment, and marine scientific research. Secondly, although voluntary in nature, they allow States to strengthen some important points or issues discussed elsewhere and raise their political profile. Finally, they constitute one of the best tools for ensuring an integrated approach because all subjects of ocean affairs are contained therein.

The Consultative Process has certainly contributed to improving the annual debate, focusing the discussion on the annual report presented by the UN Secretary-General on the current developments in all aspects of oceans and seas issues. It went further in selecting a few subjects representing key issues in need of further action. In doing so, it had the great merit of opening the discussions not only to delegations but also to representatives of intergovernmental organizations and nongovernmental organizations. The discussion panels were conducive to fruitful exchanges of views between the different actors. For all these reasons, the 57th General Assembly decided to renew the Consultative Process for another 3 years.[34]

The establishment of the Consultative Process represents a very significant breakthrough in the process of building a global system of ocean governance. Member States have sought to make positive use of the outcomes of the Process, as is evident from the discussions in the General Assembly under the agenda item "oceans and the law of the sea" and the resulting Assembly resolutions during its 55th, 56th, and 57th sessions.

---

uments can be viewed at the web site maintained by the Division for Ocean Affairs and Law of the Sea/Office of Legal Affairs—United Nations, http://www.un.org/depts/los/ (accessed September 4, 2003).

33. See de Marffy (n. 30 above).

34. See General Assembly Resolution A/Res/57/141, par. 60, online at the web site maintained by the Division for Ocean Affairs and Law of the Sea/Office

THE INSTITUTIONAL PILLAR: INTER-SECRETARIATS COORDINATION AND COOPERATION

The Consultative Process was established with an emphasis in particular on "identifying areas where cooperation and coordination at the intergovernmental levels and interagency level should be enhanced (Resolution 54/33, paragraph 2).

The inevitability of international cooperation and coordination for the effective implementation of the international regime for the oceans established by the 1982 Convention prompted the framers of the Convention to include specific provisions relating to international cooperation and coordination in various parts of the Convention. Agenda 21 in its Chapter 17, in addition to devoting an entire programme area to "strengthening international, including regional cooperation and coordination," identifies activities relating to "international and regional cooperation and coordination" under all seven programme areas.

Cooperation is quite extensive among the organizations of the United Nations system, in many cases extending to other intergovernmental bodies, government agencies, the private sector, nongovernmental organizations and stakeholders in the widest sense. For example, the Secretariat of the Convention on Migratory Species (CMS) signed a Memorandum of Understanding with the secretariat of the International Whaling Commission. The Memorandum of Understanding, which builds upon already well-established collaborative linkages between the two secretariats, aims to provide a formal framework for future collaboration. It deals with aspects such as institutional linkages, the regular exchange of information, cooperation in the preparation of documents where applicable and coordination of the respective programmes of activities. The Division for Ocean Affairs and the Law of the Sea signed in 2002 with the International Tribunal for the Law of the Sea an Agreement on Cooperation and Relationship.

Another example of cooperation is the establishment of the new Joint Technical Commission for Oceanography and Meteorology (JCOMM), an intergovernmental body acting as a constituent body of WMO and IOC to coordinate and regulate the provision of meteorological and oceanographic services worldwide and coordinate and guide an operational ocean-observing system to support those services, as well as global climate monitoring, research, and prediction. According to WMO, JCOMM represents a new paradigm in interagency cooperation in the United Nations system, in which two agencies are pooling resources and expertise in support of a more efficient, multidisciplinary approach to addressing an identified global requirement.

---

of Legal Affairs—United Nations, http://www.un.org/depts/los/ (accessed September 4, 2003).

However, if the cooperation at the interagency level, especially at the level of tasks projects has been and continues to be quite effective, the issue of coordination in particular in relation to overall ocean affairs, management, and governance requires serious consideration. For the agencies within the United Nations system, the challenges have been exacerbated recently with the discontinuation of the Subcommittee on Oceans and Coastal Areas of the Administrative Committee on Coordination. This Committee was established in 1993, with the purpose of meeting the coordination needs defined in Chapter 17 of Agenda 21.

The Secretary General, after reviewing the mechanism of cooperation within the overall United Nations system, decided that all existing bodies should cease to exist by the end of 2001, and that future interagency support would best be handled through ad hoc, time-bound, task-oriented arrangements. The third Informal Consultative Process devoted extensive time to this question and recommended to establish a new coordinating mechanism for issues relating to oceans and seas, consistent with the new arrangements[35] being developed in the United Nations.[36] This new coordinating mechanism should be transparent, effective and responsive. It should respond to continuing needs and should have continuity, regularity, and accountability. It should work at two levels: (i) through regular reviews of issues relating to oceans and seas involving core participating institutions to eliminate gaps and duplications; and (ii) through establishment of specific task forces as needed to carry out task-oriented activities.[37]

The Plan of Implementation adopted by the WSSD responded to the call of the Consultative Process and recommended in its paragraph 29(c) "to establish an effective, transparent and regular inter-agency coordination mechanism on ocean and coastal issues within the United Nations system." The draft resolution (A/57/L.48) heard also the call of the Process and invited the Secretary General to establish a mechanism taking into account paragraph 49 of the report of the Process.

Another mechanism that provides for cooperation within the United Nations system is also in the midst of big changes: the Joint Group of Experts on the Scientific Aspects of Marine Environmental Protection (GESAMP).

35. In October 2000, ACC decided to establish two high-level committees, the High-Level Committee on Management (HLCM) and the High-Level Committee on Programmes (HLCP), and mandated them, inter alia, to undertake a review of the ACC subsidiary machinery that should be zero based: the review should take as its starting point what needed to be done rather than what was currently being done; permanent bodies should be kept to a minimum and their retention should be based on rigorous criteria. In introducing the item, the Secretary-General noted that ACC would, through the establishment of High-Level Committees, have the pillars in place that would enable it to concentrate on strategic issues, a main objective that had moved the review forward.

36. A/57/80 (n. 31 above), Part A, par. 48.

37. A/57/80 (n. 31 above), Part A, par. 49B.

GESAMP, constituted in 1968 by an interagency Memorandum of Understanding, is an expert scientific advisory body supported by organizations of the United Nations system. As of May 2001, the sponsoring agencies were the United Nations, through its Division for Ocean Affairs and the Law of the Sea; UNEP; UNESCO/IOC; FAO; WHO; WMO; IMO; and IAEA.

The principal task of GESAMP is to provide independent, multidisciplinary scientific advice to the sponsoring agencies concerning the prevention, reduction, and control of the degradation of the marine environment, with a view to sustaining its life support systems, resources, and amenities. The annual reports of GESAMP and the reports of its working groups thus represent substantial contributions to the technical work of the sponsoring agencies under their respective mandates and programmes of work, including in relation to the implementation of the 1982 Convention and Chapter 17 of Agenda 21, among others, and, through the agencies, to their governing bodies and Member States, to assist them in policy and decision making with regard to the marine environment, particularly coastal areas. GESAMP published recently two reports: "A Sea of Troubles" and "Protecting the Oceans from Land-based Activities."[38]

In March 2000, the Executive Director of UNEP made a proposal to the Administrative Secretary of GESAMP for an in-depth independent evaluation to make the advisory mechanism more effective and responsive. GESAMP, through its Subcommittee, while recognizing the need for improving its functioning and effectiveness, reiterated the value of independent scientific advice on ocean issues and expressed concern that transforming GESAMP into an intergovernmental panel could threaten the independence of its work and lead to a complicated and expensive process.

The Governing Council of UNEP took the decision regarding a feasibility study for establishing a regular process for the assessment of the state of the marine environment (decision GC.21/13). An informal consultative meeting to discuss the UNEP Governing Council decision was convened in Reykjavik, Iceland, in September 2001. A consensus seems to have emerged that the goal of a regular assessment of the state of the marine environment would best be served not by the establishment of new structures or institutions but rather by the adaptation of existing mechanisms, structures, and programmes and the optimization of cooperation and coordination among them.

The question of the regular assessment of the marine environment was taken up during the negotiation of the resolution on oceans and the law of the sea. Under paragraph 45 of the draft resolution, it was decided to estab-

38. GESAMP. United Nations Environment Programme. Reports and Studies no. 70 and 71. January 2001. This information is online at the web site maintained by Joint Group of Experts on the Scientific Aspects of Marine Environmental Protection, http://gesamp.imo.org/ (accessed September 4, 2003).

lish by 2004 a regular process under the United Nations for global reporting and assessment of the state of the marine environment. It requested that the Secretary General in collaboration with member states, relevant organizations, agencies, and programmes of the UN system and relevant nongovernmental organizations to prepare proposals on modalities for a regular process drawing upon the work of UNEP and taking into account the review of GESAMP and submit these proposals to the 58th General Assembly.

The establishment of an effective mechanism for cooperation and coordination in oceans affairs, seen as a vital element for the implementation of the 1982 Convention and Agenda 21, has been requested by member States. The mandates of the mechanism and its functions will determine whether it will play the role to lead to the good governance of the oceans.

THE CAPACITY-BUILDING PILLAR

The promotion of capacity building had become an important and pressing task to enable the developing States to implement UNCLOS and to reap the benefits there-from.

Many countries, in particular developing countries, especially the least developed among them and small island developing States, simply do not have the capacity to implement the 1982 Convention, related conventions, Chapter 17 of Agenda 21, and related programmes of action. The concern about lack of capacity and the consequent need for capacity building were expressed pointedly, urgently, and repeatedly in General Assembly resolutions,[39] statements of delegations in the General Assembly and in the Consultative Process, and the reports of the Co-Chairpersons of the Consultative Process.[40]

The lack of capacity is seen in most of the components needed to govern the fisheries sector in the majority of developing countries. They need better access to relevant experience, technical support, and financial resources to implement sustainable fisheries management systems. Poor adequate hydrographic data in extended sea areas of the world affect the accuracy of a large percentage of the available navigational charts.

The true and tangible solutions to enhance good governance in the oceans lay in the development of the necessary personnel and technical capabilities so that States, especially developing States, could give effect to their rights and responsibilities.

Limitations in capacity not only hinder countries from benefiting from

39. See, for example, Resolution 56/12, paras. 6–8, and Resolution 55/7, par. 23.

40. See, for example, A/56/121 (n. 31 above), paras. 24–26, 59–63, 86–88, 155–160.

oceans and seas and their resources under the 1982 Convention and Agenda 21, such limitations may also create opportunities for others to divert the benefits to themselves. Examples of the latter category include (a) limitations of capacity to regulate resource exploitation; (b) where regulations against illegal exploitation exist, limitations in enforcing such regulations; and (c) where enforcement exists, limitations in monitoring and controlling resource exploitation, thereby allowing misreporting. In many cases, there is not only a loss of income and well being for the present generation, but future generations are also affected because the diversion of benefits can be of such an extent as to jeopardize the very sustainability of the resources.

The 1982 Convention does not refer specifically to capacity building, however, it refers to the need to assist developing states. Agenda 21 devotes the entire Chapter 37 to capacity building and Chapter 17 includes suggestions about capacity-building as a means of implementing the programme of action on oceans and seas.

"Specifically, capacity-building encompasses the country's human, scientific, technological, organizational, institutional and resource capabilities" (Agenda 21, paragraph 37.1). Both financial assistance and in-kind assistance can be useful for implementing capacity-building measures. Essentially such measures broaden and deepen the human resource base, strengthen the institutional structure and the institutions themselves, and expand the physical resource base. A wide range of measures can be relevant, which involve, inter alia, executing technical cooperation projects; undertaking educational, training, research, and public awareness programmes and strengthening institutions capable of carrying out such programmes; exchange of data, information, and experiences; creating and strengthening physical as well as institutional infrastructure; and provision and mobilization of raw materials, equipment, facilities, and vessels.

Capacity building is a major part of the work programme of almost all international organizations dealing with ocean affairs. A number of activities of IOC in the field of marine science are aimed at capacity building in developing countries. For example, capacity building continues to be a main component of the Harmful Algal Bloom (HAB) programme.

The United Nations Industrial Development Organization (UNIDO) stated that the transfer of skills and knowledge to member countries through capacity building, especially institutional strengthening, forms a cross-cutting activity of fundamental importance in each of the three areas of its work relating to environmental management planning, policy formulation and monitoring; reducing harmful emissions from industry; and pollution control and waste management.

Training and other capacity-building activities undertaken by UNIDO are designed to improve production management by providing managers and supporting service providers with the skills necessary to identify, assess, and modify those components of the manufacturing process that generate high demands for raw materials, water, and energy resources or that represent the principal sources of wastage and pollution emissions.

FAO gives practical effect to capacity building, especially institutional strengthening, in a number of different but related ways. It works closely with national fishery administrations, including those in small island developing States, to improve their operational efficiency in management and utilization and in the promotion of sustainable aquaculture. This is achieved through the dissemination of information pertinent to responsible management, and in particular through the preparation of technical guidelines that support the implementation of the Code of Conduct, country visits and the provision of advice on specific issues, and the organization of workshops and professional attachments within FAO.

The capacity-building activities in the field of marine environment carried out under the auspices of the United Nations Environment Programme (UNEP) are numerous. For example, the fourth Global Meeting of Regional Seas Convention and Action Plans recommended that regional clustering of activities carried out by global marine environmental agreements, Regional Seas Conventions and Action Plans, international organizations, and other regional bodies is needed to carry out activities in a more coordinated and cost-effective manner, particularly in areas such as technology transfer, development of supportive national legislation, assessment and monitoring, and public awareness and information exchange. In particular, greater efforts are required to pool resources for developing collective regional technology transfer centres for the protection and sustainable use of the marine and coastal environment in support of regional seas programmes, global marine environmental agreements, and other international initiatives.

Capacity building in maritime infrastructure is the focus of the International Maritime Organization (IMO) that attaches the highest priority to the need to ensure that the numerous rules and standards contained in its body of treaties are properly implemented. To facilitate this implementation, IMO focuses on the continuous strengthening of regulations to ensure that flag and port States and ship owners develop their capacities and fulfill their responsibility to the fullest. The technical cooperation of IMO has been intensified by the operation of the Integrated Technical Cooperation Programme (ITCP). IMO capacity-building activities in human resources development under ITCP are expected to produce an increased number of trained experts (both male and female) to develop and manage national programmes for maritime safety administration, marine environment protection, the development of maritime legislation, facilitation of maritime traffic, technical port operations, and training of seafarers and shore-based personnel. In the area of institutional capacity building, activities under ITCP are expected to strengthen public sector departments capable of ensuring the effective exercise of flag State, port State and coastal State jurisdiction.

The Hamilton Shirley Amerasinghe Memorial Fellowship Programme is a major part of the capacity-building activities of the United Nations Division for Ocean Affairs and the Law of the Sea. The Fellowship was established in 1982 in memory of the late President of the Third United Nations Conference on the Law of the Sea. It is administered by the Division and is a component of the United Nations Programme of Assistance in the Teaching, Study, Dissemination, and Wider Appreciation of International Law. The Fellowship is intended primarily to improve the expertise of government officials, research fellows, or academics who are involved in law of the sea or marine affairs. It assists the successful candidates in acquiring additional knowledge of the 1982 Convention to promote its wider appreciation and application and enhance specialized experience in those fields. Since the inception of the Amerasinghe Memorial Fellowship Programme, 17 Annual Fellowships and 5 Special Fellowships have been awarded.

Another important part of the Division's capacity-building activities is its TRAIN-SEA-COAST (TSC) programme. The programme was developed as part of a system-wide training strategy that emphasizes (a) building up permanent national capabilities for training; (b) sustainability of training efforts; (c) cost effectiveness; (d) responsiveness to specific training priorities of the countries involved; (e) transfer of experience and sharing of training resources; and (f) long-term impact.

The basic objective of the TSC programme is to create capacity at the local level to produce high-quality training courses to be shared among the TSC members, and at the same time to strengthen local institutions to become centres of excellence on training at the national or regional levels.

One possible solution to deal with the huge task of capacity building is to improve partnership between international financial institutions, bilateral agencies and other relevant stakeholders, and for the enhancement of existing international efforts and the coordination of approaches among States and relevant international organizations.

CONCLUSION

The greatest problem, which has been widely expressed either by renowned experts such as Elisabeth Mann Borgese or by politicians such as Simon Upton of New Zealand in his inaugural speech to CSD 7 and underlined by many reports of the Secretary-General, is the difficulty of implementing international rules. The integrated approach on ocean affairs requires a great deal of cooperation at the national level that certainly starts with the enactment of coherent national policy, allowing politicians, administrators, and other officials of a State to have a clear view of the direction countries should take in dealing with ocean affairs. The implementation of international rules, therefore, presents a tremendous challenge in need of being addressed forcefully.

The World Summit on Sustainable Development stressed that one of the cornerstones of sustainable development involved the establishment of the domestic institutional, legal, and regulatory infrastructure needed to manage natural resources effectively.

In addition to the absence of general marine policy or the lack of necessary legislation, States lack adequate institutions to deal with ocean affairs. The Brundtland report, *Our Common Future*,[41] characterized ocean governance[42] as needing to be

- Comprehensive, which means that ocean governance must reach from the local level of the coastal community through the level of provincial and national governance;
- Consistent, which means that regulation and decision-making processes and mechanisms at all levels of governance must be compatible, reinforcing the call for the adoption of national comprehensive marine policy to serve as the basis for all activities in all sectors of ocean affairs;
- Transsectoral or multidisciplinary, which means that activities in the ocean cannot be considered separately, sector by sector, but must be seen in their interreaction. This call has certainly been repeated over and over in CSD decisions, as well as in resolutions of the General Assembly, in particular resolution 54/33 establishing the Consultative Process on the oceans. It seems obvious that the call for an integrated approach at the international level would be heard only when the same call would be enforced at the national level. All actors or stakeholders shall be involved, not only from all the ministries having competencies in the field of oceans and seas, but also from the private sector, including industries as well as academic and scientific institutions.
- Participational, which means that regulations must not be imposed by the central level of government. The local communities whose livelihood depends on oceans and seas must be involved in the preparation of rules and regulations as well as in management. Local communities, which live by the coast, and are therefore in direct contact with problems occurring at that level, are very rarely involved in the search for a solution. The central power, in particular the representatives of legislative bodies, works often in isolation adopting laws and regulations not adapted to reality.

41. G. R. Brundtland, chairperson of World Commission on Environment and Development (WCED), *Our Common Future* (Oxford: Oxford University Press, 1987).

42. See Payoyo (n. 2 above), p. 369; See also de Marffy (n. 28 above), pp. 71–86.

What could be the solution to encourage governments to engage in the process of establishing true national governance of the oceans and coasts under State jurisdiction? It might be worthwhile to consider establishing a consultative process at the national level mirrored on the Consultative Process established by the General Assembly. The prime minister or a lead agency will convene the process. All actors involved in marine affairs, not only the ministries concerned, but also the regional and local constituencies, as well as the private sector—oil and gas, fisheries, shipping, and so forth—shall be invited.

As a first step, the national process shall prepare a comprehensive marine policy. It should then convene at least twice a year with two main purposes: first, to ensure that the implementation at all levels of government of the national policy is undertaken, and second, to oversee that the coordination between the competent ministries is efficiently carried out. A follow-up mechanism should be put in place to serve as a secretariat and focal point for all agencies and ensure the link with the international level. Such a mechanism would be very useful for international agencies and programmes as a focal point for contact.

The main weakness that has existed at the national level lies in the fact that marine affairs have always been dealt with at the central level of government and did not take sufficient account of the local communities living in coastal areas. A mechanism like a national consultative process could, in ensuring that all interests are taken care of, be the best tool to promote an integrated approach, which is the only solution to manage efficiently the oceans and seas under State jurisdiction.

The road to ocean governance, although still under consideration has seen substantial progress being achieved at the international level. However, at the national level, ocean governance remains in infancy and will only be achieved with strong political will.

The Law of the Sea and the Arctic: An Unfulfilled Legacy

Rob Huebert
Centre for Military and Strategic Studies, University of Calgary, Canada

INTRODUCTION

One of the greatest legacies that Elisabeth Mann Borgese left was the need to approach international problems in the spirit of goodwill, cooperation, and innovation. An individual who saw firsthand the worst of humankind, such as the Nazi regime, she never lost the ability to believe that with enough hard work and goodwill the many problems facing the world could be solved. As such, she dedicated her life to the development of a fair and equitable international ocean regime that would provide equal access for all to the world's ocean resources.[1] To do this she worked tirelessly for the creation of the United Nations Convention on the Law of the Sea.[2] The Convention was a major watershed in the development of not only international law but also a framework to conceptualize ocean management. It merged traditional maritime legal issues with new approaches to the sharing and management of ocean resources. It represents one of the most innovative advances in creating an equitable means of sharing and managing the ocean and its resources. It was by no means perfect, nor did it succeed in creating a truly fair and equitable means of sharing. But it went much further than almost any other international agreement of its day. Furthermore, there is no questioning the intent of Elisabeth Mann Borgese to make the Convention something that would bring out the best of humankind.

While the breadth of the topics covered by the Convention was substantial, it did omit and/or provide short shrift to some very important issues. One of these areas where the Convention was relatively silent was in regard

1. Elisabeth Mann Borgese produced a staggering amount of literature on the oceans. It was impressive for its quantity, quality, and vision. It is impossible to cite one as the core representative of her work. Perhaps one of the best examples of her foresight and vision of the world's seas can be found in *The Drama of the Oceans* (New York: Harry N. Abrams Inc., 1975).

2. United Nations Convention on the Law of the Sea, UN Doc. A/CONF.62/122 (1982). *International Legal Materials* 21, (1982), 1261. Adopted 10 December 1982, entered into force 14 November 1994.

Ocean Yearbook 18: 193–219

to the specific challenges of the Arctic waters. The Convention's universal clauses obviously apply to the Arctic. For example, Arctic states are now able to determine northern continental shelves, exclusive economic zones, territorial seas, and contiguous zones. Likewise the Convention's sections on scientific research and environmental protection also apply to the Arctic region. However, there was little that dealt with the unique and harsh conditions of the Arctic waters and the people that live there. In part this was due to the fact that the Third United Nations Conference on the Law of Sea (UNCLOS III) attempted to deal with a very comprehensive ocean agenda. It was impossible to give every aspect of the ocean the attention that each deserved. Given the relatively small number of Arctic states at the negotiations, it is not surprising that this region of the globe did not receive greater attention. The Arctic also received limited international attention at UNCLOS III because of the Cold War. Both the United States and the Soviet Union maintained extensive submarine and maritime forces in their northern waters. The hostility between the superpowers and the strategic importance of the Arctic region prevented the development of any meaningful international cooperation, including at UNCLOS III.

In the time since the completion of the negotiation and the successful ratification of the Convention, the Arctic has been experiencing several fundamental changes that may now offer the opportunity to create a cooperative management effort to see that its resources are developed in an equitable and sustainable fashion. This would truly encapsulate the progressive international spirit that Elisabeth Mann Borgese had championed throughout her long and successful career. However, there still remain parochial interests that may prevent a fully cooperative effort to develop to its fullest potential. There is also an inertia that is slowing new thinking on the Arctic. Unfortunately, the changes that are altering the Arctic must be responded to in a timely fashion. If not, many of the problems that are now arising may well exceed the ability of the international community to respond. Thus, if the maritime regions of the Arctic are to be utilized in a manner that is environmentally sensitive and that best serves the interests of the people who live in the region, action must be taken now. It is in this spirit that this article will look for cooperative solutions to international problems that face the Arctic and its oceans.

To best understand the fairest and most effective way forward, one should consider the following issues: 1) What are the changes to the Arctic region since the completion of the Law of Sea Convention in 1982? Specifically what new elements strengthen or weaken international maritime cooperation in the Arctic? 2) What does the Convention contribute as a starting point for the further development of international maritime cooperation in the Arctic? 3) What other international institutions, agreements, and initiatives have been created/taken that have contributed to the building of international cooperation in the Arctic? 4) What new steps can be taken to further cooperation? However, before these questions can be answered it is necessary to briefly define what is meant by the term Arctic.

DEFINING AND UNDERSTANDING THE ARCTIC

One of the greatest challenges is attempting to come to terms with a working definition of the North. There have been numerous efforts to create a definition that would provide an inclusive definition of the Arctic, but none have been completely successful. There are eight countries that are considered to either be an Arctic state or have some territory in the Arctic, namely Russia, the United States, Canada, Norway, Sweden, Finland, Iceland, and Denmark/Greenland. All eight have interests in Arctic waters. Once again there is no single definition of Arctic waters but generally these are considered to be waters that are above 60° North. But even this definition excludes the waters surrounding Iceland, which renders it incomplete.[3]

The major defining characteristic of the Arctic waters is the presence of ice for most if not all of the year.[4] The existence of ice means that many of the normal maritime activities such as shipping cannot be undertaken in their normal manner. The only vessels that can operate safely in these waters are either icebreakers or ice-strengthened vessels that sail in the company of an icebreaker.[5] In addition, any environmental damage that occurs in these waters is especially devastating, as pollutants will tend not to dissipate as they would in warmer climates.

The nearly constant presence of ice also means that the indigenous peoples that live in this northern region have adjusted their lifestyles to its existence. The traditional way of life of many of these peoples is based on a lifestyle that depends on hunting and fishing, much of which takes place on the ice. Because of this, they have developed traditional ecological knowledge (TEK) to guide their activities on the ice.[6] This is based on observations made by their ancestors. It provides the means of knowing the right time to engage in certain types of activities. This includes when the ice is safe to travel on for hunting and fishing and when it is not. While TEK was originally

3. One of the better descriptions of the Arctic can be found in Canada, House of Commons, *Canada and the Circumpolar World: Meeting the Challenges of Cooperation into the Twenty-First Century—Report of the House of Commons Standing Committee on Foreign Affairs and International Trade.* Standing Committee on Foreign Affairs and International Trade. Ottawa: Publication Service, April 1997, p. 2.

4. C. Joyner, "The Status of Ice in International Law," in *The Law of the Sea and Polar Maritime Delimitation and Jurisdiction,* ed. A. Oude Elferink and D. Rothwell (Hague: Maritinus Nijhoff, 2001), pp. 23–27.

5. A good description of the challenges in the Northwest Passage that also can be applied to the Northern Sea Route is found in F. Griffiths, "Where Vision and Illusion Meet," in *Politics of the Northwest Passage,* ed. F. Griffiths (Kingston and Montreal: McGill-Queen's University Press, 1987), pp. 3–8.

6. J. Sallenave, "Giving traditional ecological knowledge its rightful place in environmental impact assessment," *Northern Perspective* 22, no. 1 (1994). The term Traditional Ecological Knowledge (TEK) is now beginning to be changed to the term Traditional Knowledge (TK). Both terms are now used interchangeably.

scorned by Western science, it is increasingly being accepted as an alternative means of understanding the environmental conditions of the Arctic regions.[7]

TRANSFORMATION OF THE ARCTIC

Since the Law of the Sea Convention was finalized in 1982 the international system has undergone major transformations. Of the many changes, the Arctic has been particularly affected by three: 1) the end of the Cold War; 2) the impact of climate change; and 3) the increasing recognition of the right of aboriginal peoples over their land.

The End of the Cold War

Throughout the negotiation of UNCLOS III, the Cold War remained one of the most significant factors limiting international efforts to further cooperation in Arctic waters. The role that Arctic waters played as a strategic front meant that neither the Soviet Union nor the United States was willing to allow any international agreement to hinder their naval activity.

Both superpowers relied on their submarine services to carry a significant component of their nuclear deterrence capability.[8] Submarines had the ability to hide and were therefore seen as providing the best means of second-strike capability. Owing to the specific maritime geography of the Soviet Union, the majority of the Soviet submarines were based in the northern waters of the Kola Peninsula. In turn, the United States developed a submarine capability that could operate in Arctic waters to hunt Soviet submarines and hide their own missile-carrying submarines.[9] The net impact was that both the USSR and the United States resisted any effort to introduce international steps that could possibly interfere with the movement of their submarine fleet.[10]

The end of the Cold War and the subsequent implosion of the Soviet Union into Russia saw its navy and specifically its submarine force substan-

7. M. Freeman, "The nature and utility of traditional ecological knowledge," *Northern Perspective* 20, no. 1 (1992).

8. R. Huebert, "Canadian arctic security issues: Transformation in the post-cold war era," *International Journal* 54, no. 2 (1999).

9. R. Compton-Hall, *Submarine versus Submarine: The Tactic and Technology of Underwater Confrontation* (Toronto: Collins, 1988), pp. 173–80.

10. L. Alexander, "The Changing Nature of the High Seas," in *Multinational Naval Cooperation and Foreign Policy into the 21st Century*, ed. F. W. Crickard, P. Mitchell and K. Orr (Aldershot: Ashgate, 1998), pp. 33–34.

tially reduced. All older vessels were quickly decommissioned.[11] Newer ships that were retained saw their maintenance and days at sea substantially reduced because of the formidable financial problems faced by the Russian navy. It quickly became apparent that in their haste to reduce their navy, the Russians had not taken the proper steps to safely decommission their older nuclear-powered submarines. This currently remains a serious problem with a large number of submarines in Russian harbors literally rusting to pieces with their nuclear reactors still on board. The United States and Norway have provided significant funds for environmental remediation, but much more remains to be done.

However, the problem of decommissioned submarines notwithstanding, the virtual elimination of the former Soviet submarine force from Arctic waters and the improved relationship between the United States and Russia has opened the possibility for the development of new cooperative measures. As will be discussed later, this improved relationship has led directly to the creation of two new international Arctic institutions—the Arctic Environmental Protection Strategy (AEPS) and the Arctic Council. Both of these bodies were created to facilitate and improve international cooperation in the Arctic. While their success has so far been limited to environmental issues, it should be possible to go even further. The question then arises as to how international cooperation can best be facilitated.

Climate Change and the Arctic

One of the most serious environmental threats facing the entire international system, including the world's oceans, is climate change. Because the nature of this problem was not even recognized during the UNCLOS negotiations, there is no mention of climate change in the Convention. Currently, there is some controversy as to the full cause of climate change, but the vast bulk of current scientific research agrees that it is human activity that produces the carbon gases that are altering the global climate.[12] While not all of the processes are understood, scientists are beginning to come to terms with some of the core elements of the phenomenon. One of the most

11. Bellona, "The Russian Northern Fleet—Report 2: 1996," http://www.bellona.no/en/international/russia/navy/northern_fleet/report_2-1996/index.html (accessed 18 November 2002).

12. The leading organization on the overall impact of climate change is the UN's Intergovernmental Panel on Climate Change. They act as a coordinating body for research. Their most recent report is *Climate Change 2001: Synthesis Report.* IPCC. Cambridge: Cambridge University Press, 2001. There is also a small literature that challenges the main elements of the science supporting the concept of climate change. See for example: L. Johnson, ed., *Global Warming: The Science and the Politics* (Vancouver: The Fraser Institute, 1997).

significant elements for the Arctic is the finding that the polar regions are the most vulnerable to climate change.[13] As a result, many scientists believe that the polar regions will experience significant loss of ice over the coming decades.[14] While there is some disagreement with regard to the rate of ice melt, it is clear that the process has already begun. Both Western science and the observations of Northern peoples show that temperatures are increasing.[15]

A decreased ice cover in the Arctic will produce drastic changes in Arctic waters. These will range in scale from the microscopic to the international. There is evidence that changes in sea ice are introducing changes in the algae that live on the bottom of the ice. In turn, any changes in the algae then affects the entire food chain in the Arctic. Canadian researchers are already concerned that the decreasing amounts of ice is threatening some polar bear populations.

As the flora and fauna of the Arctic are increasingly disrupted, the ability of the indigenous Northern people to practice their traditional way of life becomes threatened. Changing ice conditions make hunting on ice increasingly dangerous.[16] Likewise the disappearance of some traditional species and the introduction of new ones will require adjustments in hunting and fishing techniques. In many cases adaptation simply is not possible. Thus, it remains a real possibility that for many communities the traditional way of life consisting of hunting and fishing on the ice will no longer be possible.

The diminished ice cover will also bring more southerners to the North.[17] As conditions become less harsh, there will be renewed efforts to exploit the resource wealth of the North.[18] There is already increased oil and gas exploration going on in Russian, Canadian and American northern lands, and offshore regions. Perhaps most important for the maritime regions of the Arctic is the

13. *Climate Change 2001: Impacts, Adaptation, and Vulnerability*. IPCC. Cambridge: Cambridge University Press, 2001, p. 16.1.1.

14. The rate of ice melt is generally thought to be at 3 percent per decade since the 1970s. However, the most recent satellite study of ice cover in the Arctic has found a 9 percent per decade loss. See J. C. Comiso, "A rapidly declining perennial sea ice cover in the Arctic," *Geophysical Research Letters* 29, no. 20 (October 2002), p. 1956.

15. R. Moritz, C. Bitz and E. Stieg, "Dynamics of recent climate change in the Arctic," *Science* 297 (August 2002), pp. 1497–1501. See also the related stories in the same edition.

16. S. Watt-Cloutier, "General assembly and 25th anniversary of the Inuit Circumpolar Conference," *Silarjualiriniq: Inuit in Global Issues*, nos. 12 & 13 (April–September 2002), pp. 2–4.

17. U. L. McFarling, "On Thinning Ice: Gradual Thaw is Bringing Big Changes to the Arctic," *Los Angeles Times* (3 February 2003).

18. Tyndall Centre, *Climate Change: The Arctic and the United Kingdom* (Norwich: Tyndall Centre for Climate Change Research, 2002), p. 3.

possibility of increased shipping in Northern waters. Historically, it has been the ice that has prevented the use of Northern waters for most forms of shipping.[19] As mentioned earlier, nuclear powered submarines have operated in Arctic waters since the early 1960s. However, surface vessels can only make similar voyages if they are specially constructed as icebreakers, or for short times in the late summer when the ice recedes. For the most part the Arctic has remained off limits to almost all other types of shipping.

After the completion of the Law of the Sea Convention in 1982, the limited shipping that did occur in the Arctic declined. This occurred for several reasons. First, the decrease of oil and gas sales in the mid-1980s meant that exploration and production of oil and gas decreased in northern Canada, Russia, and Alaska. There were similar downturns in other mineral resources that were mined in the North. All of these resulted in decreased Northern shipping activities to support these industries.

Since the end of the 1990s there has been a small increase in the construction of ice-capable vessels specifically designed for current conditions. Russia has ordered 10 new ice-strengthened tankers that were built for Northern service.[20] An American company is also constructing a new class of ice-strengthened tankers to carry oil from the Port of Valdez to southern American markets.[21] These ships represent an increase in Arctic capable vessels.

If the ice recedes there are at least four types of shipping that will find the Arctic waters beneficial. First, large bulk carriers would find either the Northern Sea Route along the Russian northern coast (also known as the Northeast Passage), or the Northwest Passage through the Canadian Arctic Archipelago to save substantial distances between Asia, Europe, and North America. Over 4,000 nautical miles can be saved between German and Japanese ports by sailing through the Northwest Passage instead of through the Panama Canal.[22] Additionally, both the Northern Sea Route and the Northwest Passage can accommodate ships that are too big to fit the locks in the Panama Canal. These include both supertankers and the current generation of large container vessels.[23]

In a warmer Arctic, it is also reasonable to expect more vessels that are associated with resource development and exploitation. If Canada, the

19. E. Frankel, "Arctic Marine Transport and Ancillary Technologies," in *Transit Management in the Northwest Passage: Problems and Prospects,* ed. C. Lamson and D. VanderZwaag (Cambridge: University of Cambridge Press, 1986), pp. 100–114.

20. "Four questions for Sergey Frank, Minister of Transportation of the Russian Federation," *New East: International Magazine* (4 May 2000), http://segodnya.spb.rus.net/3-4-00/eng/06 e.htm (accessed 2 April 2003).

21. B. Gavin, "Polar tankers: built to last in unforgiving waters," *American Ship Review 2002–2003* 68, pp. 20–24.

22. R. Kerr, "A warmer Arctic means change for all," *Science* 297 (August 2002), pp. 1490–92.

23. Riverdeep, "Water Woes at the Panama Canal," (8 December 2000) http://www.riverdeep.net/current/2001/12/120800_panama.jhtml (accessed 7 July 2003).

United States, and/or Russia begin to find the Northern environment less hostile it will become easier to develop their Northern land base and offshore resources. There will be a need for an increase in maritime support vessels to support these developments. These will range from offshore rigs to barges and other forms of maritime transport needed to move the resources to southern markets. As ice conditions improve, fishers will also go further north. Already, some fishers are beginning to move up the western Greenland coast to pursue both turbot and shrimp.

The third type of vessels that will increase their visits to this region is cruise vessels. Ecotourist vessels that are retrofitted icebreakers have already begun to visit polar waters. Some of the larger Russian icebreakers have carried tourists all the way to the North Pole.[24] There are already an increasing number of regular cruise vessels that are entering southern Alaskan water. As the ice recedes it can be expected that there will be an increase in the number of regular cruise vessels entering other Arctic waters.

The fourth type of vessels that will increase operation in Arctic waters as the ice recedes is the surface naval vessels. The American navy has already begun to examine the challenges of operating their surface fleet in Arctic waters.[25] If the American navy increases its operations, it seems reasonable to expect that other navies will also increase the presence of their surface vessels.

Overall, it is clear that as the ice recedes in the face of a warming Arctic, there will be an increase in maritime activity in the North. The question that then follows is what is the framework that will best allow this increase to be undertaken in a manner that will protect the environment, provide benefits to the Northern people, and be undertaken in a fair and economically viable manner? However, before considering the possible international frameworks, the last major transformation needs to be considered.

Northern Indigenous Peoples and the Arctic

During the negotiations for the Convention, international law was relatively silent on the significance and role played by indigenous peoples. Most Arctic states did not even recognize the land claims made by their respective Northern indigenous peoples. As such the Convention is silent on their rights. After the completion of the Convention, international law has slowly begun to recognize that these peoples have a special claim over the lands and waters that they have inhabited and used to maintain for a traditional way of life.

24. L. Bingham, "The Northern Sea Route, 1997," *Polar Record* 34, no. 190 (1998), pp. 219–220.

25. Office of Naval Research, Naval Ice Center, Oceanographer of the Navy, and the Arctic Research Commission, *Naval Operations in an Ice-Free Arctic Symposium* (17–18 April 2001).

Several of the Arctic states have reached land settlements with some of their Northern peoples. Canada, for example, has not only reached several land claims agreements, but has also created a new territory that has an Inuit majority. However, the overall record remains mixed.[26] A major breakthrough was made when the role of organizations representing these groups was recognized in the new Arctic institutions that developed after the Cold War. Both the AEPS and the Arctic Council created a new type of membership called "permanent participants."[27] These were to be the international organizations of the various Northern aboriginal peoples. Once approved, they would have full rights to all of the activities of both the AEPS and the Arctic Council. The one exception is that they do not have the right to vote on budgetary issues. However, because neither organization has its own budget, this issue is not as important as it might seem. The organizations do have the right to full representation on all of the working groups and main bodies, and as such have full right of participation. This is the first example in which such rights have been given to indigenous peoples.[28] However, as will be discussed later in this article, this advancement has been tempered by the limited successes of both the AEPS and the Arctic Council.

It is clear from this discussion that there have been important developments in the Arctic since the Convention was completed. It should be equally apparent that these new developments will lead to more substantial changes to the Arctic. These changes will be largely driven by the increased accessibility of the region caused by the warming temperatures of climate change. As this occurs and the ice recedes, the use of Arctic waters will increase. The question that now needs to be answered is what does the Convention provide for the management of these waters? What other institutions have been created since the Convention was completed and how do they fit with the framework of the Convention?

THE LAW OF THE SEA AND THE ARCTIC

As previously mentioned, during the negotiations of UNCLOS III, efforts were made to incorporate considerations of the Arctic needs, but for the most part they were overshadowed by other considerations. Because the

26. UNEP, "Chapter Two: The State of the Environment—The Arctic—Social and Background," in *UNEP Global Outlook 2000* (New York: UNEP, 1999), http://www1.unep.org/geo-text/0118.htm (accessed 12 May 2003).

27. R. Huebert, "The Arctic Council and Northern Aboriginal Peoples," in *Issues in the North,* vol. 3, ed. J. Oakes and R. Riewe (Edmonton: Canadian Circumpolar Institute, 1998), pp. 141–151.

28. R. Huebert, "New directions in circumpolar cooperation: Canada, the Arctic Environmental Protection Strategy and the Arctic Council," *Canadian Foreign Policy* 5, no. 2 (1998), pp. 37–57.

majority of the delegates were from the more southern regions of the globe, the Arctic did not receive much attention. At the same time, both superpowers were also determined that the negotiations would not interfere with their capability to operate their military forces in what was regarded as a central strategic front. Thus, little of direct relevance to the Arctic region is found in the final Convention, besides the one specific element found in Article 234. Commonly referred to as the "Canadian clause," this article was created to deal with a dispute between the United States and Canada. Nevertheless, Article 234 is the only article that provides guidance for considering the future development of large-scale international maritime traffic in the Arctic region.[29]

After the completion of negotiations little progress occurred in the implementation of Article 234. While it provided the international framework for coastal Arctic states to develop stricter environmental standards for the operations of international shipping in "ice-covered waters," little new legislation has been developed. Nor were there any efforts to develop greater international cooperation in terms of maritime activities in the Arctic.

However, the three changes discussed in the last section now offer the opportunity to see a truly international cooperative means of responding to the maritime challenges in the Arctic region. The question that then arises is how can these expected changes best be managed? Can Article 234 provide the starting point for an international cooperative effort to ensure that the existing changes are managed in a manner so that the benefits of international shipping in the North go beyond the shipping interests to those who live in the North? If so, what steps must be taken by the international community to develop the necessary guidelines and safeguards before shipping develops in an ad hoc and unregulated fashion?

THE DEVELOPMENT OF ARTICLE 234

The Arctic was not an area of central focus at any of the Law of the Sea negotiations. In the negotiations of 1958 and 1960 there were no specific reference to the Arctic. Instead, it was simply assumed that any of the provisions that were decided upon regarding any issue of navigation or boundaries would simply be applied to the Northern waters. However, anyone who is familiar with Northern waters will immediately understand that the ice-covered nature of the waters makes such assumptions incorrect.

Operations by surface vessels in ice-covered waters are limited to either icebreakers or ice-strengthened vessels escorted by icebreakers. The diffi-

29. R. Huebert, "Article 234 and Marine Pollution Jurisdiction in the Arctic," in *The Law of the Sea and Polar Maritime Delimitation and Jurisdiction,* ed. A. Oude Elferink and D. Rothwell (Hague: Maritinus Nijhoff, 2001), pp. 249–68.

culty of sailing through ice-covered waters has meant that there has been little effort by almost all states to develop a Northern shipping capability. The four countries that do have some interest and capability are Canada, the United States, Russia/Soviet Union, and Finland. The Canadian interest in Arctic shipping has primarily been directed towards the increase in resource development. The American interest in Arctic shipping is also focussed on the development and exploitation of oil and gas resources from Alaska. The Soviet Union/Russia have attempted to develop the Northern Sea Route as a transportation route and for the development of its Northern resources. Finland developed a specific ship building capacity that included a niche Arctic ship capability. As discussed earlier in this article the most significant ice-capable type of vessels were the nuclear powered submarines. With the end of World War II and the beginning of the Cold War, the USSR and the United States had focussed much of their maritime efforts on developing submarines that could go farther and carry larger weapons.

As a result of the Cold War, little international cooperation, maritime or otherwise, occurred among the Arctic nations. Throughout the negotiations of UNCLOS I–III, there was little attention given to changing this reality. The one exception occurred because of a dispute between Canada and the United States over the international status of the Northwest Passage. Ultimately it was this disagreement and Canada's search for a solution that led to the development of Article 234.

The Canadian government was transferred ownership of the Arctic region from the United Kingdom in 1880.[30] However, this transfer was somewhat vague as to what was being transferred. It was clear that the islands of the Arctic Archipelago were being given to the Dominion of Canada, but the status of the waterways remained vague. The governments of the United States, Denmark, and Norway did challenge some of the land territory, but these disagreements were almost completely resolved by the end of the 1930s.[31] What was not resolved was the international status of the Northwest Passage.

Initially, there was little concern about this because the extremely cold conditions of the region meant that it was almost inaccessible for the southern nonindigenous populations. The first complete transit was not made until 1904 by the explorer Roald Amundsen commanding the *Gjoa*.[32] This came only after 50 years of efforts by European explorers, many of whom lost their lives and ships attempting to find the passage. It was not until 1942 that the second transit occurred (and the first by a Canadian). It was not

30. D. Pharand, *Canada's Arctic Waters in International Law* (Cambridge: Cambridge University Press, 1988), p. 4.

31. S. Grant, *Sovereignty or Security: Government Policy in the Canadian North 1936–1950* (Vancouver: University of British Columbia Press, 1988), pp. 17–20.

32. G. Rowley, "Bringing the Outside Inside: Towards Development of the Passage," in *Politics of the Northwest Passage*, ed. F. Griffiths (Kingston and Montreal: McGill-Queen's University Press, 1987), pp. 36–37.

until after World War II that the ability was achieved to build vessels capable of entering and operating in ice-covered waters. Partly this was the result of the development of improved ship construction and partly of the development of extremely powerful engines, including those powered by nuclear reactors.

Towards the end of the 1960s, the United States attempted to use such vessels to cross both the Northern Sea Route (also known by some as the Northeast Passage) and the Northwest Passage. In the case of the Northern Sea Route, the United States sent two icebreakers in 1967.[33] However, the Soviet Union refused to allow the vessels to proceed, threatening to use military force against them if they did not cease their efforts. Two years later in 1969 and then again in 1970, the United States sent an ice-strengthened supertanker, the *Manhattan,* with an icebreaker into the Northwest Passage. The Canadian government did not threaten to use military force, but did offer unrequested "permission" and sent a Canadian icebreaker to assist and escort the two American vessels.[34]

In the case of the effort to transit the Northern Sea Route, the United States was attempting to demonstrate that the route was an international waterway. This is also partly the rationale for the voyage into the Northwest Passage. A second reason for the voyage was to determine if the oil resources that were then being developed from the Alaskan north slope could be shipped to the continental United States by tanker through the Northwest Passage. It was found that ice conditions made the transit too difficult. Hence the decision was made to build a pipeline to the southern Alaskan port of Valdez and ship the oil from there by tanker to the west coast of the United States.

In both instances, the efforts of the Americans to send vessels through the coastal ice-covered waters provoked the Soviet and Canadian governments to take action to strengthen their claims of control. The Soviet response was twofold. First, the Soviet Government stated that any future efforts to transit the Northern Sea Route without their explicit permission would be met with force. Second, the Soviets intensified their efforts to develop the use of the Northern Sea Route as a means of shipping goods along its northern communities.[35]

The Canadian response was somewhat different from that of the USSR. First, the Canadian government passed domestic legislation that established

33. W. E. Butler, *Northeast Passage* (Alphen aan den Rijin: Sijthoff and Noordhoff, 1978), pp. 122–23.

34. J. Kirton and D. Munton, "The *Manhattan* Voyages and their Aftermath," in *Politics of the Northwest Passage,* ed. F. Griffiths (Kingston and Montreal: McGill-Queen's University Press, 1987), pp. 67–97.

35. L. Tymchenko, "The Northern Sea Route," in *The Law of the Sea and Polar Maritime Delimitation and Jurisdiction,* ed. A. Oude Elferink and D. Rothwell (Hague: Maritinus Nijhoff, 2001), pp. 280–86.

extended jurisdictional zones for environmental regulations that exceeded existing international standards. The *Arctic Waters Pollution Prevention Act* (AWPPA) was passed in 1970.[36] In doing so, the Canadian government created functional control over its Arctic waters from its coast to a limit of 100 nautical miles. This legislation thus set an important precedent in the expansion of offshore coastal maritime zones. By avoiding a direct claim over the waters, the Canadian Government hoped that it could still establish its right to unilaterally set environmental and safety standards, but at the same time avoid provoking a direct response from the United States. While the American Government did not accept the Canadian claim, it did not make a direct challenge to the Canadian steps.

To consolidate its claim, the Canadian government then pursued a multilateral policy of building an international acceptance of its actions.[37] Its initial efforts to organize an international conference looking solely at the issue of Arctic waters failed to gain the necessary international support. However, by the beginning of the 1970s, it became apparent to Canadian diplomats that the commencement of the UNCLOS III would offer an opportunity for the Canadian government to build international support for its action. In part, this was due to the fact that independent of the Canadian efforts to justify its Arctic claim there were growing international pressures to extend the right of coastal states over the waters adjacent to their coasts.[38] Ultimately these pressures led to the creation of the Exclusive Economic Zone (EEZ). The novelty of the EEZ is that while it gave coastal states sovereign rights over the resources to a distance of 200 nautical miles, it did not eliminate some of the traditional international freedoms of the sea, the most important being that of navigation. However, as established in Article 56.1(b), the Convention also gave coastal states responsibilities for environmental protection within the EEZ. In short, the Convention provided a major transformation to the expansion of state control in its adjacent ocean territories.

The Canadian government attempted to take advantage of this changing international view on the creation of new zones of control by proposing the development of a clause that would call for the protection of special ocean zones in "exceptionally vulnerable areas." This protection would allow the coastal state to have the right to develop nondiscriminatory regulations that exceeded internationally agreed standards. However, there was resistance by many of the shipping nations to such a broad clause. Between the introduction of this clause by Canada at the first meeting in Caracas in 1974

36. Kirton and Munton (n. 34 above), pp. 85–93.

37. C. Sanger, *Ordering the Oceans: The Making of the Law of the Sea* (Toronto: University of Toronto Press, 1987), pp. 113–16.

38. R. Churchill and A. Rowe, *The Law of the Sea,* 2nd ed. (Manchester: Manchester University Press, 1988), pp. 133–34.

and the third meeting in New York in 1976, the clause was narrowed to only refer to ice-covered waters.[39] At the end of the 1976 meeting, an agreement was reached to include Article 43 in the Revised Single Negotiating Text. This was revised to Article 234 for the final formal agreement that became the Law of the Sea Convention. The final clause stated the following:

> Coastal States have the right to adopt and enforce non-discriminatory laws and regulations for the prevention, reduction and control of marine pollution from vessels in ice-covered areas within the limits of the exclusive economic zone, where particularly severe climatic conditions and the presence of ice covering such areas for most of the year create obstructions or exceptional hazards to navigation, and pollution of the marine environment could cause major harm to or irreversible disturbance of the ecological balance. Such laws and regulations shall have due regard to navigation and the protection and preservation of the maritime environment based on the best available scientific evidence.[40]

In effect, Canada was successful in internationalizing its efforts to control the environmental protection of its Arctic waters.

The Canadian delegation during the negotiations had endeavoured to ensure that the United States and Soviet Union would not see this clause as harming the right of navigation for their naval units. Article 236 in effect grants governmental vessels immunity from the environmental elements of the Convention. The effect of this protected the navies of both the USSR and United States from the condition of Article 234.

After the adoption of Article 234, both the USSR and Canada used the clause to bolster their claims over their respective Arctic waters. The Canadian Government cited Article 234 as a means of establishing the Canadian claims to the Northwest Passage in 1985 when an American icebreaker sailed through the Passage causing another dispute between Canada and the United States. The response of the American government to this particular line of argument was that because the *Polar Sea* is a government vessel, Article 234 had no impact.[41] This dispute was subsequently resolved through a series of political accommodations between Canada and the United States.

The Soviet Union has also incorporated Article 234 to support its claim of control over the Northern Sea Route. In 1984, 2 years after the Convention was finalized and 13 years before the USSR ratified the Convention (12 March 1997) it passed two edicts that had a direct bearing on the Soviet

39. D. McRae, "The Negotiations of Article 234," in *Politics of the Northwest Passage,* ed. F. Griffiths (Kingston and Montreal: McGill-Queen's University Press, 1987), pp. 98–114.

40. Sanger (n. 37 above), p. 114.

41. R. Huebert, "Polar vision or tunnel vision: The making of Canadian arctic waters policy," *Marine Policy* 19, no. 4 (1995), p. 357.

employment of Article 234.[42] The first edict established a Soviet EEZ and the second created Northern protected zones. Entitled "On the Strengthening of the Protection of Nature in the Extreme North and Marine Areas Adjacent to the Northern Coast of the USSR," this edict established the means for creating these zones and set the conditions for navigation in these waters. Specifically, the "Regulation for Navigation of the Seaways of the Northern Sea Route" clearly bases its right to regulate international shipping in its northern waters on Article 234. Both the edict and the regulations do not cite the article per se, but use the terminology of the article by stating that it reserves the right to regulate for the

> . . . purposes of ensuring safe navigation and preventing, reducing and keeping under control marine environmental pollution from vessels since the specifically severe climatic conditions that exist in the Arctic Regions and the presence of ice during the most part of the year bring about obstacles, or increased danger to navigation while pollution of sea ice on the Northern Coast of the USSR might cause great harm to the ecological balance or upset it irreparably, as well as inflict damage on the interests and well being of the North peoples.[43]

It is clear the Soviet Union, and subsequently the Russian Federation, have incorporated Article 234 as the international means to take specific actions in protecting Northern waters.

The Russian and Canadian governments' actions demonstrate that Article 234 has the capacity to provide a framework for the development of an international regime governing international shipping in the Arctic. It recognizes the need to develop special environmental standards, ship construction standards, and ship safety requirements. However, it also needs to be acknowledged that there has been little effort to develop an international approach to such a regime except in the case of the Polar Code. This will be discussed in the next section.

After the coming into force of the Convention, there has been little attention given by the institutions surrounding the Convention towards issues related to the Arctic. The two exceptions are with the Commission on the Limits of the Continental Shelf (CLCS) and the issue of marine protected zones.

Article 76 (8) and Annex II of the Convention established the CLCS as a means for states to determine their continental shelf. Once a state has ratified the Convention it has 10 years to determine the outer limits of its

42. Tymchenko (n. 35 above), p. 283.

43. Russian Federation, "Regulations for Navigation on the Seaways of the Northern Sea Route," reproduced in *International Challenges* 12, no. 1 (1992), pp. 121–26.

shelf. It then is required to deposit these limits to the CLCS for verification. Of the Arctic states that have a continental shelf, only Russia has submitted its claim to the CLCS.[44] Both Canada and the United States have not ratified the Convention and are thus not yet eligible to make their submission.[45] The CLCS has not yet made its ruling on the Russian claim but the United States and Norway have already issued diplomatic notes disputing elements of the Russian's claims.[46] The main significance of claims resulting from Article 76 will be in regards to future oil and gas development. Beyond the 200-nautical mile limit of the EEZ to the 350 nautical mile limit of the continental shelf, the main issue is control of the seabed and subsoil resources. However, because the continental shelf of all Arctic states extends into the most northern regions of the globe, the development of any resources even with the impact of climate change will remain far into the future.

After the coming into force of the Convention, the UN General Assembly agreed to begin an Open-ended Informal Consultative Process on Oceans and the Law of the Sea.[47] The General Assembly then decided that the main focus of these consultations would be on 1) protecting vulnerable marine ecosystems and 2) the safety of navigation.[48] Recently, this process has included discussions on the sensitivity of Arctic ecosystems. A report by Olav Orheim points out that Russian northern shipping is expected to rise substantially by 2015 due to the increase in oil and gas development in northern Russia.[49] He warns of a substantially increased risk of pollution as a result.

As important as this process is, it has not moved beyond the identification of the problem. Furthermore, the risk to the Arctic is seen as simply one more additional problem for marine sensitive areas. Overall this means that the framework provided by the Convention has not been advanced.

44. UN, Oceans and the Law of the Sea, Division for Ocean Affairs and the Law of the Sea, "Commission on the Limits of the Continental Shelf (CLCS) Outer Limits of the Continental Shelf beyond 200 nautical miles from the baselines: Submissions to the Commission: Submission by the Russian Federation," 16 June 2003, http://www.un.org/Depts/los/clcs_new/commission_submissions.htm (accessed 14 July 2003).

45. A. Oude Elferink, "The Outer Continental Shelf in the Arctic: The Application of Article 76 of the LOS Convention in a Regional Context," in *The Law of the Sea and Polar Maritime Delimitation and Jurisdiction,* ed. A. Oude Elferink and D. Rothwell (Hague: Maritinus Nijhoff, 2001), pp. 152–55. Canada subsequently ratified UNCLOS in November 2003.

46. Ibid.

47. United Nations General Assembly. Resolution 54/33. 24 November 1999.

48. United Nations General Assembly. Report on the Work of the United Nations Open-ended Informal Consultative Process on Oceans and the Law of the Sea. A/58/53. 6 June 2003, p. 3.

49. O. Orheim, "Protecting the Environment of the Arctic Ecosystem" (paper presented to the Panel on Protecting Vulnerable Marine Ecosystems – United Nations Open-ended Informal Consultative Process on Oceans and the Law of the Sea at the Fourth Meeting, New York, 2–6 June, 2003).

However, there have been some efforts outside of the Convention that have attempted to provide a multilateral framework for responding to the challenges faced by the Arctic.

DEVELOPMENT OF NEW ARCTIC INTERNATIONAL INSTITUTIONS AND INITIATIVES

The end of the Cold War has seen several attempts to develop the necessary international instruments to improve international cooperation in the Arctic. The four initiatives that are most important to the discussion of this analysis are the Arctic Environmental Protection Strategy (AEPS), the Arctic Council, the Polar Code, and the Russian Northern Sea Route.

New opportunities for the development of international cooperation in the Arctic region arose even before the Cold War ended. In 1987, Mikhail Gorbachev made the first overture for improved cooperation in a speech that he gave in Murmansk.[50] He called on Northern nations to forsake the military rivalries that had frozen circumpolar cooperation. Specifically, he called for the development of a "zone of peace" in the Arctic Ocean. Because it was the Soviet leader who made the offer, this initiative was important. However, Western leaders questioned his sincerity. This was due to his exclusion of the Soviet naval bases in the Kola Peninsula from the zone of peace. The result was that his initiative was seen as only a ploy to eliminate the presence of NATO submarines from northern waters off the Kola Peninsula.

However, Gorbachev's other reforms did act as the catalyst that ultimately led to improved international cooperation in the Arctic. Ultimately, these reforms led to the end of the Soviet Union. When this occurred, many saw the opportunity to initiate new cooperative initiatives. The focus of most of these efforts was made to address environmental issues. Well before the collapse of the Soviet Union, scientific research had discovered a paradox. Although the Arctic region had little industrial activity, researchers found substantial amounts of pollutants in the area.[51] These included a large variety of different substances, including persistent organic pollutants (fertilizers and pesticides), mercury, and radionuclide pollution. Subsequent research demonstrated that these pollutants originated from southern latitudes but were being carried to the Arctic through water and air currents. Owing to the distances that these pollutants were travelling, they became known as transboundary pollutants. Given the nature of the earth's rotation, ocean

50. D. Scrivener, *Gorbachev's Murmansk Speech: The Soviet Initiative and Western Responses* (Olso: Norwegian Atlantic Committee, 1989).

51. L. Barrie, D. Gregor, B. Hargrave, R. Lake, R. Shearer, B. Tracy, and T Bidleman, "Arctic contaminants: sources, occurrences and pathways," *Science of the Total Environment* 122 (1992), pp. 1–74.

currents and wind patterns, the pollutants did not leave the Arctic but accumulated in the North once they were deposited. Thus an area of the globe that produces no pollution was acting as a major receptacle of international sources of pollution.[52] Once the research had shown that the entire Arctic was suffering from this process, it became clear that the only manner in which the problem could be properly addressed would be through improved international cooperation.

Arctic Environmental Protection Strategy

The first step taken towards addressing these problems was made on an ad hoc and restrained basis. The Finnish government with the close cooperation of Canadian officials decided that the best course of action was to proceed quickly and cheaply.[53] Rather than deal with existing institutions or agreements such as the Law of the Sea Convention or any other similar formal agreement, it was decided that a new body would be created to deal with various aspects of transboundary pollution, including but not limited to maritime pollution. By proceeding as rapidly as possible it was hoped to lock the new Russian government into cooperative action. At the same time, the American government was not likely to accept the creation of new formal international institutions.[54] In part, this was due to the American belief that formal multilateral solutions were costly and inefficient. Equally important was the political reality that Senator Jessie Helms as chair of the Senate committee on foreign relations was not allowing any new multilateral initiatives to be placed on the Senate agenda unless it was trade related. Given the American governmental division of powers, Helm's opposition to new multilateral initiatives prevented new international treaties from passing the American Congress.

The net result of these considerations was the creation of the AEPS as an agreement and not as an international organization. Based on a Canadian model called the Arctic Environmental Strategy (AES), the AEPS was intended to achieve two main objectives. First, it was to provide a forum of discussion and cooperation for the Arctic states. Second, it was to provide a means for identifying the different environmental problems these countries were facing in their northern territory. While many hoped that the AEPS could achieve a third objective of providing remedies for the identified

52. Perhaps the most detailed assessment of these processes is found in AMAP, *AMAP Assessment Report: Arctic Pollution Issues* (Oslo: Arctic Monitoring and Assessment Programme, 1998), pp. 1–844.

53. E. Rajakoski, "Multilateral Cooperation to Protect the Arctic Environment: The Finnish Initiative," in *The Arctic: Choices for Peace and Security* (Vancouver: Gordon Soules Book Publisher, 1989), pp. 54–55.

54. Huebert (n. 28 above), p. 51. The U.S. has become a signatory to the AEPS.

problems, it was recognized that such a goal would likely be too ambitious for its initial existence.

The Finnish and Canadian governments were able to convince the five other Arctic nations to join the initiative. These included Denmark (Greenland), Iceland, Norway, Sweden, and Russia. Developing on practices pioneered by Canada in the AES, several Northern aboriginal organizations were also invited to join the AEPS as "permanent participants."[55] These included the Inuit Circumpolar Conference, the Saami Council, and the Association of Indigenous Minorities of the North, Siberia, and the Far East of the Russian Federation (now known as the Russian Association of Indigenous Peoples of the North). These three organizations were given the right to participate in all of the activities of AEPS, except in regards to budget issues. Because AEPS had no formal budget, this was not an important omission. The significance of the official inclusion of these aboriginal bodies should not be underestimated. This was the first time that aboriginal bodies were given such standing in an international body and represented a very important first step in recognizing their role in circumpolar affairs.

To organize its actions, AEPS divided its activities among working groups and a task force. Originally there were four working groups. A task group was soon added. The four working groups were the Arctic Monitoring and Assessment Program (AMAP); Protection of the Arctic Marine Environment (PAME); Emergency Prevention, Preparedness and Response (EPPR); and Conservation of Arctic Flora and Fauna (CAFF).[56] At the second annual meeting of AEPS in Nuuk, Greenland, a fifth body was added, the Task Force on Sustainable Development.[57] Each of these bodies was required to develop a workplan that identified the problem that existed within their overall mandate. The bodies were then required to develop a means by which they would attempt to respond to the problem. However, it was always made clear that the working bodies and task group could not allocate the use of resources outside of those that individual Member States were willing to volunteer.

Arctic Council

The AEPS soon demonstrated that it was an excellent body for identifying Northern international environmental problems. However, it was also soon apparent that it lacked the political clout necessary to respond to the prob-

55. D. Scrivener, *Environmental Cooperation in the Arctic: From Strategy to Council, Security Policy Library No. 1* (Oslo: Norwegian Atlantic Committee, 1996).

56. *Arctic Environmental Protection Strategy* (Rovaniemi, Finland, 14 June 1991) in *International Legal Materials* 30 (1991), pp. 1624–69.

57. The Arctic Environmental Protection Strategy: Second Ministerial Conference, *The Nuuk Declaration on Environment in the Arctic* (Nuuk, Greenland, 16 September 1993), pp. 3–4.

lems that it was finding. Thus, efforts were made to develop a body that could provide the necessary political clout. Led by Canada, this initiative was conceived to provide a high-level political forum to discuss and act on a broader range of international Arctic issues. Ultimately the Canadian efforts to develop an international body were successful and the Arctic Council was officially formed in September 1996.[58]

Unfortunately, this body suffered from many of the same problems that plagued the AEPS. While the Council was conceived as a high-level political forum to give all Arctic issues a venue for discussion, the real focus of the body remained on further developing the existing work of the AEPS. As a condition of its membership the United States specifically stated that the Council could not address military-related issues. American reluctance to the creation of new international institutions also meant that the Council would not be entrenched in a formal treaty. Instead, the Arctic Council remained an agreement and not a treaty. The Council also did not receive its own source of revenues. Thus it remains dependent on the resources that are volunteered by its Member States, as was the case for the AEPS.[59]

The focus of the Arctic Council remains in the area of environmental examination. From a structural manner, the new organization was built on the AEPS. All of the working groups were retained and continued with their mandate. The Task Force on Sustainable Development was transformed into a working group. One of the new initiatives that was added was an Action Plan to Eliminate Pollution. It was primarily designed to coordinate research by the Member State and to develop an action plan. However, in keeping with the major limitations of the other working groups, the limited resources hinder the development of an effective international strategy.

Within both the AEPS and the Arctic Council, the one working group that has been mandated to deal specifically with maritime issues in the Arctic is PAME. The focus of most of the activities of the working group is on the protection of the marine environment. There are currently nine projects that are being conducted. They include updating an overview of international agreements and arrangements pertaining to the Arctic marine environment; promoting the 1997 guidelines for offshore oil development; implementing an action plan for the protection of the Arctic marine environment from land-based activities; supporting the national plan of action for the protection of the Arctic marine environment from anthropogenic pollution in the Russian Federation-Russian Pan-Arctic; developing Arctic waters oil transfer guidelines; developing follow-up activities to

58. Huebert (n. 28 above), pp. 52–56.

59. D. VanderZwaag, R. Huebert and S. Ferrara, "The Arctic Environmental Protection Strategy, Arctic Council and Multilateral Initiatives: Tinkering while the Marine Environment Totters," in *The Law of the Sea and Polar Maritime Delimitation and Jurisdiction,* ed. A. Oude Elferink and D. Rothwell (Hague: Maritinus Nijhoff, 2001), pp. 246–48.

address ship-generated waste; and providing a report on the state of current and potential shipping activities in the Arctic.[60]

Of these activities, most remain in the realm of problem identification. They are still attempting to come to terms with the nature of the problems facing the Arctic maritime environment. Even the study on shipping will be nothing more than an attempt to provide a "snapshot" of current activities. However, the need to undertake such a study also illustrates the dearth of information that currently exists on the topic. There simply is no understanding of current Arctic shipping capability beyond the ability to provide an overview of existing ships.

Recently, there have been efforts led by the United States to use the Arctic Council to examine transportation in the Arctic. The Circumpolar Infrastructure Task Force (CITF) was created in September 2000 as a program of the Arctic Council and the Northern Forum.[61] Part of the project includes an examination of maritime linkages in the north. It is focusing on assisting the Russian Government in the development of the Northern Sea Route.[62]

Overall the AEPS and the Arctic Council both represent important first steps in the development of international cooperation in the Arctic. They play an important role in that they bring together a set of international actors that have not had the opportunity or inclination to meet. However, as important as these initial steps have been, the substantive actions taken by these bodies have been limited by several factors. First, any steps taken can only be funded through voluntary contributions by the Member States. Second, the main course of action has been the identification of environmental threats and the establishment of remedial action. While such cooperation is critical, there is a need to implement the course of action that has been identified. For example, the EPPR has done excellent work in the creation of response guides in the event of an oil spill in Arctic waters. The creation of the guide was a Canadian initiative, but the guide is based on information provided by all of the Member States. However, efforts to develop a cooperative reactive capability to an oil spill are a long way off. Each Arctic State would still have to develop its own capacity according to its own means. Even PAME, the one working group that has been specifically mandated to deal with maritime environmental issues, has not been able to develop a mandate that goes beyond the determination of the maritime environmental issues facing the Arctic region.

60. Arctic Council, "*Activities*," http://www.arctic-council.org/activities.html#70 (accessed 8 July 2003).

61. The Northern Forum was another institution that was created to facilitate and promote economic and business relationships among northern regions. Its members are not the Arctic states, but the various political sub-units such as territories, provinces etc.

62. Circumpolar Infrastructure Task Force (CITF), "Presentation to the Northern Forum General Assembly" (St. Petersburg, Russia, April 2003).

Polar Code/Guidelines for Ships Operating in Arctic Ice-Covered Waters

The Polar Code was an initiative that was launched by Canadian officials in the early 1990s.[63] By the end of the 1980s it was beginning to become clear to many of the states with an interest in shipping in the Arctic that either climate change and/or oil and gas development would soon increase the amount of shipping in the Arctic. It made more sense to develop a common set of rules and regulations for shipping before this increase made any such harmonization impossible. Beginning in the early 1990s, a series of meetings under the auspices of the International Maritime Organization were held. These included officials from all of the Northern states with an interest in shipping, as well those associated with various insurance companies.

The original intent of these meetings was to harmonize the different approaches towards polar ship construction, safety standards, and operating procedures. Over the years, countries such as Canada and the USSR/Russia had developed different but similar rules. If shipping were to increase, a common set of rules would ensure that such an increase would take place in an efficient manner. By taking such a proactive initiative, it also stood to reason that the best environmental standards could be developed. Because the negotiations involved all of the Arctic shipping nations, it was logical to believe that such an initiative was also the best means of ensuring that any resulting code could be made mandatory. If all of the relevant players were at the negotiations and all came to an agreement, it is unclear why any state would not want the code to be enforceable. Unfortunately, the United States became that objecting state.

The initial Polar Code discussions attempted to cover vessels that operated in both polar regions. There was also an initial endeavour to make the code mandatory for all vessels operating in the Arctic. However, these efforts were opposed by the United States. Eventually, the other states conceded and the negotiations were soon developing voluntary guidelines for Arctic shipping.[64]

Throughout much of the negotiations, Article 234 of the Convention acted as the cornerstone. The preamble of the draft document in 2000 stated:

> 1.2 The need to develop safety and pollution control guidelines specific to polar operations has been recognized by several of the Administrations principally affected, by a number of classification societies, by

63. L. Brigham, "Commentary: An international polar navigation code for the twenty-first century," *Polar Record* 33, no. 187 (1997), 283.

64. L. Brigham, "The Emerging International Polar Navigation Code: Bi-polar Relevance?" in *Protecting the Polar Marine Environment: Law and Policy for Pollution Prevention,* ed. D. Vidas (Cambridge: Cambridge University Press, 2000), pp. 316–18.

> international organizations concerned with the polar environment, and by the United Nations itself. *Clause 234 of the Law of the Sea Convention (UNCLOS 82) gives Coastal States with ice-covered sea areas the right to "adopt and enforce non-discriminatory laws and regulations" for pollution control within their 200 mile Exclusive Economic Zones (EEZs).* [Emphasis added][65]

However, when an agreement was finally reached in 2003, all mention of the Convention and Article 234 had been removed. In its place was the recognition that "[s]hips operating in the Arctic environment are exposed to a number of unique risks."[66] In effect, the Code had become a guide to provide advice for vessels entering Arctic waters.

The technical information and guidance that the guide provides is important and useful. However, the final guide is substantially different from the vision of a Polar Code that existed when negotiations began. It is not clear why the United States Government objected to the idea of developing a code that would be mandatory for all vessels entering polar waters. They had experience with a major oil spill in northern waters when the *Exxon Valdez* ran around in 1989, and enacted strong legislation to protect against any future spills.[67] So it is not a question of the Americans not agreeing to strong environmental standards for Arctic shipping. Therefore it remains unclear from where their opposition originates.

Northern Sea Route

During the Cold War, the Soviet Union made extensive use of its Northern Sea Route.[68] As with all of the activities of the USSR, the shipping and escort that was provided was done on a state-controlled basis. This meant that there was not a requirement to ensure that such activity was undertaken on an economic basis. At the same time, it is also evident that the Soviet regime was not particularly concerned about the impact that their activities had on the Northern environment.[69] After the collapse of the USSR, the Russian Federation then began to look for ways in which the route could be made economically viable. To this end, the Russian government has entered into a series of agreements to study the requirements of the route.

65. Transport Canada, *Guidelines for Ships Operating in Arctic Waters*, http://www.tc.gc.ca/polarcode/imo_version_of_code.html (accessed 3 July 2000), p. 3.

66. International Maritime Organization, *Guidelines for Ships Operating in Arctic Ice-Covered Waters*. MSC/Circ.1056, MEPC/Circ. 399. 23 December 2002, p. 2.

67. J. Feeble and N. Forbes, *Out of Channel: The Exxon Valdez Oil Spill in Prince William Sound* (Eastern Washington University Press, 1999).

68. Tymchenko (n. 35 above), p. 274.

69. M. Feshbach and A. Friendly, *Ecocide in the USSR* (New York: Basic Books, 1992).

The first of such studies was titled International Northern Sea Route Programme (INSROP) and took place between 1993 to 1999.[70] It was conducted through a partnership between the Fridtjof Nansen Institute of Norway, the Ship and Ocean Foundation of Japan, and the Central Marine Research and Design Institute of Russia.[71] The research undertaken was divided into four themes: 1) natural conditions and ice navigation; 2) environmental factors; 3) trade and commercial shipping aspects; and 4) political, legal, and strategic factors. These led to 167 working papers that examined a wide range of issues. The general finding was that "in spite of climatic, technological and political restraints, an increase in commercial shipping is feasible in economic, technological and environmental terms."[72]

A second study was undertaken by the European Commission and the Russian Federation and was called Arctic Demonstration and Exploratory Voyage beginning in 1997. The objective of this study was to undertake a test voyage of European and Russian vessels to determine if year-round navigation of the Northern Sea Route was possible.[73] Four vessels were used, a tanker and three icebreakers. As in the case of the INSROP study, it was found that "year-round navigation in the western part of the Northern Sea Route was economically feasible even in the harshest winter conditions for the last 33 years."[74]

A follow-up study entitled Arctic Operational Platform (ARCOP) was launched at the end of 2002 between the Russian government and European Union. It was officially launched on 31 January 2003 and will run for 3 years.[75] It will examine the transportation of oil in the Russian Arctic and will include a maritime dimension. This study is predicated on the expectation that the Russian government will be developing a new export and loading for crude oil in the Murmansk area. When this new port facility is completed it will then be joined by pipeline to Russian oil developments in its northern region. If this project is completed it will result in a substantial increase in maritime oil shipments from the western Russian Arctic and offshore Norway. The intent of the ARCOP project is to determine how this increase in traffic can be undertaken in a safe and environmentally protective fashion.

70. L. Brigham, "The Northern Sea Route, 1999–2000," *Polar Record* 37, no. 203 (2001), p. 332–34.

71. Tymchenko (n. 35 above), p. 275.

72. Ibid.

73. European Commission Transport RTD Programme, "Waterborne Research: ARCDEV" 12 December 1999, http://www.cordis.lu/transport/src/srcdev.htm (accessed 7 June 2000).

74. European Commission Transport RTD Programme of the 4th Framework Programme. *Public Summary of the ARCDEV Project* (no date), p. 3.

75. Finland, Ministry of Trade and Industry, "Press Release – ARCOT Project Launched: Finland Participating in Development of Russia's Oil Transport," (31 January 2003).

Recently, the International Arctic Science Committee (IASC) has announced that it will be commencing another study that will examine a new project on Arctic marine transport in 2003 titled Marine Transport and Changing Access in the Arctic Ocean. It will examine Arctic ice change and assess the impact of these changes on maritime transport routes in the Arctic Ocean and Baltic Sea.[76] This will include both the Northern Sea Route and the Northwest Passage.[77]

The Russians are not only engaged in extensive research with their European neighbours, but have also been increasing the size of their commercial ice-strengthened fleet. LUKOIL, a Russian company that owns Murmansk Shipping Company, placed an order to build 10 new ice-strengthened oil tankers at the end of the 1990s.[78] The first five were built in Germany and the last five are being built in Russia.[79] This means that as the Russians improve their knowledge of the challenges and opportunities to use the Northern Sea Route, they are also strengthening their ability to use it. Ultimately, however, this knowledge and capability will be Russian. As the Russians improve their capability it seems unlikely that they will be willing to agree to international rules governing ship construction, safety, and operation.

THE ROAD FORWARD

The question then arises as to where the international community goes from here. The expected impact of climate change will make the entire Arctic region considerably more accessible to southern interests and activities. Even if climate change was not occurring, the Arctic will see increased activity because of the increased development of oil and gas resources. It is not entirely clear as to what degree this activity will increase and when it will occur, but it will be sooner rather than later. The question then remains how can the international community prepare?

The two major objectives that must determine any action are that the increased activity and shipping in particular must take place in an environmentally sustainable and safe manner. Even with the reduction of the ice

76. PAME, "Program for the Protection of the Arctic Marine Environment: Working Group Meeting Report," no. I-2003, (25–27 February 2003) Stockholm, Sweden, p. 9.

77. IASC, "IASC Project Catalogue 2003—Marine Transportation and Changing Access in the Arctic Ocean" (12 March 2003), http://www.iasc.no/ProjectCatalogue/MarTrans.htm (accessed 10 July 2003).

78. Murmansk Shipping Company, "Company History" (2000), http://msco.ru/web_main/en/company.htm (accessed 10 July 2003).

79. Murmansk Shipping Company, "Fleet – Cargo Fleet – Tankers" (2000), http://www.msco.ru/web_main/en/fleet_trans2_2.htm (accessed 10 July 2003).

cover, the Arctic will remain a dangerous region for shipping activity. Second, the expansion of commercial activity must also be accomplished in a manner that does not omit those who live in the North and in particular the Northern aboriginal peoples. Communities that exist along the Northern Sea Route and the Northwest Passage need to share in the economic advantages that an increase in economic activity such as shipping will bring. These same communities must also be protected from the dangers that will accompany these new expansions.

Unfortunately, as this analysis has shown there is reason to be concerned about the international community's ability to achieve both of these objectives. There is no doubt that considerable effort has gone into some attempts to achieve both objectives. UNCLOS was designed to be the constitution for the oceans[80] and does contain articles that could act as a framing instrument for management of the Arctic waters. The AEPS and the Arctic Council were created to allow for the discussion of major issues at high political levels among Arctic states and the Northern aboriginal peoples. There have even been initiatives such as the Polar Code by which officials from Northern states have attempted to kick start regulations for the safe and environmental use of shipping in the Arctic. But the joining theme of each of these international initiatives is that they have not been able to move very far beyond individual state interests when it comes to the Arctic.

In the case of UNCLOS it is clear that the driving force for the inclusion of Article 234 came about only because of important national interests that Canada wished to pursue through multilateral means. Canada needed to gain international support for its domestic legislation, the AWPPA. Canadian officials were looking for a means to assert sovereignty over the Northwest Passage without over-aggravating the United States. The fact that the route that was taken provided protection for the environment was an added bonus for Canadian officials but was not the driving concern. The failure of any state, Canada included, to build on Article 234 since the Convention came into force demonstrates the lack of political will that exists to create a multilateral regime governing international shipping in the Arctic.

Likewise the inability of the Arctic Council to move beyond environmental issues also suggests a lack of political will. There have been no shortages of attempts to do so, but the continued under funding of the Council's activities means that such efforts almost inevitably have been unsuccessful. This is not to suggest that the current efforts of the Council to understand the environmental problems facing the North have been insignificant, but success in providing remedial action has been limited. This has been particularly true of issues relating to shipping and other related maritime activities.

80. T. Koh, "A Constitution for the Oceans," in *The Law of the Sea: United Nations Convention on the Law of the Sea with Index and Final Act of the Third United Nations Conference on the Law of the Sea* (New York: UN, 1983), pp. xxxii–xxxvii.

The Polar Code was an initiative that should have been picked up by the Arctic Council and supported by the senior leadership of all of the Arctic nations. Its potential to have provided the means to establish a sustainable set of rules and guidelines was high. But it never received the political support that it needed. As a set of guidelines it will provide important information for companies that wish to operate in the North. But because the guidelines remain voluntary, its potential impact will be more limited.

Thus the core question remains, how can the Arctic be prepared for the coming increased maritime activity? The pieces for effective and fair international actions are in place. The LOS Convention provides the international framework for an extended protection of the Arctic maritime environment; the Arctic Council provides the political framework for bringing together senior Arctic leaders and Northern aboriginal peoples; and the Polar Code/Guidelines provide the first step at working out the technical requirements of the regulations that need to govern all shipping.

The time has arrived to join these pieces by applying the ideals of Elisabeth Mann Borgese to the Arctic. Professor Borgese's demonstration of what was possible for spurring the international community into better cooperation now needs to be turned into reality in the Arctic. Her determination and success to move the world beyond parochial state interests when it came to the oceans showed this is possible. Thus it is now necessary for those who wish to see the Arctic prepared for the coming changes it will face to redouble their efforts to develop meaningful international cooperation. It is an easy prescription to describe; it is a difficult one to apply. But the need exists for all interested parties to continue their pressure on their respective governments. Cooperation needs to be developed now before the Arctic is opened to an uncontrolled explosion of shipping and maritime activity.

Participation and Compliance in International Law

M.C.W. Pinto
Attorney of the Supreme Court of Sri Lanka

My last letter to Elisabeth, and her—as usual, prompt—response to it dated 25 September 2001, concerned the thoughts that struggle for expression in this article. I do not think she would mind if wider currency were given to what she wrote:

> My first reaction to any form of weighting votes is suspicion. No matter how you do it, it will always work out in favour of the rich. Because education, health, "freedom", international activity, all are linked somehow to wealth, even though it may be difficult to establish a "cause and effect" relationship.
>
> Interestingly enough, Arvid had designed a rather intricate system of weighted voting in his Draft Ocean Space Convention of 1971. The formula was based on population, size of territory, length of coastline, use of ocean resources, and a few other things . . .
>
> I was critical of the scheme at the time. I still suspected that somehow it *must* favour the rich. I also thought it was too complex to work out in practice . . .
>
> Now, I would also add that it seems to me extremely difficult to design one system for all uses, e.g., don't you think that ocean organizations would use different criteria from an Outer Space Organization?
>
> All this does not mean that I want to reject your proposal. I think that the pages you sent me are intensely interesting and based on an experience which we have shared. I would be glad to do some work on it . . .

By the way she lived, as by her thought; by her generosity, as by her steadfastness of purpose, Elisabeth inspired, and continues to inspire us all.

DO STATES OBEY INTERNATIONAL LAW?

In an essay in 1997, Professor Harold Honju Koh asked: "Why do Nations Obey International Law?"[1] He offered a tentative response in the course of

1. H. H. Koh, "Why do nations obey international law?," *Yale Law Journal* 106 (1997): 2599 et seq.

Ocean Yearbook 18: 220–245

his review of two significant works that had then recently appeared, dealing with the subject of compliance with, or obedience to, rules of international law.[2] Having examined several analyses of rule-generating conduct among States, which place emphasis on the *legitimacy* of the originating process (and presumably also of the responsive process), as well as the fairness inherent in the *distributive outcome,* he summarizes the process by which obedience to a rule is brought about, in the following terms:

> . . . such a process can be viewed as having three phases. One or more transnational actors provokes an *interaction* (or series of interactions) with another, which forces an *interpretation* or enunciation of the global norm applicable to the situation. By doing so, the moving party seeks not simply to coerce the other party, but to *internalize* the new interpretation of the international norm into the other party's internal normative system. The aim is to "bind" that other party to obey the interpretation as part of its internal value set. Such a transnational legal process is normative, dynamic, and constitutive. The transaction generates a legal rule which will guide future transnational interactions between the parties; future transactions will further internalize those norms; and eventually, repeated participation in the process will help to reconstitute the interests and even the identities of the participants in the process.[3]

Attractive as are these analyses of the compliance process, they seem more related to the formation of rules of customary international law, where disparity of power between a strong "provoker" State and a weak "interpreter" State is likely to speed "internalization" and, ultimately, compliance. It seems less descriptive of the complexities of the multilevel negotiation of rules of international law that takes place at a plenipotentiary conference under the auspices of the United Nations. Whereas there, "internalization" would seem to remain an essential ingredient in the foundation of compliance, a rule formulated as expressing the will of the majority of States at such a conference is less likely to "provoke," in an unwilling minority of the powerful, an "interpretation" that would lead them to "internalize" and eventually to comply with, the rule so formulated. When considering the rules formulated at such conferences and intended to become international law, the observer may well be led to ask a different question: "Do States observe international law?" to which the dissident few might well respond, "But we do not hold such rules to be the law, and so do not need to comply with them." According

2. A. Chayes and H. C. Chayes, *The New Sovereignty: Compliance with International Regulatory Agreements* (Cambridge, Mass.: Harvard University Press, 1995); T. M. Franck, *Fairness in International Law and Institutions* (Oxford: Clarendon Press, 1995).
3. Koh (n. 1 above), p. 2599.

to the rules governing "internalization" (e.g., signature, ratification, and national legislation) operative today, they would be right.

The "legitimacy" of the "provoker" of the interaction (at such conferences, the majority seeking change), is founded on participation in the rule-making process. It is confronted by the "legitimacy" of the "interpreter" States, secure in the genuine independence conferred by economic and political power, and their rejection of the invitation to "internalize." Thus, rule making on the basis of the expressed will of the participating States, even of the overwhelming majority of them, continues to be subject to the power of the few. In this respect little has changed in the realities of international rule making since the Congress of Vienna,[4] or, for that matter, since Athens forced the Island of Melos to join its empire.[5]

Whereas international rule making continues to be led and controlled by a few States with the power to do so, there have been far-reaching social and political changes within those very States, which could make changes possible at the international level. The establishment of democracy within States and the phenomenal development of telecommunications technology now enables opinions to cross borders and influence whole populations. Because the technology and other resources required for dissemination lie largely within the control of the powerful, opinions are today mainly projected outwards from them to influence the rest. But progress is possible there, and if the great majority of countries, home to the overwhelming majority of the world's people, have something to say, they can now convey their message in the expectation that, in time, it will elicit a sympathetic

4. As was observed of the prototype of the modern international conference:

. . . the Congress of Vienna as a congress of all Europe was never constituted. It remained a Congress of the Great Powers, who for their convenience had summoned the smaller Powers of Europe to meet them. The idea of a constituent assembly, imagined by some . . . was found to be impossible. The large number of small States made such an assembly impracticable in any case. But the wishes of the masters of Europe were from the first clear and unbending on this point. They considered themselves as 'Europe', and at the Congress they asserted successfully the ascendancy of the Great Powers. The smaller States were only to be admitted at such times and on such terms as suited those who had great resources and armies at their command.

C. K. Webster, *The Congress of Vienna 1814–1815* (London: G. Bell & Sons Ltd., 1919), p. 77.

5. In the strikingly timeless "Melian dialogue," the Athenian negotiators explain ". . . the standard of justice depends on the equality of power to compel and that in fact the strong do what they have the power to do, and the weak accept what they have to accept." Thucydides, *The Peloponnesian War,* Book 5, para. 89 (trans. R. Warner) (London, Penguin Books, 1972), p. 402.

response from within the citadels of the powerful. But what would that message be? What message could unite those who seek change, and at the same time, be understood by, and appear persuasive to, those who are content with the quality of their lives and are not easily moved to welcome change?

Recent developments seem to offer a glimmer of hope. In recent years, in all countries, rich and poor alike, breakdown of the social order leading to violence and economic failure have led all to consider whether a remedy might lie in a new emphasis to be given, through massive educational programmes, to basic human values such as compassion, justice, forgiveness, trust, and ultimately, the treatment of others in the manner desired for oneself. Such an emphasis, frequently met with in the realms of religion and spirituality, seems now to have penetrated to the government level, and may even be about to reach the corporate sector.

If such a trend were to continue, fostered by the education policies of governments, and directed to the creation of a new generation that had firmly internalized those values, ways might be found to renew the structure of international law through rule making at universal conferences. Although State representatives at law-formulating conferences would continue to take positions that accord with self-serving national policies, decisions at such conferences could be so taken as to demonstrate clearly their foundation in human values commonly recognized, and so influence all peoples, including those within powerful States, to demand that their representatives show respect for those decisions and eventually ratify, internalize, and comply with them.

The modern practice of inviting universal participation in the negotiation and formulation of international law rules under the auspices of the United Nations has sometimes fancifully been described as "democratic." However, plenipotentiaries at such conferences represent the hierarchies of States, not necessarily their peoples. While the interests of a people may be deemed to be reflected in the pronouncements of their State's representatives, especially if the State is democratically organized, the impact of other interests, including the shared interests among leadership hierarchies, gives power a significant role that may yet frustrate the emergence of a people's view at such a gathering.

This article will offer examples of how power may operate effectively to frustrate the will of the great majority of States in relation to rule formation and rule observance. The article then suggests that, by modifying the voting systems at rule-formulating conferences or in other international bodies, their decisions could be more reflective of measures needed to give effect to the needs and aspirations of the great majority of the world's peoples, and not merely of the policies of those States which, by deploying their economic and political power, seek to prevent the slightest deviation from the status quo that keeps them firmly in control.

"DEMOCRATIC" RULE FORMATION AND COUNTERVAILING POLITICAL POWER: THE THIRD UNITED NATIONS CONFERENCE ON THE LAW OF THE SEA

The inexorable impact of the power of a State or group of States on the modern rule-making conference process may be seen in the history of initiatives pursued throughout a quarter of a century (1967–1992) in negotiations over a variety of subjects and issues concerning the law of the sea. Those negotiations took place among representatives of some 170 States at the Third United Nations Conference on the Law of the Sea, and, after signature of the resulting Convention in 1982, at a Preparatory Commission charged with laying the groundwork for giving it effect. By general agreement among the participants, the negotiations were governed by rules of procedure based on those of the United Nations General Assembly, providing for decisions to be taken by simple or qualified majorities of States' representatives present and voting, each State having one vote equal in weight or value with every other.[6]

In these complex negotiations, scientific, military, and commercial concerns in the form of draft legal rules competed for acceptance by required voting majorities, with political support from proponent groups of States motivated by both national interest and ideological considerations, the two being frequently intertwined. The fundamental issues on which the Conference was divided may be outlined as follows. On one side were the rela-

6. See the *Rules of Procedure of the Third United Nations Conference on the Law of the Sea* (adopted 27 June 1974, as amended, A/CONF.62/30/Rev.3), chapter VI (Decision-making), which provides, inter alia, for deferment of voting for specified "cooling-off" periods, notice of voting, and presidential mediation, all intended to ensure that "The Conference should make every effort to reach agreement on substantive matters by way of consensus, and there should be no voting on such matters until all efforts at consensus have been exhausted." (*Declaration incorporating the "Gentlemen's Agreement,"* made by the President and endorsed by the Conference at its 19th meeting on 27 June 1974, and approved by the UN General Assembly at its 2169th meeting on 16 November 1974). A leading authority describes the operation of this "qualified consensus rule" as follows: "It may be defined briefly as taking a decision only when no participant opposes it so strongly as to insist on blocking it; a consensus can thus bridge wide, though not all too deep, differences. But since an unqualified consensus rule still permits any participant to exercise a veto, and thus, if determined and independent enough, to exact a high price for its agreement, the now frequently used qualified rule maintains the possibility of reverting to voting if the consensus process breaks down. This alternative is, however, resorted to only if the dissenters are considered to constitute a small, unreasonable and substantively overrideable minority. In practice, the threat to revert to voting is one merely maintained in the background to prevent any egregious abuse of the general desire to do business by consensus." P. C. Szasz, "Improving the International Legislative Process," in P. C. Szasz, *Selected Essays on Understanding International Institutions and the Legislative Process* (Ardsley, N.Y.: Transnational Publishers, 2001), p. 16.

tively few economically developed industrialized countries possessing extensive merchant and naval fleets, and concerned to preserve (1) economic ascendancy and competitive advantage, as well as the source thereof, which they believed to lie in free (or minimally regulated) enterprise, guaranteeing access to the oceans' fisheries and mineral wealth; and (2) the prime means of protecting both ascendancy and its source, namely the lawfulness of free (or minimally regulated) transit by military and merchant vessels through all maritime areas not falling within recognized limits of coastal State jurisdiction. Opposed to them were an overwhelming majority comprised essentially of States at various earlier stages of economic development, advocating (1) commitment to dirigistic (or minimally free) economic policies governing access to, and exploitation of, all marine resources, inspired by the principles of a New International Economic Order based on inter-State cooperation and preferential treatment of less developed countries (instead of competition and self-help), and believed by them to be the basis for the establishment of a more humane and peaceful world; and (2) coastal State regulation of transit of all foreign vessels, both military and merchant, through generously conceived extents of national jurisdiction over adjacent marine areas.[7]

In resolving what often appeared to be an impasse of unprecedented proportions, most industrialized countries, confident of maintaining economic ascendancy through their scientific and technological superiority, conceded a system for seabed mineral exploitation embodied in Part XI of the Convention, that contained certain apparent constraints on free enterprise, and thus concessions in the direction of the economic "dirigism" favoured by the developing countries. Most developing countries, in turn, conceded the essentials of freedom of maritime transit urged by the industrialised countries. These two sets of complementary concessions formed the basis of what was agreed as a "package deal" the essence of which was described by the President of the Conference, Ambassador Tommy Koh as follows:

> . . . the provisions of the Convention are closely interrelated and form an integral package. Thus it is not possible for a State to pick what it

7. These negotiations, which in many respects laid the foundations of modern multilateral conference procedures and practices, have been documented by many scholars, for example, A. L. Hollick, *U.S. Foreign Policy and the Law of the Sea* (Princeton, N.J.: Princeton University Press, 1981); A. M. Post, *Deepsea Mining and the Law of the Sea* (The Hague: M. Nijhoff Publishers, 1983); R. C. Ogley, *Internationalizing the Seabed* (Brookfield, Vt.: Gower, 1984); J. K. Sebenius, *Negotiating the Law of the Sea* (Cambridge, Mass.: Harvard University Press, 1984); S. Mahmoundi, *The Law of Deep Sea-bed Mining: A Study of the Progressive Development of International Law Concerning the Management of the Polymetallic Nodules of the Deep Sea-bed* (Stockholm: Almquist & Wiksell International, 1987); M. G. Schmidt, *Common Heritage or Common Burden?* (Oxford: Clarendon Press, 1989); and E. L. Miles, *Global Ocean Politics: The Decision Process at the Third United Nations Conference on the Law of the Sea* (The Hague: Martinus Nijhoff Publishers, 1998).

> likes and to disregard what it does not like. It was also said that rights and obligations go hand in hand and it is not permissible to claim rights under the Convention without being willing to shoulder the corresponding obligations.[8]

It proved possible, nevertheless, for one country, the most influential and powerful of all, having participated actively and positively in the negotiations, to stand outside the package deal and to raise, with the support of some industrialized countries, the prospect of frustration of the outcome if their demands were not met. Having collaborated in the drafting of all of the Convention's provisions, including those of Part XI on seabed mining, and relying on a strategy of post-Conference adjustment of unwelcome provisions when subsequently negotiating detailed mining regulations at the Preparatory Commission stage, the United States delegation had actively sought compromise with the developing countries on the Convention's seabed mining provisions, inspired by the multilateralism that was then a feature of its Presidential policies. However, the political changes that swept President Reagan into office in 1981, and the review of United States' policies that followed, led to radical changes in the attitude of the U.S. negotiators. At the penultimate stage of the Conference, and on the threshold of formal adoption of a text representing a "package deal," a new U.S. delegation announced six objectives involving changes to the Convention's seabed mining provisions (Part XI) that would make possible U.S. support for the text. Those changes would, however, if incorporated, have resulted in complete negation of the initiatives with respect to the seabed mining regime resolutely pursued by the developing countries throughout the preceding decade.[9]

But the United States' proposals had come too late. On 29 April 1982, the draft Convention embodying the "package deal" was adopted by a vote

8. Ambassador Koh's remarks reproduced in "A Constitution for the Oceans," published by the United Nations in its handbook containing the Convention. See Official Records of the Third United Nations Conference on the Law of the Sea, vol. XVII (United Nations, 1983, Sales No. E.84.V.3), document A/CONF.62/122.

9. The Convention's provisions (a) should not deter the development of any deep seabed mineral resources to meet national and world demand; (b) should assure national access to those resources by . . . qualified entities to enhance United States security or supply, avoid monopolization of the resources by the Enterprise, and promote the economic development of the resources; (c) should provide a decision-making role in the deep seabed regime that reflects the political and economic interests and financial contributions of participating states; (d) should not allow for amendments to come into force without approval of the participating states, including . . . the advice and consent of the United States Senate; (e) should not set other undesirable precedents for international organizations; and (f) should be likely to receive the advice and consent of the Senate; the Convention should not contain provisions for the mandatory transfer of technology and participation by and funding for national liberation movements. U.S. State Department, *Current Policy*, No. 371 (Jan.–Feb. 1982).

of 130 in favour (most of the developing countries, and also Canada, France, Japan, the Nordic countries, Australia, and New Zealand), to four against (the United States, Israel, Venezuela, and Turkey), with 17 abstentions (nine socialist countries, Britain, West Germany, Belgium, The Netherlands, Luxembourg, Italy, Spain, and Thailand). The Convention was opened for signature at Montego Bay in Jamaica on 10 December 1982, and was signed by an unprecedented number of participating States that very day. On that occasion, UN Secretary-General Javier Perez de Cuellar observed:

> The new law of the sea thus created is not simply the result of a process of action and reaction among the most powerful countries but the product of the will of an overwhelming majority of nations from all parts of the world, at different levels of development and having diverse geographical characteristics in relation to the oceans, which combined to make a wind of change blow at the universal level. . . . Never in the history of international relations have such a large number of countries immediately signed the result of their deliberations thereby committing themselves to act in accordance with their obligations. This is a particularly important lesson to emerge from this Conference.[10]

But whatever the wind that blew through that decade-long conference, it would do little to bring fundamental change, or advancement of the developing countries' aspirations thought to have been embodied in Part XI of the Convention. At first, the developing countries, ignoring the critical stance maintained by the United States and some industrialised countries, treated the signed text of the Convention as immutable. The efforts of the latter to secure adjustments to the text that might have garnered some support among the developing countries, were met with legal and moral arguments that were difficult to counter: the sanctity attached to a carefully negotiated text that had been formally adopted by an overwhelming majority of participating States; had been signed by a comparable majority and already presented by many to their national legislatures for ratification; and the declared commitment to treat the outcome of the Conference as a "package deal" that a participant might accept or reject, but from which no selective withdrawal would be acceptable. One might search the 1969 Vienna Convention on the Law of Treaties in vain for some provision that would authorize selective adjustment of the text of a multilateral convention that was already well on its way to securing the number of ratifications needed for its entry into force.

It seemed, therefore, that if any radical surgery affecting Part XI of the Convention were to be attempted, it would have to secure the consent of

10. J. Perez de Cuellar, Statement made on 10 December 1982 at the final session of the Third UN Conference on the Law of the Sea.

all of the former participant States, and would have to be accomplished outside the Preparatory Commission, in a forum less prone to be influenced by the history and shared aspirations that had brought the Convention to its present stage of maturity. Commencing in July 1990, the Secretary-General of the United Nations was persuaded by the industrialised countries to provide just such a forum, by inviting concerned States to "consultations" aimed at making acceptance of the Convention "universal," a coded reference to facilitating ratification by the United States and other industrialised countries, to be brought about by expunging from the text those provisions of Part XI that they found unacceptable, or at least, by neutralizing them. Assisted by a variety of global changes, including wider acceptance of market-oriented policies and dwindling reliance on dirigism and central planning worldwide, the dissolution of the Soviet Union and its consequences for the direction and level of influence exercised by the States of eastern Europe, and an industry forecast that deep seabed mining was only likely to commence in the next century, the course of those consultations seemed promising enough to induce the United States to begin to take part in them in April 1993. The result was the preparation and submission to the UN General Assembly during its 48th extended session in July 1994 of the Agreement Relating to the Implementation of Part XI of the United Nations Convention on the Law of the Sea.[11] When in force, that Agreement "interpreted and applied together with Part XI of the Convention as a single instrument," would nullify those provisions in the original text of Part XI that had not been "universally" accepted, and pave the way for ratification of the Convention by the industrialised countries, including the United States. The resolution containing the draft Implementing Agreement and a detailed Annex was adopted on 28 July 1994 by 121 votes in favour, with no opposition, and with some seven abstentions.

Although unnecessary to rehearse here in its entirety the careful surgery whereby the many provisions of Part XI of the Convention, unacceptable to some industrialised countries, were neutralized through the "Implementation Agreement" of 1994, some changes need to be noted in connection with the discussion to follow. Thus, while the Assembly of the International Sea-Bed Authority is still described in Article 160 of the 1982 Convention as the "supreme organ" of the International Sea-Bed Authority, because all member States are represented on it, and because of its one-state-one-vote decision making, it is now required as a rule to act by consensus.[12] However, the Implementing Agreement shifts emphasis to the recommendatory role

11. The full text of the Agreement is published in UN doc. A/RES/48/263, 17 August 1994. Available online: http://www.un.org/depts/los/convention_agreements/convention_overview_part_xi.htm (accessed 2 February 2003).

12. Implementing Agreement, Annex, Section 3 (Decision-making), paras. 2, 3 and 4.

of the Council, itself redesigned[13] to ensure representation of the principal contributors to the Authority's budget, and seeks to ensure that decisions perceived as inconsistent with the interests of major contributors would not be adopted.[14] To protect those interests still further, the Agreement establishes a Finance Committee of 15 members, on which, for the foreseeable future, "the five largest financial contributors to the administrative budget of the Authority" will have assured representation.[15] The Assembly and the Council, when adopting decisions on specified financial issues are to "take into account the recommendations of the Finance Committee." The Finance Committee's decisions on matters of substance are to be taken by consensus, providing each member with a virtual power of veto. Finally, the power conferred on the Authority by Article 174(1) of the Convention, to borrow funds to finance its administrative budget, is withdrawn.[16] The Enterprise, the unique intergovernmental mining arm of the Authority, conceived as having a favoured position as an internationally financed, cooperative mining venture, and a kind of standard bearer of the New International Economic Order, is reduced to a shadow of the original concept, and is to carry out only a modest range of functions of an essentially information-gathering character.[17]

The effect of these sweeping changes to Part XI of the Convention was to eradicate those features seen by the developing country participants at the Conference as reflecting the New International Economic Order,[18] and to replace them with provisions acceptable to the industrialised countries, achieving also thereby the six objectives outlined by the United States as necessary to secure its support for the Convention.

By opening the 1994 Implementing Agreement for signature and simplified provisional application conditioned upon the consent of the industrialized countries, before the 1982 Convention had formally entered into force; by providing textual links in that Agreement that would automatically make its adherents parties to an ideologically cleansed version of the 1982 Convention while conferring primacy on the Agreement; and by bringing both treaties into force for them at the same time, the industrialized countries achieved their objective of creating a legal process whereby the rules

13. Ibid., Section 3, paras. 9, 10, and 15.

14. Ibid., Section 3, paras. 5, 9(a).

15. Ibid., Section 9, paras. 3 and 8. The Finance Committee is the subsidiary organ of the Council foreseen in article 162, par. 2(y) of the Convention.

16. Ibid., Section 1, par. 14.

17. Ibid., Section 2.

18. Other such features that were excised or nullified by the Implementing Agreement are noted by this author in "Common Heritage of Mankind: From Metaphor to Myth, and the Consequences of Constructive Ambiguity," in *Theory of International Law at the Threshold of the 21st Century: Essays in Honour of Krzysztof Skubszewski*, ed. J. Makarczyk, (The Hague: Kluwer Law International, 1996), pp. 263–5.

and structures of the 1982 Convention, put in place through the resolute efforts of the overwhelming majority over a period of some 20 years, could be nullified or excised. Perhaps even more astonishingly, the latter were then persuaded through relatively brief "consultations," to avail themselves of that legal process and abandon the results of 2 decades of their labours.

Calling the new treaty designed to bring about those changes an "Implementing Agreement" seemed to avoid arcane legalistic arguments about whether the signed text of the original Convention could be amended while in the process of being ratified by several parliaments, and concerns over the modalities of doing so. But the term contained a dual, perhaps unconscious, irony: "implementing" the 1982 Convention was to be brought about, not by giving effect to its provisions, or facilitating their operation, but by negating and nullifying many of those provisions; and it would achieve "universality" for the 1982 Convention, not by making it more acceptable to the generality of States, but by recasting it in the manner required by a few of them. Nothing had changed in 100 years: to paraphrase Lorimer's comment made a century earlier, "Universality was possible only by the majority giving way to the minority."[19]

What caused the developing countries, which had for some 20 years (1973–1993) resolutely urged and, to a modest extent achieved incorporation of certain principles of their New International Economic Order in the 1982 Convention, so swiftly (between 1992–1994) to abandon their allegiance to those principles, and turn their backs on provisions that had, in decade-long negotiations at the Conference, won "widespread and substantial support," indicating that they offered a "substantially improved prospect of consensus"?[20] That those countries, as a group (comprising the overwhelming majority represented at the Conference) were actually "coerced" into changing their positions, seems unlikely. Was it a collective failure of nerve, seeing their concept of the New International Economic Order withering under the contemptuous gaze of the States that had come to affluence by steadfast adherence to the old and tried economic order? Was it merely that they had come to realize the impossibility of implementing the prescriptions of the New International Economic Order, desirable as they were, if the augmenting resources of the industrialized countries were to be withheld? Or had they lost faith in the efficacy of those very prescriptions? Had they come to believe that this was, indeed, the permanent triumph of the

19. As one distinguished writer had remarked of decisions at international gatherings, already in the nineteenth century, "Unanimity was possible only by the majority giving way to the minority." J. Lorimer, *The Institutes of the Law of Nations*, vol. **1** (London: W. Blackwood and Sons, 1883), p. 47.

20. The criteria applied by the President's "Collegium" (a body of principal officers of the Conference) in determining whether to include in the text of the Convention, as destined for negotiation, draft legal rules proposed by one or more delegations.

free market, signaling an "end of history"? Was the Implementing Agreement, then, the result of the timely intervention of reason and common sense, represented by the efforts of the industrialized countries, saving the multitude from their disastrous pursuit of a romantic dream?

Response to such questions from social and legal anthropologists and political scientists could make a timely contribution to understanding the nature of hegemonic influence on the creation of international law. Here was an instance where rules that had gained "widespread and substantial support" among the overwhelming majority of sovereign States at an "universally" attended intergovernmental conference, had been formally adopted through a series of decisions reached in accordance with agreed vote aggregation procedures, and were destined thereby to become legally binding, were then set aside and substituted by formulations that entrenched the very principles that had been firmly and repeatedly rejected throughout the negotiations that had taken place in the immediately preceding decades.

The few industrialized countries whose efforts had wrought this radical change, (i.e., reintroducing old and tried approaches earlier opposed and rejected by the majority while eliminating features of a new order urged by them) did then become parties to the twin treaties. There was only one exception: the United States at whose insistence the generally agreed "package deal" had been abandoned, and different provisions acceptable to it put in their place, did not ratify the treaties. The most economically advanced and militarily powerful country thus stands outside the very regime that recalls in every significant aspect the influence of its leadership and persuasive power.

RULE OBSERVANCE AND COUNTERVAILING POLITICAL POWER

The foregoing outline of the course of the Third United Nations Conference on the Law of the Sea, and its aftermath, illustrates how conclusions and understandings carefully negotiated for over a decade, and embodied in a complex treaty that had been formally voted upon, adopted, and signed by the overwhelming majority of States, could be radically altered even as the ratification process brought the treaty to the threshold of its entry into force. It demonstrates the inadequacy of the simple one-state, one-vote majority as a device for the adoption of rules, leading, as it did at that Conference, to illusory triumphs that permitted external pressures to frustrate the prescribed sequential processes of signature, ratification, and enforcement through domestic parliamentary action. This was accomplished through the exercise of persuasive authority by a small group of industrialized countries that had either not signed the treaty, or had signed it in the hope of ameliorating what were, in their view, unpalatable provisions, through subsequent negotiation and interpretative action. In initiating this extraordinary procedure to amend treaty provisions that had won "widespread and substantial support," even while they were before several parliaments for ratification in reliance on understandings reached at the Conference, the industrialized countries that had not signed the treaty were acting in accordance with their sovereign right to persuade other States to accept their point of view, while remaining outside an international agreement. If questions could be raised regarding the legality of radical alteration of a treaty text in a manner not foreseen or provided for therein, and possibly inconsistent with Article 18 of the 1969 Vienna Convention of the Law of Treaties, it would be for those States that had signed the treaty to rationalize and justify that action.

But there are many instances where States, in reliance on power based on their perceived indispensability conferred by political influence or level of financial contribution to an organization, have ignored, contravened, or purported unilaterally to modify obligations imposed by the rules of the organization that they have, by treaty, already formally undertaken to observe. While such behaviour has often been supported by arguments alleging the unconstitutional nature of the rules or corresponding obligations themselves, it is better explained in more subjective terms: performance of the obligation would not have accorded with the national or international policies and programmes of the State in noncompliance.

When certain member States of the United Nations fell seriously in arrears with payment of their assessed financial contributions to the organization under Article 17 of Charter because they questioned the constitutionality of the assessment in relation to a portion of those contributions related to financing of United Nations' forces deployed in the Middle East and the Congo, the International Court of Justice in an Advisory Opinion requested by the General Assembly, declared that

> financial obligations which, in accordance with the clear and reiterated authority of both the Security Council and the General Assembly, the Secretary-General incurred on behalf of the United Nations, constitute the obligations of the Organization for which the General Assembly was entitled to make provision under the authority of Article 17 . . .[21]

Notwithstanding the court's opinion, and its subsequent adoption by the General Assembly,[22] the States that had refused to pay their assessed contributions in full, continued their noncompliance. Failure of these States to comply with the obligations as members of the organization was not, in this instance, a matter of lack of financial resources, a factor that then, as now, might have garnered sympathy among the membership, but was plainly be-

21. International Court of Justice. *Certain Expenses of the United Nations.* ICJ Reports. Advisory Opinion 1962, p. 177.

22. Resolution 1854 of the 17th session.

cause they had unilaterally determined that the particular activity for which the organization had incurred expenses did not accord with their national policies and objectives at the time.[23] The eventual acquiescence in their conduct by another powerful member State—the United States—and the inability or unwillingness of less influential States to resist, then seems to have weakened opposition to withholding of portions of budgetary contributions, and laid the foundation for similar action by others in the future.[24] In the decade of the 1980s, the United States responding to internal legislative initiatives, required reduction of its contribution to the United Nations regular budget from 25 percent to 20 percent unless the General Assembly agreed to financially weighted voting when adopting its budget. Citing inefficiency, waste, and corruption in the administration of the organization and its operations, the United States declared that it would not pay its assessed contribution until substantial reforms had been effected. Refusal to pay assessed dues in full continued until January 2001, when it was reportedly agreed that the United States contribution would be reduced from 25 percent to 22 percent of the organization's budget.

In 1974, the United States did not pay in full its assessed contribution to UNESCO (some 25 percent of the budget) and, citing "politicization" of its operations, subsequently withdrew from the organization. In 1975, the United States, again citing "politicization," gave notice of its withdrawal from the International Labour Organisation, withdrawal becoming effective in 1977, while a substantial part of its dues remained unpaid. Resuming membership in 1980, the United States accepted its obligations in respect of the organization. Reductions in contributions have been threatened, and sometimes implemented, in relation to the United Nations Development Programme, the United Nations Environment Programme, and quite recently even the United Nations Human Rights Commission. The reason for such behaviour has been displeasure at the failure of the organization to conduct its operations in accordance with the contributor's individual conception of the aims and purposes of the organization, a conception that, in turn, is a reflection of the contributor's own policy and ideology. The purpose of such behaviour is to bring pressure to bear on the organization, with a view to compelling it to interpret and carry out its mandate consistently with that

23. As to the political reasons for refusal by some countries to pay their dues, see H. G. Schermers and N. M. Blokker, *International Institutional Law: Unity within Diversity*, 3rd rev. ed. (The Hague: M. Nijhoff, 1995), p. 632 ff.

24. Schermers and Blokker (n. 23 above) observe: "The amount of contributions outstanding used to be limited in most organizations. However, since the 1970s this situation changed. The non-payment of contributions became common practice, and has brought organizations into serious difficulties." They note, inter alia, that "As at 15 August 1994, the UN member States owed $835 million to the regular budget and $2600 million for peace-keeping operations", quoting UN doc. A/49/1 at p. 13.

policy and ideology. The instrument of choice for the exercise of such pressure is the promise of financial support, or the threat that such support will be withheld as a prelude to withdrawal from the organization if the contributor's terms are not complied with. In either case, the intent of the State is generally revealed through its vote on financial issues.

DETERMINING THE VALUE OF A PREFERENCE: WEIGHTED VOTING RECONSIDERED

Simple one-state, one-vote majority decision making, thus seems not to offer an efficient method for either adopting new rules intended to become legally binding, or for maintaining compliance with the rules of a regime administered by an international organization. The outcome in each case may be substantially altered through the determined exercise of political influence by a relatively small minority of States acting within the scope of the autonomy granted them by international law. It is also clear that this "democratic" process of negotiation and compromise in the world of States could be a protracted one: in some circumstances a matter of several years. If delay of this order were necessarily to accompany the operation of "democratic" rule making within an intergovernmental organization, in the course of which decisions binding on the membership would need to be taken on a virtually continuous basis, it seems certain to impair efficiency. As the price of their membership in, and support for, such organizations, the industrialized countries therefore require that their control over the policies and management of such organizations be assured by processes more direct and expedient than unqualified one-state, one-vote aggregation of preferences.

The preponderant influence acquired and maintained by the industrialized countries is given effect through one or more of a variety of constitutional devices for the protection of their minority interests, for example (1) the requirement of a high majority of votes (2/3 or 3/4 of members present and voting, and/or of the membership as a whole) for the adoption of a decision; (2) permanent representation on decision-making organs of limited composition, the other members of which may be subject to replacement through periodic elections; (3) the right of those States to veto or forbid the adoption of a decision that, though it received majority support on a one-state, one-vote basis, nevertheless adversely affects their interests; and (4) according greater "weight" to the votes of those States on the basis of specified criteria. Put differently, these are devices to which the industrialized countries may have recourse so as to have the capability to reject the expressed preferences of the majority regarded, according to their system of values, as ill conceived or impractical, and so to preserve the status quo in which they have abiding confidence. The last of these, "weighted voting," often favoured by the industrialized countries as an expression of fairness, and as often rejected by the developing countries as "undemocratic," and the manifestation of an unwanted hegemony, may offer scope for progressive development. Such development of the device could lie in the direction of determining "weight" by reference, not to financial contribution alone, as in the past, but also to a range of factors likely to combine to produce the kind of balanced judgement that should direct the rule-forming processes of an institution conceived on cooperative, not-for-profit lines.[25]

25. One authority recalls various voting mechanisms considered from time to time in connection with plans to give more effective force to decisions of the UN General Assembly, while not ignoring the claims of those States recognized as having more "actual weight in the affairs of the community of nations." Among these mechanisms, some would give votes in proportion to population; others were based on level of education income, production, military strength, contribution to the budget of the United Nations or some combination of such factors. One such proposal which, he observes, would produce "surprising results," would assign votes according to the action to be taken, and then on the basis of the "square root of population, budget, etc.." C. Eagleton, *International Government,* 3rd ed. (New York: Ronald Press Co., 1957), p. 578, citing work on the idea by L. B. Sohn entitled "The Role of the General Assembly and the Problem of Weighted Voting," in *Commission to Study the Organization of Peace, Charter Review Conference,* Ninth Report (and papers presented to the Commission, New York, 1955), pp. 107–29; See also, G. Clarke and L. B. Sohn, *World Peace through World Law,* 2d rev. ed. (Cambridge: Harvard University Press, 1962), pp. xix–xxii; E. MacIntyre, "Weighted voting in international organizations," *International Organization* 8 (1954): 484–97. In general, most such proposals treat the factor of finance as central, if not controlling, but try to mitigate the resulting disproportionate weight allocation by reference to other factors, mainly population. Presenting proposals designed to moderate "the extreme effects of the one-state, one-vote rule in the UN General Assembly," Catherine Senf Manno suggests that, while maintaining "adequate influence in decision making to countries which carry the greater responsibility and can in large measure control the implementation of decisions," the factors to form the basis for weighting should be: "a fixed minimum per State to reflect State equality; and an increment related but not proportional to assessments in order to reflect population and its per capita contributions. Weights would be used only for decisions on budget programs with financial implications above a specified minimum, and separate weights would apply to differently assessed budgets. To assure that weights would continue to conform to the agreed criteria, they would need adjustment every three years when assessment scales are adjusted. Under the proposals offered here, Members of the Assembly would retain their equal votes for many important areas of decision making." C. Senf Manno, "Selective weighted voting in the UN General Assembly: Rationale and methods," *International Organization* 20 (1966), pp. 37–62. A proposal by the Center for War/Peace Studies, developed most recently in collaboration with an expert of the highest authority, Paul C. Szasz, would treat as binding a decision by the General Assembly based on a "binding triad" of votes, for example, a decision that attains, "notwithstanding Article 18 [of the Charter] each of the following percentages of votes cast by the members of the General Assembly present and voting: (a) a two-thirds majority, with one vote assigned to each member; (b) a [simple or qualified] majority with votes assigned to each member in proportion to its population, with no member assigned votes in excess of 15% of the world population; and (c) a [simple or qualified] majority with votes assigned to each member in proportion to its assessed con-

Organs in which weighted voting is considered essential by the industrialized countries are those that are (1) charged with managing the transfer of resources from a small minority of affluent States (perhaps 15 in a "population" of some 192 States, or less than 10 percent of their number), as economic assistance to the poor countries to raise their standards of living, (e.g., the World Bank, the International Monetary Fund, the regional banks, the International Fund for Agricultural Development), or to relieve the financial burden of performance of obligations internationally imposed or undertaken (e.g., the Global Environment Facility); *or* (2) created to balance or reconcile the competing interests of groups of States (e.g., exporters/producers and importers/consumers: the Commodity Councils and the Common Fund for Commodities; the States of investors and "host" States: the Multilateral Investment Guarantee Agreement). The voting systems in such organizations vary, but generally tend to combine the one-state, one-vote majority decision principle, with a definitive role for "weighted" voting. Thus, each member of an organ or category of membership receives (a) the same number of votes allocated on the basis of "equality" and in addition (b) a number of votes depending on the level of its interests at stake in participation in the work of the organization or the achievement of its aims. That level of interest has hitherto been measured by the level of a State's financial contribution to the maintenance of the organization.[26]

A State's financial contribution to the regular budget of a multilateral organization would generally be based, as in the case of the United Nations itself, on "ability to pay"—a formula established on the basis of per capita GNP and GDP, the resulting figure being arrived at after negotiation and political compromise within the organization. Payment of an amount so de-

---

tribution to the regular budget of the Organization, with no member assigned votes in excess of (15%) of the Budget, see R. Hudson, "Quick Calculator for Estimating Outcomes of Votes in the UN General Assembly under the Binding Triad System for Global Decision-making," in *CW/PS Special Study* No. 8 (New York: Center for War/Peace Studies, 1995).

26. For example, in the International Monetary Fund, each member is allocated 250 votes, and also receives in addition one vote for each part of its quota equivalent to 100,000 special drawing rights. Each member of the World Bank is allocated 250 votes, and also receives one additional vote for each share of stock it holds. In the International Fund for Agricultural Development there are three categories of members: Western countries, the oil producing countries and the developing countries, each category being allocated a total of 600 votes. Western countries apportion their votes by allocating 105 votes equally among themselves, and distributing 495 votes based on the level of each member's contribution to the Fund; the oil producing countries allocate 150 votes equally among themselves, and distribute 450 votes among members in that category according to the level of the financial contribution made by each. On the other hand, the developing countries by agreement, allocate an equal number of votes to each State in their category. For the adoption of a decision, a specified majority of votes, or of votes within each membership category is required, leaving control in the hands of the major contributors.

termined is not likely to have any significant effect on living standards within the member State.[27] The affluent pay more, and voting power allocated on that basis would represent the most efficient and sensitive device for placing the management of the organization under the control of the industrialized countries. Their level of "financial interest" would confer on them directly and automatically control over rule formation associated with all operational aspects of the organization, from determination of policy to the adoption of the legally binding rules and practices of the organization; from direction of the organization's day-to-day operations to appointments made to key staff positions.

The basis of the industrialized countries' claim to preponderant influence is essentially "fairness": it is only fair, they seem to contend, that the States whose citizens' productivity furnishes by far the greater proportion of the financial and perhaps technological and other resources needed for the effective functioning of the organization should, out of responsibility to those citizens, exercise decisive authority over creation and implementation of rules for the conduct of its internal and external affairs to protect their individual and collective interests. Put another way, it is only fair that a State that is too poor to contribute more than minimally to the maintenance and effective functioning of the organization, while receiving the benefits of membership, should be recognized as having a relatively low level of interest in the conduct of the business of the organization and thus should have a relatively weak influence on rule creation and implementation connected with its functioning. The developing countries question the validity of this contention. In particular, those who are accountable for the welfare of large populations and are engaged in the struggle to alleviate a crippling burden of poverty, possibly also required to maintain effective administration of

27. The impact on members is far from uniform. The powerful make their choices, and the poor accept what they must. One authority has observed: "Congress unilaterally decided in 1972 that the U.S. contribution to the regular budget be capped at 25 percent. This was at a time when the United States should have been assessed for over 35 percent of the Organization's expenses. By now a fair assessment would be 30.97 percent, nearly 6 percent more than the United States is actually charged. The difference is borne by all other members. Paradoxically the members that are truly over-assessed are the poorest ones that pay the floor rate of 0.01 percent, since that floor means that no matter how little they should actually pay under the ability-to-pay formula, they must pay *at least* 0.01 percent. Taken together with the fact that the U.S. rate of voluntary contribution, related to GNP, is the lowest among all the developed countries (a mere fraction of what the Scandinavians pay); that the United States earns some $3 billion from the mere presence of UN Headquarters in New York; and that it received an undue share of the Organization's purchase contracts, it ill behooves us to label the world organization as a hopeless profligate." P. Szasz, in "Structures of World Orders," Proceedings of the 89th Annual Meeting of the American Society of International Law, 5–8 April 1995, pp. 180–5, at 182.

large areas of land and sea, feel that their responsibilities to their citizens,[28] though different from those of major contributors, are of a nature and extent that engage their vital interests, and entitle them to a commensurate level of influence over the functioning of an institution organized on cooperative lines.[29]

Financially "weighted" voting offers powers that contemplate not merely govern*ance,* but actually the govern*ing* of the organization. As "consideration" for their cooperation in the venture, the industrialized countries receive, through that device, virtually the power of life and death over the organization. Should one or more of them withdraw from the organization —an option still open, it would appear, to all States in the exercise of their "sovereign" autonomy—the institution would either collapse, or be reduced to a shadow of what had originally been conceived. Such a prospect being politically undesirable for a variety of reasons and often impractical to contemplate, the dominance of the major contributors is likely to be allowed to continue.

The topic of withdrawal of a member from an international organization has long attracted the attention of scholars, and within that topic, the question whether, when the constituent instrument of an organization makes no provision for withdrawal, a member may nevertheless terminate its membership rights and obligations at will. Under the influence of the "realist" school, many would favour recognizing the validity of an act of denunciation of a constituent instrument even where no provision is made for it, while urging that customary international law would require the performance of institutional obligations existing at the effective date of denunciation. Appropriate emphasis on the cooperative nature of the international institution should, however, prompt reassessment of that position and invite consideration of why a member, absent inclusion of any agreed provision on withdrawal, may terminate its treaty obligations toward other members unilaterally and before the membership as a whole has adopted a decision (say by qualified majority) permitting withdrawal, and prescribing the condi-

28. An instance of "common but differentiated responsibilities" of the kind recognized by Principle 7 of the Rio Declaration?

29. A "co-operative" is an institution that is owned by those who use its services. The members of a cooperative share equally in control of the institution. They hold regular meetings to elect directors from among themselves; and the directors, in turn, hire managers to run the day-to-day activities of the co-operative. Most cooperatives function under principles adopted by the International Co-operative Alliance in 1966. These include: the cooperative is open to any person who will use its services and accept the responsibilities of membership; each member has one vote, regardless of how many shares the member holds; the co-operative helps its members to make business decisions, and helps the public to understand how cooperatives work; and cooperatives work together at the local, regional, national and international levels to promote the co-operative movement. *The World Book Encyclopedia,* 1990 ed., vol. 4, under "cooperative."

tions under which its validity would be recognized.[30] That a State may, in fact, unilaterally decide, in the exercise of its autonomy recognized by international law, to withdraw, and to implement that decision effectively by doing so is obvious; but such action need not be deemed the exercise of a right[31] unless and until the denouncing member's treaty partners have determined its legitimacy and consequences by vote; or, upon appeal, an agreed third party has made that determination.

Although favoured by the industrialized countries as representing the most direct translation of financial contribution into organizational control,

30. The constituent instruments of many organizations make express provision for unilateral termination (withdrawal or denunciation) of membership, requiring an agreed and specified period after which notice of such action would become effective, for example, 3 months, often 1 year. Where member States concede positions of special importance to one or more of their members, for example, as major contributors demanding control, as in the World Bank and the International Monetary Fund, a constitution may provide for denunciation to take effect immediately. On the other hand, constitutions may omit provisions for withdrawal or denunciation on the ground that they may encourage States to do so. Some 16 states having withdrawn from the League of Nations pursuant to such provisions, the drafters of the UN Charter, omitted specific provisions on withdrawal, but adopted an interpretative declaration contemplating the possibility of withdrawal in certain exceptional circumstances. Schermers and Blokker (n. 23 above), pp. 82–95, at 82 observe in their survey of the practice of withdrawal: "Withdrawal will be particularly harmful to an organization with a supranational character, since the members of such an organization are more closely linked than is the case for other organizations. Withdrawal by one member may have serious consequences for the entire organization. The transfer of sovereign powers to the organization by all members should not be rendered meaningless by the unilateral act of one member, neglecting the interests of the others and of the organization as a whole." While this comment may have been made with the European Union in mind, it would seem equally pertinent in relation to all "universal" organizations such as the UN and the specialized agencies, which have elements of "a supranational character," and defection from which would show a culpable disregard of the interests of the membership, as well as of undertakings on which they were justifiably entitled to rely. The constitution of an organization being a treaty, it is difficult to see why denunciation or withdrawal from it, when no provision is made therefor, should be dealt with differently from other treaties. Under the Vienna Conventions on the Law of Treaties, of both 1969 and 1986 (Article 56 in both), a treaty containing no provision regarding termination, denunciation or withdrawal is not subject to denunciation or withdrawal unless it is established that the parties intended to admit the possibility thereof, or a right thereto may be implied by the nature of the treaty, facts that would need to be independently and impartially determined before legitimacy of a withdrawal would be recognized.

31. As Schermers and Blokker (n. 23 above), pp. 91–2) observe: "The States which have withdrawn from international organizations in the absence of any appropriate constitutional provision, have in so acting contended that such a withdrawal is permissible. However, the validity of this contention can be challenged both on the basis of the organizations' reactions to the withdrawal and the subsequent resumption of membership by the States in question."

financially weighted voting has been accepted by the developing countries only with the greatest reserve. Commenting on weighted voting in the operation of the major international financial organizations, one work observes:

> In the international community, where the principle of equality of States is predominant the voting strength in the International Monetary Fund and the World Bank is so disproportionate that it produces resistance to voting. Consequently, where possible these organizations tend to avoid voting.[32]

However, the main objection to "weighted voting" as currently practiced would appear to be not so much that it gives more voting power to one State than it gives to another, but rather that it distributes that power in a manner that is not consistent with the principle of "equality": it allocates voting power merely by reference to a single criterion, namely the level of the financial contribution of each member, and does not take into account other relevant attributes that all States possess to some degree, and that should be allowed to contribute to the quality of decisions conceived as benefiting the membership as a whole.

COMPLEX WEIGHTED VOTING

The system of financially "weighted" voting may well have been transposed to the world of States from common experience with commercial practice at the national level. It is reasonable that one who invests more in a private commercial venture should expect to receive more by way of a return and should be recognized as entitled to greater influence over corporate policy and practice, with a view to both exercising vigilance for the protection of the investment and maximizing profit. The intergovernmental organization is not, however, a commercial venture and may even be seen as its polar opposite. Where such organizations do earn revenue, the "profits" accrue for application to community purposes and not to enrich any particular member State. Contributions of funds to such organizations are not made

32. Schermers and Blokker (n. 23 above), p. 520. For some, the logical development from the tendency to "avoid voting," was to concede that decisions could be made by "consensus": a proposal will be deemed to be accepted if there is no expressed objection from a participant. Elaborate procedures for reconciliation of differences could be provided in order to resolve controversies that could lead to objections, and such procedures have been effective in some UN bodies and conferences. However, the result is no different from that offered by the false "equality" of the unanimity rule: every State, powerful and weak alike, have a right to "object" and thereby to bring about rejection of a proposal. But that right as far as the majority is concerned, is of little utility. To paraphrase Lorimer's comments on the "unanimity" rule (n. 19 above): Consensus would be possible only by the majority giving way to the minority.

with a view primarily to earning a financial return, although such devices as "tied" loans and other conditional financing may produce that result; nor are there associated risks of a commercial or political nature of the type experienced in private commerce, from which protection would be needed. Such organizations are essentially cooperative institutions, and the "return" to be expected from contributing to them is not financial profit, but rather the common benefit and upliftment of all the members, taking into account the range of political, cultural, and economic preferences and aspirations they represent. Being a cooperative institution, neither the financial input nor the ideological predisposition of any one member or group of members should result in their acquiring decisive influence on its affairs, or, on the other hand, being deprived of the benefits of membership; nor should the institution be exposed to the risk of collapse or attrition from "persuasive" resource withholding or withdrawal by a disaffected member or group of members. Such modes of conduct, though endemic in a world of "sovereign equals," should be recognized for what they are: against the law.

The criteria for evaluating the quality of a State's judgement, and thus the weight to be allocated to its vote when internationally binding decisions are to be taken, are not necessarily those that would guide, for example, the choice of a commercial executive through whose attributes a company would expect to increase and prolong its profits. Financial capability, with its own set of desirable attributes, cannot alone be taken to imply possession of the kind of multidimensional and eclectic vision that should inform the judgement of those responsible for directing the affairs of global organizations conceived on cooperative lines. Financial acumen, without more, may not be seen as translating directly into the quality of judgement or leadership that that context demands.

The financial criterion was chosen in the past because it seemed fair and reasonable to the "Powers" of the time, that those who contribute more should be recognized as having a high order or level of "interest" in the organization, and thus should receive commensurate compensation in some form (profit or protection), and because it had the added advantage of being objectively assessable and thus lent itself to ease and clarity of implementation. Out of affluence would spring, fully equipped, the wisdom to order and develop the world. Today, however, such an approach may seem less than adequate in relation to the complexities with which an organization must deal, and to warrant review. Accordingly, it may be worth attempting to devise a different, perhaps generally acceptable system of weighted voting: one whereby relative "weight" would be allocated by a representative body empowered for the purpose, by reference not merely to level of financial contribution, but also to a range of other significant factors[33] enabling assess-

33. The idea is not, of course, a new one; discussed from time to time it is generally dismissed on the ground that determination and application of "other criteria" would not be feasible, since the necessary agreement on them could never be achieved. Thus, as early as 1945, Jenks noted the challenge: "Weighted voting is

ment of the likelihood that the preference of a State would be exercised on the basis of right judgement, or judgement that reflects not merely personal or corporate aspirations or predilections, or even immediate national interests, but also due regard to the social values inherent in a cooperative enterprise, values that are the foundation of everyone's "national interest" in the long term.

Reference to "right" judgement here implies a quality of judgement by a State when its consideration of the issues has been informed by, and taken fully into account, a commitment to the economic and social advancement of the greatest number over the long term; a quality of judgement such that, in recognizing the ultimate convergence of the interests of its own people with the interests of peoples everywhere, leads it to express its preference—whether by vote or otherwise—in a manner supportive of long-term humanitarian aims; a manner that we may characterize as "cooperative." However, such a quality of judgement would imply an appeal to *moral principle,* and any project to give a measure of priority to the preferences of States based upon the moral roots of "cooperation," would be open to criticism from the realists who hold that governments exercise judgement by reference exclusively to the *interests* of their State, generally conceived in terms of short-term objectives, and are not, nor should they be thought to be, influenced by moral considerations, which are held to be operative only within the conscience of the individual.[34] Although the realist position currently enjoys

---

most readily attainable in an organization the functions of which are sufficiently circumscribed and well-defined to afford some simple basis for the selection of criteria of relative importance capable of securing general acceptance. Where an organization has a wide range of responsibilities, the factors to be taken into account in assessing the relative interest of its members either in its work as a whole or in particular decisions are likely to be too varied and imponderable and the relative weight to be attached to the different factors is likely to be the subject of acute controversy." C. W. Jenks, "Some constitutional problems of international organizations," *British Yearbook of International Law* 22 (1945): 11–72, at 40–2. See also n. 25 above.

34. George Kennan would have us ". . . recognize that the functions, commitments and moral obligations of governments are not the same as those of the individual. Government is an agent, not a principal. Its primary obligation is to the *interests* of the national society it represents, not to the moral impulses that individual elements of that society may experience. No more than the attorney vis-à-vis the client, nor the doctor vis-à-vis the patient, can government attempt to insert itself into the consciences of those whose interests it represents." However, he does seem to concede that, in relation to two problems—the threat of nuclear war, and the threat to the environment—the dictates of national interest and morality seem to coincide. He asks: "Is there not, whatever the nature of one's particular God, an element of sacrilege involved in the placing of [the unique endowment of the planet] at stake for the sake of the comforts, the fears and the national rivalries of a single generation? Is there not a moral obligation to recognize in this very uniqueness of the habitat and nature of man the greatest of our moral responsibilities, and to make of ourselves, in our national personification, its guardians and protectors rather than

widespread recognition among practitioners of international law and international relations, it is open to question whether exclusive focus on financial contribution as the sole determinant, or as subsuming all other determinants of the level of a State's "interests" as a member of an organization, so as to confer a dominant position in the making of decisions on international issues, has promoted progress toward a more peaceful and ordered world.[35] It could be time to promote a change in mind-set designed to evolve into a system for allocating greater weight to the vote of the State which, on an evaluation of a range of agreed factors, is deemed likely to express its preference in the "cooperative" manner suggested earlier.

While it would not be feasible, in a brief essay, to distinguish, justify and "prioritize" a comprehensive range of factors that should form the bases for evaluating records of cooperative conduct for the purpose of allocating voting strength, nine such factors to be considered in such an endeavour may be suggested by way of example.

1. Population—implying responsibility for maintenance or improvement of the security and the economic and social well being of communities subject to its jurisdiction: the greater the number, the more onerous the responsibility and the more qualified for allocation of voting strength.
2. Territory—implying responsibility for maintenance of the security and the sustainable development of land-based, aquatic, and atmospheric resources subject to its jurisdiction: the greater the area, the more onerous the responsibility and the more qualified for allocation of voting strength.

---

its destroyers?" G. F. Kennan, "Morality and foreign policy," *Foreign Policy* (1985/6): 205–6, 217.

35. Mary Maxwell, having reviewed a range of positions adopted in the literature to the question "is there, or can there be, a moral relationship between States?" favours a positive response, though a qualified one. She concedes that six powerful factors may operate to obstruct the realization of such a relationship among States: (1) "group morality" which, through the idea of the primacy of national self-interest (raison d'etat) may contradict individual ethical standards; (2) the group's tendency to self-aggrandizement; (3) weakness of altruism in relation to strangers; (4) lack of the visible struggle of the powerless (notwithstanding the explicit images of modern television); (5) the "acceptability" of evil, that sense that cannot comprehend fighting for justice, when another value (for example, standard of living, accumulation of profit) is held to be paramount, as in the industrialized countries; and (6) the "slipperiness" or excessive flexibility of the language of moral discourse, that is the result of a lack of cultural consensus about international morality. However, drawing on insights from sociobiology, she foresees that the moral behaviour of nations will come about through the force of new circumstances such as a burgeoning population and the decline of environmental quality. M. Maxwell, *Morality among Nations: An Evolutionary View* (Albany: State University of New York Press, 1990), pp. 128–44.

3. Adherence to and implementation of specified multilateral treaties[36] enshrining core social values recognized in the world of States: the more complete the scope of implementation, the more qualified for allocation of voting strength.
4. Implementation of multilaterally agreed rules for the protection and preservation of the environment and the sustainable development of resources worldwide: the more complete the scope of implementation, the more qualified for allocation of voting strength.
5. Quality of domestic governance, as indicated by adherence to basic democratic principles regarding representation, regular elections, and administrative transparency and accountability: the higher the quality, the more qualified for allocation of voting strength.
6. Legal provision for and implementation of civil liberties: the broader the range so implemented, the more qualified for allocation of voting strength.
7. Law and policy directed at developing gender empowerment: the more comprehensive and effective, the more qualified for allocation of voting strength.
8. Level of contribution to the regular budget of the United Nations (and possibly to the budgets of the international financial institutions): the greater the level, the more qualified for allocation of

36. A starting point for determining the treaties to be taken into consideration could be the "core group of multilateral treaties deposited with the Secretary-General, representative of the organization's key objectives," so described in the UN Secretary-General's letter to Member States inviting ratification or approval of them by the close of the twentieth century, and in celebration of the dawn of the twenty-first. That group includes multilateral treaties on (1) human rights, (2) refugees and stateless persons, (3) international criminal law, (4) disarmament, and (5) the environment. But there are several other treaties that may be said to belong to such a "core group," including the two Vienna Conventions (1969, 1986) on the Law of Treaties; the Vienna Conventions on Diplomatic (1961) and Consular (1963) Relations; the 1982 United Nations Convention on the Law of the Sea, and its 1994 "Implementing Agreement"; and the four 1949 Geneva Conventions on the Laws of War, and their two 1977 Protocols. Of the relevance of legal commitment, represented by adherence to a treaty, to the existence of an "international morality," one scholar has observed: ". . . only those rules of international morality are universally relevant which are incorporated into the body of contemporary international law. In other words, they are coterminous in international relations. This understanding has a number of merits: (a) it avoids the high degree of cognitive uncertainty which would otherwise accompany international morality; international law provides well-defined procedures for reaching agreement on its content; (b) it ensures that international morality will not serve as an instrument for the subversion of the international legal system; and (c) it compensates for the weaknesses of an autonomous international morality through offering the institutionalised mechanisms of international law for their interpretation and enforcement." B. S. Chimni, *International Law and World Order: A Critique of Contemporary Approaches* (New Delhi: Sage Publications, 1993), p. 67.

voting strength. This factor being based on "ability to pay" (level of affluence) and the product of statistics and negotiated settlements where necessary, it should be balanced by. . .

9. Level of poverty (level of need), also based on statistics and negotiated settlements: the greater the level, the more qualified for allocation of voting strength.

Establishment of a Global Cooperation Index (GCI) could be made the responsibility of a subsidiary body of the United Nations' Economic and Social Council, which could also be charged with revising the Index periodically, for example, every 2 years. The Council's decisions should be guided by the results of a multidisciplinary study by an expert group constituted and operating on a broad based and thorough scientific collaboration, along the lines of the Intergovernmental Panel on Climate Change. One may conceive of a time in the future where this group, and indeed other such advisory groups whose function it is to give unfiltered expression to the opinions of the people, would be elected directly by them, and not appointed through some arcane selective process influenced by a State hierarchy. The group would be responsible, for example, for establishing the areas in which the State's performance would be relevant for factoring in to the GCI; the criteria on which to base assessment of such performance, and the relative value assigned to one factor as against another, as well as devices for equitably adjusting the factors for application.

The result should be the establishment of a system of complex weighted voting that does not merely translate money into executive wisdom, but would instead relate *voting power more responsively to the capacity to exercise mature and balanced judgement on the processes of rule-formation in the context of a global cooperative enterprise.* The existence of the GCI could, moreover, have the effect of motivating States to improve their performance in relevant areas, and so move up the ladder of influence on those processes.

Integration, Coordination, and Implementation: The World Summit on Sustainable Development and the Future of Marine Governance

Klaus Töpfer and Amy Hindman*
United Nations Environment Programme, Nairobi

INTRODUCTION

When the news came that Professor Elisabeth Mann Borgese had died in February of 2002, much of the international environmental community was taken up with preparations for the World Summit on Sustainable Development, a scant 6 months away. The question on the lips of many was what kind of memorial would be fitting for the woman who had pioneered so many initiatives in the world of marine protection? What could commemorate the work of someone who had garnered so many awards[1] for her efforts and who devoted decades to advocating practical, tangible measures to protect the world's oceans?

Perhaps the most obvious answer to that question is simply "results"—the tangible achievement of the goals that Professor Borgese's work identified, defined, and strove to reach. The World Summit on Sustainable Development (WSSD), which was convened to develop a plan of implementation for Agenda 21[2] (adopted at the Rio Summit in 1992), provided an ideal opportunity to create just such a memorial for Professor Borgese—the adoption of a plan of action to achieve what she worked toward all her life. Now that the WSSD has ended and the Plan of Implementation has been adopted

*Editors' Note.—The authors would like to thank David Osborn and Adil Karimbux for their comments and assistance.

1. Among her many other plaudits, Professor Borgese was among the first recipients of the UNEP Sasakawa Environment Prize, awarded annually to individuals who have made outstanding contributions to the management and protection of the environment.

2. Agenda 21 was adopted at the United Nations Conference on Environment and Development (UNCED), Rio de Janerio, Brazil, 3–14 June 1992, http://www.un.org/esa/sustdev/agenda21text.htm.

Ocean Yearbook 18: 246–266.

by the world's leaders,[3] the Plan's provisions may be seen as the foundation for what could be the most lasting memorial ever—the achievement of sustainable use of the world's oceans, seas, and coastal areas.

THE APPROACH TO THE WORLD SUMMIT ON SUSTAINABLE DEVELOPMENT

Chapter 17 of Agenda 21 contains a highly detailed set of provisions for the protection of oceans, seas, coastal areas, and related resources.[4] Like much of Agenda 21, it is replete with priorities and goals, both specific and general. The challenge posed by the World Summit on Sustainable Development—adopting a concise, tangible action plan that translated the lengthy and occasionally abstract Agenda 21 to an implementable programme—was daunting.

The road was made easier, however, by the many advances that took place after the Rio Summit. In the decade between Rio and Johannesburg, many of the elements for the work to come had been adopted in the form of the adoption or entry into force of legally binding instruments, the creation of adjudicating institutions, and the development of voluntary programmes. The most important of these are more than indications of advances, they are indicators of the way forward and their development and existence guided the work for the WSSD.

The most important of these advances is, of course, the entry into force of the United Nations Convention on the Law of the Sea (UNCLOS) in 1994.[5] Adopted in 1982, this ground-breaking convention is unique in several regards, most notably its integrated and comprehensive approach to addressing issues relating to the world's oceans and seas. Professor Borgese, who worked tirelessly to bring the Convention into being, hailed it as providing "the legal framework within which all activities in the ocean will be carried out—perhaps for the next three hundred years."[6] The Convention's

3. See *World Summit on Sustainable Development (WSSD) Plan of Implementation.* Report of the World Summit on Sustainable Development, Johannesburg, South Africa, 26 August–4 September 2002, A/CONF.199/20. New York: United Nations, 2002, http://www.johannesburg.org/.

4. The title of Chapter 17 of Agenda 21 reflects the level of specificity: "Protection of the oceans, all kinds of seas, including enclosed and semi-enclosed seas, and coastal areas and the protection, rational use and development of their living resources," http://www.un.org/esa/sustdev/agenda21chapter17.htm.

5. United Nations Convention on the Law of the Sea, 1982. Adopted 10 December 1982 and entered into force 14 November 1994.

6. E. Mann Borgese, "Remarks on Ocean Governance" (delivered on 7 June 2001 at the Canadian Oceans Stewardship Conference, 6–8 June 2001, Vancouver, Canada).

importance is not limited to the advancement it signaled in oceans governance; its approach must be recognized as being a forerunner of our current approach to sustainable development.

Ten years before the Rio Summit and 20 years before WSSD, the adoption of UNCLOS heralded our understanding that we cannot just address development issues, or trade issues, or environment issues individually, because these issues are all interrelated and mutually dependent. By simultaneously providing a framework for everything from the governance of exclusive economic zones to navigational rights, to deep seabed mining, and to the protection and preservation of the marine environment, the Convention provided a first glimpse of what sustainable development law should be in its broad-ranging scope. It is not a trade treaty or an environmental instrument, because the oceans and seas, just as the rest of the world, are not purely economic or environmental resources. To truly provide a legal framework for their use and protection, we had to acknowledge that they are both, and more.

Moreover, the decade between the Rio Summit and WSSD saw the creation or entry into force of no less than 20 instruments and initiatives regarding the marine environment or marine biodiversity.[7] Some of these advances took the form of nonbinding initiatives, such as the Washington Declaration establishing the Global Programme of Action for the Protection of the Marine Environment from Land-based Activities (GPA) (1995).[8] Some involved the adoption, revision, or entry into force of legally binding instruments such as the adoption of the Helsinki Convention on the Protection of the Marine Environment of the Baltic Sea Area (1992)[9] and the combining of the Oslo and Paris Conventions to create the OSPAR Convention for the Protection of the Marine Environment of the North-East Atlantic (1992).[10] Some will have an effect on the protection of the marine environment as only a part of their overall scope, such as the Stockholm Convention on Persistent Organic Pollutants (2001).[11] Many are regional in scope, such

7. P. Bernal, B. Cicin-Sain with S. Belfiore and J. Barbiére. *Ensuring the Sustainable Development of Oceans and Coasts: A Call to Action—Co-Chairs' Report from the Global Conference on Oceans and Coasts at Rio+10.* Paris, UNESCO, 3–7 December 2001, http://www.udel.edu/CMS/csmp/globaloceans/.

8. Washington Declaration and Global Programme of Action for the Protection of the Marine Environment from Land-Based Activities, adopted 3 November 1995. UNEP(OCA)/LBA/IG.2/7, http://www.gpa.unep.org/documents/.

9. The Helsinki Convention on the Protection of the Marine Environment of the Baltic Sea Area, 1992, entered into force on 17 January 2000, http://www.helcom.fi/helcom/convention.html.

10. The Convention for the Protection of the Marine Environment of the North-East Atlantic (OSPAR Convention), 22 September 1992, entered into force 25 March 1998, http://www.ospar.org/.

11. Stockholm Convention on Persistent Organic Pollutants, 22 May 2001, UNEP/POPS/CONF/4, http://www.chem.unep.ch/pops/.

as Regional Seas Conventions and Action Programmes,[12] while others are global in their approach, such as the entry into operation of the International Tribunal on the Law of the Sea (1997). They all share one thing in common, however; they all to some extent further the goals set forth in Chapter 17 of Agenda 21.

No one can argue with the need for dynamic and sustained action in this area. In the last 30 years, marine degradation has not only continued, but has intensified,[13] and this decline has not been arrested by the work done since Rio.[14] Those preparing for the WSSD were faced with a difficult dilemma. If instruments and initiatives as diverse and far-reaching as those coming into being in the last decade have been insufficient to reverse the tide of marine degradation, then what would be sufficient?

The answer seems to be clear: these initiatives have put us on the right path, but standing as independent mechanisms, and often inadequately or only partially implemented, they can only go so far. The real test for the WSSD in the area of the marine and coastal environment was for it to gather the elements of existing instruments and plans of action in a coherent and integrated fashion and promote their full and vigorous implementation so that they would be more than lofty statements of goals. Integration, coordination, and implementation were the key elements for success.

THE WORLD SUMMIT ON SUSTAINABLE DEVELOPMENT PLAN OF IMPLEMENTATION

Given the level of focus on this area, it is remarkable that initial versions of the Plan of Implementation developed in the preparatory process for the WSSD contained no specific references to oceans or coastal areas.[15] Very quickly, however, the draft evolved to not just mention these issues, but give them prominence. As we came closer to the WSSD, the United Nations Secretary-General, Kofi Annan, identified five priority areas of focus as a contribution to WSSD; water and water-related issues were featured on this list.[16]

12. UNEP regional seas convention texts, http://www.unep.ch/seas/main/hconlist.html.

13. United Nations Environment Programme, *Global Environment Outlook 3: Past, Present and Future Perspectives* (London: Earthscan, 2002), p. 180.

14. Bernal et al. (n. 7 above), p. 4.

15. B. Cicin-Sain, P. Bernal, V. Vandeweerd, S. Belfiore and K. Goldstein, *Oceans, Coasts, and Islands at the World Summit on Sustainable Development and Beyond* (Newark, Delaware: Center for the Study of Marine Policy, December 2002), http://www.udel.edu/CMS/csmp/globaloceans/pdf/WSSDGuide.pdf.

16. United Nations Press Release, 14 May 2002. The five areas identified by the Secretary-General were: Water, Energy, Health, Agriculture, and Biodiversity ("WEHAB"). The "Water" element focused on clean drinking water and sanitation, but the "Health" and "Biodiversity" elements also included references to issues like

Some months before the WSSD, a Global Conference on Oceans and Coasts at Rio+10 was convened in Paris with the goal of, among other things, laying the groundwork for the inclusion of an ocean perspective at the WSSD. At this conference, experts offered a number of possible causes for the continued degradation of the world's oceans and coastal areas in spite of the sustained and focused activity in this area. These included lack of implementation of relevant instruments and agreements and lack of coherence and cohesion among these agreements.[17]

Fortunately, the WSSD was poised to address just these deficiencies. By developing a plan of action, implementation of the overall goals set by the various agreements and conventions was made concrete and tangible. Greater coherence could be achieved by integrating into a single plan the targets and timetables set for these actions.

The WSSD achieved two distinct types of results: a binding Plan of Implementation with general/global application (implementation plan or Type I Outcomes) and a vast series of partnerships among various countries, international organizations, civil society, the private sector and other stakeholders in which these entities voluntarily agreed to join forces to undertake specific projects (Type II Outcomes).[18] Both outcome types add greater specificity and concrete elements for implementation of Agenda 21 and through their simultaneous development as WSSD outcomes, both types provide greater coherence to actions undertaken at the subregional, regional, and global level.

Section IV of the WSSD Plan of Implementation is dedicated to "Protecting and managing the natural resource base of economic and social development." This Section covers a broad array of water-related issues, from domestic wastewater and sanitation, to the protection of the marine environment. Three major pressures facing the world's oceans, seas, and coastal areas received particular attention, however: fisheries, marine biodiversity loss, and pollution to marine and coastal ecosystems.

How the Plan of Implementation addresses these pressures, with its focus on implementation of existing agreements and initiatives, improved coordination among responsible entities, and greater integration of the three elements of sustainable development (i.e., economic, social, and environmental) in the development of solutions, gives a good indication of the fu-

---

polluted water and marine issues such as coral reef protection. Of course, even those elements of WEHAB that do not appear, on first glance, to have a strong impact on oceans and marine issues have the power to affect these areas. For example, the impacts of agricultural activities on the world's oceans are undeniable: global inputs to the ocean are dominated by agricultural run-off (as well as atmospheric deposition). See UNEP (n. 13 above), p. 181.

17. Bernal et al. (n. 7 above), p. 10.

18. The WSSD also generated the Johannesburg Declaration on Sustainable Development, A/CONF.199/L.6/Rev.2, 4 September 2002.

ture of marine governance. Moreover, the Plan's call for an improvement in the level of understanding of marine and coastal ecosystems, through a global marine assessment can provide a roadmap for all future action identifying problems and formulating solutions. These portions of the Plan of Implementation warrant a closer look.

The Ecosystem Approach and Fisheries Management

The opening portion of the Plan of Implementation section regarding oceans and seas notes the importance of oceans, seas, islands, and coastal areas for global security and for sustaining economic prosperity.[19] As an "overview" section, it calls for ratification and implementation of UNCLOS, full implementation of Chapter 17 of Agenda 21, an integrated interagency coordination mechanism on ocean and coastal issues within the United Nations system, application of the ecosystem approach as highlighted in decision 5/6 of the Convention on Biological Diversity's Conference of the Parties (discussed later), integrated coastal and ocean management programmes at the national level, strengthened regional cooperation among relevant regional programmes (including the United Nations Environment Programme's [UNEP's] Regional Seas Programme), assistance to developing countries in various areas such as management of fishery resources and coastal management, and facilitation of the United Nations General Assembly's review of developments in oceans affairs.

The priorities in ocean-related issues highlighted at the WSSD thus become immediately apparent: greater cooperation among the various relevant programmes and organizations, increased integration in how these matters are approached, and improved capacity-building efforts to assist developing countries in their efforts in this regard.

Although this is more of a general section, it is notable that it does set one deadline, that is, application of the ecosystem approach by 2010. This is telling in two regards. First, the setting of particular targets and timetables is an essential element of the Plan of Implementation. Although those actions with a specific deadline are not of a higher priority than others, the level of specificity provided by a deadline underscores the practical, tangible nature of the outcomes dictated by the Plan. Second, the ecosystem approach is yet another element of developing an integrated approach to resource management. Its application as a priority in this context emphasizes the focus of the Plan of Implementation: developing integrated and coordinated methods for achieving sustainable development.

The ecosystem approach is a strategy for the integrated management of land, water, and living resources that promotes conservation and sustain-

19. WSSD Plan of Implementation (n. 3 above), par. 29.

able use in an equitable way.[20] Its application was called for in a decision of the fifth Conference of the Parties to the Convention on Biological Diversity, which noted the importance of developing practical approaches for its implementation.[21] It calls for a balance of conservation, sustainable use, and fair sharing of the benefits arising out of the use of resources. As such, it is more than an integrated approach to ecosystems in their entirety, as it takes into account social and economic aspects of resource management.

Supported by a variety of principles, such as the conviction that ecosystem managers should consider the effects of their activities on adjacent or other ecosystems and the objectives of resource management are a matter of societal choice, this approach applies to any and all ecosystems, not just oceans and seas. Its inclusion in this portion of the WSSD Plan of Implementation is highly indicative, however, of the particular resonance the ecosystem approach has regarding marine affairs.

Notably, paragraph 25(d) of the Plan of Implementation endorsing the Biodiversity Convention's Decision regarding the ecosystem approach also endorsed the Reykjavik Declaration on Responsible Fisheries in the Marine Ecosystem. This Declaration was adopted at a meeting convened by the United Nations Food and Agriculture Organization (FAO) in which governments agreed to integrate the ecosystem approach into their fisheries management strategies. The Declaration also emphasizes the importance of improving cooperation between regional and international fisheries management organizations and bodies in charge of managing and conserving the marine environment.[22]

How the Plan of Implementation thus deals with and addresses fisheries management is important for a variety of reasons. First, the depletion of fish stocks due to unsustainable practices is one of the greatest pressures on the marine ecosystem currently faces. Secondly, this is an area where the overlap between conservation and economic concerns has long been acknowledged and recently begun to be addressed in an innovative, integrated fashion.

For example, in November 2001, trade ministers from over 140 countries met at a World Trade Organization (WTO) Ministerial Conference in Doha that laid the groundwork for a sea change in the way the overlap between trade instruments and environmental instruments are addressed. The resulting Doha Declaration[23] made a commitment to commence negotiations regarding the relationship between multilateral environmental agree-

20. Convention on Biological Diversity Conference of the Parties Decision 5/6, Annex A(1).

21. Ibid., par. 2.

22. Reykjavik Declaration on Responsible Fisheries in the Marine Ecosystem, par. 3.

23. Doha Ministerial Declaration, WT/MIN(01)/DEC/1, adopted on 14 November 2001, http://www.wto.org.

ments and WTO Rules.[24] Moreover, the Declaration made a specific and express commitment to clarify and improve WTO disciplines on fisheries subsidies,[25] thereby taking the first important step in eliminating perverse subsidies that are not only trade distorting, but counterproductive to attempts to promote sustainable fisheries management.

The Plan of Implementation expressly notes the work of the WTO in this regard and in paragraph 30(f) calls for the elimination of subsidies that contribute to illegal, unreported, and unregulated fishing and to overcapacity. The Plan sets an ambitious goal in paragraph 30(a) for the maintenance and restoration of fish stocks to levels that can produce the maximum sustainable yield. This work is to be done "on an urgent basis and where possible not later than 2015."[26]

In fact, many of the fishery-related goals in the Plan note the already ongoing work in this area or call for the implementation of a particular instrument: for example, the Agreement for the Implementation of the Provisions of UNCLOS Relating to the Conservation and Management of Straddling Fish Stocks and Highly Migratory Fish Stocks,[27] the 1995 FAO Code of Conduct for Responsible Fisheries,[28] and the relevant FAO plans of action and technical guidelines. Particular urgency is applied to these last two, as the plan calls for the implementation of the plan of action for the Management of Fishing Capacity by 2005 and the Plan of Action to Prevent, Deter, and Eliminate Illegal, Unreported and Unregulated Fishing by 2004.[29]

Through endorsing the speedy implementation of existing agreements, decisions, and plans of action, through the integration of work ongoing in sectors traditionally seen as purely economic or purely environmental, and through the holistic plan of attack set forth in the principle of the ecosystem approach, the fisheries-related portions of the Plan of Implementation provide a microcosm view of the overall approach of the Plan.

Biodiversity and Marine Protected Areas

The same can be said of the section of the Plan of Implementation regarding the conservation of marine and coastal biodiversity. In paragraph 31(c),

24. Ibid., par. 31.
25. Ibid., par. 28.
26. WSSD Plan of Implementation (n. 3 above), par. 30(a).
27. The United Nations Agreement for the Implementation of the Provisions of the United Nations Convention on the Law of the Sea of 10 December 1982 relating to the Conservation and Management of Straddling Fish Stocks and Highly Migratory Fish Stocks, entered into force 11 December 2001.
28. FAO Code of Conduct for Responsible Fisheries, adopted 31 October 1995, http://www.fao.org/fi/agreem/codecond/codecon.asp.
29. The International Plan of Action for the Management of Fishing Capacity, adopted February 1999; International Plan of Action to Prevent, Deter and Elimi-

the Plan calls for the implementation of the work programme arising from the Jakarta Mandate on the Conservation and Sustainable Use of Marine and Coastal Biodiversity of the Convention on Biological Diversity.[30]

This Mandate and its Programme of Action provide unique insight into a particularly progressive approach to the management of marine and coastal resources. Adopted in 1995, the Jakarta Mandate is a decision resulting from the Second Conference of the Parties to the Convention on Biological Diversity.[31] Characterized by the Ministerial Declaration of the Conference as a "new global consensus on the importance of marine and coastal biological diversity,"[32] the Mandate led to the adoption of a plan of action in 1998 at the fourth Conference of the Parties.[33]

The Jakarta Mandate and its resulting Programme of Action recognizes the myriad of factors threatening marine and coastal biodiversity, including chemical pollution and eutrophication; fisheries operations; global climate change; and alterations in physical habitat and invasions of exotic species, and more importantly, the fact that the response to this threat demands an integrated, cohesive approach. As such, the Programme of Work calls for the participation and involvement of the governing bodies of a wide variety of Agreements: the United Nations Framework Convention on Climate Change (UNFCCC),[34] the United Nations Fish Stocks Agreement,[35] the FAO Code of Conduct on Responsible Fisheries,[36] regional seas agreements such as OSPAR,[37] and the UNEP Global Programme of Action for the Protection of the Marine Environment from Land-based Activities (GPA), just to name some of them.[38]

The Programme of Action has six major elements: integrated marine and coastal area management, marine and coastal living resources, marine and coastal protected areas, mariculture, alien species and genotypes and coral bleaching.[39] Although all are important, the work in integrated marine

---

nate Illegal, Unreported and Unregulated Fishing, adopted 2 March 2001, http://www.fao.org/fi/ipa/ipae.asp.

30. Jakarta Mandate on Marine and Coastal Biological Diversity, adopted in 1995.

31. Report of the Second Meeting of the Parties to the Conference on Biological Diversity, 30 November 1995 (UNEP/CBD/COP/2/19).

32. Ibid., par. 15.

33. Report of the Secretary. *Conference of the Parties to the Convention on Biological Diversity*. UNEP/CBD/COP/4/5. 24 February 1998.

34. United Nations Framework Convention on Climate Change (1992). Adopted 9 May 1992, entered into force 21 March 1994, http://unfcc.int.

35. United Nations Fish Stocks Agreement (n. 27 above).

36. FAO Code of Conduct (n. 28 above).

37. OSPAR Convention (n. 10 above).

38. (n. 33 above).

39. (n. 33 above). The Programme of Action originally had only five elements; coral bleaching was subsequently added.

and coastal area management and protected areas are of particular interest in this context.

Integrated Marine and Coastal Area Management (IMCAM) was promoted in the Jakarta Mandate as "the most suitable framework for addressing human impacts on marine and coastal biological diversity and for promoting conservation and sustainable use of that diversity."[40] IMCAM is a participatory process for decision making to control or prevent adverse impacts from human activities in the marine and coastal environment. Crucial components are "relevant sectoral activities, such as construction and mining in coastal areas, mariculture, mangrove management, tourism, recreation, fishing practices, and land-based activities, including watershed management."[41] Because of its integrative nature, participation in decision making comes from all levels and sectors: the private sector, nongovernmental organizations, the public, and of course, government at all levels.

This is an example of the broad-based approach necessary for sustainable development at its most fundamental level: economic, social, and conservation-related goals are all considered as a matter of course in the decision-making process. The single sector approach that formerly governed this process is quickly becoming a thing of the past, as the Programme of Action calls for the integration of the IMCAM approach at the local, national and regional level.[42]

Within the framework of IMCAM, the establishment of networks of marine and coastal protected areas is another important, independent element of the Jakarta Mandate and the Programme of Action. Such networks have the potential to provide valuable management approaches for conservation. Although an important criterion for the selection of such networks is their status as providing critical habitats for living marine resources, the protection of ecosystem functioning as a whole, as well as the wider context of IMCAM, ensures that the determination and protection of such networks is not a conservation exercise without regard to other concerns.[43]

Although the establishment of such networks is an element of the Jakarta Mandate and the resulting Programme of Action, the WSSD Plan of Implementation singles this measure out for special attention. The Plan calls for the development and facilitation of "the use of diverse approaches and tools, including the ecosystem approach, the elimination of destructive fish practices, *the establishment of marine protected areas consistent with international law and based on scientific information, including representative networks by 2012* . . ."[44]

40. See (n. 31 above), Decision II/10, par. 2.
41. See (n. 31 above), Decision II/10, Annex I(ii).
42. See (n. 33 above), Decision IV/5, Annex.
43. See (n. 31 above), Decision II/10, Annex I at par. iv.
44. WSSD Plan of Implementation (n. 3 above), par. 31(c), (emphasis added).

The establishment of such representative networks and the comparatively short deadline for this action is of particular interest given that there are currently regional instruments providing for their establishment within national jurisdiction, but no single instrument provides for their establishment beyond that. For example, several of the myriad of Regional Seas Conventions and related Action Plans administered by UNEP provide for the establishment of protected marine areas. Although no agreement precludes the establishment of such areas on the high seas, none explicitly provide for it either.

Thus, the WSSD Plan of Implementation has taken an existing concept, present in current action plans and agreements, to a new level. If the networks called for in the Plan are to be truly "representative," it stands to reason that they will not be solely limited to the confines of national jurisdiction, as areas providing threatened habitats or otherwise needing protection will not, as a matter of logic, only exist in such jurisdictions. Moreover, the Plan calls generally to "maintain the productivity and biodiversity of important and vulnerable marine and coastal areas, including in areas within and beyond national jurisdiction."[45] The potential for action in this field will be addressed further in a later section.

Pollution Prevention and the Global Programme of Action

A third major pressure on sustainable use and protection of oceans and the marine environment—pollution—is addressed in various portions of the Plan of Implementation. The Plan calls for the implementation of the International Maritime Organization's (IMO's) agreements on maritime safety and marine pollution and notes a resolution adopted at the General Conference of the International Atomic Energy Agency (IAEA) regarding radioactive wastes.[46] Perhaps the most comprehensive approach to marine pollution issues comes, however, in the paragraph devoted solely to the Global Programme of Action for the Protection of the Marine Environment from Land-Based Activities (GPA).

The Plan of Implementation calls for the advancement of the GPA, with particular emphasis in the period 2002–2006 on municipal wastewater[47] and the physical alteration and destruction of habitats and nutrients. Specific actions called for in the Plan include the facilitation of partnerships and capacity-building initiatives for the better implementation of the GPA. A

45. WSSD Plan of Implementation (n. 3 above), par. 31(a).

46. WSSD Plan of Implementation (n. 3 above), paras. 33 and 33 bis.

47. Sewage is the largest source of contamination, by volume, of the marine and coastal environment and coastal sewage discharges have increased dramatically in the past 3 decades. See UNEP (n. 13 above), p. 181.

deadline of the next GPA Conference in 2006 is set to "make every effort to achieve substantial progress . . . to protect the marine environment from land-based activities."[48]

The Global Programme of Action was adopted in 1995 to address a pervasive negative effect,[49] as approximately 80 percent of the pollutant load in the oceans comes from land-based activities. Like so many initiatives and instruments highlighted in the WSSD Plan of Implementation, it is a crosscutting, multisectoral response to a threat to the sustainable use of natural resources. The preamble to the Washington Declaration, in which some 108 governments and the European Commission adopted the GPA, expressly recognizes the importance of all three pillars of sustainable development (i.e., economic, social, and environmental). It notes that the alleviation of poverty is an essential factor in addressing both the impacts of land-based activities on coastal and marine areas and the major differences among the different regions of the world in terms of environmental, economic and social conditions.[50]

The GPA itself was developed and has been implemented with this approach guiding its focus. It is designed to be a source of conceptual and practical guidance to be drawn upon by national and regional authorities for developing and implementing action to prevent, reduce, and/or eliminate marine degradation from land-based activities. Five general aspects to the recommendations in it cover this approach, from identifying and assessing the marine pollution problem, to establishing priorities for action, to setting objectives, to selecting a response strategy, and finally to evaluating the effectiveness of that strategy.[51]

The elements to each of the recommendations reveal how fully all the concerns of sustainable development have been integrated into its approach. For example, the first step calls for governments to identify and assess the problem related to, among other things, food security and poverty alleviation, public health, coastal and marine resources, including biological diversity, and economic and social benefits and uses, including cultural values.[52]

In addition to the substance of the GPA's work, its comprehensive and crosscutting nature can be seen in its administration. Serviced by a Secretariat provided by UNEP, the GPA substantively involves the support of perhaps more partners in different areas than any other global programme—from Friends of the Earth, the International Atomic Energy Agency, the World Bank, to the Chemical Manufacturers Association. In fact, the GPA's efforts

48. WSSD Plan of Implementation (n. 3 above), par. 32.
49. Washington Declaration (n. 8 above).
50. Washington Declaration (n. 8 above).
51. GPA (n. 8 above).
52. GPA (n. 8 above).

to integrate as many stakeholders as possible in the implementation of its work resulted in the development of one of the major partnership initiatives to emerge from WSSD—the Hilltops to Oceans Partnership (discussed later).

Global Marine and Coastal Ecosystem Assessment

Scientific data, supported by a precautionary approach, provided the foundation for the identification of the three major pressures on marine and coastal ecosystems discussed earlier, as well as the development of the responses. The need for an improved scientific understanding of marine and coastal ecosystems was highlighted in the Plan of Implementation as a fundamental basis for sound decision making. As such, the Plan calls for a variety of actions to improve that understanding. Increased scientific and technical collaboration, marine science technology transfer, and marine science capacity building, including promoting the use of environmental impact assessments, are all highlighted as necessary actions.[53] Perhaps the most notable provision, however, is that which calls for the establishment by 2004 of a "regular process under the United Nations for global reporting and assessment of the state of the marine environment, including socio-economic impacts, both current and foreseeable, building on existing regional assessments."[54]

The potential for this assessment to guide and vastly improve the manner in which we approach marine-related problems cannot be overstated. Moreover, like many other aspects of the Plan of Implementation, this requirement builds upon existing work in this area, not just at the regional, but also at the global level.

In February 2001, UNEP's Governing Council directed it to cooperate "with IOC/UNESCO and other United Nations agencies, the Convention on Biological Diversity Secretariat, and the regional seas programmes to explore the feasibility of establishing a regular process for the assessment of the state of the marine environment, with active involvement by governments and regional agreements, building on ongoing assessment programmes."[55]

To implement this decision, UNEP hosted two consultative meetings, the first in Reykjavik in September 2001 and the second in Bremen in March 2002. The participants of the first meeting affirmed both the desirability of and urgent need for a global assessment of the marine environment

53. WSSD Plan of Implementation (n. 3 above), par. 34.
54. WSSD Plan of Implementation (n. 3 above), par. 34.
55. UNEP GC Decision 21/13, Article 4.

(GMA).[56] The second meeting was in the form of a technical workshop to further elaborate the key objectives and define the practical framework for developing a GMA process.[57]

Both workshops noted the plethora of existing monitoring and assessment programmes. Monitoring done pursuant to the Regional Seas Conventions and Plans of Action, the work of the Joint Group of Experts on the Scientific Aspects of Marine Environmental Protection (GESAMP), the Global International Waters Initiative under UNEP, the work of the Intergovernmental Oceanographic Commission of UNESCO, and a myriad of studies and analyses conducted by NGOs and academic institutes provide a strong foundation upon which a global approach can be formulated.[58]

As with other elements of the WSSD Plan of Implementation, the call to action regarding a global assessment is thus to coordinate and integrate existing work, filling in gaps, eliminating duplication of effort, and achieving a more comprehensive result. What precise form the global approach may take is discussed in more detail below.

IMPLEMENTATION: AFTER THE WORLD SUMMIT ON SUSTAINABLE DEVELOPMENT

The end of WSSD signaled the beginning of the next phase in our struggle for sustainable development: the Plan of Implementation identified our priorities and the framework for our plan of attack. The real test, however, and the best indication of whether we are achieving the results in marine and coastal ecosystem governance that are effective will be what happens next.

There are two paths that the action taken pursuant to the commitments made at the WSSD can take: action pursuant to the Plan of Implementation and action pursuant to the hundreds of partnerships agreed to as part of the Summit. These paths are not separate, but complementary; the partnership initiatives bring the private sector and civil society into the implementation of the Plan.

Action Pursuant to Partnerships: "Hilltops to Oceans"

Known as "Type II Outcomes," the partnerships emerging from the WSSD do not constitute the type of government-negotiated agreement reflected

56. UNEP, "Proceedings for the First Feasibility Study for Establishing a Regular Process for the Assessment of the State of the Marine Environment," Reykjavik, Iceland, 12–14 September 2001.

57. UNEP, "Proceedings for the Technical Workshop for Establishing a Regular Process for the Global Assessment of the Marine Environment," Bremen, Germany, 18–20 March 2002.

58. Ibid.

in the Plan of Implementation. Rather, they are voluntary arrangements made by governments, nongovernmental organizations, intergovernmental organizations, and the private sector to work together to implement various activities.

During the preparatory committee meeting held prior to the WSSD, there was some concern that these Type II Outcomes would come to overshadow the Plan of Implementation and take the place of binding government commitments. Instead, however, they served as a supplement and bolster to the commitments contained in the Plan. Moreover, by involving all stakeholders, they provided a unique opportunity for entities besides governments to bring their plans, concepts, and ideas to the table as part of the WSSD's overall work. The theme of integration and coordination was carried beyond the Plan of Implementation into these nonbinding outcomes.

For example, work pursuant to the Global Programme of Action (GPA) will not be limited to the dictates set forth in the Plan of Implementation. Through a broad-based partnership initiative, "Hilltops to Oceans," an integrated approach to this work, involving all levels of government, the public and private sector, and NGOs has now commenced.

The "Hilltops to Oceans" partnership is an initiative led by UNEP's GPA, IOC-UNESCO, numerous governments (notably contracting parties to the Regional Seas Conventions and Action Plans) and several nongovernmental organizations. It is built in part upon the commitment made at the First Intergovernmental Review of the GPA held in Montreal, Canada in 2001: "Taking appropriate action at the national and regional levels to strengthen institutional cooperation between, inter alia, river-basin authorities, port authorities and coastal zone managers, and to incorporate coastal zone management considerations into relevant legislation and regulations pertaining to watershed management in particular transboundary watersheds."[59]

The partnership's objectives include facilitating recognition by governments and the international community of the basic linkages between fresh water and the marine environment, assisting countries in raising new and additional financing for projects that address priority problems of river, coastal, and marine pollution, assisting in the development of partnerships and coordinating activities among governments and financial bodies like the Bretton Woods institutions and regional development banks and integrating the private sector and civil society in addressing problems of river, coastal, and ocean management and implementing the GPA.

59. Montreal Declaration on the Protection of the Marine Environment from Land-Based Activities. Adopted by the Intergovernmental Review Meeting on the Implementation of the Global Programme of Action for the Protection of the Marine Environment from Land-Based Activities, 30 November 2001, Montreal, http://www.gpa.unep.org/igr/.

One component of the partnership is a Wastewater Emission Targets (WET) initiative aimed at improving the recognition of and response to the threat posed to human health, marine, and freshwater resources caused by increasing emissions of untreated wastewater into fresh water, coastal, and marine areas. Other objectives include promoting the development and realization of internationally agreed targets for action pertaining to wastewater emissions and exploring the application of global or regional economic instruments, such as water markets, pollution reduction trading mechanisms, and multistakeholder funds.

Another component of the partnership is the promotion of the elaboration and implementation of National Programmes of Action (NPAs) for the protection of the marine and coastal environment from land-based activities and sources. This component aims at assisting developing countries to prepare and implement feasible NPAs in consultation with all relevant stakeholders, including targets and timetables.

As with so many nonbinding and voluntary initiatives connected to the marine environment, international recognition of the necessity of this action can be found in UNCLOS, which provides as follows:

> States, acting especially through competent international organizations or diplomatic conferences, shall endeavor to establish global and regional rules, standards and recommended practices and procedures to prevent, reduce and control pollution of the marine environment from land-based sources, taking into account characteristic regional features, the economic capacity of developing States and their need for economic development. Such rules, standards and recommended practices and procedures shall be re-examined from time to time as necessary.[60]

Through the creation of such nonbinding initiatives and the facilitation of voluntary partnerships and capacity-building efforts, the binding commitment made by governments in paragraph 32 of the WSSD Plan of Implementation to implement the GPA has become the responsibility and the priority of a vast array of stakeholders.

Action under the Plan of Implementation: Global Monitoring Assessment

The official mandate (and guidance) for the Global Monitoring Assessment (GMA) discussed earlier has not ended with the WSSD. The United Nations General Assembly has just adopted a Resolution providing a further impetus for this work and specific dictates for how it will proceed:

60. UNCLOS (n. 5 above), Article 207(4).

> Decides to establish by 2004 a regular process under the United Nations for the global reporting and assessment of the state of the marine environment, including socio-economic aspects, both current and foreseeable, building on existing regional assessments, and requests the Secretary-General, in close collaboration with Member States, relevant organizations and agencies and programmes of the United Nations system (United Nations Environment Programme, Intergovernmental Oceanographic Commission of the United Nations Educational Scientific and Cultural Organization, Food and Agriculture Organization of the United Nations, International Maritime Organization, World Health Organization, International Atomic Energy Agency, World Meteorological Organization and Secretariat of the Convention on Biological Diversity), other competent intergovernmental organizations and relevant non-governmental organizations, to prepare proposals on modalities for a regular process for the global reporting and assessment of the state of the marine environment, drawing, *inter alia*, upon the work of the United Nations Environment Programme pursuant to Governing Council decision 21/13, and taking into account the recently completed review by the Joint Group of Experts on the Scientific Aspects of Marine Environmental Protection, and to submit these proposals to the General Assembly at its fifty-eighth session for its consideration and decision, including on the convening of a possible intergovernmental meeting.[61]

Although many provisions of the WSSD Plan of Implementation appear in one form or another in this General Assembly Resolution on the Law of the Sea, the level of detail in this provision and its comprehensive approach to the upcoming work make it of particular interest. To begin with, the enumeration of the United Nations agencies to be involved in this work reflects its crosscutting nature and the fact that expertise in this area is spread among a vast array of different bodies. By integrating the work of United Nations programmes with mandates relating to health, the environment, energy, food supplies, cultural conservation, maritime affairs and others, the General Assembly has ensured that the resulting monitoring programme will be crafted in a manner that takes all three pillars of sustainable development into account.

Moreover, as both this Resolution and the Plan of Implementation note, the Global Monitoring Assessment (GMA) should build upon existing work in this field in the form of regional assessments and the Resolution notes that the development of modalities for the GMA should draw on the work UNEP has done in this area pursuant to its Governing Council directive.[62]

61. United Nations General Assembly, A/57/L.48/Rev.1, par. 45 (10 December 2002).

62. See (n. 57 above), and related text.

As is noted earlier, UNEP's work in this area has included two expert workshops in which a wide variety of governments, intergovernmental bodies, and NGOs participated.[63] Based on that work and the recommendations resulting from it, UNEP's Governing Council is being presented with a report by its Executive Director proposing the establishment of an open-ended ad hoc group of experts under the auspices of the proposed intergovernmental panel on global environmental change, to consider the contribution of UNEP to follow-up on the General Assembly Resolution on GMA.[64]

Based on the analysis and assessment conducted at the two UNEP workshops on GMA, a number of suggestions and proposals for the modalities of the GMA have emerged. A broad ecosystem approach based on commonly accepted ecological boundaries was strongly advocated, as was a scope of the GMA activities that fully integrates socioeconomic considerations. Possible elements for the institutional mechanism and operational arrangements include a multilateral architecture that

1. Applies a science-based approach involving national, regional, and global policy makers and provides an interface with all stakeholders, assessment users, and data providers. Regional assessments could be peer reviewed prior to their integration into the GMA.
2. Maximizes cost effectiveness by relying to the extent possible on existing mechanisms.
3. Includes a secretariat that, in cooperation with other United Nations bodies, coordinates the implementation of the GMA.

The experts attending the UNEP workshop also proposed that the expected outputs of the GMA process be subject to a transparent peer review process and be reported in a "two tier" format, consisting of a scientific or technical report and a policy-oriented report based on the same information. This approach would ensure that the outputs would be both scientifically valid and in a form that would be useful and accessible to policy makers without a scientific background.

In response to a proposal made at the second workshop, UNEP, in close consultation with the Secretariat for the Convention on Biological Diversity and other interested entities is currently conducting a review of the scope, status, and timing of existing and forthcoming assessments carried out under the various national, regional, and global organizations. This review will not only ensure that all existing work is taken into account and built upon

63. The results of these meetings were presented at the United Nations Open-Ended Informal Consultative Process on Oceans and the Law of the Sea held in New York in April 2002. The resulting recommendations were then taken into account at the Fourth Preparatory Committee for the WSSD, and the Plan of Implementation adopted the provision on the GMA.

64. UNEP, UNEP/GC/22/2/Add.5 (19 November 2002).

in the process ultimately selected for the GMA, but it should allow the identification of gaps and means by which the GMA could address them.

Action under the Plan of Implementation: The Establishment of Representative Protected Marine Networks

As noted earlier, there are currently several regional agreements that provide for the establishment of marine protected areas. Moreover, the Programme of Action adopted under the Jakarta Mandate emphasizes the importance of such areas for protecting critical habitats and ensuring ecosystem functioning. As such, the provision in the WSSD Plan of Implementation calling for the establishment of representative networks of marine protected areas by 2012 is not a mandate lacking precedent or existing examples upon which to draw. The approaches adopted in the relevant instruments and programmes for identifying such areas and ensuring their continued viability will be invaluable.

At the same time, however, there is no example of the binding establishment of such areas beyond national jurisdiction and no express binding international agreement expressly and explicitly providing the legal basis for such establishment. There is also no linking mechanism to make the marine protected areas a true system. Both the relevant Plan of Implementation provision and United Nations General Assembly Resolution note that such representative networks must be selected in a manner consistent with relevant international law, and neither indicate which, if any, United Nations body should take the lead on this initiative. Unlike the global monitoring assessment of the marine environment discussed earlier that rests on firmer footing and appears to have a clear mandate and lead for its work, this provision appears to be less grounded. The question thus emerges, will the networks established under this provision exist solely in national jurisdictions (and hence fail to be truly "representative") or does a sufficient legal basis exist for the preliminary identification of networks on the high seas as well as within national jurisdiction?

The need for multiple use marine protected areas on the high seas has been identified before, notably by the Government of Australia at the opening session of the United Nations Open-ended Informal Consultative Process on Ocean Affairs in 2000.[65] Moreover, a careful analysis conducted by Australia of the potential legal basis for such establishment suggests that the basis does exist.[66]

65. R. Warner, "Marine Protected Areas Beyond National Jurisdiction: Existing Legal Principles and Future Legal Frameworks" (prepared for the Legal and Scientific Experts Workshop on High Seas and Marine Protected Areas, Isle of Vlim, 27 February–4 March 2001). Environment Australia, Canberra.

66. Ibid.

Most notably, UNCLOS itself may provide that basis. Article 194 requires states to take all measures consistent with the Convention that are necessary to prevent, reduce, and control pollution of the marine environment, including measures necessary to protect "rare or fragile ecosystems as well as the habitat of depleted, threatened or endangered species and other forms of marine life."[67] States are required to cooperate on a global basis in creating international rules, standards, recommended practices, and procedures for the protection of the marine environment.[68]

Although there are also soft law principles supporting the establishment of marine protected areas beyond national jurisdictions (such as Principles adopted by the International Union for the Conservation of Nature and Natural Resources—IUCN),[69] it is once again the broad and far-reaching terms of UNCLOS that are likely to serve as the foundation for future work in this area. When asked if she believed an amendment to UNCLOS was necessary, Professor Borgese responded in the negative, noting that the foundation for all future action was there, but that the Convention must and would evolve and that the international community would contribute to this evolution through interpretation and implementation of useful parts.[70]

The establishment of representative networks of marine protected areas called for in the WSSD Plan of Implementation remains an area where the international community must answer Professor Borgese's call. The evolution of UNCLOS and the implementation of existing law can provide a strong basis on which to undertake this work.

CONCLUSION

As Professor Borgese observed, the sectoral approach (often applied to conservation measures in the past) does not work in the ocean and coastal environment; integrated management and governance at all levels and among all sectors is a must.[71] The emphasis on integration, coordination, and implementation in the Plan of Implementation and the partnerships adopted at the WSSD are a good indication that we are on the right track laid out for us by the principles of sustainable development and the approach advocated by Professor Borgese. The benefits provided by the vast array of instruments and initiatives regarding the oceans and seas will only be realized when they are coordinated in a comprehensive manner and fully implemented. The question of whether the roadmap provided by the Plan of Im-

67. UNCLOS (n. 5 above), Article 194(5).
68. UNCLOS (n. 5 above), Article 197.
69. Warner (n. 65 above), p. 4.
70. Borgese (n. 6 above).
71. Ibid.

plementation for this action will be effective, however, remains to be seen. The outcome of the World Summit on Sustainable Development thus provides a firm foundation for the best memorial to Professor Elisabeth Mann Borgese—the sustainable use of our oceans and seas—but the memorial itself is still under construction.

The Concept of Protection and Sustainable Development of the Marine Environment

Alexander Yankov
Vice-President of the International Ocean Institute, Member of the International Tribunal for the Law of the Sea

INTRODUCTION

The present essay is a kind of dedication to the memory of Elisabeth Mann Borgese and an expression of admiration for her outstanding contribution to the promotion of topical concepts relating to the oceans. One of these is the integrated concept of protection and sustainable development of the marine environment. This brings together in an inclusive and interdependent manner two most important aspects of sound management of the seas and oceans, namely, protection and conservation of the marine environment, on the one hand, and economic and social development of coastal and marine areas, on the other. The promotion of this concept was one of the guiding objectives in Elisabeth's activities.

My association with Elisabeth Mann Borgese dates back to the early 1970s, prior to the inauguration of the Third United Nations Conference on the Law of the Sea. I met her on the eve of the first *Pacem in Maribus* Conference in 1970, in my capacity as Vice-Chairman of the Legal Sub-Committee of the United Nations Seabed Committee. Ever since that date and over the years until her last days, we were united by common endeavours, a close friendship, and collaboration within the framework of the International Ocean Institute (IOI), the United Nations Law of the Sea Conference and the Independent World Commission on the Oceans.

Elisabeth's visionary approach to ocean perspectives and future ocean governance has been generally recognized. As Ruud Lubbers from the Club of Rome stated in his Preface to her signature work, *The Oceanic Circle,* "Elisabeth Mann Borgese proves able in this book to go one step further."[1] Indeed, her concepts on topical issues relating to the fate of the oceans and management of their resources were often ahead of her time. She was among the first personalities who, long before the United Nations Conference on Envi-

1. E. Mann Borgese, *The Oceanic Circle: Governing the Seas as a Global Resource* (Tokyo: United Nations University Press, 1998), p. xiii.

Ocean Yearbook 18: 267–283

ronment and Development (UNCED) of 1992 in Rio de Janeiro, had articulated the policy of integrated marine environmental protection and sustainable development of coastal and marine areas. The active involvement of Elisabeth Mann Borgese in major international events and activities of intergovernmental and nongovernmental organizations dealing with ocean affairs provided her with generative grounds for novel propositions and grand ideas.

Elisabeth acquired her insights on topical global issues from her active association with organizations and groups of intellectuals with advanced perceptions of the world. Major international events in the field of environment and uses of the seas contributed to shaping her concepts and her practical experience. The beginning of her career was marked by her involvement in a group of professors at the University of Chicago under the leadership of the University President Robert M. Hutchins, during the late 1940s. This group of visionaries established a Committee to Frame a World Constitution under Robert Hutchins and Giuseppe A. Borgese, who elaborated the Preliminary Draft of a World Constitution.[2] Twenty years later, President Hutchins founded the Center for the Study of Democratic Institutions in Santa Barbara, California, to which he called Elisabeth as a fellow. Her activities focused on law of the sea and related political matters, under the central idea that "[T]he oceans should, in effect become our laboratory for the making of a new world order."[3]

Elisabeth Mann Borgese's understanding of ocean governance implied that the international legal order to be established through the United Nations Convention on the Law of the Sea (UNCLOS) should, as stipulated in the Preamble of the Convention, be in conformity with the principles of the new international economic order. In addition, Elisabeth always maintained that ocean governance is an essential component of a global system. When Ambassador Tommy Koh, the President of the UN Law of the Sea Conference, described UNCLOS as "a Constitution for the Oceans," Elisabeth rejoined in her book *The Oceanic Circle* that, "We all knew it would have to be part of, and a model for, a constitution for the world in the next century,"[4] referring to the "Preliminary Draft of a World Constitution," prepared by the Chicago Committee and published by the University of Chicago Press in 1948.[5]

2. E. Mann Borgese and Krishan Saigal, *The IOI-Story: International Ocean Institute* (Hamburg: Dreiviertelverlag Verlag GmbH & Co. KG, 2000), p. 8.

3. Ibid., pp. 10–11. See also the final chapter of *The Oceanic Circle* where one of the general conclusions reads: "The ocean will be considered as a great laboratory for the making of a genuinely new international/national political, legal, and social order." (n. 1 above), p. 6.

4. Borgese (n. 1 above), p. 7.

5. R. M. Hutchins, *Preliminary Draft of a World Constitution* (Chicago: University of Chicago Press, 1948).

Elisabeth Mann Borgese, together with other members of the Center, encouraged Ambassador Arvid Pardo of Malta to submit to the XXII Session of the UN General Assembly his famous statement on the exploration and exploitation for peaceful purposes of the seabed and ocean floor and the subsoil thereof beyond the limits of national jurisdiction. The essential elements were the comprehensive regime for the international seabed area to be established, and the novel proposition for the seabed and its mineral resources beyond national jurisdiction to be treated as the Common Heritage of Mankind. This statement and the ensuing resolution[6] adopted by the General Assembly triggered the process of preparation for the United Nations Convention on the Law of the Sea, adopted in 1982 and entered into force in 1994.

Elisabeth Mann Borgese's next important contribution to the promotion of the concept of marine environment and sustainable development was her active participation in the work of the Club of Rome.[7] The fundamental methodological concept of the Club of Rome, as Elisabeth emphasized in *The Oceanic Circle*, was the "interdependence of all great issues of our time in their interaction." Therefore she believed, "[S]uch interdependence of issues and problems demands interdisciplinary approaches if solutions are to be forged."[8]

Elisabeth Mann Borgese benefited greatly from her close association with the Club of Rome in that it influenced her to apply some of the Club's

6. The Statement of Ambassador Pardo was presented on 1 November 1967 to the First Committee of the General Assembly. The General Assembly adopted Resolution 2340 (XXII) on 18 November 1967.

7. The Club of Rome is an international nongovernmental organization, a permanent group of outstanding academics, economists, sociologists, political scientists, industrialists and public figures from Europe, the United States, Japan and several other countries. The Club was established in 1968 on the initiative of the Italian industrialist Dr. Aurelio Peccei and registered with the Union of International Associations. The main objective of this organization is the research of mankind's current economic and social issues and their implications. Its main activities consist of preparing special reports containing indications of present patterns and foreseeable future trends, as well as suggestions for alternatives and proposals to alleviate potential critical situations. The first report published in 1972 was entitled *Limits to Growth* (of world population), followed in 1974 by the report *Mankind at the Turning Point* (on disparities in living standards between the developing and the developed countries). The third report, *Reshaping the International Order* (on the international economic order), was published in 1976, when the ongoing Third United Nations Conference on the Law of the Sea had already prepared for consideration the "revised single negotiating text," which was an important instrument for negotiations for the Convention on the Law of the Sea. This fact had a definite effect on the discussions which took place at the Club of Rome on the main topic of the report, since the establishment of a new legal order over the world ocean was considered within the framework of the new international economic order as one of its main components.

8. Borgese (n. 1 above), p. 6.

suggestions and conclusions in its reports, which had been prepared by eminent scientists and experts on topical issues relating to the governance of the oceans. On the other hand, as an active member of the Club of Rome, Elisabeth was able to share with her colleagues her insights and expertise on problems relating to oceans. Thus, Elisabeth Mann Borgese played an important part in bringing to the agenda of the Club of Rome the problematique of ocean governance, including protection of the marine environment and sustainable development. Together with Arvid Pardo she submitted a Report to the Club of Rome in 1976, entitled *The New International Economic Order and the Law of the Sea*,[9] which constituted a chapter of the third report of the Club of Rome *Reshaping the International Order*.

Elisabeth Mann Borgese performed her leading role in promoting of the concept of marine environment and sustainable development first and foremost in the *Pacem in Maribus* Conferences and the International Ocean Institute (IOI). She was the founder and leader of both institutions. They represented the creative realization of her belief in the ever-growing significance of nongovernmental entities within the system of ocean governance. *Pacem in Maribus* and IOI will remain a testimony to her resourcefulness and exemplary dedication to the oceans.

During the last 4 decades of Elisabeth's dynamic life she played a prominent role, participating in several international events under the auspices of the United Nations in the field of the environment and in particular on the protection and sustainable uses of marine resources. This sequence of major international initiatives started with the United Nations Conference on Human Environment of 1972 in Stockholm, followed by UNCLOS, UNCED and the Johannesburg Summit. The Stockholm Declaration[10] adopted by the Conference laid down the fundamental principles and main objectives of environmental policy, covering all parts of our planet, including the seas and oceans. Principle 1 proclaims the "solemn responsibility to protect and improve the environment for present and future generations." The element of "improvement" of the state of the marine environment as a component of this "solemn responsibility" was unfortunately not followed in subsequent formulations.

Principle 7 of the Declaration is devoted specifically to the protection of the marine environment, stipulating that:

> States shall take all possible steps to prevent pollution of the seas by substances that are liable to create hazards to human health, to harm living resources and marine life, to damage amenities or to interfere with other legitimate uses of the sea.

9. Ibid., p. 7.

10. Ed. A. C. Kiss and D. Shelton, *Manual of European Environmental Law*. UN. Doc. A/CONF.48/14/Rev.1 (UN Pub. E 73, IIA. 14) (1973). Cambridge: Grotius Publications Limited, 1993, pp. 26–28.

This provision is the genesis of Article 192 of the United Nations Convention on the Law of the Sea (UNCLOS). It lays down the general obligation of states to protect and preserve the marine environment. Indeed, it represents the first attempt in international law and practice to formalize the obligation to protect and preserve the marine environment as a general obligatory legal rule entailing legal consequences. There is no doubt that in this case a declarative statement was being transformed into a treaty provision.

Furthermore, Principle 21 of the Declaration reads:

> States have . . . the sovereign right to exploit their own resources pursuant to their own environmental policies, and the responsibility to ensure that activities under their jurisdiction or control do not cause damage to the environment of other States or of areas beyond the limits of national jurisdiction.

This principle of the Declaration was often taken into consideration during the negotiations at the Third United Nations Conference on the Law of the Sea, leading to the adoption of Article 193 of UNCLOS. Similarly, Principle 22 served as a starting point in drafting the relevant articles of UNCLOS concerning responsibility, liability, and compensation in respect of damage caused by pollution of the marine environment.[11] In these two instances, there was also a transformation of declarative principles into legally binding treaty provisions. I had the opportunity on many occasions during the UN Law of the Sea Conference, as Chairman of the Third Committee of the Conference, to share with Elisabeth my views regarding these relatively new phenomena in law making as one of the specific features of the legislative process at the Conference. Elisabeth followed closely the negotiations on environmental matters and played an important part in the Conference as a leading member of the nongovernmental organizations[12] in her capacity of IOI representative, and later as a member of the Austrian delegation in the second part of the Conference when the final draft of the Convention was negotiated and approved.

The concept of the integration of environment and sustainable development of the marine environment is the result of the interface between UNCLOS and UNCED, in particular Agenda 21's Chapter 17, the Rio Declaration on Environment and Development[13] and the conventions, agree-

11. See Article 235 of UN Convention of the Law of the Sea, UN Doc. A/CONF62/122 (1982).

12. Fifty-seven nongovernmental organizations were admitted to the Conference with observer status. See "Final Act of the Conference," in *The Law of the Sea. United Nations Convention on the Law of the Sea. With Index and Final Act of the Third United Nations Conference on the Law of the Sea.* United Nations Publication. Sales No. E. 83. V. 5. New York: United Nations, 1983, pp. 188–89.

13. See *Earth Summit (The United Nations Conference on Environment and Development [UNCED]); Agenda 21: Programme of Action for Sustainable Development; Rio Declaration on Environment and Development. Statement of Forest Principles. The Final Act of Agree-*

ments, action plans, and documents from conferences and other international instruments that followed UNCED. The elucidation of the objectives and mechanism of this interface required at the outset a brief examination of the evolving policy of protection and preservation of the marine environment under the influence of UNCLOS and special conventions and agreements relating thereto, on the one hand, and the emerging concept of sustainable development, as a follow-up to the Report of the World Commission on Environment and Development and UNCED, on the other.[14] Elisabeth Mann Borgese made a valuable contribution to this problem area through several IOI projects and most of the Pacem in Maribus Conferences since 1987–1988.[15] In addition, to complete and augment the examination of the interrelationship between the marine environment and sustainable development, the input of the Johannesburg Summit 2002 and in particular, the Johannesburg Declaration on Sustainable Development, should be noted.[16]

The following part of this paper will comprise a brief examination of the evolving concept of marine environmental protection and preservation (and conservation) under the relevant provisions of UNCLOS and ensuing conventions, agreements, and other international instruments. The latter relate to the protection of the marine environment, the emerging concept of sustainable development of marine resources under the influence of UNCED and the Johannesburg Summit 2002, and the effect of the concept of integration of environment and development, that is, the interface between UNCLOS and UNCED.

THE INTEGRATED CONCEPT OF PROTECTION AND SUSTAINABLE DEVELOPMENT OF THE MARINE ENVIRONMENT

Evolution of the Concept of Protection and Preservation of the Marine Environment under the Influence of UNCLOS

The protection and preservation of the marine environment was one of the key subjects and issues to be considered by the Third United Nations Conference on the Law of the Sea, as an essential part of the international legal

ments Negotiated by Governments at the United Nations Conference on Environment and Development (UNCED), 3–14 June 1992, Rio de Janeiro, Brazil. United Nations Publication Sales No E.93.1.11. New York, N.Y.: 1993.

14. The World Commission on Environment and Development, *Our Common Future* (Oxford: Oxford University Press, 1987), and also UN Doc. A/42/427. 1987.

15. For more details, see Borgese (n. 1 above), pp. 151–57.

16. See *Report of the World Summit on Sustainable Development, Johannesburg, South Africa, 26 August–4 September 2002.* UN Document A/CONF.199/20. 2002., *Chap. I, Resolution, Annex and Plan of Implementation on the World Summit on Sustainable Development,* and *Resolution 2, Annex, 17th Plenary Meeting and Round-Up 4 September 2002.* UN publication sales No. E.03.11.A.1.

regime for the seas and oceans under UNCLOS. The four Geneva Conventions adopted by the First UN Conference on the Law of the Sea in 1958 contained only three articles relating to the prevention of pollution of the marine environment, which were treated in a somewhat haphazard manner.[17] Two of them were in the Convention on the High Seas and one in the Convention on the Continental Shelf. They are limited in scope and do not contain any provisions for enforcement measures and liability for damage, nor do they offer a mechanism for the settlement of disputes.[18]

In contrast with its predecessors, UNCLOS provides a much broader legal framework governing the uses of the seas and the exploitation of their natural resources. The provisions of the Convention on the protection of the marine environment are concentrated in Part XII, Articles 192 to 237, but rules governing the prevention, reduction, and control of pollution of the marine environment from any source may be found in other parts of the Convention, including Article 1 (1) on definitions of pollution and dumping; Article 19 (2)(h) prohibiting "any act of willful pollution" during innocent passage in the territorial sea; and Article 21 (1)(f) on compliance with the coastal state laws and regulations for the preservation of the marine environment and the prevention, reduction, and control of pollution, when foreign vessels are exercising their right to innocent passage. Similar rules are applied in transit passage through straits used for international navigation under Article 39 (2)(b), Articles 40 and 42 (1)(b), and Article 52 on innocent passage in archipelagic waters. There are also several articles in other parts of the Convention and its Annexes, relating to various other aspects of the protection and preservation of the marine environment.[19]

17. See Articles 24 and 25 of the Convention on the High Seas. In Article 24, there is this reference: "to prevent pollution of the seas by the discharge of oil from ships or pipelines or resulting from the exploitation and exploration of the seabed and its subsoil." Article 25 of the same Convention requires States "to take measures to prevent pollution of the seas from dumping of radio-active waste." Article 5 (7) of the Convention on the Continental Shelf contains an obligation on the part of the coastal States to undertake appropriate measures in the safety zones, established around continental shelf installations, to protect living resources from harmful agents.

18. For more details, see M. H. Nordquist, *United Nations Convention on the Law of the Sea 1982: A Commentary*, vol. IV, ed. S. Rosenne and A. Yankov (Dordrecht: Martinus Nijhoff, 1991), p. 6.

19. See for instance, Article 56 (1)(b) (III), regarding the jurisdiction of the coastal State in its exclusive economic zone with respect to the protection and preservation of the marine environment; Article 145 on the prevention, reduction, and control of pollution and other hazards to the marine environment, deriving from activities in the International Seabed Area and protection and conservation of the natural resources of the Area and prevention of damage to the flora and fauna; Article 240 (d) in respect to the obligation to conduct marine scientific research in compliance with the rules and regulations for the protection and preservation of the marine environment; Article 263 (3) with regard to the responsibility and liability for damage caused by pollution of the marine environment arising out of the conduct of marine scientific research; Article 277 (c) concerning the function

One of the characteristic features of UNCLOS is its comprehensive and well-structured framework of general rules, providing an adequate background for a legal regime over all coastal and marine areas and governing all major maritime activities.[20] The preeminently piecemeal approach of the preceding attempts at codification of the law of the sea in general, and its environmental component in particular, was hereby overcome. In addition, the Convention may be considered as an attempt, though not a completely successful one, to go beyond the conservative model of the zonal and sectoral approach, that is, to confine the scope of a given convention or agreement to a specific maritime area or source of pollution. The zonal approach does not correspond well with the nature of the marine environment, which is not confined to legally established boundaries of maritime space zones. The sectoral approach also does not correspond with the integrated and interdependent features of the marine environment. The guiding principle throughout the negotiation process was the understanding that key issues were interdependent and had to be treated as a "package." This understanding is reflected in the Preamble to the Convention: "[T]he problems of ocean space are closely interrelated and need to be considered as a whole."

A distinct trait of UNCLOS is the underlying intention to move beyond the reactive approach of pollution abatement after the harm has occurred, towards prevention of the adverse effects of pollution. This intention was not completely achieved by UNCLOS, but there were indications that the new preventative orientation gained some ground. This is evident from the wording "prevent, reduce and control pollution of the marine environment" as a kind of a term of art. However, no consensus was attained on this issue initially, but the existing wording will not create legal obstacles for advancing the preventative approach. As a follow-up to UNCED and further development of strategies in the field of protection and conservation of the marine environment, the "ecosystem approach"[21] has evolved as a holistic or inclu-

---

of regional marine scientific and technological centres in study programmes related to the protection and preservation of the marine environment and the prevention, reduction and control of pollution; Article 290 (1) on provisional measures imposed by a court or tribunal in connection with a view to preserving the respective rights of the parties to the dispute, or to prevent serious harm to the marine environment, pending the final decision; and Article 1 of Annex VIII on special arbitration of disputes concerning the interpretation or application of the Convention relating to protection and preservation of the marine environment.

20. See the Transmittal Letter of the President of the United States to the Senate where Part XII of UNCLOS was recognized as ". . .the strongest comprehensive environmental treaty in existence or likely to emerge for quite some time," *United States: President's Transmittal Letter of the United Nations Convention on the Law of the Sea and Agreement Relating to the Implementation of Part XI to the US Senate with Commentary, International Legal Materials* 34 (1995): 1397.

21. See the Resolution of the General Assembly of the United Nations on Agenda item 25 (a), Oceans and the Law of the Sea: Oceans and the Law of the Sea, Doc. A/57/L.48, where states are called upon ". . . to promote the conservation and

sive treatment of environmental protection, not by a single specific source of pollution, or within a special maritime zone, but employing various available methods to prevent, reduce and control pollution.

With regard to the regime for protection of the marine environment, the provisions of UNCLOS provide favourable grounds for harmonization of UNCLOS with special agreements and conventions or national legislation. Indeed, UNCLOS had already played a constructive role to this effect even prior to its entry into force in 1994. References to UNCLOS are made in many international instruments and national legislation. The Convention had therefore already acquired acknowledgment as an authoritative source of modern law of the sea. Part XII of the Convention was also recognized as part of customary international law and that it was,

> . . . the strongest environmental treaty in existence or likely to emerge for quite some time' [and that] 'it creates a positive and unprecedented framework for environmental protection and will encourage all Parties to take their environmental obligations seriously and come together to address issues of common and pressing concern.[22]

It also acknowledged that:

> [T]he articles of the 1982 UNCLOS on the marine environment thus represent the culmination of a process of international lawmaking which has effected a number of fundamental changes in the international law of the sea.[23]

One of the positive features of Part XII is its structure. Of the 11 sections, three consecutive sections are assigned to international rules and national legislation (Section 5), their enforcement (Section 6) and further safeguards (Section 7). They are closely interrelated: the provisions on enforcement correspond exactly to the content and format of the international rules and national laws and regulations as legal means for their implementation. The safeguards are the prerequisites for compliance with the rule of law,

---

management of the oceans in accordance with Chapter 17 of Agenda 21 and other relevant international instruments, to develop and facilitate the use of diverse approaches and tools, including the ecosystem approach. . ." On the need to apply "an international ecosystem approach to ocean management," see (n. 14 above), p. 265.

22. It may be noted that the President of the United States in his Letter of Transmittal to the Senate characterized Part XII of UNCLOS as being part of customary international law. (See Transmittal Letter [n. 20 above].) References to UNCLOS are contained in several treaties at the regional and international levels adopted under the auspices of IMO, FAO, UNEP and other international organizations.

23. See P. W. Birnie and A. E. Boyle, *International Law and the Environment* (Oxford: Clarendon Press, 1992), p. 253; and related doctrinal sources (n. 7 above).

through measures to facilitate proceedings and fair administration of justice. This serves as a legal guarantee for the settlement of disputes and avoidance of adverse consequences in enforcement activities and the imposition of sanctions. In these three sections, particular emphasis is placed on global and regional cooperation.

The characteristic features taken together reveal the main elements of the concept of protection of the marine environment under the relevant provisions of UNCLOS. They were further elucidated and substantiated through special conventions and agreements and the contribution of UNCED, in particular Chapter 17 and the Rio Declaration on Environment and Development.

The Integrated Approach to Protection of the Marine Environment and Sustainable Development

The concept of sustainable development of the marine environment contains two complementary components, one environmental and the other socioeconomic. The 1972 Stockholm Conference on the Human Environment placed the emphasis on the protection and conservation of the environment. But soon after the Conference, already in the early 1980s, a new trend in environmental strategy made headway. The need for a new approach to the interrelationship between environment and development had been steadily gaining ground. The consideration of the ecological implications of economic growth and technological development raised the fundamental problem of compatibility between environmental and economic considerations. On the initiative of the United Nations General Assembly an independent World Commission on Environment and Development was established.[24]

The World Commission in its report identified the general concept of sustainable development in the following manner:

> Sustainable development is development that meets the needs of the present without compromising the ability of future generations to meet their own needs. It contains within it two key concepts:

24. UN General Assembly Resolution 38/16 of 1983, adopted at its 38th Session. The resolution called on the Secretary-General of the UN to appoint the Chairman and Vice-Chairman of the World Commission on the Environment and Development. The Secretary-General appointed Mrs. Gro Harlem Brundtland of Norway as Chairman, and Dr. Mansur Khalid from the Sudan as Vice-Chairman. The Commission produced a report in 1987 entitled *Our Common Future* (n. 14 above). The UN General Assembly in Resolution 38/1 determined the Terms of Reference of the Commission. The report of the Commission was discussed by the Governing Council of UNEP and thereafter submitted for consideration by the UN General Assembly at its 42nd Session in 1987.

- the concept of needs, in particular the essential needs of the world's poor, to which overriding priority should be given;
- and the idea of limitation imposed by the state of technology and social organization on the environment's ability to meet present and future needs.[25]

Thus, economic and environmental considerations should not be opposed to each other. On the contrary, they should be viewed as being complementary to each other, within an integrated system of decision making, united by common objectives and strategies. Economic, social, demographic, and humanitarian factors must be integrated with measures to prevent degradation of the environment. This general approach includes the marine environment, too.

The emergence of the integrated concept of environment and sustainable development generated legal and institutional changes in the policy of exploration and exploitation of the natural resources of the seas and oceans and protection of the marine environment as an important part of ocean governance. This new trend in turn affected the process of lawmaking at the national, regional, and global level, substantiated by relevant national legislation, bilateral, regional, subregional, and global agreements, action plans, and other international instruments and related institutions. The report as a whole also deals with the promotion of international cooperation as an essential requirement for integrated protection, management, and sustainable development. Among the important legal means to enhance the integrated environment and development regime, the urgent need "to reinforce existing methods and develop new procedures for avoiding and resolving environmental disputes" is noted.[26]

The main conclusions of the report of the World Commission on Environment and Development concerning the legal and institutional change are summarized in the "Proposed Legal Principles for Environmental Protection and Sustainable Development" elaborated by the Group of Experts on Environmental Law," annexed to the final report of the Commission.[27] The essential elements of the concept of environment and development were embodied in Principle 7 stating that the following:

> States shall ensure that conservation is treated as an integral part of the planning and implementation of development activities and provide assistance to other States, especially to developing countries, in support of environmental protection and sustainable development.[28]

25. See *Our Common Future* (n. 14 above), p. 43.
26. Ibid., p. 330.
27. Ibid., pp. 348–51. The "Summary of Proposed Legal Principles" sets out general principles, rights, responsibilities, and obligations of States to cooperate in implementing their rights and obligations, derived from the proposed principles.
28. Ibid., p. 349.

The following principle (Principle 8) sets out international cooperation as a general obligation of States in the field of protection and sustainable development of the marine environment. So far as the marine environment is concerned, this provision might be considered as a reflection of the relevant articles of UNCLOS on the obligation of States to cooperate on a global and regional basis and to render technical assistance to developing countries, in the protection and preservation of the marine environment.[29]

The last principle (Principle 22) is a further elaboration of the principle of peaceful settlement of disputes as a general obligation. It provides for compulsory arbitration or judicial settlement at the request of the States concerned, if no mutual agreement on a solution or on other dispute settlement arrangement is reached within 18 months.

I recall that during our work in the Independent World Commission on the Oceans (IWCO), in our conversations, Elisabeth often referred to the Report on Environment and Development with great respect and appreciation. She considered the report of the Commission to be a model that should be taken into account when preparing the report of IWCO.

The report of the World Commission on Environment and Development generated the convening of the United Nations Conference on Environment and Development (UNCED). The Conference was called by the General Assembly of the United Nations in 1989 "to devise integrated strategies that would halt and reverse the negative impact of human behaviour on the physical environment and promote environmentally sustainable economic development in all countries."[30] Agenda 21, the Programme of Action for Sustainable Development, including Chapter 17 on protection of the oceans,[31] and the Rio Declaration on Environment and Development, have all exercised their crucial influences on the regime of protection and sustainable development of the marine environment during the last decade.

Thus, UNCED made a primary contribution to the formation of the integrated notion of environmental protection and sustainable development.

THE EFFECT OF THE INTERFACE BETWEEN UNCLOS AND UNCED ON THE PROTECTION AND SUSTAINABLE DEVELOPMENT OF THE MARINE ENVIRONMENT

The United Nations Convention on the Law of the Sea is a comprehensive framework of legal rules for pursuing the uses of the sea, management of

29. See UNCLOS Articles 197–201 and 202–203.

30. United Nations. *Earth Summit. Agenda 21. The United Nations Programme of Action.* United Nations Publication Sales No E. 93.I. 11. New York: United Nations, 1993, p. 3.

31. The official title of Chapter 17 is "Protection of the oceans, all kind of seas, including enclosed and semi-enclosed seas, and coastal areas and the protection, rational use and development of their living resources."

its resources, and protection and sustainable development of the marine and coastal areas. This role of the Convention is recognized in the Introduction and several paragraphs of Chapter 17 of Agenda 21,[32] and in the reports of the Secretary-General of the United Nations on "Oceans and the Law of the Sea."[33] In these annual reports and reports of the Commission on Sustainable Development the progress of interaction between UNCLOS and Agenda 21 of UNCED was examined.[34] Therefore States, the Secretariat of the United Nations and other international organizations often tend to deal with the implementation of Agenda 21 together with the International Tribunal for the Law of the Sea (ITLOS) since there has been a close association between UNCLOS and Agenda 21, in a kind of an institutional symbiosis.

The ecological, economic, and social considerations built into the integrated concept of environment and development could be deduced from two general provisions of Part XII of UNCLOS, Articles 192 and 193. Article 193 sets out the general obligation of States to protect and preserve the marine environment. Article 193 for its part lays down the sovereign right of States to exploit their natural resources pursuant to their natural environmental policy, yet also subject to their international legal obligation to protect and preserve the marine environment. Thus the exercise of the sovereign right of exploitation of the natural resources is not unconditional, but subordinated to the State's environmental obligations. The two provisions ought to be considered as interlocked or interdependent, entailing mutual balancing of rights and obligations. Taken together they might be considered as the forerunners of the legal concept of integrated environmental and economic considerations and the legal basis of the integrated approach. Of course the integrated approach in Chapter 17 of the Agenda 21, and in the Rio Declaration, is more elaborate and better articulated. Therefore these Articles do not need detailed interpretation. The provision of Principle 4 of the Declaration provides an unambiguous statement of the purpose and content of the integrated approach, which reads:

> In order to achieve sustainable development, environmental protection shall constitute an integral part of the development process and cannot be considered in isolation from it.

The formation of the integrated concept of environment and development or integrated approach has been a long process, in which the 1972 Stockholm Declaration on the Human Environment and UNCLOS marked only

32. Agenda 21, Chapter 17, paras 17, 17.22, 17.31, 17.49, 17.50 17.79, et cetera.

33. Reports of the Secretary-General on Oceans and the Law the Sea, UN Doc. A/47/623; A/48/527; A/49/631; A/50/713; A/51/645; A/52/487.

34. Report of the Commission on Sustainable Development on the overall progress achieved in 1996–1997, in UN Doc. E/1996/28 and E/CN17/1997/Add. 16.

the beginning. In several reports of the Secretary-General on "Oceans and the Law of the Sea," prior to UNCED, there was noted the following:

> . . . a discernible, although still incipient, trend among States to move toward a comprehensive integrated approach to national policy-making and development-planning and management for their coastal and offshore areas.[35]

The interrelationship between UNCLOS, in particular Part XII (Protection and Preservation of the Marine Environment), and Agenda 21, Chapter 17 of UNCED, has been most productive in promoting new approaches in environmental and developmental policy. A critical evaluation of UNCLOS in the light of present-day perceptions and standards will reveal some substantive insufficiencies in the content and format of certain provisions regarding the integrated management and protection of the marine environment. The provisions of the Convention adopted almost 3 decades ago by consensus were the result of compromises between conflicting economic interests and divergent views on environmental issues. The measures to prevent, reduce, and control pollution of the marine environment are essentially based on the sectoral and zonal approach and governed predominantly by the polluter pays principle.

The evolution of international environmental law from UNCED through Agenda 21 and the Rio Declaration on Environment and Development has served as a corrective measure for UNCLOS. These two documents added economic, social, demographic, and human rights components to environmental policy and decision making. One of the main objectives of environmental protection and sustainable development set forth in Agenda 21 is to: ". . . integrate protection of the marine environment into relevant general environmental, social and economic development policies," for example, introducing economic incentives to apply clean technologies, and improving the living standards of coastal populations, particularly in developing countries.[36] This new trend of interdependence and integration of economic and social development and environmental protection has been emphasized in several principles of the Rio Declaration and in various UN General Assembly documents.[37]

35. UN Doc. E/1985/79, par. 7, and A/41/742, A/42/688, A/43/718, A/44/650, A/46/724, A/47/512.

36. Agenda 21, par. 17.22.

37. Principle 3 ("The right to development must be fulfilled so as to equitably meet developmental and environmental needs of present and future generations"); Principle 4 ("In order to achieve sustainable development, environmental protection shall constitute an integral part of the development process and cannot be considered in isolation from it"); and Principle 25 ("Peace, development and environmental protection are interdependent and indivisible"). See also documents from the Nineteenth Special Session of the General Assembly, UN Commission on Environment and Sustainable Development.

Both Agenda 21 and the Rio Declaration extend beyond reactive remedies, for example by advancing the precautionary principle and anticipatory approach to be applied at the stage of planning of a major project. The precautionary approach requires prior environmental assessment based on scientific knowledge and reliable data obtained through systematic observation. Under Principle 15 of the Rio Declaration "lack of full scientific certainty shall not be used as a reason for postponing cost-effective measures to prevent environmental degradation." Precaution in this context falls within the broad concept of prevention, with special emphasis on measures susceptible to avoid a significant risk of potential damage or irreversible adverse effect. These new approaches may provide grounds for amplifying the application of the relevant provisions of UNCLOS.[38] This could be the case with Article 206 of UNCLOS on the assessment of the potential effects of planned activities that may cause substantial pollution or significant, harmful changes to the marine environment. In general, other provisions of UNCLOS contemplating preventive measures against imminent threats to the marine environment may fall within the purview of the precautionary approach. Several other agreements in the field of protection of the marine environment have also referred to the application of precautionary approach or precautionary principle.[39] Thus Agenda 21, Chapter 17 has made an important input to the amplification of the scope of many provisions of UNCLOS regarding prevention of pollution. Of course it is obvious that, while UNCLOS is a binding international multilateral treaty, both Agenda 21 and the Rio Declaration are international instruments with moral and political significance, but neither carries the weight of a legally binding rule.

The report of the Independent World Commission on the Oceans,[40] like the report of the World Commission on Environment and Development, also contributed to the enhancement of the integrated concept of environment and sustainable development of the marine environment. This latter study of the oceans could benefit from the wealth of accumulated knowledge and experience of the last few decades of intensity of ocean use, increasing opportunities and new challenges on the start of the new millennium. The main topics of the report are centered on promoting peace and security in the oceans, equity challenges, sustainable development and effective ocean governance. Protection and sustainable use of coastal and marine resources count among the crucial issues relating to the fate of the oceans.

38. Agenda 21, par. 22, explicitly refers to the application of "preventive, precautionary and anticipatory approaches" in accordance with UNCLOS.

39. See Article 3/3 of the 1992 Framework Convention on Climate Change, *International Legal Materials* 31 (1992): 849; and the 1992 Convention on Biological Diversity.

40. *The Ocean, Our Future.* Report of the Independent World Commission on the Oceans. Cambridge: Cambridge University Press, 1998.

The sequence of major international events relating to environmental protection and sustainable development was marked by the Johannesburg Summit on Sustainable Development, 26 August–4 September 2002.[41] This Conference was a kind of a follow-up to UNCED, but should be distinguished by the emphasis on pressing concerns of poverty and improving people's lives, reversal of the degradation of the environment and the promotion of partnerships in solving global problems. In the words of the Secretary-General of the UN, Kofi Annan: "This Summit makes sustainable development a reality and will put us on a path that reduces poverty while protecting the environment, a path that works for all peoples, rich and poor, today and tomorrow."[42]

The main documents of the Conference, the *Report of the World Summit on Sustainable Development, Resolutions 1* and *2,* and the *Plan of Implementation on the World Summit on Sustainable Development,* contain specific references to Agenda 21, and to matters relating to the marine environment and uses of the oceans. The Report points out the following:

> Prominent in the Implementation Plan are ocean and coastal management and preservation issues. Oceans, seas, islands, and coastal areas form an integrated and essential component of the earth's ecosystem and are critical for the global good, security and well-being of many economies.[43]

The Report further states that the Conference encourages the application, by 2010, of an ecosystem approach to sustainable development of oceans, which also requires effective coordination and cooperation at the regional and global level. The Conference called on States to ratify the 1997 Kyoto Protocol to the United Nations Framework Convention on Climate Change *in a timely manner* and to undertake to reduce the emissions of greenhouse gases. The Plan of Implementation sets as a target of 2010 to halt the loss of biodiversity. All these remedies taken together constitute a broad programme of action to expand the scope of application of Agenda 21, and the relevant provisions of UNCLOS on environment and sustainable development.

*****

The overview of the evolving integrated concept of protection of the marine

41. It may be worth noting that, perhaps by a mere coincidence, since the 1972 Stockholm Conference on the Human Environment, every major international event in the field of protection and management of the marine environment has appeared regularly at 10-year intervals. The next event was the adoption of UNCLOS and its opening for accession in 1982, followed by UNCED in 1992 and the Johannesburg Summit in 2002.

42. See Press Release, Johannesburg Summit 2002, 5 February 2003, p. 1.

43. See Doc. A/CONF.199/20.

environment and sustainable development of marine resources has proved that it comprises a multitude of ecological, economic, social, demographic, and other related components. In combination, these constitute an essential prerequisite for viable ocean governance. The implementation of a new strategy based on the integrated concept urges the application of new approaches both to the protection of the marine environment and to the management of marine resources. UNCLOS and UNCED, together with the ensuing conventions and agreements, may provide appropriate legal instruments for putting this strategy into effect.

Might Future Generations Conclude that Their Interests in Whale Stocks Would Have Been Better Safeguarded by a Body Considering Ocean Space Holistically?

Patricia W. Birnie
Visiting Fellow, London School of Economics and Political Science

INTRODUCTION: THE COMPLEXITY OF INTERESTS AND DISCIPLINES INVOLVED IN THE CONSERVATION OF WHALES

Marine mammals have been hunted by various means since time immemorial.[1] Mankind's right freely to exploit the living resources of the sea was virtually unquestioned over the centuries.[2] The great whales were, however, frequently celebrated by poets as objects of wonder. Milton, for example, refers to "Leviathan, Hugest of living creatures," who "at his gills/draws in, and at his trunk spouts out a sea."[3] The Psalmists also singled them out as divinely created and succoured creatures disporting themselves in the vastness of the seas,

> . . . wherein are things creeping innumerable,
> Both small and great beasts.
> There go the ships:
> There is that Leviathan, whom thou hast made to play therein.

1. For an account of this, see P. Birnie, *International Regulation of Whaling: From Conservation of Whaling to Conservation of Whales and Regulation of Whale Watching,* 2 vols. (Dobbs Ferry, N.Y.: Oceana, 1985), Ch. II, 63–104; P. Birnie, "Intentional legal issues in the management and protection of the whale: A review of four decades of experience," *Natural Resources Journal* 29 (1989): 903–34.

2. See J. N. Tønnessen and A. O. Johnsen, *The History of Modern Whaling* (Berkeley: University of California Press, 1980). Note that "whale" is not a scientific description of the order of Cetacea, but a term used by whalers to describe the particular species that they hunted, namely the 12 great whales. It also emphasises the emergence of a conservatory approach. J. L. McHugh, "The Role and History of the International Whaling Commission," in *The Whale Problem,* ed. W. Schevell (Cambridge, Mass.: Harvard University Press, 1976); F. W. Fulton, *The Sovereignty of the Sea* (Edinburgh: William Blackwood & Sons, 1911), passim.

3. J. Milton, *Paradise Lost* (New York: Odyssey Press, 1935), bk. vii, l. 412.

Ocean Yearbook 18: 284–329

These wait all upon thee;
That thou mayest give them their meat in due season.[4]

Despite the intervening centuries of exploitation, this nonexploitative view of Leviathan is currently now strongly pressed by many people, whilst, at the same time, a few States with long traditions of whaling continue to assert their right to kill whales for industrial, cultural and socio-economic purposes, albeit in vastly reduced numbers compared to those taken in the heyday of the industry in the early twentieth century,[5] when Antarctic whaling was at its height. Most recently their views have been supported by some developing countries and indigenous peoples asserting rights to sustainable development. Any endeavour to solve the problems raised by these conflicting views, given the historical context, draws us into a moral as well as a legal maze from which no easy exit has yet been perceived. Though we now have 60 years experience of attempts to resolve the problems created by centuries of internationally unregulated whaling, the problems both of international law and the other disciplines involved have become more rather than less complex. Indeed, new disciplines have been evolving in the meantime, as well as a greater focus on environmental and, more recently, developmental aspects of living resource exploitation, especially following the requirements of the Declaration of Principles, Agenda 21 and Convention on Biological Diversity (CBD), adopted at the 1992 United Nations Conference on Environment and Development (UNCED)[6] and its recent 2002 World Summit on Sustainable Development (WSSD).[7]

Sir Robert Jennings, the former President of the International Court of Justice (ICJ) recently drew attention, indirectly, to a crucial aspect of the problems now faced within the International Whaling Commission (IWC) when he observed, in another context, that "International law is more than ever before an interdisciplinary subject"[8] and that the international lawyers

4. *Psalm* 104, verses 24–27.

5. G. Elliot, *A Whaling Enterprise: Salvesen in the Antarctic* (Norwich, UK: Michael Russel (Publishing) Ltd., 1998), p. 11.

6. Held in Rio de Janeiro, 3–14 June 1992. It adopted a Declaration on Environment and Development endorsed by UN General Assembly Resolution 47/190 (1992) and Agenda 21, A Programme of Action; Texts in S. Johnson, *The Earth Summit: the United Nations Conference on Environment and Development* (London: Graham and Trotman, 1993), at p. 117 and 125 respectively.

7. Held in Johannesburg 26th August–4th September 2002. It adopted a Declaration on Sustainable Development and a Plan of Implementation, http://www.johannesburgsummit.org/ (accessed September 4, 2003).

8. See letter from Sir Robert Jennings to the American Society of International Law, American Society of International Law Newsletter, May–June 1999, nos. 1 and 2; see also J. Scarff, "The international management of whales, dolphins and porpoises: An interdisciplinary assessment," *Ecology Law Quarterly* 6 (1977): 323–571.

therefore should seek advice from and invite scientists, engineers, economists, historians, and international relations scholars to attend their meetings, as appropriate, when developing international law. He had in mind the usefulness to the ICJ of the advice of hydrographers when the Court was sitting in cases concerning disputes about the delimitation of the continental shelf.[9] Though perception of the interdisciplinary aspects of international law making is not new, traditionally this aspect has seldom been accorded prominence in the development of international law. Instead, emphasis has been placed on the special characteristics that distinguish law from other disciplines. It is interesting to note that despite this recent observation of its former president, the ICJ, in its recent decision in the case concerning Kasikili/Sedudu Island,[10] in which it was required to evaluate a considerable amount of cartographical and hydrological evidence relating to the depth and flow of water in certain channels that was relevant to the determination of the boundary between Botswana and Namibia, did not appoint scientific experts to advise it. However, this failure to do so led Judge Oda in his separate opinion to remark that as the definition of the main channel and its location depended on scientific knowledge, it should have obtained such advice by seeking the assistance of experts appointed by it.[11] Judge Weeramantry, in a dissenting opinion, discussed, inter alia, the ambivalence of the scientific criteria for determining the main channel and considered the appropriate judicial responses to the wider issues raised in boundary delimitation, which involves the dismantling or division of an ecologically integral unit.[12] He also addressed the need for establishment of joint international regimes to safeguard the environment in cases such as these.

This case provides contemporary evidence of the problematic relationship of international law and the sciences, but nowhere are such difficulties more apparent than in the interpretation and application of the International Convention for the Regulation of Whaling (ICRW),[13] adopted in 1946, in which many disciplines are now involved.

INTERDISCIPLINARY ISSUES ARISING IN THE IWC

During the 54 years of its existence, the IWC's attempts to develop policies and resolve both past and current disputes arising in the IWC, have necessitated numerous interdisciplinary approaches though their interrelationships are still far from being resolved within the IWC.

9. Jennings (n. 8 above), p. 2.

10. ICJ Communiqué No 99/53, 13 December 1999, *Kasikili/Sedudu Island (Botswana/Namibia 1999)*, 1-12, Annex 99/53 bis, 1-5, at 2.

11. Ibid.

12. Ibid.

13. 161 U.N.T.S. 143. The ICRW entered into force on 10 November 1948.

The question arises in the context of both the development of relevant international law generally and the operations of the IWC in particular concerning which disciplines, whether referred to as multi- or interdisciplines, have proved relevant to the operation and interpretation of the ICRW. The range of disputed issues currently on the Agenda of IWC Meetings raise questions deriving, inter alia, from the following:

Moral Philosophy and Ethics.—For example, do animals have "rights" or at least "moral rights"; should humans kill animals; if so, can any of the methods for doing so be regarded as "humane"?[14] Should indigenous coastal peoples (including those already referred to in the first schedules of the ICRW as "aborigines") and those living in developing states be allowed to catch whales otherwise protected on conservation grounds?

Sociology and Economics.—For example, despite the continued setting of quotas at zero by the IWC, on scientific grounds, for all whale stocks currently regulated by it, should the cultural, social, and economic needs of small coastal communities other than aborigines (see later) be met? Should the social and economic needs of the whaling industry be taken into account in considering resumption of whaling, as well as scientific advice?[15]

Human Rights.—For example, should indigenous coastal peoples (referred to in the Schedule to the ICRW as "aborigines") in developed states who traditionally have taken whales by nonindustrial methods for noncommercial purposes, that is, for cultural or subsistence purposes or both, be allowed to do so to meet these needs from depleted stocks that otherwise would require special protection? Should a similar right be recognised for coastal communities of nonindigenous peoples in developed or developing States for whom eating whale meat or catching whales has been or allegedly become part of their culture?[16] What is the origin of such rights and are they inviolable?

Science, including Marine Biological, Environmental, Ecological, and Other Scientific Disciplines.—For example, should a broader, more integrated approach be taken to management of living resources, as now advocated by scientists, governments, and nongovernmental organisations (NGOs), especially following the UNCED, an approach that takes account not merely of

14. *Chairman's Report of the 51st Annual Meeting,* 24–28 May 1999, p. 9. See also, "Humane Killing" in the *Chairman's Report of the 51st Annual Meeting,* p. 6–10; On this, see A. Gillespie, "The Moral Considerability of Animals," in *International Environmental Law, Policy and Ethics* (Clarendon Press: Oxford, 1997), Ch. VIII, 137–49.

15. *Chairman's Report of the 51st Meeting* (n. 14 above), "5 Socio-Economic Implications and Small-Type Whaling," p. 1–2; See Gillespie (n. 14 above), "The Use of Economic Rationale as Justification for Environmental Protection," Ch. III, p. 28–61.

16. *Chairman's Report of the 51st Meeting* (n. 14 above), Aboriginal Subsistence Whaling, item #11, p. 13–15; item 5, Gillespie (n. 14 above), "Aesthetic, Cultural and Recreational Justifications," Ch. V, 83–106, p. 92–102.

catch statistics but of the status of the whales' habitat, that is, the whole marine environment; and the effect on its biodiversity not only of pollutants but of climate change? What is the role of biological science and population dynamics in relation to evaluation of the status of whale stocks and determination of catch quotas? Such questions, currently being addressed, inter alia, by the IWC's Scientific Committee, raise issues involving several scientific disciplines.[17]

History.—The format of the ICRW itself and the presence of many of the items now on the IWC's agenda, as well as the sustained opposition of many States and NGOs to the resumption of whaling following a cessation of this activity since 1984–1985, cannot be understood or evaluated without appreciation of their historical context. An understanding of the IWC's present problems and interpretation of the relevant articles of the ICRW require considerable understanding of the long historical background of the freedom of the seas, the Law of the Sea generally, whaling, the first instruments regulating whaling concluded under the League of Nations, the circumstances in which the ICRW was concluded, and its operation thereafter.[18]

In this context, comments made elsewhere by Sir Robert Jennings concerning the process of developing international law for purposes of protecting the environment, including its living resources are particularly pertinent to the development of the legal regime for the conservation of whales.[19] When an issue is perceived as "a concern," he has warned, there is often a strong temptation to regard it as "a study by a newly enlightened generation," yet a historical perspective illustrates the dangers of treating environmental law as a specialisation that can be the object of separate study, because many applicable doctrines of global international law, such as sovereignty over natural resources, "soft" and "hard" law approaches, and numerous general principles, both old and new, already exist. Of course, the historical doctrines are in many cases likely to be inadequate on their own to resolve the environmental problems created by conflicts between technological advances, especially in relation to fisheries, and the growing scientific understanding that a more ecological approach to living resource management is required to maintain a sustainable yield and in some cases

17. *Chairman's Report of the 51st Meeting* (n. 14 above), "5 Environmental Concerns," pp. 29–34, including pollution, pp. 29–30; noise; ozone depletion; habitat degradation, p. 31; ecosystem-level effects, p. 32; health effects, p. 33; Gillespie (n. 14 above), "The Law Ethic," Ch. X, p. 159–75, discusses holistic environmental ethics and deep ecology, but note that scientists themselves, when referring to "interdisciplinary," may well be using this term primarily in relation to other established scientific disciplines such as biology, physics, and engineering; J. Kress, "Leader," *NERC News* (UK Natural Environment Research Council, Autumn 1999): 3.

18. See (n. 1 and 2 above), passim.

19. Foreword by Sir Robert Jennings Q.C. in P. Sands, *Principles of International Environmental Law* (Manchester: Manchester University Press, 1995), xii–xiv.

the very survival of particular resources. Wisely Jennings noted the need to maintain flexibility in relevant laws and regulations to facilitate ready response to changes in policy. Such laws should reflect lessons learned from the natural sciences and the availability and use of new technologies, despite the fact that scientists frequently cannot reach agreement even after extended research and that new technologies can be harmful as well as useful.[20]

But history advances slowly; there may not be time for laws to evolve gradually in response to new scientific knowledge, as they did in the early years of whaling when stocks were either abundant or the industry, having overexploited some species, could move on to hitherto unexploited species. New concepts such as the precautionary principle or approach adopted at UNCED have, however, only recently gained prominence within the IWC despite the fact that the "interests of the nations of the world in safeguarding for future generations the great natural resources represented by the whale stocks" was recognised in the preamble to the ICRW.[21]

Theology.—Religious belief has played its part in the pursuit of whaling from the pre-Christian era onwards. The great whales have inspired awe in the context of most religions. The Psalmists' view of the purposes of the creation of leviathan, to which we referred in our introduction, is now regarded as preferable by many, and is more in accord with our coexistence with creatures on this planet than the story of creation outlined in the Book of Genesis in the Christian Bible that records that "God created the great whales" on the fifth day and "every living creature that moveth, which the waters brought forth abundantly" and on the sixth day made man in his image and said "let them have dominion over the fish of the sea . . . and every living thing that moveth upon the earth."[22] This view of creation is no longer acceptable to many people though, as Elliot remarks in his recent memoir of the Antarctic whaling era. Svend Foyn, the Norwegian whaler who developed ca. 1860–1870 the steam whale catcher with a heavy harpoon gun at its bow that fired a harpoon with an explosive grenade head, was inspired as much by the conviction that he was doing God's work in harvesting the seas as by commercial success. Foyn's diary chronicling his labours was interspersed with prayers to the Almighty to support him in a fruitful outcome.[23] Such diverse views are still held, though now restrained by the process of development of the legal regime for conservation of whales and whaling.

International Relations and Political Science.—These more recent disciplines endeavour to explain in theoretical terms the negotiations and alli-

20. On this, see generally, J.-P. Beurier, A. Kiss and S. Mahmoudi, eds,. *New Technologies and Law of the Marine Environment* (The Hague: Kluwer Law International, 1999).

21. ICRW, first preambular recital.

22. *Book of Genesis,* Ch. 1, verses 20, 21 and 26.

23. Elliot (n. 5 above).

ances formed and reformed over the years in the process of concluding international regimes and identify the political arguments and rationale. For our purposes this means focusing on issues arising in the IWC when adopting its Agenda, setting of quotas and adopting and operating other regulations and recommendations relating to these, for which purposes it has to build the majorities or consensus required. Scholars in these fields supplement the legal analysis of powers and events in the IWC by providing insights into the formation of nonlegal regimes within such organisations and illustrating how these could be developed further to resolve some of the problems arising, as well as their relation to development of the legal regime itself.[24] As Jennings noted, our present system of international relations makes it difficult to develop appropriate environmental regulations in a timely manner and the traditional view that international relations are based on "pluralistic separate sovereignties" is inadequate when pressures such as scientific and technological advance make such sovereignties increasingly interdependent. The need to create a new form of international society must be faced.[25] International relations and political science theory have adopted various approaches to this. Some writers argue that only world government can solve environmental problems that cross the national borders of so-called sovereign states. Others argue that mechanisms exist within the interstate system through which transborder environmental problems can be resolved by cooperation; that is, through institutional mechanisms or regime creation of increasing degrees of sophistication constituting a source of so-called "global governance," without changing the basic structure of international law and politics, but working alongside it.[26] Concomitant with these

24. See S. Buck, *The Global Commons: An Introduction* (London: Earthscan, 1998), passim; For a good overview of developing theory and a useful biblography, see M. Patterson, "Interpreting trends in global governance," *International Affairs* 75, no. 6 (1999): 793–802; For the relationship between international law and such theories, see M. Byers, *Custom, Power and the Power of Rules* (Cambridge: Cambridge University Press, 1999), passim.

25. Jennings (n. 19 above). Byers (n. 24 above), p. 20–21, reaches a similar conclusion, noting how an interdisciplinary approach accommodates the possibility of change in customary law and thus of international society. Obviously this also has relevance to the development of rules within the flexible procedures of the IWC.

26. See also, generally, O. R. Young, ed. *Global Governance: Drawing Insights from the Environmental Experience* (Cambridge, Mass.: MIT Press, 1997); J. Rosenau, *Governance Without Government: Order and Change in World Politics* (Cambridge, Mass.: Cambridge University Press, 1992); L. Hempel, *Environmental Governance: The Global Challenge* (Washington D.C.: Island Press, 1996); R. Lipschutz (with J. Magiers), *Global Civil Society and Global Environmental Governance: The Politics of Nature from Place to Planets* (Albany: SUNY Press, 1996); P. Newell, "Environmental NGOs, Transnational Corporations and the Question of Governance," in *Social Governments and Social Institutions,* ed. R. Cohen and S. Rai (London: Routledge, 1999). For a concise resume of the literature, see S. J. Toope in *The Role of Law in International Politics. Essays in International Law and International Relations,* ed. M. Byers (Oxford: Oxford University Press, 2000), p. 94–99.

new approaches is the suggestion that adversarial enforcement imposed by states is no longer the best or most preponderant form of enforcement of international laws. Rather, nowadays "softer" methods of securing "compliance" are becoming the favoured method, achieved by operating through the activities of so-called "civil society," that is, NGOs and the networking of other transnational bodies.[27]

No doubt observers of the operation and implementation of the ICRW by the IWC will be able to identify for themselves the relevance of many other disciplines—geography and oceanography, for example, but for our purposes this brief list must suffice to illustrate the relevance of other specialisms. Most important, for our purposes, is the role specifically accorded to science by the ICRW within its regulatory process and the reevaluation of this role in the light of the Declaration of Principles adopted by the United Nations Conference on Environment and Development (UNCED) held in Rio de Janeiro in 1992.[28]

THE DEVELOPMENT OF THE WHALING INDUSTRY: FROM A "NO SCIENCE" BASE TO ONE BASED ON "SCIENTIFIC FINDINGS"

Unregulated Whaling from the Seventeenth to Mid-Twentieth Centuries

Until Svend Foyn transformed the whaling industry, men had for centuries hunted whales with rowing boats and handheld harpoons. The development of steam power in the nineteenth century enabled vessels to go further afield, but the catching method remained the same. The industry was driven by the then insatiable demand for whale products, especially whale oil. The primitive techniques originally used compelled the whalers to concentrate on coastal waters and slower-moving whales that could be floated alongside the mother ship, such as the right, humpback, and sperm whales. Foyn's inventions increased in size, power, and technical refinement, and opened access to baleen whale populations. The huge blue as well as fin whales became the foundation of the twentieth century whaling industry, enabling the exploitation of vast numbers of unexploited stocks of large whales as far afield as Antarctica.[29] Hitherto, the most distant grounds had been in the

27. E. O. Brown Weiss and H. K. Jacobson, ed. *Engaging Countries, Strengthening Compliance with International Environmental Accords* (Cambridge, Mass.: The MIT Press, 1998); P. M. Haas, R. O. Keohane and M. A. Levy, *Institutions for the Earth: Sources of Effective International Environmental Protection* (Cambridge, Mass.: The MIT Press, 1993).

28. Text in Johnson (n. 6 above).

29. The first two expeditions to Antarctica set out in 1892 on a successful reconnaissance voyage from Norway and Scotland using old style ships and rowing boats, but the companies concerned were unconvinced of any economic benefit, Elliot (n. 5 above), p. 12.

Arctic exploited by the British and Dutch. The United States' whalers pursued whales not only off Massachusetts as they voyaged widely round the world, though not into the Antarctic.[30] However, by the nineteenth century, under this sustained assault, whales had become scarce in the absence of any international controls. The regulations that did exist were enacted ad hoc under a few States' national laws.[31]

The introduction of the new technology led to an explosion of whaling activity throughout the world from 1905–1922, not only in Antarctica, but off Africa, Mexico, Alaska, Labrador, Korea, and Japan.[32] However, many of these enterprises soon ended because the stocks of large whales were now as easily and quickly exhausted as they were easily and quickly caught. Nonetheless, no initiatives were taken to introduce international controls although, as we shall see, marine biologists were already concerned about the effects of such unlicensed slaughter. There is no doubt that any thoughts of introducing such controls would have been discouraged by the seminal decision of the International Tribunal established ad hoc to resolve a dispute concerning another species of marine mammal, the Bering Fur seals.[33] It held that the United States, even when such species migrated through its territorial sea to pup on United States territory and thus could be and were legitimately regulated under United States' law, could not enforce its laws against foreign vessels taking the seals on the high seas because the historic doctrine of "freedom of the high seas" prevailed.

Whaling continued during World War I, though both whales and the means of transporting the carcasses to the Antarctic land stations were more difficult to find. The war saved the U.K. industry, then threatened by an oversupply of whale oil, as new uses had not been developed pre-war; demands for glycerine for use in high explosives now arose.[34] After the war ended, the U.K. government, to ensure that the maximum oil continued to be produced, suspended its pre-war requirement that the industry ensure the full utilisation of whale carcasses. Facilitated by the development in 1925 of the stern slip, a ramp that enabled the whole whale to be hauled on deck for purposes of cutting it up, the industry gradually recovered.[35] Norway, which had diverted its whalers to the cargo trade, by use of direction finders

30. Ibid.

31. Ibid., p. 15; For further details, see Birnie (n. 1 above), Ch. II, p. 63–104.

32. Ibid., p. 13, For further details, see Tønnessen and Johnsen (n. 2 above), passim, and Birnie (n. 1 above), p. 65–74, 102–104.

33. Report of the Bering Fur Seals Arbitration 1898. I. Moore's International Arbitration I (755–961); reproduced in *International Environmental Law Reports* (1999): 43–88, 129, 137, 141, 169, 237, 649–50.

34. Elliot (n. 5 above), p. 18–19.

35. Ibid., p. 24.

and wireless soon returned to become the leader of a rapid growth in whaling.[36] Both Norway and the United Kingdom introduced national control through licensing systems; Norway's fleet increased dramatically. New floating factories were introduced bringing in much larger catches, Britain resisted pressure to give preference to British companies in licensing rounds,[37] but began to ban the taking of overexploited humpback whales[38] and set aside for scientific research part of the revenue levied by it through the licensing system as little was known about life cycle and reproductive patterns of the whales and their migratory routes.[39] It was now realised that such knowledge, obtained by conducting surveys involving the spotting and counting of whales and studying sea currents and temperatures and the complex structures of biological life at sea, was essential for assessment and effective regulation of whale stocks. These activities were not, however, popular in Norway.[40]

The Economic Approach: Intercompany Agreements and the Problem of New Entrants

In the absence of internationally established control of catches, intercompany economic measures of regulation were introduced when overproduction of whale oil led to a collapse in the market in the 1931–1932 season. The whaling companies acted privately to resolve the economic problem by reducing both the number of whaling expeditions and the total production of oil by means of intercompany agreements that limited both catch and effort.[41] This they did by establishing quotas allocated to individual expeditions but transferable between companies. However, the withdrawal of a company or vessel from the industry did not bring about a corresponding diminution of effort, yet the private system worked to the extent that the system did encourage older fleets to give up whaling. Elliot considers that the period from 1932–1937 was the only one in the whole history of the industry during which catching effort was effectively controlled because it was restricted by the companies not the governments, which might for reasons of national prestige encourage or collude in overfishing. The intercompany quotas could not be exceeded, and given that the companies had negotiated and accepted them for sound economic reasons, they did not cheat

36. Ibid., p. 25–26.
37. Ibid., p. 22.
38. Ibid., p. 23.
39. Ibid.
40. Ibid.
41. Ibid., p. 32–33.

on the number of so-called Blue Whale Units (BWUs)[42] awarded to them. The view of Harold Salvesen was that the last people to entrust with conservation of natural stocks were governments, whose interests were essentially short term—raising taxes, protecting their balance of payments, or defending national honour.[43] Nonetheless, concern about depletion of whale stocks and the wasteful processing practice now popular in the rush to extract whale oil increased at the international level. Governments thus again began to establish controls.[44]

Elliot's optimism, however, was undermined when in 1937 both Germany and Japan began whaling in Antarctic waters as the historic doctrine of freedom of fishing on the high seas, confirmed in the Bering Fur Seal Case, entitled them to do. The problems of deterring or controlling new entrants to a fishery continue to this day, both within the IWC and in relation to fisheries for straddling fish stocks and highly migratory species globally that have prompted further regulatory responses internationally.

Growth of Scientific Concern

The rapid depletion of whale stocks resulting from the pre- and post-World War I overfishing using the new technology, had not gone unremarked by concerned scientists. As early as 1910, at the Eighth Zoological Conference, they drew attention to the need to conserve the whales.[45] A Meeting of the International Commission for the Protection of Wildlife in 1913 further concluded that "this most important source of marine wealth would mathematically be exhausted in a short time."[46] In 1918, an American-Canadian Fisheries Conference called for measures to halt this decline either through international action or bilateral agreements.[47] As we have seen, the latter did not provide a stable basis for conservation in a situation of unrestricted entry. Existing Norwegian and British whaling vessels could no longer be restrained by informal arrangements that provided that they would take quotas agreed between only these two operators.

42. Whales were accorded a unit value related to their oil production; the Blue Whale had the highest value.

43. Elliot (n. 5 above); Harold Salvesen was then Managing Director of Christian Salvesen, one of the two British Whaling Companies.

44. Elliot (n. 5 above), p. 34–35.

45. P. Bock, "A Study in International Regulation: A Case of Whaling" (Ph.D. thesis, New York, University, 1966), p. 74–79; See also S. Holt, *Seas at the Millennium: An Environmental Evaluation*, vol. III, *Whales and Whaling*, ed. C. R. C. Sheppard (Amsterdam: Pergamon, 2000), Ch. 112, p. 63–88.

46. Ibid., p. 19.

47. *Report of the American-Canadian Fisheries Conference 1918* (Washington D.C.: US Government Printing Office, 1920).

THE LEAGUE OF NATIONS AND THE FIRST INTERNATIONAL AGREEMENTS

Concerns of ICES: Response to Scientific Concern

The post-World War I period had introduced a new era in international relations. The first global international institution, the League of Nations, had been established in 1919 and provided for the first time a forum whose attention could be drawn to major international issues. Many scientists began to cooperate through the International Council for the Exploration of the Sea (ICES), established by a gentleman's agreement in 1902[48] among scientists with an interest in marine biology. It took advantage of this opportunity to draw the League's attention to the problems of overexploitation of whales. ICES had originated from proposals made at a conference in Sweden in 1895[49] for a scheme for international cooperation in marine scientific research under which "a programme of scientific investigation would be accompanied by a practical exposé of the steps to be taken in order to bring exploitation of the sea fishery more in accord with the natural conditions regulating the growth and increase of fish." This would benefit European markets by ensuring sustained supplies. A further conference in 1901 resolved "that a rational exploitation of the sea should rest *as far as possible on scientific enquiry*"[50] and noted that international cooperation was the best way to achieve satisfactory results.

Once established, ICES coordinated and directed, inter alia, the appropriate biological research of participating States and published the resulting data and papers in its Bulletin. Whales were first considered in detail in 1912.[51] Its work was expanded after World War I, and in 1926 it introduced the system of dividing the ICES area into squares and collecting statistics on that basis.[52] In 1927, scientists interested in whaling problems met specially with a view to conserving the stocks. The work of this whaling committee[53] proved crucially important, facilitating cooperative international research, the results of which were reported annually to the Council. Its background lay in considerations of biology, zoology, geography, and economics and it represented an important step forward in international relations and politics in this difficult field. The independence of the scientists, who did not meet under the auspices of any political organisation, lent credibility to their findings.

48. For the origins and subsequent history of ICES, see A. E. J. Went, "Seventy Years Agrowing: A History of the International Council for the Exploration of the Sea. 1902–1972," *Rapp. P-V. Rven, Cons. Int. Explor. Mer.* (1972).

49. By the International Geographical Conference, Went (n. 48 above).

50. Ibid., (emphasis added).

51. Ibid., section 17, pp. 78–79.

52. Ibid., p. 59. The system is still used and the IWC still gathers data on this basis.

53. Le Comité International pour la Protection de la Baleine.

League of Nations Committee on the Products of the Sea

Thus when the League convened the first international conference on the Law of the Sea in 1930, the League Committee listing possible questions to be addressed by the conference, included whether it was possible to establish by way of international agreement rules regarding the exploitation of the products of the sea.[54]

The rapporteur of the relevant subcommittee, Snr. Suarez, was as progressive in his conclusions and recommendations[55] as over 60 years later was the UNCED's Chapter 17 of Agenda 21 on Protection of the Oceans, All Kinds of Seas and the Protection, Rational Use and Development of their Living Resources in 1992.[56] He noted that the migratory nature of most aquatic species created the "biologic-geographical solidarity of the species which should find its counterpart in a legal solidarity in the sphere of international law."[57] Existing ad hoc fisheries agreements were found to be a palliative, not a cure, because species migrated from regulated to unregulated areas. Going further than have any of the recent committees established by the United Nations Food and Agriculture Organization (FAO) or by the United Nations itself to consider the problems of highly migratory species, he observed that "Animals are ignorant of jurisdiction and national frontiers and observe not international law but internationalism; the sea for them is a single realm" and noted that no treaty existed to prevent the whaling industry from exterminating the whales despite technological advances and called for conclusion of an international agreement to protect them because "the riches of the sea" and the immense wealth of the Antarctic region are the "patrimony of the whole human race."[58] The "new jurisprudence should be based on the scientific and economic considerations which alone would see justice done."[59] He proposed reserved zones, establishment of general and local principles for better control and institution of methods of supervision of these controls.[60] These remain key but disputed issues within the IWC today, still entrenched on its agenda.

ICES assisted in the preparations for the 1930 Law of the Sea Conference and put forward conservatory proposals calling countries interested in

54. League of Nations Committee of Experts for the Progressive Codification of International Law 1925–1928, Annex; *American Journal of International Law* 20, Spl. Supp. (1926), pp. 230–41.

55. S. Rosenne, ed., *Report of Sub-committee on the Exploitation of the Products of the Sea,* vol. 2, (1992) p. 231–41.

56. Text in Johnson (n. 6 above).

57. Suarez Rept. *American Journal of International Law* 20, Spl. Supp (n. 54 above), p. 234.

58. Ibid.

59. Ibid., p. 235

60. Rosenne (n. 55 above), p. 240–41.

whaling, as a matter of urgency, to give serious consideration to the question of taking immediate, temporary measures for dealing with the situation.[61] It detailed the measures required, stressed the need for uniform legislation in all whaling states to give effect to them, and invited the Norwegians to establish a central institution to collect catch statistics from the whaling industry. The system still exists though the IWC itself now receives the data, which has been vital to its efforts to establish New Management Procedures (NMP) rather than responding to the call of the UN Conference on the Human Environment (UNCHE) in 1972 for a 10-year moratorium on whaling,[62] and its more recent efforts to establish a Revised Management Procedure (RMP), discussed later.

The First International Conventions and Protocols on Whaling 1931–1945

After the League's 1930 Law of the Sea Conference failed, the growing international concern about the excessive slaughter of the whales, focused through the League reports, led to the conclusion of the first International Convention for the Regulation of Whaling[63] at a conference convened by the League in 1931 specifically for that purpose. Some commentators criticised even then, as they do today, the inclusion of participants from non-whaling states in the negotiations and within the final treaty. The critics considered that this made the deliberations too unwieldy and led to a treaty that was ineffective for conservation purposes, and would, in the absence of any permanent institution or committees, have to be modified by ad hoc protocols concluded by smaller groups of concerned States.[64] The contrary criticism was also later to be levelled against the IWC; by the 1970s, its more conservationist member States considered that it would be a more effective

61. Went (n. 48 above), p. 78–79.

62. Recommendation 33, Action Plan for the Human Environment, *Report of the United Nations Conference on the Human Environment,* Stockholm, 5–16 June, 1972, UN Doc. A/CONF. 48/14/rev.1.J.

63. The League of Nations. LNTS, CLV, 349. Geneva. For an assessment, see W. R. Vallence, "International convention for the regulation of whaling," *American Journal of International Law* 31 (1937): 112–19; Tønnessen and Johnsen (n. 2 above), p. 399–401; Birnie (n. 1 above); L. Leonard, "Recent negotiations towards the international regulation of whaling," *American Journal of International Law* 35 (1946): 90–133; It was signed by 26 States, 18 of which ratified it; 10 later adhered; It thus had as wide a membership as the ICRW eventually achieved but the non-ratifying States included Japan, Germany, Chile, Argentina, and Brazil, all of which were developing their whaling industries in this period. The ratifying and adhering States included 8 non-whaling states.

64. See also P. Jessup, "The international protection of whales," *American Journal of International Law* 24 (1930): 751–52; Tønnessen and Johnsen (n. 2 above), p. 360–66.

instrument for their purpose if its membership included more non-whaling States, an objective that was eventually achieved.[65] Thus during the 1970s, the number of Contracting Governments to the ICRW was by various means, gradually increased from 14 in 1949 to 39 in 1982, and at the 51st Annual Meeting, held in Grenada, from 24–28 May 1999, it stood at 40 though only 34 Parties attended.[66] By 2002, at its 54th meeting the issue concerning whether or not the ICRW benefits from more parties remained unsettled.[67] At the time of writing it has 52 Parties as both whaling and non-whaling older members have lobbied states of their persuasion to join, hoping to increase the number of votes to support their proposals.

Although much criticised because of its regulatory scope and lack of any permanent institution (any changes in regulations required the convening of a further ad hoc conference for the adoption of another protocol, which then might be ratified by different parties), the League Convention and its Protocol had the great advantage of applying for the first time to "all the waters of the world."[68] This provision was later reflected in the 1946 ICRW's Article 1 (2), though this refers to "all waters in which whaling is prosecuted by factory ships, land stations and whale catchers." Many of the provisions of the 1931 Convention and Protocols were drawn from the existing national legislation of the States parties and the few preexisting treaties already protecting some birds, seals, and fish species. Thus enforcement was left to national means: Parties were required to license their vessels and take action in relation to their registered vessels and within their national jurisdiction.

65. P. Birnie, "The role of developing countries in nudging the international whaling commission from regulation of whaling to encouraging non-consumptive uses of whales," *Ecology Law Quarterly* 12 (1985): 937–75.

66. IWC, *Chairman's Report of the 51st Annual Meeting* (n. 14 above), p. 1.

67. Commentators do not necessarily agree on the benefit to the IWC of wider participation; S. Andresen, "The Making and Implementation of Whaling Policies: Does Participation Make a Difference?" in *The Implementation of Effectiveness of International Environmental Commitments: Theory and Practice,* ed. D. G. Victor et al. (Cambridge, Mass.: MIT Press, 1988); cf. Birnie (n. 65 above) and the now different position of recent developing country participants, for example, Oman, St. Vincent and the Grenadines, St. Lucia, Dominican Republic and the Solomon Islands, expressed support at the 51st IWC Meeting, alongside Denmark and Norway, for a resolution proposed by Japan requesting a small take of minke whales for certain of its coastal communities. They expressed interest in small-type whaling on developmental grounds. *Chairman's Report of the 51st Annual Meeting* (n. 14 above), Item 5, Socio-Economic Implications and Small-Type Whaling, pp. 1–2.

68. Leonard (n. 63 above), p. 100. He nonetheless concluded that the Convention did little more than rally the support of nations to the cause of conservation. It did no more than prohibit the taking of right whales, calves, immature or undersized whales (all of which were undefined) or females accompanied by calves. See also Tønnessen and Johnsen (n. 2 above), Ch. 22, esp. p. 399–407.

Following the failure of the intercompany agreements and further stock depletion, a new convention was negotiated in 1937[69] that included land-based stations, but proposals for more effective measures were opposed and compromised. More whales were killed than before and more oil flooded the market. Fears of extermination of some species increased and ICES drew attention to the need for stricter conservation. Proposals were put forward at a series of conferences at which further ad hoc protocols were negotiated from 1937 to 1946[70] in an attempt at introduction of uniform penalties for violations, including confiscation of whale oil and products and a ban on transfer of whale equipment to non-Parties; all were rejected.

Thus although the pre-1946 agreements made some attempt at conservation, and in that respect were better than the internationally unregulated situation that preceded them, they were insufficient, especially in their failure to address the economic problems inherent in allocating equitable shares of the catch, providing means of ensuring regulations on the basis of scientific advice, and establishing international supervision of enforcement. These inadequacies forced whaling States to readdress the problem at the end of World War II when whaling resumed and with it new problems. The war had stimulated major advances in science and technology, including ships, aircraft, and sonar locating, which the whale catchers could put to good effect. The new negotiations did, however, now take place within a climate of internationalism fostered by the establishment of the United Nations in 1945, followed by the institution of a number of other global bodies.

THE INTERNATIONAL CONVENTION FOR THE REGULATION OF WHALING, 1946

The pre-war system of ad hoc Protocols required Parties to take and enforce within their national jurisdiction through a national licensing system only the measures set out in each specific Protocol. The economic issues were not addressed publicly but left to the private intercompany schemes. The final 1946 Protocol did set a catch limit of 16,000 BWU but did not specify how it was to be distributed among the Parties. By 1946, the Protocols had required the Parties to collect statistical and biological information but also had the weaknesses described earlier,[71] although Parties had adopted a rec-

69. *Protocol Amending the International Whaling Convention 1937.* LNTS, CAC 79. The League of Nations; *American Journal of International Law* 34 (1940): supp., p. 106.

70. For a resume of these and the reasons for failure, see Birnie (n. 1 above), p. 116–41, esp. p. 136–41.

71. For details of existing precedents up to 1946 or then in process of negotiation, see Birnie (n. 1 above), vol. 1, p. 136–41.

ommendation that their registered whaling vessels should not be transferred to non-Party States. It was also accepted that coastal aborigines using canoes or similar unmotorised craft were exempted from all restrictions, as long as they took whales only for their own consumption and were not under contract to deliver the products of their whaling to any third person.

The great need concerning regulation of whaling in 1945–1946 as the industry revived was perceived to be not that the freedom of all States to harvest the resources of the high seas should be dispensed with and the activities of the whaling industry be fully internationalised, but rather that States should be free to catch whales subject to acceptance of the need to conserve them, and thus enable the preservation of the industry on a permanently sustainable basis, *as the requirements for that purpose were perceived at that date.* The most urgent needs were envisaged as restriction of the catch of those species identified as being endangered by overexploitation, relating this process to ongoing scientific advice, and establishment of a permanent commission to carry out these tasks by the means specified in a new convention.

It was recognised that the regulation of only species by measures that were accepted to be in the agreed interest of the negotiating Parties would be approved for inclusion, but that these interests could only be safeguarded, in the light of past experience, if these measures were adopted globally and reflected scientific advice. The prime need was seen to be to establish a system on the basis of which measures could be flexibly adapted as the urgency of conservation increased or, if successful, decreased.

There were few precedents to draw upon, as none of the existing fisheries commissions regulated species on a global basis,[72] although the 1930 Fraser River Convention applied to Fraser River salmon throughout their whole

72. Examples included the Provisional Fur Seal Treaty of 1911, as renewed in 1942, which continued the abstention principle, the aboriginal exemptions and the exceptions for taking of otherwise protected seals for purposes of scientific research; the International Pacific Halibut Convention 1923, as renewed in 1943, which provided the first examples, inter alia, of closed seasons and restriction of States' sovereign rights for purposes of conserving stocks and establishment of a uniform system of collecting statistics on the basis of which the complex biological problems facing catch controls could be studied without taking account of the legal boundaries and be regulated on the basis of recommendations made by its in-house independent research staff; the International Pacific Salmon Fisheries Convention 1930, which applied to all these fisheries whether found in the river, territorial waters, or the high seas and which also employed its own research staff; and the North East Atlantic Permanent Commission 1946, which was difficult to achieve through the medium of a separate ICES/NEAFC Liaison Commission. For a critique of these and other relevant conventions, see D. Johnston, *The International Law of Fisheries: A Framework for Policy-oriented Inquiries,* Pt. II (Dordrecht: M. Nijhoff, 1987), pp. 157–314, 319–440.

migratory range, which included parts of the high seas.[73] The few other fisheries conventions were more concerned with establishing the limits of national control over fisheries; none had established a fully international enforcement system, although some allowed for mutual inspection on the high seas of vessels suspected of violating the regulations. In such cases, however, only their flag States were allowed to prosecute the offending vessels. Only one purely conservatory convention existed in 1946, namely the dormant Convention on Nature Protection and Wild Life Preservation in the Western Hemisphere,[74] which aimed at creation of national sanctuaries "to protect and preserve in their habitat representatives of all species of the natural fauna in sufficient numbers and over areas extensive enough to ensure that they did not become extinct through any agency within man's control." Although the pre-1946 whaling instruments had allowed for establishment of reserved areas, this was solely for purposes of preserving overtaxed species from exploitation for a period to give them time to recover.

It is not proposed for our purposes to examine in great detail the practice of the Parties to the ICRW during its 54 years of operation, as this has been well covered by earlier commentators. Rather, the framework for action provided by the ICRW and the role and powers it assigns to the IWC for this purpose will be examined in conjunction with the interdisciplinary problems to which its interpretation and operation has given rise in the context of the UNCHE, UNCED, and WSSD and its relationship to other relevant wildlife conventions within the framework provided by the UNCLOS. Finally, conclusions will be drawn concerning the future international organsational structure for conservation of whales.

The ICRW's structure closely followed a draft prepared by the United States, a strongly conservationist State, which took account of the strengths and weaknesses of the earlier instruments. Ironically, the United States eventually became one of the strongest critics of the manner in which many of its provisions were applied. The United States provided one of its leading scientists to chair the 1946 conference and later to lead its first IWC delegation. However, as the United States was and remains committed to free enterprise, it insisted, long before establishment of the World Trade Organisation, that this freedom be protected within the ICRW. It thus insisted that any overall quotas set remained open to full competition by all, that is, that each expedition be able to take as much as it could until the total permitted catch was

73. Convention for the Protection, Preservation and Extension of the Pacific Salmon Fisheries in the Fraser River System 1930, LNTS CLXXXIV 305 (1930).

74. Convention on Nature Protection and Wild Life Preservation in the Western Hemisphere 1940, 161 U.N.T.S. No. 485 193.

taken and whaling halted. At the time of the ICRW's adoption the most important whaling grounds were still those surrounding Antarctica, and the U.S. whalers did not operate there. Though economically equitable in one sense, once the whaling fleets expanded in terms of size and the types of vessels and technology available, as they inevitably did in short-sighted efforts to increase a company's capacity to catch whales, any overall economic benefit was soon whittled down, the catching season was extended and the number of whales taken by each expedition was gradually reduced as the industry became uneconomic for most States. Elliot's recent "insider" account of the problems created by this U.S. policy and its repercussions on IWC practice, on which the following analysis is based, is a telling one.[75] Because of its surplus capacity, the industry nonetheless, over time, strongly resisted demands to cut the catch limit. It was not until 1962, when it was too late to save the industry as a whole, that this policy was abandoned and thereafter many Parties gradually gave up whaling, though most remained members of the IWC. Why has the ICRW nonetheless endured? Why did not such Parties then withdraw from the Convention? The reasons are various and often mixed. For some the goal was economic; they hoped by conservation to put the industry on a more stable footing so that whaling could be resumed. Others considered that in the light of its history the industry could never be effectively controlled or supervised and stayed in to press for purely conservationist goals. Some were opposed to whaling on religious or moral grounds that recognised the rights of animals and sought either to end killing or ensure that it was done humanely. Others were predominantly interested in ensuring that the scientific advice provided was reliable, whilst yet others thought that at the present time, given the range of potential threats, this was nonattainable and stayed or joined to press for cessation of whaling. This meant that the balance in the Commission shifted from a majority of States whose interests lay predominantly in promoting those provisions of the ICRW that preserved industrial goals, to one which, faced with the disastrous situation emerging, was more concerned to give effect to goals that emphasised conservation, scientific research, and provision of whale sanctuaries, as indicated in the discussion of and commentary on the ICRW's provisions that follows. A different version of the problem created by "new entrants" emerged under the ICRW, not in the traditional sense of new entrants to the fishery (which had endangered it in the past), but of new State entrants that sought to direct the IWC's policies to exclusively conservatory goals. Most recently however, as we shall see, some new entrants, including several small island developing states and coastal indigenous peoples, support resumption of whaling in the interest of their right to sustainable development, whether or not they had previously exploited whales. These

75. Elliot (n. 5 above).

divergences in policy goals now lead Parties, non-Parties and NGOs to interpret the relevant articles of the Convention in very different ways.

ICRW Preamble

The failure of the ICRW to conserve whales in the post-World War II (WWII) period was unfortunate as its preambular recitals were exceptionally innovative at the time of its conclusion. Though these statements are not binding they remain a useful guide for the interpretation of the Convention, which international law requires should be done in good faith and in accordance with its object and purpose.[76] These recitals, inter alia, recognise "the interest of the nations of the world in safeguarding for future generations the great natural resources represented by whale stocks" and acknowledge the past overfishing and the need to protect all whale species from further depletion.[77] Recitals 3 & 4 also acknowledged that "properly regulated" stocks would increase and thus allow increases in catch without further stock endangerment and affirmed the "common interest" in achieving the optimum stock level as rapidly as possible "without causing widespread economic and nutritional distress" (the prevalent problem at a time of post-war food and oil shortages). The Contracting Governments also expressed their desire to establish "a *system* of international regulation to ensure proper and effective conservation *and* development of whale stocks"[78] on the basis of the principles set out in the earlier agreements. The Preamble concluded by asserting that the new convention would "provide for the proper and effective conservation of whale stocks and thus make possible the orderly development of the whaling industry," a dual purpose achievement that became difficult as the industry rapidly declined.

Recognition of the global interest in safeguarding whales for "future generations" and the "common interest" are now perceived by environmentalists to be the priority post-UNCED goals. However, both the content and the purpose of these amorphous concepts are now perceived differently, with the result that some of the preambular aims are now seen to be in conflict with others, especially in the context of current theories on development of international law aimed at protection of the marine environment and its living species and species whose habitat it sustains within the overall objective of sustainable development.

76. Article 31 (1) of the Vienna Convention on the Law of Treaties, 8 ILM 1969, 679, is generally regarded as reflecting the customary international law on this. I. Brownlie, *Principles of Public International Law,* 4th ed., (Oxford: Oxford University Press, 1999), Ch. XXV, p. 603–64, esp. at p. 625–32 on interpretation. ICRW recital (emphasis added).

77. First and second preambular recitals respectively.

78. ICRW seventh preambular recital (emphasis added).

Definition of Terms: "Whales" and the "Whaling Industry"

The ICRW defines some terms[79] but not "whale" or the "whaling industry." Interpretation of its preambular goals has thus during the last 50 years led to a divergence of views. In issue, inter alia, is whether the lack of definition of "whale" allows for gradual expansion of the ICRW's scope to cover all species of cetaceans, large and small,[80] or whether it is confined to those species on whose exploitation the industry was based in 1946; and thus whether the term "whaling industry" is necessarily restricted to the commercial exploitation of those whales,[81] or whether it can be interpreted to embrace the nascent nonconsumptive "whale watching industry,"[82] which is ex-

79. Article II defines "factory ship," "land station," "whale catcher" (amended in the 1956 Protocol to include "helicopter, or other aircraft") and "Contracting Government," in terms of any government that has ratified or adhered to the convention, that is, any State whether or not whaling, can become a Party: An important factor in the building of coalitions both by the non- and pro-whaling factions within the IWC.

80. On this, see H. Nijkamp and A. Nollkaemper, "The protection of small Cetaceans in the face of uncertainty: An analysis of the ASCOBANS agreement," *Georgetown International Environmental Law Review* 10, no. 2 (Winter 1997): 281–302; P. Birnie, "Small Cetaceans and the IWC," *Georgetown International Environmental Law Review* 10, no. 1 (Fall 1997): 1–28; W. Burns, "The IWC and the Regulation of Small Cetaceans: The Critical Agenda for the 1990s," in *International Wildlife Law Occasional Paper Series*, No. 5 (Madison. W.I.: Pacific Center for International Studies, 1994); W. Burns, "The future of small Cetaceans: Problems and proposals," *Colorado Journal of International Environmental Law and Policy* 8, no. 1, (Winter 1991): 31–88; R. Churchill, "Sustaining Small Cetaceans: A Preliminary Evaluation of the ASCOBANS and ACCOBAMS Agreements," in *International Law and Sustainable Development: Past Achievements and Future Challenges*, ed. A. Boyle and D. Freestone (Oxford: Oxford University Press, 1999): 225–52.

81. The Final Act of the 1946 Conference did attach an Annex on Nomenclature of Whales, which gave the Latin names of the major species then exploited by the industry and the more popular English and French language versions used by the industry. The Conference recommended that this chart "be accepted *as a guide* by the governments represented at the Conference" (emphasis added), but it has since been claimed by some governments that the ICRW's scope is limited to the species, Annex reproduced in Birnie (n. 1 above), vol. II, p. 901. It was clearly not intended to limit regulation by the IWC to these species but to help it in setting quotas, providing statistics et cetera, clearly to identify the names of the species concerned in terms understood by all in the Commission and the industry.

82. In the absence of definition, it is suggested by like-minded States and NGOs that the term "whaling industry," as used in the ICRW, should be regarded as referring to or including the "whale watching" industry. A series of workshops sponsored by the International Fund for Animal Welfare (IFAW) et al. on all aspects of whale watching was convened. Three of the reports were presented to the IWC by concerned governments (the United States, United Kingdom, and New Zealand) and the other two were available to the SC. These Workshops were Scientific Aspects of Managing Whale Watching, Monte Castello di Vibio, Italy, 1995; (ii) Special Aspects of Watching Sperm Whales, Commonwealth of Dominica, 1996, (iii) Educational Values of Whale Watching, USA, 1997; (iv) Social and Economic Aspects of Whale

panding rapidly throughout the world. Though whale watching is conducted in both member and nonmember states and now subject to regulations or guidelines in many of them, it is not subject to regulation under any existing international convention. There is, however, growing international concern in a number of ICRW Parties that if unregulated this activity could result in disturbance and harassment of whales. It is thus now strictly regulated in some states, including when it is conducted on small cetaceans. Japan strongly opposes IWC regulation, but the topic has recently been placed on the IWC's agenda and it has established a Whale Watching Working Group and on its advice adopted Resolutions.[83]

Status of the Schedule

Breaking new ground, the ICRW established under Article I (i), as an "integral part" of the Convention, an amendable Schedule. All references to the Convention must be understood as including this, as amended annually. Thus, though no amendment procedures are provided in relation to the 11 substantive articles of the ICRW, the Schedule, because it is amendable, has become, over time, the vehicle for introduction of considerable change, reflecting advances in international law, ethics, science, and political theory, especially concerning the methods of conservation and killing, the continuation of aboriginal whaling, the status of small cetaceans under the ICRW and demands for sustainable development.

Scope of the Convention

Under Article I (2) the Convention applies to factory ships, land stations, and whale catchers under the jurisdiction of Contracting Governments and to "all waters in which whaling is prosecuted" by these. In practice, and the current form of provision for cessation of "commercial" whaling (a term not used in the ICRW) in the Schedule[84] confirms this, its Parties regard the Convention as still applying in "all waters of the world," the terminology used in some pre-WWII agreements. As far as the writer can ascertain from the IWC reports this interpretation has not been challenged.

Watching; New Zealand, 1999; (v) Legal Aspects of Whale Watching Workshop, Italy, 2000. In presenting the *Report on Legal Aspects,* the United Kingdom noted on its cover that it considered it "a useful tool for facilitating debate on whale watching." The reports are available from IFAW.

83. IWC Resolution 1996–2, *Chairman's Report of the 48th Annual Meeting,* 1999, recognises the IWC's role in monitoring and providing guidance on the sustainable development of this activity.

84. 1998 Schedule, par. 10 (e).

Composition of the IWC

Undoubtedly one of the most important articles in the Convention is Article III, which establishes an International Whaling Commission composed of one member (commissioner) from each Contracting Government (15 in all in 1949 when the ICRW entered into force; 52 at the time of writing). Each government has one vote but the Commissioner can be accompanied by an unlimited number of experts and advisors of all kinds. This has led to considerable discrepancy in the scope and strength of representation and in the ability of particular delegations fully to participate in working groups and committees and to influence events, including interpretation of the ICRW, unless they form coalitions which, of course, do not necessarily remain stable. For example, in the 1970s, following the recommendation made by participants in the 1972 UNCHE that a 10-year moratorium on whaling should be adopted by the IWC, environmental NGOs encouraged a number of developing countries to become parties to the ICRW in the expectation that they would support calls for a moratorium. Many were small island States that either had or subsequently proclaimed Exclusive Economic Zones in the process of development at UNCLOS[85] from 1973 onwards. At the 51st Annual Meeting in 1999, Antigua, Barbados, Chile and Oman were represented only by their respective Commissioners, whereas Japan had a delegation of 41 (including some whaling industry representatives); the United States fielded 21, the United Kingdom 15, Norway 12 (including some industry representatives), and Denmark 8 (including Greenlanders). Even Grenada, the host State, fielded only 3 persons.[86] The same inbalance in composition of delegations continues as the IWC's Annual Reports evidences.

The composition of the respective IWC delegations reflects the particular interests of ICRW Parties, and thus may include whalers, indigenous peoples, and NGOs. Although the larger delegations may include ministers, politicians, civil servants, scientists, and established NGOs, only a few include lawyers, despite the fact that legal issues arise, especially those concerning interpretation of the ICRW, UNCLOS, the UNCED instruments and related conservatory treaties.[87] Obviously most States will obtain preliminary legal opinions either from in-house legal advisers or consultants, as required.[88]

85. On these, see R. Churchill and A. Lowe, *The Law of the Sea*, 4th ed. (Manchester: Manchester University Press, 1999), Ch. 14, pp. 279–327, 287–89.

86. I.W.C/51/3, List of Delegates.

87. For example, CCAMLR, CITES, and Agreements concluded under the Convention on Migratory Species (CMS).

88. Some Parties and NGOs, however, commission legal opinions on particular issues that are circulated either informally or as IWC documents as appropriate. For example, Japan has circulated opinions concerning the legality of the continuation of the current cessation of whaling and on the establishment of the Southern Ocean Sanctuary. Opportunities arise for lawyers on like-minded delegations to discuss the

Japan currently continues to take the largest number of whales under research permits, since the moratorium on whaling adopted in 1982–1984 is still in place and thus has by far the largest delegation; delegations of whaling States carry appropriate representatives of their whaling interests. The United Kingdom, which abandoned whaling in 1963 when it became uncommercial, is now the leader of a "like-minded" caucus group of Parties opposed to resumption of commercial whaling, which, inter alia, includes Australia, New Zealand, the Netherlands, and the United States. Parties that are either now nonwhaling or have never whaled (e.g., Switzerland) generally support the "like-minded" approach depending on the specific issue. Switzerland, for example, recently presented a legal opinion supporting the view that small cetaceans fall within the regulatory scope of the ICRW.[89]

Relation to UN, Inter-Governmental and Non-Governmental Organisations: Creation of Observer Status

The IWC elects its own Chairman and Vice-Chairman and determines its own Rules of Procedure (Article II (2)). These represent another vehicle for change, because they govern the terms of admission of NGOs as observers at IWC meetings. Ninety-one observers, including pressure groups for "small type coastal whaling," attended the IWC's 51st Meeting, over 100 at its 54th one, but over the years efforts have been made to limit NGO representation

---

legal aspects of problems arising. Legal opinions, conference papers and articles on legal aspects of problems facing the IWC published in legal journals are often brought to the attention of delegations by IWC Members or NGOs; see for example, *Report on International Legal Workshop on Assessment of Actions of the International Whaling Commission under the International Convention for Regulation of Whaling* held at the Sixth International Whaling Symposium, which convened at the Institute of Cetacean Research (ICR), Tokyo, Japan, 7–9 January, 1996; W. Aron, W. Burke and M. Freeman, "Flouting the convention," *Atlantic Monthly* (May 1999): 22–29 (an extended version of this article, W. Burke, "The whaling issue," appeared in *Marine Policy* 24 (2000): 179–91; see also P. Birnie, "Are twentieth century marine conservation conventions adaptable to twenty-first century goals and principles," Parts I and II. *International Journal of Marine and Coastal Law* 12, no. 3-4 (1997): 307–39 and 488–532; See also W. T. Burke, Editorial Comment, "Legal aspects of the IWC decision on the Southern Ocean Sanctuary," *Ocean Development and International Law* 28 (1997): 313–27. Papers on international relations aspects may also be circulated, for example, R. L. Freidheim, "Moderation in the Pursuit of Justice: Explaining Japan's Failure in the International Whaling Negotiations" (paper presented at Panel on International Cooperative Studies on Negotiating Behaviour, Kyoto Conference on Japanese Studies, Kyoto, 19 October 1994, on file with the author).

89. Switzerland introduced a "Legal Analysis of IWC Competence to Manage Small Cetaceans" by a Swiss lawyer, A. F. Goetschel, commissioned by a Swiss NGO, The Swiss Coalition for the Protection of Whales; IWC *Chairman's Report of the 51st Meeting,* 1999; Agenda Item 19, IWC's Competence to Manage Small Cetaceans.

by establishing criteria for increasingly restricting observer status. Gradually each NGO has been limited to one representative, charged expensive admission fees, and denied access to official delegation document boxes for purposes of circulating NGO reports.[90] Environmental and pro-whaling NGOs can still distribute their papers and lobby the various delegations, however, and exercised considerable imagination in by-passing restrictions.[91] Observers from non-member governments, UN specialised agencies and other inter-governmental organisations (IGOs) can also attend[92] and submit reports. It should be noted, however, that the IWC was never brought within the scope of any UN specialised agency, though this was contemplated in Article III (b) of the ICRW, despite the fact that the UN's Food and Agriculture Organization (FAO) has competence for fisheries in general.

Voting Procedures: Recommendations and Regulatory Measures

The Commission makes its decisions by a simple majority of those voting, but decisions taken in pursuance of Article V (amendments of the Schedule) require a three-fourths majority thereof. This creates an important distinction between issues subject to binding and those subject to nonbinding procedures, of particular relevance since commercial quotas were set at zero in 1982. Building the necessary majorities when policy proposals are contentious is crucial to the outcome.

Recommendations

Thus, recently, the Commission has more often exercised its powers under Articles IV, VI, and VIII to make nonbinding recommendations in the form of resolutions to Contracting Governments. Article VI, allowing it to do so on "any matter relating to whales or whaling," has proved a particularly useful vehicle for encouraging gradual changes in practice. It is used when it is apparent that the three-quarters majority required for a Schedule amend-

90. IWC Rules of Procedure and Financial Regulation, as at September 1998; *Chairman's Report of the 51st Annual Meeting* (n. 14 above), p. 53, paras. 22–23. It was also resolved at this Meeting to dispense with transcripts of verbatim records, a decision that now severely inhibits scholarly research on the IWC Meetings; only CD oral recordings are available.

91. For example, when observers were required to have headquarters in more than 3 countries, NGOs either did so establish themselves, or "veiled" themselves within NGOs established for other purposes. For several years one well-known environmentalist represented the International Association of Rabbis.

92. At the 51st Meeting, Barbados, Canada, Iceland, Jamaica, Morocco, Namibia, and Zimbabwe were represented. At the 54th Meeting, held in Shimonoseki, Japan, 2003, new members included Gabon, Palau, Mongolia, and Benin, which voted with Japan. Kenya, which had not attended for 15 years, also attended voting to preserve the Indian Ocean Sanctuary; IWC 54th Rep. (Forthcoming).

ment does not exist or might not do so even following intensive lobbying by delegates and NGOs, both for and against contentious proposals. It is left to the IWC itself to decide on the parameters of "related" issues. At its 51st Meeting, for example, the IWC adopted resolutions raising legal, economic, political, and scientific issues.[93]

Schedule Amendments

The subject matter of Schedule regulations relating to conservation and utilisation of "whale resources," is specified in Article V, as also are the criteria on which they must be based. The IWC can, under Article V (1), inter alia, fix protected and unprotected species; open and close seasons and waters, including designate sanctuary areas; size limits of species; time methods and intensity of whaling, including the maximum catch per season; types and specifications of gear, apparatus and appliances used; measurement methods; catch returns and other statistical and biological records. Over the years from its original modest form, the IWC has built the Schedule into a formidable array of regulations. The drastic cuts in the overall quota that were required as the industry declined proved difficult to negotiate because Article V (2) places limitations on the amendment procedure. Amendments must be those "necessary" to carry out the objectives and purposes of the Convention and provide for conservation, development, and optimum utilisation of the "whale resources," all of which terms are undefined and disputatious in the light of current theories and concepts. The Commission has sought to balance these requirements because it is unclear when stocks are severely depleted whether "conservation" takes precedence over "development" of the resources or whether, in the light of scientists' increasing awareness of how little they know about the complex ecological balances of the oceans, "optimum utilisation" in the consumptive sense should be superseded by use for scientific study. Article VIII concerning scientific permits allows for both. These questions are further complicated by the addition of the pivotal requirement that the amendments be based on undefined "scientific findings." The ICRW does not specifically address the situation

93. Resolutions were adopted on a Revised Action Plan on Whale Killing Methods (matters arising from the Workshop on Whale Killing Methods), Special Permits for Scientific Research Whaling Under Special Permit, Health Effects from the Consumption of Cetaceans, the Funding of High Priority Scientific Research, Cooperation Between the IWC and CITES, Small Populations of Highly Endangered Whales, DNA Testing of Dalls Porpoise, and Amendments to the Commission's Rules of Procedure and Revised Rules of Procedures of the Scientific Committee (Appendices 12 and 13, 65–74), *Chairman's Report of the 51st Annual Meeting* (n. 14 above), IWC, 14 December 1999. The contentious issue concerning whether "whales" include small cetaceans has meant that resolutions have for many years been the vehicle for proposing management advice on particular species or populations thereof.

in which these "findings," however that phrase is interpreted, necessitate that the best conservatory approach is to suspend whaling for a period or even for ever. Greatly exacerbating the problems were (i) the continued overexploitation from 1949 to 1982, which resulted largely from the Commission's compromising on the scientific advice, and frequently adopting the highest rather than the lowest estimate of permitted catch; and (ii) its insistence on adherence to Article V (2) (c) that there must be no restrictions on the number or nationality of factory ships or land stations with no allocation of specific quotas to them and that the interests of consumers of whale products as well as the whaling industry (both now negligible in global terms) must be taken into consideration. Even in the 1950s and 1960s, the 5 Antarctic whaling States had found it necessary to meet outside the IWC, albeit unsuccessfully, to allocate the overall quota among themselves for their economic benefit. These problems were further exacerbated through unregulated whaling by some parties to the ICRW and lack of international inspection even of Parties' activities.

Objection Procedures

Under Article V (3) Parties are not bound by Schedule amendments if they object to them within a prolonged objection period (possibly up to 210 days). Several Parties have used this procedure over the years. Norway's current whaling for minke whales within its EEZ is legitimated by its objection to the "zero" quotas set in 1984–1985. Russia and Peru also sustain objections but do not whale commercially. Iceland opted for the alternative of withdrawing from the ICRW under Article X, rather than objecting as Canada had done in 1980 when it feared the IWC would attempt to regulate taking of small cetaceans taken by its indigenous populations. Iceland, however, recently controversially rejoined the convention, attempting to do so with an objection to the zero quotas, although Iceland had not lodged an objection within the required 90-day period when these quotas were first adopted and it was still a member of the IWC.

Influence of UNCLOS, UNCHE, UNCED and WSSD and Other Instruments on the Practice of the IWC and Related Conventions

Further difficulties of interpretation have arisen in the post-UNCHE and UNCED period, particularly concerning the Rio Declaration's Principle 15 advocacy of the precautionary approach.[94] The ICRW does not operate in

94. On this, see D. Freestone and E. Hey, ed. *The Precautionary Principle and International Law: The Challenge of Implementation* (The Hague: Kluwer Law International, 1996), esp. "Origins and Development of the Principle," Ch. 1, p. 3–18; K. von Moltke, "The Relationship between Policy, Science, Technology, Economics, and Law in the Implementation of the Precautionary Principle," in Freestone and Hey, ed. (this note), Ch. 6, p. 97–108; L. Mee, "Scientific Methods and the Precautionary Principle," in Freestone and Hey, ed. (this note), Ch. 7, p. 109–132; J. S. Gray, "Integrating Precautionary Scientific Methods into Decision-Making," in Freestone and Hey, ed. (this note), Ch. 8, p. 133–146; D. Freestone, "International Fish-

a legal, economic, or social vacuum. Its Contracting Governments participated in the UNCHE, UNCLOS, and UNCED negotiations and endorsed the UNCHE and UNCED Declarations and Agenda 21, the Framework Conventions on Climate Change and Biological Diversity. They also participated in the World Summit on Sustainable Development held in Johannesburg in 2002. The UNCLOS had recognised in Article 65 that both coastal States and the competent international organisation could "prohibit, limit or regulate the exploitation of marine mammals more strictly than provided for in this Part," that is, Part V creating the Exclusive Economic Zone and requiring "optimum utilisation" of its living resources. Marine mammals were thus exempted from this requirement. Article 65 also required States to "co-operate" in "conservation of marine mammals" and "in the case of cetaceans, in particular, to work through the appropriate international organisations for their conservation, management and study." The relevant organisations were not named although the IWC remains the only one exclusively focused on whales and applying in "all waters." The UNCED Agenda 21, after intensive negotiation, repeated the UNCLOS, Article 65 in Chapter 17 but recognised in paragraphs 47 and 90 (in the context of "International regional co-operation and co-ordination" in the high seas and national jurisdictional areas respectively) the responsibility of the IWC "for conservation and management of whale stocks and the regulation of whaling pursuant to the ICRW, the work of its Scientific Committee in carrying out studies of large whales in particular, as well as other cetaceans," and that of "other organisations" such as the Inter-American Tropical Tuna Commission (IATTC) and the Agreement on the Conservation of Small Cetaceans of the Baltic and North Seas (ASCOBANS).[95] The IATTC was mentioned because of its role in preventing incidental take of small cetaceans and executing UNCLOS Article 64 responsibilities concerning Highly Migratory Species and the ASCOBANS as a nonexploitative, conservatory instrument. The North Atlantic Marine Mammal Commission (NAMMCO) was not mentioned. It was not finalised until September 1992. Its inclusion was strongly opposed by mostly NGOs and conservationist ICRW parties.

As pointed out by Wolfrum, the precautionary approach advocated in the Rio Declaration necessitates that cessation of potentially harmful activities should not be postponed solely for the reason that there is no scientific proof that possible harm will materialise.[96] This formulation reflects the view

---

eries Law Since Rio: The Continued Rise of the Precautionary Principle," in Boyle and Freestone (n. 80 above), p. 135–66; D. Freestone, "Implementing Precaution Cautiously," in *Developments in International Fisheries Law,* ed., E. Hey (The Hague: Kluwer Law International, 1999), p. 287–326.

95. 1995 UKTS 52, 3187. London: Her Majesty's Stationery Office, 1995.

96. R. Wolfrum, "Precautionary Principle," in *New Technologies and the Law of the Marine Environment,* ed. J.-P. Beurier, A. Kiss and S. Mahmoudi (The Hague: Kluwer Law International, 2000), p. 203–14. He interprets the principle, as now

of the "like minded" IWC Members who oppose resumption of whaling on the grounds of uncertainty concerning present advances in scientific understanding and/or the inadequacy of the Current Schedule of the ICRW to ensure either ecosystem-based management or that the technology currently used for killing whales excludes pain and suffering. Most Member States of the IWC have participated in the negotiation of various relevant recent conventions and the updating of earlier ones[97] to take account of the Rio concepts and Agenda 21, which extended UNCHE Declaration of the Principle 21 that recognised that States have the right to pursue their own environmental policies as long as they do not harm the environment of other States or areas beyond national jurisdiction to include developmental policies. But, as Von Moltke has remarked, the formulation of environmental policy, even when not closely related to developmental policy within the UNCED goal of "sustainable development," is "a complex process in which a plethora of voices must be heard to render the environment actionable in economic and social terms."[98] He hazards that is the reason why NGOs play such an exceptional role in environmental policy making because no single group can adequately represent these complexities and NGOs may include scientists, industrialists, environmentalists, and those pursuing development and also involve the media. The present complexities of environmental threats cannot, however, be resolved solely on the basis of scientific understanding because the environment and the threats to it are now known to be too complex to be fully described in strictly scientific terms.[99] The precautionary approach offers a means of addressing this problem, taking account of the

---

refined in treaty law, as reflecting the need to take decisions where there is scientific uncertainty about the potential future harm of a particular activity with caution, but notes that others argue that the burden of proof of harm is fully reversed. He suggests that the precautionary principle overcomes the limitations of the maximum sustainable yield approach to conservation of fisheries under which States need only intervene if a crisis occurs. "States concerned now have to prove that such a crisis does not exist and that the activity will not lead to such a crisis," p. 212. See also other commentators, (n. 94 above).

97. On this, see Ch. V. "International Aspects of Marine Mammal Protection and Conservation," esp. 123–48, "Co-operation with Other Organisations," at 129, in *Annual Report to Congress,* CITES, CCAMLR, Arctic Council, Marine Mammal Commission, 31 January 2000, pub. Marine Mammal Commission, 4340 East-West Highway, Room, 9905, Bethesda, Maryland 20814; See also, *Marine Mammal Commission Compendium of Selected Treaties, International Agreements, and other Relevant Documents on Marine Resources, Wildlife and the Environment* (4 vols.). Other relevant treaties include those on Conservation of Migratory Species of Wild Animals under whose auspices the ASCOBANS and ACCOBAMS have been concluded to protect small cetaceans in the Baltic, the North and the Black and Mediterranean Seas respectively. On this, see IWC, *Chairman's Report of the 51st Annual Meeting* (n. 14 above), p. 36.

98. von Moltke (n. 94 above), p. 97.

99. Ibid., p. 98.

fact that on many scientific questions ignorance and doubt prevail in relation to the effect on whales of possible changes in their habitat or food supplies affecting dependent or related species. Moltke suggests that the precautionary approach recognises that as science will not provide clear policy prescriptions criteria need to be developed systematically to address the uncertainties in the policy process.[100] Even the precautionary approach cannot provide unambiguous grounds for action, bounded as it is by prevailing legal norms of economic analysis, its application may incur excessive costs that might involve need for financial support when applied in treaties involving developing countries, as does the ICRW.[101] This is a problem that post-UNCED is partially provided for in the United Nations Framework Convention on Climate Change (UNFCCC) and the Convention on Biological Diversity (CBD), but not in the ICRW where it does not currently arise except in relation to small type socioeconomic whaling.

The need to apply a precautionary approach has not been overlooked, however. In 1972, the IWC instructed the Scientific Committee to develop a New Management Procedure, which for the first time offered graded protection to particular species by classifying them under three categories—Protected Stocks (PS), Initial Management Stocks (IMS), and Sustained Management Stocks (SMS)—on the advice of the Scientific Committee. Exploitation was based on cautious application of the MSY principle, PS stocks being withdrawn from industrial activity. This procedure failed, largely because of the lack of reliable data on stock abundance,[102] whale characteristics, and an effective international enforcement system. The IWC then approved a temporary cessation of "commercial" whaling (a term not found in the ICRW) world-wide in 1982 by setting all quotas at zero and instructed the Scientific Committee to embark on an in-depth comprehensive assessment of whale stocks, in the light of specific management objectives and procedures and to develop a revised management procedure (RMP).[103] The original deadline for this of 1990 could be not be met given the complexities of the process, but the RMP was finally adopted at the IWC's 1994 Annual Meeting. It has not yet been put into operation, however, pending the subsequent additional requirement that a Revised Management Scheme (RMS) be concluded. This requires introduction of an effective international enforcement system and provision for more effective methods of killing whales

100. Ibid., p. 99–101, science itself needs to be constantly revised in the light of new evidence. It should be noted that this now includes evaluation of approaches that take account of the complex theories of Deep Ecology and Large Marine Ecosystems.

101. Ibid., p. 105.

102. R. Gambell, *Whaling, Science and the IWC,* obtainable from the IWC Secretariat, The Red House, Histon, (Cambridge, U.K., 1990), p. 1–3.

103. R. Gambell, *The International Whaling Commission Now,* June 1998, an information sheet obtainable from the IWC.

that reduce, to the best extent possible, their pain and suffering.[104] Both of these RMS requirements remain under discussion within the IWC, though Japan and Norway have now introduced major technological improvements in the latter.

The Scientific Committee

Under Article III (4) the Commission can establish Committees, subcommittees, working groups et cetera.[105] Most important of these Committees, as we have seen, is the Scientific Committee (SC) in view of the Article V(2)(b) requirement that Schedule amendments shall, inter alia, be based on "scientific findings." It was against the US Draft of Article III that Harold Salvesen, director of the United Kingdom's major whaling company and the industrial advisor to the U.K. delegation in the negotiation of the ICRW, significantly wrote on his personal copy of the Draft Convention "I am afraid the Commission will get into the hands of scientists and not of practical people."[106] Here the drafters did not follow the precedents presented by earlier fisheries conventions of employing their own in-house research staff, or using ICES' expertise, but left the IWC to "set up," from its own members and experts or advisers, "such Committees as it considers desirable to perform such functions as it may authorise."[107] It thus established its own SC from the scientists carried on such delegations as had them. As cetacean biology is a highly specialised field of science and no quotas are currently set for commercial whaling, the number of scientific experts currently working in this field is limited. At present, though the SC is composed only of scientists nominated by the Commissioners of each Party, representatives of other bodies specified in its Rules of Procedures (ROP), have under these Rules, either a right to attend or can be invited to do so, and their specific role is laid down in the ROP. The Rules, as revised at the 51st Meeting of the IWC provide for *participation* by scientists representing member governments and *nonvoting*

104. *Chairman's Report of the 46th Annual Meeting, 1994.* IWC. Resolution on the Revised Management Scheme, Appendix 5. Cambridge: IWC, 1995, pp. 48–50. This report accepted that the RMP, as then set out, completed the scientific component in the development of a Revised Management Scheme for Baleen Whaling.

105. Current Committees, Sub-Committees and Working Groups include a Credentials Committee, Scientific Committee, Technical Committee, Working Group on Whale Killing Methods and Associated Welfare Issues, Infractions Sub-Committee, Aboriginal Subsistence Whaling Committee, Working Group on the Revised Management Scheme, Small Cetaceans Sub-Committee, IWC, ASCOBANS Joint Working Group, Harbour Porpoise, Finance and Administrative Committee.

106. U.S. Draft Article III; document on file at Christian Salvensen Ltd., kindly made available to the writer for inspection during earlier research.

107. ICRW Article III (4). United Nations Treaty Series, N.13, viz UNTS.

participation by a scientific representative of IUCN and relevant intergovernmental organisations, and *observer status* for nonmember governments. Nongovernmental organisations accredited as observers at the IWC Meetings can nominate a scientifically qualified observer to attend the SC Meetings. Papers can be submitted, but only scientists from IWC governments can vote.[108]

The original purpose of the SC was to advise the IWC on the status of whale stocks to assist it in determining the setting of the overall quota of BWUs that could safely be taken without endangering the stocks. As overfishing and stock decline continued, the IWC, to bring its policies more in line with scientific findings, suspended its quota briefly in the 1960s.[109] Using the powers accorded to it under Article IV to recommend studies on whales and whaling, the IWC established a so-called "Committee of Three"[110] independent scientists with expertise in population dynamics and related sciences to advise on the level of sustainable yield that could be supported by the Antarctic whale stocks and the conservation measures necessary to achieve it. Its reports, based on application of the maximum sustainable yield formula, expressed grave concern and called for drastic and urgent action to control catches, abolition of the overall quota system, and establishment of species quotas.[111] The IWC's whaling members found it difficult to follow this advice. A Special Meeting of a Scientific Subcommittee recommended that the IWC should consider inviting an impartial specialist committee of economists, possibly involving FAO, to study the economic problems associated with stock assessment, as well as the biological ones,[112] but this option has never been pursued. As the economic position declined, the old figures on which stock assessment was based became increasingly unrealistic and the SC's practice, following the "Committee of Three's" advice, of putting forward a range of "best estimates" resulted in adoption of the higher rather than the lower catch limits.

The SC generally found it difficult to formulate realistic "scientific findings" given its composition and the lack of reliable data on which to base them, and when later required to follow a precautionary approach, to know what allowance should be made. The situation has much improved but given

108. "IWC Rules of Procedure and Financial Regulations," as of September 1998. Note that the "Rules of Procedure of the Scientific Committee" were amended at the 51st Meeting of the IWC; see Chairman's Report thereof, December 1999, Appendix 13, p. 69–73.

109. Because the ICRW provided only for an overall quota, these States had to meet privately outside the IWC to endeavour to agree their shares. In 1960, they failed to do so and Norway and the Netherlands gave notice of withdrawal from the Convention. Each of the 5 APW States then set their own quotas, and proposals for the introduction of an International Observer Scheme were delayed.

110. *IWC Twelfth Report,* 1961.

111. Ibid., p. 46–49.

112. This Committee was later extended to 4. Its Report is found under *Report of Ad Hoc Scientific Committee IWC/13/3.* Cambridge: 1962, Appendix VIII, p. 38.

the appalling history of overfishing and time taken to develop a precautionary approach, many States and NGOs doubt whether any formula devised by humankind to manage such unusual species migrating through such vast areas can ever be regarded as reliable. Those still whaling and some others, however, consider that scientific problems have been solved to the extent humanly possible and press for quotas now officially to be set. The tensions between the preambular aims of conservation and orderly development of the industry thus continue to dominate debate and negotiations within the IWC.

The Scientific Permit System

Article VIII of the ICRW allowed a Contracting Government to grant a "special" revocable permit to any of its nationals for scientific research purposes (Article VIII), to ensure that collection of the data required to enable "scientific findings" to be made would continue, even when particular (or all) species were protected from taking. It was left entirely to that government to issue the permit, on terms and for numbers that it thought fit. The only obligations imposed on it were to report the permit issued to the IWC and transmit to a body designated by the IWC the scientific information thus made available concerning whales and whaling and the results of its research. As the collection and analysis of biological data related to operations of factory ships and land stations were recognised to be indispensable to sound management, the Parties were also required to "take all practicable measures" to obtain it (Article VIII) and to ensure that carcasses were not discarded and wasted. Article VIII required that the whales thus taken be processed and dealt with under directions issued by the permitting government. Over the years relatively small numbers of whales otherwise banned from taking have regularly been taken for research under this Article.

However, though complying with the decision to cease "commercial whaling," Japan has since 1989 embarked on a long-term programme of lethal research on whales within the Antarctic ecosystem and, from 1994, in its coastal waters.[113] Though much useful information has been obtained, because of the large number of whales taken many IWC members and NGOs consider that Japan is using Article VIII as a loophole to evade the "zero" quotas set by the IWC. The IWC annually calls upon Japan to reconsider its programme, the take from which was 500 whales *per annum*.[114] Norway conducted a 7-year programme from 1988 studying minke whales in the Northeast Atlantic as part of an ecological programme aimed at future multi-species management in the Barents Sea.[115] As the whales must be processed

113. R. Gambell. *Fisheries*. PECH/CM/340885.EN. (speech to European Parliament, Committee, 1 December 1997).

114. Ibid.

115. Ibid.

and commercial whaling is currently banned, it is not surprising that observers are suspicious of these programmes' true purposes, despite their provision of information useful to the SC's current work programme. The IWC has continually called upon Japan (and Iceland, which also conducted research programmes, before it withdrew from the ICRW), to end these programmes and meanwhile has developed by Resolutions, detailed guidelines that enable the SC and the IWC to review their value. The IWC's criticism of Iceland's programmes precipitated its withdrawal. Meanwhile, those opposed to use of lethal research methods regularly call for "benign" research, for example, conducted solely by observing whales in the sea, or on dead stranded whales.

Enforcement

As enforcement was left under Article IX of the ICRW to national means, parties were required to "take appropriate measures" to apply it, punish infractions, withhold bonuses, et cetera, prosecute infractions and transmit details of these, as reported by inspectors, to the SC and the IWC. The Commission established an Infractions Committee to review and comment on these reports. This procedure was insufficient, especially following the decimation of whale stocks by a notorious so-called "pirate whaler," the *Olympic Challenger,* operating under a flag of convenience provided by Panama, an IWC Member, which denied all knowledge of its activities. In the absence of international inspection, the IWC could not refute this denial.[116] At the same time Chile, Ecuador, and Peru established an independent Permanent Commission for the South Pacific,[117] with authority to regulate whaling within their unilaterally established 200-M (nautical mile) exclusive economic zones.[118]

As the IWC's regulations were not fully complied with, a Protocol to the ICRW adopted in 1956,[119] which redefined some ICRW terms was also

116. Birnie (n. 1 above), vol. I, p. 218–19, 231–34. It had formerly flown the flag of Honduras, a non-Party to the ICRW. For some years, an NGO annually compiled a list of so-called "pirate whalers," available at the IWC meeting. It is feared the practice may be revising.

117. UN Legislative Series ST/LEG/SERB/6 (1956).

118. Declaration of the Maritime Zone, Agreement between Chile, Ecuador and Peru, text in R. R. Churchill, M. H. Nordquist and S. H. Lay, ed., *New Directions in the Law of the Sea, Documents* vol. I, (Dobbs Ferry, N.Y.: Oceana Publications, 1973–1981), p. 231–2.

119. Protocol to the Convention for the Regulation of Whaling 1956, 338 UNTS, created in Washington D.C., 19 November 1956, ratified by 17 States: Japan, USSR, Norway, United States of America, United Kingdom, South Africa, Australia, New Zealand, Denmark, Sweden, Netherlands, France, Mexico, Panama, Brazil, Sweden, and Canada.

the vehicle for amending Article V (1) to add "methods of inspection" to the Commission's powers to amend the Schedule.[120] Various schemes were considered between 1956 and 1963 and eventually one based on appointment by the IWC of Member State "observers" on vessels engaged in Antarctic whaling, rather than of more authoritative international inspectors, was approved and included in the Schedule. But numerous political difficulties provided pretexts to delay its implementation.[121] Eventually an International Observer Scheme (IOS) was adopted in 1967 based on appointment by the IWC of Observers nominated by all the whaling States under agreements concluded by them (the Schedule was being amended accordingly) to appoint observers in five areas (for pelagic whaling in Antarctica, the North Pacific, and North Atlantic) and from land stations in the North Pacific and the Southern Hemisphere. The Scheme was not put into practice until 1974, after the UNCHE's moratorium resolution.[122] The observers recorded infractions and reported in writing to the IWC at the end of whaling seasons, and were required to note whether or not each regulation had been complied with. The Scheme was innovatory at that date but did not, of course, cover the operations of non-Parties and, as it depended on conclusion of agreements between concerned Parties it became inoperative on the setting of quotas at zero. Efforts to deter "pirate whaling" conducted either by vessels registered in non-Parties or using flags of convenience by calling on such States to end that practice and NGO compilation of an official register of the vessels involved in this action by Member States to deter their nationals from serving on such vessels had some success to achieve. The United States resorted to use of national trade sanctions established under its national laws.[123] Parties notifying withdrawal from the ICRW, a conservation treaty to which the United States was party, were regarded as "undermining" it and threatened with possible denial of access to fishing in the U.S. EEZ or a ban on import of their fishing products into the United States, but the threat of use of these was often sufficient to induce a change of policy in the targeted States. However, the establishment of the World Trade Organisation (WTO) and conclusion of the General Agreement on Trade and Tariffs

120. IWC 15th Report, Appendix to Chairman's Report, pp. 23–26; See also Birnie (n. 1 above), p. 322–24.

121. Birnie (n. 1 above), p. 350–52; States operating in one or the other of the three areas then included Japan, Norway, USSR, Canada, Australia, United States of America, Denmark and Iceland, videlicet. 8 of the IWC's 14 Members.

122. For details, see Birnie (n. 1 above), vol. I, p. 549–74. The United States of America initiated the proposal at the IWC's 26th Meeting in 1974 and was obligated by its newly enacted Marine Mammal Protection Act 1972 to ensure that the ICRW conformed to the requirements of that Act.

123. The Packwood-Magnusson Amendment of 1979 to the U.S. Fisheries Conservation and Management Act 1976 and the Pelly Amendments to the Fishermen's Protective Act 1967, Pub. L. No. 92–219, 85 Stat. 786 (1965), as amended.

(GATT) have deterred further use of these procedures by the United States.[124]

Vehicles for Change in Means of Conserving Whales

There are various possibilities for changing the means of conserving whales, some of which are in use and others already unsuccessfully attempted.

Renegotiation

Renegotiation of the ICRW could enable any new convention to explicitly reflect developments in international environmental law or international law pertaining to sustainable development evidenced in the UNCHE and UNCED Declarations, Agenda 21, the WSSD Declaration, its Plan of Implementation and relevant new and revised conventions and contemporary State practice.[125] As the ICRW does not provide for amendment, such a proposal can be realised only if approved by consensus or achieving unanimity. There seems little likelihood, however, that there is at present sufficient support for this, given the differences in policy and on interpretation of key principles outlined herein and especially whether any renegotiation would result in a convention that would attract the support of all current Parties, as well as draw in new ones. Three attempts to develop an agreed text of a new convention foundered between 1978–1981.[126] As the ICRW did not provide for amendment, the revision meetings had to be convened ad hoc by concerned States, although the IWC Secretariat did prepare a composite text based largely on a Canadian draft and alternatives proposed by South Africa and Brazil. NGOs were not invited to attend the Meetings, but non-parties that conducted whaling attended as observers.

Although many of the proposed revisions of the ICRW were acceptable, others were not. The latter included extending its scope to include all cetaceans and renaming the convention accordingly; its application within the 200-M fisheries or exclusive economic zones then enacted by some States following their inclusion in the UNCLOS negotiating texts; redrafting and expanding the ICRW's preambular objectives to include aboriginal subsistence whaling; aesthetic and ecological values; reduction of pain and suffer-

124. On the problems of use of national trade sanctions against States allegedly undermining fisheries' conventions to which the United States is party, see T. McDorman, "Fisheries Conservation and Management and International Trade Law," in Hey, ed., (n. 94 above): 500–32, esp. pp. 530–31.

125. The WSSD aims were set out in UNGA Res 55 (1999). For its Declaration see A/CONF.199/46 (2002), and, for its Plan of Implementation, see http://www.johannesburgsummit.org/ (accessed September 4, 2002).

126. Meetings were convened by Denmark in Copenhagen, 1978; Portugal (a non-Party) in Estoril, 1979 and Iceland, in Reykjavik in 1981.

ing; limitation of scientific permits; a focus on ecological research; a conservation system based on scientific principles; a duty to notify significant adverse impacts of activities on cetaceans; and definitions of "cetacean" and "conservation." Also proposed was wider competence for the SC; a fully international system of inspection; dispute settlement procedures; and provision for the ICRW's interrelationship with other treaties. Following the failure of these "revision meetings" no further attempt has been made to re-negotiate the ICRW but the option remains, especially since the UNCED and WSSD developments. We shall return to this in our Conclusions.

Given the disagreement that still prevails in the IWC on all these issues, there seems little better prospect of a successful renegotiation of the ICRW today than there was in 1981. In the absence of agreement on such a wide range of issues, change is more likely to be effected by other means. The IWC's practice has revealed other ways of achieving this that are outlined later.

Broad Interpretation of the Convention

The ambiguity of the ICRW's terms provides many opportunities for this, albeit there is a range of views on the choices to be made and the extent to which the rules codified or introduced de novo in the Vienna Convention on Treaties[127] allow for this, as we have seen, especially in relation to the establishment of quotas under the RMP and the validity of the Southern Ocean and other Sanctuaries whose legality has been challenged by Japan and others. The arguments raised by a range of commentators concerning this[128] have recently been overviewed by Gillespie, who regards interpretation as the "core issue" and examines the legitimacy of interpretation.[129] He notes that interpretation of "science" (and hence "scientific findings" is not value free and may be rejected by policy makers on social, ethical, economic, and political considerations. He considers that there has been a paradigm shift within the international community on issues similar to those concerning the Southern Ocean Sanctuary (SOS) in the currently evolving debate on international environmental law generally following the UNCLOS, UNCED, and UN Fish Stocks Agreement[130] and their effect on interpretation of related instruments, when the rules of interpretation are unsettled and

127. Convention on the Law of Treaties, Vienna, *International Legal Materials* 8, (1969).

128. See for example those cited in n. 88 above.

129. A. Gillespie, "The Southern Ocean Sanctuary and the evolution of international environmental law," *International Journal of Marine and Coastal Law* 15, no. 3 (2000): 293–316. He draws attention to the useful list of relevant works on interpretation in P. R. Menson, *The Law of Treaties Between States and International Organisations* (Lewiston: Edwin Meller Press, 1992), p. 69–70.

130. Agreement for the Implementation of the Provisions of the United Nations Convention on the Law of the Sea of 10 December 1982 relating to the Conservation and Management of Straddling Fish Stocks and Highly Migratory Fish Stocks, adopted 4 August 1995, Cm 3125, H.M.S.O. London: HMSO, Misc. No. 12, 1993.

open to three interpretative approaches.[131] Using an "ecological approach" in interpreting terms relating to exploitation et cetera, in older treaties such as the ICRW, in their context, in his view allows them to be interpreted in nonconsumptional ways.

If all Parties are to be bound by a more liberal interpretation, major change ultimately requires arrival at an agreed view. This necessitates that the economic, social, moral, and other concerns are accorded weight in the building of political support. In this respect, Recommendations, which require negotiation of only a simple majority of Parties, are a useful method of exerting pressure on parties resistant to proposed changes. For example, despite the rejection by some Parties of the view that small cetaceans come within the IWC's regulatory scope, many are now being reserved under national laws following a series of recommendations addressing the management needs of particular species, which the SC has been instructed by the IWC to study.

Schedule Amendment[132]

As the Schedule can be altered every year, examples given provide only illustrative "snap shots" of a particular year. Bringing about change by this means is easier than doing so by revision or interpretation because it does not require unanimity or consensus, but only approval by a three-quarter majority. It was the vehicle for introducing the temporary cessation of whaling by setting all quotas at zero.[133] The Schedule has been expanded over the years to include several small cetaceans within its "interpretations," (but not regulations) including beaked, bottlenose, killer, and pilot whales.[134] Although resisting Japanese proposals that small coastal communities, as well as aboriginal ones, should be awarded quotas for socioeconomic purposes, the Schedule does recognise among its general interpretations the existence of "small type whaling," which it limits to the use for catching purposes of powered vessels with mounted harpoon guns hunting exclusively for minke and these smaller whales.[135] Meanwhile, working groups and committees have been established to consider the socioeconomic aspects of the problem.

The Schedule also provides for Aboriginal Subsistence Whaling, which is exempted from the cessation as long as the whales are taken to satisfy

131. M. Hayashi, "The Straddling and Highly Migratory Fish Stocks Agreement," in Hey, ed. (n. 94 above), p. 55–84 ; D. Nelson, "The Development of the Legal Regime of High Seas Fisheries," in Boyle and Freestone (n. 80 above), p. 225–52.

132. This paragraph is based on the IWC Schedule, as amended by the Commission at the 50th Annual Meeting 1998, replacing that dated February 1998.

133. Ibid., par. 10.

134. Ibid., 1 B.

135. Ibid., par. 1 (c).

aboriginal subsistence need and it lays down the principles for its conduct.[136] Five communities within the ICRW Parties were covered by this exception.[137]

The IOS and the SOS were created by Schedule amendment,[138] as was the use of the cold grenade harpoon, except for killing minke whales.[139] The Schedule is also the vehicle for establishing the details of supervision and controls systems.[140] It provides for carriage on factory ships and at land stations of national inspectors and still provides for the observer scheme[141] if and when it is resumed, though the "like-minded" Parties now insist on completion of a Revised Management System (RMS) including an effective International Observer or Inspection Scheme before they will lift the ban on commercial quota setting.

Following this vehicle of change, however, is open to the difficulty that the objections procedure may be activated if consensus is not arrived at and the issue will then be put to the vote. Thus again the interdisciplinary aspects cannot be avoided.

Judicial Settlement or Arbitration

Though legal opinions have been sought on rare occasions by the IWC, these have related to relatively technical issues[142] and are not, per se, binding. Legal opinions and articles have been circulated by various ICRW Parties and NGOs, but they also are not binding. Japan, still strongly opposed to the SOS, has frequently called for the issue concerning the legality of the SOS to be submitted to binding dispute settlement procedures. As the ICRW neither provides any settlement procedures nor requires submission of disputes relating to any ICRW issues to such procedures, the only possibility of recourse to this option would seem to be either, as in the Bering Fur Seal Case, for the disputing Parties to establish an ad hoc tribunal for this purpose, or to refer the question to an appropriate existing tribunal, such as the ICJ (possibly involving its environmental panel), or to invoke one of the procedures established by Article 287 of the UNCLOS: arbitration, special arbitration, the Conciliation Commission or the International Tribunal for the Law of the Sea. There are, however, formidable difficulties concerning this. For example, who would bring the case? Would the IWC itself have

136. Ibid., par. 13 (a).

137. In the United States of America in Alaska (13 (b) (1), in the Russian Federation (13 (b) (2), in Greenland (3) and the Beqias of St. Vincent and the Grenadines.

138. IWC Schedule, III Capture, paras. 7(a) and (b) respectively.

139. Ibid., par. 6.

140. Ibid., V Supervision and Control.

141. Ibid., par. 21 (c).

142. For example, opinion by Dr. D. Bowett on the Amendment to Paragraph 7 of the Schedule dated November 1976 under the 1946 International Whaling Convention, on file at IWC Headquarters, the Red House, Histon, Cambridge, as are other opinions by him.

status to do so, in the absence of any provision for dispute settlement in the ICRW? Which procedures would be available given the rules laid down in Article 287 concerning Parties choice of procedure on signing, ratifying, or acceding to the UNCLOS and the effect of this? Would the ICRW qualify as an international agreement related to the purposes of the UNCLOS concerning interpretation or application of which the UNCLOS tribunals have jurisdiction, given the exceptions and other provisions laid down in Articles 65 and 120 of UNCLOS, and the withdrawing of many fisheries disputes from compulsory settlement procedures by Article 297 (3)(a)? As conciliation would not be the objective of the putative litigants, they are unlikely to choose the option of resort to a Conciliation Commission. It seems more likely that the majority of ICRW Parties would prefer to resolve such disputes, according due weight to the interdisciplinary aspects, within the negotiating chamber of the IWC, as they have done to date. Distinguished commentators have suggested that practice reveals that international tribunals are reluctant to rule on such internal disputes.[143] For example, Judge Nelson (currently President of ITLOS) noted that the essentially bilateral nature of the judicial process does not easily lend itself to resolving disputes concerning high seas fisheries, especially in relation to conservation measures, which is why international organisations have a significant role in establishing conservation measures.[144] He cited the questions raised by Judge Gros in his dissenting opinion in the Fisheries Jurisdiction Case[145] viz. "How could such general questions of law involving at least 11 States be judicially settled between two?," and draws attention to Allott's observation that "International law has delegated to the state-societies the settlement of their disputes, as if their disputes were their own business,"[146] in stressing that the UN Fish Stocks Agreement evidences the common interest of all States in preservation of the integrity of the biodiversity of the marine environment.

CONCLUSIONS

The issues concerning exploitation of marine mammals have featured on the international agenda since they were first raised at this level in the nineteenth century in the Bering Fur Seal Case. Concern about overexploitation and stock decline and the means of controlling it in the interest of conserv-

143. See T. M. Franck, *Fairness in International Institutions* (Oxford: Oxford University Press, 1995), pp. 318, 328; M. Miyoshi, "The State's propensity for control over settlement of disputes," *Japanese Journal of International Affairs,* 104 (1996): 43–55, 56–57; A. Hurrell's conclusions concerning "International Law and the Changing Constitution of International Society," in Byers (n. 26 above), 328–347.

144. Nelson (n. 131 above), p. 113–34.

145. U.K. v. Iceland, ICJ rep. 1974, p. 138.

146. P. Allott, *Eunomia* (Oxford: Oxford University Press, 1990), p. 334.

ing stocks for future generations have, from the outset, involved a number of disciplines. In particular, scientists have struggled to refine the theoretical basis for maintaining an optimum level of stock of the particular species exploited. Economists similarly have sought to refine theories addressing the interests of the fishing and other industries concerned in ensuring their survival, in particular concerning suitable means of allocating access to the catch and its distribution among them. Whether humans have a right to exploit animals—"the moral considerability of animals"—has concerned moral philosophers and theologians for centuries, as has the right of indigenous peoples to be exempted from restrictions on exploitation and use of these species and their products.

The prolonged attempts to regulate whaling can only be understood or resolved in the context of their history and by weighing the arguments put forward. As this study has established, a solution acceptable to all States has not yet been found, but the position achieved today, by long negotiation over 57 years within the ICRW framework as variously interpreted and applied over the years, especially through the work of the Scientific Committee acting on the instructions of the IWC, has brought about remarkable progress towards a new regime and the "Whaling Olympics" conducted in past centuries appear unlikely to be held again. But the current impasse between States and NGOs that seek to end all industrial whaling and those that seek to ensure that the industry continues in some form seems at present to some observers to be irresolvable. But the history of State practice within the IWC suggests that this is not so.

The advent of a new framework of "hard" and "soft" law *outside* the IWC, built within numerous new or revised conservatory conventions and other instruments that are based on more precautionary approaches and recognise the "common interest" of all States, is now pressing upon the IWC's deliberations.[147] Many IWC members are party to these instruments and involved in the operation of the new regimes. In particular, the removal of marine mammals by Article 65 of the UNCLOS from the "optimum utilization" of these species that would otherwise be required for marine living resources, and the UNCED Declaration of Principles and Chapters 15 (Conservation of Biodiversity) and 17 (The Oceans and All Kinds of Seas) of its Agenda 21 have provided a new framework within which the IWC (whose members participated in their adoption) must now operate. Application of the "precautionary approach" and attainment of the goal of "sustainable development," strongly pressed at the WSSD, are now obviously key policy objectives; however, both are amorphous concepts whose content is nowhere clearly prescribed.[148] The IWC membership includes developed and

147. On this, see A. Boyle, "Some reflections on the relationship of treaties and soft law," *International Comparative Law Quarterly* 48, no. 4 (1999): 901–913.

148. On this, see V. Lowe, "Unsustainable Arguments," in Boyle and Freestone (n. 80 above), whose analysis is as acute as it is entertaining, p. 19–37.

developing States, some with indigenous minorities. Thus within both groups supporters of both developmental and environmental policies are found.

Recourse to courts or tribunals seems unlikely and, even if this were to take place, in the light of the case concerning the Gabcikovo-Nagymoros Project[149] it would likely result in an invitation to the disputants to conduct further negotiations. The ICJ did recognise that mankind has throughout the ages, for economic reasons, constantly interfered with nature, without regard to its effects on the environment. It is also noted that new insights into the risks for mankind of continued headlong pursuit of such policies have emerged. New norms and standards have developed through many recent instruments that now have to be considered and weighed "not only when States contemplate new activities but also when continuing activities begun in the past: this need to reconcile economic development with protection of the environment is aptly expressed in the concept of sustainable development."[150]

Leaving the current problems within the IWC, particularly those concerning "scientific findings,"[151] to be resolved through other bodies does not in this writer's view provide a satisfactory answer, as the many disputes within the CITES illustrate. The so-called "Irish Proposal" aimed at a controversial compromise, allowing the taking of whales within the EEZs of concerned States based on review by the SC, approval of quotas by the IWC and inspection under IWC auspices—waters beyond the EEZs becoming in effect a global sanctuary—still lies on the table and seems likely to do so in the foreseeable future. Canny's report on this provides a fitting comment to our survey of the IWC's progress to date: "there was some movement in understanding the different views and a will to move forward."[152] What then is the way forward?

One possibility is to reconsider, in more practical terms, the means of implementing the declared purposes of the ICRW. What is now the "common interest" in the whale stocks? Can all states agree on this question? This has not been debated, so far as the writer is aware, in any official or permanent international forum other than the IWC, although variants of this concept have been included in other treaties, for example in the UNCLOS,

149. 1997 ICJ Reports, p. 7.

150. Ibid., par. 140, 54–55.

151. On this, see L. A. Kimball, *Treaty Implementation: Scientific and Technical Advice Enters a New Stage*, Studies in Transnational Legal Policy, No. 28 (Washington, D.C.: American Society of International Law, 1996), passim, esp. Ch. 8, Conclusions, 177–185.

152. Mr. Canny, then the Irish Commissioner who had proposed it, reported to the 51st Meeting of the IWC that consensus had not been reached during informal discussions. *Chairman's Report of the 51st Annual Meeting*. Cambridge: IWC, December 1999. This remains the case.

where the resources of the deep seabed have been declared the "common heritage of mankind" to be exploited for the benefit of mankind as a whole by an International Sea-Bed Authority in the operation of which all the parties to this seminal convention can participate.[153] The UNCLOS also stresses that "the problems of Ocean Space are closely interrelated and need to be considered as a whole".[154] The UNFCCC and the CBD also acknowledge the wider interests of the whole international community. The FCCC states that the "change in the climate and its adverse effects are a common concern of mankind."[155] The CBD affirms that "the conservation of biodoversity is a common concern of human kind,"[156] and that its parties are "conscious of the intrinsic value of biological diversity and of ecological, genetic, social, economic, scientific, educational, cultural, recreational and aethestic values of biological diversity and its components".[157] Both the UNFCCC and the CBD parties express their determination to conserve or protect these values for the benefit of "present and future generations."[158] Both the UNFCCC and the CBD now have 190 parties, the difference from the ICRW thus lies in the number of their parties and thus the potentially more globally representative nature of their Conferences of the Parties (COPs), although not all their parties can afford to attend them or their numerous committees and subsidiary bodies, because problems of appropriate expertise and financial support arise. Much depends on financial support being provided by donor states through the World Bank's Global Environment Facility (GEF). Clearly, in the writer's view, the debate on conservation and use of whales, whatever the outcome, should involve the whole international community, as do these recent conventions, but the practical problems of addressing the range of issues involved—recognised in the opening words of the CBD, and equally appropriate to any rewriting of the ICRW Preamble—are formidable and without further economic and social development in the larger part of that community, unlikely to benefit the IWC in the short term.

Thus the present situation in the IWC continues. Various relevant intergovernmental organisations attend the IWC as observers and submit reports (several such "observers" are already members of their state's IWC delegation). At the 54th IWC Meeting in 2001 there were brief reports on the IATTC's 68th Meeting, ICES 89th Meeting, the 20th Meetings of CCAMLR and of its Scientific Committee; NAMMCO's 11th Council and Scientific Committee, the first meeting of Agreement on the Conservation of the Cetaceans of the Black Sea, Mediterranean Sea and Contiguous Atlantic Area

153. UNCLOS Preamble, Recital; Articles 125 (I); 136; 155 (2); 311 (6). The UNCLOS currently has 150 Parties.

154. UNCLOS Preamble, Recital 3.

155. UNFCCC Preamble, Recital 1.

156. CBD Preamble, Recital 1.

157. Ibid., Recital 3.

158. Ibid., Recital 23.

(ACCOBAMS) and the FAO's Committee on Fisheries Conference on Responsible Fisheries in the Marine Ecosystem.[159] Several States,[160] however, submitted a Resolution on "The Synergy of the IWC and Other International and Regional Bodies," which, citing UNCLOS and Agenda 21, stressed the need for other bodies to be aware that the IWC "is the universally recognised organisation for the management of cetaceans and their conservation."[161] Other states joined in proposing that a resolution be transmitted to CITES clarifying the relationship between the ICRW and CITES, stressing that the IWC has not yet completed a revised management regime and it would be premature for CITES to transfer the whale stocks concerned to its Appendix II. The number of other organisations at the international and regional level whose activities are potentially relevant to conservation of whales is currently legion because these species must now be considered in the context of conserving their contribution to oceanic biodiversity,[162] not just their economic value. Similarly in all contexts, preservation of their marine habitat from pollution (part of the UNCLOS package), including atmospheric and land-based sources of pollution, is increasingly needing attention, and many organisations are now dealing with this problem around the globe. Both regional and international conventions addressing this have proliferated, but severe problems remain, including the effect on habitat and food supply of introduction of alien species. The catching or injuring of whales as by-catch in various fisheries conducted in all waters, whether under national controls or those of regional or international fisheries bodies, is also a factor in conservation.

Thus a diffused, delegated international system is becoming increasingly unwieldy. For whales, we must now ask, is leaving sole overview to the IWC, in the light of the complexity, inter- and multidiscipliniarty of the issues involved, wise? If not, how should the international community act? Proposals for establishing constitutions for World Government do not seem realistic in present circumstances or in any foreseeable future. Elisabeth Mann Borgese advocated, at the outset of the UNCLOS, the need to approach marine science on a common heritage basis[163] and to treat ocean space as an ecological whole. She pressed for the establishment of a World Commission on Oceans: its bureaucratic approach when established disap-

159. *Cooperation with other Organizations.* IWC/54/10. Cambridge: IWC, 2002.

160. New Zealand, Argentina, Australia, Germany, Italy, the Netherlands, South Africa, and the United Kingdom.

161. *The Synergy of the IWC and other International and Regional Bodies,* draft resolution. IWC/54/46.

162. IWC/54/47, text of resolution on *Cooperation Between the IWC and CITES.*

163. "Preface, Proceedings of Pacem in Maribus Convocation," Malta, 23 June 1973, International Ocean Institute, 1974, xviii.

pointed her.[164] She thus recommended that, in the absence of an UNCLOS Conference of the Parties (COP), the UN General Assembly (UNGA) assume the role of holistic overview by establishing a Committee of the Whole serviced by the UN's Department for Ocean Affairs and the Law of the Sea (DOALOS) and including representatives of all the UN and other agencies, treaties, IGOs, NGOs, and so forth, involved.[165] Though the UNGA did establish an Informal Consultative Process on the Oceans and the Law of the Sea,[166] the very complexity of the problems involved, the now huge number of UN member states, their range of vested interests and different capacities (which has initiated the concept instituted by UNCED Principle 7 of "common but differentiated responsibility" ((CBDR) reiterated in the CBD and UNFCCC, but not, of course, included in the UNCLOS or ICRW), gives rise to considerable pessimism concerning the practicability of such visionary global approaches in the short term, however desirable. What can be done better, however, in the shorter term, is to increase and strengthen in practical ways, the mechanisms for cooperative interrelationships among relevant conventions and concerned institutions. Providing funding and practical back-up for wider and more effective participation by all ICRW parties in more inter- or multidisciplinary workshops and for more scientific understanding and research on the complexities of whale conservation would help to overcome the problems faced by many new delegations to the IWC and its Committees, which may be ill equipped in terms of finance, scientific, socioeconomic, legal, and other necessary expertise.[167] The subtleties of the calculations on which the Revised Management Procedure are based, the practicalities of establishing a fully effective system of supervision and control, the problems of monitoring the IWC's existing whale sanctuary areas

164. S. Keckes, "Review of International Programmes Relevant to the Work of the Independent World Commission on the Oceans," (1997), on file with the author.

165. E. M. Borgese, *The Oceanic Circle: Governing the Seas as a Global Resource* (Tokyo: United Nations University Press, 1998).

166. E. M. Borgese, "The first session," *Environmental Policy and Law* 30, no. 5 (2000): 224–232; E. M. Borgese, "The second session," *Environmental Policy and Law* 31 no. 4-5 (2001): 211–217.

167. See J. Swan and B. P. Satia, *Contribution of the Committee on Fisheries to Global Fisheries Governance, 1977–1997* (Rome: FAO, 1999); "Multilateral Environmental Agreements: A Summary" (Background Paper prepared by UNEP for the First Meeting of the Open-Ended Intergovernmental Group of Ministers or their Representatives on International Environmental Governance, New York 2001); UNEP/ILM/1/INF (30 March 2001), based on information supplied by 20 Secretariats of Multilateral Agreements. For an overview of such agreements, see P. Birnie and A. Boyle, *International Law and the Environment* (Oxford: Oxford University Press, 2002), Chs. 6–13; Kimball (n. 151 above); L. Kimball, "International law and institutions: The oceans and beyond," *Ocean Development and International Law* 21 (1990): 147; See, generally, the journal *International Environmental Agreements: Politics, Law and Economics,* vol. I, et seq., passim.

and exploring their values for scientific research, are formidable. Given that whales and marine mammals in general are likely to be found in the waters of all coastal states, their sustainable development could be inhibited by exploitation, whether the species are exploited for products, for scientific research, viewing by coastal tourists, or whale watchers at sea. More practical help with these aspects, on the basis of the CBDR, could be provided within the IWC and through other international institutions.

"Future generations" do not end with our own; the negotiators of the ICRW and its earlier delegates have now joined "past generations." What will future generations conclude about our wardship of the whales, if indeed they survive current threats to their existence, including the political, economic, social, and other compromises that have contributed to the weakness of the present legal regimes and their operation? Will they be able to establish a new legal regime arising from different perspectives of international relations and international laws based on more informal approaches to "ocean governance" as they become diffused through greater involvement of "civil society"? There is certainly need for this, and in the short-term, for better synergism among the many relevant conventions, but any jury constituted by the present generation must surely remain out in the light of present experience.

Whales, Submarines, and Active Sonar

Jon M. Van Dyke
William S. Richardson School of Law, University of Hawaii at Manoa

Emily A. Gardner
Graduate Ocean Policy Program, University of Hawaii at Manoa

Joseph R. Morgan
Department of Geography, University of Hawaii at Manoa

Elisabeth Mann Borgese devoted her professional life to promoting awareness about the ocean and building regimes to protect fragile marine ecosystems. This article examines a new acoustic military use of the ocean, which potentially threatens all ocean creatures, and explains how existing principles of international law and treaty regimes apply to this activity.

Professor Van Dyke worked with Elisabeth at the Center for the Study of Democratic Institutions in Santa Barbara, California in 1969–1970, where she introduced him to the emerging efforts to develop a global regime to govern ocean resources and stimulated his early interest in this topic by inviting him to the 1970 *Pacem in Maribus* meeting in Malta. Dr. Morgan worked closely with Elisabeth as co-editor of the *Ocean Yearbook* for Volumes 7–14, and Ms. Gardner was assistant editor of the *Yearbook* for Volume 12. Research support for this paper was provided by the Ocean Mammal Institute.

INTRODUCTION

On 15 July 2002, the U.S. National Marine Fisheries Service (NMFS) exempted the U.S. Navy's Low Frequency Active Sonar (LFAS) program from the requirements of the Marine Mammal Protection Act after determining that its operation would have a "negligible impact" on any species.[1] NMFS thus authorized the Navy to use two ships to transmit low frequency active sonar in about 75 percent of the world's oceans (exempting the polar ex-

1. K. R. Weiss, "Sonar Approved Despite Possible Risks to Whales," *Honolulu Advertiser*, 16 July 2002; M. Kaufman, "Navy Cleared to Use a Sonar Despite Fears of Injuring Whales," *Washington Post*, 16 July 2002, http://www.commondreams.org/headlines02/0716-06.htm (accessed 19 July 2002).

Ocean Yearbook 18: 330–363

tremes). Ten weeks later, in late September 2002, 15 Cuvier's beaked whales beached on the Canary Islands at the same time the U.S. destroyer *Mahan* was maneuvering in the area with ships from nine other members of the North Atlantic Treaty Organization.[2] Autopsies of the whales revealed brain damage consistent with an acoustic impact.[3] This mass stranding followed similar incidents near the Bahamas in March 2000 and Greece in 1996, and in the Canaries between 1985 and 1989, which are described later and which were followed by another incident in the Haro Strait near Vancouver Island.[4]

The NMFS approval of the Navy's use of LFAS was challenged by the Natural Resources Defense Council and other organizations in 2002, leading to a determination by Federal Magistrate Judge Elizabeth D. LaPorte that NMFS had violated federal law in a number of respects, but that the Navy should be permitted to continue with some limited testing because of the strong national security interest involved.[5] On August 26, 2003, Judge

2. Nine Cuvier's beaked whales were found dead on 24–25 September 2002 on the Canary Islands of Fuerteventura and Lanzarote. Six beached whales were pushed back into the sea, and another two were seen floating lifeless in coastal waters. Ships from Belgium, Canada, France, Germany, Greece, Norway, Portugal, Turkey, the United Kingdom, and the United States were conducting a multinational exercise known as Neo Tapon 2002 designed to practice securing the Strait of Gibraltar. The Cuvier's beaked whale is a toothed cetacean that ranges from 5 to 8 meters in length. J. Socolovsky, "Investigation Points to NATO Exercise in Mass Whale Beaching," *Associated Press,* 10 October 2002, posted at the Web site of the Environmental News Network, http:/www.enn.com/news/wire-stories/2002/10/10102002/ap_4866.

3. Ibid. (quoting a researcher as saying that the "the only cause which we cannot rule out . . . is acoustic impact").

4. See text at (n. 18, 21 and 24–7 below). On 5 May 2003, the U.S. Navy's guided-missile destroyer *USS Shoup* tested mid-range sonar for five hours in the Haro Strait near Vancouver Island, sending out pings louder than 200 dB, which caused a pod of 22 killer whales and a minke whale to stop their feeding and form into a tight group as far from the sound as possible and then flee the region. The dead carcasses of eight harbor porpoises washed ashore in the days after this test, and subsequent investigations indicated that they had suffered severe trauma to their brains. Tracy Vedder, "This Is Another Smoking Gun," KOMO TV, 8 August 2003, http://www.komotv.com/news/printstory.asp?id=26542 (accessed 28 August 2003); Robert McClure, "Tests on Marine Mammals to Look for Sonar Link to Injuries," *Seattle Post-Intelligencer,* 12 July 2003, http://www.seattlepi.nwsource.com/local/130609_sonar12.html (accessed 28 August 2003); Peggy Anderson, "Did Navy Tests Kill Porpoises?" CBSNEWS.com, 23 July 2003, http://www.cbsnews.com/stories/2003/07/23/tech/main564700.shtml (accessed 28 August 2003).

5. Natural Resources Defense Council, Inc. v. Evans, No. C-02-3805-EDL (N.D.Cal., Opinion and Order on Cross-Motions for Summary Judgement, 26 August 2003); Judge LaPorte's earlier Opinion and Order Granting Plaintiff's Motion for a Preliminary Injunction was issued 31 October 2002 and published at 232 F.Supp.2d 1003 (N.D.Cal. 2002). Judge LaPorte ruled that NMFS had violated the Marine Mammal Protection Act of 1972, 16 USC Chapter 31, the National Environmental Policy Act of 1969, 42 USC secs. 4321 et seq., and the Endangered Species

LaPorte issued a permanent injunction blocking the broad permit issued by NMFS, holding that it had violated several federal statutes and explaining that "the extremely loud and far traveling naval sonar system" maintains its "sound pressure level of approximately 140 dB more than 400 miles from the [transmitting] vessel" and covers broad areas because it "bounces from the ocean bottom to the surface and back again."[6] She stressed that NMFS and the Navy had ignored relevant studies, such as one prepared by Great Britain's Defense Research Agency, which reported that fish exposed to LFAS "suffered internal injuries at 160 dB, eye damage at 170 dB, auditory damage at 180 dB, and transient stunning at 190 dB."[7] The injunction requires the Navy to extend its coastal buffer zone from 12 to at least 43 nautical miles offshore (except in certain limited areas where coastal training is required), to use aerial surveys or observational vessels to monitor for nearby species when operating close to shore, and also to avoid areas of the deep ocean where marine mammals and other endangered species such as sea turtles are migrating, breeding, feeding or clustering. The court's opinion instructs the parties to meet together to agree on limited areas where the Navy's testing can continue.[8]

Act of 1973, 16 USC Chapter 35.

In her October 2002 opinion, Magistrate Judge LaPorte had explained that: "It is undisputed that marine mammals, many of whom depend on sensitive hearing for essential activities like finding food and mates and avoiding predators, and some of whom are endangered species, will at a minimum be harassed by the extremely loud and far traveling LFA sonar." 232 F.Supp.2d at 1053. Although Magistrate Judge LaPorte found that the Navy's activities violated three federal statutes designed to protect the marine environment, she accepted the testimony of the NMFS experts regarding the impact of LFAS on marine mammals over the sharply conflicting testimony presented by the plaintiff's experts. Judge LaPorte wrote that: "The law is clear . . . that when qualified experts on both sides reach carefully reasoned but different conclusions, the Court must defer to the agency's experts. . ." Order of 26 August 2003, slip op. at 49; also at 232 F.Supp.2d at 1017. Other courts dealing with ocean environmental issues have taken a more skeptical view of the scientific opinions offered by federal agencies. See, for example, Natural Resources Defense Counsel v. Daley, 209 F.3d 747, 755, 754 (D.C. Cir. 2000) (explaining that courts "do not hear cases merely to rubber stamp agency actions" and criticizing the agency's scientific conclusions as ones that could only be correct in "Superman Comics' Bizarro world, where reality is turned upside down"); Greenpeace v. National Marine Fisheries Service, 106 F.Supp.2d 1066 (W.D.Wash. 2000) (where the court treated the views of the two sides' experts as having equal credibility and issued the injunction sought by plaintiffs despite the contrary testimony of the agency's experts).

6. Ibid., Order of 26 August 2003, slip op. at 3, 11.

7. Ibid., slip op. at 40 (citing a 1994 study by Dr. Turnpenny entitled "The Effects on Fish and Other Marine Mammals of High-Level Underwater Sound").

8. After the court's October 2002 order issuing a preliminary injunction, 232 F.Supp.2d 1003 (N.D.Cal. 2002), the parties reached an agreement allowing the Navy to test its sonar in an area of the Western Pacific extending from Saipan in the Commonwealth of the Northern Mariana Islands, to Japan's Bonin Islands, south of Tokyo. D. Kravets, "U.S. Navy Agrees to Temporarily Limit Testing of New Sonar

About the same time, U.S. Magistrate Judge James Larson, also in Northern California, issued a temporary restraining order blocking geographers from the National Science Foundation, Columbia University, and the Georgia Institute of Technology from "using an array of twenty airguns to fire extremely high energy acoustic bursts into the ocean to generate geophysical data in the Gulf of California" with sound blasts "as high as 263 decibels (dB) at the source," which had apparently killed "[a]t least two Cuvier beaked whales (*Ziphius cavirostris*), a species particularly susceptible to acoustic trauma."[9] Judge Larson noted that: "These levels are significantly higher than 180 dB, which is acknowledged by the Government to cause significant injury to marine mammals."[10]

In January 2003, U.S. District Judge Samuel Conti of the Northern District of California made an additional ruling against sonar use, blocking experiments (authorized by NMFS) that were to be conducted by Woods Hole Oceanographic Institution scientist Dr. Peter Tyack to determine the effect of the sound on the gray whales migrating along the West Coast of California to their winter grounds along the coast of Mexico.[11] Judge Conti ruled that because the permits involved "major amendments" to the original project, which had generated "public controversy," it was necessary to conduct a proper environmental impact assessment under the National Environmental Policy Act before undertaking the experiments. In the process of "balancing" the "harms" to determine whether to issue an injunction, Judge Conti noted that the population of gray whales had been dropping since 1984 (from 21,942 individuals to 17,414) and that "Dr. Tyack's proposed experiments might inflict unacceptable levels of harm on the gray whales."[12]

Because of the new acoustic technologies created by the Navy and other researchers, the creatures living in the world's oceans are now facing a new form of pollution, justified by the Navy as militarily necessary, but with enormous and untested destructive potential. The controversy surrounding the use of sonar and other acoustic devices in the oceans is certain to continue into the future, and will trigger challenges by other nations and nongovernmental organizations. The three cases described earlier indicate that proper enforcement of U.S. environmental laws may protect the marine environment from the dangers posed by LFAS. But if these laws should prove to be inadequate, or if Congress should exempt LFAS from U.S. environmental

---

System Amid Marine Life Concerns," *Associated Press* (18 November 2002), http://www.planetsave.com/ViewStory.asp?ID=3299 (accessed 2 March 2003).

9. Center for Biological Diversity v. National Science Foundation, No. C02-5065 JL, 2002 WL 31548073 (N.D. Cal., Temporary Restraining Order, 30 October 2002), slip op. at 2–3.

10. Ibid., p. 3.

11. Hawaii County Green Party v. Evans, No. C-03-0078-SC (N.D.Cal., Order Granting Permanent Injunction, 24 January 2003).

12. Ibid., slip op. at 24.

laws that would otherwise govern,[13] other countries and groups concerned about the impact of this technology on their marine resources, and the ocean environment generally, will be obliged to utilize international law principles and tribunals to limit the use of low frequency active sonar by the navies and scientists of the United States and other countries. The sections that follow examine the scientific information now available about the impact of LFAS on the marine environment, address the military and scientific arguments in favor of its use, and analyze possible international strategies that might be pursued to challenge it.

THE EFFECTS OF LOW FREQUENCY ACTIVE SONAR ON MARINE BIOTA

The ocean has always been a noisy place. For billions of years, natural sounds produced by wind, waves, precipitation, ice, seismic events, and marine organisms defined the ocean's acoustic milieu. The auditory sensitivities of marine organisms surely evolved in the presence of these sounds and over time species became specially adapted to deal with the ambient sounds of the ocean environment.[14]

During the last 2 centuries, humans have significantly added to the ocean's array of sounds with the introduction of machine-driven commercial and military ships and the active exploitation of the hydrocarbons in the ocean floor. Only recently has much consideration been given to the impacts these sounds could be having on the life forms that inhabit the sea. A particular concern has arisen for marine mammals, many of which use sound as their primary sense, to communicate, to navigate, and to detect predators and prey.

The U.S. Navy's Surveillance Towed Array Sensor System (SURTASS) Low Frequency Active Sonar (LFAS) will employ very loud low-frequency sounds (less than 500 Hz with intensity levels as great as 230 dB re 1μPa at 1 m[15]), posing a significant threat to the safety and welfare of marine mam-

13. The U.S. Navy received, for instance, a congressional exemption from the requirements of the Migratory Bird Treaty Act of 1918 to permit it to continue live-fire military training exercises on the island of Farallon de Medinilla, near Saipan, in the Commonwealth of the Northern Mariana Islands. D. DePledge, "Navy Freed from Bird Protection Act," *Honolulu Advertiser,* 14 November 2002, at A11, col. 4. See also J. McQuaid, "Fight Brews Over Environmental Law; Bush Officials Consider Policy to Exempt Oceans," *Times-Picayune* (New Orleans), 16 August 2002, p. 5.

14. National Research Council, Committee on Low-Frequency Sound and Marine Mammals, Low-Frequency Sound and Marine Mammals: Current Knowledge and Research Needs (Washington, D.C.: National Academy Press, 1994), p. 2.

15. Although the Navy refuses to release the maximum source level of SURTASS LFAS, claiming it to be classified information, reports indicate the maximum source level to be 230 dB re 1 μPa. See "Quiet please. Whales navigating," *The*

mals, and possibly to other forms of marine life as well. The transmitted sound will be about 215 dB at its source, arrayed in a manner to have "an effective source level" of 230–240 dB. According to the Navy's environmental impact statement (EIS), the sound dispersion would vary somewhat according to the geography and environment but would generally be at the 180 dB level 1 km from the source, at 173 dB 2 km from the source, about 165 dB 40 nautical miles (M) from the source, at the 150–160 dB level up to 100 M from the source, and some 140 dB 400 M from the source vessel.[16] (Decibel levels are logarithmic in nature, so that a sound of 180 dB is 10 times as intense as one of 170 dB.) The sounds are not transmitted uniformly in all directions from the source, but travel in a beam that is a few hundred feet in width, which tends to expand as it leaves its source.[17] These sounds are the loudest ever put into the world's oceans by humans, with the possible exception of underground explosions. They are designed to travel great distances and are audible by humans in the water 1000 km away without any signal processing.

The threat of this active sonar to marine mammals first became evident in 1996 when an unusual stranding event took place involving 12 Cuvier's beaked whales in the Mediterranean Sea near Greece that coincided temporally and geographically with "sound detecting system trials" of LFAS by the NATO research vessel *Alliance*. The whales were exposed to sound transmitted from at least 25 km away, which was determined to have reached them at the 150–160 dB re 1 μPa at 1 m level after 238 short four-second pings of sound were released, and which caused severe tissue damage to their ear cavities.[18] Cuvier's beaked whales are a deep-diving pelagic species that rarely strands. Only seven cases of more than four individuals stranding have been recorded since 1963.[19] One commentator concluded that the probability that the mass stranding was not related to LFAS testing was less than 0.07 percent.[20] Moreover, three mass strandings involving similar species were also associated with military maneuvers in the Canary Islands between 1985 and 1989, and in 1983[21] sperm whales in the southeast Caribbean became

---

Economist (7 March 1998): 85 and A. Frantis, "Does military testing strand whales?" *Nature* 352 (5 March 1998): 29.

16. See Natural Resources Defense Council v. Evans, No. C-02-3805 EDL, 2002 WL 31445165 (N.D.Cal., Opinion and Order Granting Plaintiffs' Motion for a Preliminary Injunction, 31 October, 2002), slip op. at 12, 28.

17. Ibid., at 28.

18. See generally, Joint Interim Report Bahamas Marine Mammal Stranding Event of 15–16 March 2000. U.S. Dept. of Commerce and Secretary of the Navy. December 2001, http://www.nmfs.noaa.gov/prot_res/overview/Interim_Bahamas_Report.pdf (accessed 28 August 2003).

19. Frantzis (n. 15 above).

20. Ibid.

21. M. P. Simmonds and L. F. Lopez-Jurado, "Whales and the military," *Nature* 351 (6 June 1991): 448.

"unusually silent and dispersed" when exposed to intense military sonar from submarines operating in the area.[22]

Because of the way sound is measured and the different speed that sound travels through water, as compared to land, it is estimated that "underwater sound pressure levels numerically are about 61.5 dB greater than sound pressure levels in air for an equal intensity."[23] In other words, sound measured at 131 dB in water would have the same pressure impact as sound measured at 70 dB on land (60 dB on land is the sound generated by freeway traffic). Continuous exposure above 85 dB (on land) is likely to degrade the hearing of most humans. "Deafening" noise (on land) begins at 110 dB, with 120 dB measuring a hard rock band, 130 dB being the point at which pain is registered, and 140 dB being the point adjacent to a jet engine. The 180 dB (in water) figure said by the Navy to be "safe" for cetaceans would thus affect them at about the same extent as human hearing would be affected by standing next to a hard rock band at a rock concert, if we can assume that the hearing system of cetaceans is roughly comparable to ours.

Following the 1996 experience of the atypical mass stranding of beaked whales in the Mediterranean, efforts have been made to collect the ears of stranded animals that coincided with the nearby use of LFAS and other sonar devices. In March 2000, 17 whales of four different species, including Cuvier's beaked whales, two minke whales, and a dolphin stranded in the Bahamas in March 2000 as a result of tactical mid-frequency sonar transmitted from U.S. Navy vessels. The whales were exposed to sounds transmitted at the 223–235 dB re 1 μPa at 1 m level, with pings transmitted every 24 seconds over a 16-hour period, which were thought to have reached the whales at the 165 dB level.[24] (LFAS transmissions will be of longer duration and have more energy; its pings will last between 6 and 100 seconds and will be repeated every 6 to 15 minutes). Scientists found hemorrhaging around the brain and ear bones of the beached cetaceans, injuries consistent with exposure to extremely loud sounds. Eight of the stranded whales died, and other whales probably sank to the sea floor before they had a chance to strand.[25] The Navy has admitted that the Bahamas stranding and related

22. W. A. Watkins, K. E. Moore, and P. Tyack, "Sperm whale acoustic behaviors in the Southeast Caribbean," *Cetology* 49 (1985): 6.

23. R. C. Gisiner, "Proceedings, Workshop on the Effects of Anthropogenic Noise in the Marine Environment, 10–12 February 1998" (Marine Mammal Science Program, Office of Naval Research, 1988), p. 24.

24. Natural Resources Defense Council v. Evans, No. C-02-3805 EDL, 2002 WL 31445165 (N.D.Cal., Opinion and Order Granting Plaintiffs' Motion for a Preliminary Injunction, 31 October 2002), slip op. at 5 (citing the Navy task force's analysis of the incident).

25. Those whales whose ability to navigate was most severely damaged by the sonar would have died before they were able to make it to the nearest beach.

deaths "were most likely caused by its [mid-range] sonar transmissions,"[26] but contends that LFA sonar will affect whales differently. The Navy claims that mid-range sonar can be heard over shorter distances by many marine mammals, while LFA sonar can travel several hundred miles but is audible to fewer species.[27]

Because the Navy intends to deploy SURTASS LFAS globally, an Overseas Environmental Impact Statement and an Environmental Impact Statement (OEIS/EIS) was required under the authority of the National Environmental Policy Act, prior to the Navy's use of the technology. As part of the process of preparing the OEIS/EIS, the Navy sponsored a three-phase marine mammal research program (MMRP) to determine how representative marine mammals responded to LFAS transmissions. Phase I of the program focused on blue and fin whales and was conducted off San Nicolas Island in southern California from 5 September through 21 October 1997. Phase II focused on migrating gray whales off central California and was conducted from 8 through 27 January 1998. Phase III was conducted off the northwest coast of the Big Island of Hawaii from 26 February through 31 March 1998 and focused on male humpback whales. An environmental assessment was prepared prior to each phase of this research.

Results from each of the three phases of the LFAS MMRP indicated that the technology did have an effect on each of the representative marine mammal groups tested. The results of Phase I, in which fin and blue whales were exposed to less than full-scale LFAS sound transmissions, indicated a decrease in vocal behavior by approximately 50 percent in blue whales and approximately 30 percent in fin whales.[28] The findings from Phase II, in which gray whales migrating nearshore were exposed to LFAS source levels of 185 dB re 1 μPa at 1 m, and 170 dB re 1 μPa at 1 m (both substantially lower than the actual source level that will be utilized by the Navy), demonstrated an obvious avoidance response to the LFAS signal, particularly at the higher source level of 185 dB where whales deviated 1 km from the source.[29] The extent of deviation from the source was less at the lower

26. Center for Biological Diversity v. National Science Foundation, No. C02-5065, 2002 WL 31548073 (N.D.Cal., Temporary Restraining Order, 30 October 2002), slip op. at 8.

27. "Navy Deployment of Sonar Protested," *Honolulu Advertiser*, 6 September 2001, p. A6.

28. C. W. Clark, P. Tyack, and W. T. Ellison, "Quicklook, Low-Frequency Sound Scientific Research Program, Phase I: Responses of Blue and Fin Whales to SURTASS LFA, Southern California Bight, 5 September B 21 October, 1997" (27 February 1998), pp. 30–1, Figure 28.

29. P. Tyack and C. Clark, "Quicklook Phase II, Playback of Low-Frequency Sound to Gray Whales Migrating Past the Central California Coast, January 1998" (23 June 1998), pp. 22–5, Figures 7–9. Gray whales migrating further offshore did not display the same response.

source levels tested, but apparent nonetheless.[30] In addition, observations of sea otters near the LFAS Phase II playback site suggested a reduction in the rate of foraging success of about 11 percent and an increase in dive times by about 11 percent when all dives during acoustic playback were pooled.[31] Similar to Phase I, the results of Phase III indicated a reduction of vocal activity in male humpback whales exposed to less than full-scale LFAS signals.[32] Of 17 male humpback whales tested, 10 individuals stopped singing when exposed to received levels of the LFAS signal ranging from 121 to 151 dB re 1 μPa.[33] Four of the whales that stopped singing joined other whales during the transmissions, suggesting they may be trying to maintain normal social interactions or bonding for protection.[34] The evidence suggested that the humpback whales avoided the LFAS sound source in addition to stopping their singing.[35]

The biological significance of these changes in behavior and distribution in response to the LFAS signal cannot be summarily dismissed. Singing and migration are linked to courtship and mating activities. Disruption of these behaviors could potentially impact the reproductive success of individuals, and ultimately the size of a population. Thus, the possibility that the LFAS signal could have long-term adverse effects on marine mammal populations cannot be ruled out, particularly in the case of small populations. A U.S. Navy press release following Phases I and II of LFAS MMRP stated that although "behavioral responses were observed, none raised concern about the potential harm to animals during the playback experiments."[36] This statement is insensitive to the potential long-term impacts the disruption of courtship and migratory activities could have on a marine mammal population. If such disruptions were widespread throughout a particular habitat, they could have a greater impact on a population overall than that of a few individuals being harmed as a result of exposure to the full-scale sound source.

It is also important to emphasize that none of the three phases of the LFAS MMRP exposed animals to the sound source at the level the Navy actually plans to utilize. Scientists leading the MMRP explained that less-than-full-scale sound signals were used because it was critical to evaluate how animals thought to be particularly sensitive would respond to sonar at

30. Ibid.
31. Ibid.
32. C. Clark and P. Tyack, "Quicklook, Low-Frequency Sound Scientific Research Program, Phase III: Responses of Humpback Whales to SURTASS LFA off the Kona Coast, Big Island, Hawaii" (31 August, 1998), p. 24, figure 15.
33. Ibid.
34. Ibid.
35. Ibid.
36.. "Navy and Scientific Community Conduct Low Frequency Sound Research," United States Navy Pacific Fleet Public Affairs Office (March 4, 1998).

received levels potentially well below those thought to pose a risk of harm, and that the best way to evaluate the risk of behavioral disruption is by experiments that carefully control the sound level.[37] Given that all three groups of marine mammals tested displayed behavioral and/or distributional changes upon exposure to less-than-full-scale LFAS, it is highly probable that they will have additional and more dramatic responses to the full-scale sound source, and that other species will be affected as well. In fact, the Navy has assumed that 95 percent of the whales would be at risk of experiencing a biologically significant behavioural reaction if exposed to the LFAS at 180 dB, that 70 percent to 75 percent would be at risk of being "taken" if exposed to 173 dB, and that 50 percent would be at risk if exposed to 165 dB.[38]

The mass strandings in the Bahamas, the Canaries, and the Mediterranean coupled with the results of the MMRP establish that LFAS and other forms of active sonar are harmful to marine mammals. Because the MMRP focused on such a small sampling of species it is not possible to rule out indirect effects on marine mammal populations resulting from adverse effects of LFAS on their species of prey. Laboratory evidence strongly suggests that high intensity sounds may affect the egg viability and growth rates of fish and invertebrates.[39] It is important to recognize that adverse effects experienced at one level of the marine food chain may have repercussions throughout the chain as the delicate balance of predators and prey becomes disrupted. The LFAS MMRP, which involved three separate studies, lasted only 6 to 8 weeks in duration, and examined the effects on five species to less than full-scale LFAS signals, was insufficient to rule out adverse impacts from exposure to full-scale transmissions to the species tested or to other components of the ecosystem. It has been suggested, because the MMRP exposed whales to sounds that were much lower intensity than full-scale LFAS transmissions, that the research was designed to yield results indicating that the technology had no significant impact on marine mammals.

In any event, the National Marine Fisheries Service did exempt the LFAS system from the Marine Mammal Protection Act in July 2002, after determining it would have a "negligible impact" on any species.[40] This conclusion is directly contrary to the results of the MMRP, which showed that

37. P. Tyack, "Comments on Low-Frequency Playback Experiments to Singing Humpback Whales in Hawaiian Waters in Phase III of the LFA Marine Mammal Research Program" (MARMAM, 9 June 1998).

38. Natural Resources Defense Council v. Evans, No. C-02-3805 EDL, 2002 WL 31445165 (N.D.Cal., Opinion and Order Granting Plaintiffs' Motion for a Preliminary Injunction, 31 October 2002), slip op. at 4, 49–50 (quoting from Declaration of Dr. Kurt Fristrup).

39. National Research Council, Committee on Low-Frequency Sound and Marine Mammals (n. 14 above), pp. 53–4.

40. Dept. of Commerce, NOAA, NMFS Letter of Authorization, http://www.surtass-lfa-eis.com/Home/Dept (accessed 8 September 2002).

LFAS brought about behavioral and distributional changes in all species tested, and the 2000 incident in the Bahamas in which the Navy acknowledged that mid-range sonar caused the death of at least eight whales.

As a condition of receiving its exemption, the Navy agreed not to transmit LFAS from immediate coastal areas, but the sound will undoubtedly reach these areas and will be very loud in some locations. In its Environmental Impact Statement, the Navy stated that its transmissions would be limited to "below 180 dB within 22 km (12 M) of any coastlines and offshore biologically important areas." On its Web site, the Navy says that "The HF/M3 sonar [which is designed to be used as a preventative measure] will provide a very high probability that no marine mammal will be exposed to high sound levels in the LFA mitigation zone (at or above 180 dB)."[41] The effects of received sound levels above 151 dB on marine life have not been studied at all, by the LFAS MMRP or in any other test, and many scientists contend that transmissions above the 120 dB level are likely to cause negative effects on marine mammals and other creatures. The October 2002 federal court ruling required the Navy, in particular, to expand the areas that would be protected from its sonar.[42] Available evidence suggests that the NMFS decision to exempt the LFAS system from the Marine Mammal Protection Act should be revisited and that international legal mechanisms should be explored to better protect marine mammals and their environment from the use of LFAS and other forms of military sonar.

THE NAVY'S JUSTIFICATIONS

One of the U.S. Navy's principal missions is to detect and, when necessary, destroy enemy submarines. During the Cold War, the enemy submarines of concern were primarily nuclear powered and nuclear armed. Now, they are chiefly diesel-electric craft. Nuclear submarines can be detected by passive sonar, because of their relatively noisy propulsion machinery. The United States established a system of hydrophones placed on the sea floor connected to cables that terminated at shore stations. In the Pacific, this listening system was called Oceanographic System Pacific and for many years the "cover story," that the stations, Naval Facilities (NAVFACS), were engaged in scientific research based on oceanography, was effective. When the true nature of the system became known—the secret simply could not be maintained—the specific locations of the hydrophone arrays still remained secret.

41. See http://www.surtass-lfa-eis.com/Highlights/stage.htm (accessed 8 September, 2002).

42. Natural Resources Defense Council v. Evans, No. C-02-3805 EDL, 2002 WL 31445165 (N.D.Cal., Opinion and Order Granting Plaintiffs' Motion for a Preliminary Injunction, 31 October 2002), slip op. at 54.

The virtues of this passive sonar system were that long-range detections became possible whenever the Soviet submarines were too noisy for their own safety. Sound ranges are influenced by absorption of the sound in seawater, refraction or bending of the sound caused by changes in seawater temperature, and spreading of the sound as it proceeds from its source to the detecting hydrophones. The system of passive bottom-laid hydrophone arrays could determine bearings or directions, but not ranges. Two or more arrays detecting the target were needed to get an approximate location or fix. Even then, the location as determined was not exact and was effectively an area rather than a point. Follow-up activity by long-range surveillance aircraft was needed to "localize" the enemy submarine, and finally surface ships—destroyers or frigates—were vectored to the site to deliver what might be the final blow. The use of this system was practiced frequently by the combined passive sonar system, and a command or headquarters center was needed to put the information together. The Commander Oceanographic System Pacific was located initially at San Francisco, California (later moved to Pearl Harbor, Hawai'i) and the NAVFACS were on the U.S. west coast, at Barbers Point, Hawai'i, and in Adak, Alaska.

Commander Oceanographic System Pacific was disestablished in 1995 for reasons not disclosed. The Cold War, of course, had been over for half a decade and the threat of a nuclear attack from submarines had been greatly diminished. In addition, the Russian submarines had become quieter and detection ranges determined by the passive sonar were diminished.

What is the submarine threat today? Diesel-electric submarines are now much quieter than they were previously. The need to spend long periods of time on the surface to charge batteries, a procedure that makes the sub susceptible to visual detection, has changed. Even by the end of World War II, efforts were made by German subs to reduce or even eliminate time on the surface by means of a snorkel.[43] At present, snorkeling time is on the order of a few minutes, and can be carried out at night. Modern "enemy" boats[44] can thus escape detection from passive sonar used by the "black boxes" on the ocean floor, and the U.S. Navy decided that long-range, very high-powered, low-frequency active sonar is needed. As explained earlier, this active sonar requires the generation of a powerful sound source that bounces off the enemy ship and is returned to the source vehicle. Surface ships operating as part of the modern SURTASS LFAS can carry and

43. The snorkel is a tube that is extended vertically from a submerged submarine, enabling the submarine to obtain sufficient air to operate its diesel engines while remaining submerged at a relatively shallow depth to avoid visual detection. Use of the term snorkel as a verb, that is, to snorkel or snorkeling is common with submarine personnel.

44. Submariners refer to their craft as "boats." This is an exception to common nautical terminology, which would classify them as "ships" because of their size and importance.

monitor hydrophone arrays and generate the active sound source, and thereby increase the capability to detect enemy vessels.

Diesel-electric (conventional) submarines are operated by many countries bordering the Atlantic, Pacific, and Indian Oceans, and important smaller bodies of water such as the South China Sea and the Sea of Japan/East Sea. These submarines are particularly effective in straits where numerous sea-lanes converge and surface ships are in transit. Many carry torpedoes and long-range cruise missiles and are of the ex-Soviet Kilo class or have similarly effective designs. Some of the important sea-lanes the United States relies upon for its national security lie near or along important straits, which have become potential "choke points." Many of these choke points such as the Suez and Panama Canals, the Malacca-Singapore Straits, and the Straits of Florida are vulnerable to disruption by surface ships and submarines.

The U.S. Navy has reported that "there are 224 submarines operated by non-allied nations, and the submarines prowling the world's oceans today are much quieter and more deadly than ever before."[45] To assess numerically the danger to U.S. and allied navies now that the Cold War is over, we have consulted the authoritative *Jane's Fighting Ships*.[46] Midget subs are omitted from our list because of their obvious inability to attack U.S. ships, but all others are listed—whether operated by potential enemies or by countries presumed to be friendly. To provide a general assessment of the capabilities of the subs, the following classification is used: SS is the general classification for submarines and the other designations are in effect modifiers: N stands for nuclear; B stands for ballistic missile; G stands for guided missile; K stands for killer (i.e., subs configured for hunter-killer operations).

Australia—6 SSK
Canada—4 SSK
Chile—5 SSK
China—121 with 8 more under construction. The numbers include 1 SSBN, 1 SSB, 7 SSN, 6 SSG, and 106 SS
Colombia—2 patrol subs (SS that are not modernized or improved)
Cuba—1 Foxtrot class (SSK)
Denmark—5 coastal subs with an additional 4 under construction (SS)
Ecuador—2 type 209 class subs (SSK)
Egypt—4 patrol subs with an additional 2 under construction

45. See http://www.surtass-lfa-eis.com/WhyNeed/stage.htm (accessed 9 June 2002); see also Department of Navy Office of Legislative Affairs, Memorandum for Interested Members of Congress—Record of Decision for the Surveillance Towed Array Sensor System Low Frequency Active (SURTASS LFA) Sonar, 17 July 2002.

46. Jane's Fighting Ships, 2002–2003 (Coulsdon, Surrey, U.K.: Jane's Information Group, Sentinel House, 2002).

France—2 SSBN with an additional 4 either under construction or planned, 6 SS
Germany—14 patrol subs with an additional 4 under construction (SS)
Greece—8 patrol subs with an additional 3 under construction (SS)
India—1 SSN under construction, 17 patrol subs (SS)
Indonesia—2 SSK
Iran—3 Kilo class (SSK)
Japan—23 SSK
Malaysia—3 SS
Netherlands—4 SSK
North Korea—22 SS and 22 classified as "Coastal" and presumed to be unimproved models with limited capability
Norway—10 SSK with an additional 4 under construction
Pakistan—7 SSK with an additional 2 under construction
Poland—3 SSK
Portugal—3 SSK
Russia—17 SSBN with an additional 1 under construction, 7 SSGN with an additional 1 under construction, 17 SSN with an additional 3 under construction, 14 SSK with an additional 2 SSK under construction.
Singapore—4 SSK
Taiwan—10 (4SS, 6 SSK)
United Kingdom—4 SSBN, 12 conventional attack submarines with five more SSK under construction
Venezuela—2 SSK

Simple quantitative data cannot, of course, completely assess the threat. We are at present unable to judge the skills of the submarine crews, the state of maintenance of the boats, or, most importantly, whether the countries can be considered to be potential enemies or allies. North Korea would certainly be in the potential enemy category. In view of our current relations with China, we cannot be certain about the danger of Chinese subs, but it would be foolish to discount it. Malaysia, Indonesia, and Singapore are certainly not enemies, but their important location guarding the Strait of Malacca puts them in the category of countries of interest.

The Navy has a responsibility to try to detect potential enemy submarines, but in view of the recognized threat to marine life posed by its low frequency active sonar, passive sonar alternatives should continue to be developed and utilized wherever possible.[47] The use of active sonar, espe-

47. The Executive Summary of the Navy EIS for SURTASS LFA Sonar at ES-6 states this idea generally as "(Restricted Operation—the Navy's preferred alternative) the use of this system would include geographic restrictions and monitoring to prevent injury to potentially affected species."

cially in light of the documented damage it causes, can be justified only where the threat from a potential enemy submarine is clearly demonstrated, immediate, and severe.

DOES THE USE OF LOW FREQUENCY ACTIVE SONAR VIOLATE INTERNATIONAL LAW?

The U.S. Navy's current and projected plans to use LFAS do appear to violate international law, particularly the duty of all states to protect the marine environment from pollution, the duty to act with precaution (and to undertake environmental assessments before starting new activities), and the duty to cooperate with other affected countries.

International law is relevant because LFAS will impact areas outside the areas under the jurisdiction of the United States and the NATO countries using this technology, and also because it will impact migratory and straddling species that are in waters under U.S./NATO jurisdiction for part of their life-cycle and outside these waters for other phases of their lives.

RELEVANT TREATY REGIMES

The 1982 United Nations Law of the Sea Convention[48]

Under Article 192 of the Law of the Sea Convention, all countries have "the obligation to protect and preserve the marine environment." This principle is obligatory even for countries that have not ratified the Convention, like the United States, because it has become a binding norm of customary international law.[49] Article 65 of the Convention has particular relevance to the threats posed to marine mammals, because it requires countries to "co-

48. United Nations Convention on the Law of the Sea, 10 December 1982, entered into force 16 November 1994, UN Doc. A/CONF.62/122 (1982), *International Legal Materials* 21 (1982) at 1261.

49. As of 24 February 2003, 142 countries had ratified the Law of the Sea Convention. UN Division for Ocean Affairs and the Law of the Sea, Chronological List of Ratifications, http://www.un.org/Depts/los/reference_files/chronological_lists_of_... (accessed 1 March 2003). A few important countries like the United States and Canada had not ratified the Convention as of that date, but they both have been giving serious consideration to ratification. The United States has frequently acknowledged that the provisions in the Law of the Sea Convention, except those governing exploitation of deep seabed minerals, reflect existing norms of customary international law. See, for example, Ocean Policy Statement by the President, 10 March 1983, accompanying Proclamation No. 5030, 48 Fed. Reg. 10,605 (1983) ("the Convention . . . contains provisions with respect to traditional uses of the oceans which generally confirm existing maritime law and practice and fairly balance the interests of all States").

operate with a view to the conservation of marine mammals and in the case of cetaceans . . . in particular [to] work through the appropriate international organizations for their conservation, management and study."

The unusually loud sounds emitted in the LFAS process would certainly be considered "pollution," which is defined in Article 1(1)(4) of the Convention as:

> the introduction by man, directly or indirectly, of substances or *energy* into the marine environment, including estuaries, which *results or is likely to result* in such *deleterious effects as harm to living resources and marine life,* hazards to human health, hindrance to marine activities, including fishing and other legitimate uses of the sea, impairment of quality for use of sea water and reduction of amenities. (Emphasis added).

Sound is a "form of energy manifested by small pressure and/or particle velocity variations in a continuous medium."[50] "While the definition [of "pollution" in the Law of the Sea Convention] was . . . not drafted with acoustic pollution in mind, the inclusion of 'energy' implies that noise can be a form of pollution under the terms of the LOS Convention."[51]

Article 194(1) is quite clear that countries must do everything possible "to prevent, reduce and control pollution of the marine environment from any source." "States are required, therefore, to take preventive measures based on existing knowledge to avoid pollution, rather than to take remedial measures once it has occurred, and to apply a precautionary approach when scientific certainty about the harmful effects is not (yet) available."[52] Article 194(5) makes it clear that these duties, in particular, require countries to adopt measures "to protect and preserve rare or fragile ecosystems as well as the habitat of depleted, threatened or endangered species and other forms of marine life."

Article 196 requires countries to "take all measures necessary to prevent, reduce and control pollution of the marine environment resulting from the use of technologies under their jurisdiction or control." Articles 204–206 require the preparation and dissemination of environmental impact assessments.[53] Although the U.S. Navy did prepare an EIS, the scientific tests it relied upon, as explained earlier, were woefully inadequate and, even so,

50. W. J. Richardson et al., *Marine Mammals and Noise* (San Diego: Academic Press, 1995), p. 544.

51. H. M. Dotinga and A. G. Oude Elferink, "Acoustic pollution in the oceans: The search for legal standards," *Ocean Development and International Law* 31 (2000): 151, 158.

52. Ibid., at 161.

53. See also Law of the Sea Convention (n. 48 above), Article 165(2)(d) (also requiring environmental impact assessments for activities exploiting the resources of the deep seabed).

demonstrated that LFAS will have negative impacts on marine mammals. In addition, the Navy's EIS was not made available to other countries during its preparation for their comments and input.

The Convention on the Conservation of Migratory Species of Wild Animals[54]

Article III(4) of this treaty requires parties that are "Range States" to "endeavour" "(b) to prevent, remove, compensate for or minimize, as appropriate, the adverse effects of activities or obstacles that seriously impede or prevent the migration of the species; and (c) to the extent feasible and appropriate, to prevent, reduce or control factors that are endangering or are likely to further endanger the species . . ." The United States is not one of the 81 parties to this treaty,[55] and it has relatively weak enforcement provisions, saying only in Article XIII that disputes should be resolved through negotiation and that, if negotiations are unsuccessful, countries "may, by mutual consent, submit the dispute to arbitration . . ." Nonetheless, its substantive provisions can be viewed as reflective of the consensus of international views on this subject, and as supporting customary international law norms requiring countries to protect wild migratory species.

The Biodiversity Convention[56]

This treaty confirms in Article 3 the principle that emerged from the 1972 Stockholm[57] and 1992 Rio Declarations[58] that "States have . . . the responsibility to ensure that activities within their jurisdiction or control do not cause damage to the environment of other States or of areas beyond the limits of national jurisdiction." The treaty also contains general provisions saying

54. Convention on the Conservation of Migratory Species of Wild Animals, Bonn, 1979, reprinted in D. Hunter, J. Salzman, and D. Zaelke, *International Environmental Law and Policy—Treaty Supplement,* 2002 Edition (New York: Foundation Press, 2002), p. 320.

55. Convention on Migratory Species, http://www.wcmc.org.uk/cms/cms_banner.html (accessed 1 March 2003).

56. Convention on Biological Diversity, 5 June 1992, preamble, UNEP/Bio. Div/CONF/L.2, S. Treaty Doc. No. 103-20, *International Legal Materials* 31 (1992) at 818, 822–3.

57. Declaration of the United Nations Conference on the Human Environment (Stockholm Declaration), UN Doc. A/CONF.48/14, 7, *International Legal Materials* 11 (1972) at 1416, 1420.

58. Rio Declaration on Environment and Development, 14 June 1992, UN Doc. A/CONF.151/5/Rev.1(1992), *International Legal Materials* 31 (1992) at 874.

that countries, should, when feasible, promote and protect biological diversity.

The Biodiversity Convention utilizes what some have called a "purer form" of the precautionary principle, stating in its preamble that "where there is a threat of significant reduction or loss of biological diversity, lack of full scientific certainty should not be used as a reason for postponing measures to avoid or minimize such a threat. . ."[59] In addition, Article 14(1)(a) requires contracting parties to undertake "environmental impact assessment[s] of its proposed projects that are likely to have significant adverse effects on biological diversity with a view to avoiding or minimizing such effects and, where appropriate, allow for public participation in such procedures."

The Biodiversity Treaty has a dispute settlement provision saying that disputes should be resolved through conciliation unless the parties agree to compulsory submission to an arbitral panel or to the International Court of Justice. This treaty has achieved almost-universal acceptance, with 187 ratifications.[60] The United States signed this treaty in 1993, but the U.S. Senate refused to ratify it in 1994.

The International Whaling Convention[61]

This Convention's text does not say anything directly about acoustic impacts on whales, or indeed about pollution of the habitats of whales. But Article V does authorize the contracting parties to "adopt regulations with respect to the conservation . . . of whale resources, fixing . . . (c) open and closed waters, including the designation of sanctuary areas . . . " Various committees have examined the acoustic issues, and the 1999 Report of the Scientific Committee "stated that noise-producing activities (such as seismic surveys or sonar operations) should not be conducted in critical habitats at certain times of the year, which could greatly reduce exposing mothers and calves or breeding animals to high sound levels. It supported measures to mitigate adverse effects of noise wherever possible and stressed the need for further research."[62]

59. S. McCaffrey, "Biotechnology: Some issues of general international law," *Transnational Law* 14 (2001): 91, 97.

60. Parties to the Convention on Biological Diversity, http://www.biodiv.org/world/parties.asp (accessed 1 March 2003).

61. International Convention for the Regulation of Whaling, 2 December 1946, 161 U.N.T.S. 72, 10 U.S.T. 952.

62. Dotinga and Oude Elferink (n. 51 above), p. 169 (citing IWC/51/4, para. 11.4.1 and Annex H, para. 7.1).

Regional Cetacean Agreements

Two regional agreements designed to address small cetaceans have been adopted pursuant to the 1979 Bonn Convention on Migratory Species.[63] The Agreement on the Conservation of Small Cetaceans of the Baltic and North Sea of 17 March 1992 (ASCOBANS)[64] has been ratified by all eight countries in the region. The Conservation and Management Plan provides that the parties shall work toward "the prevention of other significant disturbance, especially of an acoustic nature" of the species involved, and various meetings and studies have been undertaken to address this issue.[65] The Agreement on the Conservation of the Cetaceans of the Black Sea, Mediterranean Sea and Contiguous Atlantic Area (ACCOBAMS)[66] has now been ratified by seven nations and signed by eight others. A number of the contracting parties to these two treaties are also members of the North Atlantic Treaty Organization (NATO).

RELEVANT PRINCIPLES OF CUSTOMARY INTERNATIONAL LAW

The Duty to Avoid Causing Harm to Shared Resources and the Common Heritage

Principle 21 of the Stockholm Declaration on the Human Environment[67] affirmed the responsibility of States "to ensure that activities within their jurisdiction and control do not cause damage to the environment of other states or areas beyond the limits of national jurisdiction."[68] The introduc-

63. See text accompanying n. 54 and 55 above.

64. Agreement on the Conservation of Small Cetaceans of the Baltic and North Seas, 17 March 1992, http://www.oceanlaw.net/texts/summaries/ascobans.htm (accessed 1 March 2003).

65. Dotinga and Oude Elferink (n. 51 above), pp. 169–70.

66. Agreement on the Conservation of the Cetaceans of the Black Sea, Mediterranean Sea and Contiguous Atlantic Area (ACCOBAMS), 24 November 1996, http://www.oceanlaw.net/texts/summaries/accobams.htm (accessed 1 March 2003).

67. Declaration of the United Nations Conference on the Human Environment, UN Doc. A/CONF.48/14, 7, *International Legal Materials* 11 (1972) at 1416, 1420. See generally L. Sohn, "The Stockholm declaration on the human environment," *Harvard Journal of International Law* 15 (1973): 423, and M. Akehurst, "International liability for injurious consequences arising out of acts not prohibited by international law," *New York Journal of International Law* (1985): 3.

68. See also Principle 2 of the 1992 Rio Declaration (n. 58 above), and Restatement (Third) of Foreign Relations Law (1987), Section 601. Philippe Sands in *Principles of International Environmental Law*, vol. I (1995), p. 186 concludes that taken together Principle 21 and Principle 2 "establish the basic obligation underlying environmental law and the source of its further elaboration in rules of greater specificity." The International Court of Justice has referred to "every State's obligation not to allow knowingly its territory to be used for acts contrary to the rights of other

tion of acoustic pollution into the ocean, which causes damage to marine mammals and other marine species in the exclusive economic zones of other nations and in the high seas beyond national jurisdiction, would certainly violate this norm of customary international law.

The Precautionary Principle

The precautionary principle, or "precautionary approach" as some countries and commentators prefer to call it, has evolved into a norm with real content.[69] It mandates that studies precede action, and that interdisciplinary environmental impact assessments be written and distributed, with public input.[70] It shifts the burden to those that would undertake a new development or use of an environmental resource, replacing the old approach that

States," Corfu Channel Case (United Kingdom v. Albania), 1949 I.C.J. 4, and this central principle is also relied upon in the Trail Smelter Arbitration, 3 R. Int'l Arb. Awards 1905, 1938 (1941), holding that "no State has the right to use or permit the use of its territory in such a manner as to cause injury by fumes in or to the territory of another."

69. The essence of this norm was articulated in the 1992 Rio Declaration as "Where there are threats of serious or irreversible damage, lack of full scientific certainty shall not be used as a reason for postponing cost-effective measures to prevent environmental degradation." Rio Declaration (n. 58 above), at 879. For detailed analysis of the precautionary principle, see, for example, D. Freestone, "The Precautionary Principle," in *International Law and Global Climate Change,* ed. R. Churchill and D. Freestone (London: Graham & Trotman/M. Nijhoff, 1991), p. 21; E. Hey, "The precautionary concept in environmental policy and law: Institutionalizing caution," *Georgetown International Environmental Law Review* 4 (1992): 303; J. E. Hickey, Jr., and V. R. Walker, "Refining the precautionary principle in international law," *Virginia Environmental Law Journal* 14 (1995): 423; G. D. Fullem, Comment, "The precautionary principle: Environmental protection in the face of scientific uncertainty," *Willamette Law Review* 31 (1995): 495; J. M. Macdonald, "Appreciating the precautionary principle as an ethical evolution in ocean management," *Ocean Development and International Law* 26 (1995): 255; J. M. Van Dyke, "Applying the precautionary principle to ocean shipments of radioactive materials," *Ocean Development and International Law* 27 (1996): 379; J. Cameron and J. Abouchar, "The Status of the Precautionary Principle in International Law" in *The Precautionary Principle and International Law: The Challenge of Implementation,* ed. D. Freestone and E. Hey (The Hague: Kluwer Law International, 1996), p. 29; M. Territo, "The precautionary principle in marine fisheries conservation and the U.S. Sustainable Fisheries Act of 1996," *Vermont Law Review* 24 (2000): 1351; R. Unger, "Brandishing the precautionary principle through the Alien Tort Claims Act," *New York University Environmental Law Journal* 9 (2001): 638; V. R. Walker, "Some dangers of taking precautions without adopting the precautionary principle," *Environmental Law Reporter* 31 (2001): 10040.

70. For a listing of international agreements requiring environmental assessments, see D. Hunter, J. Salzman, and D. Zaelke, *International Environmental Law and Policy* (New York: Foundation Press, 1998), pp. 366–70.

had imposed the burden on the environmentalists who challenged such activity.[71] It requires those countries and companies that want to undertake new developments to engage in scientific studies to determine the effect of their initiatives, and also to consider less intrusive approaches. It accords respect to ecosystems and living creatures for their own sake, without requiring that they prove themselves to be useful or to have marketplace value. It rejects the idea that risks and costs can be transferred from one region to another, or from this generation to future ones, and it requires that risks and costs be internalized in order to force decision makers to engage in a fair and sober analysis before deciding to proceed with a project. And ultimately it requires that we proceed slowly in the face of uncertainty, constantly testing and monitoring the effects of our activities.

The precautionary principle has become the foundation of a number of important recent treaties designed to manage fishing resources and to protect the marine environment, including the 1995 Migratory and Straddling Stocks Agreement[72] and the 2000 Honolulu Convention,[73] and it has also been recognized in regional and national decisions. The European courts have led the way in applying the precautionary principle,[74] and Euro-

71. Ibid., p. 360.

72. Agreement for the Implementation of the Provisions of the United Nations Convention on the Law of the Sea of 10 December 1982 Relating to the Conservation and Management of Straddling Fish Stocks and Highly Migratory Fish Stocks, 8 September 1995, UN Doc. A/CONF.164/37, *International Legal Materials* 34 (1995): 1542.

73. The Convention on the Conservation and Management of Highly Migratory Fish Stocks in the Western and Central Pacific Ocean, Honolulu, 4 September 2000, (accessed 26 March 2001); see generally V. Botet, "Filling in one of the last pieces of the ocean: Regulating Tuna in the Western and Central Pacific Ocean," *Virginia Journal of International Law* 41(2001): 787.

74. The most significant decision of the European Court of Justice occurred in 1998, when the Court upheld the European Commission's decision to ban all bovine animals and all beef and veal products from the United Kingdom, based on the EC's judgment that all risks of transmission from bovine spongiform encephalopathy (mad cow disease) could not be excluded. The Queen v. Ministry of Agriculture, Fisheries and Food, Commissioners of Customs & Excise, ex parte National Farmer's Union, David Burnett and Sons Ltd., R.S. Case C-147-96, [1998] E.C.R. I-2211. In response to the argument of the English National Farmers' Union that this decision violated the principle of proportionality, the Court acknowledged that the principle of proportionality required that the least onerous alternative be chosen, but ruled also that "[w]here there is uncertainty as to the existence or extent of risks to human health, the institutions may take protective measures without having to wait until the reality and seriousness of the risks become fully apparent." Ibid., para. 63. The Court repeated this statement in United Kingdom v. Commission of the European Communities, Case C-180/96, [1998] E.C.R. I-2265, para. 99. In another important decision, the Court of First Instance in Europe rejected a challenge to a decision that had withdrawn an antibiotic from the list of authorized animal feeds by quoting from the statement above, referring to the precautionary principle, and adding that "[t]here can be no question but that the requirements of the protection of public health must take precedence over economic considerations."

pean institutions have also fully embraced it.[75] The British government has recognized that it should be widely followed,[76] as have courts in, for instance, India, Pakistan, the Netherlands, Australia,[77] and Hawaii.[78]

Alpharma, Inc. v. Council of the European Union, Case T-70/99 R, [1999] E.C.R. II-2027, para. 3.

75. The European Community (EC) has been promoting reliance upon the precautionary principle "in the international arena, in general, and in the WTO [World Trade Organization], in particular." See, for example, Hans-Joachim Priess and Christian Pitschas, "Protection of public health and the role of the precautionary principle under WTO law: A Trojan Horse before Geneva's walls?" *Fordham International Law Journal* 24 (2000): 519, 520 (adding that "The EC relied on this principle in EC Measures Concerning Meat and Meat Products (Hormones), and it recently submitted a communication on the very same principle to the WTO Committee on Sanitary and Phytosanitary Measures. The Commission also published a communication on the precautionary principle . . . at the beginning of this year, and the Council issued a resolution on the precautionary principle at the Nice summit."). The EC issued a "Communication" in 2000 stating that the precautionary principle is "a full-fledged and general principle of international law." "Communication on the Precautionary Principle, Communication from the Commission of the European Communities, COM(2000) 1 final (2 February 2000)," http://europa.eu.int/comm/off/health_consumer/precaution.htm. See M. Geistfeld, "Reconciling cost-benefit analysis with the principle that safety matters more than money," *New York University Law Review* 76 (2001): 114, 176–8.

76. The 1990 British White Paper entitled "This Common Inheritance: Britain's Environmental Strategy," September 1990, Cm 1200, provides the following guide to all British governmental activities: "We must analyze the possible benefits and costs both of action and of inaction. Where there are significant risks of damage to the environment, the Government will be prepared to take precautionary action to limit the use of potentially dangerous pollutants, even where scientific knowledge is not conclusive, if the balance of the likely costs and benefits justifies it. This precautionary principle applies particularly where there are good grounds for judging either that action taken promptly at comparatively low cost may avoid more costly damage later, or that irreversible effects may follow if action is delayed."

77. See references in Unger (n. 69 above), p. 664 (citing Zia v. WAPDA, Human Rights Case No. 15-K (Pakistan S.C. 1992), http://www.elaw.org/custom/custompages/resourceDetail.asp?profile_ID=280; Vellore Citizens Welfare Forum v. Union of India & Ors., (1995) 5 S.C.C. 647, 703, http://www.elaw.org/custom/custompages/resourceDetail.asp?profile_ID=199; A.P. Pollution Control Board v. Prof. M.V. Nayudu (Retd.), (1999) 2 S.C.C. 718, Leatch v. National Parks & Wildlife Service, (1993) 81 L.G.E.R.A. 270; Simpson v. Ballina Shire Council, (1994) 82 L.G.E.R. 392; and Greenpeace Australia Ltd. v. Redbank Power Co., (1995) 86 L.G.E.R.A. 143). A Dutch court relied upon the precautionary principle in Vander Eudt-Louwerse B. V. et al. v. State Secretary of Transport, Public Works and Water Management, JM 2001/99 (Netherlands Administrative Law Division of the Council of State, 26 April 2001), see NILOS Newsletter, no. 19 (February 2002): 5.

78. The Hawaii Supreme Court ruled in In the Matter of Water Use Permit Applications, Waiahole Ditch Combined Contested Case Hearing, 9 P.3d 409, 466–67 (Hawaii 2000), that "the precautionary principle simply restates the [Water] Commission's duties under the [Hawaii] constitution and [Hawaii's Water] Code. Indeed, the lack of full scientific certainty does not extinguish the presumption in favor of public trust purposes or vitiate the Commission's affirmative duty to protect

When risks are anticipated, the precautionary principle requires those creating the risks to work with potentially affected nations to prepare for foreseeable emergency contingencies,[79] to create appropriate liability regimes to ensure that injured parties are properly compensated,[80] to notify other countries of situations threatening harmful effects on their environment,[81] and of course to take every appropriate precaution to prevent or limit damage to the environment.[82] "A strict application of the precautionary principle would require additional research of a broader scope to eliminate the possibility of long-term, irreversible harm to the marine ecosystem or any of its living components before the SURTASS LFAS system can be deployed globally."[83]

The Polluter-Pays Principle

Another general principle of international law is that when a State violates its international obligations, it has a duty to make reparations for the wrongs committed. The Permanent Court of International Justice (PCIJ) stated in the Chorzow Factory Case that "reparation must, as far as possible, wipe out all the consequences of the illegal act and reestablish the situation which would, in all probability, have existed if that act had not been committed."[84] The International Court of Justice (ICJ) also recognized in the Gabcikovo-Nagymoros Case that "[i]t is a well-established rule of international law that

---

such purposes wherever feasible." The Hawaii Supreme Court cited, as evidence that "'[t]he precautionary principle' appears in diverse forms throughout the field of environmental law," the cases of Ethyl Corp. v. EPA, 541 F.2d 1, 20-29 (D.C. Cir.), cert denied, 426 U.S. 941 (1976); Lead Industries v. EPA, 647 F.2d 1130, 1154-55 (D.C. Cir. 1980), cert. denied, 449 U.S. 1042 (1980); and Les v. Reilly, 968 F.2d 985 (9th Cir. 1992), cert. denied, 507 U.S. 950 (1993). "As with any general principle, its meaning must vary according to the situation and can only develop over time. In this case, we believe the [Water] Commission describes the [precautionary] principle in its quintessential form: at minimum, the absence of firm scientific proof should not tie the Commission's hands in adopting reasonable measures designed to further the public interest." 9 P.3d at 467.

79. See, for example, Law of the Sea Convention (n. 48 above), Article 199.

80. Ibid., Article 235.

81. Ibid., Article 198; Rio Declaration (n. 58 above), Principle 18.

82. See Philippe Sands, *Principles of International Environmental Law* vol. I, pp. 194–5 (1995), citing the Stockholm Declaration (n. 57 above), Principles 6, 7, 15, 18 and 24, the 1978 UNEP Draft Principles, Principle 1, the 1982 World Charter for Nature, the growing network of specific environmental conventions, the Trail Smelter Arbitration, 3 R. Int'l Arb. Awards 1905 (1941), and the Lac Lanoux Arbitration (Spain v. Fr.), 12 R. Int'l Arb. Awards 281, 24 I.L.R. 101 (1957).

83. E. Gardner, "The Precautionary Principle as Applied to Marine Acoustic Activities," in *Emerging Issues in National Ocean and Coastal Policy*, ed. H. N. Scheiber (Berkeley, California: Ocean Governance Study Group, 1999), pp. 9, 12.

84. Chorzow Factory Case, P.C.I.J., Series A, No. 17, p. 47.

an injured State is entitled to obtain compensation from the State which has committed an internationally wrongful act for the damage caused by it."[85] The emission of low-frequency-active sonar is not an inherently "wrongful act," but it can be wrongful and harmful if its operation falls short of accepted international standards and has the effect of harming the marine environment.

The Duty to Cooperate

Another principle well established in customary international law is the requirement of cooperation among States in making decisions that may substantially affect the environment. Principle 24 of the Stockholm Declaration states:

> International matters concerning the protection and improvement of the environment should be handled in a co-operative spirit by all countries, big or small, on an equal footing. Cooperation through multilateral or bilateral arrangements or other appropriate means is essential to effectively control, prevent, reduce and eliminate adverse environmental effects resulting from activities conducted in all spheres, in such a way that due account is taken of the sovereignty and interests of all States.[86]

This principle had earlier been utilized by the arbitral tribunal in the 1957 Lac Lanoux Arbitration,[87] where it was held that, as a matter of customary international law, a State that is engaging in behavior likely to impact the environment of another State significantly is obliged to involve the affected state in discussions regarding these activities. Article 197 of the Law of the Sea Convention makes this duty obligatory with regard to activities that may impact the marine environment:

> States shall co-operate on a global basis and, as appropriate, on a regional basis, directly or through competent international organizations, in formulating and elaborating international rules, standards and recommended practices and procedures consistent with this Convention,

85. Case Concerning the Gabcikovo-Nagymoros Project (Hungary / Slovakia), 1997 I.C.J. 7, 81 (Sept. 25, 1997).

86. Stockholm Declaration (n. 57 above), Principle 24, http://www.unep.org/Documents/Default.asp?DocumentID=97 (accessed 16 March 2002); see also D. Hunter, J. Salzman, and D. Zaelke, *International Environmental Law and Policy* (New York: Foundation Press, 1998), p. 287.

87. Lac Lanoux Arbitration (Spain v. Fr.), 12 R. Int'l Arb. Awards 281, 24 I.L.R. 101 (Trib. Arb. 1957).

> for the protection and preservation of the marine environment, taking into account characteristic regional features.[88]

What About the Immunity of Military Vessels?

Article 236 of the 1982 Law of the Sea Convention contains the following, somewhat confusing, language:

> The provisions of this Convention regarding the protection and preservation of the marine environment do not apply to any warship, naval auxiliary, or other vessels or aircraft owned or operated by a State and used, for the time being, only on government non-commercial service. However, each State shall ensure, by the adoption of appropriate measures not impairing operations or operational capabilities of such vessels or aircraft owned or operated by it, that such vessels or aircraft act in a manner consistent, so far as is reasonable and practicable, with this Convention.

Articles 31 and 32 provide further explanation, making it clear (in Article 32) that the warship is itself immune from seizure but also (in Article 31) that the flag State of the vessel "shall bear international responsibility for any loss or damage to the coastal State resulting from the non-compliance by a warship . . . with the provisions of this Convention or other rules of international law." It would thus be improper to seize a military vessel engaging in polluting activity, but the government that owns such a vessel is duty bound to provide compensation for damage caused by the vessel and Article 235(3) requires nations to work together to establish meaningful liability and compensation regimes to ensure that victims can recover for their losses and that the marine environment is protected.

What About the Self-Defense Purposes of LFAS?

In its Nuclear Weapons advisory opinion,[89] the International Court of Justice said, "The Court does not consider that the treaties in question could have intended to deprive a State of the exercise of its right of self-defence under international law because of its obligations to protect the environment. Nonetheless, States must take environmental considerations into account when assessing what is necessary and proportionate in the pursuit of legiti-

88. Law of the Sea Convention (n. 48 above).

89. Legality of the Threat or Use of Nuclear Weapons General List No 95, Advisory Opinion of July 8, 1996, 1996 I.C.J. 226.

mate military objectives." The Court then went on to quote from Principle 24 of the 1992 Rio Declaration,[90] which says that "Warfare is inherently destructive of sustainable development. States shall therefore respect international law providing protection for the environment in times of armed conflict and cooperate in its further development as necessary."

Although the right to self-defense permits the use of force in appropriate situations, governments are now being held liable for environmental damage caused by their acts of warfare. Examples include the United Nations Compensation Commission's rulings holding Iraq liable for the extensive environmental damage caused by its military activities during the Gulf War,[91] and Article 55 of the 1977 Protocol No. 1 to the 1949 Geneva Conventions,[92] which requires combatants to take care "in warfare to protect the natural environment against widespread, long-term and severe damage." Also relevant is Article 35(3) of Protocol I prohibiting the use of weapons that "are intended, or may be expected, to cause" such damage.

The Convention on the Prohibition of Military or Any Other Hostile Use of Environmental Modification Techniques, which the United States ratified in 1980, prohibits the use of techniques that modify the environment and cause "widespread, long-lasting or severe" destruction, damage or injury to another party.[93] The focus of this convention is on "deliberate manipulation of natural processes," but its language would also appear to prohibit actions that incidentally have the effect of altering or eliminating a species or ecosystem.[94] In its Nuclear Weapons advisory opinion, the ICJ said, refer-

90. Rio Declaration (n. 58 above).

91. The Compensation Commission was created by Security Council Resolution 687, which states that claims are to be paid from a fund generated by Iraqi oil sales after 2 April 1991. In June 2001, the Commission awarded Kuwait $108.9 million for environmental remediation efforts. C. Lynch, "Kuwaiti War Claim Approved," *Washington Post*, 28 September 2000; "Kuwait unveils plan to treat festering desert wound," *Science* 293 (2001): 1410. See generally www.unog.ch/uncc/start.htm (accessed 9 June 2002).

92. Protocol Additional to the Geneva Conventions of 12 August 1949, and Relating to the Protection of Victims of International Armed Conflicts (Protocol I), 8 June 1977.

93. Convention on the Prohibition of Military or Any Other Hostile Use of Environmental Modification Techniques (ENMOD Convention), 18 May 1977, 31 U.S.T. 33, 1108 U.N.T.S. 151. "Widespread" is defined as "encompassing an area on the scale of several hundred square kilometers;" "long-lasting" is something that lasts "for a period of months or approximately a season;" and "severe" is something "involving serious or significant disruption or harm to human life, natural and economic resources or other assets." United States Arms Control and Disarmament Agency, Arms Control and Disarmament Agreements: Texts and Histories of the Negotiations (Washington, D.C.: Arms Control and Disarmament Agency, 1990), pp. 211–13.

94. Article II of the ENMOD Convention defines "environmental modification techniques" as "any technique for changing—through the deliberate manipulation of natural processes—the dynamics, composition or structure of the Earth, includ-

ring to the language in 1977 Geneva Protocol I, that "these provisions embody a general obligation to protect that natural environment against widespread, long-term and severe environmental damage."

OPTIONS TO ADDRESS THE PROBLEM AT THE INTERNATIONAL LEVEL

If the use of this polluting active sonar in the world's oceans violates governing principles of international law, do mechanisms exist to limit the use of this technology?

Dispute-Resolution Procedures under the Law of the Sea Convention—The International Tribunal for the Law of the Sea

The Law of the Sea Convention establishes binding dispute-resolution procedures, and these could be invoked directly by an injured State against any other state that is utilizing LFAS in a manner that damages the marine resources of the victim State or the marine environment generally. The United States could argue that these procedures cannot be invoked against it until it ratifies the Convention, but they appear to have become applicable to the United States, at least in part, through the U.S. ratification of the 1995 Straddling and Migratory Stocks Agreement, as explained later.

Article 286 of the Law of the Sea Convention says that: "Subject to section 3, any dispute concerning the interpretation or application of this Convention shall . . . be submitted at the request of any party to the dispute to the court or tribunal having jurisdiction under this section." In Section 3, Article 297(1)(b) says that the compulsory jurisdiction provisions apply "when it is alleged that a State in exercising the aforementioned freedoms, rights or uses [referring to freedom of navigation and "other internationally lawful uses of the sea," that is, military activities related to self-defense] has acted in contravention of this Convention or of laws or regulations adopted by the coastal State in conformity with this Convention and other rules of international law not incompatible with this Convention." This language is thus explicit in establishing compulsory jurisdiction over claims that military activities damage coastal resources and pollute the marine environment.

Article 298(1)(b), however, allows a country to issue a written declaration saying that it does not accept compulsory jurisdiction over "disputes

---

ing its biota, lithosphere, hydrosphere and atmosphere, or of outer space." The "biota" are the flora and fauna of a region, and, therefore, a military technique that has the effect of causing damage to some or all of the marine fauna is certainly prohibited by this convention.

concerning military activities, including military activities by government vessels and aircraft engaged in non-commercial service." Argentina, Cape Verde, Chile, France Norway, Portugal, Russia, Slovenia, Tunisia, and Ukraine have issued such declarations. Those countries that have exempted military matters through a declaration are still required by Article 279 to settle their disputes through peaceful means according to the procedures listed in Article 33 of the United Nations Charter.

The 1995 Straddling and Migratory Stocks Agreement[95]

Article 30 of this Agreement (which the United States ratified in 1996 and which came into effect on 11 December 2001 when the 30th nation deposited its ratification) says that the dispute resolution provisions in the Law of the Sea Convention "apply *mutatis mutandis* to any dispute between States parties to this Agreement concerning the interpretation or application of this Agreement, whether or not they are also Parties to the [Law of the Sea] Convention." Because the 1995 Agreement has just recently come into force, it is not clear how exactly this language will be interpreted, but Canada (which, like the United States, has ratified the 1995 Agreement) recognized the potential use of the dispute-resolution procedure and issued an explicit declaration to the 1995 Agreement exempting military activities from the compulsory procedures pursuant to Article 298(1)(b) of the Law of the Sea Convention.[96] Significantly, however, the United States did not file a similar declaration when it ratified the 1995 Agreement.[97]

The dispute-resolution procedures under the 1995 Agreement could become important if a state whose resources were being damaged by LFAS sought to invoke them, because this Agreement requires all contracting parties to protect living marine resources and it is predicated explicitly on the precautionary approach. The governing principles in Article 5(d), (f), and (g) require contracting parties to "assess the impact of . . . other human activities . . . on . . . stocks and species," to "minimize pollution," and to

95. Agreement for the Implementation of the Provisions of the United Nations Convention on the Law of the Sea of 10 December 1982 Relating to the Conservation and Management of Straddling Fish Stocks and Highly Migratory Fish Stocks, UN Doc. A/CONF.164/37, 8 September 1995, *International Legal Materials* 34 (1995): 1542.

96. Declarations to 1995 Straddling and Migratory Stocks Agreement, http://www.un.org/Depts/los/convention_agreements/fish_stocks_ag... (accessed 1 March 2003).

97. Ibid. The United States did file a declaration choosing the special arbitral tribunal established in Annex VIII of the Law of the Sea Convention as its preferred mechanism for resolving disputes.

"protect biodiversity in the marine environment." And Article 6(2) says that "States shall be more cautious when information is uncertain, unreliable or inadequate. The absence of adequate scientific information shall not be used as a reason for postponing or failing to take conservation and management measures." The use of LFAS in a manner that caused damage to marine species, interfering, for instance, with their habitats or reproductive activities, would appear to violate these responsibilities.

International Court of Justice

Sixty-four countries have accepted the compulsory jurisdiction of the International Court of Justice with regard to other countries that have similarly accepted this jurisdiction. (The United States withdrew its acceptance of the Court's compulsory jurisdiction in 1986.) A country that has accepted this jurisdiction would be able to challenge the use of the LFAS system by another country that has similarly accepted the Court's compulsory jurisdiction, and a number of NATO countries have issued such declarations and thus could be named as defendants.[98] Jurisdiction against a country using LFAS in a manner that damages living resources of another country might also be obtained through another treaty, possibly through one of the "Friendship, Commerce, and Navigation" treaties that the United States signs with its trading partners.

The International Maritime Organization (IMO)

"The IMO is the competent organization to address vessel-source pollution at the international level."[99] But the IMO has not given the LFAS issue any particular attention thus far,[100] and it generally does not deal with military

98. The countries that have accepted the Court's compulsory jurisdiction are: Australia, Austria, Barbados, Belgium, Botswana, Bulgaria, Cambodia, Cameroons, Canada, Colombia, Costa Rica, Cyprus, Democratic Republic of Congo, Denmark, Dominican Republic, Egypt, Estonia, Finland, Gambia, Georgia, Greece, Guinea, Guinea-Bissau, Haiti, Honduras, Hungary, India, Ivory Coast, Japan, Kenya, Lesotho, Liberia, Liechtenstein, Luxembourg, Madagascar, Malawi, Malta, Mauritius, Mexico, Nauru, Netherlands, New Zealand, Nicaragua, Nigeria, Norway, Pakistan, Panama, Paraguay, Philippines, Poland, Portugal, Senegal, Somalia, Spain, Sudan, Surinam, Sweden, Swaziland, Switzerland, Togo, Uganda, United Kingdom, Uruguay, and Yugoslavia.

99. Dotinga and Oude Elferink (n. 51 above), p. 171.

100. But see IMO Resolution A.720(17) (adopted in 1991), which also allows areas to be designated as particularly sensitive sea areas if they fulfill designated ecological criteria such as unique or rare ecosystem, diversity, vulnerability, or scientific, recreational, or historical significance.

vessels or with living resources. It may be possible for countries concerned about potential LFAS pollution coming from ships to get the attention of the IMO and create a focus for this issue, and, if so, nongovernmental organizations (NGOs) may then also be able to play a useful supporting role.

The European Court of Human Rights

The European Convention on Human Rights protects the "right to life" in Article 2 and "the right to respect for private and family life, his home and his correspondence" in Article 8.[101] The language in Article 8 was used to protect the rights of a family that was forced to abandon its home after noxious fumes from a waste treatment facility violating environmental standards made the daughter sick.[102] In its conclusion, the European Court of Human Rights stated that the Spanish government "did not succeed in striking a fair balance between the interest of the town's economic well-being—that of having a waste-treatment plant—and the applicant's effective enjoyment of her right to respect for her home and her private and family life."

It may be possible to build upon this case to bring a broader claim on behalf of the marine environment, or on behalf of endangered cetacean species. The language used by the European Court focuses on the rights of individuals to family and home, and the right to live in a world with diverse creatures may require another step forward. Perhaps if it could be stressed that migratory cetacean species are "common property" shared by all of us, then a claim brought on their behalf, or based on the loss each of us suffers if we lose biological diversity, might be possible.

A Lawsuit in the United States?

The Alien Tort Claims Act (ATCA) provides non-U.S. citizens with an avenue to bring suits in U.S. federal courts for torts committed in violation of fundamental principles of international law.[103] The ATCA states that: "The district courts shall have original jurisdiction of any civil action by an alien for a tort only, committed in violation of the law of nations or treaty of the United States."[104] In 1980, the U.S. Court of Appeals for the Second Circuit

101. European Convention for the Protection of Human Rights and Fundamental Freedoms, 4 November 1950, 312 U.N.T.S. 222, Eur. T.S. No. 5 (1950), revised by Protocol 11.

102. Lopez Ostra v. Spain, App. No. 16798/90, 20 Eur. H.R. Rep. 277 (Eur.Ct.H.R. 1994).

103. 28 U.S.C. sec. 1350 (1994).

104. Ibid. Most recent cases utilizing the ATCA have involved gross human rights violations. See generally Unger (n. 69 above).

in Filartiga v. Peña-Irala,[105] expanded the reach of ATCA to include suit for violations of modern international law. A claim under ATCA must be brought (1) by a foreign citizen (2) for a tort (3) in violation of the laws of nations.

It might be possible for a non-U.S. citizen to bring a suit to challenge the use of LFAS in ocean areas where cetaceans and other marine species will be harmed. The substantive law would appear to be in place to support the claim that this activity violates norms of customary and treaty law, as explained above. Several difficult procedural problems would, however, have to be confronted. First, how would the plaintiff establish sufficient "injury" to satisfy the "standing" requirements in federal court? Second, how would the plaintiff overcome the claim of "sovereign immunity" that a defendant would raise, if the defendant were the U.S. government,[106] or the government of any foreign country?[107] If a private company could be identified as defendant, that would eliminate the sovereign-immunity problem, but the plaintiff would then need to establish that the private entity was bound by international law, perhaps because it was working in concert with a government.[108]

Generally, in determining whether a norm of international law is applicable, the court must look to see if the alleged violation is definable, obligatory, and universally condemned.[109] The district court in Beanal v. Freeport-McMoran, Inc.[110] set forth the following requirements:

(1) [N]o State condones the act in question and there is a recognizable

105. Filartiga v. Peña-Irala, 630 F.2d 876 (2d Cir. 1980).

106. A claim against the United States would be governed by the Federal Torts Claims Act, 28 U.S.C. sec. 2680, which allows claims for injuries resulting from "ministerial" acts, for example, negligence, but not for those resulting from "discretionary" acts. The decision to use LFAS would almost certainly be classified as a discretionary act, and thus the immunity granted to the federal government would appear to block a lawsuit filed against the federal government. But see Alvarez-Machain v. United States, 107 F.3d 696 (9th Cir. 1996) (allowing a claim to proceed against the United States for an abduction in violation of international human rights norms).

107. The Foreign Sovereign Immunities Act, 28 U.S.C. sec. 1605(a)(5)(A) permits actions to be brought in U.S. courts against foreign governments for tortious acts or omissions, but only if the damage occurs "in the United States" and is not caused by "the exercise or performance or the failure to exercise or perform a discretionary function regardless of whether the discretion be abused." For a claim to be successful, therefore, the effect of LFAS would have to occur in the territorial sea of the United States (the first 12 nautical miles from the coasts) and it would have to be concluded that the damage resulted from negligence, rather than from a discretionary decision of the foreign government.

108. See, for example, Doe I v. Unocal, 2002 WL 31063976 (9th Cir. 2002), opinion withheld pending en banc review, 2003 WL 359787 (9th Cir. 2003).

109. Filartiga, 630 F.2d at 881.

110. Beanal v. Freeport-McMoran, Inc., 969 F. Supp. 362 (E.D. La.1997).

> "universal" consensus of prohibition against it; (2) there are sufficient criteria to determine whether a given action amounts to the prohibited act and thus violates the norm; (3) the prohibition against it is nonderogable and therefore binding at all times upon all actors.[111]

The Filartiga court indicated that the Supreme Court has held that the law of nations "may be ascertained by consulting the works of jurists, writing professedly on public law; or by the general usage and practice of nations; or by judicial decisions recognizing and enforcing that law."[112] Thus, principles such as the precautionary principle, the polluter-pays principle, and the duty to cooperate could provide the basis for an ATCA claim.

The U.S. Court of Appeals for the Second Circuit rejected this approach in September 2003, however, ruling that the claim by Peruvian citizens that the activities of a U.S. copper smelting company in Peru caused severe lung disease and thus violated their rights to life, to health, and to sustainable development did not state a cause of action under the Alien Tort Claims Act, because such "rights" "are insufficiently definite to constitute rules of customary international law."[113] The court ruled that although they are recognized in international treaties and resolutions, they are "boundless and indeterminate," expressing "virtuous goals" but at such a "level of abstraction" that they "state abstract rights and liberties devoid of articulable or discernable standards and regulations."[114] This court emphasized that customary international law had not crystallized regarding acts of intranational pollution, and thus that U.S. courts should not provide judicial forums for these acts, but it may still be possible to pursue claims in U.S. courts involving acts of pollution that cross national boundaries or ones that occur in common spaces like the high seas.[115]

111. 969 F.Supp. at 370. On appeal, in Beanal v. Freeport-McMoran, Inc., 197 F.3d 161, 167 (5th Cir. 1999), the court ruled that a claim based in part on the precautionary principle did not present a cognizable claim as a violation of customary international law under the Alien Tort Claims Act, 28 U.S.C. sec. 1350, because the claimants had not shown that the principle enjoyed "universal acceptance in the international community" or had "articulable and discernable standards" sufficient to "constitute international environmental abuses or torts." See, in contrast, the opinion of the Hawaii Supreme Court in In the Matter of Water Use Permit Applications, Waiahole Ditch Combined Contested Case Hearing, 9 P.3d 409, 466–67 (Hawaii 2000), described above in n. 78.

112. Filartiga, 630 F.2d at 880.

113. Flores v. Southern Peru Copper Corporation, – F.3d –, 2003 WL 22038598 (2d Cir. 2003).

114. Ibid. at *16 (quoting from Beanal, 197 F.3d at 167).

115. Another court that refused to allow ATCA claims based solely on principles that "do not set forth any specific proscriptions, but rather refer only in a general sense to the responsibility of nations" is Amlon Metals, Inc. v. FMC Corp. 775 F. Supp. 668 (S.D.N.Y. 1991). The court would not accept a claim based solely on the alleged violation of Principle 21 of the Stockholm Declaration (n. 57 above), which confirmed that states have a responsibility to ensure that activities within their

CONCLUSION

Substantive principles of international law have evolved through treaties and the development of customary international law, and they now clearly prohibit pollution of the marine environment. Noise is polluting energy, and the incredibly loud noises that will be emitted by the navies of the United States and its NATO allies through their active sonar program, and by scientists using this technology for other purposes, have been shown to interfere with marine life and must certainly be classified as pollution. In 2002 and 2003, three judges in three different cases in the U.S. District Court for the Northern District of California issued opinions blocking and limiting the use of sonar based on violations of U.S. laws.[116] Legal challenges in U.S. courts relying on U.S. environmental laws will remain a good method of addressing the risks created by LFAS and related sonars, but, because U.S. judges do permit continued testing of LFAS and because Congress may exempt military sonar from U.S. environmental laws,[117] it is also necessary to consider international remedies. Although international law respects military activities necessary for self-defense, military decision makers must balance the military benefit against the risks to the environment. The use of untested technologies likely to have a significant impact on marine life for a limited military goal that can probably be achieved through other means would certainly be considered by most observers to be a violation of international law.

Procedural mechanisms are not always in place to protect the substantive international law norms that have emerged in recent years, but it may be possible to use existing and recently created tribunals to protect the ocean creatures threatened by LFAS. The most promising approach would be to use the dispute-resolution procedures found in the Law of the Sea Convention. Even though the United States has not ratified the Convention, it would appear to be possible for a concerned country to bring a claim against the United States pursuant to the 1995 Straddling and Migratory Species Agreement, which the United States has ratified and which is now in force.[118]

Political efforts can also be pursued, utilizing international organizations such as the International Maritime Organization and the European Parliament. Lawsuits can be filed in national and regional courts, in the United States using the Alien Tort Claims Act, and also in the European Court of Human Rights, although significant procedural barriers would need to be overcome.

---

jurisdiction do not cause environmental damage to other states. The court stated that the plaintiff's reliance on Principle 21 was "misplaced, since those Principles do not set forth any specific proscriptions, but rather refer only on a general sense to the responsibility of nations." Ibid., at 671.

116. See text at (n. 5–12 above).

117. See (n. 13 above).

118. See text at (n. 95–7 above).

The principles that have emerged in treaties and recent cases make it clear that it is impermissible to introduce pollution into the marine environment, especially not at the level presented by the planned use of low frequency active sonar, which will impose severe risks on marine life. Because of the serious and perhaps devastating impact LFAS can be expected to have on marine mammals and other ocean life, it is likely that any tribunal allowed to address the merits of this controversy would act conscientiously to restrict the use of this new technology, drawing upon the existing treaties and principles of international law described earlier.

Whales and Ice: Common Themes of Antarctica, Whaling, and the Law of the Sea

Sidney J. Holt*
International League for the Protection of Cetaceans, and Third Millennium Foundation, Umbria, Italy

Elisabeth Mann Borgese, to whose memory this special volume of the *Ocean Yearbook* is dedicated, would not, I think, have liked what has happened to the idea of the New International Order she and her close collaborator, Ambassador Arvid Pardo, so cherished. The current weakening of the United Nations system, on which "We the Peoples," individually and collectively, placed such high hopes after 1945—especially through the failures of powerful governments to enter into new binding agreements and uphold old ones, and to support existing and new international institutions, and the blatant buying of votes in decision-making bodies by a few of the most influential and richer states—does not bode well for our collective future. This is a time when those of us who worked with Elisabeth must reflect deeply on where the so-called "international community" is now going.

BACKGROUND

The late 1960s and early 1970s witnessed the beginnings of vast changes in the regimes governing the use and protection of the resources of Antarctica and the surrounding ocean. Ambassador Arvid Pardo, acting on behalf of the Government of Malta, put forward his proposals for the fundamental revision and extension of the Law of the Sea, and the Government of the United States began to press for a pause in all commercial whaling operations. For many, perhaps most, people concerned about what Elisabeth and Arvid referred to as "international ocean affairs" and human activities

*Editors' Note.—The author is grateful for the support in the preparation of this paper offered by the International Fund for Animal Welfare, Yarmouth Port, Ma, U.S.A. and Bristol, U.K. The author is also appreciative of help from the Third Millennium Foundation, Paciano (PG), Italy. The author has benefited from many conversations with colleagues throughout the world, but the views expressed here are the author's.

Ocean Yearbook 18: 364–382

in and around "ocean space," this conjunction of the vast scope of maritime governance and the regulation of a minor and now almost extinct extractive industry may seem to be a leap from the sublime to the more-or-less ridiculous. I shall later seek to correct that impression. But first let me make another conjunction—with the Antarctic. Since the International Geophysical Year in 1957, and the consequent conclusion of the Antarctic Treaty,[1] the Antarctic landmass, and to a limited degree the icy seas south of 60° S, have been the subject of a separate body of international law. Parties to the Treaty were originally the countries claiming possessions on the continent as well as the sub-Antarctic islands and/or those conducting scientific research there. The prime purposes of the Treaty were to reserve the continent to research, to exclude military activities and the exploitation of minerals, and to put territorial claims on indefinite hold. While the Treaty mechanism was applied to seal populations, it was from the beginning agreed to exclude consideration of the whales that feed in summer near the continent, with the intent that the existing International Whaling Commission (IWC)—established under the International Convention for the Regulation of Whaling 1946 (ICRW)[2]—would continue to have sole competence. Later however, as deep-sea fishing began to expand in the Southern Ocean, a new management convention was negotiated, under the sponsorship of the Antarctic Treaty Parties, the Convention on the Conservation of Antarctic Marine Living Resources (CCAMLR).[3] That Convention does not explicitly exclude the whales and other cetaceans, but by general agreement it does not for the time being deal with them.

At the time of the Maltese initiative it seemed to some of us that Antarctica, as well as the deep seabed, might be a ripe subject for application of the concept of the Common Heritage of Mankind, notwithstanding the reality that the Antarctic Treaty was de facto an exclusive club of the Consultative Parties. Wiser counsel prevailed, however, and subsequently the Treaty activities became in any case more open and involved many more States than the original signatories.

Although the Antarctic Treaty was designed to impede exploitation of, and even exploration for, mineral resources on the continent and on and under the surrounding seabed, moves began in the 1980s to open the continent to both these activities. However, in a sudden volte-face the Parties formulated the Protocol on Environmental Protection to the Antarctic

1. The Antarctic Treaty, signed 1 December 1959 in Washington, D.C., entered into force 23 June 1961, http://www.scar.org/Treaty/Treaty_Text.htm.

2. International Convention for the Regulation of Whaling, signed 2 December 1946 in Washington, D.C., entered into force 10 November 1948, http://www.iwcoffice.org/convention.htm.

3. Convention on the Conservation of Antarctic Marine Living Resources, signed 20 May 1980 in Canberra, http://www.ccamlr.org/.

Treaty that prohibits both activities for at least 50 years.[4] The Protocol came into force in 1998.

In the first decade of the 20th century imperial ambitions and personal pride energised efforts, particularly in Britain and Norway, to explore the continent, to traverse it, and especially to reach the South Pole. Hunters of seals and whales, however, had taken an interest in the Antarctic seas for many years before that and were dominant in the "discovery" of the coastlines both of the continent and of the sub-Antarctic islands, as they had earlier been of the Arctic regions. In this enterprise the British (and British Empire), and Norwegians were also dominant, though a few others maintained some interest—France, Argentina, and Chile, for example.

The Southern Ocean provides the summer feeding grounds of perhaps 80 percent or more of the world's whales, and the whaling industry there, beginning late in the 19th century, grew by the 1930s into an enormous industry. So-called "modern" whaling operations (using powered vessels and cannon firing harpoons with explosive grenades on their heads) depended on adequate supplies of fresh water; hence in the early years, when whales were towed to shore stations for flensing,[5] the island groups of, principally, South Georgia and South Shetlands provided the necessary facilities and local resources. This set geographic limits to these shore-based operations. But, partly to escape taxation by the islands' sovereigns, and partly to facilitate operations far from the few landing places, "floating factories" were built to which killed whales could be towed and processed. These were moored in sheltered locations and provided fresh water by desalination of seawater. Next these ships were provided with stern ramps up which whales could be hauled and the era of "pelagic whaling" using "expeditions" of factory ships and associated catcher boats had begun.[6]

4. Protocol on Environmental Protection to the Antarctic Treaty, signed 4 October 1991, entered into force 14 January 1998, http://www.antarctica.ac.uk/About Antarctica/Treaty/protocol.html.

5. Flensing is the technical term (from the Norwegian for 'flaying') for the process of stripping off blubber prior to the reduction of the whale by butchering and dismembering of the carcass. In rendering down the blubber for oil extraction and for processing of other valuable by-products, large quantities of fresh water are essential, just as they were for the steam engines that powered the early modern whalers.

6. For more of this history see the following: S. J. Holt, "Whales and Whaling," in *Seas at the Millennium: An Environmental Evaluation,* vol. 3 *Global Issues and Processes,* ed. C. R. C. Sheppard. (Amsterdam: Pergamon, 2000), Chapter 112, 73–88; S. J. Holt, "The Experience of Antarctic Whaling: Contribution to the International Fisheries Symposium on International Approaches to Management of Shared Stocks—problems and future directions," 2003, proceedings in press, available from CEFAS, Lowestoft, Suffolk, UK; S. J. Holt, "ICES Involvement in whaling and whale conservation, and implications of IWC actions," *ICES Marine Science Symposia* 215 (2002): 464–73.

Whale oil was the raw material from which was made most of the glycerine used in munitions by the Allied Powers in the First World War. After that war pelagic whaling expanded further, now to provide the basis for the production of a butter substitute—margarine—a German invention. Britain and Norway sought by every available means to maintain a virtual monopoly of production of the basic raw material—baleen whale oil. They competed with each other vigorously but at the same time conspired to prevent companies and ships from other countries from entering the industry. They also promoted international agreements between both companies and governments to limit oil production, which, while ostensibly aimed at resource conservation were intended primarily to maintain the market price. Whale oil again became a strategic commodity; at one point in the late 1930s the British Government threatened to destroy the industrial economy of Norway by withholding coal supplies unless Norway ceased selling whale oil to Nazi Germany.

In this period, the catches of whales in the Antarctic seas constituted nearly 20 percent by weight of the total (global) recorded production from marine living resources. This was, however, unsustainable. After World War II many countries considered going whaling in the Antarctic, particularly because of the world shortage of fats and oils for human consumption. The Netherlands was one of those—more than most other Europeans it was suffering severe shortage of fats. Germany was another but it was impeded at the time by the British role in the United Nations occupying forces. In Japan, however, the U.S. administration encouraged the resumption of whaling to meet protein and oil shortages; Japan had a tradition of human consumption of whale meat that had been almost entirely absent from Europe since the era of Basque whaling in the North Atlantic in the late Middle Ages.[7] Pre-war Germany had pioneered the construction of whaling ships with high-tech freezing and processing capacity, and the Japanese entrepreneurs efficiently exploited that technology.

Although the IWC was created in 1946 (its first annual meeting was in 1949) to conserve whales and manage whaling in the interests of future (human) generations—among other things—it did not try to limit catches to sustainable levels until 1960; up to then it set overall catch limits for Antarctic pelagic operations for the short-term benefit of the existing industry, and with virtually no scientific input. A new policy was launched that year in the light of the obvious continuing depletion of the resources at a time that whaling was still very profitable and so new entrants were tempted and

7. The Basques were the pioneers of commercial whaling. In the 11th century they searched for right whales across the North Atlantic (Probably discovering Newfoundland and perhaps the shores of New England in the process, as well as discovering—and keeping secret—the vast cod resources of the Newfoundland Banks). They salted and dried the meat and rendered blubber down to oil, which was traded all over Europe, as shown by the extant records of the Hansiatic League.

competition intensified, bringing on a deep crisis in the organisation. The move to bring catches down to levels that scientists would advise to be biologically sustainable was launched in 1959, primarily by the U.S. and U.K. Governments. While genuinely aimed at conservation, it had another important motive, particularly dear to the U.S. authorities. The United States had invested much effort in the post-war years in the creation of a network of regional, intergovernmental fisheries management organisations. At the time, "the domino effect" was a popular metaphor in international politics—if Korea or Vietnam 'fall' to communism, all the countries of south-east Asia will fall one by one. So, it was feared that if the IWC were to collapse—as seemed very likely—this would trigger catastrophic stresses in other fisheries management bodies of even greater economic importance.

Throughout the 1960s, the IWC strived for biological sustainability through its cumbersome regulations, but it failed.[8] Uncertainties in the scientific advice as to what catches would be sustainable were used to delay decisive action. And there could be no agreement on overall catches without agreement on how these would be shared among participating nations—Japan, the Netherlands, Norway, the U.K., and the USSR. (Sharing, between the British and the Norwegians, was also a critical issue in the 1930s negotiations among governments and companies.)[9] However, for sharing to be feasible a scheme involving internationally designated "observers" on all whaling ships had to be negotiated. Many years later, when the populations of Southern Hemisphere whales had been further depleted, it was revealed that at least one of the nations—USSR, with Japanese observers on its ships—had falsified catch statistics on a vast scale which, among other things, revealed why the supposedly "protected" blue, humpback and southern right whales had apparently failed to recover.[10] The coverup of the excess production of meat—including from species close to extinction—was effected by surreptitious transfer of commodities at sea from the factories to refrigerated transport vessels.

8. Part of the problem was that it refused, despite repeated recommendations by its scientists, to set catch limits by species. However, it subsequently turned out that the scientists' recommendations, which they thought at the time to be "conservative," in fact enormously overestimated the yield-capacity of baleen whales, in part due to incorrect determination of their ages.

9. See S. J. Holt, "Sharing the Catches of Whales in the Southern Hemisphere," in *Case Studies on the Allocation of Transferable Quota Rights in Fisheries,* FAO Fisheries Technical Paper 411, ed. R. Shotton (Rome: FAO, 2001), pp. 322–73.

10. See V. I. Danilov-Danilyan and A. V. Yablokov, "Foreword" in *Soviet Antarctic Whaling Data (1947–1972)* (Moscow: Centre for Russian Environmental Policy, 1996), p. 335 (for 1996 bilingual English and Russian edition of 1995 original in Russian only, pp. 4–6); Also: T. Kasuya and R. L. Brownell Jr., Illegal Japanese Coastal Whaling and other Manipulation of Catch Records. IWC Doc SC/53/RMP 24. Cambridge, UK: IWC, 2001, p. 8.

During the 1960s, Dr John Gulland and I were both engaged in this process, initiated by the IWC and supported by the Food and Agriculture Organization of the United Nations (FAO), by which it was hoped that commercial whaling in the Southern Ocean might be brought under effective control, at least with respect to the resources of blue, fin, and humpback whales. The firsthand experience that gave us of the unruly nature of the whaling industry led us to propose that those resources should be appropriated by the United Nations, which would take full responsibility for their exploitation and direct the profits to the infrastructure of management and relevant scientific research. Without describing it in those words we were effectively proposing that the whales should be designated as a Common Heritage of Mankind.[11] Nothing came of this, and the United Nations lost its opportunity for further intervention when the Stockholm Conference[12] merely invited the IWC to consider declaring a fixed-term, 10-year moratorium on commercial whaling.

The IWC did "consider" that idea in each of the following years for a decade, and rejected it! It was evident that some of the countries that had not opposed, or had even supported, the recommendation in Stockholm (while insisting that the IWC should remain responsible for such an action, rather than the United Nations itself) had fully intended to suppress any such action in a forum comprising, at the time, few countries, half of which were still engaged in whaling; any three-fourths majority there for a moratorium or other "strong" conservation measure, was out of the question. Not until 1982 did the IWC declare a moratorium of indefinite duration on all commercial whaling, to come into effect in 1985–1986.[13] It is of some inter-

11. J. A. Gulland, "The Management of Antarctic Whaling Resources," *J. Cons. Int. Explor. Mer.* 31 (3) (1968): 330–41.

12. As a staff member of FAO, I was assigned to the Secretariat of the Stockholm conference, while also serving as Professor of Ocean Affairs at the Royal University of Malta and as the first Director of the International Ocean Institute based there. The *Pacem in Maribus* convocation convened by the IOI in Malta, immediately after Stockholm, was the first of many subsequent assemblies of non-governmental organisations to welcome the Stockholm resolution on whaling.

13. See ICRW Schedule for decision, paragraph 10(e), "Notwithstanding the other provisions of paragraph 10, catch limits for the killing for commercial purposes of whales from all stocks for the 1986 coastal and the 1985/86 pelagic seasons and thereafter shall be zero. This provision will be kept under review, based upon the best scientific advice, and by 1990 at the latest the Commission will undertake a comprehensive assessment of the effects of this decision on whale stocks and consider modification of this provision and the establishment of other catch limits." Also see relevant footnotes, "The Governments of Japan, Norway, Peru and the Union of Soviet Socialist Republics lodged objection to paragraph 10(e) within the prescribed period. For all other Contracting Governments this paragraph came into force on 3 February 1983. Peru withdrew its objection on 22 July 1983. The Government of Japan withdrew its objections with effect from 1 May 1987 with respect to commercial pelagic whaling; from 1 October 1987 with respect to commercial coastal whaling for minke and Bryde's whales; and from 1 April 1988 with respect to commercial

est that another small country, the Republic of Seychelles—emulating the influence of Malta in the Law of the Sea enterprise—with a great interest in ocean affairs resulting from the agreements to extend national jurisdictions out to 200 M from coasts, succeeded in obtaining this Agreement, which is still in force. It quickly led to the cessation of all commercial whaling except by Japan and Norway.[14]

The 1982 decision was immediately preceded by a decision to halt all pelagic whaling operations except those that took the small minke whales, the exploitation of which in the Antarctic had only begun in 1971, and another to halt all catching of sperm whales by any means and for any purpose.[15] The idea that an industry utilizing renewable resources should be required to pause when it was out of control and endangering those resources, or otherwise misusing them, was at the time widely regarded as unacceptable. But since then, of course, we have seen a similar drastic approach taken with a number of overexploited and depleted fisheries.

The vote on the Seychelles' proposal was composed of three rather diverse trends in States' policies. One of these, initiated particularly by Australia, which had until recently been operating shore-based whaling stations, was that commercial whaling was no longer an acceptable activity; several reasons were given for this.[16] Another trend favoured a pause during which scientists would try to provide methods of computing catch limits that were both sustainable and precautionary. The third trend was recognition that much of the residual whaling activity would be economically unsustainable,

---

coastal sperm whaling. The objections of Norway and the Russian Federation not having been withdrawn, the paragraph is not binding upon these Governments," http://www.iwcoffice.org/Schedule.htm.

14. They have continued to the present by using loopholes in the ICRW: one, used by Norway, allows 'objections' to be lodged within a limited time of any otherwise binding decision being taken; the other, by Japan, exploits a provision that any nation may give its nationals, unilaterally, an unlimited number of special permits to kill whales as scientific specimens, and that such whales must be "processed" and the products disposed of, which the Japanese authorities interpret as "sold" to help fund further "research." (For further analysis of this, see a series of articles and letters in *BioScience* 52 (2002): 1137–40; also in *BioScience* 53 (2003): 210–12, 448–49 .

15. The sperm whale—"Moby Dick"—was caught only for its special oil, used industrially.

16. Reasons given then and since by various governments and persons for absolute opposition include, principally, that whaling is incurably inhumane, and that it cannot in practice be properly regulated and policed, especially that which is prosecuted on the high seas. This latter is based, in part, on several decades of experience of so-called "pirate whaling," by vessels operating under flags of non-member States of IWC. The IWC has sought to bring that under control—through denial of port facilities by its members, prohibition of transfers of material and skills, and by monitoring illegal trade in commodities from whales. International NGOs, particularly Greenpeace, have played a notable part in the latter; for example, packages of frozen whale meat have been found at transit points labelled as frozen shrimp or mackerel!

even if biologically sustainable catch limits were set—and in some situations even without that limitation. The IWC Members in that trend naturally favoured the 3-year "phase-out" offered in the Seychelles proposal. An additional incentive for them to pull out of the industry was that most of their whaling operations were either for the Japanese market or were actually joint ventures with Japan, the profits as well as the products from which were mostly exported.

Since 1982 the disposition of countries comprising the three trends has changed. Australia has been joined by several others in opposition to commercial whaling in principle.[17] Only Japan and Norway continue to engage in this industry, though Iceland has recently announced its intention to resume. Those in the third trend have, since the Commission accepted in principle (in 1991) the scientists' proposals for a Revised Management Procedure (RMP) for setting catch limits for baleen whales, concentrated on maintaining the 1982 "moratorium" decision until measures to ensure compliance with regulations have been agreed. These measures would include an international observer scheme more effective than that adopted in the 1960s, other monitoring procedures and, especially, the maintenance of a database of DNA samples from all legally killed whales. Negotiation of these measures is highly controversial and that is one of the reasons why the IWC has for several years made no progress in either, on the one hand, ending commercial whaling or, on the other, of permitting the resumption of regulated commercial whaling.[18]

MANAGEMENT, CONSERVATION AND PROTECTION

During the decade 1972–1982, when a general moratorium was debated annually in the IWC, a sort of compromise between contending factions emerged. Called by its proponent, the Government of Australia, "an amended moratorium," it provided for the setting of annual catch limits on each species population judged to be in numbers still over about half the initial number—that is before commercial whaling began—and the protection of all those populations judged to be below half that number. Called the New Management Procedure (NMP), this essentially introduced three

17. To the reasons for this stance, noted previously, must now be added the growing and spreading recognition that cetaceans—or at least some of them—were "special" animals, based on recent scientific discoveries about their behaviour, social structure, communication systems, and brains.

18. The problem of enforcement has not been addressed. At present, Members merely report to an Infractions Committee their own misdemeanours, and no action is taken, other than for a government occasionally to fine one of its nationals. There are no other penalties for transgressions, and independent evidence of them, particularly from "private" sources—which is the usual provenance—is not recognised.

new ideas. First, that a "stock" would be "protected" from exploitation long before it had been depleted to the level at which it was seriously threatened with extermination. This contrasted with the previous declaration of Protected Species only when the species in a particular region was thought to have been reduced close to extinction, notwithstanding the fact that there was no scientific basis for determining any such level.

Second, catch limits for stocks above the roughly 50 percent threshold would be set at sustainable levels, with the presumption that holding them at roughly 60 percent of their original number (or letting them recover towards such a number) would maximize the sustainable annual catch (MSY). Meanwhile, the concept that good management of fisheries resources entailed holding stocks at MSY levels was being sanctified in the negotiations for a new law of the sea set in train by Ambassador Pardo's speech. Unfortunately, because the Third United Nations Conference on the Law of the Sea was paying far more attention to the problems of the seabed, the creation of new maritime zones, and the governance of scientific research than to the problems of managing fisheries, it passed unnoticed that the scientific community had for some years been challenging the idea of MSY as a desirable aim of management, and even the possibility of measuring such a quantity and determining its location on the scale of animal abundance. The IWC's selection of the 60 percent level was pure guesswork dressed as "science." Furthermore, it opened the way to the argument that any population that had not yet been heavily exploited should be reduced to the MSY level, and as soon as possible, that is, that it should for the time being be exploited *unsustainably*. In fact, the Japanese delegation told the IWC during the contentious later years of the decade that it was immoral and wasteful to impede any such reduction.[19] This was particularly important because, since the history of Antarctic whaling was the depletion of one species after another, in descending order of body size, the industry's eyes were always flicking to the smaller, more numerous species that had not yet been depleted, rather than the larger and later protected ones—in the 1960s this was the sei whale, in the 1970s the minke whale. *Unsustainable* whaling was the name of the game, and it still is, as we shall see.

The third innovation was the introduction of the so-called *safety factor*, a mild precursor of the *precautionary principle*, or *approach*, which became the fashion after 1992, following the United Nations Conference on Environment and Development in Rio de Janeiro. This took the form of setting catch limits a certain percentage lower than the estimated (actually, guessed) MSY;

19. This foreshadowed debates in the proceedings of the World Conservation Union (IUCN) as to whether the accepted aim of "sustainable use of wild living resources" should be interpreted as "If a resource is used such use must be sustainable" or as "resources must be used, but sustainably." There is a world of difference in the imperative.

the percentage safety margin adopted by the IWC was a derisory 10 percent and even that was bitterly contested by the major whaling countries who argued that this would lead to whales increasing to such high numbers that the resources would be wasted!

By 1979—only 3 years after it had been put into action—the NMP was in tatters. Firstly, the commercially favoured species that were still relatively numerous (the minke whale, and the Bryde's whale of temperate and subtropical waters) were the very ones for which there were insufficient data even to make "informed guesses" as to their MSY levels. And, secondly, advances in the procedures of computer simulation had led to the demonstration that even if all the parameters of a simple population model on which the NMP was based were well estimated, and if the mathematical model then in favour was realistic, following the NMP would still allow—or even encourage—the depletion of the stocks.[20] It is therefore not surprising that there was an upsurge in the pressure for the IWC to declare a general moratorium, which it did in 1982.

Supporters of, and voters for, the moratorium included those who believed the Scientific Committee of the IWC should be given another chance to produce a "safe" method of calculating catch limits. It did labour at this task through the later 1980s and the early 1990s, giving birth to a Revised Management Procedure (RMP) of an entirely different nature from the NMP—despite the name it was not a "revision" of that. Its gestation was an interesting process in itself, especially in that it relied on computer simulations of kinds never before employed in fisheries management studies, and also was a result of intense competition between five groups of scientists each working separately but in accordance with rules set by the Commission and the Scientific Committee. This process has been described in numerous publications, including by the "winner" of the competition, Dr Justin Cooke.[21]

From our point of view, the important features of the RMP are as follows. First, its objectives were precisely defined by the Commission itself. They were three: to have a very small chance that any stock would be inadvertently reduced to arbitrarily defined low levels; to lead to as large a cumulative catch over a long period as was compatible with the first objective; and to limit changes in permitted catches from year-to-year—except for any necessary correction for major errors—for the sake of stabilizing the industry.

Thus, the idea of absolute sustainability, and with it that of aiming at MSY, was abandoned and replaced by a pragmatic goal of high cumulative

20. W. K. de la Mare, "Simulation studies on management procedure," *Reports of the International Whaling Commission* 36 (1986): 429–50.

21. J. G. Cooke, "The International Whaling Commission's Revised Management Procedure as an Example of a New Approach to Fisheries Management," in *Whales, Seals, Fish and Man,* ed. A. S. Blix, L. Walløe and O. Ulltang (Amsterdam: Elsevier, 1995).

catches over a computable period, which was 100 years (as determined by available computing power). The threshold probabilities of inadvertent depletion were set very low, thus embodying one element of the precautionary principle, while all catch limits were set at a default zero unless there was positive scientific evidence to justify doing otherwise, thus effectively reversing the burden of proof and embodying another element of the precautionary approach to management. The parameters of the RMP algorithm were set so that there would be a high probability that whale populations would rise over the management period to numbers not very much less than their preexploitation number, and certainly far higher than the NMP had sought.

The second important feature, technically, was that limited data are required, and these come from specially designed and conducted sighting surveys to count the whales independently of any whaling operations,[22] and that the algorithm used to calculate catch limits did not depend on a particular mathematical population model.

In the years of inventing the RMP, two other changes were happening. One was the quite spectacular worldwide growth of whale-watching industries as an element of ecotourism. This introduced another economic "use" of whales as resources as an alternative to whaling. Now, this benign industry is active in more places than were ever centres of whaling. The question of whether and on what terms the two can coexist has not yet been resolved, but it is already clear that without operational guidelines, or even regulation, whale watching could be damaging to the welfare of whales. The IWC has accepted responsibility—despite a very reluctant Japan—for acting as a focus for relevant scientific studies and also in helping the development of guidelines. But in doing so it has rejected any idea of engaging itself in regulation of whale watching, especially—but not only—because almost all whale-watching takes place in national exclusive economic zones (EEZs), except, of course, in the Antarctic and the Mediterranean.

The other change is the increasing interest in establishing large sea areas in which whaling is prohibited in the long term. Such areas are provided for in the ICRW, being called "sanctuaries." This term is a hangover from the early 1930s when it was thought that some of the Antarctic whales would be able to move into them for protection from intrusive and excessive whaling activities elsewhere. From 1946 to 1955, a wide swathe of the South Pacific sector, south of 40° S was so designated in relation to pelagic whaling operations (there was in any case no whaling from land stations in that sec-

22. Previously, assessments of whale stocks had depended largely on measures of the efficiency of whaling operations—"catch per unit (whaling) effort," cpue. This index of animal abundance was practically universal in fisheries assessments, but this too has recently been replaced or supplemented by direct counts of fishes, usually by techniques utilising sonar.

tor) for baleen—"whalebone"—whales. Pelagic whaling was—and still is—also prohibited in the Southern Hemisphere north of that latitude.

In 1979, a proposal by Seychelles was adopted, designating the entire Indian Ocean as a sanctuary (for all species and with respect to all types of commercial whaling), although as a compromise to secure the necessary three-fourths majority of votes, the zone south of 55° S, where minke whales were being exploited by Japan and the USSR, was excluded. In the following years various other proposals were made regarding the Mediterranean, the Northeast Atlantic, and the Northwest Atlantic, but none were acted upon. However, in 1994, a proposal by France to designate the entire Southern Ocean south of 40° S (with some small derogations near The Falklands/Malvinas and in the far southeast of the Pacific) was adopted. This effectively closed the possibility that in the future a non-zero catch limit for minke whales might be considered. This decision was formally objected to by Japan, but only insofar as it applied to minke whales.

In recent years proposals have been put forward for the designation of the South Pacific north of 40° S (launched by Australia and New Zealand) and similarly in the southwestern Atlantic (launched by Brazil), but neither has yet secured the necessary three-fourths majority of member States participating in a meeting. It is clear, however, that designation de facto of the entire Southern Hemisphere as a sanctuary is the wish of the coastal States of the hemisphere, none of whom are now engaged in whaling nor showing any inclination to do so in the future. Many of those have also declared their EEZs as closed to whaling, especially in the Indian Ocean, the South Pacific, and along the coasts of Latin America. Protection of the entire Southern Hemisphere makes biological sense because the whale populations there are biologically quite separate from those in the North Atlantic and those in the North Pacific, even though they are largely comprised of the same species. Before intensive commercial whaling began, perhaps 80 percent of the world's whales were living in the Southern Hemisphere, and if they were all allowed to recover that situation would probably be replicated.

The possible designation of sea areas as Marine Protected Areas (MPAs) is now commonplace in fisheries management discussions, as well as considerations of the protection/preservation of biological diversity. Authority to designate such areas on the high seas is unfortunately lacking from the 1982 United Nations Convention on the Law of the Sea (UNCLOS),[23] and in fact the IWC is the only body having such authority; the ICRW applies, explicitly to "all waters" in which whaling is prosecuted and by uncontested extension, in which whales live. However, although whaling, especially unregulated whaling, as at present, remains the greatest threat to the welfare of whale populations, other problems now come from impacts with surface vessels,

23. Official Records to the Third United Nations Conference on the Law of the Sea. Vol XVII, UN Document A/CONF.62/122. New York: United Nations, 1984.

pollution (including noise pollution), and contaminants (which accumulate especially in the fat and can be health hazards to the humans who eat them as well as to the whales), and in certain cases destruction of critical habitat. These cannot be addressed through sanctuaries as defined, and in fact even if definitions were changed, by amendment of the ICRW, it is obvious even a modified IWC could not itself resolve them.

The case of a cetacean sanctuary established jointly by France, Italy, and Monaco in the Ligurian Sea (northwestern Mediterranean) is an interesting one because the Mediterranean remains, like the Southern Ocean, almost all high seas. This sanctuary was created not to stop whaling—there is none—but to provide an instrument for forms of protection of the surprisingly numerous large whales—especially fin and sperm whales—that frequent the area. It is a location where whale watching can be profitable but where whales can be adversely affected by other human activities. Legal advisers to the Italian Government, particularly, have argued that the trilateral declaration accords some rights to the coastal signatories over the adjacent high seas beyond their jurisdiction, as well as over vessels flying their flags and the nearby ports.[24] In addition, the coastal states of the Mediterranean as a whole (which include Morocco and Spain, that are also IWC Members) have declared, through the UNEP-sponsored Barcelona Convention,[25] their wish that the IWC declare the Sea as a sanctuary.

WHERE NEXT?

Soon after the adoption of the three moratoria in 1980–1982 the Government of Japan began to recruit countries to vote with it against the moves by groups of other Members towards more rigorous conservation of whales by the IWC. In reinforcement of the IWC decisions, the Parties to the Convention on International Trade in Endangered Species (CITES)[26] prohibited trade in commodities from the species covered by the IWC moratorium; Japan and Norway have also regularly sought to overturn those prohibitions, so far without success. This has led to intense procedural debates as to

24. T. Scovazzi, "The Mediterranean Sanctuary for Marine Mammals," in *Report of the Closing Workshop to Review Various Aspects of Whale Watching,* Tuscany, Italy, 6–10 February 2000, (London, UK: IFAW, 2001), pp. 79–84. (Also issued as *IWC Doc.*-IWC/53/22).

25. Convention for the Protection of the Marine Environment and the Coastal Region of the Mediterranean (Barcelona Convention), adopted 16 February 1976, entered into force 12 February 1978, amended 10 June 1995 (not yet in force), http://www.unepmap.org.

26. Convention on International Trade in Endangered Species of Wild Fauna and Flora, signed 3 March 1973 in Washington D.C., entered into force 1 July 1975, http://www.cites.org/eng/disc/text.shtml.

whether actions under one international convention can or should be influenced by related actions taken under another; to date, consistency has been maintained between CITES and IWC, with the IWC effectively taking the leading role.

Japan's recruits were at first a number of Caribbean Island states that were already Members of IWC and were persuaded to change their policies in response to large "aid" packages related to fisheries development, port and processing construction, training, and the like.[27] In recent years this policy has extended to encouragement for countries never before interested in whales or whaling to join IWC and vote with Japan in return for substantial fisheries aid. (Although Seychelles, a leader among the developing countries, never accepted such inducements, it did under intense and persistent pressure eventually withdraw from the IWC). The aim was to create a situation in which the "old" non-whaling nations could never command a three-fourths majority to take binding decisions. The process continues with Japan's apparent aim being eventually to secure a three-quarter majority itself and thereby be able to overturn the moratorium and also abolish the sanctuaries, especially the crucial Southern Ocean sanctuary.

In the 1990s, the delegation of Ireland to the IWC launched an initiative to bring about a resolution of the present impasse through a negotiated compromise. The proposal was to declare all high seas as a "global sanctuary" while maintaining all existing sanctuaries; to permit some coastal whaling for baleen species within EEZs, regulated by strict application of the RMP bolstered by an observer scheme and other provisions to ensure compliance, under the RMS umbrella; and to prohibit international trade. This initiative failed as it came too late. The two whaling countries clearly saw no advantage for themselves except perhaps to escape from the opprobrium of being labeled as against environmental protection and that was insufficient reason to negotiate. Several of the non-whaling countries, on the other hand, saw the Irish proposal as a betrayal of their overall aim of bringing commercial whaling to an end. Some of those seemed also to be worried about the legalistic implications of measures to deny use of high seas resources to all states, especially as any such decision by the IWC should, according to the ICRW, have some *scientific* justification. As expectations of some resolution of the problems lapsed (there were in play, informally, a number of alternative versions of the Irish idea), Japan stepped up two notches its "scientific samplings" of whales: first by conducting them, for minkes, in the North Pacific as well as in the Antarctic (this allowed year-round deployment of the whal-

27. See *Briefing on Japan's "Vote-buying" Strategy in the International Whaling Commission* (Paciano, Italy: Third Millennium Foundation, 2002), pp. 17 + tables. Also, referred to in a broader context, S. Aga Khan, "Beyond the Limits of Sustainable Growth: Earth on the Market," in *Le Monde Diplomatique,* English language edition, (December 2002), p. 8.

ing fleet, and thus had economic advantages), and then expanding the North Pacific operation to include sperm, sei, and Bryde's whales. This expansion has been accompanied by a strategic shift towards justification of the claim that whales eat so much fish and other marine resources of interest to humans that they are a contributory cause of the decline of fish stocks that FAO, ICES and other authorities have generally attributed to overfishing plus the effects of pollution and habitat deterioration.

In the Japanese view, examination of this "whales-eat-fish" hypothesis is now a high priority and calls for the killing of large numbers of whales to examine their diets notwithstanding the fact that the stomachs of many thousands of whales were so examined in the days of large-scale commercial whaling, worldwide.[28] This would be a precursor to large-scale "culling" to prevent the recovery of whale populations or even to reduce them sharply. In terms of policy, this signifies a shift away from carefully regulated biologically sustainable operations to deliberate unsustainable depletion, under the guise of "multi-species management" or "ecosystem management." There is now a vast scientific literature on this matter but suffice to say here that while there have been interesting attempts to develop mathematical models pertaining to several species interacting through competition and/or predation, none of these is yet at a stage to be used with confidence for practical management.[29]

These considerations lead to questions about whether commercial whaling could ever be both biologically and economically sustainable. It never has been up to now. Profits—enormous profits—have come from depletion, not sustainable use.[30] The current Japanese "scientific" minke

28. This matter is discussed most recently in a series of papers and articles in the March 2003 issue of *BioScience,* including by S. J. Holt and P. Clapham et al. See also S. Altherr, "Running out of Fish . . . Who is Responsible for the Plundering of the Oceans?," (joint publication of Third Millennium Foundation, Italy, the East Caribbean Coalition for Environmental Awareness, Martinique and Pro Wildlife, Germany, 2002), p. 16.

29. In my opinion, they may never be useful except as rough guides to the kinds of things that might happen; marine ecosystems are far too complex to be dealt with in this way, and almost nothing is yet known about the mutual behaviour of predators and prey—for example, what are the dynamics of changes in diet? An early effort to do such modelling, for the Southern Ocean, including the whales, which is more of historical than of practical interest, is: R. M. May, et al., "Management of multispecies fisheries," *Science* 205 (1979): 267–77. This study did play a role however, in securing the provision in both UNCLOS and CCAMLR of the (so far neglected) requirement that fisheries management should be such as to ensure that the biological productivity of "dependent" species (i.e., predators such as whales) is not adversely affected by depletions of the smaller prey.

30. They built the city of Sandefjord, the pelagic whaling base in southern Norway, and provided the capital for Christian Salveson's, the world's biggest whaling company, based in Leith, Scotland, to become a major road transportation operator in Europe. I suppose that might be classed as "sustainable development," if not as "sustainable use."

catches in the Antarctic probably are biologically sustainable; they do not exceed in total number the catch limits that might be set under the RMP if it were applied in the sanctuary, though there are questions about whether they are satisfactorily distributed among the numerous distinct, but geographically overlapping populations thought to inhabit the Southern Hemisphere. However, these whaling operations are subsidized, and the wholesale prices of the commodities from them are set by the Institute for Cetacean Research in Tokyo that is closely associated with government and which conducts research and operates the ships, employs the crews, and markets the products. And, of course, to be economically sustainable the profits must be sufficient to accumulate capital to renew vessels and equipment as well as cover operating costs. It is possible that fully recovered stocks of blue, fin, humpback, and right whales in the Southern Hemisphere could one day support a properly managed pelagic industry, but recovery is expected to take at best decades or perhaps centuries. Thus the argument used by Japanese government spokesmen, in recent UN/FAO debates about "food security," that such security requires the immediate "use" of whales for meat, is spurious. If anything it will be for future human generations to decide this, not the present nor even the next generation, and our responsibility is therefore to ensure as best we can the protection and recovery of the whale resources.

Towards the end of 2002 the IWC Commissioner for Mexico began consultations for an initiative that was discussed at the June 2003 annual meeting of the IWC in Berlin. This is seen as an effort to bring the Commission to face the many new factors that have come into play since the ICRW was negotiated. Some of these have been mentioned earlier. The Mexican initiative has been launched, it should be noted, in the context of increasingly strident assertions by those with vested interests in whaling that the IWC is "dysfunctional."[31] Such assertions are wrong, even if superficially plausible. The IWC still holds the keys to many decisions that have ensured, and continue to ensure, if they are nurtured, that the whales will not again be driven towards extinction, for short-term profit.

The most important new factor is, naturally, the completion and coming into force of the UNCLOS. This can affect the regime for whaling and whale conservation in several ways. One has been mentioned earlier: the

31. A view of Japanese whaling interests on this is given by K. Yonezawa in *A New Focus for the International Whaling Commission,* one of a number of articles in a booklet published in March 2001 by the Institute for Cetacean Research, Tokyo, prefaced by its Director-General, S. Ohsumi. This booklet is the annual report of the Japanese Government's Overseas Fisheries Operations Public Information Task. Yonezawa, an ex-official of the Japan Fisheries Agency, is at present president of the Global Guardian Trust, a Japanese NGO that he founded. This booklet also contains an article by J. Morishita and D. Goodman entitled *Competition between Fisheries and Marine Mammals—Feeding Marine Mammals at the Expense of Food for Humans.*

requirement for fishing to be managed to protect dependent species. Another concerns the definition of "highly migratory species" (HMSs) and the special regulatory regime applicable to them. All marine cetaceans, except the coastal true dolphins (*Phocaenidae*), are listed as HMSs, thus including the true dolphins (some of which are popularly called "porpoises" in the United States), beaked whales, pilot whales, bottlenose whales, the narwhal, the beluga (white whale), and all the so-called "great whales." Management of their use and their conservation are to be provided for throughout their migratory ranges through multilateral organizations, including primarily the IWC. This could offer a solution to a problem that has plagued the IWC since the 1970s: the absence of a definition of "a whale" in the ICRW. Many—probably most—IWC Members assert its competence with respect to all marine cetaceans, while others accept competence only for species the various names of which are given in a Nomenclatural Annex to the Final Act of the 1946 negotiating conference. This latter—and logically absurd—view leads to curious anomalies. For example, there are four species of bottlenose whale, only one of which, native to the North Atlantic, is listed in the Annex; the species exploited by Japanese coastal whalers, Baird's beaked whale, is not there. But that is because Norway was at the 1946 conference and Japan, being under U.S. Military occupation was not! In practice, the IWC has not been entirely consistent in its regulatory decisions either. None of the dolphins, nor the killer whale (*Orca*) which is either a dolphin or a close relative, are listed in the Annex, but the catching of *Orca* is regulated by the IWC while the other dolphins are not. Acceptance that all the highly migratory species fall within the IWC's competence could be a defensible compromise.[32]

The UNCLOS also provides that more strict conservation measures, including full protection, can be taken for marine mammals than for other marine resource species. Thus UNCLOS provides the solution to a long-standing controversy about whether the IWC can legitimately offer long-term protection to some species and populations.

32. The debates about species' competence have been utterly confused by repeated reference to "small cetaceans" as not coming within IWC's competence (though it has been accepted that the Scientific Committee may examine and pronounce upon data and studies of all cetaceans, even including the freshwater species). Until 1970, the minke whale was consistently described as a "small cetacean;" now the IWC's competence to regulate the catching of it is unquestioned, though for a time the Government of Norway, which promotes minke whaling in the North Atlantic, argued that it had never considered the minke to be a "real" whale. Now, the Baird's beaked whale, which is larger than the minke, is regarded as a "small cetacean" outside the IWC's competence. This is especially disturbing as the Japanese coastal whaling boats catch Baird's beaked whales and minkes in the same operation, and, when the minke was protected, the Government simply authorised a comparable increase in beaked whale catches. Pilot whales are also the targets in several regions of unregulated commercial whaling.

A somewhat controversial question is whether the IWC's provision that its authority extends to "all waters" is compatible with UNCLOS, which provides for different regimes in EEZs and on the high seas. However, because the UNCLOS regime for HMSs extends seamlessly across boundaries of EEZs with the adjacent high seas, and if it were accepted that IWC's jurisdiction is limited to HMSs, then there would seem to be no legal conflict.

What is lacking from UNCLOS is any power to establish MPAs in the high seas, or indeed straddling them and national EEZs. As the United Nations embarks now on a process of first revision of UNCLOS it is to be hoped that this omission will be rectified.[33]

Another issue that might be taken up in the Mexican initiative is the IWC's relations with other intergovernmental bodies having mandates that have a bearing on the conservation and protection of whales. IMO, with its concern for surface shipping and marine pollution is an obvious example, as is FAO, with its deep involvement in fisheries management. Recognition of such other bodies and provisions for working with them are almost completely lacking from the ICRW, which envisages only exchanges of letters between secretariats. The Commission cannot even address non-Member governments directly and with authority. The ICRW originally envisaged the bringing of the IWC into the United Nations system, specifically by coming under the umbrella of FAO, but that option was rejected at the first meeting of the IWC in 1949. Strengthening of the increasingly needed cooperative and consultative relationships with other bodies could be brought about by agreement on a Protocol that effectively amends the main text of the ICRW. A protocol was adopted many years ago to make some changes in definitions and to provide for an International Observer scheme. But such changes at that time were considered to need ratification by all parties before they could come into force for anyone.[34] It may be possible now, having regard to the Vienna Convention on Treaties,[35] to find an easier route to change.

For several years concern has been expressed about the effects of changes in the ocean climate (closely connected with change in the atmospheric climate, of course) on whale populations. This alone makes coopera-

33. In 1999, the UN General Assembly accepted the need to broaden the focus of its annual review to coordinate better international action and widen debate on ocean issues. This led to a resolution in January 2000 to establish an "Open-ended Informal Consultative Process on Oceans and the Law of the Sea" (UNICPOLOS). Further information, including reports from previous meetings (four, annually to date) and press releases, can be found at http://www.un.org/Depts/los/consultative_process/consultative_process.htm.

34. In the 1970s, three diplomatic conferences were held in an effort to revise or replace the ICRW, but all failed.

35. Vienna Convention on the Law of Treaties, signed at Vienna 23 May 1969, entered into force 27 January 1980, http://www.un.org/law/ilc/texts/treaties.htm.

tion and consultation with the various bodies in the UN system concerned with this matter a necessity. For example, although the Scientific Committee has assured the Commission that the RMP is "robust" to quite large environmental changes, some doubts remain as to whether this is adequate. In particular, there is concern about what is happening to the southern polar ice edge. In fact, historical whaling records have shown that the ice edge in summer has been retreating for most of the 20th century, and this has been confirmed in recent years by satellite remote sensing.[36] It now appears that algae are trapped each year in the newly formed ice with the onset of winter, and released again as the following spring arrives. This "shower" of algae provides food for the krill (Euphausids) on which the baleen whales that tend to feed close to the ice—blue, fin, humpback, and minke—largely depend.[37] Thus it may reasonably be conjectured that the retreat of the ice edge could affect drastically, and negatively, the biological productivity of the whales. We can be sure that this and related oceanographic phenomena will be debated when, in mid-2004, the Southern Ocean sanctuary decision is to be reviewed at the IWC's annual meeting in Sorrento, Italy. Although the Scientific Committee may acquire whatever technical competence is needed (because the member States designate most of its members) it may be that cooperation could with benefit be arranged with the Scientific Committee of CCAMLR, with UNESCO's Intergovernmental Oceanographic Commission (IOC), and also with the nongovernmental advisory mechanisms under the International Council of Scientific Unions (ICSU): SCOR, the Scientific Committee on Oceanic Research, and SCAR, the Scientific Committee on Antarctic Research, which is also advisory to the Antarctic Treaty.

In conclusion, if the Mexican initiative is successful we should see in the coming years more involvement and interaction of the IWC with the diverse instruments of international ocean governance, especially as they relate to the Southern Hemisphere, removing it from the relative isolation in which it has functioned for over half a century.

36. W. K. De la Mare, "Abrupt mid-twentieth-century decline in Antarctic sea-ice extent from whaling records," *Nature* 389 (1999): 5–60.

37. A. S. Brierley, et al., "Antarctic krill under sea ice: Elevated abundance in the narrow band just south of the ice edge," *Science* 295 (2002): 1890–2.

The Law Governing High Seas Fisheries: In Search of New Principles

Francisco Orrego Vicuña
University of Chile Law School and Institute of International Studies, Santiago, Chile

INTRODUCTION

The exploitation of ocean resources has long been the subject of an increasing conflict of interest. Competing users in closely related geographical areas were at first the basic element of this conflict. Long-distance fishing versus the interests of coastal States later became an added element of this equation. While geographical aspects were of course present in this later context, the dispute had turned mostly to a question of competing economic interests and power.

Various forms of accommodation took place among users or States in order to cope with a problem that had turned into a situation menacing the orderly conduct of international relations. Bilateral treaties, followed by major international conventions, gave rise to a number of arrangements in the field. Decisions by international tribunals helped to clarify the legal and practical implications of some disputes. These developments, however, did not suffice to put an end to the progression of conflict. Exploitation versus conservation became more recently a new kind of conflict characterizing the international community in connection with ocean resources. Again, some treaty and practical developments have purported to accommodate this other kind of conflict. Principles have been laid down, but strong differences of opinions as to their meaning and implementation persist.

The question this contribution seeks to address is, what is the basic principle governing the fisheries activities on the high seas today? Historical patterns are clear, as is the evidence of past accommodation. However, there is no certainty or clarity about the state of the law at this stage. Will the approach to a long-term solution be an all-powerful and encompassing central regulatory scheme as some believe and propose, or should it be an entirely decentralized mechanism giving place to market mechanisms where the basic role will be performed by the individual interest?

Ocean Yearbook 18: 383–394

AN ISSUE LACKING CLEAR RESPONSE

What is the legal principle governing high seas fisheries today? This rather simple question does not seem to find an adequate response on the part of governments, nor in respect of the procedures for the settlement of disputes that have been undertaken in this matter at various points in time.

In each of the central periods marking the evolution of the law of the sea, there has been one basic principle serving as the reference point for fishing activities, a principle that many times finds expression in or arises from the decisions of international tribunals intervening in disputes of this kind, as happens only too frequently. At the time of unrestricted freedom of fishing on the high seas, the governing principle was the prohibition for States to interfere with such activities. But as Georges Scelle explained in the illuminating memorandum prepared by the Secretariat of the United Nations in anticipation of the codification of the law of the sea undertaken in 1950, this negative principle resulted in "les désordres, les destructions, les gaspillages."[1]

The reasonable exploitation of living resources was the first organized response by the community of States to put an end to a situation that was evidently leading toward unacceptable consequences. However, the 1958 Convention on Fishing and Conservation of the Living Resources of the High Seas[2] that embodied that principle finally failed as a regulatory mechanism.[3]

COOPERATION IN RATIONAL EXPLOITATION: A ROLE FOR THE COASTAL STATE

A second approach was then devised by coastal States. This was the time of the large national maritime claims that in the long-term led to the adoption of the Exclusive Economic Zone (EEZ). Unnecessarily, this approach pursued only the interest of the coastal State, as it was also the means for introducing a regulatory authority on the high seas capable of bringing into effect the conservation measures that otherwise were ignored by States.[4] It is on this basis that the EEZ purported to take into account both the interests of the coastal State and those of long-distance fishermen.

1. United Nations, "Memorandum on the Regime of the High Seas, prepared by the Secretariat," Doc. A/CN.4/32 (14 July 1950) in *Yearbook of the International Law Commission, II* (New York: United Nations, 1950), p. 69, par. 11.

2. Done at Geneva, 29 April 1958, 17 UST 138, TIAS No. 5969, 559 UNTS 285.

3. P. W. Birnie and A. E. Boyle, *International Law and the Environment* (Oxford: Oxford University Press, 1992), p. 425.

4. W. T. Burke, *The New International Law of Fisheries: UNCLOS 1982 and Beyond* (Oxford: Oxford University Press, 1994), p. 95.

These conceptual developments had a decisive influence on the most important arbitral and judicial decisions of the time. First, the Bering Sea Fur Seals Arbitration, while reaffirming the freedom of fishing on the high seas, required the adoption of specific conservation measures to be regulated by the States concerned.[5] Next, the fisheries jurisdiction cases, while also recognizing the rights of States on the high seas, introduced the requirement of a reasonable exploitation of resources with a view to their conservation and also accepted the preferential participation of coastal States in the allocation of catches.[6]

This conceptual evolution must be supplemented today with those elements inspired by the concern for environmental protection. Conservation also relates to the large ocean areas constituting marine ecosystems. It is not a question of enlarging coastal State claims beyond the 200 nautical mile (M) areas, but rather of who should have the authority to ensure conservation and avoid the problems arising from the competitive participation of numerous States or interests in the exploitation of fisheries. Does this function pertain to the coastal State in the vicinity of such exploitation or to the international community duly organized to this effect?

GRADUAL REGULATORY ARRANGEMENTS

Whatever might be the response to the question posed, the inevitable conclusion is that the high seas areas are not excluded from the efforts today directed toward the conservation of resources. In fact, albeit timidly, the United Nations Convention on the Law of the Sea (LOS Convention)[7] made an important contribution to the conservation of living resources on the high seas, in addition to the detailed regulation of those activities conducted in the EEZ.

The introduction of regulations adapted to the realities of different species, the relationship between stocks straddling the EEZ and the high seas, and the principles concerning the protection of the marine environment, are all conceptual innovations that allow approaching the issue of fishing on the high seas in a more orderly manner. The concepts of total allowable catch and optimal utilization of resources on a scientific basis are also elements of interest in this matter.[8]

5. Moore, *International Arbitration Awards,* vol. 1, *Bering Sea Fur Seals Arbitration* (1893), p. 755.

6. See the discussion of this decision by Birnie and Boyle (n. 3 above), p. 118.

7. United Nations Convention on the Law of the Sea, adopted 10 December 1982, entered into force 14 November 1994.

8. W. T. Burke, "Importance of the 1982 UN Convention on the Law of the Sea and its Future Developments," in *Ocean Development and International Law* 27 (Philadelphia: Taylor and Francis, 1996), p. 1.

The rules applicable to straddling fish stocks and highly migratory species are those where the new relationship between the interests of coastal States and those of long-distance fishermen can best be noted. The emphasis of the LOS Convention on cooperation and the negotiation of rules on conservation between interested States is indicative of the fact that this is no longer a question exclusively related to the high seas, but one that requires taking into account the broader interests present in a given geographical region, including the interests of coastal States.[9]

Even though the LOS Convention is rather elementary on this matter and that a number of rules require further interpretation and refinement, the international community has not failed in its duty to introduce some perfecting of the initial design. The view that fishing on the high seas is governed by unrestricted freedom, as was argued at the beginning of the noted conceptual evolution, was quickly put to rest. The view calling for a more active role of coastal States on the high seas did not find significant support, despite conceptual and conventional efforts to that end.

The decade following the signature of the LOS Convention witnessed efforts aimed at an intermediary solution in which neither unrestricted freedom of fishing nor the sovereign or jurisdictional intervention of the coastal State would have a central role.[10] This was an effort built on three pillars: the introduction of responsible fishing, sustainable development with a view to introduce an environmental reference point, and the control of activities by means of regional management arrangements. The organizations in charge of fisheries matters would soon begin their adaptation to these new more stringent requirements.

Some of these aspects, however, could not be introduced by means of an interpretation of the 1982 Convention. This would be the main task of the 1995 United Nations Fish Stocks Agreement,[11] which in spite of its title indicating the aim of interpreting the Convention, it in fact goes much further.[12]

9. E. Hey, *The Regime for the Exploitation of Transboundary Marine Fisheries Resources: The United Nations Law of the Sea Convention Cooperation between States* (Dordrecht: M. Nijhoff, 1989), Chapter 5.

10. United Nations, *The Law of the Sea. The Regime for High Seas Fisheries* (New York: Division for Ocean Affairs and the Law of the Sea, Office of Legal Affairs, 1992), p. 3.

11. The United Nations Agreement for the Implementation of the Provisions of the United Nations Convention on the Law of the Sea of 10 December 1982 relating to the Conservation and Management of Straddling Fish Stocks and Highly Migratory Fish Stocks (entered into force 11 December 2001).

12. United Nations. *International Legal Materials* 34. Doc. A/CONF.164/3, 1995. Washington, D.C.: American Society of International Law, 1995, p. 1542.

SUSTAINABLE DEVELOPMENT AS A NEW PRINCIPLE IN FISHERIES AGREEMENTS

In this new context, different principles were introduced with a view to ensuring the goal of making fisheries on the high seas compatible with the interests of the community, including those of the coastal State. The central tenet in this matter is that of long-term sustainable development. While optimal utilization is also part of the approach followed in this respect by the Agreement, environmental concerns are those that appear to predominate.

The Agreement next emphasizes the principle of prevention, with a view to the elimination and control of the overfishing characterizing the state of the matter today. More specifically, the precautionary principle born in the context of regimes of environmental protection is adapted to fisheries activities under the more flexible concept of the precautionary approach.[13]

This is not a simple play on words, as the precautionary approach reflects the need to take into account that in fisheries activities scientific uncertainty is always the rule. It follows that activities cannot be paralysed until having full scientific certainty that no environmental damage will ensue. Reference points and standards are also introduced in order to measure the compatibility of fishing efforts with the precautionary approach.

The most important contribution made by the 1995 Agreement is to ensure the management of maritime areas characterized by their biological unity, while taking into account the existence of different jurisdictional regimes, one under the authority of the coastal State in the EEZ and the other on the high seas beyond the 200-mile limit.[14] The emphasis placed by the 1995 Agreement on the objective of implementing the 1982 LOS Convention had the specific legal consequence of preventing the exercise of coastal State jurisdiction beyond the EEZ, just as activities on the high seas cannot interfere with the rights of sovereignty and jurisdiction of the coastal State. This is the essential balance that makes feasible the solution sought by the 1995 Agreement.

On the basis of this balance, the 1995 Agreement defines the area of its application as being that beyond the limits of national jurisdiction. In so doing, however, the Agreement provides for some exceptions that connect its operation with decisions adopted by the coastal State under its jurisdiction. First, the precautionary approach also applies to fishing for the species concerned within the EEZ. Secondly, the application by the coastal State of

13. D. Freestone and E. Hey, eds., *The Precautionary Principle and International Law: The Challenge of Implementation* (The Hague: Kluwer Law International, 1996).

14. M. Hayashi, "The role of the United Nations in managing the world's fisheries," in *The Peaceful Management of Transboundary Resources,* ed. G. H. Blake et al., (London: Graham & Trotman, 1995), pp. 373–93, at 379.

measures concerning compatibility in its jurisdictional areas must also be ensured. Thirdly, there are general principles that apply to fisheries both on the high seas and under national jurisdiction, in the latter case involving the exercise of sovereign rights of the coastal State. It follows that the management of the biological unit as a whole is entirely compatible with the rights set forth by the 1982 LOS Convention in the EEZ.[15]

The balanced solution sought by the 1995 Agreement becomes still more evident in connection with the principle of compatibility. In fact, while safeguarding the interests of both the coastal State and the high seas, the principle of compatibility ensures that the measures adopted by the coastal State will not be applied as such on the high seas, and conversely that those devised for the high seas will not be applied as such in the EEZ. It is rather a question for each of these two ambits to take into account the measures adopted by the other, thus ensuring comparable or similar management criteria with a view to avoiding imbalances in a system that is considered as a whole.

It follows that if the coastal State has enacted appropriate measures for the management of resources, it will be in the best position to require that the measures adopted for the high seas not be weaker. Only in the case where the coastal State does not enact appropriate measures will it not be in a position to make demands in respect of the high seas and quite possibly will be required to adopt the measures in force for the high seas for its jurisdictional areas.

The 1995 Agreement provides for a very elaborate system of international cooperation to ensure the implementation of the principles noted.[16] The participation in regional agreements and related organizations is normally reserved for States having a real interest in the fisheries, ensuring a non-discriminatory approach and what in fact amounts to a prohibition of fishing in respect of non-member States. Even in respect of States that do not participate in regional agreements or are not parties to the 1995 Agreement, there are obligations or policies that must be observed.

Although this new regime is undoubtedly the expression of more elaborate principles in respect of fisheries, particularly in connection with the high seas, the question of the implementation of these principles is more complex. There are, however, two sources of importance to evaluate the degree of real practical application of such new principles.

15. F. Orrego Vicuña, *The Changing International Law of High Seas Fisheries* (Cambridge: Cambridge University Press, 1999), Chapter 7.

16. M. Hayashi, "The 1995 Agreement on the conservation and management of straddling and highly migratory fish stocks: Significance for the Law of the Sea Convention," *Ocean and Coastal Management* 29 (1995): 58.

TREATIES ESTABLISHING NEW TRENDS

It is first the practice of States in making treaties and putting in place regional agreements that confirms that the principles and approaches indicated are not merely an intellectual or theoretical elaboration, but on the contrary respond to the need to ensure effectiveness in the management of the world's seas. If recent practice is examined, it can be noted that the role of scientific advice in the determination of allowable catches is more influential with each passing day. Also, the adoption of compatible measures becomes a regular practice both under regional agreements and broad international conventions.[17] The exercise of sovereignty in the EEZ is not an obstacle for the adoption of stricter measures for the high seas, and quite to the contrary, on many occasions the measures previously enacted by the coastal State will create the necessary pressure to adopt similar measures on the high seas.

The precautionary approach, the effective management of large ecosystems, restrictions in the access to fishing by new participants, and the allocation of catches among historical users, together with effective measures to bring into force such regimes and measures, are also trends becoming evident in contemporary international practice.

The conventions and agreements devised for the Bering Sea,[18] the Sea of Okhotsk,[19] the North Atlantic fisheries, even in situations of conflict,[20] the Barents Sea,[21] or the Convention on the Conservation of Antarctic Marine Living Resources,[22] are all specific examples of a marked evolution concerning the principles governing high seas fishing.

Two other recent conventions confirm the trends relating to principles that find their origin both in the 1982 LOS Convention and the 1995 Agreement. The Convention on migratory species of the Western and Central Pacific,[23] has established a comprehensive system of rules and institutions

17. O. S. Stokke, ed., *Governing High Seas Fisheries: The Interplay of Global and Regional Regimes* (New York: Oxford University Press, 2001).

18. D. A. Balton, "The Bering Sea Doughnut Hole Convention: Regional Solution, Global Implications," in Stokke (n. 17 above), p. 143.

19. A. G. Oude Elferink, "The Sea of Okhotsk Peanut Hole: De facto Extension of Coastal State Control," in Stokke (n. 17 above), p. 179.

20. E. Meltzer, "Global overview of straddling and highly migratory fish stocks: The nonsustainable nature of high seas fisheries," *Ocean Development and International Law* 25 (1994): p. 255.

21. O. S. Stokke, "The Loophole of the Barents Sea Fisheries Regime," in Stokke (n. 17 above), p. 273.

22. R. Herr, "The International Regulation of Patagonian Toothfish: CCAMLR and High Seas Fisheries Management," in Stokke (n. 17 above), p. 303.

23. Convention on the Conservation and Management of Highly Migratory Fish Stocks in the Western and Central Pacific Ocean, 5 September 2000, *International Legal Materials* 40 (2001): p. 278.

governing fisheries in an extended area of the Pacific Ocean with the participation of all interested States. The principles examined are recognized as having an important role in this context, while it can also be noted that the criteria of the 1995 Agreement begin to be to some extent interpreted, particularly in respect of the criteria governing the participation of States and related definitions.

The second regional convention of interest is that adopted for the South-East Atlantic on April 20, 2001.[24] While emphasizing the issue of straddling stocks, the Convention also provides for the adoption of compatible measures, the regulation of fishing activities on the high seas, and the criteria for participation in it. Again, some definitions of the 1995 Agreement seem to be generously interpreted so as to accommodate historical fishing.

In contrast with these trends, a weaker agreement was signed in Santiago on August 14, 2000 by the countries of the South-East Pacific, bearing the name of the Galápagos Islands Agreement.[25] This Agreement reaffirms the interest of coastal States in the fishing activities on the high seas, but does not seem to have clearly understood the manner how the compatibility of measures adopted under national jurisdiction with those adopted for the high seas is ensured. Problems concerning participation are also apparent. This confusion is also at the heart of the decision of this group of countries not to sign the 1995 Agreement.

SEARCHING FOR A DECISIVE DISPUTE

Two recent cases have also served the purpose of clarifying the substantive problems that need to be addressed in the context of the trends finding their origin in the United Nations Convention on the Law of the Sea and the 1995 Agreement.

First, the Southern Bluefin Tuna case[26] has been received with reactions of hope and disappointment. The consideration of this matter by the International Tribunal for the Law of the Sea with a request for provisional measures, while finding a limited response, gave rise to high hopes.[27] General

24. Convention on the Conservation and Management of Fishery Resources in the South-East Atlantic Ocean, 20 April 2001, *International Legal Materials* 41 (2002): p. 257.

25. Framework Agreement for the Conservation of Living Marine Resources of the South Pacific," 14 August 2000, http://www.oceanlaw.net/texts/galapagos.htm (accessed 28 January 2003).

26. Southern Bluefin Tuna cases (provisional measures), Australia and New Zealand v. Japan. See ITLOS Proceedings and Judgments online: http://www.itlos.org/.

27. ITLOS, Order of 16 August 1999 and Order of 27 August 1999. See the discussion by R. Goy, "L'Affaire du Thon a Nageoire Bleue," *Espaces et Ressources Maritimes* 14 (2001): 47.

measures were coupled with a few other specific measures entailing limits to fishing. Examples of the latter are the limitation of catches to the quotas that had been agreed to by the parties and the decision that all experimental fishing must be included in the national quota allocated. There are other questions that were approached in an indirect manner, particularly the role of the precautionary principle, which did not find the judicial support that the claimants proposed and some judges wished.

The results of this case would be different before an arbitral tribunal convened under the United Nations Convention on the Law of the Sea.[28] This Tribunal decided that it lacked jurisdiction in the case, thus disappointing some writers.[29] However, the Tribunal was not wrong in considering that the obligations concerning dispute settlement in a given agreement can in certain cases prevail over the broader mechanisms of the 1982 LOS Convention.

While deciding to refuse jurisdiction, the Tribunal admits two principles of great importance for the future.[30] First, it recognizes that the same dispute could arise under several treaties, which means in fact that even if a particular agreement is available, the principles and obligations of the 1982 LOS Convention are not excluded. Secondly, the Tribunal declared that if the 1995 Agreement had been in force there would have been a good number of other possibilities in this case, both in respect of substantive provisions and of those governing the settlement of disputes in regional agreements.

The fact was, however, that the 1995 Agreement was not in force and that the trends it embodies cannot simply be applied by a judge on his or her own will, independently from the consent of the parties. It is precisely this last element that is beginning to change in the law of the sea, as has become evident in the most recent international agreements following the 1995 Agreement, in particular those concerning the South-West Pacific and the South-East Atlantic. These new arrangements apply in respect of dispute settlement mechanisms of the 1982 LOS Convention and those of the 1995 Agreement, depending on the disputed species.

Another dispute has confronted Chile and the European Union in respect of swordfish fishing on the high seas in the vicinity of the Chilean EEZ. While Chile has enacted conservation measures in the EEZ for this and associated species, Spanish fishing vessels operate uncontrolled in the neighbouring areas of the high seas and export their catches through Chilean ports.

28. *Southern Bluefin Tuna Case,* Award on Jurisdiction and Admissibility, 4 August 2000, http://www.worldbank.org/icsid/bluefintuna/award080400.pdf (accessed 28 January 2003).

29. A. Boyle, "The Southern Bluefin Tuna arbitration," *International and Comparative Law Quarterly* 50 (2001): 447.

30. B. Kwiatkowska, "'Southern Bluefin Tuna,' International Decisions," *American Journal of International Law* 95 (2001): 162.

The issue posed in this case is again the regulation of high seas fishing in accordance with conservation standards that take into account the measures adopted by the coastal State most directly concerned. The precautionary principle and the principle of cooperation with the coastal State are also part of this dispute. The issue is to a large extent solved by the provisions of the 1995 Agreement, and in more general terms by those of the 1982 LOS Convention. However, again in this case the former was not applicable.

This case was brought by Chile before the International Tribunal for the Law of the Sea[31] and by the European Union before the World Trade Organization,[32] but apparently neither will come to be decided in view of a provisional agreement made by the parties on 25 June 2001 and the signature of a Free Trade Agreement in May 2002.

In any event, the principles at stake are clearer with each passing day and the role of the 1995 Agreement is also more broadly recognized. This dispute has thus also contributed to the development of the approaches that ought to govern this delicate balance between the rights and interests of the coastal State and those concerning fishing on the high seas.

LIMITS TO REGULATION AND THE ROLE OF INDIVIDUAL INTERESTS

The evolution of the basic principles of the law of the sea evidences a growing concern about overexploitation, taking into account the available scientific evidence. Up to now, the reaction has been to introduce more complex regulations each passing day, starting from the premise that cooperation as such is not sufficient to attain real solutions. In point of fact, cooperation by itself has failed as a viable alternative following the efforts in this respect embodied in the 1958 Geneva Conventions.

Which is the most appropriate form of regulation is still an open and unanswered question. The more active role of the coastal State, the development of mechanisms of regional cooperation, and the adoption of standards applicable in the areas subject to regulation, are no doubt all innovations of interest. The concern for conservation, however, cannot amount to restricting fishing beyond a reasonable point, as the activity is also a valid and legitimate economic objective. Prohibition of fishing is not a real solution, while it has been recognized that uncontrolled fishing cannot prevail any longer.

31. {International Tribunal for the Law of the Sea} {Case No. 7} {Order 2001/1} ({15 March 2001}).

32. M. Orellana, "The Swordfish in peril: the EU challenges Chilean port access restrictions at the WTO," *Bridges* (July–August 2000): 11, (November–December 2000): 5, and (January–April 2001): 9.

The kind of agreement that has been recently adopted is perhaps the last opportunity to achieve a balanced solution encompassing these fundamental interests. If the underlying values are not adequately handled in this context, it is not impossible to think that coastal State action will again forcefully emerge just as it was the right answer at the time of the enactment of 200-mile EEZ claims.[33] This is yet another reason why the 1995 Agreement should succeed.

Meanwhile, new approaches of interest have emerged, surpassing cooperation and regulation as self-contained solutions. Market mechanisms, such as individual transferable quotas, have been applied successfully in several national experiences.[34] Open access is replaced by individual fisheries rights, which requires a prior intervention of the State for the distribution of quotas, the supervision of market operations and enforcement. Regulation per se is no longer the answer underlying these approaches. The conservation of resources thus becomes an interest and a responsibility not only of public authority but also of economic operators themselves. The fishing industry is then governed by principles of effectiveness and not of depletion, as has been the case with the open access system.

This new approach may well apply to fishing on the high seas as supplementary to the efforts of cooperation and supervision introduced in the most recent fishing agreements.

CONCLUSION

Domestic experiences in some fisheries activities strongly point toward the convenience of introducing the operation of market economy principles as the guiding principle governing such activities. The efficient allocation of economic resources and the interest of the user in ensuring the conservation of the resources to be exploited are the central tenets of such an approach. On the other hand, all-encompassing regulatory schemes have ended up in the entanglement of bureaucratic self-interest, waste of resources, and finally compromising conservation in a no man's land.

This does not mean an end to the role of public authority, domestic or internationally. This authority has the ultimate responsibility of ensuring the proper working of the market, safeguarding competition and allowing for dispute resolution, tasks that in themselves are crucial for the success of the new approach.

33. Burke (n. 4 above), p. 350.

34. P. H. Pearse, "From open access to private property: Recent innovations in fishing rights as instruments of fishing policy," *Law of the Sea Institute: The Marine Environment and Sustainable Development: Law, Policy and Science* (1991): 178.

Domestic experiences now face the very serious challenge of proving themselves in the broader context of the operation of high seas fisheries, which in fact would mean the internationalisation of the experience available today.

A long evolution and constant experimentation should no doubt result in attaining reasonable solutions to an historical situation that has already over a century of confrontations. To do so would be very much within the spirit that guided the fruitful contribution of Elisabeth Mann Borgese to the law of the sea.

Operationalizing Article 82 of the United Nations Convention on the Law of the Sea: A New Role for the International Seabed Authority?*

Aldo Chircop
World Maritime University, Malmö, Sweden

INTRODUCTION

The author was one of many scholars who over a generation was challenged, inspired, and influenced by the visionary thinking of the late Elisabeth Mann Borgese. Elisabeth was a firm believer and supporter of the International Seabed Authority (Authority), established by the United Nations Convention on the Law of the Sea (LOS Convention) in Jamaica, as a new international organization responsible for the International Seabed Area (Area). That belief included a vision of the Authority as humanity's trustee for the common heritage of mankind. Elisabeth, like her mentor Arvid Pardo, saw the Area as a source of wealth that should be used to ameliorate the socioeconomic conditions of the developing world. Unfortunately, the technological and economic conditions at this time, or for the foreseeable future, are not such as to enable the full realization of that grand vision. However, a part of that visionary thinking may be realizable. The Authority is today in existence and in the foreseeable future may well play a unique role in channelling benefits from national ocean development to developing states.

In recent years, offshore oil and gas drilling technology has developed to enable exploratory and commercial activities on the slope and rise of the continental margin outside the 200-nautical mile (M) limit. State parties to the LOS Convention are entitled to claim up to 200 M of continental shelf or, where the continental margin extends beyond 200 M, up to the limits of the continental margin according to criteria set out in the Convention (extended continental shelf).[1] There may be as many as 50 or more states entitled to an extended continental shelf, and which are referred to in this article as broad

*Editors' Note.—The author wishes to acknowledge the assistance and support of the World Maritime University library.

1. Official text in *The Law of the Sea: Official Text of the United Nations Convention on the Law of the Sea* (New York: United Nations, 1983), Article 76.

Ocean Yearbook 18: 395–412

margin states.[2] Licences for exploration or discovery activities are already being issued on the Canadian Atlantic and U.S. Gulf of Mexico continental shelves, and new licences are expected to be issued as knowledge of these areas grows and deep-sea technology develops. Canada ratified the LOS Convention in 2003 and the Unites States is expected to do so in 2004. Although production on the extended continental shelf has not yet taken place, discoveries are expected, and production can thus be expected to occur, perhaps within the decade.

When such production occurs, Article 82 (Payments and Contributions with respect to the Exploitation of the Continental Shelf beyond 200 Nautical Miles), an obscure provision in the LOS Convention, will commence to operate.[3] This article is one of the most innovative provisions in the LOS Convention. It prescribes a novel duty for broad margin states to make payments or contributions in-kind on the production from nonliving resource exploitation. That revenue or in-kind contribution will be made available to developing countries through the Authority.

There are several legal and policy issues that can be expected to arise as a result, in particular the interpretation of Article 82 and the role of the Authority. Different interpretations potentially have far-reaching significance for determining whether the development of extended continental shelf resources is commercial. The precise role of the Authority and the criteria for the distribution of benefits remain to be defined. At this time it is fair to state that broad margin states are as unprepared for the implementation of Article 82 as the Authority. Article 82 contains many ambiguities and the Convention and its diplomatic history provide very little guidance on the operationalization of this provision. This paper attempts to highlight actual and potential difficulties and tentatively suggests ways how these might be addressed. The article concludes that the operationalization of Article 82 will necessitate close cooperation between the Authority and pioneering broad margin states. This article assumes that the reader is familiar with the modern regime of the continental shelf and the rules for the determination of seaward limits, and consequently focuses on the content and operational dimensions of Article 82. Similarly, the paper does not address the process of claiming an extended shelf through the United Nations Commission on the Limits of the Continental Shelf.

ARTICLE 82

Article 82 states the following:

1. The coastal State shall make payments or contributions in kind in

2. A. Chircop and B. A. Marchand, "International Royalty and Continental Shelf Limits: Emerging Issues for the Canadian Offshore" (paper presented at the Canadian Petroleum Law Foundation, Second East Coast Seminar, 18–20 September 2003, St. John's, Newfoundland and Labrador, Canada).

3. LOS Convention (n. 1 above), Article 82.

respect of the exploitation of the non-living resources of the continental shelf beyond 200 nautical miles from the baselines from which the breadth of the territorial sea is measured.

2. The payments and contributions shall be made annually with respect to all production at a site after the first five years of production at that site. For the sixth year, the rate of payment or contribution shall be one per cent of the value or volume of production at the site. The rate shall increase by one per cent for each subsequent year until the twelfth year and shall remain at seven per cent thereafter. Production does not include resources used in connection with exploitation.
3. A developing state which is a net importer of a mineral resource produced from its continental shelf is exempt from making such payments or contributions in respect of that mineral resource.
4. The payments or contributions shall be made through the Authority, which shall distribute them to States Parties to this Convention, on the basis of equitable sharing criteria, taking into account the interests and needs of developing states, particularly the least developed and the land-locked amongst them.[4]

To understand the full content and implications of this article it is necessary to recall discussions prior to the Third United Nations Conference on the Law of the Sea (UNCLOS III), and especially conference negotiations reflected in successive negotiating texts.[5] There was a close quid pro quo relationship between Article 76 (Definition of the Continental Shelf) and Article 82. The special entitlement of broad margin states to an extended continental shelf came about at the expense of the Area and the common heritage of mankind. When he launched the revolutionary concept of the common

4. Ibid.

5. For an in-depth discussion of the diplomatic history of Article 82, see Chircop and Marchand (n. 2 above); S. N. Nandan and S. Rosenne, vol. eds., *United Nations Convention on the Law of the Sea 1982: A Commentary,* vol. 2 (Dordrecht: Martinus Nijhoff Publishers, 1993), commentary on Part VI, Article 82, pp. 930–47. See also the various UNCLOS III negotiating texts: Article 69, Informal Single Negotiating Text, ISNT/Part II, A/CONF.62/WP.8, 7 May 1975, in R. Platzöder, *Third United Nations Conference on the Law of the Sea: Documents* (New York: Oceana, 1983–1988), vol. 1, p. 31; Article 70, Revised Single Negotiating Text, Part II, A/CONF.62/WP.8/Rev. 1/Part II, 6 May 1976, in Platzöder, ibid., vol. 1, p. 218; Article 82, Informal Composite Negotiating Text, A/CONF.62/WP.10, 15 July 1977, in Platzöder, ibid., vol. 1, p. 318; Article 82, Informal Composite Negotiating Text/Revision One, ICNT/Rev. 1, A/CONF.62/WP.10/Rev. 1, 28 April 1979, in Platzöder, ibid., vol. 1, p. 423; Article 82, Informal Composite Negotiating Text/Revision Two, ICNT/Rev. 2, A/CONF.62/WP.10/Rev. 2, 11 April 1980, in Platzöder, ibid., vol. 2, p. 51; Article 82, Draft Convention on the Law of the Sea (Informal Text), A/CONF.62/WP.10/Rev. 3, 22 September 1980, in Platzöder, ibid., vol. 2, p. 227; Article 82, Draft Convention on the Law of the Sea, A/CONF.62/L.78, 28 August 1981, in Platzöder, ibid., vol. 2, pp. 409–10.

heritage of mankind in 1967, Maltese Ambassador Arvid Pardo had proposed that the Area be developed in the interests and for the benefit of all mankind, but with preferential consideration for developing countries.[6] He also proposed that states that were to benefit from the new maritime zones should contribute a percentage of the revenues generated from the development of the living and nonliving resources within their jurisdiction.[7] He suggested that there be equitable sharing of the benefits generated from development in the Area and a percentage of the revenues derived from national activities. This thinking carried through the Seabed Committee and UNCLOS III, except that it eventually focused on the extended continental shelf only. Several states, in particular the land-locked and geographically disadvantaged, resisted the seaward expansion of maritime zones, which they perceived as an encroachment on the Area.[8] Proposals to subject the exclusive economic zone (EEZ) and continental shelf within the 200-M limit to this regime were eventually abandoned. The "package deal" procedure of UNCLOS III and the effort at producing consensus led to a compromise. Coastal states, and broad margin states in particular, agreed to an application of the Article 82 regime to the extended continental shelf in return for agreement on the new seaward limits of the continental shelf in Article 76. As a result, the continental shelf windfall benefit for broad margin states was accompanied by the contingent duty to make payments or contributions according to a predetermined formula based on production within national jurisdiction, but beyond 200 M.

NATURE OF PAYMENT OR CONTRIBUTION IN KIND

Article 82 is a negotiated international obligation. UNCLOS III negotiators stopped short from calling the obligation a "tax." "Tax" is a well-defined concept in a domestic context and its application in an international setting would need very careful consideration. It carries connotations that may not be relevant or helpful for application in an international setting, such as the exercise of the sovereign's right to levy monies so that government may be supported and services provided. An essential characteristic of "tax" is that

6. "Ocean Space, Seabed, Common Heritage of Mankind," First Statement to the First Committee of the General Assembly, 1 November 1967, in A. Pardo, *The Common Heritage: Selected Papers on Oceans and World Order 1967–1974* (Malta: Malta University Press, 1975), p. 1–41.

7. A. Pardo, "From Seabed Regime to Ocean Space Regime," 23 March 1972, in Pardo, *Common Heritage*, ibid., p. 219. See also Article 61 of "Draft Ocean Space Treaty," Working Paper submitted by Malta, A/AC.138/153, ibid., pp. 387–88 and 421.

8. For an overview of the debate and alternative proposals, see Nandan and Rosenne (n. 5 above), pp. 930–47.

"it is not a voluntary payment or donation, but an enforced contribution, exacted pursuant to legislative authority."[9] Also, the power to tax connotes a power to assess (i.e., assessments of tax due), and the Authority has not been duly empowered by the LOS Convention to make assessments. The broad margin state does not make the payment or contribution to the Authority, nor does it enjoy any special service entitlement as a result of the payment or contribution. Also, considering that the payment or contribution relates to activities within national jurisdiction, the utilization of "tax" to conceptualize the new international obligation would have established a precedent that state parties were not ready for at the time. Taxation of activities undertaken as sovereign rights is in itself a *sovereign* power of the state, and thus it is unlikely that negotiating states would have agreed to the creation of a taxation function in a global international organization. Even in relation to activities in the Area, there is no utilization of domestic law fiscal concepts connoting the exercise of sovereign functions, and instead reference is made to "payment," a generic concept connoting a financial obligation and no more.[10] The references to "payment" and "contribution" do not evoke ideas of sovereign prerogatives, but simply convey the content of an international obligation.

Rather than a "tax," it is probably more appropriate to treat Article 82 as a type of "international servitude." "Servitude is a civil law concept connoting a burden on real property".[11] At international law, Article 82 is akin to an economic servitude, tied to a specific type of territory (i.e., the extended continental shelf) and creating a restriction on it and which applies *erga omnes* and for the benefit of other LOS Convention State parties.[12]

From an oil and gas industry perspective, if the payment or contribution due by a state party (i.e., the duty at international law) is transferred for payment by industry (i.e., domestic implementation), it is likely to be perceived as a royalty. In general, a royalty constitutes "compensation for the use of property . . . (e.g., natural resources) . . . expressed as a percentage of receipts from using the property as an account per unit produced," and

9. *Black's Law Dictionary* (St. Paul, Minn.: West Publishing, 1979), p. 1307. Other charges comprehended by "tax" are toll, tribute, tallage, gabel, impost, duty, custom, excise, subsidy, aid, supply, etcetera. Ibid.

10. For example, LOS Convention (n. 1 above), Article 162(2)(p) and Annex III, Article 13.

11. Servitude corresponds to the concept of easement at common law, except that servitude refers to the burden, whereas easement refers to the benefit enjoyed. *Black's Law Dictionary* (n. 9 above), p. 1229.

12. "It follows from the nature of a servitude as being bound to a specific territory, that only exceptional restrictions on territorial sovereignty are meant, and not those general restrictions on territorial supremacy which, according to certain rules of international law, apply equally to all states." U. Fastenrath, in R. Bernhardt, *Encyclopedia of Public International Law,* vol. 4 (Amsterdam: Elsevier, 2000), pp. 387–90, at p. 388.

more specifically in "mining and oil operations, a share of the product or profit paid to the owner of the property."[13] In offshore development, where the "property owner" is the state rather than a private individual, a royalty is a payment to the crown in consideration for the licenced utilization of a natural resource. The oil and gas royalty regime is a complex legal and management structure, which in general is legislated, but whose implementation may also be negotiated on a per-licence basis. Much depends on the anticipated costs of the exploration, development and hopefully production from a particular field. In a deep-sea environment, such as the extended continental shelf, the technological and transportation costs are very considerable. Given the risks and associated costs, royalty expectations may well determine whether a particular discovery is in fact a commercial find at all.

In addition to the similarity of the payment or contribution to domestic royalty payments, another similarity to the royalty is the element of compensation, in the case of Article 82 for International Seabed Area "lost" to the broad margin state as a result of Article 76. However, there is also a significant difference: the payment and contribution in kind are due not to the licencing state, and not even to the Authority, but to state parties of the LOS Convention. In financing or otherwise fulfilling its obligation, one option that the broad margin state can be expected to consider is its royalty regime.

The text of Article 82 may also provide for another and more flexible interpretation, which might point to another means of fulfilment of the obligation. Although the payment or contribution would be based on the value or volume of production, there is nothing to suggest that this obligation is not equally discharged if the broad margin state elects to fulfil the obligation, to the same material extent, through some other manner, for instance the provision of Official Development Assistance (ODA). However, in this scenario, it would be important that the performance of the legal obligation does not amount to the conversion of an existing prior responsibility, but rather must be a direct expression of the obligation in Article 82. In performing the conventional obligation in good faith, the broad margin state would need to demonstrate that it is responding to the obligation consistently with what was intended by the UNCLOS III negotiators.

BASIC ELEMENTS OF ARTICLE 82

Basic Principle: Duty to Make Payments or Contributions In Kind

The choice between performing the obligation through financial payment or contribution in kind rests with the broad margin state. It is not clear who

13. *Black's Law Dictionary* (n. 9 above), p. 1195.

is responsible for the determination of the precise percentage of value or volume that may be due, that is, the broad margin state, the producer in the broad margin state, or the Authority. The licencing and broad margin state is ostensibly better informed than the Authority as to the volume or value to be taken into account. At the same time, although as seen earlier the Authority has not been mandated with an "assessment" power, it is responsible for receiving the payment or contribution. Accordingly, it is reasonable to suggest that the Authority should be informed of the basis for the calculation of the amount or payment that is due.[14]

At a domestic level there is likely to be an issue as to who is ultimately fiscally responsible for the payment or contribution in kind. While the obligation in Article 82 is one at international law, its domestic implementation may raise concerns as to where the ultimate responsibility lies. In a federal state, the answer to this question may be even more complex, especially whether a state or a provincial government may have entitlements or expectations to a share of offshore revenue, together with the federal government. This is a potential issue for Canada, where the federal and provincial governments have entered into an agreement on the levying of royalties and sharing of revenues.[15] The question that could arise is whether the obligation at international law is one that ought to be shared internally by those levels of government that benefit from offshore development. However, it would be unrealistic not to anticipate that the Article 82 obligation would not be transferred, at least to some measure, to the offshore producers. The fact that the obligation is based on the value or volume of production suggests a role for the producers. Also, it may be politically difficult to conceive of federal and possibly provincial taxpayers either footing the bill entirely or foregoing public revenues. Accordingly, it is going to be important for legislators and offshore licencing agencies to anticipate how the cost of this international obligation is going to be met. It may well be that federal, state, or provincial governments, and producers may have to reconsider the full extent associated with offshore development and production on the extended continental shelf.

Article 82 foresees the making of payments or contributions on an annual basis. Presumably, the obligation is discharged if a representative domestic public authority makes the payment on behalf of the broad margin state. It may be possible for the broad margin state to indicate that the obligation to make the payment or contribution (especially where the contribution option is exercised) is to be discharged by the domestically licensed producer directly. In any case, it is likely that the value of the payment or volume

14. On the role of the Authority in this regard, see M. W. Lodge, "The International Seabed Authority: Its Future Directions" (paper presented at the Conference on Legal and Scientific Aspects of Continental Shelf Limits, Reykjavik, Iceland, 25–27 June 2003). Paper on file with the author.

15. See Chircop and Marchand (n. 2 above).

of the contribution will vary from year to year in response to market and other conditions.

Applicable Resources

The duty applies to nonliving resources of the extended continental shelf. Early proposals in anticipation of and during UNCLOS III included all resources of the EEZ, but by the time the first negotiating text was produced it was clear that the duty would have a limited resource and spatial application.[16] Coastal states became increasingly reluctant to share resources, or the benefits therefrom, that were otherwise subject to the sovereign rights of exploration and exploitation. At the same time, those states not having a broad margin resisted an unconditional expansion of coastal state rights. Insofar as the EEZ was concerned (and continental shelf up to 200 M), the idea of sharing was whittled down to the surplus of fisheries (but not sedentary species) in that zone.[17]

In the case of the continental shelf, the idea of sharing was eventually confined to the nonliving resources of the extended continental shelf.[18] As seen earlier, the rationale was that the broad margin state was going to enjoy an additional benefit beyond that enjoyed by other coastal states and in effect at the expense of the common heritage of mankind. "Mankind," perhaps in the form of the other state parties to the LOS Convention, was entitled to benefit from this encroachment on the area, not necessarily with reference to the size of the extended shelf falling within national jurisdiction, but rather in relation to the benefits of resource development. This was consistent with the idea that benefits to be derived from the utilization of the International Seabed Area and its resources were to be undertaken for the benefit of mankind as a whole, albeit with preferential consideration for some states and peoples.[19]

Article 82 applies to transboundary nonliving resources straddling: (1) the EEZ and extended continental shelf, (2) neighbouring extended continental shelves, and (3) the extended continental shelf and International Seabed Area:

- Where (1) occurs, the producing state would need to determine what percentage of the production is proportionate to that part of the re-

16. Informal Single Negotiating Text (ISNT), 1975, Article 69, in Platzöder vol. 1 (n. 5 above), p. 31.

17. LOS Convention (n. 1 above), Articles 62, 69–72.

18. It should be remembered that the resources of the continental shelf that are subject to sovereign rights include sedentary species of living resources (e.g., lobster, crab, scallops). LOS Convention, ibid., Article 77(4).

19. LOS Convention, ibid., Article 140(1).

source located on the extended shelf. This scenario could pose considerable difficulties for producers because it may well be that only part of the production would be subject to the payment or contribution, when in reality the resource would be developed as a unit. Difficulties could be exacerbated where the payment or contribution is considered by industry as discriminatory because it would obviously not apply to offshore development within the 200-M limit.

- In the case of (2), if the transboundary resource development is unitized, presumably the duty will apply to the overall production from the unitized field or joint development zone, and the neighbouring states would have to agree on their respective shares of payments or contributions just as much as they would normally agree on benefit sharing. On the other hand, if the development is unilateral, then the payment or contribution is clearly the duty of the producing state only.
- In the case of (3), there could be two scenarios. The first is one where the broad margin state undertakes unilateral development of the transboundary resource, in which case it would have to make the payment or contribution in relation to production.[20] The second scenario is where the Authority, perhaps through a future-established Enterprise or some other mechanism, enters into joint development with the broad margin state. In this case there would have to be agreement on what proportion of the resource subject to the payment or contribution is located on the extended continental shelf. Although not the direct concern of this article, a joint development zone involving the Area in part will need to satisfy the procedures for the exploration and exploitation in Part XI, although the Authority's jurisdiction would be limited to those activities specifically occurring in the area.[21]

Basis of Assessment and Rising Scale of Payments or Contributions

Article 82 foresees a grace period of 5 years within which the producer is expected to recoup the development costs. On the 6th year the payment or contribution will commence to operate at the rate of 1 percent, and will continue to increase by 1 percent per year until the ceiling of 7 percent in the 12th year is reached. This last percentage will then continue to apply

20. There does not appear to be in the LOS Convention a duty on the broad margin state to consult the Authority on the development of transboundary resources, although there may be one at customary law. There is, however, a duty on the Authority to act with due regard to the rights and legitimate interests of the broad margin state. The duty requires consultation, including prior notification. See LOS Convention, ibid., Article 142.

21. LOS Convention, ibid., Article 153.

over the rest of the production period. This formula was probably based more on the need for a compromise than on the realities of cost recovery. There were alternative proposals at the negotiating table. Early proposals would have levied different percentages on the production depending on whether it occurred within or outside 200 M. Others included contributions of up to 5 or 10 percent.[22]

The grace period may cause difficulties for producers in two ways. First, given the very expensive modern-day offshore development environment, it remains to be seen whether 5 years is sufficient to recoup development costs in their entirety. The answer to this question will depend on the field concerned, the difficulty of the geology, market value of the product and regulatory obligations. Second, it appears that the grace period is applicable for the recovery of the development costs only. Once the payment or contribution period commences, the assessment appears to be on the gross, rather than on net value. The implications can be far reaching. This means that, although costs are significantly lower at the production stage, there is no deduction of these costs before the royalty is determined. It seems that this was a conscious addition to this provision. A proposal in a Working Paper to apply the royalty on the net did not receive sufficient support.[23] The U.S. delegation considered this proposal but felt that there would be significant difficulties in dealing with the accounting processes needed to determine the net, especially considering the differences between economies.[24]

There can be a situation where the production is so low that a broad margin state is not likely to receive a significant domestic royalty. A question that arises in such a situation is whether there is an implicit priority in Article 82 in favour of other states parties that would be expected to benefit from the payments or contributions. Will the broad margin state be expected to forgo domestic revenue? On the one hand there is the argument that the sovereign right to explore and exploit ought reasonably to include an expectation of priority benefit, otherwise exclusivity would not amount to much. On the other hand, that sovereign right is subject to an international servitude, that is, it may only be exercised with due regard to the special condition to which it is subject. Clearly, if the obligation in Article 82 is prioritized over benefits to the broad margin state, the latter margin state and licencee

22. Chircop and Marchand (n. 2 above).

23. Provision VIII, Informal Working Paper No. 4/Rev. 2, 27 August 1974, Formula A: "1. All States deriving revenues from the exploitation of the non-living resources of the . . . zone shall make contributions to the international authority at the rate of . . . per cent of the net revenues. 2. The international authority shall distribute these contributions on the same basis as the revenues derived from the exploitation of the international sea-bed area." Platzöder (n. 5 above), vol. 3, p. 362

24. M. H. Nordquist and C. Park, *Reports of the United States Delegation to the Third United Nations Conference on the Law of the Sea* (Honolulu: Law of the Sea Institute, University of Hawaii, 1983), pp. 98–100.

would need to determine whether a marginally viable field is at all commercially viable.

Eligible Contributing States

Not all broad margin states need make payments or contributions. During UNCLOS III there were differences of opinion as to whether all states should be subject to the obligation, but the compromise reached was that developing states that are net importers of the mineral resource produced on their continental shelves would be exempt.[25] Therefore, a developing state that exports the mineral resource concerned would be subject to the obligation. At the same time, a producing but net importing state may be in a position to benefit from the payments and contributions made by other states. Whether such a state would be entitled to benefit *pari passu* with other developing states will depend on the equitable sharing criteria developed by the Authority.

Role of the International Seabed Authority

Delegations participating in the Second Committee at UNCLOS III were divided over the role that an appropriate international organization would play in relation to Article 82, but there was eventual compromise in support of a role for the Authority.[26] The LOS Convention provides little guidance on the actual role of the Authority. In part this is due to the nature of the duty articulated in this provision, namely a responsibility for broad margin states, and a collateral role to be played by the Authority in fulfilling the objectives of the provision. Even so, the Authority's role and its relationship to the broad margin state needs to be clarified.

The Preparatory Commission (PrepCom) for the Authority and the International Tribunal for the Law of the Sea (Tribunal) established under Annex I of the LOS Convention did not consider this provision during its 10-year period of work.[27] The mandate of the PrepCom consisted of tasks that would enable the Authority and the Tribunal to commence functioning when that instrument came into force. Its output consisted of various recommendations, rules, procedures, agreements, and studies for (1) the Assembly and

25. See Nandan and Rosenne (n. 5 above), pp. 956–47.

26. The United States of America had proposed that the payments and contributions could be directed at a UN body or regional economic organization. Nandan and Rosenne, ibid., p. 941.

27. Final Act of UNCLOS III, Annex I, Resolution I: Establishment of the Preparatory Commission for the International Sea-Bed Authority and for the International Tribunal for the Law of the Sea, LOS Convention (n. 1 above), pp. 175–76.

Council, (2) the Secretariat, and (3) states parties. Article 82 considerations did not constitute a specifically assigned task and the PrepCom's work focussed on organizational, structural, informational, and regulation-drafting tasks that would enable the Authority to function without delay once the Convention came into force. Issues that would have required negotiation on behalf of the future Authority with specific states could only be addressed if specifically so mandated by UNCLOS III.[28] The role to be played by the Authority will need to be inferred in part by reference to Article 82 itself and its negotiating history, in part by reference to other provisions in the LOS Convention, and finally also with reference to what may be implicitly inferred from the purposes of Article 82 and the overall functions of the Authority.

The Role of the International Seabed Authority as Stated in Article 82

Paragraph 4 suggests both passive and active roles for the Authority. The passive role is with reference to the broad margin state, in the sense that it is the recipient of payments or contributions made by the broad margin state, but there is no role allocated for the determination of their nature, amount, tradable currency, and precise timing. The active role is with reference to what happens to the payments and contributions once made, but that role may appear to be limited. The Authority is to distribute these on the basis of equitable sharing criteria mentioned earlier. Clearly the responsibility to establish the criteria is a significant task. But even here, the Authority would have to perform this task within the framework of general criteria already provided. Also, it is important to note that the provision does not suggest that the Authority may retain any of the payments or contributions, for example, to cover administrative costs. There is no reference that other than the full payments or contributions (and thus not the net proceeds) must be distributed to states parties.

As noted earlier, the broad margin state's payments or contributions are to be made *through* the Authority (note: not *to* the Authority), for the purpose of distribution to state parties. Clearly, the Authority is not the final destination of these payments or contributions. Pardo's original idea before and during the Seabed Committee was that the payment would be made to the International Ocean Space Institutions that would emerge from UNCLOS III. During the negotiation of this provision, there were proposals designating the Authority as a beneficiary of the payments or contributions,

28. For example with pioneer investor states and entities specified in the Final Act of UNCLOS III, Resolution II: Governing Preparatory Investment in Pioneer Activities relating to Polymetallic Nodules, LOS Convention (n. 1 above), pp. 177–82. The Authority and its subsidiary bodies are bound by the decisions of the PrepCom under this Resolution, ibid., Article 14, p. 182.

but they did not receive significant support to enable inclusion in the negotiating texts.[29]

There is thus a fettered role that can be played by the Authority, perhaps in the form of a trustee of funds or resources. First, the Authority is the institution specifically designated to receive the payments and contributions, which presumably will be held in trust and on a temporary basis. Whether this function entails an implicit subsidiary function for the Authority to determine if and when the obligation of a broad margin state has been discharged is open to conjecture. Second, the Authority has the mandate to distribute the payments and contributions to states parties. Third, because distribution must occur on the basis of equitable sharing criteria, it is reasonable to presume that the Authority also has the authority to determine those criteria.

Powers and Functions of the International Seabed Authority in other Pertinent Provisions

The LOS Convention foresees roles for both the Assembly and Council of the Authority. The Assembly is the supreme organ of the Authority and is empowered "to establish general policies in conformity with the relevant provisions of this Convention on any question or matter within the competence of the Authority."[30] The Council is the Authority's executive organ and has the power to establish specific policies on any matter within the Authority's competence, but within the more general policies of the Assembly.[31] This mandate is further augmented by other assigned powers, including, for Article 82 purposes, the power to

> . . . recommend to the Assembly rules, regulations and procedures on the equitable sharing of financial and other economic benefits derived from activities in the Area and the payments and contributions made pursuant to Article 82, taking into particular consideration the interests and needs of developing States and peoples who have not attained full independence or other self-governing status . . .[32]

In turn, the Assembly will consider those recommendations and may approve them or "return them to the Council for reconsideration in the light of the views expressed by the Assembly."[33]

In principle, the procedure appears simple. However, it is unclear as to how differences would be resolved (other than resorting to formal dispute settlement) between a broad margin state and the Authority on the interpreta-

29. Nandan and Rosenne (n. 5 above). See especially the discussion at the Sixth Session at UNCLOS III, p. 940 et seq.
30. LOS Convention (n. 1 above), Article 160(1).
31. Ibid., Article 162(1).
32. Ibid., Article 162(2)(o)(i).
33. Ibid., Article 160(2)(f)(i).

tion of the full responsibilities of such a state, including the payment or contribution due. The Authority would need to be informed of the nature and extent of eligible activities on extended shelves, but there is no explicit duty to inform on the part of the broad margin state. Again, there is no explicit mandate for the Authority to monitor activities (other than desktop exercises) on extended shelves, or even more far-reaching, to audit production to ascertain or corroborate the full extent of the payment or contribution.[34] In effect, the Authority would have to rely on the goodwill of the broad margin state, because it is possible that the broad margin state may not be compelled to disclose.[35] Admittedly, broad margin states have an obligation to "fulfil in good faith the obligations assumed" under the LOS Convention, and not exercise their rights in a manner as to constitute an abuse of rights.[36]

It is conceivable that, although the Council has to recommend a framework to the Assembly for Article 82 purposes, there may have to be ad hoc arrangements between the Authority and an individual broad margin state. Such arrangements may need to address how the obligation will be performed (payment or contribution), the value or volume calculated, modalities of payments or contributions established, and timing determined.

Possible Implicit Functions

It is a moot point as to what powers the Authority enjoys other than what is specifically mandated in the LOS Convention. As a treaty creation, the Authority is required to function within the framework and boundaries of its empowering instrument. Article 157(2) states the following:

> The powers and functions of the Authority shall be those expressly conferred upon it by this Convention. The Authority shall have such incidental powers, consistent with this Convention, as are implicit in and necessary for the exercise of those powers and functions with respect to activities in the Area.[37]

34. In certain circumstances, it may be possible for the coastal state to argue that there is no duty under the LOS Convention, even with reference to the fulfillment of a conventional obligation, to disclose information that might be contrary to the essential interests of its security. Ibid., Article 302. There is an argument that the Authority may have to monitor activities on the extended shelf in the case of a joint development zone that includes, with its consent, the adjacent international seabed area.

35. This scenario is not as far-fetched as may appear. In the case of contributions to the International Oil Pollution Compensation Fund, several states parties have not provided to the Fund the basic information required to determine contributing oil, and thus assess contributions to the Fund. *International Oil Pollution Compensation Funds: Annual Report* 2002, p. 27.

36. Ibid., Article 300.

37. Ibid.

The incidental powers seem to be limited to activities in the Area. The receipt of payments or contributions in Article 82 may be seen as a function that is unrelated to activities in the Area and therefore the Authority may not enjoy incidental powers in this regard, other than what is specifically provided in the LOS Convention.

A possible alternative view is that although the Article 82 obligation is established outside Part XI, the Authority's role in relation to this article is also spelled out in Part XI. The interpretation of the content of Article 82(4) and other relevant provisions of the LOS Convention should be guided by the spirit behind these provisions. The Authority was given a role and will need flexibility to enable it to fulfil that responsibility pragmatically and effectively with due regard to the intent of Article 82, even though it may be argued that the Authority has no incidental powers in this regard.

Equitable Sharing: Eligible Beneficiary States

In principle, all states parties to the LOS Convention are entitled to benefit from the payments and contributions made. The sharing process is expected to be governed by equitable sharing criteria adopted by the Authority. The only LOS Convention a priori criteria to govern equitable sharing are the following: (1) the taking into account of the interests and needs of developing states; (2) the particular consideration of the interests and needs of least developed and land-locked developing states; and (3), where Article 162(2) further mentions "the interests and needs of developing States and peoples who have not attained full independence or other self-governing status." Insofar as (3) is concerned, the LOS Convention seems to contain some minor inconsistency between Articles 82(4) and Article 162(2) in the way preferential consideration is put forward.

It is not clear what "taking into account" means, but it does imply preferential consideration. Nor is the precise intent behind "interests and needs" a clear one. Is it conceivable that a hierarchy of needs may be established by the Authority as criteria to determine access (or extent of access) to the payments and contributions (e.g., states with basic livelihood needs, in comparison to states that wish to reduce their dependence on imported energy)? In theory, it is conceivable to foresee a tentative general ranking, in order of priority, as follows:

(1) least developed land-locked states (and presumably peoples who have not attained full independence or other self-governing status);
(2) other developing states (including other land-locked developing states); and
(3) other states (including newly industrialised, developed land-locked, and developed states generally).

The Authority would need to do more than this. It would need to consider which states would be considered as least developed and developing. It might have to consider socioeconomic criteria and mineral resource dependence. Since the adoption of the LOS Convention there are now also newly industrialised states, and it remains to be seen how these will be characterised for benefit-sharing purposes. Also, the negotiating history of UNCLOS III and the requirement to consider equitable criteria in a LOS Convention context suggest that the situation of developed land-locked states and geographically disadvantaged states may also have to be considered.

DISPUTE SETTLEMENT

The LOS Convention is silent on the consequences of when a broad margin state refuses to make or unreasonably delays the making of the required payment or contribution in kind. Although during the negotiation of Article 82 there were suggestions to consider the consequences of nonpayment (including when nonpayment occurs), there was no consensus on a rule that would tighten the broad margin state's obligation.[38]

It is unclear what dispute settlement mechanism should apply to a dispute between a broad margin state and the Authority. State parties have access to the dispute settlement institutions set up by the LOS Convention, but the access of the Authority to the same mechanisms is constrained: "The dispute settlement procedures specified in this Part [i.e., Part XV on dispute settlement] shall be open to entities other than State Parties only as specifically provided for in this Convention."[39] Clearly the Authority has access to the Tribunal's Seabed Disputes Chamber,[40] so long as the claim by the Authority is eligible subject matter. The jurisdiction of the Chamber is restricted to disputes with respect to activities in the international seabed area and with reference to specific categories.[41] A dispute on the interpretation or application of Article 82 does not concern activities in the Area. Even if the dispute concerns the Assembly's and Council's regulatory powers in relation to Article 82, these powers do not concern activities in the Area. In any case, even where the Chamber has jurisdiction, there is a significant limitation on the exercise of that jurisdiction. Where a dispute is concerned, the Chamber "shall not pronounce itself on the question of whether any rules,

38. See Informal Single Negotiating Text II (ISNT II), Article 69(5) proposed by the group of Land-Locked and Geographically Disadvantaged States: "If a State concerned fails to comply with the provisions of this Article the International Authority may take appropriate measures in accordance with the powers and functions conferred upon it by this Convention." Platzöder (n. 5 above), vol. 4, p. 327.

39. LOS Convention (n. 1 above), Article 291(2).

40. Ibid., Article 187 and Annex VI, Article 37.

41. Ibid., Article 187.

regulations and procedures of the Authority are in conformity with this Convention, nor declare invalid any such rules, regulations and procedures."[42] This is pertinent when the Council's and Assembly's powers to make rules, regulations, and procedures in relation to Article 82 are concerned.[43]

There is an argument for considering an Article 82 dispute as one encompassed by Article 187 only where the dispute concerns a resource that straddles an extended continental shelf and the Area. However, where differences between the broad margin state and the Authority relate to the interpretation of Article 82, the dispute settlement route is not stated. Part XV is concerned with disputes between states, as well as Part XI Section 5 disputes, including "such a dispute" involving an entity other than a state party.[44] Despite the intention of the negotiators of UNCLOS III to extend the application of Part XV Section 1 to disputes between a state party and the Authority,[45] the technical reference to "such a dispute" (i.e., qualifying the dispute to one relating to activities in the Area), seems to exclude Article 82 disputes.

Although the drafting of Article 285 might pose a technical hurdle for Article 82 disputes, what is essential is that there be willingness by the broad margin state concerned and the Authority to resolve the dispute. Article 285 was negotiated with the spirit and intention to enable state parties and the Authority to resolve their disputes in accordance with any means of their choice.[46] Further, the provisions on the Tribunal's competence anticipate the possibility of state parties and other entities appearing before it, either as provided in Part XI or "in any cases submitted pursuant to any other agreement conferring jurisdiction on the Tribunal which is accepted by all the parties."[47] This text is generic enough not to exclude the possibility that "any other agreement" could be a special agreement between a broad margin state and the Authority conferring jurisdiction on the Tribunal. In this case, there is also the possibility of resort to conciliation, but resort to arbitration under the LOS Convention is less clear.[48]

42. Ibid., Article 189: "Its jurisdiction in this regard shall be confined to deciding claims that the application of any rules, regulations and procedures of the Authority in individual cases would be in conflict with the contractual obligations of the parties to the dispute or their obligations under this Convention, claims concerning excess of jurisdiction or misuse of power, and to claims for damages to be paid or other remedy to be given to the party concerned for the failure of the other party to comply with its contractual obligations or its obligations under this Convention."

43. Ibid., Articles 160(2)(f)(i) and 162(2)(o)(i).

44. Ibid., Article 285.

45. M. H. Nordquist, S. Rosenne and L. B. Sohn, eds., *United Nations Convention on the Law of the Sea 1982: A Commentary*, vol. 5 (Dordrecht: Nijhoff, 1989), p. 36.

46. LOS Convention (n. 1 above), Article 280; Nordquist et al., ibid., pp. 35–36.

47. LOS Convention (n. 1 above), Annex VI, Articles 20(1), 21 and 22. See also Article 288 in the main text of the Convention.

48. Ibid., Article 284 read against Article 285. Article 285 extends the application of Part XV, Section 1, to entities other than state parties. The reference to

CONCLUSION

As has been seen, the LOS Convention provides relatively scarce guidance on how Article 82 should be interpreted, let alone implemented. Broad margin states with an interest in this article and the International Seabed Authority have necessarily complementary roles to play in implementing this provision. Neither individual broad margin states, nor the Authority alone will be able to make this provision work without close consultation and agreement. Insofar as the broad margin state is concerned, such a state will need to integrate Article 82 responsibilities in its domestic royalty regime. It needs to anticipate how it will fulfil its "sharing" responsibility. This needs to be done sooner, rather than later, because the time scales for offshore development tend to be over the long term, perhaps over decades. Industry needs to fully appreciate the extent of its fiscal obligations when investing in extended continental shelf activities. The fact that offshore fiscal regimes tend to be negotiated well ahead of actual production, along with the desire to avoid potential domestic discord, indicates some urgency for broad margin states that are already licencing offshore activities on the extended shelf.

The Authority, on the other hand, is potentially poised to play a more active role in channelling benefits to the developing countries than currently possible under the bulk of its mandate in Part XI. To do so, the Authority needs to start considering how it could perform its Article 82(4) responsibility by utilizing the powers granted to the Assembly and Council in Part XI. Council and Assembly members will need to interpret the explicit and implicit mandate conferred by the LOS Convention to enable the Authority's performance of its responsibility, both with regard to paying or contributing broad margin states and in relation to beneficiary states parties. The criteria for the sharing of benefits need to be developed. At the same time, and in interpreting its mandate, the Authority will need to work closely with interested broad margin states to clarify mutual expectations and minimize uncertainty that might discourage offshore development.

"party" in Annex V on Conciliation, Article 1, is not restricted to state parties. Although arbitration under Annex VII does not seem to apply to non-state entities because Article 285 does not apply to Part XV, Section 2, in reality Section 1 allows disputants (states and entities) to choose their own dispute settlement procedures. Ibid., Article 280.

(Under)Mining the Seabed? Between the International Seabed Authority Mining Code and Sustainable Bioprospecting of Hydrothermal Vent Ecosystems in the Seabed Area: Taking Precaution Seriously

Ikechi Mgbeoji*
Osgoode Hall Law School, York University, Toronto

INTRODUCTION

Over the millennia, the diverse wealth of the oceans and the critical role of marine ecosystems in the biogeochemical processes of our planet have remained important components of and catalysts to human development. Although life in the oceans is dominated by physical factors such as tides, waves, salinity, temperature, et cetera, these in turn largely determine the nature and character of biological communities. On the economic scale, the relevance of the oceans of the world is simply too vast to detail.[1] The ocean produces most of the oxygen we breathe and oceans dominate the biosphere. Put simply, we owe our existence to the oceans.

Whether in terms of transportation of goods and services, recreation, fishing, or as a source of energy, an econocentric conception of the oceans has dominated normative developments on the exploitation of both marine ecosystem resources and metallic resources lying at the abyssal plains of the oceans.[2] Interestingly, international law on ocean governance has been fo-

*Editors' Note.—The author wishes to note that the research assistance of Ekaterina Lioubar in the preparation of this article is appreciated. The usual caveat on the author's responsibility holds. This article is dedicated to the author's friend and colleague, Dr. Obiora Chinedu Okafor. *Dianyi, daalu.*

1. K. Button, "Is There an "Economics of Oceans?"," in *Ocean Yearbook 14*, ed. E. M. Borgese, A. Chircop, M. McConnell, and J. R. Morgan (Chicago: The University of Chicago Press, 2000), pp. 16–37. The intense convergence of interests in the oceans makes it a meeting spot for opposed interests. As one of the leading marine bioprospecting corporations recently lamented, "biodiversity of the oceans should be viewed as the reservoir of new products. Unfortunately, it has also become a rallying point for some environmentalists." See "Deep Sea Minerals." http://www.deepseaminerals.com (accessed 9 August 2002).

2. K. Saigal, "Knowledge and Sustainability of the Oceanic Ecosystem: Differing North-South Perspectives," in *Ocean Yearbook 15*, ed. E. M. Borgese, A. Chircop, and M. McConnell (Chicago: The University of Chicago Press, 2001), pp. 37–59; W.

Ocean Yearbook 18: 413–452

cused on the regulation of ocean resources, especially fish and mineral resources. The latter has been the primary assignment of the International Seabed Authority (ISA) created by the United Nations Convention on the Law of the Sea (UNCLOS).[3] It was apparently expected that seabed minerals would make a significant contribution to the wealth of nations and the global economy. Recent developments in marine biotechnology, however, suggest that the international community may have missed the primary or at least immediate source of products, services, wealth, and scientific insights. In spite of the focus of the ISA on seabed minerals, bioprospecting of seabed ecosystems, especially, hyperthermophiles and thermophiles[4] is increasingly becoming a profitable industry.[5]

Generally speaking, there are still a lot of things about the oceans and deep seas that modern science is yet to uncover, study, and understand. The evolution of the deep seabed, the dynamics of fluid migration, and the variables where biosphere meets geosphere are some of the fascinating aspects of the deep seabed, which scientists are currently studying. Giant and complex ecosystems in the deep seabed, the role of microbial mediation in biomineralization and calcification in particular, are some of the particular phenomena of the deep seabed that still fascinate marine scientists. The actual and potential economic benefits of hydrothermal bioprospecting and seabed microbiological resources have catalyzed greater research into deep-sea life forms and ecosystems.

Almost 6,000 bioactive metabolites from such microorganisms have been described in recent literature. Hundreds of these bioactive metabolites have novel structures and properties of commercial and industrial interest. In most cases, "these structural and functional properties may provide paradigms for chemically synthesized materials"[6] and biotechnological[7] products. Given the difficulty in reproducing their natural growth conditions in the laboratory setting, bioprospecting of some these organisms remains the only way of collecting and exploiting their unusual chemical properties.

In addition to bioprospecting of hydrothermal bioresources, modern technological development is at the threshold of devising machines and systems for mining polymetallic nodules such as sulfide and manganese deposits

---

Jones, "The international seabed authority without U.S. participation," *Ocean Development and International Law* 12 (1983): 151–72.

3. United Nations Convention on the Law of the Sea, concluded at Montego Bay, 10 December 1982. Entered into force 16 November 1994, reprinted in *International Legal Materials* 21 (1982): 1261–1354.

4. Thermophiles and hyperthermophiles are heat-loving organisms found in geothermally heated areas of the seabed.

5. See the proceedings of the 31st Underwater Mining Institute Conference, 31 October–3 November 2001. http://www.soest.Hawaii.edu/UMI2001.

6. UMI Conference (n. 5 above).

7. Biotechnology is the term used to describe the technologies devoted to the practical use of living organisms and their genetic products.

found on the seabed beyond the territorial jurisdiction of states. These developments are a fulfillment of earlier predictions that supplies of metallic ores from the international seabed may replace or at least significantly augment the land-based supply of precious metals.[8] However, the environmental impact of some of these seabed mineral mining tools remains an open question.

As modern developments in marine biotechnology and ocean mining make feasible the prospects of commercial exploitation of the resources and ecosystems of the international seabed, the question arises as to whether international law has risen to the complex challenges of developing and institutionalizing the framework for the sustainable development of the international seabed area so as to protect hydrothermal vent ecosystems.[9] These questions arise because unlike in the past, the oceans, a "global life-support system often viewed as infinitely resilient, is in a state of serious decline."[10] The environmental impact of seabed mining and bioprospecting is no longer a matter of mere academic speculation or paranoia on the part of environmentalists. There is conclusive evidence to support the dire warnings of marine environmentalists, especially in respect of the environmental impact of seabed polymetallic mining on hydrothermal vent systems.

For example, recent scientific surveys show that as polymetallic nodules are sucked up from the seabed and transported to the surface (during the mining process) sediment clouds are generated at the seabed, mid-water, and at the surface through unwanted sediment discharge. According to one commentator, the sediment activation is "extensive and continuous. For example, a German prototype mining system would mobilize 7,400 tons of sediment daily.[11] Biological, as well as geophysicochemical systems may be affected."[12] Similarly, there is abundant evidence that bioprospecting of plants and habitat destruction has driven some terrestrial plants to extinction.[13] Unless adequate safeguards are in place, there is no reason why a

8. G. Pontecorvo, "Musing about seabed mining, or why what we don't know can hurt us," *Ocean Development and International Law* 21 (1990): 117–18; M. El-Baghdadi, "The seabed's mineral resources and the conditions affecting the regime to regulate their exploitation," *Journal of World Trade* 26, no. 3 (1992): 85–97. See also, H. N. Siddique and P. S. Rao, "Exploration for polymetallic nodules in the Indian Ocean," *Ocean Development and International Law* 19 (1988): 323–35.

9. M. Lodge, "International Seabed Authority's regulations on prospecting and exploration for polymetallic nodules in the area," *Journal of Energy and Natural Resources Law* 23 (2002): 270–95.

10. P. Seligmann, "Outlook," *Frontlines* 2, no. 3 (2003).

11. T. Thiel and F. Tiefsee-Umweltschutz, "Evaluation of the environmental consequences of polymetallic nodule mining based on the results of the TUSCH Research Association," *Deep Sea Research* 48, part 2 (2001): 3433–52.

12. D. Richardson, "E.I.A. In Deep," *Environmental Focus* 11, 2001. http://www.nottingham.ac.uk/law/accessweb/elc/environmental.focus.pdf.

13. E. Newman, "Earth's vanishing medicine cabinet: Rain forest destruction and its impact on the pharmaceutical industry," *American Journal of Law and Medicine* 20 (1994): 479–511; E. Asebey and J. Kempenaar, "Biodiversity prospecting: Fulfilling

similar pattern may not occur in respect of hydrothermal life forms of the international seabed and associated habitat. It is hardly in doubt that given the considerable environmental impact of polymetallic and nodule prospecting in the seabed area, a workable regime[14] limiting the environmental impact of polymetallic nodule mining on hydrothermal vent communities is imperative.[15]

Rapid developments in marine biotechnology and the prospect of seabed mining have exposed the inadequacy of legal frameworks to regulate the exploration, exploitation, and sharing of the benefits that arise from such marine endeavors. The fact of the matter is that despite the giant strides made in and the huge financial stakes involved in bioprospecting of hydrothermal vent ecosystems, legal issues raised by profitable biotechnology development through marine scientific research (MSR) are still at an infant and underdeveloped stage.[16]

This article evaluates the extent to which the present legal order for the mining of seabed polymetallic nodules with its tangential reference to hydrothermal vent ecosystems succeeds in incorporating precautionary principles. In addition, the article queries the continued wisdom in severing the regulation of seabed mining of polymetallic nodules from the nonregulation of bioprospecting of hydrothermal vent communities of the seabed. The omission of the latter from the regulatory framework of the ISA is perhaps a reflection of the limited jurisdiction conferred on the ISA by the relevant legal instruments governing the oceans. The unfortunate situation today is that there is no existing legal order, sketchy or otherwise, regulating bioprospecting of hydrothermal vent ecosystems. Lyle Glowka has articulated the lacuna in international law of the sea as follows:

> [F]rom a practical standpoint, hydrothermal vents, their associated biological communities and the activities governing them fall into an inter-

---

the mandate of the biodiversity convention," *Vanderbilt Journal of Transnational Law* 28 (1995): 703–24.

14. Although there are various definitions of "regime," this article would adopt the definition that an international regime is a social institution comprising a set of principles, norms, rules, and decision-making procedures around which actors' expectations converge in a given issue area in international relations. For a fuller analysis of the concept of regimes, see S. D. Krasner, ed., [Special Edition] *International Organization* 36, no. 2 (1982): 1–22. See also S. Meese, "The legal regime governing seafloor polymetallic sulfide deposits," *Ocean Development and International Law* 17 (1986): 131–62.

15. J. M. Markussen and M. Drucker, "Commercial exploitation of polymetallic nodules: Comments on some central issue areas," *Proceedings of the Annual Conference of the Law of the Sea* (1992): 336–65.

16. See for example, D. Dzurek, "Marine Scientific Research and Policy Issues in East Asia," in *Ocean Yearbook 9*, ed. E. M. Borgese, N. Ginsburg, and J. R. Morgan (Chicago: The University of Chicago Press, 1991), pp. 157–87.

> national legal crack; neither UNCLOS (United Nations Convention on the Law of the Seas) nor the CBD (Convention on Biological Diversity) specifically reference them, and their application can only be inferred.[17]

Although international treaties such as UNCLOS and the Convention on Biological Diversity[18] (CBD) may apply to hydrothermal vents, the scope of applicability of each treaty is largely dependent on the nature and location of the activity in question. Hydrothermal vent ecosystems located in the Exclusive Economic Zone of States are regulated by the relevant laws of the State (including the State's legal obligations under the CBD or any other pertinent treaty to which it is a party). Where, however, hydrothermal vents and their related ecosystems occur in areas outside national jurisdictions and thus part of the "common heritage of mankind," the right to exploit such resources rests with the international community. Strangely enough, the international community has not yet articulated a legal regime for the exploitation of such resources. International law of the sea is, however, in the process of designing a new regime for the exploitation of polymetallic sulfides, which in many respects have some organic links with hydrothermal vent ecosystems. The question that arises is whether the regulation of seabed mining of polymetallic sulfides without making similar rules for hydrothermal vent ecosystems does not compartmentalize an otherwise holistic phenomenon.

This article argues that unless the proposed ISA Mining Code on seabed sulfides makes adequate provisions for the protection of seabed hydrothermal vent ecosystems, the perpetuation of a practice of compartmentalizing the seabed raises significant issues for the health and diversity of hydrothermal vent ecosystems and the seabed as a whole. If a holistic regulation of seabed governance is to emerge, international law has something to do about the legal crack in which hydrothermal vents, their associated biological communities, and the activities governing them have fallen into.

Activities on the seabed that invariably affect hydrothermal vent ecosystems need to be regulated in such a manner as to take into consideration the fact that the overall health and resilience of the oceans cannot be promoted by compartmentalizing the processes and phenomena of the seabed. Although the discovery of hydrothermal vents is a relatively new event, it can hardly be denied that seabed mining and marine bioprospecting are activities that pose serious challenges to hydrothermal vent systems. According to Lyle Glowka, "threats include not only direct physical damage

17. L. Glowka, "Testing the water: Establishing the legal basis to conserve and sustainably use hydrothermal vents and their biological communities," *InterRidge News* 8 (1999): 1–15.

18. Convention on Biological Diversity, 29 December 1992, reprinted in *International Legal Materials* 31 (1992): 818–62.

and destruction, but indirectly the possibility of sedimentation and upsetting water circulation systems."[19] In short, a major thrust of this article is that Article 145 of UNCLOS should be expansively and creatively interpreted by the ISA so that the protection of marine flora and fauna in the international area can be a reality. While it may be premature at this stage to speculate on the contents of the proposed code on seabed sulfide mining by the ISA, the provisions of the Mining Code on manganese nodules probably offers some clues on the direction of the proposed code on seabed sulfide mining. Within this context this article argues that if seabed hydrothermal vents are to be adequately protected, the ISA should seriously consider adopting a relatively liberal construction of Article 145 of UNCLOS.

Furthermore, this article suggests that the preoccupation with polymetallic nodules to the marginalization of hydrothermal vent ecosystems of the international seabed is a legacy of the founding instruments of Part XI of UNCLOS. Arguably, the drafters of the UNCLOS treaty probably did not contemplate the emergence of marine bioprospecting as a viable industry, probably yielding more immediate economic and scientific rewards than polymetallic nodules. Given recent shifts in modern technology, this narrow focus needs to be revisited.[20] More importantly, the question has to be asked, how can exploration for seabed mineral deposits benefit extremophile bioprospecting, and vice versa? And, what, if any, procedural controls are appropriate at this early stage of development of the regimes for seabed mining and bioprospecting of hydrothermal vent communities of the international seabed?

Another collateral issue pertinently articulated by Brewer is the question of the recognition to be accorded to intellectual values and skills, especially those relating to the technology relevant to the exploitation of hydrothermal vent organisms in the Area. In this context, it is important to note that the sharing of technology is not inconsistent with appropriate recognition of the rights of ownership of technology and the benefits accruing to the owners.[21] However, further analysis of the issue of intellectual property rights arising from biotechnology products derived from hydrothermal vent communities is premature and thus beyond the scope of this article.

In summary, this article broadly examines the adequacy or lack thereof of the recent Regulations on Prospecting and Exploration for Polymetallic Nodules in the Area,[22] otherwise known as the ISA Mining Code. These is-

19. Glowka (n. 17 above), p. 2.

20. The fact that some microorganisms may be found only in physically and/or chemically extreme environments makes them highly useful for the production of novel products.

21. W. Brewer, "Deep seabed mining: Can an acceptable regime ever be found?," *Ocean Development and International Law* 11 (1982): 25–67.

22. *Decision of the Assembly of the International Seabed Authority Relating to the Regulations on Prospecting and Exploration for Polymetallic Nodules in the Area.* ISBA/6A/18. (Kingston, Jamaica) 13 July 2000. (Hereafter called the Mining Code.)

sues are examined within the context of the evolving norms on sustainable development of marine ecosystems and the obligation of applying the principle or approach of precaution to activities that have the potential of impacting negatively on the marine environment, especially hydrothermal ecosystems. In the course of the analysis, attention is drawn to the fact that UNCLOS and other relevant instruments deriving their authority therefrom gives the ISA power to elaborate and adopt rules, regulations, and procedures to facilitate and govern the exploration and exploitation of seabed minerals.

Without doubt, the most significant body of rules on marine nodule mining and related activities is the Mining Code. The importance of this new regulation, its symbolism as the first mining code on the seabed, and indeed, what it omits to regulate, justifies its central place in the course of subsequent analysis in this article. Three themes run the course of analysis in this article. The first is the limited scientific knowledge of the role of fragile marine environments in the regulation or ordering of global biogeochemical processes. This reality makes a compelling case for precaution. Second, the international community should revisit the inattention to matters regarding hydrothermal vent communities. It is difficult to create a regulatory regime on the marine environment, particularly, the international seabed, and in the same breath, postpone action on regulating hydrothermal vents of the seabed.

Third, in designing the regime for sustainable utilization of the resources of the seabed and bioprospecting of hydrothermal marine ecosystems, there is a great need for flexibility and appreciation of the complexity and differences between various types of nodule deposits and hydrothermal ecosystems. These themes derive from the inherent interrelations and tensions between economic development and the integrity of the marine environment. The fundamental idea in this article is that given the unity of the oceans, serious activities in "one" ocean or part of an ocean would reverberate in other oceans and marine ecosystems.

Towards articulating these multiple but convergent ends, I have divided this article into three parts. The first part deals with the nature and characteristics of marine polymetallic nodules and extremophile ecosystems. This part also evaluates the differences between various polymetallic nodules and thermophilic ecosystems of the international seabed. In addition, issues related to the complexity and immense potential economic benefits of seabed nodules and life forms occurring in the hydrothermal vents of the seabed are addressed. Given the economics of marine resources and ecosystems, this part also examines, albeit briefly, the political economics influencing the development of a regime for deep seabed mining.

The second part examines the evolution of a regulatory regime for the international seabed. The dominant feature here is the process leading towards the emergence of the concept of common heritage of mankind as the juridical anchor for international seabed governance. This part thus evaluates the various legal doctrines competing for acceptance as the jurisprudential basis for control and regulation of activities relating to the international seabed and associated ecosystems. In this context, the ascendancy of the concept of common heritage of mankind in the development of a regime for regulating access to and exploitation of the seabed is explained on the basis of the numerical weight of third world States at the United Nations. In sum, the second part deals with the foundations, character, and scope of the jurisdiction of the ISA.[23]

The third part extends the scope of the analysis by examining the provisions of international law on sustainable exploration, exploitation, and conservation of the international seabed. It argues that while the Mining Code contains bold and imaginative procedures on dealing with seabed nodule mining, it ignores the potential and actual harmful effects of manganese nodule mining on fragile seabed ecosystems, such as hydrothermal vents. This part evaluates the probable environmental impact of seabed mining and extremophile bioprospecting vis-à-vis on hydrothermal vent ecosystems. Obvious environmental impacts of manganese nodule mining and hydrothermal bioprospecting include marine biodiversity loss, pollution from mining activities, and the possible loss of habitat for hydrothermal life forms.[24]

It seems that the regulations in the Mining Code have sufficient flexibility to adequately reflect the complexity of polymetallic nodules on the international seabed. The more difficult question, rather, disappointment with the Mining Code, is that despite its extensive and stringent nature, it makes little provision for dealing with the impact of manganese nodule mining on hydrothermal ecosystems. However, considering that seabed sulfides have closer organic relationships with hydrothermal vents, this omission may be intentional on the part of the ISA. It is hoped that the proposed Mining Code on seabed sulfide will address the question of protecting hydrothermal vent systems from the environmental impact of seabed sulfide mining. The article concludes with the suggestion that Article 145 of the Convention affords the ISA the legal authority to make provisions for the protection of seabed hydrothermal vents.

POLYMETALLIC NODULES AND HYDROTHERMAL ECOSYSTEMS

Seabed minerals include deposits of copper, sulfur, cobalt, nickel, gold, manganese, and other minerals. There are differences between the origins

23. See Article 156, UNCLOS (n. 3 above).

24. R. Wilder, "Law of the Sea Convention as Stimulus for Robust Environmental Policy: The Case for Precautionary Action," in *Ocean Yearbook 12*, ed. E. M. Borgese, N. Ginsburg, J. R. Morgan, (Chicago: The University of Chicago Press, 1996), pp. 207–22.

of manganese nodules[25] and sulfide deposits. Sulfide deposits are usually derived from hydrothermal vents, hence the close relationship between sulfide deposits and manganese nodules. Sulfide deposits are thus usually found at or near areas of active hydrothermal venting, "where hot-water mineral springs flow from the earth and deposit their mineral contents"[26]on the seabed. Hydrothermal vents open where the earth's crust is unstable and as these cracks form, seawater seeps "down into the hot rock and is then expelled again as the temperatures inside the vent causes it to boil. The temperature around such a crack can be as high as 420°C. Small particles and hot water enriched with minerals from the rock spew out the vent."[27] These volcanogenic polymetallic sulfides,[28] as they are called, occupy about 1 percent of the ocean floor.

25. These seabed minerals often accumulate in the abyssal plains of the seabed. In some cases, nodules lie exposed on the seabed. The depth of oceans where polymetallic nodules are located falls between 15,000 and 20,000 feet and distribution of the nodules across the oceans vary. These nodules contain a staggering amount of mineral deposits. Estimates of the volume of manganese nodules in the Pacific Ocean range from 1,700 billion tons to one trillion tons. A United Nations study shows that seabed nodules may contain 16.4 billion tons of nickel, 8 billions tons of copper, and 8.8 billion tons of cobalt. Although nodules occur almost everywhere on the ocean floor, the most promising finds occur in a narrow band stretching from Baja California to about 1000 miles south of Hawaii, a region called the Clarion and Clipperton Fracture Zones. Generally speaking, seabed minerals vary widely in their origins, chemical constitution, physical shapes, and appearance. The nodules are usually spherical, cannon-ball sized concentrations of metallic substance. The abyssal plains of the seabed where the nodules often occur includes mountain ranges, deep trenches, and other unexplored parts of the ocean bed formed as a result of marine geological activities spanning millions of years and extending to present-day geological activities. See H. U. Oebius, "Parameterisation and evaluation of marine environmental impacts produced by deep-sea manganese nodule mining," *Deep-Sea Research* 48, Part 2 (2001): 3453–67; J. Mero, *The Finding and Processing of Deep-Sea Manganese Nodules* (Berkeley: The University of California Press, 1959); J. Mero, *The Mineral Resources of The Sea* (Amsterdam: Elsevier Pub. Co., 1964). Although all oceans have deposits of manganese nodules, available data show that most such nodules occur in the Pacific Ocean; The Report of the U.N. Secretary General. *Marine Mineral Resources.* E/CM.20DD5. 13 January 1971. Manganese is used in the refining of steel and for scrubbing sulfur from stack gas, usually from coal burning plants. Manganese may also be used to refine copper and cobalt. The United States is the world's largest consumer of manganese.

26. Deep Sea Minerals (n. 1 above), p. 2.

27. "Exploring the Depths," http://www.europa.eu.int (accessed 29 August 2002).

28. These are deposits of sulfur-containing minerals formed by hydrothermal activity, that is, by an upwelling of hot volcanic magma and super-heated seawater from beneath the ocean floor. They are found along an active submerged volcanic mountain range that extends through all the world's ocean basins, as well as around volcanic island chains such as along the western edge of the central Pacific. See *Seabed Authority Begins Work on Scheme to Regulate Polymetallic Sulfides and Cobalt-Rich Crusts,* ISA Press Release, SEA/1764, 15/08/2002. In contrast, cobalt crusts are oxi-

Heat-loving life forms are often found in the ecosystems of such hydrothermal vents. Polymetallic sulfides have a link with hydrothermal vents and related ecosystems but their exploitation is a challenge for modern technology.[29] From the juridical perspective it would seem that the development of a legal regime for the exploitation of seabed sulfides has been contingent on their relatively lower economic value. With particular reference to manganese nodules, many states have sought to encourage mining of seabed polymetallic manganese nodules through sponsored scientific researches, tax incentives, and direct government investment.[30] However, while engineering advances in seabed mining have largely focused on manganese nodules,[31] it would seem that immediate economic benefits are flowing from bioprospecting of hydrothermal vent ecosystems.[32] This is largely a result of the fact that seabed mining is not yet commercially viable. The mining of different types of seabed minerals, especially sulfides, when it becomes commercially and technologically viable, however, raises the question of the impact of such activities on hydrothermal vent ecosystems. Given the ecological and environmental interrelationship between polymetallic sulfide deposits and hydrothermal vent ecosystems, it is pertinent to briefly examine the nature of these ecosystems before evaluating the adequacy, or lack thereof, of the new regime on mining of polymetallic manganese nodules. The nature of these ecosystems raises interesting policy questions for ocean governance.[33]

The existence of unusual life forms at great depths, pressures, and toxicity is not a recent discovery. These life forms found around oceanic hydro-

---

dized deposits of cobalt-rich and manganese layers formed by the precipitation of minerals from cold seawater onto hard seabed surfaces. They cover the submerged flanks of inactive underwater volcanoes throughout the oceans, on ridges and other seafloor elevations where currents sweep the rock floor clear of sediments. In addition to the cobalt found in both types of deposit, ferromanganese sulfides also contain manganese, iron, other metals and rare earth elements, while crusts include copper, lead, nickel, zinc, gold, and silver. See, ISA Press Release 1764.

29. E. M. Borgese, "Managerial Implications of Sustainable Development in the Ocean," in *Ocean Yearbook 12,* ed. E. M. Borgese, N. Ginsburg, and J. R. Morgan (Chicago: The University of Chicago Press, 1996), pp. 1–18; A. Marvasti, "Conceptual model for the management of international resources: The case of seabed minerals," *Ocean Development and International Law* 20, no. 3 (1989): 273–84.

30. *Report of the Secretary General of the United Nations on the Economic Implication of Sea-Bed Mineral Development in the International Area,* presented to the UNCLOS III in U.N. Document A/CONF.62/25, 25 May 1974, p. 40.

31. J. Van Dyke and C. Yuen, "Common Heritage v. Freedom of the High Seas: Which governs the seabed?," *San Diego Law Review* 19 (1981–1982): 493–551.

32. P. Willsey, "The Deep Seabed Hard Mineral Resources Act and the Third United Nations Conference on the Law of the Sea: Can the conference meet the mandate embodied in the Act?," *San Diego Law Review* 18 (1981): 509–32.

33. B. Cicin-Sain, R. W. Knecht, L. D. Bouman, and G. W. Fisk, "Emerging Policy Issues in the Development of Marine Biotechnology," in *Ocean Yearbook 12,* ed. E. M. Borgese, N. Ginsburg, and J. R. Morgan (Chicago: The University of Chicago Press, 1996), pp. 179–206.

thermal vent systems were discovered in 1977 by Jack Corliss and his group.[34] Prior to the discovery of these ecosystems, many scientists held the view that the deep seabed was devoid of biodiversity. The reverse is indeed the case. Thriving communities of many species have been found, some that are unknown elsewhere. These unusual life forms thrive in toxic and extreme environments. The base of the food web for hydrothermal vent communities is populated by a group of bacteria-like microbes, named Archaea,[35] which are genetically distinct from other species on earth.[36] Scientists are of the view that Archaea may have preceded all other life forms on Earth. These Archaea and other biota found at hydrothermal vent sites (collectively termed "extremophiles") have demonstrated incredible abilities to "conduct the basic processes of life at high temperatures and pressures and in the presence of generally toxic chemicals."[37] Over 300 species of hydrothermal organisms have been documented and studied.

The ability of these organisms to survive and thrive in such extreme environments make them prime candidates for synthesizing or developing chemical reactor systems and pollution control organisms where high temperatures, pressures, and chemical activities are necessary for efficient reactions. In this age of biotechnology,[38] these strange life forms have yielded useful medicines, enzymes, nutritional additives, and improved chemical, energy, and agricultural products. For example, two thermophile species *Thermus aquaticus* and *Thermococcus litoralis* are used as sources of the enzyme DNA polymerase for the polymerase chain reaction in DNA fingerprinting. The enzymes from these microorganisms are stable at relatively high temperatures, which is necessary for the polymerase chain reaction process. This product has a current market of about US$ 100 million and forms the basis of much of today's DNA technology industry. According to Montserrat Gorina-Ysern, "the potential market revenue for these industrial uses has

34. Hydrothermal vents occur when water seeping through cracks on the ocean floor (mid-ocean ridges where the Earth's tectonic plates meet) touch the core of the Earth's magma and are then spewed out at temperatures nearing 350°C. It has been estimated that 30 of these individual vents generate the equivalent energy of the largest nuclear power stations.

35. These organisms have the ability to create their energy without the aid of sunlight or photosynthetic processes. Instead, they use sulfide, which is plentiful in the vents, to create food, in a process called chemosynthesis. There are no plants in the deep ocean, because sunlight cannot reach them.

36. Deep Sea Minerals (n. 1 above), p. 3.

37. Ibid.

38. Biotechnology refers to a wide range of techniques for identifying, developing, and using the properties of living things to make various products and services. See S. D. Murphy, "Biotechnology and international law," *Harvard International Law Journal* 42 (2001): 47–139. Biotechnological breakthroughs include treatments for chronic anemia, hepatitis B, multiple sclerosis, kidney cancer, growth hormone deficiency, et cetera.

conservatively been assessed at US$ 3 billion per year. Another estimate puts worldwide sales of marine biotechnology related products at $100 billion in the year 2008."[39] Another thermophile, *Bacillus stearothermophilus*, which survives temperature of 75°C, "has been grown commercially to obtain the enzymes used in 'biological' washing powders."[40] The multibillion dollar market for bio-based products (potentially estimated at $13–$22 billion) is increasingly boosted by recent scientific developments in the area of new deep-diving submersibles and other modern tools. These developments and emerging potentials of the economic and industrial utility of the hydrothermal ecosystems may justify recent hopes that hydrothermal vent ecosystems would become a subocean pharmacy of the world.

It is increasingly becoming apparent in many circles that contemporary international law of the sea has no adequate provisions for sustainable bioprospecting of hydrothermal vent ecosystems. This situation is probably a result of the recent nature of marine biotechnology and more importantly the narrow focus on seabed nodules by the negotiators and drafters of UNCLOS. Thus, although the conduct of marine scientific research (MSR)[41] is regulated in Part XIII of UNCLOS and other international treaties such as the CBD (especially where such activities occur within the territorial boundaries of states), neither UNCLOS nor any other treaty deals in detail with the measures to be taken to regulate bioprospecting of hydrothermal vent communities.

In effect, the impact of treaties such as UNCLOS and CBD are greater in respect of hydrothermal vent ecosystems occurring within national jurisdiction than in areas of the international seabed. Moreover, considering that some technologically advanced States at the forefront of marine bioprospecting, such as the United States, are not party to either UNCLOS or the CBD, the prospecting of hydrothermal vent ecosystems remains a sort of no-man's land where the rule of ability, rather than of law seems to be the state of affairs. It is within these contexts that the next section examines the im-

39. M. Gorina-Ysern, "Legal issues raised by profitable biotechnology development through marine scientific research," *American Society of International Law* [Insights] (September 2003): 1–7. See also, L. Glowka, "The Deepest of Ironies: Genetic Resources, Marine Scientific Research, and the Area," in *Ocean Yearbook 12*, ed. E. M. Borgese, N. Ginsburg, and J. R. Morgan (Chicago: The University of Chicago Press, 1996), pp. 154–78.

40. Gorina-Ysern, pp 1–7.

41. Marine Scientific Research is a term applied "to a range of scientific disciplines (such as physics, biology, chemistry, geology, geophysics) concerned with the study of the ocean, its biota and its physical boundaries with the solid earth and the atmosphere." Gorina-Ysern (n. 39 above), p. 2. See also, Intergovernmental Oceanographic Commission (of UNESCO) "Ocean Science for the Year 2000" (Twelfth Session of the Assembly, Paris, 3–20 November, 1982), reprinted in *Ocean Yearbook 4*, ed. E. M. Borgese and N. Ginsburg (Chicago: The University of Chicago Press, 1983), pp. 176–259.

pact of the negotiating history of UNCLOS on the contemporary lacuna in governance of hydrothermal vent ecosystems of the seabed area.

THE DEVELOPMENT OF A SEABED NODULE MINING REGIME AND THE MARGINALIZATION OF HYDROTHERMAL VENT ECOSYSTEMS

The complexity of the legal nature of access to and property rights over seabed resources, especially hydrothermal vent ecosystems in the international seabed area, is an enduring challenge for seabed governance. The debate is often an oceanic version of the terrestrial global divide and controversy on equitable access to and equitable sharing of the resources of the planet. In a nutshell, the debate on access to the deep seabed revolves around the vexed issues of ownership, mining, production, distribution, pricing and equitable sharing of the profits from seabed resources. However, these complex problems directly implicate not only the juridical character of the ocean floor, but also governance of the fragile ecosystems of the seabed.

In a juridical sense, the heart of the matter is how best to devise an equitable and sustainable regime governing access to the seabed and its ecosystems, especially, hydrothermal vent communities. While some states, scholars, and various stakeholders in the resources and ecosystems of the seabed have sought to answer this question by positing that the international seabed is *res communis humanitatis* (common property), others have argued that the concept of *res publica* (public property) should be the operating concept. These various concepts import different legal and juridical implications.[42]

Ostensibly deriving support from the writings of Hugo Grotius, some scholars[43] and few industrialized states argued that the ocean seabed be-

42. M. Shaw, *International Law*, 2nd ed. (Cambridge: Grotius Publications, 1986), p. 276. See also, K. Saigal, "Sustainable Management of Ecosystems," in *Ocean Yearbook 13*, ed. E. M. Borgese, A. Chircop, M. McConnell, and J. R. Morgan (Chicago: The University of Chicago Press, 1998), pp. 56–79; C. Joyner, "Legal implications of the concept of the common heritage of mankind," *International and Comparative Law Quarterly* 35 (1986): 190–211.

43. See for example, D. Larson, "Foreword," *Ocean Development and International Law* 11, no. 1 and 2 (1982): 1–8; D. Larson, "The United States position on the deep seabed," *Suffolk Transnational Law Journal* 3 (1979): 1–45. It is doubtful whether Grotius meant what modern scholars attribute to him in respect to the seabed. Grotius argued, at least by inference, that title to a produce of the high seas vests in whoever was first to reduce such produce to private possession. This is quite different from the assertion of exclusive right to harvest the seabed being advanced by some scholars and a few industrialized States. While the doctrine of the freedom of the seas justifies the former, it hardly protects the latter. The latter is clearly a claim of right to the resource in situ or indeed a private claim of territorial sovereignty of the seabed itself. For a detailed analysis of this issue, see G. Biggs, "Deep seabed mining and unilateral legislation," *Ocean Development and International Law* 8, no. 3 (1980): 223–58.

longed to no one and thus its exploitation should be free to everyone and merely restrained by ability, technology, and financial strength. In other words, ocean floor minerals and ecosystems should be subject to a free-access regime (FAR).[44] In practical terms, what this position translates into is that the resources of the high seas belong to those who have the means and the will to exploit it.[45] Needless to say, in a world divided on the lines of technological abilities or lack thereof, seabed resources would practically belong to the industrialized States.[46]

Scholarly support for the FAR doctrine was anchored on scant authorities such as Article 2 of the 1958 Geneva Convention.[47] However, as Van Dyke and Yuen have clearly demonstrated, neither the text of the 1958 Geneva Convention nor the associated ambiguous commentaries affords any defensible basis for the theory that the international seabed was part of the freedom of the high seas under customary international law.[48] Not surprisingly, few States and scholars shared the opinion that the seabed should be subject to a FAR doctrine.

Although the vocal champions of the common heritage concept as applied to the seabed were mainly drawn from the industrializing world, it would be incorrect to argue that all industrialized States had always believed the international seabed to be subject to the principle of the high seas, belonging to no one[49] or *res communis.* In fact, some of the earliest proponents of the common heritage concept as applied to the international seabed were

44. Marvasti (n. 29 above), p. 274.

45. According to Charles Brewer, Acting Legal Adviser, United States Department of State "at the present time, under international law and the High Seas Convention, it is open to anyone who has the capacity to engage in mining of the seabed." Hearing Before the House Subcommittee on Oceanography of the House Committee on Merchant Marine and Fisheries, 93rd Congress, 1st Session, 50 (1974).

46. The trend in modern international law is to construe the high seas and other parts of the "global commons" as part of the common heritage of mankind. I. Brownlie, *Principles of Public International Law* (Oxford: Clarendon Press, 2003); B. Larschan and B. Brennan, "The common heritage of principle in international law," *Columbia Journal of Transnational Law* 21 (1982–1983): 305–45; C. Joyner, "Antarctica and the Law of the Sea: Rethinking the current legal dilemmas," *San Diego Law Review* 19 (1981): 415–36. For a related argument in respect to outer space see, A. Kerrest, "Outer Space: Res Communis, Common Heritage or Common Province of Mankind?," (Notes for a lecture in the Nice 2001 ECSL Summer Course). On file with the author.

47. Convention on the High Seas, done 29 April 1958, 499 U.N.T.S. 285.

48. See generally, Van Dyke and Yuen (n. 31 above).

49. There are inherent inconsistencies and inefficiencies in the res nullius argument for the seabed. For example, if the res nullius doctrine is applied to the seabed, the first occupier of a defined part of the seabed would appropriate it as private space. This would of course conflict with the high seas doctrine itself. For a res nullius argument on the seabed, see L. F. E. Goldie, "A general international law doctrine for seabed regimes," *International Law* 1 (1973): 796-825.

Presidents Lyndon Johnson[50] and President Richard Nixon of the United States of America. As Van Dyke and Yuen have correctly noted, "the United States gave significant support to the common heritage idea during the Nixon administration."[51]

Ultimately, the political economics of the ocean floor and the struggle for control and regulation of its resources is a reflection of terrestrial self-interest of States and thus it is not surprising that the industrialized States disagreed with the industrializing States on the characterization of the seabed as a common heritage of mankind. As Marvasti notes, "the developing countries support a tightly controlled state ownership regime under the United Nations.[52] The developed countries favor a market system solution administered through a licensing agency or a registry where prices will be the rationing criteria."[53] For a long time, these ideological controversies plagued the development of an acceptable regime for seabed governance.

There are some reasons why the FAR doctrine was not convincing and which made it yield to a regime of common control of the international seabed. First, the industrializing States had the preponderance of votes and were generally opposed to the "winner takes all" principle implicit in the FAR doctrine. Besides the advantage of numbers possessed by the industrializing States under the United Nations framework, the FAR regime originally proposed by some of the industrialized States presupposed that unregulated access to the seabed, even by the industrialized States alone, would not result in congestion and over-use by those possessed of the technological ability.

This supposition is far from the reality. A regime of FAR would have had enormous potential for mischief, perhaps anarchy, on access to the seabed. Furthermore, the common heritage concept was proposed at a time when the doomed movement by the industrializing States for a new international economic order was gaining intellectual and emotional ascendancy. Thus, the argument for regulated access to the international seabed was not only anchored on the common heritage concept,[54] but on the economics of effi-

50. In 1966, President Johnson had warned, "under no circumstances, we believe, must we ever allow the prospects of rich harvest and mineral wealth to create a new form of colonial competition among the maritime nations. We must be careful to avoid a race to grab and hold the lands under the high seas. We must ensure that the deep seas and the ocean bottoms, are, and remain, the legacy of all human beings." As cited to in Van Dyke and Yuen (n. 31 above), p. 527.

51. Van Dyke and Yuen (n. 31 above), p. 225.

52. E. Evriviades, "The third world's approach to the deep seabed," *Ocean Development and International Law* 11 (1982): 201–64.

53. Marvasti (n. 29 above), p. 274. See also, U.S. Department of State, Current Policy No. 371, *Law of the Sea* (1982).

54. The concept of common heritage of mankind entered the lexicon of international law a few decades ago. While some scholars attribute the origins of this concept to Ambassador Arvid Pardo in 1967, others point to Aldo Cocca's statement some months earlier at the deliberations on peaceful uses of the outer space. It seems, however, that Arvid Pardo was the first to articulate the concept of common

ciency of demarcated property rights and the prevailing temper of the times.[55] The combination of these and other factors help to explain the relative triumph[56] of the industrializing States during the process of fashioning a regime on seabed governance.[57]

The Common Heritage Concept and the International Seabed Area

While the industrializing States had argued, at least, since the late 1960s that the ocean seabed should be characterized as a common heritage of mankind,[58] normative steps were simultaneously taken to entrench this viewpoint. First, a United Nations resolution, the "Moratorium Resolution," declared as unlawful any seabed mining activity undertaken without the authorization of an international body.[59] Second, the position of the industrializing States soon gained ground as the now defunct Soviet Union,[60] China, Poland, Norway, Finland, the Netherlands, New Zealand, and Australia all voiced support for the common heritage concept.[61]

Historically, the characterization of the seabed as a common heritage of mankind may be traced to Ambassador Arvid Pardo's famous address to the United Nations General Assembly in 1967. The address, also contained in the note verbale submitted by the Maltese delegation to the General Assembly of the United Nations in 1967, probably owes a measure of debt to John Mero's landmark publication of *The Mineral Resources of the Sea* describing vast seabed resources.[62] Prior to John Mero's publication, there was little

---

heritage as a potential principle on which the proposed seabed governance would have to be anchored. For an examination of the confused thinking on the concept of common heritage concept see S. Gorove, "The concept of common heritage of mankind: A political, moral or legal innovation," *San Diego Law Review* 9 (1972): 390–403.

55. I. G. Bulkley, "Property rights and the efficient development of minerals on the ocean floor," *Research in Law and Economics* 3 (1981): 143–54.

56. An attempt by the industrializing states to characterize technology as part of the common heritage concept failed. See "The draft international code of conduct on the transfer of technology," 6 May 1980, *International Legal Materials* 17 (1970): 462–546.

57. Evriviades (n. 52 above).

58. R. Wolfrun, "The principle of the common heritage of mankind," *Heidelberg Journal of International Law* 43 (1983): 369–82.

59. Moratorium Resolution. G.A. Res. 2574, 24 U.N. GAOR, Supp. (No. 30) 10 U.N. Doc. A/7630 (1969). The vote passed with 62 affirmations and 28 abstentions.

60. See statement of the Soviet representative at U.N. Doc. A/CONF.62/SR. 109, p. 30.

61. For a treatise on the common heritage concept, see K. Baslar, *The Concept of the Common Heritage of Mankind in International Law* (The Hague: Martinus Nijhoff, 1998).

62. J. L. Mero, *The Mineral Resources of the Sea* (Amsterdam: Elsevier Science, 1965).

public knowledge of the immense mineral wealth of the seabed. The seabed was an ignored part of the planet.

In the note verbale, the Maltese Delegation posited that the seabed and ocean floor that constitutes five-sevenths of the world's area should be declared a "common heritage of mankind."[63] Riding on those forces that I have briefly elucidated on, and supported by near global unanimity, the Maltese position gained momentum as an emerging norm of international law and was adopted by the United Nations General Assembly Resolution 2749 17 December 1970.[64] Although this resolution is notoriously ambiguous, Article 1 thereof clearly states, "the seabed and ocean floor, and the subsoil thereof, beyond the limits of national jurisdiction (hereinafter referred to as the Area), as well as the resources of the Area, are the common heritage of mankind."[65]

The characterization of the seabed as a common heritage of mankind has been further entrenched in subsequent norm-bearing instruments hammered out at various international fora. For example, the Charter of Economic Rights and Duties of States adopted by the UN General Assembly on 12th December 1974 recognizes the international seabed as a common heritage of mankind.[66] Article 29 thereof provides, inter alia, that "the seabed and ocean floor and the subsoil thereof, beyond national jurisdiction, as well as the resources of the area, are the common heritage of mankind."[67] Given the large number and repeated acceptance of the common heritage concept in various international treaties and conventions, it is hardly debatable that the common heritage concept as applied to the seabed has become an entrenched principle of modern international law. However, its scope of application and defining elements or characteristics remain undetermined and sometimes controversial.

The designation of the international seabed as a common heritage of mankind imports some legal obligations on parties to such treaties and conventions. First, it delegitimizes and makes unlawful, national appropriation of the seabed by State parties or entities deriving their juridical status from

63. Note Verbale dated 17 August 1967 from the Permanent Mission of Malta to the United Nations, U.N.G.A./A/6695. The resolution was passed unanimously, by a vote of 108-0 with only 14 states from Eastern Europe abstaining. However, since the mid-1970s, Eastern European states have embraced the concept of common heritage of mankind as applied to the seabed.

64. *Declaration of Principles Governing the Seabed and the Ocean Floor, and the Subsoil Thereof, Beyond the Limits of National Jurisdiction,* 17th December 1970, 1933rd plenary meeting, UNGA 25th Session.

65. Ibid. For an analysis of the juridical status of UN General Assembly declarations, see J. Castaneda, *Legal Effects of United Nations Resolutions* (New York: Columbia University Press, 1969).

66. *Charter of Economic Rights and Duties of States.* GA Res.3281 (xxix), UN GAOR, 29th Sess., Supp. No. 31 (1974) 50.

67. Ibid.

the domestic legal framework of those State parties. Second, it forbids the militarization of the ocean floor through the establishment of fixed military installations. Third, within the context of equity and the Sisyphean attempt to redress chronic global economic apartheid, the common heritage concept abhors the exploitation and depletion "of resources of immense potential benefit to the world, for the national advantage of technologically developed countries."[68] More importantly, notwithstanding some controversies surrounding its elements and scope, the common heritage of mankind concept as applied to the international seabed imposes other legal duties on State parties to the relevant treaties and conventions.

These legal incidents include the removal of the seabed from the sphere of spaces open to national appropriation. In addition, the exploration and exploitation of the seabed would have to be done in a manner consistent with the Principles and Purposes of the Charter of the United Nations. Further, the use of the seabed and its economic exploitation would have to be undertaken with the "aim of safeguarding the interests of mankind. The net financial benefits derived from the use and exploitation of the sea-bed and the ocean floor shall be used primarily to promote the development of poor countries."[69] Furthermore, the seabed is reserved exclusively for peaceful purposes in perpetuity.[70] And finally, the common heritage concept would entail the creation of an international agency to act as a trustee for all countries over the seabed and ocean floor.[71] As the present writer has argued elsewhere, these laudable objectives and normative changes have not completely resolved considerable disagreements over the meanings of the elements of the common heritage concept and the scope of its applicability to the global commons.[72]

68. Note Verbale (n. 63 above).

69. Ibid.

70. On the basis of this principle, the use of the ocean floor as a testing ground for weapons of mass destruction was outlawed under international law. See "Treaty on the Prohibition of the Emplacement of Nuclear Weapons and Other Weapons of Mass Destruction on the Seabed and on the Ocean Floor and In the Subsoil Thereof," *International Legal Materials* 10 (1971): 145–77. Similar prohibitions or control on the use of the ocean floor have been made in respect to maritime warfare, laying of submarine cables, marine pollution, etc.

71. Strong United States' objection to these radical proposals that ultimately found their way to the UNCLOS Convention led to its nonratification by the United States. See R. Hildreth, "Legal regimes for seabed hard mineral mining: Evolution at the federal and state levels," *Ocean Development and International Law* 20, no. 2 (1989): 141–56. Other states that joined the United States in this approach are the United Kingdom and Germany.

72. I. Mgbeoji, "Beyond rhetoric: State sovereignty, common concern, and the inapplicability of the common heritage concept to plant genetic resources," *Leiden Journal of International Law* 16 (2003–2004): 700–19.

This situation may well be a result of the difficult journey towards a global regime on seabed mining that was characterized by protracted negotiations, disappointments, and compromises by various states and blocs, particularly, the notorious North-South divide.[73] From 1973 and 1982, the Third United Nations Conference on the Law of the Sea (UNCLOS III) had produced a comprehensive convention on the seas and oceans of the world.[74] Of the 9 parts of UNCLOS,[75] perhaps the most important is Part XI, which establishes the ISA.[76] The fundamental area of disagreement between the United States and the industrializing States was whether the Assembly or the Council created by UNCLOS should have authority over the proposed ISA.[77] In apparent protest against the ideological and procedural leanings of the emergent ISA and the inordinate delay in fashioning a regime acceptable to its domestic interests, the United States[78] and some other industrialized States such as Germany[79] enacted domestic laws authorizing private entities to exploit and explore the "resources"[80] of the ocean seabed.[81]

Two leading theories have been proposed in explanation for the unilateralist measure of the United States (followed by Germany and Italy) in respect of seabed mining. The first is that the United States wanted to break the deadlock in negotiations concerning the decision-making procedures of the proposed ISA. The second was the fear by the Reagan administration that the American seabed mining industry might abandon the development of seabed mining technology.[82] Some scholars have interpreted the rejection of UNCLOS by the Reagan administration as a triumph of ideology. As Ted McDorman argued, "the United States, in particular, has been unhappy with

73. E. Richardson, "The politics of the Law of the Sea," *Ocean Development and International Law* 11 (1982): 9–23.

74. UNCLOS (n. 3 above) is made up of 15 parts, 320 Articles and 9 annexes.

75. The 1982 LOS Convention which was opened for signature on 10 December 1982, entered into force on 16 November 1994, having received, according to its terms, the necessary number of ratifications or accessions.

76. Part XI of the Convention has been ratified by almost all the industrialized states except the United States.

77. Willsey (n. 32 above), p. 518–521.

78. Deep Seabed Hard Mineral Resources Act of 1980, Publ. No. 96-283, 94 Stat. 553, Art. 3 (a) (2). Signed into law by President Carter on 28 June 1980.

79. Act of Interim Regulation of Deep Seabed Mining, *Bundesgesetzblatt,* Part 1, 9080, No. 50 (22 August 1980).

80. It is significant that in the definition of the term "resources" of the seabed, only polymetallic nodules are captured by the definition. In effect, hydrothermal vent ecosystems and their allied components are not considered "resources" by the UNCLOS Treaty.

81. For a fuller analysis of this phenomenon, see Biggs (n. 43 above).

82. It is significant that of all the industrialized states of the world, only the United States has refused to ratify both UNCLOS and Part XI thereof which establishes the International Seabed Authority.

the deep sea-bed regime of the LOS Convention siding against the regime in the early 1980s primarily for ideological reasons."[83] Although these types of law were designed to be superseded by the UNCLOS treaty,[84] it is now generally agreed by scholars that unilateral legislation on deep-sea mining by individual States is arguably contrary to international law.[85]

Interestingly, unilateral legislation on seabed mining, especially the U.S. version, purport to perform at least two critical functions that may conflict with the international legal regime on deep seabed ocean governance. First, such unilateral legislation created temporary legal frameworks regulating seabed mining by citizens of the States enacting them at the period before the passage of the enactment itself and before the ratification of UNCLOS. Second, it was intended that in the event negotiations failed to produce a treaty acceptable to those States, the temporary regulatory framework created by those unilateral enactments would then become permanent.[86]

Given that new global regulatory machinery has now been instituted, albeit, without the formal participation of the United States, this leaves the question of the juridical and practical import of some of those regulatory frameworks created vis-à-vis the UNCLOS regime. Perhaps, the better question is what is the present legal status of those unilateral legislation on seabed mining? This is a question that may be resolved by reference to accepted principles of international law, particularly, whether a treaty may bind non-parties. Some delegates foresaw this problem during negotiations over the wording of the Declaration of Principles and UNCLOS itself. To avoid this conundrum, both the United States'[87] and United Kingdom's representatives had strongly argued that the emergent regime on seabed governance must derive its authority from a great majority of States traversing the various ideological, geopolitical, and economic divides.

83. T. McDorman, "The entry into force of the 1982 LOS Convention and the Article 76 Outer Continental Shelf Regime," *International Journal of Marine and Coastal Law* 10 (1995): 165–93 at 169.

84. See for example, Article 1 of Italy Law on the Exploration and Exploitation of Mineral Resources of the Deep Seabed 20 February 1985 *International Legal Materials* 24 (1985): 983–1001; C. Johnston, "Deep Seabed Mineral Resources Act," *Natural Resources Journal* 20 (1980): 163–71.

85. Biggs (n. 43 above). For an opposing view, see D. Caron, "Municipal legislation for exploitation of the deep seabed," *Ocean Development and International Law* 8, no. 4 (1980): 259–97. It is instructive that the U.S. Government rejected an attempt by Deepsea Ventures to claim exclusive mining rights over a part of the ocean seabed. See *Notice of Discovery and Claim of Exclusive Mining Rights and Request for Diplomatic Protection of Investment,* by Deepsea Ventures, filed with U.S. Secretary of State, 15 Nov. 1974, *International Legal Materials* XIV (Jan. 1975): 51–68. But see, D. Arrow, "The 'alternative' seabed mining regime," *Fordham International Law Journal* 5 (1981–1982): 1–33.

86. For a fuller argument, see Willsey (n. 32 above), p. 510.

87. See statement of John Stevenson. U.N. Doc. A/C.1/PV. 1799. p. 3.

This position is certainly a reflection of the well-known rule in international law that treaties generally bind only States that ratify them. However, there are treaties that have a universal constitutive effect, for example the UN Charter, binding on all nations, parties or not. A prime example of such a treaty would be one that brings into existence some new global entity. This is particularly the case where the constitutive entity is a product of a treaty generally agreed upon by a preponderance of States across the globe. However, treaties such as UNCLOS that enjoy support from most major political, economic, and geographical groups of the world but lack the universal character of say, for example, the United Nations, are not binding on nonparties.[88] However, the *realpolitik* of international law may dictate that the structures created by unilateral legislations on seabed mining may not be given practical effect by States that created them, in political deference to the sensibilities of other States or groups of states with mutual interests in the biotic resources of hydrothermal vent communities. Be that as it may, the unenviable situation now is that the regulation of seabed hydrothermal bioprospecting falls into a vacuum that may only be filled by the self-restraint of States and entities. In effect, the consensus of States or entities interested in hydrothermal vent bioprospecting is the crucial lynchpin for the sustainable use of resources of hydrothermal vent ecosystems.

The Jurisdiction of the ISA and Sustainable Exploitation of Seabed Hydrothermal Vent Organisms: Does Article 145 Really Matter?

Apparently taking a cue from the focus of the negotiations at UNCLOS III, the main focus of the ISA has been the regulation of the exploration for and exploitation of manganese nodules. The mandate of the ISA is thus limited, at least for the present, to the Area's mineral resources. However, there is a potential expansion of the ISA's jurisdiction, especially, where seabed mining impacts on hydrothermal vents and in cases where marine scientific research takes place in the seabed area. The potential jurisdiction of the ISA thus involves an intricate web of factors. As Lyle Glowka points out,

> [I]t only addresses marine scientific research and the Area's biological communities when seabed mining is involved. Therefore, without (1) direct measures taken by researching States to regulate the conduct of their marine scientific researchers in the Area, (2) a new international treaty or (3) voluntary oversight by the scientific community itself, there is very little that international law can directly offer at present to mini-

88. Justice Strong in *The Paquette Habana.* 175 U.S. 677.

> mize the potential use conflicts and the threats marine scientific research may pose to a hydrothermal system.[89]

Hence, to the exclusion of hydrothermal vents and other aspects of the seabed, modalities for the implementation of the rules and procedures concerning the exploitation of the seabed have largely been focused on manganese nodules, and lately, polymetallic sulfides.[90] Yet, mining of polymetallic sulfides, when it becomes technologically and commercially viable, would inevitably impact on hydrothermal vent communities. To appreciate the character of ISA's limited jurisdiction and how this limitation may be remedied or modified to deal with the realities of hydrothermal vent bioprospecting in the Area, it is perhaps necessary to examine the development of the ISA jurisdiction.

The emergence of an acceptable scientific regime for the sustainable exploitation of seabed nodules (to the exclusion of hydrothermal vent resources) may be traced to August 1993 when representatives of several industrialized and industrializing states circulated a paper among the delegates. By 1994, the final rounds of consultations focused on the paper of August 1993 had congregated around five issues, namely,

- Decision-making in the Council,
- The Enterprise, that is, the proposed ISA,
- Provisional application of the Agreement and provisional membership in the Authority,
- The treatment of pioneer investors, and
- Representation of the Eastern European Group in the Council.

At the last meeting of these consultations (31 May–3 June 1994) the draft agreement on the implementation of Part XI of the LOS Convention was

89. Glowka (n. 17 above). See also, L. Mullineaux, S. K. Juniper, and D. Desbruyères, "Deep-sea hydrothermal vents sanctuaries: A position paper," *InterRidge News* 7 (1998): 15–17.

90. D. Larson, "When will the UN Convention on the Law of the Sea come into effect?," *Ocean Development and International Law* 20, no. 2 (1989): 175–202; U. Jenisch, "Bridging the gap for seabed mining: Preparatory instruments for the New Law of the Sea," *San Diego Law Review* 18 (1981): 409–13. Resolution I that was annexed to UNCLOS in the final session of the Third UN Conference on the Law of the Sea established the Preparatory Commission (PrepCom) to draw up the rules, regulations, and the procedures for the International Seabed Authority (ISA) and the International Tribunal for the Law of the Sea (ITLOS). Resolution II designates as pioneer investors France, India, Japan, and the defunct USSR because these states signed the Convention and before 1 January 1983 expended an amount equivalent to at least US$ 30 million in pioneer activities.

adopted.[91] Given that this Agreement substantively changed certain provisions in Part XI of the LOS Convention,[92] and laid the legal framework for the Mining Code, it has the legal character of a protocol of amendment to the substantive treaty. Moreover, the Agreement and Part XI have to be interpreted and applied as a single instrument[93] and following the lex posterior principle in the interpretation of statutes or legal agreements, in the event of any inconsistency between Part XI and the Agreement, the latter will prevail. In effect, there is no dual regime on the exploitation of the seabed; rather, the terms of the Agreement would have to be reconciled with the UNCLOS treaty.[94] However, a rider is apposite here. No state or entity may establish its consent to be bound by the Agreement unless it has established or establishes its consent to be bound by the Convention itself.[95]

Although the ISA is undoubtedly a unique international organization representing interests covering nearly three-fourths of the Earth's surface,[96] the problematic question is whether the ISA would be willing to interpret its jurisdiction in such a manner as to enable it to regulate mining activities that negatively affect seabed hydrothermal vent ecosystems. This question arises because a careful reading of the pertinent provisions of UNCLOS and the texts of the Agreement and other instruments of the ISA, particularly the Mining Code, leaves the impression that the ISA jurisdiction is limited to seabed mining. In effect, notwithstanding the clear and direct potential harm that may befall hydrothermal vent ecosystems in the event of seabed sulfide mining activities, hydrothermal ecosystems are left at the mercy of the restraint, if any, that may be shown by entities engaged in seabed mining.

Beyond the potential environmental impact of seabed sulfide mining, regulating access to hydrothermal vent ecosystems of the seabed Area has not really featured in the emerging regime on seabed governance. Thus, marine scientific research or other activities directed at bioprospecting (of seabed hydrothermal ecosystems) would seem to be, prima facie at least, "an exercise of the freedom of the high seas under Article 87 of the UNCLOS

91. This Agreement was adopted at the 48th session of the General Assembly on 28 July 1994. The votes were, 12 in favour, none against, with seven abstentions. See *Agreement Relating to the Implementation of Part XI of the UNCLOS of 10 December 1982.* A/RES/48/263; reprinted in *International Legal Materials* 33 (1994): 1309–82.

92. For example, provisions on review conference, transfer of technology, production policy, and financial terms of contracts.

93. Article 2 of the Agreement (n. 91 above).

94. For a fuller examination of these issues, see Brewer (n. 21 above).

95. Article 4, par. 2 of the Agreement. This mechanism protects the interests of States who had agreed to be bound by UNCLOS.

96. M. Baghdadi, "The binding nature of the Disputes Settlement Procedure in the Third U.N. Convention on the Law of the Sea: The International Seabed Authority," *Journal of Mineral Law and Policy* 6, no. 2 (1990–1991): 173–203.

Convention."[97] The consequence of this state of affairs is that hydrothermal vents and their communities on the seabed are free for exploitation by whoever has the means or technology to exploit them. Certainly, given the fragile nature of hydrothermal vent systems, it is doubtful whether a regime of neglect of hydrothermal vent systems is consistent with sustainable use of seabed resources.[98] What is interesting here is that the ISA has limited its jurisdiction by circumscribing its regulatory ambit to exploration and exploitation of manganese polymetallic nodules leaving only a tangential responsibility in cases where such mining activities impact negatively on hydrothermal vent ecosystems. This cautious construction of its jurisdiction by the ISA is perhaps best exemplified in the Mining Code. For example, Regulation 1 of the Mining Code provides the following:

> [F]or purposes of these regulations. . .
>
> "exploration" means searching for deposits of polymetallic nodules in the area with exclusive rights, the analysis of such deposits, the testing of collecting systems and equipment, processing facilities and transportation systems, and the carrying out of studies of the environmental, technical, economic, commercial and other appropriate factors that must be taken into account in exploitation.[99]

Similarly, seabed prospecting is limited to or defined as the search for polymetallic nodules. Again, Regulation 1 of the Mining Code defines prospecting as "*the search for deposits of polymetallic nodules in the area,* including estimation of the composition, sizes and distributions of polymetallic nodule deposits and their economic values, without any exclusive rights."[100] Bioprospecting of hydrothermal vent ecosystems is clearly excluded. Clearly, the Mining Code on polymetallic nodules denies and rejects a jurisdiction over hydrothermal vents and its ecosystems. Consequently, the legal position seems to be that bioprospecting activities (not necessarily marine scientific research) in the seabed area and with particular reference to hydrothermal vent systems may proceed unsupervised and unregulated by the ISA or any other international agency.

Although the stance of the ISA on this issue is apparently justified by international law and the enabling convention granting the ISA its powers, such a conservative approach to the exercise of its jurisdiction operates on the questionable assumption that the seabed could be segmented and thus

97. *Report of the Secretary-General of the International Seabed Authority Under Article 166, Para. 4 of the United Nations Convention on the Law of the Sea,* 5–16 August 2002. ISBA/8/A/5. p. 8.

98. Saigal (n. 42 above).

99. Mining Code (n. 22 above).

100. Ibid. (Emphasis added).

regulated by piecemeal mechanisms. Unless, of course, hydrothermal vent bioprospectors show some restraint of their own volition, it would appear that no legal regulation obliges them to explore or exploit hydrothermal vent organisms in a sustainable or environmentally friendly manner. This would seem to be the legal position, notwithstanding that Article 143(1) of UNCLOS maintains the platitude that marine scientific research in the Area "shall be carried out for the benefit of mankind as a whole."[101] Interestingly, neither UNCLOS nor the Agreement defines the meaning of the phrase "benefit of mankind as a whole." Leaving aside the possible regulation of marine scientific research in the seabed area, would the commercialization of the benefits of marine bioprospecting be construed as a "benefit of mankind as a whole"?

In short, while there is something to be said for voluntary restraint,[102] it would seem that the ISA would be on a good footing if it construed the provisions of Article 145 of UNCLOS in such a manner as to enable it to regulate any activity in the Area that causes or has the potential to pollute or harm hydrothermal vent ecosystems, bioprospecting included. In making this liberal interpretation of Article 145, a few points of argument may be proposed in support. First, Article 87 of UNCLOS is not an absolute provision. The rights granted by Article 87 are to be exercised under the conditions laid down by UNCLOS itself and by other manifestations or evidences of international law on the issue. In addition, the legitimate interests of the other States qualify Article 87.

More importantly, the argument that bioprospecting of the seabed is a freedom of the seas must not be pursued in a manner that seems oblivious to the mutual vulnerabilities of various segments of the oceans. Hydrothermal vents are often linked to polymetallic sulfides. Accordingly, while it might be somewhat expansive for the ISA to make rules pertaining to hydrothermal vent ecosystems in the context of the Mining Code on polymetallic manganese nodules (which have a different origin and relationship with hydrothermal vents), the same cannot be said for hydrothermal seabed sulfides. The overlap between hydrothermal vent ecosystems and polymetallic sulfides makes it reasonable for the ISA, when the time comes, to craft a regulatory framework for the protection of hydrothermal vent ecosystems within the larger framework of the proposed regime or code on mining polymetallic sulfides.

The overlap and shared commonalities between hydrothermal vent systems and seabed sulfide deposits justify any holistic regulatory regime that deals with both types of resources as if they were intertwined and largely inseparable. As the Secretary-General of the ISA recently observed,

101. UNCLOS (n. 3 above).

102. L. Glowka, "Genetic resources, marine scientific research and the international seabed area," *Review of European Community and International Environmental Law* 8 (1999): 8–22.

> [T]he essential problem for the Authority is that the hydrothermal vent sites that are being targeted by scientific researchers and bioprospectors are also of considerable interest to prospective seabed miners. There is therefore considerable overlap, as well as potential for conflict, between the Authority's responsibilities in respect of the marine environment and activities directed at bioprospecting."[103]

Furthermore, an argument may be made that where hydrothermal vents occur at the seabed the provisions of Article 1 of Part XI of UNCLOS may be read or construed in such a manner that in conjunction with Article 145, UNCLOS empowers the ISA to regulate activities that may be harmful to the integrity and sustainability of seabed hydrothermal vent ecosystems. The territorial jurisdiction of the ISA is limited by UNCLOS to "the seabed and *ocean floor* and subsoil thereof, beyond the limits of national jurisdiction."[104] However, it has to be conceded that beyond the issue of territorial jurisdiction, the pertinent activities that the ISA may regulate in the Area are "all activities of exploration for, and exploitation of, *resources* of the Area."[105] Given that the term "resources" is further delimited or circumscribed to mineral resources, hydrothermal vent organisms are excluded. Furthermore, according to Article 133 of UNCLOS, "for the purposes of this part, (a) 'resources' means all solid, liquid or gaseous mineral resources in situ in the Area or beneath the seabed, including polymetallic nodules; (b) resources, when recovered from the Area, are referred to as 'minerals'."[106] In effect, where activities in the Area pertain to hydrothermal vents, it would seem that on a strict interpretation of UNCLOS, the ISA lacks the jurisdiction, prima facie, to regulate activities in the seabed area that pertain to bioprospecting of hydrothermal vent organisms.

However, beyond the narrow question of territory and what constitutes "resources" under UNCLOS, the larger question is whether a holistic reading of UNCLOS clearly debars the ISA from regulating activities in the Area if such activities endanger the integrity and sustainability of seabed ecosystems, even if such activities do not directly pertain to seabed polymetallic mining (whether manganese or sulfide)? The answer to this question would probably depend on how narrowly or widely one wants to construe Article 145 of UNCLOS. It would seem that the ISA has a broader regulatory role with respect to the protection and preservation of the marine environment. This jurisdiction would conceivably extend to seabed prospecting of biodiversity as well as to the regulation of marine scientific research in the Area generally.

103. Secretary General's Report (n. 97 above), p. 12.
104. Article 1, Part XI, UNCLOS (n. 3 above). (Emphasis added).
105. Ibid.
106. Article 133, Part XI, UNCLOS (n. 3 above).

This expansive construction of the ISA jurisdiction may be justified on the grounds that aside from mining activities, exploration activities for and bioprospecting of hydrothermal vent communities have huge impacts on the marine environment of the seabed. As Lyle Glowka has pointed out, it is an irony that "perhaps the most immediate threat to hydrothermal vent systems and their associated biological communities may be marine scientific research itself."[107] Mullineaux and other commentators have noted that disturbance "by researchers can have a substantial impact on vent systems" and that "anthropogenic changes in distribution and occurrence of vent fluid flows and of associated vent communities have been well documented at vents along the East Pacific Rise, on the Juan de Fuca Ridge and the TAG field on the Mid-Atlantic Ridge."[108]

In addition, depending on the circumstances, sampling of marine invertebrates occurring at hydrothermal vents may compromise the biological communities of hydrothermal vents. This may be the case in situations where alien or nonindigenous species are introduced. Furthermore, where a microorganism is not readily culturable or synthesizable, excessive collection or harvesting of such microorganisms may endanger the sustainability of such microorganisms in the pertinent hydrothermal vent community. These concerns make it imperative to rethink how Article 145 of UNCLOS is applied to hydrothermal vent communities. As provided by Article 145,

> Necessary measures shall be taken in accordance with this Convention with respect to activities in the Area to ensure effective protection for the marine environment from harmful effects which may arise from such activities. To this end the Authority shall adopt appropriate rules, regulations and procedures for inter alia:
>
> (a) the prevention, reduction and control of pollution and other hazards to the marine environment, including the coastline, and of interference with the ecological balance of the marine environment, particular attention being paid to the need for protection from harmful effects of such activities as drilling, dredging, excavation, disposal of waste, construction and operation or maintenance of installations, pipelines and other devices related to such activities;
> (b) the protection and conservation of the natural resources of the Area and the prevention of damage to the flora and fauna of the marine environment.[109]

107. Glowka (n. 17 above).
108. Mullineaux et al. (n. 89 above).
109. Article 145, Part XI, UNCLOS (n. 3 above).

Clearly, paragraph (b) of Article 145 is a potential source of legal authority for the regulation by the ISA of any activity capable of damaging life forms of hydrothermal vents. This power can best be exercised in a very nuanced and sophisticated manner. It must however be conceded that the jurisdictional ambit of the ISA that extends to marine scientific research, regulation of seabed mining, accommodation of activities in the Area and in the marine environment, protection of archaelogical and historical objects lying at the seabed, et cetera, has not yet been construed to include hydrothermal vent communities of the seabed. This lacuna may be filled by the ISA carefully crafting a mining code on sulfide deposits that takes into full account the relationship between hydrothermal vent systems and sulfide deposits.

THE ISA MINING CODE ON POLYMETALLIC NODULES: PRECAUTIONARY TALES AND THE PROSPECTIVE CODE ON SEABED SULFIDES

The vastness of the oceans may yield the mistaken impression that they are immune from human despoliation.[110] However, there is a consensus of opinion that mining activities in or affecting the ocean floor have various deleterious effects on the entire ocean ecosystem.[111] For example, in addition to direct physical damage and destruction of the seabed, there is the possibility of sedimentation and upsetting of water circulation systems. Living marine resources, their habitats and nonliving marine resources are in a constant state of interaction that may be adversely affected if adequate precautionary measures are not taken in the course of seabed mining. This makes it reasonable to adopt an ecosystem approach in the exploration and exploitation of marine resources.

Conscious of the harmful effects that may result from seabed mining and related activities, Article 145 of UNCLOS recognizes the need for protection of the marine environment.[112] As already noted, Article 145 provides that "necessary measures shall be taken in accordance with this Convention with respect to activities in the Area to ensure effective protection for the marine environment from harmful effects which may arise from such activities."[113] In addition to authorizing the ISA to deal with pollution and/or environmental damage arising from seabed mining or related activities, Arti-

110. D. Elders, "Sustainable Use of Marine Ecosystems," in *The Marine Environment and Sustainable Development: Law, Policy, and Science*, ed. A. Couper and E. Gold (Honolulu, Hawaii: Law of the Sea Institute, 1993), pp. 56–96.

111. See Preamble to Part XI of UNCLOS, par. 3, (n. 3 above).

112. M. Belsky, "Management of large marine ecosystems: Developing a new rule of customary international law," *San Diego Law Review* 22 (1985): 733–63.

113. Article 145, Part XI, of UNCLOS (n. 3 above).

cle 145 makes the protection and conservation of the flora and fauna of the Area a cardinal responsibility of the ISA.[114]

In this regard, activities in the Area are to be conducted in a policy that will achieve an "orderly, safe and rational management of the resources of the Area ... in accordance with sound principles of conservation."[115] Furthermore, Article 147 provides that "activities in the Area shall be carried out with reasonable regard for other activities in the marine environment."[116] Under Article 165 of Part XI of UNCLOS, the Legal and Technical Commission of the ISA has the power to "prepare assessments of the environmental implications of activities in the Area."[117] In addition, a close reading of Article 165 and other pertinent provisions makes it clear that the Legal and Technical Commission has the power to make regulations governing mining and related activities in the Area. Clearly, these are immense responsibilities requiring interdisciplinary cooperation, flexibility, and expertise.[118] More importantly, these provisions offer a juridical basis for an ecosystem approach in the articulation of a framework for regulating mining of polymetallic sulfides and the impact of such activities on hydrothermal vents.

Under the relevant procedures of the ISA, mining of the seabed may be undertaken if the following requirements are guaranteed: (a) the economic viability of the mining site; (b) the availability of the mining and metallurgical processing technology; (c) the existence of safe legal grounds with security of investment and assurance of access to mining sites; and (d) the availability of adequate financing. Remarkably, however, none of these criteria have a direct bearing on the issue of hydrothermal vent bioprospecting. Under the ISA guidelines, access to the minerals of the area may be gained when the prospective miner submits a workplan to the Authority's Legal and Technical Commission. The workplan submitted to the Commission should be in the form of a contract and contain not only a declaration of sponsorship by the appropriate state, but also an assurance that the applicant will comply with the provisions on the transfer of technology to the Authority and will accept that the rules and regulations of the ISA, including the Mining Code, are enforceable.

114. Pursuant to this provision, the ISA hosted 10 experts on the deep seabed environment to help make recommendations for regulations on deep seabed mining. See Marine Scientific Research Geared to Provide Suitable Environmental Databases for the Implementation of Article 145 of the Convention and of the Regulations on Prospecting and Exploration for Polymetallic Nodules in the Area of the Mining Code. 11–13 March 2002, ISBA/7/LTC/1, ISBA/7/LTC/1/Rev.1 and ISBA/LTC/1/Rev.1/Corr.1.

115. Article 150 (b), Part XI, of UNCLOS (n. 3 above).

116. Article 147, Part XI, of UNCLOS (n. 3 above).

117. Article 165 (d), Part XI, of UNCLOS (n. 3 above). Originally envisaged as having 15 members, the Legal and Technical Commission now has 22 members.

118. J. Gamble, "Assessing the reality of the deep seabed regime," *San Diego Law Review* 22 (1985): 779–92.

Upon receipt and evaluation, the legal and technical committee makes a recommendation to the ISA whether to accept or reject the workplan. Until the Agreement and Mining Code were completed and adopted, some commentators opined that such workplans need not take into serious consideration the issue of marine environmental integrity. In fact, in 1992 when Secretary-General Boutros Boutros-Ghali continued the informal consultations that had been initiated by his predecessor, "the issue of environmental consideration was removed from the list of issues since it was no longer considered to be a controversial issue in the context of deep sea-bed mining."[119] However, as already evident from the Agreement on implementation of Part XI of the LOS Convention, marine environmental protection ranks high on the concerns of the ISA. This development may not be unconnected with the development of precautionary approaches as an essential element in contemporary international environmental law.[120]

It is a necessary and welcome development in the ISA regime on marine integrity that the precautionary principle[121] or approach in international environmental law is not only recognized but also embraced by the new Mining Code. Regulation 31 paragraph 2 of the Mining Code provides that "in order to ensure effective protection for the marine environment from harmful activities which may arise from activities in the Area, the Authority and sponsoring States shall apply a precautionary approach, as reflected in Principle 15 of the Rio Declaration,[122] to such activities."[123] This is a clear and explicit adoption of the emergent principle of precaution in international law.[124]

For good reasons, the norm of precaution[125] (whether accepted as a principle or as an approach) has become one of the most powerful and

119. L. M. Nelson, "The new deep seabed mining regime," *The International Journal of Marine and Coastal Law* 10 (1995): 189–203 at 191.

120. L. Ruessman, "Putting the precautionary principle in its place: Parameters for the proper application of a precautionary approach and the implications for developing countries in light of the Doha WTO Ministerial Conference," *American University International Law Review* 17 (2002): 905–97.

121. S. Boutillon, "The precautionary principle: Development of an international standard," *Michigan Journal of International Law* 23 (2002): 429–69; S. Charest, "Bayesian approaches to the precautionary principle," *Duke Environmental Law and Policy Forum* 12 (2002): 265–85.

122. *Report of the United Nations Conference on Environment and Development*, Rio de Janeiro, 3–14 June 1991. Sales No. E.91.1.8 and corrigenda, vol. 1: Resolutions adopted by the Conference, Resolution 1, Annex 1. United Nations Publications.

123. Mining Code (n. 22 above).

124. For an exhaustive analysis of the status of the precautionary principle in international law, see H. Hohmann, *Precautionary Legal Duties and Principles of Modern International Environmental Law* (Dordrecht: Martinus Nijhoff, 1994).

125. For an overview and analysis of the nature of the concept of precaution in international environmental law, see D. VanderZwaag, "The precautionary principle in environmental law and policy: Elusive rhetoric and first embraces," *Journal of Environmental Law and Policy* 8 (1999): 355–75.

influential legal concepts in recent times for the regulation of activities that pose potential but unproven dangers to human health and the environment. It is neither an agenda for fear nor a mask for ignorance.[126] Rather, in its pragmatic simplicity, it posits that activities that have a reasonable potential of danger to the environment should be prevented even when there is not full scientific certainty to prove that such activities are actually dangerous. It emphasizes avoidance and is preventative in approach. As long as there is reasonable basis or grounds for concern, the norm of precaution requires States to prevent the occurrence of such irreversible harm. The precautionary approach is the juridification and institutionalization of caution as a fundamental postulate of international environmental law and policy.[127] While its principles are broad, it has the inbuilt advantage of permitting local flexibility and domestic discretion.[128]

In the application of the precautionary principle to mining activities on the seabed, prior understanding of the potential consequences of such activities is a condition for any rational judgement of the potential and actual impacts of such activities. In addition, it makes the application of the precautionary principle credible machinery for marine environmental sustainability, rather than an engine of recklessness and technological hubris. The embrace of the precautionary approach by the Mining Code is not a function of fear and idle speculation on the dangers of seabed mining. Rather, it is a function of knowledge of the potential and actual impacts of mining activities on the marine environment, especially the hydrothermal vents.

Exploration and testing activities on the seabed have revealed the enormous potential for environmental damage and harm. For example, scientific reports show that "impacts from full-scale mining operations could create a plume visible from space. Mining impacts on water column chemistry and biology may be of sufficient magnitude to merit serious investigation."[129] According to a recent report by scientists commissioned by the ISA to examine some of these issues, "despite decades of study, we still cannot predict the impacts of re-sedimentation from mining plumes on abyssal seafloor communities. We cannot say, for example, whether rapid accumulation of 1 cm of sediment will wipe out the benthic macro fauna or have little effect."[130] Given this mounting list of evidence, it is difficult to disagree with Thiel and Foell that "it would be reckless and possibly dangerous to initiate large-scale

126. L. Bergkamp, "Understanding the precautionary principle," *Environmental Liability* 10 (2002): 18–39.

127. E. Hey, "The precautionary concept in environmental law and policy: Institutionalizing caution," *Georgetown International Environmental Law Review* 4 (1992): 303–18.

128. D. Freestone and E. Hey, ed., *The Precautionary Principle and International Law: The Challenge of Implementation* (The Hague: Kluwer, 1996).

129. Scientific Report (n. 114 above), p. 12.

130. Ibid.

mining disturbances in the sea-bed without having achieved a fuller understanding of the potential ramifications of such activities."[131] Indeed, in instances when the consequences of such activities are not predictable, it follows, upon an application of the precautionary principle, priority should be accorded to conservation rather than reckless exploitation of poorly understood parts of the world's oceans.[132]

With respect to pollution of hydrothermal vents, the minimum threshold for precaution to be set in motion is the rather "imprecise pollution-tolerant limit encapsulated in the ocean's assimilative capacity in reference to specific substance sources responsible for its deterioration."[133] Interestingly, the resilience and assimilative capacity of the oceans seems to have been exaggerated, or better still, taken for granted for too long.[134] Given the emerging consensus among commentators that seabed mining is a potential source of ocean pollution, it is hardly deniable that the precautionary principle ought to be helpful in the formulation of any regime on seabed mining. Given the complex nature of oceans, the precautionary approach is not a plea for inaction; rather, it is a summons for interdisciplinary and intersectoral cooperation. To paraphrase Thiel and Foell, it is a task requiring the collaborative efforts of scientists, engineers, economists, and politicians. For example, while scientists would identify environmental risks, engineers would contribute their skills and knowledge towards developing environmentally safe technology. In addition, economists would consider the environment in cost accounting as politicians issue suitable environmental regulations.

From the foregoing, it is clear that the most pressing difficulty with devising a regulatory regime for seabed mining, including hydrothermal bioprospecting, is the absence of sufficient ecological knowledge necessary to adequately and quantitatively define impacts for purposes of risk assessments. The irony here is that the very knowledge and research needed to define the threshold of precaution may not be gathered or acquired without harming or endangering some hydrothermal vent ecosystems. In effect, the most immediate threat to hydrothermal vent systems and their associated biological communities is arguably, marine scientific research itself. As the Report of the ISA Secretary-General notes,

131. H. Thiel and E. Foell, "Environmental Risk Assessment for Manganese Nodule Mining and Application of the Precautionary Principle," in *The Marine Environment and Sustainable Development: Law Policy, and Science,* eds. A. Couper, E. Gold, and P. S. Vanchiswar (Hawaii: Law of the Sea Institute, 1993), pp. 226–234.

132. D. Dzidzornu, "Four principles in marine environment protection: A comparative analysis," *Ocean Development and International Law* 29 (1998): 91–123.

133. Ibid.

134. J. MacDonald, "Appreciating the precautionary principle as an ethical evolution in ocean management," *Ocean Development and International Law* 26 (1995): 265–300; A. R. Stebbing, "Environmental capacity and the precautionary principle," *Marine Pollution Bulletin* 24 (1992): 287–95.

> [O]ne specific issue which is becoming of increasing concern to the international community is the question of the management of threats to the biodiversity of hydrothermal vent fauna and in particular the legal regime to be applied to bio-prospecting (the harvesting for commercial purposes of genetic resources) in the Area. The international scientific community has concluded that deep sea hydrothermal vents are particularly sensitive because of their high percentage of endemic species and the unique nature of many of the species found there. Several such sites are already under potential threat either from *intensive scientific exploration, including bioprospecting,* or from future mining activities.[135]

Consequently, some acceptable damage to hydrothermal vent communities would have to occur if scientists are to obtain and proffer a credible and empirical basis for precaution. As the report of the scientists commissioned by the ISA to examine this issue critically observes,

> [T]he abyssal Pacific and Indian Ocean floors are thought to be major reservoirs of biodiversity, and yet the patterns and scales of this biodiversity are very poorly known. It will be extremely difficult to evaluate the threat of nodule mining to deep sea biodiversity (in particular, the likelihood of species extinctions) without knowledge of (1) the number of species residing within areas potentially perturbed by mining operations, and (2) the typical geographic ranges (and rates of gene flow) of species living within the targeted regions.[136]

However, these are not insurmountable problems. They represent challenges that could be dealt with by reevaluating the methods and scales of seabed research.[137] Newer and less destructive research models would have to be devised. These challenges make a compelling case for international cooperation in deep seabed mining risk assessment. They also point the way for interdisciplinary collaboration, specifically between industry and science. This high-level and specialized cooperation would best be pursued at both national and global levels.[138]

An extant juridical problem here is whether Article 256 of UNCLOS, which permits all states and competent international organizations to con-

135. Secretary-General's Report (n. 97 above), par. 50, p. 12.

136. Report of the Authority's Preparatory Meeting of Scientists Held at its Headquarters, 11–13 March 2002, p. 4.

137. Recently, a group of researchers at Scripps Institution of Oceanography at the University of California, San Diego, has shown that sediments in the deep sea ocean are a potential source of microbes that produce antibiotic molecules. See *Scripps News,* 17 January 2003.

138. Scientific Report (n. 114 above), p. 6.

duct marine scientific research in the Area, is a blank cheque for scientific inquiries in the Area, even when such research has the potential of damaging marine ecosystems, especially, hydrothermal vent communities. It must be noted that Article 143, paragraph 2 of UNCLOS authorizes the ISA to coordinate the results of such research. However, Articles 143 and 256 of UNCLOS hardly resolve the question as to whether marine scientific research in the Area is subject to the jurisdiction of the ISA. In seeking to resolve this argument, the Report of the ISA Secretary-General delivered on 5–16 August 2002, notes the following:

> [W]hile UNCLOS III was unable to reconcile conflicting views on the distinctions between "fundamental" and "applied" research in the various jurisdictional zones established in the Convention, it is clear that, under Article 143, marine scientific research in the Area is to be considered separate and apart from marine scientific research on the high seas and the results of such research are to be utilized for the benefit of mankind as a whole. Consequently, it will become necessary for the Authority to give more detailed consideration as to how best to realize the ideals set out in the Convention and the Agreement concerning the dissemination of the benefits of marine scientific research and technology transfer. One of the key practical questions that arise in this context is how to ensure the fair and equitable distribution of the benefits from such research without creating unreasonable obstacles to such activities as commercial biotechnological development and without limiting unreasonably commercial incentives, such as intellectual property rights, for work undertaken on the genetic resources of the Area.[139]

This article argues that the better way to resolve this impasse would be to encourage the ISA to extend its jurisdiction under Article 145 of UNCLOS to protect seabed flora and fauna from pollution. Until the ISA is permitted to exercise a jurisdiction over the seabed in a manner that recognizes the interrelatedness of seabed sulfide mining with potential pollution of seabed fauna and flora, including hydrothermal vent ecosystems, the ability of the ISA to apply the precautionary principle across the breath of the depths of the oceans, especially in respect of hydrothermal vent ecosystems, will be seriously hampered.

It may be arguable that Regulation 40 of the Mining Code extends the jurisdiction of the ISA to hydrothermal vents occurring at the seabed. Regulation 40 provides as follows:

> [I]f a prospector or contractor finds resources in the Area other than polymetallic nodules, the prospecting and exploration for and exploita-

139. Secretary-General's Report (n. 97 above), p. 9.

> tion of such resources shall be subject to the rules, regulations and procedures of the Authority relating to such resources in accordance with the Convention and the Agreement.[140]

However, it is very doubtful whether this omnibus clause in a specialized code dealing with polymetallic manganese nodules refers to or deals with hydrothermal vent ecosystems of the seabed. If the legislator had so intended, it would have been clear from the tenor and overall text of the code. No such intention is manifest on the face of the code. Moreover, UNCLOS and the Agreement clearly define or delimit the word "resources" to mean mineral resources. Therefore, it would be tardy to read into Regulation 40 an intention on the part of the ISA to exercise jurisdiction and regulatory control over hydrothermal vent ecosystems and bioprospecting of thermophilic life forms.

Beyond the inattention to hydrothermal vents, there is another problem with the Mining Code, particularly, the ambiguous way in which some aspects of the precautionary approach are provided for. For example, Regulation 2 paragraph 2 of the Mining Code stipulates, "prospecting shall not be undertaken if substantial evidence indicates the risk of serious harm to the marine environment."[141] While this provision generally resonates with contemporary understanding of the precautionary approach, neither the Mining Code nor any other instrument from the ISA defines what constitutes "substantial evidence" or "serious harm" to the marine environment. Given the general tenor of the code, it is difficult to speculate on the standard or threshold of "harm" that may trigger the precautionary principle into action. It is hoped that when the code on seabed sulfide mining is negotiated, the drafters of the code would revisit and clarify this issue.

In the search for an objective application of the precautionary principle in seabed mining activities, however, two interesting measures have been instituted by the Mining Code. The first relates to the well-known requirements of conducting environmental impact assessments of mining activities and the second deals with the principle of using the "best available technology" in such activities. This is a significant improvement on the application of the precautionary principle to seabed mining. Generally, the applicability of precautionary approaches is often tied to the ability of States to take measures necessary to prevent irreversible harm to the environment. Raising the bar to require the application of the "best available technology" by States or entities interested in seabed polymetallic mining is certainly an improvement on the prevailing minimum threshold.

The technology needed to exploit seabed minerals with minimal ecological damage must contend with and address issues related to removal

140. Mining Code (n. 22 above).
141. Ibid.

of surface sediments, the relationship between the impact on the seafloor community and the amount of sediment dropped on it. Other challenging issues include marine biological and chemical disturbances, which will arise from seabed mining activities. These challenges compel the adoption of the principle of "best available technology." If this principle were reflected in the code on sulfide mining and hydrothermal vent bioprospecting, contractors would be obliged to use best experience and technology to deal with these sensitive and fragile marine ecosystems.

Another related issue is the question of environmental impact assessment. According to the provisions of paragraph 7, Section 1 of the Annex to the Agreement,

> [A]n application for approval of a plan of work shall be accompanied by an assessment of the potential environmental impacts of the proposed activities and by a description of a programme for oceanographic and baseline environmental studies in accordance with the rules, regulations and procedures adopted by the Authority.[142]

It seems that the idea in this provision was borrowed from the unilateral legislation on seabed mining enacted by the U.S. Congress in 1980. The United States legislation that predated the Agreement requires an environmental impact assessment prior to issuance of a license or permit.[143] Under such licenses, the activities of a seabed miner may be circumscribed by concerns for marine environmental integrity.

Perhaps the most laudable and objective method of achieving a credible environmental impact assessment of seabed mining activities is the environmental baseline concept and impact reference zones articulated in Regulation 31, paragraphs 4 and 7 of the Mining Code. On the former, paragraph 4 of Regulation 31 provides as follows:

> Each contract shall require the contractor to gather environmental baseline data and to establish environmental baselines, taking into account any recommendations issued by the Legal and Technical Commission pursuant to Regulation 38,[144] against which to assess the likely effects of its programme of activities under the plan of work for exploration on the marine environment and a programme to monitor and report such effects.[145]

142. Agreement (n. 91 above).
143. See s. 109(d) of the statute.
144. This regulation empowers the Legal and Technical Commission to periodically make rules on seabed mining.
145. Mining Code (n. 22 above).

Under this regulation, when a contractor applies for exploitation rights, baseline environmental data gathered by the contractor during the exploration contract should be sufficiently representative of the exploration area for the contractor to propose areas to be set aside for impact reference zones (IRZ). According to paragraph 7 of Regulation 31,

> If the contractor applies for exploitation rights, it shall propose areas to be set aside and used exclusively as impact reference zones and preservation reference zones. "Impact reference zones" means areas to be used for assessing the effect of each contractor's activities in the Area on the marine environment and which are representative of the environmental characteristics of the Area. "Preservation reference zones" means areas in which no mining shall occur to ensure representative and stable biota of the seabed in order to assess any changes in the flora and fauna of the marine environment.[146]

As evident from these texts, the preservation reference zones and impact reference zones are areas to be used to assess the effect of the contractor's activities on the marine environment.[147] According to Nollkaemper and Kimball, "these designations provide an innovative method to assess damage by establishing with a relatively high degree of certainty what the specific effects of mining activities on the environment have been."[148]

The second innovative measure that makes practical sense in designing a code on seabed mining and related activities is the need for flexibility in both the rules and the rule-making process itself. This is particularly useful given the varieties of seabed nodules and their varied ecological demands. Considering the differences between polymetallic sulfides and cobalt-rich crusts,[149] the need for different sets of rules for exploitation of the respective resources is imperative. This has been appreciated by the ISA. According to the ISA, there is a . . .

> [N]eed for a flexible approach to the formulation of regulations for prospecting and exploration, particularly, in view of the lack of scientific knowledge relating to deep sea ecosystems. It was also clear that polymetallic sulphides and cobalt-rich crusts were different from polymetallic nodules as well as distinct from one another. Particular ecologi-

146. Ibid. See also, M. Cruikshank, "Law of the Sea and Minerals Development," in *Ocean Yearbook 13*, ed. E. M. Borgese, et al. (Chicago: The University of Chicago Press, 1998), pp. 80–106 at 87.

147. Marine Scientific Research on Mining Code, 11–13 March 2002, p. 1.

148. Ibid.

149. Nodules are scattered loosely over the sea floor. Crusts are fused to the underlying rock and sulfides occur around hydrothermal vents sprouting from volcanic areas of the seabed.

cal considerations arose with respect to polymetallic sulphides located at hydrothermal vents.[150]

Indeed, prior to the adoption of the Mining Code, the ISA noted, "particular ecological considerations arose with respect to sulfides located at active hydrothermal vents from which superheated seawater containing minerals in solution wells up from hot magma beneath the sea floor."[151]

Given the differences between polymetallic sulfides and seabed polymetallic nodules, it is a significant contribution of Regulation 31 to the jurisprudence on environmental impact assessment of seabed mining activities that the dynamism and complexity of the seabed environment is recognized as crucial factors in the formulation of legal rules on harvesting the various resources and ecosystems of the seabed. Hence, Regulation 31 paragraph 1 provides for periodic review of environmental rules, regulations, and procedures to ensure a responsive regime of protection for seabed biota. All six contractors[152] with contracts for exploration for deep seabed polymetallic nodules have agreed to these innovative guidelines.

CONCLUSION

In summary, the manganese nodule Mining Code is a welcome improvement and contribution to international environmental jurisprudence. Its evolution and development is a function of global economics and politics but in the final analysis, a measure of international consensus has developed around it. In the development of the Mining Code, the common heritage concept has played a significant role. Similarly, it would be naïve to ignore the realities of industrial and economic power and efficiency. These factors have combined to yield the Mining Code. The same embrace of realism ought to influence its approach to the growing significance of marine biotechnology to the global economy and how the oceans are perceived.

It is equally clear, at least from its embrace of the precautionary principle, that the emergent regime on exploration and exploitation of polymetallic nodules is comprehensive and stringent. Indeed, the emergent order has taken the regime of marine environmental protection one step further in its overall use of the precautionary approach. As Doug Richardson has

150. ISA Press Release, ISA/1764 (n. 28 above), p. 2.

151. Seabed Council Ends Session Devoted Mainly to Polymetallic Sulphides and Crusts, Press Release SEA/1762, 15/08/2002.

152. ISA Press Release SEA/1764 (n. 28 above). The contractors are from China, Japan, France, Korea, Poland, and Russia. All six contractors are exploring the Clarion-Clipperton fracture area. The Government of India is in the process of finalizing its contract with the ISA on the exploration of an area in the central Indian Ocean basin.

noted, this may have arisen "out of necessity, using strict guidelines to alleviate some of the potentially colossal impacts that may occur when dealing with projects of up to 150,000 square kilometers in size."[153] The perils and promises of deep-sea mining are really enormous.

But more importantly, notwithstanding the apparent limitations on the jurisdiction of the ISA, particularly in respect of hydrothermal vent communities, one can hardly disagree with the Secretary-General of the ISA on the potentially wide scope of the regulatory ambit of the ISA on matters pertaining to the sustainable use of hydrothermal vent ecosystems. In the report to the 8th session of the International Seabed Authority, the Secretary-General articulated the ambit of the jurisdiction of the ISA in such aspects as follows:

> [A]lthough the role of the Authority in the regulation of activities in the Area is directed primarily at exploration for and exploitation of mineral resources, the Authority also has a broader regulatory role with respect to the protection and preservation of the marine environment (including its biodiversity) as well as with respect to marine scientific research in the Area generally. This is made clear, *inter alia,* by (a) Article 145 of the Convention . . . and (b) other provisions within both the Convention and the Authority's regulations that enable or require the adoption of rules, regulations and procedures for environmental protection. In addition, Article 165, paragraph 2, of the Convention requires the Legal and Technical Commission to, *inter alia,* make recommendations to the Council on the protection of the marine environment, take into account assessments of environmental implications when formulating the rules, regulations and procedures for exploration and exploitation referred to Article 162, paragraph 2 (o), of the Convention, and make recommendations to the Council regarding the establishment of a monitoring programme.[154]

Clearly, the mandate of the ISA as conferred by the United Nations Convention on the Law of the Sea is broad and ample. It extends to the regulation of activities that may be harmful to the integrity and sustainability of hydrothermal vents in the seabed area. It would therefore seem that the present focus on polymetallic nodules does not necessarily mean a denial of regulatory jurisdiction over seabed hydrothermal vents if mining activities endanger the health of or pollute hydrothermal vent communities.

153. Richardson (n. 12 above), p. 13. But see, L. Kimball, "A Framework for Environmentally-Sound Development of Non-Living Resources in International Areas," in Couper and Gold (n. 110 above), p. 236.

154. Report of the ISA Secretary-General. ISBA/8/A/5. 7 June 2002, (n. 97 above), p. 12.

In summary, the Secretary-General of the ISA seems to have made a powerful argument when his report of 2002 suggested the following:

> [T]he solution to the problem of managing biodiversity in the Area is essentially one of better implementation of existing legal regimes and integration at the institutional level. While management of all the world's hydrothermal vent sites is an unrealistic goal, the possibility of developing internationally agreed criteria for the identification of sites of critical importance and sensitivity may be considered.[155]

155. Ibid.

The Unfulfilled Promise of the Seventies: Shipping and Developing Countries

Awni Behnam
United Nations Conference on Trade and Development, Geneva
President of the International Ocean Institute

PREFACE

In July 1976, I received a letter from Elisabeth Mann Borgese inviting me to participate in *Pacem in Maribus* VII, which was being held jointly with a special meeting of the Club of Rome on the New International Economic Order (NIEO) in Algeria, in October 1976. She explained the unique reason for holding *Pacem in Maribus* in conjunction with the special meeting of the Club of Rome and the Reshaping of the International Economic Order (RIEO) project. It was an attempt to integrate the RIEO proposals and the new international economic order into the specific area of ocean management, and she specifically asked me to address "The Economy of Shipping." In fact, the main question that the organizers were interested in was how to improve the participation of developing nations in international shipping business and seaborne trade. Elisabeth, very modestly, wrote that she wanted to learn as much as possible about the way liner conferences worked as a basis for discussion, and how they might be brought under public control for the benefit of poor nations.

At that time, I was lecturing at the Department of Maritime Studies, University of Wales Institute of Science and Technology (UWIST), and was only a few months away from submitting my doctorate thesis entitled "Ocean Freight Rates and the Developing Economy."[1] That invitation from Elisabeth to speak at PIM VII was to be the opening of a wonderful and rewarding friendship that endured until the day she departed in 2002.

At the time, I was not aware of the implication of that first meeting with Elisabeth and the bonds that it would build between us. It came at a time of a deepening and raging debate, both in academic circles and industry, on the subject of shipping and developing countries. Also, international organizations such as UNCTAD and IMCO (the precursor to IMO) had man-

1. A. Behnam, "Ocean Freight Rates and the Developing Economy, Volume I and II," (Ph.D. Thesis, UWIST, MAST, University of Wales, Cardiff, October 1976).

Ocean Yearbook 18: 453–487

dates and work programmes dealing with shipping questions and developing countries. Many conflicting views and proposals were being bandied about, debated and placed on the multilateral negotiating agenda. The international scene was like one large laboratory of ideas over shipping questions.

1976 was an almost pivotal year in the international debate on this subject and perhaps also the crowning point for many of the solutions to shipping issues that were being promoted. Elisabeth wished them to be brought to the forefront at the Algiers meeting. She had a reason, of course, to single out economic and commercial shipping issues for separate treatment, because she was already concerned that the law of the sea would not deal with it adequately from a perspective that was of concern to her, that is the question of justice and equity in the division of international labour in shipping and the integration of developing countries in world shipping.[2] At that time, I was not committed with UNCTAD, and I recall clearly that the paper that I delivered at the Algiers meeting, entitled "Liner Conferences, Developing Countries, and Consumer Policy," was not the paper Elisabeth expected or hoped for. This will be clarified later.

INTRODUCTION

The United Nations Conference on Trade and Development (UNCTAD)[3] was created in 1964[4] as a principal organ of the United Nations General

2. In the statement Elisabeth delivered to the opening of the meeting, she stated: "To fully integrate the work of the Law of the Sea Conference into the work of building the New International Economic Order does not mean, by any means, to distract the Law of the Sea Conference: or to ask it to try to solve all the world's problems and thereby to resolve nothing. It is a conceptual problem: it is a question of direction: of goal and purpose. In some areas the Law of the Sea Conference may indeed lead the building of the new order: it may be pattern setting. In other areas, where it depends on the building of this order by other means and fora, the very recognition of this fact may facilitate compromises at the Law of the Sea Conference. In both cases the joining of the issues would enhance both the building of the new international economic order and the making of the law of the sea. They potentiate each other." Pacem in Maribus VII, October 1976.

3. UNCTAD's main objective in the field of trade was to increase the volume of external trade of developing countries by enabling them to derive the greatest benefits from their exports and help in the developmental process of trade expansion. UNCTAD set out to tackle the international trade structure itself and could not be limited in its activities to purely addressing itself to certain needs of developing countries. For UNCTAD, that meant the comprehensive restructuring of international trade and the reorganization of international economic cooperation through rewriting the rules of the game in the establishment of a new international economic order.

4. UNCTAD held its first Conference in June 1964 in Geneva, and it has since held 10 quadrennial Conferences.

Assembly. The raison d'être of UNCTAD stemmed from that of the United Nations itself—to ensure world peace and harmony among nations. It became amply clear in the late 1950s, as many developing countries gained their independence, that peace could not be secured if there were worldwide economic disparities with consequential economic and social upheavals. Change in international economic relationships was needed, and the establishment of UNCTAD was deemed a response to that need, not only because of the growing disparity in levels of development and developing countries' declining share of international trade, but also because there existed no forum of an international character to deal with the comprehensive problems of trade and development at the global level.

Trade was envisaged as the engine of growth and development for fledgling economies and a vehicle by which developing countries could integrate themselves into the world economy so as to acquire the capacity to accumulate wealth and the capacity to deal with the kaleidoscope of development problems. In pursuit of better terms of trade and growth through trade, the economy and efficiency of the transport of trade (shipping) came under scrutiny. It was inevitable that an organization devoted to finding internationally acceptable solutions to international trade and development and facilitating the process involved therein would tackle the means of moving international trade shipping with the same vigour.

If there was to be a single landmark in the international debate on shipping, it would be UNCTAD. Had it not been for UNCTAD, there would not have been an international forum to discuss economic and commercial aspects of world shipping, and there would not have been a raging debate on the role of shipping in the developing economy. Both the debate and the role of UNCTAD led to expectations and to a promise inherent in the work of the organization, which began well before the Algiers meeting in 1976. In the early 1960s, prior to UNCTAD, the international shipping industry was on the eve of change and attracted attention and focus more than at any time in its history. It came under close scrutiny and study by academics, the media and governments.

THE TRADE AND SHIPPING SCENE—A PERSPECTIVE IN HISTORY

For most of the long haul of history prior to and even after World War II, international shipping tended to be controlled almost exclusively by a few maritime powers. That state of affairs largely reflected the main contours of international economic relations, the balance of power, colonialism, and the role of shipping in commercial policy, underscored to varying degrees by security considerations. The period 1947 to 1964 witnessed the birth and the struggle for existence of some 75 new and developing States. Those new nations watched with deep concern the decline in their terms of trade, which were being further aggravated by the heavy impact of rising ocean freight rates and the inadequacies associated with the then existing institutional mechanisms in international shipping.

Those newly independent nations became very conscious of, inter alia, the adverse impact on their balance of payments of the outflow of foreign exchange in payment for invisible transactions, the major one of which was shipping freight rates,[5] and the extent to which ocean freight rates acted as tariff and nontariff barriers to their exports.

UNCTAD, in its analysis of the shipping industry,[6] pointed out that during the latter part of the 19th century the economic power of individual shipowners on most trading routes had become greater than that of individual shippers. The organization of shipping services was determined by the needs and desires of the shipowners and the competitive pressures facing them. The weaker partner in the contract of carriage, the shipper, had to accept and conform to the services and conditions provided by the shipowner.[7]

A significant change in that balance of power between shippers and shipowners began in the second half of the 20th century. The growth in the size of enterprises that occurred in developed countries to achieve technological and managerial economies of scale had led to increases in the size of shipments. As a result, many cargoes that had formerly traveled by liner parcels began to travel in full shiploads. Where possibilities of consolidating cargoes had not been put into practice before, shippers began to realize that, if they acted collectively, they could become powerful enough to bargain with shipowners. Thus, a system of shippers' councils and consultation machinery was developed in Western Europe as a formalized machinery enabling the partners to the shipping contract to meet and talk. However, the economic strength of shippers in new and emerging developing countries in relation to that of shipowners was equivalent to that of shipowners in Western Europe in the 19th century. That's where the developing countries found themselves in the early 1960s.

Shipping remained the dominant mode of transport. Ninety percent of world cargoes were moving by sea, and the cost and quality of transport was a determining factor as to whether goods and commodities moved or not. Economic growth, which is linked to international seaborne trade

5. UNCTAD. "Ocean shipping and freight rates in developing countries," *UNCTAD I: Financing and Invisibles, Volume V.* UN Publication Sales No. 64.II.B.15. Geneva: 1964, par. 16, p. 225.

6. UNCTAD. *UNCTAD–Shipping in the Seventies.* TD/177. Geneva: 1972, p. 3.

7. Such imbalance was clearly pointed out by UNCTAD in its study on the Hague Rules which exempted shipowners from liability for loss of goods in transit, and it was discussed in full in the famous report of UNCTAD on Bills of Lading UNCTAD. *Bills of Lading.* UN publication, Sales No. E.72.II.D.2. Geneva: 1972, pp. 32–51.

growth, could not be separated or insulated from the factors affecting or induced by the international shipping industry. In fact, the structure and direction of trade and the organization of shipping services and markets were closely linked and interdependent. Developing countries were soon to discover that the structure of the world shipping market did not make it easy for them to increase their participation in the world carriage of seaborne trade, nor had they the capacity to protect their interests as shippers of cargoes.

By the mid-1960s, a raging economic discussion on the structure and efficiency of the shipping industry was in full swing in academic circles, with the virtues of the free market in shipping and particularly the level and structure of freight trade coming increasingly under scrutiny among academic and specialized media communities.

For the developing countries as well as the UNCTAD secretariat, the shipping scene was defined by a number of features: in general cargo trade, which accounted for 25 percent of world seaborne trade in tonnage and more than 50 percent in value, the dominant position was held by traditional maritime shipowners operating cartel-type organizations of liner shipping conferences,[8] and that constituted a formidable barrier to fair and free competition; in the oil and dry bulk trades, transportation took place mainly within vertically integrated concerns primarily under the control of transnational corporations, and only a very small portion of the total dry bulk and oil trade was offered at shipping exchanges located in developed market economy countries.

UNCTAD I: THE LAUNCHING OF THE PROCESS—1964 AND BEYOND[9]

Prior to the creation of UNCTAD, the shipping industry had been outside international economic regulations or action, while trade had been subject to international regulation under the General Agreement on Tariff and Trade (GATT). Prior to UNCTAD, there was no international forum in which economic and commercial questions relating to maritime transport could be discussed. IMCO (now IMO) was at the time mainly concerned with universal standard setting and had no mandate to deal with commercial and economic aspects of international shipping.

8. Liner shipping describes maritime transport by regular shipping lines that publish in advance their ports of call and tariffs. This is distinct from tramp shipping that refers to transport performed irregularly depending on demand and negotiated freight rates.

9. An unattributed version of this section was written by the author in 1984 as a contribution to the commemoration of the 20th anniversary of UNCTAD. *The History of UNCTAD, 1964-1984*. E.85.II.D.6. 1985, pp. 130–42.

At its creation in 1964, UNCTAD received a unique mandate in the area of shipping. It was the sole international organization mandated to deal with the economic and commercial aspects of international shipping. The mandate also reflected the contours of the external environment that surrounded the creation of UNCTAD—a North-South divide, a rich/poor confrontation, and the East-West Cold War. This was also the period of struggle for economic survival and a rising militancy in promoting speedy economic achievement by the newly independent nations.

The first UNCTAD Conference in 1964 provided the opportunity to raise issues related to the economic and commercial aspects of shipping in a multilateral context and in particular the level of freight rates, focusing on the impact of maritime transport on the balance of payments of developing countries.

It was not an easy matter to bring shipping under the scrutiny of a multilateral forum that itself had come into existence against the wishes of most of the developed countries, which included the traditional maritime nations, particularly since that forum was to seek ways and means of improving the participation of developing countries and integrating them in a more equitable manner into the world shipping scene.

The efforts of developing countries at the first UNCTAD Conference did not go beyond an initial agreement on "Common Measures of Understanding,"[10] an agreement representing the lowest tier of possible negotiated agreement, on how to treat the issue of shipping on the international agenda. The "Understanding" concentrated on liner trades (that were at that time the services in which developing countries were largely interested and whose operations and monopolistic practices were self-regulated by a cartel-type system of "liner conferences),[11] regarded by developing country interests as not taking enough account" of their legitimate trading and shipping concerns and needs. The "Understanding" was geared principally at securing closer consultations between shippers and conferences in regard to the adequacy of shipping services. It supported the idea of international financing and of technical assistance for the improvement of port operations and connected inland transport facilities in developing countries on favorable terms and conditions. It also encouraged the establishment and expan-

10. The Third Committee at UNCTAD I constituted a Working Party on Shipping (Document E/CONF.46/C.3/L.10) which, after 13 meetings and historically revealing animated deliberations, often with raised tempers, concluded an agreement that resulted in the celebrated document E/CONF.46/C.3/L.46 of 9 May 1964 on *Common Measures of Understanding on Shipping Questions* (Annex A.IV.22 to the Final Act of the Conference).

11. C. H. C. Mackenzie, M. E. Power, T. L. McDorman, *Liner Shipping Conferences: An Annotated Bibliography* (Toronto: D.C. Heath and Company, Lexington Books, 1985).

sion of developing countries' merchant marines on the basis of sound economic criteria[12] and as an important element in import substitution policy.

Equally important, the Common Understanding recognized the need to establish a permanent intergovernmental organ where deliberations on shipping questions could continue, providing the foundation for the Committee on Shipping in UNCTAD.

The forces emanating from the first Conference and the momentum gathered by developing countries created sufficient pressure to institutionalize shipping questions in UNCTAD. Consequently, when the Trade and Development Board[13] met at its first session in April 1965, the developing countries proposed that terms of reference be formulated for the body dealing with shipping matters. By resolution 11(I) of 29 April 1965, the Trade and Development Board decided to establish a separate committee and not, as some had anticipated, a working group of the Committee on Invisibles and Financing. The Committee on Shipping held its first regular session in Geneva in November 1965 and its first special session in July 1966.

Under its terms of reference, the Committee on Shipping was, inter alia,[14]

- To promote understanding and cooperation in the field of shipping and to be available for the harmonization of shipping policies of Governments and regional economic groupings that fall within the competence of the Trade and Development Board;
- To study and make recommendations on the ways in which and the conditions under which international shipping can most effectively contribute to the expansion of world trade, in particular of the trade of developing countries. Particular attention should be paid to economic aspects of shipping, to those shipping matters that affect the trade and balance of payments of developing countries, and to related shipping policies and legislation of Governments on matters that fall within the competence of the Trade and Development Board;
- To study measures to improve port operations and connected inland transport facilities, with particular reference to those ports whose trade is of economic significance to the country in which they are situated or to world trade;

12. The term "sound economic criteria" was never clearly defined and as a consequence it was to "haunt" the negotiations in UNCTAD in the 1970s.

13. The Trade and Development Board is the governing body of UNCTAD's intergovernmental machinery during the periods between the four yearly conferences of the organization.

14. See *Rules of Procedures of the Main Committees of the Trade and Development Board*. UNCTAD. TD/B/740. Geneva: UNCTAD, 1979.

- To make recommendations designed to secure, where appropriate, the participation of shipping lines of developing countries in shipping conferences on equitable terms;
- To promote cooperation between shippers and the conferences by establishing a well-organized consultation machinery with adequate procedures for hearing and remedying complaints by the formation of shippers' councils or other suitable bodies on a national and regional basis;
- To study and make recommendations with a view to promoting the development of merchant marines, in particular of developing countries.

It became clear that developing countries, prior to the establishment of the Shipping Committee of UNCTAD, did not play an active role in the institutional and structural developments of the world shipping industry. The dominant institutions in the organization of the world shipping remained those established by developed countries during the colonial period.

When the first UNCTAD conference met, the developed/developing countries' relationship on shipping matters was characterized by a general feeling of disappointment and frustration, with differences in viewpoints and a sharp divergence in approach. UNCTAD I launched a process with a view to bridging this gap over the long term.[15]

Historically, the domination of world shipping by the former colonial powers had served to confine developing countries to a role of passive suppliers of raw materials. Developing countries were not merely effectively excluded from participating in an economically viable activity, but also had their bargaining position weakened by controls their trading partners exercised over the processing, marketing, transportation, and distribution of their products. Foreign control of transport generally restricted the ability of exporting developing countries to influence either the competitiveness of their products or the percentage of the final consumer prices that their producers received. It was therefore not surprising that these countries embraced the Committee on Shipping and the policies developed by UNCTAD. Consequently, most of the developing countries, organized within the Group of 77,[16] began to view their main shipping problems as concerning

15. E. Gold, *Maritime Transport* (Toronto: Lexington Books, 1981), p. 271. E. Gold describes the atmosphere prevailing as that of vigorous opposition and almost shrill alarm in response to the demands and proposals put forward by developing countries at UNCTAD I. In particular the major shipping countries, all members of Group B, opposed placing any shipping matters on the Conference agenda.

16. The Group of 77 representing a coalition of developing countries was formed at the end of the UNCTAD I in 1964 when 77 developing countries signed a joint declaration of solidarity, thus officially launching the group system in multilateral diplomacy. Today, the number of members of the Group is 134.

the existence or absence of a national fleet. They further determined that their shipping policy in relation to fleet development could not be based on purely commercial rate-of-return criterion, and they argued for a wider socioeconomic criterion.

Developing countries complained that their shipping problems ranged from complete dependence on foreign flags for the sea transport of their international trade, inability to expand their national merchant marines, and the heavy burden of the freight bill on their balance of payments,[17] to the lack of guarantees for foreign exchange needed to purchase vessels, technical and commercial know-how, training facilities, and repair and maintenance facilities. Perhaps most prominent was their disquiet over conference practices; the liner conference system, in existence since 1875, characterized very clearly the power of the traditional shipowners. That monolithic structure of closed-door monopolies had become widespread and dominated every major trade route by the 1960s. Developing countries faced difficulties with respect to admission of their national shipping lines to these conferences, suffering the consequences of a system of unilateral fixing of freight rates, discriminatory practices, stifling competition by systems of tying shippers, and the refusal of conferences to hold meaningful consultations with shippers from developing countries.

Thus, the approach of developing countries to the question of shipping, which was to shape the events from UNCTAD I (1964) to UNCTAD VI[18] (1983), were based on four policy objectives:[19]

a. To influence the structure and level of freight rates to lessen the impact of high freight rates on their traditional and nontraditional exports;
b. To establish and expand their own national merchant fleets and their rights to assist such fleets in their infant stage;
c. To rewrite international shipping legislation and the basic framework of regulation;
d. To create an environment conducive to the improvement of their human resources and physical infrastructure.

In 1965, the UNCTAD Committee on Shipping provided member countries with an international, intergovernmental forum for the examination of

17. See N. Singh, *Achievements of UNCTAD I and UNCTAD II in the Field of Shipping and Invisibles* (New Delhi: S. Chand and Co., 1969), pp. 136–59.

18. As indicated later, shipping as such was not on the agenda of UNCTAD VII. At UNCTAD VIII, it was treated in the context of trade in service, and, at UNCTAD IX, there was no reference to shipping.

19. See L. M. S. Rajaw, "Trade and Shipping Needs of Developing Countries," in *Shipping and Developing Countries*, No. 582 (Washington, D.C.: Carnegie Endowment for International Peace, March 1971).

international shipping questions on a continuing basis with the aim of finding acceptable international solutions to conflicts and problems that gave rise to concerns, particularly in developing countries. The Committee, assisted by the analytical research and reports of the secretariat, addressed the structure of shipping markets and the ability of shipowners in developing countries to compete freely and on a fair and equitable basis for cargoes, particularly those generated by their own foreign trade.

The forum of the Committee on Shipping was deemed by developing countries particularly necessary because self-regulation in certain sectors of the shipping industry, especially the liner trade, did not adequately take into account the needs of shippers or the economic interests of the countries served. Moreover, it did not provide the necessary balance of negotiating power between shippers and shipowners. The work of UNCTAD towards a restructuring of the shipping industry to take into account the interests of developing countries inevitably came to focus on the elaboration and adoption of several international instruments and conventions.[20]

At its fourth session in 1970, the Committee on Shipping approved its work programme, which focused on the protection of shippers' interests, establishment or expansion of merchant marines in developing countries, development of ports, technological change, international legislation on shipping, and technical assistance.

Assisted by a proactive secretariat that produced an avalanche of research, analysis, and reports, triggering controversy at the time, UNCTAD moved very aggressively into numerous dimensions of shipping, insisting upon the need for international accountability of an industry that had remained remarkably impervious to public supervision. In particular, the liner conference system was challenged to secure admission of developing countries' merchant marines on more favorable terms than in the past. It pressed for expansion of the merchant marines of developing countries through concessionary financing for the purchase of ships, examined the value of cargo reservation to national vessels, and began a review of existing international shipping legislation.[21]

20. The shipping industry in the 1960s was showing signs of extremely grave problems. The dissatisfaction of shippers with conference pricing policies, the escalating freight rates, the arbitrary decisions on services and the imbalance in the obligations between shipowners, shippers and conferences in particular were sufficient reasons to start the dialogue between the traditional maritime nations and the newcomers—"the developing countries." The inception of the Committee on Shipping, it was thought at the time, would divert the industry from a course that could have led to chaos, unilateral actions and perhaps strife and antagonism between the traditional maritime carriers and the aspiring developing countries.

21. For a more detailed discussion, see I. Haji, "UNCTAD and shipping," *Journal of World Trade Law* 6, no. 1 (January-February, 1972): 58–118. J. J. Oyevour, "Technological Change and the Future of Shipping in Developing Countries," in

Walters,[22] in explaining the reasons for UNCTAD's impact in the field of shipping, noted that "unlike most areas of interest to UNCTAD, there was no other international organization, which viewed these types of shipping questions as falling within its mandate. Thus, UNCTAD as an international organization had the field to itself in a way that was not true of other fields such as international trade, aid, and monetary affairs, for example. The expertise developed by UNCTAD in the shipping field had enhanced the seriousness with which governments and other international organizations have responded to UNCTAD initiatives in this issue area."

In the Shipping Committee debates, developing countries strongly focused on the issue of fair share in the participation of developing countries in world shipping and consequently on the institutional barriers to such participation, namely the liner conference system, the open registry system, and the control exercised by transnational corporations (TNCs) over the carriage of bulk cargoes through vertically integrated operations.

There is no denying that other motivations also existed that propelled developing countries towards participation in fleet ownership as a policy remedy. Political factors such as economic nationalism played its role.[23] However, as traditional carriers continued to begrudge increased participation by developing countries, they aggravated the situation, with developing countries demanding greater participation beyond that of nationalist motives.

Assisted by major studies,[24] developing countries used to the full their newly found power of majority vote in UNCTAD to impose change through international legislation, with a view to leveling the playing field in international shipping and dismantling the power of shipping cartels to decide unilaterally on shipping matters that impacted the economic welfare of their countries.

It was not surprising that the first target for such action was the liner sector and the liner conference system. For a policy of national fleet expansion to succeed, collateral had to be found to obtain adequate shipping fi-

---

Shipping and Developing Countries, No. 582 (Washington, D.C.: Carnegie Endowment for International Peace, March 1971).

22. R. S. Walters, "UNCTAD: Intervener between poor and rich states," *Journal of World Trade Law* 7, no. 5 (September-October, 1973): 534.

23. See A. Behnam, "Political factors and the evolution of national fleets in developing countries," *Maritime Studies and Management* 3, no. 3 (January 1976): 131.

24. UNCTAD *Establishment or Expansion of Merchant Marines in Developing Countries.* UNCTAD. TD/26/Rev.1, Sales No. E.69.II.D.1. Geneva: UNCTAD, 1968; UNCTAD. *The Liner Conference System.* UNCTAD. TD/B/C.4/62/Rev.1, Sales No. E.70.II.D.9. Geneva: UNCTAD, 1970; UNCTAD. *The Regulation of Liner Conferences (a code of conduct for the liner conference system).* UNCTAD. TD/104/Rev.1, Sales No. E.72.II.D.13. Geneva: UNCTAD, 1972; UNCTAD. *Level and Structure of Freight Rates.* UNCTAD. TD/B/C.4/38/Rev.1, Sales No. E.69.II.D.13. Geneva: UNCTAD, 1969; UNCTAD. *Terms of Shipment.* UNCTAD. Sales No. E.69.II.14. Geneva: UNCTAD, 1968.

nancing for ship acquisition by developing countries. For the majority of developing countries, the only and obvious collateral was access to cargoes and guarantees for the carriage of such cargoes. Hence, albeit not solely for these reasons, great efforts went into the elaboration of the United Nations Convention on a Code of Conduct for Liner Conferences and the famous cargo sharing (40-40-20) formula.[25] No less important was the follow-up work aimed at phasing out open registries, which later culminated in the current United Nations convention on open registries.[26] In addition, there were numerous negotiations, resolutions, and decisions covering the bulk cargoes sector and multimodal transport.

In short, there was a deliberate policy aimed at changing the external environment and the international structure of shipping by altering the rules of the game for the economic and commercial conduct of international shipping whereby, through legal instruments, resolutions, and decisions, it would become possible for developing countries to acquire a greater and increasing share of world shipping activities and particularly ownership of national shipping fleets. This policy was complemented by two sets of targets promoted in the International Development Strategies for the 1970s[27] and 1980s. These targets stipulated that developing countries were to be assisted, inter alia, by the actions of the Committee on Shipping in acquiring 10 percent, then 20 percent of the world fleet by 1990.

DEVELOPING COUNTRIES AND WORLD SHIPPING—STRATEGIES AND EXPECTATIONS OF THE SEVENTIES

In 1976, the relative share of developing countries in world shipping showed a declining share of 6 percent, and that was more than 10 years since the establishment of the Committee on Shipping in UNCTAD. It was therefore not surprising that the proposals by Elisabeth for the New International Economic Order and the Law of the Sea at the Algiers meeting were in strong support of those aspirations of developing countries. These proposals went so far as to suggest that liner-shipping conferences be converted to public utilities and international shipping come under international register.[28] This

25. See Article 2 of the *United Nations Conference of Plenipotentiaries on a Code of Conduct for Liner Conferences, Volume II, Final Act.* Sales No. E.75.II.D.11. New York: UN Publications, 1975.

26. *United Nations Convention on Conditions for Registration of Ships.* United Nations. TD/RS/CONF/23. (adopted by the United Nations Conference on Conditions for Registration of Ships on 7 February 1986.)

27. International Development Strategy adopted by the General Assembly in Resolution 2626(XXV) (New York 24 October 1970).

28. International Ocean Institute, "The New International Economic Order and the Law of the Sea—A Projection" (Occasional Paper no. 4, 1976). "An effective international licensing system obviously would put the countries of open registry out of business. Ideally, the new law of the sea should combine the preventive and

was perhaps a remarkable example of what the debate in the 1970s was all about. In fact, during that time, developing countries, being convinced of the impediments to free and fair competition in shipping had made up their mind as to the nature and trajectory of their maritime policies, placing priority on asset ownerships and national and international intervention through legally binding instruments.

The promise of the 1970s was pervasive. As UNCTAD V (1979) in Manila unfolded with Mr. L. Fadika, Minister of Merchant Marines of Côte d'Ivoire leading the Group of 77, a comprehensive strategy was in the making that responded to the then stated aspirations of developing countries.

Targeted Fleet Development Strategy

Developing countries staked their claim to an equitable share in shipping on the basis of the direct relationship between trade generation and degree of involvement in shipping. Whereas in 1979 developing countries exported over 60 percent of world seaborne trade and accounted for 40 percent of world trade, they owned less than 10 percent of the world deadweight tonnage. In their bulk trade, developing countries owned less than 6 percent of world bulk carriers, although they exported 90 percent of world tanker cargoes and over one-third of dry bulk cargoes. The historical evolution of seaborne trade and shipping fleets is illustrated in Fig. 1-4.

Developing countries collectively had formulated a strategy within the corridors of the Committee on Shipping for the growth of their national fleet so that by the end of the second United Nations Development Decade (1980) they would achieve a target share of 10 percent of the world fleet. This was followed by a second target, set in 1980 in Resolution 35/36 of the United Nations General Assembly, for the third United Nations Development Decade. It called upon the international community, inter alia, to continue to take the necessary steps to enable developing countries to expand their national and multinational merchant fleets, so as to increase their share substantially with a view to coming as close as possible to 20 percent of the deadweight tonnage of the world merchant fleet by 1990.[29]

---

the corrective approach, and the licensing of ships should be entrusted to a strengthened IMCO. Some way would thus have to be found to bring the Liner Conference from the private to the public sector, or at least to a mixed private/public sector: either by stipulating that Liner Conference decisions, to be enforceable, have to be approved by the IMCO Assembly; or by making Liner Conferences into 'Public International Enterprises' under the political control of the IMCO Assembly. If the New International Economic Order is to become concrete, IMCO, and the Law of the Sea, will have to deal with the multinationals operating on the seabed."

29. Resolution 35/36 of the General Assembly. It is often pointed out that these targets were reached. However, only a few developing countries, particularly oil-exporting and South Asian countries, achieved successful expansion of their fleets. Also, the majority of vessels owned by developing countries were in fact qualitatively inferior to those of the competitors, the traditional shipowners.

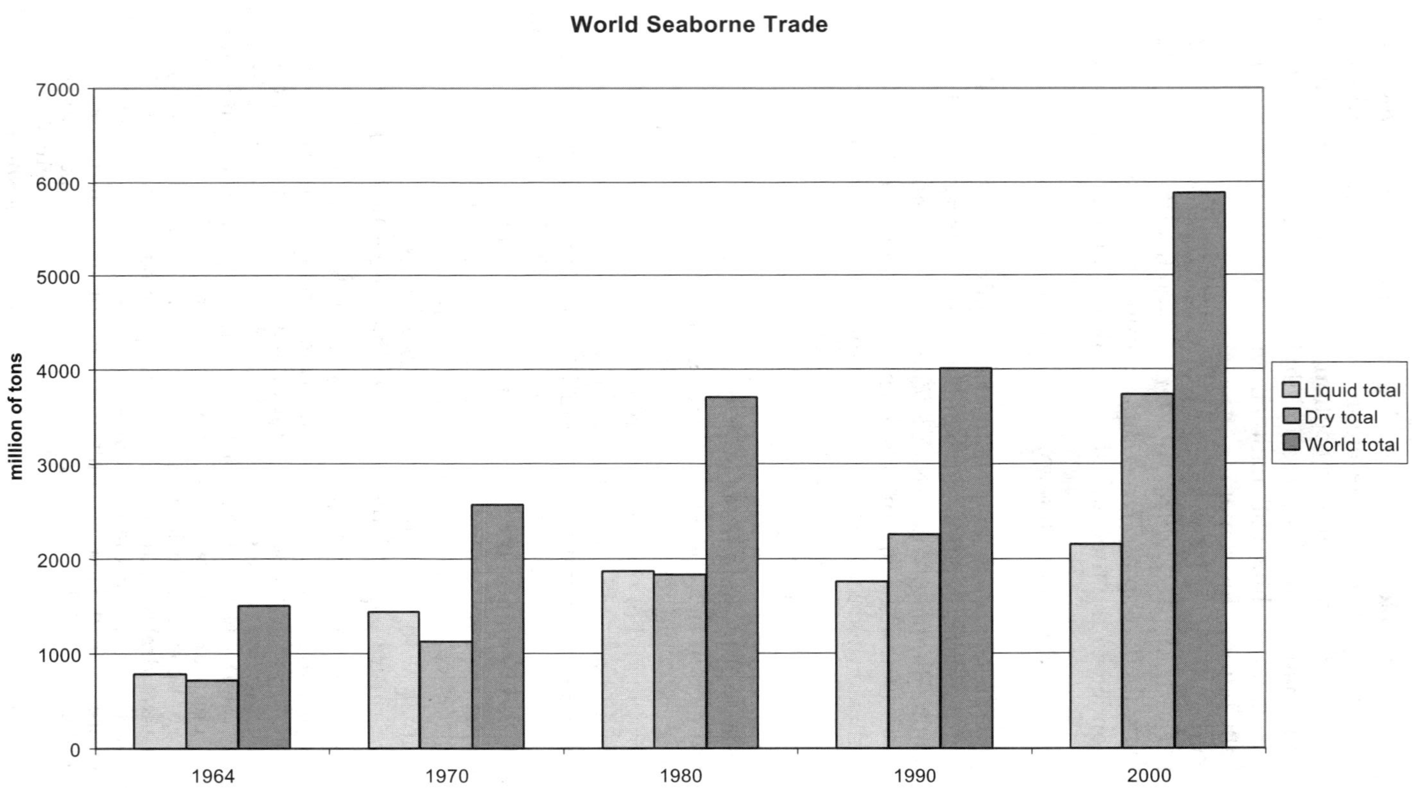

FIG. 1.—World seaborne trade, 1964–2000. SOURCE.—UNCTAD, *Annual Review of Maritime Transport,* (Geneva: UNCTAD, 2002).

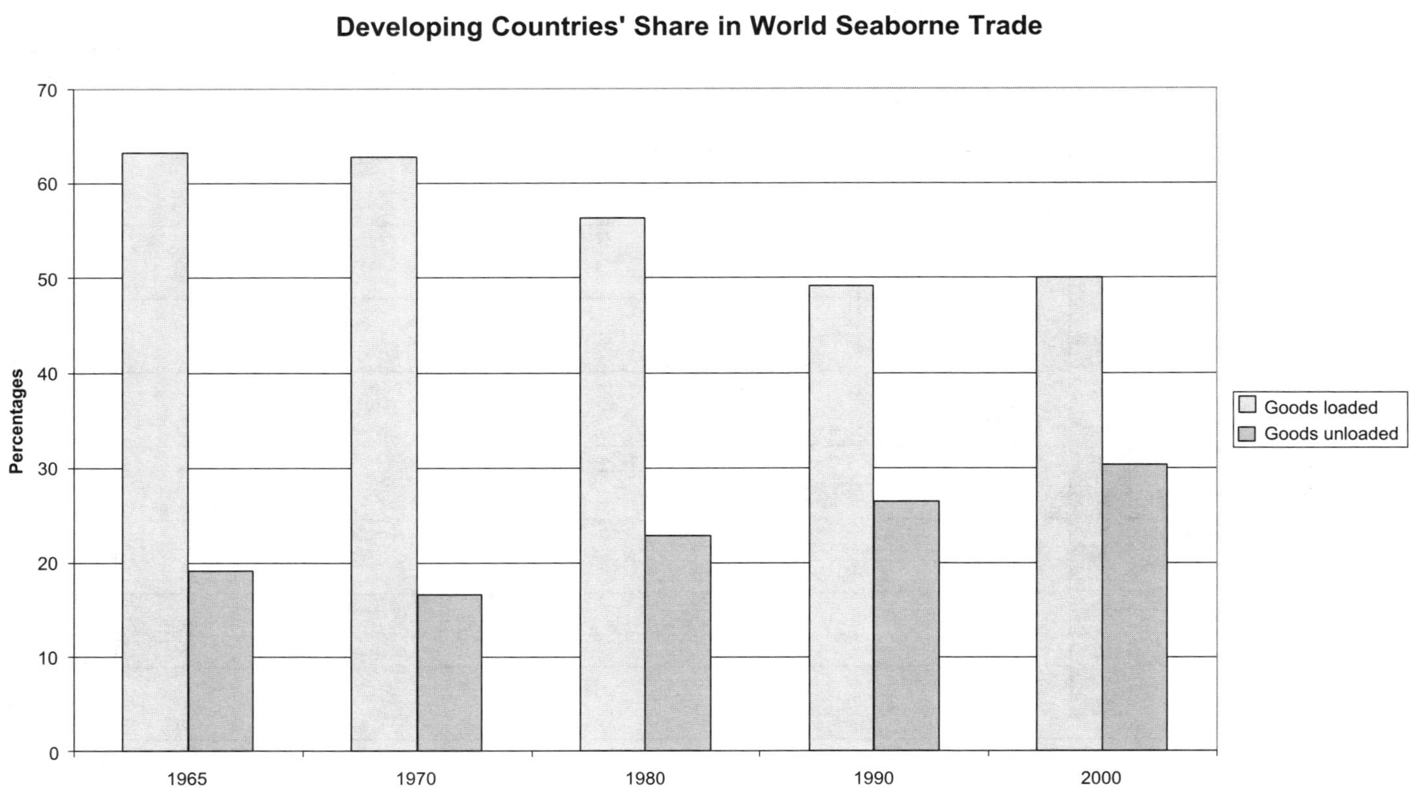

FIG. 2.—Developing countries' share in world seaborne trade, 1965–2000.
SOURCE.—UNCTAD, *Annual Review of Maritime Transport*, (Geneva: UNCTAD, 2002).

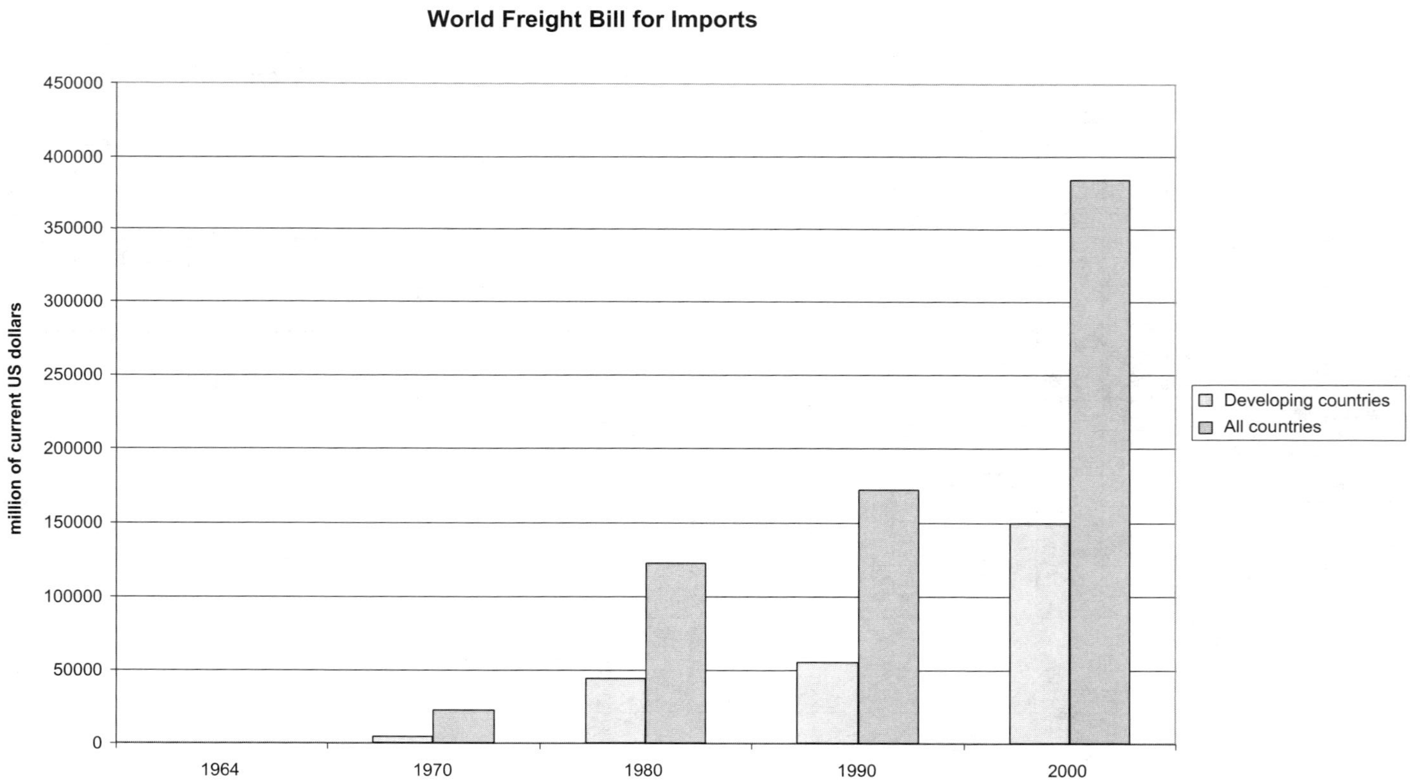

FIG. 3.—World freight bill for imports, 1964–2000. SOURCE.—UNCTAD, *Annual Review of Maritime Transport*, (Geneva: UNCTAD, 2002).

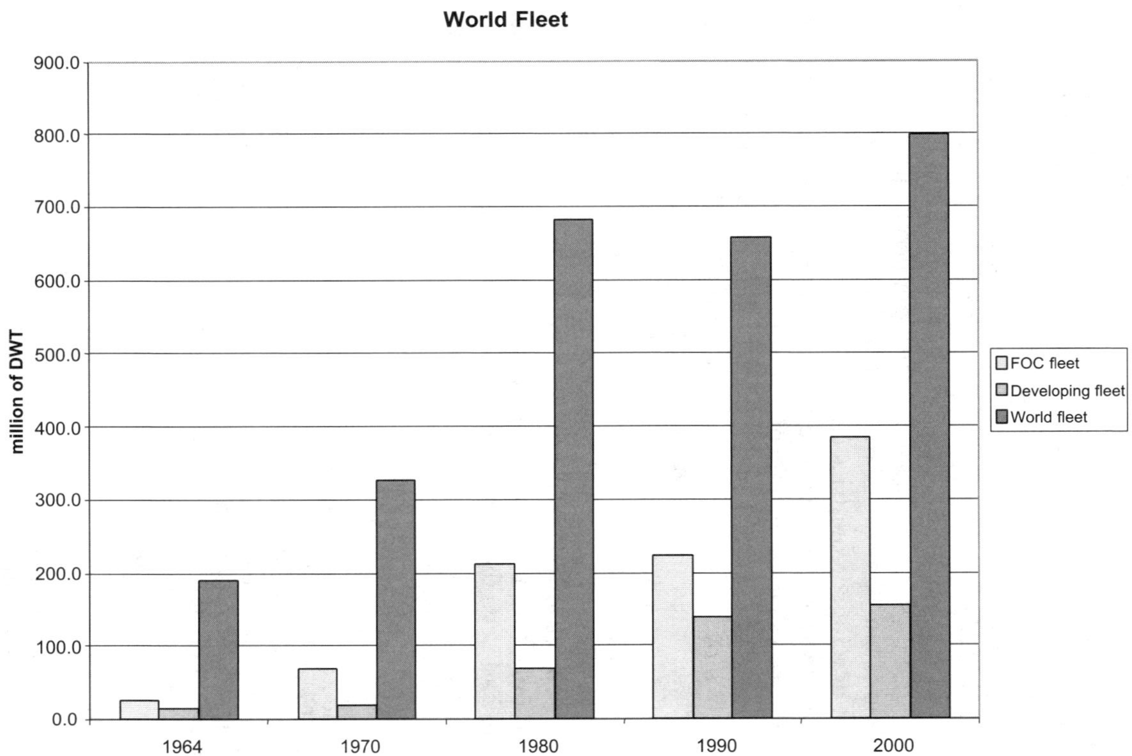

FIG. 4.—World fleet size in million dead weight tons, 1964–2000. SOURCE.—UNCTAD, *Annual Review of Maritime Transport,* (Geneva: UNCTAD, 2002).

Action in Bulk Cargo Shipping

At UNCTAD V (1979), the most untouchable of the shipping sectors, the transport of bulk cargoes, was brought to the negotiating table and placed on the agenda of the Conference. It had always been argued, particularly by traditional maritime countries, that unlike liner trade, trade in bulk cargoes was free and subject to the play of market forces.[30] It was argued that, unlike liner shipping, no institutionalized barriers existed in bulk shipping. However, the UNCTAD secretariat's views on the transport of major bulk commodities, including hydrocarbons, were markedly different. The secretariat insisted that bulk shipping was to a large extent controlled by transnational corporations and that the market was not as free as the traditional shipowners and developed countries claimed.

A bitter debate was to develop in which developing countries made claims for bulk cargo sharing arrangements not unlike those in relation to the Code of Conduct for Liner Conferences. Obligatory 50-50 sharing formulas for shuttle movement were deemed very possible. Developing countries openly declared their determination to actively pursue participation in the transport of their bulk cargoes. They made it known that—in the absence of an equitable solution—they would resort to unilateral actions that would grant them what they termed "fair access to bulk cargoes."

Developing countries felt confident that sooner or later their right to the carriage of bulk cargoes would be recognized by the traditional maritime nations, as had been the case in the Code of Conduct for Liner Conferences, and that their trading partners would no longer treat them as passive suppliers of bulk commodities. The expectations of the Group of 77 were euphorically high.[31]

30. See "The Economies of Bulking Cargoes," note by the UNCTAD secretariat, TD/B/C.4/67 and TD/B/C.4/203. It is ironic that support for UNCTAD's point of view came rather too late when Professor David Moreby, after analysing dry bulk cargo and tanker markets, also concluded that many factors distort the relative, competitive positions of owners, shippers, and charterers and confirm the fact that shipping has never been—nor ever will be—in a truly "free" market place. Mr. David H. Moresby, Professor, Polytechnic South West, U.K. in his lecture delivered at the seminar "Management Development Programme for Senior Shipping Executives," sponsored by Shipping Credit & Investment Company of India in collaboration with the Centre for Maritime Cooperation held in April 1990 in Bombay.

31. Resolution 120 (V), adopted at UNCTAD V (1979), called upon governments to take steps to ensure for developing countries equitable participation in the transport of all cargoes and more specially bulk cargoes generated by their own trade by national vessels of the respective trading countries and also recommended equitable participation in bilateral trading agreements, with the recommendation that the contracts between developing and developed countries for sale or purchase of bulk cargoes should stipulate that a substantial and increasing proportion be carried by national vessels. It is important to understand that developing countries' insistence on legally sanctioned cargo reservation measures through sharing formu-

Phasing Out Flags of Convenience

In the late 1970s, it was inevitable that UNCTAD, the Committee on Shipping, and the developing countries would focus their attention on perhaps the most unacceptable face of international maritime transport, the existence of flags of convenience. This cancerous phenomenon in world shipping had spread progressively, mainly in the bulk sector.[32] Flags of Convenience accounted for some 28 percent of the world fleet by 1978. UNCTAD was convinced that the flags of convenience phenomenon lay at the root of the irrational and erratic development of the world fleet.

In 1978, a major report on flags of convenience was produced by UNCTAD,[33] bringing the issue to the forefront of international action and scrutiny. The developing countries, supported by the UNCTAD secretariat, considered that flags of convenience constituted a major threat to international shipping and a main impediment to the transfer of shipping to developing countries in line with their comparative advantage.

Developing countries, including labour-supplying developing countries to open registries, with the exception of open registries themselves, called for the phasing out of flags of convenience. Developing countries contend that their ability to participate in world shipping was heavily impaired by the high concentration of world fleet ownership in the hands of traditional maritime owners and that that state of affairs was due to their ability to register tonnage under flags of convenience.

The expansion of flag of convenience fleets was deemed without doubt to have a detrimental effect upon the orderly expansion of fleets of developing countries. The owners of these vessels were largely faceless men who concealed their identities behind the veil of nominal holding companies.[34]

---

las such as 50-50 or the code's 40-40-20 was the only means available to them to assist and support their fledging infant fleets. Most of the fleets of traditional maritime nations grew and prospered through many forms of assistance they received and were still receiving in the form of subsidization—shipbuilding subsidies, direct operating subsidies, tax privileges, et cetera. Developing countries could not match that type of assistance because of the scarcity of financial resources available to them, and if they had resorted to unilateral cargo reservation, they would have faced brutal retaliation and withdrawal of shipping services.

32. In the late 1980s and 1990s as the conference system declined and nationality of vessels became of less consequence, the flags of convenience phenomena spread to liner shipping.

33. UNCTAD. *Report of the Ad Hoc Intergovernmental Working Group on the Economic Consequences of the Existence or Lack of a Genuine Link between Vessel and Flag of Registry*. UNCTAD. TD/B/C.4/177. Geneva: UNCTAD, February, 1978, Annex to the report, p. 1.

34. See UNCTAD. *Beneficial Ownership of Open Registry Fleets*. UNCTAD V. Document TD/222/Supp.1. Geneva: UNCTAD, May 1979, and UNCTAD. TD/B/AC.1/7. Geneva: UNCTAD, October 1979.

The consequences of flags of convenience[35] and all their ramifications, whether economic, social, environmental, or even moral, were debated. Only those who were privy to that heated debate and soul searching could understand why phasing flags of convenience out was the first choice. But this debate was the precursor to the adoption of the United Nations Convention on Conditions for Registration of Ships under the auspices of UNCTAD.[36]

Implementation of the Code of Conduct for Liner Conferences

The International Convention on a Code of Conduct for Liner Conferences was adopted in 1974 but took time to enter into force[37] because of the stringent conditions involved. There were strong indications that support for the Code was gaining momentum. The 40-40-20 formula became a brand name.

35. Developing countries, supported by the UNCTAD secretariat, argued that the main consequence of open registration is that it enables the traditional maritime countries to maintain their domination over world shipping—despite their increasing inability to operate under their own flags on account of their high labour costs and scarcity of seafarers. At the beginning of the 1970s these countries owned 86 percent of the total world dwt tonnage: they still own a very high percentage (68 percent in 1996 and 74 percent in 2000), but whereas their national flag fleets have declined from 65 to 26 percent of the world total, the percentage that they operate under flags of convenience has increased almost correspondingly. If market forces had been allowed to operate freely, much of this tonnage would have been transferred to developing countries, which can operate economically under their own flags. In other sectors of the world economy, the transnationals have been forced to set up subsidiaries in low-cost countries to obtain cheaper labour, but, in shipping, the open registry phenomenon constitutes an artificial barrier to this natural development. Further, although the transnationals benefit from the cheaper crew costs that they gain by operating under flags of convenience, these cost savings are only to a limited extent passed on to consumers, particularly in the bulk sectors, where the FOC fleets mainly operate. See UNCTAD. *The Repercussions of Phasing Out Open Registries.* UNCTAD. TD/B/C.4/AC.1/5. Geneva: UNCTAD, September 1979, p. 14, par. 43.

36. See also A. Behnam and P. Faust, "Twilight of Flag State Control," in *Ocean Yearbook 17,* ed. E. Mann Borgese, A. Chircop and M. McConnell (Chicago: University of Chicago Press, 2002), pp. 167–192.

37. The Code of Conduct was adopted at a United Nations Conference of Plenipotentiaries convened by the General Assembly and meeting under the auspices of UNCTAD in 1974. On 6 April 1983, the requirements for entry into force of the Convention on a Code of Conduct for Liner Conferences were fulfilled due to ratification by the Federal Republic of Germany and accession by the Netherlands, the 57th and 58th countries to subscribe to the instrument as Contracting Parties bringing into account 20,842,921 gross registered tons or 28.67 percent of the relevant world liner tonnage (24 countries representing 25 percent was required to bring it into force). The Code of Conduct entered into force on 6 October 1983 and has been ratified and acceded to by 78 States. UNCTAD. *UN Convention on a Code of Conduct for Liner Conferences.* TD/CODE/13/Add.1. Geneva: UNCTAD, 1975.

It was the centerpiece of developing countries' policies and strategies to achieve increasing and equitable participation in world shipping. It was the single most important structural change brought about by the sheer political will of developing countries in the late 1960s and early 1970s. While it protected the Conference cartel system itself, it nevertheless opened the door for developing countries to join their trading partners in sharing in the carriage of their liner trade without fear of retaliation.

In the minds of the majority of developing country policy makers, it was clear that the scope of application of the Code and their newly acquired right to participation were not limited to *conference trade* but covered all *liner trade.* That was a very basic premise in the aspirations of developing countries. Furthermore, the Code provided them with consultative machinery that allowed the State to be a partner in the decision making of Conferences, particularly concerning the level and structure of freight rates. Through the Code, developing countries had gained rights that would have been inconceivable prior to the establishment of UNCTAD, whether in respect of the admission of their new lines and the institutionalization of consultative machinery or in respect of the ability of their shippers to influence freight charges. A particular advantage was the mandatory machinery for the settlement of disputes and conciliations backed by an institutional machinery.[38] All that was needed was for the Convention to enter into force quickly, as developing countries prepared themselves to acquire and operate liner ships in the Conferences serving the liner trade.

The Road to the United Nations Convention on International Multimodal Transport of Goods

As early as 1973, UNCTAD began to work in earnest on the question of multimodal transport. Developing countries wished to address the economic and social consequences of new technologies and containerization of shipping, particularly the imminent advent of multimodal transport operations.[39] Developing countries sought to protect themselves and ensure that they were party to rule making in the content of a revolutionary change that was engulfing the maritime transport industry. They expected to be equal partners in formulating the new rules of the game that were evolving. Conse-

38. Articles 28–46 of the Code. Elisabeth Mann Borgese considered Article 46 as one of the more important benefits derived from the Code. She placed it, for a number of years in the 1980s, on the syllabus of the International Ocean Institute's flagship training programme in ocean management in Halifax, Canada.

39. The author, while at UWIST, prepared for the UNCTAD secretariat a report on *Technical and Financial Aspects of Modern Transport Technologies used in Multimodal Transport Operations.* UNCTAD. TD/B/AC.15/15. Geneva: UNCTAD, 1975.

quently, the debates in UNCTAD and its Committee evolved towards the formulation of an international instrument to govern multimodal transport of goods. In September 1978, the terms of reference of the Committee on Shipping were expanded to include the question of multimodal transport, and the Committee's programme was correspondingly enlarged.

Developing countries were concerned by the speed and momentum of technology change, particularly in the liner trade. Such change implied higher capital costs and increased premature technological obsolescence for developing countries' investments in containerization or new and technologically advanced methods of transport. As developing countries were forced into achieving greater technological compatibility in systems at both ends of the trade, they sought guarantees that the technology revolution would not impede their development and particularly the transport strategies that they had adopted. The results were their call for a United Nations Conference on International Multimodal Transport to bring multimodal transport and containerization under mandatory international control. Such a Convention, it was believed, would provide an element of stability and harmonization of policies in the expanding multimodal transport sector.[40]

On 24 May 1980, a United Nations Conference, convened under the auspices of UNCTAD, adopted by consensus the Convention on International Multimodal Transport of Goods.[41]

PROTECTION OF SHIPPERS' INTERESTS AND TECHNICAL ASSISTANCE

There was no denying that, in terms of shipping services, developing countries were buyers in a seller's market. Shipping costs therefore fell on shippers, the ultimate consumers of shipping services in developing countries.

40. A major concern of developing countries has been the lack of consultations between the foreign line operators and developing countries on the introduction of new transport technologies in developing countries' trades. For this reason, developing countries insisted that the UN Convention on International Multimodal Transport of Goods should cover this situation. Thus, the Convention now provides that States that are parties to the Convention: recognize "the need to have regard to the special interest and problems of developing countries, for example, as regards introduction of new technologies..." and agree "that consultations should take place on terms and conditions of services both before and after the introduction of any new technology in the multimodal transport of goods, between the multimodal transport operator, shippers, shippers' organizations and appropriate national authorities."

41. The Convention was opened for signature in New York from 1 September 1980 until 31 August 1981. It would enter into force internationally when 30 States became contracting parties to it. The text of the Convention is found in document TD/MT/CONF/16. UNCTAD. Geneva: UNCTAD.

The 1970s witnessed great awareness of the need to organize shippers to improve their shipping practices and lower transport costs. The Committee on Shipping encouraged the setting up of regional and subregional shippers' councils, commodity groups, and freight bureaus.

In UNCTAD, the preliminary and substantive work was also undertaken that led to the Hamburg Rules, aimed at providing greater balance in the obligations of shippers and shipowners and consequently contributing to the notion of protecting shippers' interests.

As was evident in UNCTAD in the 1970s, the total shipping and maritime framework had gradually been brought within the scope of international discussion and action. While there was much confrontation and controversy in the developing/developed countries' relationship in the Committee on Shipping, there was also great willingness on both sides to promote cooperation for the benefit of the international community and the shipping industry at large. Developed countries provided considerable technical assistance to developing countries in such areas as port development and management. Some 122 technical assistance projects were implemented through UNDP in the field of shipping, ports, multimodal transport, and maritime legislation.

In 1978, an innovative and imaginative project was launched to train 60,000 managers at senior, middle, and junior levels in developing countries, which came to be known as the TRAINMAR project. This involved a system of training of trainers and promoting cooperation among national and regional institutions affiliated to the project.

THE UNFULFILLED PROMISE FROM THE EIGHTIES TO THE NINETIES

There was no denying that in the 1970s expectations were high, the debate and negotiations were raging, and adrenaline levels were raised in the blood of policy makers of developing countries. Every aspect of shipping was being brought onto the development agenda, and as priority matters, by an intellectually prolific secretariat. A rhetorical question was being bandied about in the corridors and smoke-filled rooms of UNCTAD—"if developing countries cannot develop in the field of shipping, then where can they?" Shipping appeared to be the test case for timely and progressive development.

As the 1970s came to a close, the shipping prospects of developing countries were very promising and optimism was running high. However, with the opening of the 1980s, there appeared signs that the momentum of the 1970s was slowing down rapidly. Increasingly, the atmosphere in UNCTAD was becoming confrontational, with developing countries increasingly using majority votes as a means of decision making and reciprocal cooperation with their developed partners waning fast. The goodwill of the 1970s in respect of international cooperation, which might have been motivated by combinations of political and economic factors such as the oil threat, East-West rivalry, and the remnants of a guilty conscience for colonial domination of developing countries, appeared to be being replaced by antagonism, mistrust, and greater self-interest. A very different decade in multilateral cooperation began to unfold.

For developing countries, the 1980s became a decade of economic stagnation that was to be qualified as the lost decade of development, even as early as 1986. The policy of increasing the participation of developing countries in shipping through national fleet ownership and international redistribution of labour in shipping by the legal force of international legal instruments came under vicious attack from many quarters.

There was a direct challenge by the traditional maritime interests through the representatives of their countries on the policy strategies adopted by developing countries. It was a two-pronged attack. One part was an accusatory challenge addressed at the secretariat itself regarding the quality of its intellectual rigour and its philosophy, accusing it of political bias in favour of state policies.[42] The other was a negative uncooperative stand in the debates and discussions in the Committee of Shipping itself. That seemed somewhat contradictory, particularly since the 1980s saw the completion of negotiations on the United Nations Convention on Multimodal Transport, with the adoption of the Convention on 24 May 1980, and the entry into force on 6 April 1983 of the United Nations Convention on a Code of Conduct for Liner Conferences.

Two dimensions of the work of UNCTAD's secretariat were endorsed by the developing countries and placed on the work programme of the Committee on Shipping, namely the transport of bulk cargoes and the phasing out of flags of convenience. These two subjects hit a very raw nerve with the traditional maritime nations, their shipowners, and transnational corporations, and that created the first impasse. As a result, UNCTAD's secretariat and developing countries were in no position, given the resistance of their developed partners, to move on the issue of bulk sharing. It was natural then to refocus on the question of flags of convenience, where the majority of ships involved in bulk trade were registered.

42. The attack that was unleashed on the UNCTAD secretariat was conducted in the main through the specialized and general media, for example, the article by A. S. Price, Chairman of the Liberian Shipowners Council, "The great UNCTAD hustle," *Sea Trade Journal*, (June 1984): 116; B. P. Shaw, "Results and consequences from UNCTAD V," in *Report of the International Symposium* (Bremen: Institute of Shipping Economics, 1980), p. 105; "Liner Shipping in the Eighties," in *Report of the International Symposium* (Bremen: Institute of Shipping Economics, 1980); R. Pearson, "US presses UNCTAD on trade, shipping stances," *Journal of Commerce* (Monday, 26 March 1984): 3A; M. J. Strauss, "Western nations seek overhaul of UNCTAD, citing myriad ills," *Wall Street Journal* (29 March 1984); G. Corea, "On the defensive," *Journal of Commerce*, (30 April 1984); R. Righter, "Now Reagan Threatens to quit UNCTAD," *London Sunday Times* (15 April 1984).

In January 1980, a deadlock was already in the making on the issue of phasing out flags of convenience,[43] which was called for by the developing countries, in the Group of 77 with the exception of Liberia and Panama.

The developed countries, assisted by a media campaign of unprecedented proportion, predictably financed by open-registry shipowners, blocked the developing countries' proposal and promoted another proposal dealing with the symptoms of flags of convenience rather than with the root causes. In 1980, the Committee on Shipping failed to reach agreement on the phasing out of open registries. It was quite clear for the majority of developing countries that the objective of phasing out open registries had become unattainable for the simple reason that the majority of developed market economy countries were opposed to such action, and developing countries had no other option than to concede and reduce their ambitions in the hope of achieving something indirectly by bringing the issue to the table through an international agreement on conditions for the registration of ships. The General Assembly convened a conference on this subject in July 1984, and it lasted until February 1986, when the United Nations Convention on Registration of Ships was adopted. However, the Convention was a far cry from what the developing countries had hoped or wished for, and in fact it did not come into force and flags of convenience, like the cancer they were, grew to embrace half of the world fleet.

For the developing countries, having lost the battle on the carriage of bulk cargoes and on dealing effectively with flags of convenience, which was the centerpiece of their policies of the 1970s, there remained one bright spot, namely the implementation of the Code of Conduct for Liner Conferences.

Much hope had been placed in the Code of Conduct for Liner Conferences, perhaps the single most important product of the intellectual capacity and determination of the secretariat of the Shipping Division of UNCTAD. The Code had entered into force in 1983. In accordance with the provisions of Article 52 of the Convention, a Review Conference "to review the working of the Convention, with particular reference to its implementation, and to consider and adopt appropriate amendments" was held in Geneva from 31 October to 18 November 1988.

The Code had been adopted in 1974, at a time when the Shipping Conferences carried 80 percent–90 percent of the liner trade. For various reasons,

43. "Phasing out" means the gradual elimination of the practice of registering ships in countries with which the ships have no genuine link. In this context, the existence of a "genuine link" implies some form of economic linkage. "Phasing out" does not imply the immediate "abolition" of the shipping registries of countries presently offering open-registry facilities, but rather a gradual tightening of the conditions on which those countries will accept new registrations or retain vessels on their registers, as well as simultaneous restrictions on the establishment of any new open-registry facilities.

conditions had changed, and from the middle of the 1980s more than 50 percent of liner cargoes were being shipped on non-Conference Lines, and in some trades as little as 20 percent remained under conference control. As a consequence, the proportion of cargoes carried by developing countries' shipping lines generally decreased and then quickly evaporated. The developing countries' major concern was therefore the extension of the scope of application of cargo sharing provisions of the Convention to all liner trades, but that was vehemently opposed by traditional maritime countries.

The Review Conference was attended by some 21 Ministers, mainly from West and Central African countries. They were led by the Minister of Defence of the Côte d'Ivoire, who was the Chairman of the Ministerial Conference of West and Central African States on Maritime Transport (MINCOMAR). Perhaps it is relevant to point out that, due to the institutional machinery and organizational structures created in these countries, they had made considerable advances in implementing the Code and consequently had the greatest stake in the outcome of the Review Conference, particularly since they had also made serious investments in liner fleet acquisition. Their position was that the Review Conference was not intended to judge the validity of the Convention but rather to examine factors that had impeded its implementation.

The Group of 77 developing countries were basically concerned with increasing their share in liner trade controlled by nonconference lines and with other developments such as round-the-world services and the growth of consortia that undermined the benefits expected from the Code by the developing countries.

The industrialized countries interpreted the Code essentially as a self-regulatory instrument, and in their view the Convention described and limited the role of governments, which in general had to distance themselves from the activities of commercial parties. In fact, contrary to the developing countries' view they maintained that developments in containerization that had led to conference market share decline were not relevant to the Review Conference.

A deadlock developed with the demands of the developed countries that noncontracting parties to the Convention should have the right to vote, to amend, or to vote against amendments to the Convention, and to ensure that no action could be taken on the scope of application, implementation, or interpretation of the Convention without the participation and agreement of noncontracting parties to the Convention. Otherwise all decisions were to be taken by consensus. Furthermore, these countries also insisted that office bearers be elected from among the noncontracting parties to the Convention, giving further powers to noncontracting States to influence the outcome of the Review Conference.

The developing countries did not accept that stance of the developed countries. They insisted that voting rights should be exercised only by States that were contracting parties. They even questioned the secretariat action in inviting noncontracting States to the Review Conference.

Consequently, the Conference was unable to reach agreement on the majority required to adopt amendments to the Convention, as well as other business of the Conference.

Such were the difficulties encountered in the negotiations on the rules of procedure that the direct involvement of the Secretary-General of UNCTAD, Mr. K.K.S. Dadzie, became necessary. Through his good offices, a complex final compromise package was arrived at (much to the dissatisfaction of most, if not all, West African countries). In the final analysis, the agreement reached on the rules of procedure permitted noncontracting parties to participate in the Conference and gave these noncontracting States the right of participation in decision making and voting, setting a very dangerous precedent in the jurisprudence of international legal relations.

When the Review Conference on the Code of Conduct came to a close after long sessions in 1991, it represented the complete and final debacle for a rule-based approach to development and multilateral negotiating processes in UNCTAD. In fact, most of the developing countries, knowing the results in advance and that the battle was long lost, did not turn up for the resumed session of the Review Conference.

Overall, time, technology and money defeated the developing countries in their aim of making the Code an effective instrument for their participation in liner trade. The Code itself was formulated in the early 1970s, reflecting the structure of the liner shipping industries, the policies and aspirations of developing countries with regard to national merchant fleet development, and the problems encountered by developing countries in terms of both shipper protection and national fleet development vis-à-vis conference-dominated liner trades.

In the meantime, a fundamental transformation had taken place in liner shipping in terms of both technology and structural arrangements since the Code had been adopted. The growth in the size of liner vessels and containerization, the changing pattern of shipping, and particularly the huge capital investments that had become now necessary in liner shipping, for both container terminals and superliner ships, meant that participation was beyond the reach of developing countries.[44] The world liner trade came

44. The technological and structural changes that have taken place and are continuing to take place are certainly of a character and magnitude that would make it quite impractical to seek to accommodate all of them effectively within the framework of the Code. For example, the size of vessel that is economically viable in containerized trades in the context of intermodalism and transhipment renders it quite impractical for many developing countries to seek to own and operate vessels viably based on an exclusive or even preponderant dependence on national cargoes. Secondly, the patterns and magnitudes of transhipment of liner cargoes makes it virtually impracticable in many cases to administer any form of cargo sharing in the same manner as in the case of the conventional port-to-port liner services for which the

to be controlled by a few major players who were superconsortia, grand and mega alliances outside the Conference system. The pattern and magnitude of transhipment of liner cargoes made it virtually impossible, in many cases, to administer the Code sharing formula, even if it was applicable. The shipping scene had changed fundamentally and conferences were no longer relevant. Their importance had receded and the scope of application of the Code had not been extended to all the liner trade, but confined to conference services. For all practical purposes, the Code was redundant. Slowly, developing countries were pushed out of the mainstream of shipping and later even from the secondary lanes and feeder services. Consequently, the developing countries were left with a paper tiger and dashed hopes. After long years of pain and effort to negotiate the Code, today it is no more than a marginal instrument, more of historic interest than of practical use. It is, as are the fleets of developing countries, a victim of the globalization and liberalization dogma of the 1990s. The emergence of grand and global alliances in liner shipping and global mergers has set the new scene for the new millennium of dominance of the traditional operators. The question that has now to be asked is whether there will be any governance, particularly international governance, to protect the weaker parties in the globalized economy and to level the playing field of competition. (See Annex I).

The demise of the liner conferences monopolies in the era of the Washington Consensus (Reagan-Thatcher orthodoxy) of the 1980s and then the era of globalization and the knowledge economy in the 1990s has become irreversible. The new breed of shipping companies has replaced the old conferences.[45]

Code was designed. These developments are compounded by the extent of the growth of nonconference lines. Equally significant is the increasing trend towards superconferences and trade-wide stabilization agreements that are tending to eclipse the traditional conferences with regard to both tariff formation and trade sharing. Therefore, any attempt at the rationalization of liner shipping trades must necessarily address itself to the common concerns of both conference and nonconference operators.

45. In the 1990s, globalization in the widest sense had dramatically changed the demand for transport and related services. Furthermore, the twin process of liberalization and privatization provided a new basis for a concentration process that permanently changed the structure of the shipping industry. Progress in container shipping had been based on economies of scale, on improvements in transport organization, and on systemic application of information technology. As a result of this, combined with the need to respond to global transport requirements of large shippers and at the same time to rationalize the use of existing assets and new investments, shipping lines were forced to enter into global alliances. By the end 1998, the major global and trade-related alliances represented nearly 50 percent of the world fleet, with considerable impact on the ability of smaller carriers and the new service suppliers to enter markets thus dominated. The creation of global alliances marked the culmination of an evolutionary process based on cooperative mechanisms to be followed by growth through mergers and takeovers, with major shipping

Similarly, the Convention on Multimodal Transport did not afford developing countries much protection. The Convention has not entered into force to date and is very unlikely to do so.

Today, with the benefit of hindsight, it is apparent what little the developing countries got from their investment of effort in the Convention on Multimodal Transport. In any case, they wanted to ensure their participation in the new and evolving multimodal transport system, but the Convention addressed mainly the liability and documentary regime. In the meantime, multimodal transport continues to expand exponentially, and successful regulation of the liability regime remains elusive.

The backlash of the 1980s was fortified by an international economic environment that had decimated most developing countries' economies. In the aftermath of the oil money bubble came the great debt burden and then world economic recession. Developing countries had no appetite to give priority to shipping any longer. A new phase in the political economy had unfolded in the Reagan-Thatcher era, where the supremacy of unfettered market forces, liberalization and privatisation of assets, and the demise of the role of the State were in complete contradiction with the shipping policies of the 1970s.

Perhaps developing countries could have dealt with these new elements in moving the development of their shipping sector forward, but that proved impossible not only because of the technology-related centralization and concentration of capital that was needed, but also since the international shipping was an imperfect market and the State was no longer allowed to deal with market imperfections.

As pointed out by the author elsewhere, the collapse of the policies of the 1960s and 1970s was evidenced by the fact that, after 25 years of endeavour, the redistribution of ownership of vessels that had taken place within developing countries was so skewed that it favoured only a handful of devel-

---

lines increasingly moving into logistic services and implementing differentiation strategies. For developing countries, the implications were very clear. While in the past their maritime policies had been characterized by a strong bias in favour of regulatory policies affecting market access, commercialization, and then liberalization and privatization, they inevitably changed policy objectives. Lacking sufficient capital, with the majority unable to enter into alliances and having even less access to corresponding technologies, they regressed. Many still had a large component of break-bulk or multipurpose vessels in mixed break-bulk/containerized operations, but as they were basically inefficient and uncompetitive, the majority of their fleets were driven out of the markets. At the same time, unlike in the past, they had no forum, such as the Committee on Shipping of UNCTAD, to which they could resort to seek international support in taking corrective measures. In fact, the full force of globalization and its immediate effect of marginalization was best demonstrated in shipping, as most developing countries were driven out of the mainstream of the industry.

oping countries. Some eight developing countries out of 128 owned almost 80 percent of developing countries' fleet.[46] (See Annex II.)

As early as 1987, when shipping was not placed on the agenda of UNCTAD VII, the secretariat, under a new leadership, set in motion measures that were later to change the policy approaches of the work of UNCTAD in this area, and this was compounded by the cyclonic changes that occurred following the demise of the socialist camp and the fall of the Berlin Wall. The combination of the unrelenting attack on UNCTAD for its policy and work in the area of shipping and the changing political and economic international environment led to the first institutional change in UNCTAD. The Committee on Shipping was replaced by the Standing Committee on Developing Services Sector, with shipping, ports, and multimodal transport included among its main tasks.

This was only possible because of the change that also occurred among the developing countries themselves within the Group of 77. Under the pretext of shedding the legacy of confrontation as a means of opening the door to cooperation, the Group of 77 sacrificed unity for more pragmatic and flexible approaches to issues of international cooperation and the processes of negotiation.[47] The focus was now on issues that were more amenable to consensus building and on domestic policies rather than international solutions. As the process of globalization began to gain momentum, new policies were espoused for developing countries, based on the liberalization of trade in goods and services, privatization of public sector companies, and commercialization of assets and operations, particularly foreign direct investment. Market-oriented shipping policies were promoted as the new tools of development in this sector. Recommendations along these lines were now being provided to developing countries by the experts in UNCTAD, and this represented a major departure from the 1970s.

The UNCTAD Committee established in 1992 at UNCTAD VIII to deal with shipping lasted only 4 more years. It was abolished in 1996, after UNCTAD IX, and policy dialogue on shipping came to an abrupt halt in UNCTAD.[48] Developing countries were left more or less to fend for themselves in an era of globalization and liberalization, as shipping and in particu-

46. A. Behnam, "Future of shipping dialogue in UNCTAD," *Maritime Policy and Management* 21, no. 1 (January-March 1994): 17.

47. The developing countries themselves bear a considerable responsibility for not building on the promises of the 1970s. Their representatives in negotiations on shipping issues in Geneva always put on a brave face when it was obvious that there was a great schism between the rhetoric in Geneva and policy actions at the national level. Most of them never put into practice what they advocated in Geneva in the Committee on Shipping.

48. In 1999, UNCTAD took up one last remaining mandate on its agenda. On 12 March 1999, the UN/IMO Diplomatic Conference unanimously adopted the International Convention on Arrest of Ships, after 2 weeks of intensive deliberations. Representatives from almost 100 nations as well as about 20 intergovernmental and

lar fleet development was removed from the agenda of UNCTAD. Consequently, there no longer exists a dedicated United Nations forum where economic and commercial aspects of shipping can be debated. This, in the view of the author, is the greatest loss suffered by developing countries. The ensuing global governance deficit in ocean management was also a loss for the international community.[49]

Today, the majority of developing countries experience needs in their development efforts that are very similar to those of the 1970s. In fact, in the era of the new economy, their problems have become even more critical as a result of increasing marginalization. While the problems may be similar to those experienced by developing countries in the past, the approach to solutions, in both policies and concepts, have differed. Today, developing countries increasingly focus on their productive capacity. Policies aimed at capacity building, consumer protection, increasing competitiveness, and levelling the playing field take precedence over asset owning and State intervention.

For developing countries, however, one problem is as pressing as ever: without a predictable legal framework to regulate international trade and transportation of goods, equitable access to markets is not possible for small or medium players, be they companies or countries. At the same time, developing countries are often at a disadvantage even when negotiations geared at achieving agreement on international uniform legislation are conducted. The interests of developed nations tend to be much better represented through strong and well-organized industry associations, good communications between governments and industry, and high levels of expertise among decision makers. For this reason, UNCTAD's continued active involvement in international efforts at unification of laws in the field of trade and transport remains vital to assist developing nations in their "efforts to integrate into the world economy on an equitable basis," one of UNCTAD's stated main goals. Elisabeth would have said yes to this wholeheartedly.

FINAL REFLECTIONS—PIM VII (1976)

As explained in the preface to this article, 1976 was my first meeting with Elisabeth at the Algiers Conference. I delivered the paper she asked me to prepare, which was entitled "Liner Conferences, Developing Countries and Consumer Policy." The paper was based on the theory that where market

---

nongovernmental organizations participated in the Conference, which was held in Geneva from 1 to 12 March 1999.

49. A small skeleton secretariat remains active in UNCTAD in the areas of transport, transport legislation, transport logistics and port development. See A. Behnam, "Emerging Institutional Framework for Ocean Governance," in Proceedings of Pacem in Maribus XVIII, Hamburg, 2000.

discipline fails to provide protection to consumers such as shippers in the case of shipping services, either owning the means of production (ship acquisition) or the exercise of countervailing power needs to be employed. I wrote at that time that developing countries as consumers and users of such services should perhaps opt for an alternative consumer policy based on strengthening their effective countervailing power to impact on the behaviour of the shipowners. Also, such a policy focusing on improving the behaviour and practices of shipowners, traders, ports, et cetera, would make redundant restrictive legislation such as instruments for sharing of cargoes and acquisition of national fleets.

The paper attempted to treat shipping in developing countries as part of their overall transport problem, focusing on the need to reduce transport costs. It subscribed to the view that shipping could not be treated separately from the whole complex issue of total transport costs as they affected the consumer, the objective being to secure the most efficient low-cost shipping regime compatible with commercial requirements of shippers. The basic thesis of the paper was that economic efficiency should not be sacrificed at the expense of political control through restrictive legislation, and it was somewhat critical of governmental and international control over the international shipping market.

While the paper raised more questions that it answered, it provoked an angry response on the part of my host at the time for having proposed a consumer-based policy for developing countries as an alternative choice. At that time, to propose that developing countries should increase their efficiency and capacity by using foreign-provided services as a means of addressing their shipping problems must have sounded heretical.

I admit now it was the wrong proposal at the wrong time. One year later, I joined the UNCTAD secretariat and put that paper aside. In fact, it was ethically not possible to publish it, as it contradicted the stated policy of the organization. I look back with nostalgia on those days, and I liken my attitude to adopting UNCTAD policies to that of the developing countries' attitude to liner conferences. Officially, developing countries had stated that they wished to join liner conferences to change them from inside, but once they joined them, they became the system's greatest protagonists. I became a protagonist of UNCTAD policy as it evolved in the 1970s and 1980s.

During all the following years, Elisabeth always found it very amusing that our friendship had begun with such differences. I still believe that, despite all that transpired in the 25 years that I served UNCTAD, the policies of the 1970s were the right policies at the right time. The fact that they were not durable does not invalidate their intrinsic merit. The fact that the absolute power of the centres prevailed over moral values and justice and that sometimes we might have had to retreat is not something to be ashamed of. Perhaps we are retreating today into passive policies and accepting certain realities as given and working with them. Elisabeth loathed this, but she was also a pragmatist and optimist; she did not despair, but made the best of bad choices. However, she never gave up in believing in the destiny and the bright future of the mass of humanity that live in the developing countries, as well as in the abundant generosity of the ocean.

ANNEX I: THE OCEAN GOVERNANCE DEFICIT[50]

The struggle for the promotion of equity and balanced economic growth based on just social values, respect for nature and protection of the environment, including the sustainable use of the oceans, was placed on the back burner in the last decade in the pursuit of the elusive hopes and promises held out by globalization. Furthermore, the institutions that were endeavouring to provide the necessary framework for global governance were, in reality, ineffective and incapable of ensuring implementation of their policies, rules, and regulations as they lacked powers of enforcement.

Shipping is one sector in the use of the oceans where the global implications of this reality has been clearly demonstrated. It is one sector where the brutal impact of globalization is so visibly discernible. Unfettered liberalization, privatisation, massive accumulation, and concentration of capital in a few hands, unadulterated use of economic power and mastery of technology, compounded by an amazing loophole in international law—"the legal fiction of flag territory at sea"—has led to the rise of mega-operators with their integrated transport operations that are way beyond the reach of their developing country competitors.

Shipping today, continues to represent the most valuable use of the oceans. More than 90 percent of world trade moves by sea. In 1999, seaborne trade exceeded 5.2 billion tons and the world fleet reached 790 million dead weight tons. However, hidden behind this apparently healthy global growth and progress lies a very disturbing and ugly reality—at the start of the new millennium half of the world fleet is under flags of convenience. This is an epidemic that is spreading out of control. Behind the veil of efficient world shipping, with the lowest ever freight rates (as shipowners tend to claim) and sophisticated use of advanced technology, lies another darker aspect of unchecked market forces. It represents a world of unprecedented mergers and acquisitions, accumulation and concentration of capital within a small elite and the concentration of world shipping amongst a few mega-alliances and consortia that dominate world maritime commerce. They are accountable virtually to no one and exercise enormous economic power.

50. A. Behnam, "Emerging Institutional Framework for Ocean Governance—A Contribution," (paper submitted at the 28th PIM Conference. See IOI, Pacem in Maribus XXVIII, The European Challenge, Hamburg, Germany, 2000. Proceedings of this meeting were compiled by Dr. Johanna Wesnigk, June 2002, IOI, Malta, pp. 105–110).

The first victims of their onslaught were the fledgling fleets of developing countries, particularly the least developed among them, who during the silent 1990s were driven out of mainstream operations and forced into secondary roles from where they were then driven out completely. The gains of the 1970s and 1980s, when institutions such as UNCTAD placed economic justice and participatory international economic systems at the forefront of their activities in assisting developing countries to make headway in shipping, were lost in the 1990s. Africa suffered the most—the infant shipping fleets of West Africa died an early death. Globalization managed to wipe out almost all of Africa's shipping fleets but did not make even a dent in malaria eradication.

ANNEX II: WHAT SUCCESS FOR NATIONAL FLEET POLICIES?[51]

- Not a single African country is among the 35 most important maritime countries, though six Asian developing countries rank among the 20 most important maritime countries.
- In 1990, all developing countries of Africa taken together owned container tonnage with a carrying capacity of 1,810 TEU—less than the carrying capacity of a single third-generation container ship.
- A large part of the developing countries' bulk fleet is old and without the capacity to meet new safety requirements, and this implies operating outside mainstream bulk trades.
- Developing countries are not sufficiently involved in large container traffic, they do not offer related downstream back-up services and consequently they are unable to diversify into multimodal transport operations. In modern liner shipping, the concept of ownership is outdated.
- Developing countries' fleets suffer considerable structural deficiencies. A large part of the shipping tonnage is general cargo and obsolete and a large number of developing countries have failed to undertake the necessary reinvestment to replace economically redundant tonnage.
- The linkage between trade generation and participation in shipping has proved to be a self-defeating policy that has resulted in the bilateralization of maritime transport, with limiting and costly consequences. Cargo reservation laws have proved to be unimplementable, and the consequent necessary derogations have made such laws for all practical purposes redundant.

51. A. Behnam, "Future of the shipping dialogue in UNCTAD," *Maritime Policy and Management* 21, no. 1 (January-March 1994): 21.

- The scope of the Code of Conduct for Liner Conferences does not extend beyond conference trades.
- Developing countries can take several alternative approaches to shipowning to improve their maritime trade. National fleet ownership has not proved to be a feasible instrument to reduce freight rates. On the contrary, national fleets in some developing countries' trades have been proponents of higher freight rates.

Jurisdiction over Foreign Commercial Ships in Ports: A Gap in the Law of the Sea Codification

Moritaka Hayashi
Waseda University School of Law, Tokyo, Japan

INTRODUCTION

The 1982 United Nations Convention on the Law of the Sea (the LOS Convention) contains several references to "internal waters,"[1] but none of them provides for the general regime or status of internal waters as such. The only provision that gives a specific rule of substance is Article 8(2), establishing the right of innocent passage in internal waters that has been newly created through the use of straight baselines in the waters that had previously been part of the territorial sea. Nor does the Convention contain rules on the status of foreign ships in ports, except for a few provisions relating to the protection of the marine environment and the safety of ships.[2]

The lack of provisions on the status of foreign ships in ports and more broadly on the regime of internal waters in the LOS Convention was not the result of a decision upon deliberations at the Third United Nations Conference on the Law of the Sea (UNCLOS III). It was inherited from the 1958 Geneva Conference on the Law of the Sea (UNCLOS I), which adopted the Geneva Convention on the Territorial Sea and the Contiguous Zone that formed the basis of most of the relevant provisions of the LOS Convention.

In the traditional treatises on international law of the sea, the regime of internal waters and the status of foreign ships therein (as well as those in the territorial sea) occupied a substantial part. A leading law of the sea authority, Gidel, devoted a whole volume to the subject.[3] State practice, particularly in respect of the status of foreign ships, has accumulated since the beginning of the 19th century, mostly in Europe and the Americas. An attempt at codification of the subject was made in 1930 at the Hague Conference for the Codification of International Law.

1. Articles 2(1), 7(3), 8, 10(4), 18(1), 25(2), 27(2) and (5), 28(3), 35(a), 50, 111(1), 211(3) and 218. United Nations Convention on the Law of the Sea, 1982. A/CONF.62/122.

2. See, for example, Articles 211(3), 219 and 220.

3. G. Gidel, *Le Droit International Public de la Mer. Le Temps de Paix. Tome II: Les Eaux Intérieures* (Paris: Edouard Duchemin, 1932–34. Reprinted in 1981).

Ocean Yearbook 18: 488–511

One wonders why, despite such background, UNCLOS I excluded the subject of internal waters from the scope of its codification efforts. Why indeed, as Luke Lee remarked in 1961,[4] has there been only scant attention paid since UNCLOS I to the even broader subject of the jurisdiction over foreign merchant ships in the territorial sea? Lee's discussion relates mainly to Articles 19 and 20 of the Geneva Convention, but it is essentially valid also for Articles 27 and 28 of the LOS Convention.[5] Thus, one tends to agree with the observation that the general international law regime on internal waters "est assez peu développé."[6]

It is indeed unfortunate if the development of the law in this area ceased with the failure at the Hague Conference, because the problems that may be caused by the ambiguity of the regime could be potentially much greater and more serious now than in the pre-World War II period. There are at least two reasons for this. The first is the new regime of innocent passage introduced by the Geneva Convention for the areas that had not previously been internal waters but have been enclosed by straight baselines as such waters.[7] Since many States have created rather extensive areas of internal waters in that way,[8] it is now more likely that problems related to the exercise of the right of innocent passage would arise.

The other reason is the rapid increase in the last few decades of the number of ships registered with flag of convenience or open-registry States. Registries that are generally characterized as such have rapidly increased in recent years and now number nearly 30.[9] The world's top five or six registries

4. See L. T. Lee, "Jurisdiction over foreign merchant ships in the territorial sea: An analysis of the Geneva Convention on the Law of the Sea," *American Journal of International Law* 55 (1961): 77.

5. Notable exceptions are: F. Francioni, "Criminal jurisdiction over foreign merchant vessels in territorial waters: A new analysis," *Italian Yearbook of International Law* 1 (1975): 27–41; V. D. Degan, "Internal waters," *Netherlands Yearbook of International Law* 17 (1986): 3–44.

6. Nguyen Quoc Dinh, P. Dailier and A. Pellet, *Droit international public*, 6th ed. (Paris: L.G.D.J., 1999), p. 1105.

7. See the Geneva Convention on the Territorial Sea and the Contiguous Zone, Article 5(2) and the LOS Convention, Article 8(2).

8. By the time of entry into force of the LOS Convention, more than 70 States had employed straight baselines, and a number of them had made excessive claims not in conformity with the requirements of the Convention. See United Nations Division for Ocean Affairs and the Law of the Sea, *Law of the Sea: Practice of States at the Time of Entry into Force of the United Nations Convention on the Law of the Sea* (New York: United Nations, 1994), p. 6. A. Roach and R. Smith point out that many of the baseline systems have created large areas of internal waters which otherwise would legally be territorial seas or areas in which the freedom of navigation and overflight may be exercised. *Excessive Maritime Claims*, vol. 66, *International Law Studies* (Newport, RI: Naval War College, 1994), p. 44.

9. International Transport Workers' Federation, *Flags of Convenience Campaign Report 2000*, http://www.itf.org.uk/seafarers/foc/foc.htm (accessed 1 September 2002).

of fleets in gross tonnage are currently all such States. Many of these flags of convenience States are characterized by their inability or unwillingness to enforce strictly international minimum standards on their ships, including the basic flag State duties as laid down in Article 94 of the LOS Convention, and tend, generally speaking, to be more likely to cause problems than other flag States.[10]

Some of the problems and incidents caused on board foreign ships at port or in internal waters may also be of concern for the coastal State. Problems may become unnecessarily complicated and prolonged to settle and involve great costs in terms of human rights and economic loss in cases of flag of convenience vessels. This is illustrated by a recent incident involving a murder on a Japanese-owned Panamanian-flagged tanker, as discussed later.

This article will focus on only one aspect of the regime of internal waters. It will highlight the problems relating to criminal jurisdiction of the coastal State over foreign ships in ports, and examine the development of international customary law. It will further attempt to see why the subject was neglected in the post-World War II codification efforts. In the conclusion, the need will be stressed for the international community to revisit the question with a view to taking specific measures to fill the gap in the LOS Convention.

MURDER ON PANAMANIAN TANKER *TAJIMA*

On 7 April 2002, while the *Tajima*, a Panamanian-flagged VLCC tanker owned by a Japanese corporation and operated by another Japanese company, was navigating on the high seas off Taiwan, a Japanese officer disappeared from the vessel. The following day, a Filipino seaman reported to the master that he had seen two Filipino seamen beating and throwing him into the sea. The master reported the incident to the Panamanian Consulate in Tokyo, and, with the assistance of Japanese Coast Guard officers, confined the two suspects into separate rooms on the vessel on her continued voyage to Himeji port in Japan. On 12 April, upon arrival in Himeji port, a team of Coast Guard officers boarded the tanker to conduct an investigation on the basis of a request from Panama. It was reported that traces of blood were found on the deck and the two suspects admitted having committed the crime.

The report of the investigation was handed to the Panamanian Consulate on 19 April. Action by Panama was delayed, because of the time allegedly needed for translation and study of the document, until 14 May, when it

10. For the current practices and problems of substandard shipping in general, see International Commission on Shipping, *Inquiry into Ship Safety: Ships, Slaves and Competition* (Newcastle, Australia: ICONS, 2001).

requested Japanese authorities to detain provisionally the suspects. The suspects were then sent to the High Public Prosecutors Office in Tokyo. Despite repeated requests from various sources concerned, no action was taken by the Japanese authorities either to admit the suspects to land or to detain them even temporarily. Thus, the seriously abnormal situation continued for more than a month. The master and the crewmembers were compelled to stay on board together with the suspected seamen, with the ship anchored outside the port and no official assistance from any governmental authorities. The official position of the Japanese authorities was that they had no jurisdiction under the Criminal Code to institute proceedings in the case where a Japanese national was the victim of a crime committed outside the territory of Japan.[11] In fact, it abandoned the principle of passive personal jurisdiction in 1947. Under the circumstances, even the temporary detention of the suspects on land was not possible without some assurances from Panama to request their eventual extradition.

It was another month later, on 14 June, that the Panamanian Government formally requested the extradition of the suspects to Panama. Having no agreement on extradition between the two countries, Japan commenced its formal process of examination under its Law on the Extradition of Fugitive Criminals, and the case was referred to the Tokyo High Court. Finally, on 15 August, the High Court delivered its decision that the extradition may be possible under the law, and the Minister of Justice ordered the extradition.

The *Tajima* illustrates the kind of jurisdictional problems for the port State in dealing with serious incidents on board a foreign ship and the dilemma that the port State faces when shipowners of the State rely on flags of convenience abroad for their ships. If the ship flew the Japanese flag, investigations and other proceedings would have been undertaken speedily, even before she arrived at port.

Another incident potentially involving port State jurisdiction was that of the *Glory Cape*, a Panamanian registered iron-ore carrier managed out of the Republic of Korea, with Korean officers and Chinese and Indonesian ratings. When the ship was at the port of Dampier, Western Australia, in 1995, the Indonesians sought the help of the International Transport Workers' Federation (ITF) in collecting underpayment of wages. On 31 October, the master took the ship out from the loading berth and anchored, having promised that the ship would not sail until the disputes had been settled. In the early morning of 1 November, however, the master lifted the anchor and moved out to sea. The Indonesian radio operator contacted the ITF to inform of the situation, and while doing so, was attacked by other

11. See the Criminal Code of Japan, Articles 1–3. After submission of the manuscript for this article, in July 2003, a new law was passed by the Japanese Diet amending the Criminal Code to recognize jurisdiction in such a case.

seamen and beaten with an iron bar. He and his five Indonesian colleagues, in fear of their lives, and having failed to release a raft that was padlocked to the deck, jumped into the sea. At daybreak, Australian rescue services picked up the six, but the radio operator was dead. The ship continued its voyage to China, and to other ports, without coming back to Australia. It has subsequently changed its flag and name. There was apparently no serious investigation of the incident either by Panama or Australia.[12]

CRIMINAL JURISDICTION OVER FOREIGN SHIPS IN PORT

When dealing with the State practice with respect to jurisdiction over offences on board a ship that has voluntarily entered a port of the State other than the flag State, two situations, illustrated by the *Tajima* and the *Glory Cape*, may be distinguished. The first is the case where the offence takes place while the ship is outside the territorial sea of any State, that is, on the high seas, which for the purpose of the present article includes the exclusive economic zone because the rules relating to the status of ships on the high seas also apply therein. The second is the case where the offence is committed while the ship is in a port, or in other parts of the internal or territorial waters of the coastal State.

There are few internationally reported cases belonging to the first, while most of the cases cited by courts and discussed in the literature are those falling under the second category. In reviewing State practice, however, the question may be asked whether a clear distinction can or should

12. Information provided by Hon. Peter Morris, member of the Australian House of Representatives at the time of the incident, in personal correspondence of 26 August 2002. It appears that Australia considered only Panama had criminal jurisdiction over the matter under the LOS Convention and no Australian legislation covered it. In another case involving the Taiwanese-flagged freighter *Maersk Dubai*, the Canadian authorities boarded and arrested the captain and six other seamen, all from Taiwan, while she was at the port of Halifax in May 1996, after several Filipino seamen reported that three Romanian stowaways had been found and forced out of the ship on the high seas. The Canadian action was taken at the request of Romania under the bilateral extradition treaty. In March 1997, the Canadian extradition judge ruled that the treaty did not cover the alleged offences and thus he had no jurisdiction to commit the accused for extradition to Romania. The ruling was appealed, but the Canadian Minister of Justice subsequently announced that the accused, in the company of the law enforcement officers of Taiwan, would be returned to Taiwan, where the prosecution process had been initiated and assurances for a full trial were provided. See M. McConnell, "Forward this cargo to Taiwan: Canadian extradition law and practice relating to crime on the high seas," *Criminal Law Forum* 8 (1997): 335–51 and the Statement by the Minister of Justice and Attorney General of Canada Allan Rock Regarding the Seamen of the *Maersk Dubai*, http://canada.justice.gc.ca/en/news/nr/1997/dubai.html (accessed 30 December 2002).

be made between the two categories in all cases. Does it, or should it, make a material difference if, for example, a murder is committed on the high seas just before the ship enters the territorial sea or internal waters, or the trouble started while the ship was on the high seas and the actual killing took place in port? Does the nature or the degree of gravity of a serious crime or disorder on board for the port or the coastal State change depending on exactly where it took place, as far as its direct effects or impact continues after the ships enters the port?

These are the kind of questions that were precisely raised by the case of the *Tajima*. Although it was on the high seas when the murder allegedly took place, the Japanese Coast Guard assisted the vessel in searching for the victim, as well as the confinement and guarding of the suspects until it reached the port. Not only the families of the victim were Japanese, but the owners and operators of the *Tajima* were also. Serious human rights and humanitarian problems accumulated as the master and the crewmembers, together with the suspects, were obliged to stay on the vessel with no assistance from the local authorities for more than a month. There appears thus no denying that the immediate effects of the murder and the continuing situation on board disturbed the peace and public order of the port and the country.

It is worth reviewing the State practice and doctrine with these points in mind. We shall first deal with the two categories separately, but attempt to see if the distinction is really valid.

Jurisdiction over Offences Committed on the High Seas

One of the few reported cases involving criminal incidents on the high seas is U.S. v. Dixon,[13] where the defendant, a British member of the crew of the U.S. vessel, had fatally injured another member of the crew on the high seas, and was taken ashore at Ceuta, Spanish Morocco, by the master and placed under the guard of the British Consul. Dixon was subsequently placed on board another U.S. vessel and returned to the port of New York, where he was arrested and subsequently tried by the U.S. District Court. The Court held that because Dixon had signed on a U.S. ship and thereby subjected himself to the U.S. law, the trial in the United States was proper, and he was not entitled to any intervention by Spanish Morocco or Great Britain.[14]

This apparently follows the custom that had been "decisively settled" according to Hall, who earlier in the 20th century wrote the following

13. *73 F. Supp.* (E.D. N.Y. 1947).
14. M. Whiteman, *Digest of International Law*, vol. 9 (Washington, D.C.: GPO, 1968), pp. 55–6.

> If a person on board a British ship commits a crime on the high seas and is brought in custody into a foreign port, the territorial authorities will not interfere with his being kept in custody on board, nor with his being transferred to another vessel for conveyance to England.[15]

This was the situation prevailing before the Permanent Court of International Justice (PCIJ) gave the celebrated decision in the case of the *Lotus* in 1927.[16] In a collision between the French vessel and a Turkish vessel, the *Boz-Kourt*, on the high seas, the latter sank with loss of several Turkish nationals on board. The captain of the *Boz-Kourt* was taken on board the *Lotus,* which continued her voyage to Constantinople, where the Turkish authorities arrested him and a French crewmember of the *Lotus* in charge of the watch on board at the time of the collision, and convicted both for manslaughter under Turkish law. Upon the protest by France, the case was submitted to the Permanent Court of International Justice. The Court held that (1) the act committed on board the *Lotus* produced its effects on board the *Boz-Kourt,* which was, as it were, part of Turkish territory; (2) there was no rule of international law prohibiting legislation to extend the jurisdiction of national courts to offences committed outside its territory against its nationals; and (3) thus Turkey had not acted in conflict with international law in instituting the criminal proceedings.

The decision of the PCIJ was reached only by the casting vote of the President, and turned out to be controversial. As a result, the International Convention for the Unification of Certain Rules relating to Penal Jurisdiction, in Matters of Collision or Other Incidents of Navigation,[17] signed at Brussels in 1952, reversed the decision and provided for criminal or disciplinary proceedings in cases of "collision or other incident of navigation" only for the flag State of the vessel on which the suspect served or the State of which he was a national (Articles 1 and 3). The same rule was followed by the 1958 Geneva Convention on the High Seas (Article 11).

On the basis of such developments, Colombos concludes that where an offence is committed on the high seas, "there is a weighty and preponderant opinion" in favour of the rule that jurisdiction is primarily vested in the courts of the flag State of the vessel, but that the State whose national is accused of a crime on board a foreign ship is also competent to try him where he is within its jurisdiction, although such jurisdiction is not generally exercised.[18]

15. W. Hall, *Foreign Jurisdiction of the British Crown,* p. 81, quoted in A. H. Charteris, "The legal position of merchantmen in foreign ports and national waters," *British Year Book of International Law* 1 (1920–21): 73.

16. *P.C.I.J., Series A,* No. 10 (1927).

17. 439 *UNTS* 233.

18. C. J. Colombos, *The International Law of the Sea,* 6th rev. ed. (London: Longmans, 1967), pp. 306–7.

It should be pointed out, however, that the *Lotus* case as well as the 1952 Brussels Convention and the 1958 Geneva Convention, which he discusses, are all situations involving a "collision or other incident of navigation." No reference is made by Colombos to any State practice with respect to such common crimes as murder on the high seas. Nor is there anything new in the LOS Convention.[19] Despite the paucity of reported cases involving common crimes taking place on the high seas, a number of municipal court decisions and bilateral treaty provisions relating to jurisdiction over foreign ships at ports appear to recognize the coastal State jurisdiction over incidents on board even if they originated when the ship was outside the territorial sea, as we shall see later.

Jurisdiction over Offences on Foreign Ships at Port

There has been long-lasting controversy between the British and French systems or doctrines on the extent to which a foreign commercial vessel is subjected to the jurisdiction, particularly criminal jurisdiction, of the coastal State when she voluntarily enters its port.

The British System

The British system is based on the principle, adopted in statutory enactments since 1854, that the local sovereign is entitled, in the absence of any treaty stipulation, to exercise jurisdiction over foreign vessels in its ports. As a matter of general practice, however, the absolute jurisdiction is not exercised in cases involving the internal discipline of the ship and the relations between her master, crewmember, or passenger.[20] This long-standing position was further confirmed and clarified in the British Government's reply to the Questionnaire for the 1930 Hague Codification Conference, stating that a State is entitled to exercise jurisdiction over a foreign merchant vessel lying in its ports and over persons and goods on board, and that in criminal matters, it is not usual for the authorities to intervene and enforce the local jurisdiction unless their assistance is invoked by, or on behalf of, the local representative of the flag State or those in control of the ship, or a person directly concerned, or unless the peace and good order of the port is likely to be affected. It was also stressed that in every case, it is for the authorities of the State to judge whether or not to intervene.[21]

The British system was followed by several European and the Commonwealth countries. It is sometimes called the Anglo-American system, though the U.S. practice has not always been consistent.

19. Article 97(1) of the LOS Convention is an exact copy of Article 11(1) of the Geneva Convention on the High Seas.

20. Colombos (n. 18 above), p. 320.

21. Ibid., p. 322.

The French System

The French system was originally formulated by the famous *Avis* of the Conseil d'Etat of 20 November 1806. In 1805, two separate incidents involving American crewmembers occurred on board American merchant vessels, the *Sally* in the port of Marseilles and the *Newton* in the port of Antwerp, then under the French dominion. In both cases, one seaman wounded another, and the U.S. Consul claimed exclusive jurisdiction to handle the case.[22] The Conseil d'Etat decided in favor of the United States on the ground that the offences in question did not disturb the tranquility of the port. The *Avis* reasoned that (1) a neutral vessel admitted to a port of the State is completely subject to the laws of police in force at the place at which it is received; (2) the crewmembers are equally subject to the jurisdiction of the local tribunals for offences they commit, even on board, against persons other than fellow members of the crew; but (3) in cases where an offence is committed by a member of the crew against another member, the rights of the neutral power shall be respected touching the internal discipline of the vessel in which the local authorities shall not interfere unless the assistance has been invoked or the tranquility of the port has been compromised.[23]

This formula of the French system was further developed by the 1859 decision of the Cour de Cassation in the case of Jally (or the *Tempest*), where the American mate of an U.S. merchant vessel, the *Tempest*, killed one of her crew members and wounded another while she was at the port of Havre, and voluntarily surrendered to the local authorities. The Court upheld the jurisdiction of the local courts and held that the local authorities were competent

> lorsque le fait constitue un crime de droit commun que sa gravité ne permet á aucune nation de laisser impuni sans porter atteinte á ses droits de souveraineté juridictionnelle et territoriale, parce que ce crime est la violation la plus manifeste comme la plus flagrante des lois qui chaque nation est chargée de faire respecter dans toutes les parties de son territoire.[24]

22. The 1788 Consular Convention between France and the United States, then in force, authorized the Consuls to exercise policing over all vessels of their respective nations and conferred on them all powers and jurisdiction in civil matters as well as entire inspection over the said vessels and crews. On the other hand, it safeguarded the territorial sovereignty by providing in article 10 that "in case where subjects or citizens of the respective countries shall have committed any crime or violation of public tranquility, they shall be justiciable by the local judges." Quoted by Charteris (n. 15 above), pp. 49–50.

23. Quoted by Gidel (n. 3 above), p. 207, n. 1.

24. Ibid., p. 217.

The most significant aspect of this decision was its emphasis on the *intrinsic gravity of the crime* committed on board, like murder, which compels the coastal State to intervene. According to Gidel, this is an interpretation of the 1806 *Avis,* and not an expansion thereof.[25] It was thus clarified that the tranquility of the port would be considered compromised when a crime of particular gravity is committed. The French system, either in the original formula or as interpreted in the *Tempest* case, was followed by a number of European and Latin American countries. This is particularly reflected in the consular conventions they concluded bilaterally, as discussed later.

The United States Practice

The "gravity of the crime" rule was also closely followed by the U.S. Supreme Court decision in the case of Wildenhus rendered in 1887.[26] A Belgian seaman, Wildenhus, on board a Belgian ship moored at a dock in Jersey City, New Jersey, killed another Belgian crewmember. He was arrested by the local authorities and imprisoned on a charge of felonious homicide. The consular convention between Belgium and the United States, concluded in 1880, provided that the consuls shall have exclusive charge of the internal order of their merchant vessels and shall alone take cognizance of all differences that might arise between the captains, officers, and crews, and "the local authorities shall not interfere except when the disorder that has arisen is of such a nature as to disturb tranquility and public order on shore, or in the port. . ."(Article 11). The Belgian consul contended that both by this provision and by the law of nations, the State of New Jersey had no jurisdiction in the matter.[27]

The Supreme Court held that (1) when a merchant vessel of one country enters the ports of another for the purpose of trade, it subjects itself to the law of the place to which it goes unless otherwise agreed; (2) however, matters of discipline and other things done on board that affected only the vessel or those belonging to it should be left to be dealt with by the authorities of the flag State, while crimes committed on board *of a character to disturb the peace and tranquility of the port* should be dealt with by the local tribunals if they should see fit to assert their authority; and (3) the disorder in question was of a nature to disturb the public peace or public repose of the people.[28]

In the opinion, the Court stressed the gravity of the kind of crime that "every civilized nation considers itself bound to provide a severe punishment for when committed within its own jurisdiction." The Court said that if the

25. Ibid.
26. 120 U.S. 1 (1887).
27. J. B. Moore, *A Digest of International Law,* vol. II (Washington, D.C.: GPO, 1906), pp. 303–4
28. Ibid., p. 304.

crime itself was of a character to awaken public interest when it became known, it was a "disorder," the very nature of which was to disturb the quiet of a peaceful community, and to create, in the language of the above-quoted consular convention, a "disorder" that would "disturb tranquility and public order on shore or in the port." The Court concluded that all must concede that felonious homicide was precisely of such a character and therefore the consul had no right to interfere to prevent the proceedings.[29]

This ruling and the opinion were evidently influenced by the *Tempest* case, and a key element in the process was probably Article 11 of the consular convention with Belgium, which was in line with the French system. Although the U.S. position is often assimilated to the British system,[30] the Wildenhus case gave considerable influence on subsequent U.S. practice.[31]

State Practice Reflected in Consular Conventions

As indicated already in passing, the question of coastal States' rights and jurisdiction with respect to foreign commercial vessels in their ports has often been dealt with in bilateral treaties. In the 19th century, relevant provisions were contained normally in treaties of commerce, navigation, and friendship. From the latter half of that century, they appear mostly in consular conventions. These treaties reflect the positions that governments could at least accept, if not the maximum that they wished to assert. A review of major treaties of this nature shows interesting trends in the evolution of relevant provisions. Indeed, particularly among the post-World War II treaties, there is a remarkably broad similarity in their main contents. In the following, therefore, after a brief examination of the pre-War treaties, the main analysis will be focused on those concluded after the War. The pre-War treaties may generally be divided into two categories.

A group of 19th century and early 20th century treaties, mostly with the United States as a party, provided for the right of consular officers to serve as judges and arbitrators in, or take cognizance of, the differences between

29. Ibid., pp. 304–5.

30. See, for example, R. R. Churchill and A. V. Lowe, *The Law of the Sea*, 3rd ed. (Manchester: Manchester Univ. Press, 1999), p. 66.

31. See, for example, the case involving the Spanish vessel *Viviana*, 1907, and other cases summarized by G. H. Hackworth in *Digest of International Law*, vol. II (Washington, D.C.: GPO, 1941), p. 209 ff. McDougal and Burke wrote in 1962 that the test adopted by the Wildenhus' case was "still considered authoritative in the United States," M. McDougal and W. Burke, *The Public Order of the Oceans* (New Haven and London: Yale Univ. Press, 1962), p. 167. *Restatement of the Law, Foreign Relations Law of the United States, Second* (1965) also provides that the coastal State waives the right to exercise its enforcement jurisdiction over a foreign vessel in port or internal waters with regard to matters involving internal management or discipline and with regard to criminal conduct aboard the vessel, unless the consequences of the crime extend to the coastal State or "the crime is of a kind to disturb the peace of the port." Whiteman (n. 14 above), vol. 9, pp. 62–3.

the master and crewmembers, or between the latter themselves, on board the vessels of their nationality while they are in the ports of the country to which the officers are sent. While such treaties prohibited the interference of local authorities, an exception is made where the conduct of the crews "disturb the (public) order or tranquility" of the country (or in port or on shore).[32] In some cases, the term "the peace and public order" or "public peace" was substituted for "the order or tranquility."[33] Several of the treaties point to the "nature" of the differences, thus including the cases where they are likely to disturb the order or tranquility.[34] It should also be pointed out that most of these treaties either do not specify the location of occurrence of the differences concerned, or refer to all differences that may arise "at sea or in port,"[35] though some others treaties provide for the possible intervention by the local authorities in cases where such differences or disorder have arisen within the territorial waters.[36]

The other categories of treaties are modeled on Article 24 of the French-Spanish Consular Convention of 1862, which permits the local authorities to intervene voluntarily in two cases. The first case, which is virtually the same as the first category mentioned above, is "where the disorders (les désordres) caused on board the vessel are of such a nature as to disturb the tranquility and public order on land or in port." And the second case, which is new, is where a national of the coastal State *or* a person who is not the master or crewmember is involved in the disorders.[37]

Gidel states that this model has been followed by all subsequent conventions concluded by France, and cites those with Italy, Portugal, Russia, Greece, El Salvador, Dominican Republic, Bolivia, etc.[38] The same formula

32. See, for example, *Compilation of Treaties in Force* (hereinafter "*Malloy*"). U.S. Senate. U.S.-Prussia Treaty of Commerce and Navigation (1828), Article 10. Washington, DC: GPO, 1904, p. 646; Ibid. U.S.-Russia Treaty of Commerce and Navigation (1822), Article 10, p. 662; Ibid. U.S.-Sweden and Norway Treaty of Commerce and Navigation (1827), Article 13, p. 758; Ibid. U.S.-Denmark Consular Convention (1861), Article 1, pp. 236–237. Moore's *Digest* also notes that such "an express exception is usually made" in various treaties relating to consular relations to which the United States was a party as to the offences that disturb the peace or tranquility of the port. Moore (n. 27 above), p. 298.

33. *Malloy*. U.S.-Austria-Hungary Consular Convention (1870), Article 11, p. 45; Ibid. U.S.-German Empire Consular Convention (1871), Article 13, p. 283; Ibid. U.S.-Netherlands Consular Convention (1878), Article 11, p. 582.

34. The conventions which the United States concluded with Austria-Hungary, Belgium, German Empire and the Netherlands.

35. The conventions which the United States concluded with Denmark, Austria-Hungary, Belgium, German Empire and the Netherlands.

36. Ibid. U.S.-Italy Consular Convention (1878), Supplemental Art (1881) to Article 11, p. 463; Ibid. U.S.-Greece Consular Convention (1902), Article 12, p. 402; Ibid. U.S.-Spain Treaty of Friendship and General Relations (1902), Article 23, p. 738.

37. Gidel (n. 3 above), p. 225.

38. Ibid.

was also used in the US-Belgium Consular Convention of 1880 (Art. 11),[39] and the Yugoslavia-Poland Consular Convention of 1930 (Art. 16).[40] Germany, in a 1914 Port of Hamburg notification to the Consul, stated that it had concluded treaties containing similar provisions with Bulgaria, France, Greece, Honduras, Italy, Japan, Mexico, Nicaragua, Portugal, Russia, Spain and the United States.[41] Similar provisions are also contained in the consular conventions between US and Germany (1923), Italy and Czechoslovakia (1924), Germany and Soviet Union (1925), Germany and Estonia (1925), France and Poland (1925), and US and Finland (1934).[42] Again, it should be noted that in most of these treaties, the exact location where the disorders or differences occurred is not mentioned. It may therefore be interpreted that the local authorities may intervene in cases where they started on the high seas and the situation or its direct consequences are brought to the port.

Turning now to the post-War treaty practice, it should be pointed out first that relevant treaties now contain more detailed and sophisticated provisions regarding the situations in which intervention is permitted by local authorities. The relevant treaties, mostly consular conventions, may be classified into five categories.

First, in a significant rapprochement between the French and British systems, the United Kingdom and France concluded a Consular Convention in 1951,[43] which in Article 40(2) provides for the following as their common affirmation of "the international practice":

1. The Parties confirm the right of the coastal State to take cognizance of offences committed on board any vessel in its ports or in its territorial waters and cognizable under the local law or to enforce local laws applicable;
2. The Parties "affirm their approval of the international practice" under which the local authorities *should not,* except at the request or with the consent of the consular officer,
   a. concern themselves with any matter taking place on board the vessel except for the preservation of peace and order or in the interests of public health or safety; or
   b. institute prosecutions in respect of offences committed on board the vessel unless,

39. Ibid, n. 1, p. 241; Moore (n. 27 above), p. 303.
40. Gidel (n. 3 above), p. 228.
41. Charteris (n. 15 above), n. 1, p. 79. In apparent adoption of the rule laid down in the *Tempest* and the Wildenhus cases, the Hamburg notification explains that the police authorities may go on board in prosecution of offences disturbing the peace or good order ashore or in the port and mentions as examples "murder, homicide, grievous assault" in addition to mutiny of the crew and arson.
42. Lee (n. 4 above), p. 82, n. 20.
43. UN Reg. No. 4744; Cmd. 8457 (France).

i. they involve the tranquility or safety of the port or the laws of the territory regarding public health, the safety of life at sea, customs or any similar matter; or
ii. they are committed by or against persons other than the master or members of the crew, or by or against nationals of the coastal State; or
iii. an offence of a serious character.[44]

This formula has been followed by a number of consular conventions, including those between the United Kingdom and Norway (1951),[45] Article 27(2); the United Kingdom and Sweden (1952),[46] Article 27(2); the United Kingdom and Greece (1953),[47] Article 28(2); and the United Kingdom and Mexico (1954),[48] Article 29(2).

In the second category of consular conventions, the Parties confirm the same point as (1) in the earlier-mentioned U.K.-French Convention and repeat point (2) as their "common intention," rather than expressing their approval of the international practice. Another difference is that no reference is made to "laws regarding public health, the safety of life at sea, customs or any similar matter." This does not mean, however, that this element is deleted altogether, for this formula is found only in the U.S.-U.K. Convention relating to Consular Officers (1951),[49] Article 22(2), and the Japan-U.S. Consular Convention (1963),[50] Article 21(2), and the latter adds a provision explaining that crimes or offences against the laws of the coastal State regarding public health, customs, or immigration committed on board a vessel in its ports or waters shall be deemed to be included in the crimes or offences involving the tranquility of the port.

The third category of conventions provides for essentially the same circumstances as in the earlier-mentioned two categories in which the local authorities may intervene in incidents on board. These conventions, however, make it an obligation for the local authorities not to intervene unless such circumstances arise, instead of a simple exhortation to refrain from intervening under the conventions in the first and second categories. These conventions thus contain the provisions along the following lines:

44. "Offence of a serous character" is defined in the case of the U.K.-French convention as an offence for which a sentence of imprisonment for 5 years or over may be awarded for the U.K. and an offence which constitutes a "crime" under the laws of the territory in the case of France. In other similar conventions, the definition mostly refers to an offence punishable by an imprisonment for 3 to 5 years.
45. UN Reg. No. 4713.
46. UN Reg. No. 2731. 202 *UNTS* 157.
47. UN Reg. No. 2582. 191 *UNTS* 151.
48. UN Reg. No. 4750. Cmd 9162 (Mexico).
49. UN Reg. No. 2174. 165 *UNTS* 121.
50. UN Reg. No. 7495.

> The local authorities *shall not*, except at the request or with the consent of the consular officer:
>
> a. concern themselves with any matter taking place on board the vessel unless for the preservation of peace and order or in the interests of public health or safety; or
>
> b. institute prosecutions in respect of offences (or disorders) on board the vessel unless:
>
>   i. they involve the tranquility or safety of the port or the law of the territory regarding public health, immigration, the safety of life at sea, customs or any similar matters; or
>
>   ii. they involve persons other than the master or crewmembers, or nationals of the coastal State; or
>
>   iii. the offence is of a serious character.

Such provisions are also often accompanied by an additional provision that "administrative authorities" shall not intervene in relation to any matter occurring on board the vessel, except in connection with the possible judiciary intervention for prosecution or where a crewmember is detained on board in a manner unlawful under the coastal State's law or accompanied by unjustifiable severity or inhumanity.

This formula is contained in the following consular conventions: U.K.-Italy (1954),[51] Article 29(2), Sweden-France (1955),[52] Article 37, U.K.-Germany (1956),[53] Article 32(2), U.K.-Austria (1960),[54] Article 41, U.K.-Spain (1961),[55] Article 47(2), U.K.-Denmark (1962),[56] Article 27(2), U.K.-Japan (1964),[57] Article 34(2), France-Tunisia (1972),[58] Article 35(3), France-Senegal (1974),[59] Article 33, France-Algeria (1974),[60] Article 37(2) and (3), France-Poland (1976),[61] Article 46, and Belgium-Algeria (1979),[62] Article 50.

The fourth category of consular conventions start with the confirmation of "the superior right of the administrative and judicial authorities" of the coastal State to take cognizance of crimes or offences that disturb the peace of the port or to enforce its laws applicable to vessels of any State within its waters, and provide for the rights of consular officers to exercise jurisdiction over "controversies" aboard vessels of their country at port. This

51. UN Reg. No. 5798.
52. UN Reg. No. 6150.
53. UN Reg. No. 4748.
54. UN Reg. No. 7327.
55. UN Reg. No. 8198.
56. UN Reg. No. 8197.
57. UN Reg. No. 8179.
58. UN Reg. No. 13379.
59. UN Reg. No. 16158. 1061 *UNTS* 256.
60. UN Reg. No. 18952. 1183 *UNTS* 230.
61. UN Reg. No. 15886. 1054 *UNTS* 67.
62. UN Reg. No. 21948. 1318 *UNTS* 76.

is found in the consular conventions between the United States and the Republic of Korea (1963),[63] Article 7(2), and the United States and France (1966),[64] Article 2.

Lastly, a fifth category of conventions simply provides that the local authorities "may exercise jurisdiction" over the kind of offences described in the first and second categories. This formula is contained in the consular conventions between Belgium and the United States (1969),[65] Article 37(1), and Belgium and Turkey (1972),[66] Article 48(1).

Several observations may be made on the basis of this survey. The first, most important, is that the rule is now firmly established that criminal jurisdiction may be exercised by a coastal State over foreign ships in its ports in a broadly accepted set of circumstances. Because the flag States have the jurisdiction and control over all ships flying their flags,[67] there will be concurrent jurisdiction of two States in such cases.

The question may be asked, Which of the two jurisdictions prevail in case both the coastal Sate and the flag State intend to intervene? These treaties do not have clear provisions as to which of the two has the priority in the exercise of their jurisdiction, except the two treaties cited in the fourth category, which specifically confirm the "superior right" of the coastal State authorities in this regard. There is, however, a strikingly common provision in *all* the treaties cited to the effect that when conducting investigation or other enforcement measures, the coastal States shall notify the consular officer of the flag State of the vessel concerned in principle beforehand, through the master or otherwise, to enable him/her to be present, and inform him/her of the result of the measures taken. It is often provided that such measures may be taken in exceptional circumstances at the same time as the notification is being made.[68] These provisions may well be interpreted that these treaties recognize, at least tacitly, the priority of the jurisdiction of the coastal State.

63. UN Reg. No. 7211.
64. UN Reg. No. 10044.
65. UN Reg. No. 13178.
66. UN Reg. No. 15142. 1029 *UNTS* 208.
67. See the Geneva Convention on the High Seas, Article 5(1); the LOS Convention, Article 94(1).
68. Such provisions are contained in the following consular conventions: U.K.-Italy (1954), Article 29(3); Sweden-France (1955), Article 37; U.K.-Germany (1956), Article 32(5); U.K.-Austria (1960), Article 41(5); U.K.-Spain (1961), Article 47(5); U.K.-Denmark (1962), Article 27(5); U.K.-Japan (1964), Article 34(4); France-Tunisia (1972), Article 35(4); France-Senegal (1974), Article 33(2); France-Algeria (1974), Article 37(4); France-Poland (1976), Article 47(1); Belgium-Algeria (1979), Article 51(1); U.K.-France (1951), Article 40(3); U.K.-Norway (1951), Article 27(3); U.K.-Sweden (1952), Article 27(3); U.K.-Greece (1953), Article 28(3); U.K.-Mexico (1954), Article 29(3); Belgium-U.S. (1969), Article 37(2); Belgium-Turkey (1972), Article 48(2); U.S.-U.K. (1951), Article 22(3); Japan-U.S. (1963), Article 21(4); U.S.-Republic of Korea (1963), Article 7(3); and U.S.-France (1966), Article 32(3).

Secondly, there is a clear trend now to mention specifically an offence or crime of a serious character as a third situation that permits local intervention, in addition to the traditional enumeration of the disturbance of the order or tranquility and the involvement of nationals or non-crewmembers in the disorder. Exceptionally, however, such a crime or offence is considered to be one of the acts that disturbs the peace or tranquility of the port.[69]

Thirdly, it should be stressed that the traditional distinction between the French and British systems makes no longer any sense. The main substantive contents of the treaties are mostly the same. The only notable difference is that, while the treaties in the first and second categories use the term "should not," indicating the nonobligatory nature of the coastal State's abstention from intervention, those in the third category use "shall not," making such abstention obligatory. The former is closer to the traditional British system, while the latter to the French system. However, both France and the United Kingdom, as well as some other States that used to follow one of them, are no longer parties to only one of them, and reject the other. It appears that both groups of countries now accept either of the two formulas. It may thus be interpreted that the use of one of the two expressions in a treaty indicates the difference in emphasis and not the firmly established legal position of the State concerned.

Fourthly, all the conventions cited, except one, do not specify that the offence or disorder for which the coastal State may intervene has occurred while the ship is in port or even in its territorial sea.[70] In fact, a convention specifically provides for offences committed in the waters of the coastal State separately from those committed outside its waters, both of which are punishable under its laws. Thus, strong assumption may be made that, generally speaking, the coastal State may intervene even in cases where a crime or offence had been committed before the vessel entered the port or the territorial sea.

Lastly, another new trend of the post-War consular conventions is to provide for circumstances permitting local intervention by not only judicial but also administrative authorities. This clearly broadens the actions that could be taken by local authorities with respect to matters on board a ship at port beyond the traditional jurisdiction for the purpose of criminal and civil procedures. This is evidently a reflection of the growing humanitarian

69. Such provisions are contained in the consular conventions between Japan and the United States (1963), Article 21 (2)(b), and the United States and the Republic of Korea (1963), Article 7(2). In the case of the former, the provision is quite broad, stipulating that "crimes or offences against the laws of the receiving (coastal) State regarding public health, customs or immigration committed on board a vessel in the ports or waters of that State shall be deemed to be included in the crimes or offenses involving the tranquility of the port."

70. The sole exception is the convention between Japan and the United States, 1963, Article 21(2)(b).

concern of the international community for those working on board ships; a typical case mentioned by several treaties is the case where crewmembers are detained in a manner unlawful under local laws or accompanied by unjustifiable severity or inhumanity.

The Emerging Principles

The earlier review of the main trends in the practice of principal countries shows that, despite the traditional emphasis on the doctrinal dichotomy between the French and British systems, there appears to be in fact little difference in actual practice and that it is no longer possible to divide States into any distinct groups on the basis of the two systems. The salient features that characterize the contemporary practice of States with regard to criminal jurisdiction may be summarized as follows:

1. Foreign ships that enter a port are subject to the sovereignty of the coastal State, which has criminal jurisdiction thereover;
2. The coastal State, however, does not *exercise* such jurisdiction, either as a matter of principle or practice, over matters involving solely the internal discipline of the ship;
3. There will be concurrent jurisdiction exercisable by the flag State of the ship and the coastal State when an offence or disorder caused on board the ship (i) affects or is likely to affect the peace and order or the tranquility of the port or on land, (ii) is committed by or against a national of the coastal State or a person other than the master or crewmembers, or (iii) is of a serious character, usually punishable by a sentence of imprisonment for more than a few years. Such an offence or disorder includes, in principle, those that occur while the ship is on the high seas as far as the same situation or its direct effect remains when it enters a port;
4. It is solely the coastal State that may determine the presence or absence of the situation falling under (3.) above.[71]
5. Under such circumstances, the coastal State may investigate or take other enforcement measures on board the ship by giving, in principle, prior notification to the consul of the flag State;
6. Coastal State authorities may also "concern themselves" with matters taking place on board for the preservation of peace and order or in the interests of public health or safety, customs and immigration;
7. The coastal State may intervene in any incident on board when requested by the master of the ship, its flag State or its consular officers.

71. McDougal and Burke (n. 31 above), p. 168, state that "[t]here appears to be full agreement, surprisingly, that this decision is solely that of the coastal state."

It is submitted that these elements indicate emerging principles and could serve as useful bases for further development of the law on the subject.

ATTEMPTS AT CODIFICATION

The League of Nations and the United Nations held four conferences for the codification of the law of the sea, though the third one was devoted only to the question of breadth of the territorial sea. None of them produced any provision on the status of foreign ships in ports, including coastal State's jurisdiction. In fact, only the first conference, the 1930 Hague Conference for the Codification of International Law, discussed the question, without success.

In the Bases of Discussion elaborated by the Preparatory Committee for the Codification Conference, there was Basis No. 27, which read as follows:

> The criminal jurisdiction of the State to which the port belongs may not be exercised in regard to crimes or offences committed on board a foreign merchant ship lying in a port except:
> 1. where the crime or offence was committed by or against persons not forming part of the crew; or
> 2. where, in the opinion of the competent local authority, it was a nature to disturb the peace of the port; or
> 3. where the assistance of the local authorities was requested by the captain of the ship, the consul of the country whose flag the ship flies, or a person directly affected.[72]

Positions of governments were divided on this provision. Before the Conference was convened, six States (Belgium, Denmark, Finland, Germany, Italy, and the Netherlands) had expressed the view that it was not appropriate for a convention on the territorial sea to deal with the jurisdiction over foreign ships in ports, whereas 14 governments had commented affirmatively either in an express or implied manner.[73]

The negative view was apparently based on two reasons. One was the lack of the need for such provision because of the existence of a great number of conventional rules already regulating the matter. The other is the objective of the future convention, which would be the codification of the law applicable to the territorial sea and would thus exclude ports. On the other hand, a number of governments, including the United Kingdom

72. League of Nations. *Conference for the Codification of International Law. Bases of Discussion,* Vol. II, *Territorial Waters.* League of Nations, 1929, p. 101.
73. Gidel (n. 3 above), p. 252, n. 1.

and the Dominion countries, believed in the need to deal with the question even if ports are, technically speaking, not part of the territorial sea.[74]

At the Conference, the deletion of Basis No. 27 in the Bases of Discussion was proposed by Poland, Spain, and the United States, and in view of the divided views on the proposal and the lack of adequate time for a thorough examination of the subject, it was decided that no action would be taken on the provision. It was instead recommended that the 1923 Convention on the International Regime of Maritime Ports should be completed by adopting provisions regulating the extent of judicial powers of States with regard to the foreign vessels in their internal waters.[75] No attempt, however, has since been made to act on this recommendation.

UNCLOS I followed closely the work of the Hague Conference, thus excluding the question of jurisdiction over foreign ships in ports. This was intentional from the beginning of its preparatory stage, when the special rapporteur, J.P.A. François, on the regime of the territorial sea started his work in the International Law Commission (ILC). In his first report to ILC, François wrote that he was inspired largely by the report he himself had submitted on the regime of the territorial sea as the rapporteur of the Second Commission of the Hague Conference.[76] ILC as a whole also took the same attitude in completing the draft articles concerning the law of the sea. This is evident in its commentary to Article 20, which, though dealing with foreign ships passing through the territorial sea, touches upon ships at port:

> In the case of a ship lying in the territorial sea, the jurisdiction of the coastal State should be regulated by the State's own municipal law. Such jurisdiction is more extensive than in the case of ships which are simply passing through the territorial sea . . . This applies also to ships which have called at a port . . . Thus the proposed article [Article 20] does not attempt to solve conflicts of jurisdiction between the coastal State and the flag State in the matter of criminal law . . . The Commission is fully aware of the *desirability of codifying the law relating to these matters* . . . Nevertheless, *following the example set by the 1930 Conference,* the Commission refrained from formulating specific rules on this subject, because it felt that in this very broad field certain limits must inevitably be set to its work. (emphases added)[77]

74. Ibid.

75. See Lee (n. 4 above), p. 81.

76. UN doc. A/CN.4/53 (4 April 1952), reproduced in *Yearbook of the International Law Commission,* 1952, vol. II, UN Publication, Sales No. 58.V.5.Vol. II, p. 26.

77. Report of the International Law Commission Covering the Work of its Eighth Session, 23 April–4 July 1956 (UN doc. A/3159), reproduced in *Yearbook of the International Law Commission,* 1956, vol. II, p. 275.

In other words, ILC excluded from its work the subject of criminal jurisdiction over ships lying in the territorial sea and those that have called at a port, despite the desirability to include it, because it would broaden the scope of the work too much. ILC allegedly followed the example set by the Hague Conference on this point. This explanation, however, appears to be inconsistent because that Conference had not exactly reached agreement on the desirability of codifying the law on the subject. Nor did the Conference consider that the subject would broaden the scope too much. Another stated reason for ILC's reluctance to deal with the matter was that, although it was aware of the usefulness to determine what court would be competent for criminal proceedings arising out of a collision in the territorial sea, a convention on that very subject had been adopted in 1952.[78] It may be observed that the subject matter that that convention dealt with was a matter quite different from the general question of coastal State's jurisdiction over foreign ships in port. Thus the conclusion may be inescapable that ILC and UNCLOS I, which eventually were mandated to cover all aspects of the law of the sea, decided to exclude the question from the scope without coherent, logical reasons.

With regard to the LOS Convention, there was a broad understanding at the beginning of UNCLOS III that the basic provisions relating to the traditional law of the sea questions should follow as much as possible those contained in the Geneva Conventions on the Territorial Sea and the Contiguous Zone and on the High Seas. In fact, discussion in the Second Committee, which dealt with the matters covered by these Conventions, followed very closely the provisions in the two Conventions. None of the proposals submitted by governments at the beginning of the Conference nor the Main Trends working paper, a synthesized compilation of main proposals and formulations that became the basis of negotiations, contained any provision on the status of foreign ships in ports.[79]

Thus, despite the "desirability" of codifying the question expressed by ILC at UNCLOS I, no State was ready to raise it, or the question had been completely forgotten, at UNCLOS III.

CONCLUSION

The question of coastal State jurisdiction over foreign ships at its ports has gone through 2 centuries of evolution since the French Conseil d'Etat gave

78. Ibid. The convention referred to is the International Convention for the Unification of Certain Rules Relating to Penal Jurisdiction in Matters of Collisions or Other Incidents of Navigation, signed at Brussels on 10 May 1952. 439 *UNTS* 233.

79. See *Third United Nations Conference on the Law of the Sea, Official Records*, vol. III, UN publication Sales No. E.75.V.5 (New York, 1975). The Main Trends working paper is reproduced on p. 107 ff.

its famous *Avis* in 1806. For more than a century, State practice was divided between those following the French system based on the *Avis*, and those following the British system based on the absolute doctrine of the coastal States jurisdiction. But such doctrinal difference was often highlighted more than the actual conduct of governments and courts. In fact, the practice of even key States was not always consistent. The departure from traditional positions became increasingly clear, particularly in the post-War practice of bilateral consular conventions. Furthermore, such conventions generally share several common elements, on which recent State practice seems to largely converge.

Despite a rather long evolution in practice, the subject has never been successfully incorporated in any codification convention since the first attempt at the 1930 Hague Conference ended without success. UNCLOS I and UNCLOS III, which attempted to address law of the sea questions in a comprehensive manner, avoided to take up that particular subject by simply following the Hague Conference. One may wonder, however, if the approach taken by the latter two conferences was appropriate. Although the Hague Conference failed to agree on the provision on the subject, it did not consider that the subject deserved no attention. On the contrary, since the focus of the Conference was on the territorial sea, it recommended that the subject be dealt with elsewhere, that is, within the context of the 1923 Convention on maritime ports through elaboration of additional provisions. On the other hand, ILC admitted the need for codification of the subject, but decided not to take it up, with no recommendation on what should be done with the subject.

The need for codification expressed by ILC has since been neglected completely by the international community. It is submitted that the time is not only ripe for revisiting the subject with a view to codification particularly in view of the broad convergence of post-War practice; the need for such codification is getting increasingly stronger with the rapid expansion of the global shipping with ever-greater complexity in ships' nationality, ownership, management, and crew composition. The cases of the *Tajima* and the *Glory Cape* will therefore not be isolated incidents.

There are two options in any future efforts at codification of the subject. It could be part of the broader codification of the general regime of internal waters, which is the most desirable. Alternatively, codification could be focused on criminal jurisdiction over foreign ships at ports.

As far as the forum for such work is concerned, the first approach should be entrusted with a new global conference to be convened either through the amendment procedures of the LOS Convention under Article 312, or through a new initiative at the UN General Assembly. In the latter case, the new instrument to be adopted could take the form of a protocol to the LOS Convention or an independent convention, and ILC could be invited to prepare draft articles.

As regards the second, narrower approach to focus only on jurisdictional questions, a conference of the States parties to the 1923 Convention on maritime ports could be convened for the purpose of adopting an amendment thereto or an additional protocol. Such a conference, however, would be too limited in participants,[80] and would not satisfy many countries that are not parties but are interested in the subject. Thus, a better approach would be the same as for the first approach, or alternatively it could be undertaken under the International Maritime Organization's auspices.

In future efforts at codification on criminal jurisdiction, a useful model to be considered would be the Tokyo Convention on Offences and Certain Other Acts Committed on Board Aircraft.[81] The Convention is aimed at clarifying the jurisdiction of different States that would be potentially interested in exercising it in cases where certain offences and acts have been committed on board a civil aircraft "in flight."[82] The offences and acts covered are "offences against penal law" and "acts which, whether or not they are offences, may or do jeopardize the safety of the aircraft or of persons or property therein or which jeopardize good order and discipline onboard."[83] Regarding criminal jurisdiction, the Convention recognizes first that of the State of registration of the aircraft, obliging such State to take measures necessary to establish its jurisdiction over offences.[84] Other States may also interfere with an aircraft in flight in order to exercise its criminal jurisdiction over an offence committed on board in exceptional cases. These are cases where

a. the offence has effect on the territory of such State;
b. the offence has been committed by or against a national or permanent resident of such State;
c. the offence is against the security of such State;
d. the offence consists of a breach of any rules or regulations relating to the flight or manoeuvre of aircraft;
e. the exercise of jurisdiction is required under other treaties.[85]

The Tokyo Convention further contains provisions on the powers of the aircraft commander and the powers and duties of States, which are essential for the effective control of criminal acts on board.[86] Civil aircraft and ships

80. The parties to the 1923 Convention are currently 42 States, according to the information obtained from the UN Secretariat on 1 September 2002.

81. 2 *International Legal Materials* 1042 (1963).

82. The Convention considers an aircraft is "in flight" from the moment when power is applied for the purpose of take-off until the moment when the landing run ends (Article 1[3]).

83. Ibid., Article 1(1).

84. Ibid., Article 3.

85. Ibid., Article 4.

86. Ibid., Articles 5-15.

engaged in international trade or carrying passengers share many common features, with the incidence of criminal acts far greater in the latter. Drafting of similar provisions may be done without much difficulty for ships in navigation and in ports given the recent trends described earlier. It may be more difficult for States to agree on the powers and duties of masters since there have been rules and practices of long flag State tradition on them, unlike the cases of aircraft commanders. It is, however, worth trying to draft basic rules on that aspect also to facilitate the speedy and effective handling of criminal cases on board.

Maritime Regional Cooperation in South Asia: Opportunities and Challenges*

Abul Kalam Azad
Marine Affairs Program (2001–2002), Dalhousie University, Halifax, Canada
Bangladesh Institute of International and Strategic Studies, Dhaka

INTRODUCTION

In contemporary ocean management, the protection and conservation of the marine environment and its resources through regional cooperation seems to have gained momentum for a number of reasons. Among these, the most widely held is "the recognition of the fact that many ocean resources and uses are inherently trans-boundary in nature, and that not all of these are functionally manageable at a global level."[1] In a similar vein, reference is made to the limitations at the national level in tackling the multifarious ocean-related problems. As observed in the United Nations Environment Programme/Global Programme of Action (UNEP/GPA) News Forum, "coastal and marine environmental management cannot, however, be fully served by national and sub-national institutions because of the large scales, and limited human knowledge and ownership of ocean ecosystems. The spatial and jurisdictional borders of nations rarely conform to the boundaries of marine ecosystems."[2] In the face of such limitations, regional cooperation is now considered an effective means of managing ocean affairs in so far as it (i) allows for a more accurate assessment of transboundary

* Editors' Note.—This article was the winning entry in the 2002 *Ocean Yearbook* Student Paper Competition.

1. P. Saunders, "Maritime Regional Cooperation: Theory and Principles," in *Maritime Regime Building: Lessons Learned and Their Relevance for Northeast Asia,* ed. M. J. Valencia (The Hague: Martinus Nijhoff Publishers, 2000), pp. 1–16.

2. UNEP/GPA News Forum, http://gpanews.unep.org (accessed 5 September 2001). 'Most natural resource and other environmental problems are essentially limited to their ecological region or ecosystem, a condition that holds true both for land and the ocean. At the same time, a majority of the recurring international conflicts is between neighboring nations. It thus becomes eminently sensible to foster cooperation among a group of nations that share such an ecological region (often a 'sub-region' in political terminology),' A. Westing, "Environmental Dimensions of Maritime Security," in *Maritime Security: The Building of Confidence,* ed. J. Goldblat (New York: United Nations, 1992), pp. 77–98.

Ocean Yearbook 18: 512–542

problems, as well as for an appropriate identification of priorities for action, (ii) strengthens mechanisms for both regional and national capacity building, and (iii) harmonizes and adjusts measures according to national environmental, institutional and socioeconomic conditions.[3] In effect, the regional approach to ocean governance is now looked upon as an endeavor to bring all the actors—national, regional and global—in the same continuum. Elisabeth Mann Borgese remarked, "the restructuring of ocean governance at the regional level is of crucial importance for the entire global/regional/national and sub-national governance structure. Just as the coastal community is the link between national and regional communities, the regional community is the link between national and global communities."[4]

The attempt to forge maritime regional cooperation is not without its political and legal basis. While the 1982 United Nations Convention on Law of the Sea (UNCLOS)[5] lays down the basic framework for global and regional marine cooperation, efforts at the international level for such cooperation go back to the United Nations Conference on the Human Environment in 1972 at Stockholm. Various proposals and arrangements at the United Nations Conference on Environment and Development (UNCED) at Rio in 1992 and in the post-Rio period also refer to regional cooperation in solving environmental problems for attaining the goal of sustainable development, both on land and in the ocean. In particular, with respect to marine environmental protection, Chapter 17 of Agenda 21[6] of the UNCED specifically refers to strengthening international, including regional, cooperation and coordination.[7] Thus, over the years, regional cooperation has extended to living resource management, scientific research, marine transport, military activities, environmental protection, and non-living resource management, as well as broadly based regional economic development activities.[8] In this respect, "some arrangements and institutions have been 'independent' in the sense of being created within a region, while others have operated under the auspices of broader global programs sponsored by bodies such as the United Nations Food and Agriculture Organization (FAO) and the Intergovernmental Oceanographic Commission (IOC) of

3. P. Akiwumi and T. Melvasalo, "UNEP's Regional Seas Programme: Approach, Experience and Future Plans," *Marine Policy* 22, no. 3 (1998): 229–34.

4. E. M. Borgese, *Ocean Governance and the United Nations* (Halifax: Centre for Foreign Policy Studies, Dalhousie University, 1996), p. 164.

5. See UNCLOS, Division for Ocean Affairs and the Law of the Sea, United Nations, New York, http://www.un.org/depts/los/ (accessed 5 February 2002).

6. United Nations Conference on Environment and Development, *Agenda 21* (New York, NY: United Nations Dept. of Public Information, 1993). See for details, Borgese (n. 4 above), pp. 58–63.

7. See for details, T. Treves, "The Protection of the Oceans in Agenda 21 and International Environmental Law," in *The Environment After Rio: International Law and Economics*, ed. L. Campigilio, L. Pineschi, D. Sinisiscalco and T. Treves (London: Graham and Trotman/Martinus Nijhoff, 1994), pp. 161–71.

8. Saunders (n. 1 above), p. 4.

UNESCO."[9] UNEP, through its extensive Regional Seas Programme, has promoted networks of framework conventions, action plans, and other instruments in 14 regions. Despite the proliferation of regional networks, however, progress in even such advanced regions like the Baltic, the North Sea, and the Mediterranean Sea is to be noted with caution.

The purpose of this article is to study the present nature of maritime regional cooperation in South Asia. The research focus of the article consists of identifying the problems and prospects of such cooperation in a conflict-ridden area such as South Asia from a perspective that takes into account the legal, political, social, and economic elements. The inquiry is mainly based on a study of the UNEP-sponsored South Asian Regional Seas Programme, the only regional institution to deal with marine-related problems at present. However, an attempt will be made to identify whether other avenues of cooperation in the field are possible, in particular, under the aegis of the South Asian Association for Regional Cooperation (SAARC), or on the platform of a few recently proposed arrangements. The article is divided into three sections dealing with theoretical and legal aspects, maritime regional cooperation, and challenges and opportunities for maritime cooperation in South Asia.

MARITIME REGIONAL COOPERATION: THEORETICAL AND LEGAL REFLECTIONS

The ideal of regional cooperation is basically terrestrial in nature, reflecting the nation-states' penchant for meeting their geosecurity, social, and economic needs in cooperation with each other at the sub-systemic level, while still being a part of the central international system. Although a post-World War II phenomenon, evidence of regionalism is found in 19th century Europe when, for example, continental commissions were set up to ensure the freedom of navigation on the Rhine (1815) and the Danube (1856).[10] As a land-based concept, regionalism is explained by a number of theories, that is, integration, functionalism, neofunctionalism, and globalism, et cetera.[11]

9. Ibid., pp. 3–4.

10. It is interesting to see how the Rhine and Danube Commissions were formed in the midst of political situations marked by discord, strife, and tension among the European powers. See for details, P. Gerbet, "Rise and Development of International Organization: A Synthesis," in *The Concept of International Organization,* ed. G. Abi Saab (Paris: UNESCO, 1981), pp. 27–66.

11. Among all the theories, functionalism has gained its prominence in fostering regionalism. The functionalist school accepts the predominance of economics over politics, a kind of economic determinism so dear to classical liberalism and Marxism. Functionalism presumes to offer means for overcoming suspicion and distrust that have often prevented the building of peace systems. See for details, C. F. Alger, "Functionalism and Integration as Approaches to International Organization," in G. Abi Saab (n. 10 above), pp. 122–45.

The phenomenon is also rich in empiricism in so far as a vast array of regional organizations, built along the theoretical models as appropriate to the regions, serve as examples to show the success or failure in their respective functions. In effect, regionalism in the terrestrial domain received much of its stimuli from the importance accorded to regional studies in post-war international relations for reasons such as the East-West conflict; the emergence of a number of new countries after the process of decolonization; a fear of neocolonialism; the rapid advancement in science and technology; and above all, the growing expectation of the people for better and safer living, both in the developed and underdeveloped worlds.[12] Looking from this angle, one may find that regionalism in the ocean medium appears to be somewhat a belated phenomenon. This is explained not by the absence of any concept of region in the oceans, but by a late human realization that the vastness of the oceans is not a perpetual guarantee for its abundant wealth and opportunity. In other words, the absence of Westphalian concepts of sovereignty, territoriality, or ownership in a strict Roman sense in the oceanic domain did not necessarily imply a possession of carte blanche by humankind to adversely affect the oceanic resources, habitat, and environment. The excesses committed by humankind thus needed redressing. In this respect, the profligate use of marine resources, in particular, overexploitation of fisheries from the mid-1950s (made possible by rapid advances in acoustic technology, net design, and the gradual replacement of outmoded pre-war vessels), became the issue of foremost concern, followed by other issues like increasing marine pollution due to multifarious human activities in the ocean that included commercial exploitation and exploration of oil, gas, and other resources, and military uses.[13]

The reasons for such problems could not be studied from a global angle as there were significant regional differences in their causes and intensity, and hence differences in effects. The stated problems, in effect, ushered in opportunities for countries to cooperate rather than disagree. Like regionalism on the land that on many occasions was initiated in response to crisis, in the ocean domain too, a similar endeavor was taken in response to crisis. Thus, the proliferation of a number of regional fisheries management programs under the aegis of the FAO since the 1950s was essentially a move to respond to the fish crisis of the time.[14] Prior to these initiatives, the Interna-

12. Various chapters in *Regional Politics and World Order,* ed. R. A. Falk and S. H. Mendlovitz (San Francisco: W. H. Freeman and Company, 1979) describe the trends of regionalism in the post-World War II period. In particular, regionalism received its stimulus from the theoretical breakthrough in the concept provided by a number of political analysts.

13. R. P. Barston and P. W. Birnie, "Introduction," in *The Maritime Dimension,* ed. R. P. Barston and P. Birnie (London: George Allen and Unwin, 1980), pp. 1–3.

14. S. Keckes, "The Protection and Development of the Marine Environment: UNEP's Oceans and Coastal Areas Programme," in *Ocean Management in Global*

tional Council for the Exploration for the Sea (ICES) and the International Council for the Scientific Exploration of the Mediterranean (ICSEM), were the only existing regional programs to deal with fisheries in addition to associated programs for scientific research.[15] Beginning in the late 1960s, marine pollution attained a crisis dimension that drew the rapt attention of the international community; the need for cooperation in the field led to the birth of programs supported by legally binding agreements. The first agreement in this series was the Bonn Agreement (1969) that dealt with the protection of the North Sea from pollution by oil.[16] Perhaps an important trend of the period to which oceanic regionalism owes much is the quest for a new approach to ocean governance, so as to manage oceanic resources in the interests of humankind. While Hardin's 'Tragedy of the Commons' or Arvid Pardo's concept of the 'Common Heritage'[17] might have provided the philosophical basis for such a quest, impetus to it was given by the UN initiative in creating a new ocean regime to ensure that all nations and all peoples benefit from the uses of the oceans and the exploitation of its resources. This implied undertaking a series of negotiations for overcoming the deficiency of the Geneva Convention on the Law of the Sea (1958–60)[18] in many important facets of the ocean regime. It is important to note the great strides made by the United Nations in the field of preservation and protection of the marine environment by incorporating these issues into a comprehensive and elaborate manner in the final 1982 UNCLOS,[19] provisions for which

---

Change, ed. P. Fabbri (Elsevier, London and New York: Applied Science, 1992), p. 347.

15. Ibid.

16. The Bonn Agreement was followed by other regional agreements designed to control marine pollution by concerted joint action of a group of countries like the Oslo Convention 1972, Paris Convention 1974, and Helsinki Convention 1974, etc. All of these agreements were the products of direct negotiations between the interested governments, without the involvement of the UN system. Ibid., p. 348.

17. While Garett Hardin's influential article "Tragedy of the Commons," *Science* 162 (1968): 1243–1248 influenced the management of common resources from their eventual destruction, it had its implications for ocean management too. Arvid Pardo's common heritage put the entire oceanic perspective in a newer form in so far as it introduced the principles of equity and nonproperty in the ocean domain. He revolutionalized the thinking of politicians, jurists, and scientists alike when the seabed and the ocean floor were declared as common heritage to be used and exploited for peaceful purposes and for the exclusive benefit of humankind as a whole. Part XI of the UNCLOS entitled '*Area*' deals with various aspects of common heritage in Articles 136, 137, 138, 140, 141, and 142, complemented by other articles of the Convention.

18. See *Official Records of the United Nations Conference on the Law of the Sea,* vols. I to VII, United Nations publication, Sales No.: 58.V.4, vols. I to VII.

19. Part XII of the UNCLOS, entitled *Protection and Preservation of the Marine Environment,* contains what is still today the only existing comprehensive, universal, binding, and enforceable international environmental law, covering the ocean environment globally, dealing with pollution from all sources, whether oceanic, atmo-

were virtually absent in the 1958–1960 agreements.[20] Still more important to note is the role played by the United Nations in institutionalizing regional cooperation in the marine domain much before the final UNCLOS. In theory, it goes to prove that unlike in regional cooperative organizations on land where United Nations' involvement is not necessary, in marine regional arrangements, in most cases such involvement appears to be a prerequisite. Thus, one observes the regional approach to marine cooperation receiving much of its stimulus from the 1972 UN Conference on the Human Environment.[21]

The conference that outlined the priorities and the need to safeguard and improve the environment in all developmental activities could not, perhaps, remain indifferent to the marine domain in such concerns. UNEP, established in the same year, with its raison d'être well grounded in the ideals of the conference, soon realized that dealing with first-generation environment problems, namely pollution of water, air, and soil (land degradation) would not attain complete results until marine cooperation was undertaken in an institutionalized manner: hence, the initiation of the Regional Seas Programme under the aegis of UNEP in 1974.[22] This set in motion a new kind of marine cooperation with due cognizance of the fact that given the variance in the nature and the relative importance of threats to the health of the oceans from region to region, nothing less than a regional approach would be the means to combat them.

Ocean management at the regional level, in particular in the way it is envisaged under the UNEP Programme seemed to have prompted many

---

spheric, or from land-based sources, and including pollution of all kinds, whether oil, industrial, or agricultural wastes, chemicals, or other hazardous substances. E. M. Borgese, *The Oceanic Circle: Governing the Seas as a Global Resource* (Tokyo: UN University Press, 1998), p. 113.

20. Barston and Birnie (n. 13 above), p. 2.

21. The 1972 UN Conference on the Human Environment outlined a master plan for protecting the environment from degradation in which advantages of a regional approach to many of the global environmental problems were advocated. Akiwumi and Melvasalo (n. 3 above), p. 229. It may be mentioned that earlier in 1972, the UN Committee on Peaceful Uses of the Seabed stressed that "maritime pollution could effectively be dealt with by a combination of global, regional and national rules and procedures with the global one fixing the minimum provision . . . and the regional and national ones laying down particular and structural provisions as may be required . . . in a region or country." O. Okidi, *Regional Control of Ocean Pollution: Legal and Institutional Problems and Prospects* (Netherlands: Sijthoff Publications on Ocean Development, 1978), p. 3.

22. UNEP initiated the Regional Seas Programme as a global program implemented through regional components. At present, the Regional Seas Programme includes 14 regions worldwide, comprising over 140 coastal states and territories participating in the Programme. The Programme is action oriented, focusing not only on the mitigation or elimination of the consequences, but also on the causes of environmental degradation.

analysts and specialists to apply the concept of 'regime' or 'regime building' in the ocean domain too. Essentially non-oceanic in nature, the concept describes the trend towards sequentially negotiated arrangements involving mostly the same actors over a period of time.[23] It introduces the idea of a combination of formal/binding and informal/nonbinding instruments that evolve together, making up a regime, cluster, or system of commitments.[24] The value of this concept lies in the fact that cultivating cooperative arrangements does not necessarily depend on formal instruments. While the concept has been defined in various ways, its most broad definition has been epitomized/forwarded by Krasner. A regime, according to him,

> is a cluster of . . . implicit or explicit principles, norms, rules and decision-making procedures around which actors' expectations converge in a given area of international relations. Principles are beliefs of fact, causation, and rectitude. Norms are standards of behavior defined in terms of rights and obligations. Rules are specific prescriptions or proscriptions for actions. Decision-making procedures are prevailing practices for making and implementing collective choice.[25]

Saunders has also identified some of the important traits of regime building.[26] Firstly, by including soft-law instruments, institutional and social elements, nongovernmental actors, the scope of activities within a regime becomes wide. Secondly, the regime approach puts significant emphasis on knowledge that might be gathered from different sources. In this connection, Saunders refers to the role played by "epistemic communities."[27] Thirdly, the regime approach is appropriate to the management of the oceans at the regional level where as he argues, "it provides the possibility

23. O. R. Young, *International Cooperation: Building Regimes for Natural Resources and the Environment* (Ithaca: Cornell University Press, 1989), cited in D. VanderZwaag and D. M. Johnston, "Toward the Management of the Gulf of Thailand: Charting the Course of Cooperation," in *SEAPOL Integrated Studies of the Gulf of Thailand Volume 1*, ed. D. M. Johnston (Bangkok, Innomedia Co. Ltd.: South East Asian Program in Ocean Law, Policy and Management, 1998), p. 82.

24. VanderZwaag and Johnston, p. 83.

25. Saunders (n. 1 above), p. 2.

26. Ibid., p. 3.

27. P. M. Haas is the political scientist who used the term epistemic communities as an explication of why Mediterranean ocean governance came in place during the 1970s and 1980s. He defines epistemic communities as "channels through which ideas circulate from societies to governments as well as from country to country." Haas cites, "a network of professionals with recognized expertise and competence in a particular domain and an authoritative claim to policy-relevant knowledge within that domain or issue area." See T. Naess, "Epistemic Communities and Environmental Co-operation in the South China Sea," University of Oslo: Centre for Development and the Environment, http://www.prio.no/research/asiasecurity/Publications/pdf/Naess.pdf (accessed 4 February 2003).

of expanding the range of relevant regional characteristics which might be employed in determining the suitability of a particular type of cooperative activity in a region."[28] In effect, regime building is now considered as an essential component of the emerging system of ocean governance, and acts as a link between national and global communities. The national sector benefits from the convenient marriage between globalism and regionalism. In this respect, the latter tries to specify the generality of a myriad of global agreements and arrangements in a regional context.[29] The legal basis of maritime regional cooperation derived from global dispensation is, indeed, a marked feature to distinguish it from land-based regionalism where global legal dispensation is somewhat absent.[30] It is, therefore, relevant to shed, in a brief manner, some light on the legal aspects of maritime regional cooperation.

It is the UNCLOS dispensation in the field that draws one's attention. Even the initiation of the Regional Seas Programme by UNEP in 1974, much before the birth of UNCLOS in 1982, drew on the convention that was under negotiation.[31] Article 197 of UNCLOS may, perhaps, be considered as the fountain head of regionalism in the oceanic domain,[32] and it figures in Part XII of UNCLOS entitled, Protection and Preservation of the Marine Environment, that contains the only existing comprehensive, binding, environmental law, covering pollution from all sources, whether land-based, oceanic, or atmospheric. It also provides a comprehensive, binding system for the peaceful settlement of environmental issues, as well as enforcement

28. Saunders (n. 1 above), p. 3.

29 Okidi (n. 21 above), p. 166.

30. Although the UN system encourages regional political cooperation, as explicitly expressed in Article 52 of the Charter involving the Security Council, the main instruments for promoting the general welfare in economics and social areas were to be the specialized agencies, which by example from the past would have the global membership, characteristic of the ILO or UPU. However, the creation of regional commissions for economic cooperation within the UN Framework clearly reflected ideological notions about the promise of regional cooperation (Economic Commissions for Europe, Far East and Latin America, for example). L. Gordenker, "The UN and Political Cooperation in Africa," in *African Regional Organizations,* ed. D. Mazzeo (Cambridge: Cambridge University Press, 1984), pp. 15–16.

31. The Regional Seas Programme emanating from the Stockholm Conference on the Human Environment relied heavily on the universal law emerging in the nascent Part XI of UNCLOS and would be unthinkable without it. If it was UNEP's most successful undertaking, this was because it could build within the solid framework of that Convention. Other sectors of environmental programs did not enjoy this advantage. Borgese (n. 4 above), p. 185.

32. Article 197: "States shall cooperate on a global basis and as appropriate, on a regional basis, directly or through competent international organizations, in formulating and elaborating international rules, standards and recommended practices and procedures consistent with this Convention for the protection and preservation of the marine environment, taking into account characteristic regional features," UNCLOS (n. 5 above).

mechanisms, dividing enforcement responsibilities between port States, coastal States, and flag States.[33] It is important to note that, although in Article 197 regional cooperation is hinted at by taking into account characteristic regional features, nonetheless, the efforts in this direction should be in conformity with the international rules, standards, practices, and procedures as reflected in the Convention. Thus, as stated earlier, regionalism as espoused by UNCLOS is inseparable from globalism.

It is to be noted that UNCLOS does not define the term 'region' in any precise manner.[34] The result being flexibility and latitude in utilizing the terms in taking any of the following criteria: (i) geographical, to include an area of ocean waters bounded by two or more states and based upon a distinctive geographical feature or features; (ii) a functional approach in terms of the need to manage transboundary pollution or living resource issues; and (iii) a numerical sense of a cooperative marine management arrangement falling between the extremes of bilateral (involving just two countries) and global (involving the community of states).[35] Towards this end, states are urged to establish regional rules, standards, and recommended practices to prevent and control pollution of the marine environment from land-based activities, seabed activities, ocean dumping, and atmospheric sources. Various Articles deal with maritime cooperation in several dimensions.[36]

Regionalism in the ocean is also guided by soft law—a term used in Europe in the 1970s to describe environmental instruments that were legal in form, but lacked in potential litigative significance due to the usage of general and open-ended language.[37] With respect to environment, soft law began to attain new color and texture when sustainable development, the dominant theme of UNCED, became a new paradigm to guide development in harmony with the environment. The paradigmatic shift also had positive effects on the ocean domain. Chapter 17 of Agenda 21 places the entire oceanic domain in a new perspective in so far as development, preservation, and conservation of marine resources are concerned.[38] Henceforth, the

33. Borgese (n. 4 above), p. 185.

34. VanderZwaag and Johnston (n. 23 above), p. 114.

35. Ibid.

36. UNCLOS, inter alia, 122, 123, 199, 200, 207, 208, 210, 212, 276, and 277 (n. 5 above).

37. P. M. Dupey, "Soft law and the international law of the environment," *Michigan Journal of International Law* 420, no. 12 (1991), cited in VanderZwaag and Johnston (n. 23 above), p. 85.

38. "Agenda 21 is a nonenforceable 'soft law' instrument—with the exception of Chapter 17. This chapter deals with the seas and oceans, and interprets, fleshes out, develops and advances the Convention, which in turn provides a legal framework enforcement mechanism, and a dispute settlement system, thus moving the Agenda from 'soft law' in the direction of conventional international law. Imple-

important elements in ocean governance are understanding the seas in a wider sense to include the coastal areas and the living resources of the seas and considering the marine environment as an essential component of the global life-support system and a positive asset that presents opportunities for sustainable development.[39] While the legal basis of all activities in the mentioned areas would be drawn from UNCLOS, there is the need to adopt new approaches for attaining sustainable development in an integrated manner. It is here that one notices an emphasis on regional cooperation as indicated in paragraph 1 of Chapter 17.[40] That Chapter 17 had its direct influence on the modalities of ocean governance at the regional level is well reflected in the various efforts of the Regional Seas Programmes to shift from the utopian sectoral approach to environmental protection towards an integrated approach enhancing both economic development and the conservation of the environment, both having social and natural effects. Phase II of the Mediterranean Action Plan is a case in point.[41] Various post-UNCED arrangements, in particular, the Global Programme of Action for the Protection of the Marine Environment from Land-based Activities (GPA) acts as soft law to influence maritime regional cooperation in one way or another.[42] All soft law arrangements allow States to resort to non-legal forms such as action plans or to instruments that are legal in form but soft in obligatory content such as a framework convention.[43] In the post-UNCED period, this has facilitated the Regional Seas Programmes to adjust to the comprehensive perspectives of integrating environment and development in the ocean sector within a framework of sustainable development.

---

menting Chapter 17 of Agenda 21 means implementing the Law of the Sea Convention. Implementing the Law of the Sea Convention means implementing Chapter 17. At the same time, Agenda 21 covering all economic/environmental activities, whether at sea, on land, or in the atmosphere now links the Law of the Sea and ocean governance to the rest of the global system . . ." Borgese (n. 4 above), p. 185.

39. Ibid., p. 58.

40. Treves (n. 7 above), p. 165.

41. The Phase II, amended Barcelona Convention and related instruments, are guided by the Rio principles of sustainable development. It confirmed the 'shift from a sectoral approach to pollution control to integrated coastal zone planning and management as the key tool through which solutions are being sought' (UNEP MAP Phase II Instruments). See A. Chircop, "The Mediterranean: Lessons Learned," in Valencia (n. 1 above), pp. 27–49.

42. The GPA, adopted in 1995 by 109 states, urges governments to develop, within a few years, National Programmes of Action to address land-based activities, as well as to consider developing regional and subregional programmes of action. Besides, the 1995 Agreement on Straddling Fish Stocks and Highly Migratory Fish Stocks and the Code of Conduct for Responsible Fisheries encourage states to cooperate at the regional level. VanderZwaag and Johnston (n. 23 above), p. 113.

43. Ibid., p. 85.

MARITIME REGIONAL COOPERATION IN SOUTH ASIA

Any scheme for maritime regional cooperation in South Asia must take into account certain factors peculiar to the region, like physical and economic geography, demography, geopolitics, history, culture and tradition, religion, and ecology, among others. If history is any testimony, then it would not be wrong to state that, to date, the mentioned factors bear negative implications for cooperation in the region's terrestrial domain. Therefore, highlighting these facts in the following two subsections is relevant to the article, as they are likely to influence any future regime building in the oceanic arena as well.

South Asia is a distinct and widely recognized geostrategic unit consisting of seven countries: Bangladesh, Bhutan, India, Pakistan, Maldives, Nepal, and Sri Lanka.[44] The region is one of the least developed in the world, with poverty being the common regional phenomenon. Culturally, all the countries of the region share a common history flowing from the dominant Indian civilization, with social systems more or less symmetrical in nature. More important, they share a closely knit system of resources and ecology, the development of which needs a cooperative and coordinated approach for the benefit of all. This is particularly true for combating poverty—the common enemy of all.[45] Despite these similarities, regional cooperation in

44. South Asia has long continued to remain an ill-defined geopolitical unit. To many, it comprised an area that extended up to Myanmar in the east and to Afghanistan in the west. Also, the region was known as Indian Sub-continent. However, the controversy and the confusion over the area dissipated when the SAARC was formed in 1985 to include the countries mentioned above.

45. Poverty is a major problem in South Asia. Most countries in the region are included in the list of the least developed countries drawn up by the United Nations Committee for Development Planning (CDP). Except for Sri Lanka, the exclusion of some other countries in the region is because their population exceeds the identified limit, and not because of their level of development. With the exception of Sri Lanka, all South Asian countries are well below the cut-off point for income level, and the newly employed composite index called the Augmented Physical Quality of Life Index based on life expectancy, per capita calorie supplies, combined primary and secondary school enrollment ratios, and adult literacy rates. In all cases, there are problems of uneven distribution of wealth. Indeed, in most cases, the welfare benefits for the general population are so poor that they attain a very low rank in the UNDP's Human Development Index. In fact, despite an overall per capita growth rate for the region averaging at 3.1 percent over the past decade, estimates of the poor in the region varied between 330 million and 440 million in 1991. It is not surprising, therefore, that the Independent South Asian Commission on Poverty Alleviation argues, "When coupled with the multifaceted crisis currently facing South Asian counties, the problem is becoming unmanageable, not only putting democracy at risk, but also posing a threat to the fabric of South Asian societies." See M. Jaleel and A. Shaheed, "Regional Economic Trends: Security Implications for the Maldives," in *Regional Economic Trends and South Asian Security*, ed. Iftekharuzzaman (Colombo: Regional Centre for Strategic Studies, 1997), p. 108.

South Asia has been a chimera mainly due to the region's geopolitics. In this respect, it is the region's Indo-centricity that draws one's attention. With a total area of approximately 3,287,590 km^2, India straddles the region like a giant, thereby making the smaller neighbors look like dwarfs in its vicinity. The importance of India's colossal size is further accentuated by its central location in the region. In addition, India shares land borders with all her neighbors (which many refer to as a tyranny of geography[46]), whereas these latter do not share the same among themselves—a situation not found in other regions of the world with central or core powers.[47] Asymmetry is glaringly apparent between India and the other countries in terms of population, economic resources, industrial base, technology, science and skill, military might, and in all other elements of power.

In brief, it is the Indian preeminence in the region by the irreversible facts of history, geopolitics, economics, culture, and more that the smaller countries have to accept as a reality. While the neighbors have no qualms in accepting this, the problem arises when India tries to translate this preeminence into predominance through certain acts and policies. Reference is thus made to India's role as a regional hegemonic power, with specific emphasis on its Indian doctrine that regards South Asia as a single strategic unit to be controlled and managed according to the Indian order of things.[48] Also, the Indian preferred policy of bilateralism is disliked by its neighbors, as it appears in their eyes as a political means of keeping them under a short leash to gain their acquiescence to the greater Indian ambition in the region. Another factor to unnerve the psyche of the smaller neighbors is the rapid Indian weaponization program, with conventional, missile, and nuclear components. The military might of India is seen as an attempt to dominate the region by force if necessary. While India has its rationale and justification for framing out the contours of its regional policy commensurate with its own national interests, the fact remains that the constant misapprehension, mistrust, and tension between India and its smaller neighbors ultimately divided South Asian politics into two distinct poles: Indo-Pakistan and India versus the smaller countries.[49]

46. The concept of tyranny of geography was used by a Pakistani scholar, P. I. Cheema (Ex-Chairman of the Department of International Relations, Quaid-E-Azam University, Islamabad, Pakistan). Later, this idea was used by many scholars in the same field in smaller countries of the region. In particular, in Bangladesh, the concept became very popular in the context of the country's relations with India.

47. The geographical regions mentioned above pertain to South America, Southern Africa and South East Asia where Brazil, South Africa and Indonesia aspired to play the role of central powers respectively.

48. See Iftekharuzzaman, "The India Doctrine: Relevance for Bangladesh," in *Issues and Challenges Facing Bangladesh Foreign Policy,* ed. M. G. Kabir and S. Hassan (Dhaka: Bangladesh Society of International Studies, 1989), pp. 18–43.

49. The author undertook extensive research on India's regional policy vis-à-vis South Asia as part of his unpublished Ph.D. dissertation entitled "The Political

It is relevant to mention that the conflict circumscribed around the first pole involving India and Pakistan, with its roots going deep into the region's history, politics, geopolitics, economics, culture, and ecology, has from the beginning obfuscated any move towards a cooperative regime in the region. With the disputed Kashmir issue remaining unresolved between India and Pakistan, their current arms race with nuclear and missile components further exacerbates the already existing mutual antagonism and tension. Equally, the 'Indo-phobia' generated in the second pole had its negative effects on any meaningful cooperation in the region. It is the smaller neighbors' feeling that any cooperation with India would be tantamount to entering an unequal partnership with the regional giant.[50] Amidst this situation, SAARC, the existing regional organization, has not fared well in its goals and objectives.[51] Lacking any record of success to its credit, the organization

---

Role of India as a Regional Power in South Asia: Response of Pakistan and of Bangladesh" (Le Rôle Politique de l'Inde Comme Puissance Régionale dans l'Asie du Sud: La Réponse du Pakistan et du Bangladesh). The three basic contours of Indian regional policy (i) translating the Indian doctrine into a reality, (ii) the policy of bilateralism, and (iii) the rapid militarization program, in essence, reflect India's own perception of the geopolitical, economic, and social realities within an exclusive South Asian context. A deep inquiry into these aspects would reveal philosophical and moral undertones as provided by India. However, what is important to bear in mind is that in India's *realpolitik* calculation, strict adherence to these principles would maintain the existing balance of power in the region—which by all logical calculations remains perennially in her favor. Whereas, to the neighbors a change in the status quo is needed to curtail Indian influence in the region at least to a certain extent. For the smaller countries, any change would require external intervention or multilateralism that will ultimately go in India's disfavor. Judged in this light, the conflict between India and the smaller neighbors is, in fact, from a strict geostrategic angle, over the preservation and perturbation of the balance of power in the region. In this respect, the smaller powers seem to receive moral inspiration from Pakistan, the most defiant state in so far as its policy vis-à-vis India is concerned.

50. The feeling is widespread in Bangladesh, where dealing with India even on noncontroversial issues becomes problematic. In particular, in the field of trade and commerce where the balance of trade always remains in favor of India, new ventures are difficult to take. This has negative impacts on other areas of cooperation too. The partnership in all cases is felt to be unequal between the two.

51. It may be mentioned that the frequent postponement of the SAARC Summits, due to contentious bilateral issues, has put into question the very relevance and validity of the SAARC. But the redeeming fact is that SAARC has not lost its relevance in South Asia. Whatever progress made by SAARC since its launching in 1985, it has been perhaps the only forum where the South Asian leaders are brought together despite their intense political inhibitions and insurmountable national reservations on certain political issues. Despite a snail's pace for progress, one of the remarkable contributions of SAARC has been the fact that it has been able to trigger a whole range of activities outside the official SAARC forum. These activities, in the private sector, in nongovernmental organizations, and in community-level activities across the region have in fact withstood all kinds of political ups and downs. M. P. Lama, "SAARC: Shallow Regionalism, Political Abstinence and Economic Advocacy," *BIISS Journal* 21, no. 1 (January 2000): 1–35.

is now criticized by many as an institution embodying 'inverse regionalism.'[52] The need, therefore, is to remove the existing bilateral irritants between India and its neighbors as a means of confidence measures for greater cooperation on the platform of SAARC. This would also have positive implications for any future maritime cooperation on a regional basis.

The Oceanic Matrix of South Asia

Coming to the maritime environment of South Asia, one finds symmetry in so far as oceanographic features, seasonal monsoons (northern hemisphere of the Indian Ocean), fauna and flora, marine ecosystems (estuaries, mangroves and coral reefs), natural disasters, environmental management, and the patterns and spread of disease are concerned.[53] Both land-based and coastal activities of the littoral countries contribute to marine pollution for reasons like dumping of solid waste, discharge of chemicals used in agriculture, drainage from port areas, deposit of domestic and industrial effluents, construction along the coast, and tourism activities, among others. Also, discharges through out-falls and various contaminants from ships, sea-based activities, including marine transportation, offshore mineral exploration and production activities, and accidental oil spills further exacerbate pollution in the ocean.[54] Because of the open nature

52. The term 'inverse regionalism' has been used by the Pakistani economist, S. Lahari, while explaining his dismay over the current intraregional trade of the region, which is in the range of 3 percent of all foreign trade of the member countries. Thus, to him, economics that has been emphasized as a golden opportunity of regional cooperation is now wishful thinking in the region. Cited in P. Zingel, "On the Economics of Regional Cooperation in South Asia," (paper presented at the 15th European Conference on Modern South Asian Studies, Prague, September 8–11, 1998, p. 1).

53. R. Sen Gupta et al. *State of the Marine Environment in the South Asian Seas Region*. UNEP Regional Seas Reports and Studies. Report no. 123, UNEP, 1990, p. 7.

54. A report by Sustainable Development Information Service (SDIS) profiles environmental problems in the South Asian Seas Region (the Bay of Bengal, Arabian Sea, and northern Indian Ocean), emphasizing the impact of human settlement and economic activity on coastal and marine habitats. Oil pollution—due to tanker deballasting, flushing, and spillage—is common almost everywhere in the region, while organic pollution is increasing because sewage treatment is virtually nonexistent among the coastal populations. In India, for example, only cities with populations greater than 100,000 have treatment facilities. Coastal fisheries—an important source of both nutrition and employment—are being threatened by high coliform bacteria levels and by destructive fishing practices. Mangrove forests, which are found in coastal India, Pakistan, Bangladesh, and Sri Lanka play a key role in coastal environments by providing spawning and feeding areas for crustaceans and fish, as well as protection to vulnerable marine communities. These areas, however, are under threat from the increasing demand for land and fuel. Coral reef depletion is also a major concern: dynamite fishing, ornament collection, and mining are depleting coral populations throughout the region. In north Malé, for example, coral

of the ocean and continuous flow of currents, all the countries of the region feel the effects of pollution. In this respect, the common interest in combating pollution should at least be guided by concern for fisheries and other marine habitat. Leaving behind these similarities in the maritime environment, one also notices a wide asymmetry in maritime configuration of the South Asian countries. With the exception of Nepal and Bhutan, the two land-locked countries, India, Pakistan, and Bangladesh are the principal Indian Ocean littoral countries, while Sri Lanka and Maldives are the island states in the region. Like in the terrestrial domain, India's preeminence also resonates in the ocean that bears its name. Its coastline that stretches for 7,000 km where it is surrounded by the Bay of Bengal in the east, the Arabian Sea in the west, and the Indian Ocean in the south, significantly roofs the northern portion of the Indian Ocean, thereby endowing the country with a significant maritime status. The only country in the region with a well-defined ocean policy, India's main maritime interests include trade and commerce, exploitation and exploration of ocean resources, and maritime security. India has pursued an active program of exploration for manganese nodules in the Indian Ocean and has been successful in being designated a pioneer investor with respect to this area by the Preparatory Commission for the International Sea-Bed Authority, and as such is the only Third World nation to achieve this status.[55] Bangladesh and Pakistan, sharing 710 km and 960 km coastlines, respectively, do have similar interests in the region. The economy of Sri Lanka and of the Maldives is to a great extent ocean based, with particular emphasis on fishing and coastal tourism. From a geopolitical perspective, the ocean cannot be viewed to be free from tension and conflict in as much as India's powerful navy in the region creates misapprehension and speculation in the littoral countries about India's ultimate designs in the region. The maritime dispute between India and Bangladesh with respect to the delimitation of boundaries is also a factor in the ocean's geopolitical tapestry.[56] The Indo-Pak terrestrial conflict is also reflected in the

---

formations may be exhausted by 2014. Other discussions in the report include, inter alia, threatened species, tourism, protected areas, coastal erosion and sedimentation, industrial wastes, and agricultural pollution. See Asia, Regional Environmental Problems of the South Asian Seas Region: An Overview, http://www.wri.org/wdces/as87_67.html (accessed 23 February 2003).

55. A. K. H. Morshed, "Cooperation in the Maritime Zones Among and Between the SAARC Countries," *BIISS Journal* 20, no. 1 (January 1999): 1–11.

56. M. H. Kabir, "Bangladesh's Maritime Interests and Options," *BIISS Journal* 18, no. 2 (April 1997): 73–87. A detailed discussion on the maritime delimitation problem between India and Bangladesh is made in the paper entitled "Practice of SAARC Countries on the Delimitation of Maritime Boundaries: Some Pertinent Issues for Bangladesh" (presented by M. H. Rahman at the Training Workshop on the "Legal and Technical Requirements of Maritime Boundary Delimitation," jointly organized by the Bangladesh Institute of International and Strategic Studies [BIISS] and the Oceans Institute of Canada [OIC], at BIISS auditorium, Dhaka, Bangladesh, July 27–29, 1998).

ocean domain. Pakistan, which has always opted for a near parity with India in military strength, is unlikely to play second fiddle to India, as Indian naval expansion, in the calculation of the former, threatens it more than any other littoral countries of the Indian Ocean region.[57]

Whither the Maritime Institutions in South Asia?

For a long time, the building of institutions for regional cooperation on oceanic issues did not make any headway in South Asia due to the reasons cited earlier. This is explained by the failure of UNEP in establishing any Regional Seas Programme in the region during the 1970s,[58] notwithstanding the fact that the protection of the marine environment was given priority in conjunction with the overall environmental policies of countries like Bangladesh, India, Maldives, Sri Lanka, and Pakistan. While it is true that oceanic regionalism in the area is reflected in such initiatives as the Bay of Bengal Program (1979),[59] Indian Ocean Marine Affairs Cooperation (IOMAC, 1990),[60] or the Indian Ocean Rim Initiative (1995),[61] the question remains as

57. See for details, A. T. S. Ahmed, "Indian Naval Build Up: Justification, Missions and Implications," *BIISS Journal* 14, no. 1 (January 1993): 67–104. Pakistan is very critical of India's increasing rapid naval build-up. While it is near impossible for the country to match Indian naval might, nonetheless, efforts are underway to augment its naval might. An important fact to bear in mind is that with the possession of nuclear weapons by both India and Pakistan, the possibility of making the Indian Ocean a zone of peace seems to have disappeared. It may be mentioned that in May 1998 both India and Pakistan exploded nuclear bombs.

58. Report of the Workshop on "Implementation of GPA for the Protection of the Marine Environment from Land-based Activities in the South Asian Seas Region," (UNEP, 23 October 1997), p. 19.

59. *Bay of Bengal News* (September 1995). The program has implemented a number of pilot projects, studies and surveys related to stock assessment, craft and gear, coastal fisheries development, brackish aquaculture, postharvest technology, marketing, approaches to extension and socioeconomic aspects such as credits, non-financial education and fisherfolk organizations. See for details, F. Vatten, "Coastal Development in the Bay of Bengal," (December 1994).

60. A potential framework for maritime cooperation is provided by the 1990 Agreement (the Arusha Agreement) on the IOMAC. It is an interregional and trans-sectoral organization dealing specially with ocean affairs. IOMAC seeks to promote peaceful uses of the ocean in noncontroversial areas such as economic, scientific, and technical cooperation in the Indian Ocean. See for details, S. Bateman, "Prospects for Indian Ocean Cooperation," in *Ocean Yearbook* 12, ed. E. M. Borgese, N. Ginsburg and J. R. Morgan (Chicago: University of Chicago Press, 1996), pp. 306–15. Also see, B. Kwiatkowska, "Institutional marine affairs cooperation in developing state regions," *Marine Policy* 22, no. 2 (September 1990): 399–420.

61. Two significant initiatives were launched in 1995 to establish a trade-oriented economic grouping in the Indian Ocean region. In March 1995, the Mauritius government hosted a meeting known as the Indian Ocean Rim Initiative in which Australia, India, South Africa, Oman, Kenya, and Singapore participated. The second was held about 2 and a half months later on 11–15 June in 1995. Hosted by

to their actual nature and functions as regional organizations. As a fisheries organization under the FAO, the Bay of Bengal Programme with member countries on both sides of the Bay mostly concentrated on projects, studies, and surveys related to coastal fisheries, and towards this end, successes are credited to the organization as well. However, in the realm of maritime cooperation, fisheries is just one of the sectors in the overall maritime environment. This realization probably has driven the FAO to concentrate on environment and sustainable development in the third phase that began in 1996. At least, for regionalism in the area, the lesson learned from the Bay of Bengal Programme is that the regional States, if backed by political commitment, can act jointly to preserve their common resources. As far as the other two organizations are concerned, they may be viewed as geographically broad based, with a focus on a wider Indian Ocean context. They do not even include all the South Asian countries. In particular, the absence of India in the IOMAC has been a negative factor affecting its functioning. Our focus is, therefore, on the UNEP-sponsored South Asian Regional Seas Programme—the only institutional manifestation of maritime regionalism in South Asia—with a brief discussion on its emergence, the current status and functions.

Launching the Regional Seas Programme amidst a political atmosphere of tension and mutual distrust needed environmental consciousness in the region as its prelude. It was not until the creation of SACEP (South Asia Cooperative Environment Program) in 1982 that the region started moving towards a common approach to dealing with various environmental problems, including marine issues. It is out of this program that the region finally witnessed the birth of the Regional Seas Programme in 1995. Considering the prevailing South Asian politics at the time, cooperation under a nonpolitical and noncontroversial body like SACEP was a move to attenuate tension in the region to a certain degree.[62] Thus, SACEP is as well a trendsetter

---

Australia, it was a relatively more broad-based effort, with a three-tier participation, in which the government, business, and academia from 22 countries met at Perth to discuss the possibilities of establishing an International Forum for the Indian Ocean Region (IFIOR). The various proposals reflected the desire to go for a comprehensive cooperation in technical and economic matters guaranteeing the participation of all the littoral states of the Indian Ocean whether developed, underdeveloped, small or big. For details see A. Saeed, "An economic forum for the Indian Ocean Region," *Regional Studies* 10, no. 3 (August 2000): 59–75.

62. It may be mentioned that during the period, the political situation in South Asia appeared to be extremely tense in view of the arms competition between India and Pakistan. It was a period when Pakistan became, under a strategic consensus with the United States, the conduit of Western arms and ammunitions to the Afghan Mujaheedins. The rise in armament build-up in Pakistan had its impact on India during the same period in which it also accelerated its armament build-up with R&D. In addition, the bilateral problems between India and its neighbors became more problematic due to the hardline attitude of Prime Minister Indira Gandhi who viewed the open door policy in Sri Lanka as Bangladesh's attempt to interna-

for regional cooperation under the aegis of SAARC (1985). As a precursor to the South Asian Regional Seas Programme, the SACEP had to pass through a few problems in the initial stages. In particular, during the 1980s, its activities did not make any breakthrough in its goals and objectives. Most of SACEP's steps to deal with the region's shared environmental problems like atmospheric pollution, acid rain, deforestation, water scarcity, loss of biodiversity, soil degradation, the migration of toxic or hazardous wastes, climate change, marine pollution, and more seemed to remain at the proposal stage, showing a gap between the planned proposals and implementation.[63] Also, having no formal link with SAARC, SACEP could not fare well in serving the purpose for which it was launched. Already affected by interstate conflict during the period, the SAARC could not embrace the idea of broad-based regional cooperation on environmental issues as envisaged by SACEP. Beginning in the early 1990s, various post-Rio environmental arrangements had a positive impact in the region. In keeping with the reality of time, the renewed strategy and program of SACEP (1992–96) incorporating such pragmatic elements as capacity building, awareness raising, information exchange, and technology transfer, training in environmental management and institutional development, cooperative management of mountain ecosystems, watersheds, and coastal ecosystems, and conservation of wildlife and habitat bore implications for a future regional cooperation in the marine arena.[64] SACEP's strategy and program could not remain without its direct influence on the SAARC, as in 1997 the former assisted the latter in formulating a Regional Environment Action Plan that later was officially endorsed in the Male Declaration of the 9th SAARC Summit in the same year. Henceforth, environmental programs and packages in all South Asian countries put more stress than before on issues related to the marine environment.[65] Towards this end, it can probably be said that UNCLOS has

---

tionalize the Ganges water issue and Nepal's veering towards China and others as detrimental to Indian interests. This was also the period when the Tamil crisis in Sri Lanka surfaced.

63. R. Chatterjee, M. Mehera and S. Banerjee, "Environmental Security in South Asia," http://www.teriin.org/division/padiv/mea/docs/ft01.pdf (accessed 6 February 2003).

64. Ibid.

65. It should be noted that beginning in the 1990s, various global efforts for protection of the environment and intense pressure from the rich donors on the developing countries for meeting the environmental standards in their development activities created a new dent in the minds of policy makers in several Afro-Asian and Latin American countries. This too had its fallout on South Asia. 1992 was declared as the 'SAARC Year of Environment.' Having participated in various Rio arrangements with valuable contributions in many cases, the policy makers of the region became committed to environmental issues more than before. More importantly, in arousing such consciousness, the role of academic institutions, NGOs, cultural organizations, journalists, human rights activists, and others was formidable in many countries of the region. The environmental security, henceforth, was not confined

been taken as the appropriate point of departure for maritime cooperation among the South Asian countries, reinforced by other soft law arrangements.

Like all other UNEP Regional Seas Programmes, the South Asian Regional Seas Programme works through an Action Plan called the South Asian Seas Action Plan, adopted in 1995 with unqualified support of the region's five countries.[66] Its objective is to protect and manage the marine environment and ecosystems of the region in an environmentally sound and sustainable manner. The SACEP has been privileged to participate in this work, and in terms of institutional arrangements is now serving as the Action Plan secretariat, with responsibilities including formulating projects and approaching donor agencies.[67] The SAS Action Plan is possibly the first regional plan developed under the Regional Seas Programme to identify specific priority program areas in addition to the general components such as environmental assessment, environmental management, and environmental legislation, which are common to all Regional Action Plans.[68] The priority areas of activities are (i) integrated coastal zone management, (ii) national and regional oil spill contingency planning, (iii) resource development through strengthening regional centers of excellence, and (iv) protection of the coastal environment from land-based activities.[69]

While grand ambition is reflected in the priority areas of activities, in particular, in the fields of integrated coastal zone management and protection of the coastal environment from land-based activities, nonetheless, the SAS Action Plan reflects realism in so far as it tries to cope with the concepts and ethos of environment and development in the post-Rio period. In effect, it is the very timing of the SAS Action Plan that has facilitated such incorporation. As mentioned earlier, it is a period when UNEP's Action Plans covering a wide range of geographical areas started focusing not only on the ancien sectoral approach dealing with pollution control, but as well on coastal zone planning and management with consideration of social and economic aspects of development. As evidenced by the SAS Action Plan's

---

to the terrestrial domain only, as the marine environment was also a key concern. Thus, for example, in Bangladesh, in the country's first-ever environment policy enunciated in 1992, protection of the marine environment finds its expression in the section entitled 'Coastal and Marine Environment.' This is, of course, preceded by several Acts in the past like the Territorial Water and Maritime Zones Act of 1974, the Territorial Waters and Marine Zones Rules of 1977, the Marine Pollution Ordinance of 1989, the Marine Environment Act of 1990 etc. See M. Farooq and S. R. Hasan, *Laws Regulating Environment in Bangladesh* (Dhaka: Dana Printers Ltd., 1996), p. 734.

66. South Asian Regional Seas Programme: Present Status of the Implementation of Actions and Conventions. UNEP. 1 December 2000, pp. 1–5.

67. Ibid, p. 1.

68. Ibid, p. 2.

69. Ibid, p. 5.

activities, some results have already been achieved in developing the South Asian Oil Spill Contingency Plan.[70] India and Sri Lanka have already developed their plans, while the others are in the process of doing so.[71] With respect to GPA, it is important to note that the SAS Action Plan has floated another program called the Regional Program of Action directing each of the member states to draft their respective National Plans.[72] SACEP's Environment and Natural Resources Information Center (SENRIC) is engaged in capacity building with the objective of increasing the capacities of governments utilizing modern information technologies and tools to integrate biophysical and socioeconomic data. It has also established a subnational, subregional, and regional environmental information network. As a whole, it has assisted in the dissemination of holistic environmental concepts through training in Geographical Information System and Remote Sensing (GIS/RS) applications.[73] It should be mentioned that various projects have been floated on the four core areas of activities that are currently in need of financial support for materialization. Of these, only one, Development of National Water Quality Criteria for Different Uses of Sea Water (2001–02) falling under the GPA, has been taken up for support by the Norwegian Water Institute (NIVA) and the expected funding is around US$1.2 million.[74]

CHALLENGES AND OPPORTUNITIES FOR MARITIME COOPERATION IN SOUTH ASIA

The successful functioning of any maritime regional organization depends on its pragmatic choice of objectives and on other proper preparation to translate these objectives into reality. Proper preparations, in effect, connote to what extent the organization's members would be able to commit themselves politically, economically, socially, and legally to the organization's purpose. Such commitment does not necessarily need to be state centric, as contemporary environmental problems and their solutions, even more than in the past, go beyond the capacity of states to resolve. Thus, in an intergovernmental regime as envisaged by the Regional Seas Programme, the choice of actors should be a broad one so as to include a wide range of non-governmental actors like the epistemic community, the NGOs, the private enter-

70. Regional Reporting for the Intergovernmental Review of the GPA—2001, (SACEP), http://www.unep.ch/seas/dumsas.html (accessed 5 February 2002).

71. Ibid.

72. Ibid.

73. Ibid.

74. South Asia Regional Seas Programme: Present Status of the Implementation of Actions Plans and Conventions (n. 66 above), p. 5.

prises, civil society, and research institutes. Then comes the question: how would the actors prioritize the issues and actions and with what logistics and legal basis? In this respect, the challenges to the South Asian Regional Seas Programme are many, and they are mostly 'region specific,' as is the program itself. This section attempts to identify such challenges, followed by a discussion on the opportunities in two successive subsections.

Challenges for South Asian Regional Maritime Cooperation

The challenges for the countries that have adopted the South Asian Seas Action Plan fall within two levels, theoretical and operational. At the theoretical level, the adoption of priority areas of action appears to be too ambitious. Considering the fact that the countries have not gained experience and skills in the basic task of combating marine pollution in the area, the current program for integrated coastal zone management may appear to be premature. Considering the Mediterranean experience, one can probably say that efforts for such comprehensive programs should go in phases. Thus, Phase I of the MAP, with its concentration mainly on the marine pollution problem of the region, was not wider in nature, and the subsequent wider Phase II benefited by the experiences and skills gained in Phase I. In effect, the problem arises due to the involvement of a number of enterprises in any integrated coastal zone management like agriculture, industry, energy, and tourism. As mentioned earlier, all of these sectors, involving a number of stakeholders, need to be properly integrated by an efficient public policy. There is also the need to create a holistic outlook and awareness among the public about the linkage between the marine and terrestrial environment. Also, in a poverty-ridden region, the parties who are engaged in activities that harm the coastal and marine environment do not see the importance of the activities carried out for protection of the marine environment by the government or other stakeholders. This is especially true when they are bound up with other problems associated with poverty and unemployment.[75] These issues need time to remedy and should be addressed in a step-by-step process. There is also the legal problem of whether, as per the OECD principle, integrated coastal zone management includes coastal land areas and waters within national jurisdiction and the EEZ where a coastal state's rights according to international law are not uniform.[76]

75. Regional Reporting for the Intergovernmental Review of the GPA—2001 (n. 70 above). It should be mentioned here that poverty cannot remain as an excuse for people's indifference to marine problems. The ground reality, as much in Bangladesh as in other countries, is the people's ignorance. Most of the people are ignorant about what is happening in the marine environment due to illiteracy, lack of information, and inaccessibility to mass media, et cetera.

76. Treves (n. 7 above), p. 162.

The question of spearheading regional cooperation under the initiative of UNEP also raises certain other critical questions for close scrutiny. In all Regional Seas Programmes, regional Action Plans are initiated to develop capacity building to assess the marine environment and causes of its deterioration, and to develop response actions for management and development of the marine and coastal environment. These plans normally reside within a definite framework of legal arrangements that are adopted by the intergovernmental meeting of a particular region before the program becomes operational. In this respect, a convention is a legal instrument to bind the different governments of the region in activating their program.[77] The political commitment of the governments participating in the Action Plan is embodied in the Regional Seas conventions, which serve as the legal framework of the Action Plan. Also, unlike the global environmental conventions, the Regional Conventions and Action Plans are comprehensive, covering issues ranging from chemical wastes and coastal development to the protection of marine animals and conservation of ecosystems. Because each convention defines the geographic area of its application, lists the general and specific obligations of the contracting parties, and the institutional arrangements supporting the implementation of the convention, the Programme's focus can be easily drawn on channeling the energies of a wide range of interest groups into solving what are interlinked problems.[78] In fact, a convention as the constituent instrument of a regional organization not only defines the nature and function of the latter, but as well creates the scope for the organization to cope with new projects as deemed necessary. In this connection, it is important to bear in mind the role of the protocols. The protocols that supplement the conventions contain provisions related to such projects and deal with measures expected to be implemented by the contracting parties from time to time in accordance with the findings of studies and assessments.[79] In brief, protocols reflect the pragmatism of the Regional Seas Programmes to deal with issues specific to the needs at the time. If the Mediterranean Region is an example demonstrating its ability to adjust to such needs, then it is in all the protocols, besides the framework convention, that accompany the amended Barcelona Convention (1995),[80] and which reflect the region's flexibility, pragmatism, and excellence in dealing with oceanic issues in tune with the post-UNCED needs.

In South Asia, no convention has yet been signed to strengthen the operationalization of the Action Plan. Most countries in the region are of

77. Akiwumi and Melvasalo (n. 3 above), p. 230.

78. Ibid., p. 232.

79. Keckes (n. 14 above), p. 351.

80. Convention for the Protection of the Marine Environment and the Coastal Region of the Mediterranean (Barcelona Convention), adopted 16 February 1976, entered into force 12 February 1978, amended 10 June 1995 (not yet in force), http://www.unepmap.org/.

the opinion that there is adequate coverage by UNCLOS.[81] As Prasanth Dias Abeyegunaseardene remarks, "Although, we do not yet have our own regional convention, we are working diligently to apply the existing global environmental and maritime conventions to our region."[82] Such an argument may appear to be inappropriate in the case of the South Asia Regional Seas Programme, because without a convention and protocols, it is not in a position to show the Plan's conflict or cooperation with the provisions of UNCLOS. The SAARC does not set a good example in this respect. In the case of SAARC, based on a charter as a guide to its legal, institutional, administrative, and financial structures, cooperation in various noncontentious and noncontroversial areas of mutual interest is guaranteed by conventions like the Agreement on Establishing the SMRC Food Security Reserve, the Regional Convention on Suppression of Terrorism, the Convention on Narcotic Drugs and Psychotropic Substances, the Agreement on SMRC Preferential Trading Arrangement,[83] the Convention on Regional Arrangements for the Promotion of Child Welfare in South Asia,[84] and the SMRC Convention on Preventing and Combating Trafficking in Women and Children for Prostitution.[85] Signed at various points of time, these conventions have not yielded positive results, as they are nonbinding instruments and depend on the signatories' political will in rendering cooperation on the related issues. Again for the implementation of any agreed convention, the cooperation of India is crucial in terms of its size, geographical location, economy, population, and the level of its advancement in all sectors. This, however, is not forthcoming due to contentious bilateral issues between India and its smaller neighbors. Any solution to such problems on the platform of SAARC is hindered by Article X (2) of the charter that keeps bilateral and contentious issues outside the scope of SAARC.[86] More important, many States in the region not have yet incorporated the convention requirements in the domestic legislation of their respective countries. The follow-up action in most of the countries is still lacking. This clearly demonstrates that the South Asian nations are very slow in approaching a convergent point on any

81. South Asian Regional Seas Programme: Present Status of the Implementation of Action Plans and Conventions (n. 66 above), p. 2.

82. P. D. Abeyegunaseardene is the Deputy Director, Programme, SACEP.

83. S. Kchetri, "11th SAARC Summit: Just another round of talks!," *The People Review,* 13–19 December, 2001, http://www.yomari.com/p-review/2001/12/13122001/11.html (accessed 11 April 2003).

84. SAARC Convention on Regional Arrangements for the Promotion of Child Welfare in South Asia, http://www.cwin-nepal.org/resources/documents/saarc_childwelfare.htm (accessed 11 April 2003).

85. For details, see SAARC Conventions and Agreements, http://safdic.southasiafoundation.org/saf/sas/conventions.htm (accessed 11 April 2003).

86. S. K. Khan, "Bangladesh and SAARC: Security Environment and Related Issues," in *Bangladesh and SAARC: Issues, Perspectives and Outlook,* ed. Iftekharuzzaman and I. Ahmed (Dhaka: Academic Publishers, 1992), pp. 251–62.

issue, even of mutual interest. In this light, a possible explanation for the noninclusion of the convention in the South Asian Regional Seas Action Plan is the reluctance of the parties to go for a formal and legally binding instrument in view of certain constraints like uncertainty about political commitment, maritime disputes between members, fear of domestic backlash, and fear of commitment in a new field. In the absence of a convention, there is, therefore, the skepticism that political commitment might be lacking in South Asia and this even may make the existing arrangement nonviable in the future. Also, in view of the expanding agenda of UNEP to include integrated coastal zone management and the control of various land-based sources of pollution (as per the GPA), the absence of an appropriate legal framework may hinder the harmonizing process between the regional and municipal legislation. In other words, a regional convention must clarify in black and white the amendments needed in national legislation.

Next comes the question of political commitment of the participating countries—a crucial element for the success of any regional plan. It should be mentioned that regional institutions for marine environmental management need to be based on two independent attributes: shared political orientation and geographical proximity to a shared large marine ecosystem.[87] In South Asia, a number of factors already taken up for discussion earlier explain the absence of both. In a region marked by wide asymmetry in power, political, geostrategic, military, economic, and social factors between India and the other smaller neighbors, a common political orientation is still a far distant possibility. Under the circumstances, any attempt to consider their marine environment, despite few common oceanic features and problems, as a shared ecosystem would continue to remain a hostage to perennial political dissension in the region.

Funding is another challenge for the region. If the lack of funds, particularly in developing countries, is the crucial and single major impediment for a more forceful environmental protection action, then the problem attains a more serious dimension in South Asia. In a poverty-ridden region, funding for projects distant from the gravity of current issues like unemployment, shortage of food, and social and economic stresses may not be without problems in the future. Currently, there exists the SAS Trust Fund where the member countries agreed to an annual contribution according to the ratios in the SAARC Scale of Assessment agreed upon by SAARC member States (the maximum contribution from a member State being 35 percent and the minimum being 5 percent).[88] Table 1 shows the meager amount that the countries agreed upon to contribute. This also amply demonstrates that the huge financial resources that would be needed to deal with marine-

87. UNEP/GPA News Forum (n. 2 above).

88. South Asian Regional Seas Programme: Present Status of the Implementation of Actions Plans and Conventions (n. 66 above), p. 3.

Table 1.—SAARC MEMBER STATE CONTRIBUTIONS, 1997–2000

Country	Percentage	1997	1998	1999	2000
Bangladesh	14.5	US$10,367	US$11,020	US$12,120	US$13,335
India	35.0	25,025	26,600	29,260	32,185
Maldives	6.5	4,647	4,940	5,435	5,975
Pakistan	29.5	21,092	22,420	24,660	27,130
Sri Lanka	14.5	10,367	11,020	12,125	13,335
Total (US$)		71,500	76,000	83,600	91,960

Source.— South Asian Regional Seas Programme: Present Status of the Implementation of Actions and Conventions, NEP 01, December 2000.

related problems could not be met from regular government budgets. If one looks at the current sources of funds for the SAS Trust Fund, the hope for future generation of income from them remains subject to uncertainty, speculation, and failure. In particular, the sources internal to States such as user charges, polluter charges, local taxes, national taxes, private sector borrowing, national revolving fund, and private sector participation[89] are not expected to yield a significant amount given the current economic conditions in the respective countries. Also, the state-level sources now giving stress on the international private sector, export credit agency, grant and concessionary assistance, multilateral loans, multilateral equity funds, debt-for-equity swaps, and others,[90] fail to give any exact figure of income likely to be earned therefrom. What may appear to be critical in the case of Regional Actions Plans is that no appropriate budget can be envisaged for any project at any stage. For example, some 10 years back the UNEP Regional Seas Programme in the Mediterranean had only $6 million a year as against the need for $18 billion for responding to various pollution problems. It is clear therefore, that the extended program in the area would now need more money than is currently available.[91] Thanks to some of the economically prosperous members of the MAP, the region has the capacity to meet its financial requirements more than what South Asia can do in this regard. Although, the member countries are regularly contributing towards the SAS Trust Fund, SAS Secretariat has not been able to attract additional financial resources and funds from sources like UNDP, ESCAP, IMO, IOC of UNESCO, the Asian Development Bank, and other relevant organizations. To date, the major source of funding for program activities is UNEP.[92]

89. Regional Reporting for the Intergovernmental Review of the GPA—2001 (n. 70 above).

90. Ibid.

91. M. Tolba, "Policy of UNEP," *Marine Policy* 16, no. 1 (January 1992), p. 61.

92. South Asian Regional Seas Programme: Present Status of the Implementation of Action Plans and Conventions (n. 66 above), p. 5.

It should also be noted that the grand program of the South Asian Seas Action Plan envisaging integrated coastal management and actions against land-based sources of pollution now encompasses many activities within the national jurisdiction of member countries. In other words, there is the need to adopt national programs commensurate with the objectives and goals of the regional programs. While tying regional implementation with domestic implementation may pose problems for financial and technological reasons, the foremost problem would probably be with respect to the question of transforming international obligations into national legislation and administrative and court practices for political and social reasons. As Chircop remarks, "The domestic implementation of regime activities is ostensibly coordinated through national focal points. This is the weakest link, for regional efforts often find political, technological and socioeconomic stumbling blocks in domestic implementation. And indeed, it is at this level that this regime needs strengthening, more than at the regional institutional level."[93] In addition to domestic considerations, because of the oceanic features the South Asian countries may be required to cooperate with the nonmember countries, in which case the Action Plan, for functional, scientific, and technical reasons, might suggest interregional cooperation. This would naturally call for additional responsibility and commitments for the South Asian members. It may be mentioned that in the case of the Mediterranean, a semi-enclosed sea, such an imperative probably was not felt. Lastly, there might arise the problem relating to implementation and enforcement. The possibility of a joint coast guard can only be possible if the political understanding between the countries in a problematic area, as is the Indian Ocean, gets better.

Opportunities and Prospects for South Asian Regional Maritime Cooperation

The challenges to maritime regional cooperation in South Asia that are administrative, legal, institutional, and financial in nature can be met once the member States realize the advantages or opportunities likely to come of such cooperation. In South Asia, where the program is of recent origin, its effective and beneficial results are still not in sight. However, the fact that such a program exists goes to show the regional states' urge and endeavor for cooperation in areas of mutual interest beyond their terrestrial environment. It should be mentioned that cooperation within a regional framework mostly follows a step-by-step process where failure in one phase may cause problems for solving a particular issue, but it does not necessarily stop the process of cooperation. It is, therefore, the spirit and value of cooperation

93. Chircop (n. 41 above), p. 43.

and more importantly, its continuity that one should take into account in evaluating the significance of a regional organization. Thus, despite few legal and administrative loopholes in the current regional arrangement, imperatives for cooperation between and among the South Asian nations are many.

Firstly, cooperation in the marine domain may allow countries of the region to come out of the narrow confines of Indo-phobia caused by terrestrial geopolitics. While it is true that in the ocean too, it is the Indian preeminence that one cannot dispel, nonetheless, the significant maritime status of India for reasons stated earlier creates an incentive for other littoral states to cooperate with India. Experience from the Mediterranean Sea shows that epistemic communities played a significant role in changing the normative and causal beliefs of decision makers.[94] This community, which is a transnational network of scientists, provides a pool of expertise and authoritative knowledge that acts as a necessary basis for any collective action. In South Asia, therefore, the formation of such a community would depend on Indian initiative and on the cooperation of the smaller neighbors towards it. In this framework of cooperation with India, the smaller neighbors are most likely to gain rather than lose. It is also relevant here to point out that if these countries share contemporary intergovernmental oceanic management, developed states in the region could provide the opportunity not only for transfer of technological information, but also for financial cooperation.

Secondly, the current action plan that envisages multidimensional activities for sustainable use and management of marine resources would benefit the region in two ways. In the first place, the work by all governments, national institutions, civil societies, private groups, relevant stakeholders, NGOs, donors, and the international bodies under a common umbrella would resolve the differences in prioritizing issues of importance and concern. Once priority issues are identified, a comprehensive plan can be developed out of the concerted efforts of all to harmonize the national and regional legislation and policies for protection of the marine environment. As mentioned earlier, all such actors would be important components of the regime. From a political angle, this people-to-people contact can act as one of the means of Track II diplomacy to influence the terrestrial politics of the region in a positive way. Besides, several modes of cooperation can be launched before the actual operationalization of a particular project, as observed in the case of SEAPOL where steps like intergovernmental consultative mechanisms, intergovernmental task forces, and official cooperative research plans were effectuated before the project.[95] This opens the way for

94. Naess (n. 27 above), p. 29. Also see for details, Chircop (n. 41 above), pp. 27–49.

95. There are 12 modes of cooperation as envisaged by SEAPOL in the case of the Gulf of Thailand. See VanderZwaag and Johnston (n. 23 above), pp. 118–22.

more confidence building in the region.[96] In the second place, various projects in coastal and marine conservation are likely to create opportunities related to socioeconomic development, public health and food supply, and natural resource management. These opportunities are external developments that may induce, strengthen, or support the feasibility or efficiency of the projects undertaken.

Thirdly, a shared responsibility and burden sharing would create some kind of compulsion for the South Asian countries to concentrate more on marine affairs, which at present remain a low priority in their respective environmental policies. Capacity building and awareness activities on a collective basis would be conducive to research, monitoring, exchange, and sharing of data and information. More important would be the creation of a new collective social and economic consciousness in the region as the new approach of the Regional Seas Programme takes into account economic and social values in developing relevant environmental action programs.

Fourthly, working together within a cooperative framework may reduce the budgetary problem for the South Asian countries. As mentioned earlier, South Asia has difficulties in mobilizing sufficient financial resources for environmental protection. At present, the amount of funding within South Asia and other sources is insufficient to carry out all the planned environmental activities. The region, therefore, is in need of external aid and assistance and this may be forthcoming once the countries succeed in creating a positive image outside by pooling their respective available resources for a common cause.

Finally, the envisaged projects on protection and preservation of the marine environment under the Regional Seas Programme would lead to a number of interactive processes between and among the South Asian countries. While, in the terrestrial domain, issues in the interactive process become hostage to geopolitics, discordant ambitions and goals of the countries, and market dynamics, the same scenario is not expected to prevail in the oceanic domain. Here the issues are soft, noncontroversial, and technical in nature. Hence, cooperation on them would set the stage for confidence building so much needed in a conflict-ridden area such as South Asia. Benefits of functionalism are, therefore, to be reaped from maritime cooperation.

96. It may be mentioned that although SAARC has not been successful in accomplishing many of the tasks, in particular, in building a 'cooperative regime in South Asia,' nonetheless, the increasing participation of people, civil society, the business community, NGOs, private groups, et cetera, in some of the soft issues of a nonpolitical nature are sending signals of a groundwork for a South Asian community. In this light, cooperation in the ocean domain may as well create an 'oceanic community,' and the South Asian Regional Seas Programme may be instrumental in this regard. See chapters in *Confidence Building Measures in South Asia,* ed. D. Baneerjee (Colombo: Regional Centre for Strategic Studies, 1999), pp. 1–197.

CONCLUSION

The current Regional Seas Programme is a living indication of the South Asian nations' willingness to cooperate and is a launching pad for efforts for cooperation with extraregional actors on maritime issues. In this connection, the idea of the Bay of Bengal Community figured prominently in the thinking of the policy planners. A tangible step in this direction has been the establishment of BIMSTEC (Bangladesh-India-Myanmar-Sri Lanka-Thailand Economic Cooperation) in June 1998.[97] The organization, the first of its kind to bring together two ASEAN (Association of South East Asian Nations) and three SAARC countries, was prompt in identifying important areas of cooperation like communication, infrastructure, energy, trade, investment, tourism, and fisheries. By forming such an organization, "the extended neighborhood," as the Indian Ministry of External Affairs refers to these countries, "would rightly become a part of the immediate neighborhood."[98] Soon, the concept of a Bay of Bengal Community was to become a common agenda of many littoral countries. In the prevailing wave of efforts to go for marine cooperation beyond South Asia, attention was given to explore the possibility of undertaking the same under the aegis of SAARC. In this respect, opinions, voices, and plans were floated from many levels. Thus, one Indian authority remarked, "Maritime cooperation among the SAARC countries is both desirable and feasible. But to be useful and feasible, it should be promoted step by step, taking into account the sensitivity of the particular subject-matter and avoiding conflicts of jurisdiction."[99] Bangladesh, the architect of SAARC, came out with the proposal to establish a Center for Maritime Cooperation. The proposed Center envisaged, among other things, bilateral and multilateral cooperation among the regional navies on maritime surveillance, naval procurement plans, operational exercises, management of national disasters, weather prediction, pooling expertise in marine salvage, search and rescue, and on exchange of military personnel and joint actions in the enforcement of international law and order at sea. For our purpose it is relevant to mention that an incorporation of SACEP in SAARC would facilitate the functioning of the South Asia Regional Seas Programme and diversify many of its activities.[100]

The foregoing discussion clearly reveals that the prospect for marine cooperation in South Asia no longer remains in the backwater of contemporary South Asian politics. Despite a host of problems and challenges, some progress has been made in the field of regional marine cooperation,

97. V. Suryanarayan, "Prospects for a Bay of Bengal Community," http://www.india-seminar.com/2000/487/487percent20suryanarayan.htm (accessed 6 February 2003).

98. Ibid.

99. Morshed (n. 55 above), p. 8.

100. Ibid.

whether in the form of the Regional Seas Programme, the floated idea of the Bay of Bengal Community, or in the proposal to include the issue in SAARC. What one probably notices at present is a number of weaknesses like insufficient capability to prioritize the environmental issues in development activities, lack of adequate financial, institutional, and legal arrangements to ensure proper implementation of various environmental protection policies, lack of human and financial resources, and lack of political will and coordination within the concerned governments. The region does not have a ready-made solution to all such predicaments and challenges, nor is there a formula that can be provided by SAARC to address the issues for reasons explained earlier. More ominous is the current state (at the time of writing the article) of intense Indo-Pakistan tension with the threat of a possible nuclear war in the region. In these circumstances, it is not only the fate of SAARC that is at stake, but also of other regional organizations likely to face the same consequences.

Coming out of the present impasse would require tremendous political commitment from the regional governments. Along with this would be the need for a new realization that lack of cooperation on nonpolitical and noncontroversial environmental issues may lead to a rapid destruction and loss of valuable resources in the region. Such a realization would definitely not be without its political implications. Environmental degradation and unsustainable development practices, in all likelihood, would further aggravate the political tension in the region, thereby weakening the already conflict-ridden region as a whole in the global arena. Thus, a cooperative approach to answering the environmental problems both on land and in the ocean can be a foundation for environmental security, as well as a guarantee for the overall human security in the region. The expected dividends—both economic and political—of cooperation at the regional level in all sectors including the oceans, would be promising for all. At the practical level, there is, therefore, the need to develop the national environmental institutions, long-term systematic research and skills, replace narrow expertise by the epistemic community, conduct high-level intergovernmental cooperation through multilateral programs and agreements, recognize the role of the NGOs, and garner support for financial aid and assistance. In the final analysis, it should be mentioned that if the South Asian countries get bogged down in governmental and bureaucratic apparatus like in case of SAARC, the mission under the Regional Seas Programme may not reach its expected results. The better approach for the South Asian countries would be to accept the fact that all efforts towards ocean management would simply be unproductive unless they take due cognizance of two essential facts: firstly, "the problems of ocean space are closely interrelated and need to be considered as a whole,"[101] and secondly, ocean management is holistic in

101. UNCLOS (n. 5 above), Preamble.

nature involving activities not only by bureaucrats but by different sectors, organizations, NGOs, and relevant stakeholders at the local, regional and global levels. In this direction, the 1995–1996 revised Barcelona Convention can be a guideline for South Asia as well. This can also have positive effects on SAARC that till now remains captured by the governments of the member States. Finally, it can be said that cooperation on a regional basis, whether in the terrestrial or oceanic domain, would in all likelihood generate a climate of congeniality so much needed in a region marked at present by chronic political instability. Maritime cooperation is thus a new laboratory test case for South Asia.

Safety on the Seas: Human Security as an Element of Ocean Governance

François N. Bailet
Deputy Executive Director, International Ocean Institute Headquarters
Former Special Assistant to Elisabeth Mann Borgese

When the *Ocean Yearbook* editors kindly invited me to contribute a short piece for volume 18, a volume described as "a commemorative issue honoring Elisabeth Mann Borgese," I accepted with great honor and enthusiasm. However, it quickly became evident that the scope of what I would like to write about Elisabeth could fill several volumes of the *Ocean Yearbook*, not the dozen or so allocated pages.

I first met Elisabeth when I was a student in the International Ocean Institute 1996 Summer Training Program. Her patience and enjoyment of youth and its naivety, optimism, and energy were evident then and became marked features of what came to be our 6-year working relationship and friendship. She was a teacher and mentor who shared her experiences, ideas, and wisdom generously and without prejudice. She is greatly missed by those who worked with her over the last 3 decades to build the International Ocean Institute, the manifestation of her determination to contribute in a practical manner to the implementation of better ocean governance and finally to achieve Pacem in Maribus.

This article explores the very difficult problem posed by ocean-based illicit activities such as piracy and armed robbery at sea, trafficking by sea, and other maritime-based illicit activities, by non-State actors, which threaten the physical security of humans, ships, and marine activities. These illicit acts are increasing and are linked to other organized international crimes such as trafficking in illegal narcotics by terrorist organizations, an activity that has important implications for a State's security which is defined to include all components of human security.[1] This issue, and generally, the

1. International Ocean Institute, *Integrating Sustainable Development and Regional Security: Report on the Leadership Seminar on Mediterranean Basin-wide Co-development and Security* (Malta: International Ocean Institute, 2001), p. 100. For a comprehensive overview of the concept of human security, see S. Alkire, "Conceptual Framework for Human Security," background document, Commission for Human Security, http://www.humansecurity-chs.org/doc/frame.pdf (accessed 22 January 2003). Also see generally the Commission for Human Security's documents and publications, http://www.humansecurity-chs.org/doc/index.html (accessed 16 February 2003).

Ocean Yearbook 18: 543–557

need to prevent illicit use of ocean space, preoccupied Elisabeth in the last few years of her life. She saw it as essential that peace on the ocean be understood to include human security: the ability to carry out ocean activities without fear of crime and violence or other problems that might arise from the lack of a comprehensive security regime in the broader context of ocean governance. In other words, achieving Pacem in Maribus required ensuring that human security on the ocean was maintained.

The following pages represent only a broad overview of what was Elisabeth Mann Borgese's last intellectual journey in this regard. It is presented here within two sections. The first outlines the foundations of her vision for an overarching ocean governance regime, which she felt was so necessary to reach peace in the ocean. The second section enumerates the considerations she envisioned with regard to the incorporation of security considerations within the ocean governance regime on the local, national, regional, and international levels.[2] It is the ideas presented within this second section that preoccupied Elisabeth Mann Borgese's imagination and intellect during the last months of her life.

THE FOUNDATIONS OF OCEAN GOVERNANCE

It is becoming increasingly clear that the effective implementation of the United Nations Convention on the Law of the Sea[3] (UNCLOS), the United Nations Conference on Environment and Development[4] (UNCED) and the UNCED Process which ensued,[5] as well as the emerging international and regional "ocean convention regimes," all place enormous responsibilities on States if they are to be effectively implemented. It is also evident that a large majority of these States are, in fact, unable to implement even the most basic provisions contained within this plethora of ocean convention regimes.[6]

However, in an attempt to meet these obligations (responsibilities) and effectively take full advantage of the associated advantages (rights), nations worldwide are beginning to (re)formulate their national ocean policies and

2. Certain ideas presented in the brief overview of the interaction between peace, security, and ocean governance, as Elisabeth Mann Borgese perceived it, were presented to the Australia-Canada Ocean Research Network 2 meetings in Canberra, Australia (29 May–2 June 2002).

3. United Nations Convention on the Law of the Sea, A/CONF.62/121 (1982). Hereafter: UNCLOS.

4. United Nations Conference on Environment and Development, A/CONF.151/26 (Vol. I) 12 August, 2002. Hereafter: UNCED.

5. Hereafter: UNCED Process.

6. See generally, E. L. Miles et al., *Environmental Regime Effectiveness* (Cambridge, MA: The MIT Press, 2002), p. 508.

their regional disposition toward joint management of ocean spaces, resource exploitation, and marine-related activities. In response to this trend, one can also observe certain corresponding institutional and program developments within the United Nations system, as well as within national institutions and regional intergovernmental organizations. From the United Nations Environment Programme's (UNEP) Global Programme of Action for the Protection of the Marine Environment from Land-based Activities[7] (UNEP-GPA), to the creation of the United Nations Open-ended Informal Consultative Process (ICP) established by the General Assembly in its resolution 54/33 to facilitate the annual review by the Assembly of developments in ocean affairs,[8] there is a clear expression of desire, on the part of the international community, to address ocean issues with the attention they so desperately require and in a manner consistent with the holistic approach prescribed by UNCLOS.

Through this recent international mobilization, one could perhaps begin to speak of the emergence of an ocean governance regime. Although we are still far from the establishment of such a regime—or even defining the precise attributes of such a regime—it is possible to observe the development of what could be considered its seminal components, two of which were alluded to in the earlier paragraph.

The implications and the interrelatedness of economy, environment, human well-being and the need for integrated management of all components at all levels of governance for secure, sustainable development are now well-established ideas. However, the implementation of these ideas, particularly in connection with ocean governance, presents some difficult institutional and legal problems. The need for a framework or structure for comprehensive ocean governance was a primary concern of Elisabeth Mann Borgese and as she developed her ideas in this regard, she drew on what she often called the "principles of ocean governance." These guiding principles can be summarized as follows:[9]

7. Hereafter: UNEP-GPA.

8. Hereafter: ICP.

9. This summary is drawn from numerous speeches and lectures delivered by Elisabeth Mann Borgese between 1997 and 2002; see also: F. N. Bailet, "Ocean Governance: The Oceanic Circle" (Plenary Intervention delivered to the "DOALOS/UNITAR Briefing on Developments in Ocean Affairs and the Law of the Sea 20 Years after the Conclusion of the United Nations Convention on the Law of the Sea," New York, United Nations Headquarters, 25 September, 2002). Presentation available on the DOALOS website, http://www.un.org/Depts/los (accessed 3 October 2002); E. Mann Borgese and F. N. Bailet. *Ocean Governance: Legal, Institutional and Implementation Considerations.* International Ocean Institute. A report prepared for the Ship and Ocean Foundation of Japan. Halifax, Canada: Dalhousie University—International Ocean Institute, 2001, p. 213; E. Mann Borgese, *The Oceanic Circle: Governing the Seas as a Global Resource* (Tokyo: United Nations University Press, 1988), p. 240, and E. Mann Borgese, *Ocean Governance and the United Nations*, 2nd ed. (Halifax, Canada: Dalhousie University, 1996), p. 246.

Elisabeth Mann Borgese saw the Common Heritage of Mankind, as elaborated by Arvid Pardo in the early 1970s and codified within Part XI of UNCLOS, as the most important of these principles.[10] This principle is at the root of her ideas on ocean governance. The Common Heritage of Mankind principle sets forth the unprecedented notion that a State or individual may not "claim or exercise sovereignty or sovereign rights over any part of the Area or its resources. . .";[11] the 'Area' being defined as "the seabed and ocean floor and subsoil thereof, beyond the limits of national jurisdiction."[12] Furthermore, the international community is made responsible for the management of this area for the benefit of mankind as a whole and with particular consideration for the needs of the poor. The principle also reserves the Area for peaceful purposes and stipulates that it must be conserved for future generations.[13]

The Common Heritage of Mankind comprises four dimensions, all of which must be adhered to while working towards the development of ocean management regimes, including compliance and enforcement regimes, even if these do not relate directly to the Area. These four dimensions are the following:

- *economic dimension*—the development of oceanic resources is recognized;
- *environmental dimension*—the ocean must be conserved;
- *peace and security dimension*—the ocean must be reserved for peaceful purposes; and the
- *ethical dimension*—benefits derived from the ocean must be shared equitably with particular consideration for the poor.

Indeed, in the last years of her life, Elisabeth began to reflect on the implications of extending these principles to all maritime areas beyond the territorial seas of nations. She noted that this process was already set in motion with the elaboration of the numerous "ocean-related conventions" that all

10. cf. United Nations General Assembly (32nd Session). "Request for the inclusion of a supplemental item in the agenda of the twenty-second session: Declaration and treaty concerning the reservation exclusively for the peaceful purposes of the sea-bed and of the ocean floor, underlying the seas beyond the limits of present national jurisdiction, and the use of their resources in the interests of mankind." Note verbale dated 17 August 1967 from the Permanent Mission of Malta to the United Nations addressed to the Secretary-General (A/6695). Of course, this note was introduced by Ambassador Arvid Pardo of Malta, and the drafting of the accompanying text, which was to become the pierre angulaire of the Common Heritage of Mankind and Part XI of UNCLOS, was undertaken by Ambassador Pardo and Elisabeth Mann Borgese.

11. UNCLOS, Article 137.

12. UNCLOS, Part 1, s. 1(1).

13. cf. generally: UNCLOS, Part XI.

seemed to codify various elements of the Common Heritage of Mankind, if not implicitly, then at least between the lines of what she affectionately referred to as 'stuff.'

But the Common Heritage of Mankind is only one of several principles that Elisabeth drew upon in formulating her vision of an ocean governance regime.

A second guiding principle, which reinforces the importance of a holistic and integrated approach to ocean affairs, was best expressed in the preamble of UNCLOS: "Problems of ocean space are closely interrelated and need to be considered as a whole."[14] Although political compromises made during the long negotiations on the Convention meant that some elements of the Common Heritage of Mankind dimension, as well as that of the holistic approach to ocean management, were not fully achieved, they remain central to the philosophy of ocean governance.

As we move towards the development of ocean governance regimes, it is imperative that policy makers seek to reconcile peace and security with integrated approaches to the management of ocean space and activities. This becomes particularly evident when one considers the troubling trends in rising transnational criminal activity, which make use of the seas (piracy and armed robbery at sea;[15] smuggling of humans,[16] weapons, narcotics and controlled substances;[17] illegal immigration; illicit transport and dumping,

14. UNCLOS, Preamble.

15. cf. E. Mann Borgese and F. N. Bailet, "Technology Cooperation and Transfer, Piracy and Armed Robbery at Sea: A Discussion Paper in Two Parts for UNICPOLOS II," in *Ocean Yearbook* 17, ed. E. Mann Borgese, A. Chircop and M. McConnell (Chicago: University of Chicago Press, 2003); the International Maritime Bureau (IMB), Commercial Crime Services of the International Chamber of Commerce (ICC), http://www.iccwbo.org/ccs/menu_imb_bureau.asp (accessed 25 August 2002); and the work of the Marine Safety Committee (MSC) of the International Maritime Organization (IMO); particularly the MSC's circular regarding this topic: *Piracy and Armed Robbery Against Ships: Guidance to ship-owners and ship operators, shipmasters and crews on preventing and suppressing acts of piracy and armed robbery against ships.* MSC. MSC/Circ.623/REV.3 — 24/7/2002. http://www.imo.org/includes/blastDataOnly.asp/data_idpercent 3D5378/623r3.pdf (accessed 5 September 2002.)

16. cf. The UN Draft Convention Against Transnational Organized Crime, A/55/383 (November 2, 2000), http://www.odccp.org/odccp/crime_cicp_convention_documents.html and the UN Global Programme Against Trafficking in Human Beings, http://www.odccp.org/odccp/trafficking_human_beings.html?id=11705 (both accessed 11 October 2002); R. A. Pedrozo, "International Initiatives to Combat Trafficking of Migrants by Sea," in *Current Maritime Issues and the International Maritime Organization*, ed. M. H. Nordquist and J. N. Moore (London: Martinus Nijhoff, 1999), pp 53–84; and K. Best, "Migration: An international phenomenon lacking a global response," *The Federalist Debate* Year XV, no. 1, (March 2002): 20–4.

17. F. N. Bailet, "L'Approche Juridique du System International D'Interdiction du Narco-Trafic Maritime dans la Region Caraïbe Atlantic Nord-Ouest" (Ph.D. diss., Université de Nice-Sophia Antipolis, 2001), p. 500.

etc.). The urgency of the situation is even more apparent with the discovery of linkages between these organizations and terrorist organizations worldwide.[18]

The Brundtland Commission's concept of sustainable development, as further elaborated and applied through the UNCED process, is the final major founding principle from which Elisabeth based her vision of ocean governance. This concept takes the underlying ideology of UNCLOS one step further by solidifying the linkages between the economic and environmental dimensions of ocean management and maintaining the emphasis on equity through the objective of poverty eradication. All are proposed as preconditions for, or elements of, sustainable development.

It is interesting to note that despite the peace and security imperative, this dimension is omitted in all but Principle 25 of the Rio Declaration, which states that peace, development, and environmental protection are interdependent and indivisible. Clearly, it is difficult to pursue sustainable economic development while ensuring environmental protection in the best of conditions, let alone in the absence of peace and security.

Guarding the integrity of the earlier enumerated principles and indeed incorporating them into an ocean governance regime necessitates a holistic approach that takes into account all aspects of major ocean issues and calls for both horizontal and vertical integration of ocean management regimes at all levels. Although Elisabeth Mann Borgese professed this was the only way forward, she also admitted—without ever losing hope or determination—that the task at hand is enormous and necessitates considerable legal and institutional reform: its accomplishment will represent a major shift in current State thought and behavior.

HUMAN SECURITY CONSIDERATIONS IN THE IMPLEMENTATION OF OCEAN GOVERNANCE

While it may seem obvious that one cannot speak of ocean and coastal management, or ocean governance, without addressing the need to implement a legal framework in support of such regimes, these discussions rarely take place. Furthermore, full implementation of legal frameworks in this context requires effective compliance and enforcement mechanisms that are sustained by properly mandated and resourced institutions. Again, if these essential tools of implementation are not lacking altogether in the ocean context, they are all too often limited to national initiatives that are sectoral in nature and thus neglect the golden rule of the oceans: all aspects of ocean space are interrelated and should be considered as a whole.

It is through such lacunas that human security on the ocean becomes

18. See, for example, The White House, *The National Drug Control Policy 2003* (Washington: The White House, 2003), p. 160.

difficult to maintain and indeed illusive in many regions of the ocean. Effective compliance regimes and enforcement operations on the ocean must be integrated and implemented at all levels of ocean governance: the local, the national, the regional, and the global.

The Local Level

The science of criminology has long ago established a correlation between disempowered and marginalized individuals and their actions that are often not in conformity with social norms.[19] This correlation has led social scientists to conclude that the nature of decision-making systems within society should be, as much as possible, inclusive to reflect the needs and beliefs of its constituents. This approach not only allows for a higher quality of decision making, but also gives the individual a sense of importance to, and participation in, the "System."

With respect to the context of ocean governance, the implementation of this approach goes far beyond contemporary democratic institutions; for the very philosophy of ocean governance prescribes that all stakeholders must be involved in the manner in which ocean affairs are governed. However, although the local level—where the individual occupies such an important and often independent role—may be traditionally associated with certain models of governance, it is rarely the case in the realm of compliance and enforcement regimes, particularly not executive enforcement.

Increasingly, the role of the individual at this level is being recognized and accepted as it becomes incorporated into institutional aspects of ocean governance in the form of what has been called "community-based co-management."[20] But such models of management must not only occur at the institutional level, they also must be developed at the legal as well as the implementation levels. Furthermore, it is important to involve the appropriate representatives within the local level. Although the process may be difficult, these representatives must be properly selected, taking into consideration that factors of geography, occupation, religion, et cetera, may all be relevant, and furthermore, that certain important segments may not be organized and thus may be unrepresented.[21]

19. Bailet (n. 17 above), at p. 388 et suite.

20. For a comprehensive overview of theory and practice of integrated approaches to ocean management, see B. Cicin-Sain and R. W. Knecht, *Integrated Coastal and Ocean Management: Concepts and Practices* (Washington: Island Press, 1998), p. 516.

21. This trend is of particular importance to compliance and enforcement, as it is only with the integrating of the appropriate constituents within the governance structures that these structures will be able to make informed decisions. For example, it is sometimes observed that nearshore fishers are often represented by large fishing companies whose activities are concentrated in the offshore, thus alienating nearshore fisheries that often contribute much more to the well-being of the com-

Law enforcement agents have often said the "the only law is an enforceable law." Communities as well as individuals play a significant role in ensuring that a law is enforceable through their active participation in both the derivation of law and in its application. In the case of deriving law, it is clear that the appropriate constituents, individually or represented, can contribute to the development of fair and equitable rules and regulations that will be consistent with the context within which they are applied. If this integration is achieved, marginalization will be minimized thus resulting in an increase in compliant behavior.

Compliance can be further reinforced through numerous strategies that may vary in the level of State and community involvement, and include, inter alia, education, training, codes of conduct, self-regulation, and inspections, all of which come together to form a compliance and enforcement matrix.[22]

Communities and the private sector should also be involved in the application of law, including surveillance, monitoring, and control aspects of enforcement activities. In this context, surveillance means the detection and notification of any State of a condition, activity, or event of interest within an area of interest over a period of time; monitoring means the systematic observation of a specific condition, activity, or event of interest; and control means the executive enforcement act that renders effective the rule of law.[23]

Furthermore, individuals who are not agents of the State may be in a position to actively and passively contribute to these operations as they are intimately involved in community activities and thus are able to observe the occurrence of illicit acts with relative ease. Through the participation of such individuals, a network of surveillance may be established that will act as a detection and notification system for the agents of the State.[24] Such networks

---

munities. The same observation has also been made in the context of communities of fishers utilizing different gear types as legislation aimed at one group without making provisions for another, often resulting in unfair restrictions leading to marginalization. Similar examples can also be derived from all ocean industries: for example, can a shipping company, or a national delegation at the IMO, represent seafarers? Professor Alastair Couper provides some chilling insight into this question in his book *Voyages of Abuse: Seafarers, Human Rights and International Shipping* (London: Pluto Press, 1999), p. 211.

22. F. N. Bailet, "Achieving Compliance in the Maritime Sectors," (paper presented to the Maritime Institute of Malaysia [MIMA], October 2000). One of the goals of the aforementioned Dalhousie University study on maritime security within Canadian waters is to dissect the Canadian maritime enforcement matrix and gain insight into the actual and potential role of compliance measures.

23. F. N. Bailet, F. W. Crickard and G. J. Herbert, *Integrated Maritime Enforcement: A Handbook* (Halifax: Dalhousie University, 2000), p. 28.

24. Within the maritime sectors, these contributions often take the form of NGOs and industry groups who survey and monitor activities within their local areas to detect illicit activities, such as the trafficking of narcotics and humans, illegal dumping, illegal harvesting of natural resources, non-observance of safety standards and procedures, et cetera.

may be formal, such as 'Coast Watch' and 'Citizen Patrol' programs, and function as auxiliaries to State agencies, as their involvement may extend to monitoring activities and in some instances they may be competent in providing support of control operations. Informal contributions most often manifest themselves in the form of anonymous reporting of observed illicit or potentially illicit activities.[25]

It is thus through the effective involvement of constituents in the formulation and implementation of law and policy that the State will be able to increase the level of compliance within the maritime sectors, thereby decreasing the need for executive enforcement operations which bare such a high economic and human cost—a cost impossible to bear for so many nations.

National Level

The local level strategies described earlier can only be effectively implemented if they are guided and enabled by an overarching national governance structure that is inclusive and truly integrated.

At the national level, two of the most common barriers to effective enforcement action undertaken by national authorities are the lack of resources made available to enforcement agencies and the lack of cooperation among these agencies.[26] These barriers are particularly evident in the realm of interdiction of illicit maritime activities such as the trafficking of humans and narcotics, piracy and armed robbery at sea, and marine pollution.[27]

Perhaps the first two categories of illicit acts—trafficking in human and narcotics and piracy and armed robbery—represent the largest threat to

25. In this respect, it is important for the State to provide a credible, anonymous reporting system that is free of charge for the user. Such systems often include toll-free telephone numbers and mailing addresses for investigation services. This system has been particularly successful in small, coastal, isolated communities and highly unionized dockyards, often areas of frequent illicit maritime activity, and where the consequences of being labeled as an informant can be serious.

26. cf. the reports of the Meeting of Heads of National Drug Law Enforcement Agencies held under the auspices of the United Nations Office for Drug Control and Crime Prevention (UNDCP), available on the UNDCP web site, www.undcp.org (accessed 2 February 2003). Also see I. Lloyd Griffith, *Drugs and Security in the Caribbean: Sovereignty under Siege* (Pennsylvania: Pennsylvania State University Press, 1997).

27. cf. the annual reports of the UNDCP, for example, UNDCP. *World Drug Report 2000.* Oxford: Oxford University Press, 2000, p. 780; also, Focus on IMO. *Piracy and Armed Robbery at Sea.* London: International Maritime Organization, 2000, p. 8; see IMO/MSC (n. 15 above), and the work of the Inter-American Drug Abuse Control Commission of the Organization of American States (OAS/CICAD), for example, CICAD. *Evaluation of Progress in Drug Control: Hemispheric Report 1999–2000.* Washington: Organization of American States, 2001, p. 26.

maritime security as they transcend all maritime sectors and are increasing at an alarming rate in both their frequency and distribution.[28] Nonetheless, it is important to note that a State, as a subject of international law, has an obligation to enforce all provisions of customary international law as well as those of all treaties, conventions, and accords it is a party to.

This responsibility places a colossal burden on States, particularly less developed countries (LDCs) and small island developing States (SIDS), which may not even possess the most fundamental capacity necessary to effectively exercise surveillance in the maritime zones under their jurisdiction, let alone determine the outer limits of their continental shelf. Furthermore, even within nations that possess potentially adequate levels of human and financial resources, the responsibility for enforcement of laws, regulations, and standards usually falls within the jurisdiction of many ministries and agencies, most of which operate in a sectoral and competitive manner, thus fragmenting the overall effectiveness of the State's maritime enforcement capacity.

For example, the implementation of various provisions made by the IMO Conventions, and MOUs such as the inspection of vessels party to a regional Port State Control system, may fall within the mandate of the Ministry of Transport. However, within the same nation, these officials who visit many ships for the purpose of their inspections, are not habilitated to detect suspicious activities and circumstances that may indicate illicit cargo. Sadly, it is also often noted that the enforcement officials of one agency, although aware of illicit activities that do not fall within their mandates, will not report these activities to their counterparts in the appropriate agencies. This lack of cooperation often stems from longstanding rivalries between various government ministries which are all eager to justify their importance, at the expense of others, as they compete for a portion of limited and/or shrinking government budgets.

However, this lack of cooperation does not always characterize relations

28. In the case of piracy and armed robbery at sea, the latest statistics from the International Maritime Organization and the International Chamber of Commerce indicate that between 1999 and 2000 these illicit activities have risen 57 percent and between 1991 and 1999 they rose by 450 percent. It is important to note that it is also estimated that 50 percent of these illicit acts go unreported, as the shipping industry could be faced with an increase in insurance premiums as a result. Another important trend to note is that, according to these same agencies, violence utilized in realizing these acts is dramatically increasing: 24 seafarers were injured and 3 killed in 1999, and 99 seafarers were injured and 72 killed in 2000. The IMO noted that the number of acts of piracy and armed robbery against ships which had occurred in 2001, as reported to the Organization, was 370, a decrease of 101 by number and 21 percent under the figure for 2000. The total number of incidents of piracy and armed robbery against ships, reported to have occurred from 1984 to the end of April, 2002, was 2,650.

between government departments. On the contrary, although cooperation often ranges from infrequent to occasional, it is indeed present and, in some cases, yields very fruitful results. This interdepartmental cooperation often arises out of governmental initiatives that seek to rationalize operational assets thereby developing new mandates for certain well-endowed ministries to support the activities of less equipped ministries. This policy is exemplified by the increasing use of military assets in the support of constabulary operations such as fisheries patrols or environmental monitoring. These operations are usually executed according to strict guidelines that are set forth in the form of an interagency memorandum of understanding (MOU) that stipulates operational procedures and command structures. [29]

For example, the Ministry responsible for the management of living resources within the nation's jurisdiction may not possess the necessary assets to execute fisheries patrols within the EEZ. However, the nation's Ministry of Defense may be well-equipped to do so and could thus provide a manned vessel for fisheries patrol that would embark a fisheries officer to engage in EEZ patrols. Furthermore, while on ordinary military exercise or patrol, the vessels of this ministry could also be habilitated to respond to other maritime security issues. These could include safety of life at sea incidents as well as marine pollution incidents, all of which the State must react to, if not out of self-interest, then by treaty obligation under various conventions it may be party to.

The level of private sector involvement should also become a recognized and significant component of maritime compliance and enforcement activities, as not only are its interests most directly threatened by illicit activities, but it often possesses the necessary resources and management structures to implement surveillance and monitoring programs efficiently. Public-private sector cooperative arrangements also arise out of necessity, as is sometimes the case with the shipping industry where the transport of cargo is extremely time-sensitive. Comprehensive customs inspections carried out on vessels as well as their cargo may impede the ability of the shipping industry to deliver to markets in a timely manner, thus resulting in enormous losses in revenue. Equally important, and perhaps acting against effective inspections, is the structure of the global transportation network that continually seeks to minimize transaction costs.[30] It is therefore in the interest

29. For a Canadian example of this category of agreements, see the Memorandum of Understanding between the Minister of National Defense and the Solicitor-General of Canada on Counter-Narcotics Assistance Provided by the Canadian Armed Forces to the Royal Canadian Mounted Police (4 August 1999).

30. It is important to note that although the earlier example utilized the case of customs inspections and shipping, this type of situation is also very much a factor in the cruise ship industry, as well as many resource-based industries.

of both parties to elaborate integrated cooperative arrangements to maintain low 'transaction costs' without compromising the effective enforcement of maritime policy.[31]

Even though the use of nonconstabulary assets to support enforcement actions at sea has been widely debated, the motivations of the private sector are often questioned, and community involvement in governance can be very difficult, it is incontestable that these entities are often the only ones who possess the necessary knowledge and resources to effectively reinforce the limited capabilities of the State. Ocean governance structures should thus seek to include these sectors as much as possible in the elaboration and implementation of maritime enforcement regimes.

Such participation could perhaps be facilitated through the establishment of maritime advisory boards with a membership consisting of representatives from all ministries responsible for implementing ocean policy as well as stakeholder representatives. Such bodies could collectively assess the various threats to ocean security drawing on their day-to-day experiences within each of their areas of marine activity and thus propose insightful integrated approaches through which the threats could be addressed.

Regional Level

Often, issues which pose challenges to safe, secure, and sustainable governance of the ocean occur on large geographical scales. As globalization relentlessly pushes forward, it is also only normal that both licit and illicit uses of the ocean follow suit. In response to this reality, the international community has come to recognize that it is on a regional level that many initiatives, ranging from pollution control to cooperative scientific research, are most effective.

The UNEP Regional Seas Programme was perhaps one of the pioneers of this philosophy and its approach has subsequently been adopted by many regional bodies attempting to govern, survey, monitor, and control ocean issues such as shipping standards (Port State Control), sustainable develop-

31. An interesting example of this type of cooperative arrangement is the Carrier Agreements under the US Customs Carrier Initiative Program. Through these agreements, Customs Officers assist businesses and government to develop security programs and initiatives that safeguard legitimate shipments from being used to smuggle narcotics. cf. http://www.customs.gov/about/carint.htm#pg18 and http://www.customs.ustreas.gov/impoexpo/impoexpo.htm (both accessed 13 June 2002). Another interesting example is seen in the cooperation between Environment Canada (EC) and the Canada-Nova Scotia Offshore Petroleum Board (CNSOPB) to ensure the compliance to and enforcement of environmental legislation: Cooperation on gathering scientific data recording the effects of offshore oil and gas development on the marine environment, cost sharing for environmental emergency response, as well as training. See the MOU between EC and CNSOPB, 2000 (This document can be obtained by writing to either EC or CNSOPB).

ment (Barcelona Convention System), and narcotics interdiction (Organization of American States).

Unfortunately, current trends in regional approaches to ocean governance all seem to lack one of the most fundamental components: regional implementation mechanisms. Regional programs of action as well as protocols abound, and institutional bodies have been created that have effectively integrated many of the constituents of the ocean community (e.g., the Mediterranean Commission for Sustainable Development), however, they have all too often neglected to provide for the integration of surveillance, monitoring, and control measures across all ocean sectors active within the regions. This lacuna provides ample opportunity for illicit undertakings to go undetected and unpunished as the weakest members of the region are targeted at the expense of the collective.[32]

These symptoms are abundant in many regions, as substandard ships serve maritime routes where coastal states lack inspection capacities; human cargo is smuggled to remote coastlines where national authorities have no surveillance infrastructure; and narcotics transit and are transshipped in the waters of nations who do not posses the minimum means necessary to detect and interdict such activities. These examples are only a small sampling of the epidemic. All of these activities foster regional instability as the negative impact of illicit activities continues to be felt and certain States react unilaterally, and sometimes extraterritorially, to protect what is believed to be their national interests and those of the region as a whole.[33]

Recognizing the dangers of such actions, certain regions have attempted to develop cooperative frameworks, in the form of multilateral accords and MOUs, that seek to establish multilateral surveillance, monitoring, and control activities, all the while reaffirming the sovereignty of each State over its zones of maritime jurisdiction and the ships flying its flag.[34] It is

32. Mann Borgese and Bailet (n. 15 above).

33. This situation is very well-documented in the case of narcotics trafficking in the Caribbean Sea. The USA has declared that since these criminal activities present a clear and present danger to the nation's (and region's) socioeconomic well being and the neighboring nations do not possess the means to act, they will act unilaterally. In some instances, the actions undertaken by the United States have extended into the territorial seas of their neighboring nations, and the laws of the United States have been applied to individuals in these areas. See Lloyd Griffith (n. 26 above).

34. For example, for narcotics interdiction, cf. the Draft Agreement Concerning Co-operation in Suppressing Illicit Maritime Trafficking in Narcotic Drugs and Psychotropic Substances in the Caribbean Area, OEA/Ser.L/XIV.2.28, CICAD/Doc.1076/00 rev.1 (24–26 October 2000). (Background material for information briefing by the Government of the Netherlands during the 28th Regular Session of the Organization of American States); and for substandard shipping control, cf. Paris MOU http://www.parismou.org, Tokyo MOU http://www.iijnet.or.jp/tokyomou, and the Vina Del Mar MOU http://www.sudnet.com.ar/ciala. (All accessed 24 March 2002).

clear that these initiatives are critical to the successful establishment and maintenance of maritime security, as well as contributing to the development of common understanding of the issues and foster the necessary integration of national responses at the regional level.

However, these regional initiatives are limited in their application as they often only prescribe the necessity for States to 'cooperate' to find common solutions instead of erecting truly integrated maritime enforcement regimes. Once again, the majority of the responsibility and associated costs of implementation are left up to each individual nation and thus propagating insecurity within regions.

This situation has led certain scholars and policy makers to begin exploring the concept of multilateral regional Coast Guards as efficient compliance and enforcement mechanisms for certain regions.[35] Although the development of such instruments is increasingly considered to be an acceptable and necessary objective, their operationalization is still over the horizon. Furthermore, it is imperative that during the elaboration of such approaches, due consideration be given to the fundamental philosophical underpinnings of ocean governance so as to ensure both their effectiveness and their role as tools of sustainable development.

Global Level

Compliance and enforcement mechanisms, and indeed all aspects of ocean governance, must provide the international community with a global forum within which problems can be discussed and solutions sought through consensus. Furthermore, although these solutions are often only implemented at the regional, national and local levels, they must be harmonized at the global level so as to be truly effective.

This imperative is particularly apparent in the case of maritime security programs, for transnational criminal organizations are highly adaptable and will quickly modify their modus operandi to take advantage of a weakness in interdiction strategies at all levels and in all regions of the globe. The importance of a global strategy is particularly well exemplified in interdiction efforts aimed at the trafficking of narcotics and humans by sea as well as that of combating substandard shipping.

35. For example, calls for a Caribbean Coast Guard: the OAS-CICAD's Draft Agreement Concerning Co-operation in Suppressing Illicit Maritime Trafficking in Narcotic Drugs and Psychotropic Substances in the Caribbean Area (see n. 34 above) contains provisions for the establishment of regional and subregional maritime law enforcement programs that constitute the foundations of a Regional Coast Guard; G. J. Herbert and T. M. Shaw, "Oceans Governance and Human Security: Towards the End of the Century: Regional Approaches," in *The Aegean Sea after The Cold War* ed. A. Chircop, A. Gerolymatos and I. Iatrides (Houndmills, Basingstoke: International Political Economy Series, Macmillan Distribution Ltd. UK, 2000).

In the first case, the illicit use of legitimate maritime transport as a vehicle to traffic narcotics and humans is increasingly being undertaken by transnational criminal organizations. The entities behave very much like multinational corporations and are characterized by complex production, transportation, and distribution networks that are all supported by the latest information technologies.[36] In other words, the international community is faced with a dynamic and intelligent supranational actor who possesses enormous technical and financial means.

Thus, it is only through collective action that these transnational criminal organizations can be effectively countered. A global multidimensional approach must be elaborated and implemented at all levels in such a manner that no one region or nation can serve as a refuge or staging post for illicit activities: wherever substandard ships operate, they should be intercepted; whenever illegal dumping occurs, it must be detected; however illicit cargos are being taken to markets, they will be intercepted and trafficking networks shut down.

If enforcement action at a global level is difficult to envision, regional actions of this nature must be enabled through the global harmonization of laws, policies, procedures, the standardization of information collection and exchange, the provision for proceedings transfers and global admissibility of evidence, et cetera. For without global consensus and harmonized approaches, all levels of ocean governance will be undermined, as the legal and institutional aspects will not be supported by effective means of implementation.

If achieving Pacem in Maribus through the development and effective implementation of ocean governance as outlined earlier seems difficult at best, and perhaps naïve, it is important to recall one of Elisabeth's favorite sayings that she often shared with youth when they where confronted with institutional difficulties or generational challenges: "the idealist of today will become the realist of tomorrow, but the realist of today will be dead tomorrow."

36. cf. United Nations Office for Drug Control and Crime Prevention. *World Drug Report 2000*. http://www.undcp.org/world_drug_report.html (accessed 10 September 2002).

The Pacific Islands Regional Ocean Policy: The Quest for Good Ocean Governance

Joeli Veitayaki and Nathan Evans
Marine Affairs Programme, University of the South Pacific, Suva, Fiji

G. Robin South
IOI Regional Centre for Australia and the Western Pacific, Townsville, Australia

Joeli Veitayaki first met Elisabeth Mann Borgese during the International Ocean Institute Class B Training Programme at Dalhousie University in 1992. From then to their last meeting at the Oceans and Coasts at Rio+10 Conference in Paris in 2001, he was always amazed at her great knowledge and farsightedness, which never seemed affected by her advanced years. Elisabeth was years ahead of us in her thoughts, which she had a powerful and convincing way of putting across to us. The world is poorer without EMB.

Robin South first met Elisabeth Mann Borgese when she visited Fiji to discuss the foundation of IOI-Pacific Islands (then IOI-South Pacific) in 1992, and continued to work closely with her from then until he moved to Townsville in early 2002 to establish IOI-Australia. Elisabeth played a key role during the hosting of *Pacem in Maribus* in Fiji in 1999, and strongly supported the establishment of IOI-Australia. Following her death, the IOI training facility in Townsville was dedicated to Elisabeth's memory.

INTRODUCTION

The presentation of the Pacific Islands Regional Ocean Policy at the 2002 World Summit on Sustainable Development in Johannesburg marked the culmination of yet another milestone achievement in regional cooperation in the Pacific Islands. The formulation of the regional ocean policy began with a request from the 1999 Forum Leaders that a regional ocean policy be produced. This Policy is to be the basis for the harmonisation of national and regional actions in relation to oceanic and coastal resources in the

Ocean Yearbook 18: 558–577

Pacific Islands. The Policy will also offer the platform for the formulation of a Pacific Islands Regional Ocean Strategic Action Plan that will prescribe the sustainable use of the ocean and its resources. The Pacific Island countries were urged to become parties to international treaties and conventions such as the United Nations Convention on the Law of the Sea (UNCLOS).[1]

The responsibility of producing the regional ocean policy was given to the Council of Regional Organisations in the Pacific (CROP). CROP consists of regional organisations in the Pacific Island countries. This is a feature of the Pacific Islands region where individual countries are members of a number of regional technical or policy institutions. CROP outlined how the policy will be developed and implemented and designated its Marine Sector Working Group (MSWG), which consists of CROP organisations that have a marine focus, to do the drafting. The members of the MSWG include the Forum Secretariat, the Secretariat of the Pacific Community (SPC), South Pacific Applied Geoscience Commission (SOPAC), the South Pacific Forum Fisheries Agency (FFA), the South Pacific Regional Environment Programme (SPREP), and the University of the South Pacific (USP).[2]

Between 2001 and early 2002, the MSWG drafted the Pacific Islands Regional Ocean Policy. The process was coordinated by the Forum Secretariat, and began with a concept paper prepared by a consultant, followed by a detailed framework document prepared by the Forum Secretariat in collaboration with the USP and the SPC. The drafting took place during a series of dedicated meetings, as well as in the margins of other regional meetings. The MSWG gave freely of their time and, in the spirit of regionalisation, worked towards consensus in the text of the final draft. The drafting process involved extensive research, analysis, and review of all pertinent regional and global initiatives, as well as several ocean policy models, such as those of Australia and Canada.

Drafting an ocean policy for the 23 Pacific Island countries and territories was a difficult task, given that most are newly independent with large Exclusive Economic Zones (EEZ) and that there are many opportunities that now present themselves under the purview of UNCLOS, to which many are signatory.[3] In addition, the high seas present a special regional responsi-

1. United Nations Convention on the Law of the Sea, 1982. A/CONF.62/122. Adopted 10 December 1982, entered into force 16 November 1994.

2. Regional cooperation in marine resources policy and practice is a feature of how the region organizes itself. See, for example, K. Eteuati, "Regional Cooperation for Marine Environmental and Resources Management," in *Oceans Governance and Maritime Strategy,* ed. D. Wilson and D. Sherwood (Sydney: Allen and Unwin, 2000), pp. 88–95.

3. The following Pacific Island Countries and bordering countries have ratified UNCLOS: Australia (1994), Kiribati (2003), Cook Islands (1995), Fiji (1982); Marshall Islands (1991); Federated States of Micronesia (1991), Nauru (1996), New

bility on the Pacific Island countries, as is evident from the recent conclusion of the Multilateral High Level Conference (MHLC) process.[4] Given these constraints, it was understood by the MSWG that the Policy would form a blueprint, providing building blocks for the Pacific Island countries to develop national ocean policies. The Policy thus is a broad-brush policy based on a vision and five guiding principles. These principles are part of the new era of ocean governance from UNCLOS and the agreements and conventions originating from the United Nations Conference on Environment and Development, Agenda 21,[5] Chapter 17,[6] the Barbados Programme of Action,[7] and the World Summit on Sustainable Development's Plan of Implementation.[8]

After endorsement from the CROP Heads, the draft Policy was then circulated through the governing bodies of the different regional organisations for comments from the stakeholders throughout the region. At the 33rd Pacific Islands Forum in Suva in August 2002, the region's Heads of State and Governments endorsed the Pacific Islands Regional Ocean Policy (Annex 1).[9] The leaders at the Suva meeting included the Heads of State and Government of Australia, the Cook Islands, the Federated States of Micronesia, Fiji, Kiribati, Nauru, New Zealand, Niue, Palau, Papua New Guinea, the Republic of the Marshall Islands, Samoa, Solomon Islands, Tonga, Tuvalu, and Vanuatu.

Zealand (1996), Palau (1996), Papua New Guinea (1997), Samoa (1995), Solomon Islands (1997), Tonga (1995), and Vanuatu (1999).

4. The Multilateral High Level Conference on fisheries has been well reported elsewhere; see S. Tarte, "A Duty to Cooperate: Building a Regional Regime for the Conservation and Management of Highly Migratory Fish Stocks in the Western and Central Pacific," in *Ocean Yearbook 16,* ed. E. Mann Borgese, A. Chircop and M. McConnell (Chicago: University of Chicago Press, 2002), pp. 261–99.

5. Agenda 21 was adopted at the United Nations Conference on Environment and Development (UNCED), Rio de Janerio, Brazil, 3–14 June 1992. http://www.un.org/esa/sustdev/agenda21text.htm (accessed 5 June 2003).

6. Chapter 17 of Agenda 21, "Protection of the Oceans, All Kinds of Seas, Including Enclosed and Semi-Enclosed Seas, and Coastal Areas and the Protection, Rational Use and Development of Their Living Resources," http://www.un.org/esa/sustdev/agenda21chapter17.htm (accessed 5 June 2003).

7. Programme of Action for the Sustainable Development of Small Island Development States and the Barbados Declaration, A/CONF.167/9, http://www.un.org/documents/ga/conf167/aconf167-9.htm (accessed 5 June 2003).

8. Plan of Implementation was adopted at the World Summit on Sustainable Development (WSSD), Johannesburg, South Africa, 26 August 4 September 2002, http://www.johannesburg.org/ (accessed 5 June 2003).

9. The full text of the Pacific Islands Regional Ocean Policy is provided to publicise it so that interested people can have a copy of the document. The emphasis in the Pacific Island countries is to publicise the Policy and invite comments and action. It must be remembered that the Policy is a living document that can be revisited as often as necessary.

The endorsement of the Policy by the leaders was accompanied by a call for follow-up action from the region and individual countries. In line with the call from the Pacific Islands Forum Leaders, the MSWG is planning a Pacific Regional Oceans Forum in February 2004 to develop an implementation framework for the Policy. The planned Forum should allow for further consultation between regional and national stakeholders, government, and civil society. This will provide a platform for new partnerships within the region. This paper is part of the follow-up action and aims to publicize and promote the Policy and its adoption and explore ways in which it can be effectively implemented.

THE RATIONALE AND CONTEXT

The Pacific Islands Regional Ocean Policy presents a vision for "A healthy ocean that sustains the livelihoods and aspirations of Pacific Islands communities." In an age when the oceans are subjected to unsustainable exploitation and usage, the call for a healthy ocean from the region is reassuring. The Pacific Ocean, as the world's largest and one of the last remaining sources of healthy fisheries and habitats should be managed effectively to ensure its continued survival and use.

The Policy demonstrates the commitment within the Pacific Islands region to take care of their ocean, which has been the most dominating feature of their environment since their forefathers settled the islands after their epic journeys across the ocean. The Policy is predicated on the principle that Pacific Island countries are custodians of 12 percent of the world's oceans, that the vast resources of this ocean space are finite, and that the Pacific Island countries have the daunting task of managing these resources for future generations. Indeed, the very survival and future of these is inexorably linked to that of the ocean and its resources. The Policy also recognizes that the oceans are a continuum—that the Pacific is a part of the global ocean system. Finally, the Policy recognizes the need for partnerships if it is to be properly implemented, because the Pacific Island countries are small and severely lack the capacity to sustainably manage their ocean space.

If the ocean's resource potentials are realized, the people in these resource-strapped islands in the Pacific Ocean will have very bright futures. However, there are many constraints that need to be addressed. Most of the hazards are extreme natural events such as tidal waves, earthquakes, and cyclones. Pollution and illicit and illegal human activities also threaten the ocean's resources and its life-supporting services. For these reasons, Pacific Island countries need to take proper care of their ocean starting now.

The Pacific Islands Regional Ocean Policy is not legally binding but is founded on international and regional conventions, treaties, and instruments. The Policy is intended as a framework that can guide the formulation and implementation of sustainable ocean development within the region. Individual countries must formulate more specific and appropriate policies and strategies. However, in many of the countries where local capacity is limited or nonexistent, the Policy is a welcomed development that will prompt countries to look after the ocean and its resources in the areas under their jurisdiction.[10]

Particular issues require special consideration in the Pacific Island countries because they influence the implementation of the Policy. These issues are capacity building, vulnerability, and the enjoyment of rights and responsibilities. Capacity building is required to provide the knowledge base necessary to generate information about the ocean upon which life is dependent. The region requires a cadre of scientists and policy makers who can formulate the most appropriate strategies for utilizing and managing the ocean and its resources. Regional organisations and the countries can enhance the process by providing the support and opportunities for developing local capacity.

Vulnerability is manifested in terms of environmental, economic, and social circumstances. Examples of environmental vulnerability include climate change, sea-level rise, and extreme natural events. Economic vulnerability is associated with the nature of Pacific Island countries and their place within the global economy. Pacific Island countries are economically vulnerable because they have small economies that are isolated from the main markets and are dependent on the export of primary produce.[11] These countries lack the high skill and capital requirements of oceanic development activities. Social vulnerability is related to population growth and distribution, food security, and the loss of traditional knowledge. These vulnerabilities have been successfully addressed in many instances and should be the case in the Pacific Island countries if good, innovative policies and strategies are put in place.

The enjoyment of rights and responsibilities is a feature of international law such as UNCLOS. Whilst the Pacific Islands are given the rights to claim different maritime zones and resources, they are expected to undertake marine resource surveys and organize management regimes for different resources in these areas within their jurisdiction. These regimes may require the countries to collaborate and form partnerships to improve performance. Countries are encouraged to conduct scientific research and to collaborate

10. At the end of 1998, the International Year of the Ocean, Australia released Australia's Oceans Policy as an instrument to maintain the integrity of oceanic waters while simultaneously promoting the development of maritime industries. Since then, a number of countries have commenced oceans policy planning, including New Zealand and the United States. See G. Wescott, "The development and initial implementation of Australia's 'integrated and comprehensive' Oceans Policy," *Ocean and Coastal Management* 43, no. 10–11 (2000): 853–78.

11. Annex 2 provides an outline of Pacific Island countries' land and Exclusive Economic Zone (EEZ) areas and population. The small areas and economies, cou-

with those that have the resources and capacity. In return, countries are to allow the conduct of research within their waters and be willing to share the information and technology.

With the Policy, the Pacific Island countries are renewing their commitment to sustainably use the resources of the ocean. The Pacific Island countries expect other countries, entities, and individuals to respect their rights to manage their resources and promise to support other management initiatives that are instituted by others. This is a sign of goodwill that will enhance the acceptance of the Policy. Pacific Island countries have demonstrated their capacity for collaborative work that augurs well for new partnerships. Good stewardship and the involvement of communities are emphasized because local communities should be responsible for the care of their resources. Strengthened involvement at these different levels should result in the effective implementation of the Policy.

THE POLICY

The goal of the Policy is to "ensure the future sustainable use of our ocean and its resources by Pacific Islands communities and external partners." The goal emphasizes the wise use of the ocean and its resources. At present and in the future, the most pressing threat to Pacific Island countries will be from outsiders who ship oil, nuclear materials, or fish in the Pacific Ocean. In addition, as marine resources in many parts of the world are fully utilized or are no longer available, Pacific Islanders and their partners will need to formulate effective policy and strategies for ensuring the future sustainability of their own resources.[12]

The guiding principles to the Policy reflect the most important features of the ocean and its use. These principles are purposely kept at a high level with general and encompassing statements that highlight the importance of the ocean to Pacific Islanders and emphasize why it must be properly managed. It was determined early in the policy development process to elevate the Policy in this way to maximize the likelihood of reaching concurrence on its content. Moreover, there is now a period of reflection for the countries and people to consider the types of actions that can be pursued to deliver on the Policy's vision. These general statements therefore serve as the basis for all types of activities that are undertaken in the ocean, coasts and islands in the future.

---

pled with the large EEZ areas that the countries are responsible for, are indicative of the challenges that face the Pacific Island countries.

12. The experience of another developing part of the world (the Caribbean) and its quest for sustainable oceans use is described in M. Miller, "Third world states and fluid sovereignty: development options and the politics of sustainable ocean management," *Ocean and Coastal Management* 42 (2000): 235–53.

Principle 1—Improving our Understanding of the Ocean

Understanding the ocean is a huge call for humanity let alone the developing Pacific Island countries. However, Pacific Islanders need knowledge of the ocean, how it functions, and how it is affected by the changes caused by human activities. This knowledge will provide the basis for planning "sustainable uses of the ocean and its resources, for the amelioration of pollution and harmful practices and for the prediction of weather, climate and ocean variability."

Effective resource management principles should be applied at all levels using all available methods. While the local communities should be involved in these management exercises, there are also specific roles for the district, national, and regional stakeholders and institutions. The multiple uses of the ocean require collaboration and partnerships between the users. Integration of traditional knowledge with contemporary scientific information is critical if the decision makers of the region are to have a better understanding of ocean processes and ecosystems. This critical knowledge is "dependent on access to science and technology, to enable research, exploration and development of both living and non-living marine resources, and of long-term monitoring and observation."

To provide effective solutions, Pacific Island countries need to understand the threat of pollution from all sources and the best ways of addressing them. With increased human activities, pollution is likely to worsen. This poses threats to the long-term health of coastal systems and ecological processes, public health and the social and commercial use of ocean resources.

Principle 2—Sustainably Developing and Managing the Use of Ocean Resources

Pacific Island communities are heavily reliant on their marine resources and the services that the ocean provides. The resources include the extractive uses of living and nonliving resources, as well as the nonextractive uses such as transport and communication, waste disposal, recreation, cultural activities, and life support systems. Research and modern technology are expected to create new opportunities for developing ocean resources and managing the impacts of natural and human activities in the ocean. The future of Pacific Island communities is dependent on how the people maintain the health of the ocean. It is therefore imperative that principles such as the precautionary approach, integrated development, and adaptive management are articulated and implemented to ensure the sustainable use of the ocean and its resources.

Pacific Island countries are responsible for the sustainable management of the world's largest tuna resources. These resources now supply an estimated one-third of all landed tuna, 40 percent to 60 percent of total supply to tuna canneries, and 30 percent of tuna to the valuable Japanese sashimi market.[13] Yet Pacific Islands countries are receiving less than 10 percent of the value of the tuna that is fished from their waters. In addition, ocean resource management is based on the maximum sustainable yield, which risks over-exploitation if harvests are beyond this level (either due to poor enforcement of regulations or a lack of information on what the maximum sustainable yield is). Pacific Island countries need to explore new and suitable ways of getting a better return from the use of their tuna fisheries. For instance, it has been argued that the maximum economic yield (the harvest rate that maximizes economic returns from the fishery) is almost always less than the maximum sustainable yield (the most that can be harvested without reducing long-term stock size) and therefore should be used in the management of the region's fisheries.[14] According to these experts, economic returns to the countries will increase and its sustainability will be better protected if the resources are managed according to their maximum economic yield.

Principle 3—Maintaining the Health of the Ocean

The health and productivity of the ocean is dependent upon the preservation of its ecosystem and the minimization of the impact of human activities. The health and integrity of the marine ecosystem should be maintained so that it continues to provide the life-support services it performs. In addition, the ocean is the final repository of all the substances that enter the environment. In trying to maintain the health of the ocean, Pacific Island countries need to have policies and strategies that address the threats from all their activities whether these are land based, air borne, or in the high seas.

Ocean and coastal systems must be protected from degraded water quality caused by "accidental and deliberate dumping of fuels, chemicals and ballast water from ships, aircraft and satellite launches, and non sustainable resource use." Pacific Island countries must also guard against resource depletion that threatens the natural state of equilibrium in the world's ocean.

Pacific Island countries must effectively control outsiders' activities in the region. This may require innovative policies and strategies that pass more responsibility for surveillance and control to their external partners.

13. R. Gillett, M. McCoy, L. Rodwell and J. Tamate, *Tuna: A Key Economic Resource in the Pacific* (Manila: Asian Development Bank, 2001).

14. M. King, *Fisheries, Biology, Assessment and Mangagement,* (Oxford: Fishing New Books, 1995).

Principle 4—Promoting the Peaceful Use of the Ocean

Peaceful uses of the ocean "means discouraging unacceptable, illicit or criminal activities that contradict regional and international agreements." Pacific Island countries have to exercise control and enforcement over their maritime zones. They must also seek the support of other users such as shipping nations, distant water fishing nations, and naval powers. Again, it will not be possible to do this alone. International collaboration and partnership will be required. The uses of technology such as the satellite monitoring system that is now used by the South Pacific Forum Fisheries Agency will provide more effective options.

Educating the people to support the policies and strategies can be a useful tool. People will act properly if they know what is occurring and understand what they need to do. The peaceful use of the ocean can be a polemic debate to settle but the strategies should spell out the appropriate course of action in a given situation.

Principle 5—Creating Partnerships and Promoting Cooperation

Pacific Island countries have demonstrated effective partnerships and cooperation in the sustainable management of the ocean. This should be strengthened and extended to include new and emerging partners from outside the region. Partnership and cooperation are emphasized in UNCLOS and Agenda 21 but need to be specifically articulated in the policies, strategies, and action plans of Pacific Island countries. Joint development and joint ventures are examples of partnerships that have been attempted in the past and can be the basis for future collaboration.

Pacific Island countries need to "maintain sovereign rights and responsibilities in managing, protecting and developing the ocean." This is complex and requires innovative and creative ideas that should be transformed into policies and strategies. The countries must work with reputable international organisations to assist in capacity building and creating fundamental databases.

Strategic Actions

Under each of the guiding principles the Policy lists the strategic actions that can be taken by the Pacific Island countries. There is no sequence or order, but the activities are designed to help achieve the Policy's vision. The strategic actions are directly related to the guiding principles and should provide direction for regional and national activities. Pacific Island countries can identify and prioritize their needs and then identify their appropriate action plans.

AVENUES OF DEVELOPMENT

In developing the Policy, Pacific Island countries can pride themselves on another notable regional achievement. The challenge now is for the countries to embrace the Policy, as their leaders have done, and make it the basis for articulating their national policies, strategies, and actions for the sustainable development and management of their ocean resources. The Policy provides the basis for reconciling national and regional actions, while the implementation will require a commitment by all stakeholders.

The avenues of development outlined here provide ideas about the types of activities that can be undertaken across the region within this framework. Existing regional organizations provide a valuable platform that should be built upon in taking the Policy forward. Many of the proposed development avenues are activities that fall within the remit of one or more of the CROP agencies. It therefore follows that either the MSWG or a new dedicated body should be charged with creating both a momentum for delivering on the Policy and coordinating efforts to this end.

Specific actions that can be undertaken under Principle 1 are the following:

- Establish a harmonized regional regime for marine scientific research in conformity with Part XIII of UNCLOS.
- Develop a region-wide information gathering and data collection programme to provide coherence to the research and outreach activities of CROP bodies.
- Conclude the determination of the maritime boundaries of Pacific Island countries.
- Examine the potential for new marine industries and activities such as biotechnology and deep seabed exploration, addressing the scientific, economic, and legal aspects.
- Articulate a regional research agenda to enable external research providers to align their activities with priorities defined within and for the region.
- Develop capacity within the region.

Under Principle 2, some of the activities that can be undertaken include the following:

- Develop ecosystem-based marine plans for the Pacific Island countries as the vehicle for integrating uses across marine sectors and between user groups.
- Ensure that legislation and policies regulating marine activities reflect international standards, are transparent, and provide for stakeholder input.

- Devise and apply a common environmental impact assessment regime to marine activities within the Pacific Island countries.
- Formulate legislation, policies, and strategies that emphasize integrated and adaptive management.

Actions that can be formulated under Principle 3:

- Determine oceanic water quality standards for the Pacific Islands region.
- Protect and where necessary restore critical habitats and at-risk species through legal and other effective means.
- Review national policies and laws for conformity with agreed international and regional undertakings relating to peaceful and lawful ocean use. Enact new legislation, where necessary.
- Ensure that hazardous or undesirable practices are prohibited while ensuring the maintenance of safety standards including the safety of seafarers and other maritime workers.

Principle 4 activities:

- Enhance at-sea observation of ocean uses within the region to ensure that the South Pacific Ocean is used lawfully and peacefully in accordance with agreed goals.
- Evaluate the worth of the marine asset base and scope options for future use, including possible alternative uses.
- Formulate innovative policies, strategies, and plans to exercise control.

Some activities that can be undertaken under Principle 5 include the following:

- Identify areas or uses of the regional ocean that would benefit from regional management, including in relation to impacts generated from outside the region.
- Align existing institutional arrangements to promote a holistic ecosystem approach to marine management.
- Review the practices of adjacent jurisdictions, CROP bodies, and Pacific Island countries for consistency with this Policy and establish dialogues to remedy inconsistencies.

CONCLUSION

There are signs that the Policy is widely accepted. Regional Heads of Government and States have approved the Policy. CROP agencies have also endorsed the Policy and are consulting extensively through their governing bodies. Regional organizations are committed to its successful delivery. Nevertheless, the successful delivery of the Policy's principles requires the commitment and endorsement of the member governments.[15] After all, good governance in the ocean ultimately is the responsibility of the States and their people.

The dynamic nature of the Policy also needs to be emphasised. In any setting, but perhaps especially in a developing part of the world, such an authoritative document must be interpreted and applied in a manner that reflects the evolving status of institutional and community capacity. The vision and principles provide the guidance for future delivery against which specific initiatives and undertakings should always be planned.

The Ocean Forum being planned represents the first exciting step in realizing the Policy. It is hoped that activities of the kind suggested here find currency at this important event. Endorsement of these or similar initiatives will represent a demonstrable move towards the future sustained use of the Pacific Ocean.

ANNEX 1: PACIFIC ISLANDS REGIONAL OCEAN POLICY

THIS IS OUR OCEAN

The care of the ocean is the responsibility of all people. The oceans are interconnected and interdependent, covering seventy percent of the world's surface. They are the last great frontier, and their conservation and sustainable use is vital to the well being and survival of the human race.

Pacific Island communities inhabit the islands scattered throughout an ocean across which some of the greatest migrations in human history have taken place over many thousands of years. The ocean unites Pacific Island communities more than anything else. It has supported generations of Pacific Island communities, not only as a medium for transport but also as a source of food, tradition, and culture.

Our ocean and island ecosystems contain high biological diversity that has sustained the lives of Pacific Island communities, since first settlement.

15. The role of CROP agencies in pursuing regional approaches to marine planning and management is outlined in R. J. Morrison, "Coastal and maritime zone planning and management: Relationships between Australia and the South-west Pacific," in *Coastal and Maritime Planning and Management: Transnational and Legal Considerations*, Wollongong Papers on Maritime Policy No. 2, ed. M. Tsamenyi, S. Bateman and J. Delaney (Wollongong: Centre for Maritime Policy, University of Wollongong, 1995), pp. 75–98.

It contains the most extensive coral reefs in the world, globally important fisheries, significant seabed mineral resources, and high number of threatened species. These ecosystems may contain many undiscovered resources of potential use to humankind.

Many thousands of islands and atolls are entirely coastal in nature.

The ocean is not only a lifeline, it is also a source of hazards. These hazards can be increased by the impact of human activities both within and external to the Pacific Islands region.

Our ocean provides the greatest opportunities for economic development. Responsibly managed, it has the potential to support Pacific Island communities in perpetuity.

As Pacific Island communities we are acutely aware that over 98 percent of the 38.5 million square kilometres of the Earth's surface over which we have influence is ocean.

But concerns for the long-term health of the ocean are not confined to the areas covered by sovereign rights, they extend equally to adjacent areas of high seas.

Our commitment to the development of a common Policy for this ocean stems from our collective awareness of an increasing number and severity of threats to its long-term integrity. This Policy presents a framework for the sustainable management and conservation of the resources and habitats within the region. It provides guiding principles for individual and collaborative action that will promote responsible stewardship of this large ocean for regional and global benefit.

This Policy is intended to promote the Pacific region as an ocean environment in support of sustainable development. It is not a legal document, however its guiding principals are founded on international law, as reflected in the United Nations Convention on the Law of the Sea and other international and regional agreements.

These guiding principles are: improving our understanding of the ocean; sustainably managing the ocean resource use; maintaining the health of the ocean; promoting the peaceful use of the ocean; and creating partnerships and promoting cooperation.

We invite others to recognise our commitment to these guiding principles and support our strategies to implement this Policy to help ensure our ocean remains healthy and sustains the livelihoods and aspirations of Pacific Island communities.

WHY A REGIONAL OCEAN POLICY?

The need for a Policy is based on our collective awareness of the transboundary and dynamic nature of our ocean, the increasing number and severity of threats to its long-term integrity and the reality that sustainable economic and social development will be dependent on wise use of the ocean and its resources. It is also based on our awareness of the potential for fragmentation of programmes and for conflicting commitments in different sectors as ocean-related activities increase. This requires increased regional collaborative arrangements among Pacific Island communities.

PACIFIC ISLANDS REGION

For the purpose of this Policy, the "region" includes that part of the Pacific Ocean over which the island countries and territories (Pacific Island communities), that are members of the organisations comprising the Council of Regional Organisations of the Pacific (CROP) are found. As such, the extent of the region includes not only the area within the 200 nautical mile Exclusive Economic Zone (EEZ) boundaries circumscribing these island countries, but also the ocean areas and coastal areas that encompass the extent of the marine ecosystems that support the region.

The "ocean" is defined to include the waters of the ocean, the living and nonliving elements within, the substrate beneath and the ocean-atmosphere and ocean-island interfaces.

Pacific Islands are often referred to as Small Island Developing States. They may also be thought of as Large Ocean Developing States.

Capacity Building

In order to replenish and sustain our knowledge base, it is necessary to generate new knowledge about the oceans upon which our way of life depends. Fundamental to the sustained generation of new knowledge is the continuing education of a cadre of scientists and policy makers. Educating and training people within the region is the best strategy for ensuring the continuity of marine understanding and replenishment of knowledge.

Vulnerability

Pacific Island communities are vulnerable to environmental, economic and social factors. Environmental factors include: climate variability; climate change and sea-level rise; other natural hazards such as earthquakes, tsunamis and volcanic events; fragile ecosystems; and geographic isolation.

Economic factors include: limited land area and fresh water resources; limited local markets; high import dependencies; fluctuating world prices for commodities and isolation, including large distances to world markets.

Social factors include population growth and distribution; human and food security; external influences; cultural dilution and loss of traditional knowledge and practices.

Rights and Responsibilities

The ocean has been the major influence in the history of Pacific Island communities. Throughout the region, customary association with the sea forms the basis of present-day social structures, livelihoods, and tenure systems, and traditional systems of stewardship governing its use.

International law and instruments confer rights of Pacific Island communities relating to the use of the ocean and its resources. With these rights come responsibilities, especially for sustainable management and conservation of the ocean's living resources and for the protection of the ocean environment and its biodiversity.

Pacific Island communities have established national laws, based on international principles, which provide for responsible management and use of the ocean and its resources within their area of jurisdiction.

The Pacific communities will work with other partners to promote the application of compatible policies by those partners in areas subject to their jurisdiction and surrounding waters, and with all other countries having interests in the region.

Island communities respect the rights and interests of others to participate in legitimate activities. With this sharing comes the expectation that they will meet their obligations and responsibilities to our ocean.

This Policy promotes stewardship in addition to ownership. Good stewardship captures the element of trusteeship, which refers to active engagement by communities in caring for the oceans. It draws upon ideas, policies, institutions and enforcement procedures needed to protect the oceans from abuse including the effects of land-based activities.

VISION

A healthy ocean that sustains the livelihoods and aspirations of Pacific Island communities.

GOAL

The goal of this Policy is to ensure the future sustainable use of our ocean and its resources by Pacific Islands communities and external partners.

The Guiding Principles to achieve this Goal are:

- Improving our understanding of the ocean
- Sustainably developing and managing the use of ocean resources
- Maintaining the health of the ocean
- Promoting the peaceful use of the ocean
- Creating partnerships and promoting cooperation

PRINCIPLE 1—IMPROVING OUR UNDERSTANDING OF THE OCEAN

Contemporary and traditional understanding of the ocean provides the basis for sustainable use of the ocean and its resources, for the amelioration of pollution and harmful practices, and for the prediction of weather, climate and ocean variability.

Resource management approaches based purely on scientific information have had limited success in the region over the last 50 years. The cost of obtaining scientific information, in all but a few highly commercialized systems, is beyond the capacity of many islands. As a result resource managers in the Region advocate precautionary management approaches that are more robust where comprehensive scientific understanding and intensive monitoring are difficult. This includes an enhanced role for community groups and customary resource owners in the development and application of local management arrangements for local resources.

Whilst community approaches are essential for implementing effective resource management in many cases, the long-term maintenance of exploited systems, particularly transboundary systems, still requires better science. Increased scientific understanding of ocean processes and ecosystems is critically dependent on access to science and technology, to enable research, exploration and development of both living and non-living marine resources, and of long-term monitoring and observation. The result will be improved ability to effectively conserve marine biological diversity and predict the impact of climate variation and human use patterns on the health of the ocean.

Strategic Actions

- To identify and prioritise information needs and the co-operative mechanisms for acquiring, accessing and disseminating this information.
- To strengthen national and regional capacity, encourage partnerships between regional and international organisations, and the

public and private sectors, to improve our understanding of the ocean.

- To facilitate access to this information, encourage its wide application in the implementation of this Policy and any compatible national ocean policies that may be developed in association with it.
- To have regard for traditional knowledge and its potential to contribute to better understanding the ocean and to the effective management of contemporary issues.
- To promote further formal education and training of local people in marine science and marine affairs disciplines.

PRINCIPLE 2—SUSTAINABLY DEVELOPING AND MANAGING THE USE OF OCEAN RESOURCES

Pacific Island communities are heavily reliant on the wide range of resources and services that the ocean provides for their social, cultural and economic security. This includes not only the existing extractive uses of its living and non-living resources but also the non-extractive uses such as transport and communication, waste disposal, recreation and tourism, and cultural activities. New research and technologies are creating opportunities for accessing and using the ocean and its resources.

To safeguard Pacific Island communities and maintain the health of our ocean, in perpetuity, it is imperative that we adopt a precautionary management approach to ensure the use of the ocean and its resources are sustainable.

Strategic Actions

- To identify, prioritise and implement resource development and management actions and regimes, in accordance with the precautionary approach.
- To encourage equitable sharing of resource access and benefits at local, national and regional levels.
- To engage, as appropriate, local communities in resource management decision-making.
- To build capacity of Pacific Island communities for sustainable resource development and management.
- To establish and protect traditional knowledge rights.
- To establish and protect intellectual property rights.

PRINCIPLE 3—MAINTAINING THE HEALTH OF THE OCEAN

The health and productivity of our ocean is driven by regional-scale ecosystem processes. It is dependent upon preserving ecosystem integrity and minimising the impact of human activity.

Threats to ocean and coastal health and productivity, reflected in a degradation in water quality and resource depletion include accidental and deliberate dumping of fuels, chemicals and ballast water from ships, aircraft and satellite launches, and nonsustainable resource use.

Pollution from the land contributes up to eighty per cent of all ocean pollution and is a major threat to the long-term health of nearshore systems affecting ecological processes, public health and social and commercial use of ocean resources.

Strategic Actions

- To adopt an integrated transboundary approach, through harmonised institutional arrangements, including existing international and regional agreements to manage marine ecosystems for long-term sustainable benefit.
- To incorporate sound environmental practices into social and economic development activities.
- To protect and conserve biological diversity of the ocean ecosystem at local, national and regional scales.
- To reduce the impact of all sources of pollution on our ocean environment.

PRINCIPLE 4—PROMOTING THE PEACEFUL USE OF THE OCEAN

Peaceful uses of the ocean have environmental, political, social, economic, and security dimensions. Promoting peaceful use means discouraging and reducing unacceptable, illicit or criminal or other activities contrary to regional and international agreements. Such activities threaten the major source of livelihood for Pacific Island communities.

Strategic Actions

- To ensure that all activities carried out in our ocean meet all relevant international and regional safety standards, and do not cause environmental damage, social economic hardship to the region.

- To seek remedial actions in the event of an incident resulting from nonpeaceful use of the ocean.
- To ensure that the ocean is not used for criminal activities nor for other activities that breach national or international laws.
- To encourage cooperation amongst law enforcement agencies.

PRINCIPLE 5—CREATING PARTNERSHIPS AND PROMOTING COOPERATION

Partnerships and cooperation provide an enabling environment and are essential for the sustainable management of our ocean. As a group, Pacific Island communities achieve economies of scale, a united voice for international advocacy, a regional power bloc with increased international influence and a forum for developing coordinated action on ocean issues of mutual interest or with transboundary implications.

In pursuit of creating partnerships and promoting cooperation, Pacific Island communities will seek to maintain sovereign rights and responsibilities in managing, protecting and developing the ocean.

Strategic Actions

- To foster partnerships and cooperation in the areas of security, monitoring, enforcement and the sustainable use of resources.
- To make fullest possible use of regional and international partnerships and collaboration, such as regional organisations, ocean-related treaties, and bilateral arrangements as appropriate.
- To have regard for the ocean policies of ocean jurisdictions adjoining our own, and advocate that their policies have regard for this Policy.
- To encourage Pacific Island communities to develop national ocean policies that complement and are consistent with this Policy.

FUTURE

This Policy is the result of a regional effort to achieve responsible ocean governance. It is based on existing international and regional agreements that establish a broad framework for regional cooperation and coordination to sustainably manage and conserve the ocean ecosystem in the region. It provides the basis for the harmonisation of national and regional action for the next five years. The implementation process will require a commitment by all stakeholders.

This Policy articulates guiding principles and strategic actions that will define a regional Pacific Ocean Initiative. The initiative will include a Pacific Islands Regional Ocean Summit to define the status of current knowledge and activities, and a review process to define progress, and will provide an integrated framework to include existing programmes, and identify and prioritise future Action Plans.

ANNEX 2: PACIFIC ISLAND COUNTRY STATISTICS

Country	Land Area (km^2)	EEZ Area (km^2)	Population
American Samoa	*197*	*434,700*	*54,800*
Commonwealth of Northern Mariana Islands	*478*	*777,000*	*56,700*
Cook Islands	240	1,830,000	18,000
Federated States of Micronesia	700	2,978,000	95,000
Fiji	18,376	1,290,000	737,000
Guam	*541*	*218,000*	*140,000*
Kiribati	822	3,550,000	72,000
Marshall Islands	181	2,131,000	48,000
Nauru	21	310,000	9,000
Niue	258	390,000	3,000
New Caledonia	*22,405*	*1,230,891*	*190,000*
Palau	428	616,000	17,500
Papua New Guinea	476,500	3,120,000	4,100,000
Pitcairn	*5*	*800,000*	*50*
French Polynesia	*3,521*	*5,030,000*	*218,000*
Samoa	2,934	120,000	163,000
Solomon Islands	29,785	1,340,000	325,000
Tokelau	*12*	*319,000*	*1,700*
Tonga	747	700,000	101,000
Tuvalu	26	900,000	9,250
Vanuatu	14,763	680,000	150,000
Wallis and Futuna	*255*	*242,700*	*14,400*

Note.— Members of both the Pacific Islands Forum and the Pacific Community. The countries and territories in Italics are members of the Pacific Community only.

Marine Resources Management: Ocean Governance and Education

Gunnar Kullenberg*
International Ocean Institute, Malta

It was my great fortune and pleasure to work closely with Elisabeth Mann Borgese in particular during the period 1998 until her passing away. I learned much from this collaboration, and the present article is based thereon. Also before 1998 I had many contacts and exchanges with Elisabeth. We had similar objectives. I wish to pay tribute to her and thank her for the inspiration and encouragement she gave, and for her unfailing trust and willingness to always share her knowledge and spirit with others.

INTRODUCTION

This article presents an overview of the role of the ocean and its resources in the new global service-oriented economy and the associated need for adequate ocean governance and education and awareness of ocean-related issues.

The importance of shipping has increased. Sea transport remains by far the most cost-effective way of moving goods and raw materials around the world, including economically important cargo such as grain, oil, and gas. Food production is the oldest service that the ocean provides, and one of the most important. According to the United Nations Food and Agriculture Organization (FAO) approximately half of the global marine resources are fully exploited; one quarter has some potential for increasing catches, while the remaining quarter is over exploited.[1]

The ocean plays a role in the climate system that is complementary and of comparable importance to that of the atmosphere. Evaporation from the

*Editors' Note.—The author wishes to acknowledge with thanks many interesting discussions on the subjects of this article with Dr. François Bailet. A slightly different version of the text was presented at the Techno-Ocean 2002 Conference, Japan, November 2002.

1. FAO, 2000, *State of World Fisheries and Aquaculture*, http://www.fao.org/DOCREP/003/X8002E/X8002E00.htm.

Ocean Yearbook 18: 578–599

ocean is the major source of water vapour, providing approximately 60 percent of the annual freshwater input to land. The ocean absorbs approximately 30 percent to 40 percent of the excess carbon dioxide (CO_2) that society is injecting annually into the atmosphere.[2]

The coastal zone is a very large national resource. Approximately 50 percent of the global population lives within 150 km of the sea on approximately 10 percent of the total land surface.[3] The Exclusive Economic Zone (EEZ) has added another province to the coastal state. The ocean, the coast, and small islands provide the basis for many recreational and tourism activities. Tourism is the single largest growing industry globally; the cruise line industry is growing the most rapidly.[4]

Emerging uses of ocean space and their associated consequences are closely coupled to the service economy: new classes of marine contaminants, new energy sources, and new uses of the recently discovered deep seabed ecosystem. Thus, the ocean and its resources have a dominating influence on economy, development, and security.

The ocean also provides a model on how to achieve adequate governance. For the coast it has been realized that integrated management is required. However, this is necessary also for the ocean as a whole. The model has been specified through the United Nations Convention on the Law of the Sea (UNCLOS) of 1982,[5] and provides a "constitution of the ocean." UNCLOS has been made comprehensive through the additional conventions and agreements resulting from the United Nations Conference on Environment and Development (UNCED) in 1992 and the related ongoing processes. Together, these provide a legal and institutional framework. Tools for their implementation include educational, technological, and financial resources, and means for monitoring, surveillance, and enforcement.

The International Ocean Institute's (IOI) vision is to address the need for education through the establishment of an internationally recognized interdisciplinary and intersectoral programme of study that will not only serve to facilitate the integration of ocean knowledge, but also will allow access to any professional or student in the world. To realize this vision, the IOI Virtual University is being developed. This is constituted as a network of education, training, and research centers of expertise in ocean, coastal,

2. IPCC, *Third Assessment Report on Climate Change, Volumes I, II and III* (Cambridge: Cambridge University Press, 2001).

3. GESAMP 2001. *Third State of the Marine Environment Report.* UNEP. Nairobi.

4. A. Behnam, "Shipping and Ports in Developing Countries—A Historical and Development Perspective" (presented at IOI, Centre for Marine Tropical Ecology and Hanse Institute for Advanced Studies Workshop on: Ocean Resources, Services and Products, 2001 [to be published by IOI]).

5. United Nations Convention on the Law of the Sea, 1982, adopted 10 December 1982, entered into force 14 November 1994, http://www.un.org/depts/los/.

and marine-related affairs and governance, joined together in partnership to provide an interdisciplinary and comprehensive coverage of the subject areas.

This article presents an overview of three aspects: the role of the ocean; the model of ocean management; and the education tool required for implementation.

THE ROLE OF THE OCEAN IN THE ECONOMY AND RELATED ISSUES

Our service economy relies on services, distributions, transportations, global connections, and communications. The ocean provides a multitude of services for our society and the economy, and thus has a role in the reduction of poverty. The most important services include maritime transport, regulation of climate and the hydrological cycle, recreation and tourism, and wastes depository; products include, inter alia, food, fresh water, oil, and gas.

Wealth is very unevenly distributed with approximately 83 percent of the world's income going to the richest 20 percent. Trade is a major process for poor countries to develop to obtain a growing economy. Maritime transport has a major impact on the poorest countries and people.

Maritime Transport

The importance of shipping has increased. Sea transport remains by far the most cost-effective way of moving goods and raw materials around the world. The role of the transportation sector for our economy is crucial. Shipping and trade are large shares of the GDP: 14 percent in United States of America; 24 percent in Japan; 60 percent in Nigeria; and 94 percent in The Gambia. The European Union (EU) has approximately 14 percent of the global trade by ships. Ninety percent of the EU international trade and 40 percent of the EU intra-trade is transported by ships.[6] The EU is very sensitive to shipping issues, as the maritime transport sector influences decisions of the member countries and the regional political bodies.

Developing countries generate a huge amount of world trade, but they have been marginalized in the management of maritime transport. Efforts to increase the involvement of developing countries in shipping have failed, largely because of flags of convenience. Flag States no longer maintain control of shipping; this is done by five or six leading companies or alliances.

6. A. Behnam (n. 4 above).

For example, there are no African states among the 30 leading shipping countries.

Maritime fraud is an increasing problem and includes piracy; illegal fishing; the illegal transport of people, hazardous wastes, and drugs; professional scuttling crews; abuse of seafarers; arson; insurance fraud; and the sale of nonexistent cargoes. Flag State control does not work, as it is an abuse of sovereignty, and Port State control is only possible in developed countries. Freedom of navigation no longer applies. There is a lacuna in ocean governance with respect to the shipping sector. It is imperative that all countries participate and play an active role in the distribution system for the benefits of globalization to reach all and to generate equity.

Fishing vessels carry out many violations, opposing fisheries management and conservation. There is a strong need for more surveillance and enforcement. Regional cooperation can help address all of these problems.

Food from the Ocean

Over the last 50 years the annual harvest of food from the ocean has increased by approximately a factor of five, due to a large and rapid geographical expansion of the areas being harvested and technological advancements in fishing methods.[7] Now, however, marine fisheries are at a crossroads. According to FAO, approximately half of the global marine resources are fully exploited; one quarter has some potential for increased catches, while the remaining quarter is over exploited.[8]

Overfishing has reached serious levels not only in many coastal areas, particularly regions with high population densities, but also in many high seas fisheries. Without effective action by both governments and users it appears that overfishing and long-term decline in production will continue. The socioeconomic pressures are very large. Indeed, FAO has estimated that by 2010 the contribution of marine fisheries to the supply of human food could fall to approximately 40 Mmt per year. By-catch and discards are a problem in most fisheries, amounting to approximately 30 Mmt annually. The illegal unreported and unregulated fisheries also constitute a very serious problem.

There is a need for a new management approach, and the sector is realizing this. The fisheries situation in many poor developing countries in Africa and elsewhere is of great social concern. The pressure from industrialized fishing by foreign fleets in the EEZs is enormous. The countries are unable to control these fisheries, and the allocated quotas are often surpassed. Instead, many of the fisheries on the coasts and shelf seas could be

7. FAO (n. 1 above).
8. Ibid.

managed through a community-based system using small vessels for fishing that could provide high levels of employment for the local peoples. This would address increasing poverty as well as human health issues. Fishing provides a great human impact on many shelf areas, for example, the depletion of leading predators in the ecosystem. Fishing and fish production are vulnerable to ecosystem and climate changes.

Ocean in Climate and Hydrological Cycles

The ocean plays a critical role in the regulation of the world's climate. It transports heat in amounts of the same magnitude as that carried by the atmosphere. Evaporation from the ocean is the major source of water vapour, the main greenhouse gas, and the ocean absorbs and releases CO_2.

The importance of the North Atlantic Ocean circulation to the climate of Europe is well known. The air-sea interaction in the northern North Atlantic Ocean cools the saline surface layer water sufficiently to make it more dense than the underlying water, even causing this layer to sink to the bottom in some conditions. The sinking water mixes with the deep water and spreads out, flowing southward. This thermohaline circulation, driven by the combination of the salt and heat content of the water and the atmosphere-ocean interaction, provides an enormous northward heat flux of the same or greater magnitude than that found in the atmosphere.

In the northern Pacific Ocean the thermohaline circulation is not as developed, partly due to the less intense atmosphere-ocean interaction and the lower salt content in the surface layer relative to the deeper water. In particular in the North Atlantic, the thermohaline circulation has been most clearly identified as one part of the climate system that might be significantly modified by small changes. If the salinity of the surface layer is reduced, the cooling may not be sufficient to produce water dense enough to sink to the depths let alone to the bottom. This could happen during present conditions in the northern North Atlantic and North Pacific Oceans.

The ocean takes up CO_2 from the atmosphere through direct absorption from the air in contact with the sea surface. Carbon dioxide thus dissolved in the surface water can be used by phytoplankton (plants), which convert it to organic matter and oxygen in the presence of sufficient sunlight. The carbon moves higher in the food chain when these plants are consumed by zooplankton and other animals, which in turn are consumed by higher-level organisms. The sinking of cool surface water with large amounts of dissolved carbon dioxide, together with the organic debris that falls from the surface layer, can transfer considerable amounts of carbon to the depths of the ocean. Through these processes the ocean absorbs approximately 30 percent to 40 percent of the excess CO_2 produced annually from our fossil fuel-driven society. If the rate of injection of CO_2 into the atmosphere was sufficiently smaller, the ocean could possibly cope and maintain an equilibrium. This is an enormous service the ocean is giving our economy.

Global climate change is presently considered our most important environmental problem. The third assessment of the IPCC[9] stated clearly that there is solid scientific foundation behind the statement that the global climate does change due to human impact. Recent research has made it possible to simulate with adequate accuracy the evolution of the most important global climate parameters, and to show that it is only when the models take into account both natural and anthropogenic factors affecting the climate that the simulations satisfactorily resemble the past changes. The projections of CO_2 levels in the atmosphere show that with a business-as-usual scenario, CO_2 will be approximately 700 ppm by about 2100 (i.e., approximately 3 times as much as in 1850). With CO_2 emissions frozen as of today, the level will be approximately 400 ppm, and only with Draconian measures will there be a decrease of the CO_2 level, initiated from around 2050.[10] The models project that the corresponding average temperature increases would be 2°C −3°C and approximately 1°C, for both frozen emissions and Draconian measures, respectively. This is for a 100-year time scale. However, the climate system has a very large inertia, and we should consider the evolution over larger time scales, of the order of 1000 years. According to recent tested models, the Kyoto Protocol[11] requirements would, over such time scales, lead to potentially unacceptable temperature changes. The frozen emission scenario would yield an average temperature increase of 5°C and the business-as-usual scenario, an 8°C increase. These are similar to the changes the Earth experienced during the last deglaciation of approximately 12,000 years ago.

The Intergovernmental Panel on Climate Change (IPCC) report of 2001[12] states that most models over the 100-year time scale show a weakening of the ocean thermohaline circulation as a result of the expected global warming. The models also show an increase in sea surface temperature in the tropical areas of at least 1°C−2°C over the coming 50 years, and in some areas of the Indian Ocean and the western Atlantic Ocean, an increase of at least 2°C−3°C. The impacts of such changes are still to be elucidated. However, one effect we know is a potential increase in evaporation over these parts of the ocean. Satellite observations of the radiation budget combined with surface observations have shown that the greenhouse effect increases significantly with sea surface temperature. This constitutes an exam-

9. IPCC (n. 2 above).

10. M. Latif and K. Hasselman, "Climate Change Scenarios," (presented at IOI, Centre for Marine Tropical Ecology and Hanse Institute for Advanced Studies Workshop on: Ocean Resources, Services and Products, 2001 [to be published by IOI, Malta and printed in 2003/2004]).

11. Kyoto Protocol to the United Nations Framework Convention on Climate Change, 1992, adopted 11 December 1997, http://unfccc.int/.

12. IPCC (n. 2 above).

ple of a positive feedback involving the ocean. A potential negative feedback for the climate of Western Europe is given by the possible weakening of the North Atlantic thermohaline circulation, which would imply a decrease in temperature. However, this will probably not compensate for the potential temperature increase due to the warming.

There are many elements in the oceans that are still very unsatisfactorily known and not included in existing models. The capacity of the ocean to take up CO_2 is not sufficiently known; the processes and effects thereof at high latitudes in the Arctic Basin and the Antarctic-Southern Ocean are even less well known.

Evidence of massive transformation of Arctic and Antarctic ice is recalled. Dwindling Arctic ice cover and weakening of the permafrost layer will have serious consequences for local coasts, for circulation at large scales, and for the ecosystem.

The impacts of the temperature increase on the tropical and subtropical zones are also of large concern. The most vulnerable natural systems are the glaciers, coral reefs and atolls, mangroves, polar ecosystems, and estuaries; they are all at interfaces. The most serious present problems associated with climate change are inundation and flooding; fresh water availability; security of food sources, including fisheries; and impacts on coastal zones and all related activities.

It should be stressed that we are discussing scenarios, not forecasts of global climate changes. We cannot make such forecasts. At present we can make predictions of such phenomena as El Niño over the coming 6 months or so, and we can provide scenarios for the development of various climate factors over longer time scales.

The Coastal Zone and the Exclusive Economic Zone

The coastal zone is a very large national resource. About 50 percent of the global population live within approximately 150 km of the sea-land interface, corresponding to approximately 10 percent of the global land area. About 70 percent of all marine food products result from the coastal zone. According to FAO, 20 percent–30 percent of the total animal protein intake in poor countries of Asia and Africa comes from fish. The coastal ecosystems also serve as cleaning agencies for much of our waste products, most of which ultimately end up in the sea. The impact of society on the marine environment is most seriously felt and is most obvious in the coastal areas. The coastal zone has seen an enormous urbanization over the last couple of decades. About two-thirds of all cities over 2.5 million inhabitants are coastal. Coastal megacities with populations over 8 million will number approximately 35 by 2015, with 30 in the developing world. These megacities are very large, urban economic power centers generating by far most of the

GNP, in particular in middle- and high-income countries. At the same time, they contain enormous poverty.

The EEZ has added another dimension to the coastal zone.[13] The EEZ adds a new province to the country and provides the potential for an added dimension to its development. About 90 percent of all known and estimated hydrocarbon reserves under the sea fall into some national jurisdiction as a result of the EEZ. The same is the case for almost all known and potential offshore mineral resources. The most valuable fishing grounds are predominantly in coastal zones and hence in EEZ waters. It was also the desire of coastal States to control the fisheries in their adjacent waters that was the major driving force behind the creation of the EEZ. The benefits to individual States brought by the EEZs are evident, and most coastal States have established an EEZ. Hence, almost 90 percent of the world's fisheries now fall under national jurisdiction of coastal States. Land-locked States are excluded, and the establishment of the EEZ concept has taken away a very large part of the seabed proposed by Arvid Pardo, Ambassador of Malta to the United Nations in the 1960s, to become the Common Heritage of Mankind.

The ocean, the coastal zones, and small islands provide the basis for many recreational and tourism activities. Tourism is the single largest industry globally (approximately US$500 billion/year), the largest employer (260 million jobs) and is still growing fast and is expected to double over the first decade of the 21st century.[14] The forecasts of the World Tourism Organization suggest 1.2 billion international arrivals by around 2015. The cruise ship industry is growing most rapidly. Environment and climate conditions together with security and stability are major requirements for tourism development. The events during the fall of 2001 certainly demonstrate the vulnerability of this leading industry to security and stability factors.

The ocean is used as a waste recipient. This is having very serious consequences for the coastal environment in many areas, impacting marine food production and human health, with negative effects on tourism, local living conditions, and amenities. Other land-based activities of society also have large impacts on the coastal zone. These impacts include habitat destruction, changes in biological diversity, erosion, and alterations of river inputs of both water and particulate matter.

Integrated coastal zone management is the adopted approach to address these problems. This is also linked to the Global Programme of Action to Protect the Marine Environment against Land-based Activities (GPA-LBA).[15] The increased vulnerability and uncertainties regarding implications of man-

13. See Part V, Articles 55-75, UNCLOS (n. 5 above).

14. Behnam (n. 4 above).

15. Global Programme of Action for the Protection of the Marine Environment from Land-based Activities, adopted 3 November 1995, http://www.gpa.unep.org/documents/.

agement and development actions have implied that both risk assessment and risk management are essential elements in integrated coastal area management. This of course brings in the precautionary principle, as part of any insurance scheme. The impacts of natural hazards have led to many severe losses and concerns about insurability.

New Needs and Emerging Issues

Creating, injecting, or applying new financial mechanisms to help address the implementation of international conventions dealing with environment and development are major problems. However, all the conventions point to the application of the precautionary principle in different ways. It should be possible to learn how to make this principle operational and at the same time inject an alternative financial mechanism by cooperating with the insurance industry, making this a partner, and introducing insurance principles as one element of development, resource use, and management. This has been suggested by the IOI, particularly concerning coastal zone management in developing countries. This would constitute a financial services model originating from the ocean. It should be recalled that the insurance principle was conceived and applied originally in the context of maritime transport.

There are a number of emerging uses of ocean space and related issues closely coupled to the service economy. These include new classes of marine contaminants; influence on populations of marine organisms, reproduction, genetics, and endocrine functions; accumulation of persistent pollutants in deep sea sediments; exploitation of the deep seabed with respect to hydrothermal ecosystems, gas hydrates (clathrates), and deep sea drilling for oil and gas; and the potential for storing CO_2 in the deep ocean, using it as a repository. These and other issues require considerable scientific attention to be addressed adequately. In conclusion, it is clear that the ocean and its resources have an enormous influence on our society in terms of economy, development, and security.

OCEAN MANAGEMENT

It was Arvid Pardo who formulated the seminal idea by stating in his speech to the United Nations General Assembly in 1967 that "all aspects of ocean space are inter-related and should be treated as a whole." Arvid Pardo also injected how to achieve this through his other seminal idea that "the resources of the deep seabed constitute the common heritage of mankind."[16]

16. E. Mann Borgese, *Ocean Governance and the United Nations* (Halifax: Centre for Foreign Policy Studies, Dalhousie University, 1995), p. 246.

The Legal Framework[17]

The basis for the legal framework is the 1982 United Nations Convention on the Law of the Sea, referred to as a "Constitution for the Ocean." The Convention includes a number of innovations:[18]

- replacing often conflicting claims by coastal States with universally agreed limits on the territorial sea, on the contiguous zone, on the exclusive economic zone and on the continental shelf;
- an elaborate system for mandatory peaceful settlements of disputes, the most advanced so far ever designed and accepted by the international community;
- the introduction of the principle of the Common Heritage of Mankind as a new principle of international law;
- the establishment of a framework for the development of international environmental law in Part XII of the Convention: Protection and Preservation of the Marine Environment; this has had a profound influence including for the UNCED process; and
- the creation of a new regime for the conduct of marine scientific research in Part XIII: Marine Scientific Research, striking an equitable balance between interests of the research States and the coastal States.

The Law of the Sea Convention should be seen as a "process," capable of interacting with changing conditions and providing for integration. The Convention provides for regulation of economic activities, and thus can make a contribution to economic security and food security. If ocean-based and ocean-dependent goods and services were managed sustainably and equitably, the positive impact on economic security would be very large. The oceans' services influence all sectors of our current service economy. Part XII of the Convention is the most comprehensive and binding instrument to protect the ocean ecosystems and their services, thus providing a great contribution to environmental security. Part XII also provides the legal framework for the ocean-related parts of all subsequent treaties, agreements, and programmes resulting from the UNCED process. This framework includes enforcement of rules, regulations, and standards; the Convention includes enforcement also in other parts. The Convention includes the requirement for coastal States to promote and cooperate in the establishment, operation, and maintenance of an adequate and effective search and rescue

17. Most of this part is based on an unpublished manuscript prepared for the Ship & Ocean Foundation in Tokyo, Japan by E. Mann Borgese and F. Bailet, "Ocean Governance," International Ocean Institute, 2001, p. 68.

18. E. Mann Borgese, *The Oceanic Circle: Governing the Seas as a Global Resource* (Tokyo: United Nations University Press, 1998), p. 240.

service by way of mutual regional arrangements. Implementation requires institutions in harmony with the integrated approach.

The Institutional Framework

The basis for this component of ocean management is found in the Law of the Sea and in the results of the 1992 UNCED process, in particular Agenda 21.[19]

United Nations Convention on the Law of the Sea

The UNCLOS established four institutions: the International Sea-Bed Authority; the Commission on the Limits of the Continental Shelf; the International Tribunal for the Law of the Sea, with associated arrangements permitting conciliation commissions, arbitral tribunals; and the Meeting of States Parties.

The Convention also mandated the establishment of regional centres for the advancement of marine science and technology. These have not yet been implemented, whereas the four institutions have been established. Each of these institutions are currently functioning and are gradually adjusting to changing situations. For instance, the International Sea-Bed Authority is having a dialogue with the Secretariat for the Convention on Biological Diversity[20] with respect to the management of deep seabed ecosystems. New discoveries of resources in the seabed from the mid-1970s have given the seabed a very high economic potential for pharmaceuticals and for hydrates for fossil fuel energy. These assets should be made part of the Common Heritage of Mankind—they are not as yet.

The Commission on the Limits of the Continental Shelf has encountered two major difficulties, both related to the complexity of the definition of the limits of the continental shelf in Article 76 of the Convention. The first is that it is very costly and difficult to prepare the required declaration, and the second is that a number of States have already advanced claims exceeding the boundaries, as defined in Article 76. More such claims may well emerge. If boundaries cannot be agreed upon, this threatens to destabilize the Convention and the efficiency of ocean governance.

The system for peaceful settlements of disputes is a fundamentally important part of ocean governance, with the International Tribunal for the Law of the Sea, the International Court of Justice, arbitration and special arbitration tribunals, and conciliation commissions. The Tribunal has had a number of cases and has delivered judgments swiftly and competently. There are some very important loopholes in the system, for example, con-

19. Text of Agenda 21, http://www.un.org/esa/sustdev/agenda21text.htm.

20. Convention on Biological Diversity, 1992, adopted 5 June 1992, http://www.biodiv.org/.

cerning shipping as regards the open registries and the responsibilities of the flag States. The globalization of the shipping industry makes it difficult or impossible to identify the real criminal or culprit. The globalization of crimes constitutes another increasing problem. The number of cases of piracy and armed robbery at sea is rising at an alarming rate. These crimes can be connected with the drug trade, illegal transport of people or goods such as hazardous wastes. The enhanced emphasis on implementation, compliance, and enforcement, including through joint regional enforcement and surveillance mechanisms, should help in achieving control. There is a need emerging for an international tribunal for international crimes at sea, to which all such cases could be mandatorily submitted. The International Tribunal for the Law of the Sea could become such a tribunal.

The UNCED Process

The legal framework for ocean governance developed through the 1992 UNCED process includes essentially seven other conventions, agreements, and programmes: Agenda 21;[21] the United Nations Fish Stocks Agreement;[22] the Convention on Biological Diversity;[23] the United Nations Framework Convention on Climate Change;[24] the FAO Code of Conduct for Responsible Fisheries;[25] the Global Programme of Action for the Protection of the Marine Environment from Land-based Activities;[26] and the Programme of Action for the Sustainable Development of Small Island Developing States.[27] All these provide essential elements toward achieving sustainable development, all have strong association or interfaces with the ocean and coasts, all are part of a comprehensive ocean governance, and all are the building blocks for achieving integration of sustainable development and comprehensive security.

The impact of the 1992 UNCED process on the UNCLOS process is clearly large. First, it extends the scope of the "Constitution for the Ocean" to the coastal land areas where the majority of humankind lives. This is ex-

21. See n. 19 above.

22. The United Nations Agreement for the Implementation of the Provisions of the United Nations Convention on the Law of the Sea of 10 December 1982 relating to the Conservation and Management of Straddling Fish Stocks and Highly Migratory Fish Stocks (entered in force 11 December 2001), http://www.un.org/depts/los/.

23. See n. 20 above.

24. United Nations Framework Convention on Climate Change, 1992, adopted 9 May 1992, entered into force 21 March 1994, http://unfccc.int/.

25. FAO Code of Conduct for Responsible Fisheries, 1 November 1995, http://www.fao.org/fi/agreem/codecond/ficonde.asp.

26. See GPA (n. 15 above).

27. Programme of Action for the Sustainable Development of Small Island Developing States and the Barbados Declaration, A/CONF.167/9, http://www.un.org/documents/ga/conf167/aconf167-9.htm.

tremely important. For one thing, 80 percent–90 percent of marine pollution originates from our activities on land. Secondly, the problems of the densely populated coastal zone, including conflicts between various users of the space and resources, the sustainability of living resources, human health, and food and water security, all require an integrated approach. This is now referred to as "integrated coastal area management." This reflects the seminal idea of Arvid Pardo that "the problems of ocean space are closely inter-related and need to be considered as a whole." It was also realized that management must be done in conditions of uncertainty and risk. The precautionary principle became a substantial element for sustainable development in conditions of uncertainty.

Integrated coastal area management cannot be applied without proper linkages between institutions at all levels: the community, the State, the region, and the global developments must work together in harmony at all levels of ocean management.

At the global level, the newly created United Nations Informal Consultative Process on Oceans and the Law of the Sea is an integrating institution at the highest level. It has addressed such problems as illegal, unregulated, and unreported fishing; the economic and social impact of pollution from land-based activities; marine science development and transfer of marine technology; and piracy and armed robbery at sea. At the regional level, a similar all-embracing mechanism is required.

Tools for Implementation

The legal and institutional frameworks will not function or will be very ineffective if there is a lack of material tools for implementation. These tools include education, technology, financing, and means for monitoring, surveillance, and enforcement. Here I will focus on the educational requirements.

EDUCATION AND AWARENESS CREATION

An education and training system is required to help change attitudes, to enhance understanding, and to help achieve participation, awareness, and responsibility. An advocacy mechanism/institution should be part of this system.

Motivation for the IOI Virtual University[28]

An internationally agreed upon framework exists that when properly implemented and enforced would lead to adequate ocean and coastal area manage-

28. A complete presentation of the concept, idea and development process of the IOIVU is given in the *Report on the IOIVU*, (International Ocean Institute, Malta, March 2001), p. 93.

ment and development for the benefit of society, including the developing countries. However, the international agreements are not being implemented. The major reason for this is ignorance and lack of understanding of the significance and importance of adequate management and protection of the whole marine system for our society and its survival. Education and the provision of reliable information are needed to overcome this obstacle.

During the period since World War II there has been a very large migration of people to the coastal strip of land. Now, approximately 50 percent of the global population is living near the coast, and more people are moving there. Most of these people are totally ignorant of the conditions at the coast, the hazards that may come from the sea, and about the need to take care of the resources there. Education, enhancement of public awareness, and training in different fields are needed to change these attitudes, so as to gradually turn the population to become more ocean- and seas-minded or oriented, and thereby more responsible.

Not only does a large part of the population live at the coast, but most of our activities occur there, involving all sectors of society, and much of this also concerns the seas and the ocean. Thus, there is a need for a broad and intersectoral education for those who are going to be responsible for the adequate management and protection of these areas, resources, and the activities of society.

Recent decades have seen an enormous development of information technology. At the same time, sensors and equipment have been developed that can make observations of the ocean and seas, both at the surface and below it and transmit data in near real time. When provided to tested models, the data can generate forecasts of various conditions, with degrees of uncertainty. These forecasts should be used in the management and decision-making schemes for the protection of resources, human lives, economic investments, and for management of several basic activities on land, for example, agriculture, transportation, and freshwater systems. This also calls for education and training as regards the use of tools and services that the observations and models provide. The enhanced knowledge about the ocean and seas and conditions in the coastal zone, which the research in recent decades has provided, makes all of this possible.

Technology transfer and related capacity building are required and are of special concern to UNCLOS and UNCED follow-up and implementation. Today's technology is knowledge- and information-based; it cannot be bought and transferred, it has to be learned. It calls for an ongoing relationship between the producer of the technology and the user. Joint ventures have been recommended by the Commission on Sustainable Development in their review of the implementation of related agreements.

The development of information technology has also made it possible to radiate the information to the population. It is no longer necessary for all the people to migrate temporarily for several years to a schoolhouse to become educated and trained. The education and training can be brought to the people.

The International Ocean Institute Virtual University (IOIVU) aims to address these points: provision of an adequate, intersectoral education to as many as possible and in particular to those who are dealing with the management of the ocean, seas, and coasts, or who intend to do so or who should do so.

The goal of the IOIVU is to enhance the abilities of, particularly, developing countries to manage and govern their own marine and coastal resources and environment sustainably for the benefit of their people and in harmony with related international conventions and agreements. This is to be achieved through the establishment of an internationally recognized programme of education, leading to a master's degree. The programme is based on a global network of universities and training and research centres of expertise in ocean, coastal, and marine-related affairs and governance working together in partnership to provide for an interdisciplinary and comprehensive coverage of the required subject areas. The IOIVU has its Charter, its Board of Governors, its Chancellor and Rector, and its technical infrastructure is in place at IOI-Southern Africa, at the University of the Western Cape in Cape Town. The development phase is guided by a Development Committee, which is composed of a group of academic experts, and a Technical Committee whose membership includes individuals with expertise in information technology and distance education systems.

The primary target groups are mid-level and young professionals working in sectors associated with ocean and coastal affairs. Since much of our present service economy, socioeconomic development, and vulnerability are coupled to the ocean and coastal resources, processes, and conditions, the target groups are fairly large, involving most sectors of society. The students entering the IOIVU are expected to have an initial university degree or equivalent or corresponding study, some professional experiences, confirmed dedication, identified need for the education, sponsorship or permission from the employer, and required practical computer and language knowledge.

The IOIVU will deliver courses through the Knowledge Environment for Web-based Learning (KEWL) course delivery platform, which was developed by IOI Southern Africa and the University of Western Cape. The KEWL platform offers many advantages over commercially available software as it is open source in nature, thus enabling it to be distributed freely at no cost and to be customized and expanded according to specific needs without the impediments inherent in software copyrights. This software is also particularly user friendly, participatory, and student oriented more than teacher oriented. These characteristics render KEWL not only ideologically well suited for the IOIVU, but will also provide the University with a sound and economical technical solution for online course delivery.

Experiences of the IOI

Training and education are basic activities of the IOI. These actions have developed over the decades to include not only regular courses with required participation, spanning over days to months, but also distance learning courses, postgraduate education, internships, upgrading of skills, community-based training and awareness creation with active participation, information dissemination, and on-the-job training. In parallel, the subject range covered by the training has expanded, so that it presently includes ocean governance at the global level with education about UNCLOS, UNCED and the related processes, regional perspectives, and national-local concerns. The subjects are also specific, for instance, as regards mariculture or artisanal fisheries developments, marine pollution, and coastal zone conditions. The community-based training done by the IOI through the Eco-villages and Sustainable Livelihoods approaches always includes all relevant sectors so as to be of use in creating self-sustainability and co-management actions. In these programmes, a certain focus is given to the participation and training of women.

The new institutional academic arrangement proposed by the IOI should respond to a number of challenges and new opportunities:

1. The interdisciplinary character of contemporary knowledge, which transcends the departmental division of traditional universities. Traditional universities in many parts of the world are struggling to overcome the structural impediments to interdisciplinary learning. The IOI Virtual University could be a pilot experiment toward new approaches to this problem.
2. Globalisation and the communications revolution, facilitating global communication among universities and between universities and students, but still largely inaccessible to students in poor countries.
3. Financial constraints on students, especially in developing countries, which in most cases prevent them from extended sojourns in foreign countries to obtain a well-recognized degree; and where they succeed, the resulting brain drain will detract from, rather than add to, the transfer of knowledge to developing countries.
4. Financial restraints on academia, globally entailing more and more downsizing and privatization of universities, which may endanger academic freedom as well as public higher education as a pillar of genuine democracy.

The IOIVU concept provides for a structure and approach by which the educational activities and programmes of the IOI Network of Operational Centres and of their prestigious Host institutions can be combined into one focused mechanism and purpose, coupled with activities of other academic centers of excellence, to provide a truly international and interdisciplinary curriculum.

The IOIVU

The Objectives

1. The fundamental objective of the University is to contribute to the sharing of knowledge on the oceans and their potential wealth and challenges as a Common Heritage of Mankind, with special consideration for the needs of developing countries.
2. The University shall promote interdisciplinary education, training, and research reflecting the complex nature of ocean space and maritime activities, where the multiplicity of related problems have to be considered as a whole in their interface.
3. Through its unique structure, accumulated global experience in education, training, and capacity building, the IOI Network of Operational Centres and Host institutions through the University shall enhance the abilities of developing countries to manage and govern in a sustainable manner their marine and coastal resources, for their peoples, in harmony with the principles of modern international law and relevant international conventions and agreements.
4. The University shall provide the academic framework for encouraging and assisting students from any part of the world, and in particular from developing countries, to obtain postgraduate-level education and advanced training, upgrading and supplementing their previous education and work experience, as well as internationally recognized academic degrees.
5. It shall be a continuous objective of the University to advance innovative approaches toward solving some of the major problems besetting higher education at the end of the last century and the beginning of this century.

The overall capacity-building objective is to help address poverty eradication and establish self-reliance through enabling countries to develop and govern their own marine resources and create an enhanced solidarity and equity between developed and developing countries within the framework provided by the UNCLOS and UNCED outputs and follow-up processes. At the same time, the action will support the institutional capacity-building of the participating institutions, and foster partnerships and the development of joint ventures. This responds well to the World Summit on Sustainable Development (WSSD) 2002 approach.

Through the IOIVU project we aim for the following results:

- Education at a master/postgraduate level in the area of marine affairs and management to become available to students from all countries of the world almost irrespective of their financial capabilities.
- The IOIVU to set a new standard in distance learning in marine affairs. Through the capability to select courses from different sources, the student will be able to acquire not only good knowledge of the subject of his or her interest, but in particular become aware of the interdisciplinary issues and interdependences involved, and learn how to address these.
- The ideas of Common Heritage and humanitarian values of peace and culture will find a new audience and media.
- Successful implementation of the project and launch of the IOIVU operations will lead to better return on investments in the University. At the early stages, the need for additional investments cannot be excluded, but in the longer-term perspective the University should become self-sustainable.
- The increasing population of IOIVU graduates will form a factor in better management of ocean resources. In the long-term perspective, this should facilitate sustainable development of states operating at seas and at coasts and lead to healthier ocean and coastal environments.

The Curriculum

The Curriculum will be interdisciplinary, comprehensive, and responding to the purposes and objectives. The structure is specified as the following:

1. Postgraduate or advanced graduate levels (from 3 years of other university study onwards): core courses, optional courses; thesis (research) work; and examination. This part aims at providing a Master's degree.
2. Advanced training in specific subjects through existing or new courses of IOI or the Host institutions of the Operational Centres. As an option, the participation in such advanced training could be given a certificate and a credit, provided there is an examination.
3. Upgrading or supplementary education and training in the form of professional development through individual courses, with examination and certificate as an option. This part could respond to expressed needs for short and specified courses.

The Master's Degree Programme of the IOI Virtual University will have three components:

1. A number of courses will have to be completed, each one with an established number of credits. These courses can be taken through any one of the IOI Operational Centres and/or in their host institutions. They also can be taken through distance-learning arrangements, which should become the primary learning method of the IOIVU.
2. There will be an internship of one quarter, which can be completed in any of the IOI Operational Centres or Host institutions. However, internships in other institutions including UN bodies may also be considered, provided it can be practically arranged and scheduled.
3. There is a thesis requirement. Students can select their supervisor and thesis committee from the roster of the Virtual University Faculty.

Any degree awarded by the Virtual University shall be comparable to and have the quality of current mainstream degrees at the same level awarded by any of the participating institutions hosting the IOI Operational Centres. Regular courses from an endorsed partner university can be accepted as part of the curriculum in the local national language. The thesis work is anticipated to be in English, French, or Spanish. Available courses will be listed in a database so as to be easily found and assessed. Students would select from this list, in consultation with their individual advisor, so as to obtain sufficient course credits. A list of existing courses within the IOI Centres and Host institutions has been compiled and categorized.

The online courses will cover at least the following topics:

- UNCLOS and UNCED: Ocean Governance and the Law of the Sea;
- Integrated coastal area management;
- Sustainable development in coastal communities;
- Marine and coastal resources economics;
- Integrated management of marine pollution, in particular related to land-based sources;
- Spatial information management and decision-making support;
- Coastal and oceanic ecosystems and processes;
- Introduction to living and nonliving marine resources;
- Matters related to maritime transport and issues at sea; to be prepared in cooperation with UNCTAD, WMU and IMLI of IMO;
- Public-private partnerships in ocean management;

KEWL as a Basic Software Platform

A team of educational researchers and programmers, lead by Professor Derek Keats at the IOI-Southern Africa based at the University of the Western Cape, has developed an open source, free, educational software package called the Knowledge Environment for Web-based Learning (KEWL).

KEWL is a suite of integrated software tools for developing, delivering, and managing online courses. The Centre has been running undergraduate courses in an online environment for a number of years, during which time it has been researching best practices for online learning, and it was this that led to the development of KEWL.

KEWL was built around the idea of constructivist learning, where students are placed at the centre of the learning process and are expected to construct their own knowledge by using a variety of resources and tools. Although there is a little bit of open source code in KEWL, most of the code for KEWL was created from scratch by Derek Keats and Martin Cocks at IOISA. Other people are now making contributions as well, and KEWL is starting to attract people who share the open source philosophy from other parts of the world.

KEWL can be used by an institution or a department to run a site that delivers online learning via the Internet. Using the built-in tools, the average person can probably have an online course up and running in a short time if the content already exists in text and related formats.

Hardware Systems

The hardware systems for the IOIVU will be based on the experiences that have been developed while designing and building the online courseware system for the University of Western Cape. This system was designed and developed within IOISA under contract to the University's Teaching and Learning Technology Unit.

CONCLUSION

This is an age of transformation, information, and uncertainty. Transformation and information generate uncertainty. This calls for risk management, the application of the precautionary principle, use of insurance, enhanced public awareness, participation, and education.

The globalization process provides for potential benefits in that growth may be accelerated and prosperity more evenly distributed than before with enhanced equity and solidarity. Education, skills, and technology can be spread and shared much more than before, and opportunities likewise. However, equity must also be achieved.

The overview of the role of the ocean and its resources in the new global service-oriented economy is intended to present a case for the need for adequate ocean management. Such must include an ocean observing system able to provide required data inputs for models. The models must also be an integral part of the ocean management system. These models should be able to analyze various management and development scenarios at regional and subregional scales, feeding into management models at the local level. The models need to include the circulation and the ecosystem dynamics. The basis for development of such model tools is available and public models are being produced. Society must ensure that adequate factual information about the conditions, observations, and data are regularly provided. The case for this has already been made in the context of climate change analysis.

We operate now in a truly global situation. In the words of the Secretary-General of the United Nations: "Globalization has been made possible by the progressive dismantling of barriers to trade and capital mobility, fundamental technological advances, steadily declining costs of transport, communication and computing." This has fostered an interdependency and interrelationship between peoples and regions at a global scale not experienced before. We are now really all in the same ship. Global change has impacts everywhere. The most significant global change over the past 50 years is the rise of the human population from 2 to 6 billion people. Climate change is another issue of great concern, coupled to population growth. Both of these global changes are irreversible, at least over the 100-to-1000-year time scale.

At the same time, our society has become more vulnerable: local-regional disturbances, including epidemics, can have global impacts whereas earlier they could be contained. Management decisions must be made in scenarios with considerable uncertainties. The knowledge base has been transformed into a more stochastic and much less deterministic paradigm. However, this scenario provides for coincidences to turn into opportunities. Progress in development essentially occurs only when the interests of idealism and realism can coincide, especially in the economic sphere. Because we are now in the same ship, cooperation and solidarity are required. We face the convergence of impacts from global changes and economic and ecological crises. The regional scale of cooperation, which can link local-national and global interests, is emerging as the most promising. At the same time, the community-based co-management and co-development model is gaining ground for sustainable development and security at the local level.

All sectors of society are influenced by the ocean and coastal services. In the case of the coast, it has been realized that an integrated management approach is needed. This is needed also for the ocean as a whole. An accepted global ocean governance mechanism must be put in place. The legal and international agreements are in place through UNCLOS and the Conventions and Agreements reached through UNCED. These together give an internationally agreed and comprehensive framework for ocean governance—a comprehensive ocean constitution. However, it must all be implemented and enforced. This has not yet been achieved. At the global level, the United Nations General Assembly has established an open-ended and comprehensive consultative mechanism that reports to the General Assembly, with the potential to develop into a global ocean governance mechanism.

At the regional level, we have the Regional Seas Conventions established through UNEP, and several other regional conventions, for example, for the Baltic and North Seas. The problem with these, however, is that they are not comprehensive. They are focused on the environmental aspects. The fisheries management conventions and bodies are also sectoral. This is not sufficient. A comprehensive mechanism is needed that can involve all relevant parties (or stakeholders) and sectors, as well as various parts of society: governments, private industry, and the civil society, including NGOs.

Presently, it seems that the coincidence of idealism and realism is at hand through the enormous role of the ocean and the marine environment, including the coast, for our current service economy.

Education, including the creation of public awareness, is a key factor. The need to develop an interdisciplinary and integrated culture of knowledge that is inclusive and accessible for all is the principal challenge faced by traditional forms of education. This challenge is nowhere more evident than in the realm of ocean affairs. Education, research, management, and exploitation of the ocean and its resources are pursued at all geopolitical scales; here knowledge must be truly integrated and interdisciplinary. As stated by Arvid Pardo, "all aspects of ocean space are inter-related and should be treated as a whole."

The IOIVU responds to the strong call for efforts in education and capacity building expressed in Agenda 21 as a whole, and in particular in Chapters 36 on Education and 37 on Capacity Building. The issue of education is a priority, now even more pronounced than in 1990. This is realized by many decision and policy makers. The approach adopted by IOI in pursuing the development of the IOIVU takes into account the social, scientific, technological, and economic developments that have occurred over the last decade.

The IOIVU will support the implementation of international agreements concerning the coasts and the ocean and will help in the outreach by enhancing public awareness and participation. The cooperation with UN bodies, other NGOs, and the association of IOIVU with the Host institutions furthermore ensures an intersectoral education, taking into account cultural and social differences. Education plays a basic role in the eradication of poverty and in achieving enhanced solidarity and equity, which are all fundamental prerequisites for reaching larger scale sustainable development, as well as comprehensive security.

The IOIVU aims at providing this education as regards the ocean governance and using this as a model for education as regards other elements of the life-supporting system. Environmentally sound management and transfer of clean technologies, for example, through joint ventures, are likewise basic requirements for sustainable development that the IOIVU will help achieve.

The World Summit on Sustainable Development in 2002 provided the opportunity to pursue the quest for sustainable development and achieve a comprehensive approach, including the elements of equity, responsibility, education, and partnership in management and governance. The IOI is responding to the challenge through pursuing the development of the IOIVU.

The Importance of Education and Capacity-building Programs for Ocean Governance*

Hiroshi Terashima
Institute for Ocean Policy, Ship & Ocean Foundation, Tokyo, Japan

"And just what might you mean by 'comprehensive,' Terashima-san?," Professor Borgese asked abruptly, with some merriment in her eyes but in a voice that carried unmistakable conviction.

It was June 1999 and I was visiting the International Ocean Institute headquarters in Malta to explain the new think tank I was organizing in Japan. To her question, I answered that we intend to study ways in which comprehensive ocean policies might be carried out, within the framework of UNCLOS and Agenda 21 regarding development, the environment, peaceful uses, and equity in resources. I said that we wanted to contribute to the efforts needed to make sustainable development an accepted idea in Japan and the conservation and protection of the ocean a reality. After my rather self-conscious recital, she smiled and nodded, as if I had passed my oral exam.

I had the good fortune afterwards of meeting with Professor Borgese several times a year. Our discussions ranged over many issues in ocean governance, and I never failed to leave her without having gained a new insight or inspiration. Our last meeting was in Paris in December 2001, during the Oceans and Coasts at Rio +10 Conference, when our table talk centered as always on how to implement the ocean governance education and capacity-building plans she was so passionately proposing.

In August 2002, I joined the Ship & Ocean Foundation as Executive Director of its Ocean Policy Institute, the think tank that I had helped to launch several years previous. To my profound regret, I could not report this good news to my friend, nor benefit from her expected admonishments or words of encouragement. After leading the world to a vision of ocean governance, Professor Borgese left us suddenly in February 2002. As a tribute to her memory, I am privileged to offer the following thoughts and findings on ocean governance education and capacity building, a subject she worked for so tirelessly to the very end.

*Editors' Note.—Translated from the Japanese by John A. Dolan.

Ocean Yearbook 18: 600–611

INTRODUCTION

The vast area we collectively call the ocean covers 71 percent of our planet and has an average depth of 3,800 meters. Twenty years ago, representatives from all over the world came together at the Third United Nations Conference on the Law of the Sea to deliberate on the optimum development, use, protection, and conservation of this area, and adopted the United Nations Convention on the Law of the Sea (UNCLOS).[1] It has been almost 10 years since, after overcoming numerous hurdles, UNCLOS came into force. Building on the momentum generated by UNCLOS and the adoption of Agenda 21,[2] and guided by the principle of sustainable development that informed the Rio Summit, countries around the world began to undertake ocean initiatives from the mid-1990s. Progress, however, has been slow. A primary goal for human society in the 21st century, as it sets out to take responsibility for the vast ocean, will be the implementation of 'consistent and coherent' governance at all levels of global society. To do this, effective implementation of existing conventions and treaties within the overall framework of UNCLOS and action plans for sustainable development are required. In this article, I would like to address what I consider the most indispensable elements for realization of genuine ocean governance: education and capacity building.

A NEW PARADIGM: OCEAN GOVERNANCE

In recent years, our view of the oceans as a source of endless bounty and the paradigm based on that view, which regulates human activities on the oceans, has undergone a major change. In the last half-century, driven by scientific and technological advances, the desire for affluent lifestyles, and the burgeoning world population, development and encroachment on the oceans has taken place around the globe. At the same time, marine pollution, decreases in fish stocks, and the degradation of coastal environments has proceeded apace. As a result, we have been forced to revise the conception we long held that the oceans were immune to any adverse activities inflicted by humans, including the dumping of wastes.

The time has come for us to construct a new paradigm, recognizing the degree to which human activities affect the ocean environment and ocean

1. United Nations Convention on the Law of the Sea, (1982). Adopted 10 December 1982, entered into force 14 November 1994, http://www.un.org/depts/los/.

2. Agenda 21 was adopted by more than 178 governments at the United Nations Conference on Environment and Development (UNCED) held in Rio de Janeiro, Brazil, 3–14 June 1992. The full text is available online: http://www.un.org/esa/sustdev/agenda21text.htm.

resources, and based on the awareness that "ocean problems are closely interrelated and need to be considered as a whole." This paradigm, which will come to regulate future activities on the oceans, should therefore consider human activities in their totality when assessing the degree to which they affect the oceans. Faced with these circumstances, the conclusion now drawn by more and more people is that to feed an ever-growing world population, improve standards of living, and conserve our natural resources for future generations, effective governance of our life-giving oceans is an absolute necessity. From this viewpoint, humankind's major successes in ocean governance initiatives have been the Third United Nations Conference on the Law of the Sea, which resulted in the 1982 United Nations Convention on the Law of the Sea, and the Rio Earth Summit, which resulted in the principle of sustainable development and the Agenda 21 Plan for Action. Over the last half-century, there have been various other international agreements aside from UNCLOS and Agenda 21, regarding ocean governance. Since the Rio process especially, international agreements important to ocean governance and integrated coastal zone management have been the United Nations Framework Convention on Climate Change[3] and the Kyoto Protocol,[4] Convention on Biological Diversity,[5] and the Global Programme of Action for the Protection of the Marine Environment from Land-based Activities.[6] However, regardless of the number of international agreements signed, if they are not effectively implemented they are worth no more than the paper they are printed on.

Even though individual countries have been given mandates over certain ocean areas, in actuality, given the vast unknown and uninhabited spaces of the oceans, managing them effectively is not an easy task in either the scientific, the economic, or the institutional realms. And yet, we must continue in our cooperative efforts to implement these agreements on a global scale. Reliable implementation of these conventions and action plans, in a 'consistent and coherent' manner, should be our primary goal in the 21st century.

WHAT IS OCEAN GOVERNANCE?

I would now like to consider what steps we should take to realize consistent and coherent ocean governance through the sure implementation of conventions and programs of action.

3. United Nations Framework Convention on Climate Change, (1992). Adopted 9 May 1992, entered into force 21 March 1994, http://unfccc.int/.

4. Kyoto Protocol to the United Nations Framework Convention on Climate Change, (1992). Adopted 11 December 1997, http://unfccc.int/.

5. Convention on Biological Diversity, (1992). Adopted 5 June 1992, http://www.biodiv.org/.

6. Global Programme of Action for the Protection of the Marine Environment from Land-based Activities. Adopted 3 November 1995, http://www.gpa.unep.org/documents/.

The usual principals in conventions and action plans are States. However, if we simply leave these instruments to be dealt with as State problems, we may very well be accused of not understanding the importance of the problem and of being careless as well. To avoid these strictures, we must recognize the need to think deeper about what serves as the backbone of UNCLOS and Agenda 21, the concept of ocean governance.

First of all, a useful perspective on the nature of ocean governance, can, I believe, be obtained from the words of the late Professor Elisabeth Mann Borgese, who earned the affectionate appellation 'mother of the sea' for her work in ocean governance, as one of the drafters of UNCLOS and as someone who contributed greatly to the capacity building of ocean governance professionals in developing countries. The following quotes are from a speech delivered by Professor Borgese at a seminar in Tokyo.

> In the Club of Rome's literature, a distinction is made between government and governance. Government is the governance of the state. Governance comprises far more. It includes the way families are organized, or businesses, or schools, or churches are run . . . This model of ocean governance begins with the local coastal community. This is where they are actually involved in marine activities; this is where they are directly exposed to the ravages of nature and the deadly impact of pollution. It is at this level that we see new forms of cooperation and organization emerging. These new forms are spelled out in Agenda 21, which was adopted at the Rio Earth Summit in 1992. 'Community-based management' means both 'horizontal integration,' i.e., the participation of ocean users (fishing organizations, harbor masters, tourist organizations, consumers, NGOs, scientists, etc.) in local decision making, as well as 'vertical integration,' i.e., fora for joint decision making between local, provincial and national organs . . . The need for horizontal integration is as pressing at the national as it is at the local level . . . The regional level is the optimum level for the solution of many problems which transcend the limits of national jurisdiction but are not necessarily global in scope . . . Thus a system of ocean governance is taking shape that is consistent, coherent, participatory and bottom-up . . . Borrowing from Gandhi, I like to call this emerging form of ocean governance the 'oceanic circle,' as it reaches from the individual to the local community, to the nation, to the region, and to the United Nations General Assembly.[7]

In other words, effective implementation of consistent and coherent ocean governance requires not only the participation of state governments, but

7. Address by Professor Elisabeth Mann Borgese at the "Nippon Foundation Ocean Governance Seminar 2000," 13 July 2000, Tokyo, Japan Proceedings.

also a broader range of ocean stakeholders at the local, national, and regional levels. As Professor Borgese points out, Agenda 21 also calls for wide participation of ocean stakeholders in the integrated management of oceans and coasts: "Each coastal State should consider establishing, or where necessary strengthening, appropriate coordinating mechanisms (such as a high-level policy planning body) for integrated management and sustainable development of coastal and marine areas and their resources, at both the local and national levels. Such mechanisms should include consultation, as appropriate, with the academic and private sectors, non-governmental organizations, local communities, resource user groups, and indigenous people."[8]

THE NEED FOR A COMPREHENSIVE APPROACH TO OCEAN GOVERNANCE EDUCATION AND CAPACITY BUILDING

If ocean governance calls for a comprehensive involvement of all sectors of society, education and capacity building, as the guarantors of effective implementation, also demand a comprehensive approach. Agenda 21 calls for implementation of such broad and comprehensive education and training to develop human resources:

> Coastal States should promote and facilitate the organization of education and training in integrated coastal and marine management and sustainable development for scientists, technologists, managers (including community-based managers) and users, leaders, indigenous peoples, fisherfolk, women and youth, among others. Management and development, as well as environmental protection concerns and local planning issues, should be incorporated in educational curricula and public awareness campaigns, with due regard to traditional ecological knowledge and socio-cultural values.[9]
>
> States individually or in cooperation with each other and with the support of international organizations, whether subregional, regional or global, as appropriate, should:
>
> a) Provide training for critical personnel required for the adequate protection of the marine environment as identified by training needs' surveys at the national, regional or subregional levels;

8. Paragraph 17.6 of Chapter 17, Agenda 21. "Protection of the oceans, all kinds of seas, including enclosed and semi-enclosed seas, and coastal areas and the protection, rational use and development of their living resources," http://www.un.org/esa/sustdev/agenda21chapter17.htm.

9. Paragraph 17.15 of Chapter 17, Agenda 21 (n. 8 above).

b) Promote the introduction of marine environmental protection topics into the curriculum of marine studies programs;. . ."[10]

IMPORTANT AGENDAS IN EDUCATION AND CAPACITY BUILDING

I would next like to consider what practical measures we might take in education and capacity building that would work towards the implementation of effective ocean governance.

As we all know, since 1994, when the United Nations Convention on the Law of the Sea came into force, there have been great changes in the ocean regime that covers 71 percent of our planet. While UNCLOS removed many long-standing problems by standardizing the breadth of territorial waters at 12 nautical miles, instituting an archipelagic water regime and an Exclusive Economic Zone regime, it also recognized coastal countries' rights for the Continental Shelf up to 200 nautical miles regardless of its shape, preventing further claims to increase those areas. It also designates the deep seabed and the mineral resources therein to be the common heritage of mankind. By virtue of this, coastal countries were given sovereign mandates over the natural resources in vast areas of the ocean, as well as the responsibility to protect and conserve the marine environments therein. It is said that the total area within these countries' Exclusive Economic Zones now totals almost half the world's ocean area. It follows that ocean governance will depend greatly on the degree to which coastal states implement the various ocean-related treaties in the areas of their mandate.

If ocean governance, as Professor Borgese points out, is a combination of horizontal and vertical integration and begins by including the various stakeholders in a community in the decision-making process, and if various countries are to responsibly oversee the ocean areas within their mandate, there is a necessity for ocean governance education and capacity building to be based on universal ideals and frameworks, and at the same time for individual countries to carry these out in an autonomous fashion adapted to the unique conditions adhering in their countries and regions. With these goals in mind, I would suggest that the following are fields in which future strengthening efforts are especially needed.

Enhancement of Marine and Maritime Education Opportunities for Youth

As argued earlier, there is a need for ocean governance to be based on the relevant knowledge and understanding of people from all sectors of society.

10. Paragraph 17.38 of Chapter 17, Agenda 21 (n. 8 above).

Furthermore, for the sustainable development of society, more emphasis needs to be placed on our environment and ecosystems and less on activities encouraging our selfish appetites for material consumption. The obvious conclusion to be drawn, then, is the necessity for a philosophy of ocean governance, incorporating these goals and aimed at passing on a healthy marine environment and marine resources to the next generation, to be understood by people in all sectors of society. Also, while far-sighted leadership into how much human life and survival is dependent on the oceans is essential, it can be effectively exercised only after knowledge and understanding of ocean governance is widespread and interest in active participation reaches a high level.

It is therefore of the utmost urgency that countries enhance their maritime education and public awareness initiatives, especially toward youth, with the goal of improving understanding and awareness and encouraging active interest in coexistence with the ocean. The youth-oriented initiatives should be undertaken both in the schools and community. In concrete terms, ocean and coastal zone topics should be included in the curricula of elementary, junior high, and high schools, adequate textbooks and teaching materials developed, and teachers' interest and knowledge promoted. Moreover, the oceans' catalogue of uniqueness means that many of its aspects must be experienced directly to be grasped. Opportunities for fieldwork must therefore be increased, including visits to nearby ports, museums, and oceanographic and onboard facilities.

As noted earlier, Agenda 21 calls on all countries to promote the introduction of curricula on marine environmental protection. Regarding this, there is a need for each individual country to seriously consider how it will implement this increased maritime education within its general curriculum. I also propose that, internationally, UNESCO take the lead in actively promoting the exchange and sharing of information on ocean education, as well as the cooperation and exchange of personnel working in ocean education.

Enhancement of Comprehensive and Interdisciplinary Ocean Education and Research

As stated in the preamble to UNCLOS, there is a necessity for a comprehensive approach toward ocean problems: "the problems of ocean space are closely interrelated and need to be considered as a whole." Likewise, ocean governance education and capacity building also deserve a comprehensive approach. In other words, to build capacity for an ocean governance inclusive of the economic dimension of development, the environmental dimension of protection and conservation, and the security dimension of peaceful uses, there is a need for a comprehensive and interdisciplinary approach to university and research institute work, which constitutes the core of the work being done in professional training and capacity building. It goes without saying that to accomplish this we must promote exchanges within the natural sciences, but also a strengthening among interdisciplinary education and research carried out between the natural sciences, social sciences, and humanities.

In the areas for which each country has a mandate, ocean governance must consist of a responsible system based on universal principles and a common framework, which is yet responsive to regional conditions. This being so, the ideal situation would be for ocean education and research to be conducted by universities and research institutes in the area where ocean governance and coastal zone management are to be carried out. Moreover, given that ocean governance requires expertise and technical capabilities and an internationalization that means real interdependence and simultaneous implementation within a common framework, it would be desirable if universities and research institutes engaged in ocean governance education were able to draw on a common curriculum at the basic levels.

In looking at professional ocean governance and coastal zone education around the world, however, there are currently few universities and graduate schools outside of the United States, Canada, and Australia where this kind of comprehensive and interdisciplinary approach to ocean governance is being undertaken. At most universities, conditions presently range from a total lack of courses in ocean governance and coastal zone management to a great variance in the aims and levels among courses that are indeed offered, with the latter often noticeably lacking in the interdisciplinary approach the subject demands. The danger resulting from this is that if current conditions are allowed to persist, bottlenecks may arise obstructing effective ocean governance implementation in those countries and regions where such education and research are absent.

A most important challenge for us in the near future, therefore, is reformation of higher education in ocean governance, with a particular emphasis on meeting the needs of the state and region where such institutions are located, while at the same time raising the course content and incorporating a certain level of curricula harmonization at the basic levels. The following are areas that I believe are important in bringing this about:

Government Relationships with Universities

Institutes of higher education should recognize the importance of ocean governance by taking a greater interest in the ocean governance and coastal zone issues in the community, country, and region where they are located. These proactive efforts should in turn be guided by stimuli provided by needs from outside. One form this might take would be for State and regional governments to make a point of encouraging a relationship with universities in which the results of their ocean governance education and research are actively incorporated into government ocean initiatives. Such an approach would also be in line with the provision in Agenda 21 cited earlier.

Effective Relationships between Academia and Practitioners

To facilitate effective ocean governance relationships between academia and practitioners, internships in various sectors of society need to be a part of ocean education. Conversely, programs should be developed where members of society already employed in industry, administration, and testing research areas have the opportunity to attend lectures and continue their research in ocean-related fields.

Academic Exchange Agreements

As noted at the beginning of this section, ocean governance is by definition an international undertaking. With this in mind, there is a need to open up and internationalize ocean governance education by forming academic exchange agreements among universities around the world for the exchange of faculty and students and the mutual recognition of academic credits earned. Exchange among universities will be a critical element in the reform of higher-level ocean governance education.

Interdisciplinary Postgraduate Courses and Programs

With the implementation of UNCLOS and other conventions and action plans being a major challenge for the 21st century, it is necessary to promote a comprehensive ocean governance education that includes the Law of the Sea, environment and resource issues, and integrated coastal zone management. To accomplish this, interdisciplinary postgraduate courses and programs should be established and joint research between universities encouraged.

Marine Policy Research Centers

At the national and regional level, there is a need to establish marine policy research centers for the study of individual countries' ocean policies and laws. Such a center should also make policy recommendations based on the analysis and evaluation of ocean policy from an academic standpoint.

Creation of Networks among Mid-Level Ocean Affairs Administrators

At present, there are many relatively short-term education and training programs in ocean governance, operated mainly by international or regional organizations, or as part of the overseas development programs of the developed countries. What is lacking among these programs, however, and what is urgently necessary for promoting ocean governance, are education and training programs designed specifically for mid-level ocean affairs administrators of developing states.

As the deliberations that produced UNCLOS were aimed at achieving a consensus that would allow for the participation of the greatest number of States, many of the provisions in it remain abstract and await the efforts of those involved in ocean affairs as to how they should be implemented. For this reason, it is no exaggeration to say that although many ocean and coastal zone initiatives have begun around the world, they are still operating by trial and error in implementation matters.

In the interest of promoting ocean governance implementation, the exchange of ideas and information and the sharing of experience among mid-level ocean administrators of individual countries will therefore be extremely important and effective. At present, unfortunately, not only are some ocean administrators in various countries less than expert in their area of responsibility, there is no professional network that they may access, nor do they have sufficiently close working relationships with the appropriate United Nations agencies.

In addition, as 12 years were required from the time the Third United Nations Conference on the Law of the Sea adopted UNCLOS until it came into force, and another 10 years have passed since then, many of the international lawyers, politicians, and administrators who represented their countries in the Conference deliberations have now retired. In other words, the cadre of specialists and networks built up nationally and internationally through the UNCLOS deliberations is now rapidly disappearing.

For this reason, to effectively implement ocean governance in individual countries, we must respond to the urgent need for measures whereby national mid-level administrators in ocean affairs from around the world are afforded the same knowledge base, understanding, and techniques, and are able to maintain close collaborations. It would therefore be most desirable, if the United Nations Division for Ocean Affairs and Law of the Sea, in cooperation with leading universities and research institutes, could provide short-term intensive education and training programs in ocean governance for mid-level ocean affairs administrators, thus contributing to the rebuilding of a professional international network.

Regional Cooperation

In looking over the various ocean governance initiatives being undertaken around the world, regional initiatives in ocean governance implementation, education, and capacity building are proving to have the biggest effect.

Oceans circulate as regional systems, within which are to be found a variety of cultures, lifestyles, and customs that are directly related to the ocean and share many common elements. These circumstances, along with the fact that ocean governance requires specialized knowledge, expertise, and large amounts of funding, make obvious the advantages to be had when countries that share a common sea culture work together in international regional efforts at managing regional and sub-regional seas. When a developed State is among the countries of a region, knowledge sharing, technology transfer, and, importantly, financial cooperation are easier to carry out.

It also seems realistic to believe that progress can be made in ocean governance education and capacity building, in the present circumstances, by working through such a regional initiative. A good example of this is the GEF/UNDP/IMO Partnerships in Environmental Management for the Seas of East Asia (PEMSEA).[11] The PEMSEA program, in which 12 East Asian countries participate, has succeeded by organically combining its efforts at the regional, national, and local levels. It has carried out its localized approach in education and training, working with local universities and with the cooperation of state and local governments, to implement necessary capacity-building measures at various environmental 'hot spots' among regional coastal zones and semi-enclosed seas. The integration of local government-led initiatives with local universities, and guidance and back-up support by national governments in tandem with regional cooperation, are key to successful implementation of ocean governance and ocean education and capacity building and deserve to be strengthened.

CONCLUSION

In conclusion, I would like to emphasize the following points:

In light of the earlier noted concerns, I believe the ideal form of ocean governance will be bottom-up participatory initiatives that combine horizontal integration, in which ocean stakeholders participate in the decision-making process of autonomous community initiatives, and vertical integration, in which organizations at the local, provincial, and State levels cooperate to provide a forum for decision making. Furthermore, if this kind of comprehensive and integrated approach is adopted, our initiatives in ocean governance education and capacity building will have to be expanded and improved far beyond current levels, where education and training programs are conceived largely to meet immediate needs, giving little thought to the comprehensive character of ocean governance. Future enhancement of ocean governance education initiatives must therefore be based on long-range goals, and, at the university level, be comprehensive and multidisciplinary in character.

11. Partnerships in Environmental Management for the Seas of East Asia (PEMSEA) was launched in October 1999. See additional details online: http://www.pemsea.org/.

Next, given the difficulty of adapting technological, economic, and institutional arrangements, it is obvious that international cooperation at the appropriate level, especially the regional level, will be necessary to foster implementation of ocean governance at various locations worldwide. Learning from previously successful examples, I would like to emphasize the importance of giving regional initiatives precedence, which I believe the recent World Summit on Sustainable Development (WSSD) Plan of Implementation[12] also encourages.

However, at the same time, when implementing such initiatives, care must be taken not to weaken the autonomous initiatives of regional communities and developing countries, as the essence of ocean governance lies in voluntary and autonomous participation in management. It is clear from the examples noted earlier that an ocean governance that has lost the spontaneous and voluntary participation at the local level is one that has fallen short of its goal.

As we set out to accomplish the comprehensive implementation of ocean governance, the words of the late Professor Elisabeth Mann Borgese should serve as our guide:

> Borrowing from Gandhi, I like to call this emerging form of ocean governance the 'oceanic circle,' as it reaches from the individual to the local community, to the nation, to the region, and to the United Nations General Assembly.[13]

I believe the time has come to put our best and combined efforts into education and capacity building efforts to meet this goal.

12. See WSSD Plan of Implementation in *Report of the World Summit on Sustainable Development, Johannesburg, South Africa, 26 August–4 September 2002.* United Nations. A/CONF.199/20. New York, 2002. Available online at http://www.johannesburgsummit.org/.

13. See n. 7 above.

Annual Report of the International Ocean Institute

Report of the International Ocean Institute, 2001–2002*

INTRODUCTION

The International Ocean Institute (IOI) has continued the implementation and development of system-wide training programmes, with the International Ocean Institute Virtual University (IOIVU) being a flagship one. Activities of the IOI "Women and the Sea" and "Youth" Programmes have been continued by several centres. The first phase of these Programmes came to an end by 31 December 2002 and there are plans to continue and extend the Programmes. The IOI Executive Committee meeting in April 2002 recommended that the possibility of launching a "Children and the Sea" programme be explored and the findings reported to the Governing Board meeting in December 2002.

The work of the IOI among coastal communities has continued to take into account the recommendations of the IOC Conference "Oceans and Coasts at Rio+10," Paris, 3–7 December 2001, which was co-sponsored by the IOI. A number of leading IOI experts took part at the Conference and contributed to its success. The IOI has improved its links of co-operation in integrated coastal zone management with the Caspian Environment Programme, the Land-Ocean Interactions in the Coastal Zone (LOICZ) Project, and MEDCOAST by implementing joint training courses and workshops.

New IOI Operational Centres were created in Australia, Brazil, Chile and Germany. The establishment of the IOI Operational Centres in the Islamic Republic of Iran, Sweden, Bulgaria, Mexico and Greece is under negotiation.

TRAINING AND EDUCATION

In accordance with its mission, IOI has been conducting recurrent training programmes at individual Operational Centres. For almost three decades IOI has implemented a standing, annual intensive training programme in ocean governance. This has been run first in Malta and later in Canada at the IOI-Canada Operational Centre. The programme covers ocean law and governance in the broadest sense and is intended to assist developing countries in the implementation of the UNCLOS-UNCED process. This programme has trained on the order of 1000 mid-career civil

*Editors' Note.—This report has been edited for publication in the *Ocean Yearbook* and is based on the "Annual Report of IOI Institutional Activities up till 2002," provided by IOI Headquarters in Malta.

servants from developing countries. It has always attracted strong interest. The participants, however, have repeatedly brought out the shortcoming of this activity: It does not lead to a university degree. A consolidated version of the individual IOI courses would form the basis for a university degree. Such an integrated programme would be interdisciplinary and holistic.

The IOI Virtual University – IOIVU

IOI is responding to the need for a university degree in ocean management or ocean governance by endeavouring to integrate the training efforts and experiences obtained over two to three decades into the innovative initiative—the establishment of the IOI Virtual University (IOIVU). Through such a mechanism it should also be possible to consolidate and fully utilise the unique structure of the IOI network and its accumulated experiences in education, training, research and related integrated capacity building. The aim is to achieve a truly international and interdisciplinary postgraduate education in ocean management and ocean governance.

The IOIVU has been posted on the International Waters: Learn on-line information catalogue.[1] There have also been many expressions of interest from potential students, mainly from developing countries.

Training and Education Activities of the IOI Centres

Training and capacity building are parts of all IOI activities and programmes. The formal flagship training course is given annually in Canada on Ocean Governance: Policy, Law and Management, focusing on the combined UNCLOS and UNCED 1992 comprehensive international legal and constitutional package. This course is aimed at middle level professionals, mainly coming from developing countries and economies in transition.

Other training courses and capacity building actions during the period include:

- Lectures and on-site training on set net fishing technology given by fishermen from Himi City, Japan to fishermen in Costa Rican coastal communities;
- A Yokohama City university lecture series for citizens on the theme "The Ocean and Mankind" was initiated in spring 2001, with lectures by Professor Fuse, Chair of the IOI Planning Council, and Professor Rajagopalan, Director, IOI-India, among others.
- A training course on integrated coastal area management was implemented by the IOI-Caspian Sea Operational Centre in collaboration with the Execu-

1. See the International Waters Learning Exchange and Resource Network, http://www.iwlearn.org/.

tive Director and with support from the Caspian Environment Programme of UNDP-GEF, in April 2002. A similar course with lecturers from IOI Operational Centres was subsequently run by the Executive Director in the Caspian Sea part of Iran.

- IOI-Caspian Sea jointly with the IOC of UNESCO implemented in October 2002 a training cruise within the Caspian Floating University programme, with the goal to make students and researchers acquainted with modern methods of sample collection for the study of the ctenophore *Mnemiopsis leidyi* and other jellyfish in the Caspian Sea.
- A training course on integrated coastal zone (area) management is being organized in December 2002 by the IOI-China Operational Centre for participants from China.
- Training in seaweed farming was given by IOI-Eastern Africa (IOI-EA) as part of the Women and the Sea Programme.
- The IOI-Southern Africa Operational Centre is pursuing the programme entitled "Education Through Technology." This programme develops and delivers training courses to a wide range of audiences in ocean and coastal management. The training courses range from fully computer-based to fully classroom-based. The IOI-Southern Africa (IOI-SA) is also continuing the development of the Knowledge Environment for Web-based Learning (KEWL). This allows for the creation, delivery, management and administration of online courses by teachers with only moderate computer skills. IOI-SA is very active in developing courses for IOIVU, and in the IOIVU development overall. IOI-SA also cooperates with the Train-Sea-Coast Programme of UN-DOALOS for the Benguela Current system. The course on Marine Pollution Control has been developed and tested in 2001–2002. Another course on Ballast Water Management is under development, jointly with the Train-Sea-Coast Programme in Brazil.
- IOI-Pacific Islands is also cooperating with the Train-Sea-Coast Programme. Intensive course preparation workshops have been held during the period for the course Responsible Fisheries in the Pacific Islands Region. The course validation was initiated in mid-2002, but not completed. The IOI-PI also serves as a partner in the programme called SEREAD–Scientific Educational Resources and Experiences Associated with the Development of Argo drifting floats in the South Pacific Ocean. This project is aimed at introducing education on ocean conditions in schools of the Pacific islands.
- Within the Coastal Eco-Villages Programme run by the IOI-India Operational Centre much capacity building is ongoing. Training is given in new skills, development issues, vocations and ecology. A series of training programmes for children on biological diversity, herbal plants and their uses has been given with support from Japan.
- IOI-Russia, Moscow, delivered a series of lecturers at Moscow University on marine resources management.
- Several Operational Centres, e.g., IOI-Indonesia, IOI-Russia, IOI-Costa Rica,

IOI-Western Africa, IOI-Senegal, IOI-Thailand, IOI-Brazil, and IOI-Black Sea have organized workshops or seminars that include training, education and awareness creation on marine resources, coastal management, ocean governance, maritime enforcement, conflict management, and sustainable development. IOI-Russia has developed a dedicated awareness creating and education programme for children.

DEVELOPMENT ACTIVITIES OF OPERATIONAL CENTRES

Apart from the development of human resources, the IOI system is involved with other development issues in most of the Centres, addressing: poverty eradication; generation of self-reliant development in local coastal communities; resources management, development of eco-friendly technologies and use of traditional environmental knowledge; co-development and co-management with a focus on integrated coastal area management; sustainable livelihoods; mitigation of and adaptation to natural hazards, e.g., cyclones, storm-surges; and empowerment of developing country communities to manage their coastal and EEZ resources.

Problems of coastal communities are addressed in an integrated way, with social, economic, environmental and survival aspects all taken into account in community driven projects, guided by IOI Centres in co-operation with local NGOs, and in consultation with local and national authorities as required. The basic approach involves co-management and sustainable livelihood considerations. The innovative part lies in addressing the links between social, survival, economic and environmental needs, in a balanced fashion. The impacts on local communities include improved living conditions, increased self-reliance and confidence, establishment of local community-driven enterprises, e.g., mariculture, food processing, tree planting and gardening, and increased interest in education.

These issues are tackled through a system-wide approach. It is recognized that conservation and management of the sea and the coastal zone involves managing people who live in the coastal zone as much as the coastal resources themselves.

Women and the Sea Programme

The Programme was established in 2000 for a three-year period and funded through private donation. During the first two years, seven Operational Centres dedicated their efforts to enhancing the capacity and participation of women from poor developing countries in ocean and coastal affairs. The Programme activities included training women decision-makers, coastal community-based sustainable development projects, and development of sustainable livelihoods and education in management, conservation and use of marine resources.

The International Oceans Institute of Canada (IOIC) offered an intensive ten-week training programme (May 27–August 2, 2002) in Halifax at Dalhousie University. The title of this interdisciplinary course was Ocean Governance: Policy, Law and Management. It provided a foundation programme in a new and very important field of development strategy and ocean and coastal area management. It was designed to benefit developing country mid-career professionals, with a focus on training women, with the interest of helping these countries to form a core of decision-makers aware of ocean management issues and able to contribute to tackling them.

IOI-Costa Rica implemented the project with the aim to improve the quality of life of a group of women living in a poverty-stricken island community in the Gulf of Nicoya. Several small projects have been implemented with the aim of increasing family income and decreasing unemployment. Training and education actions were also ongoing components of the project.

IOI-India continued working on the eco-village project. Taking into account the survey of needs, the implementation of three components of the project have been facilitated: further development of sanitation facilities; creation of home gardens for nutrition; and setting up a multipurpose centre for training women in income-generation activities. The proposal is to set up a centre for extended regular training in product manufacture, marketing and business skills for women from the villages. The training centre will be a long-term asset to the people and will also be used for meetings of women leaders, environmental education, exhibitions and competitions for women and children.

IOI-Eastern Africa activities in 2002 included the establishment of pilot and demonstration seaweed farms at two sites, Gazi and Shimoni, to serve as training centres for field-testing, production and extension work. The purpose was to train women in the pilot phase of the project in actual seaweed growing. It also included awareness campaigns and mobilization of the local community leaders/politicians, government institutions, NGOs and other stakeholders on seaweed farming in Kenya; organization of an aggressive marketing strategy, including exchange visits, exchange of results, etc.; and conducting livelihood investigations to assess the socio-economic conditions of the coastal communities at the sites with suitable conditions for seaweed farming.

IOI-South Africa was implementing a project on sustainable livelihoods at the coast by working with a community in St. Helena Bay.

IOI-Senegal, West Africa re-centred its activities on the development of a one-year project to reinforce feminine understanding in the sector of skilled transformation of fishing products in Fass Baye, Senegal. Two main activities were conducted: the formation of women transformers and the financing of communal equipment (sanitation). This project is integrated to some degree with the projects being implemented in India, Costa Rica and Eastern Africa.

IOI-South Pacific had good progress in the women in fisheries project through implementing training activities, organizing mangrove planting, and issuing a book to be used as resource material to advance the role of women in the marine sector. The work continued on mangrove areas around Suva and other urban centres with the aim to set up a marine protected area (MPA). Baseline surveys in the Namena District continued and further workshops and training on MPAs and ecotourism were organized.

Coastal Management and Mariculture Development

IOI-South West Atlantic Ocean (SWAO) supported a research project RECOS (Coastal Resources Project), which was approved at the end of 2001 by the Brazilian authorities as part of the Millennium Initiative.[2]

The main objective of the project is to help identify conflicts in the coastal zone, covering all 8,500 km of the Brazilian coastline using the best practices and scientific knowledge. The key issue is solving or attenuating such conflicts based on objective, integrated information, and within acceptable costs and deadlines. To do that, a significant increase in our ability to detect and predict the changes occurring in the coastal zone is required. In order to be able to offer elements for the solution of conflicts derived from the use of the coastal zone, it is necessary to construct an integrated monitoring system and provide required data and knowledge for:

- protecting the population and contributing to the improvement of the quality of life and safety of human activities in coastal regions;
- managing and restoring healthy coastal systems and their resources;
- predicting and mitigating effects of natural disasters and catastrophic events; and
- detecting changes in coastal systems associated with global climate change phenomena.

The RECOS Project resulted from the decision of several federal universities to form a consortium to start joint work in various areas, particularly in ocean sciences. It was recognised that such problems could only be appropriately addressed in a joint and co-ordinated fashion, with the formation of a network of researchers/institutions from north to south. This partnership attracted researchers from several universities and agencies, who have assimilated the work's philosophy. The proposed strategy implies the realisation of standard studies of several coastal systems covered by an observation network, with the objective of monitoring, understanding, and predicting problems related to fishing, mariculture, biodiversity, environmental quality, erosion and coastal land use and occupation.

Following the approval of the project, the meeting of the Monitoring, Modelling and Land Use Working Group of the RECOS project was locally organized through the Operational Centre with all local arrangements and support implemented by the IOI-SWAO Secretariat. Almost 40 researchers, covering the entire Brazilian coast from North to South, were present in Pontal do Sul, 4–7 July 2002. The group produced a final report and procedures manual for the coastal studies that will be performed during the project. The Group also performed a training fieldwork during the meeting.[3] This project has full involvement of IOI-SWAO and can be considered at present as its main activity.

2. See more details about RECOS, http://www.cem.ufpr.br/milenio/icapa.htm.
3. See online, http://www.cem.ufpr.br/milenio/RelatoWIMMOC.htm.

IOI-Costa Rica reported that the first phase of the community-based coastal resource management has come to an end. Results of this phase have been published in the book *Balancing People and Resources: Interdisciplinary Research and Coastal Areas Management in the Wider Caribbean.*[4] The second phase has started. It consists of 15 projects in the Wider Caribbean integrating natural and social science interdisciplinary research leading to the empowerment of the involved coastal communities. The second phase will last until December 2003. In September 2002, a training course is to be organized for the project leaders in Costa Rica. As a follow-up action and taking into account the first phase experience, visits to the project areas by the academic community will take place.

IOI-China prepares jointly with the IOC and IOI-HQ an international workshop on the coastal megacities to be held in China in the fall of 2003.

IOI-SA has drawn up a new mission in coastal zone management which now reads: "IOI-SA promotes the peaceful and sustainable use of ocean space and resources in the southern African context by facilitating sustainable livelihoods of coastal peoples through awareness creation, education, information dissemination, research, community initiatives." The focus is on South Africa's needs and coastal communities. IOI-SA assists coastal communities by offering capacity building and research programmes that assist with poverty alleviation and the fostering of sustainable livelihoods within these communities, and by implementing community initiatives and projects. In 2001–2002, the following projects have been implemented:

St. Helena Bay Seaweed Mariculture Project

The St. Helena Bay seaweed mariculture project has been assisting the local community to initiate a seaweed mariculture operation. IOI-SA assisted in the establishment of a company of community shareholders, Maribus industries, which will run the mariculture operations. Maribus industries and IOI-SA are now keen to continue with the seaweed mariculture project, and will be putting effort into further operational (divers, boat skippers) and business skills training for the remainder of 2002. A field-trip for Maribus industries shareholders to a working Gracilaria farm in Luderitz, Namibia, is also envisaged for later in 2002. It is hoped to raise funds and to establish the infrastructure for the pilot Graciliaria farm, and to make this operational in a pilot phase during 2003.

West Coast Cookbook Project

The West Coast cookbook is a project being done in conjunction with the Bergrivier Vissersvroue Vereeniging, a women's group on the South African west coast, Mrs. Ina Paarman, a South African cooking celebrity, and Struik Publishers. During 2001 and 2002, the Bergrivier Vissersvroue Vereeniging gathered recipes from communities along the West Coast. Recipes for the book were selected by Mrs. Paarman, and testing of these recipes has been completed by women from the community. In

4. *Balancing People and Resources: Interdisciplinary Research and Coastal Areas Management in the Wider Caribbean.* IOI-CFU-Laval-IDRC. 2002.

addition to the recipes, the book will also contain information on the history of the West Coast. A local historian was contracted to compile this, and this was completed in 2002. The manuscript is now with Struik Publishers, who are doing the editing, design, and photography with the assistance of Mrs. Paarman. Struik Publishers are hoping that the book will be on the shelves in June 2003.

Bait Mariculture Project

This year the bait mariculture project has started up. This project is based on the culture of two species of polychaete worms that are commonly used for bait in South Africa. The ultimate goal is to develop a community mariculture operation on the West Coast that will be responsible primarily for breeding the worms. Young worms will then be transported on other centres along the South African coast, where local people can augment their livelihoods by growing these out and selling them to fishermen in the area. During 2001, the directors of the SeaBait Ltd, a highly successful company established at Newcastle University in the United Kingdom for the purposes of marine worm culture, visited IOI-SA with the view to establish links between their operations and the project in South Africa. IOI-SA discovered that much groundwork would need to be done before such an operation could be contemplated. As a beginning, a grant was thus sought from the National Research Foundation (NRF) to fund the basic research on the reproductive biology of these worms. The project is planned until 2004, although there is a need to source additional funds for the project, as the NRF grant is only available for one year.

IOI-EA initiated a study on coastal livelihood in the Lamu Mpeketoni area with technical support from IOI India. The main livelihood issues were identified. High levels of poverty in an environment rich in resources, lack of adequate health facilities, clean water and poor infrastructure were identified as the main issues that hinder economic growth, and result in a deterioration in the livelihood status in the area. A project proposal has been developed to address the key issues. In the Kenyan South Coast under the coastal livelihood initiative, IOI is supporting integrated aquaculture. The IOI component in the project covers seed production and involves adoption of simple hatchery technology in developing a hatchery to supply rice farmers with fish seed. The other component of the project covers promotion of fish culture through pilot projects in key rice growing areas in the South Coast.

Jointly with IOI-SA and with partners from Europe and South America, IOI-EA is involved in the Seaweed Africa project. Its objective is to develop a database for all useful seaweeds. Basic equipment has been purchased and work is in progress. The Kenya Marine and Fisheries Research Institute (KMFRI) is providing the manpower to execute the project. IOI is providing coordination and management.

IOI-Western Africa Operational Centre (WAOC) organized a two-day conference on integrated coastal area management (ICAM) in July 2002. The objectives included, among others:

- Further announcement of the establishment of an IOI-Western Africa Operational Centre;
- Promotion of awareness on the structure, goals and activities of the IOI worldwide; and
- Dissemination of information on ICAM to bodies and organizations whose activities involve dealings with or can potentially influence the socio-economic life of local coastal communities.

There were four technical sessions. The sessions examined the boundaries, characteristics and opportunities in the coastal zone, resources of the zone and their rational management. Other issues examined included the scope of ICAM, threats to coastal resources, national and regional perspectives of coastal zone management and proposals for future collaboration. A report on the conference has been lodged with the Headquarters of IOI.

Recommendations arising from the conference included several measures aimed at promoting rational and sustainable management of the coastal space and the resources therein. These recommendations will be made available to appropriate agencies and bodies and will, as much as possible, be taken into account in the future activities at IOI-WAOC.

Biodiversity and Fisheries

The Biodiversity and Conservation Programme recognises the need to research and understand marine and coastal biodiversity in order to achieve sustainable use of resources. IOI Centres also support the FAO efforts in advertising the FAO Code of Conduct for Responsible Fisheries and related conventions and agreements.

IOI-Costa Rica, jointly with IOI-Japan, is involved in a cultural exchange between the fishing community of Himi Prefecture, Japan and Costa Rica. The experiment has taken place at Tarcoles, Pacific Coast of Costa Rica. This cooperative effort promotes the transfer of set net fishing, eco-friendly Japanese traditional fishing technology. The results are satisfactory and will be submitted to "Trap Net Summit" in Himi in November 2002. There will be key talks and panel discussions about the set net fishing or fishing in general for the sustainable and eco-friendly usage of the living marine resources at the global level. A similar action from this cooperation and favouring the Twin Cities declaration between Puntarenas and Himi is being proposed to the Himi and Puntarenas local governments.

IOI-Australia is engaged in a marine biodiversity project looking at the impact of marine protected areas on the conservation of marine biodiversity. The staff of the Centre conducted field-work at the Palolo Deep National Marine Reserve jointly with a biological consultant from Fiji. Data and field results are now being analysed. Plans are progressing well for the field work in Sulawesi, at the Bunaken National Park, Manado. Contacts have been established with Sam Ratulangi University, USAID project and through the Queensland Department of Primary Industries

(Cairns), who are conducting part of their seagrass watch programme at the Bunaken National Park. The first Progress Report was completed and delivered electronically at the end of July 2002.

IOI-Pacific Islands continues to support the Women in Fisheries Network, the Post-Harvest Fisheries Programme and the Node Coordination Unit for the Global Coral Reef Monitoring Network established for seven countries in the South West Pacific with funding from IOI-PI. In August 2001, the three-year project funded by C-SPODP II (CAD$343,000) came on stream and is implemented now by the Institute of Marine Resources.

The translation of the FAO's "What is the Code of Conduct for Responsible Fisheries" into nine Pacific Island languages was undertaken and completed. The materials are now being distributed to the island countries and to the FAO offices in the region as well as in Rome.

IOI-SA involvement in the biodiversity research was primarily related to marine algae, and coralline algae, in particular. A grant application has been made to the National Research Foundation (NRF) for a project that will deal with the evolutionary biology and speciation mechanisms in a group of southern African endemic coastal fishes for 2003–2004.

IOI-SA is collaborating with the National University of Ireland in Galway, the University of Cape Town, the Division of Marine and Coastal Management of the Department of Environmental Affairs and Tourism in South Africa, the University of Namibia, IOI-East Africa, the University of Stockholm, and the University of Porto in Portugal in implementing the Seaweed Africa project—a global biodiversity database of seaweed information. This includes information on the ecology, distribution, potential and realized uses, correct harvesting methods and mariculture procedures, as well as information on the legal framework within which seaweeds are used. IOI-SA's role is in the development of the technology behind the database, which will be accessible and managed, via the Internet. Thus far the web portal is complete, and the programming that powers the database is nearing completion.

During 2001, IOI-SA developed a computer-based network system for the International Marine Biodiversity Initiative (IMBI). This is based on the software platform developed by IOI-SA for online learning. Through this network, biodiversity professionals remain in contact, can upload relevant documents, have online discussions and share views related to marine biodiversity issues.

IOI-SA is assisting in developing a web portal for providing public access to GIS related to the Cape Floral Kingdom. This initiative is led by the Conservation Planning Unit of the Western Cape Nature Conservation Board and is to curate, utilize and share information regarding local biodiversity to support bio-regional planning and land-use decision making. The initiative is funded by GEF, WWF, Conservation International (CI), and the Cultural Ecosystems Partnership Fund (CEPF).

A profile on Orimedu fishing community was prepared by IOI-WAOC and submitted as a contribution to a global IOI initiative in line with agreements reached during the IOI Planning Council meeting in Hamburg in December 2000. The profile describes the demographic and social structure, occupations and traditions of the community. Present community and governmental initiatives are also evaluated. Areas of possible intervention identified in the profile will form the basis of some IOI programmes from which this community stands to benefit in the future.

IOI-Ukraine prepared a project proposal on the recovery of the brown trout population in the coastal rivers of Crimea. The recovery plan contains not only preservation measures for such endangered species as brown trout but also proposals on restoration of original wild stock, including creation of special farms. Implementation of the project will help to provide additional aquaculture product and employment for the coastal community.

OCEAN GOVERNANCE

The development, promotion and implementation of ocean governance continue to be among core objectives of the IOI Network. These objectives are pursued by various elements of the IOI Network through active participation in the various United Nations fora, national and international academic conferences, the delivery of leadership seminars, and the publication of the *Ocean Yearbook.*

Participation in UN System Ocean Governance Events

Global Forum on Oceans, Coasts and Islands (New York, January 29, 2002)
Early in the preparatory process for the World Summit on Sustainable Development (WSSD), it became evident that issues relating to oceans, islands and coasts were not going to be properly recognized throughout the Summit process. In response to this grave lacuna, IOI joined forces with several key oceans-related organizations, researchers, government officials and international civil servants (participating in their personal capacities). This informal alliance met for the first time at the United Nations Headquarters in New York to hold an "Oceans Round Table in Preparation for the WSSD."

From this meeting emerged an informal "WSSD Coordinating Group on Oceans, Coasts and Islands," whose primary mandate was to ensure that oceans figured prominently during the WSSD and that the Process would yield concrete outcomes with respect to ocean issues. The Coordinating Group remained very active throughout the four WSSD PrepComs and during the WSSD itself through lobbying delegations and holding meetings and side events on oceans, coasts and islands. Through its activities, the Coordinating Group achieved considerable success in influencing the WSSD Process in such a manner as to recognize the importance of oceans, coasts and islands as distinct and requiring particular attention in the WSSD Plan of Implementation.

IOI participated in all meetings and related events, and will continue to be an active member of what has now been officially named the Global Forum on Oceans, Coasts and Islands. In the post-WSSD implementation phase, the Global Forum will work to facilitate the implementation of commitments made during WSSD, including the Type II initiatives: raise the international profile of issues relating to Oceans, Coasts and Islands; and serve as a clearinghouse and focal point for all stakeholders.

Third United Nations Open-Ended Informal Consultative Process on Oceans and Law of the Sea (UNICPOLOS) (New York, April 8–15, 2002)

In 2002, IOI was asked by UN-DOALOS and the UNICPOLOS Co-chairs to contribute to UNICPOLOS through the delivery of an intervention during the UNIC POLOS plenary session on the topic of Capacity Building for Ocean Governance. Through this intervention, the IOI's credibility and standing was reinforced within the United Nations System as a global leader in capacity building and in pursuit of ocean governance.

Participation in UNICPOLOS also provided IOI with the opportunity to meet with various members of the 'international ocean community' in order to discuss the latest trends in ocean governance and possibilities for future cooperation. These discussions are summarized in the Deputy Executive Director's Report (DED/02/01, dated April 2002).

WSSD PrepCom 4 (Bali, Indonesia, 27 May–7 June, 2002)

IOI actively participated in the fourth PrepCom for the WSSD. IOI's contribution in this process took the form of direct participation in the multilateral negotiation process within the Oceans Contact Group, thematic side-events and informal discussions with individuals representing nations, IGOs and NGOs. Through these activities, IOI was able to directly contribute to the elaboration of the paragraphs related to ocean governance contained within the WSSD Plan of Implementation.

The Founder and Honorary Chair Prof. Elisabeth Mann Borgese had been invited to the Conference entitled "Sea and Human Security," organized by UNITAR and Hiroshima Prefecture, in Hiroshima, Japan, 5–8 March 2002, to present a keynote speech at the opening of the Conference. After the sad February event, the organizers insisted that an IOI high-level personality attend the Conference and deliver a keynote speech. The Senior Executive Director attended and presented a paper entitled "Integrating sustainable development and security," built on the ocean governance model of Elisabeth Mann Borgese.

The Deputy Executive Director participated in "Advancing Human Development and Security in Africa 1" and "Advancing Human Development and Security in Africa 2" meetings, organized by the Centre for Foreign Policy Studies (Dalhousie University), ISROP (DFAIT, Government of Canada), and the Institute of Commonwealth Studies (University of London) in March 21, 2002 and May 8–9, 2002, and presented papers on the IOI vision of the African strategy.

Regional Intergovernmental Ocean Governance Meetings

IOI participated in the APEC Integrated Oceans Management Forum 2 (APEC-IOMF2 in Canberra, Australia, 3–7 June, 2002), which was held immediately following the Second Australia Canada Oceans Research Network meeting (ACORN2 in Canberra, Australia, May 31–2 June, 2002) in which IOI also participated.

Through participation in both the ACORN2 and APEC-IOMF2, IOI was able to promote the notion of maritime security as an integral component of ocean governance and the IOI's visibility and credibility was enhanced within senior academic and governmental circles in the Asia-Pacific region. Concurrent informal discussions held with participants further served to reinforce the IOI's profile and provided opportunities for discussions on future collaboration in areas of research and capacity building.

Ocean Yearbook

The *Ocean Yearbook* continues to be edited by Dr. Aldo Chircop and Dr. Moira McConnell, and published by the University of Chicago Press. Volume 17 is practically finished (expected publication by the mid-2003) and work on Volume 18 (expected publication in 2004) is well under way. Volume 18 will be a commemorative volume dedicated to Elisabeth Mann Borgese. The feeling of the Yearbook editors is that they are committed to the current Editorial Board until Volume 18 and expect to start work on Volume 19 in the spring of 2003 (publication in 2005).

RESEARCH AND SCIENCE APPLICATION

The Operational Centres are associated with universities or other research- and technology-oriented institutions as their Host-institutions. The IOI activities in this area include policy-oriented research, studies in governance mechanisms and legal, economic and social orders, as well as natural and social science research.

GIWA (Global International Waters Assessment)

GIWA is designed to provide GEF with a global framework of priority environmental issues related to transboundary waters. One of the unique features of GIWA is that the impacts of environmental degradation are assessed not only in the natural, but also in the socio-economic environment, and the interplay between these is highlighted. For the purposes of GIWA, the assessments are being done in 66 subregions around the world. Scaling and scooping assessments have been received from 30 different subregions. Several IOI Operational Centres are involved in the assessment studies. IOI-SA has acted as the subregional focal point for the Benguela Current during 2001 and 2002. The scoping, detailed assessment, causal chain and policy options analysis have all been completed for the Benguela Current, and the scoping report is available as a model report on the GIWA web site. IOI-SA has been involved in the Methods Task Team for GIWA, and has participated in methodology training workshops. The Director of the Centre was also involved in preparation of the GIWA subregional report for sub-Saharan Africa that was presented to WSSD.

The IOI-PI and Australia are also part of GIWA. The scaling and scoping exercises for sub-region 62 (Pacific Islands) and 56 (Sulu–Celebes) have been completed and the work is being undertaken on the causal chain analysis. For subregion 62 the work was concluded with a two-day workshop held in Suva, Fiji in August 2002.

SEREAD (Scientific Educational Resources and Experiences Associated with the Deployment of Argo Drifting Floats in the South Pacific Ocean)

The project was launched in the Pacific in early 2001 as part of a global project to improve understanding of the interaction between the ocean and the atmosphere. This is a multi-agency funded project aimed at awareness raising of the Argo Project, and the importance of climate change and measuring the physical parameters of ocean climate, specially focused on Pacific Island schools. Activities include the development of curriculum materials, an "adopt a float" programme, and development of a web site.

During the year, the following activities were undertaken as part of the project:

(i) Produced and approved SEREAD logo in September 2001.
(ii) Produced SEREAD brochure in October 2001.
(iii) Produced and circulated to SEREAD Steering Committee members, three draft teaching modules.
(iv) Trial the modules and promote the project activities.
(v) First school visit to Tonga by the Project leader took place in November 2001.
(vi) School visit to Samoa in December 2001.
(vii) School visit to Kiribati in April 2002.
(viii) Meeting with Argo Data Centre manager, March 2002 to develop SEREAD web site under http://argo.jcommops.org/.
(ix) Hands-on training on Argo data retrieval to 5 postgraduate diploma students from the Physics Department who were taking an oceanography course. They have carried out a small individual project based upon ARGO data and part of their reports could be used for the future teaching modules for SEREAD.
(x) One more draft teaching module on Argo float and access to Internet was written.

Until April 2002 the SEREAD activities were coordinated by the IOI-PI and led by Dr. Than Aung of the Department of Physics. However, in April 2002 the Third SEREAD Steering Committee meeting decided to shift the SEREAD project management and base to NIWA in New Zealand.

The future involvement of USP and IOI-PI in SEREAD is uncertain, although Robin South and Than Aung are still listed as Steering Committee members of SEREAD for the future. The issue will be discussed at the meeting of the SEREAD Steering Committee in October 2002 as the USP was not represented at the previous meeting and was not able to defend its position. It seems that the coordination of the project through NIWA is a temporary arrangement and that there is no plan to coordinate the Pacific Islands part from there.

Waste and Sewage

IOI-Costa Rica is negotiating with German and Spanish NGOs on the development of a regional project for the Caribbean Islands and Riparian countries on the application of solar energy, on organic waste treatment, on potable water facilities, treatment of the infectious/contagious hospital waste and hog farms waste.

In January 2001, IOI-SA began working with an environmental consulting firm, ARUP Environmental, to complete baseline and monitoring surveys to evaluate the effects of a newly constructed sewage outfall on the benthic fauna and flora of Robbin Island. The baseline survey was completed in January 2001, and the first of the monitoring surveys in June 2002. Two further monitoring surveys are planned for September 2002 and January 2003. This project is being done with the co-operation of the Zoology and Chemistry Departments of the University of the Western Cape.

IOI-Ukraine conducted studies on marine disposal of wastewater. The results contain analysis of the international legal framework on marine disposal of wastewater in the Black Sea region and identify the Ukrainian national perspective on this issue. The results were presented at the Second International Conference on Marine Wastewater Discharges.

Mangrove Research Initiative

In association with the Australian National University, IOI-PI is sponsoring a Fiji mangrove research initiative. The initiative builds on a regional mangrove workshop held at the USP in 2001, which concluded that more multidisciplinary research is required in the area of mangroves. Under the initiative, a research assistant was hired to build an Internet library that gathers under one location all materials that have been written about mangrove forests, their uses and management. This Internet library is now functional and should be used to promote more research.

IOI-PI is currently looking for funds to have a national workshop where representatives from different stakeholder groups are invited to present commissioned papers. The papers will be published in a book, while the data and information will be used to calculate, in a realistic manner, the value and contribution of mangrove resources and uses to the national economy. A field survey is also planned as a follow up to the national workshop. The pilot study will be duplicated in the other countries of the Pacific Islands if this is deemed suitable.

Pollution Studies

In 2002, IOI-SA was awarded a tender by the International Maritime Organization (IMO) to develop an online network for aquatic pollution in southern and eastern Africa? "SeaWaste." The SeaWaste network will provide an online forum for people involved in aquatic pollution at all levels, from scientific research to oil spill contingency planning. Through this network, those with an interest in aquatic pollution will be able to share documents with other members, enter discussion fora, and share news and other information relating to aquatic pollution. The first step in the process is to develop a web portal. Work on this has begun, and it is expected to have the portal up by September 2002. IOI-SA is also investigating the possibility of attracting additional funds to hold a workshop of marine pollution professionals in order to gain greater insights into the needs and requirements of users and to request input from them into the design of the network. It is envisaged that the SeaWaste project will be completed by December 2003.

IOI-SA is also involved in the Globallast Programme, from assisting with baseline diver surveys in the port of Saldanha Bay to the development of the Globallast web site, and is collaborating with the Centre for Marine Studies at the University of Cape Town and the Train-Sea-Coast Brazil Course Development Unit in developing training materials for the Globallast Programme. Globallast (the Global Ballast Water Management Programme) is an IMO Initiative aimed at identifying and minimizing the risks of translocation of marine aliens around the globe. Such aliens can have devastating effects on local marine resources and ecosystems. It is a three-year programme focusing on five demonstration ports around the world, with Saldanha Bay in South Africa being one of those.

IOI-Indonesia reported on the development of an information system and database about risk assessment and management of oil spills at Lombok Strait waters caused by oil tankers. With these instruments, calculation of economic loss caused to natural resources and environment destruction can be done easily and fast.

IOI-India, in collaboration with the University of Madras, completed in June 2002 the project entitled "Citizen Action, Water Pollution and Public Health: An Analysis of Administrative and Implementation Dimensions." The project explored the responses of citizens to the issue of water pollution through the use of legal mechanisms like consumer's courts and green benches.

Risk Management and Natural Hazards

Risk management, assessment and reduction problems have been studied through different actions. IOI-Japan co-organized the Symposium on Risk Management of

Coastal Mega Cities in December 2001 sponsored by Yokohama City University. Following the Symposium, a proposal for Risk Management of the Coastal Mega City in the Case of Yokohama City was submitted to the IOI-HQ in February 2002 as a contribution to the Swiss Re IOI proposal.

IOI-China continued the research programs in impoverished coastal areas and its strategic research on poverty migration and risk management.

IOI-Costa Rica is involved in the feasibility assessment of the project proposal on climate hazards, which is being negotiated by the Regional Committee of Hydrological Resources as part of a bigger program that Sweden plans to develop for Central America. An integral part of the project will be control and sustained management of water basins in the region. IOI-Russia supported the IOC Workshop on local tsunami mitigation held in Retropavlovsk–Kamachatski, Russia in September 2002 by funding two experts from Japan and Russia to give talks on tsunami risk assessment studies and on risk reduction of natural hazards.

Insurance Project

The project aimed at integrating insurance into integrated coastal management was initiated in 1999. The first phase included a partnership with Swiss Re-insurance based in Zurich and contained three components: preparation and delivery of a training module on risk management in integrated coastal zone management, given as part of the Ocean Governance course in Canada; a seminar to open a dialogue between the ocean and coastal management community and the insurance industry, held at the Bermuda Biological Station for Research in spring 2000, co-sponsored by the IOI and Swiss Re; and coastal community case studies carried out by several IOI Operational Centres. This first phase was concluded in 2001 and a report prepared, published through IOI Headquarters in 2002.

Through this effort a notable convergence of interests in the coastal zone was identified: risk reduction. This could lead to an alliance between the ocean and coastal management community and the insurance industry. The second phase of the project is aimed at establishing such an alliance. The Founder and Honorary Chair prepared a concept paper for the second phase which was presented to an insurance industry workshop in October 2001, organized by the Geneva Association. The concept was well received and basically endorsed. The proposal focused on implementation of a few selected case studies covering rural coastal communities, a coastal megacity, a small island developing state, and a sub-region. IOI Operational Centres in Japan, India, Fiji, South Africa and Costa Rica were invited at the end of 2001 to prepare or outline proposals for such case studies. Proposals were received by middle of 2002 from Japan, India and South Africa. The project idea was also included in the IOI package for WSSD. The project is still under development and specification. It can fit well with the WSSD Type II partnership initiative idea.

GOOS

IOI-Costa Rica participated in the GOOS-IOCARIBE process. The IOI-Malta continued to host the MedGOOS Secretariat and provided administrative support and assistance to the coordination of MedGOOS activities. The MedGOOS aims to facilitate the development of an operational ocean observing and forecasting system at a regional-to-coastal scale to the benefit of a wide group of users in the region. One of the main tasks undertaken by the MedGOOS Secretariat was related to the implementation of the first MedGOOS project, the Mediterranean Network to Assess and Upgrade Monitoring and Forecasting Activity in the region (MAMA), launched in January 2002. The MedGOOS Secretariat of IOI-Malta supported the networking between the MAMA partners and also made provisions for the logistic arrangements and organization of the two project meetings held so far. In the first six months of the project, IOI-Malta conducted surveys to identify the present capabilities and gaps in ocean/coastal observation and forecasting and developed a questionnaire for the inventory of operational ocean monitoring activities and forecasting. The database of key marine institutions and national organizational structure is being prepared, as well as a MAMA / MedGOOS web site and guidelines for the organization of national awareness meetings. A MedGOOS brochure and a MAMA flyer were produced and published in English.

Other Research Projects

IOI-Ukraine, in cooperation with the host institute, conducted research on the application of Black Sea fish species' physiological parameters as bio-indicators for evaluation of marine environment status in the coastal zone. The set of bio-indicators of environmental conditions is being developed. A promising preliminary result was received from the study of the changes of fish blood physiological parameters in response to different natural and anthropogenic impacts.

The Physical Oceanography Unit of IOI-Malta undertakes fundamental research in coastal meteorology, hydrography and physical oceanography with a main emphasis on the experimental study of the hydrodynamics of the sea in the vicinity of the Maltese Islands. The main endeavour of the Unit in this period consisted of the following:

- The collection of sea-level data from the station in the marina at the Malta Hilton Portomaso and from coastal tide gauge in Mellieha Bay. The station in Portomaso forms part of a regional network of sea-level stations (MedGLOSS) and constitutes the first real-time monitoring station for oceanographic observations in Malta.
- The collection of meteo data from the station in Ramla tal-Bir overlooking the southern Comino Channel.

- Development of new sea-level pre-processing and quality control software.
- Identification and rescue oceanographic data sets by third parties.

ADVISORY SERVICES

All activities of IOI include some elements of provision of advice (consultation) to users, including authorities and other organizations. The PIM Conferences represent a considerable advisory service, operating also as a think-tank where new ideas can be ventilated and formulated into recommendations and declarations. The IOI Leadership Seminar mechanism also provides advice and generates awareness. IOI is also providing advisory services through its interaction with different governmental and non-governmental organizations. The policy-oriented research results in advice on, inter alia, ocean governance and coastal area management. Advisory services are provided to national institutions directly or through the Host-institutions.

Oceans and Coasts at Rio+10

IOI co-sponsored and participated with several invited presentations in the Global Conference on Oceans and Coasts at Rio+10, held at UNESCO, Paris, 3–7 December 2001. The Founder and Honorary Chair gave a plenary visionary presentation on ocean governance for this century. Several Operational Centre Directors and the Executive Director gave presentations in different conference panels. The Executive Director chaired the Working Group 3 entitled 'Assessing and Managing the Marine Environment.' The Conference resulted in two documents that were presented at the WSSD, namely the *Reports of the 8 Conference Working Groups* and the Co-Chair's report entitled *Ensuring the Sustainable Development of Oceans and Coasts: A Call for Action.* This can serve as guidance for the IOI programme specifications.

World Summit on Sustainable Development (WSSD)

IOI representatives attended the Preparatory Committee meetings and the WSSD itself. IOI was registered as an NGO. At the last Preparatory Committee meeting, the IOI representative, the Deputy Executive Director, participated in and made significant contributions to the theme on SIDS, Coasts and Oceans.

Following that PrepCom, the Informal WSSD Coordinating Committee on Oceans, Coasts and Islands was formed. IOI is represented on this Committee by the Executive Director and the Deputy Executive Director. This Committee met several times during WSSD and coordinated the specification of the so-called Type II initiatives. This is an ongoing process, with evolving partnership programmes. The basic idea is the partnership requirement. IOI also presented its initiatives or programme package specifically formulated for WSSD. The specification of this package was initiated at the meeting of the Executive Committee, Bremen, 4–6 September 2001. A paper was accordingly prepared by the Senior Executive Director, circulated to Operational Centres, reviewed and endorsed by the meeting of the Executive Committee, Board members and Directors, Malta, 24–27 April 2002. The package of IOI focused on:

(i) Training and Education partnership through the IOIVU;
(ii) Scientific and technological capacity-building partnership through implementation of Articles 276 and 277 of UNCLOS, at national and regional levels;
(iii) Risk management, reduction and insurance in coastal areas, partnership with the insurance industry;
(iv) Specification of an African Strategy for ocean and coastal areas focusing on local and sub-regional partnership actions with communities and local NGOs.

These activities are ongoing within IOI. Through the WSSD process, IOI can continue to broaden the partnerships in these efforts. The Coordinating Committee formed for WSSD appears to continue, in the shape of a global forum on oceans, coasts and islands. The IOI representatives will continue to be members of this informal forum.

The formal statements by executive heads of UN agencies at WSSD were all similar in calling for action without being very specific. The IOI representatives met with many individuals, quite apart from attending several plenary sessions. These were focusing on the difficult and delicate issues of poverty-reduction, freshwater, and energy. The small islands, coasts and ocean theme had been essentially completed at the last PrepCom. The IOI individual meetings with partners, foundations and private enterprise representatives concerned IOI Operational Centres; interest for establishing new Centres; development of IOIVU and association with a global ocean university network; cooperation with IOC, UNEP and national institutions through national representatives. All these exchanges will be followed up through Headquarters.

At a special ocean high-level event, co-sponsored by IOI, an award was presented by UNEP in memory of Elisabeth Mann Borgese, from Ambassador Slade and Dr. Vanderweerd, Director of UNEP-GPA Office.

PIM Conferences and Leadership Seminars

PIM XXIX was held between 8–14 December 2002 in Cape Town, South Africa under the auspices of IOI-Southern Africa / University of Western Cape. The theme of the XXIXth PIM conference, *Oceans in the New Economy*, sought to explore problems created within the ocean by the new economy and, more importantly, to identify opportunities for sustainable use that arise out of interactions between the new economy and the Global Ocean. The proceedings of this PIM conference can be obtained from the University of the Western Cape, Cape Town, South Africa.

In conjunction with PIM XXIX, IOI held an African Leadership Seminar that has, as its primary objective, to specify the African Strategy for oceans and coasts focusing on the needs in coastal areas and on sustainable use of these areas and their resources. The aim was to address the gap in ongoing efforts including those of public awareness creation, education and training at the local and regional level, as well as to identify the role of IOI in these processes. The Seminar was mainly a follow-up action to the WSSD and PACSICOM recommendations.

In September 2002, the Leadership Seminar "Sustainability Conscious Development: Team Input and Multi-professional Approach" took place in Mamaia, Romania. It was organized by IOI-Black Sea with the objective to strengthen global/regional links, to exchange experience, to foster new contacts, to identify new projects for concrete environment focused approaches aimed at sustainable development of the Black Sea Region. The result of the seminar was the development of a project proposal on algae and sustainability to be submitted to the EU and of the steps to be taken for the improvement of the national marine co-ordination infrastructure and strengthening the IOI-Black Sea visibility at the national and regional levels.

Establishment of an IOI-African Ministerial Conference on the Environment (AMCEN) Partnership

The establishment of an IOI-AMCEN partnership is under development. The common interest of AMCEN and IOI in sustainable environmental development has a convergence especially where the coastal area is concerned. Such contact at the ministerial level will also promote governmental appreciation and co-operation, while positively influencing policies as and when necessary.

Oceans and the Law of the Sea Report of the Secretary-General, 2002*

CONTENTS

Paragraphs

*Editors' Note.—This document was provided by the United Nations Division for Ocean Affairs and the Law of the Sea (DOALOS) and is extracted from the United Nations General Assembly, Fifty-Seventh Session, Item 25 of the preliminary list A/57/50, UN document A57/57, 7 March 2002, http://www.un.org/Depts/los/. Annex 1 of this document on the First Intergovernmental Review Meeting on the Implementation of the Global Programme of Action for the Protection of the Marine Environment from Land-based Activities has been omitted, as Parts A and B of Annex 1 are published in *Ocean Yearbook* Volume 17. The document has been edited for publication in the *Ocean Yearbook*.

Annexes

ABBREVIATIONS

ABLOS	Advisory Board on Geodetic, Hydrographic and Marine Geo-Scientific Aspects of the Law of the Sea (Advisory Board on the Technical Aspects of the Law of the Sea)
APFIC	Asia-Pacific Fishery Commission
ARGO	Array for Real-time Geostrophic Oceanography
CARICOM	Caribbean Community
CCAMLR	Commission for the Conservation of Antarctic Marine Living Resources
CCSBT	Commission for the Conservation of Southern Bluefin Tuna
CLIVAR	Climate Variability and Predictability Study
CNES	Centre Nationale d'Études Spatiales (France)
COLREG	Convention on the International Regulations for Preventing Collisions at Sea, 1972
ECLAC	Economic Commission for Latin America and the Caribbean
EUMETSAT	European Organization for the Exploitation of Meteorological Satellites
FFA	Forum Fisheries Agency
GCOS	Global Climate Observing System
GCRMN	Global Coral Reef Monitoring Network
GEF	Global Environment Facility
GESAMP	Joint Group of Experts on the Scientific Aspects of Marine Environmental Protection
GFCM	General Fisheries Commission (formerly General Fisheries Council) for the Mediterranean
GIS	Geographic Information System
GMDSS	Global Maritime Distress and Safety System
GODAE	Global Ocean Data Assimilation Experiment
GOOS	Global Ocean Observing System
GPA	Global Programme of Action for the Protection of the Marine Environment from Land-based Activities
GTOS	Global Terrestrial Observing System
HELCOM	Baltic Marine Environment Protection Commission (Helsinki Commission)
IAEA	International Atomic Energy Agency
I-ATTC	Inter-American Tropical Tuna Commission
IBSFC	International Baltic Sea Fishery Commission
ICAM	integrated coastal area management
ICC	International Chamber of Commerce
ICCAT	International Commission for the Conservation of Atlantic Tunas
ICRI	International Coral Reef Initiative
ICJ	International Court of Justice
ICSPRO	Inter-Secretariat Committee on Scientific Programmes relating to Oceanography
ICSU	International Council for Science

IGOS	Integrated Global Observing Strategy (GOOS, GTOS and GCOS)
IHO	International Hydrographic Organization
INF Code	International Code for the Safe Carriage of Packaged Irradiated Nuclear Fuel, Plutonium and High-Level Radioactive Wastes on Board Ships
IOC	Intergovernmental Oceanographic Commission (UNESCO)
IODE	International Oceanographic Data and Information Exchange programme
IOTC	Indian Ocean Tuna Commission
IPCC	Intergovernmental Panel on Climate Change
IPHC	International Pacific Halibut Commission
ISM Code	International Safety Management Code
IUCN	The World Conservation Union
IUU fishing	illegal, unreported and unregulated fishing
IWC	International Whaling Commission
LL	International Convention on Load Lines
MARPOL 73/78	International Convention for the Prevention of Pollution from Ships, 1973, as modified by the Protocol of 1978 relating thereto
MEPC	IMO Marine Environment Protection Committee
MSC	IMO Maritime Safety Committee
NAFO	Northwest Atlantic Fisheries Organization
NASA	National Aeronautics and Space Administration (United States of America)
NASCO	North Atlantic Salmon Conservation Organization
NEAFC	North-East Atlantic Fisheries Commission
NOAA	National Oceanic and Atmospheric Administration (United States)
NODCs	National Oceanographic Data Centres
OECD	Organisation for Economic Cooperation and Development
OSPAR	Commission for the protection of the Marine Environment of the North-East Atlantic
PAME	Protection of the Arctic Marine Environment (Arctic Council)
PERSGA	Regional Organization for the Conservation of the Red Sea and the Gulf of Aden
POPs	persistent organic pollutants
ROPME	Regional Organization for the Protection of the Marine Environment
SAR Convention	International Convention on Maritime Search and Rescue
SBSTTA	Subsidiary Body on Scientific, Technical and Technological Advice (Conference of Parties to Convention on Biological Diversity)
SCOR	Scientific Committee on Ocean Research (ICSU)
SOCA	Subcommittee on Oceans and Coastal Areas of the Administrative Committee on Coordination

SOLAS	International Convention for the Safety of Life at Sea
SOPAC	South Pacific Applied Geoscience Commission
SPREP	South Pacific Regional Environment Programme
STCW Convention	1978 International Convention on Standards of Training, Certification and Watchkeeping for Seafarers
STCW-F	1995 International Convention on Standards of Training, Certification and Watchkeeping for Fishing Vessel Personnel
SUA Convention	1988 Convention for the Suppression of Unlawful Acts against the Safety of Maritime Navigation
UNCED	United Nations Conference on Environment and Development
UNCTAD	United Nations Conference on Trade and Development
UNDP	United Nations Development Programme
UNEP	United Nations Environment Programme
UNIDO	United Nations Industrial Development Organization
UNU	United Nations University
VDRs	voyage data recorders
VMS	vessel monitoring system
VOS	Voluntary Observing Ships scheme (WMO)
WHO	World Health Organization
WOCE	World Ocean Circulation Experiment
WSSCC	Water Supply and Sanitation Collaborative Council

1. OVERVIEW

1. "The importance of the world ocean as a potential supplier of goods (food, fibre, genetic resources, metals, minerals), services (trade routes, tourism), energy, and as a repository of national, regional, and global security cannot be overstated. Above all, however, the world ocean is an essential part of the biosphere; it is a crucial factor in the carbon cycle and a determinant of the planet's climate . . . The ocean's contribution of 'ecosystem services' is very much larger than that of terra firma."[1]

2. This year is a significant year for the world's oceans and seas: it marks the twentieth anniversary of the opening for signature of the United Nations Convention on the Law of the Sea (UNCLOS), "a Constitution for the oceans," and the tenth anniversary of the adoption of Agenda 21, a programme of action for sustainable development, Chapter 17 of which puts forward a programme of action for the sustainable development of the world's oceans and seas and their resources. The United Nations General Assembly decided to devote two days of plenary meetings at its fifty-seventh session, on 9 and 10 December 2002, to the consideration of the item entitled "Oceans and the law of the sea" and the commemoration of the twentieth anniversary of the opening for signature of the Convention. The World Summit

1. E. M. Borgese, *The Oceanic Circle: Governing the Seas as a Global Resource* (Tokyo: United Nations University Press, 1998), p. 50. Professor Mann Borgese, a leading member of the international ocean community, passed away in February 2002 (see United Nations press release SEA/1730).

on Sustainable Development, to be held in Johannesburg, South Africa, in August 2002, will carry out a 10-year review of Agenda 21, including, expectedly, the programme of action on "oceans and seas" in the context of natural resources and in connection with the theme relating to small island developing States.

3. Today, 20 years after the adoption of the Convention, it is fast approaching universal participation. One hundred twenty-one coastal States, 16 landlocked States and one international organization are parties to the Convention, 138 in total. All regions are represented: of a total of 53 African States, 38 are parties; of 59 Asian States, 40 are parties; Europe and North America is represented by 32 parties a total of 48 States, and by the European Community; while of 33 Latin American and Caribbean States, 27 are parties. The compliance with the provisions of the Convention, especially regarding the limits of maritime zones under national jurisdiction, is also remarkable.

4. The three institutions created by the Convention are operational and functioning effectively. The International Seabed Authority, which deals with the international seabed area beyond national jurisdiction (the Area) and its resources, has approved the plans of work of seven registered pioneer investors for exploration of polymetallic nodules in the Area and issued contracts for exploration to all but one of them. The International Tribunal for the Law of the Sea, a court dealing with the interpretation or application of the Convention, has already heard 10 cases. The Commission on the Limits of the Continental Shelf, which deals with the outer limits of the outermost maritime zone under national jurisdiction, the continental shelf, beyond 200 nautical miles from the baselines, has received its first submission.

5. The Meeting of States Parties to the Convention has already had 11 sessions and is showing increasing interest in the issues relating to the implementation of the Convention. With the entry into force of the Convention, the General Assembly assumed the role of overseeing developments relating to the Convention, law of the sea and ocean affairs in general, and carries out an annual review of such developments under a consolidated agenda item entitled "Oceans and the law of the sea." Furthermore, in 1999, the General Assembly, consistent with the legal framework provided by UNCLOS and the goals of Chapter 17 of Agenda 21, established an open-ended informal consultative process in order to facilitate its annual review, in an effective and constructive manner, of developments in ocean affairs. This year, the Assembly is to review the effectiveness and utility of this process. The United Nations is fulfilling efficiently the responsibilities entrusted to it by the Convention and the related resolutions of the General Assembly, and is functioning as the de facto secretariat of the Convention.

6. International instruments emanating from the Convention and Agenda 21 are many and varied. Two that are directly related to the implementation of the Convention have already entered into force: the Agreement relating to the implementation of Part XI of the United Nations Convention on the Law of the Sea of 10 December 1982 ("Agreement on Part XI of UNCLOS") and the Agreement on the implementation of the provisions of the United Nations Convention on the Law of the Sea of 10 December 1982 relating to the conservation and management of straddling fish stocks and highly migratory fish stocks ("1995 Fish Stocks Agreement").

7. Today, 20 years after the adoption of the Convention and 10 years after the adoption of Agenda 21, including its Chapter 17, the accomplishments are impres-

sive. But the challenges are also formidable—of implementing the legal and programmatic frameworks, of executing actions, at the global, regional and national levels, to realize benefits from these frameworks. Many countries are finding their awareness and knowledge to be scanty and unfocused, their resources scarce, their capacity limited and their means of implementation inadequate.

8. Thus, in this anniversary year, the international community should focus its efforts on actions that would contribute to the realization of optimal benefits from the world's oceans and seas, at the same time minimizing the problems that have arisen, especially with regard to the limitations in harnessing the marine potential and the degradation of the marine environment and resources.

9. At the national level, for example, the Director of a leading ocean institute, the Woods Hole Oceanographic Institution in Massachusetts, United States of America, states: "The newly created [United States] Ocean Commission, established last year by the Oceans Act of 2000, will have the opportunity to make the study of our oceans a national priority. The Commission, made up of scientists and representatives of government and business, will soon begin meeting and making recommendations to the president and Congress for new policies relating to our oceans."[2]

10. At the regional level, as an example, the South Pacific Applied Geoscience Commission (SOPAC) reports: "Regional priorities for the marine sector are . . . set by Governments of the Pacific region and are reflected in work programmes of the respective ministries (at the national level) and regional intergovernmental agencies (at the regional level). In the regional context these priorities are consolidated within the Committee on Regional Organizations of the Pacific "Regional Strategy."

11. At the global level, oceans occupy an important part of the work of the United Nations system. The newly established consultative process on oceans and the Millennium Ecosystem Assessment constitute two significant examples. The latter, which was initiated in June 2001, will examine the processes that support life on Earth, such as the world's grasslands, farmlands, forests, rivers and lakes, and oceans. It is intended to improve the management of the world's natural and managed ecosystems by helping meet the needs of decision makers in government and the private sector as well as the public for peer-reviewed policy-relevant scientific information on the condition of ecosystems, the consequences of ecosystem change and options for response.

2. THE UNITED NATIONS CONVENTION ON THE LAW OF THE SEA AND ITS IMPLEMENTING AGREEMENTS

A. Status of the Convention and its Implementing Agreements

12. The importance of increasing the number of States parties to the Convention and the Agreement relating to the implementation of Part XI of the Convention in order to achieve the goal of universal participation was stressed yet another time by the General Assembly in its resolution 56/12 of 28 November 2001. The General

2. R. Gagosian, "What the seas can offer," *The New York Times*, 4 August 2001.

Assembly has traditionally reiterated its call upon all States that have not done so to become parties to these instruments. Since the issuance of the most recent report (A/56/58/Add.1), Hungary ratified UNCLOS in February 2002; the number of States parties has thus increased to 138, including one international organization.[3]

13. There is little doubt that over the years the legal regime established by the Convention has reached almost universal acceptance. However, further efforts need to be expended in order for the goal of universal participation to be realized. Thirty (30) coastal States out of 151 are not yet parties to the Convention: 5 States in the African region (Congo, Eritrea, Liberia, Libyan Arab Jamahiriya and Morocco); 12 States in the Asian and Pacific region (Cambodia, Democratic People's Republic of Korea, Iran (Islamic Republic of), Israel, Kiribati, Niue, Qatar, Syrian Arab Republic, Thailand, Turkey, Tuvalu and United Arab Emirates); 7 States in Europe and North America (Albania, Canada, Denmark, Estonia, Latvia, Lithuania and United States of America); and 6 States in the Latin American and Caribbean region (Colombia, Dominican Republic, Ecuador, El Salvador, Peru and Venezuela). More than a half of the landlocked States—26 States out of 42—also remain outside the legal framework, despite the unquestionable benefits provided to them by the provisions of Part X of UNCLOS. These States are: Afghanistan, Andorra, Armenia, Azerbaijan, Belarus, Bhutan, Burkina Faso, Burundi, Central African Republic, Chad, Ethiopia, Holy See, Kazakhstan, Kyrgyzstan, Lesotho, Liechtenstein, Malawi, Niger, Republic of Moldova, Rwanda, San Marino, Swaziland, Switzerland, Tajikistan, Turkmenistan and Uzbekistan.

14. In 1994, the Agreement relating to the implementation of Part XI of UNCLOS became an inseparable part of the Convention. Adopted on 28 July 1994 by the General Assembly in its resolution 48/263 and in force since 28 July 1996, the Agreement is to be interpreted and applied together with UNCLOS as a single instrument. In the event of any inconsistency between the Agreement and Part XI of UNCLOS, the provisions of the Agreement prevail. After 28 July 1994, any ratification of or accession to UNCLOS represents consent to be bound by the Agreement as well. Furthermore, no State or entity can establish its consent to be bound by the

3. Algeria, Angola, Antigua and Barbuda, Argentina, Australia, Austria, Bahamas, Bahrain, Bangladesh, Barbados, Belgium, Belize, Benin, Bolivia, Bosnia and Herzegovina, Botswana, Brazil, Brunei Darussalam, Bulgaria, Cameroon, Cape Verde, Chile, China, Comoros, Cook Islands, Costa Rica, Côte d'Ivoire, Croatia, Cuba, Cyprus, Czech Republic, Democratic Republic of the Congo, Djibouti, Dominica, Egypt, Equatorial Guinea, European Community, Fiji, Finland, France, Gabon, Gambia, Georgia, Germany, Ghana, Greece, Grenada, Guatemala, Guinea, Guinea-Bissau, Guyana, Haiti, Honduras, Hungary, Iceland, India, Indonesia, Iraq, Ireland, Italy, Jamaica, Japan, Jordan, Kenya, Kuwait, Lao People's Democratic Republic, Lebanon, Luxembourg, Madagascar, Malaysia, Maldives, Mali, Malta, Marshall Islands, Mauritania, Mauritius, Mexico, Micronesia (Federated States of), Monaco, Mongolia, Mozambique, Myanmar, Namibia, Nauru, Nepal, Netherlands, New Zealand, Nicaragua, Nigeria, Norway, Oman, Pakistan, Palau, Panama, Papua New Guinea, Paraguay, Philippines, Poland, Portugal, Republic of Korea, Romania, Russian Federation, Saint Kitts and Nevis, Saint Lucia, Saint Vincent and the Grenadines, Samoa, Sao Tome and Principe, Saudi Arabia, Senegal, Seychelles, Sierra Leone, Singapore, Slovakia, Slovenia, Solomon Islands, Somalia, South Africa, Spain, Sri Lanka, Sudan, Suriname, Sweden, the former Yugoslav Republic of Macedonia, Togo, Tonga, Trinidad and Tobago, Tunisia, Uganda, Ukraine, United Kingdom of Great Britain and Northern Ireland, United Republic of Tanzania, Uruguay, Vanuatu, Viet Nam, Yemen, Yugoslavia, Zambia and Zimbabwe.

Agreement unless it has previously established or establishes concurrently its consent to be bound by UNCLOS. The Agreement had been negotiated to address certain outstanding issues relating to the deep seabed mining provisions of UNCLOS which prevented some States from ratifying or acceding to the Convention, and thereby to facilitate the widest possible participation in the Convention.

15. One hundred and four States parties to UNCLOS are now parties to that Agreement. The difference between the number of States parties to the Convention and the number of States parties to the Agreement is explained by the fact that 34 States which became parties to the Convention prior to the adoption of the Agreement on Part XI have not yet expressed their consent to be bound by the Agreement. Those States, however, participated in the work of the International Seabed Authority and its organs established on the basis of the Agreement. As such, they are considered to be applying the Agreement de facto. Those States are: Angola, Antigua and Barbuda, Bahrain, Bosnia and Herzegovina, Botswana, Brazil, Cameroon, Cape Verde, Comoros, Cuba, Democratic Republic of the Congo, Djibouti, Dominica, Egypt, Gambia, Ghana, Guinea-Bissau, Guyana, Honduras, Iraq, Kuwait, Mali, Marshall Islands, Mexico, Saint Kitts and Nevis, Saint Lucia, Saint Vincent and the Grenadines, Sao Tome and Principe, Somalia, Sudan, Tunisia, Uruguay, Viet Nam and Yemen.

16. The 1995 Agreement for the implementation of the provisions of UNCLOS relating to the conservation and management of straddling fish stocks and highly migratory fish stocks entered into force on 11 December 2001, six years after its opening for signature. The requirements for its entry into force had been met 30 days earlier, on 11 November 2001, when Malta deposited its instrument of accession (the thirtieth instrument required by Article 40) with the Secretary-General.

17. The entry into force of the 1995 Fish Stocks Agreement was a result of important efforts undertaken by international organizations and States with a view to enhancing the legal regime established by the Convention with respect to the straddling fish stocks and highly migratory fish stocks. A particularly important role in the promotion of the Agreement was played by the Food and Agriculture Organization of the United Nations (FAO) and a number of States, inter alia, Norway, the United States of America and States members of the Pacific Islands Forum Group. Although few, if any, of the current parties to the Agreement could be considered as belonging to the group of important distant-water fishing countries, it is expected that, with a forthcoming simultaneous action by the European Community and its members, there will be a big qualitative change in the participation and its representativeness.

18. In anticipation of the entry into force of the Agreement, the General Assembly, in its resolution 56/13 of 28 November 2001, requested the Secretary-General to consult with States that have either ratified or acceded to the Agreement, for the purposes and objectives of, inter alia, considering the regional, subregional and global implementation of the Agreement; making any appropriate recommendation to the General Assembly on the scope and content of the annual report of the Secretary-General relating to the Agreement; and preparing for the review conference to be convened by the Secretary-General pursuant to Article 36 of the Agreement. Another possible agenda item for the consultation may be the facilitation of the establishment of a programme of assistance within the Agreement. Such consultations should take place within the first six months of 2002 and the information about the outcome will appear in the addendum to the present report.

19. Currently, there are 31 parties to the Agreement, including the United Kingdom of Great Britain and Northern Ireland, which ratified it on behalf of its Overseas Territories. There are 10 States from the South Pacific region that are parties (Australia, Cook Islands, Fiji, Micronesia (Federated States of), Nauru, New Zealand, Papua New Guinea, Samoa, Solomon Islands and Tonga), 2 from North America (Canada and United States of America), 6 from the Latin American and Caribbean region (Bahamas, Barbados, Brazil, Costa Rica, Saint Lucia and Uruguay), 5 from among European States (Iceland, Malta, Monaco, Norway and Russian Federation), 4 from among African States (Mauritius, Namibia, Senegal and Seychelles) and 3 from among Asian States (Iran (Islamic Republic of), Maldives and Sri Lanka).

20. Thus, owing to the level of participation and various geographical factors, the regime established by the Agreements already covers substantial parts of the zones adjacent to the exclusive economic zones of States parties in the South Pacific, the North-West and South-West Atlantic, the northern part of the North Pacific Ocean, as well as the Arctic Ocean.

B. Declarations and Statements under Articles 310 and 287 of UNCLOS

21. The General Assembly in its resolution 56/12 repeated its call upon States to ensure that any declarations or statements that they have made or make when signing, ratifying or acceding to the Convention are in conformity therewith and, otherwise, to withdraw any of their declarations or statements that are not in conformity. To this day, no action by States parties in this connection has been reported.

22. Pursuant to Article 310, States may, when signing, ratifying or acceding to the Convention, make declarations or statements, provided that such declarations or statements do not purport to exclude or to modify the legal effect of the provisions of UNCLOS in their application to that State. Article 309 prohibits any reservations or exceptions to UNCLOS unless expressly permitted by other UNCLOS Articles. It is recalled that several States had noted during the General Assembly debates on oceans and the law of the sea that certain declaration and statements appeared not to be in conformity with Article 309. The categories of such declarations and statements were listed in the 1999 report (A/54/429, par. 16); they include: (a) those which relate to baselines not drawn in conformity with UNCLOS; (b) those which purport to require notification or permission before warships or other ships exercise the right of innocent passage; (c) those which are not in conformity with the provisions of UNCLOS relating to: (i) straits used for international navigation, including the right of transit passage; (ii) archipelagic States' waters, including archipelagic baselines and archipelagic sea-lane passage; (iii) the exclusive economic zone or the continental shelf; and (iv) delimitation; and (d) those which purport to subordinate the interpretation or application of UNCLOS to national laws and regulations, including constitutional provisions.

23. The Secretary-General considers that any appropriate action by States concerned, with a view to responding to the General Assembly's appeal, would represent a substantial step towards a uniform and consistent application of the Convention.

On the other hand, it must be recognized that some of the above declarations and statements were motivated by certain underlying and legitimate concerns of States. The need for alleviating such concerns should not be ignored. They should be identified and addressed in an effective manner within the framework of competent international organizations or bodies.

24. Article 287 of UNCLOS allows States, when signing, ratifying or acceding to UNCLOS or any time thereafter, to choose, by means of a written declaration, one or more of specific means for the settlement of disputes concerning the interpretation or application of the Convention. Since the issuance of the last report (A/56/58 and Add.1), two declarations have been made pursuant to that Article. Slovenia declared that it had chosen an arbitral tribunal constituted in accordance with Annex VII for the settlement of disputes concerning the interpretation or application of the Convention. Hungary declared that it had chosen, pursuant to Article 287 of UNCLOS and in order of preference, (a) the International Tribunal for the Law of the Sea; (b) the International Court of Justice; and (c) a special tribunal constructed in accordance with Annex VIII for all the categories of disputes specified therein.

25. Under Article 298, a State may, when signing, ratifying or acceding to UNCLOS or at any time thereafter, declare in writing that it does not accept any one or more of the compulsory procedures entailing binding decisions provided for in section 2 of Part XV of UNCLOS with respect to one or more of specific categories of disputes. Since the issuance of the most recent report, Slovenia declared that it did not accept an arbitral tribunal constituted in accordance with Annex VII for any of the categories of disputes mentioned in Article 298. Also, Equatorial Guinea declared that it does not recognize any of the procedures mentioned in section 2 of Part XV as compulsory "ipso facto" in regard to the categories of disputes listed in paragraph 1 (a) of Article 298 (disputes concerning the interpretation or application of Articles 15, 74 and 83 relating to sea boundary delimitations, or those involving historic bays or titles).

26. In total, declarations upon ratification, accession or formal confirmation of UNCLOS have been made by 50 States and the European Community. All declarations and statements with respect to UNCLOS and to the Agreement relating to the implementation of Part XI of UNCLOS made before 31 December 1996 have been analysed and reproduced in a United Nations publication in the Law of the Sea series; full texts of those made after that date have been circulated to Member States in depositary notifications and have been published in Law of the Sea Bulletins, Nos. 36–47. They are also available at the web site of the Division for Ocean Affairs and the Law of the Sea of the United Nations Office of Legal Affairs (www.un.org/Depts/los) as well as that of the Treaty Section of the United Nations (www.un.org/Depts/Treaty). The information concerning the choice of procedure, as provided for in Article 287, is reflected, among others, in Law of the Sea Information Circulars Nos. 14 and 15.

27. Concerning the 1995 Fish Stocks Agreement, Malta made a declaration upon accession on 11 November 2001. Among other things, Malta stated its view that the requirements of implementing the 1995 Agreement ought to be in conformity with the 1982 United Nations Convention on the Law of the Sea and that no provision of this Agreement might be interpreted in such a way as to conflict with the principle of freedom of the high seas, and of flag State exclusive jurisdiction over its vessels on the high seas as recognized by international law.

28. Malta's declaration also contained other paragraphs of an interpretative nature regarding Articles 21 (Subregional and regional cooperation in enforcement) and 22 (Basic procedures for boarding and inspection pursuant to Article 21). Its declaration also referred to the statement by the European Community made at the time of signature of the Agreement regarding the transfer of competences to it by its member States with regard to certain aspects of the Agreement and indicated that such transfer would also become applicable to Malta when it joins the European Community.

29. Thus, as at February 2002, eight States had made declarations upon ratification of or accession to the 1995 Fish Stocks Agreement.

30. In another development, on 10 December 2001, the depositary accepted a ratification of the 1995 Fish Stocks Agreement by the United Kingdom in respect of its Overseas Territories. Originally, the depositary was not in a position to accept the original instrument, lodged in December 1999, as a ratification, since it differed from the United Kingdom's practice, which consisted of ratifying certain treaties in respect of the United Kingdom's metropolitan territory and later extending them to its Overseas Territories. In this particular case, the instrument of ratification of December 1999 related only to the Overseas Territories, while the metropolitan territory falls under the procedure to be followed regarding the transfer of competence to the European Community.

31. However, after thorough examination, the Legal Counsel, taking into account special circumstances, decided to accommodate the United Kingdom approach, provided that the United Kingdom made a formal declaration explaining the legal constraints on ratification in respect of its metropolitan territory flowing from the United Kingdom's membership in the European Community and stating its intention to ratify the Agreement simultaneously with the European Community and the other member States.

32. Such additional declaration was provided by the United Kingdom on 10 December 2001. In the declaration the United Kingdom noted its keen support of the 1995 Fish Stocks Agreement. It also stated that legislation of the European Communities (Council decision 10176/97 of 8 June 1998) bound the United Kingdom as a matter of European Community (EC) law to deposit its instrument of ratification in relation to the metropolitan territory simultaneously with the Community and the other member States. The declaration explained that the constraints imposed by the Council decision only applied in respect of the United Kingdom metropolitan territory and those Overseas Territories to which the EC treaties applied. It further noted the strong wish of the United Kingdom to implement the Agreement in respect of those Overseas Territories to which the EC treaty did not apply so as to enable those territories to enjoy the rights and obligations accruing under the Agreement.

C. Meeting of States Parties

33. Eleven Meetings of States Parties to UNCLOS have been held so far, in accordance with Article 319, paragraph 2 (e), of UNCLOS.[4] The eleventh Meeting of States Parties was held in New York from 14 to 18 May 2001. For details of the work

4. Detailed reports on the issues dealt with in previous Meetings of States Parties are contained in documents SPLOS/3, SPLOS/4, SPLOS/5, SPLOS/8, SPLOS/14, SPLOS/20, SPLOS/24,

of the Meeting, see the most recent report (A/56/58/Add.1, paras. 15–23). The Meeting, inter alia, dealt with the following issues: the budget of the International Tribunal for the Law of the Sea for the year 2002, the Financial Regulations of the Tribunal, matters related to the continental shelf, and matters related to Article 319 of the Convention. The Meeting also elected Xu Guangjian (China) to serve the remainder of the term of Judge Lihai Zhao, who passed away on 10 October 2000. One of the most significant decisions of the eleventh Meeting has a positive bearing on the implementation of certain aspects of the Convention by a number of countries, especially developing countries: The Meeting decided that for a State for which the Convention entered into force before 13 May 1999, the date of the commencement of the 10-year time period for making a submission to the Commission on the Limits of the Continental Shelf with regard to the outer limits of its continental shelf beyond 200 nautical miles would be 13 May 1999.

34. In another important decision, the Meeting provided for an open-ended working group to be established as a matter of priority during the Meetings of States Parties at which financial and budgetary matters of the Tribunal will be discussed. The open-ended working group, to be chaired by the President of the Meeting, will review the proposed budget of the Tribunal and make recommendations to the Meeting. Decisions on budgetary and financial matters taken by the Meeting shall be based on those recommendations.

35. A significant development was the consideration by the Meeting of matters related to Article 319 of UNCLOS, and in that connection, issues relating to the implementation of the Convention. Many delegations expressed their support for an expanded role for the Meeting of States Parties beyond budgetary and administrative matters. In their view, the Meeting had the competence to discuss issues of implementation of the Convention bearing in mind the need to avoid duplication of the work in other forums. Other delegations stated that the interpretation of Article 319 of the Convention did not support an expanded role for the Meeting of States Parties. The mandate of the Secretary-General in Article 319, paragraph 2 (e), to convene necessary meetings of States Parties was qualified in two respects: first, it was limited to meetings that were "necessary;" and secondly, the mandate was linked to the provisions of the Convention, which clearly specified the matters to be considered by Meetings of States Parties. In the light of the various views expressed, the eleventh Meeting of States Parties decided to retain the current agenda item entitled "Matters related to Article 319 of the United Nations Convention on the Law of the Sea" for its next Meeting.

36. The twelfth Meeting of States Parties will be held from 16 to 26 April 2002 at United Nations Headquarters (see resolution 56/12, par. 9).

3. MARITIME SPACE

A. Recent Developments

37. Among the most important recent developments regarding maritime space and maritime delimitation were the preparations for the convening of a Caribbean Conference on Maritime Delimitation. The initiative to convene the conference was

SPLOS/31, SPLOS/48, SPLOS/60 and SPLOS/73, as well as the reports of the Secretary-General to the General Assembly on the law of the sea (A/50/713, paras. 14–21 and 48–58; A/51/645, paras.

announced at the twenty-second Summit Meeting of the Caribbean Community (CARICOM) held in Nassau, Bahamas, in July 2001, by the President of Mexico, Vicente Fox. The goal of the conference is to offer, within the context of regional mechanisms of cooperation and in fostering confidence-building and preventive diplomacy, a diplomatic forum to encourage and facilitate negotiations of maritime boundary delimitation in the region.

38. Many benefits are expected to be derived from a clear definition of maritime boundaries in the region, in particular a number of economic benefits, such as those related to oil and gas exploitation and to the exercise of jurisdiction over fisheries zones. It is also apparent that unresolved boundary issues and the consequent lack of cooperation contribute to the aggravation of a number of ocean-related problems, such as maritime pollution, unsustainable and unregulated fisheries, use of maritime spaces for narcotic drug trafficking, and the transport of dangerous or harmful substances in violation of applicable international rules and standards.

39. The Preparatory Committee for the Conference met in Mexico City in January 2002. Among other things, the participating States approved the draft Rules of the Conference, including the definition of its mandate. The Division for Ocean Affairs and the Law of the Sea was invited as observer. The Division made a substantial presentation on the issues related to maritime delimitation and described the technical assistance it can provide. The first session of the Conference is scheduled to be held in Mexico City from 6 to 9 May 2002.

40. The draft Rules of the Conference establish, inter alia, a Registry of the Delimitation Negotiations, for informative purposes. Participating States with opposite or adjacent coasts may mutually agree to enter into the Registry the delimitation of one or more of their maritime zones, the negotiation of which they wish to undertake or continue within the context of the Conference. The draft Rules further foresee that the Division will be invited, at the first session of the Conference, to give a presentation on the technical assistance it can offer, acting within the mandate given to it by the relevant United Nations resolutions. Such assistance may be requested by a common accord of parties involved in corresponding negotiations and shall be rendered by the Division on an impartial basis. Furthermore, the draft Rules contain provisions concerning the establishment of an assistance fund, to be managed by the Division in accordance with the terms of reference adopted on the basis of the Financial Regulations and Rules of the United Nations.

41. Regarding the mandate of the conference, the States participating in the Preparatory Committee agreed that the Conference should facilitate, mainly through technical assistance, the voluntary undertaking of maritime delimitation negotiations between the Caribbean coastal States, based on the principle that the negotiations shall take place at the time and according to terms agreed freely by the parties, and without any external intervention.

42. During the period under review, several other developments have been brought to the attention of the Division of Ocean Affairs and the Law of the Sea. In the African region, negotiations between Angola and Namibia, which started in 1993 with a view to analysing the common border, resulted in the conclusion of a treaty for

---

24–25 and 54–84; A/52/487, paras. 25–55; A/53/456, paras. 29–78; A/54/429, paras. 29–67; A/55/61, paras. 18–30; A/56/78, paras. 25–38 and 52/82).

the delimitation of the maritime border between the two States. Also, Algeria and Tunisia signed a protocol agreement on cooperation between the two countries. The agreement concerns, inter alia, arrangements for the demarcation of Algerian-Tunisian maritime borders.

43. In the Latin American and Caribbean region, Honduras and the United Kingdom concluded an agreement on the delimitation of the maritime zones between Honduras and the Cayman Islands.

44. Two cases are pending before the International Court of Justice, namely, *Maritime Delimitation between Nicaragua and Honduras in the Caribbean Sea (Nicaragua v. Honduras)*, and proceedings against Colombia with regard to "legal issues subsisting" between the two States "concerning title to territory and maritime delimitation" in the western Caribbean, initiated by Nicaragua (also see paras. 564–567). In another development, Honduras requested the Security Council, in January 2002, to make recommendations to ensure the execution of the judgement of the International Court of Justice of 11 September 1992 in the land, island and maritime frontier dispute between Honduras and El Salvador.

45. The Government of Saint Kitts and Nevis protested the status granted to the Venezuelan territory known as "Isla Aves" in certain maritime boundary treaties concluded by Venezuela. Those treaties appeared to grant "Isla Aves" full status of territorial sea, exclusive economic zone or continental shelf. Saint Kitts and Nevis pointed out that, according to customary international law and as reflected in UNCLOS, rocks which cannot sustain human habitation or an economic life of their own shall have no exclusive economic zone or continental shelf. It also pointed out that the artificial installation and structure erected adjacent to "Isla Aves" should not possess the status of an island and shall have no territorial sea of its own and its presence should not affect the delimitation of the territorial sea, the exclusive economic zone or the continental shelf. It is recalled that similar protests were made in 1997 by Antigua and Barbuda, Saint Kitts and Nevis, Saint Lucia and Saint Vincent and the Grenadines (see A/52/487, par. 74).

46. Guyana addressed protests to Trinidad and Tobago and Venezuela in connection with the Treaty on Delimitation of Marine and Submarine Areas between Trinidad and Tobago and Venezuela signed at Caracas on 18 April 1990, which entered into force on 23 July 1991. Referring to a review of its provisional maritime boundaries and of its potential claims to its extended continental shelf, Guyana stated that the Treaty purported to give to its parties rights over certain maritime areas which are a portion of Guyana's maritime space.

47. Among other unresolved maritime boundary delimitations in the Latin American and Caribbean region were delimitations between Guyana and Suriname, Colombia and Venezuela, Trinidad and Tobago and Barbados, and Guatemala and Belize. It appears, however, that at least in some of these cases, significant efforts have been made and progress has been achieved with a view to finding negotiated, mutually agreeable solutions. It also appears that in the region other negotiations and processes relating to maritime boundary delimitations may have been initiated or are under way. The Caribbean Conference on Maritime Delimitation is also expected to facilitate the search for agreeable solutions (see paras. 37–41).

48. In the European region, reports were received, inter alia, on the attempts to reach an agreement on the maritime boundary and continental shelf delimitation between Romania and Ukraine in the Black Sea.

49. No major developments have recently been reported in the Asian region, where the unresolved maritime delimitations are in a large number of cases tied to complex issues of sovereignty over islands.

50. As referred to in the most recent report (A/56/58/Add.1, par. 24), the Division is in the process of reviewing and enhancing its collection of information regarding legislative measures undertaken by States parties in implementing UNCLOS. In this context, the Division has circulated a questionnaire to all signatories of and States parties to the Convention, requesting input and seeking any other relevant information concerning steps taken by States parties to harmonize their national legislation with UNCLOS. The questionnaire has also been placed on the Division's web site (www.un.org/Depts/los). It is noted that the web site already contains a set of national legislation acts and references to maritime boundary delimitation treaties (in English) organized by regions and by States. The Division intends to prepare an analysis of the information received and share the results with States as soon as practicable as part of an overall assessment of the implementation of UNCLOS 20 years after its adoption.

B. National Claims to Maritime Zones

51. Twenty years after the adoption of the Convention, there is almost a universal acceptance of maritime zones as well as of their maximum extent and of the respective regime for them as established by UNCLOS. The statistics about national claims are presented in the table entitled "Summary of national claims to maritime zones" (see A/56/58, Annex II); they have remained mostly unchanged during the reporting period (see also A/56/58, paras. 49–51). Despite extensive research, however, the table may not always reflect the latest developments, owing to the lack of regular updates from Governments.

52. Regarding claims with respect to the continental shelf, it should again be noted that their status may appear in certain cases rather ambiguous, especially where the claims and legislation were initially based on the Convention on the Continental Shelf, adopted at Geneva on 29 April 1958, and where the State concerned subsequently became a State party to UNCLOS. States parties to UNCLOS concerned may wish to continue reviewing their legislation on the continental shelf with a view to bringing it into harmony with the provisions of current international law.

C. Continental Shelf Beyond 200 Nautical Miles and the Work of the Commission on the Limits of the Continental Shelf

53. *Work of the Commission on the Limits of the Continental Shelf.*—The Commission has held nine sessions since it was established in June 1997.[5] The tenth session of the Commission will open on 25 March 2002. It will be of three weeks' duration in

5. More detailed information regarding the work of the Commission can be found in the recent annual reports of the Secretary-General (A/56/58, paras. 52–82, and Add.1, paras. 19, 30–

order to allow time for the Commission to examine the submission of the Russian Federation, which was made on 20 December 2001 (see par. 55).

54. In view of the forthcoming second election of 21 members of the Commission at the twelfth Meeting of States Parties, to be held from 16 to 26 April 2002, the Commission proposed that the eleventh session of the Commission in its new composition should be held from 24 to 28 June 2002. The term of office of the current members of the Commission expires on 15 June 2002.

55. *Submission to the Commission by the Russian Federation.*—On 20 December 2001, the Russian Federation made a submission to the Commission on the Limits of the Continental Shelf, pursuant to Article 76, paragraph 8, of the Convention. The submission contains the information on the proposed outer limits of the continental shelf of the Russian Federation beyond 200 nautical miles from the baselines from which the breadth of the territorial sea is measured. It is noted that the Convention entered into force for the Russian Federation on 11 April 1997.

56. In accordance with rule 49 of the Rules of Procedure of the Commission (CLCS/3/Rev.4 and Corr.1), the Secretary-General circulated on that date a note verbale to all States Members of the United Nations, including States parties to the Convention, to make public the proposed outer limits of the continental shelf pursuant to the submission. The list of geographical coordinates of points proposed for the outer limits of the continental shelf and illustrative maps included in the submission, showing the proposed limits, were attached to the communication.

57. The note verbale informed the States Members that the consideration of the submission made by the Russian Federation shall be included in the agenda of the tenth session of the Commission, to be held in New York from 25 March to 12 April 2002. Upon completion of the consideration of the submission, the Commission shall make recommendations in accordance with Article 76, paragraph 8, of the Convention. Similar notification was also communicated to the members of the Commission.

58. *Reaction of States to the Russian submission.*—In response to the note verbale of the Secretary-General, communications were received from Canada, Denmark, Japan, Norway and the United States of America. The contents of these communications are being circulated to all Member States and will be communicated to the Commission at its tenth session.

59. *Second election of the members of the Commission.*—The second election of the 21 members of the Commission will be held at the twelfth Meeting of States Parties at United Nations Headquarters (16–26 April 2002). The nomination of candidates was opened on 11 December 2001 for any State party. States in the process of becoming a party to the Convention may also nominate candidates. The closing date for nominations was 11 March 2002.

60. The members of the Commission serve in their personal capacity, and are elected by the States parties to the Convention from among their nationals in accordance with Article 2, paragraph 1, of Annex II to the Convention, having due regard to the need to ensure equitable geographical representation.

61. In addition to the election of the members of the Commission, the twelfth

---

49; A/55/61, paras. 25–29; A/54/429, paras. 55–69; A/53/456, paras. 55–69; A/52/487, paras. 43–53; and A/51/645, paras. 77–84).

Meeting of States Parties will also consider the possibility of granting observer status to the Commission. The possibility of observer status for the Commission, one of the three bodies established under the Convention and the only one of the three to which that status has not yet been accorded, was suggested at the last session by the President of the Eleventh Meeting of States Parties.

62. *Trust Fund for preparation of submissions to the Commission.*—The Trust Fund for the purpose of facilitating the preparation of submissions to the Commission on the Limits of the Continental Shelf for developing States, in particular the least developed countries and small island developing States, and compliance with Article 76 of the United Nations Convention on the Law of the Sea, was established by the General Assembly in its resolution 55/7 of 30 October 2000 upon the recommendation of the tenth Meeting of States Parties. The terms of reference of the Trust Fund are contained in Annex II to the resolution.

63. Its purpose is: (a) to provide assistance to States parties to meet their obligations under Article 76 of the Convention, and (b) to provide training to countries, in particular, the least developed among them and small island developing States, for preparing submissions to the Commission with respect to the outer limits of the continental shelf beyond 200 nautical miles, as appropriate (SPLOS/59). The fund currently contains over US$ 1 million, from two contributions of Norway.

64. One of the uses of the fund may be to provide both training to the appropriate technical and administrative staff of the coastal State making a submission to enable them to perform initial desktop studies and project planning, and to prepare the final submission documents when the necessary data have been acquired. The fund also may be used to provide for advisory assistance or consultancies, if needed. The data acquisition campaigns themselves, however, are not the object of the fund.

65. Submissions to the Commission must be prepared in conformity with the provisions of Article 76 and Annex II to the Convention (and for some States, Annex II of the Final Act), on the basis of the Scientific and Technical Guidelines prepared by the Commission. The training provided should take these requirements into account and should aim at enabling the submitting State's personnel to prepare most of the required documents themselves. The preparation of the submission may entail other costs that may also be met through the fund (e.g., software and hardware equipment, technical assistance, etc.).

66. In order to qualify for monies from the fund, developing States should address their applications to the Division for Ocean Affairs and the Law of the Sea, Office of Legal Affairs, United Nations. In applications for financial assistance to the fund, the requirements of section 4 of Annex II to resolution 55/7 must be satisfied. Section 4 states both the purposes for which financial assistance may be sought and the detailed information to be provided by the State for each purpose.

67. All applications will be considered by the Division with the assistance of an independent panel of experts, who will examine them on the basis of information given according to section 4 of the terms of reference and will recommend the amount of financial assistance to be given. The Division has already sent invitations to the permanent missions of Brazil, Japan, Norway, Papua New Guinea, Slovakia and South Africa to nominate their representatives to the panel of experts. Positive responses have been received from all of them.

68. The Secretary-General will provide financial assistance from the fund on the basis of the evaluation and recommendations of the Division. The decision by

the Secretary-General will be based solely on the financial needs of the requesting developing State and the availability of funds, with priority given to least developed countries and small island developing States. Payments will be made against receipts evidencing actual expenditures for approved costs.

69. This Trust Fund is not intended to be used to finance activities conducted by an international organization; however, reimbursements may be requested from the fund for airfare and per diem (presumably based on United Nations rates) for the participants from developing countries in appropriate training courses.

70. The Division has already received queries regarding the use of the Trust Fund monies from governmental and non-governmental institutions of Federated States of Micronesia, Fiji, Gambia, Guyana, India, Indonesia, Mozambique, Papua New Guinea and Solomon Islands. Formal applications are expected soon and are scheduled to be considered by the panel of experts in March 2002.

71. *Training courses and symposia (2001–2002).*—In its resolution 55/7, the General Assembly encouraged coastal States and relevant international organizations and institutions to consider developing and making available training courses on the delineation of the outer limits of the continental shelf beyond 200 nautical miles and for the preparation of submissions to be presented to the Commission.

72. Although it is not part of its mandate to conduct or organize training, the Commission decided at its eighth session in September 2000 to design an outline for a five-day training course for the delineation of the outer limits of the continental shelf beyond 200 nautical miles and for the preparation of a submission of a coastal State to the Commission (CLCS/24). The Commission undertook this work with a view to facilitating the preparation of submissions, especially by developing States, in accordance with the letter and spirit of the Convention, as well as with the guidelines of the Commission. It was also felt that the use of the outline would ensure a uniform and consistent practice among the courses.

73. Several regional training courses were conducted in 2001 and are scheduled for 2002 using this outline as the basis for the core curriculum. The practice of offering regional courses appears to be cost-effective for developing countries in the same region and allows the courses to take into account the wide variation in types of continental margins in different areas of the oceans.

74. The Government of Brazil hosted a five-day training course at Rio de Janeiro from 3 to 9 March 2002 on the delineation of the outer limits of the continental shelf beyond 200 nautical miles and for the preparation of submissions by interested coastal States. The course will be structured in accordance with the training modules and criteria developed by the Commission on the Limits of the Continental Shelf. The Government of Brazil, in compliance with the Convention, began in 1987 an intensive programme of acquisition, processing and interpretation of marine geophysical data with a view to defining the outer limits of its continental shelf. The training course is being offered as a result of the experience gained by Brazil in preparing its submission.

75. The second five-day training course is being organized jointly by the Southampton Oceanography Centre and the Hydrographic Office of the United Kingdom from 26 to 30 March 2001 in Southampton. The course will emphasize both the delineation of the outer limits of the extended continental shelf and the practical aspects of completing a submission to the Commission, and represents a modification of the core outline for a five-day training course, designed by the Commission.

A similar course was given in March 2001 (see A/56/58, par. 81). Information about the course is available on the Internet at www.soc.soton.ac.uk/COURSES/UNCLOS/index.html.

76. Sixty-five scientists and lawyers from 27 countries took part in the Conference on Accuracies and Uncertainties in Maritime Boundaries and Outer Limits, organized by the Advisory Board on Geodetic, Hydrographic and Marine Geo-Scientific Aspects of the Law of the Sea (ABLOS) (regarding the mandate and composition of ABLOS, see A/56/58, par. 75, endnote 11). The conference was convened at the International Hydrographic Bureau in Monaco on 18 and 19 October 2001. The conference proceedings, containing the 23 papers presented, are available at the ABLOS web site: http://www.gmat.unsw.edu.au/ablos/ablos01_papers.htm.

77. This was the second of the biannual international conferences sponsored by ABLOS. The first conference was hosted by the International Hydrographic Bureau in September 1999 (see A/56/58, paras. 65–68). The third conference is planned to be convened in 2003.

D. Deposit of Charts and/or Lists of Geographical Coordinates and Compliance with the Obligation of Due Publicity

78. Coastal States, under Article 16, paragraph 2, Article 47, paragraph 9, Article 75, paragraph 2, and Article 84, paragraph 2, of UNCLOS, are required to deposit with the Secretary-General of the United Nations charts showing straight baselines and archipelagic baselines as well as the outer limits of the territorial sea, the exclusive economic zone and the continental shelf; alternatively, lists of geographical coordinates of points, specifying the geodetic datum, may be substituted. Coastal States are also required to give due publicity to all these charts and lists of geographical coordinates. Furthermore, under Article 76, paragraph 9, coastal States are required to deposit with the Secretary-General charts and relevant information permanently describing the outer limits of the continental shelf extending beyond 200 nautical miles. In this case, due publicity is to be given by the Secretary-General. Together with the submission of their charts and/or lists of geographical coordinates, States parties are required to provide appropriate information regarding original geodetic datum.

79. In this connection, it should be noted that the deposit of charts or of lists of geographical coordinates of points with the Secretary-General of the United Nations is an international act by a State party to UNCLOS in order to conform with the deposit obligations referred to above, after the entry into force of UNCLOS. This act is addressed to the Secretary-General in the form of a note verbale or a letter by the Permanent Representative to the United Nations or other person considered as representing the State party. The mere existence or adoption of legislation or the conclusion of a maritime boundary delimitation treaty registered with the Secretariat, even if they contain charts or lists of coordinates, cannot be interpreted as an act of deposit with the Secretary-General under the Convention.

80. In its resolution 56/12, the General Assembly once again encouraged States parties to the Convention to deposit with the Secretary-General such charts and lists of geographical coordinates. So far, only 24 States have fully or partially complied

with their deposit obligations (see A/56/58, Annex III). No new deposits have been received since the issuance of the most recent report (A/56/58/Add.1). Descriptions of the deposits are published by the Division periodically in its Law of the Sea Information Circular.

E. Access to and from the Sea by Landlocked Developing Countries and Freedom of Transit

81. In its resolution 56/180 of 21 December 2001, entitled "Specific actions related to the particular needs and problems of landlocked developing countries," the General Assembly recognized that the lack of territorial access to the sea, aggravated by remoteness and isolation from world markets, and prohibitive transit costs and risks impose serious constraints on the overall socio-economic development efforts of the landlocked developing countries. In that context, the Assembly reaffirmed the right of access of landlocked countries to and from the sea and freedom of transit through the territory of transit countries by all means of transport, as set forth in Article 125 of UNCLOS, and called upon the landlocked developing countries and their transit neighbours to implement measures to strengthen further their cooperative and collaborative efforts to deal with transit transport issues, including bilateral and, as appropriate, subregional cooperation, inter alia, by improving the physical infrastructure and non-physical aspects of transit transport systems, strengthening and concluding, where appropriate, bilateral and subregional agreements to govern transit transport operations, developing joint ventures in the area of transit transport, and strengthening institutions and human resources dealing with transit transport.

82. The General Assembly also requested the Secretary-General to convene in 2003 an International Ministerial Meeting of Landlocked and Transit Developing Countries and Donor Countries and International Financial and Development Institutions on Transit Transport Cooperation to review the current situation of transit transport systems, including the implementation of the Global Framework for Transit Transport Cooperation of 1995, and to formulate, inter alia, appropriate policy measures and action-oriented programmes aimed at developing efficient transit transport systems.

83. A recent example of subregional cooperation is the "North-South" transport corridor agreement signed by the Russian Federation, the Islamic Republic of Iran, India and Oman at St. Petersburg on 12 September 2000. The agreement should provide tax-free access to the existing transportation infrastructure, inter alia, to the countries of the Caspian region; the estimated cost of transportation via this corridor is reported to be 15 percent to 20 percent less than via the Suez Canal, with a reduction of the transportation period by up to 20 days. It appears that a number of landlocked countries of Central Asia have expressed their interest in participating.

4. SHIPPING AND NAVIGATION

84. An unstable global economy and recent security concerns have exerted tremendous pressure on an industry which already offers a fairly low return on investment

generally. Some industry sectors are already showing an oversupply of tonnage, with a consequent downward pressure on freight rates. Since so many shipping companies throughout the world are operating on the margins of financial viability, there is a concern that declining economic conditions will eventually lead to deterioration in quality and a decline in standards.[6]

85. *Ship recycling/dismantling.*—An ageing world fleet and higher costs associated with the introduction of stricter requirements regarding ship construction may motivate many owners to send their ships for recycling primarily for their steel content. The projected increase in the number of ships being sent for recycling, and the poor health and environmental conditions at some of the major scrapping sites has focused public attention on an industry which has traditionally been self-regulatory.

86. The Commission on Sustainable Development in its decision 7/1 (par. 35 [h]) had noted that scrapping of ships represents an issue of concern with regard to the pollution of the environment and therefore called upon the IMO to look into the issue and encouraged States to ensure that responsible care is applied with regard to the disposal of decommissioned ships. IMO in its contribution to the present report stated that the IMO Marine Environment Protection Committee (MEPC) had an extensive exchange of views on how recycling of ships should be handled by IMO in cooperation with relevant organizations, including the International Labour Organization (ILO) and the United Nations Environment Programme (UNEP)/ Basel Convention and agreed that IMO had a role to play. It established a correspondence group to undertake further work on identifying the role of IMO and to recommend possible courses of action, including the development of an IMO Assembly resolution on ship recycling, for a more in-depth discussion at the forty-seventh session of MEPC in March 2002.[7]

87. The shipping industry has recently completed a Code of Practice on Ship Recycling, which establishes a series of best practices for shipping companies to adopt in respect of ships being sold for recycling.[8] Technical guidelines for the environmentally sound management of the dismantling of ships are under development within the framework of the Basel Convention in cooperation with ILO and IMO. The Technical Working Group of the Basel Convention, which is charged with the task of developing the guidelines, plans to finalize them for adoption at the sixth meeting of the Conference of the Parties to the Basel Convention in December 2002.[9]

88. There are a number of conditions which must be met before a vessel can be considered safe for navigation. Safe and efficient navigation also depends on safe, secure and crime-free navigational routes (see also par. 111). Effective implementation and enforcement of the body of law that governs all aspects of navigation is of fundamental importance not only for the safety of navigation, but also for the protection and preservation of the marine environment (see also paras. 123–127).

6. See opening address by the Secretary-General of IMO to the 22nd regular session of the IMO Assembly, available on the web site of IMO, at www.imo.org/HOME.html.

7. The report of the Correspondence Group is contained in document MEPC/47/3/3.

8. The Code is annexed to document MEPC 47/3/2.

9. For information on progress made by the Technical Working Group of the Basel Convention, see www.basel.int.

In the 20 years since the adoption of UNCLOS, this body of law has become increasingly substantial and broad in scope, thus posing a tremendous challenge to those responsible for its implementation.

A. Safety of Ships

89. UNCLOS balances the rights of the flag State to exercise exclusive jurisdiction over ships flying its flag and to enjoy rights of navigation with the duty to effectively exercise jurisdiction and control in administrative, technical and social matters over ships flying its flag. The flag State, in its exercise of jurisdiction, must take such measures as are necessary to ensure safety at sea with regard, inter alia, to the construction, equipment and seaworthiness of ships and the manning of ships, labour conditions and the training of crews (see Article 94, paragraphs 3, 4 and 5). Pursuant to the provisions of Articles 194 (3) (b) and 217 (2), flag State jurisdiction is to be exercised not only for the purposes of safety, but also to ensure the protection and preservation of the marine environment.

Ship Construction, Equipment and Seaworthiness

90. *Ship construction and equipment.*—The generally accepted international regulations, procedures and practices governing ship construction, equipment and seaworthiness which States have developed and are required by Article 94 and other provisions of UNCLOS to observe are basically those contained in SOLAS, the International Convention on Load Lines (LL Convention), MARPOL 73/78 (for oil tanker design) and in numerous IMO recommendations, guidelines and codes. Construction and equipment requirements for the safety of fishing vessels are contained in the 1977 Torremolinos Convention as amended by the 1993 Protocol.

91. Since the adoption of UNCLOS in 1982 and since UNCED in 1992 (Agenda 21, chap. 17, par. 17.30 (a) (viii)), IMO has adopted a range of measures aimed at improving ship construction. The most significant include: safety standards for roll-on/roll-off passenger ferries (adopted in 1988 and 1995); safety standards for oil tankers (double hulls) (adopted in 1992 and 2001); safety standards for bulk carriers (adopted in 1997); the harmonized system of survey and certification (adopted in 1988); and the International Safety Management Code (adopted in 1994).

92. A major advance in maritime communications took place when the Global Maritime Distress and Safety System (GMDSS), a worldwide network of automated emergency communications for ships at sea, was adopted in 1988. Furthermore, new requirements for the installation of navigational systems and equipment, such as the Global Navigation Satellite System (GNSS), the Electronic Chart Display and Information System (ECDIS), the Automatic Identification System (AIS) and the Voyage Data Recorder (VDR), will apply as of 1 July 2002, when the revised SOLAS Chapter V, which was adopted in 2000, enters into force. IMO reported that the IMO Assembly, at its 22nd session in November 2001, in preparation for the entry into force of the new SOLAS Chapter V requirements, adopted guidelines for recording events related to navigation (resolution A.916(22)) and guidelines for the operational use of shipborne automatic identification systems (resolution A.917(22)).

93. *Safety of fishing vessels.*—In the 2001 report on oceans and the law of the sea (A/56/58, paras. 126–131), attention was drawn to the high number of fatalities among fishers at sea: more than 70 per day. Reasons for the occurrence of fatal accidents identified by FAO[10] include the lack of entry into force of the 1993 Protocol to the Torremolinos Convention, which superseded the 1977 Torremolinos Convention; the lack of national regulations or, where they exist, their enforcement; lack of experience with offshore fishing operations and lack of knowledge about essential issues such as navigation, weather forecasting, communications and the vital culture of safety at sea. FAO has also drawn attention to the fact that more than 97 percent of the 15 million fishers employed in marine capture fisheries worldwide are working on vessels which are less than 24 metres in length and thus largely beyond the scope of international conventions and guidelines. The 1993 Protocol to the Torremolinos Convention only applies to fishing vessels more than 24 metres in length.

94. The IMO Assembly at its 22nd session (November 2001), in its resolution A.925(22), urged Governments to consider becoming a party to both the 1993 Protocol to the Torremolinos Convention and the 1995 International Convention on Standards of Training, Certification and Watchkeeping for Fishing Vessel Personnel (STCW-F Convention) and invited Governments experiencing difficulties in the process of becoming parties to inform IMO of the circumstances thereof, so that consideration might be given to appropriate action being taken in that respect, including the provision of necessary technical assistance. The Maritime Safety Committee (MSC) was requested to review the situation concerning entry into force of the said instruments and, in the light of such review, to take action as it deemed appropriate.

95. *Small fishing vessels and small ships.*—The safety of small fishing vessels, that is, those less than 24 metres in length, and of small ships, that is, ships too small to be covered by SOLAS and the LL Convention, is also receiving increasing attention at the regional level. The South Pacific, for example, has adopted several safety measures, including regulations covering the Safety of Small Boats and Small Fishing Vessels (see Annex II to the present report). Common safety rules for small ships were adopted in 1996 by Bangladesh, China, Indonesia, the Islamic Republic of Iran, Malaysia, the Philippines, the Republic of Korea, Singapore and Thailand. In the Mediterranean region, work is continuing on the development of an instrument to regulate the navigation of pleasure craft.

Training of Crew and Labour Conditions

96. UNCLOS, Article 94, requires flag States to take measures to ensure safety at sea with regard to the manning of ships, labour conditions and the training of crews, taking into account applicable international instruments. The measures must conform to generally accepted international regulations, procedures and practices and the flag State must take any steps which may be necessary to secure their observance.

97. *Training of crew.*—The international regulations, procedures and practices applicable to the training of crews are set out in the International Convention on Standards of Training, Certification and Watchkeeping for Seafarers (STCW Convention), as amended in 1995. A significant feature of this Convention is that it gives

10. FAO report on the State of World Fisheries and "Aquaculture 2000."

IMO some responsibility for ensuring that its requirements are met. By 1 February 2002, all seafarers must have been trained in compliance with the 1995 amendments to STCW and carry certificates to that effect. In spite of the 1 February deadline, it appears that many seafarers have not yet been able to obtain the necessary certification required by STCW and parties to the Convention have had difficulties in concluding the arrangements required to process reciprocal recognition endorsements.[11]

98. *Labour conditions.*—The enquiry into ship safety by the International Commission on Shipping, published in March 2001, concluded that "for thousands of today's international seafarers, life at sea is modern slavery and their workplace is a slave ship." In its report the Commission makes a number of recommendations, mainly on crew issues and port State control activities, which are directed for action by flag States, coastal States, shippers' councils, classification societies, the United States Government, the European Commission, IMO, ILO, FAO, the International Group of P&I Clubs, international shipping organizations and owners.[12]

99. The international instruments governing labour conditions referred to in Article 94 of UNCLOS consist of the body of maritime labour standards adopted by ILO, better known as the International Seafarers Code, which comprises numerous Conventions and Recommendations, of which the Merchant Shipping (Minimum Standards) Convention, 1976 (No. 147) is the most far-reaching and applies to the majority of the world merchant fleet.

100. ILO reported that at its 29th session, in January 2001, the ILO Joint Maritime Commission agreed to consolidate the existing ILO maritime instruments into a single instrument. It also agreed that the new instrument should be easily ratifiable by a large majority of ILO member States; be clear enough to be rapidly implemented into national legislation; enable port State control officers to check its effective application on board vessels; be easily understandable by seafarers and shipowners; and be rapidly amendable, to take account of the accelerated pace of change in the industry. At its 280th session, in March 2001, the Governing Body of ILO accepted these recommendations and decided to convene a series of preparatory meetings with a view to the adoption of a new Convention in 2005.

101. The first such preparatory meeting, the High-level Tripartite Working Group on Maritime Labour Standards, held in December 2001, endorsed the proposal to consolidate the maritime labour standards and exchanged preliminary ideas on various points to be taken into account in elaborating the new instrument. A tripartite subgroup was established, which will meet in June 2002. The next meeting of the Working Group will be held in October 2002.[13]

102. *Provision of financial security for seafarers' claims.*—The IMO Assembly at its 22nd session, in November 2001, adopted two resolutions devoted solely to seafarers: resolution A.930(22), adopting "Guidelines on provision of financial security in case

11. For further information, see Circular STCW.7/Cir.12, available on the web site of IMO, at www.imo.org/HOME.html.

12. The report of the Commission is available on its web site, at www.icons.org.au.

13. The reports prepared by ILO for the Working Group and the report of the meeting are available on the web site of ILO at www.ilo.org/public/english/standard/rclm/gb/ docs/gb283/pdf/lils-7.pdf.

of abandonment of seafarers," and resolution A.931(22), adopting "Guidelines on shipowners' responsibilities in respect of contractual claims for personal injury to or death of seafarers." Both resolutions contain a human rights clause, and one contains a model release form. The guidelines were approved by the ILO Governing Body at its 282nd session, in November 2001, and took effect on 1 January 2002. Their implementation is to be monitored by the Joint IMO/ILO Ad Hoc Expert Working Group on Liability and Compensation regarding Claims for Death, Personal Injury and Abandonment of Seafarers, which will also assess the need for further action.[14]

B. Transport of Cargo

103. The volume of goods transported by sea has increased significantly over past 20 years since the adoption of UNCLOS. It has been estimated, according to IMO criteria, that more than 50 percent of packaged goods and bulk cargo transported by sea today can be regarded as dangerous, hazardous or harmful to the environment.

104. UNCLOS does not specifically address the carriage of dangerous goods by ships, except in Articles 22 (2) and 23.

105. SOLAS Chapter VI deals with the carriage of all types of cargo except liquids and gases in bulk. The carriage by sea of dangerous and hazardous substances is regulated in SOLAS Chapter VII, MARPOL 73/78, Annexes II and III (see paras. 381–382), and in several IMO Codes.[15]

106. *Radioactive material.*—The 1979 Convention on the Physical Protection of Nuclear Material requires all Contracting Parties to ensure the protection of nuclear material in their territory or on board their ships while in international nuclear transport. Carriage requirements for highly radioactive cargo, for example, design, fabrication, maintenance of packaging, handling, storage and receipt, which are applicable to all modes of transport, are contained in the International Atomic Energy Agency (IAEA) Regulations for the Safe Transport of Radioactive Material. The regulations were most recently revised in 1996[16] and became mandatory on 1 January 2002.

107. The development of the INF Code, as also encouraged by UNCED in Agenda 21, Chapter 17, paragraph 17.30 (a) (ix), was completed in 1993. The Code regulates the construction, equipment and operation of ships carrying irradiated nuclear fuel. It was amended in 1997 to require shipboard emergency plans and

14. See terms of reference of the Working Group in the report of their third session, document IMO/ILO/WGLCCS 3/9, annex 4.

15. International Maritime Dangerous Goods (IMDG) Code, International Code for the Construction and Equipment of Ships Carrying Dangerous Chemicals in Bulk (IBC Code), Code for the Construction and Equipment of Ships Carrying Dangerous Chemicals in Bulk (BCH Code), International Code for the Construction and Equipment of Ships Carrying Liquified Gases in Bulk (IGC Code), Code for Safe Practice for Solid Bulk Cargoes (BC Code), and Code for the Safe Carriage of Irradiated Nuclear Fuel, Plutonium and High-level Radioactive Waste in Flasks on Board Ships (INF Code). SOLAS Chapter VII provides for the mandatory application of the IBC and IGC Codes, and most recently also the INF Code. The IBC and BCH Codes are mandatory under MARPOL 73/78.

16. IAEA Safety Standards Series No. TS-R-1 CST-1, Revised.

notification in the event of an accident involving INF materials. The Code was made mandatory in 1999 by virtue of the adoption of amendments to SOLAS Chapter VII, which entered into force on 1 January 2001.

108. The shipments of mixed oxide fuel (MOX) between the United Kingdom and France and Japan continue to be of great concern to the coastal States along the routes currently being used for those shipments.[17] The Commission on Sustainable Development, in paragraph 21 (h) of its decision 9/1, on "Energy for sustainable development," adopted in April 2001, and the IAEA General Conference, in its resolution GC(45)/RES/10 adopted at its 45th session, in September 2001, called for further efforts, at the international, regional and bilateral levels, to examine and further improve measures and international regulations relevant to the international maritime transport of radioactive material and spent fuel, consistent with international law, and stressed the importance of having effective liability measures in place to ensure against harm to human health and the environment as well as actual economic loss due to an accident. The IAEA General Conference urged member States shipping radioactive material and spent fuel to provide, as appropriate, assurances to potentially affected States that their national regulations were in accord with the IAEA Transport Regulations. It welcomed the practice of some shipping States and operators of undertaking timely consultations with relevant coastal States in advance of shipments and invited others to do so.

109. IAEA is planning to convene a Conference on the Safety of Transport of Radioactive Material early in 2003. The Conference will establish a platform for discussing all aspects of safety in the international transport of radioactive material.

C. Safety of Navigation

110. Ships are required by UNCLOS to observe the applicable rights of passage in the various maritime zones, as well as the measures which coastal States may take in regulating maritime traffic. Detailed rules governing safety of navigation and the prevention of collisions at sea, with which compliance is required by UNCLOS, have been developed by IMO. SOLAS Chapter V and the International Regulations for Preventing Collisions at Sea (COLREG) constitute the main instruments in that regard.

111. *Promoting navigational safety by adequate charting.*—UNCLOS requires States to give appropriate publicity to any danger to navigation of which they have knowledge within their territorial sea (Article 24), in straits used for international navigation (Article 44), or in archipelagic sea lanes (Article 54). The International Hydrographic Organization (IHO) and IMO have in the past pointed to the need for coastal States to discharge their responsibilities with respect to surveying and charting waters under their jurisdiction with a view to improving the safety of navigation and the protection of the marine environment. The General Assembly, in its resolution 56/12 on "Oceans and the law of the sea," invited IHO, in cooperation with

17. The text of recent declarations by some States and regional groups regarding safety in the maritime transport of radioactive material were presented to the IAEA General Conference at its forty-fifth session (September 2001) by the Chairman of the Latin American and Caribbean Group, in document GC(45)/INF/18.

other relevant international organizations and interested Member States, to provide the necessary assistance to States, in particular to developing countries, in order to enhance hydrographic capability to ensure, in particular, the safety of navigation and the protection of the marine environment.

112. PERSGA in its contribution to the report (via UNEP) provided information on its Strategic Action Programme (SAP) for the Red Sea and Gulf of Aden. With support from the World Bank, a full hydrographic analysis has been undertaken covering 750 square nautical miles in the Red Sea, and the correct location of rocks and other hazards have been identified for the first time and several areas which were previously thought to be shallow areas have been proved not to be (for details of the PERSGA activities in this regard, see paras. 479–480).

113. IMO is currently executing a GEF/World Bank project in the East Asian Sea aimed at developing a regional network of electronic navigational charts to enhance navigational safety and environmental management. The first phase of the project has been executed in the Straits of Malacca and Singapore.[18]

D. Assistance at sea

Rescue of Persons in Distress

114. The duty to render assistance to any person found in distress at sea is clearly established as a principle of maritime law and enshrined in Article 98 of UNCLOS, SOLAS, Article 10 of the 1989 Salvage Convention, and in the 1979 International Convention on Maritime Search and Rescue. Article 98 of UNCLOS requires both flag States and coastal States to act in order to enforce the duty of assistance: the flag State, by requiring vessels flying its flag to assist any person in danger at sea; and the coastal State, by creating an adequate and effective search and rescue service.

115. The 1979 International Convention on Maritime Search and Rescue (SAR Convention), as amended in 1998,[19] defines the term rescue as "an operation to retrieve persons in distress, provide for their initial medical or other needs, and deliver them to a place of safety." The Convention does not address what constitutes a place of safety.

116. After the incident involving the vessel *Tampa* in August 2001, the IMO Assembly, in its resolution A.920(22), entitled "Review of safety measures and procedures for the treatment of persons rescued at sea," requested the IMO committees to review, on a priority basis, the international conventions referred to in the resolution (i.e., those listed in par. 114 above) and other IMO instruments under their scope, for the purpose of identifying any existing gaps, inconsistencies, ambiguities, vagueness or other inadequacies and, in the light of such review, to take action as appropriate so that: (a) survivors in distress incidents might be provided assistance regardless of nationality or status or the circumstances in which they are found; (b) ships which have retrieved persons in distress at sea might be able to deliver the survivors to a place of safety; and (c) survivors, regardless of nationality or status, including undocumented migrants, asylum-seekers and refugees, and stowaways might be treated, while on board, in the manner prescribed in the relevant IMO

18. See IMO document MEPC 46/INF.35.

19. The amendments entered into force on 1 January 2000.

instruments and in accordance with relevant international agreements and long-standing humanitarian maritime traditions.

117. *Search and rescue facilities.*—Coastal States are required by Article 98 of UNCLOS and by the SAR Convention to provide for the establishment of search and rescue facilities. IMO has in the past drawn attention to the fact that search and rescue (SAR) facilities are insufficient for effective operations globally, because a considerable number of States have not identified and made available responsible authorities to receive and act upon distress alerts. Only 66 States have become parties to the SAR Convention and many States have not concluded agreements establishing SAR regions in compliance with the annex to the Convention. The IMO Assembly at its 22nd session, in November 2001, in its resolution A.919(22), invited Governments to consider providing technical assistance for the provision and coordination of SAR services to States requesting such assistance.

118. The United Nations Office for Outer Space Affairs in its contribution to the present report provided information on the international COSPAS-SARSAT satellite system for search and rescue, which provides distress alert and location information for maritime, aviation and land users and supports the search and rescue objectives of IMO and the International Civil Aviation Organization. The system is available to any country on a nondiscriminatory basis and free of charge for the end-user in distress.[20]

Vessels in Distress

119. The incident last year involving the vessel *Castor,* in which the salvors of the fully laden tanker (carrying 29,500 tonnes of unleaded gasoline) were unable to find a sheltered place to effect cargo transfer and repairs for some 35 days, raised a great deal of concern about the provision of places of refuge for ships in distress.

120. As a result, IMO has decided to address as a matter of priority the issue of providing places of refuge to vessels in distress at sea, from the "operational safety" point of view, by preparing guidelines for the identification and designation of suitable places of refuge; the evaluation of risks associated with the provision of places of refuge; and actions a master of a ship should take when in need of places of refuge.[21] Legal issues, such as jurisdiction, rights of coastal States, liability, insurance and bonds, will be considered by the Legal Committee.[22]

E. Implementation and Enforcement

121. IMO reports that at present, between 110 and 143 States (depending on the treaty) have become parties to the main IMO Conventions. Since the general degree of acceptance of these shipping Conventions is mainly related to their implementation by flag States, it is of paramount importance to note that States parties to these

20. For further information, see www.cospas-sarsat.org.

21. See report of the forty-seventh session of the Subcommittee on Safety of Navigation, document NAV 47/13, paras. 12.28–12.33, and Annexes 18 and 19.

22. See report of the eighty-third session of the IMO Legal Committee, LEG 83/14, paras. 170–174.

Conventions in all cases represent more than 90 percent of the world's merchant fleet.

122. With many of the international rules and standards in place, the emphasis has shifted in recent years from the development of new rules to the effective implementation of those which have already been adopted. The adoption of the ISM Code, the establishment of the IMO Subcommittee on Flag State Implementation, the expanded role that has been given to the IMO Secretariat in monitoring the implementation of the STCW Convention, and the growing number of Memoranda of Understanding on port State control at the regional level, all attest to this change in emphasis.

123. *Flag State implementation.*—The responsibility for ensuring that the global rules and standards are actually put in place on all ships rests with the flag State. Indeed, safety of navigation and the prevention of pollution from vessels depend on the exercise of its effective jurisdiction. In recognition of the central role of the flag State and in view of the fact that some States may lack the skills and resources to carry out their responsibilities effectively, IMO has over the years developed measures which, inter alia, strengthen the management of shipping companies and assist flag States in assessing their performance. IMO provides technical assistance to individual States upon request. It has also been very active in strengthening port State control.

124. The International Safety Management (ISM) Code, which provides a framework for shipping companies' management and operation of their fleet, will become mandatory for all ships on 1 July 2002. Passenger ships, oil tankers, chemical tankers, gas carriers, bulk carriers and high-speed cargo craft of 500 gross tonnage and above have been required to implement the Code since 1998, when it entered into force. The IMO Assembly adopted "Revised Guidelines on the implementation of the ISM Code by Administrations" in November 2001 (resolution A.913[22]) to take account of the second phase of ISM implementation, as well as the amendments to the Code on certification and verification, which were adopted in 2000.

125. In preparing for the implementation of the second phase of the Code, IMO provided assistance to maritime administrations through technical cooperation activities and requested the assistance of port State control systems in assessing the level of implementation. In addition, IMO started working on issues related to the registration of ships and the transfer of flag in order to assess the need for introducing international procedures and requirements supporting the goals of IMO, taking into account previous considerations of these issues within and outside IMO. The IMO Assembly, in its resolution A.923(22), on "Measures to prevent the registration of 'phantom' ships," invited Governments to exhaust all means available to them to obtain evidence that a ship previously registered under another State's flag has been deleted from the register, or that the consent to the transfer of the ship has been obtained from that State's register.

126. In order to assist flag States in assessing their capabilities, IMO revised the procedures for the self-assessment of flag State performance to incorporate criteria and performance indicators (IMO Assembly resolution A.912[22]) and invited flag States to collect more detailed information on the authorizations granted to recognized organizations to work on their behalf.

127. IMO also approved an Assembly resolution on "Measures to further strengthen flag State implementation" (resolution A.914[22]) as part of the develop-

ment of a culture of safety and environmental conscience in activities undertaken by IMO. Such initiative complemented the ongoing work on the invitation of the Commission on Sustainable Development in its decision 7/1, paragraph 35 (a), to develop binding measures to ensure that ships of all flag States meet international rules and standards so as to give full and complete effect to UNCLOS, especially Article 91 (Nationality of Ships), as well as provisions of other relevant conventions.

128. As regards measures to strengthen flag State implementation in the area of fisheries, IMO reported that it had considered the report of the first meeting of the Joint FAO/IMO Working Group, containing proposed measures relating to the member States' responsibility either as flag Sates or as port States. It recognized that, although measures relating to fisheries management were outside its competence, there were many safety and environmental protection issues relating to the IUU fishing which were within the purview of IMO, and that the consideration of these issues would be of assistance to FAO. It recognized that the transfer of ships was also a problem in relation to illegal fishing activities.

129. *Port State control.*—While never removing the primary obligation on flag States for ensuring compliance with standards, port State control is an important part of the safety net and an effective weapon to be used against substandard operators. One of the strengths of port State control is that the standards it upholds are the same throughout the world. The objective is to secure a high level of quality universally and to remove the non-compliers from the scene.

130. IMO has adopted comprehensive guidelines and recommendations on port State control procedures in respect of ships that are required to comply with SOLAS, the LL Convention, MARPOL 73/78, STCW and the International Convention on Tonnage Measurement for Ships (IMO Assembly resolution A.787[19], as amended by resolution A.882[21]).

131. Building upon the increased involvement of States, other than the flag States, in the inspection of ships and the investigation of casualties, IMO in its contribution noted that it has worked towards the development of a harmonized global regime for port State control activities through the renewed support to regional Memoranda of Understanding on port State control by the training of port State control officers, assistance to port State control committees and the promotion of communication and exchange of information between flag and port States. To date, eight regional agreements on port State control have been signed and are currently in operation. The 1982 Paris Memorandum of Understanding on Port State Control is the first such agreement. The others cover the following regions: Latin America, Asia-Pacific, the Caribbean, the Mediterranean, the Indian Ocean, West and Central Africa and the Black Sea. A regional Memorandum of Understanding for the Gulf region is being prepared for consideration and adoption.

132. Given the success of the port State control concept in the area of maritime safety and pollution prevention, consideration has been given to its application in the fisheries sector. The 1995 Fish Stocks Agreement provides for the exercise of port State jurisdiction to promote the effectiveness of subregional, regional and global conservation and management measures. IMO notes that while there was no legal basis for extending existing port State control provisions in IMO instruments to fishing vessels, since the 1993 Protocol to the Torremolinos Convention and the STCW-F Convention are not yet in force, encouraging member States to ratify those instruments at an early date would be a positive means of dealing with the problem.

IMO has also offered to cooperate with FAO to develop a port State control regime of its own through sharing of experience and expertise on the matter.

5. CRIMES AT SEA

133. Maritime security can be threatened by a terrorist attack and also as a result of other criminal activities at sea, for example, acts of piracy and armed robbery against ships, smuggling of migrants, illicit traffic in narcotic drugs or psychotropic substances and illicit traffic in firearms. Many of these crimes are the work of organized criminals whose global reach and evasion of national controls threaten the security and stability of all States and make effective national measures and global action imperative.

134. In the 20 years since the adoption of UNCLOS, crimes at sea have become more prevalent and are increasing. Indeed, the framers of the Convention never envisaged many of the crimes which exist today and, as a result, either included only a general provision (e.g., in the case of illicit traffic in narcotic drugs and psychotropic substances) or none at all (e.g., in the case of hijacking or smuggling of migrants by sea), regarding their suppression. Since 1982, a number of conventions have been adopted which are aimed at the suppression and combating of specific criminal activities, including those which take place at sea.[23] However, it is important to note that the objectives of these conventions are in turn supported by other provisions of UNCLOS, for example, those relating to the status of ships, duties of the flag State and the right of visit with respect to ships without nationality. Indeed, it must be borne in mind that if flag States were to comply with the obligations set out in UNCLOS and exercise their jurisdiction and control over ships flying their flag and ensure that they comply with relevant international rules and regulations, it would greatly help prevent their illegal use for criminal activities. The United Nations Department of Political Affairs, in its contribution to the present report, highlighted the importance of full flag State control in the context of conflict prevention and peace-building in order to prevent the illegal use of ships for arms and diamond trafficking. They suggested that a comparative study of the degree of control of flag States could be instructive.

135. Major obstacles for coastal States in the suppression and combating of crimes at sea include the lack or shortage of trained personnel and equipment; the obsolescence or inadequacy of most national legislation; and weak maritime law enforcement capability of national agencies. A necessary first step in addressing some

23. The 1988 United Nations Convention against Illicit Traffic in Narcotic Drugs and Psychotropic Substances includes an Article on illicit traffic by sea, which builds upon the general requirement in Article 108 of UNCLOS to cooperate in the suppression of illicit traffic in narcotic drugs and psychotropic substances engaged in by ships on the high seas. The 1988 IMO Convention for the Suppression of Unlawful Acts against the Safety of Maritime Navigation (1988 SUA Convention), its 1988 Protocol for the Suppression of Unlawful Acts against the Safety of Fixed Platforms Located on the Continental Shelf (1988 SUA Protocol) and the 2000 Protocol against the Smuggling of Migrants by Land, Sea and Air, supplementing the United Nations Convention against Transnational Organized Crime, provide a legal regime for dealing with criminal activities taking place on the high seas or in the exclusive economic zone, which are not specifically addressed in UNCLOS.

of these problems is for States to become parties to the relevant conventions that govern the suppression and combating of these crimes and ensure that they have the necessary legislation in place. Some States may require technical assistance in this regard. The General Assembly in its resolution 56/120 of 19 December 2001, entitled "Action against transnational organized crime: assistance to States in capacity-building with a view to facilitating the implementation of the United Nations Convention against Transnational Organized Crime and the Protocols thereto," noting that the fight against organized crime is a common and shared responsibility of the international community necessitating cooperation at the bilateral and multilateral levels, encouraged Member States to make voluntary contributions to the United Nations Crime Prevention and Criminal Justice Fund for the provision to developing countries and countries with economies in transition of technical assistance they might require for the implementation of the Convention and the Protocols thereto, including assistance for the preparatory measures needed for their implementation.

136. Cooperation among States is also very important in the area of enforcement. The harmonization of legal approaches to enforcement at the bilateral or regional level clearly facilitates and promotes cooperation. In addition, cooperative law enforcement training can lead to common maritime law enforcement procedures that can be extremely beneficial in combating maritime crime.[24]

137. This part of the report focuses on some of the most serious crimes at sea, such as acts of terrorism, piracy and armed robbery against ships, smuggling of migrants, stowaways and illicit traffic in narcotic drugs or psychotropic substances. However, it should be borne in mind that violations of international rules and standards for the protection or preservation of the marine environment, such as illegal dumping or illegal discharge of pollutants from vessels, or the violation of rules regulating the exploitation of the living marine resources, such as illegal fishing, can also constitute criminal acts and threaten maritime security.

A. Prevention and Suppression of Acts of Terrorism against Shipping

138. Maritime security has been placed high on the agenda of the international community following the terrorist attacks on the United States of America on 11 September 2001. Attention has focused on the adequacy of measures to prevent acts of terrorism, which threaten the security of passengers and crews and the safety of ships.

139. Over the years, a number of measures have been adopted by IMO to prevent unlawful acts which threaten the safety of ships and the security of their passengers and crews, the most significant of which are the 1988 SUA Convention and the 1988 SUA Protocol.[25]

140. Both the General Assembly (resolution 56/12) and the IMO Assembly

24. See cooperative measures recommended by the Council for Security Cooperation in the Asia Pacific in its Memorandum No. 5.

25. See also IMO Assembly resolution A.584(14), entitled "Measures to prevent unlawful acts which threaten the safety of ships and the security of their passengers and crews;" MSC/Circ.443 on "Measures to prevent unlawful acts against passengers and crews;" and MSC/Circ.754, "Passenger ferry security."

(resolution A.924[22]) have urged States to become parties to the 1988 SUA Convention and its Protocol and to ensure their effective implementation. The IMO Assembly in its resolution A.924(22) also requested the relevant IMO committees to review, as a matter of high priority, whether any of the existing IMO measures needed to be updated or whether there was a need to adopt new security measures. The Secretary-General of IMO has been requested to take appropriate measures, within the Integrated Technical Cooperation Programme, to assist Governments in assessing, putting in place or enhancing, as the case may be, appropriate infrastructure and measures to strengthen port safety and security to prevent and suppress terrorist activities directed against ports and port personnel as well as ships in port areas, passengers and crews.

141. A Conference on Maritime Security will be held by IMO in December 2002 to consider any new or amended regulations to enhance ship and port security. An inter-sessional working group met from 11 to 15 February 2002. Measures proposed for consideration include: (a) review of issues relating to the installation of automatic identification systems on ships; (b) consideration of the need for security plans on ships, port facilities and offshore terminals; (c) review of the need for identification verification and background security checks for seafarers; (d) ensuring a secure chain of custody for containers from their port of origin to their destination;[26] and (e) introduction of a mandatory requirement to provide details on the beneficial owner of a vessel prior to entry into port.[27]

B. Piracy and Armed Robbery against Ships

142. The General Assembly, at its fifty-sixth session, in its resolution 56/12 on "Oceans and the law of the sea," expressed its deep concern once again at the "continued increase in the number of incidents of piracy and armed robbery at sea, the harm they cause to seafarers, and the threats they pose to the safety of shipping and to the other uses of the sea, including marine scientific research and, consequently, to the marine and coastal environment, which are exacerbated further by the involvement of transnational organized crime."

1. Reports on Incidents

143. *The situation in 2000.*—IMO compiles and distributes monthly, quarterly and annual reports on piracy and armed robbery against ships submitted by Governments and international organizations. Monthly reports list all incidents reported to IMO. Quarterly reports are composite reports accompanied by an analysis, on a regional basis, of the situation and an indication whether the frequency of incidents is increasing or decreasing and advising on any new feature or pattern of significance.

26. Proposed by the United States. See IMO document FAL 29/2/1, par. 5.

27. Proposed by the International Confederation of Free Trade Unions in a submission to the seventy-fifth session of the Maritime Safety Committee, to be held in May 2002.

144. Based on the periodical reports and additional information provided orally by the IMO secretariat, the IMO Maritime Safety Committee (MSC) at its 74th session, in 2001, noted with deep concern that the number of acts of piracy and armed robbery against ships which were reported to have occurred in 2000 was 471, representing an increase of 162 (52 percent) over the figure for 1999; and that the total number of incidents of piracy and armed robbery against ships reported to have occurred from 1984 to the end of May 2001 was 2,309 (see also A/56/121, par. 253). Most of the attacks worldwide were reported to have occurred in territorial waters while the ships were at anchor or berthed. The Committee was particularly concerned that, during the same period, the crews of the ships involved in the reported incidents had been violently attacked by groups of 5 to 10 persons carrying knives or guns, as a result of which 72 crew members had been killed, 129 had been wounded and 5 had been reported missing.[28]

145. MSC decided that a more precise distinction in the reporting of piracy and armed robbery attacks was needed to distinguish between actual attacks and attempts (threats) thereof, so that a more accurate picture of the situation might be drawn. The Committee also once again invited all Governments (of flag, port and coastal States) and the industry to intensify their efforts to eradicate those unlawful acts. It urged: (a) flag States to make reports on attacks or threats thereof using the agreed format; (b) coastal States to report on action they have taken when informed of such unlawful acts having taken place within their national waters; (c) the industry to ensure reporting of all incidents to flag/coastal States; and (d) coastal States to put in place national legislation for dealing with incidents piracy and armed robbery.

146. *The situation in 2001.*—According to the annual report on piracy for the year 2001 issued by the International Maritime Bureau (IMB) of the International Chamber of Commerce (ICC) on the basis of statistics of incidents of piracy and armed robbery reported to its Piracy Reporting Centre, during 2001, the total number of reported attacks worldwide dropped to 335, compared to 469 in 2000, but still remained higher than the 300 attacks reported in 1999. Most of the attacks took place while the ships were at anchor. However, there has been a significant rise in incidents of hijackings, which normally involve organized crime syndicates. During 2001, 16 incidents took place, compared to 8 the previous year. Another new trend which is emerging in the northern part of the Malacca Straits involves kidnapping of crew members for ransom. This "kidnap and ransom" trend previously was confined to Somali waters. The amount demanded by the attackers is normally not exorbitant and shipowners pay the amount to avoid complications. IMB believes that there may be more incidents which may have gone unreported because owners are being threatened and warned not to report to the authorities.[29]

147. The industry continues to express its concerns regarding the frequency and the ferocity of piracy and armed robbery attacks, recognizing that many coastal States are unable or ill-equipped to counter this menace. They believe that pirates and armed robbers are very well aware of the weaknesses in enforcement and the

28. Report of the seventy-fourth session of the Maritime Safety Committee, document MSC 74/24, par. 17.2.

29. See excerpts from the report on the web site of ICC at www.iccwbo.org.

law, and cross maritime jurisdictions intentionally to evade arrest. There is now an increasing fear that the rise in piracy and armed robbery may undermine sea transport in the areas where most of the incidents take place.[30] In this regard, it can be noted that so far there are basically no insurance premiums for vessels operating in such areas.[31]

148. The industry has called upon the United Nations to encourage its Members to take preventive action, such as allocating sufficient manpower in the form of law enforcement personnel; instituting national legislation addressing specific crimes and enforcing appropriate punishment of offenders; establishing an environment of partnership and cooperation involving coastal States, flag States and the shipping industry in confronting these risks; and instituting robust security measures around terminals and installations, including patrols around all vessels entering and leaving, at anchor or lying alongside in a port, as well as restrictions aimed at only allowing authorized personnel to enter port areas.[32]

2. *Actions Taken at the Global and Regional Levels*

149. *The Consultative Process and the General Assembly.*—The need for capacity-building and the cooperation of all States and relevant international bodies, at both regional and global levels, as well as the business sectors to prevent and combat piracy and armed robbery was emphasized at the second meeting of the Consultative Process during the discussions on coordination and cooperation in combating piracy and armed robbery at sea[33]—one of the areas of focus—and reinforced by the General Assembly at its fifty-sixth session (see resolution 56/12, paras. 29–32).

150. *International Maritime Organization.*—IMO will consider the General Assembly resolution and the report of the Consultative Process at the forthcoming session of MSC in May 2002. IMO reported that the IMO Assembly at its 22nd session, in November 2001, adopted the Code of Practice for the Investigation of the Crimes of Piracy and Armed Robbery against Ships (resolution A.922(22)) and "Measures to prevent the registration of 'phantom' ships" (resolution A.923[22]). (Details on these resolutions are provided in the 2001 report, A/56/58, paras. 196–201.) Other measures under consideration in IMO to reduce the operation of phantom ships are to mark ships indelibly and visibly with the IMO ship identification number externally and provide access to the Lloyds Maritime Information Services database.

151. As regards developments at the regional level, the IMO Secretariat in its contribution provided information on the evaluation and assessment missions it had undertaken during 2001. The assessment missions follow up on previous IMO piracy seminars and workshops and examine, with responsible governmental representatives, what measures the national authorities responsible for anti-piracy activities had taken to implement the relevant IMO guidelines; where such measures had not

30. Report of the IMB Fourth International Meeting on Piracy and Phantom Ships, 26 and 27 June 2001, Kuala Lumpur.

31. There may be a basic war premium of 0.1 percent, which can be raised on a seven-day basis, but it appears that incidents of piracy have little effect.

32. Measures proposed by the Baltic and International Maritime Council in a letter to the Secretary-General of the United Nations and the Secretary-General of IMO.

33. The report of the second meeting is contained in A/56/121.

been successful and what had impeded their implementation; and, eventually, how IMO could assist in overcoming any difficulties encountered in the process.

152. IMO conducted three evaluation and assessment missions in 2001: one in Indonesia (13 and 14 March 2001); one in Singapore for selected countries bordering the Indian Ocean, the Malacca Straits and the South China Sea/Pacific Ocean (15 and 16 March 2001), and one in Ecuador for selected countries of the Latin American region (25 and 26 September 2001). The next evaluation and assessment mission to be conducted by IMO will be for West Africa and will be held in Ghana in March 2002.

153. IMO reported that the main problems identified by the participants at the assessment missions in Indonesia and in Singapore meetings were: (a) the continuing economic situation prevailing in certain parts of the region; (b) the resource constraints on law enforcement agencies; (c) the lack of communication and cooperation among the various national agencies involved; (d) the slow response time after an incident has been reported to the coastal State concerned by affected ships; (e) general problems of incident reporting, for example, alerting the nearest coastal States as well as other ships in the areas of a ship under attack or threat of attack; (f) the need for the timely and proper investigation into reported incidents; (g) the need for the prosecution of pirates and armed robbers once they are apprehended; and (h) the lack of regional cooperation. With respect to the latter, the Singapore Regional Meeting invited the Secretary-General of IMO to undertake consultations with Governments in the region for the purpose of convening, at an appropriate time, a meeting to consider concluding a regional agreement on cooperation against piracy and armed robbery against ships.[34]

154. The regional meeting in Ecuador identified the same main problem areas as the Singapore meeting. The participants agreed on the importance of strengthening subregional and regional cooperation and coordination among countries in the region by such means as exchange of intelligence, patrolling certain vulnerable areas, joint and/or coordinating exercises, and also agreed that the Operative Network for Regional Cooperation among Maritime Authorities of South America, Mexico, Panama and Cuba (ROCRAM) should be used as a coordinating body for developing a regional strategy on cooperation and coordination.[35]

155. The Department of Political Affairs in its contribution to the present report suggested that a comparative assessment of the degree of compliance by Governments with the series of actions recommended by IMO and other international organizations and forums for preventing and suppressing acts of piracy and armed robbery against ships could greatly help to determine the most efficient measures and the level of awareness of Governments of the dangers posed to national and regional interests by acts of piracy and armed robbery against ships.

C. Smuggling of Migrants

156. Incidents involving illegal migration are escalating and defy an easy solution. Poverty, lack of opportunities, political and social violence in the countries of origin,

34. The report of the assessment missions is contained in document MSC 74/17/1.

35. The report of the assessment mission in Ecuador is contained in document MSC 75/18/1.

which are mainly developing countries, are among the root causes leading people to migrate, often illegally, from one country to another. The preferred destinations for many of these people are developed countries. Where legal entry to another country proves impossible or is not expected, those seeking a new life will risk everything to escape, either by themselves or with the help of criminal networks.

157. Criminal networks provide the market for fraudulent travel documents, clandestine transportation and border-crossing. Smuggling of people is considered by organized crime groups to be such a highly profitable market that many have transferred their knowledge, facilities and networks for smuggling drugs and other goods to this illegal activity. High profits are maintained by hiding people in traditional modes of transport, including sealed containers on board vessels, or by hiding people in the holds of ships, which are often unseaworthy or not equipped to carry large numbers of passengers. Whatever the means of transport, the conditions are normally equally dangerous and unsafe.

158. The victims of the smuggling activity are often seen as parties to a criminal transaction. In reality, they are often victimized economically, physically or otherwise. They are often deceived about their country of destination and are sometimes forced to engage in criminal activities in the country of destination in order to reimburse the expenses incurred. Women and children in particular are often enslaved by the criminals in the country of destination. The vulnerability of migrants, in particular irregular or illegal migrants, as a result of their precarious situation in society often leads to violations of their most basic human rights.

159. The incident involving the rescue by the Norwegian vessel *Tampa* (a container vessel built to accommodate 40 people) in August 2001 of more than 400 illegal migrants from a sinking Indonesian ferry and the difficulty of finding a place to disembark them not only brought to the fore the range and complexity of the issues surrounding the problem of illegal migration, but also raised concerns that the very complexity of the issues might act as a deterrent in the future for those on board a ship to exercise the fundamental duty to render assistance to people in distress at sea. The incident raised two main maritime issues which need to be addressed: (a) the suppression and combating of smuggling of migrants by sea; and (b) the rescue at sea of persons in distress and their delivery to a place of safety (addressed in greater detail in par. 116 above).

160. With respect to the former issue, it may be noted that a new instrument has been developed providing for the suppression and combating of smuggling of migrants by sea, that is, the United Nations Protocol against the Smuggling of Migrants by Land, Sea and Air, supplementing the United Nations Convention against Transnational Organized Crime adopted in 2000. The Protocol has not yet entered into force. It has been signed so far by 97 States and ratified by 5.[36] Its provisions are based to a great extent on the 1988 United Nations Convention against the Illicit Traffic in Narcotic Drugs and Psychotropic Substances, UNCLOS and the IMO Interim Measures for Combating Unsafe Practices Associated with the Trafficking or Transport of Migrants by Sea, adopted in 1998 and revised in 2001 (for a more detailed description, see A/56/58, par. 228). The Protocol and the IMO Interim

36. For the most recent status of the Protocol, see the web site of the Centre for International Crime Prevention of the United Nations Office for Drug Control and Criminal Justice, at www.odccp.-org/crime_cicp.html.

Measures provide cooperative mechanisms for the interception of a vessel suspected of carrying illegal migrants by a State other than the flag State. The IMO Interim Measures advise Governments of measures they can take pending the entry into force of the Protocol. Unsafe practices are defined for the purposes of the IMO Interim Measures as any practice which involves operating a ship in violation of SOLAS, including the carriage of more than 12 persons on board a cargo ship. Port States are recommended to prevent a vessel engaged in unsafe practices from sailing. Neither the Protocol nor the IMO Interim Measures address the rescue of illegal migrants in distress at sea and their subsequent disembarkation. The Protocol contains a savings clause in its Article 19.

161. While not specifically dealing with the issue of the smuggling of migrants, UNCLOS grants the coastal State the right to adopt laws and regulations to prevent the infringement of its immigration laws and regulations in its territorial sea (Article 21). In straits used for international navigation and in archipelagic sea lanes, foreign ships must comply with the laws and regulations of the States bordering the strait or the archipelagic States regarding the loading or unloading of any person in contravention of immigration laws and regulations (Articles 42 and 54). In the contiguous zone, the coastal State has the right to prevent and punish the infringement of its immigration laws and regulations committed within its territory or territorial sea (Article 33).

162. The problem of illegal migration falls within the realms of peace and security, economic and social development, human rights, organized crime, law of the sea and maritime law. The importance of a comprehensive approach to the problem and a coordinated approach to its resolution is therefore very important.

163. Following the *Tampa* incident, the Secretary-General of IMO brought the issue of persons rescued at sea and/or asylum-seekers and refugees to the attention of a number of competent specialized agencies and programmes of the United Nations pointing out the need for a coordinated approach to all attendant aspects at the United Nations inter-agency level. He proposed an inter-agency review of the existing mandates and programmes with a view to identifying gaps, inconsistencies, duplications or overlaps, and the establishment of a coordinating mechanism to ensure that the response of the United Nations in any future emergency can be coordinated in a consistent manner. The IMO Assembly at its 22nd session, in resolution A.920(22), "Review of safety measures and procedures for the treatment of persons rescued at sea" (see par. 116 above), requested the Secretary-General of IMO to pursue his initiative and inform the competent IMO bodies of developments in due course.

D. Stowaways

164. A stowaway is defined in the IMO Guidelines for the Allocation of Responsibilities to Seek the Successful Resolution of Stowaway Cases, adopted by the IMO Assembly in its resolution A.871(20) in 1997, as a person who is secreted on the ship or in cargo which is subsequently loaded onto the ship, without the consent of the shipowner or the master or any other responsible person, and who is detected on board after the ship has departed from a port and reported as a stowaway by the master to the appropriate authorities.

165. The IMO Guidelines were developed to provide an internationally agreed procedure for dealing with stowaways, since the 1957 International Convention relating to Stowaways had not entered into force and it did not appear that it would. The basic principles contained in the Guidelines have now been reflected in amendments to the IMO Convention on the Facilitation of International Maritime Traffic in the form of new standards and recommended practices, following their adoption at the 29th session of the IMO Facilitation Committee (7–11 January 2002), and are expected to enter into force on 1 May 2003.

166. The new measures in the Facilitation Convention call upon public authorities, port authorities, shipowners and their representatives, as well as shipmasters, to cooperate in preventing stowaway incidents. Among other things, port areas are to be regularly patrolled, special storage facilities for cargo particularly susceptible to stowaway access are to be established and persons and cargo entering these areas are to be continuously monitored. Contracting Governments must require ships entitled to fly their flag to undergo a thorough search in accordance with a specific plan or schedule when departing from a port where there is a risk that stowaways may be boarded. Passenger ships are to be exempted from the requirement.

167. The new measures also refer specifically to the problem of smuggling of people and call for cooperation between port authorities and relevant authorities such as police, customs and immigration to combat the practice.

168. Where stowaways do manage to get on board and remain undetected until the voyage is well under way, the masters of ships are required to take appropriate measures to ensure the security, general health, welfare and safety of any stowaway while on board, including providing them with adequate provisions, accommodation, proper medical attention and sanitary facilities.

169. With regard to disembarkation, the new measures state that public authorities shall urge all shipowners operating ships entitled to fly their flag to instruct their masters not to deviate from the planned voyage to seek the disembarkation of stowaways discovered on board the ship after it has left the territorial waters of the country where the stowaways embarked, unless permission to disembark the stowaway has been granted by the public authorities of the State to whose port the ship deviates or repatriation has been arranged elsewhere with sufficient documentation and permission for disembarkation, or if there are extenuating security, health or compassion-related reasons. Stowaways found inadmissible in the country of disembarkation should be returned from their point of disembarkation to the country where they boarded the vessel. The new measures are to be applied in accordance with international protection principles as set out in international instruments, such as the 1951 Convention relating to the Status of Refugees and the 1967 Protocol relating to the Status of Refugees and relevant national legislation.

170. The Convention on Facilitation of International Maritime Traffic (FAL Convention) provides that any contracting Government which finds it impracticable to comply with any international standard, or deems it necessary to adopt differing regulations, must inform the Secretary-General of IMO of the "differences" between its own practices and the standards in question.

E. Illicit Traffic in Narcotic Drugs and Psychotropic Substances

171. The United Nations International Drug Control Programme (UNDCP) reported that the Commission on Narcotic Drugs at its forty-fourth session (March

2001) continued to express its concern over the increasing prevalence of illicit traffic by sea in narcotic drugs, psychotropic substances and precursors. In order to further the obligation of all States parties to the 1988 United Nations Convention against Illicit Traffic in Narcotic Drugs and Psychotropic Substances to cooperate to the fullest extent possible in suppressing illicit traffic at sea (Article 17), the Commission in its resolution 44/6, entitled "Enhancing multilateral cooperation in combating illicit traffic by sea," requested UNDCP to provide technical assistance and training on maritime cooperation to interested States against illicit drug traffic by sea. It identified as possible technical assistance activities the development of a user-friendly reference guide to assist parties when making requests for verification of nationality and for consent to board, search and take appropriate action under Article 17 of the 1988 Convention and to assist competent authorities who have the responsibility to receive and respond to such requests pursuant to Article 17; the development of model reference formats to facilitate the exchange of information between the requesting and requested State; and the collection of information on bilateral and regional agreements for reference purposes. In addition, the Commission urged UNDCP to cooperate with States parties to the 1988 Convention and encouraged States to contribute their maritime expertise to the formulation of technical assistance and training.[37]

172. During 2001, UNDCP developed the first draft of a manual for competent national authorities designated pursuant to paragraph 7 of Article 17 of the 1988 Convention. The manual details the necessary legislative framework for effective cooperation and makes recommendations on the functions, powers, administrative capacity, channels of communication and procedures essential to enable the designated competent authority to receive and respond to Article 17 requests from another party. The draft manual was reviewed by an Expert Group (Vienna, 22–24 January 2002) and will be completed during 2002. It will serve as a companion to the Maritime Drug Law Enforcement Training Guide, produced by UNDCP in 1999. Upon completion of the manual, UNDCP plans to hold training courses for States that request help in establishing their Article 17 competent national authorities.

173. UNDCP also reported that considerable progress has been made in the negotiation of a regional agreement concerning cooperation in suppressing illicit maritime and aeronautical trafficking in narcotic drugs and psychotropic substances in the Caribbean area. The agreement will seek to enhance the effectiveness of the provisions of Article 17 of the 1988 Convention. It is anticipated that the negotiations will be completed and the agreement opened for signature in 2002.

6. SUSTAINABLE DEVELOPMENT OF MARINE RESOURCES, UNDERWATER CULTURAL HERITAGE

A. Conservation and Management of Marine Living Resources

174. During the reporting period, of paramount importance were the actions taken to implement and enforce binding or non-binding instruments. However, one im-

37. See *Official Records of the Economic and Social Council, 2001, Supplement No. 8* (E/2001/28), available on the web site of UNDCP at www.undcp.org/cnd_documents.html.

portant development occurred in the search for better conservation and management of marine living resources, namely the Reykjavik Declaration on Responsible Fisheries in the Marine Ecosystem, adopted by the joint FAO-Government of Iceland Conference on Responsible Fisheries in the Marine Ecosystem in October 2001. The Declaration expressed the firm intention of the Conference participants to incorporate ecosystem considerations into fisheries management in an effort to reinforce responsible and sustainable fisheries. To that end, the document urged the international community to undertake the following actions: (a) continuation of the effective implementation of the FAO Code of Conduct, the International Plans of Action (IPOAs) and the Kyoto Declaration; (b) adoption of effective management plans with incentives that would encourage responsible fisheries and the sustainable use of marine ecosystems, including mechanisms for reducing excessive fishing efforts to sustainable levels; (c) strengthening, and where appropriate establishment of Regional Fisheries Management Organizations (RFMOs) that would incorporate in their work ecosystem considerations, and improvement of cooperation between RFMOs and regional bodies in charge of protecting the marine environment; and (d) prevention of adverse effects of non-fisheries activities on the marine ecosystems and fisheries.

175. Moreover, the Reykjavik Declaration stressed that in addition to the immediate application of the precautionary approach, it was important to advance the scientific basis for incorporating ecosystem considerations into fisheries management, building on existing and future scientific knowledge. It also urged the international community to strengthen international cooperation with a view to supporting developing countries in incorporating ecosystem considerations into fisheries management. It further encouraged technology transfer contributing to sustainable management, sound regulatory frameworks, including where necessary removal of trade distortions, and promotion of transparency. FAO and other relevant technical and financial organizations were invited to cooperate in providing States with access to technical advice and information about effective management regimes and about experience for such arrangements, as well as other support, devoting special attention to developing countries. FAO was also encouraged to work with scientific and technical experts from all different regions to develop technical guidelines for best practices with regard to introducing ecosystem considerations into fisheries, and to present them at the next session of the FAO Committee on Fisheries.

176. In its contribution to the present report, the Economic Commission for Latin America and the Caribbean (ECLAC) stated that a regional expert group meeting on responsible fishing in the marine ecosystem was held from 3 to 5 December 2001 to analyse the result of the Reykjavik Conference, vis-à-vis the work being undertaken by ECLAC and the FAO regional office for Latin America and the Caribbean on the implementation of the Convention on Biological Diversity to the marine environment.

Implementation of Instruments

177. The adoption of international instruments alone, whether legally binding or of a voluntary nature, is not sufficient to ensure the conservation and sustainable use of marine living resources. To be effective, they must be translated into concrete measures at the regional, subregional and national levels and implemented by all stakeholders. Thus, States would have to use their prescriptive and enforcement

jurisdictions to implement through domestic legislation the relevant provisions of these international instruments. RFMOs would be required also to incorporate into their fisheries management such new tools as, inter alia, the precautionary approach, the ecosystem approach and the use of trade-related schemes to prevent illegal, unreported and unregulated fishing (IUU fishing). In addition, while on the one hand competent intergovernmental organizations would be invited to implement operational activities mandated by these instruments, on the other hand, NGOs are expected to monitor, on behalf of the general public, the conservation and sustainable use of the marine living resources of the world's oceans and seas as well as the implementation of all relevant instruments to ensure such conservation and sustainable use.

178. *Implementation of the 1995 Fish Stocks Agreement and General Assembly resolutions.*—In order to give effect to the relevant provisions of the 1995 Fish Stocks Agreement and General Assembly fisheries resolutions to ensure the long-term sustainability of marine living resources, and in recognition of the fact that effective flag State control is fundamental to ensure the effectiveness of fisheries management, many flag States have taken steps to ensure that fishing vessels entitled to fly their flag do not engage in any activity which undermines the effectiveness of international conservation and management measures or in any activity that constitutes unauthorized fishing in areas under the national jurisdiction of other States. Measures have been introduced also to prohibit fishing on the high seas without a proper authorization by the flag State. Under a number of regulations, a fishing vessel may be registered or granted a licence only if sufficient links exist between the flag State and the vessel.[38] Similarly, a number of regulations prohibit reflagging[39] or stipulate that the national flag may be granted only to vessels that have surrendered their flag of origin.[40]

179. Moreover, fisheries regulations in a growing number of States provide that conditions for granting fishing permits to vessels for high seas fishing require compliance by vessels with applicable international measures for conservation and management.[41] Most of such fisheries laws require flag States to maintain a record of fishing vessels entitled to fly their flag and authorized by them to fish on the high seas.[42] They also provide that fishing vessels must be marked in accordance with the FAO Standard Specifications for the Marking and Identification of Fishing Vessels.[43] Some of them even stipulate that licence applications may be denied or withdrawn if the vessel or its owner had taken part in IUU fishing on the high seas[44] or if a previous licence for high seas fishing granted to the vessel by a foreign State had

38. See A/55/386, par. 118, Mauritius Fisheries and Marine Resources Act of 1998, for example.

39. See A/53/473, par. 122; A/55/386, paras. 112, 114, 126, 129, 138; and A/56/357, par. 37.

40. See A/55/386, par. 126.

41. See A/53/473, paras. 124–127; A/55/386, paras. 111, 115, 120, 131, 135; and A/56/357, paras. 12, 15, 18, 32.

42. A/53/473, paras. 76, 117, 120, 126; A/54/461, paras. 19, 27; A/55/386, paras. 77, 112, 115, 127; A/56/357, paras. 11, 37.

43. A/53/473, paras. 117, 126; A/55/386, par. 133.

44. A/53/473, paras. 121, 126; A/54/461, par. 28; A/55/386, paras. 115, 130.

been suspended or withdrawn because the vessel had undermined the effectiveness of international conservation and management measures.[45]

180. Furthermore, a number of States have introduced provisions that make it mandatory for vessels flying their flag to submit catch reporting and other fishery data from their high seas fishing operations or to have on board national observers or vessel monitoring systems (VMS) as means of enhancing national monitoring, control and surveillance.[46] These fisheries regulations also provide for sanctions of sufficient severity for high seas fisheries violations, which may include the imposition of fines, suspension or withdrawal of fishing permits or licences, and the cancellation of registration of the fishing vessels.[47] Also, some States have placed restrictions on the export of vessels decommissioned from their national fishing fleets, to avoid exporting excess fishing capacity and reflagging.[48] Other States have indicated that they have joined or intended to join, as full members, competent RFMOs in order to give effect to their duty to cooperate in the conservation and management of high seas fisheries.[49]

181. As part of their growing role in ensuring compliance with subregional and regional fisheries conservation and management measures, a number of States have begun to implement port State control in respect of foreign fishing vessels calling voluntarily at their ports or at offshore terminals through, inter alia, the monitoring of trans-shipments and landings, and the collection of data on catch and effort.[50] They have also enacted legislation establishing restrictions or prohibition of landings or requiring the issuance of licences for fishing vessels to enter a port.[51] Under these national regulations, they have denied port access to vessels known to have engaged in illegal fishing or have closed off to their owners or operators access to markets by prohibiting landings to catches that have not been harvested in conformity with agreed regional conservation and management measures.[52] Of particular relevance are those regulations which prohibit not only landings, but also the supplying of services in ports to fishing vessels previously engaged in high seas activities that might have an adverse impact on fishery conservation and management in the exclusive economic zone of the State concerned,[53] as well as other regulations which

45. A/55/386, par. 131; A/56/357, par. 12.

46. A/53/473, paras. 116, 118, 120; A/54/461, paras. 19, 27; A/55/386, paras. 73, 110, 133, 135; A/56/357, paras. 10, 11, 43.

47. A/53/473, paras. 120, 126, 129; A/54/461, paras. 13, 28; A/55/386, paras. 115, 127, 130; A/56/357, paras. 9, 12, 37.

48. A/55/386, paras. 114, 116.

49. A/52/555, paras. 6, 16, 25, 28, 33; A/54/461, paras. 7, 11, 21; A/55/386, paras. 121, 129; A/56/357, paras. 14, 23.

50. A/52/555, par. 5; A/56/357, par. 16.

51. FAO Fishery and Agricultural Legislation: United Kingdom, Fishery Limits Act 1976, sect. 3 (6), vol. 26, No. 2, 1997, p. 89; Sri Lanka, Fisheries Act No. 59 of 1979, Regulation of Foreign Fishing Boats, vol. 29, No. 1, 1980, p. 89; Trinidad and Tobago, Archipelagic Waters and Exclusive Economic Zone Act 1986, sect. 32, vol. 36, No. 2, 1987, p. 107.

52. FAO contribution to the report of the Secretary-General on oceans and the law of the sea (December 2000).

53. Law No. 18.892 of 1989 and Amendments, General Law on Fisheries and Aquaculture, art. 165, Library of the National Congress of Chile, Juridical-Legislative System, Most consulted law, web site at: www.congreso.cl/biblioteca/leyes/otras/pesca13.htm.

prohibit the importation of fish caught illegally in areas under the national jurisdiction of other States.[54]

182. In addition, several coastal States have taken measures to control foreign fishing operations in areas under their national jurisdiction through the adoption of laws and regulations governing fishing activities and the implementation of monitoring, control and surveillance (MCS) systems for fishing operations in their exclusive economic zones. These include requirements for fishing authorization or fishing permits, types of gear, daily maintenance of logbooks, daily reporting of catches and vessel geographical positions, statistical data reporting, vessel monitoring systems, prior authorization for trans-shipments at sea, obligation to land all or part of the catch, prohibition of discard of by-catches, and obligation to stow fishing gear when fishing vessels are in transit in areas under national jurisdiction. Measures have also been taken to enforce those fisheries laws and regulations in areas under their national jurisdiction.[55]

183. However, limited resources and the large size of the ocean space over which they exercise control have had an adverse impact on the ability of many developing coastal States to enforce their conservation and management measures against unauthorized fishing. For these countries, unauthorized fishing activities had been carried out through, inter alia, the use of flags of convenience, illegal fishing on the ocean areas between the exclusive economic zones and the high seas, and misreporting of catch. Developing coastal States dependent on access fees for their economic development are particularly vulnerable because of distortions to fee levels, which are conditional upon the volume of catch.[56]

184. Consequently, in regions such as the South Pacific, coastal States have established a regional register of foreign vessels with a common database of all relevant information about vessels, updated annually, and containing information about their owners, operators and masters, call sign and port of registry. The regional register is used not only as a source of information on fishing vessels but also as a tool to ensure compliance with coastal States' laws and regulations. Coastal States have also taken additional measures, such as harmonization of the terms and conditions of access, and adoption of an agreement, which permits a party to extend its fisheries surveillance and law enforcement activities to the territorial sea and archipelagic waters of another party (see the report by SOPAC in Annex II to the present report).

185. At the regional level, a number of RFMOs have started to work within the legal framework provided for in UNCLOS for the conservation and management of marine living resources and have undertaken to strengthen their role in fisheries management, as required by developments in international fisheries law.[57] These developments have compelled these RFMOs to ensure, inter alia, the long-term sustainability of marine living resources; to apply the precautionary approach; to follow an ecosystem-based management approach; to enhance scientific advice; to stress the importance of the collection and exchange of adequate data; to implement

54. Information provided by the South Pacific Applied Geoscience Commission (SOPAC).

55. Coastal State Requirements for Foreign Fishing Database, FAO Legal Office: http://www.faolex.fao.org/cgibin/fishery.

56. Information provided by SOPAC.

57. Adoption of the 1995 Fish Stocks Agreement and the Code of Conduct for Responsible Fisheries.

effective monitoring, control and surveillance systems; to agree on decision-making procedures which facilitate the timely adoption of conservation and management measures, as well as on effective mechanisms for the settlement of disputes.

186. For these purposes, a number of FAO regional fishery bodies have already begun to strengthen their role in the management of fisheries in areas under their respective competence. Some have converted their advisory functions into regulatory ones.[58] In this respect, reference should be made to the General Fisheries Council for the Mediterranean (GFCM), which has become a "Commission" with an autonomous budget and a new Scientific Advisory Committee to secure scientific advice in the management of Mediterranean fisheries. At its sessions in 1999 and 2000, the GFCM Scientific Advisory Committee addressed such issues as the definition of management units, the definition of parameters for measuring fishing effort, the identification of the actual state of resources and methodologies for determining such status, as well as the definition of required fleet data to be included in the regional register of vessels, as a necessary starting point to monitor fishing effort.[59] In addition, the Asia-Pacific Fishery Commission (APFIC) has also amended its constitution and updated its terms of reference to take into full account the recent fundamental changes in world fisheries and, in particular, to become equipped to play its role in the implementation of UNCLOS.[60]

187. In the Indian Ocean region, the Indian Ocean Tuna Commission (IOTC) has also endeavoured to strengthen its role in the conservation and management of highly migratory fish stocks in its area of competence. On the advice of its Scientific Committee, it has implemented mandatory requirements for IOTC members to provide timely, standardized statistical data for catch, effort and size for all species covered by the Commission, as well as data for catches of non-target species. It has also recommended a substantial reduction of the fishing capacity of distant long-line tuna fleets operating in the region, as well as registration and exchange of information on vessels, including flag-of-convenience vessels fishing for tropical tunas in IOTC area of competence.[61]

188. Non-FAO regional fishery bodies and arrangements have also implemented or are in the process of implementing the new approaches to fisheries conservation and management. For example, the International Commission for the Conservation of Atlantic Tunas (ICCAT), the Northwest Atlantic Fisheries Organization (NAFO) and the North-East Atlantic Fisheries Commission (NEAFC) have considered developing the precautionary approach as a tool for fisheries management.[62] The ecosystem-based approach[63] and precautionary total allowable catch[64] have already been inte-

58. Progress Report on the Implementation of Conference Resolution 13/97 (Review of FAO Statutory Bodies) and the Strengthening of FAO Regional Fisheries Bodies, Committee on Fisheries, Twenty-third Session, Rome, 15–19 February 1999, document COFI/99/4, par. 4.

59. Report of GFCM, Twenty-fourth Session, Alicante, Spain, 12–15 July 1999 (GFCM Report 24), paras. 27–28.

60. COFI/99/4, par. 5.

61. Report of the Third Session of IOTC, Mahe, Seychelles, 9–12 December 1998, document IOTC/03/98/R [E], Appendix H.

62. A/54/461, paras. 33 and 44; Summary Report of the Eighteenth Annual Meeting of NEAFC, 22–25 November 1999, par. 7.

63. Report of the Fifteenth Meeting of CCAMLR, Hobart, Australia, 21 October–1 November 1996, document CCAMLR-XV, pp. 7–20.

64. Ibid., Conservation measures adopted in 1996: Conservation measure 103/XV, p. 54.

grated into the fisheries conservation and management programmes of the Commission for the Conservation of Antarctic Marine Living Resources (CCAMLR) and the Commission for the Conservation of Southern Bluefin Tuna (CCSBT).[65] Moreover, organizations such as CCAMLR, NAFO and NEAFC have adopted MCS schemes to enforce their conservation and management measures. A number of RFMOs, including CCAMLR, CCSBT and ICCAT, have introduced catch documentation schemes and nondiscriminatory trade restriction measures to combat IUU fishing in their convention areas.[66]

189. Furthermore, the agreements adopted recently for the establishment of new RFMOs in various regions of the world to regulate previously unmanaged fisheries, in accordance with the relevant provisions of UNCLOS and Agenda 21, Chapter 17, have also incorporated most of the fisheries conservation and management principles provided in the international instruments. Among those agreements, attention should be drawn to the Convention on the Conservation and Management of Highly Migratory Fish Stocks in the Western and Central Pacific,[67] the Convention on the Conservation and Management of Fishery Resources in the South-East Atlantic Ocean (SEAFO)[68] and the Framework Agreement for the Conservation of Living Marine Resources on the High Seas of the South-East Pacific ("Galapagos Agreement"),[69] which include provisions underlining the requirement of long-term sustainability of fish stocks, compatibility of measures within and beyond areas under national jurisdiction, ecosystem-based management and application of the precautionary approach, as well the important role of scientific information in fisheries management. These new agreements also include strong provisions enhancing flag States' responsibilities as required, inter alia, in the 1995 Fish Stocks Agreement as well as monitoring, control and surveillance and enforcement schemes involving reciprocal boarding and inspection by States parties, and port State measures modelled along those in the 1995 Fish Stocks Agreement. Moreover, the future establishment in the Indian Ocean region of the South-West Indian Ocean Fisheries Commission to promote the conservation, rational management and best utilization of non-tuna species will likely contribute to the objectives and purposes stated in Agenda 21, Chapter 17.[70]

190. In addition, particular reference should be made to the biennial meeting of FAO and non-FAO regional fishery organizations and arrangements initiated by FAO in 1999 with a view to providing a forum for coordination and cooperation between those organizations and arrangements and allowing them to discuss topics of common interest, such as major issues affecting the performance of regional fish-

65. A/54/429, par. 298.

66. A/55/386, paras. 144, 147 and 151.

67. Convention on the Conservation and Management of Highly Migratory Fish Stocks in the Western and Central Pacific, Article 5 (a), (d) and (f); Article 6; Articles 12 and 13.

68. Convention on the Conservation and Management of Fishery Resources in the South-East Atlantic Ocean, Article 2; Article 3 (e) and (g); Articles 7, 10 and 19, http://www.fao.org/Legal/default.htm.

69. Framework Agreement for the Conservation of the Fisheries Resources on the High Seas of the South-East Pacific ("Galapagos Agreement"), Article 5 (a), (b), (c) and (e), Article 7 (e), (f) and (g).

70. Draft Agreement for the Establishment of a South-West Indian Ocean Fisheries Commission, Second Intergovernmental Consultation on the Establishment of the South West Indian Ocean Fisheries Commission, Antananarivo, 25–28 September 2001.

ery bodies; the multifaceted approach to fishery status and trends; and the role of RFMOs as vehicles for good fishery governance.[71] At their second meeting in 2001, they deliberated on a number of issues of importance, such as the review of external factors that might affect the performance of fisheries bodies; regional fishery bodies performance indicators; IUU fishing; developments in the Convention on International Trade in Endangered Species (CITES) criteria for listing commercially exploited aquatic species; and ecosystem-based management of fisheries. At a recent meeting in January 2002, these fishery bodies addressed the issue of catch certification schemes and reviewed possibilities for a greater degree of coordination among fishery bodies on existing and potential schemes.[72]

191. In spite of the efforts to strengthen the role of RFMOs and arrangements in fisheries governance, progress is being hindered by the failure by States to accept and implement relevant international instruments, a lack of willingness by those States to delegate sufficient responsibility to regional bodies and the lack of effective enforcement of management measures at both national and regional levels.[73] The performance of many RFMOs is also adversely affected by inadequate financial resources, particularly in respect of FAO fishery bodies, ineffective decision-making procedures that allow non-compliance by members with management decisions, inadequacy of scientific advice and IUU fishing by vessels flying flags of convenience.

192. Nevertheless, recent developments seem to provide some indications of progress towards a progressive implementation of the objectives of the Rio Conference.[74] The most noteworthy development is the recent entry into force of the 1995 Fish Stocks Agreement (see paras. 16–20) and its impact on the conservation and management of capture fisheries in general, as well as its impact on the conservation and management of the straddling fish stocks and highly migratory fish stocks in particular. It is believed that the Agreement, among other benefits, will strengthen the ability of RFMOs to carry out their conservation and management responsibilities, including incorporation of the new approaches to fisheries management. Reference should also be made to the dramatic decline in recent years of large-scale pelagic drift-net fishing activities on the high seas, as evidenced by the number of reported incidents; to measures taken by States to prevent unauthorized fishing in areas under the national jurisdiction of other States; and to efforts undertaken by States and RFMOs to reduce by-catches and discards through the use of turtle excluding devices, mesh size limitations, confiscation of catches, a ban on landing of juveniles and/or discards, levies on by-catch, and season/area closures of fishing grounds to limit by-catches and discards, which are reported periodically to the Secretary-General pursuant to General Assembly resolutions 46/215 of 20 December 1991 and 49/116 and 49/118 of 19 December 1994.

193. *Implementation of the FAO Compliance Agreement.*—In 1995, FAO sent a circular letter to all States which had accepted the Agreement informing them that it had developed a High Seas Vessel Registration Database System (HSREG) to facilitate

71. Report of the Meeting of FAO and non-FAO Regional Fishery Bodies or Arrangements, Rome, 11–12 February 1999, FAO Fisheries Report No. 597 (FIPL/R597).

72. Information provided by FAO.

73. Report of the Meeting of FAO and non-FAO Regional Fishery Bodies or Arrangements, Rome, 11–12 February 1999, document X1212/E, par. 27.

74. Agenda 21, chap. 17, paras. 17.49, 17.70.

monitoring of vessels licensed to fish on the high seas and requested States to provide data in the database. The FAO initiative was in compliance with Article VI of the Compliance Agreement, which entrusted FAO with the establishment of an international database of information relating to fishing vessels entered into the record of each party which are entitled to fly its flag and authorized by it to be used for fishing on the high seas. To date, Canada, the European Community, Japan, Norway and the United States have provided vessel data to the database. Currently, information about more than 1,200 vessels has been entered in the database and work is continuing to update its content. This information will be of great value to States and regional fishery bodies and arrangements.[75]

194. As noted above, even though the Compliance Agreement has not yet entered into force, a number of States have already taken measures to ensure that they are able to exercise control over fishing activities of vessels flying their flag on the high seas, so that such vessels comply with the conservation and management measures established by RFMOs in their regulatory areas.

195. *Implementation of the FAO Code of Conduct for Responsible Fisheries and related IPOAs.*—Although the Code is not a legally binding instrument, all FAO members nonetheless have undertaken a serious commitment to implement it and to act in a responsible manner, and to address urgent management and related sectoral issues. At the national level, many countries are focusing on selected key areas without losing the overall holistic perspective of the Code and several of them have stressed the need for an integrated and comprehensive approach in addressing, inter alia, capture fisheries issues. An increasing number of countries have adopted, on the basis of the Code, enabling fisheries regulations and policy measures to promote or enhance sustainable fisheries management. While some countries have adapted the Code to national or local conditions and have produced guidelines to facilitate its application, others have elaborated codes of best practices for government agencies and producers.[76]

196. In addition, several countries have developed fisheries management plans for marine fisheries, with an average of more than 60 percent of these plans having been implemented. Such management plans contain the key fishery management tools, such as measures to: (a) ensure that the level of fishing is commensurate with the state of fishery resources; (b) prohibit destructive fishing methods; and (c) address fishing capacity, including the economic conditions under which the fishing industry operates. They have also indicated that the precautionary approach is applied continually in the provision of management advice, through attention to target reference points, implementation of objective-based fisheries management principles and reduction of quotas.[77] In small-scale fisheries, the fishing communities themselves (through participatory management) and NGOs (because of their grassroots fisheries affiliations) are involved in facilitating and supporting the implementation of the Code.[78] NGO contributions have been through the issuance of perti-

75. Information provided by FAO.

76. Ibid.

77. FAO Committee on Fisheries, Twenty-fourth Session, Rome, 26 February–2 March 2001, Progress in the Implementation of the Code of Conduct for Responsible Fisheries and Related International Plans of Action (COFI/2001/3), paras. 13–18.

78. Information provided by FAO.

nent technical publications, translation of the Code into local languages, the conduct of workshops and seminars, and the development of a code of best practices.[79]

197. Concerning the integration of fisheries into coastal area management, findings have shown that while the legal framework for such integration exists in many developed countries, most developing countries lack a specific legal framework for this purpose. Therefore, conflicts are reported to be common in many of these countries. In this connection, conflicts between coastal and industrial fisheries, as well as between gear types operating in the coastal fisheries, are expected to be widespread and severe.[80]

198. At the regional level, intergovernmental organizations have played important roles in assisting their members in the implementation of key elements of the Code. Indeed, regional action is essential, especially where fisheries are shared, jointly exploited, or where there are problems of common concern that can be most effectively and efficiently addressed through regional activities.[81] In 1998, the first regional workshop on the adaptation of the Code was organized for 22 coastal States of West Africa (Morocco to Namibia) under the FAO Regional Programme for Integrated Development of Artisanal Fisheries (IDAF) in West Africa. Similar workshops were planned for countries of the South Pacific and the Indian Ocean.[82] Moreover, the Southeast Asian Fisheries Development Centre (SEAFDC) is reported to be working on the regionalization of several Articles of the Code. SEAFDC is also producing materials for responsible fishing operations, undertaking research on juvenile and trash fish excluding devices, and has organized consultations on fishing gear selectivity. Furthermore, several RFMOs have indicated that, as a result of steps they had taken to implement substantively the Code through their members and within their areas of competence, their existing fisheries management plans or measures contained the necessary key management tools recommended in the Code.[83]

199. Pursuant to the objectives of the Code, FAO implemented in 1999 the Sustainable Fisheries Livelihoods Programme (SFLP),[84] a five-year programme funded by the United Kingdom aimed at assisting 25 participating countries of West Africa in reducing poverty in coastal and inland fisheries communities by improving the livelihoods of people dependent on fishery and aquatic resources. SFLP intended to reach its objectives through: (a) the development of social and human capital in fisheries-dependent communities; (b) the enhancement of the natural assets of those communities; and (c) the development of appropriate fisheries policy and institutional environments. The main beneficiaries of the programme would be the resource-users in artisanal fisheries communities, focusing on the most vulnerable groups: fishers and small-scale traders and fish processors, most of whom are women.

200. At the end, the programme expects to achieve a lasting impact in governance at the central and local levels, and in policy formulation and execution at

79. FAO Committee on Fisheries (COFI/2001/3), par. 46.

80. Ibid., par. 24.

81. Ibid., par. 37.

82. Committee on Fisheries, Twenty-third Session, Rome, 15–19 February 1999, Progress Report on the Implementation of the Code of Conduct for Responsible Fisheries (COFI/99/3), par. 5.

83. COFI/2001/3, paras. 37–38.

84. http://www.fao.org/fi/projects/sflp/index.html.

both national and international levels. Sustainability within the area of government policy and planning would be improved after the successful incorporation of relevant elements of the Code into national fisheries development and management plans. Sustainability at the local level would be enhanced with local communities participating in the planning and management of the marine living resources, and with the improvement, in many areas, of livelihoods of poor people. The experience and knowledge would be disseminated elsewhere in the region and in the wider international sphere with beneficial consequences.

201. At the global level, FAO in 1998 started an interregional programme to support activities relating to the implementation of the Code (IRP-CCRF), with Norwegian funding for two subprogrammes: MCS and assistance in improving the provision of scientific advice for fishery management. As a result, a workshop on MCS was organized in Malaysia for countries covering the Bay of Bengal and South China Sea fisheries. Under the second subprogramme, assistance to the management of small pelagics was provided to Malaysia, Indonesia and Thailand, and programmes of activities were implemented for the Brazil-Guyana shrimp and groundfish fisheries, as well as for shrimp fisheries in Madagascar, Mozambique and the United Republic of Tanzania.[85]

202. Moreover, FAO has promoted the implementation of the Code by taking the following steps:

(a) preparation of technical guidelines designed to provide practical direction for government officials and other stakeholders on *how* to implement it; (b) wide dissemination of information relating to responsible fisheries and its relationship to the Code; (c) provision of national advice through country visits; and (d) organization of national and regional training workshops. Progress in implementing the Code is monitored by the biennial sessions of the FAO Committee on Fisheries (COFI) and self-assessment information provided by Governments and stakeholders is collated and analysed by FAO and in turn presented to COFI for review.[86]

203. With respect to the implementation of the IPOAs, FAO has indicated that it had requested information from Governments, international organizations and RFMOs on activities they had undertaken to implement the IPOAs, in view of the fact that each IPOA calls upon Governments to implement national plans of action to address the problems identified therein, in accordance with agreed international measures.

204. *International Plan of Action to Prevent, Deter and Eliminate Illegal, Unreported and Unregulated Fishing* (IPOA-IUU).—FAO has initiated a number of activities to support the implementation of the IPOA-IUU, which was adopted in March 2001. These activities include: (a) dissemination of the IPOA at international forums and meetings concerning fisheries management; (b) preparation of a technical guideline explaining, inter alia, the steps that countries should take to implement the IPOA; and (c) provision of ad hoc advice to countries on implementation of the IPOA.

205. *International Plan of Action for Reducing Incidental Catch of Seabirds in Longline Fisheries* (IPOA-Seabirds).—FAO stated that during 2001 it worked with members to promote information about the IPOA-Seabirds and to facilitate its implementation,

85. Committee on Fisheries, Twenty-third Session, (COFI/99/3), par. 4.

86. Information provided by FAO to the Secretary-General, January 2002.

especially in those fisheries and regions where the by-catch of seabirds in fisheries was most problematic. In addition, it has received reports from several countries indicating that the incidental catch of seabirds was not an issue for them. Other countries have reported that longline fishing was practised but that an assessment of the situation indicated that a national plan was not required. A number of other countries have undertaken an assessment and have developed or are developing or planning to develop a national plan of action. Mitigation measures already being applied by some countries to minimize the catch of seabirds include observer coverage on longline vessels, the use of tori-streamers and other bird-scaring devices, night setting, the strategic dumping of offal, the use of fully thawed baits, removal of hooks from discarded offal, and mandatory handling and release of birds that come on board alive.

206. In this respect, particular reference should be made to CCAMLR, which has effectively pioneered a set of measures on the reduction of incidental mortality in longline fisheries and has requested its members to elaborate and implement national plans. Similarly, CCSBT and the International Pacific Halibut Commission (IPHC) require their members to use devices and fishing techniques to minimize the incidental taking of seabirds. NAFO has also endorsed IPOA-Seabirds.

207. *International Plan of Action for the Conservation and Management of Sharks* (IPOA-Sharks).—FAO indicated that it had prepared technical guidelines to implement the IPOA and support the development of national plans of action.[87] In 2001 a first assessment of the status of shark stocks was conducted by a number of countries. Several other countries reported that they had completed their national shark plans in 2001. IPOA-Sharks has also been addressed by the Inter-American Tropical Tuna Commission (I-ATTC) in the purse seine fisheries for tuna, while ICCAT has started an assessment of pelagic sharks in its convention area.[88]

208. *International Plan of Action for the Management of Fishing Capacity* (IPOA-Capacity).—FAO has developed two sets of technical guidelines in support of the IPOA on the management of capacity, one dealing specifically with the management of fishing capacity and the other on the measurement of fishing capacity.[89] In addition, in 2001, a number of countries began a preliminary assessment of their national fishing capacity.[90] The analytical methods used included assessments of fishing permits and licences, selected analyses of capacity utilization, development of indicators of excess capacity, and data envelopment analysis.

209. In their effort to maintain or reduce capacity, some countries reported the use of the following management methods: the application of individual transferable quotas (ITQs), the use of restrictive entry, vessel and permit buy-out, the scrapping of a specified percentage of large-scale tuna long-line fishing vessels, prohibition of the use of subsidies to increase capacity and the determination of fishing capacity requirements by the fishing industry itself in the light of their quota holdings. IPOA-Capacity is also being addressed by I-ATTC, the International Baltic Sea Fishery Commission (IBSFC), ICCAT, IPHC and CCSBT, SEAFDC, the Subregional

87. See COFI/2001/3, par. 8.
88. Information provided by FAO.
89. See COFI/2001/3, paras. 1–8.
90. Information provided by FAO to the Secretary-General, January 2002.

Commission on Fisheries (CSRP) and has been endorsed by the North Atlantic Salmon Conservation Organization (NASCO).

210. As a preliminary assessment, it is reasonable to conclude that efforts seem to be made by States, intergovernmental organizations, RFMOs and NGOs to implement the Code of Conduct for Responsible Fisheries and its related IPOAs. However, a number of developing countries have identified, as major constraints, inadequate institutional and technical capacity; inadequate funding; lack of information and inadequate access to information, as well as inadequate participation of all stakeholders; inappropriate legislative framework; socio-economic implications of reducing fishing effort; and difficulties of implementing such concepts as the precautionary approach in the context of reduced human and financial resources.[91]

211. In addition, NGOs have pointed to various constraints in the implementation of the Code, such as lack of knowledge and "ownership" of the Code among fisheries authorities and fishing communities; inadequate visible support by Governments and professional associations to the application of the Code; the open characteristic of many fisheries; and insufficient information on stock status and fish habitats.[92]

212. *Implementation of the ecosystem approach to fisheries management.*—Almost all international instruments adopted after the Rio Conference make reference to ecosystem-based fisheries management as a new approach which provides a more holistic and integrated view of the management of marine living resources, with the potential to complement the traditional fisheries management approach, under which each fish stock or each fish species is considered in isolation within the wider marine environment. The new approach calls for multi-species management of fish stocks, wherein the interrelationships between different stocks are accounted for in addition to each stock's internal dynamics. In addition, it recognizes that heavy fishing of target species may change the relative abundance of associated species as competitors for food, prey or predators in the marine environment. It also recognizes that because both land-based and sea-based sources of pollution can affect the productivity of fishing resources, fishery management should include not only measures to regulate fishing activities, but also measures to promote the reduction and elimination of pollution and degradation of critical habitats from non-fisheries activities in the marine environment.

213. However, due to the limited scientific understanding of the actual functioning of marine ecosystems and the lack of a scientific basis for incorporating ecosystem considerations into fisheries management, especially in many developing countries, ecosystem-based fisheries management, or, as was agreed at the Reykjavik Conference, incorporating "ecosystem considerations into fisheries management", has been the least implemented conceptfor fisheries management among those recommended for ocean governance at the Rio Conference. It is believed that the recent adoption of the Reykjavik Declaration on Responsible Fisheries in the Marine Ecosystem could provide an impetus for the effective implementation of this important approach to fisheries conservation and management. As required, the ecosystem approach, as a cross-cutting concept, may be extended to other aspects of ocean

91. COFI/2001/3, par. 47.

92. Ibid., par. 44.

governance in view of the multisectoral nature of marine activities, and could be the basis of a closer cooperation between RFMOs and UNEP regional seas programmes in the conservation and sustainable use of the oceans and their resources.

214. *Implementation of international instruments for the conservation and study of marine mammals. West African Cetaceans Research and Conservation Programme* (WAFCET).—The Convention on the Conservation of Migratory Species of Wild Animals (CMS) secretariat undertook in 1997–1998 a first survey of the status of cetaceans in Senegal, Gambia and Guinea-Bissau, as part of a long-term international effort to stimulate broad regional involvement in research and conservation of West African cetaceans. A second phase of the programme was initiated in Senegal and Gambia in November 1999. CMS provided operating funds and equipment for the implementation of field activities in both Senegal and Gambia. These field activities revealed a previously unknown population of endangered Atlantic hump-backed dolphins, *Sousa teuszii.* A third phase of the programme was started in September 2001, focusing on the interaction of small cetaceans with fisheries in Ghana and Togo.

215. *Investigation of cetaceans in the Gulf of Tonkin.*—The project, aimed at investigating the status of cetaceans in the Gulf of Tonkin and strengthening the capabilities of Chinese and Vietnamese researchers to conduct marine mammal surveys, included training, research and awareness components. Researchers from seven scientific institutions in China and Viet Nam were trained in marine mammal research techniques in October 1999. Two surveys were conducted in the Vietnamese portion of the Gulf of Tonkin, which besides cetacean sightings included data collection of fishing vessels and interviews with fishers.

216. *Small cetaceans: distribution, migration and threats. A review.*—The study was mainly aimed at providing an up-to-date and comprehensive review of available information on small cetacean migration and related conservation issues on a worldwide scale, pointing in particular to: (a) geographic areas and species for which currently available knowledge suggests the opportunity of strengthening cooperation among the range States, notably through the conclusion of new ad hoc agreements under the auspices of CMS; and (b) areas and species for which important gaps in information are evident and for which research and monitoring efforts are to be recommended as a matter of priority in order to provide the scientific/technical background for species management and, where appropriate, the conclusion of agreements under CMS.

217. *Survey for small cetaceans in the Timor Sea* (coastal waters between Indonesia and Australia).—The project is being carried out by Environment Australia in collaboration with the Indonesian Central Research Institute for Fisheries. Main activities to be undertaken include the organization of a training workshop on ship-based observation, two ship-based surveys, biopsy sampling and analysis, establishment of a locational database and geographic information system (GIS), and analysis of newly gathered and bibliographic data. In addition, Philippine and Indonesian institutions, with technical and financial support from CMS, were planning to jointly implement a marine mammal survey in the Celebes Sea.

218. *Workshop for the coordination of research on and conservation of Franciscana* (*Pontoporia blainvillei*) *in the south-western Atlantic* (Buenos Aires, 26–28 November 1997).—The workshop was co-sponsored by the CMS secretariat within its activities to promote collaborative action on the conservation of the species between the countries concerned.

219. *Workshop on the Conservation and Management of Marine Mammals in West Africa (Conakry, 8–12 May 2000).*—The goal of the workshop was to develop a collaborative regional plan for conducting basic research on the local marine mammalian fauna and identifying populations in need of coordinated management efforts. The workshop was attended by governmental representatives from Benin, Côte d'Ivoire, Equatorial Guinea, the Gambia, Guinea and Senegal.

220. *Second Conference on the biology and conservation of small cetaceans in South-East Asia.*—The conference is tentatively scheduled to be held in the Philippines in July 2002. The main objectives of the conference include: (a) updating the 1995 review of existing knowledge of general biology, including distribution and ecology, with emphasis on by-catch, of small cetaceans in South-East Asia; (b) updating the 1995 review of existing conservation measures and legislation at the regional and national levels; (c) identification of remaining significant gaps in scientific knowledge and assessment of the threats that must be met to ensure effective conservation; (d) development of recommendations and priorities for research and conservation action at the regional and national levels; and (e) consideration of the potential for development of formal regional cooperation, including review of a draft CMS regional agreement.

221. *Implementation of the Jakarta Mandate on Marine and Coastal Biological Diversity.*—In 1998, the Fourth Meeting of the Parties to the Convention on Biological Diversity adopted decision IV/5 containing a multi-year programme of work for the conservation and sustainable use of marine and coastal biological diversity, including the consideration of the issue of coral reefs and the special needs of small island developing States.[93] In a progress report to the Fifth Meeting, the Convention secretariat indicated that the implementation of the work programme was well under way, with concrete outputs emerging from it. These include: (a) tools for assisting the implementation of the work programme (a Jakarta Mandate web site and databases); (b) methodology for ecosystem evaluation (indicators); (c) materials to guide the work of experts; (d) expert analysis of coral bleaching; (e) an information document on marine and coastal genetic resources; and (f) a review of instruments related to integrated marine and coastal area management, marine and coastal protected areas, and marine and coastal alien species and genotypes.[94]

222. In its decision V/3, the Fifth Meeting of the Parties to the Convention on Biological Diversity encouraged the Convention secretariat and SBSTTA to complete, as soon as possible, the implementation of decision IV/5 dealing with the programme of work on marine and coastal biodiversity. It also requested the secretariat to explore the possibility of further collaboration with the secretariats of regional seas programmes and action plans in the implementation of the Jakarta Mandate.[95] A further progress report on the implementation of the Mandate, including the outcome of the first meeting of the Ad Hoc Technical Expert Group on Marine and Coastal Protected Areas (Leigh, New Zealand, 22–26 October 2001),[96] is ex-

93. COP-4 decision IV/5, "Conservation and sustainable use of marine and coastal biological diversity," including a programme of work, UNEP/CBD/COP/4/27, pp. 84–96.

94. UNEP/CBD/COP/5/10.

95. UNEP/CBD/COP/5/23, annex, p. 74.

96. Information provided by the secretariat of the Convention on Biological Diversity to the Secretary-General dated 21 January 2002.

pected to be submitted to the Sixth Meeting of the Parties to the Convention in April 2002.

223. *Implementation of the International Coral Reef Initiative* (ICRI).[97]—Following the recommendation of the first ICRI International Workshop in 1995, seven ICRI regional workshops were held between 1995 and 1997 throughout various regions of the world designated under the UNEP regional seas programme. In 1998, the second ICRI International Workshop was held in Australia. Various countries attending the International Tropical Ecosystems Management Symposium (ITMEMS) reported that the status of coral reefs worldwide had not improved and that more urgent action was required to reverse the alarming trend in reef degradation (see the report of SOPAC in Annex II to the present report). Accordingly, ITMEMS participants reaffirmed the "Call to Action" and "Framework for Action" of the first ICRI International Workshop and formulated a "Renewed Call for Action." They also added a series of urgent tasks for ICRI.

224. As to future directions for its efforts, ICRI is of the view that it should continue to focus the world's attention on the need for action, at the local, national and international levels, to protect and manage coral reefs. To this end, its key objectives would be as follows: (a) focusing global attention on the declining status of the world's coral reefs and promotion of practical solutions for immediate implementation to reverse this decline; (b) establishing operational networks at the international and regional levels to coordinate the key objectives of implementing integrated coastal management, building capacity, conducting effective research and monitoring, promoting awareness among all stakeholders and involving the private sector, especially the tourism industry; and (c) increasing the funding of regional programmes and projects through these networks to allow ICRI partners to cooperate in the conservation and sustainable development of coral reefs and related ecosystems. The success of ICRI would be measured in terms of its ability to turn the international momentum into concrete action at all levels and in all regions.

225. Ten years after Agenda 21, Chapter 17, was formulated, a preliminary assessment of developments affecting the conservation and sustainable use of marine living resources and marine biodiversity indicate that a large number of international instruments, whether legally binding or voluntary, global or regional, have been adopted by the international community to further the conservation and sustainable use of these resources. They cover almost all aspects of the conservation and management of marine living resources, and in doing so they have introduced new concepts and approaches to improve such conservation and management. However, conventions, agreements, resolutions, guidelines and plans of action are only as good as they are effectively implemented, at the global, regional or national level, as appropriate. Some of these instruments are in the early phase of implementation. Implementation of others has not yet been initiated and needs more time. It is thus believed that the forthcoming World Summit on Sustainable Development does not need to adopt new international instruments to assist in the conservation and management of marine living resources; a number of international instruments are in place for these purposes. What the conference may wish to consider is to encourage the international community to pursue effective implementation of the existing international instruments.

97. http://www.environnement.gouv.fr/icri/index.html.

B. Non-living Marine Resources

226. Non-living marine resources, in particular polymetallic nodules found on the deep seabed at a water depth of 5,000 to 20,000 feet, occupied a significant place in the deliberations at the Third United Nations Conference on the Law of the Sea. In 1970, the General Assembly declared that the area of the seabed and ocean floor and the subsoil thereof, beyond the limits of national jurisdiction, as well as its resources, are the common heritage of mankind. UNCLOS in its Article 136 reconfirmed the concept, and in Article 140 stipulated that activities in the international seabed area beyond national jurisdiction (the Area) shall be carried out for the benefit of mankind as a whole, and provided for the equitable sharing of financial and other economic benefits derived from such activities.

227. Today, 20 years after the adoption of the Convention, exploration contracts for polymetallic nodules in the international seabed area have been issued to six pioneer investors, and a seventh contract will be forthcoming. Consideration is also being given to regulations for the exploration and exploitation of polymetallic sulphides and cobalt-rich crusts, two other types of minerals to be found in the Area. Within national jurisdiction, two contracts for exploration for polymetallic sulphides have been issued by the Government of Papua New Guinea.

228. Also, within national jurisdiction, the offshore oil and gas industry has been growing at a remarkable pace during the past 20 years. Gold, tin, diamonds, and sand and gravel are important offshore mineral industries within national jurisdiction.

229. *Offshore oil and gas.*—Offshore oil production worldwide grew from about 13,500 million barrels per day in the early 1980s to about 18,600 million barrels per day in the mid-1990s, an increase of 37 percent. Offshore oil production accounted for about 30 percent of world oil production in the mid-1990s, as opposed to only 25 percent in the early 1980s. In the same period, offshore gas production worldwide grew from about 28,300 to 35,900 million cubic feet per day, an increase of 27 percent. Due to the same rate of growth of the on-land gas industry, the share of the offshore gas industry remained more or less the same during the period, at about half.[98]

230. With the increasing demand for oil and gas, offshore exploration and development have been shifting to the frontiers in remote and difficult places where little search and discovery activities have taken place in the past, into the deepwater provinces and selected areas where salt strata once obscured what lay beneath them. The four regions of greatest recent activity are the Gulf of Mexico, the North Sea, and offshore West Africa and South-East Asia.

231. The movement of the offshore oil and gas industry to deeper waters was characterized, inter alia, by the new record reached in 2001 in water depth for exploration, 9,743 feet. This record in the Gulf of Mexico surpassed the previous depth of 9,157 feet off the shore of Gabon, earlier in 2001.

232. Environmental considerations relating to offshore oil and gas exploration

98. Figures for 1982 are from the *International Petroleum Encyclopedia.* Figures for 1995 are from the American Petroleum Institute as well as communications with an expert, Tom Kelleck of ODS-Petrodata Group.

and exploitation and to the installations used for the industry are discussed in paragraphs 402 to 406. It is commonly held that environmental considerations can be dealt with at the national level, and under certain circumstances at the regional level; there are currently no global regulations.

233. *Methane hydrates.*—Research interest is being directed towards the recovery of methane hydrates, that is, frozen compounds of methane gas. Vast deposits are held at high pressure 600 to 1,500 feet below the ocean floor on continental margins throughout the world. Scientists have estimated that the amount of organic carbon bound up in ocean-floor methane hydrates is twice that found in all recoverable and non-recoverable oil, gas and coal deposits on earth.

234. The International Committee on Maritime Hydrates held its first workshop in Honolulu in March 2001. The primary objective of the workshop was to develop a road map for international collaboration on methane hydrates research and development. Representatives from government agencies, academia and industry in the United States, Canada, Japan, India, Norway, the Republic of Korea, Russia and the United Kingdom, were among the attendees. At the national level, at the United States Congressional hearings in July 2001, the Methane Hydrates Research and Development Act of 2000 (Public Law 106-193) was considered to be "a good first step that should prove very beneficial now and in the years to come for evaluating investments in the [United States] ocean and energy future."[99]

235. *Sand and gravel.*—Sand and gravel extraction continued to be a major marine mineral industry. The issue of climate change and sea level rise "has increased the concerns of many island countries that their coastlines may be at risk and new sites for sand resources offshore are being sought."[100] SOPAC has been active in this effort. At the same time, SOPAC is studying the potential environmental effects of marine mineral development in the Pacific islands.

236. *Freshwater.*—In view of the urgency that about two thirds of the world's population is projected to face shortages of clean freshwater over the coming decades, tapping the world's seas to produce freshwater is gaining momentum. According to IAEA, nuclear desalination is a promising technology.[101] The technology of desalination, or desalting seawater, is not new. Over the past 50 years, its use has grown, particularly in the Middle East and North Africa, where freshwater is scarce. The facilities are energy-intensive and usually draw energy they need from conventional fossil-fuelled plants. However, with growing environmental concern over greenhouse gas emissions, other cleaner sources of energy are being sought. The technology of coupling nuclear energy and desalination plants already has taken hold in Japan and Kazakhstan, where commercial facilities have been operating since the 1970s. India is seeking to expand the base of national and international experience through a demonstration plant it is building in the south-east of the country, by coupling a nuclear power plant to a desalination facility, working through international cooperation projects supported by IAEA. Other countries involved in nuclear desalination projects include the Republic of Korea, the Russian Federation, Pakistan, the Islamic Republic of Iran, Egypt, Saudi Arabia, Indonesia,

99. M. J. Cruickshank, "Globally significant events in the ocean mining industry during 2001," *Sea Technology*, January 2002, vol. 43, No. 1, p. 40.

100. Ibid., p. 40.

101. See www.iaea.org/worldatom.

Morocco, Tunisia, Argentina, Canada, France and China. In 2002, IAEA is planning an international symposium to review and update the global status of nuclear desalination. As more experience is gained and shared, the technology's use could help more countries meet rising demands for electricity and for freshwater.

237. *Deep-sea minerals within national jurisdiction.*—With respect to polymetallic sulphides, in addition to Nautilus Minerals of Australia working in the maritime zone of Papua New Guinea (see A/56/58, par. 316), a United States industrial corporation, Deep Sea Minerals, has been active on a global basis.[102]

238. Work on the Norway-Cook Islands joint initiative in polymetallic nodules offshore Cook Islands (see A/56/58, par. 315) appears to be in abeyance. A business case study was carried out under phase I of the project to determine the economic viability of mining the nodule deposits and evaluated the need to build up support institutions, formulate law and regulations, and study the environmental impacts of mining. After the completion of phase I, a review was made of the findings; no further plans are under way for the time being.

239. *Deep-sea minerals in the international seabed area and the work of the International Seabed Authority.*—The issuance of six contracts for exploration for polymetallic nodules in the international seabed area and the consideration of issues relating to regulations for prospecting and exploration for polymetallic sulphides and cobalt-rich crusts were mentioned above. The latter was initiated during the seventh session of the International Seabed Authority held in Kingston, Jamaica, from 2 to 13 July 2001. (For details about the issuance of contracts and the work of the Authority during the seventh session, see A/56/58/Add.1, paras. 74–77.)

240. There is a growing emphasis in the work of the Authority on the environmental considerations relating to the exploration and exploitation of minerals in the Area. Details of such considerations and the work of the Authority in this context are discussed in paragraphs 415 to 417.

241. Further work of the Authority includes the development of a central data repository relating to marine resources and the marine environment, the review and evaluation of additional data for the reserved areas for the Authority for polymetallic nodules, and the investigation of a geological model of the Clarion-Clipperton Zone, the area where the six contract-holders will carry out exploration for polymetallic nodules.

242. In its contribution to the present report, ECLAC stated that as a follow-up to a document issued during the previous biennium, a new document on the work of the Authority was prepared. It deals with the provisions of the Mining Code, highlighting certain issues deserving special attention from a regional standpoint, especially that of the ECLAC region.

C. Sustainable Development of Small Island Developing States

243. The sustainable development of small island developing States, especially in their efforts towards the alleviation and eradication of poverty, is intrinsically linked with the sustainable development and protection and preservation of the oceans

102. M. J. Cruickshank, op. cit.

and seas. Agenda 21 highlights that, for small island developing States, the ocean and coastal environment is of strategic importance and constitutes a valuable development resource.[103]

244. The characteristics that highlight the economic vulnerabilities and environmental fragility of small island developing States are widely accepted. In recognition of this, specific provisions catering to the special geographic characteristics and vulnerabilities of small island developing States are entrenched in UNCLOS and other international legal instruments in Agenda 21, Chapter 17, and other major non-binding instruments.[104]

245. The two resolutions adopted by the General Assembly at its fifty-sixth session (resolutions 56/12 and 56/13) under the agenda item "Oceans and the law of the sea" contained relevant paragraphs that are specific to small island developing States in their application.

246. Currently 34 of the 41 small island developing States (for a list of those States, see A/56/58, Annex VI) have ratified UNCLOS with three signatories.[105] A further 21 ratifications by small island developing States of the Agreement on Part XI of UNCLOS have been registered.[106] Of the current total of 30 ratifications of the 1995 Fish Stocks Agreement, 14 are small island States.

247. The creation of exclusive economic zones and the rights and obligations attached to their management has been a major factor for small island developing States becoming parties to UNCLOS. With their comparatively smaller land mass and consequentially severely limited land resources, small island developing States enjoy sovereign rights to exploit and manage marine resources in their respective exclusive economic zones in accordance with the provisions of UNCLOS. For many small island developing States, this UNCLOS development opened the way for economic opportunities. The adoption of the UNCLOS provisions concerning archipelagic baselines[107] meant that archipelagic States could potentially exercise jurisdiction over large ocean spaces. As a result the jurisdiction of small island developing States in the South Pacific region, for example, covers some 30 million square kilometres,[108] leading regional experts to conclude that perhaps the most suitable label for the region may be "large ocean developing States".

248. Delineation of the various maritime boundaries and zones in accordance with UNCLOS is an important requirement under the Convention, as such zones and boundaries relate to legal jurisdiction and rights and obligations of UNCLOS parties. Implementation of these provisions of UNCLOS, however, requires survey

103. Agenda 21, Chap. 17.G, par. 17.128.

104. UNCLOS Arts. 6, 7(1), 13, 47(1), 47(4), 121(2) re archipelagic States; Arts. 46, 47(1), 53(5) re regime of islands; Arts. 121 re Island States, AGXI/A/S3 (15) (d): United Nations Framework Convention on Climate Change, Agenda 21, Chap. 17.G; 1994 Declaration of Barbados and Programme for the Sustainable Development of Small Island Developing States, which includes chapter I, "Climate change and sea level rise" and chapter IV, "Marine and coastal development," respectively. Barbados 1994.

105. As at 31 January 2001.

106. As at 31 January 2001.

107. UNCLOS, Art. 47.

108. J. Kotobalavu, "Extended maritime jurisdiction in the Pacific: maximizing benefits from marine resources," in *The International Implications of Extended Maritime Jurisdiction in the Pacific*, Honolulu, Law of the Sea Institute, 1988, p. 117.

and monitoring technologies, and access to such high technology to allow small island developing States to implement these UNCLOS provisions needs to be addressed.

249. The limited resources and lack of technical capacity and know-how, coupled with limited financial resources and technological capability and other inherent disadvantages of small island developing States, including remoteness in many cases continue to pose challenges in their efforts to explore and exploit marine resources and thus to fully implement UNCLOS.

250. UNCLOS further provides procedures by which continental shelves beyond 200 nautical miles can be claimed. The number of small island developing States that may make submissions under the procedures set forth in UNCLOS is not expected to be large. However, this highly technical area calls for a coordinated approach from the international community. It should be noted that a Trust Fund to assist developing States, in particular small island developing States, has been established. Small island developing States may benefit from assistance from the Fund.

251. Small island developing States continue to attach great importance to issues concerning the conservation, protection and preservation of coastal and marine resources and the overall health of the marine environment. Flowing from the general obligations that States have to protect and preserve the marine environment, UNCED and its Agenda 21 set out the guidelines for the sustainable development of the world's marine resources. Chapter 17 addressed the issue of the protection of the oceans, and Chapter 17.G addressed the issue of small island developing States. Agenda 21 recognized small island developing States as a "special case," for both environment and development. Their small size, limited resources, geographic dispersion and isolation from markets and unique vulnerabilities place them at a disadvantage economically and prevent economies of scale.

252. The Global Conference on the Sustainable Development of Small Island Developing States and its primary outcome, the Programme of Action for the Sustainable Development of Small Island Developing States[109] (Barbados Programme of Action) which was adopted at the Conference continues to serve as the blueprint for the sustainable development of small island developing States. Part IV, "Coastal and marine resources," of the Barbados Programme of Action sets out the basis for action to be taken and policies to be adopted at the national, regional and international levels. Although the Barbados Programme of Action is a non-binding document, it should be noted that with regard to the actions called for at the international level, its contents are in conformity with the general obligations outlined in UNCLOS as they apply to, in particular, global and regional cooperation in the protection and preservation of the marine environment[110] and the conservation and management of the living resources of the high seas.[111]

109. Report of the Global Conference on the Sustainable Development of Small Island Developing States, Bridgetown, 25 April–6 May 1994 (United Nations publication, Sales No. E.94.I.18 and corrigenda).

110. Part IV.C, par. (i), (iii), (v) and (vi) of the Barbados Programme of Action share elements that reflect aspects of Article 197 of Part XII of UNCLOS, which deals with "Cooperation on a global or regional basis."

111. UNCLOS Arts. 61, 62, 63, 64 and 1995 Fish Stocks Agreement.

253. The Barbados Programme of Action underwent a review and appraisal in 1999 during the twenty-second special session of the United Nations General Assembly. Coastal and marine resources issues[112] were categorized under "sectoral areas requiring urgent action." Fishery activities and the sustainable development of such activities within the exclusive economic zone and areas under national jurisdiction of small island developing States was one of the issues addressed in the review and appraisal of the Barbados Programme of Action.[113]

254. Fishery activities, especially in the exclusive economic zones of small island developing States, are an important source of foreign income in many of these countries. In some, it is the only viable source of foreign income. The importance placed on the development of the fisheries capacity of small island developing States was recognized by the General Assembly in resolution 56/13. In paragraph 9 of the resolution, the Assembly invited States and international financial institutions of the United Nations system to provide assistance according to Part VII of UNCLOS including, if appropriate, the development of special financial mechanisms or instruments to assist small island developing States to enable them to develop their national capacity to exploit fishery resources, including developing their domestically flagged fishing fleets, value-added processing and expansion of their economic base in the fishing industry, consistent with the duty to ensure the proper conservation and management of these fisheries resources.

255. Small island developing States continue to strengthen their regional fisheries management bodies. In the South Pacific, following the adoption of the Convention on the Conservation and Management of Highly Migratory Fisheries Stocks in the Western and Central Pacific (WCPC), signatories to WCPC convened in Christchurch, New Zealand, from 23 to 28 April 2001 for the first meeting in a series of preparatory conferences to undertake preliminary work that the new Tuna Commission established by WCPC will be required to assume upon entry into force. The second in this series of meetings will be held in Madang, Papua New Guinea, from 21 to 25 February 2002.

256. In the Caribbean, the CARICOM Regional Fisheries Mechanism (CRFM) is a recent initiative that replaces the CARICOM Fisheries Resources Assessment and Management Programme (CFRAMP),[114] a 12-year programme that commenced in 1991. The CRFM objectives include the consolidation and enhancement of regional cooperation and the promotion of sustainable fisheries management in the region, which requires a broad-based multidisciplinary approach.

257. The strengthening of national, subregional and regional capacity for negotiating fishing agreements was one of the issues which was identified during the review and appraisal of the Barbados Programme of Action as needing support from the international community. Such support to address this issue is built on the premise of a strong and committed partnership between small island developing States

112. Official Records of the General Assembly, Twenty-second Special Session, Supplement No. 2 (A/S-22(2), p. 8).

113. Ibid., paras. 14 and 15 (a), (d) and (f).

114. In January 1991, CFRAMP was officially launched with support from the Government of Canada to promote the sustainable use and conservation of the fisheries resources of CARICOM States. The development and establishment of CRFM will provide support to CARICOM States after the conclusion of the CFRAMP.

and the international community, one that was reiterated during the review of the Barbados Programme of Action. In the context of treaty negotiations, Pacific small island developing States have been involved in negotiations for the renewal of the multilateral treaty between the United States and the 16 Pacific Islands Forum States.[115] Forum Fisheries Agency (FFA) members, which include 14 small island developing States, met with the United States in Apia, Samoa, from 26 to 29 March 2001 to commence formal negotiations on the extension of the Treaty on Fisheries between Certain Pacific Island States and the United States of America. The Treaty currently provides a framework for access to the Western Pacific region by 50 United States purse seine vessels at a fee of US$ 18 million per annum for 10 years. The current arrangements expire on 15 June 2003.

258. The review and appraisal of the Barbados Programme of Action also identified, among other things, the need for greater regional coordination in management and monitoring, control and surveillance, including the management of straddling fish stocks and highly migratory fish stocks.[116]

259. There have been a number of recent developments that may provide assistance to small island developing States in managing their marine ecosystems. The United Nations Foundation announced on March 2001 that it would fund a pioneering project aimed at reversing the decline of the world's coral reefs. The International Coral Reef Action Network (ICRAN), which has secured up to $10 million from the United Nations Foundation, the largest to date in the Foundation's environment portfolio, will support "flagship" coral reef management demonstration sites in four regional seas: these include regions such as the wider Caribbean and the South Pacific. It is expected that the sites within these regions will become blueprints for managing threatened coral reefs worldwide, protecting them from overfishing, pollution, oil spills and the impacts of growing coastal populations (see also par. 434).

260. The Conference of Plenipotentiaries on Specially Protected Areas and Wildlife in the Wider Caribbean (SPAW), held in Kingston from 15 to 18 January 1990, adopted the SPAW Protocol to the Cartagena Convention, which came into force on 18 June 2000. The first SPAW Meeting was convened in Havana on 24 and 25 September 2001. Reflecting the unavoidable integrated approach in dealing with oceans issues, one of the Meeting's objectives was to review the scope of the SPAW Protocol and its relationship with the work of the Convention on Biological Diversity and SBSTTA.

261. In the Pacific region, the Convention to Ban the Importation into Forum Island Countries of Hazardous and Radioactive Wastes and to Control the Transboundary Movement and Management of Hazardous Wastes within the South Pacific Region (Waigani Convention) entered into force on 21 October 2001 following the tenth ratification. The Convention obligates its parties to take appropriate legal, administrative and other measures within areas under their jurisdiction to ban the import of all hazardous wastes and radioactive wastes from outside the Convention area.

262. Small island developing States have been engaged in preparation for the World Summit on Sustainable Development, to be held in Johannesburg, South

115. 14 States of the Pacific Islands Forum are small island developing States.

116. Official Records of the General Assembly, Twenty-second Special Session, Supplement No. 2 (A/S-22/2), p. 9, par. 15 (i).

Africa, from 24 August to 4 September 2002. The Pacific Subregional Preparatory Commission meeting was hosted by the South Pacific Regional Environment Programme (SPREP) in Apia, Samoa, from 5 to 7 September 2001. The Caribbean subregion met in Havana on 28 and 29 June 2001. These meetings were followed by an interregional preparatory meeting for the Summit at Singapore from 7 to 11 January 2002. A Declaration adopted at the Singapore meeting, among other things, called for the establishment or strengthening of policies and programmes to manage the ocean resources in a sustainable manner, the development of holistic island system management and ecosystem-based management approaches at the national level, and the promotion of an integrated management approach through a regional oceans and seas policy with access to appropriate technology, data management systems and related research and capacity building.

263. Furthermore, the Global Conference on Oceans and Coasts at Rio+10, held at UNESCO headquarters in Paris from 3 to 7 December 2001, made key recommendations specific to small island developing States which pointed to the need to: integrate economic, environmental, and social vulnerable factors into a vulnerability index with special applicability to small island developing States; secure greater and sustainable returns from ocean resources through improved domestic policies and legislation, improved terms of trade in ocean resources and higher levels of domestic and foreign investment; build capacity for the sound management of the exclusive economic zones of small island developing States; call for the convening of a Barbados Programme of Action+10 conference for a full and comprehensive review to focus on achievements, constraints and new initiatives necessary to significantly advance sustainable development within small island developing States.

264. The continued financial assistance through such international financial mechanisms as the Global Environment Facility (GEF) supports initiatives that have assisted small island developing States in their sustainable development programmes. The Country Dialogue Workshops programme is designed to promote country "ownership" of GEF co-financed activities, facilitate national coordination on countries' GEF programmes and enhance awareness of GEF. In 2001, Indian Ocean region workshops were held in the Comoros, Mauritius and Seychelles from 10 to 13 July and, for Pacific small island developing States, from 17 to 20 September in Apia, Samoa.

265. GEF reported that some 32 small island developing States have been participating in GEF-supported projects such as the GEF Large Marine Ecosystem projects and other international waters projects. The three regions of involvement with the international waters projects concerning small island developing States are Africa, Asia and the Pacific, and Latin America and the Caribbean.

266. In the Pacific region, 14 small island developing States [117] are participating in the Strategic Action Programme (see Annex II to the present report).

267. A recently initiated World Bank-supported project for small island developing States of the Western Indian Ocean is aimed at contributing to their capacity to address ship-related oil spills and to enhance their activities under a ship-related

117. Cook Islands, Fiji, Kiribati, Marshall Islands, Micronesia (Federated States of), Nauru, Niue, Palau, Papua New Guinea, Samoa, Solomon Islands, Tonga, Tuvalu and Vanuatu.

annex to the Nairobi Convention (the UNEP regional seas convention for the region).

268. FAO reported that it has continued to assist small island developing States in their capacity-building efforts (see par. 605). A project currently being developed by FAO under its FishCODE component, scheduled to start in early 2002, is on "Responsible Fisheries for Small Island Developing States." The aims of the project include enhancing the capabilities of fisheries administrations to improve the conservation, management, development and utilization of fisheries resources through technical assessments and the development of institutional guidelines; identifying the opportunities and formulating plans for enhancing existing fisheries industries and, where appropriate, establishing new ones; and promoting fishing fleet and shore facility privatization.

269. Climate change and its negative impacts, including sea-level rise, continue to pose great threats to small island developing States in terms of their environments, economies, livelihoods, the areas in which they may exercise sovereignty and sovereign rights, and in some cases, their very survival. In the United Nations Framework Convention on Climate Change, small island developing States are covered by the principle of "common but differentiated responsibility,"[118] which is accorded to developing States under the Convention. The Marrakesh Ministerial Declaration adopted at Marrakesh, Morocco, in November 2001 at the seventh session of the Conference of the Parties to the Convention[119] stated that the Parties remained deeply concerned that all countries, particularly developing countries, including the least developed countries and small island States, face increased risk of negative impacts of climate change.

270. Capacity-building to ensure that small island developing States are able to implement UNCLOS and benefit from the sustainable development of the oceans and seas[120] remains of utmost importance to small island developing States. The UNCLOS provisions in Articles 202, 203 under Part XII and the provisions on the development and transfer of marine technology under Part XIV may need to be fully implemented to enable developing States, including small island developing States, to be in a position to better perform the obligations expected of them as parties to UNCLOS.

271. For example, Article 276 of UNCLOS calls for the establishment of regional marine scientific and technological research centres, particularly in developing States, in order to stimulate and advance the conduct of marine scientific research by developing States and foster the transfer of marine technology. Currently no regional centres have been established in any of the small island developing States African, Caribbean, Indian Ocean and Pacific regions. The establishment of such regional centres to perform the functions, inter alia, that are outlined in Article 277 of UNCLOS may encourage and promote better implementation of UNCLOS in small island developing States regions. In many of these regions, where

118. United Nations Framework Convention on Climate Change, Article 3, "Principles," par. 1.2.

119. Marrakesh Ministerial Declaration, decision 1/CP.7, document FCCC/CP/2001/13/Add.1, chap. I.

120. General Assembly resolution 56/12, twelfth preambular paragraph.

marine-related national capacities are limited, the establishment of such regional centres is a viable option where their collective resources and strengths can be harnessed to, in turn, assist in the strengthening and building of national capacities of small island developing States parties to UNCLOS.

272. The issue of food security is an important element in the efforts of small island developing States towards achieving sustainable development. In this context, a holistic approach taking into account the management of the ocean's resources, the impact of climate change and sea-level rise, the pollution of the coasts of small island developing States from land-based sources and other socio-economic factors needs to be promoted and strengthened.

D. Underwater Cultural Heritage

273. On 2 November 2001, the 31st General Conference of UNESCO adopted the *UNESCO Convention on the Protection of the Underwater Cultural Heritage* (UCH Convention) by 87 affirmative votes, 4 against and 15 abstentions. No amendments were made to the text, which had been submitted to the Conference by the meeting of governmental experts. As a unique procedure, the President of the General Conference and the Director-General of UNESCO signed the certified copies in the six authoritative languages in lieu of signatures of member States. Member States can deposit their instrument of ratification, acceptance, approval or accession. Certain non-member States have the right to accede to the Convention (Article 26, par. 2), or may be invited to do so. The new Convention, which seeks to cover "all traces of human existence having a cultural, historical or archaeological character, which have been partially or totally under water, periodically or continuously for at least 100 years,"[121] will enter into force three months after the deposit of the twentieth instrument of ratification, acceptance, approval or accession.

274. Apart from restricting the activities of treasure hunters, those nations that adopt the UCH Convention will be expected to "impose sanctions for violations" which "shall be adequate in severity in securing compliance" (Article 17). The instrument binds States parties to "prevent the entry into their territory, the dealing in, or the possession of, underwater cultural heritage illicitly exported and/or recovered" (Article 14) and gives them power to seize such booty (Article 18).

275. One of the most important features of the UCH Convention is the annex, containing the rules concerning activities directed at underwater cultural heritage, which, in accordance with Article 33 of the Convention, form an integral part of it.

276. It should be noted that Article 3 of the UCH Convention stipulates that "nothing in this Convention shall prejudice the rights, jurisdiction and duties of States under international law, including the United Nations Convention on the Law of the Sea. This Convention shall be interpreted and applied in the context of and in a manner consistent with international law, including the United Nations Convention on the Law of the Sea." Attention should also be drawn to Article 25, paragraphs 3 to 5, on "Peaceful settlement of disputes" and the use of the mecha-

121. See UNESCO web site press release: www.unesco.org.

nisms established in UNCLOS under Part XV and, for the purpose of conciliation and arbitration, under Annexes V and VII of UNCLOS.

7. MARINE ENVIRONMENT

A. Protection and Preservation of the Marine Environment

277. In the years before the adoption of UNCLOS, a number of general multilateral agreements had been concluded to regulate specific sources of pollution, such as vessel-source pollution, dumping at sea, intervention in cases of maritime casualties and civil liability for vessel-source pollution. Ratification and enforcement of these instruments were unsatisfactory. At the same time other important problems, such as land-based sources of marine pollution and airborne pollution, were left unresolved.[122]

278. The recommendations of the United Nations Conference on the Human Environment (Stockholm, 1972) on marine pollution recognized the inadequacies of the existing regimes and underlined the need for a more comprehensive approach to the protection of the marine environment from all forms of pollution. UNCLOS provisions, in particular those contained in Part XII, represent the first attempt to create a general framework for a legal regime that establishes on a global basis the obligations, responsibilities and powers of States in all matters of marine environmental protection.[123]

279. UNCLOS creates a comprehensive, binding and directly enforceable regime for the protection and preservation of the marine environment, providing for general legal obligations coupled with a call for the development and implementation of detailed rules dealing with specific concerns. At the same time, it establishes a balance between economic development, social development and environmental protection, and in this sense foresees the concept of sustainable development. The Convention serves as a unifying framework for a growing number of more detailed international agreements on marine environmental protection and the utilization, conservation and management of marine resources. It provides for a dynamic interaction with these agreements by calling upon all States to harmonize national measures, elaborate global and regional rules, and periodically re-examine this body of law as necessary. The relationship between UNCLOS and other instruments on the protection and preservation of the marine environment is defined in Article 237. The Article provides that Part XII is without prejudice to the specific obligations assumed by States under special conventions concluded previously and which may be concluded in the future, as long as those obligations are carried out in a manner consistent with the general principles and objectives of UNCLOS. The Convention has also permitted the development of non-binding instruments (soft law), such as recommended practices, guidelines and criteria, which establish benchmarks for the development of national laws and policies.

122. A. E. Boyle, "Marine pollution under the Law of the Sea Convention," *American Journal of International Law,* vol. 79, no. 2 (1985): 347–372.

123. Ibid.

280. UNCED further developed the regime for the protection and preservation of the marine environment, building upon UNCLOS. Chapter 17 of Agenda 21 deals with "the protection of the oceans, all kinds of seas, including enclosed and semi-enclosed seas, and coastal areas and the protection, rational use and development of their living resources." UNCLOS and Agenda 21 are complementary to each other: UNCLOS provides the legal framework upon which Chapter 17 of Agenda 21 has built a programme of action. Paragraph 17.1 of Chapter 17 of Agenda 21 reaffirms that "the 1982 Convention sets forth the rights and obligations for States and provides the international basis upon which to pursue the protection and sustainable development of the marine environment and its resources."

1. Legal Regime for the Protection and Preservation of the Marine Environment

281. *Definition of pollution.*—UNCLOS defines pollution of the marine environment as "the introduction by man, directly or indirectly, of substances or energy into the marine environment, including estuaries, which results or is likely to result in such deleterious effects as harm to living resources and marine life, hazards to human health, hindrance to marine activities, including fishing and other legitimate uses of the seas, impairment of quality for use of sea water and reduction of amenities."

282. Chapter 17 of Agenda 21 introduced new terminology: the term "degradation" substituted for the term "pollution." Degradation is considered to include all deleterious effects resulting from anthropogenic modification of the physical, chemical or biological characteristics of the environment, as well as environmental impacts of technology (see A/49/631, par. 75).

283. *General obligations.*—Article 192 of UNCLOS establishes that States are under an obligation to protect and preserve the marine environment. This fundamental obligation embodies a radical change from the piecemeal approach previously applied to the protection and preservation of the marine environment. Chapter 17 of Agenda 21 recognizes that in order to achieve the goal of protection and preservation of the marine environment, States have to apply preventive, precautionary and anticipatory approaches; ensure prior assessment of activities that may have significant adverse impacts upon the marine environment; integrate protection of the marine environment into relevant general environmental, social and economic development policies; develop economic incentives to apply clean technologies and other means consistent with the internalization of environmental costs, such as the polluter pays principle, so as to avoid degradation of the marine environment; and improve the living standards of coastal populations, particularly in developing countries, so as to contribute to reducing the degradation of the coastal and marine environment (par. 17.22).

284. The general obligation under UNCLOS to protect and preserve the marine environment is qualified by Article 193, which provides that "States have the sovereign right to exploit their natural resources pursuant to their environmental policies and in accordance with their duty to protect and preserve the marine environment." The attempt to balance sovereign rights over natural resources and the duty to protect the environment is a precursor of the concept of sustainable development.

285. Moreover, the general obligation to protect and preserve the marine environment is given specific content in the other Articles of Part XII. Article 194 specifies the duty of States to take all measures necessary to prevent, reduce and control

the pollution of the marine environment from any source. States are required to take all necessary measures using "the best practicable means at their disposal and in accordance with their capabilities" (Article 194, par. 1). This qualification can be interpreted as an early application of the concept of "common but differentiated responsibility" (Rio Declaration, principle 7), aimed at balancing the common responsibility to conserve, protect and restore the environment with the differences in economic strength and in the extent of capacity. Agenda 21 (par. 17.2) confirms that the implementation of the instrument by developing countries shall be commensurate with their technological and financial capacities and priorities in allocating resources for development needs, and ultimately depends on capacity-building, technology transfer and financial resources.

286. The balance between the need to protect the marine environment and the need to avoid unjustifiable interference with activities carried out by other States in the exercise of their rights and duties (for example in relation to international navigation) is laid out in Article 194, paragraph 4. The concept is further elaborated in Part XII, section 7, of UNCLOS, which provides a series of safeguards with respect to the exercise of enforcement powers by both port and coastal States vis-à-vis flag States (see Articles 223–233).

287. Attempts to create a balance between the rights of coastal States to protect and preserve the marine environment under their jurisdiction and the rights of navigation and uses of the seas are found in various other instruments, such as the Basel Convention on the Control of Transboundary Movements of Hazardous Wastes and their Disposal, the Joint Convention on the Safety of Spent Fuel Management and on the Safety of Radioactive Waste Management, and the Code of Practice on the International Transboundary Movement of Radioactive Waste.

288. The primary duties contained in Article 194 provide the basis for a complex structure of rights and duties covering the control of pollution, the adoption and enforcement of laws and regulations, global and regional cooperation and assistance, monitoring and environmental assessment, notification and intervention, and State responsibility. The measures to be taken by States in order to fulfil their obligation to protect and preserve the marine environment include, inter alia, those necessary for the minimization of: the release of toxic, harmful or noxious substances from land-based sources, from or through the atmosphere or by dumping (Article 194, par. 3 [a]); pollution from vessels (Article 194, par. 3 [b]); pollution from installations and devices used for the exploration and exploitation of the natural resources of the seabed and subsoil (Article 194, par. 3 [c]); and pollution from other installations and devices operating in the marine environment (Article 194, par. 3 [d]). The measures shall also include those necessary to protect and preserve rare or fragile ecosystems as well as the habitat of depleted, threatened or endangered species and other forms of marine life (Article 194, par. 5); and to prevent, reduce and control pollution of the marine environment resulting from the use of technologies or the intentional or accidental introduction of species, alien or new, into a particular part of the marine environment (Article 196, par. 1).

289. Besides rules that apply to specific sources of pollution originating from activities on land and at sea, an integrated approach, viewing all sources of marine pollution as a whole, has also been developed. The duty not to transfer damage or hazards or transform one type of pollution into another, incorporated in UNCLOS by Article 195, is an example.

290. Some other principles emanated from UNCED, in particular, the now widely recognized principle of the precautionary approach and the principle that polluters should bear the cost of pollution. The ecosystem approach to the sustainable use of the environment and its resources, implicit in UNCLOS, and articulated throughout Agenda 21, offers a rational basis for assessing the effects of activities on the marine environment and the way they interact with other activities.

291. *Cooperation on global and regional basis.*—Article 197 of UNCLOS sets the general obligation of States to cooperate on a global basis and, as appropriate, on a regional basis, directly or through competent international organizations, in formulating and elaborating international rules, standards and recommended practices and procedures consistent with the Convention.

292. Agenda 21 dedicates a programme area to "Strengthening international, including regional, cooperation and coordination". Paragraph 17.115 specifies that the role of international cooperation is to support and supplement national efforts, and that the implementation of strategies and activities under the programme areas relative to marine and coastal areas and seas requires effective institutional arrangements at the national, subregional, regional and global levels in order to ensure the effective implementation of strategies and activities. Institutions at all levels are required to improve coordination and strengthen links among them.

293. *Cooperation in notification and response measures in cases of imminent or actual danger by pollution.*—The concept of cooperation under UNCLOS encompasses the duty of notification of imminent or actual danger, as well as the duty to cooperate to eliminate the effects of pollution and prevent and minimize the damage.

294. Under Article 198, when a State becomes aware of cases in which the marine environment is in imminent danger of being damaged or has been damaged by pollution, it shall immediately notify other States it deems likely to be affected by such damage, as well as competent international organizations. Article 211, paragraph 7, provides that the international rules and standards to prevent, reduce and control pollution from vessels should include, inter alia, those relating to prompt notification to coastal States, whose coastline or related interests may be affected by incidents, including maritime casualties, which involve discharges or the probability of discharges.

295. Principle 18 of the Rio Declaration reaffirms that States shall immediately notify other States of any natural disasters or other emergencies that are likely to produce sudden harmful effects on the environment of those States, and that every effort shall be made by the international community to help States so afflicted.

296. Several global instruments include provisions for notification, among them MARPOL 73/78; the Oil Pollution Preparedness, Response and Cooperation Convention (OPRC Convention); the Convention on Early Notification of a Nuclear Accident; the International Code for the Safe Carriage of Packaged Irradiated Nuclear Fuel, Plutonium and High-Level Radioactive Wastes on Board Ships (INF Code); the Convention on Biological Diversity; and the International Seabed Authority Mining Code.

297. UNCLOS provisions to the effect that States shall take measures in relation to pollution from vessels, pollution from installations and devices used in the exploration or exploitation of the natural resources of the seabed and subsoil, and pollution from other installations and devices operating in the marine environment, refer, inter

alia, to measures for preventing accidents and dealing with emergencies (Article 194, par. 3 [b], [c], [d]). UNCLOS also provides for States to cooperate in establishing contingency plans against pollution (Article 199). In particular, it requires States, in accordance with their capabilities, and the competent international organizations to cooperate in eliminating the effects of pollution and preventing or minimizing damage. To this end States are under a duty to develop and promote contingency plans for responding to pollution incidents. Article 221 reiterates the right of States to take and enforce proportionate measures beyond the territorial sea to protect their coastline, or related interests, from pollution arising after a maritime casualty or acts relating to such a casualty, which may reasonably be expected to result in major harmful consequences (see par. 395). Article 202 (b) requests States to provide appropriate assistance, especially to developing States, for the minimization of the effects of major incidents, which may cause serious pollution of the marine environment.

298. Agenda 21 requires States to establish coordinating mechanisms for integrated management and sustainable development, which shall include contingency plans to deal with degradation and pollution of anthropogenic origin, including spills of oil and other materials (par. 17.6 [e]). States are also invited to intensify international cooperation to strengthen or establish regional oil/chemical response centres or mechanisms in cooperation with subregional, regional or global intergovernmental organizations and industry-based organizations.

299. In the field of trade and maritime transport of nuclear materials and radioactive waste, the 1993 International Code for the Safe Carriage of Packaged Irradiated Nuclear Fuel, Plutonium and High-Level Radioactive Wastes on Board Ships (INF Code) (mandatory under SOLAS as of 1 January 2001) provides for measures on preparedness on board ships: Chapter 10, on "Shipboard emergency plan," establishes that every ship carrying INF cargo shall carry on board a shipboard emergency plan.

300. In the field of nuclear safety, the Convention on Assistance in the Case of a Nuclear Accident or Radiological Emergency (1986) sets out an international framework for cooperation among States parties and with IAEA to facilitate prompt assistance and support in the event of nuclear accidents or radiological emergencies.

301. In the field of pollution from vessels,[124] the need for emergency preparedness and response to marine pollution was developed at first in relation to oil spills at sea and to the response measures needed to be implemented by land-based personnel in order to protect the coast. The 1969 International Convention relating to Intervention on the High Seas in Cases of Oil Pollution Casualties together with its 1973 Protocol provides that the parties to the Convention have a right to take proportionate measures on the high seas as may be necessary to prevent, mitigate or eliminate grave and imminent danger to their coastline or related interests from pollution or the threat of pollution of the sea by oil, following upon a maritime casualty or acts related to such a casualty, which may reasonably be expected to result in major harmful consequences. The Protocol relating to Intervention on the High Seas in Cases of Marine Pollution by Substances other than Oil was adopted in 1973 to extend the regime of the 1969 Intervention Convention to substances which are either listed in the annex to the Protocol or which have characteristics substantially similar to those substances. The list of substances included in the annex

124. The information on pollution from vessels was mostly taken from www.imo.org.

to the Protocol was updated in 1991 and 1996. The Marine Environment Protection Committee of IMO at its 47th session will consider the development of a draft amendment to the annex to the 1973 Protocol to include a simple cross-reference to the criteria and lists of chemicals included in existing instruments, in order to ensure the most expeditious means of maintaining information on chemicals covered by the Protocol.

302. In recent years the number of agreements covering measures for emergency preparedness and response has increased enormously, to cover accidents involving oil as well as other hazardous and noxious substances. The measures include those relating to preparedness on board ships and at offshore and shore-based facilities, as well as shore-based centres set up to respond to emergencies. Such instruments include OPRC, the Protocol on Preparedness, Response and Cooperation to Pollution Incidents by Hazardous and Noxious Substances (2000) (HNS Protocol), the International Convention on Salvage, and the Draft Wreck Removal Convention (WRC).

303. At the regional level, most of the regional conventions have adopted protocols on cooperation in combating pollution from vessels in cases of emergency. Agenda 21 in paragraph 17.34 invited States to intensify international cooperation to strengthen or establish regional oil/chemical response centres and/or mechanisms in cooperation with relevant organizations. Recognizing the progress made by IMO and UNEP regional seas programmes in strengthening their collaborative approach to issues of oil-spill preparedness and response, the Fourth Global Meeting of Regional Seas Conventions and Action Plans (Montreal, November 2001) recommended that further collaboration should be developed, especially in the form of developing and amending existing relevant protocols, establishing regional activity centres, developing regional contingency plans and investing in regional training and exercises. Exploration and implementation of interlinkages with potential partners (e.g., the oil and shipping industry) was also encouraged.

304. *Integrated approach as part of cooperation at national, regional and international levels.*—In the preamble to UNCLOS, the fundamental principle is laid out "that the problems of ocean space are closely interrelated and need to be considered as a whole." The comprehensive regime created under the Convention, dealing with all sources of marine pollution (Article 194, par. 3), placing a duty on States to cooperate for the formulation of relevant international laws (Article 197) as well as to implement them at the national level (Article 194, par. 2), constitutes the basis for an integrated approach to the protection and preservation of the marine environment (see also paras. 646–675 below).

305. Chapter 17 of Agenda 21 states from the outset that the marine environment, including the oceans and all kinds of seas and adjacent coastal areas, forms an integrated whole that is an essential component of the global life-support system and a positive asset that presents opportunities for sustainable development. This requires new approaches to marine and coastal area management and development, at the national, subregional, regional and global levels, approaches that are integrated in content and precautionary and anticipatory in nature. Programme area A of Chapter 17 requests that coastal States create appropriate coordinating management mechanisms, improve their capacity to collect, analyse, assess and use information for sustainable use, including environmental impacts of activities affecting the coastal and marine areas, and underlines the role of international and regional

cooperation and coordination. The provisions of Part XII of UNCLOS on global and regional cooperation, monitoring and environmental assessment as well as those on studies, research programmes and exchange of information and data provide the legal framework for States to implement such requirements.

306. *Scientific research.*—In recognition of the need to gather information and data on marine pollution in order to expedite the analysis of the problem and the determination of the appropriate response measures, UNCLOS places a duty upon States to cooperate in order to promote studies, undertake programmes of scientific research and encourage the exchange of information and data acquired about pollution of the marine environment. States are under a duty to participate actively in regional and global programmes to acquire knowledge for the assessment of the nature and extent of pollution, exposure to it, and its pathways, risks and remedies (Article 200). On the basis of such data, States are under a duty to cooperate in establishing appropriate scientific criteria for the formulation and elaboration of rules, standards and recommended practices and procedures for the prevention, reduction and control of the pollution of the marine environment (Article 201).

307. Agenda 21 places a great emphasis on the importance of scientific research in relation to the protection of the marine environment. To this end States are required to cooperate in the development and establishment of the necessary systematic observation, research and information management systems, regularly exchange information on marine degradation, establishing clearing-house mechanisms on marine pollution control information, and establish global profile databases providing information on the sources, types, amounts and effects of pollutants reaching the marine environment (e.g., paras. 17.13 and 17.35) (see also A/56/121, part B, paras. 161–171).

308. *Monitoring and environmental assessment.*—A marine environmental assessment is a compilation of current knowledge about a defined area of the sea, an evaluation of this information in relation to agreed criteria for environmental quality and a statement of the prevailing condition of the area. Assessments should be regarded by managers and scientists as a normal part of the environmental protection process, whether at the local, national, regional or international level.[125]

309. The formal process known today as environmental impact assessment is the result of the enhanced awareness in the 1950s and 1960s that many industrial and other projects were producing undesirable effects on the environment. In response many Governments developed mechanisms to ensure that the environmental consequences of all major projects and plans were estimated before their execution was formally authorized.[126]

310. UNCLOS requires States, as far as practicable, to observe, measure, evaluate and analyse, by recognized scientific methods, the risks or effects of pollution of the marine environment, and in particular they must keep under surveillance the effects of activities under their control (both within and beyond national jurisdiction) and determine whether they are likely to pollute the marine environment (Article 204). The results so obtained must be published at appropriate intervals to

125. "Guidelines for Marine Environmental Assessments," GESAMP Reports and Studies No. 54, 1994.

126. "An approach to environmental impact assessment from projects affecting the coastal and marine environment," UNEP Regional Seas Reports and Studies No. 122, 1990.

the competent international organization, which should make them available to States (Article 205). Moreover, when States have reasonable grounds for believing that planned actions under their jurisdiction or control may cause substantial pollution or significant and harmful changes to the marine environment, they shall, as far as practicable, assess the potential effects of such activities and report the results of such assessments (Article 206).

311. The qualification "as far as practicable" included in Articles 204 and 206 covers the situations in which States are not in a position to carry out assessments or monitor these activities. In order to redress this eventuality, UNCLOS provides that States shall provide advice on and assistance in developing facilities for research, monitoring, educational and other programmes (Article 202, par. [a] [v]), as well as appropriate assistance, especially to developing States, concerning the preparation of environmental assessments (Article 202, par. [c]).

312. Agenda 21 contains throughout Chapter 17 a request that States engage in prior environmental impact assessment, systematic observation and follow-up of major projects, including the systematic incorporation of results in decision-making, ensuring prior assessment of activities that may have significant adverse impacts upon the marine environment and establishing monitoring programmes in relation to all sources of pollution. States are required to improve their capacity to collect, analyse, assess and use information for the sustainable use of resources, including on the environmental impacts of activities affecting the coastal and marine areas (par. 17.8).

313. Monitoring and environmental impact assessment requirements are provided for in most regional seas conventions, some of them (e.g., the Helsinki Convention on the Protection of the Marine Environment in the Baltic Sea Area [HELCOM Convention] and the Antarctic Treaty), are even more advanced in requiring consultations with potentially affected States. The full participation of institutions and experts from developing countries is facilitated by the intensive training of local personnel and considerable technical assistance provided to the institutions participating in the programme.

314. It is especially important to ensure the comparability of the data generated by monitoring programmes. For this reason, UNEP has worked from the beginning to ensure that monitoring in the regional seas is based on a common methodology, which is mandatory for all participating labs. A series of publications entitled Reference Methods for Marine Pollution Studies was developed in cooperation with IOC, FAO, WHO and WMO and under the technical coordination of the IAEA Monaco Laboratory. In order to ensure the proper use of the Reference Methods and to provide a reliable basis for intercalibration exercises and quality control of data, reference materials (i.e., standards, certified reference materials, intercomparison samples and research materials) have been prepared and made available to the users of the Reference Methods. The participants in the monitoring programmes also frequently attend workshops where sampling and analytical techniques are tested and compared using a hands-on approach.

315. At the global level, a number of organizations and programmes have been monitoring the marine environment and assessing the threats to its health on a global and regional scale. One of the first organizations concerned with ocean science was the International Council for the Exploration of the Sea (ICES). Others include the IOC Marine Pollution Monitoring Pilot Programme (MAPMOPP, 1975–

1980), which later evolved into the IOC Marine Pollution Monitoring Programme (MARPOLMON); the Joint Group of Experts on the Scientific Aspects of Marine Environmental Protection (GESAMP) (for details on the work of GESAMP, in particular in relation to marine environmental assessment, see paras. 668–674 below); the Global Investigation of Pollution in the Marine Environment (GIPME), an international cooperative programme of scientific investigation focused on marine contamination and pollution; and the Global Coral Reef Monitoring Network (GCRMN), recently established by UNEP, IOC, WMO and IUCN to assess the status of and threats to coral reefs. There is also a recent initiative, the Global International Waters Assessment (GIWA), led by UNEP and funded by the Global Environment Facility, to assess the state of international waters, including marine, coastal and inland areas.

316. At its twenty-first session, held at Nairobi in February 2001, the UNEP Governing Council adopted a decision (decision 21/13) on a global assessment of the state of the marine environment, in which it requested the Executive Director of UNEP, in cooperation with IOC/UNESCO and other United Nations agencies, the secretariat of the Convention on Biological Diversity, and the regional seas programmes, to explore the feasibility of establishing a regular process for assessment of the state of the marine environment. The decision was based on a discussion paper presented by the Government of Iceland to the Governing Council at the session. In the paper it was underlined that although there was a wealth of information available about the marine environment, there was a lack of an overview, in particular on the links between the state of the marine environment and cross-cutting issues of human health, seafood safety and sustainable fisheries. Regular assessments of the impact of human activity (climate-related, pollution, physical alteration and destruction of habitats) on the state of the marine environment at the national, regional and global level were needed, in particular to inform decision makers.[127]

317. Following the adoption of the UNEP Governing Council decision, a meeting was convened in Reykjavik from 12 to 14 September 2001 to determine whether an assessment process was needed and to deliberate on related issues. During the meeting, country representatives insisted that any proposals for a new mechanism would not receive support from their Governments. It was suggested that a reformed GESAMP, provided with adequate funding, might be the best option, largely because of its strong scientific expertise.[128] The next meeting in this connection is to be held in Bremen, Germany, from 18 to 20 March 2002 (see also par. 673).

318. It is important to note in this context the launching in June 2001 of the Millennium Ecosystem Assessment, an initiative designed to improve the management of the world's natural and managed ecosystems through the gathering of policy-relevant scientific information.[129] The United Nations as well as other international agencies, scientific groups, Governments, foundations and NGOs are involved in the initiative. Coastal ecosystems and oceans were identified as components of the assessment.

127. The full text of the paper can be found at www.unep.org/marineassessment/.

128. The report of the meeting can be found at www.unep.org/marineassessment/reports/iceland_report/FinalReportNovember2001a.doc.

129. The report on the Millennium Ecosystem Assessment can be found at: www.un.org/millennium/sg/report/full.

319. Several agencies of the United Nations system, in particular IOC, WMO and UNEP, recognized the need for a comprehensive, long-term, global monitoring programme to observe phenomena related to climate change and began preparations for such a programme, taking advantage of ongoing international, regional and national programmes in this area. Such programmes include: World Climate Research Programme (WCRP), including the World Ocean Circulation Experiment (WOCE) and Tropical Oceans and Global Atmosphere (TOGA); Joint Global Ocean Flux Study (JGOFS); Global Ocean Observing System (GOOS), including the Integrated Global Ocean Service System (IGOSS) and the Global Sea Level Observing System (GLOSS); and Land-Ocean Interactions in the Coastal Zone (LOICZ).

320. In 1990, the United Nations agencies submitted to experts for consideration a draft proposal for a "Long-term global monitoring system of coastal and near-shore phenomena related to global climate changes." As a follow-up, currently the integrated global observing systems, three interrelated global systems to observe the environment of the planet (GCOS, GOOS and GTOS), are being organized by United Nations organizations in cooperation with the scientific community and national Governments to become the main elements of the United Nations system-wide Earthwatch.

321. *Technical assistance.*—The duty to assist developing countries in their effort to protect and preserve the marine environment is clearly spelled out under UNCLOS in Section 3 of Part XII, entitled "Technical assistance." Article 202 requires States to: (a) promote programmes of scientific, educational, technical and other assistance to developing States, which should include training of scientific and technical personnel, facilitating their participation in relevant international programmes, supplying them with the necessary equipment and facilities, enhancing their capacity to manufacture such equipment, advice on and developing facilities for research, monitoring, educational and other programmes; (b) provide appropriate assistance, especially to developing States, for the minimization of the effects of major incidents which may cause serious pollution of the marine environment; and (c) provide them with appropriate assistance concerning the preparation of environmental assessments.

322. The Convention further requests international organizations to grant preference to developing countries for the purpose of the prevention, reduction and control of pollution of the marine environment in the allocation of appropriate funds and technical assistance and in the utilization of their specialized services (Article 203).

323. States are also obliged to promote international technical and scientific cooperation with regard to activities in the Area either between the parties concerned or by developing training, technical assistance and scientific cooperation programmes in marine science and technology and the protection and preservation of the marine environment (Agreement relating to the Implementation of Part XI of the United Nations Convention on the Law of the Sea of 10 December 1982, Annex, sect. 5, Art. 1 [c]).

324. Agenda 21 underlined, throughout Chapter 17, the importance of providing support especially to developing countries in relation to the protection and preservation of the marine environment. States are invited to provide access to and transfer environmentally safe technologies and methodologies (par. 17.13); coastal States are invited to promote and facilitate the organization of education and training for

all interested parties, and international organizations should support them in such efforts, devoting special attention to developing countries (paras. 17.15 and 17.16); full cooperation should be extended to coastal States in their capacity-building efforts and, where appropriate, capacity-building should be included in bilateral and multilateral development cooperation (par. 17.17). States also agreed that the provision of additional financial resources, through appropriate international mechanisms, as well as access to cleaner technologies and relevant research, are necessary to support action by developing countries in relation to marine environmental protection (par. 17.23). Transfer of technology, allocation of funds for capacity-building and training programmes to ensure the full participation of developing countries in initiatives aimed at ensuring marine environmental protection from all sources of pollution are also provided for (paras. 17.35 (f), 17.37, 17.38 (f) and 17.40–17.43).

325. *Liability, compensation and sovereign immunity.*—Article 235 of UNCLOS provides that States are responsible for the fulfilment of their international obligations concerning the protection and preservation of the marine environment (it is worth noting that the provision is not limited to obligations vis-à-vis the marine environment under the jurisdiction of other States) and that they shall be liable in accordance with international law.[130]

326. States are under a duty to ensure the availability of prompt and adequate compensation or other relief in respect of damage caused by pollution of the marine environment by natural or juridical persons under their jurisdiction. In order to ensure prompt and adequate compensation, States are under a duty to cooperate in the implementation of existing international law and the further development of international law relating to responsibility and liability for the assessment of and compensation for damage, the settlement of related disputes and the development of criteria and procedures for payment of adequate compensation (e.g., compulsory insurance or compensation funds). In fact the Convention states that its provisions regarding responsibility and liability for damage are without prejudice to the application of existing rules and the development of further rules regarding responsibility and liability under international law (Article 304).

327. Sovereign immunity is granted to warships, naval auxiliaries and other vessels or aircraft owned or operated by a State and used for government non-commercial service. However, flag States are responsible for ensuring that such vessels or aircraft act in a manner consistent with the Convention (Article 236).

328. Under principle 13 of the Rio Declaration, States shall develop national law regarding liability and compensation for the victims of pollution and other environmental damage. States shall also cooperate in an expeditious and more determined manner to develop further international law regarding liability and compensation for adverse effects of environmental damage caused by activities within their jurisdiction or control to areas beyond their jurisdiction.

329. Examples of major specific global agreements on liability for damage to the marine environment are provided below.

330. In 1969, the International Convention on Civil Liability for Oil Pollution

130. It is important to note that the International Law Commission at its fifty-third session (2001) adopted new draft Articles on responsibility of States for internationally wrongful acts. The General Assembly, in its resolution 56/83 of 12 December 2001, took note of the Articles and com-

Damage (CLC) was adopted to deal with the civil liability of the ship or cargo owner for damage suffered as a result of a pollution casualty. The purpose of the Convention was to ensure that adequate compensation was paid to victims and the liability was placed on the shipowner.

331. The liability limits established were considered to be too low, and the compensation made available in some cases, therefore, might have proved to be inadequate. As a result, the convention establishing the International Fund for Compensation for Oil Pollution Damage (Fund Convention) was adopted. Unlike the Civil Liability Convention, which puts the onus on the shipowner, the Fund is made up of contributions from oil importers. The idea is that if an accident at sea results in pollution damage which exceeds the compensation available under the Civil Liability Convention, the Fund will be available to pay an additional amount, while the burden of compensation will be spread more evenly between shipowner and cargo interests.

332. The limits of liability in the two conventions were greatly increased through amendments adopted by a conference held in 1992, and again during the 82nd session of the Legal Committee, held from 16 to 20 October 2000 (these amendments are expected to enter into force on 1 November 2003).

333. In 1996, the International Convention on Liability and Compensation for Damage in Connection with the Carriage of Hazardous and Noxious Substances (HNS) by Sea was adopted (not yet in force). It has generally been agreed that it would not have been possible to provide sufficient cover through shipowner liability alone for the damage that could be caused in connection with the carriage of HNS cargo (such as chemicals). Shipowner liability is therefore supplemented by the HNS Fund, financed by cargo interests.

334. IMO in its contribution to the present report stated that the one significant gap remaining in the international regime for compensating victims of oil spills from ships in accordance with Article 235 of UNCLOS was addressed with the adoption by IMO of a new convention on liability and compensation for pollution from ships' bunkers. A diplomatic conference held from 19 to 23 March 2001 at IMO headquarters in London reached agreement on the details of the convention. The International Convention on Civil Liability for Bunker Oil Pollution Damage, 2001, will establish a liability and compensation regime for spills of oil, when carried as fuel in ships' bunkers. Current regimes covering oil spills do not include bunker oil spills from vessels other than tankers.

335. The adoption of a bunkers convention completes the task initiated by the Legal Committee when it was established by IMO more than 30 years ago, namely, the adoption of a comprehensive set of unified international rules governing the award of prompt and effective compensation to all victims of ship-sourced pollution.

336. The Basel Protocol on Liability and Compensation for Damage Resulting from Transboundary Movements of Hazardous Wastes and their Disposal was adopted at the Fifth Conference of the Parties to the Basel Convention on 10 Decem-

---

mended them to the attention of Governments (for the text of the Articles, see Resolution 56/83, annex).

ber 1999. The Protocol negotiations began in 1993 in response to the concerns of developing countries about their lack of funds and technologies for coping with illegal dumping or accidental spills. The objective of the Protocol is to provide for a comprehensive regime for liability as well as adequate and prompt compensation for damage resulting from the transboundary movement of hazardous wastes and other wastes, including incidents occurring because of illegal traffic in those wastes (Article 1). The Fifth Conference of the Parties also adopted a decision for an interim arrangement to cover emergency situations until the Protocol enters into force.

337. Article 15 (Responsibility and liability) of the 1996 Protocol to the Convention on the Prevention of Marine Pollution by Dumping of Wastes and Other Matter (1972 London Convention) establishes that "in accordance with the principles of international law regarding State responsibility for damage to the environment of other States or to any other area of the environment, the Contracting Parties undertake to develop procedures regarding liability arising from the dumping or incineration at sea of wastes or other matter."

338. In September 1997, Governments took a significant step forward in improving the liability regime for nuclear damage by adopting the Protocol to Amend the 1963 Vienna Convention on Civil Liability for Nuclear Damage (not yet in force) and the Convention on Supplementary Compensation for Nuclear Damage (not yet in force). The Protocol contains, inter alia, a better definition of nuclear damage (now also addressing the concept of environmental damage and preventive measures), extends the geographical scope of the Vienna Convention and extends the period during which claims may be brought for loss of life and personal injury. The Convention on Supplementary Compensation defines additional amounts to be provided through contributions by States parties on the basis of installed nuclear capacity and the United Nations rate of assessment. Taken together, the two instruments should substantially enhance the global framework for compensation well beyond that foreseen by existing conventions.

339. Before these developments occurred in 1997, the international liability regime for nuclear damage consisted of the Vienna Convention on Civil Liability for Nuclear Damage of 1963 and the Paris Convention on Third Party Liability in the Field of Nuclear Energy of 1960 (as amended by the 1963 Brussels Supplementary Convention), linked by the Joint Protocol relating to the Application of the Vienna Convention and the Paris Convention on Civil Liability for Nuclear Damage of 1988. Under these Conventions, inter alia, liability is channelled exclusively to the operators of the nuclear installations; liability of the operator is absolute; liability is limited in amount and time; the operator must maintain insurance of other financial security for an amount corresponding to his liability; if such security is insufficient, the installation State is obliged to make up the difference up to the limit of the operator's liability. The Joint Protocol of 1988 established a link between the Conventions, combining them into one expanded liability regime.

340. In 1971, IMO, in association with the International Atomic Energy Agency and the European Nuclear Energy Agency of the Organisation for Economic Cooperation and Development, convened a conference which adopted the Convention relating to Civil Liability in the field of Maritime Carriage of Nuclear Material to regulate liability in respect of damage arising from the maritime carriage of nuclear substances.

341. *Settlement of marine environmental disputes under UNCLOS.*—Under UNCLOS any dispute not settled in accordance with Article 2, paragraph 3, of the Charter of the United Nations, can be settled by recourse to the International Court of Justice, the International Tribunal for the Law of the Sea, arbitral tribunals or special arbitral tribunals (see Article 287). Special arbitral tribunals may receive a submission only in relation to four categories of disputes, among them protection and preservation of the marine environment, and navigation, including pollution from vessels and by dumping.[131] The members of such tribunals are drawn from lists of experts, maintained for each of the four fields by FAO, UNEP, IOC and IMO respectively, as opposed to being drawn from a single list of experienced persons.[132]

342. The court or tribunal, having duly received a submission, may prescribe any provisional measures which it considers appropriate under the circumstances to, inter alia, prevent serious harm to the marine environment, pending the final decision.[133]

343. The settlement of disputes mechanisms provided for in UNCLOS have the potential to play an important role in the development of international law relating to the protection and preservation of the marine environment. Such a case is already before the International Tribunal for the Law of the Sea, the MOX Plant Case (Ireland v. United Kingdom) (see paras. 557–563).

344. *Current challenges.*—Significant advances have been made in the development of international rules and standards for the protection and preservation of the marine environment. However, ratification and implementation of multilateral agreements as well as implementation of soft-law instruments, need to be broader.

345. Implementation at the national level is also a key issue for reaching the goal of sustainable development of oceans and seas. Although the past decade has witnessed the development of a number of initiatives at the national level, regional differences are significant. SOPAC reported that not many States in the region have actually enacted legislation to give full effect to a number of multilateral conventions and make the provisions enforceable in national law. This is due to the limited expertise (especially in legislative drafting) and human and financial resources in the area of marine pollution and its prevention. Moreover, the prevention of pollution is not a priority on the political agenda, especially in the light of the fact that the national institutions that deal with marine matters are often a small branch of larger departments dealing with other issues.

346. As a result, ocean resources and environmental conditions are continuing to decline. The most serious threats to the marine environment worldwide have been identified by GESAMP[134] and by the Global Conference on Oceans and Coasts at Rio+10.[135] They include: (a) the destruction and alteration of habitats—at least half of the world's mangrove forests have been lost over the last century, 70 percent of coral reefs are threatened and important seagrass habitats are rapidly being destroyed; (b) overfishing and the effects of fishing on the environment—47 percent of global fisheries are fully utilized and 28 percent are overutilized, while 75 percent

131. UNCLOS, Annex VIII, Article 1.
132. UNCLOS, Annex VIII, Article 2.
133. UNCLOS, Article 290, par. 1.
134. "A Sea of Troubles," GESAMP Reports and Studies No. 70, 2001.
135. Paris Conference, op. cit.

require urgent management to freeze or reduce capacity; (c) the effects of sewage and chemicals on human health and the environment—while the presence in the marine environment of some pollutants has been reduced, research shows that sewage pollution has a massive effect on health worldwide and some chemicals are suspected of causing cancer, disrupting reproduction and altering behaviour; (d) increasing eutrophication—excessive growth of marine plant life is seriously disrupting ecosystems and threatening life throughout the world; (e) changes to hydrology and the flow of sediments caused by such developments as building dams and causeways, creating reservoirs, establishing large-scale irrigation schemes and changing the way land is used; (f) the introduction of alien species—it is estimated that 3,000 species of animals and plants are transported every day around the world in the ballast water of ships, or in their hulls, while other species enter the sea after being released from aquaria and fish farms; (g) climate changes—Intergovernmental Panel on Climate Change projections show that continued use of fossil fuels will exacerbate global climate changes, with severe consequences for the oceans and coastal ecosystems.

2. Prevention, Reduction and Control of Pollution

(a) Land-based activities: The Global Programme of Action[136]

347. Land-based sources are responsible for 80 percent of the pollution of the oceans and affect the most productive areas of the marine environment. Article 207 of UNCLOS requires States to adopt laws and regulations to prevent, reduce and control pollution from land-based sources and to endeavour to establish global and regional rules, standards and recommended practices and procedures, acting especially through competent international organizations and diplomatic conferences.

348. Two international documents were adopted by an Intergovernmental Conference in November 1995: the Washington Declaration on the Protection of the Marine Environment from Land-based Activities and the Global Programme of Action for the Protection of the Marine Environment from Land-based Activities (A/51/116). The Global Programme of Action (GPA) addresses the impacts of land-based activities on the marine and coastal environment, including contaminants, physical alteration, point and non-point sources of pollution, and such areas of concern as critical habitats, habitats of endangered species and protection of ecosystem components such as breeding and feeding grounds.

349. In 2001, the GPA underwent its first intergovernmental review, which examined the accomplishments to date and focused on opportunities and barriers with respect to its implementation. The conclusions of the Co-Chairs of the First Intergovernmental Review on the Implementation of the Global Plan of Action for the Protection of the Marine Environment from Land-based Activities, held at Montreal, Canada, from 26 to 30 November 2001, along with the Montreal Declaration adopted by the ministerial/high-level segment of the meeting, are presented in Annex I to the present report.

136. The information presented in this section is excerpted from the contribution of the GPA Coordination Office.

350. The General Assembly, in its resolution 51/189 of 16 December 1996, designated UNEP as the lead agency in the implementation of the GPA. Under the auspices of UNEP, the GPA Coordination Office was established at The Hague in 1997. The Montreal intergovernmental meeting also reviewed the work of the GPA Coordination Office and formulated a work programme for it for the period 2002–2006.

351. In 2001, among other activities, the GPA Coordination Office continued to implement the UNEP/WSSCC/WHO/Habitat Strategic Action Plan on Municipal Wastewater. A number of regional meetings were held, organized in collaboration with the regional offices and the regional seas secretariats, respectively, to consider, inter alia, the GPA Guidance on Municipal Wastewater. During 2002, the GPA Coordination Office will build upon the approach taken for municipal wastewater to develop a strategic action plan for a second pollutant source category, namely the physical alteration and destruction of habitats.

352. With the support of donors, the GPA Coordination Office will also fund projects for the development of national programmes of action for the protection of the marine environment from land-based activities in Egypt, Nigeria, Sri Lanka, the United Republic of Tanzania and Yemen during 2002. The projects strongly advocate dialogue among key stakeholders and represent a direct step towards the establishment of national capabilities and institutional strengthening.

353. As regards the specialized agencies, FAO has taken a number of initiatives to implement the GPA, including, notably, addressing the impact of coastal degradation on fishery resources.

354. GEF continues to play a vital role in funding projects in a variety of environment-related issues. An example of a GPA-related initiative is in the Black Sea region, where a GEF-funded project has been developed to address the problem of land-based nitrogen pollution leading to accelerated eutrophication. Another example of GEF activity in GPA-related matters and its marine science implications is the Baltic LME initiative, which features GEF assistance for nitrogen pollution reduction from agricultural sources consistent with Helsinki Convention obligations.

355. Furthermore, with regard to implementation of the GPA, the United Nations Industrial Development Organization (UNIDO) executes major projects addressing regional transboundary problems of large marine ecosystems and their associated river basins, wetlands and coastal zones within the International Waters focal area of the Global Environment Facility (see par. 602).

(b) Pollution by dumping; Waste management

356. The relative contribution of dumping to the overall input of potential pollutants in the oceans is estimated at 10 percent. Control of pollution of the marine environment by dumping is very much dependent on finding solutions to land-based sources of marine pollution and proper waste management in general.

357. *The legal regime.*—Dumping is defined in Article 1 of UNCLOS as "any deliberate disposal of wastes or other matter from vessels, aircraft, platforms or other man-made structures at sea; and any deliberate disposal of vessels, aircraft, platforms or other man-made structures at sea." States are required by Article 210 to adopt

national laws, regulations and measures which must be no less effective in preventing, reducing and controlling pollution by dumping than the global rules and standards to be established by States acting through competent international organizations or diplomatic conference. Dumping within the territorial sea and the exclusive economic zone or onto the continental shelf is to be carried out only with the express prior approval of the coastal State. The obligation to enforce laws and regulations adopted in accordance with the Convention and international rules is assigned by Article 216 not only to the flag State but also to the affected coastal State and the State in which the waste was loaded.

358. The global rules and standards referred to in UNCLOS are contained in the 1972 Convention on the Prevention of Marine Pollution by Dumping of Wastes and Other Matter (London Convention) and its 1996 Protocol. The relationship between UNCLOS and the London Convention was discussed formally by the Contracting Parties to the London Convention in 1988 and again in 1994 when they assessed the implications of the entry into force of UNCLOS for the application of the London Convention.[137]

359. In the past 20 years since the adoption of UNCLOS, and since UNCED in 1992, great progress has been made in strengthening the globally applicable rules on the dumping of wastes and other matter.[138] The most significant developments include the adoption in 1993 of amendments to the annexes to the London Convention with a view to: phasing out dumping of industrial waste; prohibiting incineration at sea of industrial waste and sewage sludge; and prohibiting the dumping of radioactive waste and other radioactive matter. Parties to the London Convention had been encouraged in Agenda 21, paragraphs 17.30 (b) and 22.5 (b), to take such measures.

360. In 1996, following a detailed Article-by-Article review of the London Convention, a Special Meeting of Contracting Parties adopted a Protocol to the London Convention, which will eventually replace the Convention. The Protocol represents a major change of approach from the 1972 Convention regarding how to regulate the use of the sea as a depository for waste materials. The Protocol introduces a wider definition of dumping than that contained in UNCLOS. It includes within the definition the expressions "any storage of wastes or other matter in the seabed and the subsoil thereof from vessels, aircraft, platforms or other man-made structures at sea" and "any abandonment or toppling at site of platforms or other man-made structures at sea, for the sole purpose of deliberate disposal."

361. The Protocol requires parties to apply a precautionary approach and the polluter-pays principle. The dumping of any waste except those listed in the Protocol is prohibited,[139] as is the export of wastes and other matter for the purpose of dump-

137. See "Implications of the entry into force of the United Nations Convention on the Law of the Sea on the 1972 London Convention," Comments by the Division for Ocean Affairs and the Law of the Sea, United Nations Office of Legal Affairs. IMO document LC/AM 2/3/1, dated 18 March 1994.

138. See report of the Twenty-third Consultative Meeting of Contracting Parties to the London Convention 1972, in connection with the World Summit on Sustainable Development, document LC23/16.

139. The wastes or other materials that may be considered for dumping under the Protocol are: dredged material; sewage sludge; fish waste, or material resulting from industrial fish processing operations; vessels and platforms or other man-made structures at sea; inert, inorganic geological material; organic material of natural origin; and bulky items, primarily composed of iron, steel, etc.

ing at sea. The Contracting Parties to the London Convention have developed guidelines for all waste materials which may be considered for disposal at sea.

362. Issues which the Contracting Parties to the London Convention have identified as part of their future activities include the review of emerging practices regarding ocean disposal of CO_2 from fossil fuel production and use (see also A/56/58/Add.1, par. 83).

363. At the regional level, progress has been made in the harmonization of approaches regulating the disposal of wastes at sea. Specific instruments or special provisions have been adopted for the Baltic Sea region, the Black Sea, the Mediterranean Sea, the North-East Atlantic, the South-East Pacific, the South Pacific and Antarctica.

364. *Implementation and enforcement.*—Only a small percentage of Contracting Parties to the London Convention have been meeting their notification and reporting requirements under Article VI (4) of the Convention and have sent reports with regard to their dumping activities to the secretariat (Article 9 of the 1996 Protocol contains a similar obligation to report). The Contracting Parties, noting that reporting constitutes a first step in the process which includes compliance assessment and subsequently effectiveness review, have given priority attention to developing measures for compliance promotion, including technical cooperation and assistance (see A/54/429, par. 389). The Contracting Parties approved a questionnaire on compliance issues for distribution to all Contracting Parties in 1999 and 2000 to obtain a record of the views and needs of Contracting Parties with regard to compliance; developed guidance on the implementation of the 1996 Protocol at the national level, which is aimed at States interested in becoming parties to the Protocol; and prepared a project concept document for submission to the Global Environment Facility to identify barriers to compliance with the provisions of the London Convention and the 1996 Protocol and to develop and implement solutions. In addition, one of the aims of the Long-term Strategy for Technical Cooperation and Assistance under the London Convention 1972, adopted at the most recent Consultative Meeting of Contracting Parties in October 2001, is to assist those parties which lack the technical capacity to comply with the Convention.

365. Finally, in order to address problems of illegal dumping, the Contracting Parties are developing reporting procedures for vessels or aircraft observed to be dumping in alleged contravention of the London Convention.

366. *Waste management. Hazardous wastes.*—The 1989 Basel Convention on the Control of Transboundary Movements of Hazardous Wastes and Their Disposal strictly regulates the transboundary movements of hazardous wastes and requires the parties to ensure that such wastes are managed and disposed of in an environmentally sound manner. The main principles of the Basel Convention are that: (a) transboundary movements of hazardous wastes should be reduced to a minimum consistent with their environmentally sound management; (b) hazardous wastes should be treated and disposed of as close as possible to their source of generation; and (c) hazardous waste generation should be reduced and minimized at source. The Convention introduced a prior informed consent regime for the import/export of hazardous wastes and their passage through third countries.

367. The Convention was amended in 1995, to provide for the prohibition of all transboundary movements of hazardous wastes destined for recycling or recovery operations from OECD to non-OECD countries, and in 1999 the Protocol on Liabil-

ity and Compensation for Damage resulting from the Transboundary Movements of Hazardous Wastes and their Disposal was adopted.

368. The Basel Convention has been further elaborated at the regional level and specific regimes have been adopted for Africa, Central America, the South Pacific, the Mediterranean Sea, the Commonwealth of Independent States, the area covered by the Kuwait Regional Convention for Cooperation on the Protection of the Marine Environment from Pollution, and Antarctica.

369. Recent activities under the Basel Convention have, as in the case of the London Convention, been focused on promoting the implementation of the Convention and its amendments worldwide. A 10-year Strategic Plan for the Basel Convention is being developed for approval at the Sixth Meeting of the Conference of the Parties, to be held in December 2002. The plan includes a mission statement, one overarching goal, namely the environmentally sound management of hazardous waste, and a set of operational objectives.[140]

370. *Waste management. Radioactive wastes.*—The Joint Convention on the Safety of Spent Fuel Management and on the Safety of Radioactive Waste Management was adopted by IAEA in 1997 and entered into force on 18 June 2001. It is the first international instrument to address the safety of management and the storage of radioactive wastes and spent fuel in countries with or without nuclear programmes. One of its main objectives is to ensure that during all stages of spent fuel and radioactive waste management there are effective defences against potential hazards. The Convention contains requirements related to the transboundary movement of spent fuel and radioactive waste, which are based on the 1990 IAEA Code of Practice on the International Transboundary Movement of Radioactive Waste. The State of origin must ensure that it obtains the prior notification and consent of the State of destination. The Convention provides that "transboundary movement through States of transit shall be subject to those international obligations which are relevant to the particular modes of transport utilized."

371. The Convention establishes a mechanism whereby each Contracting Party is obliged to submit for review by meetings of Contracting Parties a report on the measures taken to implement each of the obligations under the Convention. This includes reporting on national inventories of radioactive wastes and spent fuel.

372. IAEA in its contribution to the present report describes the progress it has made in collecting information on all inputs of radioactive materials in the world oceans for its Clearing House on Radioactive Substances to be launched in 2002 and linked to the GPA main node. A report on accidents and losses of radioactive materials at sea was published in September 2001. The Coordinated Research Programme on Worldwide Radioactivity Studies has been completed by the IAEA Marine Environment Laboratory (IAEA-MEL) and provides the most comprehensive information on radionuclide levels in the world oceans. The results will be used as the international reference source on the average levels of anthropogenic radionuclides in the marine environment so that any further contributions from nuclear reprocessing plants, radioactive waste dumping sites, nuclear bomb test sites and possible nuclear accidents can be identified.

140. The text of the draft Strategic Plan is posted on the web site of the Secretariat of the Basel Convention at www.basel.int.

(c) Pollution from vessels

373. Threats to the marine environment from shipping activities can arise from (a) accidents (e.g., groundings, spills and collisions); (b) operational discharges (i.e., oil, noxious liquid substances (chemicals), harmful substances carried in bulk, sewage, garbage as well as air emissions); and (c) physical damage to marine habitats, such as coral reefs or organisms (i.e., damage caused by anchors, ship strikes of marine mammals or the smothering of species/habitats). Normal shipping operations can also be responsible for the introduction of unwanted aquatic organisms into the marine environment. The use of toxic anti-fouling paints on ships' hulls seriously harms marine life. Damage to the marine environment can also be caused by an illegal discharge, or by an accident which happened as result of the ineffective enforcement of international safety-related rules and standards, for example, those relating to ship construction, equipment, training of crew, etc. (see also paras. 96–97).

374. In tonnage terms, the main pollutant entering the marine environment resulting from shipping operations is oil, which is introduced predominantly as a result of routine tanker operations, such as discharges of machinery wastes and tank washings. However, currently the greatest threat to the marine environment from shipping activities arises from the introduction of harmful alien species into new environments through ships' ballast water. The Global Environment Facility has identified this as one of the four greatest threats to the world's oceans (the other three are land-based sources of marine pollution, over-exploitation of living marine resources and physical alteration/destruction of marine habitats).

375. *The legal regime in UNCLOS.*—Article 194 (3) (b) of UNCLOS requires States to take measures to minimize to the fullest possible extent pollution from vessels, in particular measures for preventing accidents and dealing with emergencies, ensuring the safety of operations at sea, preventing intentional and unintentional discharges, and regulating the design, construction, equipment, operation and manning of vessels.

376. States are required by Article 211 to establish, through the competent international organization or a general diplomatic conference, international rules and standards to prevent, reduce and control pollution of the marine environment from vessels and to re-examine them from time to time as necessary. States must also promote the adoption, in the same manner, and wherever appropriate, of routeing systems designed to minimize the threat of accidents. For the flag State the global rules and standards constitute the minimum standard which it must adopt for vessels flying its flag. Coastal States can adopt stricter rules and standards than the generally accepted global standards for application in their territorial sea, so long as such standards do not apply to the design, construction, manning or equipment of foreign ships, or hamper innocent passage. In the exclusive economic zone, the generally accepted international rules and standards apply, except where the coastal State has adopted more stringent measures pursuant to Article 211 (6) (for more details, see par. 389).

377. Enforcement rights regarding vessel-source pollution are set out in Articles 217 to 221. The primary obligation is placed on the flag State to ensure that vessels flying its flag comply with applicable international rules and standards and with national legislation adopted in accordance with the Convention. It must prohibit its vessels from sailing until they can comply with the requirements of the interna-

tional rules and standards (Article 217 [2]). The duties of the flag State are set out in general terms in Article 94 of the Convention (see paras 123–128).

378. A significant feature of UNCLOS is the enforcement rights it grants to both port and coastal States (discussed in detail in paras. 129–132). Section 7 of Part XII (Articles 223–233) sets out a series of safeguards with regard to the exercise of enforcement powers and the institution of proceedings against foreign ships.

379. States are required by Article 198 to notify affected States in the event of actual or imminent danger to the marine environment (see par. 294). They must also jointly develop and promote contingency plans for responding to marine pollution incidents (Article 199) (discussed in more detail in paras. 298–303). UNCLOS furthermore requires States to ensure that recourse is available in accordance with their legal systems for prompt and adequate compensation or other relief in respect of damage caused by pollution of the marine environment. The Convention in Article 235 places particular emphasis on the need to develop international law relating to responsibility and liability for damage caused by pollution of the marine environment (discussed in more detail in paras. 325–340).[141]

380. *International rules and standards governing the prevention and control of pollution from vessels.*—The measures which States are required to take pursuant to Article 194 (3) (b) of UNCLOS to prevent, reduce and control pollution from vessels are contained in a number of instruments. Part IV, "Shipping and navigation," of the present report describes many of the international rules and standards which have been developed in respect of all aspects of navigation, for example, ship construction and equipment, training of crew and labour conditions, transport of cargo and safety of navigation. Measures to prevent intentional as well as unintentional discharges are contained in the International Convention for the Prevention of Pollution from Ships, 1973, as modified by the Protocol of 1978 relating thereto (MARPOL 73/78). Measures for dealing with emergencies have been developed at the global and regional levels and are set out in the OPRC Convention, its 2000 Protocol and in a number of regional instruments (described in paras. 296 and 302).

381. Many of the international rules and standards for the prevention, reduction and control of pollution from vessels are contained in MARPOL 73/78, which regulates discharges from ships in six annexes: oil (Annex I); noxious liquid substances (chemicals) carried in bulk (Annex II); harmful substances carried by sea in packaged form (Annex III); sewage (Annex IV); garbage (Annex V); and air pollution (Annex VI). Annexes IV and VI have not yet entered into force. The use of harmful anti-fouling systems is regulated in the 2001 International Convention on the Control of Harmful Anti-fouling Systems on Ships (see par. 387).

382. IMO in its contribution to the present report states that it has decided to undertake a review of Annexes I and II of MARPOL 73/78 in order to update them and also to simplify their implementation. Annex I will be restructured so that there is a complete version for each generation of tanker. The revision of Annex II, which is expected to be completed by 2003, will focus on the criteria for defining pollution categories and ship types.

383. As regards Annex III, it can be noted that the International Maritime Dangerous Goods (IMDG) Code, an implementation vehicle for Annex III, has recently

141. For a detailed presentation of the legal regime in UNCLOS regarding the prevention, reduction and control of pollution from vessels, see the report of the Secretary-General on the law of the sea: protection and preservation of the marine environment, document A/44/461.

been revised and reformatted to make it more user-friendly. IMO has also decided, in principle, to make some of its chapters mandatory, aiming at an entry-into-force date of 1 January 2004.

384. Routeing systems designed to minimize the threat of accidents which might cause pollution of the marine environment, as called for in Article 211 of UNCLOS, have been developed under SOLAS, the International Regulations for Preventing Collisions at Sea and the IMO General Provisions on Ships' Routeing.

385. It is important to bear in mind that the "generally accepted" or "applicable" international rules and standards which UNCLOS requires States to "conform to" and "give effect to" under Article 211, and enforce under Articles 217, 218, 219 and 220, can comprise international rules and standards contained in conventions, as well as those in recommendations adopted, for example, by the IMO Assembly or by MSC or MEPC. The extent to which parties to UNCLOS are required to implement and enforce those rules and standards depends on the degree of their international acceptance. Unlike the parties to the London Convention, the appropriate bodies of IMO or the parties to UNCLOS have not yet formally addressed the relationship between UNCLOS and the various instruments which regulate pollution from vessels and identified what are the "generally accepted" or "applicable" international rules and standards.[142] It may be noted that some of the more recent instruments do include a reference to a specific Article in UNCLOS. In 1997, a study on the implications of the entry into force of UNCLOS for IMO was prepared by the IMO secretariat in consultation with the Division for Ocean Affairs and the Law of the Sea, pursuant to a request of the IMO Council and the General Assembly.[143] The IMO Council took note of the study and recommended that the various organs and bodies of IMO should keep the study in mind as a reference document in the context of their work.

386. Over the past 20 years since the adoption of UNCLOS, significant progress has been made in developing the measures called for in Article 194 (3) (b), the international rules and standards required by Article 211, and in implementing a number of the specific measures which were identified by UNCED in Agenda 21, Chapter 17, paragraph 17.30 (a), and at the fourth session of the Commission on Sustainable Development, the nineteenth special session of the General Assembly, to review and appraise the implementation of Agenda 21 (Earth Summit+5), and the seventh session of the Commission on Sustainable Development, as necessary for the prevention, reduction and control of the degradation of the marine environment from shipping. Apart from the safety-related measures, including routeing measures, which are presented in part IV of the present report, the following recent regulatory developments can be highlighted.

387. *Organotin compounds used in anti-fouling paints.*—UNCED in Agenda 21, Chapter 17, paragraph 17.32, had requested States to take measures to reduce pollution caused by organotin compounds used in anti-fouling paints (see also Commission on Sustainable Development decision 7/1, par. 35 (f)).[144] In October 2001,

142. The Division for Ocean Affairs and the Law of the Sea is currently engaged in preparing a study, in the form of a matrix, on the obligations of States under UNCLOS and those originating from other conventions to which UNCLOS refers as international rules, norms, standards and regulations.

143. The study is contained in document LEG/MISC/2.

144. See Official Records of the Economic and Social Council, 1999, Supplement No. 9 (E/1999/29), Chap. I, Sect. C.

IMO adopted the International Convention on the Control of Harmful Anti-fouling Systems on Ships. In its contribution to the present report, IMO explained that the Convention sets 1 January 2003 as the date from when the ban on the application of organotin-based anti-fouling systems on all ships will come into effect, and 1 January 2008 as the date commencing on which ships, with some exceptions, will not be allowed to bear such systems, or will need to have their existing organotin-based anti-fouling system coated over to prevent it from leaching out. The Convention not only bans the use of organotin-based anti-fouling systems, but also provides a mechanism through which other harmful anti-fouling systems may be banned or regulated in the future.

388. *Harmful aquatic organisms in ballast water.*—The development of requisite measures to address the spread of non-indigenous organisms through ballast water discharge, as required in Article 196 of UNCLOS (see also par. 440) and recommended by UNCED in Chapter 17, paragraph 17.30 (a) (vi), and by the Commission on Sustainable Development in its decision 7/1, paragraph 35 (e)[145] has proved a challenging task. Guidelines for the control and management of ships' ballast water to minimize the transfer of harmful aquatic organisms and pathogens were adopted by the IMO Assembly in 1997, but mandatory regulations have been under development since 1994. The task of determining acceptable standards for the effectiveness of ballast water treatment and determining treatment options which meet the "agreed" criteria of ship safety, environmental acceptability and cost-effectiveness, has proved to be very complex because of the enormous engineering and scientific difficulties involved.[146] IMO is developing the legal instrument on the basis of a two-tier approach: (a) mandatory requirements applicable to all ships; and (b) special requirements applicable in certain areas. A Diplomatic Conference to adopt the new instrument is tentatively planned for the biennium 2002–2003.

389. *Protection of special areas and particularly sensitive sea areas.*—In addition to international rules and standards regulating operational discharge which are applicable in all maritime areas, IMO has established more stringent discharge requirements for application only in "special areas" designated under MARPOL 73/78, or as a protective measure for particularly sensitive sea areas (PSSAs), or as a measure for a clearly defined area of the exclusive economic zone pursuant to Article 211 (6) of UNCLOS. The measures which can be adopted for a PSSA or for a clearly defined area of the exclusive economic zone are not restricted to discharge requirements, but can also include navigational measures (for details see paras. 472–485).

390. *Implementation and enforcement.*—Over the past 20 years since the adoption of UNCLOS, significant progress has been made in developing the legal regime for the prevention, reduction and control of pollution from vessels. Moreover, many of the instruments which set out the applicable regime have been widely ratified.

391. However, some States have experienced problems incorporating what constitutes a significant body of law into their national legislation, because of, inter alia, limited experience in the area of marine pollution and its prevention and/or little or no experience with legislative drafting in this area (see the SOPAC contribution in Annex II to the present report). Other problems of implementation experienced

145. Ibid.

146. See *Ballast Water News*, issue 3, October–December 2000.

by States relate to difficulties in meeting the obligation in MARPOL 73/78 to provide adequate reception facilities for dirty ballast water, cargo residues and garbage for ships calling at their ports (see paras. 397–401).

392. Since 1992, IMO has provided technical assistance to 77 member States on safety and pollution matters through its Technical Assistance Programme, which has as one of its main objectives to facilitate ratification and implementation of the appropriate maritime legislation.

393. Other measures adopted by IMO to enhance the implementation of international rules and standards have been aimed predominantly at strengthening flag State implementation, in recognition of its central responsibility for the prevention of pollution from vessels, for example, the International Safety Management (ISM) Code, and the introduction of procedures for the self-assessment by flag States of their performance (for a detailed description of all issues relating to flag State implementation, see paras. 123–128).

394. *Enforcement by port States and coastal States.*—While recognizing that the primary responsibility for implementing the international rules and standards rests with the flag State, both UNCLOS and the main IMO instruments do not leave compliance enforcement to the flag State alone. UNCLOS grants States jurisdictional powers over foreign vessels voluntarily in their ports in connection with the implementation of international rules and standards. Article 218 provides measures port States can take with respect to a vessel in the event of a discharge committed in violation of international rules and standards on the high seas, or in the internal waters, territorial sea or exclusive economic zone of another State, if requested by that State, or if the violation has caused or is likely to cause pollution in its own internal waters, territorial sea or exclusive economic zone. Article 219 provides measures a port State can take if a vessel is in violation of applicable international rules and standards relating to seaworthiness. The latter provision can be considered together with the IMO regulations relating to the exercise of port State control. SOLAS, the Load Line Convention and MARPOL 73/78 provide for the exercise of port State jurisdiction for the purpose of correcting deficiencies in the implementation of applicable standards for maritime safety and pollution prevention (for further details, see paras. 129–132).

395. Several provisions in UNCLOS, in particular Article 220, regulate the enforcement measures which a coastal State can take with respect to a vessel which has violated its laws and regulations adopted in accordance with the Convention or applicable international rules and standards for the prevention, reduction and control of pollution from vessels. The enforcement rights of the coastal State differ according to where the violation took place and the degree of pollution caused or threatened. Article 221 gives States enforcement rights beyond the territorial sea to protect their coastline or related interests, including fishing, from pollution or threat of pollution following upon a maritime casualty or acts relating to such casualty, which may reasonably be expected to result in major harmful consequences. This provision echoes the main features of the right of intervention by coastal States regulated in the 1969 Intervention Convention and its 1973 Protocol (for further details on this Convention, see par. 301).

396. However, many coastal States are unable to exercise their enforcement rights, since they have limited enforcement capacity and therefore find it difficult to undertake effective monitoring and surveillance operations to control marine pollution from ships. Some States have therefore entered into cooperative enforce-

ment arrangements with other States, as also called for in Agenda 21, Chapter 17, paragraph 17.30 (a) (iii).

397. *Facilities in ports for the reception of wastes from ships.*—All Parties to MARPOL 73/78 are obliged to provide adequate reception facilities for ships calling at their ports. This requirement is especially necessary in "special areas" where, because of the vulnerability of these areas to pollution, more stringent discharge restrictions have been imposed. These reception facilities should, in each case, be "adequate" for the reception of wastes from ships without causing undue delay to the ships using them.

398. UNCED in Agenda 21, Chapter 17, paragraph 17.30 (d), had called upon States to facilitate the establishment of port reception facilities for the collection of oily and chemical residues and garbage from ships, especially in MARPOL special areas, and to promote the establishment of smaller-scale facilities in marinas and fishing harbours.

399. Since 1992, IMO has developed a number of guidelines on port reception facilities. The most recent include the Comprehensive Manual on Port Reception Facilities, reissued in 1999, and the guidelines for ensuring the adequacy of reception facilities, published in 2000. IMO has also provided technical assistance to a number of countries, for example, to States in the Gulf area and in the wider Caribbean region, with a view to bringing into effect the regions' special area status under MARPOL 73/78.

400. In spite of these efforts, progress in the provision of adequate reception facilities worldwide has not been satisfactory. It is a matter of extreme complexity, which involves the shipping industry, port operators, oil and chemical companies and Governments. It is widely recognized that, if the problem is to be satisfactorily resolved, it will be necessary to address the economic as well as the technical aspects of the issue.

401. Meanwhile many cruise ships' favourite destinations cannot cope with the vast amount of wastes they generate. In the light of the phenomenal growth of the cruise ship industry, the search for a solution to this problem becomes even more pressing.

(d) Pollution from seabed activities subject to national jurisdiction

402. For most States the only seabed activity currently taking place within their areas of national jurisdiction is the exploration and exploitation of offshore oil and gas, which is still predominantly concentrated in waters near the coast and on continental shelves. Different views have been expressed with regard to the level of pollution caused by the exploration and exploitation of oil and gas.[147]

147. The Group of Experts on the Scientific Aspects of Marine Environmental Protection (GESAMP) has expressed the view that, while exploratory drilling, extracting oil and transporting and refining petroleum all produce waste, these activities have had relatively minor effects on coastal and seabed ecosystems. The Group considers the potential for contamination from the exploitation of oil and gas to be greater in deeper waters—since for example a blow-out in deep water would be difficult to control quickly and have serious ecological effects. ("A Sea of Troubles," GESAMP Report and Studies No. 70). IMO considers that offshore oil and gas exploration and production activities are significant sources of marine pollution and has cited as an example the North Sea, where it is estimated that between 1984 and 1990 some 14 to 27 per cent of oily pollutants originated from offshore oil and gas activities. (IMO report to the Conference on Sustainable Development in connection with the World Summit on Sustainable Development [Background Paper No. 9]).

403. The legal regime governing the prevention and control of pollution of the marine environment from seabed activities subject to national jurisdiction is set out in UNCLOS. Articles 208 and 214 require States to adopt and enforce national laws and regulations to prevent, reduce and control pollution of the marine environment arising from or in connection with seabed activities subject to their jurisdiction and from artificial islands, installations and structures under their jurisdiction, pursuant to Articles 60 and 80, which must be no less effective than international rules, standards and recommended practices and procedures. States are also required to endeavour to harmonize their policies at the appropriate regional level.

404. Any legislative activity that has taken place in this area since the adoption of UNCLOS has been focused only on the oil and gas industry. However, that industry has remained essentially self-regulatory. No global measures have been adopted regulating the discharges directly arising from the exploration, exploitation and associated offshore processing of oil and gas. Harmonized regulations with respect to the exploration and exploitation of oil and gas have been developed in four regions: the Baltic Sea area, the Mediterranean, the North-East Atlantic and in the area covered by the Kuwait Regional Convention for Cooperation on the Protection of the Marine Environment from Pollution.

405. The need for global measures to address pollution from offshore oil and gas activities has been discussed in IMO and in the Commission on Sustainable Development. Views have been divided in IMO on the issue. Those in favour of international regulations or guidelines have argued that there are still many oil-producing regions which do not have the capacity to develop either national or regional standards and that some kind of international regulations or guidelines would help them. Those who have argued against global measures contend that offshore oil and gas activities only pose a threat of local pollution, which can be dealt with through national regulations or regional agreements.[148]

406. The Commission on Sustainable Development in its decision 7/1, in noting the outcome of an international expert meeting on environmental practices in offshore oil and gas activities, held in 1997 (see A/53/456, par. 258), had recommended that the primary focus of action on the environmental aspects of offshore oil and gas operations should continue to be at the national, subregional and regional levels, and noted that in support of such action, there was a need to share information on the development and application of satisfactory environmental management systems.

407. *Prevention, reduction and control of pollution of the marine environment from artificial islands, installations and structures.*—Coastal States are required in Articles 208 and 210 of UNCLOS to adopt and enforce national laws and regulations to prevent, reduce and control pollution of the marine environment from artificial islands, installations and structures under their jurisdiction pursuant to Articles 60 and 80. Furthermore, Article 194 (3) (c) of UNCLOS contains a general obligation for States to adopt measures to minimize to the fullest possible extent pollution from installations and devices used in the exploration or exploitation of the natural resources of the seabed and subsoil. The provision therefore also applies on the high seas.

408. In 1992, UNCED called upon States to assess existing regulatory measures to address discharges, emissions and safety and to assess the need for additional

148. Report of IMO to the Conference on Sustainable Development at its seventh session.

measures to address degradation of the marine environment from offshore oil and gas platforms (Agenda 21, par. 17.30 [c]).

409. As noted in paragraph 404 above, measures regulating discharges from offshore installations which arise directly from oil and gas exploration and exploitation activities, such as oil in produced water, contaminated drill cuttings and production chemicals, have only been adopted in some regions. (For OSPAR's actions, see paras. 467–469.)

410. Discharges from offshore installations originating in machinery space are regulated by MARPOL 73/78, as are accidental discharges to some extent. Requirements regarding oil pollution emergency plans on installations are set out in the 1990 OPRC Convention. Regulations regarding the dumping of wastes or other matter from offshore installations are provided for in the London Convention and its 1996 Protocol.

411. Developments in offshore activities over the past 30 years have produced mobile offshore craft, such as floating production, storage and offloading units, which do not easily fall within the definition of an installation or a ship, and it is therefore sometimes difficult to discern the applicable legal regime (see A/54/429, paras. 358–360). Some of the measures which have been developed by IMO in relation to the safe operation of offshore installations and structures apply generally to mobile offshore units, for example, the 1989 Code for the Construction and Equipment of Mobile Offshore Drilling Units and the 1999 Recommendations on Training of Personnel on Mobile Offshore Units. The applicability of ILO labour standards to personnel working on offshore installations requires consideration.

412. *Removal and disposal of offshore installations and structures.*—Requirements regarding the removal of abandoned or disused offshore installations or structures are addressed in UNCLOS in Article 60 and, by reference, Article 80. Entire removal is not specified. The Convention recognizes the need for the competent international organization to establish international standards to be taken into account by States when removing an installation or structure. Guidelines and standards for the removal of offshore installations or structures were established by the IMO Assembly in 1989 (resolution A.672 [16]).

413. If dumping at sea is considered an option for disposing of a decommissioned installation or structure, then Article 210 of UNCLOS, read together with Article 1 (5) (a), which defines dumping as any deliberate disposal of, inter alia, platforms or other man-made structures at sea, applies; and the coastal State is required to adopt laws and regulations to prevent, reduce and control pollution by dumping which are to be no less effective than the global rules and standards. Those global rules and standards are contained in the 1972 London Convention and its 1996 Protocol. Provisions on the removal and disposal of offshore installations are included in some regional agreements, e.g., the States in the Baltic Sea area must ensure that abandoned or disused offshore units are entirely removed and brought ashore.

(e) Pollution from activities in the area

414. Articles 145 and 209 of UNCLOS set forth the basic framework for the protection of the marine environment from the harmful effects of exploration for and exploitation of the mineral resources of the international seabed area. Annex III to the Convention also contains relevant provisions.

415. *Mineral activities.*—As the deep seabed mineral activities move from prospecting to exploration, greater attention is being paid to environmental considerations. The Regulations for Prospecting and Exploration for the Polymetallic Nodules in the Area (ISBA/6/A/18, Annex) elaborate on the provisions of UNCLOS, and devote an entire part, Part V, to the protection and preservation of the marine environment. In its contribution to the present report, the International Seabed Authority states that, in 2001, the Authority's Legal and Technical Commission issued a set of recommendations for the guidance of contractors for the assessment of the possible environmental impacts arising from exploration for polymetallic nodules (ISBA/7/LTC/1/Rev.1 and Corr.1). These recommendations are designed to help contractors to fulfil their obligations under the contract as they relate to the protection of the marine environment from potential harmful effects which may arise from activities in the Area. The purpose of the recommendations is to describe the procedures to be followed in the acquisition of baseline data by contractors, including the monitoring to be performed during or after any activities having the potential to cause serious harm to the environment, and to facilitate reporting by contractors. The recommendations are based upon the outcomes of an international workshop held by the Authority in 1998, which were then given detailed scrutiny by the Legal and Technical Commission. They represent, therefore, an analysis based on the best available scientific knowledge of the deep ocean environment and the technology to be used in exploration.

416. The International Seabed Authority also adds that one of its most important functions in the future will be to monitor the implementation of plans of work for exploration and to review the reports and other data and information submitted by contractors. In this regard, a group of scientific experts convened by the Authority in March 1999 recommended the development of a standardized system of data interpretation. To continue this task further, and with a view to preparing proposals on standardization of environmental data for consideration by the Legal and Technical Commission, the Authority convened in June 2001 the fourth in its series of international workshops on issues relating to deep seabed mining. The subject of the workshop, which was attended by a number of eminent scientists and researchers, was the standardization of data collection and evaluation from research and exploratory activities undertaken in the deep seabed, both in respect of the mineral resources and in respect of protection and preservation of the marine environment. The specific objectives of the workshop were: (a) to propose standards for the measurement of the biological, chemical, geological and physical components of the marine environment that are required to establish environmental baselines in exploration areas; (b) to recommend sampling designs for acquiring these data and for monitoring tests of mining equipment; and (c) to facilitate the conversion of data acquired by the registered pioneer investors to a common basis for comparison and for the development of a database to enable the Authority to better manage impacts from future mining for polymetallic nodules.

417. The International Seabed Authority concludes that it is clear from the discussions that took place during the above workshop as well as previous ones that considerable further research is required to bridge the gaps in current knowledge of deep ocean ecosystems to enable the Authority to effectively manage impacts from future mining.

418. *Marine scientific research. Genetic resources.*—In its contribution to the present

report, the International Seabed Authority points out that the Authority has an important role to play both as a global repository of data and information relating to marine resources and to the marine environment and as a catalyst for collaborative research at the international level. In July 2002, immediately prior to the opening of its eighth session, the Authority will convene a workshop which will focus on the prospects for international cooperation and collaboration in marine scientific research on the deep oceans and address critical issues for the sediment biota and biota living on polymetallic nodules in potential mining areas.

419. The subject of marine scientific research is a matter of great concern to the Authority, which has a duty under the Convention to promote and encourage the conduct of marine scientific research in the international seabed area and to coordinate and disseminate the results of such research.

420. Two of the particular issues which will need to be addressed through better coordination are the need to clarify certain aspects of the regime for marine scientific research and the question of how to deal with newly discovered genetic resources.

421. The basic principle set out in the Convention is that all States and competent international organizations have the right to conduct marine scientific research subject to the rights and duties of other States as provided for in the Convention. This broad principle is justified by the need to increase current knowledge of the marine environment and the benefit of such knowledge to mankind as a whole. In the context of the International Seabed Authority, for example, marine scientific research will be an essential tool in providing it with the information it needs to fulfil its obligations to protect and preserve the marine environment under Article 145 of the Convention, as well as to provide the basic information necessary to effectively regulate prospecting, exploration and exploitation of the resources of the Area.

422. According to the Authority, the problem is that, while there is a freedom to engage in marine scientific research on the high seas and in the seabed, mineral resource prospecting and exploration in the Area are regulated through the Authority. The Convention does not adequately distinguish between the terms "marine scientific research," "prospecting" and "exploration," nor does it make a distinction between "pure" and "applied" scientific research. (In fact, Article 251 of UNCLOS provides that States shall seek to promote through competent international organizations the establishment of general criteria and guidelines to assist States in ascertaining the nature and implications of marine scientific research.) The problem becomes more acute in the case of new scientific discoveries that have been made in recent years, particularly the deep sea vents, which comprise both mineral resources (polymetallic sulphides) and genetic resources in the form of rich biological communities of unknown potential use to science. Here there is a real conflict between true marine scientific research and mineral prospecting, and the potential for multiple use conflicts between, for example, deep seabed miners, so-called bioprospectors, and the proper conservation and management of the deep ocean environment.

423. There is a close relationship between the conduct of activities relating to non-living resources, for which the Authority has responsibility, and the sustainable use of living resources of the deep ocean. Indeed, the Authority has the duty, under Article 145 of the Convention, to adopt appropriate rules, regulations and procedures for the protection and conservation of the natural resources of the Area and

the prevention of damage to the flora and fauna of the marine environment. Article 145 implies that protection of the environment is indeed a core concern of the Authority, to be balanced against the need to promote effective utilization of the resources of the Area. In this regard, it is therefore critical at this early stage that the various interests and agencies involved cooperate to the maximum extent possible.

424. To this end, the Authority is actively engaged in studying the need for further environmental regulation of the Area in accordance with the Convention and the Agreement on Part XI of UNCLOS and the environmental protection tools that might be available for this purpose. These studies will also examine how the Authority might give practical and meaningful effect to the environmental provisions of the Convention and the Agreement as they relate to the Area as well as the relationship between the responsibilities of the Authority and other international instruments.

(f) Other concerns

425. *Pollution from installations or devices not used in the exploration or exploitation of natural resources.*—UNCLOS in its Article 194 (3) (d) requires States to take the necessary measures to minimize to the fullest possible extent pollution from other installations or devices (i.e., other than those used in exploration or exploitation of the natural resources) operating in the marine environment.

426. While offshore installations and structures are most frequently associated with the offshore oil and gas industry, they are not limited to that industry alone. Past reports on oceans and the law of the sea by the Secretary-General have drawn attention to the use of offshore installations and structures for fish farming, energy production, tourism and recreation, and aerospace support (satellite launching). Their use has also been proposed for floating aerodomes for both commercial and military purposes and for offshore logistical bases (see A/53/456, par. 459 and A/54/429, paras. 556–558).

427. Under UNCLOS, a determination as to who has the responsibility for implementing Article 194 (3) (d) must take into account the location of the installation or device and the purpose for which it is used. On the high seas, the State of registry has jurisdiction with regard to installations or devices, irrespective of their intended use. In the exclusive economic zone, the right of the coastal State to exercise jurisdiction depends upon the purpose of the installations or devices. UNCLOS provides that only installations and structures that serve economic purposes and which interfere with the exercise of the rights of the coastal State in the zone are subject to the authorization and jurisdiction of the coastal State (Article 60 [1]). The coastal State also has jurisdiction with respect to the deployment and use in the exclusive economic zone of the scientific research installations or equipment referred to in Article 258.

428. Requirements regarding the safety of navigation around artificial islands, installations or structures and on the establishment of safety zones are set out in Articles 60, 260, 261 and 262 of UNCLOS. Only MARPOL 73/78, with respect to discharges, and the London Convention and its 1996 Protocol, with respect to

dumping, apply generally to offshore installations and structures, and not just those relating to oil and gas activities.

429. Removal and disposal requirements with respect to offshore installations and structures are provided for, respectively, in the 1989 IMO Guidelines and Standards for the Removal of Offshore Installations or Structures on the Continental Shelf and in the Exclusive Economic Zone, and in the London Convention and its 1996 Protocol (discussed in more detail in paras. 359–363).

430. *Measures to protect and preserve rare or fragile ecosystems as well as the habitat of depleted, threatened or endangered species and other forms of marine life.*—UNCLOS provides that the measures taken by States to prevent, reduce and control pollution of the marine environment shall include those necessary to protect and preserve rare or fragile ecosystems as well as the habitat of depleted, threatened or endangered species and other forms of marine life.[149] Agenda 21 in its Chapter 17 reiterates the need for these measures in paragraphs 17.46 (f) and 17.74 (f). (See also section C below, on "Protection of specific marine areas.")

431. It is important to note in this respect that UNCLOS provides for the right of coastal States to adopt and enforce non-discriminatory laws and regulations relating to pollution from vessels in ice-covered areas within the limits of the exclusive economic zone.[150]

432. A number of global instruments and programmes deal with the protection of special geographic areas, including: the International Whaling Convention;[151] the Convention on Wetlands of International Importance, especially for Waterfowl (Ramsar Convention); the Convention Concerning the Protection of the World Cultural Heritage (World Heritage Convention); the Convention on Biological Diversity; the Action Plan for Biosphere Reserves (1984) and the Seville Strategy and Statutory Framework for the World Network of Biosphere Reserves (1995) of UNESCO; and the International Coral Reef Initiative (ICRI).

433. In its contribution to the present report, the secretariat of the Ramsar Convention stated that there are currently 519 sites worldwide (of a total of 1,126) in the Ramsar List of Wetlands of International Importance which include coastal wetland types. The Ramsar Convention has recognized that some coastal wetland types are underrepresented in the list and the Contracting Parties have been urged to address this through the "Strategic framework and guidelines for the future development of the List of Wetlands of International Importance" adopted by the 7th Meeting of the Conference of the Contracting Parties in 1999. Joint actions by the Ramsar Convention and the Convention on Biological Diversity on marine and coastal biodiversity focus on marine and coastal protected areas, the development of guidance on integrated marine and coastal area management, and methodologies for the rapid assessment of marine and coastal biological diversity.

434. In its contribution to the present report, UNEP stated that the International Coral Reef Action Network (ICRAN)[152] has launched its Action Phase in June

149. UNCLOS Article 194, par. 5.

150. UNCLOS Article 234.

151. The International Whaling Commission designated the Indian Ocean (1979) and the Southern Ocean (1994) as sanctuaries where commercial whaling is prohibited.

152. ICRAN is a collaboration between the UNEP World Conservation Monitoring Centre (WCMC); the regional seas programmes for the Caribbean, Eastern Africa and East Asia; the World Fish Center (ICLARM); the World Resources Institute (WRI); the International Coral Reef Initiative

2001. The project supports coral reef management in four regional seas programmes: the wider Caribbean, East Africa, East Asia and the South Pacific, which will become blueprints for managing threatened coral reefs worldwide. A meeting of regional seas coral reef coordinators was held in September 2001 in Bonaire, Netherlands Antilles to refine the regional seas work plans for implementing the Action Phase (see also par. 259).

435. Protection for species designated as threatened or endangered is dealt with by a number of international agreements, both global and regional. Examples of global conventions are: Convention on International Trade in Endangered Species of Wild Fauna and Flora (CITES); Convention on the Conservation of Migratory Species of Wild Animals (CMS or Bonn Convention); Convention on Biological Diversity; and, in the specific case of marine mammals, UNCLOS and the International Whaling Convention.

436. The CITES and the CMS Conventions have created lists of species (included in the annexes) threatened with extinction or under risk of becoming threatened. Several marine species are included in the lists. The same approach has been adopted by several regional conventions. IUCN also maintains a Red List of Threatened Species.

437. In its contribution to the present report, the CMS secretariat indicated that within the current CMS activities of relevance to marine mammals, several regional agreements have been developed and implemented (for details, see paras. 214–220).

438. *Use of new technologies.*—Since technological developments in ocean uses could be quite rapid indeed, Article 196 of UNCLOS provides for necessary measures to be taken to prevent, reduce and control pollution of the marine environment resulting from the use of technologies.

439. *Introduction of alien or new species.*—Every day, it has been estimated, 3,000 species of animals and plants are being transported around the world in the ballast water of ships, or in their hulls. Other species enter the sea after escaping or being released from aquaria and fish farms. Most alien species are introduced near coasts, and these waters are particularly vulnerable to them.[153] The invasion of alien species is ranked second to habitat loss as the major threat to biodiversity, and there is growing evidence that the rate of invasion is accelerating with the expansion of international trade.[154]

440. Article 196 of UNCLOS imposes on States the duty to take measures to combat pollution of the marine environment resulting from the intentional or accidental introduction of new or alien species which may cause significant and harmful changes thereto. This obligation was reiterated in Agenda 21, Chapter 17, where it is requested that States should adopt measures in relation to pollution from shipping on ballast water discharge to prevent the spread of non-indigenous organisms (par. 17.30 (vi)).

---

secretariat (ICRI); the Global Coral Reef Monitoring Network (GCRMN); the Coral Reef Alliance (CORAL) and the South Pacific Regional Environment Programme (SPREP).

153. GESAMP, "A Sea of Troubles," GESAMP Reports and Studies No. 70, p. 13.

154. L. A. Kimball, International Global Governance—Using International Law and Organizations to Manage Marine Resources Sustainably, IUCN, 2001, p. 65.

441. The Convention on Biological Diversity recognizes that alien species pose one of the greatest threats to biodiversity, and therefore underlines the need to prevent their introduction, to control them or to eradicate them when they threaten ecosystems, habitats or species (Article 8, par. h). The Biosafety Protocol to the Biodiversity Convention, by establishing a regime for the import of genetically modified organisms, also deals with the threats posed by the import and the introduction into the marine environment of genetically modified live fish.

442. Marine aquaculture is another increasingly significant activity in coastal areas. Badly managed aquaculture has destroyed key habitats such as mangrove forests and has allowed selectively bred fish to escape to open waters and interbreed with their relatives, with unknown consequences.[155] A number of instruments attempt to deal with the impact of aquaculture, inter alia: Code of Practice on the Introduction and Transfer of Marine Organisms (1994), developed by the International Council for the Exploration of the Sea; Code of Conduct on the Import and Release of Exotic Biological Control Agents (1996); Code of Conduct for Responsible Fisheries (1995), developed by FAO; and draft Guidelines for the Prevention of Biodiversity Loss due to Biological Invasion (2000), developed by IUCN.

443. In view of the severe threat posed by alien species to the ecological character of wetlands, and, if they become invasive, to both terrestrial and marine wetland species, in 1999, the 7th Meeting of the Conference of the Contracting Parties to the Ramsar Convention adopted a resolution on invasive species and wetlands (resolution VII.14), in which the Contracting Parties were requested to address the environmental, economic and social impact of invasive species on wetlands within their jurisdictions, wherever possible.

444. At the regional level, several protocols to the regional conventions have been adopted in order to deal, inter alia, with the problem of alien invasive species.

B. Regional Cooperation

1. Review of UNEP Regional Seas Programmes and Action Plans[156]

445. The regional approach is an extremely effective—in may cases the most effective—way to protect and preserve the marine environment. This was the basis for the development of its regional seas programme by UNEP. UNCLOS highlighted regional cooperation and Chapter 17 of Agenda 21 specifically pointed to the UNEP regional seas programme as a significant activity promoting the objectives of sustainable development of the oceans and seas and their resources. The programme is based upon periodically revised action plans adopted at high-level intergovernmental meetings and implemented, in most cases, in the framework of legally binding regional seas conventions under the authority of the respective contracting parties or intergovernmental meetings.

446. Since its initiation in 1974, the regional seas programme, which is currently undergoing a revitalization, has expanded to cover the marine environment of more

155. GESAMP, "A Sea of Troubles," GESAMP Reports and Studies No. 70, p. 22.

156. The information presented in this section is excerpted from the contribution of UNEP to the report. For more details about the UNEP regional seas programme, see www.unep.ch/seas/.

than 140 of the world's coastal countries.[157] It has remained the central UNEP initiative providing the major legal, administrative, substantive and financial framework for the implementation of Agenda 21 and its Chapter 17 on oceans.

447. There are currently 13 regional seas conventions and/or plans of action in operation. Ten of them had been adopted prior to UNCED in 1992, and of these, six had been adopted prior to the conclusion of UNCLOS in 1982. Since UNCED, on the other hand, four regional seas conventions and action plans[158] have either been adopted or have seen the entry into force of protocols to them concerning land-based sources of pollution. In addition, four regional seas conventions[159] have been either adopted or have seen the entry into force of protocols to them dealing with specially protected areas. Another regional seas programme of action is currently being negotiated.[160]

448. The main objectives of the regional seas conventions and action plans include promotion of the integrated management and sustainable development of coastal areas and associated river basins and their living aquatic resources, promotion of the implementation of appropriate technical, institutional, administrative and legal measures for the improved protection of the coastal and marine environment, and facilitation of assessments of the coastal and marine environment, including their conditions and trends.

449. *Fourth Global Regional Seas Meeting.*—Regional seas stakeholders and secretariats from around the world have met on four occasions. All four of these global regional seas meetings were held during the period since the adoption of the GPA in 1995. The Fourth Global Meeting of Regional Seas Conventions and Action Plans was held in Montreal, Canada, from 21 to 23 November 2001.

450. A number of recommendations were made at the Montreal meeting. An important outcome was the decision that the regional seas programmes should consider the necessary steps to be taken towards the adopion of an ecosystem-based management of the marine and coastal environment. In that connection, particular importance was attached to the issues of integrated coastal area management and the ecosystem-based approach to fisheries management.

451. Emphasis was also placed on the need to strengthen cooperation between regional seas programmes and the GPA, as the programmes were the principal implementation platforms for GPA projects and activities at the regional level. Such cooperation should proceed from an identification of problems and the setting of priorities by the regional seas programmes, while the GPA could serve as the principal instrument for identifying partners and donors and forming links with them.

157. It should be noted that not all 140 of the countries are parties to UNCLOS.

158. Convention for the Protection of the Mediterranean Sea against Pollution; Kuwait Regional Convention for Cooperation on the Protection of the Marine Environment from Pollution; Convention for the Protection and Development of the Marine Environment of the Wider Caribbean; and Convention on the Protection of the Black Sea Against Pollution.

159. Convention for the Protection of the Mediterranean Sea against Pollution; Convention for the Protection of the Marine Environment and Coastal Area of the South-East Pacific; Convention for the Protection and Development of the Marine Environment of the Wider Caribbean; and Convention for the Protection, Management and Development of the Marine and Coastal Environment of the Eastern African Region.

160. Upper South-West Atlantic.

452. The meeting recommended that the conduct of the feasibility study establishing a regular process for the assessment of the state of the marine environment mandated by the Governing Council of UNEP at its twenty-first session (see par. 316 above) should be facilitated and that the regional seas programmes should become full participants in the consultations carried out in the context of that study.

453. The Montreal meeting further agreed that oceans governance would be strengthened through the following actions, bearing in mind that regional seas conventions and action plans are the best placed platforms for promoting the protection and sustainable use of the marine and coastal environment:

(a) Because of their multisectoral nature, regional seas programmes can provide complimentary regional frameworks for the implementation of global multilateral environmental agreements and global conventions relevant to the environment, including the biodiversity-related conventions, the hazardous chemicals and wastes conventions, the GPA, the UNCED-related conventions, the IMO marine pollution conventions and protocols and UNCLOS;
(b) Horizontal cooperation among regional seas conventions and action plans on issues of common concern, including the provision of technical cooperation by the more developed regional seas programmes to those that are less developed, needs to be promoted further;
(c) Increased cooperation of the regional bodies of international organizations, including UNEP (specifically the regional seas programmes), FAO, IOC/UNESCO, IMO and IAEA, among others, is required for enhanced governance and management of the marine and coastal environment;
(d) Regional clustering of activities carried out by global multilateral environmental agreements, regional seas conventions and action plans, international organizations and other regional bodies is needed to carry out activities in a more coordinated and cost-effective manner, particularly in areas such as capacity-building, technology transfer, development of supportive national legislation, assessment and monitoring, and public awareness and information exchange;
(e) In particular, greater efforts are required to pool resources for developing collective regional technology transfer centres for the protection and sustainable use of the marine and coastal environment in support of regional seas programmes, global multilateral environmental agreements and other international initiatives.

454. The Fifth Global Meeting of Regional Seas Conventions and Action Plans is scheduled to be held in Toyama, Japan, in 2002.

455. *Implementation of UNEP regional seas programme.*—[161] In the Mediterranean region, after a number of years dedicated to the assessment of marine pollution, its causes and effects, and with a view to ameliorating and completing the legal system for the protection of the marine and coastal environment, during the biennium 2000–2001 there was a shift of interest towards the issue of concrete control of pollution and enforcement of the existing legislation.

456. With regard to pollution from land-based activities, following the important initiatives of the GPA at the global level, efforts were concentrated on the formu-

161. The information presented in this section is excerpted from the contribution of UNEP to the report.

lation of an operational strategy, including practical guidelines and methodology, related to the practical implementation of the Strategic Action Programme to Address Pollution from Land-based Activities. The action programme, which was adopted in 1997 and is expected to soon become a binding legal instrument, foresees the achievement of a number of practical actions to combat pollution, and in particular the implementation and the tracking of concrete reductions of releases of industrial pollutants into the sea.

457. The system that was formulated and adopted by the countries foresees the establishment of the year 2003 as the base year for calculating the national budget of polluting releases and a series of supporting activities to ensure the implementation of the pollution reductions starting from that year. These activities include a large cooperative, multi-donor project, largely financed by GEF and the Fonds Français pour l'Environnement Mondial (FFEM) and other donors. The project, which encompasses the participation of Governments, international bodies, intergovernmental bodies and NGOs, contains a large capacity-building programme, at both the technical and managerial levels, and includes the identification of financial instruments to ensure the financial sustainability of the pollution control measures to be taken by the countries.

458. In the Red Sea and Gulf of Aden region, the Regional Organization for the Conservation of the Environment of the Red Sea and the Gulf of Aden (PERSGA) is executing the Strategic Action Programme (SAP) for the Red Sea and Gulf of Aden, which was developed over a period of three years by PERSGA and the three GEF implementing agencies, namely UNDP, UNEP and the World Bank. The implementing agencies, together with the Islamic Development Bank, have provided the necessary financial and technical support. The Strategic Action Plan provides a cooperatively developed framework for the long-term conservation and management of the coastal and marine resources of the region. A programme of activities is being carried out through six complementary components. Furthermore, PERSGA is establishing a network of marine protected areas which will serve to assist in conserving representative examples of regional biodiversity and have the potential to benefit both migratory species that require scattered habitats and transboundary or straddling stocks. In the area of training, a new training course for marine protected area managers has been prepared in association with the United Nations TRAIN-SEA-COAST programme, and the first course was delivered in January 2002. New public awareness centres have been established in several countries and provided with equipment and materials.

459. A Strategy on Biodiversity and the Establishment of Protected Areas for PERSGA and ROPME has been prepared, in cooperation with ROPME and the UNEP Regional Office for West Asia (UNEP-ROWA) and with the support of the European Commission. This has led to the drafting of a Protocol concerning the Conservation of Biological Diversity and the Establishment of Protected Areas for both the PERSGA and the ROPME regions. Furthermore, a Protocol on the Protection of the Marine Environment from Land-based Sources of Pollution in the Red Sea and Gulf of Aden has been prepared.

460. Regional capacity in marine sciences has been improved through numerous workshops and training courses, including: basic GIS, shark identification and fisheries data collection methods, principles of biodiversity conservation, standard survey methods for habitats and species, diving and environmental education.

461. After a long period of almost no activity, the UNEP Division of Environmental Conventions, Regional Seas Branch, acting as the interim Secretariat for the North-west Pacific Action Plan (NOWPAP), organized several technical meetings. The Sixth Intergovernmental Meeting (Tokyo, December 2000) decided to establish a Regional Coordinating Unit. Japan and the Republic of Korea both expressed their willingness to co-host the Regional Coordinating Unit and developed a detailed plan to co-host the NOWPAP Regional Coordinating Unit in Toyama, Japan, and Pusan, Republic of Korea, in full consultation with China, the Russian Federation, and UNEP. The Regional Coordinating Unit is expected to be established during 2002.

462. During the Tokyo meeting NOWPAP member States decided to develop a new project on the assessment and management of land-based activities within the NOWPAP programme framework. UNEP, as interim secretariat for NOWPAP, was requested to assist in further developing the GEF proposal on "Formulation of a strategic action programme for the North-west Pacific region to address pollution of the marine environment from land-based activities." The project covers the eastern half of the NOWPAP region, extending from the southern extremities to the south-westernmost Japanese islands.

463. The most recently established regional seas programme covers the North-east Pacific region. The first Intergovernmental Meeting of the Plan of Action for the Protection and Sustainable Development of the Marine and Coastal Environment of the North-east Pacific was held in Guatemala City from 19 to 22 February 2002. The Convention for Cooperation in the Protection and Sustainable Development of the Marine and Coastal Environment of the North-east Pacific (Antigua Convention) was signed at Antigua, Guatemala, on 18 February 2002. The Convention establishes the framework of operation of the plan of action and is the first regional seas convention since the adoption of the GPA in 1995 to integrate GPA implementation within its framework.

464. As noted above, the GEF continues to be one of the major financial mechanisms for funding specific projects under the regional seas programme. (For GEF-funded regional seas projects, see paras. 579–592.)

2. Other Regions

465. *Baltic Marine Environment Protection Commission (HELCOM).*—In 1974, seven Baltic coastal States signed the 1974 Baltic Sea Convention, which entered into force on 3 May 1980. In the light of the political changes and developments in international environmental and maritime law, the Convention on the Protection of the Marine Environment of the Baltic Sea Area, 1992 (Helsinki Convention), was open for signature in 1992 by all the States bordering the Baltic Sea and the European Community just prior to UNCED. The Convention, which entered into force on 17 January 2000, covers the whole of the Baltic Sea area including inland waters as well as the seabed. Measures were also taken in the whole catchment area of the Baltic Sea to reduce land-based pollution. According to Article 15 (Nature conservation and biodiversity), the Contracting Parties agree to conserve natural habitats and biological diversity and to protect ecological processes.

466. A major project that was recently undertaken is the Baltic Sea Regional Project (2001–2006). Because pollution and marine life do not respect national boundaries, marine environments must be managed at a higher regional level. The

project, partly funded by the Global Environment Facility (GEF), involves environmental monitoring and assessment as well as ecosystem and fisheries management. The actions involved include coordination of regional monitoring and assessment, development of ecosystem management tools for application in the whole of the Baltic marine ecosystem, management of pollution hot-spots, such as the coastal lagoons of the eastern Baltic, reduction of nutrient discharges from diffuse sources, mainly farmland, and promotion of ecological sustainability in fisheries management.

467. *OSPAR Commission for the Protection of the Marine Environment of the North-East Atlantic.*—Following its ratification by seven Contracting Parties, Annex V to the OSPAR Convention came into force on 30 August 2000. This gives the Commission competence to adopt programmes and measures to control all human activities that may adversely affect the marine environment of the North-east Atlantic, except for questions relating to the management of fisheries. For questions relating to maritime transport, preference is given to action through IMO. Remaining signatories have declared their intention of ratifying the OSPAR Convention, and by the end of 2001 a further three had done so.

468. At its annual meeting, held in Valencia, Spain, from 25 to 29 June 2001, the Commission revised its List of Chemicals for Priority Action, adopted background documents on policies for the control of a number of hazardous substances, drew the attention of the regional fisheries management authorities to the conclusions of the Quality Status Report 2000 on the need for action on certain questions, especially deep-sea fish species, and agreed on conclusions to improve cooperation with the European Community.

469. The Commission also adopted a recommendation on the management of produced water from offshore installations.

470. *Programme for the Protection of the Arctic Marine Environment (PAME).*—In the 1998 Iqaluit Declaration, the Arctic Council[162] Ministers adopted the Regional Programme of Action for the Protection of the Arctic Marine Environment from Land-based Activities. The programme of action was given the following five goals: to promote public health; to reduce the degradation of the marine environment; to promote the sustainable use of marine resources; to promote biodiversity; and to provide remedies for persistent organic pollutants (POPs), heavy metals and radionuclides which present an immediate and concrete threat to the Arctic marine environment. The GPA outlines the basic principles of the Regional Programme of Action. The Regional Programme of Action builds on existing and planned activities and is intended, in part, to provide a mechanism for improving coordination among existing programmes as well as to identify additional actions needed.

471. A recent Arctic Council circumpolar overview report on biodiversity draws attention to various threats caused by human beings to nature and wildlife in the Arctic. Climate change is taking place, with strong, variable and largely unpredictable effects on nature and communities in the Arctic. The Arctic Council has launched an ambitious project to assess the environmental, social and economic

162. The Arctic Council is a high-level intergovernmental forum that provides a mechanism to address the common concerns and challenges faced by the Governments of States bordering the Arctic and the people of the Arctic. Members of the Council are Canada, Denmark, Finland, Iceland, Norway, the Russian Federation, Sweden and the United States of America.

consequences of climate variability and change and the effects of increased UV and UVB radiation in the Arctic. The project will pay special attention to the impacts of climate change on indigenous peoples.

C. Protection of Specific Marine Areas

472. Marine protected areas are useful management tools which can be established for a wide variety of management objectives, such as: the protection of ecologically or biologically important areas, specific marine organisms, important geological or geomorphological processes, beautiful seascapes, cultural or historic sites, and recreation. In accordance with the provisions of UNCLOS, the measures a State may wish to adopt to protect an area and its species depend upon the activities which it seeks to regulate. Marine protected areas can range from areas of strict protection to areas zoned for multiple uses. The maintenance of networks of protected areas, rather than just individual sites, is widely supported.

473. Chapter 17 of Agenda 21 calls upon States to undertake measures to maintain biological diversity and productivity of marine species and habitats under national jurisdiction, through, inter alia, the establishment and management of protected areas (par. 17.7). The Convention on Biological Diversity requires parties to establish a system of protected areas where special measures need to be taken to conserve biological diversity and to develop guidelines for the selection, establishment and management of such areas (Article 8 [a] and [b]). At its second meeting, the Conference of the Parties to the Convention on Biological Diversity endorsed marine and coastal protected areas as one of the five thematic issues and areas for action under the Jakarta Mandate on Marine and Coastal Biological Diversity.

474. The secretariat of the Convention on Biological Diversity, in its contribution to the present report, stated that at its fourth meeting, the Conference of the Parties had called for the establishment of an Ad Hoc Technical Expert Group on Marine and Coastal Protected Areas to assist the Subsidiary Body on Scientific, Technical and Technological Advice (SBSTTA) in its work on the topic of marine and coastal protected areas.

475. At its 1st meeting, held from 22 to 26 October 2001 in New Zealand, the Expert Group reviewed and discussed the status of marine and coastal protected areas globally; the value of marine and coastal protected areas and their effects on marine and coastal biological diversity; criteria for the selection of marine and coastal protected areas; the identification of linkages between marine protected areas and the sustainable use of marine and coastal biodiversity; and the identification of knowledge gaps, particularly in understanding the value and effects of marine and coastal protected areas on the sustainable use of marine and coastal living resources and on population size and dynamics, and the identification of existing efforts to fill those gaps.

476. The Expert Group identified key issues for further work and will meet for a second time in May 2002 to finalize its work for further consideration at the eighth meeting of SBSTTA.

477. One key issue which was identified for future development was the concept of a comprehensive and global representative system of marine and coastal protected

areas, in which the full range of marine and coastal ecosystems would be managed to maintain their structure and functioning and to provide benefits for present and future generations. The Expert Group identified marine protected areas in zones beyond national jurisdiction as an issue where there was a knowledge gap. It may be noted that when the protection of high seas areas was addressed at the seventh session of the Commission on Sustainable Development (decision 7/1), some delegations also proposed the development of a global representative system of marine protected areas within and across national jurisdictions, while others voiced a more cautious approach to the concept of marine protected areas on the high seas.

478. *Developments at the regional level.*—Several regional agreements include provisions relating to the designation of marine protected areas (for details see A/56/58, paras. 404–407). UNEP, in its contribution to the present report, noted that its Mediterranean Action Plan had created the Network of Specially Protected Areas of Mediterranean Importance. The Meeting of the Contracting Parties to the Barcelona Convention brought the network into operation with the inclusion of 12 areas of outstanding importance off the coasts of Spain, France, Tunisia, together with the Sanctuary for the Conservation of Marine Mammals (Monaco, France and Italy).

479. PERSGA reported that it is establishing a network of marine protected areas that will assist in conserving representative examples of regional biodiversity and have the potential to benefit both migratory species that require scattered habitats and transboundary or straddling stocks.

480. A Strategy on Biodiversity and the Establishment of Protected Areas for PERSGA and ROPME has been prepared, in cooperation with ROPME and UNEP-ROWA and with the support of the European Commission, which in turn has led to the drafting of a Protocol concerning the Conservation of Biological Diversity and the Establishment of Protected Areas for both the PERSGA and the ROPME regions.

481. *Measures to protect specific marine areas from shipping activities.*—The provisions of UNCLOS relating to the prevention, reduction and control of pollution of the marine environment from vessels strike a crucial balance between the measures which coastal States can take in the territorial sea and in the exclusive economic zone and the navigational rights of foreign vessels in those maritime zones. This balance is reflected in Article 211 (Pollution from vessels), which recognizes not only the primacy of international rules and standards but also the interests of coastal States to the extent that they are compatible with the global legal regime.

482. In the territorial sea, the coastal State is permitted by UNCLOS to adopt special protective measures affecting international navigation, provided that they do not have the practical effect of hampering innocent passage and do not apply to the design, construction, manning or equipment of foreign ships (see Articles 21 and 22). With respect to the exclusive economic zone, Article 211, paragraph 6, of UNCLOS recognizes that there may be clearly defined areas of a coastal State which, owing to their oceanographical and ecological conditions, as well as the utilization or the protection of their resources and the particular character of their traffic, require special mandatory measures more stringent than what is provided by the generally accepted international rules and standards for the prevention, reduction and control of pollution of the marine environment from vessels. In these circumstances, UNCLOS grants the coastal State the right to adopt laws and regulations for the prevention, reduction and control of pollution from vessels implement-

ing such international rules and standards or navigational practices as are made applicable, through the "competent international organization", that is, IMO, for "special areas" (Article 211 [1] [a]). Additional national laws and regulations relating to discharges and navigational practices may be adopted for the same area by the coastal State under paragraph (6) (c) of Article 211, provided they are agreed to by the competent international organization.

483. Measures which have been developed by IMO for the purpose of protecting specific marine areas from pollution from ships include the establishment of a special area under MARPOL 73/78 in which special discharge restrictions apply; or the adoption of navigational measures, such as areas to be avoided; and ship reporting systems (these measures are discussed in more detail in par. 389). IMO furthermore introduced the concept of a particularly sensitive sea area in 1978 and developed guidelines for the identification of a marine area as a particularly sensitive sea area in 1991.

484. Over the past 20 years since the adoption of UNCLOS, and since UNCED in 1992, IMO has designated a number of sea areas as special areas under MARPOL 73/78. Two particularly sensitive sea areas have been approved by IMO to date: the Great Barrier Reef of Australia and the Sabana-Camagüey Archipelago of Cuba. Two further particularly sensitive sea areas, the marine areas around the Florida Keys of the United States and the Malpelo Islands off Colombia, were expected to be designated at the session of MEPC in March 2002.

485. New revised Guidelines for the Identification and Designation of Particularly Sensitive Sea Areas and Guidelines for the Designation of Special Areas under MARPOL 73/78 were adopted by the IMO Assembly at its 22nd session, in November 2001.

D. Climate Change and Sea-level Rise

486. Scientific studies reveal that the interaction of the ocean and the atmosphere affects global and regional climatic features. Such effects include the unknown risk of sudden and large-scale "surprises," such as the reversal of the Gulf Stream or the collapse of the Greenland and West Antarctic ice sheets. While the likelihood of such devastating events may be very low, it increases with the rate and scale of global warming.[163]

487. The oceans store an immense amount of heat energy, much more than the atmosphere, and consequently play a crucial role in the regulation of the global climate. As in the atmosphere, currents assist in the transfer of heat from low to high latitudes. Warm water moves poleward while cold water returns towards the equator.[164]

488. Heat exchanges also occur vertically within the oceans—between surface water, usually the uppermost 200 metres or so, and the deep water. Sea water in the high latitudes readily sinks, forming deep-water currents. As in the atmosphere, the surface and deep-water currents of the world's oceans are interlinked, forming the global ocean circulation. Scientists have postulated that changes in this global

163. *Encyclopedia of the Atmospheric Environment* www.doc.mmu.ac.uk/aric/eae/Climate/Older/Oceans.html.

164. Ibid.

ocean circulation influence climate changes over hundreds and thousands of years.[165]

489. The United Nations Framework Convention on Climate Change was adopted at UNCED in 1992. The Convention was signed by 154 States (plus the European Community) and entered into force on 21 March 1994. It is the centrepiece of global efforts to combat global warming. Its ultimate objective is the "stabilization of greenhouse gas concentrations in the atmosphere at a level that would prevent dangerous anthropogenic (man-made) interference with the climate system. Such a level should be achieved within a time frame sufficient to allow ecosystems to adapt naturally to climate change, to ensure that food production is not threatened and to enable economic development to proceed in a sustainable manner."

490. Two notable guiding principles were enshrined in the Climate Change Convention. The principle of the "common but differentiated responsibilities"[166] of States assigns the lead in combating climate change to developed countries. The other is the precautionary principle.[167]

491. The Convention was followed by the Kyoto Protocol, adopted at the third Conference of the Parties in December 1997. Under the Protocol, industrialized countries have a legally binding commitment to reduce their collective greenhouse gas emissions by at least 5 percent compared to 1990 levels by the period 2008–2012.

492. The seventh session of the Conference of the Parties to the Climate Change Convention was convened in Marrakesh, Morocco, in November 2001. A major portion of the decisions adopted at the session contained both the rules of implementation for the Kyoto Protocol and new arrangements for technical and financial support. In the Marrakesh Ministerial Declaration, adopted at the session, the Conference of the Parties noted that the decisions adopted, constituting the Marrakesh Accords, paved the way for the timely entry into force of the Protocol.[168]

493. The Third Assessment Report of the Intergovernmental Panel on Climate Change,[169] released in 2001, confirms that "an increasing body of observations gives a collective picture of a warming world" with "new and stronger evidence that most of the warming observed over the last 50 years is attributable to human activities." The global average sea level has risen by 10 to 25 centimetres over the past 100 years. It is likely that much of this rise is related to an increase of 0.3–0.6° C in the lower atmosphere's global average temperature since 1860.

494. Models project that sea levels will rise another 15 to 95 cm by the year 2100

165. Ibid.

166. United Nations Framework Convention on Climate Change, Article 3.1.

167. Ibid.

168. Marrakesh Ministerial Declaration, document FCCC/CP/2001/13/Add.1, Chap. I, decision 1/CP.7, par. 1.

169. Recognizing the problem of potential global climate change, the WMO and UNEP established the Intergovernmental Panel on Climate Change (IPCC) in 1988. The Panel is open to all members of UNEP and WMO. Its role is to assess the scientific, technical and socio-economic information relevant for understanding the risks of human-induced climate change. It does not carry out new research, nor does it monitor climate-related data. It bases its assessment mainly on published and peer-reviewed scientific technical literature.

(with a "best estimate" of 50 cm). This will occur due to the thermal expansion of ocean water and an influx of freshwater from melting glaciers and ice. The projected rise is two to five times faster than the rise experienced over the past 100 years. The rate, magnitude and direction of sea-level change will vary locally and regionally in response to coastline features, changes in ocean currents, differences in tidal patterns and sea-water density, and vertical movements of the land itself. Sea levels are expected to continue rising for hundreds of years after atmospheric temperatures stabilize.

495. The overall consequences of such sea-level rise include the following: coastal zones and small islands will become extremely vulnerable; flooding and coastal erosion will worsen; sea-level rise could damage key economic sectors and threaten human health; valuable coastal ecosystems will be at serious risk; and ocean ecosystems may also be affected.[170]

496. With regard to implementation of the provisions of the Convention and the Protocol, the United Nations Industrial Development Organization (UNIDO) is assisting developing countries with technical cooperation, training and awareness-building programmes for industry, information, technology transfer, the development of innovative financing mechanisms, and sound regulatory programmes for emissions control.

E. Ten-year Review of the Implementation of Agenda 21

497. Ten years after the adoption of Agenda 21, a review is to be undertaken at the World Summit on Sustainable Development, to be held in Johannesburg, South Africa, from 26 August to 4 September 2002, of the progress achieved in the implementation of the outcome of the United Nations Conference on Environment and Development (UNCED). The tenth session of the United Nations Commission on Sustainable Development is serving as an open-ended intergovernmental preparatory committee for the 10-year review. (For details on preparations for the Summit in 2001, see the previous annual reports (A/56/58 and A/56/58/Add.1).) One of the aims of the Summit, including its preparatory process, is to ensure a balance between economic development, social development and environmental protection.

498. Four meetings have been scheduled during the tenth session of the Commission on Sustainable Development in preparation for the Summit during 2001–2002: the first three held in New York, from 30 April to 2 May 2001, from 28 January to 8 February 2002 and from 25 March to 4 April 2002, and the fourth in Jakarta from 27 May to 7 June 2002.

499. At the end of 2001 subregional and regional preparatory committees were held in Africa, Asia and the Pacific, Europe and North America, Latin America and the Caribbean, and West Asia. The regional preparatory committees assessed the key challenges, opportunities and constraints relating to sustainable development faced by each region over the past 10 years, and identified future priorities, new initiatives and the commitments needed to make progress in the coming years.

500. While there were some differences in regional priorities, the following

170. See www.unfccc.int/.

areas emerged as issues of common concern: implementation of the Rio Principles; globalization; poverty eradication; sustainable consumption and production; management of natural resources (including ocean resources); agriculture and food security; energy; freshwater and sanitation; sustainable human settlements; health; human development; financing of sustainable development; trade and market access; transfer of technology and capacity-building; governance/institutional structure for sustainable development; and decision-making and information requirements.

501. An informal brainstorming session was held on 16 and 17 January 2002 in New York to provide for an open, informal exchange of views in preparation for the second session of the preparatory committee. The second session (New York, 28 January–8 February 2002) was attended by over 1,000 representatives of Governments, United Nations agencies and convention secretariats, international organizations, and the nine major groups. Its purpose was to conduct a comprehensive review and assessment of progress achieved in the implementation of Agenda 21, including the Programme for the further Implementation of Agenda 21;[171] and to agree on a document that could form the basis of negotiations at PrepCom 3 in March.

502. The Commission heard reports on a number of intergovernmental meetings and processes, including the UNESCO presentation of the resolution adopted by the IOC Executive Council at its meeting on 10 and 11 December 2001,[172] outlining the commitments of IOC to raising awareness of the importance of oceans and to the Summit. In addition, the Executive Secretary of IOC discussed the deliberations and outcomes of the Global Conference on Oceans and Coasts at Rio+10, held in Paris, from 3 to 7 December 2001.

503. The Paris Conference was convened to assess global progress in the implementation of Chapter 17 of Agenda 21 and related instruments. It was attended by 424 participants from 61 countries. The Conference highlighted the fact that sustainable development and poverty reduction cannot be achieved without healthy oceans and coasts. A key question identified was how to best sustain the natural resource base and the integrity of coastal and ocean ecosystem services while continuing to expand economically. It was strongly recommended that the United Nations should make sustainable development of oceans, which comprise 70 percent of the Earth's surface, a central feature of the World Summit on Sustainable Development.

504. Among the main conclusions of the Conference were that: poverty reduction during the coming decade requires greater access to sustainable economic livelihoods and wealth derived from the ocean and the development of safer, healthy coastal communities; there is a need for capacity-building for good governance of coastal and ocean use; the health of the oceans and coasts is directly linked to the proper management of river basins, including freshwater flows to the marine environment; the protection of coastal and marine areas and biodiversity demands an ecosystem approach; strengthening science-based monitoring and assessment of the oceans is essential for managing the long-term sustainability of marine ecosystems; and it is necessary to address the special problems and issues of small island developing States.

171. General Assembly resolution S/19-2, annex.
172. E/CN.17/2002/PC.2/Misc.1.

505. During the debates at the Conference, many delegations expressed the view that greater attention should be given to the oceans, which are of central importance for human development, poverty reduction and food security. Concerns expressed focused on the protection and sustainable management of fisheries as well as coasts, and on coastal zone management. Reference was also made to the vital importance of shipping to global development and the safety of the seas.

506. Small island developing States urged a renewed commitment to the Barbados Programme of Action and requested support for a comprehensive 10-year review of its implementation in 2004.

507. The need for an integrated approach to marine and coastal management was also stressed, as requested by the Commission on Sustainable Development at its seventh session. Moreover, concerns were expressed that Governments and international institutions often followed a fragmented approach, based on sectoral issues. In that connection, consideration was given to the idea that oceans must be considered as a whole and not in a piecemeal fashion. Many delegations urged more effective implementation of the GPA, as called for in the Montreal Declaration of 2001.

508. Attention was given to the necessity for better scientific information on and assessment of the interaction between the atmosphere, oceans and climate change, especially with respect to coastal areas and small island developing States. On the other hand, it was recognized that the major constraint for small island developing States in implementing the Barbados Programme of Action was not lack of information but inadequate financial and technical resources. Many coastal developing countries lacked financial and technical support and required capacity-building, with regard to both institutions and human resources.

509. The Chairman's paper[173] is one of the major outcomes of the second session of the preparatory committee. Oceans issues, including those pertaining to the implementation of UNCLOS, are grouped under the key thematic area "Protecting and managing the natural resource base of economic and social development" (Chap. IV). A separate thematic area is dedicated to "Sustainable development of small island developing States" (Chap. VII). The Chairman's paper will be the basis for negotiations at future sessions of the preparatory committee.

510. The Chairman's paper focuses on a number of issues, such as providing financial and technological assistance, in particular to support the full implementation of the GPA, and to enable developing countries to develop the capacity for the integrated management and sustainable use of fisheries; implementing sustainable fisheries as a basis for food security and sustainable livelihoods, through relevant agreements; supporting the implementation of the IMO conventions on marine safety and prevention of marine pollution, and finalizing and implementing conventions relating to vessel-based pollution; promoting the sustainable use and conservation of marine and coastal biodiversity, as stipulated under the Convention on Biological Diversity; strengthening regional cooperation and encouraging better coordination, including raising public awareness of the importance of the protection of the marine environment; strengthening capacities in marine science; and promoting more effective coordination and cooperation.

511. The economic and environmental vulnerability of small island developing States is referred to in chapter VII of the Chairman's paper. Issues underlined in-

173. A/CONF.199/PC/L.1, annex.

clude: implementation of the Barbados Programme of Action, as well as its review in 2004; the need to support relevant regional fisheries management organizations and arrangements; the importance of providing assistance in the sustainable management of exclusive economic zones and extended continental shelf areas; the need to support the early operationalization of economic and environmental vulnerability indices; and the need to promote a global initiative to assist in the adaptation to climate change.

8. MARINE SCIENCE AND TECHNOLOGY

512. In UNCLOS, Chapter XIII on marine scientific research, Chapter XIV on development and transfer of marine technology, and some parts of chapter XII, on the protection of the marine environment, form the global regime for marine science and technology and provide the basis for relevant bilateral, regional and other international agreements for the promotion of scientific research on the ocean and its resources.

513. Agenda 21, and in particular Chapter 17, includes action-recommendations which in large part aim at implementing effectively UNCLOS provisions for the protection and preservation of the marine environment and the rational use and development of its living resources. In its chapters 34 and 35, Agenda 21 stipulates that the availability of scientific and technological information and access to and the transfer of environmentally sound technologies are essential requirements for sustainable development.[174]

514. In the years since the holding of the Rio Conference and the adoption of Agenda 21, UNCLOS has come into force (November 1994), as have a number of other important international legal instruments which have a bearing on marine scientific research. Most of these instruments recognize that sustainable development must be science-based and supported by the appropriate technology.[175]

515. In this regard, the UNESCO Intergovernmental Oceanographic Commission (IOC) has been called upon to assume the main responsibilities in promoting marine scientific research, in particular with the publication and dissemination of marine science information and knowledge, the coordination of international marine scientific research projects, the provisions of basic scientific information towards the protection of the marine environment and the transfer of technology.[176]

516. Over the years, the IOC has experienced significant evolution, from an organization devoted mostly to the coordination of scientific programmes to one that has expanded its role in order to serve the multiple needs of its members States, assisting them in developing their own capabilities to use science for the development and management of the uses of the oceans.[177] In the revised statutes of the

174. Agenda 21, Chap. 34, par. 34.7.

175. See "Towards the 2002 World Summit on Sustainable Development: Ensuring the Sustainable Development of Oceans and Coasts—A Call to Action," Co-Chairs' reports from the Global Conference on Oceans and Coasts at Rio+10, held at UNESCO headquarters, Paris, 3–7 December 2001.

176. A/56/58, paras. 452–547, and IOC document IOC/INF-961.

177. See IOC Annual Report 2000, at ioc.unesco.org/iocweb/.

Commission,[178] adopted to reflect the new international context created by UNCED and the associated new global conventions as well as the entry into force of UNCLOS, the mission of the IOC is defined as: "to promote international cooperation and to coordinate programmes in research, services and capacity-building, in order to learn more about the nature and resources of the ocean and coastal areas and to apply that knowledge for the improvement of management, sustainable development, the protection of the marine environment and the decision-making process of its member States" (Article 2 [1]).

517. Other competent international organizations also play an important role vis-à-vis marine science and technology.[179]

518. Recently, the Second United Nations Open-ended Informal Consultative Process on Oceans established by the General Assembly in its resolution 54/33 dealt with the issue of marine science and marine technology and stressed the important role they play in promoting the sustainable management and uses of the oceans and seas as part of efforts to eradicate poverty, to ensure food security and to sustain economic prosperity and the well-being of present and future generations. The need was identified to ensure access for decision makers to advice and information on marine science and technology, the appropriate transfer of technology and support for the production and diffusion of factual information and knowledge for end-users (see A/56/121).

519. Following the entry into force of UNCLOS, IOC established the Advisory Body of Experts on the Law of the Sea (ABE-LOS) to give advice, upon request, to the executive bodies of the IOC and the IOC Assembly with regard to the possible role of the Commission in the implementation of UNCLOS.[180] (For information about the 1st meeting of ABE-LOS, held in June 2001, see A/56/58/Add.1, paras. 104–113.) ABE-LOS will hold its 2nd meeting in El Jadida, Morocco, from 6 to 9 May 2002. In accordance with the recommendations adopted at the 1st meeting,[181] the 2nd meeting will continue discussions on the criteria and guidelines for the transfer of marine technology, issues pertaining to the consent regime (Article 246 of UNCLOS) and appropriate internal procedures related to the effective and appropriate use of UNCLOS Article 247. As specified in the recommendations, two open-ended subgroups, one on transfer of marine technology[182] and the other on procedures under Article 247 of the Convention, have been established and are working in close cooperation with the Division for Ocean Affairs and the Law of the Sea.

520. In its review of major accomplishments and constraints at the global level since UNCED, the Co-Chairs of the Global Conference on Ocean and Coasts at Rio+10 (Paris, 3–7 December 2001) stated in their report[183] that in the past 10 years there has been a turning point in terms of understanding and measuring the role of the oceans in global climate change and in developing the observational tools

178. Revised statutes of IOC adopted by the General Conference of UNESCO at its thirtieth session, document IOC/INF-785 Corr.

179. For further details, see paras. 521–551 below as well as A/55/274 and A/56/121.

180. A/56/58/Add.1, par. 104.

181. Ibid., para 113.

182. Document IOC/INF-1054.

183. Ibid.

needed to forecast change. Significant improvements have been made in the models and technology for monitoring climate changes; and the scientific community has succeeded in narrowing the level of uncertainty regarding many ocean processes. The collection of previously unavailable information is now being organized and utilized through a concerted inter-agency and intergovernmental effort to continuously monitor the major planetary processes. The building of the institutional framework for developing Earth system science is well under way and recent success stories include the establishment of programmes such as the World Climate Research Project and the International Geosphere and Biosphere Programme on Global Environmental Change. This is due in part to the existence of high-quality observational networks worldwide, which need to be maintained and sustained over time. The full and open exchange of environmental data which is essential for the protection of life-supporting natural systems, is a principle that calls for universal recognition.[184]

A. Marine Science Programmes in the United Nations System

521. The progress achieved in marine science in recent times is quite remarkable. A number of large-scale projects exemplify the current efforts being made to study the marine environment from a wider perspective. The details of several of these projects, which are described in the following paragraphs provide a broad picture of significant recent developments.

522. Scientists from a number of research institutes are planning to place sensors and lay fibre-optic cables to provide electric power and communications to the sensors to cover an entire tectonic plate, the 80,000-square-mile Juan de Fuca Plate, in the Pacific off the north-west coast of the United States and the south-west coast of Canada. Project Neptune, at a cost of $200 million, is expected to be operational in four or five years, and will allow scientists to study the dynamic processes that drive plate tectonics.

523. Plans are under way to undertake another large-scale project, to study the entire Mid-Atlantic Ridge, the world's largest mountain range, albeit underwater, spanning the whole Atlantic Ocean. The objective would be to study how new crust is being formed where the large tectonic plates are grinding against each other.

524. Another large-scale project is the Census of Marine Life, a $1 billion international project to inventory all marine living beings. Its objective is to assess and explain the diversity, distribution and abundance of marine life in the world's oceans (see also A/56/121, par. 20).

525. The international Argo programme is well known to the international community. It is part of the integrated Global Ocean Observing System (GOOS), under the auspices of IOC and WMO, working with UNEP and ICSU. Using 3,000 profiling floats, its goal is to profile the complete upper ocean over the entire world, in real time by 2005, providing various types of oceanographic data (physical, chemical and biological) (see par. 533 below, as well as A/55/61, par. 257; A/56/58, par. 513; and A/56/121, paras. 223–226).

184. Ibid.

526. IOC has been the lead agency in the United Nations system with regard to ocean science and services, especially in the sphere of global ocean observations, through its GOOS programme.

Ocean science[185]

527. *Climate Variability and Predictability Study (CLIVAR), and World Ocean Circulation Experiment (WOCE).*—CLIVAR and WOCE are the projects of the World Climate Research Programme (WCRP) with the most significant involvement and dependence on ocean science. Activities include GODAE, the joint WCRP-SCOR Working Group on Air-Sea Fluxes, the Surface Ocean/Lower Atmosphere Study (SOLAS), the Climate and Cryosphere (CliC) project, the Arctic Climate System Study (ACSYS) and the Coordinated Enhanced Observing Period (CEOP) and Global Atmospheric Boundary Layer Study of the Global Energy and Water Cycle Experiment (GWEX).

528. The year 2001 was the penultimate year of WOCE as a part of WCRP. Major publications marking the significant achievements of this 20-year project have begun appearing, among them: "Ocean Circulation and Climate—Observing and Modelling the Global Ocean;" a series of four atlases (one for each major ocean) presenting the results of the unprecedented global hydrographic survey of the physical and chemical properties of the oceans. The WOCE high-quality data sets will also continue to be mined by future researchers and the steady flow of results will continue to have an impact on the understanding of the physics of ocean circulation and its role in climate. WOCE science will be the focus of a major international conference to be held in San Antonio, Texas, in November 2002, marking the end of the WOCE programme as a separate element of WCRP.

Global Ocean Observing System (GOOS)[186]

529. GOOS is influencing national thinking and planning. Many countries are currently planning, or conducting their own coastal and ocean observations in line with the GOOS Strategic Plan and Principles. Many countries have created GOOS Committees with a view to developing contributions to GOOS at the national or regional level by improving their operational oceanography methods and practices so as to meet management needs and address policy issues. The user community is being consulted regularly about GOOS design through stakeholder workshops, to ensure that the end products meet user needs.

530. To a fair extent, GOOS implementation will depend upon the success of the newly created Joint WMO/IOC Technical Commission for Oceanography and Marine Meteorology (JCOMM), which will hold its first intergovernmental meeting in Akureyri, Iceland, from 19 to 29 June 2002.[187]

531. In 2001, the GOOS Initial Observing System (GOOS-IOS), a collection of existing observing subsystems, expanded with the inclusion of two new subsystems.

185. The information presented in this section is excerpted from the contribution of IOC to the present report.

186. The information presented in this section is excerpted from the contribution of IOC to the present report.

187. See the contribution by the WMO (paras. 543–547).

532. GOOS is also being implemented through pilot projects such as the Global Ocean Data Assimilation Experiment (GODAE).[188] The most significant recent development is the establishment of the GODAE server operated by the United States in Monterey, California. The site will provide access to all GODAE data, either directly or via distributed access, as well as providing a range of products. A similar facility is being established in France.

533. GODAE itself has pilot projects. The largest GODAE pilot project is the Argo project[189] to seed the ocean with 3,000 profiling floats that will all be operational during the period 2003–2005. This will provide the first global coverage ever of the temperature and salinity of the upper ocean, an essential ingredient in the improvement of numerical models and forecasts of the behaviour of the ocean, weather and climate systems. The existing multinational commitments to Argo include 984 floats already funded and 2,274 proposed over the next three years, which suggests that the project goals will be met on time. A regional implementation planning for Argo for the Indian Ocean was held in Hyderabad, India, in July 2001.

534. Regional meetings[190] were held to advance the development of GOOS in the Caribbean, GOOS-Africa, Indian Ocean GOOS, and South-East Asia and North-East Asia GOOS. MedGOOS attracted major funding from the European Commission to expand development of the observing system in the Mediterranean. NEAR-GOOS has embarked on a strategic planning exercise that should lead to the structured inclusion of chemical and biological parameters.

535. In January 2001, the partners in the Integrated Global Observing Strategy (IGOS)[191] published an "ocean theme" document indicating the capabilities and developments needed in space-based measurements to make GOOS fully operational. A major development in this context was the announcement at the last IGOS meeting in Kyoto, Japan, of the intention of NASA, NOAA, CNES and EUmetsat to jointly start the planning and development, as requested in the ocean theme Intergovernmental Oceanographic Commission, of a high-precision oceanographic altimetry mission, to follow Jason I, which had been successfully launched from Vandenberg Air Force Base in California on 7 December 2001.

536. GOOS, through its climate and ocean component GCOS, and a number of other agencies and observing systems presented to the Conference of the Parties to the United Nations Framework Convention on Climate Change, a summary of current global requirements in the area of climate observations. As a result, the Conference of the Parties is requiring the Parties to develop action plans to implement climate-monitoring systems, including ocean components that will form part of GOOS. The goal is to meet the urgent need to improve the quality, coverage and management of the global ocean observing system, and especially to support the increase in the number of ocean observations, particularly in remote locations, called for by the Conference of the Parties.

537. *International Oceanographic Data and Information Exchange (IODE).*—The IODE system was established in 1961 to enhance marine research, exploitation and development by facilitating the exchange of oceanographic data and information

188. See A/56/58, par. 513.

189. Ibid.

190. See also A/56/58, par. 514.

191. A/56/58, par. 515.

between participating member States and by meeting the needs of users for data and information products. The IODE system is a worldwide, service-oriented network consisting of designated national agencies, national oceanographic data centres and world data centres oceanography. During 2001, Cameroon and Togo joined the IODE system, which now has 64 members.

538. *(a) IOC data and information management: the regional projects and activities.*—Through the regional networks, IODE has established close working relationships with other IOC programmes such as the Ocean Science Programme (e.g., to provide ocean data and information to assist the ICAM programme), GOOS, as well as with other non-IOC programmes and projects, providing them with ocean data and information services with expertise.

539. Implementation of the Ocean Data and Information Network for Africa (ODINAFRICA) project[192] started in 2001. The Ocean Data and Information Network for the IOC Subcommission for the Caribbean and Adjacent Regions (IOCARIBE) and South America Regions (ODINCARSA) is the newly established (July 2001) network to implement a regional ocean data and information programme for these regions. Fourteen countries attended the first ODINCARSA planning workshop (Guayaquil, Ecuador, 24–26 October 2001).

540. *The UNESCO/IOC Ocean Portals (African Ocean Portal-Caribbean/South American Ocean Portal)* will provide access to information and data on all aspects of ocean/coastal research and management for the benefit of various communities such as decision makers, the private sector, the education community and the general public. The Ocean Portal is a high-level directory of ocean data and information-related web sites, launched in July 2001, containing descriptions of over 3,000 sites. The development of regional portals will provide for increased ownership of the portal by the target audiences and will enable a more targeted focus on national and regional issues.

541. *(b) General Bathymetric Chart of the Oceans (GEBCO) and Ocean Mapping Programme (OMP).*—The main goal of GEBCO and OMP is to cover the world ocean with bathymetric and geological/geophysical charts in order to provide decision makers, scientists, students and a wide range of users with information about the bottom relief and geological parameters of the open part of the world ocean and exclusive economic zone. GEBCO and OMP provide a useful framework for many IOC programmes.

542. At the end of December 2001, the third version of the GEBCO Digital Atlas CD-ROM was released. Furthermore, all seven regional bathymetric projects within OMP were developed successfully during 2001. They covered the following areas: Western Indian Ocean; Caribbean Sea and Gulf of Mexico; Arctic Ocean; Central Eastern Atlantic; and Western Pacific. In accordance with a request of the IOC member States from the South-East Pacific region, a new project for a bathymetric chart on the region was established in 2001.

543. *World Meteorological Organization.*—In its contribution to the present report, WMO notes that while data from the ocean data buoys, both drifting and moored, are of considerable value to States, some coastal States have expressed concerns regarding those platforms that drift into territorial waters and exclusive eco-

192. Ibid., par. 518.

nomic zones. Measures need to be taken to address these concerns and enhance understanding of the nature of the platforms and the applications and value of the data.

544. In addition, for a number of reasons, the availability of meteorological and oceanographic observations made by ships at sea (WMO Voluntary Observing Ships (VOS) scheme) and transmitted to shore in real time has been stagnant or decreasing for several years. Since such observations are critical to an enhanced scientific understanding of fluxes at the air-sea interface and eventually for modelling and prediction of such fluxes in coupled atmosphere-ocean climate models, efforts are required to enhance data quality.

545. WMO still continues to point to the lack of capacity of many developing countries, which inhibits their ability to participate in and contribute to the major marine observation and services programmes of WMO and IOC, or to benefit from the data and products which these programmes generate.[193]

546. In response to the above issues, WMO, in close cooperation with IOC, has undertaken a number of activities: (a) A JCOMM in situ observing platform support (JCOMMOPS) working primarily through a database accessed through a dedicated web site (http://www.jcommops.org), has been launched, providing a wealth of operational information and technical support to the operators as well as the users of ocean data buoys and subsurface floats. It also provides real-time information to coastal States regarding the positions and status of all such platforms in operation; (b) A VOS Climate project has been established and made operational to provide a subset of high-quality air-sea flux data to be used as a reference data set for coupled atmosphere-ocean models and the calibration of satellite-sensed ocean data; and (c) a South-East Asian Centre for Atmospheric and Marine Prediction (SEACAMP) Project and a Western Indian Ocean Marine Application Project (WIOMAP) have been set up for the enhancement of marine observing networks, data management and services in both ocean regions. These are regional cooperative projects involving both meteorological and oceanographic agencies and institutions.

547. In a major cooperative initiative to pool the resources and expertise of the meteorological and oceanographic communities, both nationally and internationally and in support of programmes addressing major global concerns, IOC and WMO established JCOMM jointly in 1999 (see also A/54/429, par. 622). At its meeting in June 2001,[194] the Commission established a comprehensive work plan which in particular seeks to implement a fully integrated ocean observing and data management system to support maritime safety, global climate studies and marine environmental protection.

B. Marine Technology Programmes in the United Nations System

548. At the special session of the General Assembly to review and appraise the implementation of Agenda 21, in 1997, the Assembly noted that provision of adequate and predictable financial resources and the transfer of environmentally sound tech-

193. See also A/56/58, par. 529.

194. See par. 530 above.

nologies to developing countries are critical elements for the implementation of Agenda 21. It further noted: "However, while some progress has been made, much remains to be done to activate the means of implementation set out in Agenda 21, in particular in the areas of finance and technology transfer, technical assistance and capacity-building."[195]

549. UNIDO, as a global forum on industrialization, has a particular mandate to strengthen industrial capacities in developing countries and countries in transition. In this regard, its activities are grouped in two main programmes: (a) "Strengthening of industrial capacities," which includes, inter alia, (i) promotion of investment and related technologies; (ii) institutional capacity-building at the country and sectoral levels; and (iii) industrial information through networking, including information on the transfer of technology; and (b) "Cleaner and sustainable industrial development," in order to (i) support programmes on environmentally sustainable industrial development strategies and technologies, including on transfer of environmental technologies within industrial subsectors assigned high priority; and (ii) development of specific norms and standards relating to environmentally sustainable industrial development strategies and technologies, and implementation of international protocols, agreements and conventions. (For further details on the capacity-building activities of UNIDO, see paras. 596–603.)

550. The ninth session of the UNIDO General Conference was held at Vienna from 3 to 7 December 2001. The Conference suggested that the UNIDO industrial capacity-strengthening work should focus on areas such as institutional capacity-building for the application of technical standards, investment promotion and technology transfer for enhanced productivity and competitiveness, closer North-South cooperation and the extension of technology foresight activities.[196]

551. Discussions on the issue of transfer of technology also took place within the Commission on Investment, Technology and Related Financial Issues of the United Nations Conference on Trade and Development (UNCTAD) Trade and Development Board. An expert meeting was held on "International arrangements for transfer of technology: best practices for access to and measures to encourage transfer of technology with a view to capacity-building in developing countries, especially in least developed countries."[197] During the discussions, the experts were of the view that measures should be taken to prevent anti-competitive practices by technology rights holders or the resort to practices which unduly impede the transfer and dissemination of technology. They noted, however, that although control of such practices was common in developed countries, there was a lack of legislative measures in this regard in many developing countries. The development of relevant legislation at either the national or the regional level was considered to be a promising option. Countries should be encouraged to create a hospitable domestic regulatory environment for foreign investment, along with intellectual property protection for access to the newest technologies. They suggested that supporting capacity-building, in particular in the least developed countries should be carried out through specific projects and programmes and by establishing scientific and technological infrastructure on a cooperative basis for both public and private research facilities to enable

195. General Assembly resolution S-19/2, annex, par. 17.

196. See UNIDO web site: www.unido.org.

197. See TD/B/COM.2/33-TD/B/COM.2/EM.9/3.

them to assess, adopt, manage, apply and improve technologies.[198] Another important suggestion of the experts was that the relevant international instruments should contain built-in implementation mechanisms, including financial provisions and monitoring arrangements.[199]

9. SETTLEMENT OF DISPUTES

552. Under Part XV, section 1, of UNCLOS, States parties are required to settle their disputes concerning the interpretation or application of the Convention by peaceful means in accordance with Article 2, paragraph 3, of the Charter of the United Nations. However, when States parties to UNCLOS involved in a dispute have not reached a settlement by peaceful means of their own choice, they are obliged to resort to the compulsory dispute settlement procedures entailing binding decisions, subject to limitations and exceptions, provided for under the Convention (Part XV, sect. 2).

553. The mechanism established by the Convention provides for four alternative procedures for the settlement of disputes, that is, the International Tribunal for the Law of the Sea; the International Court of Justice; an arbitral tribunal constituted in accordance with Annex VII to UNCLOS; or a special arbitral tribunal constituted in accordance with Annex VIII to UNCLOS. States parties may choose one or more of the procedures by written declaration made under Article 287 of UNCLOS and deposited with the Secretary-General of the United Nations.

554. UNCLOS entered into force on 16 November 1994 and the International Tribunal for the Law of the Sea was inaugurated in October 1996. In its brief history to date, the Tribunal has heard 10 cases that have been brought before it regarding issues of direct relevance to the application or interpretation of UNCLOS by States parties.

555. During the period under review, the Tribunal was seized of the Mox Plant case (Ireland v. United Kingdom); and the International Court of Justice was seized of the cases concerning Sovereignty over Pulau Ligitan and Pulau Sipadan (Indonesia/Malaysia) and Territorial and Maritime Dispute (Nicaragua v. Colombia). Further details on these cases may be found at the web sites of the Tribunal and the International Court, respectively, at: www.itlos.org/ and www.icj-cij.org/.

556. *Trust Fund.*—It is recalled that pursuant to paragraph 9 and Annex I to General Assembly resolution 55/7, the Secretary-General established a Trust Fund for the purpose of assisting States in the settlement of disputes through the International Tribunal for the Law of the Sea. No formal requests have been received by the Secretariat as yet for assistance from the Fund. To date, contributions to the Trust Fund amount to $24,865 (United Kingdom).

A. Case before the International Tribunal for the Law of the Sea[200]

557. *Mox Plant case (Ireland v. United Kingdom).*—On 9 November 2001, a request for prescription of provisional measures, pending the constitution of an arbitral

198. Ibid.

199. Ibid.

200. The information presented in the following section has been excerpted from documents of the Tribunal.

tribunal to be established under Annex VII of the United Nations Convention on the Law of the Sea, was submitted to the Tribunal.

558. The dispute, according to the request, stems from the authorization of the United Kingdom to open a new "Mox" plant in Sellafield, United Kingdom. The plant is designed to reprocess spent nuclear fuel containing a mixture of plutonium dioxide and uranium dioxide into a new fuel, which is known as mixed oxide fuel or "Mox." The Government of Ireland is concerned that the operation of the plant will contribute to the pollution of the Irish Sea and underlines the potential risks involved in the transportation of radioactive material to and from the plant.

559. On 25 October 2001, Ireland notified the United Kingdom that it was requesting that their dispute be submitted to an arbitral tribunal in accordance with Annex VII of UNCLOS. In addition and pending the constitution of such an arbitral tribunal, Ireland requested, in its application to the International Tribunal for the Law of the Sea, the prescription of provisional measures.

560. The United Kingdom requested the Tribunal to reject Ireland's request for provisional measures and to order Ireland to bear the United Kingdom's cost in the proceedings.

561. A hearing was held on 19 and 20 December 2001. The Tribunal, based on Article 282 of UNCLOS, examined the United Kingdom argument that the Tribunal was not competent to prescribe provisional measures since the main elements of the dispute were governed by regional agreements, including European treaties, which provide for binding means of resolving disputes. However, the Tribunal took the view that the dispute concerned the interpretation and application of UNCLOS only. The United Kingdom also maintained that the requirements of Article 283 had not been satisfied since no exchange of views had taken place between the parties before the case was submitted to the Tribunal. The Tribunal considered that a State Party was not obliged to continue with an exchange of views if it concluded that the possibility of reaching an agreement had been exhausted. Therefore, it found that an Annex VII arbitral tribunal would prima facie have jurisdiction over the dispute.

562. As regards whether provisional measures were required pending the constitution of an Annex VII arbitral tribunal, the Tribunal noted that, in accordance with Article 290, paragraph 5, of UNCLOS, it might prescribe provisional measures if it considered that the urgency of the situation so required. The Tribunal found that the urgency of the situation did not require the prescription of provisional measures, as requested by Ireland, in the short period before the constitution of an Annex VII arbitral tribunal.

563. Nonetheless, the Tribunal considered the duty to cooperate as a fundamental principle in the prevention of the pollution of the marine environment under Part XII of UNCLOS and general international law and that rights arose therefrom which the Tribunal might consider appropriate to preserve under Article 290 of UNCLOS. Accordingly, it prescribed a provisional measure, pending a decision by an Annex VII arbitral tribunal, to the effect that Ireland and the United Kingdom were to cooperate and enter into consultations in order to exchange further information with regard to possible consequences for the Irish Sea arising out of the commissioning of the Mox plant; monitor the risks or the effects of the operation of the Mox plant for the Irish Sea; and devise, as appropriate, measures to prevent the pollution of the marine environment which might result from the operation of

the Mox plant. Moreover, the Tribunal decided that each party was to submit an initial report on compliance with the provisional measure prescribed by 17 December 2001 and authorized the President of the Tribunal to request such further reports and information as might be deemed necessary after that date.

B. Cases before the International Court of Justice[201]

564. *Territorial and Maritime Dispute (Nicaragua v. Colombia).*—Nicaragua instituted proceedings against Colombia on 6 December 2001 and invoked, as a basis for the Court's jurisdiction, Article XXXI of the 30 April 1948 American Treaty on Pacific Settlement (Pact of Bogotá), to which both Nicaragua and Colombia are parties. Nicaragua also referred to the declarations under Article 36 of the Statute of the Court, by which Nicaragua (1929) and Colombia (1937) had accepted the compulsory jurisdiction of the Court.

565. Nicaragua claimed that the islands and keys of San Andrés and Providencia islands pertained to the group of islands and keys that in 1821, date of independence from Spain, became part of the newly formed Federation of Central American States, and that in 1838, after the dissolution of the Federation, became part of Nicaragua. Moreover, Nicaragua considered that the Barcenas-Esguerra Treaty of 24 March 1928, which is not a treaty of delimitation, lacked legal validity and consequently could not provide a basis for Colombian title to San Andrés. Accordingly, Nicaragua requested the Court to adjudge and declare that Nicaragua had sovereignty over the islands concerned and on that basis to determine the course of the single maritime boundary between the areas of continental shelf and exclusive economic zone appertaining to Nicaragua and Colombia in accordance with equitable principles and relevant circumstances recognized by international law.

566. Nicaragua indicated that it reserved the right to claim compensation for elements of unjust enrichment consequent upon Colombian possession, in the absence of lawful title, of the islands of San Andrés and Providencia as well as the keys and maritime spaces up to the 82nd meridian. Also, Nicaragua reserved the right to claim compensation for interference with fishing vessels of Nicaraguan nationality or vessels licensed by Nicaragua.

567. By an Order dated 26 February 2002, the International Court, taking into account the views expressed by the parties, fixed 28 April 2003 as the time limit for the filing of a Memorial by Nicaragua and 28 June 2004 as the time limit for the filing of a Counter-Memorial by Colombia.

568. *Sovereignty over Pulau Ligitan and Pulau Sipadan (Indonesia/Malaysia).*—On 23 October 2001, the Court delivered its judgment on the application of the Philippines for permission to intervene in the case and found that it could not grant such permission since the Philippines had failed to show that it had an interest of a legal nature specific to its claim that might be affected by the final judgment in the case. It is recalled that the Court had been requested to determine whether sovereignty

201. Excerpted from the contribution of ICJ to the present report. See also the annual report of the Court to the General Assembly, *Official Records of the General Assembly, Fifty-sixth Session, Supplement No. 4* (A/56/4), and the ICJ web site: www.icj-cij.org.

over Pulau Ligitan and Pulau Sipadan, two islands in the Celebes Sea, belonged to either Indonesia or Malaysia. On 13 March 2001, the Philippines filed an application with the Court to intervene in the case in order to preserve its historical and legal rights arising from its claims to dominion and sovereignty over North Borneo.

10. CROSS-CUTTING ISSUES

569. The General Assembly, in its resolution 56/12, paragraph 48, recommended that one of the two areas around which the Consultative Process should organize its discussion at its third meeting should be "capacity-building, regional cooperation and coordination, and integrated ocean management, as important cross-cutting issues to address ocean affairs, such as marine science and the transfer of technology, sustainable fisheries, the degradation of the marine environment and the safety of navigation."

570. Cross-cutting issues are relevant across various marine and coastal sectors, and encompass multiple aspects of ocean affairs, from a number of aspects. An excellent example of the significance and interrelations of cross-cutting issues in ocean affairs is provided by General Assembly resolution 55/203 of 20 December 2000, in which the Assembly recognized "the importance of adopting an integrated management approach to the Caribbean Sea area in the context of sustainable development", encouraged States, in that regard, "to continue to develop regional cooperation in the management of [the Caribbean countries'] ocean affairs in the context of sustainable development", and called upon "the international community, the United Nations system and the multilateral financial institutions . . . to support actively the above-mentioned approach."[202]

A. Capacity-building

571. Many countries, in particular developing countries, especially the least developed among them and small island developing States, simply do not have the capacity to implement UNCLOS, related conventions, Chapter 17 of Agenda 21 and related programmes of action. The concern about lack of capacity and the consequent need for capacity-building were expressed pointedly, urgently and repeatedly in, among others, General Assembly resolutions (see, for example, resolution 56/12, paras. 6–8, and resolution 55/7, par. 23); statements of delegations in the General Assembly and in the Consultative Process; and the reports of the Co-Chairpersons of the Consultative Process (see for example, A/56/121, paras. 24–26, 59–63, 86–88, 155–160).

572. Limitations in capacity not only hinder countries from benefiting from oceans and seas and their resources under UNCLOS and Agenda 21; such limitations may also create opportunities for others to divert the benefits to themselves. Examples of the latter category include: (a) limitations of capacity to regulate resource exploitation; if (b) where regulations against illegal exploitation exist, limita-

202. General Assembly resolution 55/203, paras. 1, 3 and 8.

tions in enforcing such regulations; if (c) where enforcement exists limitations in monitoring and controlling resource exploitation, thereby allowing misreporting. In many cases, there is not only a loss of income and well-being for the present generation, but future generations are also affected because the diversion of benefits can be of such an extent as to jeopardize the very sustainability of the resources.

573. The framers of UNCLOS were keenly aware of the need for capacity-building, especially in the absence of any fund or assistance programme embedded in the Convention itself. As the Co-Chairpersons of the Consultative Process have pointed out, "Although the United Nations Convention on the Law of the Sea does not use the phrase 'capacity-building,' it contains about 25 references to the need to help developing States and take their concerns into account" (A/AC.259/L.3, appendix II, par. 6). In addition to devoting an entire chapter, Chapter 37, to capacity-building, Agenda 21 in its Chapter 17 includes suggestions about capacity-building as a means of implementing the programme of action on oceans and seas, listed under each of the seven identified programme areas (for a brief summary of the suggestions, see A/56/58, paras. 550–556).

574. "Specifically, capacity-building encompasses the country's human, scientific, technological, organizational, institutional and resource capabilities" (Agenda 21, par. 37.1). Both financial assistance and in-kind assistance can be useful for implementing capacity-building measures. Essentially such measures broaden and deepen the human resource base, strengthen the institutional structure and the institutions themselves, and expand the physical resource base. A wide range of measures can be relevant which involve, inter alia, executing technical cooperation projects, including those related to transfer of technology and know-how; undertaking educational, training, research and public awareness programmes and strengthening institutions capable of carrying out such programmes; exchange of data, information and experiences; creating and strengthening physical as well as institutional infrastructure; and provision and mobilization of raw materials, equipment, facilities and vessels.

575. With a view to facilitating the deliberations in the General Assembly and in the Consultative Process, the following paragraphs provide information, in brief, about the capacity-building measures of international organizations relating to oceans and seas, starting with the provision of financial resources. It should be added that measures of national agencies and institutions, both in developed countries and developing countries as well as in countries whose economies are in transition, can contribute significantly to capacity-building in other countries. (For example, during the second meeting of the Consultative Process, mention was made of the provision of financial resources, technical assistance, equipment and vessels, education and training by national agencies and institutions (see A/56/121, Part B, par. 88). At the regional level, the work of many regional organizations involves the capacity-building of their respective member countries; the regional projects of many global organizations also include elements of capacity-building. For example, the secretariat of the Pacific Communities assisted the maritime training institutions in the Pacific island countries in complying with the requirements of the STCW 95 Convention. It also has an extensive mentoring programme for raising the awareness of non-technical personnel, at operational and policy levels, about the many aspects of the maritime sector. (For further details, see the SOPAC contribution in Annex II to the present report.)

576. Capacity-building is a major part of the work programme of almost all international organizations dealing with ocean affairs. Many of their activities, although strictly speaking capacity-building measures, can still contribute to enhancing the capacity of member States. For example, the provision of information and analysis through information systems, databases, web sites, publications, handbooks, etc., can expand the capacity of national experts. Many other activities have a component of providing advice which, broadly speaking, can be interpreted as technical assistance and transfer of knowledge and know-how.

577. In 2000, UNDP carried out a preliminary survey of the capacity-building activities of the organizations of the United Nations system related to oceans and seas. The survey findings show that the range of activities is quite wide and the scope quite diverse. Focusing on education, training and field projects, the survey found that fellowships in ocean affairs are awarded by UNESCO, IMO, the United Nations and UNU; training programmes are carried out by IOC, IMO, FAO, IAEA and the United Nations; field projects are executed by FAO, IAEA, IMO, UNDP and UNIDO. (For further details on the survey findings, see A/56/58, paras. 557, 568–569.) In its contribution to the present report, the Department of Political Affairs of the United Nations Secretariat commented that FAO, IMO and UNDP appear to be engaged extensively in capacity-building activities in matters relating to oceans and seas, with remarkable results. It would therefore be useful, the Department suggested, to carry out a comparative study of the socio-economic impact of the wide range of capacity-building activities undertaken by those organizations as well as by UNU, UNESCO and its IOC, and IAEA, to see what should be done further to promote capacity-building.

578. As to financing, the report of the Co-Chairs of the Global Conference on Oceans and Coasts at Rio+10 (paras. 3–7, December 2001) stated: "In the last decade, significant new funding for coastal and marine programmes and activities has been provided by many multilateral and national donors, and financial institutions such as the World Bank, the Asian Development Bank, the Inter-American Development Bank, and SIDA, CIDA, JICA, DANIDA, USAID, among many others."[203] The report goes on to provide data about funding: in the past decade, World Bank funding for projects related to coastal and marine areas was in the order of $500 million in Africa and $175 million in the Asia-Pacific region; the Asian Development Bank funded marine projects in the Asia-Pacific region to the extent of $1.2 billion; in Latin America and the Caribbean, funding by international donors in coastal and marine projects amounted to about $1.3 billion. The report also discusses funding by GEF for projects related to international waters, biodiversity and climate change, all of which have major marine components.

579. *Global Environment Facility.*—In its contribution to the present report, GEF stated that it views the ever expanding degradation of coastal and marine ecosystems to be of critical concern to the global community. Since its establishment in 1991,

203. Co-Chairs' Summary, p. 8. The Co-Chairs' Summary, entitled "Ensuring the Sustainable Development of Oceans and Coasts: A Call to Action," may be accessed at www.udel.edu/cms/csmp/rio+10/pdf/cochairsreport.pdf. SIDA (Swedish International Development Agency); CIDA (Canadian International Development Agency); JICA (Japanese International Cooperation Agency); DANIDA (Danish International Development Agency); USAID (United States Agency for International Development).

it has supported 83 projects requested by GEF recipient States that directly address coastal and marine protection, at a total cost exceeding $1.1 billion ($0.480 billion in GEF grants). About 110 recipient countries are participating in approved international waters projects and 24 countries are involved with approved biodiversity projects focusing on coastal and marine ecosystems. An additional 20 international waters projects and 16 biodiversity projects are under preparation by GEF, and new developments in the area of persistent organic pollutants can be relevant to them. The international waters area of GEF has been particularly active in supporting projects in ocean affairs for 36 small island developing States and for 32 of the United Nations-designated least developed countries.

580. With its decade of experience in providing catalytic assistance to developing States and those in economic transition, GEF, in its contribution, presented a summary of its work since UNCED relating to coastal and marine ecosystems.

581. GEF projects are implemented by UNDP, UNEP and the World Bank and expanded opportunities exist for other executing agencies. Since 1991, GEF has allocated $4.2 billion in grant financing, supplemented by more than $10 billion in additional financing, for more than 1,000 projects in 156 developing countries and those in economic transition. All six thematic areas of GEF—biodiversity loss, climate change, degradation of international waters, ozone depletion, persistent organic pollutants, and land degradation—have implications for coastal and marine ecosystems. Of the six areas, the biodiversity and international waters focal areas have been utilized by developing States more than the other areas to address coastal and marine issues.

582. *International waters.*—The international waters focal area of GEF was established to help recipient nations address concerns of bodies of water that are transboundary in nature. Over 95 percent of all capture fisheries of the oceans are taken from the 50 large marine ecosystems (LMEs—an LME is an extensive region with a unique hydrographic regime, distinguishable biological productivity and trophically dependent populations). In 1995, the GEF Council included the concept of LMEs in its GEF Operational Strategy as a vehicle for promoting the ecosystem-based management of coastal and marine resources in the international waters focal area within a framework of adaptive management. GEF allocations to this focal area are limited; consequently it has played a modest, catalytic role during the past decade in order to test approaches and demonstrate strategies for reversing degradation and restoring biomass.

583. The GEF Operational Strategy recommends that nations begin to address coastal and marine issues by jointly undertaking strategic processes for analysing factual, scientific information on transboundary issues, setting priorities, and then determining the policy/legal/institutional reforms and investments needed to address the priorities in a country-driven strategic action programme.

584. The recommended GEF processes in LME projects foster "learning by doing" and capacity-building as "enabling activities" do in other GEF focal areas. They allow the scientific community to become engaged and provide interim outputs that may serve as vehicles for stimulating stakeholder participation. These processes foster cross-sectoral integration so that a truly ecosystem-based approach to improving management institutions may be pursued. This builds confidence among different sectoral interests in a State (through establishing a GEF inter-ministerial committee in each State) and then among participating States sharing the LME. The process

of producing the strategic action programme facilitates the further development of country driven, politically agreed ways for commitments to action that address the priorities in a framework that encourages adaptive management. This shared commitment and vision for action has proved essential in GEF projects that have completed the processes in securing commitments for policy, legal, and institutional reforms in different economic sectors. GEF may then fund an implementation project to assist countries in addressing the country-driven priorities for reform and investments. These LME projects were designed for consistency with Chapter 17 of Agenda 21, and they also promote consistency with UNCLOS, the 1995 Fish Stocks Agreement, the FAO Code of Conduct for Responsible Fisheries, the GPA, regional seas agreements and regional fisheries agreements.

585. In the first decade of GEF (1991–2001), the GEF Council approved 46 international waters projects addressing the degradation of coastal and marine ecosystems, of a total cost of $850 million ($361 million in GEF grants).

586. According to GEF, its LME projects are revolutionizing ways of implementing the integrated management of oceans, coasts, estuaries and freshwater basins through an ecosystem-based approach. Ten LMEs and their adjacent freshwater basins, where appropriate, have been approved for funding. In order to integrate freshwater basin States contributing pollutants to the LME, a number of projects have been "nested" or focused in a programmatic approach to provide a greater chance of success. In all, 25 approved international waters projects have been developed to address the 10 LMEs and their transboundary priority concerns. The projects represent a total cost of $520 million ($224 million in GEF grants). While 72 GEF recipient countries are participating in the projects related to the 10 LMEs, non-recipient OECD countries also share these LMEs or are located in contributing basins, such as Germany and Austria in the Danube Basin draining to the Black Sea. Emphasizing the global situation in which both developed and developing nations must cooperate in order to reverse the continuing degradation of coastal and marine ecosystems, a total of 18 non-recipient developed States are collaborating with the GEF recipient States in those LME projects on the particular high-priority concerns relevant for each body of water: depletion of fisheries in some, habitat restoration/protection in others, and reduction of pollution from land-based sources in still others.

587. *Biodiversity.*—GEF is the largest financier of activities that protect global biodiversity in developing States and those with transitional economies. The projects are driven by country needs, priorities and actions as expressed through the Convention on Biodiversity. In its early years, GEF supported many protected areas projects. To date, it has funded 37 biodiversity projects directly addressing coastal and marine ecosystems, at a total cost of the $289 million ($116 million in GEF grants) and with the involvement of 24 nations. A number of country-wide projects for protected areas management also include marine ecosystems. Overall, there are 24 projects of a total cost of $125 million ($79 million in GEF grants) for assisting States in managing protected areas containing coral reefs. Capacity-building components are normally included within the projects. A further 16 biodiversity projects addressing coastal and marine issues are under preparation. Altogether, approved projects and those under preparation cover 12 least developed countries. These biodiversity projects represent important interventions to help improve the protection and preservation of the marine environment because sustainable use of the ecosystems provides the key to livelihoods and food security for coastal communities.

588. As examples, a series of two projects with UNDP assistance helped Argentina and NGOs along the Patagonia coast to conserve the fragile coastal ecosystems, while GEF support is helping Belize, Ghana and Indonesia shield the undersea beauty and rich biodiversity of the barrier reefs and coastal wetlands. The creation of marine protected areas has allowed depleted fisheries to recover, with improvements in stocks of lobster, conch, and reef fish.

589. *Persistent organic pollutants (POPs).*—Following the adoption of the GPA, the GEF Operational Strategy identified among the priority concerns to be addressed under international waters the "control of land-based sources of surface and groundwater pollution that degrade the quality of the international waters," with special emphasis on the "prevention of releases of persistent toxic substances and heavy metals."

590. The Stockholm Convention on Persistent Organic Pollutants, was adopted; in May 2001, it designated GEF as the interim financial mechanism for the Convention. Also in May 2001, the GEF Council approved the first actions designed to support the implementation of the Convention: (a) approval of initial guidelines for enabling activities on POPs, and (b) the joint GEF/UNEP project entitled "Development of National Implementation Plans to Manage Persistent Organic Pollutants," aimed at testing the guidelines in the field and building the capacity of States to meet their obligations under the Convention.

591. As of January 2002, a number of GEF-eligible countries have requested and obtained GEF assistance for the preparation of their national implementation plans for the Stockholm Convention ("enabling activities" in GEF terminology). In several of those countries implementation has already started. The total GEF funding for enabling activities is so far approximately $18 million.

592. The countries involved ensure geographic balance and diversity of characteristics. Each of the pilot countries is to become a regional centre for capacity-building and exchange of experiences. To that end, funds have been allocated specifically to involve neighbouring States in the project with a view towards enhanced coordination, convention ratification and improved quality of the national implementation plans.

593. *Intergovernmental Oceanographic Commission.*—A number of activities of IOC in the field of marine science are aimed at capacity-building in developing countries. For example, capacity-building continues to be a main component of the Harmful Algal Bloom (HAB) programme. The backbone in the implementation of the capacity-building effort is the IOC Science and Communication Centres on Harmful Algae in Copenhagen, Denmark, and Vigo, Spain, which provide annual training courses for 30 to 40 people, as well as a number of regional training courses. In this context, in IOC/WESTPAC, cooperation with the University of Tokyo on HAB capacity-building plays the same role as does the work of the IOC HAB centres for the international courses. A regional training workshop was also held in Accra, Ghana, in November 2001, which had as an addition the objective formulation of a project for a regional survey of the occurrence of potentially harmful microalgae. Moreover, in September 2001, IOC assisted at a FAO-ROPME training course for the Gulf region in Kuwait. The two IOC HAB centres provide, in addition to the short-term training courses, a mechanism for North-South institutional twinning and cooperative research, and specific projects are ongoing with countries in South-East Asia, Africa and Latin America. Within WESTPAC, a training course on the

ecology and physiology of harmful algae was held in March 2001, with the participation, for the first time, of scientists from the Democratic People's Republic of Korea. The experience obtained will be used by the trainees in designing and conducting research on the ecology and physiology of harmful microalgae in their respective home countries.

594. The regional meetings to advance the development of GOOS, through the exchange of information and experiences among regional member countries and between IOC and the region, also serve to strengthen regional capacity. Such regional meetings were held in 2001 for the Caribbean, Black Sea, South-East Asia, Africa and Indian Ocean regions.

595. The activities under the IOC Committee on Oceanographic Data and Information Exchange (IODE) are in themselves of a capacity-building nature. A good example is the Marine Environment Data Information Referral Catalogue (MEDI), a directory system for data sets, data catalogues and data inventories developed by IODE. Capacity-building is a major priority area of the IODE programme. IODE provides capacity-building assistance at the national level (assisting member States in developing and updating national ocean data and information management facilities) as well as the regional level (e.g., through the development and maintenance of regional ocean data and information management networks such as the Ocean Data Information Network (ODIN)). The capacity-building programme also includes regional training courses, travel and training grants, equipment support, etc.

596. *United Nations Industrial Development Organization.*—In its contribution to the present report, UNIDO stated that the transfer of skills and knowledge to member countries through capacity-building, especially institutional strengthening, forms a cross-cutting activity of fundamental importance in each of the three areas of its work: relating to environmental management planning, policy formulation and monitoring; reducing harmful emissions from industry; and pollution control and waste management.

597. UNIDO executes major projects addressing regional transboundary problems of LMEs and their associated river basins, wetlands and coastal zones within the international waters focal area of GEF. These projects bring together Governments of the region and scientists from different disciplines to assess the complex interactions of industrial development and performance with the international waters and to establish baseline conditions against which future actions can be evaluated. Such cooperation provides the solid foundation for fundamental capacity-building and institutional strengthening at national and regional levels, for the setting of appropriate environmental and developmental goals, and for the implementation of priority actions to maintain or restore environmental productive capacity.

598. Of prime importance in these regional projects is involvement and ownership by Governments and the successful cooperation among those Governments participating in the projects. In turn, cooperation at the operational level underpins regional governance structures, enhancing, for example, the implementation of regional seas conventions and, ultimately, UNCLOS.

599. UNIDO attributes much of the success of its Gulf of Guinea Large Marine Ecosystem project to the strong sense of commitment and community of the six participating Government partners. Indeed, that ownership has now generated a successor project drawing in 10 additional Governments to the consortium. This new project will combine new regional marine surveys of the Guinea Current ecosys-

tem with a series of land-based projects demonstrating different approaches to the reduction of pollutant fluxes to those coastal and marine environments.

600. Training and other capacity-building activities undertaken by UNIDO are designed to improve production management by providing managers and supporting service providers with the skills necessary to identify, assess and modify those components of the manufacturing process that generate high demands for raw materials, water and energy resources or that represent the principal sources of wastage and pollution emissions.

601. UNIDO delivers these capacity-building services through demonstration projects, often as part of integrated programmes of industry support to member countries, and through a global network of National Cleaner Production Centres, established jointly with UNEP. Over 20 such centres are in operation worldwide, with a significant number of additional ones in the process of being set up. The centres provide practical technical assistance and training to industry as well as access to information from the global network of centres and related institutions around the world.

602. Each signatory country to the Stockholm Convention, which seeks to reduce and ultimately eliminate the production and use of the identified organo-halogen chemicals, is expected to undertake so-called "enabling activities", financed by the GEF, leading to the development of a national implementation plan (see also paras. 590–592 above). These activities include the preparation of an inventory of the sources and emissions of POPs and a preliminary assessment of stockpiles of POPs and of waste products contaminated with POPs. An action plan for their careful management, reduction, control or disposal can then be developed. The expertise and long experience of UNIDO with industry has earned it the status of "executing agency with expanded opportunities" with regard to GEF, the financial instrument for the Convention. This status allows UNIDO to assist developing countries and those with economies in transition in preparing and executing the enabling activities and building the capacity necessary to be able to report country progress towards ratification of the Convention. To date, over 50 countries have requested the assistance of UNIDO. The organization is currently assisting developing countries with technical cooperation, training and awareness-raising programmes for industry, information, dissemination, technology transfer, development of innovative financing mechanisms, and development of sound regulatory programmes for emissions control.

603. UNIDO programmes seek to build capacity to deal with a wide range of waste management and pollution control issues among decision makers working in public authorities and industrial and commercial enterprises, including companies in the commercial pollution control and waste management sectors. Such training includes: developing tools and methodologies for identifying and evaluating pollution-control and waste-management options based on technological, risk and compliance criteria and analysis of the waste streams that are collected; financial and economic analysis of waste management options as a precursor to seeking investment; operation of pollution control and waste management technologies; and estimation of demand for services, at the city level for municipalities and at the city, regional, or even national levels for commercial pollution control and waste management sectors. Remediation technologies, such as bio- and phytoremediation, are also demonstrated at the pilot level to increase awareness and highlight alternative options for pollution control and contaminated land remediation.

604. *Food and Agriculture Organization of the United Nations.*—FAO stated that capacity-building, especially institutional strengthening, in developing countries is the key element in facilitating long-term sustainability in the fisheries sector. It is stressed in all aspects of the FAO programme of work in fisheries. Moreover, the 1995 FAO Code of Conduct for Responsible Fisheries explicitly recognizes the importance of enhancing human and institutional capacity and urges action to be taken to that end.

605. FAO gives practical effect to capacity-building, especially institutional strengthening, in a number of different but related ways. It works closely with national fishery administrations, including those in small island developing States, to improve their operational efficiency in management and utilization and in the promotion of sustainable aquaculture. This is achieved through the dissemination of information pertinent to responsible management, and in particular through the preparation of technical guidelines that support the implementation of the Code of Conduct; country visits and the provision of advice on specific issues; and the organization of workshops and professional attachments within FAO.

606. Developing countries face particular challenges in fisheries management owing to the number of international instruments and initiatives adopted since UNCED and the requirement to implement them. Moreover, these instruments contain a number of new concepts and approaches, such as ecosystem management, the precautionary approach, sustainable indicators for management, and catch certification. The implementation of these concepts is crucial for the achievement of responsible fisheries and as a result they are being addressed routinely by FAO in its capacity-building activities.

607. Effective monitoring, control and surveillance (MCS) is an essential part of fisheries management. FAO has an ongoing programme of technical assistance in MCS which, principally through regional workshops, seeks to enhance national MCS capacity while encouraging regional MCS cooperation. FAO also provides, on a request basis, technical inputs to national MCS programmes.

608. One evident difficulty being faced by a number of fisheries administrations is how to diagnose the situation and a lack of firm advice on what management decisions to apply in the case of a fishery. Certainly MCS can provide information of use to scientists as well as to fishery managers in their assessment of what is happening to a fishery, and on what problems need to be faced so that decisions can be taken. In 2001, a national MCS workshop was held in India, attended by 30 participants from maritime States and associated territories. Issues addressed covered information collection; procedures for inspection onshore and at sea; vessel identification; patrol platforms; gear selectivity; and vessel monitoring systems.

609. FAO is also involved in an MCS project financed by the Government of Luxembourg assisting Senegal, Mauritania, Cape Verde, the Gambia, Guinea-Bissau, Guinea and Sierra Leone. FAO has given its support to the establishment of the International Network for the Cooperation and Coordination of Fisheries-related Monitoring, Control and Surveillance Activities, with a view to promoting the exchange of information on MCS among countries.

610. *United Nations Environment Programme.*—The capacity-building activities in the field of marine environment carried out under the auspices of UNEP are numerous. The Fourth Global Meeting of Regional Seas Convention and Action Plans recommended that regional clustering of activities carried out by global MEAs,

Regional Seas Conventions and Action Plans, international organizations and other regional bodies is needed to carry out activities in a more coordinated and cost-effective manner, particularly in areas such as capacity-building, technology transfer, development of supportive national legislation, assessment and monitoring, and public awareness and information exchange. In particular, greater efforts are required to pool resources for developing collective regional technology transfer centres for the protection and sustainable use of the marine and coastal environment in support of regional seas programmes, global MEAs and other international initiatives.

611. Many of the activities under the regional seas programmes of UNEP contribute to capacity-building in the member countries. For example, in PERSGA, in executing the Strategic Action Programme for the Red Sea and Gulf of Aden, mobilized financial resources from GEF and the Islamic Development Bank and technical cooperation from the three executing agencies, UNDP, UNEP and the World Bank. Financing was obtained through the World Bank for a hydrographic analysis of the southern Red Sea for the long-term conservation and management of the coastal and marine resources of the region, with technical cooperation for the project provided by the United Kingdom Hydrographic Office. In a demonstration programme under way to promote sustainable lobster fishing, lobster traps are being made available to replace the gillnets that are currently in use. Two regional fisheries training centres are being upgraded, one in Aden, and the other in Jeddah, Saudi Arabia. Addressing the problems that can arise if methods of surveying species are not standardized, PERSGA developed a set of standard survey methods for key habitats and key species that are being used in studies on coral reefs, mangroves, seagrass beds, marine mammals, turtles and seabirds.

612. A new training course for marine protected area managers has been prepared by PERSGA in association with the TRAIN-SEA-COAST programme of the United Nations Division for Ocean Affairs and the Law of the Sea; the first course was delivered in January 2002. PERSGA is also implementing a pilot project for integrated central zone management in Aden. Under the auspices of PERSGA, new public awareness centres have been established in several countries and provided with equipment and materials, and a public awareness campaign was conducted throughout the PERSGA region in 2001. Several training courses on environmental education have also been held, leading to the establishment of nature conservation clubs in schools in Somalia, the Sudan and Yemen. Furthermore, a social marketing survey was carried out within the region to determine people's attitudes and understanding of environmental issues and a microgrants programme has been prepared to promote community participation in environmental improvement. Under PERSGA, regional capacity in marine sciences has been improved through numerous workshops and training courses, in such areas as basic GIS, shark identification and fisheries data collection methods, principles of biodiversity conservation, standard survey methods for habitats and species, diving, and environmental education.

613. *International Maritime Organization.*—Within the United Nations system, capacity-building in maritime infrastructure is the focus of IMO. IMO attaches the highest priority to the need to ensure that the numerous rules and standards contained in its body of treaties are properly implemented. To facilitate this implementation, IMO focuses on the continuous strengthening of regulations to ensure that flag and port States and shipowners develop their capacities and fulfil their responsi-

bility to the fullest. The technical cooperation of IMO has been intensified by the operation of the Integrated Technical Cooperation Programme (ITCP), aimed at ensuring that funds from different donor sources are properly channelled towards the execution of projects under the supervision of IMO as executing agency, with the objective of strengthening the maritime infrastructure of developing countries.

614. In a previous contribution, IMO had reported that the importance of technical assistance to developing countries and the form that such assistance would take are reflected in IMO Assembly resolution A.901(21), entitled "IMO and technical cooperation in the 2000s" (see also A/55/61, paras. 245–246, and A/56/58, par. 561). The resolution urges parties to IMO instruments containing provisions on technical cooperation to respond to their commitments and invites member States to use IMO as a coordination mechanism for technical cooperation in the maritime sector. It also invites member States, the shipping industry and partner organizations to continue and, if possible, to increase their support for ITCP and affirms that ITCP can and does contribute to sustainable development. The resolution also urges IMO to give priority to technical assistance programmes that focus on human resources development, particularly through training and institutional capacity-building.

615. With respect to human resources development, IMO capacity-building activities under ITCP are expected to produce an increased number of trained experts (both male and female) to develop and manage national programmes for maritime safety administration; marine environment protection; the development of maritime legislation; facilitation of maritime traffic; technical port operations; and training of seafarers and shore-based personnel. In the area of institutional capacity-building, activities under ITCP are expected to strengthen public sector departments capable of ensuring the effective exercise of flag State, port State and coastal State jurisdiction.

616. Priority global programmes within the ITCP framework include the development of administrative, legal and technical advisory services to Governments on the implementation of IMO safety and anti-pollution conventions, enhancement of training institutions and provision of fellowships, integration of women in the maritime sector, harmonization of the operation of various regional agreements on port State control, enhancement of maritime safety, prevention and control of illicit drug-trafficking and enhancement of port security. The main constituent programmes foreseen within the ITCP framework include regional programmes for Africa, Arab States/Mediterranean, Asia and the Pacific Islands, the Commonwealth of Independent States and Eastern Europe, and Latin America and the Caribbean.

617. The training of crews of ships is an essential capacity-building measure. The requirements regarding the training of crews which the flag State must implement under Article 94 of UNCLOS are those contained in the STCW Convention and the STCW Code (see par. 97).

618. In addition, many of the new instruments adopted by IMO in recent years have capacity-building measures built into them; in many cases, while adopting a convention the conference also adopts a number of resolutions, some of which address capacity-building. For example, a resolution accompanying the recently adopted (5 October 2001) International Convention on the Control of Harmful Anti-fouling Systems on Ships addresses the promotion of technical cooperation related to the ratification, implementation and enforcement of the Convention.

619. IMO also reports that it has, in the course of 2001, developed and executed further measures aimed at supporting capacity-building regarding maritime safety issues falling under the responsibility of maritime administrations.

620. Regarding the enhancement of flag State capabilities to work towards safer shipping, IMO made preparations for the implementation of the second phase of the International Safety Management (ISM) Code, which should become mandatory for all types of ships on 1 July 2002. Assistance was provided to maritime administrations through technical cooperation activities in this regard.

621. In order to assist flag States in the assessment of their capabilities, IMO revised the procedures for the self-assessment of flag State performance to incorporate criteria and performance indicators and invited flag States to collect more detailed information on the authorizations granted to recognized organizations to work on their behalf.

622. Building upon the increased involvement of States, other than the flag States, in the inspection of ships and the investigation of casualties, IMO worked towards the development of a harmonized global regime for port State control activities through renewed support to regional memoranda of understanding on port State control through the training of port State control officers, assistance to port State control committees and the promotion of communication and exchanges of information between flag and port States.

623. Similarly, IMO provided assistance through training activities for the implementation of increased cooperation among substantially interested States in the conduct of investigations into casualties on the basis of a specific model course based on the Code for the investigation of marine casualties and incidents.

624. In identifying some of the safety and marine pollution problems affecting non-convention ships, that is, those which are not covered by existing international instruments, because of their type or their size or their area of trade, a need for assistance to developing countries was also identified, since these ships constitute the vast majority of the fleets of such countries. IMO, therefore, developed a programme of activities relating to these problems, based on consultancy and seminars, which focused on the East African and Maghreb regions in the course of 2001.

625. *United Nations University.*—The capacity-building activities of UNU with respect to multilateral environmental agreements are developed under a strategic "Inter-linkages Initiative," the underlying concept of which is that sustainable development requires an approach that promotes greater interlinkage between ecosystems and societal actions. The initiative consists of two fundamental elements: synergism and coordination. On a practical level this involves greater cohesion among institutional, environmental issue-based, and development-focused responses to the challenges of sustainable development.

626. UNU views capacity-building as affecting not only the level of response and effectiveness of implementation of multilateral environmental agreements, but also the level of negotiation and ratification capability of countries. Capacity-building at the thematic and institutional levels is addressed. The thematic approach is followed so as to ensure the synergies that exist in particular areas, such as the cluster of multilateral environmental agreements relating to oceans, are identified and utilized. The institutional approach is followed, ensuring that knowledge and capacity are not only developed and transferred but also sustained.

627. The UNU Fisheries Training Programme offers six-month postgraduate

training in six fisheries and fisheries-related fields in Iceland, covering fishery policy and planning, marine and inland water resource assessment and monitoring, and environmental assessment and monitoring. The programme started in 1998 and is offered annually. It has grown gradually from 6 participants in the first year to 14 in 2001. To date, a total of 43 participants from 15 countries have completed the training.

628. Participants are from developing countries with considerable fisheries potential (nationally or provincially) who are already working as professionals in their disciplines. The training in Iceland is practical in its approach and tailored to suit the needs of the individual participants. After a six-to-seven week introductory course, the fellows undergo specialized training in their fields. This part consists of a five-week structured course followed by a project and work attachment. The programme is run in cooperation with several institutions and universities in Iceland, under the coordination of the Marine Research Institute in Reykjavik. (More information about the programme can be obtained at www.hafro.is/unuftp/.)

629. UNU adds that the activities at the UNU Centre are most relevant to the topic of "Marine resources, the marine environment and sustainable development" within the framework of UNCLOS. Capacity-building is central to these activities, which primarily focus on management of coastal resources and the control of land-based sources of pollution.

630. Of note is the UNU project entitled "Environmental Monitoring and Governance in the East Asian Coastal Hydrosphere." One of the major components of the project deals with monitoring of the pollution of marine and coastal environments from land-based sources of endocrine disruptor chemicals. Monitoring is conducted in the coastal waters off nine East Asian countries, namely China, Indonesia, Japan, the Republic of Korea, Malaysia, Singapore, Thailand, Viet Nam and the Philippines. Significant capacity-building for coastal monitoring has been included in the project. The monitoring programme has clearly indicated an increasing trend in pollution from land-based sources, particularly pesticides and herbicides from agricultural sources. Urban areas also are major contributors to this pollution. Some encouraging signs of decreasing DDT levels in coastal areas have also been observed in the region, which indicates an improved control of DDT application in East Asia. A comprehensive GIS-based database of the monitoring data, called LandBase, has been developed for data coordination and dissemination, and can be accessed at http://landbase.hq.unu.edu/.

631. *International Atomic Energy Agency.*—IAEA states that its Marine Environment Laboratory responds regularly to requests for technical assistance. It has recently developed strategies to apply nuclear techniques to address coastal zone management issues. In particular, projects using nuclear techniques have focused on quantifying the rates of coastal ocean processes and understanding the distribution and transport of contaminants in the near-shore environment. New technical cooperation projects are being initiated which greatly improve the ability to assess the problem of harmful algal blooms and their impact on aquaculture and on the overall health of seafood consumers.

632. *United Nations Division for Ocean Affairs and the Law of the Sea.*—The Hamilton Shirley Amerasinghe Memorial Fellowship Programme is a major part of the capacity-building activities of the United Nations Division for Ocean Affairs and the Law of the Sea. The Fellowship was established in 1982 in memory of the late Presi-

dent of the Third United Nations Conference on the Law of the Sea. It is administered by the Division and is a component of the United Nations Programme of Assistance in the Teaching, Study, Dissemination and Wider Appreciation of International Law. The programme encompasses all training and fellowship programmes of the United Nations and of UNESCO in the field of international law and is coordinated by the Office of Legal Affairs of the United Nations.

633. The Fellowship is intended primarily to improve the expertise of government officials, research fellows or academics who are involved in law of the sea or marine affairs. It assists the successful candidates in acquiring additional knowledge of UNCLOS in order to promote its wider appreciation and application and enhance specialized experience in those fields. Since the inception of the Amerasinghe Memorial Fellowship Programme, 16 Annual Fellowships and 4 Special Fellowships have been awarded. The recipients of the Fellowship come from 15 developing countries and two countries in transition, including 8 small island developing States and 2 landlocked countries, representing all the developing regions of the world, as well as the States with economies in transition. An informal survey has shown that the enhanced capacity of Fellowship recipients is being utilized for the purposes of addressing marine-related issues in their own countries.

634. In December 2001, upon the recommendation of the High-level Advisory Panel, Mr. Kamran Hashemi of the Islamic Republic of Iran, was given the Sixteenth Annual Fellowship award and Mr. Boris Danailov of Bulgaria was granted the Fourth Special Fellowship award, funded by a grant from the United Kingdom of Great Britain and Northern Ireland.

635. Information regarding the participating universities and the membership of the High-level Advisory Panel, may be obtained from press release SEA/1728 as well as from the web site of the United Nations Division for Ocean Affairs and the Law of the Sea, at www.un.org/Depts/los/HSA.htm.

636. Another important part of the Division's capacity-building activities is its TRAIN-SEA-COAST (TSC) programme. The programme was developed as part of a system-wide training strategy that emphasizes: (a) building up permanent national capabilities for training; (b) sustainability of training efforts; (c) cost-effectiveness; (d) responsiveness to specific training priorities of the countries involved; (e) transfer of experience and sharing of training resources; and (f) long-term impact.

637. The basic objective of the TSC programme is to create capacity at the local level to produce high-quality training courses to be shared among the TSC members, and at the same time to strengthen local institutions to become centres of excellence on training at the national or regional levels. (For more details about the programme, see A/56/58, paras. 579–585.)

638. In 2001, two training courses were successfully delivered and validated according to the TSC standards. They were tailored to and delivered within the framework of two GEF international waters projects, namely, the Benguela Current Large Marine Ecosystem (BCLME) programme and the Strategic Action Programme for the Red Sea and the Gulf of Aden. A total of 20 individuals from South Africa, Angola and Namibia participated in a course on marine pollution control developed by the TSC Benguela Current Course Development Unit, in Cape Town, South Africa. The course was designed to provide technical knowledge and specific skills to environmental officers, government officials and environmental specialists from the BCLME countries. A total of 23 individuals from Djibouti, Egypt, Eritrea, Jordan,

Saudi Arabia, Somalia, the Sudan and Yemen participated in a one-week course on management of marine protected areas. The course was developed by the TSC Red Sea Course Development Unit in Port Sudan. The objective was to provide current and future marine protected area managers in the Red Sea and Gulf of Aden region with an array of knowledge, skills and approaches for marine protected area planning and management.

639. For 2002, the planned activities under the TSC programme include the delivery of seven training courses prepared by GEF-associated Course Development Units. Other non-GEF-associated TSC Course Development Units will also deliver new courses. The TSC Central Support Unit at the Division will present a Course Developers Workshop in March to reinforce existing TSC units through the training of new course developers. It is expected that a number of training courses will be shared, adapted and delivered between TSC units during 2002.

B. Regional Cooperation and Coordination

640. "The advantages of regional cooperation and organization are threefold. . . : first of all, the regional sea approximates most closely what is now called the 'large marine ecosystem' (LME), and this facilitates fisheries management as well as pollution control from most sources. Second, the regional level offers economies of scale, facilitating, among other things, the advancement of marine scientific research and the development and transfer of technologies. Third, the States bordering regional seas often have developed a commonality of interests. This may facilitate the advancement of regional security, through the kind of cooperation required for the suppression of piracy and other crimes at sea."[204] Additional advantages of a regional approach include the mobilization of synergies among various marine and coastal sectors within a region and the realization of benefits from twinning of the region with a more advanced region, which in turn furthers international cooperation.

641. The advantages of a regional approach in ocean affairs are so evident that both UNCLOS and Agenda 21 have respectively enshrined regional cooperation in hard law and soft law, especially in relation to the conservation and management of marine living resources, the protection and preservation of the marine environment, the development and transfer of marine science and technology, and responses to emergencies at sea. Likewise, the international instruments and the plans of action that emanated from UNCLOS and Agenda 21 prescribed or recommended a regional approach in many instances; special mention can be made of the 1995 Fish Stocks Agreement, the Convention on Biological Diversity and the Global Programme of Action for the Protection of the Marine Environment from Land-based Activities.

642. In fact, the regional approach in ocean affairs had been pursued by States and international organizations at the global and the regional levels even prior to the conclusion and adoption of UNCLOS. A number of regional fisheries management organizations or arrangements, regional seas programmes (dealing with the

204. E. M. Borgese, "UNICPOLOS: The second session," *Environmental Policy and Law*, August 2001. vol. 31, Nos. 4–5, p. 212.

marine environment), regional marine science organizations as well as regional organizations dealing with regional cooperation in marine affairs in general were already in existence before the advent of the Convention. But in the past 20 years, the growth of regional programmes and regional organizations in the field of ocean affairs has been phenomenal.

643. Within the United Nations system, under the auspices of the UNEP, there are currently 13 regional seas programmes in operation, and an additional one is currently under development (for a list of UNEP regional seas conventions and protocols, see A/56/58/Annex V). Four regional seas organizations which were developed independently are today working closely with UNEP. (For details of the work carried out under the regional seas programmes, see paras. 445–464.) FAO has developed five regional fisheries management organizations or arrangements while there are 23 non-FAO regional fisheries bodies. (For a list of regional fisheries management organization and arrangements, see A/56/58, Annex IV.) Recently, periodic joint meetings have been held among them. (For details of the work of regional fisheries bodies, see paras. 185–191). There are 11 regional bodies dealing with marine science under the auspices of IOC. Although IMO does not have any formal regional body, a number of its programmes and projects are implemented at the regional level. The regional commissions of the United Nations themselves have marine and coastal programmes involving the member countries in their respective regions. Outside the United Nations system, but in many cases working closely with it, there are a number of regional marine organizations, especially in the South Pacific and the Caribbean.

644. It is to be noted that the second meeting of the Consultative Process highlighted "a need to establish or strengthen, as appropriate, regional cooperation, including that between regional fisheries organizations and arrangements, regional seas programmes and other regional marine environment bodies . . . and the regional marine science organizations, including those under the auspices of the Intergovernmental Oceanographic Commission" (A/56/121, part A, par. 6). Although this need was mentioned in relation to ensuring an intersectoral approach to marine scientific research, it is applicable to all marine and coastal fields, especially the sustainable development of oceans and seas and their resources.

645. The contribution of the South Pacific Applied Geoscience Commission (SOPAC) to the present report exemplifies the application of the regional approach in overall ocean affairs, with emphasis on sustainable marine development. With a view to facilitating the deliberations of the General Assembly and the Consultative Process on the cross-cutting issue of regional cooperation and coordination in ocean affairs, SOPAC's contribution is presented in its entirety in Annex II to the present report.

C. Integrated Ocean Management

646. "The Law of the Sea Convention provides for the first time a single Convention of such a comprehensive and diverse nature which, in one stride, has brought about changes of such complexity and magnitude that national Governments have been required to formulate new policy, review their marine-related legislation and make

new administrative arrangements. . . . The complexity of the Convention and the regime governed by it involves an interplay between rights and duties, and there is a need for a comprehensive approach."[205]

647. The need for a management approach to ocean affairs and for ocean management to be of an integrated nature is also underscored in Chapter 17 of Agenda 21, which devotes the very first programme area to "Integrated management and sustainable development of coastal and marine areas, including exclusive economic zones." The General Assembly in its annual resolution on "Oceans and the law of the sea" also calls for such an approach.

648. There is a vast literature on integrated ocean management, and it is defined and applied in various ways. The central element is moving away from a fragmented, sectoral and unidimensional approach to the development and implementation of overall policy and a management strategy. In doing so, there is not only a synthesis of national priorities, but also an integration of the marine dimension with overall national policy, taking into account the interdependence of environment and development and the complex interplay between national interests and concerns and rights and duties in the international context. The decision-making and implementation processes should involve all stakeholders, usually in a vertically integrated framework, from the bottom up. Finally, there is spatial integration across all maritime areas under the jurisdiction of a State, combining coastal areas and maritime zones, and in many cases, watersheds, river basins and sea areas.

649. The challenges of developing and applying integrated ocean management cannot be overstated. In most cases, the limiting factor is capacity, but in many cases, the obstacles are at the conceptual or political level. Yet the imperatives of an integrated management approach are so overwhelming that in spite of the daunting problems of full integration, there is a growing movement towards achieving some degree of integration.

650. In its contribution to the present report, IOC has provided information about its integrated coastal area management (ICAM) programme. The ICAM programme is intended to assist IOC member States in their efforts to build marine scientific and technological capabilities in the field of integrated coastal area management as a follow-up to Agenda 21, Chapter 17, and to help to ensure that marine sciences are integrated into the development of national and regional ICAM programmes and plans, particularly in assisting, through the exchange of experiences, in developing a trans-sectoral decision-making process and the corresponding institutions for the sustainable development of coastal areas.

651. The objectives of the ICAM programme are to address coastal zone problems through activities of a more cooperative, coordinated and interdisciplinary nature and ensure good coordination among existing IOC efforts related to the coastal zone. The programme also aims to provide a mechanism to promote interaction between IOC programmes related to ICAM and those of other international organizations between marine natural scientists and social scientists, as well as between scientists and coastal managers and policy makers. After several years of wide practice around the world, ICAM is in a position to attempt to codify these practices into methodological tools. Following the publication by IOC of the first *Methodologi-*

205. "Ocean Management: A Regional Perspective," report by a Commonwealth Group of Experts, London (Commonwealth Secretariat, 1984), p. 57.

cal Guide on Integrated Coastal Management in 1997, a second methodological manual was published in 2001, entitled *Steps and Tools towards Integrated Coastal Area Management.* While the first edition mainly focused on the use of natural science tools, in particular the process of building up an information system, the 2001 edition emphasizes and integrates the socio-economic aspects of ICAM. The ICAM planning steps and cycle are described and analysed in detail through a number of selected case studies with practical recommendations for ICAM operators and managers.

652. In terms of full integration, recent developments in three countries— Australia, Canada and South Korea—can offer valuable insight and guidance.

653. Australia's development of an ocean policy was driven by two underlying motives: to assert its sovereign rights over its exclusive economic zone and to ensure the ecologically sustainable development of the nation's ocean resources, both for wealth creation and environmental protection. In addition, there has been an intrinsic need for efficient coordination of the nation's utilization of the oceans given the broad range of sectoral agencies having responsibilities for various aspects of its planning and management.

654. Australia's oceans policy commits the Government to implement it through an integrated and ecosystems-based ocean planning and management system aimed at ensuring the maintenance of ecological processes, biological diversity and viable functioning populations of native species. The ecosystems-based approach is to be implemented through a regional marine planning process outlined in the policy, with the aim of improving linkages between different sectors and across jurisdictions. These regional marine plans are based on large marine ecosystems derived from the Interim Marine and Coastal Regionalization for Australia. A national system of marine protected areas is to be the major component of the implementation.

655. While Australia has proceeded along a policy pathway for the development of its oceans policy and implementing it through a regional marine planning process, Canada has proceeded along a legislative pathway, with the proclamation of the Oceans Act in 1997, as a precursor to the development of an oceans management strategy that is to be implemented through integrated management plans.

656. The objective of the Oceans Act is to establish a framework for ocean resource management and marine environmental protection in Canada by defining the ocean areas that Canada proposes to manage and protect; establishing guiding principles and assigning the authority to negotiate partnerships for the development of an oceans management strategy; and consolidating and defining some oceans programmes to improve the effectiveness of Canada's conservation and protection initiatives.

657. The Oceans Management Strategy section of the Oceans Act outlines a new approach to managing oceans and their resources. The concept is based on the premise that oceans must be managed as a collaborative effort among stakeholders and that ocean management should be based on the principles of sustainable development, integrated management of activities occurring in or effecting oceans, and the precautionary approach.

658. The Republic of Korea has proceeded along an institutional reform pathway by establishing the Ministry of Marine Affairs and Fisheries in 1996, thus integrating the ocean-related functions from 10 government authorities in order to ensure consistent and effective marine policy.

659. Three major factors have shaped the Republic of Korea's marine policy: the geopolitical situation of the country and its ocean-borne trade strategies; the lack of land area and natural resources which spurred the country to put more emphasis on maritime policy; and the continuous prominent position occupied by marine policy since the mid-1960s, though it was since 1982 that emphasis has been placed upon the expansion of national interests from coastal seas to pelagic oceans, environmental concerns in coastal areas as a result of massive coastal reclamation, landfilling, increased coastal uses and sporadic oil-spill accidents, and governmental reforms on deregulation, liberalization and globalization.

660. Beginning with its early efforts in defining an approach to ocean governance, the Republic of Korea has been searching for an influential and permanent organizational device for providing policy direction, high-level inter-ministerial coordination to harmonize the disparate goals and programmes of existing agencies, and more authority in order to raise the profile of marine affairs. The current Ministry of Marine Affairs and Fisheries integrates almost all marine administrations into one "super-agency."

11. INTERNATIONAL COOPERATION AND COORDINATION

661. The advantages, and in some cases the inevitability, of international cooperation and coordination for the effective implementation of the international regime for the oceans established by UNCLOS prompted the framers of the Convention to include specific provisions relating to international cooperation and coordination in various parts of the Convention. In its Chapter 17, in addition to devoting an entire programme area to "Strengthening international, including regional, cooperation and coordination," Agenda 21 identified activities relating to "international and regional cooperation and coordination" under all seven programme areas.

662. Emphasis on international cooperation and coordination in ocean affairs was placed, inter alia, by the Commission on Sustainable Development in its deliberations and decisions, by the Consultative Process in its work and recommendations, and by the General Assembly in its debates and resolutions. In fact, the mandate of the Consultative Process includes "suggesting particular issues to be considered by [the General Assembly], with an emphasis in *identifying areas where cooperation and coordination at the intergovernmental and inter-agency levels should be enhanced*" (General Assembly resolution 54/33, par. 2, emphasis added).

663. While cooperation at the intergovernmental and inter-agency levels, especially at the levels of tasks, projects or even programmes, has been and continues to be quite effective, in many cases because of the very nature of the activities, the issue of coordination, in particular in relation to overall ocean affairs management and governance, requires serious consideration. The issues in this context are similar to those faced by integrated ocean management (see par. 649). While frameworks for coordination are provided by UNCLOS in a legislative context and by Chapter 17 of Agenda 21 in a programmatic context, putting these frameworks into effect poses major challenges: the nature and degree of coordination in ocean affairs at the national level, which is considered to be a sine qua non for coordination at the international levels; attitudes towards internationalism and, more importantly,

towards coordination with extra-national entities; acceptance of the frameworks of UNCLOS and Chapter 17 of Agenda 21 as the basis for actions at the national and international levels; allocation of resources to achieve coordination; and functioning of effective mechanism(s) for coordination. It is interesting to note that almost all these challenges prevail in the case of inter-agency coordination in ocean affairs, albeit mutatis mutandis.

664. For the agencies within the United Nations system, the challenges have been exacerbated recently with the discontinuation of the Subcommittee on Oceans and Coastal Areas of the Administrative Committee on Coordination.

A. International Cooperation: Existing Programmes

665. As pointed out in the 2000 annual report (A/55/61, par. 280), in the field of ocean affairs and the law of the sea, formal as well as informal cooperation is quite extensive among the organizations of the United Nations system, in many cases extending to other intergovernmental bodies, government agencies, the private sector, non-governmental organizations and stakeholders in the widest sense. For example, the CMS secretariat reports that in July 2000 it signed a Memorandum of Understanding with the secretariat of the International Whaling Commission. The Memorandum of Understanding, which builds upon already well-established collaborative linkages between the two secretariats, aims to provide a formal framework for future collaboration. It deals with aspects such as institutional linkages, the regular exchange of information, cooperation in the preparation of documents where applicable and coordination of the respective programmes of activities. The CMS secretariat adds that collaboration with UNEP regional seas conventions and action plans has been limited to date owing mainly to a lack of capacity. The most active cooperation has been with the Mediterranean Action Plan. There is scope for extending cooperation in other regions, particularly Latin America and the Caribbean, East Asia and Africa. IUCN has been a collaborator in many of the projects undertaken to date with sponsorship from CMS.

666. In its contribution to the present report, WMO re-emphasized the nature of the new Joint Technical Commission for Oceanography and Meteorology (JCOMM), an intergovernmental body established recently as a constituent body of WMO and IOC to coordinate and regulate the provision of meteorological and oceanographic services worldwide and coordinate and guide an operational ocean-observing system to support those services as well as global climate monitoring, research and prediction (see also par. 547). According to WMO, JCOMM represents a new paradigm in inter-agency cooperation in the United Nations system, in which two agencies are pooling resources and expertise in support of a more efficient, multidisciplinary approach to addressing an identified global requirement. Significantly, both agencies have not only obtained mandates from their respective governing bodies, but have also obtained approval of budgetary provisions. JCOMM is expected to lead to enhanced efficiency and cost-effectiveness at the intergovernmental institutions dealing with meteorology and oceanography. It has already spurred coordination at the national level as well, among the oceanographic and the meteorological communities.

667. In their contributions to the present report, the respective organizations have provided information about a wide range of cooperative and collaborative projects and programmes at the international level, most of which have also been described in the previous reports on oceans and the law of the sea. At the second meeting of the Consultative Process, delegations themselves enumerated a number of cooperative international projects and programmes relating to oceans and seas (see A/56/121, part B, par. 65). These include: the IOC programme on the international exchange of data and information; GOOS, a cooperative programme of States and the organizations of the United Nations system and the related Argo project; the Global International Waters Assessment (GIWA); the efforts of FAO relating to information on status and trends with respect to fisheries and marine living resources, including the development of an international plan of action and assistance in national capacity-building in fishery statistics; the IOC-WMO Joint Technical Commission on Oceanography and Marine Meteorology; the development and implementation jointly by UNIDO and the United States of America of GEF-supported ecosystem-based international waters projects involving 16 countries in Africa; the United Nations University Fisheries Training Programme for practising professionals from the fisheries sectors in developing countries; the European Union (EU) Programme for Scientific and Technological Cooperation with Developing Countries and, within its framework, research on oceans and seas by the Research and Development Programme of EU (INCODEV); the multilateral programme, Census of Marine Life, to assess and explain the diversity, distribution and abundance of marine life in the world's oceans, and its component, Ocean Biogeographic Information System (OBIS), designed to be an online, worldwide atlas of marine life; existing regional and global mechanisms to promote the access of developing countries to science and technology; regional cooperation along the lines of active scientific cooperation in the North-East Atlantic within the International Council for the Exploration of the Sea (ICES); training and technical assistance available in developed States, for example, the United States, including educational and training programmes, fellowships and scholarships, clearing houses, databases and web sites; the Canadian International Development Agency's "Strategy for Ocean Management and Development;" Norway's programme of assistance in developing national regulations relating to the conduct of marine scientific research in waters under national jurisdiction and its contribution to the trust fund for facilitating the preparation of submissions to the Commission on the Limits of the Continental Shelf by developing States; and the International Marine Projects Activity Centre (IMPAC) of the Cooperative Research Centre for the Great Barrier Reef World Heritage Area of Australia, facilitating cooperation in the areas of fisheries management, coastal planning, management and research, and policy development for oceans governance.

668. *Joint Group of Experts on the Scientific Aspects of Marine Environmental Protection (GESAMP)* is one important cooperative body within the United Nations system. Constituted in 1969 under an inter-agency Memorandum of Agreement, GESAMP is an expert scientific advisory body within and supported by the United Nations system, namely by: the United Nations through its Division for Affairs and the Law of the Sea of the Office of Legal Affairs, UNEP, UNESCO/IOC, FAO, WHO, WMO, IMO and IAEA. Its principal task is to provide scientific advice to the sponsoring agencies concerning the prevention, reduction and control of the degradation of the marine environment. The annual reports of GESAMP and the reports of its

working groups thus represent substantial contributions to the technical work of the sponsoring agencies under their respective mandates and programmes of work, including in relation to the implementation of Chapter 17 of Agenda 21.

669. As noted in the previous report of the Secretary-General on oceans and the law of the sea (A/56/58/Add.1, paras. 132 and 133), at its thirty-first session, in August 2001, GESAMP considered the final report of the independent evaluation team that it had established at its thirtieth session to recommend ways to make it more effective, more inclusive and more responsive to emerging problems and to the needs of policy makers and decision makers. At the session, following considerable discussion, GESAMP responded positively and constructively to the evaluation team's recommendations, some of which contained substantial financial implications.

670. Follow-up actions have since been undertaken, among them, to date, the convening of a GESAMP Intersecretariat meeting at WHO headquarters in Geneva, on 7 and 8 February 2002, the main purpose of which was to develop the key elements of a new framework for GESAMP in response to the evaluation team's recommendations. The meeting was convened following a very extensive exchange of information and ideas among the GESAMP Intersecretariat, comprising the Technical Secretaries and the IMO Administrative Secretary, and encompassing the input of the GESAMP Chairperson and Vice Chairperson. In addition to the Technical Secretaries, the GESAMP Chairperson and Vice Chairperson and two other participants from WHO and FAO, the meeting was attended by Mr. Magnus Johannesson (Iceland) and Mr. Chris Tompkins (United Kingdom) attended the meeting on the second day in an observer capacity.

671. In the light of an exchange of views on the future functions of GESAMP, and in particular whether it should continue to prepare periodic reviews and assessments of the state of the marine environment, the meeting formulated three goals/functions for GESAMP, as follows: (a) at the request of one or more sponsoring agency or Government, to conduct sectoral/topic-specific assessments and scientific syntheses, ensuring that there is an interdisciplinary review and endorsement of those assessments; (b) to provide advice and an oversight capability relative to the monitoring and assessment and related activities being carried out by the sponsoring agencies, considering, in particular, ways in which the agencies and Governments can interact and cooperate in these assessments, integrate and synthesize their results and contribute to global assessments of the state of the marine environment; and (c) to address the scientific aspects of new and emerging issues regarding marine environmental protection that are of concern to the sponsoring agencies and/or Governments.

672. Most attention was given to the second goal, assigning an oversight capability to GESAMP relative to monitoring and ocean assessment activities carried out by the United Nations agencies. It was considered that the agencies should confirm that they needed such an oversight capability and also that the needs of agencies should be based on the needs of Governments. It was suggested that GESAMP, in its oversight role, should prepare succinct annual reports on the coordination between agencies on their assessment activities and submit these reports, inter alia, to all United Nations agencies involved in marine assessments, the Secretary-General of the United Nations and the Consultative Process. It was unclear how the outcome of the UNEP feasibility study for establishing a regular assessment process might

influence the further development of the role of GESAMP as defined in the second goal. The governmental observers expressed the view that, irrespective of the outcome of the UNEP feasibility study, GESAMP should play a role in global assessments as formulated, and that the ideas developed at the meeting would be a valuable input for the next stage of the feasibility study, that is, the UNEP Technical Workshop (Bremen, Germany, 18–20 March 2002).

673. Among other issues, the meeting assessed the process for the selection of GESAMP experts; funding arrangements for GESAMP; the involvement of Governments; membership of GESAMP working groups; and the GESAMP web site. It also conducted a review of the recommendations of the GESAMP evaluation team for the purpose of developing a GESAMP "business plan" encompassing all aspects of the recommendations.

674. It is quite clear from an analysis of the existing cooperative arrangements that, through cooperation, coordination in relation to the scientific aspects of the world's oceans and seas is also being achieved to a large extent. However, while dealing with administrative, legal and developmental issues, coordination still remains a challenge.

B. Mechanism(s) for International Coordination

675. In 1993, the Administrative Committee on Coordination (ACC), acting on a proposal of the Inter-Agency Committee on Sustainable Development, established the Subcommittee on Oceans and Coastal Areas (SOCA),[206] with the purpose of meeting the coordination needs defined in Chapter 17 of Agenda 21.

676. Those needs, as elaborated in various sections of Chapter 17 of Agenda 21, are quite extensive. In particular, under the heading "Strengthening international, including regional, cooperation and coordination," Chapter 17 sets out a number of objectives, among them, to "promote the effective operation of coordinating mechanisms for the components of the United Nations system dealing with issues of environment and development in marine and coastal areas, as well as links with relevant international development bodies." (par. 17.116 [d]).

677. Among the management-related activities enumerated to serve this end, the Secretary-General, the agencies and organizations are requested to: "strengthen coordination and develop improved arrangements among the relevant United Nations organizations with major marine and coastal responsibilities, including their subregional and regional components"; "improve representation of United Nations agencies dealing with the marine environment in United Nations system-wide coordination efforts;" and "promote, where necessary, greater collaboration between the

206. The Subcommittee, now defunct, was a subsidiary body reporting to the Inter-Agency Committee on Sustainable Development under the Administrative Committee on Coordination (ACC). At its resumed 2001 substantive session in October 2001, the Economic and Social Council agreed to change the name of ACC to "United Nations System Chief Executives Board for Coordination" (CEB), without a change in its mandate. The Council also requested CEB to submit a comprehensive report on the reform of its machinery to the Council at its next session, bearing in mind the relevant reports of the Committee for Programme and Coordination. (decision 2001/321).

United Nations agencies and subregional and regional coastal and marine programmes." (par. 17.117).

678. At its session at United Nations Headquarters, on 27 and 28 October 2000, ACC decided to establish two high-level committees, the High-Level Committee on Management (HLCM) and the High-Level Committee on Programmes (HLCP), and mandated them, inter alia, to undertake a review of the ACC subsidiary machinery that should be zero-based: the review should take as its starting point what needed to be done rather than what was currently being done; permanent bodies should be kept to a minimum and their retention should be based on rigorous criteria. In introducing the item, the Secretary-General noted that ACC would, through the establishment of High-Level Committees, have the pillars in place that would enable it to concentrate on strategic issues, a main objective that had moved the review forward. The Secretary-General noted further that a third key element towards this objective was the consolidation of the ACC secretariat, and emphasized two main considerations in this regard. One was to ensure that, without prejudice to current procedures and the provision of dedicated services to the different interagency committees, ACC could count on coherent and well-coordinated support from both United Nations Headquarters and the United Nations Office at Geneva. The second was to consolidate secretariat capacities to promote a more effective exchange and dissemination of comprehensive information on the work of the system and to maximize support for the "task manager" and "lead agency" approaches that should guide the functioning of the reformed ACC machinery.[207]

679. In his most recent report on oceans and the law of the sea (A/56/58/Add.l, par. 128), the Secretary-General, in discussing the results of the deliberations of SOCA at its eleventh session (United Nations Headquarters, 3–4 May 2001), noted the view of the Subcommittee that "international coordination and cooperation is of vital importance in addressing all aspects of oceans and coastal areas. The cooperation between the relevant parts of the United Nations Secretariat for the purpose of ensuring better coordination of United Nations work on oceans and seas is thus considered imperative. The existence of a mechanism such as ACC/SOCA is needed." The Subcommittee had also expressed its conviction that the most productive course of future action lay in "building on existing mechanisms through innovative and more integrated approaches for effective coordination and cooperation."

680. At its fifty-sixth session, the General Assembly also considered the report on the work of the second meeting of the United Nations Open-ended Informal Consultative Process established by the General Assembly in its resolution 54/33 in order to facilitate the annual review by the Assembly of developments in ocean affairs (A/56/121) in which it was suggested "that the General Assembly should continue to invite the Secretary-General to include in his annual report on oceans and the law of the sea material on the progress of the processes of collaboration and coordination between the relevant parts of the United Nations Secretariat and the United Nations system as a whole, as described in paragraph 8 of resolution 54/33 and paragraph 42 of resolution 55/7" (ibid., part A, par. 70).

681. Furthermore, in its resolution 56/12 on "Oceans and the law of the sea," adopted on 28 November 2001, the General Assembly requested the Secretary-General "to ensure more effective collaboration and coordination between the rele-

207. See ACC/2000/20, Summary, p. 2; and par. 32.

vant parts of the Secretariat of the United Nations and the United Nations as a whole, in particular in ensuring the effectiveness, transparency and responsiveness of the mechanism for coordination on ocean issues" (par. 49).

682. At its session in 2001 held at United Nations Headquarters on 19 and 20 October, ACC, in carrying out its review of its subsidiary bodies in light of the report its High-Level Committee on Programmes,[208] "concluded by endorsing the view . . . *that all existing subsidiary bodies should cease to exist by the end of the year, and that future inter-agency support requirements of HLCP would best be handled through ad hoc, time-bound, task-oriented arrangements, using a lead agency approach, or by addressing requests to existing inter-agency networks or expert groups.* The Secretary-General requested HLCP to finalize expeditiously its review on that basis. In supporting the general approach to coordination favoured by HLCP, ACC reaffirmed its decision that the review of the subsidiary machinery should be zero-based. *It decided to move away from the concept of permanent subsidiary bodies with fixed periodicity of meetings and rigid reporting requirements, and, instead, to rely increasingly on ad hoc, time-bound and task-oriented coordination arrangements.* At the same time, ACC recognized the need for a number of inter-agency bodies to pursue their coordination work as expert bodies rather than as subsidiaries of ACC. Such expert bodies should also function on a task-oriented basis, using lead agency arrangements. It was noted that lead agency arrangements were an effective means of strengthening inter-agency consultative processes, instilling a greater sense of ownership, tapping the relevant competences of the system, and enhancing the substantive content of inter-agency cooperation."[209]

683. In the light of that decision, the members of the now defunct SOCA have engaged in substantial dialogue regarding the most effective approach to inter-agency cooperation and coordination within the new framework set out by ACC (CEB).[210] Arrangements to that end are a priority concern, for the members, in view of a number of ongoing projects that are being carried out under the Subcommittee's auspices, inter alia, such task-oriented projects as the United Nations Atlas of the Oceans, the role of the Subcommittee in the implementation of the GPA, and preparations for the World Summit on Sustainable Development. In addition, there are other issues relating to the implementation of UNCLOS and Chapter 17 of Agenda 21 that had not yet been addressed by the Subcommittee. It is expected that the former members of the Subcommittee would meet informally in conjunction with the third meeting of the Consultative Process.

684. In its contribution to the present report, FAO observed that ACC/SOCA had been highly beneficial in dealing with ocean matters requiring broader inter-agency policy discussion and joint implementation. That need remains. However, since a decision has been taken to terminate this coordinating mechanism, its functions should be continued through other mechanisms. Output-based ad-hoc mechanisms have been suggested and could be useful for projects requiring interaction to implement very specific projects (e.g., the Atlas technical meeting implementing the United Nations Atlas of the Oceans). For more policy-orientated debates, the use of ICSPRO, which had been dormant after the creation of ACC/SOCA, with adequately revised terms of reference, might be considered an option.

208. HLCP-ACC/2001/11.

209. See ACC/201/5, Summary, pp. 4–5; emphasis added.

210. See note 206.

685. In the view of FAO, enhanced coordination by countries at the national level will be useful so that delegations participating in meetings of different United Nations agencies will have consistent and mutually reinforcing positions on issues (e.g., between fisheries and maritime/shipping matters as they pertain to the operation of fishing vessels).

686. FAO furthermore suggested the establishment of a funding mechanism and related administrative and financial rules that would enable different United Nations agencies to contribute to and participate in jointly funded activities. Such a mechanism does not exist at present and it was felt that the absence of such a mechanism acts as an obstacle to the implementation of cooperative activities among agencies, even in cases where funds are available.

C. Review by the General Assembly of Developments in Ocean Affairs: United Nations Open-ended Informal Consultative Process Established by the General Assembly in Its Resolution 54/33 in Order to Facilitate the Annual Review by the Assembly of Developments in Ocean Affairs

687. The General Assembly, by its resolution 54/33 of 24 November 1999, decided to establish an open-ended informal consultative process in order to facilitate, in an effective and constructive manner, its own review of overall developments in ocean affairs. In this connection it should be noted that, at its fifty-seventh session, the General Assembly intends to review the effectiveness and utility of the Consultative Process.

688. Consistent with the legal framework provided by UNCLOS and the goals of Chapter 17 of Agenda 21, the Consultative Process discusses the annual report of the Secretary-General on oceans and the law of the sea and suggests particular issues to be considered by the General Assembly, with an emphasis on identifying areas where coordination and cooperation at the intergovernmental and interagency levels should be enhanced.

689. Thus far, the Consultative Process has held two meetings, one in 2000 and another in 2001. The third Meeting of the Consultative Process will be held from 8 to 15 April 2002.

690. The second Meeting of the Consultative Process was held at United Nations Headquarters from 7 to 11 May 2001. Pursuant to paragraph 3 (e) of General Assembly resolution 54/33 and after consultations with Member States, the President of the General Assembly reappointed Tuiloma Neroni Slade (Samoa) and Alan Simcock (United Kingdom of Great Britain and Northern Ireland) as Co-Chairpersons of the second Meeting of the Consultative Process (see A/56/58/Add.1, paras. 138–142).

691. At the fifty-sixth session of the General Assembly, during the general debate on agenda item 30 (a), entitled "Oceans and the law of the sea," delegations expressed appreciation for the work of the second Meeting of the Consultative Process and were in general agreement that since its establishment only two years earlier it had become invaluable, especially as regards the informal consultations conducted in preparation of the General Assembly resolution.

692. The two resolutions adopted by the General Assembly on 28 November 2001 (resolutions 56/12 and 56/13) incorporate many of the issues discussed at the

first and second meetings of the Consultative Process. These issues were, inter alia, the need for capacity-building for the implementation of UNCLOS; transfer of marine science and technology; coordination and cooperation in combating piracy and armed robbery at sea; the problems of illegal, unreported and unregulated fishing; and protection and preservation of the marine environment, marine resources and sustainable development.

693. In paragraph 48 of its resolution 56/12, the General Assembly recommended that the third Meeting of the Consultative Process, to be held at United Nations Headquarters from 8 to 15 April 2002, should organize its discussions around the following areas of focus: (a) protection and preservation of the marine environment; and (b) capacity-building, regional cooperation and coordination, and integrated ocean management, as important cross-cutting issues to address ocean affairs, such as marine science and the transfer of technology, sustainable fisheries, the degradation of the marine environment and the safety of navigation.

694. At the 86th plenary meeting of the fifty-sixth session of the General Assembly, on 14 December 2001, after extensive consultations with delegations, the President of the General Assembly, Han Seung-Soo (Republic of Korea), made an announcement reappointing as Co-Chairpersons of the third Meeting of the Consultative Process, Tuiloma Neroni Slade, Permanent Representative of Samoa to the United Nations, and Alan Simcock of the United Kingdom. Both were highly praised for their excellence as mediators and as consensus builders.

695. The third Meeting of the Consultative Process is the last meeting of the Consultative Process in keeping with General Assembly resolution 54/33. In that resolution, the General Assembly had further decided "to review the effectiveness and utility of the consultative process at its fifty-seventh session" (par. 4). Therefore, the General Assembly, at its fifty-seventh session, will evaluate the Consultative Process and take a decision on how, in the long term, to ensure more comprehensive, integrated and coordinated policies in matters relating to the oceans and the law of the sea.

ANNEX 1. (OMITTED)

For Parts A and B of Annex 1 on the First Intergovernmental Review Meeting on the Implementation of the Global Programme of Action for the Protection of the Marine Environment from Land-based Activities, Montreal, Canada, 26–30 November 2001, see Appendix B, Selected Documents and Proceedings, *Ocean Yearbook* Volume 17:

A. Conclusions of the Co-Chairs from the First Intergovernmental Review Meeting on the Implementation of the Global Programme of Action for the Protection of the Marine Environment from Land-based Activities
B. Montreal Declaration on the Protection of the Marine Environment from Land-Based Activities

ANNEX 2. OCEAN ISSUES IN THE PACIFIC REGION IN 2001: INITIATIVES AND PRIORITIES

(Contribution of the South Pacific Applied Geoscience Commission)

Regional Priorities in the Marine Sector

The Pacific region is well aware of the constant challenges and opportunities, which it faces with regard to issues relating to the management of its ocean resources. As well it recognizes the need for adopting more cost effective options for the delivery of regional project activities through regional cooperation and collaboration due to limited available funding resources to the sector. In response to these issues, the Council of Regional Organizations of the Pacific (CROP) agreed in September 1997 that a Working Group for Marine Sector Coordination be set up to formulate strategies and review progress of regional initiatives in the marine sector.

The Marine Sector Working Group (MSWG) comprises regional organizations (FFA, PIF, SOPAC, SPC, SPREP, SPTO USP)[211] with similar mandates to promote and enhance marine development in Pacific island countries (PICs) through research, technical assistance, project management and capacity-building. It meets regularly to discuss how cooperation and complementarity can be achieved to maximize the region's limited funding resources and optimize programme and project outputs.

Experience in the Pacific region.—Regional priorities for the marine sector are usually set by Governments of the Pacific region and are reflected in work programmes of the respective ministries at the national level and regional intergovernmental agencies at the regional level. In the regional context these priorities are consolidated within the CROP "Regional Strategy" and include ocean resources living and non-living; nearshore resources (coastal living and non-living resources); and cross-cutting themes such as environment, law of the sea, trade and globalization, capacity-building and information management issues.

Regional agencies involved in promoting and enhancing marine development in PICs must continue to be coordinated and engage in complimentary programmes to improve the cost effectiveness and impact of regional activities of the marine sector. Further, it is essential that donors be encouraged to fill any gaps in coverage of the marine sector, thus not directing resources to areas that are already adequately resourced. In this regard, donors should be encouraged to use the MSWG for screening, assessing and prioritizing regional projects in the marine sector.

Measures being undertaken to address these issues in the Pacific region.—The MSWG meets twice annually and communicates on a regular basis to review its progress, streamline relevant CROP agencies work programmes, coordinate project formulation between agencies, guide the development of work programmes and project activities and consider the needs to the member countries and the policy objectives of donors.

211. FFA (Forum Fisheries Agency); PIF (Pacific Islands Forum); SOPAC (South Pacific Applied Geoscience Commission); SPC (Secretariat of the Pacific Communities); SPREP (South Pacific Regional Environment Programme); SPTO (South Pacific Tourism Organization); USP (University of the South Pacific).

Regional Ocean Policy

The South Pacific Regional Follow-up Workshop on the Implementation of the United Nations Convention on the Law of the Sea 1982, held in August 1999 in Vava'u, Tonga,[212] resulted in the identification of six priority areas with recommendations having been made for each of these. The priority areas included: national and regional ocean policy and legislation; marine scientific research and cooperation; delimitation of maritime zones including continental shelves; human resource development, special technical assistance, and support and cooperation of regional institutions; ratification of UNCLOS and linkages to relevant treaties; and surveillance and information exchange.

The 1999 Pacific Islands Forum Leaders Meeting endorsed the conclusions and recommendations of the workshop, in particular the six priority areas identified. The Leaders also urged members, who are already parties to UNCLOS, to implement the Convention and particularly focus on the outcomes and conclusions relating to the six priority areas identified above.

A key recommendation of the Workshop articulated the need for developing an integrated ocean policy both at the regional and the national levels, with the overriding objective being to ensure the sustainability of ocean resources.

Experience of the Pacific region.—A Regional Ocean Policy has not been formally implemented in any part of the world and therefore to a large extent, the Pacific will be setting the international trend. In the Pacific context, the idea of a regional ocean policy is not new. The existing regional institutions supported by a large number of conventions and policies, provide the framework for such a policy.[213]

The possible advantages of a regional ocean policy include the consolidation of current achievements of regional institutions, the precise definition of roles and efficient allocation of scarce resources, assisting CROP agencies to develop compatible and transparent ocean programmes and providing international leadership.

Measures being undertaken to address these issues in the Pacific region.—The MSWG has prepared a draft Pacific Islands Regional Ocean Policy in July 2001. A regional consultative forum with key stakeholders, the Pacific Island Countries and Territories, is now necessary to ensure their commitment and endorsement of the Policy.

The Regional Ocean Policy aims to enhance the benefits that have so far accrued to Pacific Island Countries and Territories from their pursuit of marine regionalism. Additional benefits from harmonizing these various agreements into a coherent framework include: making it easier to identify gaps or loopholes in existing regional policy. The Regional Ocean Policy would include mechanisms for

212. This workshop, the second regional workshop on UNCLOS, was organized by the Commonwealth Secretariat and the regional organizations.

213. The draft Policy seeks to draw together all the various regional decisions, recommendations and legal instruments that have already been agreed by Pacific Islands Countries and Territories, to cover the management of Pacific Ocean-related activities. It recognizes that a high degree of regional solidarity and consensus already exists on many ocean issues, through existing regional institutions and conventions including: marine environmental protection; marine pollution; highly migratory fisheries management; integrated coastal zone management; marine scientific research; sea level rise; and shipping. It acknowledges that, to a large extent, most of the requirements for what may be covered in a Regional Ocean Policy already exist in the Pacific.

developing and agreeing to further refinements with the involvement of stakeholders; strengthening the current functional task-oriented approach to regional marine cooperation and coordination; providing a more solid justification and strategic basis for donor and project support, both nationally and regionally, based on the Policy's coordinated long-term focus; and providing a reference point for developing national ocean policies, and regional positions on ocean-related issues in international forums.

Summary of National Claims to Maritime Zone

According to UNCLOS, each PIC has exclusive jurisdiction over the living and non-living resources of the adjacent water column, seabed and subsoil to a minimum of 200 nautical miles from its coast, or to boundaries agreed with neighbouring countries. As most PICs have offshore boundaries with neighbours the delimitation of these boundaries is crucial for coastal States to define the area that is at their disposal for purposes of ocean development. Further, some PICs[214] have been identified as having the potential to establish continental shelf limits beyond 200 nautical miles.

Experience of the Pacific region.—The Maritime Boundaries Delimitation Project[215] has made significant progress in assisting individual PICs towards determining their baselines and delimitation of their territorial sea, contiguous zone and exclusive economic zone. To date, the Project has received funding assistance from the European Union and Australia. In December 2000, it was agreed that the Project be transferred from the Secretariat of the Forum Fisheries Agency (FFA) to the South Pacific Applied Geoscience Commission (SOPAC).

There are a total of 45 shared boundaries between SOPAC/FFA member countries and neighbouring countries. To date 16 have been negotiated, with a requirement for further work on three of these before they can be ratified. Three are currently under negotiation and 26 boundaries have yet to be negotiated. Three member countries have yet to complete surveys for determination of baselines.

Article 76 of the Convention may become particularly significant to the Federated States of Micronesia, Fiji, Papua New Guinea, Solomon Islands and Tonga, should sound technical evidence enable them to lay legitimate claim to extension of their maritime limits beyond their 200 nautical mile exclusive economic zone.

Although decision SPLOS/72 of the Eleventh Meeting of States Parties to the Convention allows the commencement of the 10-year time period for submission of such claims to the Commission on the Limits of the Continental Shelf in May 1999 rather than November 1994 in the case of PICs which became parties to the Convention prior to May 1999, a sense of urgency must still prevail among States Parties to prepare and submit their claims.

The costs required for acquiring the technical evidence required to substantiate such claims and the costs required to prepare appropriate legal argument are ac-

214. The following Pacific Island Countries have been identified as having the potential to claim an extended continental shelf: Federated States of Micronesia; Fiji; Papua New Guinea; Solomon Islands; and Tonga.

215. The Maritime Boundaries Delimitation Project was implemented by the Forum Fisheries Agency in 1990 until December 2000. It has since been transferred to SOPAC. Funding assistance from the Government of Australia for the Inception Phase of the Project was approved in October 2001.

knowledged as being prohibitively high for developing States. Consequently reliable external support urgently needs to be secured to review existing data (desktop assessments) to determine the nature of the continental shelf and its limits, identify data gaps, collect new data, and prepare and submit claims to the Commission.

Measures being undertaken to address these issues in the Pacific region.—At the regional level SOPAC has been tasked with identifying and securing funds for the continuation of the implementation of the Maritime Boundaries Delimitation Project. It is envisaged that the Project will be used to complete surveys for the purpose of baseline determination and delimitation of maritime zones; strengthen capacity and skills in negotiation and dispute resolution; and assist in the delivery of partial elements of determining continental shelf extension, as it is generally acknowledged that the acquisition of any new technical data and information for such claims will be costly.

Matters requiring further action and suggested actions for enhancing coordination and cooperation at the intergovernmental and inter-agency levels.—For developing PICs, especially those which meet the definition of being a small island developing State, preambular paragraphs 15, 16, 18 and 20 and the corresponding operating paragraphs of the General Assembly resolution A/RES/55/7 hold particular relevance and significance. PICs are mindful that they need to seek both financial and in-kind assistance to build their national capacity for delineation of their continental shelf limits and enable them to prepare and submit claims to the Commission due to the technical complexities, high costs and restricted time availability associated with claims preparation. Consequently, arrangements to access funds such as the CLCS voluntary trust funds, other bilateral, regional and international funding mechanisms, as well as in-kind technical support are being actively pursued, to assist potential PIC beneficiaries.

The Pacific region strongly encourages developed States to support and assist SIDS in their efforts to prepare and submit claims to delineate their continental shelf limits beyond 200 nautical miles, either through voluntary contributions to the trust funds or provision of in-kind technical assistance.

For the region, delimitation of maritime boundaries is being coordinated, at the regional level, by SOPAC in close collaboration with FFA.

Maritime Safety in the Pacific Region

Shipping is the primary means of transport in the Pacific region for both persons and cargo. Many people live on islands away from the main centres of population. So it is by ship that they send their produce to market; it is by ship that their supplies come in; and it is by ship that they travel to visit relatives, attend weddings, funerals and other important social events. Often these vessels are small cargo ships, but in many cases they are made of fibreglass, powered by small outboard engines and are often only about 19 to 25 feet long.

Any number of large ships transit the region, some stopping in ports such as Port Moresby, Honiara, and Port Vila en route to and from eastern Asia, and some putting into Suva, Apia and Nuku'alofa bound for the Panama Canal from Australia or New Zealand. There are also regional shipping companies, either bringing goods to hubs such as Suva, or returning with fresh produce for the burgeoning Pacific Island communities in Auckland, Sydney and Melbourne. Tankers bring gasoline, kerosene, aviation spirit and other fuels into the main ports of the region.

In addition to the cargo and passenger ships in the Pacific region, there are numerous fishing vessels of all sizes. They range from large American-owned purse seiners to Korean and Taiwanese long-liners, and from local commercial fishing vessels to aluminium twin-hulled catamarans, and sail-propelled outrigger canoes fishing in the many lagoons or even venturing out into the ocean.

Experience in the Pacific region.—Shipping and seafaring is of utmost importance in PICs, both as a means of transportation and a provider of employment. It is therefore necessary for PICs to have the necessary legal and administrative elements in place for the correct administration and oversight of shipping (and fishing vessels) for the safety of life and property at sea and the preservation of the marine environment.

The types of craft are numerous: from small boats, to salvage tugs, to fishing vessels to large container carriers, to small parcel tankers. The size of these vessels varies tremendously, as does the skill, experience and knowledge of their crews.

There are several international maritime conventions dealing with ship safety and safety of navigation, for example, SOLAS, Load Lines Convention, Tonnage Convention, COLREG, CSC, INMARSAT and INMARSAT Operating Agreement and Amendments, STCW and SAR of which SOLAS is the primary one.

Most PICs have Shipping Acts, many of which incorporate SOLAS by reference. The difficulty is that SOLAS is continually changing, and many maritime administrations do not have sufficient staff to monitor these changes or change their domestic legislation or regulations as necessary.

Furthermore, in recent years PICs have had to adopt Port State control requirements of various conventions, in addition to carrying out their Flag State responsibilities. This also places an additional burden on maritime administrations.

Measures being taken to address these issues in the Pacific region.—It has been agreed in various forums that the Regional Maritime Programme (RMP) of SPC has the mandate for initiatives in the area of maritime safety. Over the years, the Shipping Acts in a large number of PICs have been reviewed and in many PICs the original Shipping Acts have been replaced with an SPC model. In other cases, the existing Shipping Acts have been amended on a chapter-by-chapter basis. The net result is that most PICs have legislation incorporating by reference the above-noted conventions. Many PICs are now in the process of developing regulations to give more detailed effect to the provisions of the conventions.

To date, the RMP has developed regulations incorporating the provisions of the Load Lines, Tonnage and COLREG Conventions, and is in the process of developing regulations for the safety of convention vessels, the safety of non-convention vessels, and the safety of fishing vessels.

While many of the larger vessels transiting the Pacific region have excellent safety records, the same cannot be said for various classes of local fishing vessels or for small outboard-powered vessels carrying passengers between islands. What is required here to improve this situation is a combination of education, training and legislation/regulations requiring that vessels be fitted with various safety equipment and appliances.

The RMP has developed training course materials for navigation of smaller vessels, survival at sea, firefighting and occupational health and personal safety. The Programme has also developed regulations for the safety of small fishing vessels and the safety of small boats.

Matters requiring further action.—The RMP is preparing seminars and workshops on: the Global Maritime Distress and Safety System (GMDSS), a global radio-communications system for safety and distress related radio transmissions, together with a regional Search and Rescue capability; implementation of the International Safety Management (ISM) Code and related Safe Ship Management (SSM) and Ship's Operating Plan (SOP) systems for medium and small vessels respectively; and the carriage of dangerous goods, deck cargoes and containers on board ships operating in the Pacific region.

Maritime Training in the Pacific Region

Most of the 14 PICs rely on the sea as a form of sustenance (fisheries), coastal transportation and employment on local shipping or fishing vessels. Many of the seafarers from the PICs find employment on ships trading overseas. These seafarers earn relatively good wages by international standards and remit to their extended families monies that collectively contribute significantly to the national economy.[216]

Furthermore, the ability to gain employment on ships trading overseas reduces unemployment, which in turn reduces pressure on governments to provide assistance, and alleviates potential social problems. It allows families to remain in their traditional land-owning units and/or villages without having to flock to major centres for employment or support by family members who are employed there in the public or private sectors.

The 1978 International Convention on Standards of Training, Certification and Watch-keeping for Seafarers underwent a major revision in 1995 (STCW 95), with the amendments entering into force on 1 February 1997. STCW 95 stipulates certain standards that countries must ensure for ships sailing international waters under their flags (that is, these standards do not apply to domestic fleets). It also stipulates standards for seafarers on foreign-going vessels. In other words, to enable its nationals to work on such vessels, a country must ensure its training institution and maritime authorities meet these standards. Standards relate to: maritime training (such as curricula, teacher qualifications, workplace assessments); certification (quality audit procedures, documentary evidence, approved certificate structure) and watch-keeping (on the bridge, in the engine room, in port).

The Regional Maritime Programme (RMP) of SPC has assisted the 10 PICs that operate Maritime Training Institutions to be included on the IMO "White List," which indicates full and complete compliance with the provisions of STCW 95.

Experience in the Pacific region.—Regular remittances from seafarers working on overseas foreign-going vessels contribute greatly to the economies of most Pacific Island countries. For example, in Kiribati the remittances of approximately 1,700 seafarers amount to close to 12 million Australian dollars per annum, and in Tuvalu, the remittances of about 600 seafarers amount to about 3 million Australian dollars per annum. These remittances provide another source of cash income for village

216. This is estimated to be approximately 25 percent and 30 percent of GNP in Kiribati and Tuvalu respectively. Seafarers from Fiji, Papua New Guinea, Samoa and Tonga also sail on foreign ships and remit funds to support their families, which are still important, although contributing less to GNP in relative terms. Seafarers in the Marshall Islands, Solomon Islands and Vanuatu also obtain employment on local and foreign fishing vessels, thereby contributing to the national economy.

economies that otherwise tend to rely on the sale of fish and agricultural produce such as copra. Unlike these traditional sources that can be affected by bad weather, remittances provide a relatively steady income to meet basic needs such as food, education and clothing. Remittances have also become the major source of capital for small-scale businesses, particularly in the outer islands, and are used to build concrete houses, which require less maintenance than traditional dwellings.

The aim of the RMP to maintain the inflow of remittances by building the capacity of Pacific Island countries to maintain a supply of qualified seafarers. Among PICs, there are 10 maritime training institutions providing training at various levels, plus two institutions providing fisheries training. By 2002, ship owners and employers will require their workers to be seafarers whose qualifications are endorsed by STCW 95. Such qualifications in turn require the country's maritime authorities and colleges to meet the STCW 95 standards.

Measures undertaken to address these issues in the Pacific region.—All seafarers on international ships will need to have completed upgrade training by February 2002 in compliance with the STCW 95 Convention. Not all seafarers serving on domestic trade ships will complete their training by this deadline and will have to complete STCW 95 Upgrade Courses after February 2002. To date, over 1 million U.S. dollars has been spent to upgrade the region's seafarers.

In addition to STCW 95 upgrade requirements additional STCW 95 short courses need to be developed for seafarers serving on different classes of vessels. For example, seafarers serving on tankers must undergo a tanker familiarization course and seafarers serving on passenger ships must have completed an approved crisis management and crowd control course.

Since the 1960s, the legal regime governing shipping has become increasingly global, with the IMO developing over 25 major international maritime conventions as well as numerous codes and regulations. However, there prevails a general lack of knowledge about maritime matters in the region, and often governments are not fully aware of the overall nature of the shipping industry. Knowledge, awareness and experience among those involved in and concerned with the maritime sector are key to enhancing their contribution to, and their dealings with, maritime matters.

Non-technical personnel, at operational and policy levels, need to be aware of the many aspects of the maritime sector. The dissemination of information and its exchange at this initial level needs to be aimed at: general staff of transport departments or ministries; senior civil servants of transport and planning departments and ministries; staff of port authorities and departments; ship owners and operators, both in the public and the private sectors; and users of shipping services.

The RMP has developed the following mentoring programmes in an effort to strengthen regional capacity in the maritime sector: (a) the Administrators' Mentoring Programme provides an avenue for building up knowledge and increasing the awareness and experience in maritime matters of government officials at policy and operational levels, through attachments to relevant organizations, within the region; (b) the Port State Control Inspectors' Secondment Programme offers the region's maritime inspectors a weeklong "on-the-job training" attachment with the New Zealand Maritime Safety Authority at either their Auckland or Tauranga Ports. To date 17 PIC nationals have benefited from the Programme; (c) a Heads of School Mentoring Programme, established to enable Heads of Schools the opportunity to spend a week each at the New Zealand Maritime School and the Papua

New Guinea Maritime College to discuss topical issues and challenges facing their respective schools.[217] This interchange assists in upgrading both the skills and knowledge of these key personnel in the maritime sector; (d) the Tutor Exchange Programme is necessary for developing the professional competence of the region's maritime tutors as many of them come straight from a sea-going career into a teaching position and therefore have no formal training in education, curriculum development or delivery skills.[218] It is a collaborative programme involving maritime colleges in the PICs, New Zealand and Australia. The RMP has also developed several tutor-training programmes in basic teaching skills and additional technical skills; and (e) the Accident Investigation Secondment Programme allows the region's maritime inspectors the opportunity for on-the-job training on international obligations, legal frameworks for investigation, and types of investigation.

The dissemination of information throughout the region on matters relating to developments in the maritime industry and in international maritime legislation is an important function of the RMP. Raising awareness of safety and environmental protection issues are also key objectives. The more the maritime administrations in PICs know about the risks associated with operating in the maritime environment, the better placed they are to make informed decisions concerning the safety of those in their care. Consequently, the RMP produces a quarterly newsletter and maintains a STCW-95 compliant regional database system. Further, with the increased outreach opportunities provided by the Internet, the RMP has built a web site to help facilitate the dissemination of information to PICs. The site contains all RMP publications, generic legislation, contact details of maritime administrations and maritime schools in the region and information on the region's maritime industry and seafarers.

The Association of Pacific Islands Maritime Training Institutions and Maritime Administrations was established to promote cooperation between maritime training institutions, maritime authorities and ship owners in implementing uniform standards of training, examination and certification of seafarers within the region in accordance with international maritime conventions and regional codes. The Association consults closely with other interested government departments and maritime industries and holds an annual meeting.

Illegal, Unreported and Unregulated (IUU) Fishing

Illegal, unreported and unregulated (IUU) fishing has severe negative impacts for the economy of developing countries, especially those small island developing States whose economies are overwhelmingly dependent on the exploitation of fisheries resources. The challenge posed by IUU fishing requires a global response. Developing countries such as those in the western and central Pacific experience greater

217. The Director of the New Zealand Maritime School and the Principal of the PNG Maritime College are both senior maritime education professionals who are willing to act in a mentoring role. Other schools in the region are also available for this programme, in particular Vanuatu whose head of school is also a senior education professional.

218. Future developments may include teaching the course "in country" and running tutor exchange programmes within the region to allow tutors to broaden their experience. Individual tutors are now also understudying tutors from New Zealand and Australia when they undertake RMP funded training in the region.

difficulties in dealing with IUU fishing because of their limited resources. Their problems are exacerbated by the large area of ocean space that they have to control and the migratory nature of fish stocks, and the mobility of the fishing vessels that target these stocks. The fishing industry has also become more highly organized and sophisticated. Countries cannot unilaterally respond to the problems of IUU fishing because of the transnational nature of the fishery and the vessels that exploit the fishery. Thus, international cooperation is called for to address the problems of IUU fishing.

In recognition of the limitations suffered by developing countries in dealing with IUU fishing, various international instruments have called for special assistance to be given to developing countries. The 1995 UN Fish Stocks Agreement specifically calls on States to assist developing countries in monitoring, control and surveillance (MCS) and to provide funding for national and regional observer programmes. The FAO Code of Conduct for Responsible Fishing also enjoins States and intergovernmental organizations to give full recognition to the special requirements of developing countries. Any international plan of action on IUU fishing must reiterate the call to give special assistance to developing countries.

The problem of IUU fishing for developing countries has been manifested through the use of flags of convenience, reflagging of fishing vessels to the licensing State to avoid stringent conservation and management controls, illegal fishing on the margins of the EEZ and the high seas, and misreporting of catch. Developing countries who are dependent upon access fees for their economic development are particularly vulnerable because of distortions to the fees levels, which are conditional upon the volume of catch. There are a number of tools available to developing countries to deal with IUU fishing. These include, port State enforcement, effective exercise of flag State responsibilities, harmonization of regulations so that fishing vessels are not subjected to different regulatory regimes, and transforming international fisheries law so that it is responsive to the needs of modern fisheries management.

Measures being undertaken to address these issues in the Pacific region.—The South Pacific region has had a long history of cooperation and coordination in the development of MCS, conservation and management measures, which could provide a useful starting point for considering how developing countries deal with IUU fishing. Developing countries can learn from the experiences of the small island States in the South Pacific region who have developed low-cost, non-conventional yet innovative means of controlling the activities of foreign fishing vessels. Although the measures have not been developed to deal with IUU fishing per se, their broad application is pertinent in combating IUU fishing. These measures include the following: (a) Harmonization of terms and conditions of access for fishing vessels provides a framework for all fishing vessels to operate under uniform regulations. The framework includes provisions for: licensing; prohibition on transshipment at sea; maintenance of catch logs; access by authorized officers of the licensing State to catch logbook data and other information; regular catch reporting; use of observers; and requirements for vessel marking and identification; (b) The Regional Register of Foreign Fishing Vessels encapsulates in a common database all the relevant information about a vessel including its owner, operators and masters, call sign and port of registry. The information is updated annually so that changes to a vessel can be monitored. The Regional Register is not only used as a source of information; it is a useful tool in ensuring compliance by vessels that have violated coastal State laws but have left the jurisdiction of that State. No fishing vessel can be licensed unless it has good standing on the Regional Register. Good standing is a status which is automatically conferred on a vessel upon registration. The status may be withdrawn or suspended in certain circumstances, including where the vessel has committed a serious fishery offence. Once good standing is withdrawn or suspended, the vessel is effectively prevented from fishing in the region; (c) Effective flag State responsibility is fundamental to fisheries management. The exercise of flag State responsibility must not be limited to ensuring the application by vessels of agreed conservation and management measures; it should also encompass assistance in enforcement where there are allegations of violations; (d) Port State enforcement is recognized as an effective tool in ensuring compliance with conservation and management measures. Its manifestation in the South Pacific region is through enactment of legislation prohibiting the importation of fish caught illegally in another State's waters. The deterrent in such prohibition is that illegal fishing can be detected and prosecuted by a third party; (e) the Violations and Prosecutions Database contains information on vessels that have been involved in violations of the fisheries laws of the FFA member countries. This initiative responds to the lack of comprehensive information about the previous background and compliance records of fishing vessels, especially where the vessels have fished in other regions. Generally, licensing authorities are not aware of the historical record of fishing vessels that apply for a fishing licence and the information is not readily available or accessible to the licensing authorities; (f) Cooperation in fisheries surveillance and law enforcement is an effective means of dealing with IUU fishing especially where the fishery is transboundary. PICs cooperate under the framework of the Niue Treaty on Cooperation in Fisheries Surveillance and Law Enforcement;[219] (g) Satellite-based Vessel Monitoring System (VMS) is capable of providing near real time position reports and is a tool that is available to licensing authorities to monitor the activities of fishing vessels. The VMS is an effective means of monitoring fishing vessels for developing countries. However, the VMS currently applies to licensed vessels only. Therefore a gap remains in the monitoring of the activities of all vessels operating in a region.

Matters requiring further action and suggested actions for enhancing coordination and cooperation at the intergovernmental and inter-agency levels.—It will take some time for an effective framework to control IUU fishing to be developed. However, the development of a global database on fishing vessels, and a global violations and prosecutions database, both incorporating information held by existing regional fisheries bodies could be a first step in this process. The provision of technical assistance to strengthen boarding and inspection skills in developing countries would also be of assistance.

In the medium term the promotion of harmonized fisheries management and

219. The Niue Treaty allows a Party, by way of a subsidiary agreement, to permit another Party to extend its fisheries surveillance and law enforcement activities to the territorial sea and archipelagic waters of that Party. The Treaty also allows two or more Parties by way of a subsidiary agreement to cooperate in the provision of personnel and the use of aircraft or other items of equipment used for fisheries surveillance and law enforcement purposes. In recognition of the need to share the use of surveillance personnel, the Treaty permits the cross-jurisdictional exercise of enforcement powers of surveillance officers.

conservation schemes, the strengthening of regional and international fisheries management organizations to deny vessels access if they do not comply with agreed conservation and management measures and insistence on full flag State responsibility are actions that need to be considered.

In the longer term principles need to be developed that include making access to high seas resources conditional upon compliance with conservation and management measures prescribed by regional and international fisheries management organizations.

Status of Coral Reefs in the Region

Coral reefs are one of the most important and extensive ecosystems within the Pacific region. Pacific coral reefs are globally significant in terms of biodiversity. When considered in conjunction with the interrelated coastal habitats, mangrove, seagrass and beach systems, their importance to the well-being of the Pacific people and their island environments cannot be overstated. They are a critical element of the complex and vulnerable tropical small island environment and are essential to the food security and economic development of PIC communities.

Most people in the region are strongly dependent upon coral reefs for food resources, cash income from reef fisheries, coastal protection, aggregates for building of roads and housing, as well as upon healthy reefs to support a growing tourism industry. Consequently, the social, cultural and economic prosperity of the Pacific region has been, and will continue to be, directly dependent upon the health of coral reefs and related ecosystems.

The International Coral Reef Initiative (ICRI) launched in 1995, the ICRI Renewed Call to Action (1998) and the Global Coral Reef Monitoring Network (GCRMN)—Pacific Network are focused on the fact that coral reef systems are under threat globally and that urgent action is needed to reverse this decline. These real and potential threats are many and of varied origins, and range from global climate change and related increase in severity and frequency of cyclones and coral bleaching, to over-fishing, pollution, sedimentation and habitat destruction and crown-of-thorn outbreaks.

Experience in the Pacific region.—All PICs recognized the need to conserve marine habitats in their National Environment Strategies developed in preparation for the 1992 UNCED in Rio and in the more recently developed National Biodiversity Strategic Action Plans (NBSAPS). SPREP now assists these countries in implementing the NBSAPS and in their compliance with conventions and agreements relating to marine conservation and sustainable development.

Reef conservation is specifically reinforced in the Activity Plan for the Conservation of Coral Reefs in the Pacific Islands Region (1998 to 2002). The Plan is a partnership between countries and regional organizations and focuses on five areas: education and awareness; monitoring, assessment and research; capacity-building; legislation; and networking and linkages across people and programmes. SPREP has also organized coral reef monitoring training in several countries and coordinates the GCRMN Pacific Network, which is comprised of three Nodes, Micronesia, Polynesia and Central Pacific.

Coral reef monitoring capacity in the region varies. Countries have considerable interest in setting up monitoring programmes and improving coral reef management, but there is a critical lack of expertise and funding. There is also a strong need to involve the principal resource owners in the monitoring and management of their local reef areas. Therefore raising awareness of conservation and management ethics is of paramount importance.

There is no legislation in the Pacific that is dedicated to conserving coral reefs, although some governing fisheries resources may include coral reefs. Consequently, management of coral reefs is usually covered by several government departments in most counties. Traditional tenure systems remain strong and effective in many countries (Fiji, Samoa, Tokelau, Tuvalu, Solomon Islands and Vanuatu, Cook Islands), with customary management systems being revived to complement state legislation for better management of marine resources. The Pacific Regional Strategy for ICRI, which is endorsed by governments of the region, identifies 20 substantive issues which are grouped into five broad areas: coastal management; capacity-building; research and monitoring; coordination and review; and mechanisms for implementation. The strategy also provides a useful summary of issues and threats, which include: pollution from sewage, fertilizers, biocides, toxic wastes, oil spills, solid wastes, freshwater runoff and other land-based sources of pollution; siltation due to soil erosion from inappropriately conducted land use practices (agriculture, forestry, mining, road building, site clearance); over-exploitation of coral reef resources (for example, commercially valuable species such as beche-de-mer, giant clams, trochus, certain fish and shell fish; live coral harvesting for aquariums and the tourist trade; mining coral heads for construction; subsistence fishing pressure); destructive fishing and collecting methods (for example poisons, explosives); land reclamation (including mangrove and reef-flat destruction), inappropriate coastal protection works, and unsound mariculture practices; coastal and marine development projects progressing without environmental impact assessment (EIA), or with inadequate EIAs; channel blasting and dredging activities; mining of beach and reef materials; coastal erosion and accretion; tourism activities and related developments; military testing, training and dumping (for example, nuclear testing, munitions disposal); and catastrophic events (for example, tropical cyclones, volcanic eruptions, earthquakes, tsunamis, coral bleaching, crown-of-thorns starfish infestations, severe El Niño-Southern Oscillation (ENSO) events, and possible climate change and sea-level rise).

Matters requiring further action and suggested actions for enhancing coordination and cooperation at the intergovernmental and inter-agency leve.—To address the threats and stresses identified in the Pacific Regional Strategy for ICRI, new approaches to management must be developed which draw upon the foundations of traditional use and practices and incorporate the understanding and procedures developed through relevant science and technology.

Capacity-building is a high priority for the region to set up coral reef monitoring in a series of long-term monitoring sites. This needs to be addressed at all levels, including local community stakeholders, NGOs, governments and the private sector. Further capacity-building and institutional strengthening is required in training marine taxonomists and strengthening the Marine Biodiversity Centre at the University of the South Pacific, to enable documenting of the biodiversity of coral reefs in all countries. This will improve knowledge and understanding of the biology of reef food fishes and result in sound sustainable fisheries management practices being introduced. The framework for the Pacific GCRMN was identified at the ICRI Regional Symposium on Coral Reefs held in New Caledonia in May 2000. Four Pacific Sub-regional Nodes and Node Coordinators were identified with SPREP responsible for over-all coordination. These Node Coordinators are responsible for supporting National Coordinators and local monitoring programmes. The Sub-regional Nodes are comprised of Polynesia Mana Node, IOI Pacific Islands Node, MAREPAC Node covering the Micronesian countries, and U.S. Coral Reef Task Force-US Territories Node. Funding support had been acquired for the MAREPAC Node (USAID) and the IOI Pacific Island Node (Canada C-SPOD), but funding is urgently required to continue support to these activities and also for other Nodes.

There is an urgent need to establish community based marine protected areas (MPAs) throughout the region. This is partly being addressed by the Pacific International Coral Reef Action Plan (ICRAN)—Action Phase Implementation. ICRAN Pacific is coordinated by SPREP and will concentrate on supporting a series of demonstration and target sites focusing on community based management of coastal resources as part of a Global Network of MPA sites within the UNEP Regional Seas Framework. ICRAN supported projects are currently being established in Marshall Islands, Fiji, Samoa, Tokelau and Solomon Islands. Implementation of the Global Action Phase of ICRAN is funded by the UN Foundation and will hopefully provide seed funding support for expansion of community based marine and coastal resource management initiatives in the region.

The development of appropriate national coastal zone management plans and policies is urgently required for all countries in the region, and legislation and regulations for the management of coral reefs need urgent upgrading to incorporate integrated coastal management and sustainable fisheries management.

Further, regional and national strategies for preservation of intellectual property rights on marine biodiversity must be developed.

Seabed Minerals: Marine Scientific Research

PAC was established in 1972, originally as a United Nations project "The Committee for the Coordination of Offshore Prospecting in the Pacific," which essentially dealt with the coordination of marine scientific research of non-living resources in the Pacific. Although SOPAC's role has since broadened with regard to ocean issues, to now include: developing resource policy and providing advice on the management and development of onshore and offshore mineral and aggregate resources; assisting decision makers and planners to develop coastal zones and extract resources while protecting them from degradation; assisting decision makers and planners to understand ocean processes, develop ocean areas and extract resources while protecting the ocean from over-exploitation and pollution. However, SOPAC still coordinates marine scientific research in the region for its island member countries.

Experience in the Pacific region.—It is acknowledged that although the non-living marine resources currently contribute much less than the living resources to PIC economies, there is considerable potential for this situation to change. Cooperative research programmes over the last three decades have discovered occurrences of deep-sea minerals, such as polymetallic massive sulphides, cobalt-rich manganese crusts and polymetallic manganese nodules, within the EEZs of many PICs. Other non-living resources include hydrocarbons, which are currently important in Papua New Guinea and for which potentials may exist in coastal and offshore areas of the

Solomon Islands, Fiji, Tonga and Vanuatu. However, extensive exploration is still required to prove this.

Major constraints to development and exploitation of these mineral deposits are the development of suitable and cost-effective deep-sea mining technology, as well as the resolution of the legal and boundary issues related to the ownership of the resources. These and other economic factors could be enhanced through better understanding and knowledge. It therefore follows that both ocean science and technology continue to have a clear and vital role to play. PICs can achieve this increased understanding of their resources, through encouraging researching States to continue to conduct research activities within their EEZs, actively participate in these activities, and ensure that they develop and maintain robust oceanographic databases.

In the context of deep-sea non-living resources, exploration licenses covering more than five thousand square kilometres, which were granted in 1998 by the Government of PNG, have been re-let for a further term of two years. Applications for exploration licenses have been lodged for other areas in PNG, as well as areas within the EEZs of other PICs. These developments have led to some conflicts between the public and private sectors and it is acknowledged that this needs to be addressed and resolved to enable both activities to continue in the region.

At the offshore mineral policy workshop, held in Papua New Guinea in February 1999, the following recommendations, which have implications for marine scientific research were agreed to: (a) Coastal States should establish a consent regime for marine scientific research (MSR) in accordance with the provisions of UNCLOS and the United Nations model guidelines on MSR. The regime should take into account the interests of the State in obtaining research data and information as well as the interests of investors in protecting the confidentiality of data regarding the resources obtained during exploration; (b) Measures should be taken to minimize potential conflict between offshore mining and other traditional and non-traditional uses of the sea; (c) Measures should be taken to minimize adverse impacts of offshore mining to the marine environment; (d) Coastal States should maintain a clear policy for the promotion of MSR in their EEZ and extended continental shelf; and (e) Relevant government representatives should participate in all phases of MSR, exploration and evaluation.

The Regional Workshop on the Issues and Challenges of Marine Scientific Research in the Pacific was convened in Port Moresby, Papua New Guinea in February 2001 to increase PIC's awareness of the value of marine scientific research and the legal and technical issues relating to marine scientific research within their exclusive economic zone. Key recommendations of the meeting were clustered under the following issue areas: the legal framework for conduct of MSR; capacity-building; transfer of marine science and technology, including data; and marine mineral exploration and MSR as parallel activities. They include: (a) Where appropriate SOPAC should facilitate the development, with inputs from PICs and other CROP agencies, appropriate regional marine scientific research guidelines within the framework of UNCLOS, and when requested assist in the development of national marine scientific research guidelines; (b) PICs should, when necessary and appropriate, develop and support MSR Committees/Agencies to provide oversight of MSR activities within their EEZs; (c) PICs should recognize the logistical limitations of some researching States and acknowledge that some researching States may request special treatment of their applications if there are constraints that prohibit them from meeting the required deadlines; (d) As part of capacity-building the researching State is encouraged to provide opportunities for participants to broaden their experiences with scientists from other countries. Wherever possible the nominated participant should be part of the Science Team and actively involved in the actual research programme; (e) A regional standard should be established for digital data to ensure regional consistency in the provision of processed data and ensure that these data are provided in formats that fit regional needs. Detailed acquisition parameters should accompany all raw data provided by the research organization; (f) A regional metadata database should be established for all regional non-living marine resource data, including physical oceanographic data, to ensure that coastal and researching States can access the data; (g) PICs should adopt a flexible and facilitating policy with respect to biological prospecting. However, it should retain ownership of all samples in order to ensure that it may subsequently participate in any commercial benefits that might occur; (h) Within the context of marine mineral development SOPAC, as part of its participation in the CROP Regional Ocean Policy initiative, should promote the development of appropriate guidelines to assist member States in the formulation of policy and legislation that simultaneously provides for mineral development and parallel MSR; (i) PICs should adopt a proactive policy in defining the priorities of MSR and commercial development activities within their EEZs to minimize ad hoc decision-making; (j) PICs should be encouraged to review the applicability of their existing policy and legislation and where necessary modify or create new policy and legislation that provides for (i) a more comprehensive evaluation of the capacity of commercial investors in addition to (ii) encouraging a moratorium on selected commercial activities or (iii) allowing MSR to proceed prior to the licensing of areas for commercial purposes, in order to establish a comprehensive marine data base for decision-making, or (iv) allowing MSR and commercial activities to proceed in parallel.

Matters requiring further action and suggested actions for enhancing coordination and cooperation at the intergovernmental and inter-agency levels.—International marine scientific research has been instrumental in improving the region's understanding of the types of non-living marine resources that occur in the Pacific Ocean. However, there is still a need to promote and encourage further international research in the Pacific region, both in areas already researched to ensure a better understanding of the nature and extent of already discovered mineral deposits as well as into new areas to locate other deposits.

As marine scientific research is costly, collaboration and cooperation between national, regional and international organizations is imperative if PICs are to be able to collect the data and information that is necessary to understand their non-living marine resource base. Consequently, PICs need to be receptive towards MSR requests for access to their waters. However, at the same time PICs need to develop and strengthen their internal procedures for handling MSR requests, to ensure that measures are taken to avoid the abuse of such access and to ensure compliance with relevant provisions of UNCLOS.

With regard to the issuing of deep-sea mineral exploration licenses, support from the international community is urgently needed to assist national and regional efforts in the Pacific to assess resource information and to develop appropriate policies and legislative regimes for this activity. As it is a recent development, national capacity needs to be built to ensure that deep-sea mineral exploration is managed, regulated and monitored effectively.

Marine Pollution in the Pacific Region

The ocean is a valuable resource to the people of the Pacific Region as an important source for food, a means of transportation and an opportunity for employment. Furthermore, clean beaches and clean and clear waters promote tourism, which in turn creates employment and generates foreign exchange. However, this pristine environment is often marred by marine pollution, much of it from land-based sources, but some of it from ships. This ship-based pollution comes in the form of oil, whether intentional or accidental discharges, or hazardous materials released from shipwrecks on the coral reefs. Other marine pollution comes from waste products from ships transiting the region, such as packaging material, food wastes, and abandoned fishing nets and lines. Other hazards to the marine environment come from the introduction of exotic species contained in ballast water taken on in distant discharging ports as well as anti-fouling paints containing toxic substances.

There are a number of international conventions dealing with the prevention of marine pollution, such as, MARPOL 73/78, 1969 Intervention Convention and its 1973 Protocol, London Dumping Convention and its 1996 Protocol and OPRC with respect to marine pollution; and CLC, 1992 Fund, HNS and Bunkers Convention with respect to liability and compensation.

In order for these marine pollution prevention conventions to be put into effect, they have to be incorporated into domestic legislation, together with the creation of mechanisms to deal with offences and stipulation of penalties. Only those States may accede to the convention in a meaningful manner.

Experience in the Pacific region.—Some PICs are parties to the MARPOL 73/78 Convention and the Intervention Convention, while very few are parties to the London or OPRC Conventions. Some PICs are Parties to one or two of the conventions dealing with liability and compensation for marine pollution. However, not many States in the region have actually enacted legislation to give full effect to these conventions and make the provisions enforceable in national law.

The lack of national legislation relating to marine pollution and its prevention can be attributed to the limited expertise in this field within the PICs. Further, there is little or no experience in legislative drafting. Moreover, with limited human and financial resources, PIC governments tend to defer the issue of marine pollution, and it is not treated as a national priority.

Another reason that acceptance of any model legislation has been slow is that many of the government departments that deal with maritime matters are often small branches of much larger portfolios, often dealing with matters such as public works, communications, or land transport. Consequently, the shipping and marine pollution issues are lost in these larger, more politically sensitive sectors.

Shipping and ship-based marine pollution and the international conventions dealing with it are complex, technical documents. In many cases, senior decision makers are not familiar with the subject-matter and are hesitant to take these complex technical issues to the Cabinet or the Parliament and are equally hesitant to answer questions put to them in public forums. Hence, there is a tendency to put marine pollution and its prevention into the "too hard" basket.

Measures being taken to address these issues in the Pacific region.—The Secretariat of the Pacific Community (SPC) and the South Pacific Regional Environment Programme (SPREP) have produced a model Marine Pollution Prevention Act for PICs to use as a precedent for their own domestic legislation. In addition to the conventions noted above, the model legislation deals with the problem of anti-fouling paints, the introduction of alien marine species and the removal of wrecks.

The SPC/SPREP model legislation has been circulated to all PICs and some of the territories, but enactment of the model into national legislation has been slow. Follow-up missions have been conducted to some countries, and in some PICs the appropriate marine pollution legislation is being developed and being moved through the legislative process.

Matters requiring further action.—Tentative discussions have taken place between SPREP and SPC for information materials to be prepared and distributed to stakeholders and decision makers, explaining the need to develop and enact legislation dealing with marine pollution and its prevention, and simplifying some of the technical matters.

The recent CROP Legal Officers Meeting decided to take steps to provide background information to legal officers in local governments in several areas, including marine pollution and its prevention, as part of the larger effort to implement provisions of UNCLOS in PICs.

The SPC Regional Maritime Legal Internship Programme has been provided with funds for 2002 and will be reactivated. This provides a vehicle for both maritime administrators and government legal officers to gain experience in maritime matters, including marine pollution and its prevention.

International Waters Programme in the Pacific Region

The Strategic Action Plan for International Waters of the Pacific Small Island Developing States (SAP) is a five-year programme that commenced in February 2000. The Programme is funded by the Global Environment Facility (GEF), implemented by UNDP and executed by SPREP. The SAP has both coastal and oceanic components.

The basis for developing a programme focus in these areas is found in the Action Plan for Managing the Environments of the South Pacific Region (1997–2000), the joint regional position prepared by the PICs for the 1992 UNCED and the National Environment Management Strategies (NEMS) prepared by PICs between 1990 and 1996.

The broad objective of the SAP is to achieve global benefits by developing and implementing measures to conserve, sustainably manage, and restore coastal and oceanic resources in the Pacific. The SAP identifies four high priority areas for immediate intervention: improved waste management; better water quality; sustainable fisheries; and effective marine protected areas.

Targeted action within these activity areas is proposed in management, capacity-building, awareness/education, research/information for decision-making, and investment, with institutional strengthening being considered an important element of both the management and capacity-building categories.

The oceanic component being executed through the SPC and FFA is to address issues associated with the conservation and management of the South Pacific regional tuna resource.

Highlights, in 2001, for the coastal component of the programme being executed through SPREP, include: acceptance of the inception report by UNDP; convening of the first Regional Task Force for the International Waters Programme (IWP); strengthened relations with the implementing agency, UNDP; completion of consultations with 13 of the 14 participating countries on IWP implementation; development of guidelines for the implementation of IWP demonstration projects; and development of a communications strategy for the programme.

Global Ocean Observing System (GOOS)

Scientific understanding provides the basis for sustainable use of the sea and its resources, for the amelioration of pollution and harmful practices, and for the prediction of weather, climate and ocean variability both regionally and globally. However, applying scientific understanding for these purposes depends critically on continuing observation, the scale and extent of which requires the close and integrated cooperation of individual economies in the pooling and enhancement of their observing systems.

The success of the cooperative international approach for research and observation in the equatorial Pacific over the past two decades resulting in the capacity to predict El Nino and La Nina events and to produce associated seasonal atmospheric forecasts provided the motivation for the Global Ocean Observing System (GOOS). GOOS is intended to provide a comprehensive framework for the regional and global coordination of ocean observations of many kinds and purposes. A priority for GOOS and its implementation has been the physical observations that are needed for improving weather and climate prediction capabilities. The benefits of enhanced observations are already identifiable.

Particularly important aspects of GOOS to PICs and territories are: fisheries (coastal and oceanic fisheries, mariculture developments); coastal management (health of reefs, beaches, water quality, mangroves); and weather and climate forecasts (extreme events, conditions for coastal zone management, and support for longer-term climatic forecasts).

Experience in the Pacific region.—A GOOS capacity-building meeting for the Pacific was identified in the GOOS 1998 Plan, approved by the UNESCO/IOC Assembly and at the SOPAC Governing Council Meeting in 1997. The purpose of the meeting, held in February 1998, was to explore the possibility for developing GOOS in the region, identify capacity-building needs, and ascertain the interests of organizations serving the region, as well as the interests in GOOS, of the PICs.

An observing system in the Pacific Ocean, PacificGOOS, was formed in 1998 with SOPAC being designated the regional contact point for GOOS activities,[220] as the critical activities within the GOOS design framework relating to data gathering and database development are acknowledged as areas of expertise within SOPAC.

PacificGOOS, the Pacific regional component of GOOS, convened its second regional workshop in August 2000. The main objective of this workshop was to design concept documents for pilot projects for the coastal component of GOOS, with a view to developing, implementing and operationalizing them. Three pilot project

220. A signed memorandum of understanding exists between SOPAC and UNESCO/IOC.

concept documents on mariculture development, coastal water quality in port areas, and coral reef monitoring of key dive sites, which fit the design requirements for CoastalGOOS, were developed.

The workshop recommended that attention be accorded to other regional GOOS initiatives, such as the development of a strategic plan to provide guidance and overall direction to PacificGOOS and, the promotion of the International ARGO Programme for the region.[221]

Since the PacificGOOS meeting in August 2000, all PICs and territories have provided their concurrence for autonomous ARGO floats to be deployed within their exclusive economic zones. Other regional contributions to the ARGO Programme include: facilitating port calls, as needed, for the ships and aircraft coming into the region for float deployment; providing assistance, as needed, in identifying and linking with regional organizations which might assist float deployment from vessels of opportunity such as fisheries vessels and patrol craft; providing a regional focal point for the deployment, science and applications aspects of the Programme. Furthermore, a PacificGOOS Strategy has been drafted to establish a GOOS Regional Alliance (PacificGOOS GRA). The Strategy seeks to: establish the mandate and procedures enabling a stable operating environment for the PacificGOOS GRA; review the contribution and participation of PICs and territories in the International ARGO Project, which is an important component of GODAE; build awareness amongst the wider global community about the needs for GOOS data and products in PICs and territories, to engender interest, and to widen support and assistance to the PacificGOOS GRA; develop detailed design documents for the three CoastalGOOS pilot project concepts outlined above, and actively seek funds for their implementation; fill knowledge gaps prevailing in the Pacific region concerning existing GOOS components (such as identifying all relevant GOOS data and products relevant to oceanic fisheries).

Matters requiring further action and suggested actions for enhancing coordination and cooperation at the intergovernmental and inter-agency levels.—It has already been widely acknowledged at the international level that operational ocean observing initiatives will require substantial international collaboration if they are to be successful, as no single economy can afford to cover one ocean basin on its own. This is especially true for the Pacific Ocean, the largest ocean in the world with the majority of its custodians being small island/large ocean developing States. It is therefore imperative that collaboration, cooperation, and both financial and in-kind support be accorded to the region, if GOOS is to become a viable and successful resource planning and management mechanism in the future.

221. PICs recognize that the ARGO Programme will result in significant improvements in our understanding of global climate and ocean processes, and will also contribute to a better understanding of the currently under-observed Pacific Ocean. For PICs, ARGO will widen the scope for more detailed prediction of the frequency and geographic incidence of tropical cyclones, coastal rainfall (and its effect on nearshore ocean health), variation in boundary currents, and ocean-climate related changes in fish populations, algal blooms and reef ecology. It will also contribute to the more certain detection and anticipation of regional climate change both in the atmosphere and the oceans as well as the profound implications such changes must have for the viability of Pacific livelihoods and economies.

At the regional level the following GOOS issues have been identified as requiring attention: securing financial and in-kind support and assistance to commence implementation of key components of the PacificGOOS Strategy, as articulated above; completion of an inventory of GOOS related data, currently being collected in the region by national and regional organizations, and by countries and organizations outside the region to facilitate development of the PacificGOOS GRA. This cannot be undertaken with existing resources and will need to be carried out as a consultancy. Funds are urgently needed to initiate this programme prior to the next PacificGOOS meeting planned for the last quarter of 2002; securing international financial and in-kind support to convene an important Pacific regional workshop on Applications of Ocean Observations for Pacific Island Countries and Territories, currently scheduled for the last quarter of 2002, in Nadi, Fiji. The purpose of the workshop would be to: review potential applications of subsurface ocean observations, including those to be collected by new sources such as ARGO profiling floats, which can be of benefit to the Pacific Island Countries. Applications include: seasonal to inter-annual climate forecasting; understanding sea-level change; assessment and prediction of the health of coral reefs; fisheries population modelling; basic research in ocean variability and atmosphere-ocean interaction; and secondary education, advocacy and awareness; (b) identify appropriate data products and services requirements, for each of these applications, determine timeliness criteria for their delivery, and assess the extent to which these requirements are presently being met, with regard to requirements for improvements and particularly in instances where the International ARGO Project can contribute; and (c) establish linkages between the developers and the users of (more improved and appropriate) products and services.

Oceans and the Law of the Sea Report of the Secretary-General, 2002*

ADDENDUM

Summary

The present report has been prepared as an addendum to the main report (A/57/57) and should be read in conjunction with it, as well as with the report on the work of the third meeting of the United Nations Open-ended Informal Consultative Process established by the General Assembly in its resolution 54/33 in order to facilitate the annual review by the Assembly of developments in ocean affairs (A/57/80), and with the report of the twelfth Meeting of States Parties to the Convention, at which the elections to the International Tribunal for the Law of the Sea and to the Commission on the Limits of the Continental Shelf were held. This addendum covers the period from the date of publication of the main report, 7 March 2002, to mid-October 2002. It contains information on the status of the United Nations Convention on the Law of the Sea and its implementing Agreements, and declarations and statements made by States under Articles 287 and 298 of the Convention. In spring and summer 2002, the Commission considered the first submission by a coastal State regarding the outer limits of its continental shelf beyond 200 nautical miles and adopted its recommendations to the State on the matter. The Consultative Process conducted its third meeting and adopted recommendations to the General Assembly. The first informal meeting of States parties to the 1995 Fish Stocks Agreement was convened; it recommended certain actions to be undertaken by the General Assembly. The present addendum also contains a summary of the results of the World Summit on Sustainable Development, held in Johannesburg, South Africa, in particular as they relate to the oceans and seas.

CONTENTS

*EDITORS' NOTE.—This document was provided by the United Nations Division for Ocean Affairs and the Law of the Sea (DOALOS) and is extracted from the United Nations General Assembly, Fifty-seventh session, Item 25(a), UN document A/57/57/Add.1, 8 October 2002. Available online at the DOALOS web site, http://www.un.org/Depts/los/.

1. INTRODUCTION

1. In its annual resolutions on "Oceans and the law of the sea," the General Assembly continues to reaffirm the importance of the annual consideration and review of overall developments relating to ocean affairs and the law of the sea. The annual debate on these issues at the fifty-seventh session of the General Assembly has become even more important, since the year 2002 marks the twentieth anniversary of the adoption and opening for signature of the 1982 United Nations Convention on the Law of the Sea (UNCLOS or Convention).

2. In 1999, in its resolution 54/33 of 24 November 1999, the General Assembly established an open-ended informal consultative process in order to facilitate its annual review, in an effective and constructive manner, of developments in ocean affairs by considering the Secretary-General's report on oceans and the law of the sea. Accordingly, the Secretary-General's report on oceans and the law of the sea for the fifty-seventh session of the General Assembly was submitted to the third Meeting of the Consultative Process, held from 8 to 15 April 2002 (A/57/57).

3. The present report has been prepared as an addendum to the main report and should be read in conjunction with it, as well as with the report on the work of the Consultative Process at its third meeting (A/57/80)[1] and the report of the

1. The report of the third meeting of the Consultative Process is contained in document A/57/80. It is recalled that by a letter dated 17 July 2002, the co-chairpersons informed the permanent representatives to the United Nations in New York that the report of the third meeting of the Consultative Process would not contain, as had been previously agreed, either the summary of the panel discussions or the statements made at the first plenary session by the Under-Secretary-General for Legal Affairs, the Legal Counsel, and by the Director, Division for Sustainable Development, Department of Economic and Social Affairs, representing the Under-Secretary-General of that Department. The Division for Ocean Affairs and the Law of the Sea had been informed by the Department of

twelfth Meeting of States Parties to the United Nations Convention on the Law of the Sea, held in New York from 16 to 26 April 2002 (SPLOS/91). The present report contains a short overview of the results of both the third meeting of the Consultative Process and the twelfth Meeting of States Parties.

4. The attention of the General Assembly is also drawn to another report, entitled "Large-scale pelagic drift-net fishing, unauthorized fishing in zones of national jurisdiction and on the high seas, fisheries by-catch and discards, and other developments," submitted to the General Assembly at the current session pursuant to General Assembly resolution 55/8 of 30 October 2000.[2]

2. THE UNITED NATIONS CONVENTION ON THE LAW OF THE SEA AND ITS IMPLEMENTING AGREEMENTS

A. Status of the Convention and its Implementing Agreements

5. There have been no changes in the status of the Convention since the report of the Secretary-General (A/57/57) was issued and, as at mid-September 2002, the total number of States Parties, including one international organization, continued to stand at 138. However, it is expected that additional States may express their final consent to be bound by it at the time of the commemoration of the twentieth anniversary of the opening of the Convention for signature.

6. In August 2002, two States, Cameroon and Kuwait, expressed their consent to be bound by the Agreement of 28 July 1994, relating to the implementation of Part 11 of UNCLOS. The number of parties to that Agreement has thus risen to 107.

7. As for the 1995 Agreement for the Implementation of the Provisions of the United Nations Convention on the Law of the Sea of 10 December 1982 relating to the Conservation and Management of Straddling Fish Stocks and Highly Migratory Fish Stocks (the 1995 Fish Stocks Agreement), one new instrument of accession has been deposited by Cyprus since the issuance of the main annual report. Thus, nine months after the entry into force of that Agreement, on 11 December 2001, the number of States Parties to the Agreement stands at 32.

B. Declarations and Statements under Articles 287 and 298 of the Convention

8. Since February 2002, three States Parties made declarations under Articles 287 and 298 of UNCLOS. Under Article 287, which allows States to choose, by means

General Assembly Affairs and Conference Services, responsible for processing documents, that a new directive was in force at the Secretariat according to which reports emanating from intergovernmental bodies, such as the Consultative Process, could not exceed 25 pages in length for purposes of translation and reproduction as official United Nations documents. The draft Consultative Process report was 62 pages long. Accordingly, it was necessary to remove from the report the summary of the panel of discussions and the two statements, which are set out instead, together with the text of document A/57/80, on the web site of the Division, at www.un.org/Depts/los.

2. The four reports mentioned in paragraphs 2 to 4 are available to the General Assembly when it considers the item on "Oceans and the law of the sea" at the fifty-seventh session.

of written declaration, one or more specific means for the settlement of disputes concerning the interpretation or application of the Convention, Australia declared on 21 March 2002 that it had chosen the International Tribunal for the Law of the Sea and the International Court of Justice, without specifying that one has precedence over the other. Honduras declared, on 18 June 2002, that it had chosen the International Court. Honduras also reserved the possibility of considering any other means of peaceful settlement, including the Tribunal, as agreed on a case-by-case basis. In a declaration of 19 July 2002, Spain stated that it had chosen both the Tribunal and the International Court.

9. Under Article 298 a State may declare in writing that it does not accept any one or more of the compulsory procedures entailing binding decisions provided for in section 2 of Part 15 of UNCLOS with respect to one or more of specific categories of disputes. With reference to the provisions of that article, Australia declared that it did not accept any of the procedures provided for in section 2 of Part 15 (including the procedures it had selected under Article 287) with respect of disputes concerning the interpretation or application of Articles 15, 74 and 83 relating to sea boundary delimitations as well as those involving historic bays or titles. Spain made a similar declaration with regard to sea boundary delimitations.

10. Since the issuance of the main annual report, no States have made a declaration or statement pursuant to Article 30, paragraphs 3 and 4, of the 1995 Fish Stocks Agreement.

C. Meeting of States Parties (Twelfth Meeting)

11. The twelfth Meeting of States Parties to the United Nations Convention on the Law of the Sea was held in New York from 16 to 26 April 2002.[3] Ambassador Don MacKay of New Zealand was elected President of the twelfth Meeting. The Meeting, inter alia, considered the following issues: the budget of the International Tribunal for the Law of the Sea for the year 2003; the annual report of the Tribunal to the Meeting of States Parties; the Financial Regulations of the Tribunal; and the election of members of the Tribunal and of the Commission on the Limits of the Continental Shelf. The Meeting also dealt with the granting of observer status to the Commission, issues with respect to Article 4 of Annex 2 to UNCLOS and matters related to Article 319 of UNCLOS. The annual report of the Tribunal addressed both the administrative and the judicial functioning of the Tribunal. It also addressed the relationship between the host country and the Tribunal, including the status of the negotiations on the Headquarters Agreement (see SPLOS/74).

12. *Budget of the Tribunal.* The Meeting approved for the Tribunal a budget of US$ 7,798,300. This included a recurrent expenditure of $6,710,400 and a non-recurrent expenditure of $100,000, essentially for the acquisition of equipment. In addition, the Meeting also approved $987,900 as contingency funds to be utilized in the event of cases being submitted to it in 2003. A further amount of $500,000 was also approved to be appropriated to the Working Capital Fund of the Tribunal

3. See document SPLOS/91 for a comprehensive report of the twelfth Meeting of States Parties.

on an exceptional basis. These funds are to provide the Tribunal with the necessary financial means to consider cases to the extent that the expenditure could not be met from the contingency funds or from transfer of funds between appropriation sections. The amount was derived from savings from the financial period 2001. The total budget was based on an evolutionary approach and on the principle of zero growth.

13. *Financial Regulations.* A significant development during the Meeting was the adoption of the Financial Regulations of the Tribunal in the informal working group, with one pending issue remaining for further negotiations, the scale of assessment relating to the floor rate and a ceiling rate to be applied to contributions made by States Parties to the budget of the Tribunal. For the 2003 budget, the Meeting decided that a floor rate of 0.01 per cent and a ceiling rate of 25 per cent would be used in establishing the rate of assessment for States Parties. With regard to future budgets, it was agreed that the issue would have to be further discussed at the thirteenth Meeting.

14. Another important decision taken by the Meeting relating to the Financial Regulations was the issue of the "split currency system." The Meeting agreed that the euro would be used for the presentation of the Tribunal's budget, the determination of the annual contributions and for advances. However, it decided that payments could be made either in United States dollars or in euros. Some delegations emphasized that although the agreement reached was in conformity with the principles of savings and practicality and in line with United Nations rules, the decision should nevertheless not constitute a precedent for all international organizations to use the currency of their headquarters.

15. *Elections to the Tribunal.* The twelfth Meeting of States Parties was to elect the seven members of the Tribunal to fill the seats of those judges whose term of office was to expire on 30 September 2002. In accordance with Article 6 of the Statute of the Tribunal, Lennox Fitzroy Ballah of Trinidad and Tobago was elected to fill the vacancy and complete the term of office which became vacant as a result of the passing away on 11 September 2001 of Judge Edward Laing of Belize. The Meeting then elected Lennox Fitzroy Ballah (Trinidad and Tobago), Guangjian Xu (China), Hugo Caminos (Argentina), Jean-Pierre Cot (France), Tullio Treves (Italy), Tafsir M. Ndiaye (Senegal) and Alexander Yankov (Bulgaria) to replace those judges whose term of office was to expire.

16. *Elections to the Commission.* The Meeting also dealt with the election of 21 members of the Commission on the Limits of the Continental Shelf, in accordance with Article 2, paragraphs 3 and 4, of Annex 2 to UNCLOS (see sect. 3 on the work of the Commission).

17. *Work of the International Seabed Authority.* Pursuant to the decision of the ninth Meeting of States Parties (SPLOS/48, par. 53, and rule 37 of the Rules of Procedure for Meetings of States Parties), the Secretary-General of the International Seabed Authority, Satya N. Nandan, provided an oral report to the Meeting on recent developments with regard to the work of the Authority. He pointed out that the most significant milestone for the Authority in 2001 had been the conclusion of 15-year exploration contracts with six former pioneer investors, in accordance with the Regulations on Prospecting and Exploration for Polymetallic Nodules in the Area, approved by the Assembly of the Authority in 2000 (ISBA/6/A/18). The issuance by the Authority's Legal and Technical Commission of a set of recommen-

dations for the guidance of contractors for the assessment of possible environmental impacts arising from exploration for polymetallic nodules, was another significant achievement in the year under review. The Secretary-General outlined the main areas of focus as regards the future work of the Authority. He also introduced three scientists who made presentations in the context of the work of the Authority on cobalt-rich ferromanganese crusts and polymetallic sulphides, as well as the ecosystems in which those minerals were found.

18. *Article 319 of UNCLOS.* On matters related to Article 319 of UNCLOS, two main differing views were expressed as to the role of the Meeting of States Parties in considering issues relating to the implementation of the Convention. One view was that the Meeting should receive and consider every year a report from the Secretary-General on issues of a general nature that had arisen with respect to the Convention. Another view was that there was no legal basis in the Convention for such a role of the Meeting, and that issues relating to the implementation of the Convention were being dealt with in other forums, especially by the General Assembly. In the light of the various views expressed, the Meeting decided to retain the current item on matters related to Article 319 of UNCLOS on the provisional agenda for the thirteenth Meeting.

19. *Other matters.* In accordance with rule 18, paragraph 4, of the Rules of Procedure for Meetings of States Parties, the representative of the Seamen's Church Institute, a non-governmental organization, was invited to address the Meeting as an observer. In his statement, he drew attention to two issues: the duty to rescue persons in distress at sea and the safety of fishing vessels.

20. The Meeting also took note, with appreciation, of the decision of the General Assembly at its fifty-sixth session to devote two days of plenary meetings at the fifty-seventh session of 9 and 10 December 2002, to the commemoration of the twentieth anniversary of the opening for signature of the 1982 United Nations Convention on the Law of the Sea.

21. The thirteenth Meeting of States Parties will be held from 9 to 13 June 2003 at United Nations Headquarters.

3. MARITIME SPACE

Continental shelf beyond 200 nautical miles and work of the Commission on the Limits of the Continental Shelf

22. Since its establishment in June 1997, the Commission has held 11 sessions at United Nations Headquarters in New York. The tenth session, which took place from 25 March to 12 April 2002, was the last of the first five-year term of the Commission. The eleventh session, inaugurating the newly elected membership of the Commission, was held from 24 to 28 June 2002. The session was opened by the representative of the Secretary-General of the United Nations, Ralph Zacklin, Assistant Secretary-General in charge of the Office of Legal Affairs, who then presided over the election of the new chairman. Following consultations, Peter F. Croker was elected as Chairman by acclamation. The Commission also elected three Vice-Chairmen, Osvaldo Pedro Astiz, Lawrence Folajimi Awosika and Mladen Juracic;

and as Rapporteur, Yong-Ahn Park. All officers were elected to a term of two and a half years.[4]

23. In accordance with rule 10 of its Rules of Procedure, each member of the Commission present at the eleventh session made a solemn declaration in regard to the performance of his duties in the Commission at a ceremony convened for the occasion.

24. In addition to the election of its officers, the Commission renewed the composition of two of its standing subsidiary bodies, the Standing Committee on provision of scientific and technical advice to coastal States and the Committee on confidentiality. Upon nomination by the regional groups, the Commission elected the members of those bodies, who met and elected their officers. Philip Alexander Symonds was elected Chairman of the former Committee, and A. Bakar Jaafar as the Chairman of the latter.[5]

25. The Commission also elected the Chairmen of its two standing open-ended bodies, the Editorial Committee and the Training Committee. Harald Brekke was elected as Chairman of the Editorial Committee, and Indurlall Fagoonee was elected Chairman of the Training Committee.

26. At its eleventh session, the Commission decided not to hold the session which had originally been scheduled to be convened from 26 to 30 August 2002. Two sessions would be held in 2003, the twelfth session from 28 April to 2 May, followed by two weeks of meetings of a subcommission, in the event that a submission were to be received by the Commission. The thirteenth session was scheduled to be held from 25 to 29 August 2003.[6]

27. *Consideration of the submission made by the Russian Federation.* Although the Commission had usually held its sessions for either one or two weeks, the tenth session was of three weeks' duration in order to allow sufficient time to review the submission of the Russian Federation, which had been received by the Secretary-General on 20 December 2001.

28. The Commission had begun its tenth session formally only after the required quorum had been achieved. Mr. Yong-Ahn Park, Vice-Chairman, replaced the Chairman of the Commission, Mr. Yuri Kazmin, during the consideration of the Russian submission. The Deputy Minister of Natural Resources of the Russian Federation, Ivan Gloumov, accompanied by other experts, had been invited to make a presentation[7] of the submission to the Commission, followed by a question-and-answer period.

29. Mr. Gloumov was also requested to present the position of his Government regarding communications in respect of the Russian submission addressed to the

4. For more details on the election of the Commission, see SPLOS/91, paras. 95–101.

5. CLCS/34, paras. 15–17.

6. More detailed information regarding the work of the Commission can be found in the recent annual reports of the Secretary-General (A/57/57, paras. 53–77, A/56/58, paras. 52–82 and Add. 1, paras. 19, 30–49; A/55/61, paras. 25–29; A/54/429, paras. 55–69; A/53/456, paras. 55–69; A/52/487, paras. 43–53; and A/51/645, paras. 77–84, as well as in the report of the twelfth Meeting of States Parties (SPLOS/91, paras. 95–101), and in the statements of the Chairman of the Commission on the progress of work in the Commission, at the tenth (CLCS/32) and eleventh (CLCS/34) sessions.

7. For the text of the presentation, see CLCS/31.

Secretary-General by Canada, Denmark, Japan, Norway and the United States of America, which had been circulated by the Secretariat to States Members of the United Nations as well as to all members of the Commission.[8] He was of the view that the communications did not constitute obstacles to the consideration of the submission by the Commission.

Establishment and work of the Subcommission

30. In accordance with Article 5 of Annex 2 to the Convention, following informal consultations, a subcommission was elected to examine the Russian submission and formulate the recommendations. The Subcommission was composed of seven members, appointed in a balanced manner and taking into account specific scientific elements of the Russian Federation's submission. The composition of the Subcommission was as follows: Alexandre Tagore Medeiros de Albuquerque (Brazil), Lawrence Folajimi Awosika (Nigeria), Galo Carrera Hurtado (Mexico), Peter F. Croker (Ireland), Karl H. F. Hinz (Germany), Iain C. Lamont (New Zealand) and Yong-Ahn Park (Republic of Korea). The Subcommission elected Mr. Carrera as its Chairman, Mr. Hinz Vice-Chairman and Mr. Croker as Rapporteur.

31. Taking into account the complexity and volume of the data involved, the Subcommission considered that it was not in a position to complete the preparation of the recommendations by the end of the tenth session. The Subcommission then commenced the detailed examination of the submission and continued its work through the end of the tenth session. It met twice daily and convened 20 meetings, including 6 meetings devoted to consultations in the form of questions and answers between its members and the experts of the delegation of the Russian Federation. It requested additional information from the Russian Federation on certain elements of its submission.

32. The Subcommission reconvened from 10 to 14 June 2002, before the expiration of the term of office of the current membership of the Commission on 15 June 2002. It continued the examination of the data and other materials contained in the submission, including the additional information received on 15 May 2002. On 14 June, the Subcommission completed the recommendations and forwarded them to the eleventh session of the Commission, which was scheduled to be held from 24 to 28 June following the election of the new membership of the Commission by the Meeting of States Parties.[9]

33. The Commission at its eleventh session continued the consideration of the Russian submission. Regarding the issue of whether the representatives of the Russian Federation had a right to be present during the deliberations,[10] one member of the Commission expressed the view that, pursuant to rule 51 of the Rules of Procedure of the Commission (CLCS/3/Rev.3), Article 5 of Annex 2 to the Conven-

8. CLCS/32, paras. 1–10. The text of those communications are available on the web site of the Division for Ocean Affairs and the Law of the Sea, at www.un.org/Depts/los/clcs_new/commission_submissions.htm.

9. For more details on the establishment and work of the subcommission, see CLCS/32, paras. 12–20, and CLCS/34, paras. 29–32.

10. Rule 51 stipulates, inter alia, that "the coastal State shall, in accordance with article 5 of Annex II to the Convention, be invited to send its representatives to participate, without the right to vote, in the proceedings deemed relevant by the Commission".

tion and paragraph 16 of section 7 of the Modus Operandi of the Commission (CLCS/L.3), the representatives of the coastal State were entitled to participate in the proceedings, without the right to vote, since the discussion of the recommendations was part of the relevant proceedings referred to in Article 5. He also pointed out that, should the Rules be interpreted as preventing the participation of that State's representatives during the Commission's discussion of the recommendations of the Subcommission, the provisions of the Convention should prevail over the Rules of Procedure of the Commission.

34. An opposing view was expressed that, since the Rules of Procedure constituted a further development of the provision of Article 5 of Annex 2 and had been widely distributed, made available to all States and had met with no objections, the Commission should continue to be guided in its work by those Rules. It was emphasized that rule 51 of the Rules of Procedure provided for the participation of the coastal State "in the proceedings deemed relevant by the Commission." In addition, the representatives of the coastal State had already been invited by the Commission on two separate occasions during the tenth session to make a presentation on the submission, and furthermore, the Subcommission had held six meetings of consultations in the form of questions and answers between the members of the Subcommission and the representatives of the coastal State.

35. Moreover, in accordance with rule 4 of Annex 2 to the Rules of Procedure, as amended by the Commission at its ninth session in May 2001, "the deliberations of the Commission and subcommission on all submissions made in accordance with Article 76, paragraph 8, of the Convention shall take place in private and remain confidential." Therefore, it was stated, at the current, final stage, the Commission should consider and adopt the recommendations at a private meeting.

36. In view of the clear impossibility of achieving a consensus on the issue, the Chairman put to the vote the following question: "Do you agree that the Commission may discuss the recommendations of the subcommission and Commission in a closed meeting, and consider those proceedings as 'not relevant' for the purposes of inviting the coastal State pursuant to Article 5 of Annex 2 to the Convention and rule 51 of the Rules of Procedure of the Commission?" The vote was conducted by secret ballot, and, out of 18 members present and voting, the question was answered positively by 15 votes against 3 negative responses.

37. The Commission continued its deliberations on the recommendations in closed meetings,[11] at which the Chairman of the Subcommission, Mr. Carrera, made a presentation on its work and on its recommendations. The Commission made several amendments and adopted the recommendations by consensus. In conformity with the provisions of the Convention, the recommendations of the Commission were submitted in writing to the coastal State that had made the submission, the Russian Federation, and to the Secretary-General of the United Nations.

Recommendations of the Commission in regard to the submission made by the Russian Federation

38. The recommendations contain the results of the examination of the data and information submitted by the Russian Federation, with particular reference to the

11. The Commission also invited two former members of the Commission and the subcommission, Karl H. F. Hinz and Iain C. Lamont, as experts, to attend those parts of the proceedings of

question of the entitlement of the Russian Federation to the continental shelf beyond 200 nautical miles, as well as whether the formulae and the constraints had been applied as required by Article 76 of the Convention. The Commission presented its recommendations to the Russian Federation regarding the four areas relating to the continental shelf extending beyond 200 nautical miles contained in the submission: the Barents Sea, the Bering Sea, the Sea of Okhotsk and the Central Arctic Ocean.

39. In the case of the Barents and Bering seas, the Commission recommended to the Russian Federation, upon entry into force of the maritime boundary delimitation agreements with Norway in the Barents Sea, and with the United States of America in the Bering Sea, to transmit to the Commission the charts and coordinates of the delimitation lines as they would represent the outer limits of the continental shelf of the Russian Federation extending beyond 200 nautical miles in the Barents Sea and the Bering Sea respectively.

40. Regarding the Sea of Okhotsk, the Commission recommended to the Russian Federation to make a well-documented partial submission for its extended continental shelf in the northern part of that sea. The Commission stated that this partial submission shall not prejudice questions relating to the delimitation of boundaries between States in the south for which a submission might subsequently be made, notwithstanding the provisions regarding the 10-year time limit established by Article 4 of Annex 2 to the Convention. In order to make this partial submission, the Commission also recommended to the Russian Federation to make its best efforts to effect an agreement with Japan in accordance with paragraph 4 of Annex 1 to the Rules of Procedure of the Commission.

41. As regards the Central Arctic Ocean, the Commission recommended that the Russian Federation make a revised submission in respect of its extended continental shelf in that area based on the findings contained in the recommendations.

42. *Twelfth Meeting of States Parties to UNCLOS (16–26 April 2002) and issues relating to the Commission.* Upon the invitation of the President of the twelfth Meeting, the Chairman of the Commission, Yuri Kazmin, informed the Meeting on the work of the Commission. He also referred to the remarks made by the President of the eleventh Meeting regarding the advisability of granting observer status to the Commission (SPLOS/73, par. 60), a status that had already been granted to the Tribunal and the Authority. A number of delegations at that Meeting had expressed their belief that granting observer status to the Commission would be beneficial for the work of the Commission as well as that of the Meeting of States Parties. The members of the Commission consequently had requested the Chairman to address a letter to the President of the twelfth Meeting, conveying the view of the Commission that it would welcome its granting of observer status at the Meeting (CLCS/29, par. 22). The twelfth Meeting had this letter before it (SPLOS/76).

43. After consideration of the issue, the Meeting adopted a decision granting observer status to the Commission (SPLOS/86). A new paragraph 3 bis of rule 18 regarding the observer status of the Commission was added to the Rules of Procedure for Meetings of States Parties.

---

the eleventh session of the Commission pertinent to the work of the subcommission, which had recommended their participation in order to answer questions and provide explanations, as necessary, during the Commission's consideration of the subcommission's recommendations.

44. *Election of the members of the Commission.* According to Article 2, paragraph 3, of Annex 2 to the Convention, no less than three members of the Commission shall be elected from each geographical region. After consultations and in accordance with the understanding reached by the twelfth Meeting on 18 April 2002, for the purpose of conducting this election, the members of the Commission were elected as follows: four members from the Group of African States; six members from the Group of Asian States; three members from the Group of Eastern European States; four members from the Group of Latin American and Caribbean States; and four members from the Group of Western European and Other States.

45. One round of balloting took place. The following 21 candidates were elected: Hilal Mohamed Sultan Al-Azri (Oman), Alexandre Tagore Medeiros de Albuquerque (Brazil), Osvaldo Pedro Astiz (Argentina), Lawrence Folajimi Awosika (Nigeria), Samuel Sona Betah (Cameroon), Harald Brekke (Norway), Galo Carrera Hurtado (Mexico), Peter F. Croker (Ireland), Indurlall Fagoonee (Mauritius), Noel Newton St. Claver Francis (Jamaica), Mihai Silviu German (Romania), Abu Bakar Jaafar (Malaysia), Mladen Juracic (Croatia), Yuri Borisovitch Kazmin (Russian Federation), Wenzheng Lu (China), Yong-Ahn Park (Republic of Korea), Fernando Manuel Maia Pimentel (Portugal), Philip Alexander Symonds (Australia), Kensaku Tamaki (Japan), Naresh Kumar Thakur (India) and Yao Ubuènalè Woeledji (Togo).

46. *Trust Fund for preparation of submissions to the Commission.* Upon the recommendation of the tenth Meeting of States Parties, the General Assembly, in its resolution 55/7 of 30 October 2000, established the Trust Fund for the purpose of facilitating the preparation of submissions to the Commission on the Limits of the Continental Shelf by Developing States, in particular the least developed countries and small island developing States in compliance with Article 76 of the United Nations Convention on the Law of the Sea. The terms of reference of the Trust Fund are contained in Annex 2 to the resolution. Norway donated $1 million to the Trust Fund in 2000.[12] No reimbursements have yet been made from the Fund, although several applications to the Fund have been approved and disbursement is awaiting the completion of submission of required documents. As of the end of the six-month period of the biennium 2002–2003 (30 June 2002), the estimated balance of the Fund was $1,039,972.[13]

47. In general terms, the purpose of the Fund is to provide assistance to the developing States Parties to meet their obligations under Article 76 of the Convention, and in particular, to assist in financing the training of personnel of developing countries, to enable them to prepare submissions to the Commission with respect to the outer limits of the continental shelf beyond 200 nautical miles, as appropriate.[14]

12. See A/56/58/Add.1, par. 36.

13. The estimated balance for the Trust Fund for preparation of submissions to the Commission, as well as for other trust funds, was provided to the Division for Ocean Affairs and the Law of the Sea by the United Nations Office of Programme Planning, Budget and Accounts. The balance for the Trust Fund for attending the Consultative Process was estimated at $164,828. The balance for the Trust Fund to assist States in the settlement of disputes through the International Tribunal for the Law of the Sea was estimated at $40,956.

14. For details regarding the establishment, purpose and terms of reference of the Fund, see A/57/57, paras. 62–70.

48. Developing States that wish to apply to the Fund should address their applications to the Division for Ocean Affairs and the Law of the Sea, Office of Legal Affairs, United Nations.[15]

49. The first meeting of the panel to review applications to the Trust Fund was held in April 2002. The panel was composed of representatives from the permanent missions of Brazil, Japan, Norway, Slovakia and South Africa; applications had been received from Fiji, the Federated States of Micronesia, Papua New Guinea, Solomon Islands, Tonga, Mozambique and the Seychelles. On the basis of the recommendations of the panel, the Division approved the amounts for reimbursement for seven nominees—one national from each State which had applied—of the costs associated with the training course on the establishment of the outer limits of the continental shelf beyond 200 nautical miles in accordance with UNCLOS to be given at the Southampton Oceanography Centre, United Kingdom, from 13 to 17 May 2002. With the exception of the Micronesian candidate, all the pre-approved candidates attended the course.

50. Requests were also tentatively approved for the funding of desktop studies from four South Pacific States—Fiji, Micronesia (Federated States of), Papua New Guinea and Solomon Islands.

Workshops, training courses and symposia (2002)

51. In its resolution 55/7, the General Assembly had encouraged coastal States and relevant international organizations and institutions to consider developing and making available training courses on the delineation of the outer limits of the continental shelf beyond 200 nautical miles and on the preparation of submissions to be presented to the Commission.

52. *Training course in Brazil.* A five-day training course organized according to the outline developed by the Commission (CLCS/24) was held at Rio de Janeiro from 3 to 9 March 2002 (A/57/57, par. 74). Participants included experts from 23 countries (Angola, Argentina, Chile, Colombia, Cuba, Ecuador, Gabon, Guinea-Bissau, Guyana, Indonesia, Jamaica, Mauritius, Mozambique, Namibia, Nigeria, Papua New Guinea, Peru, Portugal, Suriname, South Africa, Trinidad and Tobago, Uruguay and Venezuela). The course was organized by Brazilian scientists directly involved in activities relating to the delineation of the outer limits of the national continental shelf, as well as by the Brazilian member of the Commission, Alexandre T. M. de Albuquerque.

53. *Southampton Oceanographic Centre.* A second training course on the establishment of the outer limits of the continental shelf beyond 200 nautical miles in accordance with UNCLOS was conducted at the Southampton Oceanography Centre from 13 to 17 May 2002. This course, partially based on the training modules developed by the Commission, had been offered for the first time in 2001. This year it was attended by 21 participants from 12 countries (Australia, Democratic Republic

15. In applications for financial assistance to the Fund, the requirements of section 4 of Annex II to General Assembly resolution 55/7 must be satisfied. Section 4 states both the purposes for which financial assistance may be sought and the detailed information to be provided by the State for each purpose. It must be emphasized that, according to the terms of reference, reimbursement may only be given upon proof of payment by the State in the form of original receipts evidencing actual expenditures for pre-approved costs.

of the Congo, Denmark, Fiji, Mauritius, Morocco, Mozambique, Papua New Guinea, Seychelles, Solomon Islands, Tonga and United States of America). Six participants were nominees of developing coastal States, primarily small island States in the Pacific region, whose expenses were authorized to be defrayed from monies from the Trust Fund for the preparation of submissions to the Commission.

54. *Workshop in Malaysia.* The Kuala Lumpur Workshop on the Delineation of the Outer Limits of the Continental Shelf was held from 8 to12 July 2002. The training module of the Kuala Lumpur Workshop was also based on the five-day training course outline prepared by the Commission (CLCS/24). The Minister for Foreign Affairs of Malaysia, Datuk Seri Syed Hamid Albar, officiated at the Workshop, which was attended by 52 participants from 15 countries (Bangladesh, Brunei Darussalam, Cambodia, Fiji, India, Indonesia, Malaysia, Mauritius, Myanmar, Pakistan, Papua New Guinea, Philippines, Maldives, Thailand and Viet Nam). It was the first workshop of its kind to be held in the Asia-Pacific region. The organizers were the National Security Division of the Prime Minister's Department, the Ministry of Foreign Affairs and the Maritime Institute of Malaysia, with the financial support of the National Petroleum Corporation of Malaysia (PETRONAS).

55. The Workshop was conducted by two current members of the Commission on the Limits of the Continental Shelf, Harald Brekke of Norway and A. Bakar Jaafar of Malaysia, together with a former member of the Commission, Karl H. F. Hinz of Germany. Two local experts, First Admiral Mohd. Rasip Hassan, formerly the Director-General of the Royal Malaysian Navy Hydrographic Department, and Tan Ah Bah of the Survey and Mapping Department, Malaysia, also participated in conducting the workshop.

56. The Kuala Lumpur Workshop also emphasized the need for coastal States, especially those bordering the South China Sea, to work jointly on activities with a view to determining the outer limits of the continental shelf beyond 200 nautical miles. It was hoped that shared arrangements would help facilitate the optimization of available limited resources through the sharing of data and expertise aimed at ensuring that the deadline of 13 May 2009 for submission to the Commission of the coastal States of the Association of South-East Asian Nations region could be met.

4. CONSERVATION AND MANAGEMENT OF MARINE LIVING RESOURCES

57. The implementation of international instruments adopted subsequent to the 1992 United Nations Conference on Environment and Development, including those relating to the conservation and management of marine living resources, has been a major focus of attention of the international community. In particular, specific reference should be made to the 1995 Fish Stocks Agreement, which, as a consequence of its entry into force, led to the informal meeting of States parties to that Agreement.

Informal meeting of States parties to the 1995 Fish Stocks Agreement

58. An informal meeting of the States parties to the 1995 Fish Stocks Agreement was held in New York from 30 to 31 July 2002, pursuant to paragraph 6 of General

Assembly resolution 56/13 of 28 November 2001, in which the Assembly had requested the Secretary-General to consult with the States parties, upon the entry into force of the Agreement, with a view to, inter alia, considering the regional, subregional and global implementation of the Agreement; making any appropriate recommendations to the General Assembly on the scope and content of the annual report of the Secretary-General relating to the Agreement; and preparing for the review conference to be convened by the Secretary-General pursuant to Article 36 of the Agreement.

59. Following the adoption of the agenda of the meeting, States parties were given the opportunity to provide information on actions they had taken to implement the Agreement at the national and international levels. While many States parties detailed the development of domestic implementation measures they had taken, it was also noted that, in general, implementation of the Agreement was still in its early stages. A number of States parties cited the Western and Central Pacific Fisheries Convention as an example of a new regional fisheries management organization incorporating principles contained in the Agreement. Several States parties also noted the impact that effective implementation of the Agreement could have on deterring and eliminating illegal, unreported and unregulated fishing activities.

60. *Provisions of Part 7 of the Agreement.* At the informal meeting an extensive discussion was also conducted on the provisions of Part 7 of the Agreement concerning the requirements of developing States, including specific calls for cooperation with and assistance to developing States. All participants in the meeting agreed that effective implementation of Part 7 would be crucial to the successful implementation of the Agreement generally. A number of States parties described bilateral, subregional, regional and global programmes of assistance currently under way. The participants considered that such a multi-tiered approach would need to continue and expand as part of a coordinated programme of assistance. The States parties agreed on a set of recommendations aimed at facilitating the implementation of Part 7 of the Agreement in respect of the special requirements of developing States, including the provision of financial and technical assistance to developing States parties to assist them in realizing their rights and meeting their obligations under the Agreement, and in general to assist them in deriving benefits from participating in the Agreement.

61. *Scope and content of the biannual report.* With reference to the scope and content of the biannual report of the Secretary-General in the light of the entry into force of the Agreement, participants recognized the usefulness of the report of the Secretary-General as a tool to monitor the effective implementation of the Agreement. It was suggested that future reports could include an analysis of the status of implementation as well as a summary of submissions received from States and intergovernmental organizations. Participants recognized that an analytical approach would require that additional resources be allocated to the Secretariat. The meeting also considered whether the Secretary-General should request reports from States on an annual or a biannual basis. Some delegations suggested that non-parties as well as parties should be encouraged to increase their reporting on implementation of the Agreement.

62. *Questionnaire.* In addition, participants agreed to recommend that the General Assembly consider the creation of a questionnaire to be disseminated among States, soliciting more detailed information on their implementation of the Agree-

ment. The questionnaire would be similar to that used by the Food and Agriculture Organization of the United Nations (FAO) to monitor implementation of the Code of Conduct for Responsible Fisheries. It was considered that future reports of the Secretary-General on the implementation of the Agreement adopting such a format might facilitate an ongoing exchange of views on implementation strategies.

63. *Review conference.* With respect to preparations for the review conference called for in Article 36 of the Agreement, to take place four years after its entry into force, delegates considered that it was premature to address that issue at the informal meeting, as the conference would likely be held in late 2005 or early 2006. The Secretariat clarified that if additional resources were required for the review conference, a request could be included in the appropriate General Assembly resolution in 2004.

64. *Future resolutions of the General Assembly.* As to the periodicity of the future General Assembly resolutions on fisheries-related issues, many delegates noted the heavy schedule of that body for its regular session in Fall 2002, where it would have to consider simultaneously both the resolution on the 1995 Fish Stocks Agreement and the resolution on the global moratorium on large-scale pelagic drift-net fishing and associated issues. There was general support for the General Assembly to move to one fisheries-related resolution negotiated on an annual basis after 2002. However, views differed on the future direction for such a resolution.

65. *Range of topics for the next informal meeting.* In relation to the timing of the next informal meeting of the States parties to the Agreement, the delegates participating in the meeting recommended that a second meeting be held in approximately one year's time in New York. They also expressed the view that the details of the terms of reference for the voluntary trust fund on the implementation of Part 7 would be a key item on the agenda of the next meeting. Consequently, one prerequisite for such a meeting would be the availability of information from the background study on the implementation of Part 7, including a study of current activities.

66. Delegates also recommended that the next informal meeting of States parties include a broader range of topics relevant to the Agreement. Provisions relating to the precautionary approach and Part 6 of the Agreement (Compliance and Enforcement) were two issue areas suggested by some delegations. In addition, Canada announced its intention to host an international conference on the Agreement sometime in 2004 or 2005, with results to be forwarded to the review conference. It was agreed that future informal meetings of States parties to the Agreement should coordinate their activities with those of the conference to be organized by Canada to maximize the utility and supportiveness of these meetings.

67. As indicated in paragraph 6 of General Assembly resolution 56/13, the purposes and objectives of the informal meeting of States parties are to contribute to the subregional, regional and global implementation of the Fish Stocks Agreement.

68. *Summary of recommendations.* For these purposes, the meeting adopted a summary of recommendations concerning the implementation of Part 7, including a recommendation to the General Assembly to explore the establishment of a voluntary trust fund at the global level to support the implementation of Part 7. It was noted that the voluntary trust fund, as part of the broader programme of assistance, would enable developing States parties to exercise their right more fully and fulfil their obligations under the Agreement. Participants identified the background study

on the implementation of Part 7 called for in paragraph 8 of resolution 56/13, as a critical prerequisite to the establishment of a voluntary trust fund. To facilitate early completion of such a study, the United Kingdom offered to provide technical assistance to the Division for Ocean Affairs and the Law of the Sea, which is the secretariat of the Agreement.

69. In accordance with the recommendations of the informal meeting of States parties to the 1995 Fish Stocks Agreement, the General Assembly should undertake the following actions:

(a) A programme of assistance with multiple components in favour of developing States parties should be established under Part 7 of the Agreement to complement existing programmes at the bilateral, regional and global levels;
(b) One component of such a programme should be the establishment of a voluntary trust fund dedicated to the implementation of the objectives set forth in Articles 25 and 26 in Part 7 of the Agreement, to be managed by FAO in consultation with the Division for Ocean Affairs and the Law of the Sea of the Office of Legal Affairs;
(c) The following activities might be considered for early implementation through the voluntary trust fund:
   (i) Facilitation of participation by developing States in regional and subregional fisheries management organizations and arrangements, e.g., by defraying their membership dues and travel costs to such meetings;
   (ii) Provision of travel costs for the participation of developing States in meetings of relevant global organizations;
   (iii) Capacity-building activities in key areas such as monitoring, control and surveillance, data collection and scientific research;
   (iv) Support for ongoing and future negotiations to establish new regional or subregional fisheries management organizations and arrangements in areas without such bodies currently in place, and to strengthen existing subregional and regional fisheries management organizations and arrangements;
   (v) Exchange of information and experience in the implementation of the Agreement;
(d) The Secretary-General should convene a second informal meeting of States parties to the 1995 Fish Stocks Agreement in 2003, for the purposes and objectives of following up discussions initiated at the informal meeting in July 2002 on the implementation of Part 7 of the Agreement, including the establishment of the trust fund to assist developing States parties, and with a view to implementing other key provisions of the Agreement;
(e) The Secretary-General should invite the United Nations Development Programme, FAO and other specialized agencies, the Commission on Sustainable Development, the World Bank, the Global Environment Facility and other relevant international financial institutions, regional fishery bodies and arrangements, and relevant non-governmental organizations to attend the next informal meeting of the States parties to the Agreement.

5. REVIEW BY THE GENERAL ASSEMBLY OF DEVELOPMENTS IN OCEAN AFFAIRS: UNITED NATIONS OPEN-ENDED INFORMAL CONSULTATIVE PROCESS ESTABLISHED BY THE GENERAL ASSEMBLY IN ITS RESOLUTION 54/33 IN ORDER TO FACILITATE THE ANNUAL REVIEW BY THE ASSEMBLY OF DEVELOPMENTS IN OCEAN AFFAIRS

70. It is recalled that the General Assembly, by its resolution 54/33 of 24 November 1999, decided to establish an open-ended informal consultative process in order to facilitate the annual review by the Assembly, in an effective and constructive manner, of overall developments in ocean affairs.

71. Pursuant to paragraph 3 (e) of resolution 54/33 and after consultations with Member States, the President of the General Assembly reappointed Tuiloma Neroni Slade (Samoa) and Alan Simcock (United Kingdom) as co-chairpersons of the third meeting of the Consultative Process, which was held at United Nations Headquarters from 8 to 15 April 2002.

72. *Third meeting of the Consultative Process: format and agenda.* The co-chairpersons held an informal preparatory meeting on 15 February 2002 at United Nations Headquarters in order to consult with delegations on the format and agenda of the third meeting of the Consultative Process. Following the practice of the two previous meetings, the third meeting adopted its format and agenda by consensus. The format of the meetings provided, among other things, the opportunity to receive input from major groups, as identified in Agenda 21, especially non-governmental organizations, and worked through plenary sessions and two discussion panels, having each a specific subject area of concentration. The areas of focus for each of the two discussion panels were as follows:

(a) Protection and preservation of the marine environment:
- Integrated approach to the protection and preservation of the marine environment, and to the conservation and management of its resources
- International rules and standards and their enforcement
- Practical measures to underpin States' activities—monitoring and assessment; collective response to emergencies and regional considerations;

(b) Capacity-building, regional cooperation and integrated ocean management.

73. The third meeting of the Consultative Process took up once again the subject of the protection and preservation of the marine environment (previously discussed at the first meeting in 2000) in order to better coordinate the work of the Process with the World Summit on Sustainable Development.

74. Consistent with the legal framework provided by UNCLOS and the goals of chapter 17 of Agenda 21, the third meeting of the Consultative Process discussed the annual report of the Secretary-General on oceans and the law of the sea and suggested particular issues to be considered by the General Assembly, with an emphasis on identifying areas where coordination and cooperation at the intergovernmental and inter-agency levels should be enhanced.

6. WORLD SUMMIT ON SUSTAINABLE DEVELOPMENT

75. The World Summit on Sustainable Development was held at Johannesburg, South Africa, from 26 August to 4 September 2002. In accordance with General Assembly resolution 55/199, the conference was organized in the context of a 10-year review of progress achieved in the implementation of the outcome of the United Nations Conference on Environment and Development in 1992 at the summit level to reinvigorate the global commitment to sustainable development.[16]

76. *Two main documents of the Summit.* The Summit negotiated and adopted two main documents: the Johannesburg Declaration on Sustainable Development[17] and the Plan of Implementation of the World Summit on Sustainable Development.[18] Oceans issues, including those pertaining to the implementation of UNCLOS, are dealt with in part 4 of the Plan of Implementation, under the key thematic area "Protecting and managing the natural resource base of economic and social development." Part 7 of the Plan of Implementation addresses the thematic area of "Sustainable development of small island developing States."

77. *The Summit and the Consultative Process.* As part of an integrated effort to assist in the negotiations at the Summit, the General Assembly, in its resolution 56/12 of 28 November 2001, recommended that in its deliberations on the report of the Secretary-General on oceans and the law of the sea, the third meeting of the Consultative Process should organize its discussions on: (a) protection and preservation of the marine environment; and (b) capacity-building, regional cooperation and coordination, and integrated ocean management, as important cross-cutting issues to address ocean affairs, such as marine science and transfer of technology, sustainable fisheries, the degradation of the marine environment and the safety of navigation (see par. 81 below). The Plan of Implementation of the World Summit on Sustainable Development in fact takes note of the work of the Consultative Process and of the upcoming review of its effectiveness and utility, to be held at the fifty-seventh session of the General Assembly. The report on the work on the Consultative Process at its third meeting was in fact made available to the Fourth Summit Preparatory Committee, held from 27 May to 7 June 2002 in Bali, Indonesia.

78. In the context of oceans and seas, the outcomes of both the World Summit on Sustainable Development and the third meeting of the Consultative Process identified in the majority of cases common issues and areas where action is needed.

79. Both the Plan of Implementation and the report of the Consultative Process underlined the importance of oceans and seas as essential components of the Earth's ecosystem and critical elements for global food security and for sustaining economic prosperity and the well-being of many national economies, particularly in developing countries. In this context the need for coordination and cooperation in integrated ocean management at all levels, within the context of UNCLOS and chapter 17 of Agenda 21, was recognized as essential. The need to establish an effective,

16. For details on preparations for the Summit, see A/57/57, paras. 497–511.

17. *Report of the World Summit on Sustainable Development, Johannesburg, South Africa, 20 August–4 September 2002.* A/CONF.199/20, chap. I, resolution 1, Annex.

18. Ibid., resolution 2, Annex.

transparent and regular inter-agency coordination mechanism on ocean and coastal issues within the United Nations system was particularly highlighted.

80. *Coastal and ocean management.* The promotion of integrated, multidisciplinary and multisectoral coastal and ocean management at the national level is at the core of both documents, with special attention to the need to build capacity in order to assist developing countries and countries with economies in transition in this endeavour. The importance of regional cooperation and coordination, especially between the relevant regional organizations and programmes, the regional seas programmes of the United Nations Environment Programme (UNEP), regional fisheries management organizations and other regional science, health and development organizations, was also emphasized.

81. *Sustainable fisheries.* In the context of sustainable fisheries, the Summit document required action to be taken in order to maintain or restore stocks to levels that can produce the maximum sustainable yield, with the aim of achieving these goals for depleted stocks on an urgent basis and, where possible, not later than in the year 2015. To achieve an improvement in the regulation of all aspects of fisheries management, both the Summit and the Consultative Process called for the implementation of an ecosystem-based approach and underlined the importance of ratifying, acceding to and implementing the relevant international instruments and putting into effect the FAO international plans of action. Both documents underline the central role of regional fisheries organizations and arrangements and the necessary actions needed on their part to achieve sustainable fisheries. The Summit document also focused on the need to eliminate subsidies that contribute to illegal, unreported and unregulated fishing and to over-capacity; to strengthen donor coordination and partnerships between international financial institutions, bilateral agencies and other relevant stakeholders to enable developing countries to develop their national, regional and subregional capacities for infrastructure and integrated management and the sustainable use of fisheries; and to support the sustainable development of aquaculture.

82. *Conservation and management of the oceans.* In the context of the conservation and management of the oceans, the need to maintain the productivity and biodiversity of important and vulnerable marine and coastal areas, including in areas within and beyond national jurisdiction, was addressed both by the Summit and by the Consultative Process. The ecosystem approach, the elimination of destructive fishing practices, the establishment of marine protected areas consistent with international law and based on scientific information, and the integration of marine and coastal areas management into key sectors were some of the approaches and tools identified to achieve this goal. The Summit document established a time frame for representative networks of marine protected areas to be set up by 2012.

83. *Protection and preservation of the marine environment.* In the context of the protection and preservation of the marine environment, actions at all levels to prevent, reduce and control pollution from land-based sources were identified as a priority. An essential requirement in this respect was the implementation of the 1995 Global Programme of Action and the 2001 Montreal Declaration on the protection of the marine environment from land-based activities. In order to prevent, reduce and control the pollution of the marine environment from all sources, it was underlined that existing international instruments and regulations, in particular those developed in the context of the International Maritime Organization (IMO),

needed to be ratified and implemented. The need to expedite the development of new measures, such as the IMO International Convention on the Control and Management of Ships' Ballast Water and Sediments, was also emphasized.

84. *Assessment of marine and coastal ecosystems.* The important role of scientific information and the need for the regular assessment of marine and coastal ecosystems was identified as a fundamental basis for sound decision-making. In particular, a request was put forward for the establishment of a mechanism for global reporting and assessment of the state of the marine environment, including socio-economic aspects, both current and foreseeable, building on existing regional assessments: the Plan of Implementation of the World Summit on Sustainable Development indicated 2004 as a deadline for the establishment of such a mechanism. The need for capacity-building in marine science, especially to help to meet the special needs of developing countries and countries with economies in transition, was also stressed.

85. *Small island developing States.* In relation to the sustainable development of small island developing States, chapter 7 of the Plan of Implementation, identifies small island developing States as a special case for both environmental and developmental reasons. The document calls for action in a number of areas, such as: implementation of chapter 17 of Agenda 21[19] and the Programme of Action for the Sustainable Development of Small Island Developing States (Barbados Programme of Action); implementation of sustainable fisheries management and improvement of financial returns from fisheries, by supporting and strengthening relevant regional fisheries management organizations; elaboration of specific initiatives, in delimiting and managing in a sustainable manner their coastal areas and exclusive economic zones and the continental shelf, as well as relevant regional management initiatives within the context of UNCLOS and the UNEP regional seas programmes; provision of support, including for capacity-building, for example for programmes of work on marine and coastal biological diversity; and implementation of the Global Programme of Action for the Protection of the Marine Environment from Land-based Activities by 2004.

7. CONCLUSIONS

86. The year 2002 marks the twentieth anniversary of the opening for signature of the 1982 United Nations Convention on the Law of the Sea. This year the Commission on the Limits of the Continental Shelf considered the first submission by a coastal State, the Russian Federation, regarding the outer limits of its continental shelf beyond 200 nautical miles, and adopted its recommendations on the matter. This event is further evidence of the successful functioning of the mechanisms established by the Convention. Several coastal States are also at an advanced stage of preparation of their submissions to the Commission, thus making further progress towards securing maritime boundaries.

87. The third meeting of the Consultative Process revisited the subject of the protection and preservation of the marine environment in order to better coordi-

19. Chapter 17, sect. G, of Agenda 21 relates specifically to the sustainable development of small island developing States.

nate the work of the Process with the World Summit on Sustainable Development, which was convened in Johannesburg. During the current session, the General Assembly will undertake its annual review and evaluation of the implementation of the Convention and other developments relating to ocean affairs and the law of the sea, and will assess the effectiveness of the consultative process.

88. The Plan of Implementation of the World Summit on sustainable Development emphasized once again the importance of addressing the sustainable development of oceans and seas and provided for the further implementation of chapter 17 of Agenda 21. The Plan of Implementation sets out commitments to actions at all levels to ensure the sustainable development of the oceans, including sustainable fisheries, the promotion of the conservation and management of the oceans, the enhancement of maritime safety, the protection of the marine environment from pollution and the improvement of scientific understanding and assessment of marine and coastal ecosystems as a fundamental basis for sound decision-making.

89. The first informal meeting of States parties to the 1995 Fish Stocks Agreement was convened in July 2002; it recommended a number of actions to be undertaken by the General Assembly, including the establishment of a programme of assistance with multiple components in favour of developing States parties to complement existing programmes at the bilateral, regional and global levels.

90. It is remarkable to see that different forums, including the World Summit, have finally adopted a unified approach to oceans and seas under the general framework of UNCLOS and the goals of chapter 17 of Agenda 21.

United Nations Convention on the Law of the Sea, Report of the Twelfth Meeting of States Parties, from 16–26 April 2002[†]

CONTENTS

[†]EDITORS' NOTE.—This document was provided by the United Nations Division for Ocean Affairs and the Law of the Sea (DOALOS) and is extracted from United Nations Convention on the Law of the Sea: Meeting of the States Parties, Twelfth Meeting, SPLOS/91, 13 June 2002, available online at the DOALOS Web site: http://www.un.org/Depts/los/.

1. INTRODUCTION

1. The twelfth Meeting of States Parties to the United Nations Convention on the Law of the Sea was convened at United Nations Headquarters from 16 to 26 April 2002, in accordance with Article 319, paragraph 2 (e), of the Convention and the decision taken by the General Assembly at its fifty-sixth session (resolution 56/12, par. 9).

2. Pursuant to that decision and in accordance with rule 5 of the Rules of Procedure for Meetings of States Parties (SPLOS/2/Rev.3), invitations to participate in the Meeting were addressed by the Secretary-General of the United Nations to all States Parties to the Convention. Invitations were also addressed to observers in conformity with rule 18 of the Rules of Procedure (SPLOS/2/Rev.3/Add.1), including to the President and the Registrar of the International Tribunal for the Law of the Sea and the Secretary-General of the International Seabed Authority.

2. ORGANIZATION OF WORK

A. Opening of the Twelfth Meeting of States Parties and Election of Officers

3. The twelfth Meeting of States Parties was opened by the President of the eleventh Meeting, Ambassador Cristián Maquieira (Chile).

4. The Meeting elected by acclamation Ambassador Don Mackay (New Zealand) as President of the twelfth Meeting of States Parties.

5. The Meeting also elected the representatives of Honduras, Indonesia, Sierra Leone and Ukraine as Vice-Presidents.

B. Introductory Statement by the President

6. In his opening statement, the President extended a welcome to all delegations participating in the Meeting and in particular, to Bangladesh, Madagascar and Hungary which, since the eleventh Meeting, had become States Parties to the United Nations Convention on the Law of the Sea, bringing the total number of Parties to 138. He urged the reaffirmation of the commitment of all Parties to reach the common objective of universal participation in the Convention.

7. Noting the presence of the President of the International Tribunal for the Law of the Sea and its Registrar, the Secretary-General of the International Seabed

Authority and the Chairman of the Commission on the Limits of the Continental Shelf, the President emphasized that the institutions created under the United Nations Convention on the Law of the Sea continued to carry out their mandates effectively. He stated that the Tribunal had had two cases submitted to it since May 2001; the Authority had signed 15-year contracts for exploration for polymetallic nodules with all seven registered pioneer investors as of March 2002; and the Commission on the Limits of the Continental Shelf had received and begun the consideration of its first submission. The submission was from the Russian Federation.

8. As a follow-up to some of the recommendations made at the previous Meeting regarding the four trust funds which had been recommended by the tenth Meeting of States Parties and approved by the General Assembly, the President informed the Meeting that the financial statements on three of the trust funds would be made available to delegations upon request. The fourth trust fund, to defray the cost of participation of the members of the Commission on the Limits of the Continental Shelf from developing countries in the meetings of the Commission, had not as yet received any contribution.

9. The President then outlined the provisional agenda for the Meeting (SPLOS/L.23), noting that a number of the items dealt with matters related to the International Tribunal for the Law of the Sea, and that three items related to the Commission on the Limits of the Continental Shelf.

10. With respect to elections, he recalled that three elections were scheduled during the meeting:

(a) One to elect a member of the Tribunal to fill the vacancy created as a result of the passing away of Judge Edward Laing of Belize, which sad event had taken place on 11 September 2001. The documents relating to that election were SPLOS/77 and SPLOS/78;

(b) Another to elect seven members of the Tribunal to replace the members whose term of office would end in September 2002. The documents relating to that election were SPLOS/77 and SPLOS/78 and Corr.1;

(c) Finally, an election of all 21 members of the Commission on the Limits of the Continental Shelf. The relevant documents are SPLOS/79, SPLOS/80 and SPLOS/81.

11. Following the statement by the President, a number of delegations made general as well as congratulatory statements.

C. Adoption of the Agenda and Organization of Work

12. The Meeting considered the provisional agenda for the twelfth Meeting (SPLOS/L.23). The agenda as adopted is contained in document SPLOS/83.

3. REPORT OF THE CREDENTIALS COMMITTEE

13. The Meeting of States Parties appointed a Credentials Committee consisting of the following nine members: Angola, Fiji, Grenada, Malta, Mexico, Monaco, Philippines, Poland and Uganda.

14. The Credentials Committee held three meetings, on 18, 19 and 23 April 2002. The Committee elected Piotr Ogonowski (Poland) as Chairman. At its meetings, the Committee examined the credentials of representatives to the twelfth Meeting of States Parties. It accepted the credentials submitted by the representatives of all Parties to the Convention, including the European Community (138). On 19 April 2002, the Meeting of States Parties approved the first report of the Committee (SPLOS/84 and Add.1). The second report of the Committee (SPLOS/85) was approved on 23 April 2002.

4. MATTERS RELATED TO THE INTERNATIONAL TRIBUNAL FOR THE LAW OF THE SEA

A. Annual Report of the Tribunal

15. The annual report of the Tribunal for the calendar year 2001 (SPLOS/74) was submitted to the Meeting of States Parties under rule 6, paragraph 3 (d), of the Rules of Procedure for Meeting of States Parties.

16. P. Chandrasekhara Rao, President of the Tribunal, introduced the report, on behalf of the Tribunal.

17. He officially informed the Meeting that Judge Edward Arthur Laing, had passed away in Belize on 11 September 2001 and expressed condolences. Judge Laing's term was due to expire on 30 September 2002. He had made an active contribution to the work of the Tribunal. In particular, he was chairman of its Information Technology Committee.

18. The President of the Tribunal informed the Meeting that the Tribunal on 20 September 2001 had elected Philippe Gautier of Belgium as its Registrar following the resignation of Gritakumar Chitty. Mr. Gautier had first been elected Deputy Registrar of the Tribunal in 1996. Following the same procedure, the Tribunal on 12 March 2002 elected Doo-Young Kim of the Republic of Korea as its Deputy Registrar.

19. Prior to the election of the Registrar, the Tribunal, after due consideration of the practice of other similar bodies, amended article 32 of the Rules of the Tribunal, reducing the term of office of the Registrar and of the Deputy Registrar from seven to five years.

20. On the judicial side of the work of the Tribunal, the President stated that during 2001 the Tribunal had been seized of three cases: the "Grand Prince" case between Belize and France; the "Chaisiri Reefer 2" case between Panama and Yemen; and the MOX Plant case between Ireland and the United Kingdom of Great Britain and Northern Ireland. The judgment in the "Grand Prince" case, delivered

on 20 April 2001, underlined the importance of the need to establish the status of the applicant as the flag State at all relevant times before an application for the release of a vessel or its crew from detention was made in accordance with Article 292 of the Convention. As regards the "Chaisiri Reefer 2" case, at the request of the parties, the proceedings were discontinued and the case was removed from the list submitted to the Tribunal. This was a case, the President stated, in which the availability of relief by the Tribunal had helped to promote an out-of-court settlement.

21. The third case, the MOX Plant case, under Article 290, paragraph 5, of the Convention, included a request for provisional measures. It involved issues concerning the protection of the marine environment. In its Order of 3 December 2001, the Tribunal found that the situation did not require the prescription of the provisional measures as requested by Ireland. However, the Tribunal did prescribe certain provisional measures in the matter of cooperation between the parties and declared, among other things, that "the duty to cooperate is a fundamental principle in the prevention of pollution of the marine environment under Part XII of the Convention and general international law and that rights arise therefrom, which the Tribunal may consider appropriate to preserve under Article 290 of the Convention." The President of the Tribunal also informed the Meeting that the parties had appointed Judge Mensah, a former President of the Tribunal, as President of the arbitral tribunal in the MOX Plant case, established under Annex VII to the Convention.

22. The President of the Tribunal recalled General Assembly resolution 56/12 of 28 November 2001, in which the Assembly had underlined what it referred to as the Tribunal's "important role and authority concerning the interpretation or application of the Convention." While the Tribunal's accomplishments had not been insignificant, it was obvious that the Tribunal had not been put to full use. The Tribunal would be able to live up to the expectations of the international community only when litigants, especially States, made full use of the institution. He hoped that States would make declarations under Article 287 of the Convention choosing the Tribunal as the means for the settlement of disputes concerning the Convention.

23. The General Assembly, the President continued, had made recommendations of interest to the Tribunal, three of which required special mention. First, under the heading "Effective functioning" of the Tribunal, the Assembly had made an appeal to all States Parties to pay their assessed contributions to the Tribunal in full and on time. The President reported that, as of 28 February 2002, there was an unpaid balance of assessed contributions in relation to the budgets of the Tribunal for the years 1996 to 2001 in the amount of US$ 1,189,879; the outstanding amount in relation to the 2002 budget was $5,677,976.

24. The General Assembly had also called upon States that had not done so to consider ratifying or acceding to the Agreement on the Privileges and Immunities of the Tribunal. It was a matter of special satisfaction that the Agreement had entered into force on 30 December 2001 after the ratification of 10 States. The vast majority of States had yet to take steps to become parties to the Agreement, which had a bearing on the effective functioning of the Tribunal.

25. Thirdly, the General Assembly had underlined the importance of the Trust Fund established by the Secretary-General of the United Nations, pursuant to General Assembly resolution 55/7 of 30 October 2000, for the purpose of assisting States in the settlement of disputes through the Tribunal. The Assembly had invited States and others to make voluntary contributions to the Trust Fund. The President hoped that contributions would be forthcoming to make the Fund useful. He emphasized that financial hardship should not stand in the way of seeking recourse to the Tribunal. Steps should also be taken to see that wide publicity was given to the Fund.

26. The President informed the Meeting that by an exchange of letters in May and June 2001, the Tribunal and the United Nations had entered into an agreement extending the competence of the United Nations Administrative Tribunal to the staff members of the Tribunal. More recently, in March 2002, it was agreed, by a further exchange of letters, that the Division for Ocean Affairs and the Law of the Sea of the Office of Legal Affairs of the United Nations would act as the liaison office for the Tribunal, whereby the Division would provide all the administrative services of the Tribunal required in New York.

27. Agreements on cooperation in information-sharing were also entered into by the Registry with the Appellate Body Secretariat of the World Trade Organization (WTO), the Legal Affairs Division of the WTO Secretariat and the International Hydrographic Organization.

28. In conclusion, the President noted that the relations between the Tribunal and the host country, the Federal Republic of Germany, had remained very cordial. However, the Headquarters Agreement had yet to be finalized. He hoped that the outstanding issues would be resolved soon, in accordance with well-established international conventions and practices in that regard.

29. The Meeting took note with appreciation of the report of the Tribunal.

B. Budget of the Tribunal for 2003

30. The President of the Tribunal, in introducing the draft budget of the Tribunal for 2003 (SPLOS/WP.16), underlined that the budget proposals had been prepared on the basis of the evolutionary approach, in accordance with the decisions of the Meeting of States Parties. He emphasized that the proposals, amounting to $7.81 million, were based on the principle of zero growth and in fact represented a slight decrease compared with the approved budget for 2002.

31. He identified budget items for which an increased level of funds was being requested compared with the 2002 level. These were: the Judges' Pension Scheme; maintenance of premises; library; general temporary assistance; and the contingency fund.

32. With regard to the Judges' Pension Scheme, he noted that in 2002, the terms of seven judges would expire, five of whom would be entitled to receive a pension if they were not re-elected. Existing provisions had only been made for

meeting obligations in respect of four retiring judges. The provisions would also continue to cover pensions currently being paid.

33. With respect to the maintenance and security of its new premises, the President stated that at the time of preparation of the budget for 2002, the Tribunal had only had four months' experience in assessing the costs required for the maintenance of the new premises. The Tribunal had currently been occupying the new premises for an entire year. In the light of the experience gained, it was now necessary to increase the provision for maintenance of premises in 2003. As regards the library of the Tribunal, while the start-up costs had been set at the seventh Meeting of States Parties at $60,000 per year for the first five years, an increase in this provision was now required to cover operational costs, in order to maintain the acquisition of serial publications and to continue to develop the library's collections.

34. The President also stated that, for 2003, a new post of Archivist was proposed at the P-2 level. The new post was necessitated by the large number of documents involved in the work of the Tribunal and the technical nature of the task of managing the Tribunal's documents and archives.

35. He drew attention to the increase in the appropriation proposed for contingency. On the basis of the experience gained in 2001, provision had been made for two judges ad hoc in contingency, compared to one judge ad hoc in 2002. As in the past, the sum provided for in contingency would only be used when cases were submitted to the Tribunal.

36. In order to maintain a zero-growth approach, the President stated, it had become necessary to decrease the amount of several budget lines. This had been achieved by reassessing needs and by postponing certain expenditures.

37. The budget proposals were first considered in an open-ended working group under the chairmanship of the President of the Meeting. Delegations expressed their appreciation to the President of the Tribunal on maintaining a zero-growth budget, which was indicative of an efficiently run organization. One delegation requested more background information on various proposals contained in the new budget. Concerning the new post of Archivist, it was explained that while in the past the Tribunal had merely classified its own documents, currently it was producing as well as receiving an increasing number of administrative and case-related documents, which required a well-developed archiving system. On a question relating to the library, it was recalled that the library was a primary facility in a court environment and that it needed to be well equipped to serve its purpose. Taking into account the fact that the library of the Tribunal had just completed its initial development phase, a number of factors necessitated the increase in budgetary allocation, including the higher price of many periodicals and the need to acquire monographs, many of which were expensive. With regard to the maintenance of premises, the requested increase was attributed mainly to the fact that since the inauguration of its new modern and sophisticated premises, the Tribunal was now fully responsible for the maintenance of its buildings and services. This included in particular the necessity to maintain existing warranties on equipment until their

expiration date. At such time, the Tribunal would renegotiate different contracts which might involve reduced costs and better terms and conditions.

38. The Working Group agreed on the draft budget of the Tribunal for 2003, as proposed by the Tribunal in document SPLOS/WP.16. On the basis of the agreement in the Working Group (SPLOS/L.27), the Meeting approved the budget of the Tribunal for 2003, which is contained in document SPLOS/90.

39. The approved budget amounted to a total of $7,798,300, including: (a) a recurrent expenditure of $6,710,400; and (b) a non-recurrent expenditure of $100,000, essentially for the acquisition of equipment. With a view to providing the Tribunal with the necessary financial means to consider cases in 2003, the Meeting of States Parties approved $987,900 as contingency funds of the Tribunal, which shall only be used in the event of cases being submitted to the Tribunal. The contingency funds include an amount intended to meet the compensation of two judges ad hoc when required.

40. Further, the Meeting of States Parties approved (SPLOS/89), on an exceptional basis, an additional amount of $500,000 to be appropriated to the Working Capital Fund of the Tribunal, to provide the Tribunal with the necessary financial means to consider cases to the extent that the expenditure could not be met from the contingency funds or from transfer of funds between appropriation sections. The funds were derived from savings from the financial period 2001, and were to be used only in the event of a temporary shortfall in funds.

41. During discussions on the above issue, one delegation emphasized that its agreement with the decision in document SPLOS/89 was based on the caveat that such appropriation was only to prevent future bottlenecks for the Tribunal. He called upon the Tribunal to stay alert and to aim at providing a long-term forecast of its caseload. He cautioned that any type of increase in the contingency fund would have a negative impact.

42. With respect to savings from the budgets of the Tribunal for 1998, 1999 and 2000, the Meeting, on the basis of a working paper prepared by the Tribunal (SPLOS/WP.18), decided that the Tribunal should surrender the savings from those years, as indicated in the working paper, in compliance with the Financial Regulations of the United Nations. The Meeting furthermore decided that a deduction of the amount of such savings should be made from the assessed contributions of States Parties for 2003, (SPLOS/87).

43. With respect to a proposed staff assessment fund, the Meeting had before it a working paper prepared by the Tribunal (SPLOS/WP.19). The Meeting decided that the Tribunal should continue with its current practice with regard to staff assessment pending the adoption of a decision based on a detailed proposal to be submitted by the Tribunal to the thirteenth Meeting of States Parties (SPLOS/88).

44. The budget of the Tribunal for 2003, including its contingency fund and the appropriation to its Working Capital Fund, are to be financed by all States and international organizations that are party to the United Nations Convention on the Law of the Sea. The contributions to be made by States Parties are to be based upon the scale of assessment for the regular budget of the United Nations for the

corresponding financial year, adjusted to take account of participation in the Convention (see also paras. 50–53). The European Community indicated that its contribution to the budget would amount to $77,000.

C. Financial Regulations of the Tribunal

45. The Financial Regulations of the Tribunal (SPLOS/WP.17) were discussed in an open-ended working group which was chaired by the President of the Meeting. Document SPLOS/WP.17, which had been prepared by the Secretariat, contained the provisions proposed by the Tribunal and the corresponding provisions from the United Nations and the International Seabed Authority, as requested by the eleventh Meeting of States Parties (SPLOS/73, par. 40). The document also reflected some of the proposals contained in SPLOS/CRP.19 and SPLOS/CRP.27. In considering the working paper, delegations took into account two informal papers: (a) an informal paper dated 18 May 2001, as circulated by the President at the eleventh Meeting of States Parties, containing regulations that had been tentatively agreed upon by the working group at that Meeting; and (b) an informal paper dated 15 March 2002, containing proposals presented by the Tribunal. The Working Group had before it document SPLOS/CRP.29, which also contained a number of proposals by the Tribunal relating to an earlier version of the Financial Regulations (SPLOS/WP.14). The examination of the matter further benefited from references to similar rules adopted for the International Criminal Court (PCNICC/2001/1/Add.2).

46. The Working Group held five meetings and reached an agreement on all provisions as contained in the "Draft Financial Regulations of the International Tribunal for the Law of the Sea: informal working paper by the President of the Meeting of States Parties, dated 26 April 2002." In view of the lack of time and last-minute negotiations on the issue of the currency for the scale of assessment, the Meeting was unable to formally adopt the document. It was agreed that the document would be forwarded to the thirteenth Meeting of States Parties for adoption.

47. During the discussions on the Financial Regulations, the following issues were highlighted: (a) the use of a "split currency system" by the International Tribunal for the Law of the Sea; and (b) change to the scale of assessments for the budget of the Tribunal.

Split Currency System

48. It should be recalled that at the tenth Meeting the delegation of Germany had put forward a proposal that a "split currency system" should be used in the presentation of the budget of the Tribunal (SPLOS/60, par. 37). The proposal was reintroduced by the representative of the European Union at the current Meeting. It was stated that, after the dollar, the euro constituted the second most important currency of the world, and that at least 70 percent of the Tribunal's expenses were incurred in euro, the currency of the host country. It was also mentioned that there were already certain precedents for using the euro as the currency, such as in the

case of the recently established International Criminal Court. It was added that the United Nations rules in this regard were also flexible.

49. After a lengthy negotiation, the Meeting agreed that the euro currency would be used for the presentation of the Tribunal's budget (see regulation 3.2 of the Draft Financial Regulations of the Tribunal). The euro would also be used for the determination of the annual contributions and advances; however, payments could be made either in United States dollars or in euros (see regulation 5.6 of the Draft Financial Regulations of the Tribunal). This agreement was reached on the understanding that it was to conform to the principles of savings and practicality, and was also in accordance with the United Nations rules. Some delegations stated that such a decision should be made on an ad-hoc basis, and that such an agreement should not constitute a precedent for all international organizations to use the currency of their headquarters.

Scale of Assessment

50. With respect to the scale of assessment, the delegation of Japan, following up on an agreement reached at the eleventh Meeting (SPLOS/73, par. 35), proposed that contributions made by States Parties to the budget of the Tribunal should be subject to a floor rate of 0.01 percent and a ceiling rate of 22.00 percent. The proposal included a lowering of the ceiling rate, but not a lowering of the floor rate, as compared to the current situation. The essential aim of Japan's proposal would be to avoid a situation in which the stability and soundness of the finances of the Tribunal were jeopardized because of an excessive dependency upon one country's contribution. It was recalled that such a proposal would reflect a recently adopted change to the scale of assessments for the regular budget of the United Nations. The delegation of Japan was of the view that General Assembly resolution 55/5 of 6 November 2000, lowering the ceiling rate for contributions to the United Nations budget, was neutral in that it respected the autonomy of other United Nations agencies to adopt a similar decision.

51. Some delegations pointed out that the resolution specifically stated that it should not constitute a precedent for other United Nations specialized agencies. Many delegations were of the view that they still needed more time to study Japan's proposal, especially with regard to its feasibility and the financial implications for each individual State Party, and in particular developing countries. It was also emphasized that such consideration would have to take into account the financial status of the Tribunal and its future needs.

52. Despite several new proposals, in particular, to ensure that there would be no increase in the contributions of States in case of a reduction of the ceiling rate, delegations were not in a position at the twelfth Meeting to agree on the lowering of the ceiling rate. It was requested that the proposals of Japan should be issued as official documents for the thirteenth Meeting of States Parties.

53. The Meeting decided that a floor rate of 0.01 percent and a ceiling rate of 25 percent would be used in establishing the rate of assessment for States Parties for the budget of the Tribunal for 2003. However, the Meeting also agreed that

there should be further discussion of the rate at the thirteenth Meeting of States Parties with regard to future years (see SPLOS/90, par. 4).

D. Report of the External Auditors and Financial Statements of the Tribunal for 2000

54. Following an introduction by the Registrar, the twelfth Meeting of States Parties considered and took note of the report contained in SPLOS/75.

E. Election of one member of the Tribunal

55. As a result of the passing away on 11 September 2001 of Judge Edward Laing of Belize, whose term of office would have ended on 30 September 2002, a vacancy occurred in the Tribunal. In accordance with Article 6, paragraph 1, of the Statute of the Tribunal, vacancies shall be filled by the same method as that laid down for the first election of the members of the Tribunal. Article 6, paragraph 2, of the Statute, provides that a member of the Tribunal elected to replace a member whose term of office has not expired shall hold the office for the remainder of the predecessor's term.

56. An invitation calling for nominations was addressed to all States Parties in accordance with the provisions of the Statute. One candidate, Lennox Fitzroy Ballah, was nominated by Trinidad and Tobago (SPLOS/77, annex I). Based on consultations between the President of the Tribunal and the President of the eleventh Meeting of States Parties, the election was scheduled to take place during the twelfth Meeting of States Parties. The election took place on 19 April 2002.

57. There was one round of balloting, during which the representatives of Algeria, Bolivia, Finland, Singapore and Yugoslavia acted as tellers. Out of 134 ballots cast, with 5 abstentions and no invalid ballots, a majority of 86 votes was required for election. Mr. Lennox Fitzroy Ballah obtained 129 votes, and was elected to serve the remainder of the term of the late Judge Laing. On behalf of the Meeting of States Parties, the President congratulated Mr. Lennox Fitzroy Ballah on his election.

F. Election of seven members of the Tribunal

58. On 19 April 2002, the Meeting held the election of seven members of the Tribunal to replace those members whose terms of office would expire on 30 September 2002 (see SPLOS/14, par. 30 (b)).

59. An invitation calling for nominations was addressed to all States Parties in accordance with the provisions of the Statute of the Tribunal. Thirteen candidates were nominated (see list of candidates, SPLOS/77, Annex II).

60. The representative of the Democratic Republic of the Congo withdrew the candidature of Mr. Mukadi Bonyi.

61. The same representatives as in the election of one member acted as tellers. At the first round, out of 134 ballots cast, with 7 invalid ballots and no abstentions, a majority of 85 was required for the election. The following candidates were elected: Lennox Fitzroy Ballah (Trinidad and Tobago) (121 votes), Guangjian Xu (China) (119 votes), Hugo Caminos (Argentina) (117 votes), Jean-Pierre Cot (France) (105 votes) and Tullio Treves (Italy) (105 votes).

62. At the second round, 133 ballots were cast. There was one abstention and no invalid ballot. With a required majority of 88 votes, Mr. Tafsir M. Ndiaye (Senegal) (100 votes) was elected.

63. A third ballot was carried out for the remaining seat. A total of 130 ballots were cast. There was one abstention and no invalid ballot. With a required majority of 86, Mr. Alexander Yankov (Bulgaria) (90 votes) was elected.

64. On behalf of the Meeting of States Parties, the President congratulated the candidates on their election to the Tribunal.

5. RULES OF PROCEDURE FOR MEETINGS OF STATES PARTIES

65. Pursuant to a discussion on the possibility of granting observer status to the Commission on the Limits of the Continental Shelf at the Meeting of States Parties (see chap. VII. C below), the Meeting decided to include a new paragraph 3 bis under rule 18 of the Rules of Procedure for Meetings of States Parties (SPLOS/2/Rev.3), to the effect that the Commission may participate as an observer in a manner consistent both with its functions as an expert body under Article 76 and Annex II to the Convention, and with the independence of its members (SPLOS/86). The Meeting requested the Secretariat to make the necessary amendments to the Rules of Procedure for Meetings of States Parties.

6. INFORMATION ON THE ACTIVITIES OF THE INTERNATIONAL SEABED AUTHORITY

A. Work of the Authority

66. The ninth Meeting of States Parties agreed that the Secretary-General of the International Seabed Authority would be given an opportunity to address the Meetings and provide information with respect to the activities of the Authority (SPLOS/48, par. 53).

67. Pursuant to that decision and in accordance with rule 37 of the Rules of Procedure for Meetings of States Parties, the Secretary-General of the Authority, Satya Nandan, provided the Meeting with an oral report on recent developments with regard to the work of the Authority.

68. The Secretary-General started by recalling the importance of the twelfth Meeting of States Parties being held on the twentieth anniversary of the adoption of the Convention and he reminded the Meeting that the General Assembly would celebrate the occasion on 9 and 10 December 2002.

69. He reported that the most significant milestone for the Authority in 2001 had been the conclusion of 15-year exploration contracts with six former registered pioneer investors, in accordance with the Regulations on Prospecting and Exploration for Polymetallic Nodules in the Area approved by the Assembly in 2000. In March 2002, the Authority had also concluded an exploration contract with the Government of India, the remaining registered pioneer investor. As a result, the Authority was now in a contractual relationship with all seven pioneer investors that had been registered under resolution II of the Third United Nations Conference on the Law of the Sea.

70. Another significant achievement in 2001 was the issuance by the Legal and Technical Commission of the Authority of a set of recommendations for the guidance of contractors for the assessment of the possible environmental impacts arising from exploration for polymetallic nodules. The recommendations were based upon the outcomes of an international workshop held by the Authority in 1998.

71. The Secretary-General reported that in 2001, at its seventh session, in response to a request made by the Russian Federation, the Council of the Authority had commenced work on the consideration of the appropriate type of regulations for prospecting and exploration for hydrothermal polymetallic sulphides (seafloor massive sulphides) and cobalt-rich ferromanganese crusts. Consideration of issues relating to the elaboration of such regulations would be continued at the forthcoming session of the Council, in 2002. To assist in that work, the Secretariat had organized a seminar, open to all members and observers, as well as members of the Legal and Technical Commission, which would be held in Kingston on 7 August 2002, during the eighth session of the Authority.

72. The Secretary-General announced that, as a prelude to the seminar, the Authority, with the help of three experts, would make a presentation on the topic during the twelfth Meeting of States Parties, providing, inter alia, background information on the metallogenesis of marine minerals, on seafloor massive sulphides and cobalt-rich ferromanganese crusts, and on the biodiversity associated with those mineral resources.

73. He further underlined that, over the past five years, the Authority had successfully established itself as a functional international organization. Over the past two years, its work had become increasingly technical. As a consequence, States members might need to consider, during the eighth session in August 2002, the current pattern of meetings of the Authority to see if it fully met the needs of the various organs and bodies involved and whether it represented the most efficient mechanism for carrying out the technical work required.

74. He stated that the future work of the Authority had three main areas of focus. The first was supervisory functions with respect to the contracts for exploration. The annual reports of contractors would need to be analysed and given detailed

consideration by the Legal and Technical Commission. The reporting requirements constituted a mechanism whereby the Authority could be provided with the information required to ensure that the responsibilities of the contractors under the Convention and the Agreement were carried out, including those related to the protection of the marine environment.

75. The second area of focus was the promotion and encouragement of the conduct of marine scientific research in the international seabed area, and coordination and dissemination of the results of such research and analysis. Since 1998, the Authority had established a pattern of workshops and seminars on specific aspects of deep seabed mining, with participation by internationally recognized scientists, experts, researchers and members of the Legal and Technical Commission as well as representatives of contractors, the offshore mining industry and member States. In August 2002, the Authority would convene the next in its series of workshops.

76. The third area of focus was information-gathering and the establishment and development of databases of scientific and technical information, for the purpose of obtaining a better understanding of the deep ocean environment. The workshops conducted by the Authority highlighted the need to agree on international standards for relevant data and information, allowing for exchange and comparison. Such standardization was essential to enable the Authority to reconcile, evaluate and draw conclusions from data and information.

77. Finally, the Secretary-General reminded States Parties that the eighth session of the Authority would be held at Kingston from 5 to 16 August 2002, to be preceded by a workshop from 29 July to 2 August 2002. One of the important matters to be taken up during the session would be the biennial election of one half the membership of the Council. In addition, the Authority would need to consider and adopt its budget for the period 2003–2004.

78. In conclusion, he urged all member States to participate in the eighth session of the Authority. Failure to achieve the required quorum would frustrate the ability of the Authority to take important decisions.

79. The Meeting took note with appreciation of the statement of the Secretary-General.

B. Presentations by Experts Called Upon by the Authority

80. The Secretary-General of the International Seabed Authority introduced the three scientists who would make presentations in the context of the work of the Authority on cobalt-rich ferromanganese crusts and polymetallic sulphides, as well as the ecosystems in which these minerals were found.

81. It was explained that whereas during the negotiations of UNCLOS, in the 1970s and 1980s, the ocean basins were considered "passive containers" of resources, currently they were seen to be characterized by processes generating continuous change (e.g., plate tectonics). In particular, it had been discovered that metals were continuously "inserted" into the oceans through a process whereby sea water infiltrated up to 300 metres into the ocean crust in high-temperature reaction zones

(magma centres being the heating source). Through chemical reactions the water mixed with metals found in the rocks to form a hydrothermal fluid, which then sprang out from beneath the floor and combined with sea water to form metal sulphides. The precipitation of the minerals thus dissolved in the water formed "high smokers" (also called hydrothermal vents) rich in polymetallic sulphides. Polymetallic sulphides contained, inter alia, gold, whose presence was of great scientific as well as economic interest, and indium, a metal used for the production of computers, for which sources on land were scarce.

82. Research had also shown that hydrothermal vents were rich in biodiversity (500 species had been identified, more than 90 percent of which were unique to these areas) and had a very high biomass (amount of live material per square metre), as opposed to the deep ocean floor, which was often compared to a desert. Hydrothermal vent ecosystems functioned on the basis of a process known as chemosynthesis (as opposed to photosynthesis, which characterized most other life forms), through which hydrogen sulphide gas was transformed into energy by microbes, which in turn constituted the basis of the food chain of the ecosystem. These novel biochemical systems were attracting the interest of scientists, especially in the light of the extreme conditions under which the systems functioned. For example, the special haemoglobin developed by tube worms inhabiting such ecosystems, which might lead to the production of artificial blood, was one promising area of research. There was also growing interest in the commercial value of the extreme-conditions enzymes and bioactive compounds that could be extracted from microbes living in such ecosystems and would then be used in a number of industrial processes (seven or eight enzymes currently being marketed had been developed from microbes found in hydrothermal vents).

83. It was stressed that the close relationship between the mineral deposits and the micro-organisms inhabiting the vents and the nearby biota should be taken into account when considering the possibility of exploiting the mineral resources. Removal of minerals would entail the destruction of the habitats and food sources of those living resources.

84. Other newly discovered resources in the form of cobalt-rich ferromanganese crusts were found in seamounts. They were found both within and outside the limits of national jurisdiction (200 nm) at depths of 200 to 2,000 metres.

85. Finally, it was pointed out that only 5 percent of the deep ocean floor had been systematically explored.

7. MATTERS RELATED TO THE CONTINENTAL SHELF AND THE COMMISSION ON THE LIMITS OF THE CONTINENTAL SHELF

A. Statement by the Chairman of the Commission on the Limits of the Continental Shelf

86. In accordance with the practice of the Meeting of States Parties, the President invited the Chairman of the Commission on the Limits of the Continental

Shelf, Yuri Kazmin, to provide information on the work of the Commission and its recent activities.

87. The Chairman informed the Meeting that, on 20 December 2001, the Commission had received its first submission, from the Russian Federation, and had begun the consideration of the submission at its tenth session (25 March–12 April 2002). He expressed his concerns regarding the lack of attendance at the sessions of the Commission by a number of members of the Commission, which had made it difficult to achieve a quorum.

88. The Commission had begun its tenth session formally only after the required quorum had been achieved. Park Yong-Ahn, Vice-Chairman, replaced Mr. Kazmin in assuming the chair for following up the consideration of the submission by the Russian Federation. Mr. Kazmin informed the Meeting that Ivan Gloumov, Deputy Minister of Natural Resources of the Russian Federation, accompanied by other experts, had been invited to make a presentation of the submission (CLCS/31) to the Commission, followed by a question-and-answer period. Mr. Gloumov was also requested to present the position of his Government regarding communications addressed to the Secretary-General by Canada, Denmark, Japan, Norway and the United States of America, which had been circulated by the Secretariat to all members of the Commission as well as to States Members of the United Nations. Mr. Gloumov was of the view that those communications did not constitute obstacles to the consideration of the submission by the Commission. At the end of his presentation he stated that, if required, members of the Commission were welcome to visit the Russian Federation with a view to examining relevant databases in situ.

89. Following informal consultations and in accordance with article 5 of Annex II to the Convention, a subcommission composed of seven members, appointed in a "balanced manner and taking into account the specific elements" of the Russian Federation's submission, was established with the following composition: Alexandre Tagore Medeiros de Albuquerque (Brazil), Lawrence Folajimi Awosika (Nigeria), Galo Carrera Hurtado (Mexico), Peter F. Croker (Ireland), Karl H.F. Hinz (Germany), Iain C. Lamont (New Zealand) and Yong-Ahn Park (Republic of Korea). Mr. Carrera was appointed Chairman, Mr. Hinz Vice-Chairman and Mr. Croker Rapporteur of the subcommission.

90. The subcommission continued its work through the end of the tenth session of the Commission; it met twice daily and convened 20 meetings, including 6 meetings devoted to consultations in the form of questions and answers between members of the subcommission and the experts of the delegation of the Russian Federation. Taking into account the complexity and volume of the data involved, the Commission had not been in a position to make a recommendation by the end of its tenth session.

91. It was decided that the subcommission would reconvene from 10 to 14 June 2002 before the expiration of the term of office of the current membership of the Commission on 15 June 2002. Mr. Kazmin informed the Meeting that additional information requested would be provided by the Russian Federation by mid-May. Upon the completion of its work, the subcommission was to submit its recommenda-

tions through the United Nations Secretariat to the newly elected membership of the Commission, which will hold the eleventh session of the Commission from 24 to 28 June 2002.

92. The Chairman of the Commission expressed his appreciation to the Secretary-General of the United Nations and to the Division for Ocean Affairs and the Law of the Sea in particular, for all the work done in preparation for dealing with submissions, including providing the subcommission with the use of a conference room equipped with the latest technology. He also wished to acknowledge the invaluable contribution to the work of the Commission of some of his colleagues who had not been nominated for the upcoming election of the membership of the Commission: Aly I. Beltagy (Egypt); André C. W. Chan Chim Yuk (Mauritius); Kazuchika Hamuro (Japan); Karl H. F. Hinz (Germany); Iain C. Lamont (New Zealand); Chisengu Leo M'Dala (Zambia); Daniel Rio (France); and K. R. Srinivasan (India).

93. Regarding the submission made by the Russian Federation to the Commission on the Limits of the Continental Shelf, the representative of the Russian Federation referred to the note verbale dated 25 February 2002 from the Permanent Representative of Japan to the United Nations addressed to the Secretary-General of the United Nations (SPLOS/82). He was of the view that the map included in the communication of Japan presented a partial position and pointed out that constructive consultations were taking place between their two Governments on the issue. He regretted that such a document had been circulated in the Meeting of States Parties.

94. The representative of Japan agreed that bilateral consultations were being carried out on the technical matter. He emphasized that document SPLOS/82 was not an attempt at politicizing the issue, but only at highlighting a technical matter.

B. Election of Members of the Commission

95. In conformity with Article 2, paragraph 4, of Annex II to the United Nations Convention on the Law of the Sea, the members of the Commission on the Limits of the Continental Shelf shall be elected for a term of five years. In accordance with rule 7, paragraph 2, of the Rules of Procedure of the Commission, the terms of office of the members of the Commission elected at the first election began on the date of the first meeting of the Commission, that is, 16 June 1997. The terms of office of the 21 members of the Commission will thus expire on 15 June 2002.

96. An invitation calling for nominations was addressed to all States Parties. The list of candidates nominated by States and the curricula vitae of those candidates were circulated in documents SPLOS/80 and SPLOS/81. The election was held on 23 April 2002.

97. In accordance with Article 2, paragraph 3, of Annex II to the Convention, no less than three members of the Commission shall be elected from each geographical region. After consultations and in accordance with the understanding reached by the twelfth Meeting on 18 April 2002, for the purpose of conducting the second election, the members of the Commission on the Limits of the Continental Shelf

were elected as follows: four members from the Group of African States; six members from the Group of Asian States; three members from the Group of Eastern European States; four members from the Group of Latin American and Caribbean States; and four members from the Group of Western European and Other States.

98. Elections were held in accordance with article 2, paragraph 3, of Annex II to the Convention, which states that two thirds of the States Parties shall constitute a quorum for election and that the persons elected to the Commission shall be those nominees who obtain a two-thirds majority of the votes of the represented States Parties present and voting.

99. The representatives of Algeria, Bolivia, Finland, Singapore and Yugoslavia acted as tellers for the election.

100. There was only one round of balloting. Out of 134 ballots cast, with 10 invalid ballots and no abstentions, a majority of 83 votes was required for election. The following 21 candidates were elected: Noel Newton St. Claver Francis (Jamaica) (118 votes), Lawrence Folajimi Awosika (Nigeria) (117 votes), Indurlall Fagoonee (Mauritius) (117 votes), Yuri Borisovitch Kazmin (Russian Federation) (117 votes), Alexandre Tagore Medeiros de Albuquerque (Brazil) (116 votes), Galo Carrera Hurtado (Mexico) (113 votes), Mihai Silviu German (Romania) (113 votes), Yao Ubuènalè Woeledji (Togo) (113 votes), Osvaldo Pedro Astiz (Argentina) (112 votes), Samuel Sona Betah (Cameroon) (112 votes), Mladen Juračić (Croatia) (111 votes), Naresh Kumar Thakur (India) (105 votes), Peter F. Croker (Ireland) (102 votes), Wenzheng Lu (China) (102 votes), Fernando Manuel Maia Pimentel (Portugal) (101 votes), Kensaku Tamaki (Japan) (101 votes), Hilal Mohamed Sultan Al-Azri (Oman) (97 votes), Yong-Ahn Park (Republic of Korea) (97 votes), Harald Brekke (Norway) (95 votes), Abu Bakar Jaafar (Malaysia) (93 votes) and Philip Alexander Symonds (Australia) (84 votes).

101. On behalf of the Meeting of States Parties, the President congratulated all the newly elected members of the Commission on the Limits of the Continental Shelf.

C. Observer Status of the Commission at the Meeting of States Parties

102. At the twelfth Meeting, the Chairman of the Commission addressed the Meeting of States Parties in relation to item 15 of the agenda of the Meeting, relating to the observer status of the Commission at the Meeting of States Parties. He noted that, as pointed out by the President of the eleventh Meeting of States Parties (SPLOS/73, par. 60), no formal relationship existed between the Meeting of States Parties and the Commission, as it did with the International Tribunal for the Law of the Sea and the International Seabed Authority, both of which enjoyed observer status at the Meeting. This was due to the fact that the Commission had not been established when the Meeting of States Parties had adopted its rules of procedure. He observed that, since the States Parties had displayed great interest in the activities of the Commission, the Meeting might wish to establish such a relationship and grant observer status to the Commission.

103. Mr. Kazmin underlined that the members of the Commission viewed the Meeting of States Parties as playing an important role in the implementation by States of Article 76 and Annex 2 to the Convention. In the past the Commission had consulted the Meeting of States Parties on important issues, such as submissions in cases of a dispute between States with opposite or adjacent coasts or other cases of unresolved land and maritime disputes. He also underlined that the Commission was grateful for the role played by the Meeting of States Parties in establishing two voluntary trust funds pertaining to the work of the Commission (General Assembly resolution 55/7, paras. 18 and 20).

104. In conclusion, he highlighted that at its ninth session, the members of the Commission had agreed that granting it observer status might be beneficial to the relationship between the Commission and the Meeting of States Parties and had requested him to address a letter to the President of the Meeting of States Parties, seeking observer status for the Commission. He noted that the President of the Meeting, in his opening statement, had acknowledged receipt of the letter.

105. A number of delegations expressed their support for granting the Commission observer status at the Meeting of States Parties. It was pointed out that it would be beneficial for the work of the Commission as well as for the work of the Meeting of States Parties.

106. A number of delegations underlined that the status of the Commission was different from that of the International Tribunal for the Law of the Sea or of the International Seabed Authority. The latter were autonomous bodies under the Convention, while the Commission was a technical body. The proposal was made that the Commission should therefore report to the Meeting of States Parties on its activities, so that the Meeting might make relevant recommendations. One delegation pointed out that while it would be logical for the Commission to inform the Meeting of States Parties about the work done and the results achieved, the Meeting of States Parties was not in a position to request reports from the Commission, which was an independent technical body. Some delegations were not supportive of the proposal that the Commission should report to the Meeting, although not opposing the granting of observer status to the Commission.

107. In that regard, the Meeting adopted a decision regarding the inclusion of paragraph 3 bis of rule 18 of the Rules of Procedure for Meetings of States Parties, granting observer status to the Commission (SPLOS/86) (see par. 65 above), and requested the Secretariat to issue the necessary corrigendum to the Rules of Procedure for the Meetings of States Parties.

D. Issues with Respect to Article 4 of Annex II to the United Nations Convention on theLaw of the Sea

108. Under Article 4 of Annex II to the Convention, a coastal State intending to establish the outer limits of its continental shelf beyond 200 nautical miles is obligated to submit particulars of such limits to the Commission on the Limits of the Continental Shelf, along with supporting scientific and technical data as soon

as possible, but in any case within 10 years of the entry into force of the Convention for that State.

109. The eleventh Meeting of States Parties decided that, for a State for which the Convention had entered into force before 13 May 1999, the date of commencement of the 10-year time period for making submissions to the Commission was 13 May 1999; therefore the submission should be made by 13 May 2009 (SPLOS/72).

110. At the twelfth Meeting, the Chairman referred to paragraph 102 of the report of the eleventh Meeting (SPLOS/73), pointing to the need to retain the item on issues with respect to Article 4 of Annex II to the United Nations Convention on the Law of the Sea on the agenda for the twelfth Meeting. In recognition of the continuing need for the consideration of the item, the Meeting decided to retain the item on the provisional agenda for the thirteenth Meeting.

8. Matters related to Article 319 of the United Nations Convention on the Law of the Sea

111. At the tenth Meeting, Chile had proposed that the Meeting of States Parties consider issues relating to the implementation of the Convention and that the Meeting should receive a report every year from the Secretary-General on issues of a general nature that had arisen with respect to the Convention (see SPLOS/CRP.22 and SPLOS/60, paras. 73–78).

112. At the twelfth Meeting, a number of delegations referred to the views they had expressed at the eleventh Meeting of States Parties regarding the role of the Meeting in considering issues relating to the implementation of the Convention (SPLOS/73, paras. 85–92).

113. Some delegations, which did not support the view that the Meeting of States Parties had the competence to consider issues relating to the implementation of the Convention, proposed that the item be removed from the agenda of the Meeting of States Parties. They were of the view that there was no legal basis in the Convention for such a role. It was pointed out that issues relating to the implementation of the Convention were being dealt with in other forums, especially by the General Assembly. In that regard, one delegation referred to the mandate of the General Assembly as reflected in Assembly resolution 49/28 of 6 December 1994.

114. In response to the above proposal, several delegations expressed support for the retention of the agenda item, pointing out that its retention was essential in order to enable delegations to consider issues relating to the implementation of the Convention at future Meetings, should the need arise. In their view, the Meeting did have the competence to consider issues relating to the implementation of the Convention; to say otherwise would, in the view of one delegation, contradict Article 319 of the Convention and the law of treaties. According to some delegations, the consideration of ocean issues by the General Assembly and the Informal Consultative Process did not imply that the Meeting of States Parties had no role in relation to the Convention. It was pointed out that the eleventh Meeting of States Parties

had already considered an issue relating to the implementation of the Convention and had taken a decision regarding the date of commencement of the 10-year period for making submissions to the Commission on the Limits of the Continental Shelf. In response, some delegations emphasized that the decision taken by the Meeting of States Parties at its eleventh Meeting was of an organizational and not a substantive nature and represented, according to one delegation, an extension of the administrative powers of the Meeting of States Parties.

115. One delegation proposed that, in view of the lengthy discussions that had already taken place on the issue, the Meeting should take a decision regarding its role at the current Meeting. Another delegation suggested that it should begin considering how it envisaged its role in relation to the implementation of the Convention. A third delegation was of the view that there was no need to formalize a monitoring role for the Meeting of States Parties, but that the door should rather be left open for any need that might arise. Some delegations proposed that the consideration of the role of the Meeting of States Parties should be postponed until the following year. One delegation noted that the Meeting would be in a better position to take a decision on the issue after the General Assembly had completed its review of the effectiveness and utility of the Informal Consultative Process.

116. In the light of the various views expressed, including that of the President that the issue constituted a very broad agenda item relating to depositary functions, the Meeting of States Parties decided to retain the current item entitled "Matters related to Article 319 of the United Nations Convention on the Law of the Sea" on the provisional agenda for its next Meeting.

9. OTHER MATTERS

A. Statement by the Representative of a Non-governmental Organization Regarding Seafarers

117. In accordance with rule 18, paragraph 4, of the Rules of Procedure for Meetings of States Parties, the Seamen's Church Institute was invited to address the Meeting as an observer. In his statement, the representative of the Institute drew attention to two issues: the duty to rescue persons in distress at sea and the safety of fishing vessels.

118. The representative underlined that one of the most cherished and protected maritime traditions was a mariners' obligation to go to the aid of all persons in distress at sea. The duty to rescue persons in distress at sea was also a legal duty under customary maritime law, international conventions and domestic law. In particular, he underlined the provisions contained in Article 98 of UNCLOS and Chapter V, Regulation 10 of the International Convention for the Safety of Life at Sea (SOLAS). Caution was expressed that no action should be taken by any State that might create a disincentive for vessels to respond to a distress at sea. There had been reports of cases in which port States had placed unreasonable financial burdens on

ships that had gone to the aid of persons in distress at sea, either by refusing them entry or by imposing on them financial responsibility for feeding, housing and repatriating the shipwrecked persons who had been allowed entry. This had resulted in a negative precedent for masters and shipowners not to comply with their moral and legal obligation to rescue persons in distress at sea.

119. Turning to the question of fishing vessel safety, the representative of the Institute pointed out that commercial fishing was one of the most dangerous occupations in the world. Nevertheless, a fragmented fishing industry coupled with a lack of political will by States had resulted in few, if any, national or international fishing vessel safety regulations. The International Maritime Organization, the International Labour Organization and the Food and Agriculture Organization of the United Nations had attempted to address some of the fishing vessel safety issues in the Torremolinos Convention and the STCW-F Convention, but neither of those conventions had come into force because of insufficient ratifications. He stressed that the international community should no longer tolerate such human losses. In that context, the obligation of States under UNCLOS must be fulfilled. In situations where UNCLOS did not address a particular need, States Parties should use the framework provided by the Convention to develop specific areas of the law of the sea. He underlined that when one flag State did not honour its obligations under UNCLOS, all States Parties were affected.

120. He concluded by pointing out that the community of nations, as well as individual nations, must step in to protect the seas' most valuable resource: the human beings who lived and worked on ships.

B. Statement by the President at the Closure of the Twelfth Meeting of States Parties

121. In his closing statement, the President of the Meeting began by pointing out that, according to the Credentials Committee, all States Parties to the Convention had participated in the twelfth Meeting. This confirmed the unique place of the Convention in international law, as the cornerstone of all modern efforts to develop and implement the legal framework for the oceans and seas and their resources.

122. The President continued by reviewing the work carried out by the Meeting. He observed that the swift approval given to the budget proposed by the Tribunal for 2003, reflected the efficient and serious manner in which the Tribunal had approached the matter. In the area of budgetary and financial matters, the Meeting had also reviewed and taken decisions on issues ranging from savings from previous budgets of the Tribunal and the staff assessment fund of the Tribunal to the transfer of funds between appropriation sections of the budget and the Working Capital Fund when necessary to deal with cases. He underlined the need to ensure that the assessed contributions to the Tribunal and the Authority were paid in full and

in a timely fashion, so that they might discharge their functions effectively and efficiently. He also urged States whose experts served on the Commission on the Limits of the Continental Shelf to facilitate their participation in meetings of the Commission.

123. Among the most important accomplishments of the Meeting, he pointed to the elections to the International Tribunal for the Law of the Sea and elections to the Commission on the Limits of the Continental Shelf. He extended his congratulations to those members who had been elected to the Tribunal and to the Commission. With regard to future elections, he observed that while the previous practice was to present an alphabetical list of candidates on the ballots, future elections would be based on geographical representation so as to make it easier to conduct them.

124. Another important task carried out by the Meeting was the adoption of the Financial Regulations of the Tribunal, on the basis of a previously drafted text, based in turn on a working paper prepared by the Secretariat, as well as on the rules adopted for the International Criminal Court. With respect to the issue of currency, it was agreed that annual contributions and advances would be determined in euros, while the contributions themselves might be paid either in United States dollars or in euros.

125. With respect to the rules of procedure of the Meeting, a rule had been adopted granting the Commission on the Limits of the Continental Shelf observer status at Meetings of States Parties.

126. The discussion on matters relating to Article 319 of the Convention had been resumed by the Meeting. Several delegations had expressed the view that the item should be removed from the Meeting's agenda, while others held that the Meeting should maintain the item on the agenda so as not to foreclose the possibility for the States Parties to discuss issues that might be of importance in the context of the law of the sea. The Meeting had also agreed to maintain on its agenda issues with respect to article 4 of Annex II to the Convention.

127. The President thanked the Secretary-General of the International Seabed Authority for introducing three eminent scientists to make presentations in the context of the work of the Authority on polymetallic sulphides and cobalt-rich ferromanganese crusts, including the impacts that activities relating to those resources might have on the relevant ecosystems.

128. He also noted the statement by the representative of the Seamen's Church Institute and thanked him for drawing the attention of the Meeting to the issues of the duty to rescue and fishing vessel safety.

129. The President outlined the agenda items for the thirteenth Meeting (see paras. 130–131 below) and noted that the year 2002 marked the twentieth anniversary of the adoption and opening for signature of the Convention. He concluded by stating that the fact that all institutions created by the Convention had completed the initial set-up period and were now fully functioning was rooted in the international community's acceptance of the Convention as the globally recognized universal standard for conduct by States with respect to the oceans.

C. Dates and Programme of Work for the Thirteenth Meeting of States Parties

130. The thirteenth Meeting of States Parties will be held in New York from 9 to 13 June 2003.

131. The thirteenth Meeting will have on its agenda, inter alia, the following items:

(a) Report of the International Tribunal for the Law of the Sea for 2002;
(b) Draft budget of the Tribunal;
(c) Scale of assessment for the contribution of States Parties to the budget of the International Tribunal for the Law of the Sea;
(d) Adoption of the Financial Regulations of the International Tribunal for the Law of the Sea;
(e) Report of the External Auditors for the financial year 2001, with financial statements of the Tribunal as of 31 December 2001;
(f) Issues with respect to Article 4 of Annex II to the United Nations Convention on the Law of the Sea;
(g) Matters related to Article 319 of the United Nations Convention on the Law of the Sea;
(h) Other matters.

Report on the Work of the United Nations Open-ended Informal Consultative Process Established by the General Assembly in its Resolution 54/33 in Order to Facilitate the Annual Review by the Assembly of Developments in Ocean Affairs at its Third Meeting, Held at United Nations Headquarters from 8 to 15 April 2002*

Letter dated 20 May 2002 from the Co-Chairpersons of the Consultative Process addressed to the President of the General Assembly

Pursuant to General Assembly resolution 54/33 of 24 November 1999, you appointed us for the third time as the Co-Chairpersons of the Open-ended Informal Consultative Process on ocean affairs established to facilitate the review by the General Assembly, in an effective and constructive manner, of developments in ocean affairs by considering the report of the Secretary-General on oceans and the law of the sea and by suggesting particular issues to be considered by the General Assembly, with an emphasis on identifying areas where coordination and cooperation at the intergovernmental and inter-agency levels should be enhanced.

We now have the honour to submit to you the attached report on the work of the Consultative Process at its third meeting, which was held at United Nations Headquarters from 8 to 15 April 2002.

In this connection it is recalled that, in view of the forthcoming World Summit on Sustainable Development and in order to prepare for the General Assembly debate to celebrate the twentieth anniversary of the opening for signature of the United Nations Convention on the Law of the Sea, the General Assembly, in its resolution 56/12 of 28 November 2001, recommended that in its deliberations on the report of the Secretary-General on oceans and the law of the sea the third meeting of the Consultative Process should organize its discussions on: (a) protection and preservation of the marine environment; and (b) capacity-building, regional cooperation and coordination, and integrated ocean management, as important cross-cutting issues to address ocean affairs, such as marine science and transfer of technology, sustainable fisheries, the degradation of the marine environment and the safety of navigation.

The Consultative Process has suggested a number of issues for consideration by the General Assembly and, in accordance with paragraph 3 (h) of resolution

*Editors' Note.—This document was provided by the United Nations Division on Ocean Affairs and Law of the Sea (DOALOS) and is extracted from the United Nations General Assembly, Fifty-seventh session, Item 25 of the preliminary list (A/57/50/Rev.1), UN document A /57/80, 2 July 2002. Available online at the DOALOS web site: http://www.un.org/Depts/los/.

54/33 and bearing in mind General Assembly resolutions 56/12 and 56/13 of 28 November 2001, has proposed a number of elements for the consideration of the General Assembly in relation to its resolutions under the agenda item entitled "Oceans and the Law of the Sea." Those elements are, of course, not intended as an exhaustive list of material relevant to the General Assembly's consideration of the item "Oceans and the Law of the Sea."

We wish to point out that this year also marks the end of the initial three-year period of the Consultative Process. Later this year, the General Assembly will need to decide on the future handling of work on oceans and the law of the sea in the light of its review of the effectiveness and utility of the Consultative Process.

(*Signed*) Tuiloma Neroni Slade and Alan Simcock, Co-Chairpersons

CONTENTS

PART A

Issues to be suggested and elements to be proposed, to the general assembly

Cross-cutting Issues

Issue A
The high value and crucial role of the world's oceans and seas, especially as a vital input to sustainable development

1. The input of the Consultative Process this year is to the resolution to mark the twentieth anniversary of the opening for signature of the United Nations Convention on the Law of the Sea (UNCLOS). The Convention is approaching universal participation. Its implementation, however, remains crucial to the sustainable development and use of the oceans and seas and thus to the whole world.

2. The importance of the world's oceans and seas as a vital component of the web of life, as a supplier of goods, services and energy, and as a foundation of security, including food security, at the national, regional and global levels for present and future generations cannot be overestimated. But despite significant progress in some fields, the resources and environmental condition of those oceans and seas continue to decline in many areas. Furthermore, the accumulated impacts of the

many various uses can threaten unpredicted change as a result of the complex interactions of natural processes in the ecosystems.

3. It is therefore proposed that the General Assembly should emphasize the high value and crucial role of the world's oceans and seas as a vital input to sustainable development in all parts of the world, should stress the need for all States to be able to play their part in ensuring that the world makes sustainable use of the oceans and seas, and should call upon the whole international community to work towards this goal, including through an enhanced effort in implementing existing international agreements and arrangements.

Issue B

The need for integration in the management of oceans and seas

4. An integrated, interdisciplinary, intersectoral and ecosystem-based approach to oceans management, consistent with the legal framework provided by UNCLOS and the goals of chapter 17 of Agenda 21, is not just desirable, it is essential. Economic development, social development and environmental protection are mutually supportive components of the sustainable development of the oceans and seas.

5. It is proposed that the General Assembly should reiterate the need for oceans management at all levels to incorporate the principles adopted by the United Nations Conference on Environment and Development (Rio Declaration on Environment and Development), to be based on the best available scientific and traditional knowledge, accompanied by efforts to make it available to all decision makers, to involve all relevant stakeholders, to provide the necessary means for resolving conflicting pressures and objectives, to be underpinned by high-level political commitment and to be part of an overall system of good and effective governance.

6. These approaches need detailed, consistent development across all the many relevant sectors. Many of the details relevant to the protection and preservation of the marine environment are taken up under the subsequent issues in the present report. Regular reviews by the General Assembly, as the global institution having the competence to undertake such reviews, will continue to be needed for all aspects of collaboration and coordination in integrated oceans management at all levels. These may be supported by reviews by all competent organizations of their contributions to such collaboration and coordination.

Issue C

The need to build capacities around the world for integrated management of oceans and seas

7. Since the world's oceans and seas are ultimately a single complex system, successful integrated management requires every State to play its part. In the interest of everyone, therefore, all States need to ensure that policy makers have a sound understanding of the oceans and of the importance of the marine environment, and to achieve adequate capacity to acquire and use the necessary information and to manage effectively the State's interests in the oceans and seas. Building the capacities of States needs to be paralleled by steps to promote public awareness and partici-

pation, including through promoting ocean-related studies within their education systems, creating networks of practitioners and other stakeholders and eliminating obstacles to good governance at all levels. Because of the scale of the tasks, international cooperation is essential, involving all actors, including States, agencies of the United Nations system, non-governmental organizations and the private sector, not least at the regional level and through networks of regional organizations. This cooperation must include mobilizing assistance, including through twinning arrangements, to developing countries for capacity-building, especially for the least developed countries and for small island developing States, whose duties in managing the oceans are often disproportionately large in comparison to their populations.

8. It is proposed that the General Assembly should:

(a) Reiterate the call in paragraph 23 of General Assembly resolution 55/7 of 30 October 2000 for reviews by the relevant international organizations and financial institutions and the donor community of the efforts to build capacity in order to identify the gaps that may need to be filled for ensuring consistent approaches, both nationally and internationally, in order to implement UNCLOS;
(b) Stress the need to intensify efforts in capacity-building for integrated oceans management and the requirement for adequate support for this purpose as foreseen in UNCLOS and Agenda 21 to developing countries, especially for the least developed countries and for small island developing States, to enable them to harness science and technology for the sustainable management and use of their marine resources and to minimize the negative impacts of the growing pressures on oceans;
(c) In particular in relation to the fisheries sector, urge the strengthening of partnerships among international financial institutions, bilateral agencies and other relevant stakeholders, with the aim of offering developing countries the best knowledge, experience and financial resources for sustainable fisheries;
(d) Emphasize the need for States to integrate the protection of marine and coastal areas into their policies for key sectors, mobilizing resources for this purpose from domestic and international sources.

Issue D
The central role of regional cooperation and coordination

9. The sheer scale of oceans space, the economies that can result from sharing and pooling resources and the need for coherent approaches between States whose activities affect the same part of the oceans and seas, all underline the central role of regional cooperation and coordination.

10. It is proposed that the General Assembly should:

(a) Emphasize the importance of regional organizations and arrangements for cooperation and coordination in integrated oceans management;

(b) Where there are separate regional structures for different aspects of oceans management, such as environmental protection, fisheries management, navigation and scientific research, call for those different structures, where appropriate, to work together for optimal cooperation and coordination; such collaboration could involve regional conferences, joint meetings, exchange of observers and shared staff.

The protection and preservation of the marine environment: Integration of ocean management, including action to preserve and protect the marine environment

Issue E

Data and information for decision-making on ocean management

11. Consistent, high-quality information is a prerequisite for effective, science-based decision-making at all levels, subject to the principle of the precautionary approach.

12. It is proposed that the General Assembly should emphasize the need to improve systems for collecting and reporting data and information relevant to the marine environment. To this end, it is proposed that the General Assembly should, at the global level, invite all relevant United Nations agencies:

(a) Individually to review their arrangements for collecting information and data relevant to the marine environment and for assuring the quality of that data, using to the fullest possible extent what is available at the regional level;
(b) Collectively to consider how to ensure that the resulting information and data sets provide, within the constraints of existing resources, an acceptably consistent, coherent and comprehensive basis for international decision-making.

13. It is proposed that the General Assembly should also invite all regional organizations concerned with the marine environment, navigational safety, fisheries management and marine science to consider how they could, within their available resources, enable themselves and their member States both to collect the information necessary for decision-making on the marine environment within their regions, and to organize management systems to share the available information and data with those who need it, particularly through the use of the Internet. The relevant United Nations agencies should further be invited to consider how they could help to meet the special needs of developing countries and countries whose economies are in transition.

14. It is proposed that the General Assembly should also invite States with capabilities for satellite surveillance to assist those States which are suffering vandalism to their monitoring equipment located in the maritime area to identify those committing such vandalism.

Issue F

Assessments of the marine environment at global and regional levels

15. In order to enable the international community to address the problems of the marine environment in a comprehensive, coherent and consistent manner, there is a need for a global marine assessment mechanism based on existing programmes to provide on a regular, timely and scientific basis the necessary assessments of the state and trends of all aspects of marine ecosystems, taking into account all relevant socio-economic factors. Such a mechanism should ensure the full participation of, and be used on a voluntary basis by, member States and international organizations as well as by policy makers and all stakeholders. In particular, the assessment should address those marine areas and/or human activities which currently are not sufficiently covered by assessment activities as well as less understood eco-systems, communities and species. The assessment should involve a two-tiered mechanism, consisting of a scientific/technical assessment and a policy-oriented report based on the same information.

16. It is proposed that the General Assembly should welcome the work of the United Nations Environment Programme (UNEP) in exploring the feasibility of a global marine assessment process. It is further proposed that the General Assembly should urge UNEP and the Intergovernmental Oceanographic Commission (IOC) of the United Nations Educational, Scientific and Cultural Organization (UNESCO) and other bodies, as appropriate, to consider further how to organize effectively such assessments of the marine environment, urge completion of that work on the proposed timetable while stressing the importance of making the fullest possible use of information collected, and assessments made, under existing arrangements, especially by regional organizations concerned with the marine environment, navigational safety, fisheries management and marine science.

17. As with the collection and sharing of information, it is proposed that the General Assembly should invite the regional organizations concerned with the marine environment, navigational safety, fisheries management and marine science in each region to consider how to achieve coordination between the marine environment monitoring programmes of their member States and appropriate management of the resulting data and information and to prepare assessments of the marine environment within their regions covering all its aspects.

18. It is proposed that the General Assembly should further invite the relevant United Nations agencies:

(a) To collectively prepare guidance and to provide assistance on how to make environmental assessments by different regions consistent with each other, thus contributing to global assessments (for example by revising the existing guidance on Quality Status Reports from the Group of Experts on the Scientific Aspects of Marine Protection [GESAMP]);

(b) To consider how they could help in making such assessments to meet the special needs of developing countries and countries whose economies are in transition.

Issue G

Moving from diagnosis to action on the marine environment

19. Existing assessments show that seamounts (isolated elevations which do not rise above the sea surface), together with certain other underwater features, have high levels of endemic species (species not found elsewhere). They therefore constitute a large, but as yet unevaluated, reservoir of biological diversity. The fauna and flora of such seamounts and other underwater features, particularly those which are not migratory, may be threatened by human activities in those areas. Such threats would emphasize the need for a precautionary approach.

20. It is proposed that the General Assembly should invite the Food and Agriculture Organization of the United Nations (FAO), the International Hydrographic Organization (IHO), the International Maritime Organization (IMO), IOC, the International Seabed Authority, the Secretariat of the Convention on Biological Diversity, the United Nations Secretariat (Division for Ocean Affairs and the Law of the Sea, Office of Legal Affairs), the United Nations Environment Programme (UNEP) and the World Meteorological Organization (WMO), with the assistance of regional and subregional fisheries bodies and other organizations in regions and subregions where the fauna and flora of seamounts and certain other underwater features may be under threat, to consider urgently how to integrate and improve on a scientific basis the management of risks to such fauna and flora within the framework of the United Nations Convention on the Law of the Sea and to make suggestions for this purpose on appropriate management action.

21. Ongoing marine scientific research activities and existing assessments also emphasize the unique and fragile nature and the rich biological diversity of the ecosystems around deep-sea hydrothermal vents.

22. It is proposed that the General Assembly should welcome the actions which national governments and regional organizations (in respect of areas within, respectively, their jurisdiction or competence) and the Intergovernmental Oceanographic Commission are taking to protect these ecosystems.

23. It is further proposed that the General Assembly should reiterate the importance of the ongoing elaboration by the International Seabed Authority, pursuant to Article 145 of UNCLOS, of recommendations to ensure the effective protection of the marine environment from harmful effects that may arise from activities in the Area.

24. It is proposed in addition that the General Assembly should invite FAO, IHO, IMO, IOC, the International Seabed Authority, the Secretariat of the Convention on Biological Diversity, the United Nations Secretariat (Division for Ocean Affairs and Law of the Sea, Office of Legal Affairs; and the Division for Sustainable Development, Department of Economic and Social Affairs), UNEP and WMO to consider, with any other United Nations agencies or regional organizations that may be involved, what action, consistent with UNCLOS, should be suggested to address priority problems in the marine environment, in particular any highlighted by future global marine assessments.

25. In order to complement such global action at the regional level, it is further proposed that the General Assembly should invite regional and subregional organi-

zations, where appropriate, concerned with the marine environment, navigational safety, fisheries management and marine science to consider how to establish specific regional targets for managing marine and coastal ecosystems in an integrated manner. The range of regional action that could be considered could include, taking into account the particular situation of each region, arrangements such as networks of marine protected areas already established in some regions, the protection of fragile coastal ecosystems, such as coral reefs, support for traditional marine management systems and methods, and, where appropriate, participation in the International Coral Reef Initiative.

International regulation and programmes

Issue H

Bringing into force agreed international agreements at the global and regional levels to prevent, reduce and control pollution

26. Much has already been achieved by States to fulfil the requirements of the United Nations Convention on the Law of the Sea in establishing at the global and regional levels rules, standards and/or recommended practices and/or procedures for the prevention, reduction and control of pollution from land-based sources, from seabed activities both within the Area and within national jurisdictions, from dumping and from vessels and airborne pollution. Nevertheless, a number of important instruments have not yet entered into force.

27. It is proposed that the General Assembly should call for action by States to bring into force:

(a) Annexes IV (sewage) and VI (air pollution) to the International Convention for the Prevention of Pollution from Ships, as modified by the Protocol of 1978 relating thereto (MARPOL 73/78);
(b) The 1996 Protocol to the London Convention on the Prevention of Marine Pollution by Dumping of Wastes and Other Matter, 1972;
(c) The International Convention on Liability and Compensation for Damage in connection with the Carriage of Hazardous and Noxious Substances by Sea, 1996;
(d) The Protocol on Preparedness, Response and Cooperation to Pollution Incidents by Hazardous and Noxious Substances, 2000;
(e) The International Convention on the Control of Hazardous Anti-Fouling Systems on Ships, 2001;
(f) The International Convention on Civil Liability for Bunker Oil Pollution Damage, 2001;
(g) The Stockholm Convention on Persistent Organic Pollutants, 2001, and to consent to the amendments, adopted in 2000, to the 1992 Protocol to the International Convention on Civil Liability for Oil Pollution Damage, 1969, and to the 1992 Protocol to the International Convention on the

Establishment of an International Fund for Compensation for Oil Pollution Damage.

28. It will also be appropriate for all interested States to become parties to various existing regional agreements for the prevention, reduction and control of marine pollution. It is furthermore proposed that the General Assembly should call upon interested States that have not done so to become parties to those agreements.

Issue I

Enhancing regional action to prevent, reduce and control pollution

29. Action at the regional level is particularly important for the prevention, reduction and control of pollution from land-based sources. All States in the region concerned should be encouraged to cooperate and to commit resources to such work. Such commitments also need to be endorsed at a high political level.

30. It is proposed that the General Assembly should invite regional seas conventions and action plans to develop regionally shared goals and time-tables in pursuance of the Global Programme of Action for the Protection of the Marine Environment from Land-based Activities (GPA), as reviewed in Montreal in November 2001. In this respect, the General Assembly should welcome the 2002 Antigua Convention, which is the first regional agreement to integrate the implementation of the GPA within its framework.

31. In view of the significance of municipal wastewater as a component of land-based pollution, it is proposed that the General Assembly should also invite regional seas conventions and action plans:

(a) To assist their member States, where necessary, in developing the components addressing municipal wastewater of their national action plans under the GPA;
(b) To provide a forum for discussion and agreements on how to mobilize public and private resources, both domestic and external, for investment in this field; in this context, approaches based on support through "payment by results" may be of particular value.

32. In order to pursue the 1999 recommendation of the Commission on Sustainable Development that "the primary focus of action on the environmental aspects of offshore oil and gas operations continue to be at the national, subregional and regional levels,"[1] it is proposed that the General Assembly should recommend that regional seas conventions and action plans in regions where offshore oil and gas industries are developing or are in prospect, and where programmes and measures relating to offshore installations do not exist, should develop programmes and/or measures to prevent, reduce and control pollution from offshore installations. It is

1. *Official Records of the Economic and Social Council, 1999, Supplement No. 9* (E/1999/29), chap. I.C, decision 7/1, par. 36 (a).

further proposed that the General Assembly should invite regional seas conventions and action plans that have developed such programmes and measures to make their information and experience available for this process.

Issue J

Developing new international agreements and guidance at the global level to prevent, reduce and control marine pollution

33. Action to prevent, reduce and control marine pollution from vessels is most appropriately achieved at the global level.

34. It is proposed that the General Assembly should welcome the progress on the negotiation of an international convention for the control and management of ships' ballast water and sediments and urge the International Maritime Organization to carry these negotiations through to completion according to the intended timetable.

35. It is proposed in addition that the General Assembly should also invite the International Maritime Organization to consider further how to facilitate the phasing out of single-hulled vessels carrying oil and hazardous substances in bulk.

36. As well as developing regional regulation of offshore oil and gas installations, it is also important to ensure that adequate national and regional plans are developed for responding to emergencies threatening marine pollution arising from accidents on such offshore installations.

37. In order to provide assistance in the development of such national and regional plans, it is proposed that the General Assembly should invite IMO, UNEP and WMO to undertake an initiative, involving the relevant regional organizations as well as the oil and gas industry, to develop guidance on the best environmental practices to prevent and control pollution from accidents on offshore installations and to mitigate their effects.

Issue K

Integration of policies on fisheries management and the conservation of biological diversity as an aspect of integrated ocean management

38. As the General Assembly has emphasized, the problems of ocean space are closely interrelated and need to be considered as a whole through an integrated, interdisciplinary and intersectoral approach.

39. In order to give effect to this approach in relation to fisheries, it is proposed that the General Assembly should invite each of the relevant regional fisheries bodies, including regional fisheries management organizations and regional fisheries arrangements, to review the implications for their work of an ecosystem approach to the management of the oceans, and to invite FAO to facilitate such reviews for the relevant regional fisheries organizations that they support.

40. It is furthermore proposed that the General Assembly should also invite each of the relevant regional fisheries bodies which have responsibilities for the management of fisheries on the high seas under Article 118 of UNCLOS and/or, where applicable, the Agreement for the Implementation of the Provisions of

UNCLOS relating to the Conservation and Management of Straddling Fish Stocks and Highly Migratory Fish Stocks (1995 Fish Stocks Agreement) to consider how to improve the regulation of all aspects of fisheries management in their areas, taking into account the ecosystem approach, and how to facilitate the implementation of their obligations by member States with respect to management within their national jurisdictions under the Convention on Biological Diversity and commitments under the Jakarta Mandate, and to invite FAO to facilitate such consideration in the relevant regional fisheries organizations that they support.

41. It is proposed in addition that the General Assembly should call upon all those States fishing on the high seas in regions where no regional fisheries organizations or arrangements have responsibility for managing such fisheries, to develop agreements or arrangements for the effective implementation of Part VII of UNCLOS and, where applicable, the 1995 Fish Stocks Agreement, and for that purpose to invite FAO and other relevant organizations, where necessary, to facilitate such negotiations.

Implementation

Issue L

Improving implementation

42. International agreements and programmes of action alone will not improve the status of the marine environment. It is essential that they are implemented and enforced to achieve the required goals. There is, however, an implementation gap: there needs to be more commitment to this less glamorous task. There also needs to be greater transparency with regard to the level of implementation and enforcement which is being achieved.

43. It is proposed that the General Assembly should emphasize very strongly the essential need to improve the implementation of both the binding and the non-binding instruments and, for all international organizations, to consider how they can assist such implementation. Such assistance could take as a model the work of IMO in assisting flag States in meeting their obligations under UNCLOS, and should include:

(a) Preparing and publishing periodic evaluations of progress;
(b) Where appropriate, providing training to personnel from developing countries in enforcement techniques;
(c) Where appropriate, providing for technical cooperation and financial assistance.

44. It is also proposed that the General Assembly should invite IMO, in respect of its conventions and protocols, and all regional organizations that support international agreements in their regions, to develop appropriate systems to evaluate the level of compliance with the requirements of those conventions, protocols and agreements.

45. It is further proposed that the General Assembly should also invite the Secretary-General and those regional organizations able to do so to explore the possibilities of collecting data on the degree of compliance and enforcement being achieved under such global and regional agreements, collected under cooperative arrangements with States and/or regional organizations.

46. Measures to prevent, reduce and control pollution cannot always prevent pollution from accidents. Implementation of cooperation agreements for the prevention of pollution from ships in the case of emergencies is encountering difficulties due to the lack of contingency plans and appropriate equipment and facilities in various States.

47. It is therefore proposed that the General Assembly should invite IMO, with the cooperation of the other relevant United Nations agencies and international financial institutions and donors, to review the programmes for supporting regional cooperative capabilities for planning responses to emergencies and to train staff to handle such emergencies, to undertake initiatives to develop such capabilities in regions where regional cooperative arrangements do not exist, and to assist developing countries in developing their national capabilities in this field.

Issue M

Ensuring cooperation and coordination between international organizations

48. As UNCLOS affirms, "the problems of ocean space are closely interrelated and need to be considered as a whole." Since these problems range across many fields, it is inevitable that many international institutions are involved in them. Particularly at the global level, cooperation and coordination are needed as a priority if effective interdisciplinary and intersectoral action is to be achieved. As more and more emphasis is placed upon implementation, the need for effective executive cooperation and coordination becomes ever stronger. This coordinating role had been undertaken since 1993 by the Subcommittee on Oceans and Coastal Areas (SOCA) of the Administrative Committee on Coordination (ACC), but that body was dissolved with effect from 1 January 2002. It is therefore essential to establish a new coordinating mechanism for issues relating to oceans and seas, consistent with the new arrangements being developed in the United Nations system.

9. It is proposed that the General Assembly should invite the Secretary-General, as chairman of the United Nations System's Chief Executives Board for Coordination, to consider establishing a new coordinating mechanism for issues relating to oceans and seas, taking into account the decisions of the World Summit on Sustainable Development in this regard, and should recommend that this new mechanism should be transparent, effective and responsive and could be based upon the following approaches:

(a) The new mechanism should include, as a core, all the United Nations departments, funds, programmes and agencies and international financial institutions that are regularly involved in issues relating to oceans and seas; other members of the United Nations system should be able to participate when that is desirable; the new mechanism would be responding to a continuing need and should have continuity, regularity and accountability;

(b) The new mechanism should be established in a way that sets up a clear mandate and demonstrates the commitment to cooperation and coordination of the core participating institutions at the highest level;
(c) The new mechanism should be able to work at two levels:

  (i) Through regular reviews of issues relating to oceans and seas which involve several core participating institutions, and of the mandates and work plans of the core participating institutions relating to them, in order to eliminate gaps, inconsistencies and unnecessary overlaps; such reviews would also be aimed at identifying newly emerging problems and devising ways to tackle them; such reviews would need adequate support; the cost of such support should be offset by the savings that would result from improved cooperation and coordination;
  (ii) Through the establishment of a specific task force, as needed, to carry out task-oriented activities; such task force should report to the new coordinating mechanism; as and when the planning and budgetary cycles of United Nations agencies are made more compatible, such task force might be charged with managing joint actions;

(d) As part of the process of improving coordination, as recommended by the General Assembly in paragraph 49 of its resolution 56/12, to ensure cooperation and coordination on issues relating to oceans and seas, each member of the United Nations system involved with such issues should nominate a fully interactive focal point for those issues; the details of those focal points should be readily available both inside and outside the United Nations system;
(e) The mechanism should establish a means of liaison with regional organizations, including those dealing with development finance, fisheries management, marine science, navigation and the protection of the marine environment;
(f) The mechanism should be transparent in its work, inter alia, by making readily available the issues that it is considering and the results of that consideration.

50. It is also proposed that the General Assembly should recommend that every State and, as appropriate, every regional economic cooperation organization should identify a focal point for coordination and cooperation on issues relating to oceans and seas, and should ensure that the United Nations Secretariat has those details so that they can be made available in the same way for focal points within the United Nations system.

PART B

Co-chairpersons' summary of discussions

Agenda item 1: Opening of the meeting
1. The discussions at the first and the second plenary sessions of the third meeting of the United Nations Open-ended Informal Consultative Process established by the

General Assembly in its resolution 54/33 in order to facilitate the annual review by the Assembly of developments in ocean affairs were based on General Assembly resolutions 54/33, 56/12 and 56/13, on the material for the annual report of the Secretary-General on oceans and the law of the sea, as well as on other documents before the meeting, including written submissions by States and international organizations.

2. The overall legal framework for the discussions was provided by the United Nations Convention on the Law of the Sea of 10 December 1982 (UNCLOS) and its two implementing Agreements,[2] while chapter 17 of Agenda 21 provided the programme of action for the sustainable development of oceans and seas, which was re-emphasized in decision 7/1 adopted by the Commission on Sustainable Development at its seventh session, in 1999.

3. The meeting was opened by Alan Simcock (United Kingdom of Great Britain and Northern Ireland), Co-Chairperson, who called for a minute of silence in memory of the late Elisabeth Mann Borgese, who had devoted her life to enriching humankind's relationship with the oceans and actively participated in the work of the Consultative Process at its two first meetings.

4. The discussions were opened, on behalf of the Secretary-General of the United Nations, by Hans Corell, Under-Secretary-General for Legal Affairs, The Legal Counsel, and Joanne DiSano, Director of the Division for Sustainable Development, who represented the Department of Economic and Social Affairs in the absence of Nitin Desai, Under-Secretary-General for Economic and Social Affairs.

5. In his introductory statement, Mr. Corell noted the significance of the year 2002 for ocean affairs, since the year marks the twentieth anniversary of the opening for signature of UNCLOS, and also the tenth anniversary of the adoption of Agenda 21, the United Nations programme of action from the Earth Summit, chapter 17 of which put forward a programme of action for the sustainable development of the world's oceans, seas and coasts. He noted that, despite major accomplishments, the potentials of the oceans and their resources remained unrealized for a large part of the community of nations and that, despite the formulation of a multitude of instruments and measures for governance, good governance in the case of the world's oceans and seas was still far from a reality, nationally, regionally or globally. In that connection, he emphasized that the suggested measures to address the limitations identified in the past were in most cases those already embedded in UNCLOS and Agenda 21.

6. Mr. Corell continued his statement by highlighting the importance of international cooperation and stressing the fact that "international cooperation," including regional cooperation, was a clear obligation both under the treaty law of UNCLOS and under the soft law of Agenda 21. Recognizing that the accomplishments in international cooperation to date had been quite commendable indeed, he sug-

2. Agreement relating to the implementation of Part XI of the Convention and Agreement for the Implementation of the Provisions of the Convention relating to the Conservation and Management of Straddling Fish Stocks and Highly Migratory Fish Stocks.

gested that the way forward was to strengthen the existing measures of international cooperation, build upon them and add to them to address the identified gaps.

7. On the issue of inter-agency coordination, Mr. Corell noted that a search for new ideas, approaches or mechanisms with regard to such coordination had become extremely essential in view of the fact that the Subcommittee on Oceans and Coastal Areas (SOCA) had ceased to exist as of December 2001, pursuant to a decision of the United Nations System Chief Executives Board for Coordination (CEB), the successor to the Administrative Committee on Coordination (ACC). The Board had decided to move away from the concept of permanent subsidiary bodies with fixed periodicity of meetings and rigid reporting requirements and, instead, to rely increasingly on ad hoc, time-bound and task-oriented coordination arrangements. Mr. Corell pointed out that the efficacy of the latter type of arrangements needed to be studied in the case of oceans in view of the interrelated nature of its problems and the need to consider them as a whole.

8. He suggested that inter-agency coordination arrangements would be facilitated if each agency designated a focal point for oceans and the law of the sea. The involvement of the liaison offices of the agencies in New York in enhancing coordination in ocean matters could be explored. He also suggested that CEB could initiate an exercise that would look into the mandates and the work plans of the departments, funds, programmes and agencies of the United Nations system in the field of oceans and the law of the sea with a view to eliminating areas of duplication, setting out work in important areas that was not currently being performed and terminating outputs that no longer served their intended purpose.

9. Finally, in the context of coordination and cooperation, he stressed the importance of coordination of ocean affairs at the national level.

10. Ms. DiSano referred in her statement, made on behalf of Mr. Nitin Desai, Under-Secretary-General for Economic and Social Affairs, to the forthcoming World Summit on Sustainable Development to be held in Johannesburg, South Africa. The summit would review progress achieved in the implementation of the Programme of Action from the United Nations Conference on Environment and Development (UNCED), held in Rio de Janeiro 10 years ago.

11. She noted that during the third session of the Preparatory Committee for the Summit held recently, there was considerable interest among participants in the issues related to the oceans. Significant work had been undertaken to give oceans, coasts and islands a higher political profile in the Summit process and at the Summit itself, with discussions on issues related to capacity-building, the sustainable use and conservation of marine living resources, marine pollution, the protection and management of coastal zones and marine ecosystems, ocean science and the need for better coordination and cooperation among Governments and international and regional organizations. She noted that much of the momentum for a focus on oceans in the Summit process might be due to the excellent inputs provided by various preparatory events sponsored by Governments and United Nations agencies, in particular the Global Conference on Oceans and Coasts at Rio+10, held at UNESCO headquarters in Paris in December 2001.

12. She also recalled other important recent meetings that had provided inputs to the Preparatory Committee for the Summit, such as the First Intergovernmental Review Meeting on Implementation of the Global Programme of Action for the Protection of the Marine Environment from Land-based Activities, organized by UNEP and held in Montreal in November 2001, and the Reykjavik Conference on Responsible Fisheries in the Marine Ecosystem, co-sponsored by Iceland, Norway and FAO in October 2001. In addition, UNEP annual meetings of regional seas conventions and action plans, and the ongoing work of the respective United Nations organizations related to oceans have contributed to Summit preparations. Ms. DiSano added that the third meeting of the Consultative Process, coming between the two last and critical sessions of the Preparatory Committee for the World Summit on Sustainable Development, provided the opportunity for a very useful input and guidance to the Summit on very important and cross-cutting issues.

13. On the subject of inter-agency coordination and collaboration within the United Nations system, Ms. DiSano stated that the Department for Economic and Social Affairs and the Commission on Sustainable Development placed great importance on the mechanisms established through SOCA, which had been set up to coordinate inter-agency activities related to oceans and coasts and to serve as task manager for chapter 17 of Agenda 21. However, she noted that the ACC subsidiary bodies had been abolished and the members of SOCA and the other inter-agency committees had been urged to consider how inter-agency cooperation could be handled through ad hoc, time-bound, task-oriented arrangements and other means of information-sharing.[3]

14. Mr. Simcock, Co-Chairperson of the meeting, highlighted that the discussions of the third meeting of the Consultative Process would take place against the background of the preparatory work for the World Summit on Sustainable Development and that there was a parallelism between the two processes, one of which would culminate with the General Assembly debate and resolution and the other would lead to the Summit. He also noted that in view of recent developments, the discussion on inter-agency cooperation and coordination would be a particularly difficult task.

15. Ambassador Tuiloma Neroni Slade (Samoa), Co-Chairperson of the meeting, underscored that a number of developing States lacked the capacity for the implementation of the Convention. He also expressed the hope that the discussion on cooperation and coordination would clearly reveal the direction for further action.

Agenda item 2: Approval of the format of the meeting and adoption of the agenda

16. Mr. Simcock, Co-Chairperson of the meeting, presented the proposals of the Co-Chairpersons for the format and annotated agenda of the third meeting (A/

3. For the complete text of the statements (in English) made by the Under-Secretary-General for Legal Affairs, the Legal Counsel, and the Director of the Division for Sustainable Development, representing the Department of Economic and

AC.259/L.3). In the light of the results of the informal consultations preceding the meeting,[4] he proposed that the meeting should adopt its format and annotated agenda. The meeting then adopted by consensus the format and annotated agenda (A/AC.259/5).

Agenda item 3: Exchange of views on areas of concern and actions needed

The Consultative Process

17. Many delegations have emphasized that it was imperative that the Process should take place within the framework established by UNCLOS and they stressed the importance of full implementation of UNCLOS and the need for the preservation of its integrity.

18. In that connection, one delegation reiterated its position and its approach to the informal Consultative Process as a whole, namely that the international legal instruments, including conventions, were binding upon their parties only, and they did not affect the rights and obligations of non-parties.

19. A number of delegations stressed the importance of the efficient use of time, the avoidance of generalities and repetition of previous statements. They called for a focused debate on the subjects and the formulation of concrete recommendations.

20. Some delegations noted the absence of an item devoted to the review of the Consultative Process, in view of the provision in General Assembly resolution 54/33 that the Assembly had decided "to review the effectiveness and utility of the consultative process at its fifty-seventh session." In their opinion, comments regarding the future of the Process might be of considerable help to the General Assembly at its fifth-seventh session, when it would perform the review and make a decision about the future of the Process.

21. Despite the absence of such an item, many statements contained elements of assessment of the Consultative Process and an overwhelming majority of delegations noted its usefulness. They stated, inter alia, that the Process had a reinvigorating effect on the General Assembly's debates on oceans and the law of the sea, which as a result had become more focused and relevant. In their view, the Process had achieved its goal: to facilitate an in-depth annual review by the General Assembly of developments in ocean affairs in a constructive and effective manner. Delegations also added that in addition to the widened and deepened debate in the General Assembly on oceans and the law of the sea, the enriched resolutions of the Assembly on the item were testimony to the value of the work of the Process.

22. Some delegations noted that the Process was the only forum where the multiple aspects of ocean issues could be examined and discussed in an integrated manner and that it had provided substantial input for a better understanding of the oceans, highlighting issues for common action.

Social Affairs, see the web site of the Division for Ocean Affairs and the Law of the Sea: www.un.org/Depts/los.

4. One round of informal consultations was held on 15 February 2002.

23. At the same time, it was noted that there was room for improvement and enhancement, both in the substantive and procedural aspects, for the Process to yield better results. Among specific suggestions, it was mentioned that the various regional cooperation mechanisms and agreements in the field of oceans and the conservation of marine resources must provide input to the substantive discussions of the Process and participate in the implementation of its results. It was also mentioned that it was indispensable to promote the participation of the landlocked States in the Process, taking into account their special circumstances and needs. In addition, it was proposed that the Consultative Process should review the progress made on issues discussed at previous meetings, as a regular agenda item.

24. The European Union (EU) made suggestions that the Process should not become institutionalized or bureaucratic. It should maintain its informality and flexibility and continue to search for the best ways and means to address, in an integrated manner, the legal, political, economic, social and environmental aspects of ocean affairs. The Consultative Process should focus on identifying areas where coordination and cooperation within the United Nations system should be enhanced and defining how concrete improvements could be achieved, with a view to proposing particular issues for consideration by the General Assembly. The Process should not be of a permanent character. The General Assembly could renew it for a fixed period and, after reviewing its performance at the end of that time, decide then on its continuation, with the same or modified terms of reference. The synergy between the Secretary-General's report, the deliberations in the Process and the debates of the General Assembly should be maintained. For that purpose, feedback was required. The Secretary-General should inform the Process about the follow-up to its recommendations, in particular those reflected in the resolutions of the General Assembly.

25. One delegation stated that the Process itself had no mandate to undertake its own review and that it was important that the outcome of the review by the General Assembly should not be prejudged. However, another delegation noted that while it was not possible for the Consultative Process to review itself, the third meeting could make appropriate recommendations to the General Assembly as to its effectiveness and efficiency.

The Consultative Process and the World Summit on Sustainable Development

26. A number of delegations addressed the relationship and the need for coordination between the Consultative Process and the World Summit on Sustainable Development, to be held in Johannesburg. They noted that the two areas of focus of the third meeting of the Process—protection and preservation of the marine environment; and capacity-building, regional cooperation and coordination, and integrated ocean management—were relevant to the work of the Summit and its preparatory meetings and that there had already been opportunities to present initiatives to highlight the intended ocean-related activities at the third session of the Preparatory Committee for the Summit. Those delegations supported the idea that efforts ought to be made at the third meeting of the Process with a view to contributing to the

Summit deliberations, in particular by making the conclusions available to participating delegations, and that the Summit should foster capacity-building, and cooperation and coordination, in particular at the regional level, as means of attaining the comprehensive management of the oceans.

Implementation of UNCLOS, the related Agreements and relevant international instruments

27. Delegations observed that the third meeting of the Process was taking place in the year of the twentieth anniversary of the opening for signature of UNCLOS and re-emphasized that the various activities carried out in the oceans and seas should be in conformity with the legal regime established by the Convention, as well as with the objectives and programmes incorporated in chapter 17 of Agenda 21, and that the integrity of the Convention should be maintained.

28. In that context, the representative of the United States of America, which is not a party to the Convention, stated that her Government accepted the Convention's provisions on traditional uses of the oceans as reflecting existing customary international law and practice and that the current Administration supported United States accession to the instrument.

Report of the Secretary-General

29. Delegations expressed their appreciation to the Secretary-General and to the Division for Ocean Affairs and the Law of the Sea for the excellent and comprehensive report on oceans and the law of the sea, as well as for the efforts deployed to make available the unofficial English version of the report, in spite of the complications owing to the advancement of the dates of the third meeting of the Consultative Process. They noted the extensive nature of the report and the detailed account of the latest developments in ocean affairs, as well as the useful information contained in the annexes. They expressed particular interest in the report of the South Pacific Applied Geoscience Commission (SOPAC) on "Ocean issues in the Pacific region in 2001: initiatives and priorities" and commended its inclusion in the report.

30. On the other hand, a number of delegations noted with regret the fact that the report of the Secretary-General was not available in all official languages and that it had not been available in a definitive format and printed form in due time. They underscored the unacceptability of such a situation since it had created grave difficulties for the work of non-English-speaking delegations and put them at a serious disadvantage. They requested that such a situation should not occur in the future.

31. The representative of the European Union made a number of additional specific comments and suggestions with respect to the report, requesting, inter alia, the reproduction of annexes included in previous reports concerning the status of UNCLOS and its implementing Agreements, national claims to maritime areas and the description of treaties adopted under the auspices of UNEP, as well as the inclusion of additional information containing the description of maritime treaties

adopted under the auspices of other international organizations, such as FAO or IMO.

32. Commenting on the synergies between the report, the deliberations in the Consultative Process and the debate in the General Assembly, which concluded with the adoption of the "omnibus" resolution on oceans and the law of the sea, and with the purpose of avoiding repetition in the annual resolution, the European Union proposed that the accomplishments in the field of oceans and the law of the sea should be consolidated in a framework resolution and, so that only the latest developments would be introduced in the yearly resolution.

33. One representative commented on certain specific issues in the report. He stated, with reference to the subsection dealing with the access to and from the sea by landlocked developing countries and freedom of transit, that his Government was opposed to an approach that unconditionally favoured the access of landlocked countries to seas through the shortest possible route, since such an approach might run the risk of disregarding the outstanding problems prevailing in the region or, in some circumstances, might not be feasible due to geographical or socio-economic factors. Concerning the subsection on underwater cultural heritage, he indicated that his Government considered such heritage as a natural resource and therefore had voted against the adoption of the UNESCO Convention on the Protection of the Underwater Cultural Heritage in November 2001.

34. The representative of the Intergovernmental Oceanographic Commission of UNESCO referred to the IOC contribution to the report of the Secretary-General on oceans and the law of the sea and pointed out that it usefully reflected the significant work on and resources devoted to ocean issues by the United Nations system as a whole. Proposing an improved approach, he noted that the report was an excellent compilation and, at the same time, a post facto exercise, after each agency and programme had forwarded its own report. Thus, it lacked the element of an integrated approach, which would highlight the interactive effects of the different uses of the ocean and coasts under the stewardship of the different agencies and programmes and could not address cross-sectoral issues, such as between transport and fisheries, between fisheries and habitat protection, and between land-based pollutants, fisheries and the marine environment. He suggested that there was a need to know and analyse the complex matrix of interactions between the different uses and recalled the objectives of the Consultative Process, one of which was to identify ways to integrate the different sectoral aspects.

Areas of focus

35. Delegations expressed their general satisfaction with the two areas of focus for the third meeting of the Consultative Process, namely: (a) the protection and preservation of the marine environment, and (b) capacity-building, regional cooperation and coordination, and integrated ocean management. A number of speakers noted the overlapping of these areas of focus, which was due, among other things, to the cross-sectoral nature of the issues of capacity-building and integrated oceans management, in particular.

36. The areas of focus were dealt with in depth in Discussion Panels A and B, respectively. For the summary of the Discussion Panels (in English), see the web site of the Division for Ocean Affairs and the Law of the Sea: www.un.org/Depts/los.

(a) Protection and preservation of the marine environment

37. As regards the protection of the marine environment, it was noted that the international community had made considerable progress on marine environmental protection and other oceans issues since UNCED in Rio de Janeiro in 1992. Among significant developments, mention was made of the entry into force of UNCLOS in 1994, providing a framework for negotiation and implementation of agreements affecting the marine environment, and the adoption of a number of other instruments, such as the 1995 Global Programme of Action on the Protection of the Marine Environment from Land-based Activities, the International Coral Reef Initiative, and Protocols to the Cartagena Convention. The Arctic Council and the South Pacific Regional Environmental Programme were highlighted as models of regional cooperation to protect human health, prevent or control pollution and ensure sound environmental management of oceans and coastal areas.

38. Delegations pointed out with disappointment that, despite achievements, there was continuing degradation of the marine environment from both shipping activities and land-based sources of pollution, information about which is contained in the report of the Secretary-General. For coastal and island States, the degradation of watersheds and marine ecosystems entailed reduced fisheries and biodiversity, loss of food security, increased risks to public health and missed opportunities for sustainable economic development. Owing to the transboundary nature of marine ecosystems, this vulnerability extended to neighbouring States reliant on the fisheries resources of shared seas, making marine ecosystem degradation a regional concern and its control a regional responsibility.

39. Many delegations called for the effective implementation of Part XII of UNCLOS in order to protect and preserve the marine environment and its living resources against pollution and degradation, and to promote the implementation of the various international agreements designed to prevent the contamination of the marine environment. Importance was attached by many to the implementation of existing international treaties rather than to the need to negotiate and adopt new instruments.

40. It was noted that implementation required (a) strengthening national and regional institutional capacity to use advanced science and technology and other tools in support of cross-sectoral approaches to watershed and marine ecosystem management; (b) facilitating the availability, transparency and harmonization of scientific data within and among Governments and scientific bodies, so that decision-making could more readily be based on scientific information; (c) strengthening regional governance capacity by increasing collaboration among regional seas and fisheries organizations through mechanisms, including joint meetings and programmes; and (d) strengthening legal systems and structures so that international plans of action could be effectively executed at the national and local levels.

41. It was stated that efforts to address the problems of the marine environment and reverse the current trends should be given continued priority, and should be implemented in an integrated, intersectoral and interdisciplinary manner.

42. Several delegations referred to the adoption of UNEP Governing Council decision 21/13, in which the Executive Director of UNEP was requested to explore the feasibility of establishing a regular process for the assessment of the state of the marine environment, with the active involvement of Governments and regional agreements. That decision was based on the growing recognition that there was an urgent need to improve communication between scientists and government policy makers and the public alike, regarding information on the state of the marine environment and its socio-economic aspects.

43. It was suggested that the functions of competent international organizations should be better exercised and that cooperation and coordination among those organizations should be strengthened, e.g., the cooperation between UNEP and IOC in the development of a scientific approach for ensuring both coastal management and protection of marine environment. It was further suggested that the role of several bodies should be reinforced, e.g., the role of UNEP in the implementation of the GPA, and that the role of existing conventions and plans of action on marine environmental protection should be strengthened. Relevant international organizations should be encouraged to develop feasible plans to promote capacity-building in developing countries in the area of marine environmental protection.

44. In addition, reference was made to the need to foster horizontal as well as vertical technical cooperation for the purpose of attaining the conservation and sustainable use of the marine resources. It was noted that it was indispensable to increase research on the relationship between coastal and marine areas to design preservation and management programmes that would respond to the real needs of populations. It was also noted that it was necessary to increase intergovernmental cooperation to reduce and prevent marine pollution and to respond adequately to accidents that endangered the environment and the living resources of oceans and seas.

45. Emphasis was placed in particular on the importance of effective regional cooperation for the protection and preservation of the marine environment and the importance of concerted endeavours among the States sharing specific marine areas. The unique features and problems of regional ecosystems and the shared nature of their resources were highlighted and the need for regional solutions was underscored. A view was expressed that much could be done to promote an integrated approach to the marine environment at the regional level, through, inter alia, more education and training opportunities on the regional marine environment, preparing management guidelines at the regional level and creating synergy through the cooperation and coordination among various marine environment programmes targeting the same regional seas. A possibility for creating partnerships through "twinning" between various regional programmes was mentioned as well. An example was the partnership which OSPAR was endeavouring to create with the Abidjan Convention for West and Central Africa.

46. Some delegations expressed the view that the key objective in regional cooperation should be the development of a framework for regional management programmes that promoted efficient use of resources and addressed the entire scope of watershed and marine ecosystem management from forests to the sea.

47. In order to ensure a comprehensive approach with regard to the marine environment, it was suggested that the discussions of Panel A should take into account a number of aspects, such as the pollution in oceans and seas and its impact on freshwater resources; impacts of pollution on fragile ecosystems; ballast water and its impact on the marine environment; dumping of wastes; hazardous wastes; radioactive and chemical wastes; marine pollution in coastal areas and its effect on agriculture and freshwater; and crisis management in emergency situations.

48. As regards increasing protection of the marine environment from transboundary movement of radioactive material, a substantial number of States pointed to the need for the elaboration of an international legal regime for the transboundary movement of radioactive material, taking into account the protection of the marine environment and human health. One group of States opposed such a process.

49. Among areas where specific and urgent action was needed, the following were mentioned: improving global and regional oceans governance; greater emphasis on marine scientific research and monitoring; taking further steps to conserve marine biodiversity; and tackling unsustainable fishing practices.

50. At the national level, several examples of an integrated approach to the protection of the marine environment were offered, such as the 1998 Oceans Policy of Australia, reflecting ecological, economic and social objectives, and the soon-to-be-published first Marine Stewardship Report of the United Kingdom, based on an ecosystem-based approach to marine management. The Great Barrier Reef Marine Park of Australia was cited as a practical example of integrated planning and management at the local level.

51. One delegation pointed out that there was an increasing awareness of the need to improve the conservation and management approach in areas beyond national jurisdiction, which did not attract much attention, and underscored the impacts of human activity on the ecological systems of the high seas. Some of the serious problems cited were: overfishing and subsequent extinction of species; benthic trawling and devastation of the diverse ocean floors; illegal, unreported and unregulated (IUU) fishing—the equivalent of ecological piracy; and pollution and the introduction of marine pests.

(b) Capacity-building

52. The topic of capacity-building was considered crucial and of special significance by all delegations. Many pointed out that the promotion of capacity-building had become an important and pressing task in order to enable the developing States to implement UNCLOS and to reap the benefits therefrom. Moreover, it was mentioned that true and tangible solutions lay in capacity-building so that States, especially developing States, might develop the necessary personnel and technical capabilities to give effect to their rights and responsibilities.

53. The lack of capacity in many areas was noted by a number of delegations. Examples included the lack of capacity in most of the components needed to govern the fisheries sector in the majority of developing countries, as well as the need for better access for developing countries to relevant experience, technical support and financial resources to implement sustainable fisheries management systems, and the lack of adequate hydrographic data in extended sea areas of the world, affecting the accuracy of a large percentage of the available navigational charts.

54. On the other hand, various successful examples for fostering capacity-building were noted. They included a training course in Rio de Janeiro, from 3 to 8 March 2002, focusing on the preparation by interested coastal States of submissions to the Commission on the Limits of the Continental Shelf, which had been developed from the technical expertise and practical experience acquired by Brazil in preparation for its own submission; and the United Nations University Fisheries Training Programme, established in Iceland in 1998, which provided capacity-building in the area of sustainable fisheries management through postgraduate training for professionals from the fisheries sectors of developing countries.

55. During the general discussion, priority areas of capacity-building for developing countries were identified: ocean monitoring, marine environmental protection, integrated ocean management and marine resource development. It was noted that in order to address such priorities, financial assistance, technological support and personnel training were needed. Many delegations, including those representing the Rio Group, called for an increase in transfer of technology and capital to developing countries in order to facilitate better management and preservation of marine environment and fishing resources in the light of the latest progress in science and technology, and to foster the capacity of the developing countries for marine research as well as the development of their human resources. One delegation suggested the development of demonstration projects of capacity-building and called for an active role to be played by developed countries in promoting the transfer of marine technology to developing countries under fair and reasonable terms and conditions.

56. Delegations highlighted the necessity of the efficient management of marine science and technology by developing countries in order to achieve the sustainable development of ocean resources. It was also noted that efficient marine resources management could maximize benefits to resource owners and communities and assist in achieving national goals.

57. Among various possible solutions to the problems of capacity-building, delegations called for improved partnership between international financial institutions, bilateral agencies and other relevant stakeholders, and for the enhancement of existing international efforts and the coordination of approaches among States and relevant international organizations. It was also considered important to create a mechanism to ensure that national and regional institutions engaged in marine scientific research in areas under the jurisdiction of a coastal State made available to that State information, reports, data, conclusions and assessments in a comprehensible and compatible format.

58. Making available and accessible the results of integrated marine assessments to policy makers and refocusing the efforts of IOC to facilitate its mission were proposed as a solution that might be recommended to the General Assembly at its fifty-seventh session. The use of the IOC system of regional centres to provide training and access to expertise, i.e., through regional workshops on data and other resources, and the possibility for developing countries to access those resources were also mentioned. Other suggestions included closer cooperation between IOC, UNEP, WHO, FAO and regional bodies carrying out marine and fisheries programmes.

59. In addition, some delegations stressed the importance of good governance—e.g., rooting out corruption, upholding human rights and adhering to the rule of law—for successful sustainable development and noted that that theme was a central focus of the World Summit on Sustainable Development, adding that one of the cornerstones of sustainable development involved the establishment of the domestic institutional, legal and regulatory infrastructure needed to manage natural resources effectively.

International cooperation and coordination

60. During the discussion in the plenary meetings of the Consultative Process, it was noted that relevant international organizations and regional mechanisms had played an important role in dealing with maritime issues and that inter-agency coordination on ocean issues was of critical importance.

61. Many delegations expressed disappointment with the abolition of the Subcommittee on Oceans and Coastal Areas (SOCA) of the Administrative Committee on Coordination (ACC), especially in the light of the recommendations included in General Assembly resolution 56/12. It was noted that the explanations on the matter included in the Secretary-General's report were not entirely satisfactory. There was general agreement that occasional inter-agency meetings might not suffice and that there should be a better mechanism to ensure coordination among the various agencies and programmes. One delegation proposed that the coordination functions of SOCA could be continued in a workable and practical way, through the strengthening of the Division for Ocean Affairs and the Law of the Sea.

62. A number of delegations called for the enhancement of the functions of the relevant international organizations, for strengthened coordination and cooperation among relevant international organizations and for an increase in assistance by those organizations to developing countries.

63. One delegation proposed that a "coordinating network" should be developed for the consideration of the issues of oceans and the law of the sea within the framework of the General Assembly and suggested that the third meeting of the Process should make a corresponding recommendation to the General Assembly at its fifty-seventh session. The function of the coordinating network would be to continue reviewing the issues related to oceans and the law of the sea and to strengthen cooperation and coordination among existing international organizations.

64. Regarding cooperation among States, many delegations emphasized the importance of regional cooperation as a way to deal more effectively with oceans

issues, in particular with the protection of the marine environment and the promotion of the sustainable development of the oceans. Furthermore, it was suggested that benefits could be derived from enhancing the coordination and cooperation between regional seas arrangements or action plans and the global conventions or relevant agreements and from promoting horizontal cooperation among relevant regional seas arrangements or action plans. In this connection, one delegation stated that since the objective of regional cooperation was to enhance confidence among States and to maintain stability in the region, regional cooperation should be carried out with due respect for territorial sovereignty and the maritime rights of coastal States, without incurring maritime disputes among coastal States.

65. In particular, it was noted that a regular and coordinated approach to the assessment of the marine environment was required to promote a closer relationship between marine science and policy-making. In that connection, the question was raised of how the regional marine conventions, such as the OSPAR Commission for the Protection of the Marine Environment of the North-East Atlantic, the Baltic Marine Environment Protection Commission (Helsinki Commission/HELCOM), and the Convention for the Protection of the Marine Environment and the Coastal Region of the Mediterranean (Barcelona Convention), could be encouraged to share knowledge, expertise and experience, since such partnerships were a key part of the GPA implementation process. An innovative and constructive way forward was suggested: the promotion of twinning arrangements, e.g., between OSPAR and the Abidjan regional seas Convention for West and Central Africa.

66. Regarding regional cooperation, it was further suggested that States in the different regions should be encouraged to define their own cooperative projects according to specific circumstances in the region and that the best way to approach regional cooperation projects could be to start with areas such as marine information exchange, marine scientific research, education and training.

67. During the debate, delegations cited a number of examples of successful regional cooperation and referred to a wealth of ideas which were being explored.

68. The Asia-Pacific Economic Cooperation (APEC) Marine Resource Conservation Working Group was highlighted as having stimulated a sense of ownership and leadership among its member economies and its regional organizations.

69. One delegation mentioned a plan to develop a broad partnership in the Caribbean region to promote improved coordination and collaboration in integrated watershed, coastal and marine ecosystem management, bringing together partners from among countries in the region, developed countries outside the region and private sector entities. The ideas being explored in that connection included holding a major conference of Caribbean region stakeholders that would include observers from Africa and the South Pacific; developing a regional web site database listing national, bilateral and multilateral cross-sectoral projects; and organizing workshops for training on Geographic Information Systems (GIS) and other remote-sensing capabilities to facilitate access to geographic information through a programme of Global Information for Sustainable Development. The progress on those plans would be announced at the Johannesburg Summit.

70. Within a regional context, several accomplishments were mentioned from among activities being carried out in the Pacific region, such as the recent adoption of the Convention on the Conservation and Management of Highly Migratory Fish Stocks in the Western and Central Pacific Ocean, which provided a comprehensive regime for the management of the region's highly migratory fish stocks and was based on the model of the 1995 Fish Stocks Agreement. The work on developing and finalizing guiding principles for regional oceans management in one region, e.g., a Pacific Islands Regional Ocean Policy, was also cited. Developed within the context of the Marine Sector Working Group of the Council of Regional Organizations in the Pacific, such a policy might form the framework for future regional ocean-related initiatives.

71. Cooperation in the conservation and management of the fishery resources among States of the Indian Ocean region through the Indian Ocean Tuna Commission and the Western Indian Ocean Tuna Organisation was mentioned, as well as cooperation, through agreements on port State control in implementing and enforcing national and international standards for the reduction of pollution from ships and for enhancing their safety.

72. The representative of IOC described a protocol, that had been quite successful in the past and was still in effect: for the Intersecretariat Committee on Scientific Programmes relating to Oceanography (ICSPRO), signed by the heads of various agencies and programmes of the United Nations system, which had been very successful in coordinating the joint activities in marine scientific research within the common system. ICSPRO had coordinated the execution of the first global assessment of the ocean in response to the recommendation emanating from the Stockholm Conference on the Human Environment in 1972.

73. One delegation proposed, with support from a number of other delegations, that IOC and UNEP should develop intergovernmental global information databases to ensure effective management arrangements for data on the marine environment. In particular, it was proposed that the Global Resource Information Database (GRID) of UNEP might be a suitable candidate to host and develop a centre for research data from the outer continental margin intended to serve the needs of coastal States and developing countries.

74. Managing and sharing information was particularly highlighted in the context of international cooperation and coordination and was referred to as a key to improving collaboration and cooperation. It was noted that, at the international level, IOC was uniquely placed to facilitate the flow of technology and aid the provision of ocean assessments and that the role of IOC in sharing information deserved further consideration.

75. The responsibility of individual Governments to share information on oceans with their citizens was mentioned as well. As an example of a special effort to develop web-based tools to allow for the involvement of all ocean stakeholders, mention was made of the web-based mechanism of Canada for informing the citizens and engaging them in integrated ocean management activities, as Canada moves forward with the implementation of its Ocean Strategy and the National Programme of Action.

Integrated ocean management

76. As regards integrated ocean management, it was emphasized, in addition to the above-mentioned examples of national ocean policies and programmes, that integrated ocean management was of common concern to all countries since chapter 17 of Agenda 21 provided that coastal States should establish integrated ocean management to ensure the sustainable utilization of marine resources and the rational development of marine industries.

77. In that connection, the Oceans Stewardship Conference in Vancouver, Canada, in June 2001 was cited as having provided an excellent opportunity for participants from around the world to share experiences and ideas on balanced and integrated approaches to ocean management.

78. The view was expressed that integrated ocean management mainly referred to the management of coastal zones and marine areas under the national jurisdiction of coastal States, with a focus on coastal zone management. In that context, it was suggested that coastal States should be encouraged to establish and strengthen the agencies responsible for integrated ocean management, to develop demonstration programmes of integrated ocean management and to establish a regime for integrated ocean management. Furthermore, relevant United Nations agencies should make every effort in assisting coastal States to formulate and implement integrated ocean management plans. It was also mentioned that transfer of technology to and the training of personnel for the developing countries should be promoted.

Fisheries and IUU fishing

79. In the fisheries area, delegations made reference to the developments over the last decade, including the adoption of the 1993 FAO Compliance Agreement, the 1995 FAO Code of Conduct for Responsible Fisheries and the 1995 Fish Stocks Agreement, the moratorium on large-scale high seas driftnet fishing, which took effect pursuant to a General Assembly resolution,[5] as well as several new regional regimes, such as the 1992 Convention on Anadromous Stocks in the North Pacific, the 1994 Convention on Pollock Resources in the Central Bering Sea, the 2000 Convention on Highly Migratory Fish Stocks in the Western and Central Pacific Ocean, and the 2001 Convention on Fisheries Resources in the South-East Atlantic.

80. However, it was pointed out that despite a decade of progress in establishing instruments and programmes related to oceans, the international community continued to confront urgent and serious challenges and that sustainable fisheries was a further area for priority action, owing to the fact that approximately 75 per cent of the world's fisheries were either fully exploited or overexploited.

81. The need to ensure the implementation of the above-mentioned instruments and programmes was emphasized in order for the international community to be able to exercise the stewardship of the world's oceans and marine resources necessary for sustainable development, the protection of human health, the alleviation of poverty and enhancement of food security. Delegations also underscored

5. General Assembly resolution 46/215 of 20 December 1991.

the necessity of securing a global consensus on reversing the decline in stocks and taking coordinated steps to address overfishing and the continuing problem of illegal, unreported and unregulated (IUU) fishing.

82. One delegation stated that fisheries were being dealt with primarily at FAO and regional fisheries organizations and that the United Nations should therefore respect those specialized organizations, possessing in-depth and technical knowledge of fisheries, as the primary forums for the consideration of fisheries-related issues.

Piracy and other crimes at sea

83. It was pointed out that maritime safety and security should also be given high priority, and that various types of crimes at sea, such as terrorist attacks, piracy, smuggling of migrants and illegal traffic in narcotic drugs, could become serious threats to the peaceful uses of the oceans. Delegations underscored the importance of the harmonization of legal approaches and procedures, cooperative law-enforcement training and information-sharing among States.

Agenda item 4

Exchange of views on collaboration and coordination on ocean issues

84. Patricio Bernal, Executive Secretary of IOC/UNESCO and former Chairman of the now defunct Subcommittee on Oceans and Coastal Areas (SOCA) of the Administrative Committee on Coordination (ACC), opened the discussion on agenda item 4 and presented an overview of the situation following the abolition of SOCA by the United Nations System Chief Executives Board for Coordination (CEB), the successor to ACC. He further presented ideas for the modalities of future inter-agency coordination and cooperation arrangements on oceans and coastal areas by United Nations programmes and agencies that had participated in the former SOCA.

85. At the outset of his presentation, Mr. Bernal stated that the United Nations system had a primary responsibility with respect to oceans and that its status should remain high on the priority list of Member States. He placed the abolition of SOCA in the context of the reforms under way in the United Nations and the abolition of the former ACC substructure, including its various subcommittees. In that connection, he recalled that the General Assembly in 1994 had called for enforcing inter-agency coordination and cooperation and that SOCA represented the only venue where high-level coordination had occurred. Consequently, United Nations programmes and agencies participating in the former SOCA had agreed to continue their coordination and had met independently, on several occasions, outside the previous formal structure. The various Secretariat bodies and United Nations programmes and agencies also continued to exercise the role of lead agencies: the Department of Economic and Social Affairs was monitoring the implementation of chapter 17 of Agenda 21; FAO was working on the United Nations Atlas of the Oceans; UNEP was responsible for the GPA; IMO was leading the review process of GESAMP; and the Division for Ocean Affairs and the Law of the Sea was responsi-

ble for reporting annually on oceans and the law of the sea. In addition, the United Nations system continued to set up task forces in response to specific needs, for example, the task force on illegal migration in the Indian and Pacific oceans set up by the Division for Ocean Affairs and the Law of the Sea, IMO and the Office of the United Nations High Commissioner for Refugees and the task force on scrapping of vessels. Mr. Bernal also recalled the establishment of the Joint WMO/IOC Technical Commission for Oceanography and Marine Meteorology (JCOMM) as the first single technical commission reporting simultaneously to two governing bodies.

86. With regard to new inter-agency coordination arrangements on oceans and coastal areas, Mr. Bernal informed the third meeting of the Consultative Process that many of the United Nations programmes and agencies participating in the coordination of oceans and coastal areas (ILO, FAO, IOC/UNESCO, WMO, IMO, UNIDO, UNDP, UNEP, United Nations (Department of Economic and Social Affairs and Division for Ocean Affairs and the Law of the Sea)) had met informally at United Nations Headquarters on 9 and 11 April 2002 and conducted consultations on the future coordination mechanism they would use as a result of the elimination of the subsidiary machinery of the former ACC.

87. All the programmes and agencies represented, as well as the World Bank representative, who was consulted separately, had expressed their willingness to continue their active participation in the system-wide coordination of ocean activities on a task-oriented basis, using lead-agency arrangements.

88. Addressing future needs, Mr. Bernal stressed two aspects of the work of programmes and agencies and the World Bank: (a) the need to exchange information on the wide range of activities implemented by programmes and agencies and the evolving mandates from their respective governing bodies; and (b) the potential for an effective coordination of the planning-budgeting cycle to move towards the joint design and implementation of activities in the field. He noted that the scope of coordination needs in ocean activities extended across the social, economic and environmental aspects of sustainable development and responded to the principle enunciated in the preamble to UNCLOS: ". . . the problems of ocean space are closely interrelated and need to be considered as a whole."

89. He further stated that the informal group of the former SOCA members had agreed that it would be useful to have a two-tier approach to coordination. Firstly, an open-ended group of representatives of programmes and agencies at the level of experts should meet regularly, at least once a year, to review ongoing joint activities; and secondly, a series of task-oriented groups should be formed, which would lead and implement specific time-bound initiatives.

90. An obstacle to the implementation of cooperative activities was the lack of a funding mechanism and attendant administrative and financial rules that would enable different United Nations agencies to contribute to and participate in jointly funded activities. The establishment of such a structure would require adjustments in the planning and budgeting cycles of agencies and programmes and would entail aligning mandates with resources across several budgets. He mentioned three areas as potential candidates for future task-oriented activities:

(a) Integrated global assessments of the ocean which would encompass social, economic and environmental factors;
(b) Assisting in efforts to improve regional ocean governance;
(c) Establishing guidelines for the application of the ecosystem approach.

91. He noted that the modalities of this new coordination phase would include an intensive use of electronic communication; the establishment of agreements among heads of agencies or responsible managers; and an open dialogue with actors from outside the United Nations system and transparent communication with all partners. He informed the meeting that it had been agreed that the former SOCA informal group would undertake an initiative to complete an across-the-board identification of the portfolios of ongoing, approved and proposed projects in oceans and coastal areas.

92. In concluding his presentation, Mr. Bernal pointed out the difference between "coordination," which would involve exchange of information and ad hoc partnerships, and "strong coordination," which required the use of managerial tools for the United Nations system to operate in a coordinated manner and entailed the alignment of budget cycles and programme planning. The latter type of coordination was necessary in order to keep the United Nations system relevant.

93. Responding to the question of the relationship between "strong" and "weak" coordination and the establishment of task forces and coordinating planning exercises, Mr. Bernal noted the existence of various lines of authority and the fact that the primary duty of each agency and programme was to respond to its governing body from which it received its mandate. Such conflicts or disparities might create internal governance problems within the United Nations system, which might need to be addressed through an inter-agency agreement similar to ICSPRO.

94. Manuel Dengo, Chief of the Water, Natural Resources and Small Island Developing States Branch of the Department of Economic and Social Affairs and former Chairman of the ACC Subcommittee on Water Resources, shared with the third meeting of the Consultative Process information on the modalities of cooperation between agencies involved in the field of freshwater resources since the abolition of the ACC substructure. Such agencies, on the basis of a recommendation by an external consultant, discussed joint programming to avoid duplication and proceeded with a selection of areas of common interest, where increased cooperation and stronger coordination were needed. One delegation noted with appreciation that the link between freshwater resources and oceans and seas had been highlighted in the context of the Consultative Process.

95. Delegates expressed their appreciation to Mr. Bernal for his presentation and recalled the provisions in the General Assembly resolutions and statements at previous meetings of the Consultative Process calling for more effective coordination and cooperation on global management of the oceans and for an increase in the effectiveness, transparency and responsiveness of SOCA. They underscored that it was imperative for the United Nations ocean-related agencies and international financial institutions to coordinate and harmonize their work so as to achieve maximum impact for good oceans governance. Moreover, delegations pointed out that

the United Nations system was ideally placed to provide such coordination. The United Nations system should set an example in that regard by duly coordinating the programmes and activities of the various bodies within the common system dealing with ocean and maritime affairs.

96. Delegations also stated that the High-level Committee on Programmes of CEB, which had recommended moving away from the concept of permanent subsidiary bodies and relying instead solely on "ad hoc" coordination arrangements, had ignored those recommendations, which had been spelled out in resolutions of the General Assembly. A number of delegations expressed their dissatisfaction with those developments and requested the Secretariat to offer explanations.

97. Expressing their disagreement with the arguments leading to the suppression of SOCA and with the way that body had been dissolved, delegations pointed out that in order to achieve effective coordination, a permanent body was needed. Such a body should meet regularly, should have continuity and be endowed with sufficient authority to coordinate autonomous agencies and bodies. In the view of delegations which spoke on the matter, "ad hoc," task-oriented arrangements and occasional meetings were not sufficient to carry out the tasks of an efficient coordinating mechanism and would lead to a lack of coordination, especially in view of the overreaching interrelatedness of ocean issues.

98. There was wide support for the proposal to establish an inter-agency forum which would bring together, on a regular basis, all the agencies and institutions of the United Nations system involved in ocean affairs. Another alternative mentioned was establishing a standing group that would link the relevant United Nations agencies and international financial institutions involved in ocean affairs, as an ocean principals group with its own secretariat. However, it was noted that that option might present institutional and budgetary difficulties. Yet another alternative would be for the agencies and institutions to form a partnership or partnerships through "memoranda of understanding" among all the entities. The necessary coordinating role of the partnership could be assigned to one of the partners or to the Division for Ocean Affairs and the Law of the Sea. It was noted that such "memoranda of understanding" would clearly set out the responsibilities for functions that would reflect the different types of expertise in the United Nations system. In that connection, several delegates noted that the Intersecretariat Committee on Scientific Programmes Related to Oceanography (ICSPRO), while useful as an example, was not in a position to fulfil the coordinating role, owing to its specialized nature.

99. It was pointed out that any coordinating mechanism established should link the United Nations, international financial institutions as well as other global institutions, such as the International Seabed Authority, the secretariat of the Convention on Biological Diversity and the secretariat of the United Nations Framework Convention on Climate Change, and that its functions should be expanded, as compared to those of SOCA. Among the purposes and guidelines proposed for the coordinating mechanism were the following: (a) contributing to reviewing programmes and activities and identifying grey areas of issues needing to be explored or addressed, with a view to updating and enriching the relationship between UNCLOS and Agenda

21; (b) carrying out a factual review of the mandates, capacities and activities of the relevant bodies of the United Nations and of the relationship between them (a task proposed initially for SOCA at the previous meeting of the Consultative Process); (c) coordinating and harmonizing the agencies' activities related to oceans, eliminating duplication, redundant outputs and overlap in planning and implementation, and expanding cooperation; (d) synchronizing the timing of agency budget cycles and governing body reviews to allow for the undertaking of jointly funded activities; (e) undertaking joint activities through the creation and operation of task forces or ad hoc working groups, as appropriate, on topics such as the Global Marine Assessment; or overseeing particular activities, such as the implementation of the United Nations Atlas of the Oceans or the GPA; (f) ensuring integrated ocean management at the international level; (g) coordinating inputs to the annual report of the Secretary-General on oceans and law of the sea; (h) ensuring that adequate resources are available to oversee the joint work and the meetings of the participants; and (i) operating in a transparent manner, with opportunities for input by governments, NGOs and the private sector. The agenda of the meetings of the participants should be made available before the meetings on a web site and a summary of actions taken should be posted on such a web site following the meetings.

100. It was also noted that the criteria of effectiveness, transparency, accountability and responsiveness should be applied with respect to any new inter-agency coordination and cooperation mechanism, with particular emphasis on the transparency aspect.

101. Several delegations noted that the new inter-agency coordination and collaboration mechanism would need to be incorporated within operational plans and budgets and that there was no need for new resources to be allocated since an overarching emphasis on coordination among agencies should result in savings through, inter alia, eliminating duplication.

102. Other delegations pointed to the need for coordination between programmes and agencies operating at the global level and international organizations and programmes operating at the regional level, in particular with respect to the Global Marine Assessment.

103. The importance of coordination between ministries and agencies at the national level was also strongly emphasized to reflect the intersectoral and interdisciplinary nature of ocean-related problems. Coordinated national positions in various governing organs of international organizations, agencies and programmes would make it easier to achieve coordination at the global level, since those governing organs formulated the mandates of the organizations from which their work programmes emanated.

104. Delegations also noted with appreciation the ideas set out in the statement by Mr. Corell regarding agency focal points and the use of liaison offices for the purposes of coordination and concluded that they deserved serious consideration. The focal points would need to be fully interactive in both directions, so as to send out information and also become the building blocks for a dynamic coordinating function among agencies.

105. Many delegations expressed their interest in the two-tier approach to coordination, as laid out in the presentation by Mr. Bernal. Some delegations pointed out that the goal of coordination should also be viewed in the context of the Preparatory Committee for the World Summit on Sustainable Development.

106. Summarizing the discussions on this item and in order to identify the elements of an emerging consensus, Mr. Simcock noted that the new mechanism should reflect the principle embodied in UNCLOS that the problems of ocean space were closely interrelated and needed to be considered as a whole. He said that since those problems ranged across many fields, many international institutions were involved and, particularly at the global level, cooperation and coordination were needed for effective multidisciplinary and multisectoral action to be achieved. With increased emphasis on implementation, the need for effective executive cooperation and coordination would become stronger.

107. In the absence of SOCA, the Consultative Process was an important tool enabling a dialogue between States and international programmes and agencies to take place. Such dialogue, as with any new international cooperation mechanism, should involve international financial institutions.

108. As for the approach to be followed, he stated, inter alia, that the new mechanism should include all the United Nations departments, funds, programmes and agencies and international financial institutions involved in issues relating to oceans and seas. The new mechanism should be established in a way as to set up a clear mandate and demonstrate the commitment of the core participating institutions at the highest levels. It should be able to work both through regular reviews of issues relating to oceans and seas and mandates and work plans of the core participating institutions, in order to eliminate gaps, inconsistencies and unnecessary overlaps, and through the establishment of specific task forces to carry out ad hoc, time-limited, task-oriented activities, and the planning and budgetary cycles of United Nations agencies should be made more compatible for that purpose. Furthermore, the mechanism should ensure transparency and should seek appropriate means for an exchange of views with States Members of the United Nations.

Agenda item 5

Identification by the Co-Chairpersons of issues that could benefit from attention in future work of the General Assembly on oceans and law of the sea in the light of the Assembly's review of the effectiveness and utility of the Consultative Process

109. Mr. Simcock, Co-Chairperson, recalled the report of the second meeting (2001) on issues for future consideration (A/56/121, Part C).

110. Delegations commented on the list of issues contained therein. The Co-Chairperson's summary of the conclusions based on those comments is set out in Part C of the present report.

PART C

Issues that could benefit from attention in future work of the general assembly on oceans and the law of the sea

1. There was agreement that it would not be appropriate to suggest any particular issues to the General Assembly for any future meeting. It was for the General Assembly to determine what issues needed attention in the light of its review of the effectiveness and utility of the Process.

2. Delegations considered that concrete and practical topics, rather than broad issues, would provide a more focused discussion.

3. There was agreement that the following list, being the topics identified for future consideration at the second meeting of the Consultative Process, remained valid as a list of topics meriting attention from the General Assembly:

(a) Marine protected areas;
(b) Review of the national, regional and global implementation of Part XII of the United Nations Convention on the Law of the Sea;
(c) Potential and new uses of the oceans;
(d) Development and transfer of marine technology;
(e) Oceans stewardship/ecosystem-based integrated management of the marine environment;
(f) Food security and mariculture;
(g) Cooperation and coordination between regional fisheries organizations and regional seas programmes of the United Nations Environment Programme;
(h) Impact of the activities in the international seabed area as a source of contamination of the marine environment;
(i) Effect of fishery subsidies on the conservation of marine living resources;
(j) Marine debris;
(k) Convergence of the legal and programmatic dimensions of international cooperation;
(l) Navigation in ecologically sensitive areas;
(m) Protection of coastal areas from the introduction of non-native species;
(n) Possibility of reviewing progress on issues discussed at meetings of the Consultative Process.

4. Further topics suggested for identification were:

(a) The science underlying the identification and management of marine protected areas;
(b) Implementation of existing international instruments;
(c) Competing uses of the continental shelf, including mariculture, the laying of cables and pipelines, and exploitation of non-living marine resources;
(d) Protecting the biological diversity of the seabed;

(e) Protecting vulnerable coastal ecosystems;
(f) Security of navigation, including the production of nautical charts;
(g) Capacity-building for the collection of marine geographic data.

5. One delegation did not support the inclusion of issues relating to marine protected areas and suggested instead the issue of the application of ecosystem-based approaches to the management of oceans, seas and coasts.

Excerpts from the Plan of Implementation of the World Summit on Sustainable Development, Johannesburg, South Africa, 26 August–4 September 2002*

4. Protecting and Managing the Natural Resource Base of Economic and Social Development

30. Oceans, seas, islands and coastal areas form an integrated and essential component of the Earth's ecosystem and are critical for global food security and for sustaining economic prosperity and the well-being of many national economies, particularly in developing countries. Ensuring the sustainable development of the oceans requires effective coordination and cooperation, including at the global and regional levels, between relevant bodies, and actions at all levels to:

(a) Invite States to ratify or accede to and implement the United Nations Convention on the Law of the Sea of 1982,[1] which provides the overall legal framework for ocean activities;
(b) Promote the implementation of chapter 17 of Agenda 21, which provides the programme of action for achieving the sustainable development of oceans, coastal areas and seas through its programme areas of integrated management and sustainable development of coastal areas, including exclusive economic zones; marine environmental protection; sustainable use and conservation of marine living resources; addressing critical uncertainties for the management of the marine environment and climate change; strengthening international, including regional, cooperation and coordination; and sustainable development of small islands;
(c) Establish an effective, transparent and regular inter-agency coordination mechanism on ocean and coastal issues within the United Nations system;
(d) Encourage the application by 2010 of the ecosystem approach, noting the Reykjavik Declaration on Responsible Fisheries in the Marine Ecosystem[2]

* Editors' Note.—This document contains oceans-related paragraphs 30–36 and 58–61 from the Plan of Implementation of the World Summit on Sustainable Development, extracted from the *Report of the World Summit on Sustainable Development, Johannesburg, South Africa, 26 August–4 September 2002.* UN document A/CONF.199/20, http://www.johannesburgsummit.org/.

1. Official Records of the Third United Nations Conference on the Law of the Sea, vol. XVII. United Nations publication, Sales No. E.84.V.3. Document A/CONF.62/122.

2. See Food and Agriculture Organization of the United Nations document C200/INF/25, Appendix I.

and decision V/6 of the Conference of Parties to the Convention on Biological Diversity;[3]

(e) Promote integrated, multidisciplinary and multisectoral coastal and ocean management at the national level and encourage and assist coastal States in developing ocean policies and mechanisms on integrated coastal management;

(f) Strengthen regional cooperation and coordination between the relevant regional organizations and programmes, the regional seas programmes of the United Nations Environment Programme, regional fisheries management organizations and other regional science, health and development organizations;

(g) Assist developing countries in coordinating policies and programmes at the regional and subregional levels aimed at the conservation and sustainable management of fishery resources and implement integrated coastal area management plans, including through the promotion of sustainable coastal and small-scale fishing activities and, where appropriate, the development of related infrastructure;

(h) Take note of the work of the open-ended informal consultative process established by the United Nations General Assembly in its resolution 54/33 in order to facilitate the annual review by the Assembly of developments in ocean affairs and the upcoming review of its effectiveness and utility to be held at its fifty-seventh session under the terms of the above-mentioned resolution.

31. To achieve sustainable fisheries, the following actions are required at all levels:

(a) Maintain or restore stocks to levels that can produce the maximum sustainable yield with the aim of achieving these goals for depleted stocks on an urgent basis and where possible not later than 2015;

(b) Ratify or accede to and effectively implement the relevant United Nations and, where appropriate, associated regional fisheries agreements or arrangements, noting in particular the Agreement for the Implementation of the Provisions of the United Nations Convention on the Law of the Sea of 10 December 1982 relating to the Conservation and Management of Straddling Fish Stocks and Highly Migratory Fish Stocks[4] and the 1993 Agreement to Promote Compliance with International Conservation and Management Measures by Fishing Vessels on the High Seas;[5]

(c) Implement the 1995 Code of Conduct for Responsible Fisheries,[6] taking note of the special requirements of developing countries as noted in its Article 5, and the relevant international plans of action and technical guidelines of the Food and Agriculture Organization of the United Nations;

3. See UNEP/CBD/COP/5/23, Annex 3.

4. See International Fisheries Instruments. United Nations publication, Sales No. E.98.V.11. sect. 1; see also A/CONF.164/37.

5. Ibid.

6. Ibid., sect. 3.

(d) Urgently develop and implement national and, where appropriate, regional plans of action, to put into effect the international plans of action of the Food and Agriculture Organization of the United Nations, in particular the International Plan of Action for the Management of Fishing Capacity[7] by 2005 and the International Plan of Action to Prevent, Deter and Eliminate Illegal, Unreported and Unregulated Fishing[8] by 2004. Establish effective monitoring, reporting and enforcement, and control of fishing vessels, including by flag States, to further the International Plan of Action to Prevent, Deter and Eliminate Illegal, Unreported and Unregulated Fishing;

(e) Encourage relevant regional fisheries management organizations and arrangements to give due consideration to the rights, duties and interests of coastal States and the special requirements of developing States when addressing the issue of the allocation of share of fishery resources for straddling stocks and highly migratory fish stocks, mindful of the provisions of the United Nations Convention on the Law of the Sea and the Agreement for the Implementation of the Provisions of the United Nations Convention on the Law of the Sea of 10 December 1982 relating to the Conservation and Management of Straddling Fish Stocks and Highly Migratory Fish Stocks, on the high seas and within exclusive economic zones;

(f) Eliminate subsidies that contribute to illegal, unreported and unregulated fishing and to over-capacity, while completing the efforts undertaken at the World Trade Organization to clarify and improve its disciplines on fisheries subsidies, taking into account the importance of this sector to developing countries;

(g) Strengthen donor coordination and partnerships between international financial institutions, bilateral agencies and other relevant stakeholders to enable developing countries, in particular the least developed countries and small island developing States and countries with economies in transition, to develop their national, regional and subregional capacities for infrastructure and integrated management and the sustainable use of fisheries;

(h) Support the sustainable development of aquaculture, including small-scale aquaculture, given its growing importance for food security and economic development.

32. In accordance with chapter 17 of Agenda 21, promote the conservation and management of the oceans through actions at all levels, giving due regard to the relevant international instruments to:

(a) Maintain the productivity and biodiversity of important and vulnerable marine and coastal areas, including in areas within and beyond national jurisdiction;

(b) Implement the work programme arising from the Jakarta Mandate on

7. Rome, Food and Agriculture Organization of the United Nations, 1999.

8. Ibid., 2001.

the Conservation and Sustainable Use of Marine and Coastal Biological Diversity of the Convention on Biological Diversity,[9] including through the urgent mobilization of financial resources and technological assistance and the development of human and institutional capacity, particularly in developing countries;

(c) Develop and facilitate the use of diverse approaches and tools, including the ecosystem approach, the elimination of destructive fishing practices, the establishment of marine protected areas consistent with international law and based on scientific information, including representative networks by 2012 and time/area closures for the protection of nursery grounds and periods, proper coastal land use and watershed planning and the integration of marine and coastal areas management into key sectors;

(d) Develop national, regional and international programmes for halting the loss of marine biodiversity, including in coral reefs and wetlands;

(e) Implement the Ramsar Convention,[10] including its joint work programme with the Convention on Biological Diversity,[11] and the programme of action called for by the International Coral Reef Initiative to strengthen joint management plans and international networking for wetland ecosystems in coastal zones, including coral reefs, mangroves, seaweed beds and tidal mud flats.

33. Advance implementation of the Global Programme of Action for the Protection of the Marine Environment from Land-based Activities[12] and the Montreal Declaration on the Protection of the Marine Environment from Land-based Activities,[13] with particular emphasis during the period from 2002 to 2006 on municipal wastewater, the physical alteration and destruction of habitats, and nutrients, by actions at all levels to:

(a) Facilitate partnerships, scientific research and diffusion of technical knowledge; mobilize domestic, regional and international resources; and promote human and institutional capacity-building, paying particular attention to the needs of developing countries;

(b) Strengthen the capacity of developing countries in the development of their national and regional programmes and mechanisms to mainstream the objectives of the Global Programme of Action and to manage the risks and impacts of ocean pollution;

(c) Elaborate regional programmes of action and improve the links with strategic plans for the sustainable development of coastal and marine resources, noting in particular areas that are subject to accelerated environmental changes and development pressures;

(d) Make every effort to achieve substantial progress by the next Global Pro-

9. See A/51/312, Annex 2, decision II/10.

10. Ramsar Convention on Wetlands of International Importance Especially as Waterfowl Habitat. United Nations, Treaty Series, vol. 996. No. 14583.

11. See United Nations Environment Programme, Convention on Biological Diversity. Environmental Law and Institution Programme Activity Centre. June 1992.

12. A/51/116, Annex 2.

13. See E/CN.17/2002/PC.2/15.

gramme of Action conference in 2006 to protect the marine environment from land-based activities.

34. Enhance maritime safety and protection of the marine environment from pollution by actions at all levels to:

(a) Invite States to ratify or accede to and implement the conventions and protocols and other relevant instruments of the International Maritime Organization relating to the enhancement of maritime safety and protection of the marine environment from marine pollution and environmental damage caused by ships, including the use of toxic anti-fouling paints, and urge the International Maritime Organization (IMO) to consider stronger mechanisms to secure the implementation of IMO instruments by flag States;
(b) Accelerate the development of measures to address invasive alien species in ballast water. Urge the International Maritime Organization to finalize its draft International Convention on the Control and Management of Ships' Ballast Water and Sediments.

35. Governments, taking into account their national circumstances, are encouraged, recalling paragraph 8 of resolution GC (44)/RES/17 of the General Conference of the International Atomic Energy Agency, and taking into account the very serious potential for environment and human health impacts of radioactive wastes, to make efforts to examine and further improve measures and internationally agreed regulations regarding safety, while stressing the importance of having effective liability mechanisms in place, relevant to international maritime transportation and other transboundary movement of radioactive material, radioactive waste and spent fuel, including, inter alia, arrangements for prior notification and consultations done in accordance with relevant international instruments.

36. Improve the scientific understanding and assessment of marine and coastal ecosystems as a fundamental basis for sound decision-making, through actions at all levels to:

(a) Increase scientific and technical collaboration, including integrated assessment at the global and regional levels, including the appropriate transfer of marine science and marine technologies and techniques for the conservation and management of living and non-living marine resources and expanding ocean observing capabilities for the timely prediction and assessment of the state of marine environment;
(b) Establish by 2004 a regular process under the United Nations for global reporting and assessment of the state of the marine environment, including socio-economic aspects, both current and foreseeable, building on existing regional assessments;
(c) Build capacity in marine science, information and management, through, inter alia, promoting the use of environmental impact assessments and environmental evaluation and reporting techniques, for projects or activi-

ties that are potentially harmful to the coastal and marine environments and their living and non-living resources;

(d) Strengthen the ability of the Intergovernmental Oceanographic Commission of the United Nations Educational, Scientific and Cultural Organization, the Food and Agriculture Organization of the United Nations and other relevant international and regional and subregional organizations to build national and local capacity in marine science and the sustainable management of oceans and their resources.

7. Sustainable Development of Small Island Developing States

58. Small island developing States are a special case both for environment and development. Although they continue to take the lead in the path towards sustainable development in their countries, they are increasingly constrained by the interplay of adverse factors clearly underlined in Agenda 21, the Programme of Action for the Sustainable Development of Small Island Developing States[14] and the decisions adopted at the twenty-second special session of the General Assembly. This would include actions at all levels to:

(a) Accelerate national and regional implementation of the Programme of Action, with adequate financial resources, including through Global Environment Facility focal areas, transfer of environmentally sound technologies and assistance for capacity-building from the international community;

(b) Implement further sustainable fisheries management and improve financial returns from fisheries by supporting and strengthening relevant regional fisheries management organizations, as appropriate, such as the recently established Caribbean Regional Fisheries Mechanism and such agreements as the Convention on the Conservation and Management of Highly Migratory Fish Stocks in the Western and Central Pacific Ocean;

(c) Assist small island developing States, including through the elaboration of specific initiatives, in delimiting and managing in a sustainable manner their coastal areas and exclusive economic zones and the continental shelf, including, where appropriate, the continental shelf areas beyond 200 miles from coastal baselines, as well as relevant regional management initiatives within the context of the United Nations Convention on the Law of the Sea and the regional seas programmes of the United Nations Environment Programme;

(d) Provide support, including for capacity-building, for the development and further implementation of:

   (i) Small island developing States-specific components within programmes of work on marine and coastal biological diversity;

14. *Report of the Global Conference on the Sustainable Development of Small Island Developing States*, Bridgetown, Barbados, 25 April–6 May 1994. United Nations publication, Sales No. E.94.I.18 and corrigenda, Chap. 1, resolution 1, Annex 2.

(ii) Freshwater programmes for small island developing States, including through the Global Environment Facility focal areas;

(e) Effectively reduce, prevent and control waste and pollution and their health-related impacts by undertaking initiatives by 2004 aimed at implementing the Global Programme of Action for the Protection of the Marine Environment from Land-based Activities in small island developing States;

(f) Work to ensure that, in the ongoing negotiations and elaboration of the World Trade Organization work programme on trade in small economies, due account is taken of small island developing States, which have severe structural handicaps in integrating into the global economy, within the context of the Doha development agenda;

(g) Develop community-based initiatives on sustainable tourism by 2004 and build the capacities necessary to diversify tourism products, while protecting culture and traditions and effectively conserving and managing natural resources;

(h) Extend assistance to small island developing States in support of local communities and appropriate national and regional organizations of small island developing States for comprehensive hazard and risk management, disaster prevention, mitigation and preparedness, and help relieve the consequences of disasters, extreme weather events and other emergencies;

(i) Support the finalization and subsequent early operationalization, on agreed terms, of economic, social and environmental vulnerability indices and related indicators as tools for the achievement of the sustainable development of the small island developing States;

(j) Assist small island developing States in mobilizing adequate resources and partnerships for their adaptation needs relating to the adverse effects of climate change, sea level rise and climate variability, consistent with commitments under the United Nations Framework Convention on Climate Change, where applicable;

(k) Support efforts by small island developing States to build capacities and institutional arrangements to implement intellectual property regimes.

59. Support the availability of adequate, affordable and environmentally sound energy services for the sustainable development of small island developing States by, inter alia:

(a) Strengthening ongoing and supporting new efforts on energy supply and services, by 2004, including through the United Nations system and partnership initiatives;

(b) Developing and promoting efficient use of sources of energy, including indigenous sources and renewable energy, and building the capacities of small island developing States for training, technical know-how and strengthening national institutions in the area of energy management.

60. Provide support to small island developing States to develop capacity and strengthen:

(a) Health-care services for promoting equitable access to health care;
(b) Health systems for making available necessary drugs and technology in a sustainable and affordable manner to fight and control communicable and non-communicable diseases, in particular HIV/AIDS, tuberculosis, diabetes, malaria and dengue fever;
(c) Efforts to reduce and manage waste and pollution and building capacity for maintaining and managing systems to deliver water and sanitation services, in both rural and urban areas;
(d) Efforts to implement initiatives aimed at poverty eradication, which have been outlined in section 2 of the present document.

61. Undertake a full and comprehensive review of the implementation of the Barbados Programme of Action for the Sustainable Development of Small Island Developing States in 2004, in accordance with the provisions set forth in General Assembly resolution S-22/2, and, in this context, requests the General Assembly at its fifty-seventh session to consider convening an international meeting for the sustainable development of small island developing States.

Statement by Ugo Mifsud Bonnici (Malta) at the Commemoration of the Twentieth Anniversary of the Opening for Signature of the 1982 United Nations Convention on the Law of the Sea, 9 December 2002*

The Acting President: I now call on His Excellency Mr. Ugo Mifsud Bonnici, former President of Malta, to pay special tribute to the late Ambassador Arvid Pardo of Malta.

Mr. Bonnici (Malta): Our globalized times cannot perhaps be best described as the result of the work contributed jointly and severally by a handful of visionaries. Millions upon millions of workers, hundreds of thousands of businessmen, managers and operators, an imprecise number of criminals also, thousands of politicians, functionaries, officials and diplomats have been, ant-like, constructing and deconstructing the present state of our planet, which is not the realization of a plan. We do not have a new world order. We have a state of fact—with some logic perhaps, some justice, continuous progress in some quarters, marvelous scientific discoveries and new miraculous technological applications, some spread of democracy and some respect for human rights and the rule of law, mostly the result of the exertions of men and women of vision.

This state of fact contains in addition, however, a more than tolerable dose of illogic, injustice, waste, hunger and disease, neglect, strife and destruction, mostly the work of confusion, inaction, ignorance, greed, craft and sheer ill-will. We need visionaries to lead peoples out of labyrinths, to inject reason, to work day in and day out for justice and to enlighten us on ways of avoiding waste, neglect and the exhaustion of resources, of achieving a better distribution of wealth, of the availability of cure and care, of the solution of conflicts and of the curbing of madness in government. We need visionaries to continue to inspire hope—and also to give an example of love. We will not, however, be satisfied with visionaries who will merely inspire hope and charity. We will not even be satisfied with visionaries who are merely fired by faith. We now require men and women who are not only endowed with prophetic vision; our visionaries must provide concrete answers. Our visionaries must now be persuaders, men and women who not only possess insight but are also good conductors of their institutions. Their talents must include competence in their field, in addition to intuition. Our visionaries have a greater task to perform than the prophets of previous centuries.

We need visionaries with determination and patience, as the world has become too complex for simple, immediate, easily implemented solutions. Education and

* Editors' Note.—Verbatim Records of the Plenary Meetings of the United Nations General Assembly, Fifty-seventh Session, 72nd Plenary Meeting, Item 25 on the provisional agenda. UN document A/57/PV.70. 9 December 2002. http://www.un.org/ga/57/pv.html (accessed 22 April 2003).

knowledge have spread but invincible ignorance as well as self-beguiling, little knowledge still bedevils the judgment of whole masses of people. We need visionaries *in loco*: we cannot afford to have them preaching in the deserts. We need visionaries in the universities as well as in the corridors of power. We need visionaries in diplomacy, in international organizations, in the boardrooms of international corporations, in parliaments, in government.

Arvid Pardo was such a visionary. His great competence as a jurist and as an international diplomat was combined with very wide human and work experience. He was of Maltese and Swedish parentage and was brought up in the Rome of the thirties. While he cherished his Maltese nationality and identity, he felt that he was also a citizen of the world. He studied law at Rome University and considered himself fundamentally molded by the legal discipline. But he was also a man of the physical and human sciences, and the future of man and of our natural environment were foremost among his anxieties and hopes. Perhaps I should have used the singular, as indeed he saw the fate of the generations to come and of our planet's physical well-being, as being one and the same.

The vicissitudes of the 1939–1945 war in Italy and his own precarious peregrinations and survival endowed him with indomitable perseverance in the face of all kinds of adversity and the unpredictable turns of the wheel of fortune. His service with the United Nations provided him with inside knowledge of the workings of the system and made him very much aware of the feelings within the milieu of international diplomacy. As a visionary he was extremely well prepared by his family history, working life and academic background. The United Nations was of course by no means a desert. But it was his appointment in the middle sixties as Ambassador Extraordinary by newly independent Malta that provided him with the loco through which he could exercise his visionary function of trying to bring about more logic, more justice, more legal order in a particular area of man's dealings and interchange with nature, as well as in the generational succession.

Pardo saw his opportunity, as Malta's seat at the United Nations provided him with the first pulpit from which to proclaim his vision of a new law of the sea, and a new way of exploiting the natural riches of the ocean bed. It was Pardo who proposed to the then Prime Minister of my country, Giorgio Borg Olivera, that Malta should take the initiative and propose the adoption of certain principles with regard to the exploitation of the ocean floor and its subsoil beyond the limit of national jurisdiction. Some doubt was expressed about the wisdom of trying to get the limelight so early in our post-independence debut in the international congress of nations. The Government of Malta, however, saw the objective need and wholeheartedly embraced it.

Pardo proceeded to deliver his memorable speech to the twenty-second session of the General Assembly in the autumn of 1967. His ardour was not dampened by the initial negative reactions of some representatives of major Powers. He continued to pursue his proposal through the adoption of resolutions by the General Assembly in December 1967, 1968 and 1969, reserving the ocean floor and its subsoil for purely peaceful purposes. The Ad Hoc Committee was established in 1967 and confirmed and enlarged in 1968. Finally, on 17 December 1970, the General Assembly approved not only resolution 2749 (XXV) incorporating the principles, but also resolution 2750 (XXV) convening in 1973 a law of the sea conference. A 35-, then 41- and finally a 91-member strong committee was entrusted with the task of preparing drafts of the convention.

Pardo took part in various Pacem in Maribus convocations together with another departed, Elisabeth Mann Borgese, and Pardo provided much of the juridical raw material. I recall visiting his home in Washington in September 1970 and had long discussions with him concerning the prospect of the realization of his initiative. Even though he was totally engrossed in what he considered was his most important mission, his interest in the future was not limited to the sea and its seabed. From the angle of a seer he was reflecting on the great technological changes, the bioethical challenges, the geopolitical rearrangements that mankind would have to face in the twenty-first century still 30 years away but substantially already with him in his mind's eye. Then lowering his gaze to the present and very mundane particular circumstances, he made me promise to suggest to the Finance Ministry when I returned to Malta that they should provide some money for the repair of the roof of the Ambassador's residence.

There was however a change of government in Malta in 1971 and Pardo had to contend with a diminished enthusiasm on the part of his home country. His determination was put to the test as he was removed from his ambassador's pulpit. Thereafter he could serve the cause laterally through his influence with the experts, fellow diplomats and academics. Even when the new Government eventually appointed him Special Envoy for the purpose, he no longer had the clout he had enjoyed with the former Government of Malta and Malta's interest itself flagged. Pardo, however, continued to prod, to encourage, and to suggest alternatives and formulations. Pardo's grand design included aspects that were considered too daring at the time, and perhaps even today. The commonality of the heritage of man could be accepted readily in the flourish of declarations but when the logical conclusions are drawn amounting to the setting up of an international organization for the exploration of seabed resources for the benefit of all, using the technical means available only to the richest and most advanced of nations, the project encountered major obstacles. These were only surmounted by substantial compromise, redimensioning most of the original proposals.

Pardo soldiered on and was happy to see the conclusion of the exercise in the final act, the opening for signature of the Convention in Montego Bay, Jamaica, on 10 December 1982. He was of course not completely satisfied with the outcome but continued to work for the acceptance of the concepts embodied in the text of the Convention on the Law of the Sea, and towards further progress in the study of this area of international law as well as in the science and technology connected with the protection of the seas, the seabed and the marine environment, and their exploitation for exclusively peaceful purposes. The last time I met him in 1997, when I was then President of the Republic, he had come to Malta to attend the formal grant of a post-graduate scholarship to an academic from a developing country in this field of study.

No one of us lives and dies as if he had never been. We, however, have a depth of gratitude towards people of vision who see a civilizing project to its conclusion. It would have made a great difference to all humanity if visionaries had never been born, or had succumbed to the fatigue of indifference, incomprehension, and inertia. I pay tribute to a great man from a small nation who contributed a part of the mosaic which makes sense in the great mural of our civilization, in large part, alas, still unfinished or unscrambled.

Statement by Robert Hage (Canada) at the Commemoration of the Twentieth Anniversary of the Opening for Signature of the 1982 United Nations Convention on the Law of the Sea, 10 December 2002*

Mr. Hage (Canada): Anniversaries are a time to celebrate, a time to look back at past accomplishments, as well as an occasion to look to the future. For many of us in this great Hall, it is amazing how fast 20 years have gone by. Indeed, for a number here today 20 years is but a moment in the law of the sea. Some were here at the inception of the Third United Nations Conference on the Law of the Sea in 1973, and indeed a few here today began with the United Nations Seabed Committee in the 1960s. Law of the sea for them was more than a United Nations conference; it was a vocation. At the signing ceremony for the United Nations Convention on the Law of the Sea (UNCLOS) 20 years ago, Canada's Minister for Foreign Affairs, Allan MacEachen, stated that the Convention "must stand as one of the greatest accomplishments of the United Nations."

The architects of UNCLOS deserve applause for their wisdom and hard work. In this respect, I would like to recognize the contribution of Alan Beesley, Canada's Ambassador to the law of the sea negotiations, who is with us here today. He is one of that select group who were present at the creation of the Law of the Sea Conference, and as Chair of the Conference Drafting Committee he ensured the precision and coherence of the Convention we celebrate today.

Like the oceans themselves, the rules and mechanisms by which we govern the oceans are dynamic. We know from our yearly discussions on the law of the sea resolution that the Law of the Sea Convention has not resolved all the problems of man's use of the seas. In the past 20 years, the bright prospects for what seemed to be an abundant supply of fish have turned dim as fish stocks around the world have collapsed, including groundfish stocks off the Atlantic coast and salmon off the Pacific coast of Canada. The sinking of the tanker *Prestige* last month off the coast of Spain has brought home once again the realization that our use of the ocean highway can lead to environmental tragedy.

In the area of fisheries, I think it fair to say no one expected the Law of the Sea Convention to be a panacea for all the world's fishing problems. However, the Convention has demonstrated resilience in serving as a basis for necessary conservation and management measures. Canada was one of a core group of States that pursued the need for an agreement to supplement UNCLOS in order to manage straddling fish stocks. Some people say that the title of the resulting instrument in 1995 is an agreement with 63 words in it. This is a bit of an exaggeration. It is "Agreement for the Implementation of the Provisions of the United Nations Con-

*Editors' Note.—Verbatim Records of the Plenary Meetings of the United Nations General Assembly, Fifty-seventh Session, 72nd Plenary Meeting, Item 25 on the provisional agenda. UN document A/57/PV.72. 10 December 2002, http://www.un.org/ga/57/pv.html (accessed 22 April 2003).

vention on the Law of the Sea of 10 December 1982 relating to the Conservation and Management of Straddling Fish Stocks and Highly Migratory Fish Stocks."

The United Nations Fish Stocks Agreement is a significant achievement, and we all welcomed its entry into force last year. The wide adoption and effective implementation of that Agreement is key to achieving sustainable management of the world's fisheries. In this regard, the work of regional fisheries management organizations is crucial. There are problem signs already. The Convention for the Conservation and Management of Highly Migratory Fish Stocks in the Western and Central Pacific Ocean was one of the first fisheries conventions to be negotiated after the adoption of the United Nations Fish Stocks Agreement. It embodies many of its principles and provisions.

We are also pleased by the continuing attention being paid by the Food and Agriculture Organization and other United Nations bodies, regional institutions and individual States to illegal, unreported and unregulated (IUU) fishing. IUU fishing cuts at the core of global and regional efforts to attain sustainable management of fish stocks. I would like to pay tribute to the Spanish Government for organizing the recent conference on IUU fishing, which made a valuable contribution in the search for solutions. Charting a way forward to minimize IUU fishing remains a challenge, one which will and can be met within the Law of the Sea Convention.

The elaboration of the United Nations Fish Stocks Agreement within that framework demonstrated an essential strength of UNCLOS. It is a structure capable of further development, one showing great foresight on the part of the law of the sea architects. There are additional areas, such as marine pollution, where the international framework is not as well developed as it could be in light of new and growing menaces to the life of the world's oceans. What is needed in these instances might well be an elaboration of law of the sea provisions in the same way as that for the United Nations Fish Stocks Agreement.

I should emphasize, however, that our own experience has shown us that no number of international instruments will be able to deal effectively with the challenges posed by our competing use of the seas, unless these agreements are implemented and complied with. The political will to comply is an essential ingredient. One way of addressing these challenges is through the Open-ended Informal Consultative Process on Oceans. These open-ended consultations have proven to be a very useful part of the international oceans architecture. By bringing together a broad range of governmental and non-governmental stakeholders to focus on oceans issues, the process serves a unique and essential function: to find the best and most creative ways to coordinate and cooperate in the management of the world's oceans. We are very encouraged by the decision to continue with the consultative process for the next three years. Let us put it to good use.

I said at the beginning of my remarks that anniversaries are also a time to remember. Every delegation will have names of those who have passed away—as we heard the other day in the cases of Austria and Germany. Elisabeth Mann Borgese of Canada, who died this year, was along with Arvid Pardo, the father of the Conference, one of the founders of Pacem in Maribus, peace on the oceans. She was fond of saying that she had always looked at the sea as a laboratory in the making of a new world order. I believe we are all privileged to be part of that laboratory. Let us celebrate both the commitment of States and the remarkable individuals they sent to negotiate our constitution of the oceans. Happy twentieth anniversary, UNCLOS!

Pacem in Maribus Conference 2002—The Ocean in the New Economy*

The 130 participants from 31 countries gathered in Cape Town, South Africa on December 8–14, 2002 to celebrate Pacem in Maribus XXIX, have agreed on the following declaration.

DECLARATION

The PIM XXIX Conference pays homage and tribute to Elisabeth Mann Borgese, the founder of Pacem in Maribus and the International Ocean Institute (IOI) for her invaluable contribution to the oceans.

She raised the standard in the struggle for the promotion of equity and balanced economic growth based on just social values, respect for nature and the protection of the environment, and in particular the sustainable use of the ocean. In this context, she was a champion of the developing countries and the marginalized communities.

The Conference recalls the unique role of Elisabeth Mann Borgese and Arvid Pardo in the elaboration of the concept of the Common Heritage of Mankind—the foundation of the United Nations Convention on the Law of the Sea (UNCLOS).

The Conference celebrates the 20th anniversary of UNCLOS, which has become a truly universal instrument with the ratification and accession of 138 countries, and calls on all those who have not yet done so to ratify or accede to the Convention—the principal legal framework for ocean governance.

The Conference is cognisant of the need for continued and reinforced international, regional and national efforts to ensure peace and security in the oceans and the seas, effective conservation and management of all ocean resources and protection, and preservation of the marine environment in order to achieve balanced and equitable sustainable development.

The Conference is convinced that the IOI and its Regional and National Operational Centres will continue to play an important and effective role in assisting all countries, particularly the developing countries, in meeting the old and new challenges of "The Ocean in the New Economy."

The Conference continues to uphold the objectives and vision of its founder and supports and encourages the International Ocean Institute–Headquarters in

* EDITORS' NOTE.—This document was accessed through the International Ocean Institute's Web site, http://www.ioinst.org/ioisa/pim2002/declaration.htm (accessed 31 January 2003).

taking action to revitalize and strengthen the Institute by implementing a coherent strategy for the coming decade.

The Conference, in addressing its principle theme, "The Ocean in the New Economy," recognises that the new economy, which is driven by information and communication technologies, has propelled the integration process to unprecedented heights. These developments combined with an ocean governance deficit create major challenges and opportunities, particularly for the majority of developing countries and their capacity to take advantage of the new opportunities to integrate themselves into the world economy and benefit from the generosity of the ocean.

In this regard, the Conference is making a contribution to the follow-up and implementation of the outcome of the World Summit on Sustainable Development in Johannesburg, 2002 through the recommendations and decisions emerging from the thematic and sectoral discussions and debate covering:

Resource Management

Ocean and coastal resource usage systems are in need of enhanced governance mechanisms that incorporate stakeholder involvement, foster partnerships, and promote co-management. There is a strong requirement for resource management systems to add value to natural products and to promote indigenous capacity-building. Issues of ethics, equity and corporate responsibility must be at the forefront of this. In so doing, the vulnerability of nations and economic sectors reliant on the utilisation of natural ocean resources can be reduced.

Transport

The Conference is concerned with the continued growth of substandard flags of convenience fleets and their implication for the security and environment of the oceans, and recommends the entry into force of the United Nations Convention on Ship Registration adopted in 1986, which would bring to international shipping transparency, identifiability and accountability to prevent abuse and environmental disasters. The Conference commends UNCITRAL, CMI and UNCTAD for their co-operation in evolving and elaborating an international transport legal instrument to govern the operations of multi-modal transportation that take into account the interests of developing countries. Furthermore, it strongly recommends greater public-private partnerships and the collegial co-operation of international organizations to develop a universal enabling environment that has roots in legislative, contractual and voluntary measures for the adoption and use of modern methods of information and communication technology and E-commerce.

Living Space

Planning is essential to ensure that a balance is achieved between economic development activities and the integrity of coastal living space. Particular attention should be paid to land-based sources of pollution, not only from coastal megacities, but all urban areas, which together are the major contributors to ocean pollution. Planning must also ensure equitable access to coastal zones and draw on principles of integrated coastal zone management in helping to mitigate user conflicts in coastal zones.

Communication

The technology available in the new economy provides an unparalleled opportunity, if used wisely, to reduce inequities, share knowledge globally and to educate about the ocean. We recognize that technology can provide a powerful complement to face-to-face interactions. Therefore, the Conference commits IOI to build on its strength in face-to-face communication and information exchange by using technology creatively to share knowledge and build capacity to manage the oceans for a sustainable future. The Conference further commits IOI to make information available according to open content license arrangements wherever possible, and calls on others active in creating knowledge about the ocean to help create a knowledge common heritage that can be built upon by current and future generations.

Industry

The new economy presents unparalleled opportunities for sustainable, shared prosperity for all humanity. It also presents unparalleled challenges. In an increasingly interdependent world, the contemporary knowledge and technological revolution impact on human endeavours ranging from high technology exploitation of offshore resources to improving the quality of life in isolated coastal communities. The tempo, magnitude and complexity of industrial change are increasing rapidly and are likely to continue to do so. Used wisely, sophisticated industrial and information technology can be agents of change for the good of all humanity. Misused, they have the potential to do irreparable harm. Managing the forces of the new industrial economy requires more than good governance. It requires active co-operation between governments at all levels, industry and empowered, informed individual citizens. With responsible, co-operative governance and management, ocean industries can be not only a benefit to this generation, but also responsible stewards of the ocean for future generations.

Security

Security is a vital pre-requisite to the effective functioning of the new economy. Enhanced technology is a double-edged sword and can equally be beneficial or destructive. The roots of genuine and lasting security, therefore, reside in human behaviour and relationships, not in increased technical ingenuity. True security requires mutual confidence. The world maritime community has long experience and sound credentials in building international confidence and co-operation. The IOI, with its multinational, inter-disciplinary and eclectic nature, has considerable potential for contributing to global mutual confidence, and thus security.

Recreation

The Conference recognises the importance of the rapidly growing ecotourism industry, including cultural tourism, and the significant contribution that it makes to the peaceful use of the ocean in the new economy. We further recognise that eco-tourism may affect vulnerable communities and sensitive ecosystems, but if properly planned and managed, eco-tourism has an important role in conservation. We recognise the need for youth and women to participate in all programmes and projects, especially those in coastal communities, to allow them to become ecological entrepreneurs, thus strengthening sustainability of the environment and economy and social equity. The Conference strongly endorses the plan of implementation for tourism agreed by the World Summit on Sustainable Development.

Food

The Conference recognises the importance of integrating mariculture for food production with sustainable practices and with community involvement in order to promote social equity and sustainable livelihoods.

The African Leadership Preparatory Committee, established on the occasion of Pacem in Maribus 2002, recognises the need to assist African countries in the implementation of the agreed plans of action contained within national frameworks, the African Process, the World Summit on Sustainable Development and NEPAD, especially in the area of ocean governance. The implementation of these commitments will be key in achieving sustainable development of oceans and coasts in Africa, and should be supported by all stakeholders. The African Leadership Preparatory Committee commits itself to establishing a process to contribute towards effective implementation of the agreed plans of action at regional and national levels through the development of an African Implementation Action Plan for Oceans and Coasts.

Directory

DIRECTORY OF OCEAN-RELATED ORGANIZATIONS

This directory was updated in December 2003. Additions and amendments are welcomed and should be sent by e-mail to ocean.yearbook@dal.ca.

THE EDITORS

1. GLOBAL INTERGOVERNMENTAL ORGANIZATIONS

Alliance of Small Island States (AOSIS)
Permanent Mission of Samoa to the United Nations
800 Second Avenue, 4th floor
New York, NY, 10017, USA
Contact: Chairman
Tel: 1 212 599-6196
Fax: 1 212 599-0797
E-mail: samoa@un.int
http://www.sidsnet.org/aosis/

Basel Convention on the Control of Transboundary Movements of Hazardous Wastes and Their Disposal (Basel Convention)
International Environment House
13-15, chemin des Anémones
CH-1219 Châtelaine, Geneva, Switzerland
Contact: Secretariat
Tel: 41 22 917 8218
Fax: 41 22 797 3454
E-mail: sbc@unep.ch
http://www.basel.int/

Commission on Science and Technology for Development
Division on Investment, Technology and Enterprise Development
United Nations Conference on Trade and Development (UNCTAD)
Palais des Nations, Building E, 9th Floor
CH-1211 Geneva 10, Switzerland
Contact: Chief, Technology for Development Section
Tel: 41 22 917 5069
Fax: 41 22 907 0197
E-mail: stdev@unctad.org
http://www.unctad.org/stdev/

Commission on Sustainable Development (CSD)
Department of Economic and Social Affairs
Two United Nations Plaza, Room DC2-2220
New York, NY, 10017, USA
Contact: Secretariat
Tel: 1 212 963-2803
Fax: 1 212 963-4260
E-mail: dsd@un.org
http://www.un.org/esa/sustdev/csd.htm

Commission on the Limits of the Continental Shelf
Division for Ocean Affairs and the Law of the Sea
Office of Legal Affairs
Room DC2-0450, United Nations
New York, NY, 10017, USA
Contact: Secretariat
Tel: 1 212 963-3966
Fax: 1 212 963-5847
E-mail: doalos@un.org
http://www.un.org/Depts/los/clcs_new/clcs_home.htm

Committee on International Oceanographic Data and Information Exchange (IODE)
IOC-UNESCO
1, rue Miollis
F-75732 Paris Cedex 15, France
Contact: Head, Ocean Science
Tel: 33 1 4568 4046
Fax: 33 1 4568 5812
E-mail: p.pissierssens@unesco.org
http://ioc.unesco.org/iode/

Convention on Biological Diversity
World Trade Centre
393 St Jacques Street, Office 300
Montréal, QC, H2Y 1N9, Canada
Contact: Secretary General
Tel: 1 514 288-2220
Fax: 1 514 288-6588
E-mail: secretariat@biodiv.org
http://www.biodiv.org/

Convention on International Trade in Endangered Species of Wild Fauna and Flora (CITES)
International Environment House
13-15, chemin des Anémones
CH-1219 Châtelaine, Geneva, Switzerland
Contact: Secretariat
Tel: 41 22 917 8139/40
Fax: 41 22 797 3417
E-mail: cites@unep.ch
http://www.cites.org/

Convention on Migratory Species
United Nations Premises in Bonn
Martin-Luther-King-Str. 8
D-53175 Bonn, Germany
Contact: UNEP/CMS Secretariat
Tel: 49 228 815 2401/2

Fax: 49 228 815 2449
E-mail: cms@unep.de
http://www.wcmc.org.uk/cms/

Division for Ocean Affairs and the Law of the Sea (DOALOS)
Office of Legal Affairs
United Nations
Room DC2-0450
New York, NY, 10017, USA
Contact: Director
Tel: 1 212 963-3962
Fax: 1 212 963-5847
E-mail: doalos@un.org
http://www.un.org/Depts/los/

Food and Agriculture Organisation of the United Nations (FAO)
Viale delle Terme di Caracalla
I-00100 Rome, Italy
Contact: Director General
Tel: 39 06 5705 1
Fax: 39 06 5705 3152
E-mail: FAO-HQ@fao.org
http://www.fao.org/

Global Biodiversity Information Facility (GBIF)
Universitetsparken 15
DK-2100 Copenhagen, Denmark
Contact: Secretariat
Tel: 45 35 32 14 70
Fax: 45 35 32 14 80
E-mail: gbif@gbif.org
http://www.gbif.org/

Global Environment Facility (GEF)
1818 H Street NW
Washington, DC, 20433, USA
Contact: Secretariat
Tel: 1 202 473-0508
Fax: 1 202 522-3240 or 522-3245
E-mail: secretariat@TheGEF.org
http://www.gefweb.org/

Global International Waters Assessment (GIWA)
Kalmarsund Laboratory
Barlastgatan 1
SE-391 82 Kalmar, Sweden
Tel: 46 480 44 73 53
Fax: 46 480 44 73 55
E-mail: info@giwa.net
http://www.giwa.net/

Global Programme of Action for the Protection of the Marine Environment from Land-based Activities (GPA)
GPA Coordinating Office, UNEP
PO Box 16227
NL-2500 BE, The Hague, The Netherlands
Contact: Coordinator
Tel: 31 70 311 4460
Fax: 31 70 345 6648
E-mail: gpa@unep.nl
http://www.gpa.unep.org/

GLOBEFISH
FAO, Fishery Industries Division
Viale delle Terme di Caracalla
I-00100 Rome, Italy
Tel: 39 06 5705 6313/5594
Fax: 39 06 5705 5188
E-mail: globefish-web@fao.org
http://www.globefish.org/

Intergovernmental Oceanographic Commission (IOC)
UNESCO
1, rue Miollis
F-75732 Paris Cedex 15, France
Contact: Head, Ocean Science
Tel: 33 1 4568 4046
Fax: 33 1 4568 5812
E-mail: p.pissierssens@unesco.org
http://ioc.unesco.org/iocweb/default.htm

Intergovernmental Panel on Climate Change (IPCC)
c/o World Meteorological Organisation
7, bis Avenue de la Paix
CP 2300
CH-1211 Geneva 2, Switzerland
Contact: Secretariat
Tel: 41 22 730 8208 84
Fax: 41 22 730 8025 13
E-mail: ipcc_sec@gateway.wmo.ch
http://www.ipcc.ch/

International Continental Scientific Drilling Program
GeoForschungsZentrum Potsdam
ICDP-OSG
Telegrafenberg
D-14473 Potsdam, Germany
Contact: Research Coordinator
Tel: 49 331 288 1020
Fax: 49 331 288 1002

E-mail: lau@gfz-potsdam.de
http://www.icdp-online.org/

International Coordination Group for the Tsunami Warning System in the Pacific (ICG/ITSU)
IOC
1, rue Miollis
F-75732 Paris Cedex 15, France
Contact: Secretariat
Tel: 33 1 4568 4046
Fax: 33 1 4568 5812
E-mail: p.pissierssens@unesco.org
http://ioc.unesco.org/itsu

International Court of Justice (ICJ)
Peace Palace
NL-2517 KJ, The Hague, The Netherlands
Tel: 31 70 302 2323
Fax: 31 70 364 9928
E-mail: information@icj-cij.org
http://www.icj-cij.org/

International Hydrographic Organisation (IHO)
4, Quai Antoine 1er
BP 445
MC-98011 Monaco Cedex, Principality of Monaco
Contact: IH Bureau
Tel: 377 93 10 81 00
Fax: 377 93 10 81 40
E-mail: info@ihb.mc
http://www.iho.shom.fr/

International Labour Organization (ILO)
4, route des Morillons
CH-1211, Geneva 22, Switzerland
Contact: International Labour Office
Tel: 41 22 799 6111
Fax: 41 22 798 8685
E-mail: ilo@ilo.org
http://www.ilo.org/

International Maritime Organisation (IMO)
4 Albert Embankment
London, SE1 7SR, United Kingdom
Contact: Secretary General
Tel: 44 207 735 7611
Fax: 44 207 587 3210
E-mail: info@imo.org
http://www.imo.org/

International Mobile Satellite Organisation (IMSO)
99 City Road
London, EC1Y 1AX, United Kingdom
Contact: Customer Care
Tel: 44 207 728 1000
Fax: 44 207 728 1044
E-mail: customer_care@inmarsat.org
http://www.inmarsat.org/

International Oil Pollution Compensation Funds (IOPC)
Portland House, Stag Place
London, SW1 5PN, United Kingdom
Tel: 44 207 592 7100
Fax: 44 207 592 7111
E-mail: info@iopcfund.org
http://www.iopcfund.org/

International Satellite System for Search and Rescue
c/o INMARSAT
99 City Road
London, EC1Y 1AX, United Kingdom
Contact: Cospas-Sarsat Secretariat
Tel: 44 207 728 1391
Fax: 44 207 728 1170
E-mail: cospas_sarsat@imso.org
http://www.cospas-sarsat.org/

International Sea-Bed Authority (ISA)
14-20 Port Royal Street, 2nd floor
Kingston, Jamaica, West Indies
Contact: Secretary General
Tel: 1 876 922-9105
Fax. 1 876 922-0195
E-mail: snandan@isa.org.jm
http://www.isa.org.jm/

International Tribunal for the Law of the Sea
Am Internationalen Seegerichtshof #1
D-22609 Hamburg, Germany
Contact: President
Tel: 49 40 3560 70
Fax: 49 40 3560 7245
E-mail: itlos@itlos.org
http://www.itlos.org/

International Tsunami Information Center (ITIC)
Grosvenor Center, Mauka Tower
737 Bishop Street, Suite 2200
Honolulu, HI, 96813-3213, USA
Contact: Director
Tel: 1 808 532-6422

Fax: 1 808 532-5576
E-mail: itic.tsunami@noaa.gov
http://www.prh.noaa.gov/itic/

International Whaling Commission
The Red House
135 Station Road, Impington
Cambridge, CB4 9NP, United Kingdom
Contact: Secretary
Tel: 44 1223 23 3971
Fax: 44 1223 23 2876
E-mail: secretariat@iwcoffice.org
http://www.iwcoffice.org/

IOC Science and Communication Centre on Harmful Algae
University of Copenhagen
Øster Farimagsgade 2 D
DK-1353 Copenhagen K, Denmark
Contact: IOC HAB Programme Coordinator
Tel: 45 33 13 44 46
Fax: 45 33 13 44 47
E-mail: hab.ioc@unesco.org
http://ioc.unesco.org/hab/act5.htm

IOC-IEO Science and Communication Centre on Harmful Algae
Instituto Español de Oceanografía
Centro Oceanografico de Vigo, Cabo Estay-Canido
E-36390 Vigo, Spain
Tel: 34 986 492 111
Fax: 34 986 492 003
E-mail: vigohab@vi.ieo.es
http://ioc.unesco.org/hab/act4.htm

IOC-WMO-UNEP Committee for Global Ocean Observing System (I-GOOS)
c/o GOOS Project Office
IOC-UNESCO
1, rue Miollis
F-75732 Paris Cedex 15, France
Contact: Director
Tel: 33 1 4568 4042
Fax: 33 1 4568 5812
E-mail: c.summerhayes@unesco.org
http://ioc.unesco.org/goos/

Joint Group of Experts on the Scientific Aspects of Marine Environmental Protection (GESAMP)
c/o International Maritime Organisation
4 Albert Embankment
London, SE1 7SR, United Kingdom
Contact: Administrative Secretary
Tel: 44 207 587 3119
Fax: 44 207 587 3210
E-mail: ksekimizu@imo.org
http://gesamp.imo.org/

Joint IOC/IHO Guiding Committee for the General Bathymetric Chart of the Oceans (GEBCO)
c/o Challenger Division of Seafloor Processes
Southampton Oceanography Centre
Empress Dock
Southampton, SO14 3ZH, United Kingdom
Contact: Permanent GEBCO Secretariat
Tel: 44 23 8059 3052
Fax: 44 23 8059 6564
E-mail: bob.whitmarsh@soc.soton.ac.uk
http://www.ngdc.noaa.gov/mgg/gebco/

Joint WMO/IOC Technical Commission for Oceanography and Marine Meteorology (JCOMM)
c/o WMO/OMM
7, bis Avenue de la Paix
CP 2300
CH-1211 Geneva 2, Switzerland
Tel: 41 22 730 8473
Fax: 41 22 730 8021
E-mail: oca@gateway.wmo.ch
http://www.wmo.ch/

Paris Memorandum of Understanding on Port State Control
PO Box 90653
NL-2509 LR, The Hague, The Netherlands
Contact: Secretariat
Tel: 31 70 351 1508
Fax: 31 70 351 1599
E-mail: office@parismou.org
http://www.parismou.org/

Ramsar Convention on Wetlands
28, rue Mauverney
CH-1196 Gland, Switzerland
Contact: Ramsar Convention Bureau
Tel: 41 22 999 0170
Fax: 41 22 999 0169
E-mail: ramsar@ramsar.org
http://www.ramsar.org/

Small Island Developing States Network (SIDSNET)
Division for Sustainable Development
United Nations Department of Economic and Social Affairs (UN/DESA)
Two United Nations Plaza, DC2-2020
New York, NY, 10017, USA
Contact: SIDS Unit Team
Tel: 1 212 963-4135
Fax: 1 917 367-3391
E-mail: sidsnet@sdnhq.undp.org
http://www.sidsnet.org/

Stockholm Convention on Persistent Organic Pollutants (POPs)
11-13, chemin des Anémones
CH-1219 Châtelaine, Geneva, Switzerland
Contact: Interim Secretariat
Tel: 41 22 917 8193
Fax: 41 22 797 3460
E-mail: ssc@chemicals.unep.ch
http://www.pops.int/

Tokyo Memorandum of Understanding on Port State Control
Tomoecho Annex Building 6F, 3-8-26,
Toranomon Minato-ku
Tokyo 105-0001, Japan
Contact: Secretariat
Tel: 81 3 3433 0621
Fax: 81 3 3433 0624
E-mail: secretariat@tokyo-mou.org
http://www.tokyo-mou.org/

United Nations Commission on International Trade Law (UNCITRAL)
Vienna International Centre
PO Box 500
A-1400 Vienna, Austria
Contact: Secretariat
Tel: 43 1 26060 4061
Fax: 431 26060 5813
E-mail: uncitral@uncitral.org
http://www.uncitral.org/

United Nations Conference on Trade and Development (UNCTAD)
8-14, avenue de la Paix
Palais des Nations
CH-1211 Geneva 10, Switzerland
Contact: External Relations and Communications
Tel: 41 22 907 1234
Fax: 41 22 907 0043
E-mail: info@unctad.org
http://www.unctad.org/

United Nations Development Programme (UNDP)
One United Nations Plaza
New York, NY, 10017, USA
Tel: 1 212 906-5558
Fax: 1 212 906-5364
E-mail: aboutundp@undp.org
http://www.undp.org/

United Nations Environment Programme (UNEP)
UN Avenue, Gigiri
PO Box 30552
Nairobi, Kenya
Contact: Executive Director
Tel: 254 2 621234
Fax: 254 2 624489/90
E-mail: eisinfo@unep.org
http://www.unep.org/

United Nations Framework Convention on Climate Change (UNFCCC)
PO Box 260124
D-53153 Bonn, Germany
Contact: Secretariat
Tel: 49 228 815 1000
Fax: 49 228 815 1999
E-mail: secretariat@unfccc.int
http://unfccc.int/

United Nations Industrial Development Organization (UNIDO)
Vienna International Centre
PO Box 300
A-1400 Vienna, Austria
Tel: 43 1 26026 0
Fax: 43 1 26926 69
E-mail: unido@unido.org
http://www.unido.org/

World Meteorology Organisation (WMO)
WMO Building
7, bis Avenue de la Paix
CP 2300
CH-1211 Geneva 2, Switzerland
Tel: 41 22 730 8111
Fax: 41 22 733 8181
E-mail: ipa@wmo.int
http://www.wmo.ch/

World Tourism Organization
Capitán Haya, 42

E-28020 Madrid, Spain
Tel: 34 91 5678 100
Fax: 34 91 5713 733
E-mail: omt@world-tourism.org
http://www.world-tourism.org/

World Trade Organization (WTO)
Centre William Rappard
154, rue de Lausanne
CH-1211 Geneva 21, Switzerland
Contact: Committee on Trade and Environment
Tel: 41 22 739 5111
Fax: 41 22 731 4206
E-mail: enquiries@wto.org
http://www.wto.org/

2. GLOBAL NONGOVERNMENTAL ORGANIZATIONS

Advisory Committee on Protection of the Sea (ACOPS)
11 Dartmouth Street
London, SW1H 9BN, United Kingdom
Contact: Director
Tel: 44 207 799 3033
Fax: 44 207 799 2933
E-mail: info@acops.org
http://www.acops.org/

Association Internationale Villes et Ports
(International Association Cities and Ports - AVIP/IACP)
45, rue Lord Kitchener
F-76600 Le Havre, France
Tel: 33 2 3542 7884
Fax: 33 2 3542 2194
E-mail: bureau@aivp.com
http://www.aivp.com/

Baltic and International Maritime Council (BIMCO)
Bagsvaerdvej 161
DK-2880 Bagsvaerd, Denmark
Contact: Secretary General
Tel: 45 44 36 68 00
Fax: 45 44 36 68 68
E-mail: mailbox@bimco.dk
http://www.bimco.org/

Baltic Marine Biologists
Department of Evolutionary Biology-Plant Ecology
Uppsala University
Villavägen 14
SE-75236 Uppsala, Sweden
Contact: General Secretary
Tel: 46 18 471 28 85
Fax: 46 18 55 34 19
E-mail: pauli.snoeijs@ebc.uu.se
http://www.smf.su.se/bmb/

Cephalopod International Advisory Council (CIAC)
c/o FRS Marine Laboratory Aberdeen
PO Box 101, Victoria Road
Aberdeen, AB11 9DB, United Kingdom
Contact: Executive Secretary
Tel: 44 1224 29 5507
Fax: 44 1224 29 5511
E-mail: hatfielde@marlab.ac.uk
http://www.nbs.ac.uk/public/mlsd/ciac/index.html

Charles Darwin Foundation for the Galapagos Islands
Av. 6 de Diciembre N 36-109 y Pasaje California
PO Box 17-01-3891
Quito, Ecuador
Tel: 593 5526 147
E-mail: galapagosinfo@darwinfoundation.org
http://www.darwinfoundation.org/

Comité International Radio-Maritime (CIRM)
(International Association for Marine Electronics Companies)
Southbank House
Black Prince Road
London, SE1 7SJ, United Kingdom
Contact: Secretary General
Tel: 44 207 587 1245
Fax: 44 207 587 1436
E-mail: secgen@cirm.org
http://www.cirm.org/

Comité Maritime International (CMI)
(International Maritime Committee)
Mechelsesteenweg, 196
B-2018 Antwerp, Belgium
Tel: 32 3 227 3526
Fax: 32 3 227 3528
E-mail: admini@cmi-imc.org
http://www.comitemaritime.org/

Commission for Cooperation with Developing Countries
c/o Mariculture and Fisheries Division
Kuwait Institute of Scientific Research
PO Box 1638
22017 Salmiya, Kuwait
Contact: President
Tel: 965 575 1984
Fax: 965 571 1293
E-mail: sdurva@kisr.edu.kw
http://www.olympus.net/IAPSO/comm.html

Commission for the Geological Map of the World (CGMW)
77, rue Claude-Bernard
F-75005 Paris, France
Contact: Secretary General
Tel: 33 1 4707 2294
Fax: 33 1 4336 9518
E-mail: ccgm@club-internet.fr
http://perso.club-internet.fr/ccgm/

Commission on Ecosystem Management (CEM)
IUCN—The World Conservation Union
Private Bag 300
Gaborone, Botswana
Contact: Secretariat IUCN Botswana
Tel: 267 3159 417
Fax: 267 3971 584
E-mail: cem@iucnbot.org
http://www.iucn.org/themes/cem/cem/

Commission on Education and Communications (CEC)
IUCN—The World Conservation Union
28, rue Mauvernay
CH-1196 Gland, Switzerland
Contact: Chair
Tel: 41 22 999 0000
Fax: 41 22 999 0002
E-mail: wjg@hq.iucn.org
http://info.iucn.org/cec/

Commission on Environmental, Economic and Social Policy (CEESP)
c/o CENESTA (Centre for Sustainable Development)
5 Lakpour Lane, Suite 24
IR-16936 Tehran, Iran
Contact: Executive Officer
Tel: 98 21 295 4217
Fax: 98 21 253 9925
E-mail: ceesp@iucn.org
http://www.iucn.org/themes/ceesp/

Commission on Environmental Law (CEL)
IUCN—The World Conservation Union
Environmental Law Centre
Godesberger Allee 108-112
D-53175 Bonn, Germany
Contact: Secretariat
Tel: 49 228 2692 231
Fax: 49 228 2692 250
E-mail: secretariat@elc.iucn.org
http://www.iucn.org/themes/law/

Commission on Mean Sea Level and Tides
Director de Recherche
Laboratoire d'Oceanographie et de Geophysique Spatiale
GRGS/ Observatoire Midi Pyrenees
14, avenue Edouard Belin
F-31400 Toulouse, France
Tel: 33 5 6133 2923
Fax: 33 5 6125 3205
E-mail: leprovos@pontos.cst.cnes.fr
http://www.olympus.net/IAPSO/comm.html

Commission on Sea Ice
Scott Polar Research Institute
Lensfield Road
Cambridge, CB2 1ER, United Kingdom
Contact: President
E-mail: pw11@cus.cam.ac.uk
http://www.olympus.net/IAPSO/comm.html

Coral Cay Conservation
The Tower, 13th Floor
125 High Street
London, SW19 2JG, United Kingdom
Tel: 44 870 750 0668
Fax: 44 870 750 0667
E-mail: info@coralcay.org
http://www.coralcay.org/

Coral Reef Alliance (CORAL)
417 Montgomery Street, Suite 205
San Francisco, CA, 94105, USA
Tel: 1 415 834-0900
Fax: 1 415 834-0999
E-mail: info@coral.org
http://www.coral.org/

Det Norske Veritas
Veritasveien 1

N-1322 Høvik, Norway
Contact Head Office
Tel: 47 67 57 99 00
Fax: 47 57 67 99 11
http://www.dnv.no/

Earth Action Network
17 The Green
Wye, Kent, TN25 5AJ, United Kingdom
Contact: Executive Director
Tel: 44 123 381 3796
Fax: 44 123 381 3795
E-mail: wye@earthaction.org.uk
http://www.oneworld.org/earthaction/

Earth Council
PO Box 319-6100
San José, Costa Rica
Contact: Secretariat
Tel: 1 506 205-1600
Fax: 1 506 249-3500
E-mail: ecouncil@ecouncil.ac.cr
http://www.ecouncil.ac.cr/

Engineering Committee on Oceanic Resources
Ocean Engineering Research Centre
Faculty of Engineering and Applied Science
St. John's, NL, Canada, A1B 3X5
Contact: Executive Secretary
Tel: 1 709 737-3284
Fax: 1 709 737-2116
E-mail: nbose@engr.mun.ca
http://www.engr.mun.ca/ECOR/index.html

Estuarine Research Federation
PO Box 510
Port Republic, MD, 20676, USA
Tel: 1 410 586-0997
Fax: 1 410 586-9226
E-mail: webmaster@erf.org
http://www.erf.org/

EUROFISH (ex-EASTFISH)
UN Centre Midtermolen 3
PO Box 0896
DK-2100 Copenhagen Ø, Denmark
Tel: 45 35 46 71 80
Fax: 45 35 46 71 81
E-mail: info@eurofish.dk
http://www.eurofish.dk/

Federation of National Associations of Ship Brokers and Agents (FONASBA)
Ground Floor North
85 Gracechurch Street
London, EC3V 0AA, United Kingdom
Contact: Secretariat
Tel: 44 207 623 1111
Fax: 44 207 623 8118
E-mail: fonasba@ics.org.uk
http://www.fonasba.com/

Fish for All
PO Box 500, GPO
10670 Penang, Malaysia
Tel: 60 4 626 1606
Fax: 60 4 626 5530
E-mail: fishforall@cgiar.org
http://www.fishforall.org/

Friends of the Earth—International
PO Box 19199
NL-1000 GD Amsterdam, The Netherlands
Contact: International Secretariat
Tel: 31 20 622 1369
Fax: 31 20 639 2181
E-mail: foei@foei.org
http://www.foei.org/

Global Aquaculture Alliance
5661 Telegraph Road, Suite 3A
St. Louis, MO, 63129, USA
Tel: 1 314 293-5500
Fax: 1 314 293-5525
E-mail: homeoffice@gaalliance.org
http://www.gaalliance.org/

Global Coral Reef Monitoring Network (GCRMN)
c/o Australian Institute of Marine Science
PO Box 772
Townsville, MC 4810, Australia
Contact: Coordinator
Tel: 61 7 4772 4314
Fax: 61 7 4772 2808
E-mail: c.wilkinson@aims.gov.au
http://www.gcrmn.org/

Global Ocean Ecosystem Dynamics (GLOBEC)
Plymouth Marine Laboratory
Prospect Place
Plymouth, PL1 3DH, United Kingdom
Contact: International Project Office
Tel/Fax: 44 1752 63 3160

E-mail: globec@pml.ac.uk
http://www.pml.ac.uk/globec/

GLOBE International
1636 R Street NW, Third Floor
Washington, DC, 20009, USA
Contact: Secretariat
Tel: 1 202 293-9090
Fax: 1 202 293-9098
E-mail: info@globeinternational.org
http://www.globeinternational.org/

Greenpeace International
Keizergracht 176
NL-1016 DW, Amsterdam, The Netherlands
Contact: Executive Director
Tel: 31 20 523 6222
Fax: 31 20 523 6200
E-mail: supporter.services@ams.greenpeace.org
http://www.greenpeace.org/

Hydrographic Society
PO Box 103
Plymouth, PL4 7YP, United Kingdom
Contact: Manager
Tel: 44 1752 22 3512
E-mail: helen@hydrographicsociety.org
http://www.hydrographicsociety.org/

ICC Committee on Maritime Transport and Logistics
c/o International Chamber of Commerce
38 Cours Albert 1er
F-75008 Paris, France
Contact: Policy Manager
Tel: 33 1 4953 2895
Fax: 33 1 4953 2859
E-mail: viviane.schiavi@iccwbo.org
http://www.iccwbo.org/home/transport/maritime_transport_committee.asp

ICHCA International Limited (IIL)
85 Western Road, Suite 2
Romford, Essex, RM1 3LS, United Kingdom
Contact: International Secretariat
Tel: 44 1708 73 5295
Fax: 44 1708 73 5225
E-mail: info@ichcainternational.co.uk
http://www.ichcainternational.co.uk/

IGU Commission on Coastal Systems
Department of Marine and Coastal Sciences
71 Dudley Road
Cook College
Rutgers University
New Brunswick, NJ, 08901, USA
Contact: Executive Secretary
Tel: 1 732 932-6555, ext. 506/500
Fax: 1 732 932-1820
E-mail: psuty@imcs.rutgers.edu
http://igu-ccs.ucc.ie/

IGU Commission on Marine Geography
c/o Department of Geographical Sciences
University of Plymouth
Plymouth, Devon, PL4 8AA, United Kingdom
Contact: Chairman
Tel/Fax: 44 1752 23 3051
E-mail: dapinder@plymouth.ac.uk
http://www.geog.plymouth.ac.uk/marine/

Industrial Shrimp Action Network
14420 Duryea Lane
Tacoma, WA, 98444, USA
Tel: 1 253 539-5272
Fax: 1 253 539-5054
E-mail: isanet@shrimpaction.org
http://www.shrimpaction.org/

Institute for Fisheries Management and Coastal Communities Development (IFM)
North Sea Center
PO Box 104
DK-9850 Hirtshals, Denmark
Tel: 45 98 94 28 55
Fax: 45 98 94 42 68
E-mail: ifm@ifm.dk
http://www.ifm.dk/

Institute of Chartered Shipbrokers (ICS)
85 Gracechurch Street
London, EC3V 0AA, United Kingdom
Tel: 44 207 623 1111
Fax: 44 207 623 8008
E-mail: info@ics.org.uk
http://www.ics.org.uk/

Institute of International Container Lessors (IICL)
555 Pleasantville Road, Suite 140 South
Briarcliff Manor, NY, 10510, USA
Tel: 1 914 747-9100
Fax: 1 914 747-4600

E-mail: info@iicl.org
http://www.iicl.org/

International Arctic Social Sciences Association (IASSA)
University of Alaska Fairbanks
PO Box 757730
Fairbanks, AK, 99775-7730, USA
Contact: Secretariat
Tel: 1 907 474-6367
Fax: 1 907 474-6370
E-mail: fyiassa@uaf.edu
http://www.uaf.edu/anthro/iassa/

International Association for the Study of Maritime Mission (IASMM)
School of Education Theology
York St. John College
Lord Mayor's Walk
York, YO31 7EX, United Kingdom
Contact: Secretariat
Tel: 44 1904 716861
Fax: 44 1904 612512
E-mail: s.friend@yorksj.ac.uk
http://www.iasmm.org/

International Association for the Study of Common Property (IASCP)
Indiana University
PO Box 2355
Gary, IN, 47409, USA
Contact: Executive Director
Tel: 1 219 980-1433
Fax: 1 219 980-2801
E-mail: iascp@indiana.edu
http://www.iascp.org/

International Association for the Physical Sciences of the Ocean (IAPSO)
PO Box 820440
Vicksburg, MS, 39182-0440, USA
Contact: Secretary General
Tel: 1 601 636-1363
Fax: 1 601 629-9640
E-mail: camfield@vicksburg.com
http://www.olympus.net/IAPSO/

International Association of Aquaculture Economics and Management (IAAEM)
Department of Economics
University of Queensland
Brisbane, QLD 4072, Australia
Contact: Secretariat
Tel: 61 7 3365 6570
Fax: 61 7 3365 7299
E-mail: aqem@economics.uq.edu.au
http://www.uq.edu.au/aem/

International Association of Aquatic and Marine Science Libraries and Information Centers (IAMSLIC)
c/o Harbor Branch Oceanographic Institution Library
5600 US 1 North
Fort Pierce, FL, 34946, USA
Tel: 1 561 465-2400 ext. 201
Fax: 1 561 465-2446
E-mail: metzger@hboi.edu
http://www.iamslic.org/

International Association of Biological Oceanography (IABO)
c/o Scottish Association for Marine Science
PO Box 3
Argyll, PA34 4AD, United Kingdom
Contact: President
Tel: 44 1631 56 7853
Fax: 44 1631 56 5518
E-mail: dmlsec@dml.ac.uk

International Association of Classification Societies (IACS)
5 Old Queen Street
London, SW1H 9JA, United Kingdom
Contact: Permanent Secretariat
Tel: 44 207 976 0660
Fax: 44 207 976 0440
E-mail: permsec@iacs.org.uk
http://www.iacs.org.uk/

International Association of Dredging Companies (IADC)
Duinweg 21
NL-2585 JV, The Hague, The Netherlands
Contact: Secretary General
Tel: 31 70 352 3334
Fax: 31 70 351 2654
E-mail: info@iadc-dredging.com
http://www.iadc-dredging.com/

International Association of Dry Cargo Shipowners (INTERCARGO)
4 London Wall Buildings, 2nd Floor
Blomfield Street
London, EC2M 5NT, United Kingdom
Contact: Secretary General
Tel: 44 207 638 3989
Fax: 44 207 638 3943

E-mail: info@intercargo.org
http://www.intercargo.org/

International Association of Geodesy
Central Bureau
c/o Department of Geophysics
Juliane Maries Vej 30
DK-2100 Copenhagen Ø, Denmark
Tel: 45 35 32 06 00
Fax: 45 35 36 53 57
E-mail: iag@gfy.ku.dk
http://www.iag-aig.org/

International Association of Hydrogeologists (IAH)
PO Box 9
Kenilworth, CV8 1JG, United Kingdom
Contact: Secretary General
Tel: 44 1926 450677
Fax: 44 1926 856561
E-mail: iah@iah.org
http://www.iah.org/

International Association of Independent Tanker Owners (INTERTANKO)
Bogstadveien 27B
PO Box 5804
Majorstua
N-0308 Oslo, Norway
Tel: 47 22 12 26 40
Fax: 47 22 12 26 41
E-mail: oslo@intertanko.com
http://www.intertanko.com/

International Association of Institutes of Navigation (IAIN)
The Royal Institute of Navigation
1 Kensington Gore
London, SW7 2AT, United Kingdom
Contact: Secretary General
E-mail: prentpage@aol.com
http://www.iainav.org/

International Association of Marine Aids to Navigation and Lighthouse Authorities (IALA/AISM)
20 ter rue Schnapper
F-78100 St. Germain-en-Laye, France
Contact: Secretary General
Tel: 33 1 3451 7001
Fax: 33 1 3451 8205
E-mail: gwenola.josse@wanadoo.fr
http://www.iala-aism.org/

International Association of Maritime Institutions
South Tyneside College
St. George's Avenue
Tyne and Wear, NE34 6ET, United Kingdom
Contact: Honorary Secretary
Tel: 44 1914 273505
Fax: 44 1914 273653
E-mail: chris.may@iami.info
http://www.iami.info/

International Association of Maritime Universities
c/o Kobe University of Mercantile Marine
5-1-1, Fukae-minami, Higashi-nada
Kobe 658-0022, Japan
Contact: Secretariat
E-mail: k-inoue@cc.kshosen.ac.jp
http://www.iamu-edu.org/

International Association of Maritime Economists (IAME)
IAME Permanent Secretariat (H12-11)
Erasmus University
PO Box 1738
NL-3000 DR, Rotterdam, The Netherlands
Tel: 31 10 408 1490
Fax: 31 10 408 9156
E-mail: rhv-iame@few.eur.nl
http://www.iame.nl/

International Association of Meiobenthologists
c/o Department of Zoology
The Natural History Museum
London, SW7 5BD, United Kingdom
Contact: Chair
http://www.meiofauna.org/

International Association of Ports and Harbours (IAPH)
5th Floor, North Tower
New Pier Takeshiba
1-11-1 Kaigan
Minato-Ku, Tokyo, 105-0022, Japan
Contact: Secretary General
Tel: 81 3 5403 2770
Fax: 81 3 5403 7651
E-mail: info@iaphworldports.org
http://www.iaphworldports.org/

International Cable Protection Committee (ICPC)

PO Box 150
Lymington, SO41 6WA, United Kingdom
Contact: Secretary
Tel: 44 15 9068 1673
Fax: 44 87 0052 6049
E-mail: secretary@iscpc.org
http://www.iscpc.org/

International Cartographic Association (ICA)
PO Box 80115
NL-3508TC Utrecht, The Netherlands
Contact: Secretary General
Tel: 31 30 253 1373
Fax: 31 30 254 0604
E-mail: f.ormeling@geog.uu.nl
http://www.icaic.org/

International Centre for Earth Tides (ICET)
Observatoire Royal de Belgique
Avenue Circulaire 3
B-1180 Brussels, Belgium
Contact: Executive Officer
Tel: 32 2 373 0248
Fax: 32 2 374 9822
E-mail: b.ducarme@oma.be
http://www.astro.oma.be/ICET/index.html

International Chamber of Shipping (ICS)
Carthusian Court
12 Carthusian Street
London, EC1M 6EZ, United Kingdom
Contact: Secretary General
Tel: 44 207 417 8844
Fax: 44 207 417 8877
E-mail: chris.horrocks@marisec.org
http://www.marisec.org/

International Christian Maritime Association (ICMA)
s-Gravendijkwal 64
NL-3014 EG, Rotterdam, The Netherlands
Contact: Secretariat
Tel: 31 10 225 1799
Fax: 31 10 225 0692
E-mail: icma@wanadoo.nl
http://www.icma.as/

International Coalition of Fisheries Associations (ICFA)
1907 North Fort Myers Drive
Arlington, VA, 22209, USA
Contact: Executive Secretariat
E-mail: info@icfa.net
http://www.icfa.net/

International Collective in Support of Fishworkers (ICSF)
27 College Road
600006 Chennai, India
Contact: Executive Secretary
Tel: 91 44 2827 5303
Fax: 91 44 2825 1145
E-mail: icsf@vsnl.com
http://www.iscf.net/

International Commission on Polar Meteorology (ICPM)
Ohio State University
1090 Carmack Road
Columbus, Ohio, 43210-1002, USA
Contact: President
E-mail: bromwich@polarmet1.mps.ohio-state.edu
http://www.antarctica.ac.uk/met/ICPM/

International Commission on Remote Sensing (ICRS)
c/o 11 Innovation Boulevard
National Water Research Institute
Saskatoon, SK, S7N 3H5, Canada
Contact: President
E-mail: al.pietroniro@ec.gc.ca
http://www.cig.ensmp.fr/~iahs/

International Commission on Snow and Ice (ICSI)
c/o INRS EAM
CP 7500
2700 Einstein
Ste-Foy, QC, G1V 4C7, Canada
Contact: President
Tel: 1 418 654-2533
Fax: 1 418 654-2600
E-mail: jones@inrs-eau.uquebec.ca
http://geowww.uibk.ac.at/research/icsi/

International Committee on Seafarers' Welfare (ICSW)
Cassiobury House
11-19 Station Road
Watford, Hertfordshire, WD17 1AP, United Kingdom
Contact: Executive Secretary
Tel: 44 1923 22 2653
Fax: 44 1923 22 2663

E-mail: icsw@icsw.org.uk
http://www.icsw.org.uk/

International Committee on the Underwater Cultural Heritage
Western Australian Maritime Museum
Cliff Street
Fremantle, WA 6160, Australia
Contact: Secretariat
Tel: 61 08 9431 8488
http://www.mm.wa.gov.au/Museum/public/ICOMOS.html

International Congress of Maritime Museums (ICMM)
PO 326
Mystic, CT, 06355, USA
Contact: Secretary General
E-mail: thomas@marinpro.com
http://www.icmmonline.org/

International Cooperative Fisheries Organization
National Federation of Fisheries
Co-operative Association (ZENGYOREN)
Co-operative building, 7th floor
1-1-12 Uchikanda, Chiyoda-ku
Tokyo 101, Japan
Contact: Chairman
Tel: 81 3 3294 9617
Fax: 81 3 3294 9602
E-mail: icfo@zengyoren.jf-net.ne.jp
http://www.coop.org/ica/ica/sb/fish.html

International Coral Reef Action Network (ICRAN)
c/o UNEP-World Conservation Monitoring Centre
219 Huntingdon Road
Cambridge, CB3 0DL, United Kingdom
Contact: ICRAN Assistant Director
Tel: 44 1223 27 7314
Fax: 44 1223 27 7136
E-mail: icran@icran.org
http://www.icran.org/

International Coral Reef Initiative c/o Roberto Jara
Department of Environment and Natural Resources (DENR)
2nd Floor, FASPO Building
DENR Compound
Visayas Avenue
Diliman, Quezon City, The Philippines
Tel: 632 928 1215
Fax: 632 928 1225
E-mail: icri_secretariat@hotmail.com
http://icriforum.org/

International Council of Cruise Lines (ICCL)
2111 Wilson Boulevard, 8th Floor
Arlington, VA, 22201, USA
Contact: President
Tel: 1 703 522-8463
Fax: 1 703 522-3811
E-mail: info@iccl.org
http://www.iccl.org/

International Council of Marine Industry Associations (ICOMIA)
Marine House
Thorpe Lea Road
Egham, Surrey, TW20 8BF, United Kingdom
Contact: Secretariat
Tel: 44 1784 22 3700
Fax: 44 1784 22 3705
http://www.icomia.com/

International Council of Scientific Unions (ICSU)
51, boulevard de Montmorency
F-75016 Paris, France
Contact: Secretariat
Tel: 33 1 4525 0329
Fax: 33 1 4288 9431
E-mail: secretariat@icsu.org
http://www.icsu.org/

International Council on Monuments and Sites (ICOMOS)
49-51, rue de la Fédération
F-75015 Paris, France
Contact: International Secretariat
Tel: 33 1 4567 6770
Fax: 33 1 4566 0622
E-mail: secretariat@icomos.org
http://www.icomos.org/

International Desalination Association
PO Box 387
Topsfield, MA, 01983, USA
Contact: Secretary General
Tel: 1 978 887-0410
Fax: 1 978 887-0411
E-mail: info@idadesal.org
http://www.idadesal.org/

International Dolphin Watch (IDW)
10 Melton Road
North Ferriby
East Yorkshire, HU14 3ET, United Kingdom
Contact: Secretary
Tel: 44 1482 64 5789
Fax: 44 1482 63 4914
E-mail: info@idw.org
http://www.idw.org/

International Ecotourism Society
733 15th Street NW, Suite 1000
Washington, DC, 20005-2112, USA
Tel: 1 202 347-9203
Fax: 1 202 387-7915
E-mail: ecomail@ecotourism.org
http://www.ecotourism.org/

International Federation of Shipmasters' Associations (IFSMA)
202 Lambeth Road
London, SE1 7JY, United Kingdom
Contact: General Secretary
Tel: 44 207 261 0450
Fax: 44 207 928 9030
E-mail: hq@ifsma.org
http://www.ifsma.org/

International Fishmeal and Fish Oil Organization (IFFO)
2 College Yard
Lower Dagnall Street
St. Albans, Hertfordshire, AL3 4PA, United Kingdom
Contact: Director General
Tel: 44 1727 84 2844
Fax: 44 1727 84 2866
E-mail: secretariat@iffo.org.uk
http://www.iffo.org.uk/

International Game Fish Association (IGFA)
300 Gulf Stream Way
Dania Beach, FL, 33004, USA
Contact: President
Tel: 1 954 927-2628
Fax: 1 954 924-4299
E-mail: igfahq@aol.com
http://www.igfa.org/

International Hydrofoil Society
PO Box 51
Cabin John, MD, 20818, USA
Contact: President
E-mail: president@foils.org
http://www.foils.org/

International Institute for Sustainable Development (IISD)
161 Portage Avenue East, 6th Floor
Winnipeg, MB, R3B 0Y4, Canada
Contact: President & CEO
Tel: 1 204 958-7700
Fax: 1 204 958-7710
E-mail: info@iisd.ca
http://www.iisd.org/

International Loran Association
ILA Operations Center
741 Cathedral Pointe Lane
Santa Barbara, CA, 93111, USA
Tel: 1 805 967-8649
Fax: 1 805 967-8471
E-mail: ila@loran.org
http://www.loran.org/

International Marine Contractors Association (IMCA)
Carlyle House
235 Vauxhall Bridge Road
London, SW1V 1EJ, United Kingdom
Contact: Secretary
Tel: 44 207 931 8171
Fax: 44 207 931 8935
E-mail: imca@imca-int.com
http://www.imca-int.com/

International Marine Minerals Society (IMMS)
c/o Marine Minerals Technology Center
University of Hawaii
1000 Pope Road, MSB 303
Honolulu, HI, 96822, USA
Contact: Administrative Office
Tel: 1 808 956-6036
Fax: 1 808 956-9772
E-mail: imms@soest.hawaii.edu
http://www.soest.hawaii.edu/HURL/IMMS/

International Marinelife Alliance
Hawaii Time Building, Suite 307
928 Nuuanu Avenue
Honolulu, HI, 96817, USA
Contact: International Headquarters
Tel: 1 808 523-0143
Fax: 1 808 523-0140

E-mail: info@marine.org
http://www.marine.org/

International Maritime Arbitration Organisation (IMAO)
38 Cours Albert 1er
F-75008 Paris, France
Contact: Secretariat of the ICC/CMI Standing Committee of the IMAO
Tel: 33 1 4953 2828
Fax: 33 1 4953 2933
E-mail: arb@iccwbo.org
http://www.iccwbo.org/court/english/maritime/all_topics.asp

International Maritime Bureau (IMB)
Maritime House
1 Linton Road
Barking, Essex, 1G11 8HG, United Kingdom
Contact: Director
Tel: 44 208 591 3000
Fax: 44 208 594 2833
E-mail: imb@icc-ccs.org.uk
http://www.icc-ccs.org/

International Maritime Economic History Association
Maritime History Publications
Memorial University of Newfoundland
St. John's, NL, A1C 5S7, Canada
Contact: President
Tel: 1 709 737-2602
Fax: 1 709 737-8427
E-mail: mhp@mun.ca
http://www.mun.ca/mhp/imeha.htm

International Maritime Pilots' Association (IMPA)
HQS Wellington
Temple Stairs
Victoria Embankment
London, WC2R 2PN, United Kingdom
Contact: Secretary General
Tel: 44 207 240 3973
Fax: 44 207 240 3518
E-mail: secgen@impahq.org
http://www.impahq.org/

International Navigation Association (PIANC/AICPN)
Graaf de Ferraris Building, 11th Floor
Boulevard du Roi Albert II, 20 - Box 3
B-1000 Brussels, Belgium
Contact: General Secretariat
Tel: 32 2 553 7160
Fax: 32 2 553 7155
E-mail: info@pianc-aipcn.org
http://www.pianc-aipcn.org/

International Network of Basin Organisations
c/o Office international de l'eau/ International Office for Water
21, rue de Madrid
F-75008 Paris, France
Contact: Secretariat
Tel: 33 1 4490 8860
Fax: 33 1 4008 0145
E-mail: riob2@wanadool.fr
http://www.inbo-news.org/

International Ocean Institute (IOI)
University of Malta
PO Box 3
Gzira, GZR 01, Malta
Contact: Executive Director
Tel: 356 21 346529
Fax: 356 21 346502
E-mail: ioihq@ioihq.org.mt
http://www.ioinst.org/

International Ombudsman Centre for Environment and Development (OmCED)
PO Box 319-6100
San José, Costa Rica
Tel: 1 506 205-1600
Fax: 1 506 249-3500
E-mail: omced@ecouncil.ac.cr
http://www.omced.org/

International Organization for Standardization (ISO)
1, rue de Varembé, Case postale 56
CH-1211 Geneva 20, Switzerland
Contact: Secretariat
Tel: 41 22 749 0111
Fax: 41 22 733 3430
E-mail: central@iso.org
http://www.iso.org/

International Organization of Masters, Mates and Pilots (IOMMP)
700 Maritime Boulevard
Linthicum Heights, MD, 21090-1941, USA
Contact: Secretary-Treasurer
Tel: 1 410 850-8700, ext. 21
Fax: 1 410 850-0973

E-mail: info@bridgedeck.org
http://www.iommp.org/

International Petroleum Industry Environmental Conservation Association (IPIECA)
209-215 Blackfriars Road, 5th floor
London, SE1 8NL, United Kingdom
Contact: Executive Secretary
Tel: 44 207 633 2388
Fax: 44 207 233 2389
E-mail: info@ipieca.org
http://www.ipieca.org/

International Salvage Union (ISU)
PO Box 32293
London, W5 1WZ, United Kingdom
Contact: Secretary General
Tel: 44 207 345 5122
Fax: 44 207 345 5722
E-mail: isu@randell.fsnet.co.uk
http://www.marine-salvage.com/

International Seaweed Association
Instituto de Biociências
Universidade de São Paulo
CP 11461
São Paulo, SP 05422-970, Brazil
Contact: Secretary
Fax: 55 11 3091 7547
E-mail: euricodo@usp.br
http://www.intseaweedassoc.org/

International Ship Managers' Association (ISMA)
Suite 202, Eastlands Court
St. Peter's Road
Rugby, CB21 3QP, United Kingdom
Tel: 44 207 417 8844
Fax: 44 207 417 8877
E-mail: alan.ward@isma-london.org
http://www.isma-london.org/

International Ship Suppliers Association (ISSA)
The Baltic Exchange
St. Mary Avenue
London, EC3A 8BH, United Kingdom
Contact: Secretariat
Tel: 44 207 626 6236
Fax: 44 207 626 6234
E-mail: issa@dial.pipex.co.uk
http://www.shipsupply.org/

International Shipping Federation (ISF)
Carthusian Court
12 Carthusian Street
London, EC1M 6EZ, United Kingdom
Contact: Secretary General
Tel: 44 207 417 8844
Fax: 44 207 417 8877
E-mail: chris.horrocks@marisec.org
http://www.marisec.org/

International Society for Environmental Protection (ISEP)
Marxergasse 3/20
A-1030 Vienna, Austria
Tel: 43 1 71528 280
Fax: 43 1 71528 2819
E-mail: office@isep.at
http://www.isep.at/

International Society for Microbial Ecology (ISME)
c/o Center for Microbial Ecology
Michigan State University
East Lansing, MI, 48824, USA
Tel: 1 517 353-9021
Fax: 1 517 353-2917
E-mail: isme@msu.edu.
http://microbes.org/

International Society for Reef Studies (ISRS)
PO Box 1897
Lawrence, Kansas, 66044-8897, USA
Contact: President
E-mail: smiller@gate.net
http://www.uncwil.edu/isrs/

International Society for the Prevention of Water Pollution
Little Orchard, Bentworth
Alton, Hampshire, GU34 5RB, United Kingdom
Contact: Chairman
Tel: 44 1420 56 2225

International Society of Acoustic Remote Sensing of the Atmosphere and Oceans (ISARS)
Physics Department
University of Auckland
Private Bag 92019
Auckland, New Zealand
Contact: Chairperson
Tel: 64 9 3737999
Fax: 64 9 3737445

E-mail: s.bradley@auckland.ac.nz
http://www.boku.ac.at/imp/isars/

International Society of Offshore and Polar Engineers (ISOPE)
PO Box 189
Cupertino, CA, 95015-0189, USA
Tel: 1 650 254-1871
Fax: 1 650 254-2038
Contact: Executive Director
E-mail: info@isope.org
http://www.isope.org/

International Support Vessel Owners' Association (ISOA)
12 Carthusian Street
London, EC1M 6EZ, United Kingdom
Tel: 44 207 417 8844
Fax: 44 207 417 8877
E-mail: isoa@marisec.org
http://www.marisec.org/isoa/

International Tanker Owners Pollution Federation (ITOPF)
Staple Hall
Stonehouse Court
87-90 Houndsditch
London, EC3A 7AX, United Kingdom
Contact: Managing Director
Tel: 44 207 621 1225
Fax: 44 207 621 1783
E-mail: central@itopf.com
http://www.itopf.com/

International Transport Workers' Federation (ITF)
ITF House
49-60 Borough Road
London, SE1 1DR, United Kingdom
Tel: 44 207 403 2733
Fax: 44 207 357 7871
E-mail: mail@itf.org.uk
http://www.itf.org.uk/

International Union of Biological Sciences (IUBS)
51, boulevard de Montmorency
F-75016 Paris, France
Contact: Executive Director
Tel: 33 1 4525 0009
Fax: 33 1 4525 2029
E-mail: secretariat@iubs.org
http://www.iubs.org/

International Union of Geodesy and Geophysics (IUGG)
c/o CIRES
Campus Box 216
University of Colorado
Boulder, CO, 80309, USA
Contact: Secretary General
Tel: 1 303 497-5147
Fax: 1 303 497-3645
E-mail: jjoselyn@cires.colorado.edu
http://www.iugg.org/

International Union of Geological Sciences (IUGS)
Geological Survey of Austria
Rasumofskygasse 23
PO Box 127
A-1031 Vienna, Austria
Contact: Secretary General
Tel: 43 1 71256 74180
Fax: 43 1 71256 7456
E-mail: wjanoschek@cc.geolba.ac.at
http://www.iugs.org/

International Union of Marine Insurance (IUMI)
Swiss Re
Mythenquai 50/60
CH-8022 Zurich, Switzerland
Contact: General Secretary
Tel: 41 43 285 2126
Fax: 41 43 282 9699
E-mail: Fritz_Stabinger@swissre.com
http://www.iumi.com/root/navigation1.htm

International Water Association
Alliance House
12 Caxton Street
London, SW1H 0QS, United Kingdom
Contact: Executive Director
Tel: 44 207 654 5500
Fax: 44 207 654 5555
E-mail: water@iwahq.org.uk
http://www.iawq.org.uk/

Islamic Shipowners' Association (ISHA)
PO Box 14900
Jeddah 21434, Saudi Arabia
Contact: Secretary General
Tel: 966 2 665 3379
Fax: 966 2 660 4920
E-mail: oisa@saudionline.com.sa

IUGG Inter-associations Commission on Geophysical Risk and Sustainability
CSIRO Environmental Risk Network
Private Bag 1
Aspendale, VIC 3195, Australia
Contact: Chair, GeoRisk Commission
Tel: 61 3 9239 4546
Fax: 61 3 9239 4444
E-mail: tom.beer@dar.csiro.au
http://www.mitp.ru/georisk/

Lloyd's Register of Shipping
71 Fenchurch Street
London, EC3M 4BS, United Kingdom
Contact: Enquiries
Tel: 44 207 709 9166
Fax: 44 207 488 4796
E-mail: lloydsreg@lr.org
http://www.lr.org/

Marine Aquarium Council
923 Nu'uanu Avenue
Honolulu, HI, 96817, USA
Contact: Executive Director
Tel: 1 808 550-8217
Fax: 1 808 550-8317
E-mail: info@aquariumcouncil.org
http://www.aquariumcouncil.org/

Marine Technology Society
5565 Sterrett Place, Suite 108
Columbia, MD, 21044, USA
Contact: Executive Director
Tel: 1 410 884-5330
Fax: 1 410 884-9060
E-mail: mtsmbrship@erols.com
http://www.mtsociety.org/

Multiport Ship Agencies Network
14 Greenwich Quay, 2nd Floor
Clarence Road
London, SE8 3EY, United Kingdom
Contact: Secretary General
Tel: 44 208 469 9188
Fax: 44 208 469 9189
E-mail: multiport@dial.pipex.com
http://www.multiport.org/

National Shellfisheries Association, Inc.
Department of Marine Sciences
University of Connecticut
1980 Shennecossett Road
Groton, CT, 06340, USA
Contact: President
Tel: 1 860 405-9282
Fax: 1 860 405-9153
E-mail: sshumway@uconnvm.uconn.edu
http://www.shellfish.org/

Ocean Drilling Program (ODP)
Joint Oceanographic Institutions
1755 Massachusetts Avenue, NW, Suite 700
Washington, DC, 20036-2102, USA
Contact: Program Manager
Tel: 1 202 232-3900
Fax: 1 202 462-8754
E-mail: joi@joiscience.org
http://www.oceandrilling.org/

Ocean, Offshore and Arctic Engineering Division (OOAE)
American Society of Mechanical Engineers
ASME International
Three Park Avenue, MS22W 3
New York, NY, 10016, USA
Contact: Chair
E-mail: chair@ooae.org
http://www.ooae.org/

Oceana
2501 M Street, NW
Washington, DC, 20037-1311, USA
Contact: Executive Director
Tel: 1 202 833-3900
Fax: 1 202 833-2070
E-mail: info@oceana.org
http://www.oceana.org/

Oil Companies International Marine Forum (OCIMF)
27 Queen Anne's Gate
London, SW1H 9BU, United Kingdom
Tel: 44 207 654 1200
Fax: 44 207 654 1205
E-mail: enquiries@ocimf.com
http://www.ocimf.com/

Ornamental Fish International
Apartado de Correos 129
E-29692 Sabinillas, Manilva, Málaga, Spain
Tel: 34 952 891 975
Fax: 34 952 890 895
E-mail: secretariat@ornamental-fish-int.org
http://ornamental-fish-int.org/

Partnership for Observation of the Global Oceans (POGO)
Bedford Institute of Oceanography
1 Challenger Drive
Dartmouth, NS, B2Y 4A2, Canada
Contact: Executive Director
Tel: 1 902 426-8044
Fax: 1 902 426-9388
E-mail: pogo@sio.ucsd.edu
http://www.ocean-partners.org/

Passenger Shipping Association (PSA)
Walmar House
288-292 Regent Street
London, W1R 5HE, United Kingdom
Tel: 44 207 436 2449
Fax: 44 207 636 9206
E-mail: admin@psa-psara.org
http://www.psa-psara.org/

Permanent Service for Mean Sea Level
Bidston Observatory
Birkenhead, Merseyside, CH43 7RA, United Kingdom
Contact: Director
Tel: 44 1516 53 8633
Fax: 44 1516 53 6269
E-mail: psmsl@pol.ac.uk
http://www.nbi.ac.uk/psmsl/index.html/

Pew Center on Global Climate Change
2101 Wilson Boulevard, Suite 550
Arlington, VA, 22201, USA
Tel: 1 703 516-4146
Fax: 1 703 841-1422
http://www.pewclimate.org/

Pew Oceans Commission
2101 Wilson Boulevard, Suite 550
Arlington, VA, 22201, USA
Contact: Executive Director
Tel: 1 703 516-0619
Fax: 1 703 516-9551
E-mail: tulouc@pewoceans.org
http://www.pewoceans.org/

Reef Ball Foundation
603 River Overlook Road
Woodstock, GA, 30188, USA
Tel: 1 770 752-0202
Fax: 1 770 360-1328
E-mail: reefball@reefball.com
http://www.reefball.org/

Scientific Committee on Antarctic Research (SCAR)
Scott Polar Research Institute
Lensfield Road
Cambridge, CB2 1ER, United Kingdom
Contact: Executive Secretary
Tel: 44 1223 36 2061
Fax: 44 1223 33 6549
E-mail: info@scar.org
http://www.scar.org/

Scientific Committee on Oceanic Research (SCOR)
Department of Earth and Planetary Sciences
Olin Hall, San Martin Drive
Johns Hopkins University
Baltimore, MD, 21218, USA
Contact: Executive Director
Tel: 1 410 516-4070
Fax: 1 410 516-4019
E-mail: scor@jhu.edu
http://www.jhu.edu/~scor/

Scientific Committee on Problems of the Environment (SCOPE)
51, boulevard de Montmorency
F-75016 Paris, France
Contact: Executive Director
Tel: 33 1 4525 0498
Fax: 33 1 4288 1466
E-mail: secretariat@icsu-scope.org
http://www.icsu-scope.org/

Sea Shepherd Conservation International
PO Box 2670
Malibu, CA, 90265, USA
Tel: 1 360 370-5650
Fax: 1 360 370-5651
E-mail: seashepherd@seashepherd.org
http://www.seashepherd.org/

Seacology
2009 Hopkins Street
Berkeley, CA, 94707, USA
Tel: 1 510 599-3505
Fax: 1 510 599-3506
E-mail: islands@seacology.org
http://www.seacology.org/

Seas at Risk Federation
Drieharingstraat 25
NL-3511 BH Utrecht, Netherlands
Contact: Secretariat
Tel: 31 30 670 1291

Fax: 31 30 670 1292
E-mail: secretariat@seas-at-risk.org
http://www.seas-at-risk.org/

Sir Alister Hardy Foundation for Ocean Science
The Laboratory
Citadel Hill
Plymouth, PL1 2PB, United Kingdom
Tel: 44 1752 60 0016
Fax: 44 1752 60 0015
E-mail: sahfos@mail.pml.ac.uk
http://www.sahfos.org/

Society for Underwater Technology (SUT)
80 Coleman Street
London, EC2R 5BJ, United Kingdom
Contact: Executive Secretary
Tel: 44 207 382 2601
Fax: 44 207 382 2684
E-mail: ian.gallett@sut.org.uk
http://www.sut.org.uk/

Society of Environmental Toxicology and Chemistry
SETAC North America
1010 North 12th Avenue
Pensacola, FL, 32501-3367, USA
Tel: 1 850 469-1500
Fax: 1 850 469-9778
E-mail: setac@setac.org
http://www.setac.org/

Society of International Gas Tanker and Terminal Operators (SIGTTO)
17 St. Helen's Place
London, EC3A 6DG, United Kingdom
Contact: Secretariat
Tel: 44 207 628 1124
Fax: 44 207 628 3163
E-mail: secretariat@sigtto.org
http://www.sigtto.org/

Society of Naval Architects and Marine Engineers (SNAME)
601 Pavonia Avenue
Jersey City, NJ, 07306, USA
Contact: Executive Director
Tel: 1 201 798-4800
Fax: 1 201 798-4975
E-mail: ccali-poutre@sname.org
http://www.sname.org/

Species Survival Commission (SSC)
IUCN—The World Conservation Union
28, rue Mauvernay
CH-1196 Gland, Switzerland
Contact: Chair
Tel: 41 22 999 0000
Fax: 41 22 999 0015
E-mail: ssc@iucn.org
http://www.iucn.org/themes/ssc/

Stockholm Environment Institute
Lilla Nygatan 1
Box 2142
SE-103 14 Stockholm, Sweden
Contact: Director
Tel: 46 84 12 14 00
Fax: 46 87 23 03 48
E-mail: postmaster@sei.se
http://www.sei.se/

The Nature Conservancy
4245 North Fairfax Drive, Suite 100
Arlington, VA, 22203-1606, USA
Tel: 1 703 841-5300
E-mail: comment@tnc.org
http://www.nature.org /

The Nautical Institute
202 Lambeth Road
London, SE1 7LQ, United Kingdom
Contact: Secretary
Tel: 44 207 928 1351
Fax: 44 207 401 2817
E-mail: sec@nautinst.org
http://www.nautinst.org/

The Reef-World Foundation (UK)
Linton House
Danesbury Park Road
Welwyn, Hertfordshire, AL6 9SH, United Kingdom
Contact: General Manager
Tel: 44 1438 71 8881
Fax: 44 1438 71 8880
E-mail: amiller@reef-world.org
http://www.reef-world.org/

The World Conservation Union—International Union for the Conservation of Nature (IUCN)
28, rue Mauverney
CH-1196 Gland, Switzerland
Contact: Director
Tel: 41 22 999 0001
Fax: 41 22 999 0002
E-mail: mail@iucn.org
http://www.iucn.org/

Tsunami Laboratory
IUGG Inter-Association Tsunami Commission (IACT)
Institute of Computational Mathematics and Mathematical Geophysics, Siberian Division
Russian Academy of Sciences
6, Pr. Lavrentieva
Novosibirsk 630090, Russia
Contact: Chairman
Tel: 7 3832 342070
Fax: 7 3832 343783
E-mail: gvk@omzg.sscc.ru
http://omzg.sscc.ru/tsulab/

UNEP World Conservation Monitoring Centre
219 Huntingdon Road
Cambridge, CB3 0DL, United Kingdom
Tel: 44 1223 27 7722
Fax: 44 1223 27 7136
E-mail: info@unep-wcmc.org
http://www.unep-wcmc.org/

Water Environment Federation
(WEF)
601 Wythe Street
Alexandria, VA, 22314-1994, USA
Contact: Executive Director
Tel: 1 703 684-2400
Fax: 1 703 684-2492
E-mail: techinq@wef.org
http://www.wef.org/

Wetlands International
International Coordination Unit
PO Box 471
NL-6700 AL, Wageningen, The Netherlands
Tel: 31 31 747 8854
Fax: 31 31 747 8850
E-mail: post@wetlands.org
http://www.wetlands.org/

World Aquaculture Society (WAS)
Louisiana State University
143 J.M. Parker Coliseum
Baton Rouge, LA, 70803, USA
Contact: Secretary
Tel: 1 225 578-3137
Fax: 1 225 578-3493
E-mail: wasmas@aol.com
http://www.was.org/

World Commission on Protected Areas (WCPA)
IUCN—The World Conservation Union
28, rue Mauvernay
CH-1196 Gland, Switzerland
Contact: Head, Programme on Protected Areas
Tel: 44 22 999 0165
Fax: 44 22 999 0115
E-mail: jce@iucn.org
http://wcpa.iucn.org/

World Conservation Trust (IWMC)
3, Passage Montriond
CH-1006 Lausanne, Switzerland
Tel/Fax: 41 21 616 5000
E-mail: iwmc@iwmc.org
http://www.iwmc.org/

World Fish Center (ex-ICLARM)
PO Box 500, GPO 10670
Penang, Malaysia
Contact: Director General
Tel: 60 4 626 1606
Fax: 60 4 626 5530
E-mail: worldfishcenter@cgiar.org
http://www.worldfishcenter.org/

World Fisheries Trust
#204 1208 Wharf Street
Victoria, BC, V8W 3B9, Canada
Contact: President
Tel: 1 250 380-7585
Fax: 1 250 380-2621
E-mail: bharvey@worldfish.org
http://www.worldfish.org/

World Glacier Monitoring Service (WGMS)
Department of Geography
University of Zurich-Irchel
Winterthurerstrasse 190
CH-8057 Zurich, Switzerland
Contact: Director
Tel: 41 1 635 5120
Fax: 41 1 635 6848
E-mail: wgms@geo.unizh.ch
http://www.geo.unizh.ch/wgms/

World Resources Institute
10 G Street, NE, Suite 800
Washington, DC, 20002, USA
Tel: 1 202 729-7600
Fax: 1 202 729-7610

E-mail: front@wri.org
http://www.wri.org/

World Ship Trust
202 Lambeth Road
London SE1 7JW, United Kingdom
Contact: Chairman
Tel: 44 207 385 4267
E-mail: worldship@lynnmallet.demon.co.uk
http://www.worldshiptrust.org/

World Travel and Tourism Council
1-2 Queen Victoria Terrace
Sovereign Court
London, E1W 3HA, United Kingdom
Tel: 44 207 481 8007
Fax: 44 207 488 1008
E-mail: enquiries@wttc.org
http://www.wttc.org/

World Watch Institute
1776 Massachusetts Avenue, NW
Washington, DC, 20036-1904, USA
Tel: 1 202 452-1999
Fax: 1 202 296-7365
E-mail: worldwatch@worldwatch.org
http://www.worldwatch.org/

World Wide Fund for Nature (WWF)
Avenue du Mont-Blanc
CH-1196, Gland, Switzerland
Contact: Director General
Tel: 41 22 364 9111
Fax: 41 22 364 8836
E-mail: members@wwfint.org
http://www.panda.org/

3. GLOBAL ACADEMIC ORGANIZATIONS

Chartered Institute of Logistics and Transport (CILT)
11/12 Buckingham Gate
London, SW1 6LB, United Kingdom
http://www.citrans.org.uk/

Circumpolar Universities Association
The Roald Amundsen Centre of Arctic Research
University of Tromsø
N-9037 Tromsø, Norway
Tel: 47 77 64 52 41
Fax: 47 77 67 66 72
E-mail: igor.zhevagin@arctic.uit.no
http://www.arctic.uit.no/cua.html

Dangerous Goods Advisory Council
Suite 301, 1101 Vermont Avenue NW
Washington, DC, 20005, USA
Tel: 1 202 289-4550
Fax: 1 202 289-4074
E-mail: info@dgac.org
http://www.dgac.org/

Institute of Marine Engineering, Science and Technology (IMarEst)
80 Coleman Street
London, EC2R 5BJ, United Kingdom
Contact: Secretariat
Tel: 44 207 382 2600
Fax: 44 207 382 2670
E-mail: info@imarest.org
http://www.imarest.org/

International Marine Simulator Forum (IMSF)
Tokyo University of Mercantile Marine
Etchujima 2-1-6 Koto-Ku
Tokyo 135, Japan
Contact: Chairman
Tel: 81 3 5245 7392
Fax: 81 3 5245 7392
E-mail: kobayasi@ipc.tosho-u.ac.jp
http://www.imsf.org/

International Maritime Law Institute (IMLI)
PO Box 31
Msida MSD 01, Malta
Contact: Director
Tel: 356 21 319343
Fax: 356 21 343092
E-mail: info@imli.org
http://www.imli.org/

International Maritime Lecturers' Association (IMLA)
c/o World Maritime University
PO Box 500
Citadellsvagen 29
SE-201 24 Malmö, Sweden
Contact: President
Tel: 46 40 35 63 67
Fax: 46 40 12 48 27
E-mail: rajendra.prasad@wmu.se
http://www.wmu.se/imla/

United Nations University (UNU)
53-70 Jingumae 5-chome Shibuya-ku

Tokyo 150-8925, Japan
Tel: 81 3 3499 2811
Fax: 81 3 3499 2828
E-mail: mbox@hq.unu.edu
http://www.unu.edu/

World Maritime University (WMU)
PO Box 500
Citadellsvagen 29
SE-201 24 Malmö, Sweden
Contact: President
Tel: 46 40 35 63 00
Fax: 46 40 12 84 42
E-mail: info@wmu.se
http://www.wmu.se/

4. REGIONAL INTERGOVERNMENTAL ORGANIZATIONS

4.1 Africa

African Organisation of Cartography and Remote Sensing (AOCRS)
(Organisation Africaine de Cartographie et Télédétection—OACT)
BP 102
16040 Hussein Dey
Algiers, Algeria
Contact: Chairman
Tel: 213 21 23 1717
Fax: 213 21 23 3339
E-mail: oact@wissal.dz
http://www.oact.dz/

Association of African Maritime Training Institutes (AAMTI)
PO Box 1029
Alexandria, Egypt
Contact: Secretary General
Tel: 20 3 560 0245
Fax: 20 3 560 2144
E-mail: aaen0038@aast.egnet.net

Conférence Ministérielle sur la Coopération Halieutique des Etats Africains Riverains de l'Océan Atlantique COMHAFAT)
(Ministerial Conference on Fisheries Cooperation Among African States Bordering the Atlantic Ocean)
Ministère des Pêches Maritimes
BP 476, Nouvelle cité administrative
Agdal, Rabat, Morocco
Contact: Permanent Secretariat
Tel: 212 37 68 83 28
Fax: 212 37 68 83 29
E-mail: alahlou@mp3m.gov.ma
http://www.mpm.gov.ma/conference/index_conf.htm

FAO Regional Office for Africa (RAF)
PO Box 1628
Accra, Ghana
Tel: 233 21 701 0930
Fax: 233 21 668427
E-mail: fao-raf@fao.org
http://www.fao.org/regional/africa/default.htm

FAO Regional Office for the Near East (RNE)
11 El Eslah El Zerai Street
12311 Dokki, Cairo, Egypt
Tel: 20 2 337 2229
Fax: 20 2 749 5981
E-mail: fao-rne@fao.org
http://www.fao.org/world/Regional/RNE/index_en.htm

FAO Sub-Regional Office for North Africa
PO Box 300
Tunis, Tunisia
Tel: 216 1 847 553
Fax: 216 1 791 859
E-mail: fao-snea@fao.org

FAO Subregional Office for Southern and East Africa
PO Box 3730
Harare, Zimbabwe
Tel: 263 4 791407
Fax: 263 4 703497
E-mail: fao-safr-registry@fao.org

Fishery Committee for Eastern Central Atlantic (CECAF)
c/o FAO Regional Office for Africa
PO Box 1628
Accra, Ghana
Contact: Assistant Director-General
Tel: 233 21 675000
Fax: 233 21 668427
E-mail: fao-raf@field.fao.org
http://www.fao.org/fi/body/rfb/CECAF/cecaf_home.html

Indian Ocean Commission
Q4, avenue Sir Guy Forget
Quatre Bornes, BP 7, Mauritius
Contact: Secretary General
Tel: 230 425 1652
Fax: 230 425 2709
E-mail: coi7@intnet.mu
http://www.coi-info.org/

Indian Ocean Rim Association for Regional Cooperation (IOR-ARC)
c/o Indian Ocean Rim Business Network (IORNET)
Federation House, Tansen Marg
New Delhi 110001, India
Tel: 91 11 3325110
Fax: 91 11 3721504
E-mail: iornet@ficci.com
http://www.iornet.com/newiornet/index.htm

INFOPECHE (Intergovernmental Organization for Marketing Information and Technical Advisory Services for Fishery Products in Africa)
Tour C, 19éme étage, Cité Administrative
BP 1747
Abidjan 01, Côte d'Ivoire
Contact: Director
Tel: 225 2022 8980
Fax: 225 2021 8054
E-mail: infopech@africaonline.co.ci
http://www.globefish.org/entry_infopeche.htm

INFOSAMAK (Centre for Marketing Information & Advisory Services For Fishery Products in the Arab Region)
71, boulevard Rahal El Meskini
16243, Casablanca, Morocco
Tel: 212 22 540856
Fax: 212 22 540855
E-mail: info@infosamak.org
http://www.infosamak.org/english/

INFOYU
18 Maizidian Street, Room 203
Chaoyang District
Beijing 100026, People's Republic of China
Tel: 86 10 6419 5140
Fax: 86 10 6419 5141
E-mail: infoyu@agri.gov.cn
http://www.globefish.org/entry_infopeche.htm

Inter-governmental Standing Committee on Shipping (ISCOS)
Bima Tower, 9th floor
Digo Road, PO Box 89112
Mombasa, Kenya
Tel: 254 11 312196
Fax: 254 11 316387

Intergovernmental Authority on Development (IGAD)
P.O. Box 2653
Djibouti, Republic of Djibouti
Contact: Secretariat
Tel: 253 354050
Fax: 253 356994
E-mail: igad@intnet.dj
http://www.igad.org/

IOC Regional Committee for the Central Eastern Atlantic (IOCEA)
Nigerian Institute for Oceanography and Marine Research
PMB 12729
Victoria Island, Lagos, Nigeria
Tel/Fax: 234 1 2619517
E-mail: l.awosika@unesco.org
http://ioc.unesco.org/iocweb/activities/regions/iocea.htm

IOC Regional Committee for the Cooperative Investigation in the North and Central Western Indian Ocean (IOCINCWIO)
PO Box 95832
Mombasa 80106, Kenya
Contact: IOCINCWIO Project Office
Tel: 254 11 472527
Fax: 254 11 475157
E-mail: m.odido@unesco.org
http://ioc.unesco.org/iocincwio/

Maritime Organisation of West and Central Africa (MOWCA)
BP V 257
Abidjan, Côte d'Ivoire
Contact: Secretary General
Tel: 225 217115
Fax: 225 224532
E-mail: minconmar@africaonline.co.ci

Niger Basin Authority (NBA)
BP 729
Niamey, Niger
Contact: Executive Secretary

Tel: 227 723102
Fax: 227 724208
E-mail: abnsec@intnet.ne
http://www.abn.ne/

Pan-African Association for Port Cooperation (PAPC)
12 Park Lane
PO Box 1113
Apapa, Lagos, Nigeria
Tel/Fax: 234 1 587 4108
E-mail: papc@afriports.org
http://www.afriports.org/

Port Management Association of West and Central Africa (PMAWCA/AGPAOC)
12 Park Lane
Box 1113
Apapa, Lagos, Nigeria
Contact: Secretary General
Tel: 234 1 587 4108
Fax: 234 1 587 7977
E-mail: secgen@pmawac-agpaoc.org
http://www.pmawca-agpaoc.com/

Port Management Association of Eastern and Southern Africa (PMAESA/AGPAEA)
PO Box 99209
Mombassa, Kenya
Contact: Secretary General
Tel: 254 11 223245
Fax: 254 11 228344
E-mail: pmaesa@africaonline.co.ke
http://www.pmaesa.org/

Regional Activity Centre for Specially Protected Areas (RAC/SPA)
Boulevard de l'Environnement
PB 337 Cedex
1080 Tunis, Tunisia
Contact: Director
Tel: 216 1 795760
Fax: 216 1 797349
E-mail: car-asp@rac-spa.org.tn
http://www.rac-spa.org.tn/

Regional Co-ordinating Unit for Eastern African Action Plan (EAF/RCU)
UNEP Secretariat of the Nairobi Convention & Related Action Plan
PO Box 487, Ste. Anne Island
Mahe, Seychelles
Tel: 248 322 945
Fax: 248 324 573
E-mail: uneprcu@seychelles.net
http://www.unep.org/eaf/

Regional Fisheries Committee for the Gulf of Guinea (COREP)
BP 161
Libreville, Gabon
Contact: Secretariat
Fax: 241 73 7149
http://www.fao.org/fi/body/rfb/COREP/corep_home.html

Secretariat for Eastern African Coastal Area Management (SEACAM)
874, Av. Amílcar Cabral, 1st Floor
Caixa Postal 4220
Maputo, Mozambique
Contact: Secretariat
Tel: 258 1 300641/2
Fax: 258 1 300638
E-mail: seacam@virconn.com
http://www.seacam.mz/

Southeast Atlantic Fisheries Organisation (SEAFO)
Ministry of Fisheries and Marine Resources
Private Bag X13355
Windhoek, Namibia
Contact: Interim Secretariat
Tel: 264 6120 5911
Fax: 264 6122 4566
E-mail: mfmr@mfmr.gov.na
http://www.mfmr.gov.na/seafo/seafo.htm

Southern African Development Community
Marine Fisheries and Resources Sector Coordinating Unit
SADC House
Private Bag 0095
Gaborone, Botswana
Tel: 267 3951 863
Fax: 267 3972 848
E-mail: registry@sadc.int
http://www.schoemans.com.na/sadc/default.asp

Southern African Transport and Communications Commission (SATCC)
Avenida Martires de Inhaminga 170, 2nd floor
SATCC-TU CP 2677
Maputo, Mozambique
Contact: Director

Tel: 258 1 420214
Fax: 258 1 420213
E-mail: director@satcc.org
http://www.satcc.org/

Sub-Regional Commission on Fisheries—SRCF
(La Commission sous-régionale des pêches—CSRP)
Km 10 Boulevard de Centenaire de la Commune de Dakar-Senegal
BP 20505
Dakar, Senegal
Contact: Secretariat
Tel: 221 345580
Fax: 221 238720
E-mail: sp_csrp@metissacana.sn
http://www.csrp-afrique.org/

UNEP Regional Office for Africa
PO Box 30552
Nairobi, Kenya
Contact: Director
Tel: 254 20 624279
Fax: 254 20 623928
E-mail: sekou.toure@unep.org
http://www.unep.org/roa/

West and Central African Regional Coordinating Unit (UNEP WACAF/RCU)
Abidjan Convention
c/o Ministry of the Environment and Forests
BP 650
Abidjan 20, Côte d'Ivoire
Contact: Coordinator
Tel: 225 2021 1183
Fax: 225 2021 0495
E-mail: biodiv@africaonline.co.ci
http://www.unep.ch/seas/dumwacaf.html

4. REGIONAL INTERGOVERNMENTAL ORGANIZATIONS

4.2 The Americas

Caribbean Community (CARICOM)
PO Box 10827
Georgetown, Guyana
Contact: Secretariat
Tel: 592 226 9280
Fax: 592 226 7816
E-mail: webmaster@caricom.org
http://www.caricom.org/

Caribbean Environment Programme Regional Coordinating Unit (CAR/RCU)
(Cartagena Convention)
14-20 Port Royal Street
Kingston, Jamaica
Contact: Coordinator
Tel: 1 876 922-9267
Fax: 1 876 922-9292
E-mail: uneprcuja@cwjamaica.com
http://www.cep.unep.org/

CARICOM Regional Fisheries Mechanism
PO Box 642
Princess Marquaret Dr.
Belize City, Belize
Tel: 501 234 444
Fax: 501 234 446
E-mail: cframp@btl.net
http://www.caricom-fisheries.com/

Central American Commission on Maritime Transport
(Comision Centroamericana de Transporte Maritimo—COCATRAM)
Contiguo a Mansíon de Teodolinda
Apartado Postal 2423
Managua, Nicaragua
Contact: Executive Director
Tel: 505 222 3560
Fax: 505 222 2759
E-mail: cocatram@cocatram.org.ni
http://www.cocatram.org.ni/

Centro del Agua del Trópico Húmedo para América Latina y el Caribe (CATHALAC)
(Water Center for the Humid Tropics of Latin America and the Caribbean)
801 City of Knowledge
Clayton, Panama
PO Box 873372
7 Panama
Contact: Director
Tel: 507 317 0053
Fax: 507 317 0127
E-mail: emilio.sempris@cathalac.org
http://www.cathalac.org/

Comisión de Pesca Continental para América Latina (COPESCAL)
c/o FAO Regional Office for Latin America and the Caribbean

Avenida Dag Hammarskjold 3241
Vitacura
Casilla 10095
Santiago, Chile
Tel: 56 2 337 2100
Fax: 56 2 337 2101
E-mail: rlc-webmaster@fao.org
http://www.rlc.fao.org/organos/copescal/copescal.htm

Comisión Permanente del Pacífico Sur (CPPS)
Edificio Inmaral, ler piso
Av. Carlos Julio Arosemena, Km. 3
Guayaquil, Ecuador
Contact: Secretariat
Tel: 593 4 2221 202
Fax: 593 4 2221 201
E-mail: cpps@ecuanex.net.ec
http://www.cpps-int.org/

Comisión Técnica Mixta del Frente Marítimo (COFREMAR)
1355 Juncal, oficina 604
11000 Montevideo, Uruguay
Contact: President
Tel: 598 2 916 1973
Fax: 598 2 916 1578
http://www.cofremar.org/

Commission for the Conservation and Management of Highly Migratory Fish Stocks in the Western and Central Pacific
Contact: Interim Secretariat
E-mail: interimsec@isa.org.jm
http://www.ocean-affairs.com/

FAO Regional Office for Latin America and the Caribbean
Avenida Dag Hammarskjold 3241
Vitacura
Casilla 10095
Santiago, Chile
Tel: 56 2 337 2100
Fax: 56 2 337 2101
E-mail: german.rojas@fao.org
http://www.fao.org/Regional/LAmerica/

FAO Subregional Office for the Caribbean (SLAC)
PO Box 631-C
Bridgetown, Barbados
Tel: 854 426 7110
Fax: 854 427 6075
E-mail: fao-slac@fao.org

Gulf of Maine Council on the Marine Environment
c/o New Hampshire Department of Environmental Services
PO Box 95
Concord, NH, 03302-0095, USA
Contact: Council Coordinator
Tel: 1 603 796-2615
Fax: 1 603 796-2600
E-mail: info@gulfofmaine.org
http://gulfofmaine.org/

INFOPESCA (Centro para los servicios de información y asesoramiento sobre la comercialización de los productos pesqueros en América Latina y el Caribe)
Julio Herrera y Obes 1296
Casilla de Correo 7086
CP 11200
Montevideo, Uruguay
Tel: 598 2 902 8701
Fax: 598 2 903 0501
E-mail: infopesc@infopesca.org
http://www.infopesca.org/

Inter-American Institute for Global Change Research (IAI)
Av. dos Astronautas, 1758
CEP 12227-010 São José dos Campos
São Paulo, Brazil
Contact: IAI Directorate—Brazil
Tel: 55 12 3945 6855
Fax: 55 12 3941 4410
E-mail: iaibr@dir.iai.int
http:// www.iai.int/

Inter-American Tropical Tuna Commission (IATTC)
8604 La Jolla Shores Drive
La Jolla, CA, 92037-1508, USA
Contact: Secretariat
Tel: 1 858 546-7100
Fax: 1 858 546-7133
E-mail: info@iattc.org
http://www.iattc.org/

International Association of Fish and Wildlife Agencies (IAFWA)
444 North Capitol Street NW, Suite 544
Washington, DC, 20001, USA
Contact: Executive VP

Tel: 1 202 624-7890
Fax: 1 202 624-7891
E-mail: iafwa@sso.org
http://www.iafwa.org/

International Pacific Halibut Commission (IPHC)
PO Box 95009
Seattle, WA, 98145-2009, USA
Contact: Director
Tel: 1 206 634-1838
Fax: 1 206 632-2983
E-mail: info@iphc.washington.edu
http://www.iphc.washington.edu/

IOC Sub-Commission for the Caribbean and Adjacent Regions
(IOCARIBE)
Casa del Marqués de Valdehoyos
Centro, Calle de la Factoría No. 36-57
Apartado Aéreo 1108
Cartagena de Indias, Colombia
Contact: Senior Assistant
Tel: 57 5 664 6399
Fax: 57 5 660 0407
E-mail: iocaribe@col3.telecom.com.co;
iocaribe@cartagena.cetcol.net.co
http://ioc.unesco.org/regcar/

North American Commission for Environmental Cooperation (CEC)
393, rue St-Jacques Ouest, Suite 200
Montréal, QC, H2Y 1N9, Canada
Contact: Executive Director
Tel: 1 514 350-4300
Fax: 1 514 350-4314
E-mail: info@ccemtl.org
http://www.cec.org/

North Atlantic Treaty Organization (NATO) Maritime Headquarters
RHQ EASTLANT/HQ NAVNORTH
Northwood Headquarters
Northwood
Middlesex, HA6 3HP, United Kingdom
Tel: 44 1923 84 3763
Fax: 44 1923 84 3762
E-mail: pio@eastlant.nato.int
http://www.eastlant.nato.int/

North East Pacific Action Plan
Secretario del Plan de Acción del Pacífico Nordeste
Contiguo al Hotel Mansión Teodolinda, Bolonia
Managua, Nicaragua
Tel: 505 222 2754
Fax: 505 222 2759
E-mail: geinfrae@cocatram.org.ni
http://www.unep.ch/seas/rshome.html

North Pacific Anadromous Fish Commission (NPAFC)
889 West Pender Street, Suite 502
Vancouver, BC, V6C 3B2, Canada
Contact: Executive Director
Tel: 1 604 775-5550
Fax: 1 604 775-5577
E-mail: secretariat@npafc.org
http://www.npafc.org/

North Pacific Marine Science Organization (PICES)
c/o Institute of Ocean Sciences
PO Box 6000
Sidney, BC, V6L 4B2, Canada
Contact: PICES Secretariat
Tel: 1 250 363-6366
Fax: 1 250 363-6827
E-mail: secretariat@pices.int
http://www.pices.int/

Northwest Atlantic Fisheries Organization (NAFO)
2 Morris Drive
PO Box 638
Dartmouth, NS, B2Y 3Y9, Canada
Contact: Executive Secretary
Tel: 1 902 468-5590
Fax: 1 902 468-5538
E-mail: info@nafo.int
http://www.nafo.ca/

Organización Latinoamericana de Desarrollo Pesquero (OLDEPESCA)
(Latin American Organization for Fisheries Development)
Avenida Petit Thouars 115
Tercer piso
Lima 1, Peru
Contact: Executive Director
Tel: 511 330 8741
Fax: 511 332 2480
E-mail: direc@oldepesca.org
http://www.oldepesca.org/

Pacific Salmon Commission (PSC)
1155 Robson Street, Suite 600

Vancouver, BC, V6E 1B5, Canada
Contact: Executive Secretary
Tel: 1 604 684-8081
Fax: 1 604 666-8707
E-mail: kowal@psc.org
http://www.psc.org/

Programa Hidrológico Internacional (PHI)
Dr. Luis Piera 1992, 2o.piso
Avda. Brasil 2697
CP 11200
Montevideo, Uruguay
Tel: 598 2 413 2075
Fax: 598 2 413 2094
E-mail: phi@unesco.org.uy
http://www.unesco.org.uy/phi/

South East Pacific Action Plan
Comisión Permanente del Pacífico Sur (CPPS)
Edificio Inmaral, lerpsiso
Av. Carlos Julio Arosemena, Km. 3
Guayaquil, Ecuador
Contact: Secretariat
Tel: 593 4 2221 202
Fax: 593 4 2221 201
E-mail: cpps@ecuanex.net.ec
http://www.plandeaccion.cpps-int.org/

South West Atlantic Action Plan
Division of Environmental Conventions
United Nations Environment Programme
PO Box 30552
Nairobi, Kenya
Contact: Director, DEC
Tel: 254 2 624052
Fax: 254 2 624618
E-mail: Jorge.Illueca@unep.org
http://www.unep.ch/seas/dumswa.html

UNEP Regional Office for Latin America and Caribbean
Boulevard de los Virreyes No. 155
Lomas de Virreyes
CP 11000
México, D.F. Mexico
Contact: Regional Representative
Tel: 52 55 5202 6394
Fax: 52 55 5202 0950
E-mail: registro@pnuma.org
http://www.rolac.unep.mx/

UNEP Regional Office for North America (RONA)
1707 H Street NW, Suite 300
Washington, DC, 20006, USA
Tel: 1 202 785-0465
Fax: 1 202 785-2096
E-mail: info@rona.unep.org
http://www.rona.unep.org/

United States Coast Guard International Ice Patrol
1082 Shennecossett Road
Groton, CT, 06340-6095, USA
Contact: Commander
Tel: 1 860 441-2626
Fax: 1 860 441-2773
E-mail: iipcomms@rdc.uscg.mil
http://www.uscg.mil/lantarea/iip/home.html

Western Central Atlantic Fisheries Commission (WECAFC)
FAO Sub-Regional Office for Latin American and the Caribbean
PO Box 631C
Bridgetown, Barbados
Tel: 1 246 426-7110
Fax: 1 246 426-7111
E-mail: bisessar.chakalall@fao.org
http://www.fao.org/fi/body/rfb/wecafc/wecafc_home.html

4. REGIONAL INTERGOVERNMENTAL ORGANIZATIONS

4.3 Asia

Arab Federation of Shipping
PO Box 1161, W Baghdad Stn
Baghdad, Iraq
Tel: 964 1 717 4504
Fax: 964 1 717 7243

Arab Fisheries Company
PO Box 17604
Jeddah 21494, Saudi Arabia
Contact: Chairman and Director-General
Tel: 966 2 651 9140
Fax: 966 2 651 0528

ASEAN Council on Petroleum (ASCOPE)
Petronas
International Business Ventures
Level 45, Tower 1, Petronas Twin Towers

50088 Kuala Lumpur, Malaysia
Tel: 60 3 233 14804
Fax: 60 3 233 11203
Contact: Secretariat
E-mail: ascopesec@petronas.com.my
http://www.ascope.com.my/

ASEAN Fisheries Federation (AFF)
Association of Southeast Asian Nations (ASEAN)
ASEAN Secretariat Building, 3rd floor
Jalan Sisingamangaraja 70A
Jakarta 12110, Indonesia
Tel: 62 21 726 2991
Fax: 62 21 725 7916
E-mail: aff@asean.sec.org
http://www.aff.or.id/

ASEAN Ports Association
c/o Philippine Ports Authority
Marsman Building South Harbour
Port Area, Manila, The Philippines
Contact: Permanent Secretariat
Tel: 632 301 9074
Fax: 632 527 4749
E-mail: aida@ppa.com.ph
http://www.ppa.com.ph/apa-2002/default.htm

Asia-Pacific Economic Cooperation (APEC)
35 Heng Mui Keng Terrace
Singapore 119616
Contact: APEC Secretariat
Tel: 65 6275 6012
Fax: 65 6275 6023
E-mail: info@mail.apecsec.org.sg
http://www.apecsec.org.sg/

Asia-Pacific Fisheries Commission (APFIC)
FAO Regional Office for Asia and the Pacific
39 Phra Atit Road
Bangkok 10200, Thailand
Contact: Secretariat
Tel: 66 2 280 7844
Fax: 66 2 280 0445
E-mail: veravat.hongskul@fao.org
http://www.fao.org/fi/body/rfb/apfic/apfic_home.html

Asian-African Legal Consultative Organization (AALCO)
E-66 Vasant Marg
Vasant Vihar
New Delhi, 110057, India
Tel: 91 11 26152 251
Fax: 91 11 26152 041
E-mail: aalcc@vsnl.com; mail@aalco.org
http://www.aalco.org/

Coordinating Committee for Geoscience Programmes in East and Southeast Asia (CCOP)
Thai CC Tower, 24th Floor, Room 244-5
889 Sathorn Tai Road
Sathorn
Bangkok 10120, Thailand
Contact: Director
Tel: 66 2 672 3080-1
Fax: 66 2 672 3082
E-mail: ccopts@ccop.or.th
http://www.ccop.or.th/

East Asian Seas Action Plan (EAS)
United Nations Building, 10th floor
Rajdamnern Nok Avenue
Bangkok 10200, Thailand
Contact: Regional Coordinating Unit
Tel: 66 2 288 1860
Fax: 66 2 281 2428
E-mail: kirkman.unescap@un.org
http://www.easrcu.org/

FAO Regional Office for Asia and the Pacific (RAP)
Maliwan Mansion
Phra Atit Road
Bangkok 10200, Thailand
Tel: 66 2 697 4000
Fax: 66 2 697 4445
E-mail: fao-rap@fao.org
http://www.fao.or.th/

Indian Ocean Tuna Commission (IOTC)
PO Box 1011
Victoria, Mahé, Seychelles
Contact: Secretariat
Tel: 248 225 494
Fax: 248 224 364
E-mail: iotcsecr@iotc.org
http://www.iotc.org/

INFOFISH (Intergovernmental Organization for Marketing Information and Technical Advisory Services for Fishery Products in the Asia and Pacific Region)
1st Floor, Wisma PKNS

Jalan Raja Laut
PO Box 10899
50728 Kuala Lumpur, Malaysia
Tel: 60 3 2691 4466
Fax: 60 3 2691 6804
E-mail: infish@po.jaring.my
http://www.infofish.org/

IOC Sub-Commission for the Western Pacific (WESTPAC)
c/o National Research Council Thailand
196 Phaholyothin Road, Chatujak
Bangkok 10900, Thailand
Tel: 66 2 561 5118
Fax: 66 2 561 5119
E-mail: westpac@samart.co.th
http://ioc.unesco.org/westpac/index.htm

Mekong River Commission
364 M.V. Preah Monivong Boulevard
PO Box 1112
Phnom Penh, Cambodia
Contact: Secretariat
Tel: 855 23 720 979
Fax: 855 23 720 972
E-mail: mrcs@mrcmekong.org
http://www.mrcmekong.org/

Network of Aquaculture Centres in Asia-Pacific (NACA)
Kasetsart Post Office Box 1040
Bangkok 10903, Thailand
Contact: Secretariat
Tel: 66 2 561 1728
Fax: 66 2 561 1727
E-mail: naca@enaca.org
http://www.enaca.org/

Northwest Pacific Action Plan (NOWPAP)
Northwest Pacific Region Environmental Cooperation Centre
Tower111 Building, 6th floor
5-5 Ushijimashin-machi, Toyama city, Japan
Contact: Director
Tel: 81 7 6445 1571
Fax: 81 7 6445 1581
E-mail: oritani@npec.or.jp
http://www.unep.ch/seas/dumnwp.html

NOWPAP Marine Environmental Emergency and Preparedness Re-sponse Regional Activity Centre (MERRAC)
PO Box 23
Yusung, Taejon 305-600, Republic of Korea
Contact: Director
Tel: 82 42 868 7281
Fax: 82 42 868 7738
E-mail: nowpap@kriso.re.kr
http://merrac.nowpap.org/

Partnership in Environmental Management for the Seas of East Asia (PEMSEA)
PO Box 2502
Quezon City 1165, The Philippines
Tel: 632 920 2211
Fax: 632 926 9712
E-mail: info@pemsea.org
http://www.pemsea.org/

Regional Organisation for the Protection of the Marine Environment (ROPME)
PO Box 26388
13124 Safat, Kuwait
Contact: Coordinator
Tel: 965 531 2140
Fax: 965 533 5243
E-mail: ropme@quality.net
http://www.unep.ch/seas/kapcap.html

Regional Organization for the Conservation of the Environment of the Red Sea and Gulf of Aden (PERSGA)
PO Box 53662
Jeddah, 21583, Saudi Arabia
Contact: Deputy Secretary-General
Tel: 966 2 657 3224
Fax: 966 2 652 1901
E-mail: information@persga.org
http://www.persga.org/

South Asia Co-operative Environment Programme (SACEP)
No. 10 Anderson Road
Colombo 5, Sri Lanka
Contact: Director
Tel: 941 596 442
Fax: 941 589 369
E-mail: pd_sacep@eureka.lk
http://www.sacep.org/

Southeast Asian Fisheries Development Center (SEAFDEC)
Suraswadi Building
PO Box 1046, Kasetsart Post Office
Bangkok 10903, Thailand
Tel: 66 2 940 6326
Fax: 66 2 940 6336
Contact: Secretariat

E-mail: sg@seafdec.org
http://www.seafdec.org/

UNEP Regional Office for West Asia (UNEP/ROWA)
PO Box 10880
Manama, Bahrain
Contact: Regional Director
Tel: 973 826600
Fax: 973 82510
E-mail: myunrowa@unep.org.bh
http://www.unep.org.bh/

UNEP Regional Office for Asia and the Pacific (UNEP/ROAP)
United Nations Building
Rajadamnern Nok Avenue
Bangkok 10200, Thailand
Contact: Regional Information Officer
Tel: 66 2 288 1870-4
Fax: 66 2 280 3829
E-mail: highham@un.org
http://www.roap.unep.org/

United Nations Economic and Social Commission for Asia and the Pacific (ESCAP)
United Nations Building
Rajadamnern Nok Avenue
Bangkok 10200, Thailand
Tel: 66 2 288 1234
Fax: 66 2 288 1000
E-mail: webmaster@unescap.org
http://www.unescap.org/

Western Indian Ocean Tuna Organization (WIOTC)
c/o Seychelles Fishing Authority
PO Box 449
Victoria, Mahé, Seychelles
Tel: 248 224 597
Fax: 248 224 508
E-mail: sfasez@seychelles.net
http://www.fao.org/fi/body/rfb/wiotc/wiotc_home.htm

4. REGIONAL INTERGOVERNMENTAL ORGANIZATIONS

4.4 Europe

Arc Manche
c/o West Sussex County Council
County Hall
Chichester, PO19 1RQ, United Kingdom
Contact: English Group Coordinator
Tel: 44 1243 77 7927
Fax: 44 1243 77 7697
E-mail: rachel.gapp@westsussex.gov.uk
http://www.arcmanche.com/

Baltic 21
Strömborg
PO Box 2010
SE-103 11 Stockholm, Sweden
Contact: Secretariat
Tel: 46 84 40 19 38/41
Fax: 46 84 40 19 44
E-mail: marek.maciejowski@cbss.st
http://www.ee/baltic21/

Baltic Environment Forum (BEF)
26/28 Peldu Street, Room 505
LV-1050, Riga, Latvia
Tel: 371 7 357555
Fax: 371 7 507071
E-mail: bef@latnet.lv
http://www.bef.lv/index.htm

Black Sea Environmental Programme
Black Sea Commission
Domabahce Sarayi
II. Harekat Kosku
80680 Besiktas
Istanbul, Turkey
Contact: Coordinator
Tel: 90 212 227 9927
Fax: 90 212 227 9933
E-mail: rmihnea@dominet.in.com.tr
http://www.blacksea-environment.org/

Blue Plan Regional Activity Centre (BP/RAC)
15, rue Beethoven
Sophia Antipolis
F-06560 Valbonne, France
Contact: Director
Tel: 33 4 9238 7130
Fax: 33 4 9238 7131
E-mail: planbleu@planbleu.org
http://www.planbleu.org/

Bonn Agreement
New Court
48 Carey Street
London, WC2A 2JQ, United Kingdom

Contact: Secretary
Tel: 44 207 430 5200
Fax: 44 207 430 5225
E-mail: secretariat@bonnagreement.org
http://www.bonnagreement.org/

Central Commission for the Navigation of the Rhine (CCNR)
2, place de la République
Palais du Rhin
F-67082 Strasbourg Cedex, France
Contact: President
Tel: 33 3 8852 2010
Fax: 33 3 8832 1072
E-mail: ccnr@ccr-zkr.org
http://www.ccr-zkr.org/

Centre for Environment and Development for the Arab Region and Europe (CEDARE)
2 El Hegaze Street, CEDARE Building,
PO Box 1057
Heliopolis Bahary
Cairo, Egypt
Tel: 20 2 451 3921
Fax: 20 2 451 3918
E-mail: email@cedare.org.eg
http://www.cedare.org.eg/

Committee on the Challenges of Modern Society (CCMS)
North Atlantic Treaty Organization (NATO)
Public Diplomacy Division
B-1110 Brussels, Belgium
Contact: CCMS Secretariat
Tel: 32 2 707 4850
Fax: 32 2 707 4232
E-mail: ccms@hq.nato.int
http://www.nato.int/ccms/index.html

Commonwealth Secretariat
Marlborough House
Pall Mall
London, SW1Y 5HX, United Kingdom
Tel: 44 207 747 6500
Fax: 44 207 930 0827
E-mail: info@commonwealth.int
http://www.thecommonwealth.org/

Conference of Peripheral Maritime Regions (CPMR)
6, rue Saint-Martin
F-35700 Rennes, France
Contact: Secretary General
Tel: 33 2 9935 4050
Fax: 33 2 9935 0919
E-mail: secretariat@crpm.org
http://www.crpm.org/

Council of Europe
F-67075 Strasbourg Cedex, France
Tel: 33 3 8841 2033
Fax: 33 3 8841 2745
E-mail: infopoint@coe.int
http://www.coe.int/

Council of the Baltic Sea States (CBSS)
PO Box 2010
SE-103 11 Stockholm, Sweden
Contact: Secretariat
Tel: 46 84 40 19 20
Fax: 46 84 40 19 44
E-mail: cbss@cbss.st
http://www.cbss.st/

Danube Commission
(Donaukommission)
Benczúr utca 25
H-1068 Budapest, Hungary
Contact: General Director
Tel: 36 1 461 8023
Fax: 36 1 352 1839
E-mail: secretariat@danubecom-intern.org
http://www.danubecom-intern.org/

Directorate-General for Fisheries
Communication and Information Unit
European Commission
Rue de la Loi 200
B-1049 Brussels, Belgium
Fax: 32 2 299 30 40
E-mail: fisheries-info@cec.eu.int
http://europa.eu.int/coml/fisheries/

Emergency Response Activity Centre (ERAC)
1, Slavejkov Sq., Port Complex, IVT
Varna 9000, Bulgaria
Contact: Coordinator
Tel: 359 52 221407
Fax: 359 52 602594
E-mail: erac-varna@bitex.com

Environment Remote Sensing Regional Activity Centre (ERS/RAC)
2 Via G. Giusti

I-90144 Palermo, Italy
Contact: Managing Director
Tel: 39 091 342368
Fax: 39 091 308512
E-mail: ctmrac@tin.it; ctm.ersrac@ctmnet.it
http://www.ctmnet.it/

European Commission
200, rue de la Loi
B-1049 Brussels, Belgium
Tel: 32 2 2999 1111
E-mail: address-information@cec.eu.int
http://europa.eu.int/comm/

European Conference of Ministers of Transport (ECMT)
2, rue André Pascal
F-75775 Paris Cedex 16, France
Tel: 33 1 4524 9710
Fax: 33 1 4524 9742
E-mail: ecmt.contact@oecd.org
http://www.oecd.org/cem/

European Environment Agency (EEA)
Kongens Nytorv 6
DK-1050 Copenhagen K, Denmark
Tel: 45 33 36 71 00
Fax: 45 33 36 71 99
E-mail: eea@eea.eu.int
http://www.eea.eu.int/

European Group on Ocean Stations (EGOS)
Christian Michelsen Research A/S
PO Box 6031 Postterminalen
N-5892 Bergen, Norway
Contact: Technical Secretariat
Tel: 47 55 57 42 64
Fax: 47 55 57 40 41
E-mail: anne.hageberg@cmr.no
http://www.meteo.shom.fr/egos/

European Inland Fisheries Commission (EIFAC)
Viale delle Terme di Caracalla
I-00100 Rome, Italy
Contact: Chair
Tel: 39 06 5705 2944
Fax: 39 06 5705 3020
E-mail: rudolf.mueller@eawag.ch
http://www.fao.org/fi/body/eifac/eifac.asp

FAO Regional Office for Europe (REU)
Viale delle Terme di Caracalla
I-00100 Rome, Italy
Tel: 39 06 5705 4963
Fax: 39 06 5705 5634
E-mail: REUD-RegRep@fao.org
http://www.fao.org/world/regional/REU/index_en.htm

FAO Subregional Office for Central and Eastern Europe (SEUR)
Benczur utca 34
H-1068 Budapest, Hungary
Tel: 36 1 461 2000
Fax: 36 1 351 7029
E-mail: fao-seur@fao.org
http://www.fao.org/regional/seur/default.asp

General Fisheries Commission for the Mediterranean (GFCM)
FAO, Room F-211
Viale delle Terme di Caracalla
I-00100 Rome, Italy
Contact: Secretary
Tel: 39 6 5705 6435
Fax: 39 6 5705 6500
E-mail: alain.bonzon@fao.org
http://www.faogfcm.org/

Helsinki Commission (HELCOM)
Baltic Marine Environment Protection Commission
Katajanokanlaituri 6 B
FIN-00160 Helsinki, Finland
Contact: Executive Secretary
Tel: 358 9 6220 220
Fax: 358 9 6220 2239
E-mail: helcom@helcom.fi
http://www.helcom.fi/

Institute for Environment and Sustainability
Joint Research Centre of the European Commission
Via Fermi
TP 263
I-21020 Ispra (VA), Italy
Contact: Inland and Marine Waters Unit
Tel: 39 0332 786660
Fax: 39 0332 789222
E-mail: steven.eisenreich@jrc.it
http://ies.jrc.cec.eu.int/

International Baltic Sea Fishery Commission (IBSFC)
Hozastrasse 20
PL-00-528 Warsaw, Poland

Contact: Secretariat
Tel: 48 22 628 8647
Fax: 48 22 625 3372
E-mail: ibsfc@polbox.pl
http://www.ibsfc.org/

International Commission for Scientific Exploration of the Mediterranean Sea (ICSEM)
16 boulevard de Suisse
MC-98000 Monte Carlo, Monaco
Contact: Director General
Tel: 377 93 30 38 79
Fax: 377 92 16 11 95
E-mail: comments@ciesm.org
http://www.ciesm.org/

International Commission for the Conservation of Atlantic Tunas (ICCAT)
Calle Corazón de María, 8, 6th Floor
E-28002 Madrid, Spain
Contact: Executive Secretary
Tel: 34 91 4165 600
Fax: 34 91 4152 612
E-mail: info@iccat.es
http://www.iccat.es/

International Commission for the Protection of the Danube River (ICPDR)
Vienna International Center
D0412 PO Box 500
A-1400 Vienna, Austria
Contact: Permanent Secretariat
Tel: 43 1 26060 5738
Fax: 43 1 26060 5895
E-mail: icpdr@unvienna.org
http://www.icpdr.org/

International Commission for the Protection of the Rhine (ICPR)
Postfach 200253
D-56002 Koblenz, Germany
Tel: 49 261 12495
Fax: 49 261 36572
E-mail: sekretariat@iksr.de
http://iksr.firmen-netz.de/

International Council for the Exploration of the Sea (ICES)
Palaegade 2-4
DK-1261 Copenhagen K, Denmark
Contact: General Secretary
Tel: 45 33 15 42 25
Fax: 45 33 93 42 15
E-mail: info@ices.dk
http://www.ices.dk/

Interreg III—North Sea Programme
Jernbanegade 22
DK-8800 Viborg Denmark
Tel: 45 87 27 19 99
Fax: 45 86 60 16 80
E-mail: info@interregnorthsea.org
http://www.interregnorthsea.org/

Joint Research Centre of the European Commission (JRC)
SDME 10/78
B-1049 Brussels, Belgium
Tel: 32 2 295 7624
Fax: 32 2 295 6322
E-mail: jrc-info@cec.eu.int
http://www.jrc.org/

Kommunenes Internasjonale Miljøorganisasjon (KIMO)
Local Authorities International Environmental Organisation
Shetland Islands Council
Infrastructure Services
Grantfield
Lerwick, Shetland, ZE1 0NT, United Kingdom
Contact: Secretariat
Tel: 44 1595 74 4800
Fax: 44 1595 69 5887
E-mail: kimo@zetnet.co.uk
http://www.zetnet.co.uk/coms/kimo/

Marine Environment Laboratory
International Atomic Energy Agency
4, Quai Antoine 1er
BP 800
MC-98012 Monaco
Contact: Director
Tel: 377 97 97 72 72
Fax: 377 97 97 72 73
E-mail: mel@iaea.org
http://www.iaea.org/monaco/

Maritime Policy
European Commission
Directorate-General Energy and Transport
DM28, office 3/76
B-1160 Brussels, Belgium
E-mail: maritime-policy@cec.eu.int
http://europa.eu.int/comm/transport/maritime/

REGIONAL INTERGOVERNMENTAL ORGANIZATIONS

Maritime Safety
European Commission
Directorate-General Energy and Transport
Maritime Safety Unit
DM28, office 2/36
B-1160 Brussels, Belgium
E-mail: maritime-safety@cec.eu.int
http://europa.eu.int/comm/transport/maritime/

Mediterranean Action Plan Regional Coordinating Unit (MEDU)
UNEP/MEDU
48 Vassileos Konstantiou Avenue
PO Box 18019
GR-116 10 Athens, Greece
Tel: 30 210 727 3123
Fax: 30 210 725 3196
E-mail: unepmedu@unepmap.gr
http://www.unepmap.org/

NATO SACLANT Undersea Research Centre
Viale San Bartolomeo 400
I-19138 La Spezia, Italy
Tel: 39 0187 527 1
Fax: 39 0187 527 700
E-mail: registry@saclantc.nato.int
http://www.saclantc.nato.int/

Nordic Council of Ministers
Store Strandstraede 18
DK-1255 Copenhagen K, Denmark
Contact: Senior Advisor for Fisheries Affairs
Tel: 45 33 96 02 55
Fax: 45 33 93 20 47
E-mail: jh@norden.org
http://www.norden.org/fisk/

North Atlantic Marine Mammal Commission (NAMMCO)
Polar Environmental Centre
N-99296 Tromsø, Norway
Contact: General Secretary
Tel: 47 77 75 01 80
Fax: 47 77 75 01 81
E-mail: nammco-sec@nammco.no
http://www.nammco.no/

North Atlantic Salmon Conservation Organisation (NASCO)
11 Rutland Square
Edinburgh, Scotland, EH1 2AS,
United Kingdom
Tel: 44 131 228 2551
Fax: 44 131 228 4384
E-mail: hq@nasco.int
http://www.nasco.int/

North Atlantic Treaty Organization (NATO)
Scientific and Environmental Affairs Division
B-1110 Brussels, Belgium
Tel: 32 2 707 4111
Fax: 32 2 707 4232
E-mail: science@hq.nato.int
http://www.nato.int/science/

North-East Atlantic Fisheries Commission (NEAFC)
22 Berners Street
London, W1T 3DY, United Kingdom
Tel: 44 207 631 0016
Fax: 44 207 636 9225
E-mail: info@neafc.org
http://www.neafc.org/

Organisation for Economic Cooperation and Development (OECD)
2, rue Andre Pascal
F-75775 Paris Cedex 16, France
Tel: 33 1 4524 8200
Fax: 33 1 4524 8500
E-mail: webmaster@oecd.org
http://www.oecd.org/

OSPAR Commission for the Protection of the Marine Environment of the North-East Atlantic (OSPAR)
New Court
48 Carey Street
London, WC2A 2JQ, United Kingdom
Contact: Secretariat
Tel: 44 207 430 5200
Fax: 44 207 430 5225
E-mail: secretariat@ospar.org
http://www.ospar.org/

Priority Actions Programme Regional Activity Centre (PAP/RCU)
Kraj sv. Ivana 11
HR-21000 Split, Croatia
Contact: Director
Tel: 385 21 340 470
Fax: 385 21 340 490

E-mail: pap@gradst.hr
http://www.pap-thecoastcentre.org/

Regional Activity Centre for Cleaner Production (CP/RAC)
C/París, 184—3ª planta
E-08036 Barcelona, Spain
Contact: Director
Tel: 34 93 4151 112
Fax: 34 93 2370 286
E-mail: cleanpro@cema-sa.org
http://www.cema-sa.org/

Regional Activity Centre for Specially Protected Areas (RAC/SPA)
Boulevard de l'Environnement
PB 337
Cedex 1080 Tunis, Tunisia
Contact: Director
Tel: 216 1 795 760
Fax: 216 1 797 349
E-mail: car-asp@rac-spa.org.tn
http://www.rac-spa.org.tn/

Regional Marine Pollution Emergency Response Centre for the Mediterranean Sea (REMPEC)
Manoel Island
Gzira GZR 03, Malta
Contact: Director
Tel: 356 21 337296
Fax: 356 21 339951
E-mail: rempec@rempec.org
http://www.rempec.org/

The North Sea Conference
Ministry of Environment
SE-103 33 Stockholm, Sweden
Contact: North Sea Secretariat
Tel: 46 84 05 10 00
E-mail: registrator@environment.ministry.se
http://www.dep.no/md/nsc/

UNEP Regional Office for Europe (ROE)
International Environment House
11-13, chemin des Anémones, 6th floor
CH-1219 Châtelaine, Geneva, Switzerland
Tel: 41 22 917 8279
Fax: 41 22 917 8024
E-mail: roe@unep.ch
http://www.unep.ch/roe/

Vision and Strategies Around the Baltic Sea 2010 (VASAB 2010)
Dlugi Targ 8-10
PL-80 828 Gdansk, Poland
Tel: 48 58 301 8255
Fax: 48 58 305 4005
E-mail: infov@vasab.org.pl
http://www.vasab.org.pl/

Western European Union
15, rue de l'Association
B-1000 Brussels, Belgium
Tel: 32 2 500 4412
Fax: 32 2 500 4470
E-mail: ueo.secretariatgeneral@skynet.be
http://www.weu.int/

4. REGIONAL INTERGOVERNMENTAL ORGANIZATIONS

4.5 Australia, New Zealand and Oceania

Commission for the Conservation of Southern Bluefin Tuna (CCSBT)
PO Box 37
Deakin West, ACT 2600, Australia
Contact: Secretariat
Tel: 61 2 6282 8396
Fax: 61 2 6282 8407
E-mail: bmacdonald@ccsbt.org
http://www.ccsbt.org/

FAO Subregional Office for Pacific Islands (SAPA)
FAO Private Mail Bag
Apia, Western Samoa
Tel: 685 22127
Fax: 685 22126
E-mail: fao-sapa@fao.org
http://www.fao.or.th/

Forum Fisheries Agency (FFA)
PO Box 629
Honiara, Solomon Islands
Contact: Director
Tel: 677 21124
Fax: 677 23995
E-mail: info@ffa.int
http://www.ffa.int/

Marine Resources Pacific Consortium
c/o University of Guam Marine Laboratory
UOG Station
Mangilao, GU, 96913, USA
Contact: Secretariat
Tel: 671 735 2175

Fax: 671 734 6767
http://www.uog.edu/marepac/

Pacific Islands Development Program
East-West Center
1601 East-West Road
Honolulu, HI, 96848-1601, USA
Tel: 1 808 944-7778
Fax: 1 808 944-7670
E-mail: pidp@EastWestCenter.org
http://www.eastwestcenter.org/pidp-ab.asp

Pacific Islands Marine Resources Information System (PIMRIS)
Marine Studies Building
Lower Campus
University of the South Pacific
Suva, Fiji
Contact: Coordinator
Tel: 679 321 2934
Fax: 679 330 0830
E-mail: pimris@usp.ac.fj
http://www.usp.ac.fj/library/informationcentres/pimris/pimris.htm

Secretariat of the Pacific Community (SPC)
BP D5
98848 Noumea Cedex, New Caledonia
Contact: Secretary General
Tel: 687 262000
Fax: 687 263818
E-mail: spc@spc.int
http://www.spc.org.nc/

South Pacific Applied Geoscience Commission (SOPAC)
Private Mail Bag GPO
Suva, Fiji
Contact: Director
Tel: 679 338 1377
Fax: 679 337 0040
E-mail: director@sopac.org
http://www.sopac.org.fj/

South Pacific Forum Secretariat (ForumSec)
Private Mail Bag
Suva, Fiji
Contact: Secretary General
Tel: 679 331 2600
Fax: 679 330 5573
E-mail: info@forumsec.org.fj
http://www.sidsnet.org/pacific/forumsec/

South Pacific Regional Environment Programme (SPREP)
PO Box 240
Vaitele, Apia, Western Samoa
Contact: Director
Tel: 685 21929
Fax: 685 20231
E-mail: sprep@sprep.org.ws
http://www.sprep.org.ws/

Treaty of Waitangi Fisheries Commission (Te Ohu Kai Moana)
48 Mulgrave Street
Thorndon
PO Box 3277
Wellington, New Zealand
Tel: 64 4 499 5199
Fax: 64 4 499 5190
E-mail: hinerangi.barr@tokm.co.nz
http://www.tokm.co.nz/

4. REGIONAL INTERGOVERNMENTAL ORGANIZATIONS

4.6 Polar Regions

Arctic Council
c/o Ministry for Foreign Affairs of Iceland
Raudararstigur 25
IS-150 Reykjavik, Iceland
Tel: 354 545 9900
Fax: 354 562 2373
E-mail: arctic.council@utn.stjr.is
http://www.arctic-council.org/

Arctic Monitoring and Assessment Programme (AMAP)
Stromsveien 96
PO Box 8100 Dep.
N-0032 Oslo, Norway
Contact: Secretariat
Tel: 47 23 24 16 30
Fax: 47 22 67 67 06
E-mail: amap@amap.no
http://www.amap.no/

Barents Euro-Arctic Council
c/o Ministry of Foreign Affairs
PO Box 8114
N-0032 Oslo, Norway
Contact: Secretariat
Tel: 47 22 24 20 08

Fax: 47 22 24 35 70
E-mail: barents@mfa.no
http://www.beac.st/

Commission for the Conservation of Antarctic Marine Living Resources (CCAMLR)
PO Box 213
North Hobart, TAS 7002, Australia
Tel: 61 3 6231 0366
Fax: 61 3 6234 9965
E-mail: ccamlr@ccamlr.org
http://www.ccamlr.org/

Conservation of Arctic Flora and Fauna (CAFF)
Hafnarstraeti 97
IS-600 Akureyri, Iceland
Contact: International Secretariat
Tel: 354 462 3350
Fax: 354 462 3390
E-mail: caff@caff.is
http://www.caff.is/

International Arctic Science Committee (IASC)
Middelthunsgate 29
PO Box 5156 Majorstua
N-0302 Oslo, Norway
Contact: Secretariat
Tel: 47 22 95 99 00
Fax: 47 22 95 99 01
E-mail: iasc@iasc.no
http://www.iasc.no/

Protection of the Arctic Marine Environment (PAME)
Hafnarstraeti 97
IS-600 Akureyri, Iceland
Contact: International Secretariat
Tel: 354 461 1355
Fax: 354 462 3390
E-mail: pame@pame.is
http://www.pame.is/

The Northern Forum
716 W 4th Avenue, Suite 100
Anchorage, AK, 99501, USA
Contact: Secretariat
Tel: 1 907 561-3280
Fax: 1 907 561 6645
E-mail: NForum@northernforum.org
http://www.northernforum.org/

5. REGIONAL NONGOVERNMENTAL ORGANIZATIONS

5.1 Africa

African Association of Remote Sensing of the Environment (AARSE)
Geological Survey Division, ITC
PO Box 6
NL-7500AA Enschede, The Netherlands
Contact: Secretary General
Tel: 31 53 4874 279
Fax: 31 53 4874 336
E-mail: worldai@itc.nl
http://www.itc.nl/personal/aarse/aboutus.html

Arab Institute of Navigation
El Sebaei 45th Street
Zahret El Sebaei Building
Miami, Alexandria, Egypt
Contact: President
Tel: 20 3 550 9824
Fax: 20 3 550 9686
E-mail: ain@aast.edu
http://www.aast.edu/ain/

Empowerment for African Sustainable Development
PO Box 165
Green Point
Cape Town 8051, South Africa
Tel: 27 21 434 6012
Fax: 27 21 434 6134
E-mail: info@easd.org.za
http://easd.org.za/

Fondation International du Banc d'Arguin
La Tour du valat
Le Sambuc
13 200 Arles, France
Tel: 33 4 9097 2926
Fax: 33 4 9097 2242
E-mail: fiba@tourduvalat.org
http://www.tourduvalat.org/news_806.htm

International Ocean Institute—Eastern Africa
Kenya Marine and Fisheries Research Institute (KMFRI)
Box 81651
Mombasa, Kenya
Contact: Director

Tel: 254 11 475527
Fax: 254 11 475157
E-mail: ioi-ea@recoscix.com; kmfri@recoscix.com
http://www.ioinst.org/

International Ocean Institute—Senegal
Centre de Recherches Oceanographiques de Dakar-Thiaroye (CRODT)
BP 2241
Dakar, Senegal
Contact: Director
Tel: 221 8 34 8041
Fax: 221 8 34 2792
E-mail: dtoure@crodt.isra.sn

International Ocean Institute—Southern Africa
Department of Biodiversity and Conservation Biology
University of the Western Cape
P Bag X17
Bellville 7535, South Africa
Contact: Director
Tel: 27 21 959 2594
Fax: 27 21 959 1213
E-mail: kprochazka@uwc.ac.za
http://www.ioinst.org/ioisa/

International Ocean Institute West African Operational Centre of NIOMAR
Wilmat Point Road
Big Beach, Victoria Island
PMB 12729
Lagos, Nigeria
Fax: 234 1 261 9517
E-mail: niomar@linkserve.com.ng

South African Association for Marine Biological Research
PO Box 10712
Marine Parade
Durban 4056, South Africa
Contact: Director
Tel: 27 31 337 3536
Fax: 27 31 337 2132
E-mail: seaworld@saambr.org.za
http://www.seaworld.org.za/

South African Network for Coastal and Oceanic Research (SANCOR)
c/o National Research Foundation
PO Box 2600
Pretoria 0001, South Africa
Contact: Secretariat
Tel: 27 12 481 4107
Fax: 27 12 481 4005
E-mail: annette@nrf.ac.za
http://www.botany.uwc.ac.za/sancor/

Western Indian Ocean Marine Science Association (WIOMSA)
PO Box 3298
Zanzibar, Tanzania
Tel: 255 24 223 3472
Fax: 255 24 223 3852
E-mail: wiomsa@yahoo.com; secretary@wiomsa.org
http://www.wiomsa.org/

5. REGIONAL NONGOVERNMENTAL ORGANIZATIONS

5.2 The Americas

Alliance for Marine Remote Sensing Association
NSCC, 5685 Leeds Street
PO Box 1153
Halifax, NS, B3J 2X1, Canada
Contact: Systems Manager
Tel: 1 902 491-2160
Fax: 1 902 491-2162
E-mail: amrsadmin@waterobserver.org
http://www.waterobserver.org/

American Association of Petroleum Geologists
Box 979
Tulsa, OK, 74101-0979, USA
Contact: Executive Director
Tel: 1 918 584-2555
Fax: 1 918 560-2694
E-mail: postmaster@aapg.org
http://www.aapg.org/

American Association of Port Authorities
1010 Duke Street
Alexandria, VA, 22314-3589, USA
Tel: 1 703 684-5700
Fax: 1 703 684-6231
E-mail: info@aapa-ports.org
http://www.aapa-ports.org/

American Boat and Yacht Council (ABYC)
3069 Solomons Island Road

Edgewater, MD, 21037, USA
Contact: President
Tel: 1 410 956-1050
Fax: 1 410 956-2737
E-mail: rmation@abycinc.org
http://www.abycinc.org/

American Bureau of Shipping (ABS)
ABS Plaza
16855 Northchase Drive
Houston, TX, 77060, USA
Contact: President
Tel: 1 281 877-5800
Fax: 1 281 877-5803
E-mail: abs-worldhq@eagle.org
http://www.eagle.org/

American Cetacean Society
PO Box 1391
San Pedro, CA, 90733-1391, USA
Tel: 1 310 548-6279
Fax: 1 310-548-6950
E-mail: info@acsonline.org
http://www.acsonline.org/

American Coastal Coalition
5460 Beaujolais Lane
Fort Myers, FL, 33919, USA
Contact: President
Tel: 1 941 489-2616
Fax: 1 941 489-9917
E-mail: info@coastalcoalition.org
http://www.coastalcoalition.org/

American Fisheries Society
5410 Grosvenor Lane, Suite 110
Bethesda, MD, 20814, USA
Contact: Executive Director
Tel: 1 301 897-8616
Fax: 1 301 897-8096
E-mail: main@fisheries.org
http://www.fisheries.org/

American Geological Institute (AGI)
4220 King Street
Alexandria, VA, 22302-1502, USA
Tel: 1 703 379-2480
Fax: 1 703 379-7563
E-mail: agi@agiweb.org
http://www.agiweb.org/

American Geophysical Union (AGU)
2000 Florida Avenue NW
Washington, DC, 20009, USA
Contact: Executive Director
Tel: 1 202 462-6900
Fax: 1 202 328-0566
E-mail: service@agu.org
http://www.agu.org/

American Institute of Fishery Research Biologists (AIFRB)
c/o 6211 Madawaska Road
Bethesda, MD, 20816, USA
Contact: President
Tel: 1 301 320-5202
E-mail: DickSchaef@aol.com
http://www.aifrb.org/

American Littoral Society
Building 18
Sandy Hook
Highlands, NJ, 07732, USA
Contact: Executive Director
Tel: 1 732 291-0055
Fax: 1 732 291-3551
E-mail: als@netlabs.net
http://www.littoralsociety.org/

American Marinelife Dealers Association
c/o Island Aquarium Services
PO Box 2342
Key West, FL, 33045, USA
Contact: Secretary
E-mail: IslandAquarium@yahoo.com
http://www.amdareef.com/

American Maritime Congress
1300 Eye Street NW, Suite 250 W
Washington, DC, 20005, USA
Contact: Executive Director
Tel: 1 202 842-4900
Fax: 1 202 842-3492
E-mail: info@us-flag.org
http://www.us-flag.org/

American Maritime Officers
2 West Dixie Highway
Dania Beach, FL, 33004, USA
Contact: National President
Tel: 1 954 921-2221
Fax: 1 954 926-5112
http://www.amo-union.org/

American Meteorological Society
45 Beacon Street
Boston, MA, 02108-3693, USA
Contact: Executive Director
Tel: 1 617 227-2425
Fax: 1 617 742-8718

E-mail: amsinfo@ametsoc.org
http://www.ametsoc.org/AMS/

American Petroleum Institute
1220 L Street, NW
Washington, DC 20005-4070
Tel: 1 202 682-8000
http://www.api.org/

American Polar Society
PO Box 464
Iowa City, IA, 52242-0464, USA
Contact: Membership Center
E-mail: ampolars@aol.com
http://www.oaedks.net/amerpolr.html

American Shore and Beach Preservation Association (ASBPA)
1724 Indian Way
Oakland, CA, 94611, USA
Contact: Business Office
Tel: 1 510 339-2818
Fax: 1 510 339-6710
E-mail: business@asbpa.org
http://www.asbpa.org/

American Society of International Law (ASIL)
2223 Massachusetts Avenue, NW
Washington, DC, 20008, USA
Tel: 1 202 939-6000
Fax: 1 202 797-7133
E-mail: services@asil.org
http://www.asil.org/

American Society of Limnology and Oceanography
5400 Bosque Boulevard, Suite 680
Waco, TX, 76710, USA
Contact: Business Office
Tel: 1 254 399-9635
Fax: 1 254 776-3767
E-mail: business@aslo.org
http://www.aslo.org/

American Society of Naval Engineers (ASNE)
1452 Duke Street
Alexandria, VA, 22314-3458, USA
Tel: 1 703 836-6727
Fax: 1 703 836-7491
E-mail: asnehq@navalengineers.org
http://www.navalengineers.org/

American Sportfishing Association
225 Rainekers Lane, Suite 420
Alexandria, VA, 22314, USA
Contact: President
Tel: 1 703 519-9691
Fax: 1 703 519-1872
E-mail: info@asafishing.org
http://www.asafishing.org/

American Waterways Operators
801 North Quincy Street, Suite 200
Arlington, VA, 22203, USA
Tel: 1 703 841-9300
Fax: 1 703 841-0389
E-mail: aburns@vesselalliance.com
http://www.americanwaterways.com/

Aquacultural Engineering Society
c/o Freshwater Institute
PO Box 1889
Shepherdstown, WV, 25443, USA
Contact: Secretary/Treasurer
Tel: 1 304 876-2815
Fax: 1 304 870-2208
E-mail: b.vinci@freshwaterinstitute.org
http://www.aesweb.org/

Aquaculture Association of Canada
16 Lobster Lane
St. Andrews, NB, E5B 3T6, Canada
Tel: 1 506 529-4766
Fax: 1 506 529-4609
E-mail: aac@mar.dfo-mpo.gc.ca
http://www.aquacultureassociation.ca/

Association of Canadian Port Authorities
85 Albert Street, Suite 1502
Ottawa, ON, K1P 6A4, Canada
Contact: Executive Director
Tel: 1 613 232-2036
Fax: 1 613 232-9554
E-mail: leroux@acpa-ports.net
http://www.acpa-ports.net/

Association of Coastal Engineers
c/o Applied Technology and Management Inc.
2770 NW 43rd Street, Suite B
Gainesville, FL, 32606, USA
Contact: Executive Secretary
E-mail: pehrman@appliedtm.com
http://www.coastalengineers.org/

Association of Environmental and Resource Economists (AERE)

1616 P Street NW, Suite 410, Room 400
Washington, DC, 20036, USA
Contact: Secretary
Tel: 1 202 328-5077
Fax: 1 202 939-3460
E-mail: voigt@rff.org
http://www.aere.org/

Association of Pacific Ports
PO Box 11087
Olympia, WA, 98502, USA
Contact: Executive Director
Tel: 1 360 943-4142
E-mail: PortsWest@aol.com
http://www.associationofpacificports.com/

Association of Ship Brokers and Agents-USA, Inc.
510 Sylvan Avenue, Suite 201
Englewood Cliffs, NJ, 07632, USA
Contact: Executive Director
Tel: 1 201 569-2882
Fax: 1 201 569-9082
E-mail: asba@asba.org
http://www.asba.org/

Atlantic Coastal Zone Information Steering Committee (ACZISC)
International Oceans Institute of Canada
Dalhousie University
1226 LeMarchant Street
Halifax, NS, B3H 3P7, Canada
Contact: Secretariat
Tel: 1 902 494-3879
Fax: 1 902 494-1334
E-mail: aczisc@is.dal.ca
http://www.dal.ca/aczisc/

Atlantic Salmon Federation
PO Box 5200
St. Andrews, NB, E5B 3S8, Canada
Contact: President
Tel: 1 506 529-1034
Fax: 1 506 529-1075
E-mail: asf@nb.aibn.com
http://www.asf.ca/

Bay of Fundy Ecosystem Partnership (BoFEP)
Acadia Centre for Estuarine Research
Acadia University
PO Box 115
Wolfville, NS, B0P 1X0, Canada
Contact: Secretariat
Tel: 1 902 585-1113
Fax: 1 902 585-1054
E-mail: secretariat@bofep.org
http://www.bofep.org/

Canadian Aquaculture Industry Alliance (CAIA)
907-75 Albert Street
Ottawa, ON, K1P 5E7, Canada
Tel: 1 613 239-0612
Fax: 1 613 239-0619
E-mail: caiaoffice@aquaculture.ca
http://www.aquaculture.ca/

Canadian Centre for Fisheries Innovation
PO Box 4920
St. John's, NL, A1C 5R3, Canada
Tel: 1 709 778-0517
Fax: 1 709 778-0516
E-mail: ccfi@mi.mun.ca
http://www.ccfi.ca/

Canadian Centre for Marine Communications
155 Ridge Road
PO Box 8454
St. John's, NL, A1B 3N9, Canada
Tel: 1 709 579-4872
Fax: 1 709 579-0495
E-mail: ccmc@ccmc.nf.ca
http://www.ccmc.nf.ca/

Canadian Coastal Science and Engineering Association (CCSEA)
c/o National Water Research Institute
Canada Centre for Inland Waters
PO Box 5050
865 Lakeshore Road
Burlington, ON, L7R 4A6, Canada
Tel: 1 905 335-4736
Fax: 1 905 336-4420
E-mail: michael.skafel@ec.gc.ca
http://www.cciw.ca/ccsea/

Canadian Council of Professional Fish Harvesters (CCPFH/CCPP)
102 Bank Street, Suite 202
Ottawa, ON, K1P 5N4, Canada
Contact: Executive Director
Tel: 1 613 235-3474
Fax: 1 613 231-4313
E-mail: fish@ccpfh-ccpp.org
http://www.ccpfh-ccpp.org/

Canadian International Freight Forwarders' Association (CIFFA)
1243 Islington Avenue, Suite 706
Toronto, ON, M8X 1Y9, Canada
Tel/Fax: 1 416 234-5100
E-mail: info@ciffa.com
http://www.ciffa.com/

Canadian Maritime Law Association
1000 de Gauchetière Street West, Suite 200
Montreal, QC, H3B 5H4, Canada
Tel: 1 514 954-3116
Fax: 1 514 954-1905
E-mail: cmla@cmla.org
http://www.cmla.org/

Canadian Nature Federation
1 Nicholas Street, Suite 606
Ottawa, ON, K1N 7B7, Canada
Tel: 1 613 562-3447
Fax: 1 613 562-3371
E-mail: cnf@cnf.ca
http://www.cnf.ca/

Canadian Nautical Research Society (CNRS)
PO Box 511
Kingston, ON, K7L 4W5, Canada
Contact: President
E-mail: jp@post.queensu.ca
http://www.marmus.ca/cnrs/

Canadian Shipowners Association
350 Sparks Street, Suite 705
Ottawa, ON, K1R 7S8, Canada
Tel: 1 613 232-3539
Fax: 1 613 232-6211
E-mail: csa@shipowners.ca
http://www.shipowners.ca/

Canadian Water and Wastewater Association
5330 Canotek Road, 2nd Floor, Unit 20
Ottawa, ON, K1J 9C3, Canada
Contact: Executive Director
Tel: 1 613 747-0524
Fax: 1 613 747-0523
E-mail: admin@cwwa.ca
http://cwwa.ca/

Canadian Wildlife Federation
350 Michael Cowpland Drive
Kanata, ON, K2M 2W1, Canada
Tel: 1 613 599-9594
Fax: 1 613 599-4428
E-mail: info@cwf-fcf.org
http://www.cwf-fcf.org/

Caribbean Alliance for Sustainable Tourism
1000 Ponce de Leon Avenue, 5th Floor
San Juan, Puerto Rico, 00907, USA
Tel: 1 787 725-9139
Fax: 1 787 725-9108
E-mail: cast@caribbeanhotels.org
http://www.cha-cast.com/

Caribbean Community Ocean Sciences Network (CCOSNET)
c/o Institute of Marine Affairs
PO Box 3160
Carenage Post Office
Trinidad and Tobago
Contact: Coordinator
Tel: 1 868 634-4291/4
Fax: 1 868 634-4433
E-mail: director@ima.gov.tt
http://www.ima.gov.tt/ccosnet.htm

Caribbean Conservation Association (CCA)
Chelford
The Garrison
St. Michael, Barbados
Contact: Executive Director
Tel: 1 246 426-5373
Fax: 1 246 429-8483
E-mail: execdirector@ccanet.net
http://www.caribbeanconservation.org/

Caribbean Natural Resources Institute (CANARI)
Fernandes Industrial Centre
Administrative Building
Eastern Main Road
Laventille, Trinidad
Tel: 1 868 626-6062
Fax: 1 868 626-1788
E-mail: info@canari.org
http://www.canari.org/

CEDAM International
1 Fox Road
Croton-on-Hudson, NY, 10520, USA
Contact: President
Tel: 1 914 271-5365
Fax: 1 914 271-4723
E-mail: cedam@bestweb.net
http://www.cedam.org/

Center for Coastal Studies
59 Commercial Street

PO Box 1036
Provincetown, MA, 02657, USA
Contact: Executive Director
Tel: 1 508 487-3622
Fax: 1 508 487-4495
E-mail: ccs@coastalstudies.org
http://www.coastalstudies.org/

Center for International Environmental Law (CIEL)
1367 Connecticut Avenue, NW, Suite 300
Washington, DC, 20036, USA
Contact: Executive Director
Tel: 1 202 785-8700
Fax: 1 202 785-8701
E-mail: info@ciel.org
http://www.ciel.org/

Center for SeaChange
2101 Wilson Boulevard, Suite 550
Arlington, VA, 22201, USA
Tel: 1 703 516-0632
Fax: 1 703 516-9551
E-mail: contactus@seachangecenter.org
http://www.seachangecenter.org/

Centro Ecuatoriano de Derecho Ambiental (CEDA)
(Center for Environmental Law)
Eloy Alfaro 1770 y Rusia, 3rd Floor
Quito, Ecuador
Tel: 593 2 223 1410
Fax: 593 2 223 8609
E-mail: comercio-e@ceda.org.ec
http://www.ceda.org.ec/

Chamber of Maritime Commerce
350 Sparks Street, Suite 704A
Ottawa, ON, K1R 7S8, Canada
Tel: 1 613 233-8779
Fax: 1 613 233-3743
E-mail: info@cmc-ccm.com
http://www.cmc-ccm.com/

Chamber of Shipping
100—1111 West Hastings Street
Vancouver, BC, V6E 2J3, Canada
Tel: 1 604 681-2351
Fax: 1 604 681-4364
E-mail: csbc@chamber-of-shipping.com
http://www.chamber-of-shipping.com/

Chilean Maritime League
(Liga Marítima de Chile)
Arda Errázuriz 471, 2° piso
Casilla Postal 117-V
Valparaíso, Chile
Tel: 56 32 235280
Fax: 56 32 255179
E-mail: ligamar@terra.cl
http://www.ligamar.cl/

Circum-Pacific Council on Energy and Mineral Resources (CPCEMR)
12201 Sunrise Valley Drive, MS-917
Reston, VA, 20192, USA
Contact: Secretariat
Tel: 1 703 648-6645
Fax: 1 703 648-4227
E-mail: nzeigler@usgs.gov
http://www.circum-pacificcouncil.org/

Clean Islands International
8219 Elvaton Drive
Pasadena, MD, 21122-3903, USA
Tel: 1 410 647-2500
Fax: 1 410 647-4554
E-mail: cii@islands.org
http://islands.org/

Coast Alliance
600 Pennsylvania Avenue, SE, Suite 340
Washington, DC, 20003, USA
Contact: Executive Director
Tel: 1 202 546-9554
Fax: 1 202 546-9609
E-mail: coast@coastalliance.org
http://www.coastalliance.org/

Coastal Communities Network
PO Box 1613
Pictou, NS, B0K 1H0, Canada
Contact: Executive Director
Tel: 1 902 485-4754
Fax: 1 902 752-9844
E-mail: coastalnet@ns.sympatico.com
http://www.coastalcommunities.ns.ca/

Coastal Community Network
#3-502 Dallas Road
Victoria, BC, V8V 1B2, Canada
Tel: 1 250 383-1923
Fax: 1 250 383-1903
E-mail: coastcom@island.net
http://www.coastalcommunity.bc.ca/

Coastal Conservation Association (CCA)
6919 Portwest, Suite 100
Houston, TX, 77024, USA
Contact: Chairman

Tel: 1 713 626-4234
E-mail: ccantl@joincca.org
http://www.joincca.org/

Coastal Research and Education Society of Long Island, Inc. (CRESLI)
Division of Natural Sciences and Mathematics
Kramer Science Center
Dowling College
Oakdale, NY, 11769-1999, USA
Tel: 1 631 244-3352
E-mail: information@cresli.org
http://www.cresli.org/

Coastal Zone Canada Association
Bedford Institute of Oceanography
PO Box 1006
Dartmouth, NS, B2Y 4A2, Canada
Contact: Secretariat
Tel: 1 902 429-9497
Fax: 1 902 429-9491
E-mail: coastalz@mar.dfo-mpo.gc.ca
http://www.czca-azcc.org/

Consortium for Oceanographic Research and Education
1755 Massachusetts Avenue, NW, Suite 800
Washington, DC, 20036-2102, USA
Tel: 1 202 332-0063
Fax: 1 202 332-8887
E-mail: core@coreocean.org
http://www.coreocean.org/

Cruise Lines International Association (CLIA)
500 Fifth Avenue, Suite 1407
New York, NY, 10110, USA
Tel: 1 212 921-0066
Fax: 1 212 921-0549
E-mail: info@cruising.org
http://www.cruising.org/

David Suzuki Foundation
2211 West 4th Avenue, Suite 219
Vancouver, BC, V6K 4S2, Canada
Tel: 1 604 732-4228
Fax: 1 604 732-0752
E-mail: solutions@davidsuzuki.org
http://www.davidsuzuki.org/

Dredging Contractors of America
311 North Washington Street
Alexandria, VA, 22314, USA
Contact: Executive Director
Tel: 1 703 518-8408
Fax: 1 703 518-8490
E-mail: jimrausch@dredgingcontractors.org
http://www.dredgingcontractors.org/

Earth Island Institute
300 Broadway, Suite 28
San Francisco, CA, 94133-3312, USA
Tel: 1 415 788-3666
Fax: 1 415 788-7324
http://www.earthisland.org/

Ecological Society of America
1707 H Street NW, Suite 400
Washington, DC, 20006-3915, USA
Contact: Executive Director
Tel: 1 202 833-8773
Fax: 1 202 833-8775
E-mail: esahq@esa.org
http://www.esa.org/

Ecology Action Centre
1568 Argyle Street, Suite 31
Halifax, NS, B3J 2B3, Canada
Tel: 1 902 429-2202
Fax: 1 902 422-6410
E-mail: eac@ecologyaction.ca
http://www.ecologyaction.ca/

Fisheries Council of Canada
38 Antares Drive, Suite 110
Ottawa, ON, K2E 7V2, Canada
Contact: President
Tel: 1 613 727-7450
Fax: 1 613 727-7453
E-mail: info@fisheriescouncil.org
http://www.fisheriescouncil.org/

Friends of the Earth (FOE)
1025 Vermont Ave NW, Suite 300
Washington, DC, 20005, USA
Contact: President
Tel: 1 202 783-7400
Fax: 1 202 783-0444
E-mail: foe@foe.org
http://www.foe.org/

Geoscience Information Society
c/o Geology Library 100-23
Caltech
Pasadena, CA, 91125, USA
Contact: Secretary
Tel: 1 626 395-2199
Fax: 1 626 568-0935

E-mail: jimodo@caltech.edu
http://www.geoinfo.org/

Global Programme of Action Coalition for the Gulf of Maine (GPAC)
c/o Atlantic Coastal Action Program Saint John
PO Box 6878, Station A
Saint John, NB, E2L 4S3, Canada
Contact: Coordinator
Tel: 1 506 652-2227
Fax: 1 506 633-2184
E-mail: acapsj@fundy.net
http://www.gpac-gom.org/

H. John Heinz III Center for Science, Economics and the Environment
1001 Pennsylvania Ave, NW, Suite 735 South
Washington, DC, 20004, USA
Contact: President
Tel: 1 202 737-6307
Fax: 1 202 737-6410
E-mail: lovejoy@heinzctr.org
http://www.heinzctr.org/

Huntsman Marine Science Centre
1 Lower Campus Road
St. Andrews, NB, E5B 2L7, Canada
Tel: 1 506 529-1200
Fax: 1 506 529-1212
E-mail: huntsman@huntsmanmarine.ca
http://www.huntsmanmarine.ca/

IEEE Geoscience and Remote Sensing Society
c/o IEEE Operations Centre
445 Hoes Lane
PO Box 1331
Piscataway, NJ, 08855-1331, USA
Tel: 1 732 981-0060
Fax: 1 732 981-1721
E-mail: grss@ieee.org
http://ewh.ieee.org/soc/grss/

IEEE Oceanic Engineering Society
2403 Lisbon Lane
Alexandria, VA, 22306-2516, USA
Contact: President
Tel: 1 703 768-9522
E-mail: t.wiener@ieee.org
http://www.oceanicengineering.org/

Institute of Navigation
3975 University Drive, Suite 390
Fairfax, VA, 22030, USA
Tel: 1 703 383-9688
Fax: 1 703 383-9689
E-mail: membership@ion.org
http://www.ion.org/

International Marina Institute
PO Box 7197
Jupiter, FL, 33468, USA
Contact: President
Tel: 1 561 741-0626
Fax: 1 561 741-0676
E-mail: info@imimarina.org
http://www.imimarina.org/

International Ocean Institute—Costa Rica
Universidad Nacional
PO Box 86
Heredia 3000, Costa Rica
Contact: Director
Tel: 506 277 3594
Fax: 506 260 2546
E-mail: ioicos@una.ac.cr
http://www.una.ac.cr/ioi/

Inuit Tapiriit Kanatami
170 Laurier Avenue West, Suite 510
Ottawa, ON, K1P 5V5, Canada
Tel: 1 613 238-8181
Fax: 1 613 234-1991
E-mail: info@itk.ca
http://www.itk.ca/

Island Resources Foundation
6292 Estate Nazareth No. 100
St. Thomas, US Virgin Islands, 00802-1104
Tel: 1 340 775-6225
Fax: 1 340 779-2022
E-mail: etowle@irf.org
http://www.irf.org/

Lake Carriers' Association
Suite 915, Rockefeller Building.
614 Superior Avenue West
Cleveland, OH, 44113-1383, USA
Contact: President
Tel: 1 216 621-1107
Fax: 1 216 241-8262
E-mail: ggn@lcaships.com
http://www.lcaships.com/

Latin American Shipowners' Association (LASA)
(Asociación Latinoamericana de Armadores)

Blanco 869, Piso 3
Valparaíso, Chile
Contact: Executive Secretary
Tel: 56 32 212057
Fax: 56 32 212017
E-mail: armadore@entelchile.net

Liberian Shipowners' Council Ltd.
99 Park Avenue, Suite 1700
New York, NY, 10016, USA
Contact: General Secretary
Tel: 1 212 973-3896
Fax: 1 212 994-6763
E-mail: jl@liberianshipowners.com
http://www.liberianshipowners.com/

Marina Operators Association of America (MOAA)
1819 L Street NW, Suite 700
Washington, DC, 20036, USA
Contact: Executive Director
Tel: 1 202 721-1630
Fax: 1 202 861-1181
E-mail: moaa@nmma.org
http://www.moaa.org/

Marine Conservation Biology Institute
15806 NE 47th Court
Redmond, WA, 98052, USA
Tel: 1 425 883-8914
Fax: 1 425 883-3017
E-mail: mcbiweb@mcbi.org
http://www.mcbi.org/

Marine Environment Research Institute (MERI)
Center for Marine Studies
55 Main Street
PO Box 1652
Blue Hill, ME, 04616, USA
Tel: 1 207 374-2135
Fax: 1 207 374-2931
E-mail: meri@downeast.net
http://www.meriresearch.org/

Marine Retailers Association of America (MRAA)
PO Box 1127
Oak Park, IL, 60304, USA
Contact: President
Tel: 1 708 763-9210
Fax: 1 708 763-9236
E-mail: mraa@mraa.com
http://www.mraa.com/

Maritime Security Council
3471 N. Federal Highway, Suite 611
Fort Lauderdale, FL, 33306, USA
Tel: 1 954 567-2536
Fax: 1 954 567-2511
E-mail: mailbox@maritimesecurity.org
http://www.maritimesecurity.org/

Monterey Bay Aquarium Research Institute
7700 Sandholdt Road
Moss Landing, CA, 95039-9644, USA
Contact: President
Tel: 1 831 775-1700
Fax: 1 831 775-1620
E-mail: mcnutt@mbari.org
http://www.mbari.org/

Mote Marine Laboratory
1600 Ken Thompson Parkway
Sarasota, FL, 34236, USA
Tel: 1 941 388-4441
Fax: 1 941 388-4312
E-mail: info@mote.org
http://www.mote.org/

National Aquaculture Association
111 W. Washington Street, Suite 1
Charles Town, WV, 25414, USA
Tel: 1 304 728-2167
Fax: 1 304 728-2196
E-mail: naa@intrepid.net
http://www.natlaquaculture.org/

National Association for the Marine Assistance Industries (C-PORT)
1600 Duke Street, Suite 400
Alexandria, VA, 22314, USA
Contact: Executive Director
Tel: 1 703 519-1713
Fax: 1 703 519-1716
E-mail: c-port@wpa.org
http://www.c-port.org/

National Association of Marine Services (NAMS)
5458 Wagonmaster Drive
Colorado Springs, CO, 80917, USA
Contact: Executive Director
Tel: 1 719 573-5946
Fax: 1 719 573-5952
E-mail: nams@namsshipchandler.com
http://www.namsshipchandler.com/

National Association of Marine Surveyors, Inc. (NAMS)

PO Box 9306
Chesapeake, VA, 23321-9306, USA
Contact: Office Manager
Tel: 1 757 488-9538
Fax: 1 757 488-0584
E-mail: office@nams-cms.org
http://www.namsurveyors.org/

National Coalition for Marine Conservation (NCMC)
3 North King Street
Leesburg, VA, 20176, USA
Contact: Executive Director
Tel: 1 703 777-0037
Fax: 1 703 777-1107
E-mail: christine@savethefish.org
http://www.savethefish.org/

National Fisheries Institute
1901 North Fort Myer Drive, Suite 700
Arlington, VA, 22209, USA
Contact: President
Tel: 1 703 524-8880
Fax: 1 703 524-4619
E-mail: tressler@nfi.org
http://www.nfi.org/

National Marine Charter Association (NMCA)
1600 Duke Street, Suite 400
Alexandria, VA, 22314, USA
Contact: Executive Director
Tel: 1 703 519-1714
Fax: 1 703 519-1716
E-mail: info@marinecharter.org
http://www.marinecharter.org/

National Marine Distributors Association (NMDA)
37 Pratt Street
Essex, CT, 06426-1159, USA
Contact: Executive Director
Tel: 1 860 767-7898
Fax: 1 860 767-7932
E-mail: info@nmdaonline.com
http://www.nmdaonline.com/

National Marine Educators Association
College of Marine Sciences
PO Box 7000
Ocean Springs, MS, 39566-7000, USA
Contact: National Office
Tel: 1 228 374-5550
Fax: 1 228 374-5559
E-mail: sharon.walker@usm.edu
http://www.marine-ed.org/

National Marine Electronics Association (NMEA)
7 Riggs Avenue
Severna Park, MD, 21146, USA
Contact: Executive Director
Tel: 1 410 975-9425
Fax: 1 410 975-9450
E-mail: info@nmea.org
http://www.nmea.org/

National Marine Manufacturers Association (NMMA)
200 East Randolph Drive, Suite 5100
Chicago, IL, 60601, USA
Contact: President
Tel: 1 312 946-6200
Fax: 1 312 946-0388
E-mail: webmaster@nmma.org
http://www.nmma.org/

National Maritime Historical Society (NMSH)
5 John Walsh Boulevard
Peekskill, NY, 10566, USA
Tel: 1 914 737-7878
Fax: 1 914 737-7816
E-mail: nmhs@seahistory.org
http://www.seahistory.org/

National Ocean Industries Association (NOIA)
1120 G Street NW, Suite 900
Washington, DC, 20005, USA
Contact: President
Tel: 1 202 347-6900
Fax: 1 202 347-8650
E-mail: tom@noia.org
http://www.noia.org/

National Shellfisheries Association
c/o PO Box 350
VIMS Eastern Shorelab
Wachapreague, VA, 23480, USA
Tel: 1 757 787-5816
Fax: 1 757 787-5831
E-mail: nlewis@vims.edu
http://www.shellfish.org/

Natural Resources Defense Council
40 West 20th Street

New York, NY, 10011, USA
Contact: Headquarters
Tel: 1 212 727-2700
Fax: 1 212 727-1773
E-mail: nrdcinfo@nrdc.org
http://www.nrdc.org/

Naval Officers' Association of Canada
324 Sunset Drive
Salt Spring Island, BC, V8K 1G2, Canada
Contact: Executive Director
Tel: 1 250 537-8791
Fax: 1 250 537-8792
E-mail: ExecDir@naval.ca
http://www.naval.ca/maritimeaffairs/

Newfoundland Ocean Industries Association
Atlantic Place, Suite 602
215 Water Street
St. John's, NL, AIC 6C9, Canada
Contact: President
Tel: 1 709 758-6610
Fax: 1 709 758-6611
E-mail: noia@noianet.com
http://www.noianet.com/

North American Association of Fisheries Economics
c/o IIFET
Department of Agriculture and Resource Economics
Oregon State University
Corvallis, OR, 97331-3601, USA
Contact: Business Office
Phone: 1 541 737 1416
Fax: 1 541 737 2563
E-mail: ann.l.shriver@oregonstate.edu
http://oregonstate.edu/Dept/IIFET/NAAFE/Home.html

North American Native Fishes Association, Inc. (NANFA)
1107 Argonne Drive
Baltimore, MD, 21218, USA
Contact: Secretary
Tel: 1 410 243-9050
E-mail: nanfa@att.net
http://www.nanfa.org/

Northwest Marine Trade Association (NMTA)
1900 N. Northlake Way, Suite 233
Seattle, WA, 98103-9087, USA
Contact: Executive Director
Tel: 1 206 634-0911
Fax: 1 206 632-0078
E-mail: info@nmta.net
http://www.nmta.net/

Oceanic Society
Fort Mason Center, Building E,
San Francisco, CA, 94123, USA
Tel: 1 415 441-1106
Fax: 1 415 474-3395
E-mail: office@oceanic-society.org
http://www.oceanic-society.org/

Oceans Blue Foundation
405-134 Abbott Water Street
Vancouver, BC, V6B 2K4, Canada
Contact: Executive Director
Tel: 1 604 684-2583
Fax: 1 604 684-6942
E-mail: sails@oceansblue.org
http://www.oceansblue.org/

Offshore Marine Service Association (OMSA)
990 N. Corporate Drive, Suite 210
Harahan, LA, 70123, USA
Contact: President
Tel: 1 504 734-7622
Fax: 1 504 734-7134
E-mail: robert@offshoremarine.org
http://www.offshoremarine.org/

Pacific Coast Federation of Fishermen's Associations (PCFFA)
PO Box 29370
San Francisco, CA, 94129-0370, USA
Contact: Executive Director
Tel: 1 415 561-5080
Fax: 1 415 561-5464
E-mail: fish1ifr@aol.com
http://www.pcffa.org/

Pacific Maritime Association
PO Box 7861
San Francisco, CA, 94120-7861, USA
Tel: 1 415 576-3200
Fax: 1 415 989-1425
http://www.pmanet.org/

Pan-American Institute of Naval Engineering (IPEN)
Instituto Panamericano de Ingenieria Naval

Avenida Presidente Vargas 542—S913
20071-000 Rio de Janeiro, Brazil
Tel/Fax: 55 21 2536263
E-mail: ipen@terra.com.br
http://www.ipen.org.br/

Passenger Vessel Association
801 North Quincy Street, Suite 200
Arlington, VA, 22203, USA
Contact: Executive Director
Tel: 1 703 807-8360 ext 255
Fax: 1 703 807-0103
E-mail: jgroundwater@vesselalliance.com
http://www.passengervessel.com/

Reef Care Curaçao
PO Box 676
Curaçao, Netherlands Antilles
Contact: President
Tel: 1 599 869-5285
E-mail: reefcare@cura.net
http://www.reefcare.org/

Reef Relief
Reef Relief Environmental Center
PO Box 430
Key West, FL, 33041, USA
Tel: 1 305 294-3100
Fax: 1 305 293-9515
E-mail: info@reefrelief.org
http://www. reefrelief.org/

Shipbuilders Council of America (SCA)
1455 F Street, Suite 225
Washington, DC, 20005, USA
Contact: President
Tel: 1 202 347-5462
Fax: 1 202 347-5464
E-mail: jmccluer@de.bjllp.com
http://www.shipbuilders.org/

Shipping Federation of Canada
300 rue de Sacrement, Suite 326
Montreal, QC, H2Y 1X4, Canada
Tel: 1 514 849-2325
Fax: 1 514 849-8774
E-mail: info@shipfed.ca
http://www.shipfed.ca/

Sierra Club
85 Second Street, 2nd Floor
San Francisco, CA, 94105, USA
Contact: Executive Director
Tel: 1 415 977-5500
Fax: 1 415 977-5799
E-mail: information@sierraclub.org
http://www.sierraclub.org/

Sierra Club of Canada
412-1 Nicholas Street
Ottawa, ON, K1N 7B7, Canada
Tel: 1 613 241-4611
Fax: 1 613 241-2292
E-mail: info@sierraclub.ca
http://www.sierraclub.org/canada/

Society of Exploration Geophysicists
8801 South Yale
PO Box 702740
Tulsa, OK, 74170-2740, USA
Contact: Executive Director
Tel: 1 918 497-5500
Fax: 1 918 497-5557
E-mail: mfleming@seg.org
http://seg.org/

Sustainable Development Institute
3121 South Street, NW
Washington, DC, 20007, USA
Tel: 1 202 338-1017
E-mail: susdev@igc.org
http://www.susdev.org/

The Coastal Society
PO Box 25408
Alexandria, VA, 22313-5408, USA
Contact: President
Tel: 1 703 768-1599
Fax: 1 703 768-1598
E-mail: coastalsociety@aol.com
http://www.thecoastalsociety.org/

The Cousteau Society
710 Settlers Landing Road
Hampton, VA, 23669, USA
Contact: President
Tel: 1 757 722-9300
Fax: 1 757 722-8185
E-mail: cousteau@cousteausociety.org
http://www.cousteau.org/

The Ecological Society of America
1707 H Street NW, Suite 400
Washington, DC, 20006-3915, USA
Tel: 1 202 833-8773
Fax: 1 202 833-8775
E-mail: esahq@esa.org
http://www.esa.org/

REGIONAL NONGOVERNMENTAL ORGANIZATIONS

The Ocean Conservancy
1725 DeSales Street NW, Suite 600
Washington, DC, 20036, USA
Tel: 1 202 429-5609
Fax: 1 202 872-0619
E-mail: info@oceanconservancy.org
http://www.oceanconservancy.org/

The Oceanography Society (TOS)
PO Box 1931
Rockville, MD, 20849-1931, USA
Contact: Executive Director
Tel: 1 301 251-7708
Fax: 1 301 251-7709
E-mail: info@tos.org
http://www.tos.org/

West Gulf Maritime Association
1717 East Loop, Suite 200
Houston, TX, 77029, USA
Contact: President
Tel: 1 713 678-7655
Fax: 1 713 672-7452
E-mail: waniemand@wgma.org
http://www.wgma.org/

Western Dredging Association
PO Box 5797
Vancouver, WA, 98668-5737, USA
Contact: Executive Director
Tel: 1 360 750-0209
Fax: 1 360 750-1445
E-mail: weda@comcast.net
http://www.westerndredging.org/

Wildlife Conservation Society
2300 Southern Boulevard
Bronx, NY, 10460, USA
Contact: President
Tel: 1 718 220-5100
E-mail: nyageneral@wcs.org
http://www.wcs.org/

Women's Aquatic Network, Inc.
PO Box 4993
Washington, DC, 20008, USA
Contact: Secretariat
E-mail: info@womensaquatic.net
http://orgs.womensaquatic.net/

World Shipping Council
1015 15th Street NW, Suite 450
Washington, DC, 20005, USA
Tel: 1 202 589-1230
Fax: 1 202 589-1231
E-mail: info@worldshipping.org
http://www.worldshipping.org/

Yacht Brokers Association of America
105 Eastern Avenue, Suite 104
Annapolis, MD, 21403, USA
Contact: Executive Director
Tel: 1 410 263-1014
Fax: 1 410 263-1659
E-mail: jmt@ybaa.com
http://yachtworld.com/ybaa/

5. REGIONAL NONGOVERNMENTAL ORGANIZATIONS

5.3 Asia

Asian Fisheries Society
PO Box 2725
Quezon City Central Post Office
1167 Quezon City, The Philippines
Tel: 63 2 921 1914
Fax: 63 2 920 2757
E-mail: afs@compass.com.ph
http://www.compass.com.ph/~afs/

China Society for Fisheries
Building 22, Maizidian Street
Chaoyang District
Beijing, People's Republic of China
Contact: President
Tel: 86 10 6419 4233
Fax: 86 10 6419 4231
E-mail: cnscfish@public.bta.net.cn
http://www.fisheries.moa.gov.cn/

Chinese Ports and Harbours Association (CPHA)
12 Zhong Shan Road (E2)
Shanghai 200002, People's Republic of China
Contact: Secretary General
Tel: 86 21 6311 5654
Fax: 86 21 6374 2473
E-mail: spaws@public4.sta.net.cn

Chinese Society of Naval Architects and Marine Engineers (CSNAME)
5 Yuetan Beijie Street
Beijing 100861, People's Republic of China
Contact: President
Tel: 86 10 6803 8833
Fax: 86 10 6803 1560

E-mail: b24@csname.org
http://www.csname.org/

Coastal Development Planning Centre
25 Vasundhara Colony, Gulbai Jkrd
Ahmedabad
Gujurat, 380006, India
Tel: 91 79 656 8421
Tel: 91 79 642 0056

Eastern Dredging Association (EADA)
c/o Port Klang Association
Mail Bag Service 202
42009 Port Klang, Malaysia
Contact: Secretary General
Fax: 60 3 3157 0211
E-mail: david@pka.gov.my

Environmental Engineers Association of Thailand
122/4 Soi Rawadee, Rama VI Road
Samsen Nai, Phayathai
Bangkok 10400, Thailand
Contact: President
Tel: 66 2 617 1530
Fax: 66 2 279 9720
E-mail: info@eeat.or.th
http://www.eeat.or.th/

Federation of ASEAN Shipowners' Associations (FASA)
456 Alexandra Road #14-02
NOL Building
Singapore 119962
Contact: Secretary General
Tel: 65 6278 3464
Fax: 65 6274 5079
E-mail: fasa@pacific.net.sg

Haribon Foundation
4/F Fil Garcia Tower
140 Kalayaan Avenue
Cor Mayaman St.
Diliman, Quezon City, The Philippines
Tel: 632 920 7430
Fax: 632 924 8976
E-mail: info@haribon.org.ph
http://www.haribon.org.ph/

Institute of Chartered Shipbrokers
GPO Box 12292
Hong Kong
Contact: Secretary
Tel: 852 2866 1488
Fax: 852 8106 1480
E-mail: icshk@netvigator.com
http://www.ics.org.hk/

International Cetacean Education Research Centre—Japan
3-37-12, Nishihara
Shibuya-ku
Tokyo, 151, Japan
Tel: 81 3 5712 3480
Fax: 81 3 5712 3481
E-mail: info@icerc.org
http://www.icerc.org/

International Ocean Institute—China
c/o National Marine Data and Information Service (NMDIS)
State Oceanic Administration
93 Liuwei Road, Hedong District
Tianjin 300171, People's Republic of China
Contact: Director
Tel: 86 22 2430 1292
Fax: 86 22 2430 4408
E-mail: houwf@netra.nmdis.gov.cn

International Ocean Institute—India
Indian Institute of Technology (IIT Madras)
IC & SR Building
Chennai 600036, India
Contact: Director
Tel: 91 44 2257 0338
Fax: 91 44 2257 0559
E-mail: ioi@vsnl.com

International Ocean Institute—Japan
Intercom Inc.
4034-20-14 Minami-Aoyama
Minato-ku
Tokyo, Japan
Contact: Director
Tel: 81 3 5775 0181
Fax: 81 3 5775 0180
E-mail: intercom@qb3.so-net.ne.jp

International Society for Mangrove Ecosystems (ISME)
c/o Faculty of Agriculture
University of Ryukyus
Okinawa 903-0129, Japan
Contact: Secretariat
Tel: 81 98 895 6601
Fax: 81 98 895 6602
E-mail: mangrove@ryukyu.ne.jp
http://www.mangrove.or.jp/

REGIONAL NONGOVERNMENTAL ORGANIZATIONS

Jordan Royal Ecological Diving Society
PO Box 831051
Amman 11183, Jordan
Tel/Fax: 962 6 06 5676183
E-mail: information@jreds.org
http://www.jreds.org/

Malaysian Shipowners' Association (MASA)
Menara Dayabuni, 17th Floor
Jalan Sultan Hisamudi
PO Box 10371
50712 Kuala Lumpur, Malaysia
Tel: 60 3 2275 2136
Fax: 60 3 2260 2575
E-mail: masa_kl@tm.net.my
http://www.malaysianshipowners.org/

Nippon Kaiji Kyokai (Class NK)
4-7 Kioi-cho
Chiyoda-ku
Tokyo 102-8567, Japan
Contact: Chairman and President
Tel: 81 3 3230 1201
Fax: 81 3 5226 2012
E-mail: bnd@classnk.or.jp
http://www.classnk.or.jp/

Small Fishers Federation of Sri Lanka
Pambala, Kakkapalliya
PO Box 01
Chilaw, Sri Lanka
Contact: Director
Tel: 94 032 48707
Fax: 94 032 47960
E-mail: sffl@sri.lanka.net
http://www.shrimpaction.com/titlessffl.html

Southeast Asia START Regional Committee (SARCS)
National Central University
Chung-Li 320, Taiwan, ROC
Contact: Secretariat
Tel: 886 3 426 2726
Fax: 886 3 426 2640
E-mail: sarcs@sarcs.org.tw
http://www.sarcs.org.tw/

Telapak Indonesia
Jl. Palem Putri III no. 1-3
Kompleks Taman Yasmin Sektor V
Bogor, Indonesia
Tel/Fax: 62 21 9154296
E-mail: info@telapak.org
http://www.telapak.org/

Yadfon Association
16/4 Rakchan Road
Tambon Tabtieng, Amphur Muang
Trang 92000, Thailand
Tel: 66 75 219 737
Fax: 66 75 219 327
E-mail: yadfon@loxinfo.co.th
http://www.shrimpaction.com/yadfon.html

5. REGIONAL NONGOVERNMENTAL ORGANIZATIONS

5.4 Europe

Alliance of Maritime Regional Interests in Europe (AMRIE)
20B22, rue de Commerce
B-1000 Brussels, Belgium
Contact: Secretariat
Tel: 32 2 736 1755
Fax: 32 2 735 2298
E-mail: info@amrie.org
http://www.amrie.org/

Association for the Preservation of Underwater Historical Heritage
(Association pour la Mise en Valeur du Patrimoine Historique Sous-Marin)
20, rue de Verdun
F-29000 Quimper, France
Contact: President
Tel/Fax: 33 9895 2007

Association of European Shipbuilders and Shiprepairers (AWES)
Rue Marie de Bourgogne 52-54, 3rd floor
B-1000 Brussels, Belgium
Contact: Director
Tel: 32 2 230 2791
Fax: 32 2 230 4332
E-mail: info@awes-shipbuilding.org
http://www.awes-shipbuilding.org/

Association of Port Health Authorities (APHA)
Dutton House
46 Church Street
Runcorn, Cheshire, WA7 1LL, United Kingdom

Contact: Executive Secretary
Tel: 44 8707 444505
Fax: 44 1928 581596
E-mail: apha@cieh.org.uk
http://www.apha.org.uk/

Association of River Waterworks (Vereniging van RivierWaterbedrijven—RIWA)
PO Box 402
NL-3430 AK Nieuwegein, The Netherlands
Tel: 31 30 600 9030
Fax: 31 30 600 9039
E-mail: riwa@riwa.org
http://www.iawr.org/

Atlantic Salmon Trust
Moulin, Pitlochry
Perthshire, Scotland, PH16 5JQ, United Kingdom
Contact: Director
Tel: 44 1796 47 3439
Fax: 44 1796 47 3554
E-mail: salmontrust@aol.com
http://www.atlanticsalmontrust.org/

Atlantic Whale Foundation
St Martins House
59 St Martins Lane
Covent Garden
London, WC2N 4JS, United Kingdom
Tel: 44 207 240 6604
Fax: 44 207 240 5795
E-mail: edb@huron.ac.uk
http://www.whalefoundation.f2s.com/

Baltic Ports Organization (BPO)
c/o Ports of Stockholm
PO Box 27314
SE-102 54 Stockholm, Sweden
Contact: Secretariat
Tel: 46 86 70 26 00
Fax: 46 86 70 26 45
E-mail: bpo@stoports.com
http://www.bpoports.com/

British Marine Life Study Society
Glaucus House
14 Corbyn Crescent
Shoreham-by-Sea, BN43 6PQ, United Kingdom
Tel/Fax: 44 1273 465433
E-mail: glaucus@hotmail.com
http://ourworld.compuserve.com/homepages/BMLSS/homepage.htm

British Maritime Law Association
c/o Ince & Co.
Knolly's House
11 Byward Street
London, EC3R 5EN, United Kingdom
Contact: Secretary & Treasurer
Tel: 44 207 623 2011
Fax: 44 207 623 3225
E-mail: patrick.griggs@ince.co.uk
http://www.bmla.org.uk/

British Ports Association
Africa House
64-78 Kingsway
London, WC2B 6AH, United Kingdom
Contact: Director
Tel: 44 207 242 1200
Fax: 44 207 405 1069
E-mail: info@britishports.org.uk
http://www.britishports.org.uk/

Central Dredging Association (CEDA)
Radex Building
Rotterdamseweg183c
NL-2629 HD, Delft, The Netherlands
Contact: General Manager
Tel: 31 15 268 2575
Fax: 31 15 268 2576
E-mail: ceda@dredging.org/
http://www.dredging.org/

Centre for Documentation, Research and Experimentation on Water Pollution Accidents (CEDRE)
715, rue Alain Colas
CS 41836
F-29218 Brest Cedex 1, France
Contact: Director
Tel: 33 2 9833 1010
Fax: 33 2 9844 9138
E-mail: contact@le-cedre.fr
http://www.le-cedre.fr/

Cetacea Defence
PO Box 78
Shaftesbury
Dorset, SP7 8ST, United Kingdom
E-mail: cetaceadefence@hotmail.com
http://www.cetaceadefence.org/

Chamber of Shipping
Carthusian Court

12 Carthusian Street
London, EC1M 6EB, United Kingdom
Contact: Director General
Tel: 44 207 417 2800
Fax: 44 207 600 1534
E-mail: postmaster@british-shipping.org
http://www.british-shipping.org/

Coalition Clean Baltic
Östra Agatan 53
SE-753 22 Uppsala, Sweden
Contact: Secretariat
Tel: 46 18 71 11 70
Fax: 46 18 71 11 75
E-mail: secretariat@ccb.se
http://www.ccb.se/

Coastwatch Europe
Civil and Environmental Engineering
Trinity College, Dublin
Dublin 2, Ireland
Contact: International Coordination
Tel: 353 55 25843
Fax: 353 55 25842
E-mail: coastwatch@eircom.net
http://www.coastwatch.org/

Committee of European Shipowners' Associations (CESA)
52-54, rue Marie de Bourgogne, 3rd floor
B-1000 Brussels, Belgium
Contact: Secretary General
Tel: 32 2 230 2791
Fax: 32 2 230 4332
E-mail: info@cesa-shipbuilding.org
http://www.cesa-shipbuilding.org/

Council of European and Japanese National Shipowners' Associations (CENSA)
12 Carthusian Street
London, EC1M 6EB, United Kingdom
Contact: Secretary General
Tel: 44 17 1600 5405
Fax: 44 17 1600 5398
E-mail: censa@marisec.org

Deltalinqs
PO Box 54200
NL-3008 JE Rotterdam, The Netherlands
Tel: 31 10 4020 399
Fax: 31 10 4120 687
E-mail: info@deltalinqs.nl
http://www.deltalinqs.nl/

ESF Consortium for Ocean Drilling (ECOD)
ESF Management Committee for the ODP (EMCO)
European Science Foundation
1, quai Lezay-Marnésia
F-67080 Strasbourg Cedex, France
Contact: Scientific Secretary
Tel: 33 3 8876 7122
Fax: 33 3 8837 0532
E-mail: jdalton@esf.org
http://www.esf.org/ecod/

ESF Marine Board
European Science Foundation
1, quai Lezay Marnésia
F-67080 Strasbourg, France
Contact: Secretariat
Tel: 33 3 8876 7141
Fax: 33 3 8825 1954
E-mail: marineboard@esf.org
http://www.esf.org/marineboard/

Estuarine and Coastal Sciences Association (ECSA)
Department of Biological Science
University of Hull
Hull, HU6 7RX, United Kingdom
Contact: Secretary
http://www.ecsa.ac.uk/

EUCC—The Coastal Union
PO Box 11232
NL-2301 EE Leiden, Netherlands
Contact: International Secretariat
Tel: 31 71 512 2900
Fax: 31 71 512 4069
E-mail: admin@eucc.nl
http://www.eucc.nl/

European Aquaculture Society (EAS)
Slijkensesteenweg 4
B-8400 Oostende, Belgium
Tel: 32 59 323 859
Fax: 32 59 321 005
E-mail: eas@aquaculture.cc
http://www.easonline.org/

European Association for Aquatic Mammals
c/o Särkänniemi
FIN-33230 Tampere, Finland
Contact: Secretary/Treasurer
Tel: 358 3 2488 111
Fax: 358 3 2121 279

E-mail: info@eaam.org
http://www.eaam.org/

European Association of Fisheries Economists
c/o Centre for Fishery ECS Research Ltd
125 Mill Lane
Saxilby, Lincoln, LN1 2HN, United Kingdom
Contact: President
E-mail: phil@cferltd.com
http://www.eafe-fish.org/

European Association of Remote Sensing Laboratories (EARSeL)
2 avenue Rapp
F-75340 Paris Cedex 07, France
Contact: Secretariat
Tel: 33 1 4556 7360
Fax: 33 1 4556 7361
E-mail: earsel@meteo.fr
http://www.earsel.org/

European Cetacean Society
Unidad de Investigación para la Conservación de los Mamíferos Marinos
Departamento de Morfología
Facultad de Veterinaria
Universidad de Las Palmas de Gran Canaria
Trasmontaña,
E-35416 Arucas, Grand Canary, Spain
Contact: Chairman
Tel: 34 928 451 103
E-mail: ecs-board@JISCmail.ac.uk
http://web.inter.NL.net/users/J.W.Broekema/ecs/

European Coastal Association for Science and Technology (EUROCOAST)
Department of Earth Sciences
Cardiff University
PO Box 914
Cardiff, Wales, CF10 3YE, United Kingdom
Contact: Secretariat
Tel: 44 2920 874830
Fax: 44 2920 874326
E-mail: eurocoast@cf.ac.uk
http://www.eurocoast.org/

European Community Shipowners' Associations (ECSA)
45 rue Ducale
B-1000 Brussels, Belgium
Contact: Secretariat
Tel: 32 2 511 3940
Fax: 32 2 511 8092
E-mail: mail@ecsa.be
http://www.ecsa.be/

European Desalination Association
Science Park of Abruzzo
via Antica Arischia, 1
I-67100 L'Aquila, Italy
Contact: Secretariat
Tel: 39 0862 3475 308
Fax: 39 0862 3475 213
E-mail: balaban@desline.com
http://www.edsoc.com/

European Dredging Association (EuDA)
2-4 rue de Praetere
B-1000 Brussels, Belgium
Contact: Secretariat
Tel: 32 2 646 8183
Fax: 32 2 646 6063
E-mail: info@euda.be
http://www.european-dredging.info/

European Federation of Sea Anglers (EFSA)
Inglewood, Braal Road
Halkirk, Caithness, KW12 6XE, United Kingdom
Contact: Secretary
Tel/Fax: 44 1847 831985
E-mail: enquiries@efsa.co.uk
http://www.efsa.co.uk/

European Geophysical Society (EGS)
Max Planck Strasse 13
D-37191 Katlenburg-Lindau, Germany
Contact: EGS Office
Tel: 49 5556 1440
Fax: 49 5556 4709
E-mail: egs@copernicus.org
http://www.copernicus.org/EGS/

European Maritime Pilots' Association (EMPA)
St. Aldegondiskaai 36-38
B-2000 Antwerp, Belgium
Contact: Secretary General
Tel: 32 3 205 9436
Fax: 32 3 205 9437
E-mail: empa@skynet.be
http://www.empa-pilots.org/

European Polar Board (EPB)
European Science Foundation
1, quai Lezay-Marnésia
F-67080 Strasbourg, France
Contact: Secretariat
Tel: 33 3 8876 7166
Fax: 33 3 8876 7181
E-mail: pegerton@esf.org
http://www.esf.org/epb/

European Science Foundation (ESF)
1, quai Lezay-Marnésia
F-67080 Strasbourg, France
Contact: Secretary General
Tel: 33 3 8876 7100
Fax: 33 3 8837 0532
E-mail: esf@esf.org
http://www.esf.org/

European Sea Ports Organisation (ESPO)
Treurenberg 6
B-1000 Brussels, Belgium
Contact: Secretary General
Tel: 32 2 736 3463
Fax: 32 2 736 6325
E-mail: mail@espo.be
http://www.espo.be/

European Shippers' Council (ESC)
Park Leopold
Rue Wiertz 50
B-1050 Brussels, Belgium
Contact: Secretary General
Tel: 32 2 230 2113
Fax: 32 2 230 4140
E-mail: secretariat@europeanshippers.com
http://www.europeanshippers.com/

European Society for Marine Biotechnology
School of Life Sciences
Heriot-Watt University
Edinburgh, EH14 4AS, United Kingdom
Contact: Publications and Information
E-mail: j.g.burgess@hw.ac.uk
http://www.esmb.org/

European Union of Geosciences (EOST)
5 rue René Descartes
F-67084 Strasbourg Cedex, France
Contact: Executive Secretary
Tel: 33 3 9024 0058
Fax: 33 3 8860 3887
E-mail: eug@eost.u-strasbg.fr
http://eost.u-strasbg.fr/EUG/Accueil.htm

European Water Association
Theodor-Heuss-Allee 17
D-53773 Hennef, Germany
Contact: Chairman
Tel: 49 22 42 872189
Fax: 49 22 42 872135
E-mail: ewa@atv.de
http://www.ewaonline.de/

EUROPECHE
(Association of National Organisations of Fishing Enterprises of the EC)
23-25, rue de la Science, bte. 15
B-1040 Brussels, Belgium
Contact: Secretary General
Tel: 32 2 230 4848
Fax: 32 2 230 2680
E-mail: europeche@free.way.net

Federation of European Aquaculture Producers (FEAP)
30, rue Vivaldi
B-4100 Boncelles, Belgium
Contact: Secretary General
Tel: 32 4 338 2995
Fax: 32 4 337 9846
E-mail: secretariat@feap.info
http://www.feap.info/feap/

Federation of European Microbiological Societies
Poortlandplein 6
NL-2628 BM Delft, The Netherlands
Contact: Central Office
Tel: 31 15 278 5604
Fax: 31 15 278 5696
E-mail: info@fems-microbiology.org
http://www.fems-microbiology.org/

Fisheries Society of the British Isles
c/o Granta Information Systems
82A High Street
Sawston, Cambridge, CB2 4HJ, United Kingdom
Contact: President
Tel: 44 1223 830665
Fax: 44 1223 839804
E-mail: fsbi@grantais.demon.co.uk
http://www.le.ac.uk/biology/fsbi/index.html

Fridtjof Nansen Institute
PO Box 326
N-1326 Lysaker, Norway
Contact: Director
Tel: 47 67 11 19 00
Fax: 47 67 11 19 10
E-mail: post@fni.no
http://www.fni.no/

Geographical Information Systems (GISIG) International Group
Via Piacenza 54
I-16138 Genova, Italy
Tel: 39 010 8355 588
Fax: 39 010 8357 190
E-mail: gisig@gisig.it
http://www.gisig.it/

German Institute of Navigation (DGON)
Kölnstrasse 70
D-5311 Bonn, Germany
Tel: 49 228 201970
Fax: 49 228 2019719
E-mail: dgon.bonn@t-online.de
http://www.dgon.de/

German Shipbuilding and Ocean Industries Association
(Verband für Schiffbau und Meerestechnik—VSM)
An der Alster 1
D-20099 Hamburg, Germany
Tel: 49 40 28 01520
Fax: 49 40 28 015230
E-mail: info@vsm.de
http://www.vsm.de/

Hellenic Marine Environment Protection Association (HELMEPA)
5 Pergamou Street
GR-17121 Athens, Greece
Tel: 3 210 9343088
Fax: 3 210 9353847
E-mail: helmepa@helmepa.gr
http://www.helmepa.gr/

High North Alliance
PO Box 123
N-8390 Reine i Lofoten, Norway
Contact: Chair
Tel: 47 76 09 24 14
Fax: 47 76 09 24 50
E-mail: hna@highnorth.no
http://www.highnorth.no/

Institute of Fisheries Management
22 Rushworth Avenue
West Bridgford, Nottingham, NG2 7LF, United Kindom
Tel: 44 11 5982 2317
Fax: 44 11 5982 6150
E-mail: v.holt@ifm.org.uk
http://www.ifm.org.uk/

Institute of Shipping Economics and Logistics
(Institut für Seeverkhvswirtschaft und Logistik— ISL)
Universitätallee GW 1, Block A
D-28359 Bremen, Germany
Tel: 49 421 220960
Fax: 49 421 2209655
E-mail: info@isl.org
http://www.isl.uni-bremen.de/

International Association for the Rhine Vessels Register (IVR)
Vasteland 12E
NL-3011 BL, Rotterdam, Netherlands
Tel: 31 10 411 6070
Fax: 31 10 412 9091
E-mail: info@ivr.nl
http://www.ivr.nl/

International Association of Waterworks in the Rhine Basin (IAWR)
(Internationale Arbeitsgemeinschaft der Wasserwerke im Rheineinzugsgebiet)
PO Box 402
NL-3430 AK Nieuwegein, The Netherlands
Tel: 31 30 600 9030
Fax: 31 30 600 9039
E-mail: iawr@riwa.org
http://www.iawr.org/

International Commission for Protection of the Rhine Against Pollution (ICPR)
(Internationale Kommission zum Schutze des Rheins Gegon Verunreinizung—IKSR)
Hohenzollernstrasse 18
Postfach 200253
D-56002 Koblenz, Germany
Tel: 49 261 12495
Fax: 49 261 36572
E-mail: sekretariat@iksr.de
http://www.iksr.de/

International Marine Certification Institute (IMCI)

rue Abbé Cuypers 3
B-1040 Brussels, Belgium
Tel: 32 2 741 6836
Fax: 32 2 741 2418
E-mail: info@imci.org
http://www.imci.org/

International Ocean Institute—Black Sea
National Institute for Marine Research and Development "Grigore Antipa"
Boulevard Mamaia 300
RO-8700 Constanta 3, Romania
Contact: Director
Tel: 40 241 543 288
Fax: 40 241 831 274
E-mail: abologa@alpha.rmri.ro

International Ocean Institute—Ukraine
2 Nakhimov Street
Sevastopol 99011, Ukraine
Tel: 380 692 545 249
Fax: 380 692 555 477
E-mail: radalpin@ibss.iuf.net

International Ocean Institute—Malta
The Farmhouse—Mediterranean Institute
University of Malta
Msida MSD 06, Malta
Contact: Director
Tel: 356 3290 2430
Fax: 356 320 717
E-mail: mzam2@um.edu.mt

Marine Biological Association of the United Kingdom
The Laboratory
Citadel Hill
Plymouth, Devon PL1 2PB, United Kingdom
Contact: Director
Tel: 44 1752 633207
Fax: 44 1752 633102
E-mail: sec@mba.ac.uk
http://www.mba.ac.uk/

Marine Conservation Society
9 Gloucester Road
Ross-on-Wye
Herefordshire, HR9 5BU, United Kingdom
Contact: Secretary
Tel: 44 1989 566017
Fax: 44 1989 567815
E-mail: info@mcsuk.org
http://www.mcsuk.org/

Marine Mammal Council
Nachimovskiy Avenue 36
117218 Moscow, Russia
Tel/Fax: 7 095 124 7290
E-mail: support@2mn.org
http://www.2mn.org/

Marine Society
202 Lambeth Road
London, SE1 7JW, United Kingdom
Contact: General Secretary
Tel: 44 207 261 9535
Fax: 44 207 401 2537
E-mail: enq@marine-society.org
http://www.marine-society.org.uk/

Marine Studies Group
The Geological Society of London
c/o British Antarctic Survey
High Cross
Madingley Rise
Cambridge, CB3 0ET, United Kingdom
Contact: Secretary
Tel: 44 1223 22 1573
Fax: 44 1223 36 2616
E-mail: rdla@pcmail.nerc-bas.ac.uk
http://www.ocean.cf.ac.uk/people/neil/MSG/

Maritime Development Center of Europe
Amaliegade 33
DK-1256 Copenhagen K, Denmark
Tel: 45 33 33 74 88
Fax: 45 33 33 75 88
E-mail: info@maritimecenter.dk
http://www.maritimecenter.dk/

MEDCOAST
Middle East Technical University
06531, Ankara, Turkey
Tel: 90 312 210 5429
Fax: 90 312 210 1412
E-mail: medcoast@metu.edu.tr
http://www.medcoast.org.tr/

Mediterranean Association to Save the Sea Turtles (MEDASSET/GR)
c/o Park Towers
2 Brick Street
London, W1J 7DD, United Kingdom
Contact: President
Tel: 44 207 629 0654
E-mail: medasset@medasset.org
http://www.euroturtle.org/

Mediterranean Marine Bird Association (MEDMARAVIS)
PO Box 2
F-83470 Saint Maximin, France
Tel: 33 4 9459 4069
Fax: 33 4 9459 4738
E-mail: medmaraxm@aix.pacwan.net
http://www.geocities.com/med_avis/

National Federation of Fishermen's Organisations (NFFO)
Marsden Road
Fish Docks
Grimsby, DN31 3SG, United Kingdom
Contact: Secretary
Tel: 44 1472 349009
Fax: 44 1472 242486
E-mail: dbevan@nffo.org
http://www.nffo.org.uk/

National Union of Marine, Aviation and Shipping Transport Officers (NUMAST)
Oceanair House
750-760 High Road Leytonstone
London, E11 3BB, United Kingdom
Contact: General Secretary
Tel: 44 208 989 6677
E-mail: enquiries@numast.org
http://www.numast.org/

Netherlands Institute of Navigation
Seattleweg 7 (Haven 2801)
NL-3195 ND Pernis, The Netherlands
Contact: Director
Tel: 31 010 498 7518
Fax: 31 010 452 3457
E-mail: r.vanrhee@loodswezen.nl
http://www.nlr.nl/nin/

Nordic Marine Insurance Pool (NMIP)
(Nordisk Sjoforsikringspool—NSP)
c/o Swedish Association of Marine Underwriters
Klara Norra Kyrkogata 33
SE-111 22 Stockholm, Sweden
Contact: Secretary
Tel: 46 87 83 98 50
Fax: 46 87 83 98 95
E-mail: sten.gothberg@sjoass.se

Northern Shipowners' Defence Club
(Nordisk Skipsrederforening)
Kristinelundveien 22
Postboks 3033 El.
N-0207 Oslo 9, Norway
Contact: General Manager
Tel: 47 22 13 56 00
Fax: 47 22 43 00 35
E-mail: post@nordisk.no
http://www.nordisk.org/

Offshore Pollution Liability Association
Bank Chambers
29 High Street
Ewell, Surrey, KT17 1SB, United Kingdom
Contact: Managing Director
Tel: 44 208 786 3640
Fax: 44 208 786 3641
E-mail: opol@compuserve.com
http://www.opol.org.uk/

Royal Institute of Navigation
1 Kensington Gore
London, SW7 2AT, United Kingdom
Contact: Director
Tel: 44 207 591 3130
Fax: 44 207 591 3131
E-mail: info@rin.org.uk
http://www.rin.org.uk/

Royal Institution of Naval Architects
10 Upper Belgrave Street
London, SW1X 8BQ, United Kingdom
Contact: Secretary
Tel: 44 207 235 4622
Fax: 44 207 259 5912
E-mail: hq@rina.org.uk
http://www.rina.org.uk/

Royal Meteorological Society
104 Oxford Road
Reading, Berkshire, RG1 7LL, United Kingdom
Contact: Executive Director
Tel: 44 1189 568500
Fax: 44 1189 568571
E-mail: execdir@royalmetsoc.org
http://www.royal-met-soc.org.uk/

Scottish Fishermen's Federation
14 Regent Quay
Aberdeen, AB11 5AE, United Kingdom
Tel: 44 1224 582583
Fax: 44 1224 574958
E-mail: ssf@ssf.co.uk
http://www.sff.co.uk/

Sea Watch Foundation

36 Windmill Road
Headington, Oxford, OX3 7BX, United Kingdom
Contact: Director
Tel: 44 1865 764794
Fax: 44 1865 764757
E-mail: info@seawatchfoundation.org.uk
http://www.seawatchfoundation.org.uk/

Shetland Fish Processors' Association
Shetland Seafood Centre
Stewart Building
Lerwick, Shetland, ZE1 0LL, United Kingdom
Tel: 44 1595 693644
Fax: 44 1595 696126
E-mail: sfpa@fishuk.net
http://www.fishuk.net/sfpa/index.htm

Shetland Salmon Farmers' Association
Shetland Seafood Centre
Stewart Building
Lerwick, Shetland, ZE1 0LL, United Kingdom
Contact: Chairman
Tel: 44 1595 69 5579
Fax: 44 1595 69 4494
E-mail: ssfa@fishuk.net
http://www.fishuk.net/ssfa/index.htm

Ship Suppliers Organization of the European Community (OCEAN)
Van Stolkweg 31
NL-2585 JN, The Hague, Netherlands
Contact: Secretariat
Tel: 31 70 358 9137
Fax: 31 70 358 4538
E-mail: secretariaat@vanstolkweg.nl

Shipbuilders and Shiprepairers' Association (SSA)
Marine House
Thorpe Lea Road
Egham, Surrey, TW20 8BF, United Kingdom
Contact: Director
Tel: 44 1784 223770
Fax: 44 1784 223775
E-mail: office@ssa.org.uk
http://www.ssa.org.uk/

Society for Nautical Research (SNR)
National Maritime Museum
Greenwich, London, SE10 9NF, United Kingdom
Contact: Honorary Secretary
Tel: 44 208 312 6772
Fax: 44 208 312 6661
http://www.snr.org/

Society of Consulting Marine Engineers and Ship Surveyors (SCMES)
202 Lambeth Road
London, SE1 7JW, United Kingdom
Contact: Secretary
Tel: 44 207 261 0869
Fax: 44 207 261 0871
E-mail: sec@scmshq.org
http://www.scmshq.org/

Society of Maritime Industries
30 Great Guildford Street, 4th Floor
London, SE1 0HS, United Kingdom
Tel: 44 207 928 9199
Fax: 44 207 928 6599
E-mail: info@maritimeindustries.org
http://www.maritimeindustries.org/

Station biologique de la Tour du Valat
Le Sambuc
FR-13200 Arles, France
Tel: 33 4 9097 2013
Fax: 33 4 9097 2019
E-mail: secretariat@tourduvalat.org
http://www.tourduvalat.org/contact.html

Swedish Shipowner Employers' Association
Box 1621
SE-111 86 Stockholm, Sweden
Tel: 46 87 62 71 71
Fax: 46 86 11 46 99
E-mail: info@transportgruppen.se
http://www.transportgruppen.se/

Tethys Research Institute
c/o Municipal Aquarium
Viale G.B. Gadio 2,
I-20121 Milano, Italy
Tel: 39 02 5831 4889
Fax: 39 02 5831 5345
E-mail: tethys@tethys.org
http://www.tethys.org/

The Netherlands Shipbuilding Industry Association (VNSI)
PO Box 138
NL-2700 AC, Zoetermeer, The Netherlands

Tel: 31 79 353 11 65
Fax: 31 79 353 11 55
E-mail: info@vnsi.nl
http://www.vnsi.nl/

Whale and Dolphin Conservation Society
Brookfield
38 St. Paul Street
Chippenham, Wiltshire, SN15 1LY, United Kingdom
Tel: 44 1249 449500
Fax: 44 1249 449501
E-mail: info@wdcs.org
http://www.wdcs.org/

5. REGIONAL NONGOVERNMENTAL ORGANIZATIONS

5.5 Australia, New Zealand and Oceania

Australian Conservation Foundation
60 Leicester Street, Floor 1
Carlton, VIC 3053, Australia
Tel: 61 03 9345 1111
Fax: 61 03 9345 1166
http://www.acfonline.org.au/

Australian Coral Reef Society
c/o Centre for Marine Sciences
University of Queensland
St. Lucia, QLD 4072, Australia
Contact: Secretary
Tel: 61 07 3365 1475
Fax: 61 07 3365 4755
E-mail: acrs@jcu.edu.au
http://www.australiancoralreefsociety.org/

Australian Marine Conservation Society
PO Box 3139
Yeronga, QLD 4104, Australia
Contact: National Coordinator
Tel: 61 07 3848 5235
Fax: 61 07 3892 5814
E-mail: amcs@amcs.org.au
http://www.amcs.org.au/

Australian Marine Sciences Association (AMSA)
PO Box 902
Toowong, QLD 4066, Australia
E-mail: inquiries@amsa.asn.au
http://www.amsa.asn.au/

Australian Water Association
PO Box 388
Artaman, NSW 1570, Australia
Tel: 61 02 9413 1288
Fax: 61 02 0413 1047
E-mail: info@awa.asn.au
http://www.awa.asn.au/

Cawthron Institute
Private Bag 2
98 Halifax Street East
Nelson, New Zealand
Tel: 64 3 548 2319
Fax: 64 3 546 9464
E-mail: info@cawthron.org.nz
http://www.cawthron.org.nz/

International Ocean Institute—Pacific Islands
c/o Marine Studies Programme
University of the South Pacific
PO Box 1168
Suva, Fiji
Contact: Director
Tel: 679 330 5272
Fax: 679 330 1490
E-mail: veitayaki_j@usp.ac.fj
http://www.usp.ac.fj/marine/

International Ocean Institute Regional Operational Centre for Australia and Western Pacific (IOI-Australia)
P.O. Box 1539
Townsville, QLD 4810, Australia
Tel: 61 07 4729 8460
Fax: 61 07 4729 8449
E-mail: robin.south@impac.org.au

Marine and Coastal Community Network (MCCN)
PO Box 3139
Yeronga, QLD 4104, Australia
Contact: National Coordinator
Tel: 61 07 3848 5360
Fax: 61 07 3892 5814
E-mail: nat-off@mccn.org.au
http://www.mccn.org.au/

Maritime Union of Australia
365 Sussex Street, Level 2
Sydney, NSW 2000, Australia
Contact: General Secretary
Tel: 61 02 9267 9134
Fax: 61 02 9261 5897

E-mail: muano@mua.org.au
http://www.mua.org.au/

New Zealand Marine Sciences Society
42 Carlyon Rd, RD1
Upper Moutere
Nelson, New Zealand
Contact: Secretary
Tel: 643 543 2109
E-mail: secretary@nzmss.rsnz.org
http://nzmss.rsnz.org/

Oceania Project
PO Box 646
Byron Bay, NSW 2481, Australia
Tel: 61 02 6685 8128
Fax: 61 02 9225 9176
E-mail: trish.wally@oceania.org.au
http://oceania.org.au/

Pacific Ocean Research Foundation
PO Box 4800
74-381 Kaeakehe Pkwy, Suite C
Kailua-Kona, HI, 96740, USA
Contact: Chairman
Tel: 1 808 329-6105
Fax: 1 808 329-1148
E-mail: porf@aloha.net
http://holoholo.org/porf/

PACON International
PO Box 11568
Honolulu, HI, 96828-0568, USA
Tel: 1 808 956-6163
Fax: 1 808 956-2580
E-mail: pacon@hawaii.edu
http://www.hawaii.edu/pacon/

Seafriends Marine Conservation and Education Centre
7 Goat Island Road
Leigh R.D.5., New Zealand
Tel: 64 9422 6212
Fax: 64 9422 6245
E-mail: floor@seafriends.org.nz
http://www.seafriends.org.nz/

South Pacific Tourism Organization (SPTO)
PO Box 13119
Suva, Fiji
Tel: 679 330 4177
Fax: 679 330 1995
E-mail: info@spto.org
http://www.tcsp.com/

5. REGIONAL NONGOVERNMENTAL ORGANIZATIONS

5.6 Polar Regions

Antarctic and Southern Ocean Coalition (ASOC)
The Antarctica Project
1630 Connecticut Avenue, NW, 3rd Floor
Washington, DC, 20009, USA
Contact: Director
Tel: 1 202 234-2480
Fax: 1 202 234-2482
E-mail: antarctica@igc.org
http://www.asoc.org/

Antarctic Institute of Canada
PO Box 1223, Main Post Office
Edmonton, AB, T5J 2M4, Canada
Contact: Executive Officer
Tel/Fax: 1 780 452-7392
E-mail: mardon@freenet.edmonton.ab.ca

Arctic Ocean Science Board (AOSB)
UCAR-JOSS
PO Box 3000-FLY
Boulder, CO, 80307, USA
Contact: Secretariat
Tel: 1 303 497-8636
Fax: 1 303 497-8633
E-mail: aosb_info@joss.ucar.edu
http://www.aosb.org/

Barrow Arctic Science Consortium
PO Box 577
Barrow, AK, 99723, USA
Contact: Executive Director
Tel: 1 907 852-4881
Fax: 1 907 852-4882
E-mail: basc@arcticscience.org
http://www.arcticscience.org/

Canadian Arctic Resources Committee (CARC)
1276 Wellington Street, 2nd floor
Ottawa, ON, K1Y 3A7, Canada
Contact: Executive Director
Tel: 1 613 759-4284
Fax: 1 613 759-4581
E-mail: info@carc.org
http://www.carc.org/

Institute for Environmental Monitoring and Research
PO Box 1859, Station "B"
Happy Valley-Goose Bay, NL, A0P 1E0, Canada
Tel: 1 709 896-3266
Fax: 1 709 896-3076
E-mail: iemr@iemr.org
http://www.iemr.org/

International Polar Heritage Committee
c/o Directorate for Cultural Heritage
PO Box 8196 Dep
N-0034 Oslo, Norway
Contact: Secretary General
Tel: 47 22 94 04 00
E-mail: pchaplin@online.no
http://www.polarheritage.com/

Inuit Circumpolar Conference (ICC)
c/o ICC (Greenland)
PO Box 204
3900 Nuuk, Greenland
Contact: President
Tel: 299 3 23632
Fax: 299 3 23001
E-mail: iccgreenland@inuit.org
http://www.inuit.org/

6. REGIONAL ACADEMIC ORGANIZATIONS

6.1 Africa

Académie régionale des Sciences et Techniques de la Mer
(Regional Maritime Academy)
BP V158
Abidjan, Côte d'Ivoire
Contact: Director General
Tel: 225 371823

Arab Academy for Science and Technology and Maritime Transport
Gamal Abdel Naser Street
PO Box 1029
Alexandria, Egypt
Contact: Director General
Tel: 20 3 556 1497
Fax: 20 3 548 7786
http://www.aast.edu/

Benguela Environment Fisheries Interaction and Training Programme (BENEFIT)
PO Box 912
Swakopmund, Namibia
Contact: Secretariat
Tel: 264 64 4101164
Fax: 264 64 405913
E-mail: nsweijd@benguela.org
http://www.benefit.org.na/

Centre de Recherches Océanolographiques (CRO)
Département des Ressources Halieutiques Vivantes
29, rue des Pêcheurs BP V18
Abidjan, Côte d'Ivoire
Tel: 225 2135 5014
Fax: 225 2135 1155
E-mail: postmaster@cro.orstom.ci
http://www.ci.refer.org/ivoir_ct/rec/cdr/cro/accueil.htm

Centre for Documentation, Research and Training on the South West Indian Ocean (CEDREFI)
PO Box 91
Rose-Hill, Republic of Mauritius
Contact: Director
Tel: 230 465 5036
Fax: 230 465 1422

Centre for Marine Studies
University of Cape Town
Oceanography Annexe
Residence Road
Private Bag
Rondebosch 7701, South Africa
Contact: Director
Tel: 27 21 650 3283
E-mail: cms@physci.uct.ac.za
http://www.sea.uct.ac.za/cms/

Department of Environmental and Geographical Science
University of Cape Town
Private Bag
Rondebosch 7701, South Africa
Tel: 27 21 650 2873/4
Fax: 27 21 650 3791
E-mail: admin@enviro.uct.ac.za
http://www.egs.uct.ac.za/

Department of Natural Resources and Conservation
Faculty of Agriculture and Natural Resources
University of Namibia
Private Bag 13301
Windhoek, Namibia
Tel: 264 61 206 3890
Fax 264 61 206 3013
E-mail: jpmsangi@unam.na
http://www.unam.na/faculties/agriculture/nrc.htm

Department of Oceanography
University of Cape Town
Private Bag
Rondebosch 7701, South Africa
Tel: 27 21 650 3278
Fax: 27 21 650 3979
E-mail: scifac@science.uct.ac.za
http://www.uct.ac.za/

Faculty of Law
University of Namibia
Private Bag 13301
Windhoek, Namibia
Contact: Dean
Tel: 264 61 206 3998
E-mail: mhinz@unam.na
http://www.unam.na/faculties/law/

Henties Bay Marine and Coastal Resources Research Centre
University of Namibia
Private Bag 13301
Windhoek, Namibia
E-mail: fmolloy@unam.na
http://www.unam.na/research/henties/

Institut des Sciences de la Mer et de l'Aménagement du Littoral (ISMAL)
BP 54
Sidi-Fredj
42321 d'Alger, Algeria
Tel: 213 2 377076
Fax: 213 2 376806
E-mail: info@ismal.net
http://www.ismal.net/

Institut Fondamental d'Afrique Noire (IFAN)
Cheikh Anta Diop University
BP 5005
Dakar, Senegal
Tel: 221 825 7528
Fax: 221 825 3724
E-mail: info@ucad.sn
http://www.ucad.sn/tdmat.html

Institut Scientifique
Université Mohammed V
Ave Ibn Batouta
BP 703 Rabat-Agdal
10106 Rabat, Morocco
Contact: Directeur
Tel: 212 37 77 45 48
Fax: 212 37 77 45 40
http://www.israbat.ac.ma/

Institute of Marine and Environmental Law
University of Cape Town
Private Bag
Rondebosch 7701, South Africa
Contact: Director
Tel: 27 21 650 5642
Fax: 27 21 650 5607
E-mail: lawmar@law.uct.ac.za
http://www.uct.ac.za/depts/pbl/imel/intro.htm

Institute of Marine Biology and Oceanography
Fourah Bay College
University of Sierra Leone
Mount Aureol
Freetown, Sierra Leone
Contact: Director
Tel: 232 22 227 924
Fax: 232 22 224 260
E-mail: fbcadmin@sierratel.sl
http://fbcusl.8k.com/index.html

Institute of Marine Sciences
University of Dar es Salaam
PO Box 668
Zanzibar, Tanzania
Contact: Director
Tel: 255 24 2232128
E-mail: director@ims.udsm.ac.tz
http://www.ims.udsm.ac.tz/

Institute of Oceanography
University of Calabar
PMB 1115
Calabar, Cross River State, Nigeria
Contact: Coordinator
Tel: 234 222855

Fax: 234 224996
E-mail: root@unical.anpa.net.ng

Nigerian Institute for Oceanography and Marine Research (NIOMR)
Wilmot Point Road
Bar Beach
PO Box 12729
Lagos, Nigeria
Tel/Fax: 234 1 617385
E-mail: niomr@linkserve.com.ng

Regional Maritime Academy
PO Box 1115
Accra, Ghana
Contact: Director General
Tel: 233 21 712343
Fax: 233 21 712047
E-mail: regisrma@africaonline.com.gh
http://www.rma-edu.com/

School of Life and Environmental Sciences
University of Natal
Durban 4041, South Africa
Tel: 27 31 260 2300
Fax: 27 31 260 1391
E-mail: diab@nu.ac.za
http://www.sles.und.ac.za/

School of Maritime Studies
University of Natal
Durban, 4041, South Africa
Tel: 27 31 260 2994
Fax: 27 31 260 3163
E-mail: maritime@nu.ac.za
http://www.maritime.und.ac.za/

Shipping Law Unit
University of Cape Town
Private Bag
Rondebosch 7701, South Africa
Contact: Director
Tel: 27 21 650 3065
Fax: 27 21 650 5607
E-mail: shiplaw@law.uct.ac.za
http://www.uctshiplaw.com/

UNESCO Chair in Integrated Coastal Management and Sustainable Development
Departement de Geographie
Faculté des Lettres et des Sciences Humaines
Cheikh Anta Diop Université
BP 5005
Dakar-Fann, Senegal
Contact: Chef de Departement
Tel: 221 825 7528
Fax: 221 825 3724
E-mail: info@ucad.sn
http://www.ucad.sn/

6. REGIONAL ACADEMIC ORGANIZATIONS

6.2 The Americas

Acadia Centre for Estuarine Research
Acadia University
Campus Box 115
Wolfville, NS, B4P 2R6, Canada
Contact: Director
Tel: 1 902 585-1113
Fax: 1 902 585-1054
E-mail: amanda.tree@acadiau.ca
http://ace.acadiau.ca/science/cer/home.htm

AquaNet
c/o Ocean Sciences Centre
Memorial University of Newfoundland
St. John's, NL, A1C 5S7, Canada
Contact: Administrative Centre
Tel: 1 709 737-3245
Fax: 1 709 737-3500
E-mail: info@aquanet.ca
http://www.aquanet.mun.ca/

Association of Marine Laboratories of the Caribbean (AMLC)
Mote Marine Laboratory
1600 Ken Thompson Parkway
Sarasota, FL, 34236, USA
Contact: Executive Director
Tel: 1 941 388-4441
Fax: 1 941 388-4312
E-mail: slegore@mote.org
http://amlc.uvi.edu/

Atmospheric and Oceanic Sciences
McGill University
805 Sherbrooke Street West
Montreal, QC, H3A 2K6, Canada
Contact: Chair
Tel: 1 514 398-3764
Fax: 1 514 398-6115
E-mail: ornella@zephyr.meteo.mcgill.ca
http://www.mcgill.ca/meteo/

Bamfield Marine Station
Bamfield, BC, V0R 1B0, Canada
Contact: Director
Tel: 1 250 728-3301
Fax: 1 250 728-3452
E-mail: info@bms.bc.ca
http://www.bms.bc.ca/

Bellairs Research Institute
Holetown, St. James, Barbados
Tel: 1 246 422-2087
Fax: 1 246 422-0692
E-mail: bellairs@caribsurf.com
http://www.mcgill.ca/bellairs/

Belle W. Baruch Institute for Marine Biology and Coastal Research
University of South Carolina
607 EWS Building
Columbia, SC, 29208, USA
Contact: Director
Tel: 1 803 777-5288
Fax: 1 803 777-3935
E-mail: fletcher@sc.edu
http://inlet.geol.sc.edu/

Bermuda Biological Station for Research
17 Biological Station Lane
Ferry Reach
St. George's, GE01, Bermuda
Contact: Director
Tel: 1 441 297-1880
Fax: 1 441 297-8143
E-mail: webmaster@bbsr.edu
http://www.bbsr.edu/

Bodega Marine Laboratory
University of California at Davis
2099 Westside Road
PO Box 247
Bodega Bay, CA, 94923-0247, USA
Tel: 1 707 875-2211
Fax: 1 707 875-2009
E-mail: ucdbml@ucdavis.edu
http://www.bml.ucdavis.edu/

Canadian Coast Guard College
PO Box 4500
Sydney, NS, B1P 6L1, Canada
Tel: 1 902 567-3208
Fax: 1 902 567-3233
E-mail: registrar@cgc.ns.ca
http://www.cgc.ns.ca/

Canadian Institute for Climate Studies
University of Victoria
130 Saunders Annex
PO Box 1700 Sta CSC
Victoria, BC, V8W 2Y2, Canada
Tel: 1 250 721-6236
Fax: 1 250 721-7217
E-mail: climate@uvic.ca
http://www.cics.uvic.ca/

Canadian Institute of Fisheries Technology (CIFT)
Faculty of Engineering
Dalhousie University
PO Box 1000
1360 Barrington Street
Halifax, NS, B3J 2X4, Canada
Tel: 1 902 494-6030
Fax: 1 902 420-0219
E-mail: food.science@dal.ca
http://www.dal.ca/~cift/

Caribbean Marine Research Center
Perry Institute for Marine Science
100N US Highway 1, Suite 202
Jupiter, FL, 33477-5122, USA
Tel: 1 561 741-0192
Fax: 1 561 741-0193
E-mail: cmrc@cmrc.org
http://www.cmrc.org/

Center for Coastal and Land-Margin Research (CCALMR)
Department of Environmental and Biomolecular Systems
OGI School of Science and Engineering
Oregon Health & Science University
20000 NW Walker Road
Beaverton, OR, 97006, USA
Contact: Director
Tel: 1 503 690-1147
Fax: 1 503 690-1273
E-mail: baptista@ccalmr.ogi.edu
http://www.ccalmr.ogi.edu/

Center for Coastal Studies
Scripps Institution of Oceanography
University of California, San Diego
La Jolla, CA, 92093-0209, USA
Contact: Director
Tel: 1 858 534-4333
Fax: 1 858 534-0300
E-mail: rtg@coast.ucsd
http://www.ccs.ucsd.edu/

REGIONAL ACADEMIC ORGANIZATIONS

Center for Oceans Law and Policy
University of Virginia School of Law
580 Massie Road
Charlottesville, VA, 22903, USA
Contact: Director
Tel: 1 434 924-7441
Fax: 1 434 924-7362
E-mail: colp@virginia.edu
http://www.virginia.edu/colp/

Center for the Study of Marine Policy
University of Delaware
301 Robinson Hall
Newark, DE, 19716, USA
Contact: Director
Tel: 1 302 831-8086
Fax: 1 302 831-3668
E-mail: bcs@udel.edu
http://www.udel.edu/CMS/cmsp/

Centre for Asian Legal Studies
Faculty of Law
University of British Columbia
1822 East Mall
Vancouver, BC, V6T 1Z1, Canada
Tel: 1 604 822-3151
Fax: 1 604 822-8108
E-mail: borthwick@law.ubc.ca
http://www.law.ubc.ca/centres/index.htm

Centre for Community-based Management
St. Francis Xavier University
PO Box 5000
Antigonish, NS, B2G 2W5, Canada
Tel: 1 902 867-2433
E-mail: ccbm@stfx.ca
http://www.stfx.ca/institutes/ccbm/

Centre for Earth and Ocean Research (CEOR)
University of Victoria
Petch Building, Room 169
PO Box 3055, Stn CSC
Victoria, BC, V8W 3P6, Canada
Contact: Director
Tel: 1 250 721-8848
Fax: 1 250 472-4100
E-mail: ceor@uvic.ca
http://ceor.seos.uvic.ca/

Centre for Indigenous Peoples' Nutrition and Environment (CINE)
Macdonald Campus of McGill University
21,111 Lakeshore Road
Ste-Anne-de-Bellevue, QC, H9X 3V9, Canada
Tel: 1 514 398-7544
Fax: 1 514 398-1020
E-mail: cine@cine.mcgill.ca
http://cine.mcgill.ca/

Centre for Marine Sciences
University of the West Indies, Mona Campus
Mona, Kingston 7, Jamaica
Tel: 1 876 977-0262
Fax: 1 876 977-1033
E-mail: cms@uwimona.edu.jm
http://www.uwimona.edu.jm/cms/

Centre for Tourism Policy and Research
Simon Fraser University
8888 University Drive
Burnaby, BC, V5A 1S6, Canada
Contact: Director
Tel: 1 604 291-3074
Fax: 1 604 291-4968
E-mail: peterw@sfu.ca
http://www.sfu.ca/%7edossa/

Centro de Investigaciones Marinas
Calle 16 #114, entre 1era y 3era
Miramar Playa.
Ciudad de la Habana, Cuba
E-mail: cim@nova.uh.cu
Tel: 537 23 0617
Fax: 537 24 2087
http://www.uh.cu/centros/cim/index.htm

Charles Darwin Research Station
Puerto Ayora, Santa Cruz, Galapagos Islands, Ecuador
Contact: Director
Tel: 593 5526 147/8
E-mail: galapagosinfo@darwinfoundation.org
http://www.darwinfoundation.org/

Chesapeake Biological Laboratory
Center for Environmental Science
University of Maryland
PO Box 38
1 Williams Street
Solomons, MD, 20688, USA
Contact: Director
Tel: 1 410 326-4281
Fax: 1 410 326-7264

E-mail: tenore@cbl.umces.edu
http://www.cbl.umces.edu/

Coastal and Oceanic Geological Research Centre
(Centro de Estudos de Geologia Costeira e Oceânica—CECO)
Universidade Federal do Rio Grande do Sul
Av. Bento Gonçalves, 9500 Prédio 43125
Porto Alegre, RS, Brazil
Tel: 55 3316 6373
Fax: 55 3316 7302
E-mail: sergio.dillenberg@ufrgs.br
http://www.ufrgs.br/ceco/

Coastal Fisheries Institute
Louisiana State University
218 Wetland Resource Building
Baton Rouge, LA, 70803, USA
Tel: 1 255 578-6455
Fax: 1 255 578-6513
E-mail: rshaw@lsu.edu
http://www.cfi.lsu.edu/

Coastal Institute
Narragansett Bay Campus
University of Rhode Island
Narragansett, RI, 02882, USA
Tel: 1 401 874-6513
Fax: 1 401 874-6869
E-mail: ci@edc.uri.edu
http://www.ci.uri.edu/

Coastal Resources Center
Narragansett Bay Campus
University of Rhode Island
Narragansett, RI, 02882, USA
Tel: 1 401 874-6224
Fax: 1 401 789-4670
E-mail: communications@crc.uri.edu
http://www.crc.uri.edu/

Coastal Resources Institute
ECMAR-UNA
Universidad Nacional
Facultad de Ciencias Exactas y Naturales
Heredia, Costa Rica
Tel: 506 277 3313
Fax: 506 277 3485
Tel/Fax: 506 661 2394
E-mail: ecmar@una.ac.cr
http://www.una.ac.cr/ecmar/

Coastal Studies Institute
Old Howe Russell Building
Louisiana State University
Baton Rouge, LA, 70803, USA
Tel: 1 225 578-2395
Fax: 1 225 578-2520
E-mail: ahawk1@unix1.sncc.lsu.edu
http://www.csi.lsu.edu/

College of Ocean and Fishery Sciences
University of Washington
1492 NE Boat Street
PO Box 355350
Seattle, WA, 98195-5350, USA
Contact: Dean
Tel: 1 206 543-6605
Fax: 1 206 543-6393
E-mail: webmaster@cofs.washington.edu
http://www.cofs.washington.edu/

College of Oceanic and Atmospheric Sciences
Oregon State University
104 Ocean Administration Building
Corvallis, OR, 97331-5503, USA
Tel: 1 541 737-3504
Fax: 1 541 737-2064
E-mail: www@coas.oregonstate.edu
http://www.oce.orst.edu/

Cooperative Institute for Arctic Research (CIFAR)
University of Alaska Fairbanks
PO Box 757740
Fairbanks, AK, 99775-7740, USA
Contact: Administrator
Tel: 1 907 474-5698
Fax: 1 907 474-6722
E-mail: slynch@iarc.uaf.edu
http://www.cifar.uaf.edu/

Darling Marine Center
University of Maine
193 Clark's Cove Road
Walpole, ME, 04573, USA
Contact: Director
Tel: 1 207 563-3146
Fax: 1 207 563-3119
E-mail: darling@maine.edu
http://www.dmc.maine.edu/

Department of Earth and Ocean Sciences
University of British Columbia
6339 Stores Road
Vancouver, BC, V6T 1Z4, Canada

REGIONAL ACADEMIC ORGANIZATIONS

Contact: Department Head
Tel: 1 604 822-2449
Fax: 1 604 822-6088
E-mail: webmaster@eos.ubc.ca
http://www.eos.ubc.ca/

Department of Marine Sciences
Marine Sciences Building
University of Georgia
Athens, GA, 30602-3636, USA
Contact: Director
Tel: 1 706 542-7671
Fax: 1 706 542-5888
E-mail: aquadoc@arches.uga.edu
http://alpha.marsci.uga.edu/

Department of Oceanography
0102 OSB, West Call Street
Florida State University
Tallahassee, FL, 32306-4320, USA
Contact: Academic Coordinator
Tel: 1 850 644-6700
Fax: 1 850 644-2581
E-mail: admissions@ocean.fsu.edu
http://www.ocean.fsu.edu/

Department of Oceanography
Fundação Universidade do Rio Grande
Caixa Postal, 474
96201-900, Rio Grande, RS, Brazil
Tel: 55 532 33 6534
Fax: 55 532 33 6601
E-mail: docosta@super.furg.br
http://www.furg.br/ciencias.marinhas

Department of Oceanography
Dalhousie University
1355 Oxford Street
Halifax, NS, B3H 4J1, Canada
Tel: 1 902 494-3557
Fax: 1 902 494-3877
E-mail: oceanography@dal.ca
http://www.dal.ca/~wwwocean/index.html

Department of Oceanography
Texas A&M University
College Station, TX, 77843-3146, USA
Tel: 1 979 845-7211
Fax: 1 979 845-6331
E-mail: web@ocean.tamu.edu
http://www-ocean.tamu.edu/

Duke University Wetland Center
Nicholas School of the Environment and Earth Sciences
Box 90333
Durham, NC, 27708-0333, USA
Contact: Director
Tel: 1 919 613-8009
Fax: 1 919 613-8101
E-mail: randyn@duke.edu
http://www.env.duke.edu/wetland/

Escuela Nacional de Marina Mercante (ENAMM)
Av. Progreso 632
Chucuito-Callao, Peru
Tel: 511 4298210
Fax: 511 4298218
E-mail: informes@enamm.edu.pe
http://www.enamm.edu.pe/

Faculty of Law
University of Victoria
PO Box 2400, STN CSC
Victoria, BC, V8W 3H7, Canada
Tel: 1 250 721-8150
Fax: 1 250 721-6390
E-mail: lawrecep@uvic.ca
http://www.law.uvic.ca/

Faculty of Marine Engineering and Marine Sciences
Escuela Superior Politécnica del Litoral
Campus Gustavo Galindo Velasco
Km. 30,5 Via Perimetral
Apartado: 09-01-5863
Guayaquil, Ecuador
Tel: 593 4 2 269269
Fax: 593 4 2 854629
E-mail: httpd@goliat.espol.edu.ec
http://www.espol.edu.ec/

Faculty of Marine Sciences
Universidad Católica del Norte
Campus Guayacán
Casilla 117
Coquimbo, Chile
Tel: 56 51 209736
Fax: 56 51 209750
E-mail: faculmar@ucn.cl
http://www.ucn.cl/facultadesInstitutos/Fac_Ciencias_de_mar.asp

Faculty of Marine Sciences
Universidad de Valparaíso
Av. Borgoño s/n, Montemar
Casilla 13-D
Viña de Mar

Valparaíso, Chile
Tel: 56 32 507829
E-mail: montemar@uv.cl
http://www.uv.cl/

Fisheries Centre
University of British Columbia
NW Marine Drive Research Station
6660 NW Marine Drive, Building 022
Vancouver, BC, V6T 1Z4, Canada
Contact: Director
Tel: 1 604 822-2731
Fax: 1 604 822-8934
E-mail: office@fisheries.ubc.ca
http://www.fisheries.ubc.ca/

Five College Coastal and Marine Sciences Program
Smith College
Northampton, MA, 01063, USA
Tel: 1 413 585-3799
E-mail: marinesci@smith.edu
http://websci.smith.edu/departments/MARINE/

Florida State University Marine Laboratory
034 Montgomery Building
Tallahassee, FL, 32306-2300, USA
Tel: 1 850 644-8436
Fax: 1 850 644-2581
E-mail: buclp@mailer.fsu.edu
http://www.marinelab.fsu.edu/

Graduate College of Marine Studies
University of Delaware
111 Robinson Hall
Newark, DE, 19716-3501, USA
Contact: Office of the Dean
Tel: 1 302 831-2841
Fax: 1 302 831-4389
E-mail: dean@cms.udel.edu
http://www.ocean.udel.edu/

Graduate School of Oceanography
University of Rhode Island
South Ferry Road
URI Bay Campus Box 52
Narragansett, RI, 02882-1197, USA
Contact: Dean
Tel: 1 401 874-6222
Fax: 1 401 874-6889
E-mail: TheDean@gso.uri.edu
http://www.gso.uri.edu/

Gulf and Caribbean Fisheries Institute
c/o Florida Marine Research Institute
2796 Overseas Highway, Station 119
Marathon, FL, 33050, USA
Contact: Executive Secretary
Tel: 1 305 289-2330
Fax: 1 305 289-2334
E-mail: leroy.creswell@gcfi.org
http://www.gcfi.org/

Harbor Branch Oceanographic Institution
5600 US 1 North
Fort Pierce, FL, 34946, USA
Tel: 1 772 465-2400
Fax: 1 772 465-2446
E-mail: education@hboi.edu
http://www.hboi.edu/

Hopkins Marine Station of Stanford University
Oceanview Boulevard
Pacific Grove, CA, 93950-3094, USA
Tel: 1 831 655-6200
Fax: 1 831 375-0793
E-mail: rmation@marine.stanford.edu
http://www-marine.stanford.edu/

Ibero-American Institute of Maritime Law
c/o Asociacion Chilena de Derecho Maritimo
Prat 827, Piso 12
Casilla 75
Valparaiso, Chile
Tel: 56 32 2525 35
Fax: 56 32 2526 22
E-mail: acgvalparaiso@entelchile.net

Inland Seas Education Association (ISEA)
PO Box 218
Suttons Bay, MI, 49682, USA
Contact: Executive Director
Tel: 1 231 271-3077
Fax: 1 231 271-3088
E-mail: info@greatlakeseducation.org
http://www.schoolship.org/

Institut des sciences de la mer de Rimouski (ISMER)
Université du Québec à Rimouski
300, allée des Ursulines
Rimouski, QC, G5L 3A1, Canada
Tel: 1 418 724-1650
Fax: 1 418 724-1842

E-mail: ismer@uqar.qc.ca
http://www.pqm.net/ismer/index.html

Institut maritime du Québec
53, rue Saint-Germain Ouest
Rimouski, QC, G5L 4B4, Canada
Tel: 1 418 724-2822
Fax: 1 418 724-0606
E-mail: institut@imq.qc.ca
http://www.imq.qc.ca/

Institute of Marine Sciences
University of North Carolina at Chapel Hill
3431 Arendell Street
Morehead City, NC, 28557, USA
Contact: Director
Tel: 1 252 726-6841
Fax: 1 252 726-2426
E-mail: john_wells@unc.edu
http://www.marine.unc.edu/organization/IMS.html

Institute of Nautical Archaeology
PO Drawer HG
College Station, TX, 77841-5137, USA
Tel: 1 979 845-6694
Fax: 1 979 847-9260
E-mail: ina@tamu.edu
http://ina.tamu.edu/

Interdisciplinary Studies in Aquatic Resources (ISAR)
St. Francis Xavier University
PO Box 5000
Nicholson Hall
Antigonish, NS, B2G 2W5, Canada
Contact: Program Officer
Tel: 1 902 867-3933
Fax: 1 902 867-2448
E-mail: lpatters@stfx.ca
http://iago.stfx.ca/people/aqua_res/

International Institute of Fisheries Economics and Trade (IIFET)
Department of Agricultural and Resource Economics
Oregon State University
Corvallis, OR, 97331-3601, USA
Contact: Executive Director
Tel: 1 503 737-1416
Fax: 1 503 737-2563
E-mail: Ann.L.Shriver@oregonstate.edu
http://www.orst.edu/Dept/IIFET/

REGIONAL ACADEMIC ORGANIZATIONS

Joint Oceanographic Institutions for Deep Earth Sampling (JOIDES)
University of Miami
RSMAS
600 Rickenbacker Causeway
Miami, FL, 33149, USA
Contact: JOIDES Office
Tel: 1 305 361-4668
Fax: 1 305 361-4632
E-mail: joides@rsmas.miami.edu
http://joides.rsmas.miami.edu/

Marine Affairs Programme
Dalhousie University
1376 LeMarchant Street
Halifax, NS, B3H 3P9, Canada
Contact: Coordinator
Tel: 1 902 494-3555
Fax: 1 902 494-1001
E-mail: marine.affairs@dal.ca
http://www.dal.ca/mmm/

Maine Maritime Academy
Castine, ME, 04420-5000, USA
Tel: 1 207 326-2206
E-mail: admissions@mma.edu
http://www.mainemaritime.edu/

Marine and Environmental Law Programme
Dalhousie Law School
6061 University Avenue
Halifax, NS, B3H 4H9, Canada
Contact: Director
Tel: 1 902 494-3495
Fax: 1 902 494-1316
E-mail: melp@dal.ca
http://www.dal.ca/~wwwlaw/melp/

Marine and Environmental Programs
Woodward Hall
University of Rhode Island
Kingston, RI, 02881, USA
Contact: Office of Marine Programs
Tel: 1 401 874-2957
Fax: 1 401 874-4017
E-mail: omp@gso.uri.edu
http://omp.gso.uri.edu/urime/

Marine Ecology Station
Port Sydney Marina
9835 Seaport Place
Sydney, BC, V8L 4X3, Canada
Tel: 1 250 655-1555

Fax: 1 250 655-1573
E-mail: info@mareco.org
http://www.mareco.org/

Marine Institute
Fisheries and Marine Institute of Memorial University of Newfoundland
PO Box 4920
St. John's, NL, A1C 5R3, Canada
Tel: 1 709 778-0200
Fax: 1 709 778-0346
E-mail: coordinator_advanced_programs@mi.mun.ca
http://www.mi.mun.ca/

Marine Invasion Research Laboratory
Smithsonian Environmental Research Center
PO Box 28
Edgewater, MD, 21037-0028, USA
Tel: 1 443 482-2200
Fax: 1 443 482-2380
E-mail: lylesk@si.edu
http://invasions.si.edu/

Marine Law Institute
University of Maine
School of Law
246 Deering Avenue
Portland, ME, 04102, USA
Contact: Director
Tel: 1 207 780-4474
Fax: 1 207 780-4239
E-mail: jduff@usm.maine.edu
http://www.law.usm.maine.edu/mli/

Marine Policy Center
Woods Hole Oceanographic Institution
Crowell House
Woods Hole, MA, 02543-1138, USA
Contact: Director
Tel: 1 508 289-2449
Fax: 1 508 457-2184
E-mail: asolow@whoi.edu
http://www.whoi.edu/mpcweb/

Marine Resource Management Program
College of Oceanic and Atmospheric Sciences
Oregon State University
104 Ocean Administration Building
Corvallis, OR, 97331-5503, USA
Contact: Coordinator
Tel: 1 541 737-1339
Fax: 1 541 737-2064
E-mail: good@coas.oregonstate.edu
http://www.oce.orst.edu/mrm/

Marine Science Center
Northeastern University
430 Nahant Road
Nahant, MA, 01908, USA
Contact: Director
Tel: 1 781 581-7370
Fax: 1 781 581-6076
E-mail: e.maney@neu.edu
http://www.marinescience.neu.edu/

Marine Science Institute
Department of Marine Science
University of Texas at Austin
750 Channel View Drive
Port Aransas, TX, 78373-5015, USA
Contact: Director
Tel: 1 361 749-6711
Fax: 1 361 749-6777
E-mail: gardner@utmsi.utexas.edu
http://www.utmsi.utexas.edu/

Marine Sciences Program
University of North Carolina
12-7 Venable Hall, CB# 3300
Chapel Hill, NC, 27599-3300, USA
Contact: Director
Tel: 1 919 962-1252
Fax: 1 919 962-1254
E-mail: cisco_werner@unc.edu
http://www.marine.unc.edu/organization/MASC.html

Marine Sciences Research Center
Stony Brook University
Endeavour Hall, Room 145
Stony Brook, NY, 11794-5000, USA
Tel: 1 631 632-8700
Fax: 1 631 632-8915
E-mail: jcosgrove@notes.cc.sunysb.edu
http://www.msrc.sunysb.edu/

Naval Postgraduate School
1 University Circle
Monterey, CA, 93943-5001, USA
Tel: 1 831 656-2441/2
Fax: 1 831 656-2337
http://www.nps.navy.mil/

Naval War College
686 Cushing Avenue
Newport, RI, 02841, USA
Tel: 1 401 841-3089

REGIONAL ACADEMIC ORGANIZATIONS

E-mail: qdeck@nwc.navy.mil
http://www.nwc.navy.mil/

Nicholas School of the Environment and Earth Sciences
Duke University
PO Box 90328
Durham, NC, 27708, USA
Contact: Dean
Tel: 1 919 613-8000
Fax: 1 919 684-8741
E-mail: schlesin@duke.env
http://www.env.duke.edu/

Ocean and Coastal Law Center
School of Law
University of Oregon
1221 University of Oregon
Eugene, OR, 97403-1221, USA
Contact: Director
Tel: 1 541 346-3845
Fax: 1 541 346-1564
E-mail: dbass@law.uoregon.edu
http://oceanlaw.uoregon.edu/

Ocean and Coastal Law Program
University of Miami School of Law
PO Box 248087
Coral Gables, FL, 33124-8087, USA
Contact: Director, International and Foreign Law Programs
Tel: 1 305 284-5402
Fax: 1 305 284-5497
E-mail: intl-llm@law.miami.edu
http://www.law.miami.edu/ifp/

Ocean Engineering Program
Department of Civil Engineering
3136 Texas A&M University
College Station, TX, 77843-3136, USA
Tel: 1 979 845-4515
Fax: 1 979 862-8162
E-mail: lori@civil.tamu.edu
http://edge.tamu.edu/

Ocean Engineering Research Centre (OERC)
Faculty of Engineering and Applied Science
Memorial University of Newfoundland
St. John's, NL, A1B 3X5, Canada
Contact: Director
Tel: 1 709 737-8805
Fax: 1 709 737-2116
E-mail: cdaley@engr.mun.ca
http://www.engr.mun.ca/OERC/

Ocean Sciences Centre
Memorial University of Newfoundland
St. John's, NL, A1C 5S7 Canada
Contact: Director
Tel: 1 709 737-3708
Fax: 1 709 737-3220
E-mail: wsparkes@mun.ca
http://www.osc.mun.ca/index.html

Office of Marine Programs
University of Rhode Island, North Bay Campus
Narragansett, RI, 02882-1197, USA
Tel: 1 401 874-6211
Fax: 1 401 874-6486
E-mail: omp@gso.uri.edu
http://omp.gso.uri.edu/

Rosenstiel School of Marine and Atmospheric Science (RSMAS)
University of Miami
4600 Rickenbacker Causeway
Miami, FL, 33149-1098, USA
Contact: Dean
Tel: 1 305 361-4000
Fax: 1 305 361-4711
E-mail: dean@rsmas.miami.edu
http://www.rsmas.miami.edu/

School for Field Studies
10 Federal Street
Salem, MA, 01970-3853, USA
Contact: President
Tel: 1 978 741-3544
Fax: 1 978 741-3551
E-mail: admissions@fieldstudies.org
http://www.fieldstudies.org/

School of Aquatic and Fisheries Sciences
University of Washington
Box 355020
Seattle, WA, 98195-5020, USA
Tel: 1 206 543-4270
Fax: 1 206 685-7471
E-mail: frontdesk@fish.washington.edu
http://www.fish.washington.edu/

School of Fisheries and Ocean Sciences
University of Alaska Fairbanks
245 O'Neill Building
Fairbanks, AK, 99775-7220, USA
Tel: 1 907 474-7824

REGIONAL ACADEMIC ORGANIZATIONS

Fax: 1 907 474-7204
E-mail: fysfos@uaf.edu
http://www.sfos.uaf.edu/

School of Marine Affairs
University of Washington
3707 Brooklyn Avenue, NE
Seattle, WA, 98105-6715, USA
Tel: 1 206 543-0106
Fax: 1 206 543-1417
E-mail: uwsma@u.washington.edu
http://www.sma.washington.edu/

School of Marine Sciences
University of Maine
214 Libby Hall
Orono, ME, 04469-5741, USA
Contact: Director
Tel: 1 207 581-4367
E-mail: davidt@maine.edu
http://www.marine.maine.edu/

School of Oceanography
University of Washington
Box 357940
Seattle, WA, 98195-7940, USA
Contact: Director
Tel: 1 206 543-5060
E-mail: frost@ocean.washington.edu
http://oceanweb.ocean.washington.edu/ocean_web/

School of the Coast and Environment
Louisiana State University
153 Howe-Russell Geosciences
Baton Rouge, LA, 70803, USA
Tel: 1 225 578-6308
Fax: 1 225 578-6307
E-mail: ocean@lsu.edu
http://ww.sc&e.lsu.edu/

Scotiabank Marine Geology Research Laboratory
Department of Geology
University of Toronto
22 Russell Street
Toronto, ON, M5S 3B1, Canada
Tel: 1 416 978-5424
Fax: 1 416 978-3938
E-mail: scottsd@geology.utoronto.ca
http://www.geology.utoronto.ca/marinelab/

Scripps Institution of Oceanography
University of California, San Diego
8602 La Jolla Shores Drive
La Jolla, CA, 92037, USA
Contact: Director
Tel: 1 619 534-2826
Fax: 1 619 453-0167
E-mail: siodir@sio.ucsd.edu
http://sio.ucsd.edu/

Sea Education Association
PO Box 6
Woods Hole, MA, 02543, USA
Contact: President
Tel: 1 508 540-3954
Fax: 1 508 457-4673
E-mail: admission@sea.edu
http://www.sea.edu/

Sea Grant Law Center
University of Mississippi
Kinard Hall, Wing E, Room 262
PO Box 1848
University, MS, 38677-1848, USA
Tel: 1 662 915-7775
Fax: 1 662 915-5267
E-mail: sealaw@olemiss.edu
http://www.olemiss.edu/orgs/SGLC/

Shoals Marine Laboratory
Cornell University
G-14 Stimson Hall
Ithaca, NY, 14853-3717, USA
Contact: Director
Tel: 1 607 255-3717
Fax: 1 607 255-0742
E-mail: shoals-lab@cornell.edu
http://www.sml.cornell.edu/

Smithsonian Tropical Research Institute
Roosevelt Avenue, Ancon
PO Box 2072
Balboa, Panama
Contact: Director
Tel: 507 212 8000
Fax: 507 232 6197
E-mail: webmaster@stri.org
http://www.stri.org/

The Oceanic Institute
41-202 Kalanianaole Highway
Waimanalo, HI, 96795, USA
Tel: 1 808 259-3145
Fax: 1 808 259-5971
E-mail: jcrawford@oceanicinstitute.org
http://www.oceanicinstitute.org/

REGIONAL ACADEMIC ORGANIZATIONS

The Reef Check Foundation
1362 Hershey Hall, 149607
University of California at Los Angeles
Los Angeles, CA, 90095-1496, USA
Tel: 1 310 794-4985
Fax: 1 310 825-0758
E-mail: rcheck@ucla.edu
http://www.reefcheck.org/

Tulane Law School
Weinmann Hall
6329 Freret Street
New Orleans, LA, 70118-6231, USA
Tel: 1 504 865-5939
Fax: 1 504 865-6710
E-mail: admissions@law.tulane.edu
http://www.law.tulane.edu/

Urban Harbors Institute
University of Massachusetts
100 Morrissey Boulevard
Boston, MA, 02125, USA
Tel: 1 617 287-5570
Fax: 1 617 287-5575
E-mail: urban.harbors@umb.edu
http://www.uhi.umb.edu/

US Naval Institute (USNI)
291 Wood Road
Annapolis, MD, 21402, USA
Contact: CEO
Tel: 1 410 268-6110
Fax: 1 410 269-7940
E-mail: jbeitler@usni.org
http://www.usni.org/

Virginia Institute of Marine Science
College of William and Mary
PO Box 1346
Gloucester Point, VA, 23062, USA
Contact: Director
Tel: 1 804 684-7000
Fax: 1 804 684-7097
E-mail: wright@vims.org
http://www.vims.edu/

Whale Research Lab
Department of Geography
University of Victoria
Box 3050, Stn CSC
Victoria, BC, V8W 3P5, Canada
Tel: 1 604 721-7327
Fax: 1 604 721-6216
E-mail: whalelab@office.geog.uvic.ca
http://office.geog.uvic.ca/dept/whale/wrlmp.html

Woods Hole Oceanographic Institution
Co-op Building, MS #16
Woods Hole, MA, 02543-1050, USA
Contact: Information Office
Tel: 1 508 289-2252
Fax: 1 508 457-2034
E-mail: information@whoi.edu
http://www.whoi.edu/

6. REGIONAL ACADEMIC ORGANIZATIONS

6.3 Asia

Akademi Laut Malaysia (ALAM)
(Malaysian Maritime Academy)
Window Delivery 2051, Masjid Tanah
78300 Melaka, Malaysia
Tel: 60 6 387 6201
Fax: 60 6 387 6700
E-mail: mma@alam.edu.my
http://www.alam.edu.my/

Aquaculture and Aquatic Resources Management Program (AARM)
School of Environment, Resources and Development (SERD)
Asian Institute of Technology
PO Box 4, Klong Luang
Pathumthani 12120, Thailand
Tel: 662 524 5456
Fax: 662 524 6200
E-mail: amara@ait.ac.th
http://www.serd.ait.ac.th/field02.htm

Aquaculture Department
Hue University of Agriculture and Forestry
24 Phung Hung
Hue, Viet Nam
Contact: Dean, Faculty of Natural Sciences
Tel: 84 54 525439
Fax: 84 54 524923
E-mail: khvndhnl@dng.vnn.vn
http://www.ire.ubc.ca/hong_ha/university/university.htm

Aquatic Resources Research Institute
9th floor, Institute Building No.3
Chulalongkorn University
Phayathai Road, Pathumwan,

Bangkok 10330, Thailand
Tel: 662 218 81603
Fax: 662 254 4259
E-mail: arri@chula.ac.th
http://www.arri.chula.ac.th/

Asia-Pacific Centre for Environmental Law
Faculty of Law
National University of Singapore
13 Law Link
Singapore 117590
Tel: 65 874 6246
Fax: 65 872 1937
E-mail: lawapcel@nus.edu.sg
http://law.nus.edu.sg/apcel/

Asian Institute of Tourism
Commonwealth Avenue
Diliman, Quezon City, The Philippines
Contact: Office of Academic Affairs
Tel: 632 926 9077
E-mail: upait@compass.com.ph
http://www.upd.edu.ph/

Centre for Coastal Pollution and Conservation
City University of Hong Kong
83 Tat Chee Avenue, Kowloon Tong
Kowloon, Hong Kong
Tel: 852 2788 7404
Fax: 852 2788 7406
E-mail: bhrolin@cityu.edu.hk
http://www.cityu.edu.hk/bch/rcp/intro/default.htm

Centre for Transportation Research
Faculty of Engineering
National University of Singapore
10 Kent Ridge Crescent
Singapore 119260
Tel: 65 777 0170
Fax: 65 777 0994
E-mail: cvefwatf@nus.edu.sg
http://www.eng.nus.edu.sg/civil/C_CTR/index.html

Centre for Transportation Studies
c/o School of Civil and Environmental Engineering
Nanyang Technical University
Block N1#1a-29
Singapore 639798
Tel: 65 6790 5328
Fax: 65 6792 3886
E-mail: wwwcts@ntu.edu.sg
http://www.ntu.edu.sg/home/cshlam/cts/centre.html

Centre of Excellence in Marine Biology
University of Karachi
Karachi 75270, Pakistan
Contact: Director
Tel: 92 43 230 2256
Fax: 92 21 924 3677
E-mail: huss@cyber.net.pk
http://www.ku.edu.pk/research/cemb/intro.html

Coastal Resources Institute (CORIN)
Prince of Songkhla University
Hat Yai
Songkhla 90112, Thailand
Tel: 66 74 212800
Fax: 66 74 212782
E-mail: corin@ratree.psu.ac.th
http://www.psu.ac.th/corin

Coastal Resources Management
Department of Biology
Silliman University
Dumaguete City, 6200, The Philippines
Tel: 63 35 422 6002 ext 314
Fax: 63 35 422 4776
E-mail: biology@su.edu.ph
http://www.su.edu.ph/cas/biology/biology.html

College of Fisheries
Central Luzon State University
Nueva Ecija 3120, The Philippines
Tel/Fax: 63 44 456 0107
E-mail: clsu@mozcom.com
http://mozcom.com/~clsu/

College of Fisheries and Ocean Sciences
University of the Philippines in the Visayas
Miag-ao, Iloilo, The Philippines
Contact: Dean
Tel: 632 033 338 1534
E-mail: upv_oc@up.edu.ph
http://www.upv.edu.ph/academicinfo/cfos/cfos.htm

College of Fisheries Sciences
Pukong National University
599-1 Daeyundong, Namgu
Pusan 608-737, Republic of Korea
Contact: Dean
Tel: 82 51 620 6134

REGIONAL ACADEMIC ORGANIZATIONS

Fax: 82 51 625 1808
E-mail: dsbyun@pknu.ac.kr
http://www.pknu.ac.kr/eng/depart/coll.htm

College of Marine Aquaculture and Fisheries
Can Tho University, Campus II
3/2 Street
Can Tho City, Vietnam
Tel: 84 71 838237
E-mail: webmaster@ctu.edu.vn
http://www.ctu.edu.vn/index_e.htm

College of Ocean Science and Technology
Kunsan National University
san 68, Miryong-dong
Kunsan Jeollabuk-do 573-701 Korea
Tel: 63 469 4114
E-mail: webmaster@ks.kunsan.ac.kr
http://www.kunsan.ac.kr/english/index.htm

Dalian Maritime University
1 Linghai Road
Dalian 116026, Liaoning Province,
People's Republic of China
Tel: 86 41 1472 7874
Fax: 86 41 1472 7395
E-mail: faodmu@dlmu.edu.cn
http://www.dlmu.edu.cn/

Department of Marine Science
Science Faculty
Chulalongkorn University
Bangkok 10330, Thailand
Contact: President
Tel: 662 218 5394
Fax: 662 255 0780
E-mail: marine@chula.com
http://www.chula.ac.th/

Faculty of Fisheries
Bangladesh Agricultural University
Mymensingh 2202, Bangladesh
Tel: 880 91 52236
Fax: 880 91 55810
E-mail: ffbau@mymensingh.net
http://agri-varsity.tripod.com/fish/fisfac.html

Faculty of Fisheries
Kasetsart University
Chatuchak, Bangkok 10900, Thailand
Tel: 66 2 5791202
Fax: 66 2 9428364
http://www.fish.ku.ac.th/

Faculty of Marine Sciences
Cochin University of Science and Technology
Aathira Justice Lane
Janatha Road
Kochi 682 019, India
Contact: Dean
Tel: 91 484 351957
Fax: 91 484 577595
E-mail: damu@cusat.ac.in
http://www.cusat.ac.in/

Faculty of Marine Sciences and Fisheries
Universitas Hasanuddin
Jalan Perintis Kemerdekaan km 10
Kampus Tamalanrea
Makassar, Indonesia
Tel: 62 411 584002
Fax: 62 411 585188
E-mail: cio@unhas.ac.id
http://www.unhas.ac.id/

Faculty of Ocean Technology
Sepuluh Nopember Institute of Technology
Jl. Arief Rahman Hakim
Kampus ITS Sukolilo
Surabaya 60111, Indonesia
Tel. 62 31 5927939
Fax. 62 31 5923411
E-mail: pr_4_its@its.ac.id
http://www.its.ac.id/

Far East Oceanic Fracture Society
c/o Department of Mechanical Engineering
Pohang University of Science & Technology
San31 Hyoja-dong
Nam-gu, Pohang, 790-784, Korea
Tel: 82 54 279 2163
Fax: 82 54 279 2845
E-mail: feofs@postech.ac.kr

Fisheries University
2 Nguyen Dinh Chieu
Nha Trang City, Khanh
Hoa Province, Vietnam
Tel: 84 58 831145
Fax: 84 58 831147
E-mail: dhtsnt@dng.vnn.vn

Institut Kelautan Malaysia (IKMAL)
(Malaysian Maritime Institute)

47A, Lorong Cungah
42000 Port Klang
Selangor Darul Ehsan, Malaysia
Tel: 60 3 3166 2472
Fax: 60 3 3166 2870
E-mail: president@ikmal.org
http://www.ikmal.org/

Institute of International Maritime Affairs
Korea Maritime University
1 Dongsam-dong
Yeongdo-ku Pusan 606-791, Korea
Tel: 82 051 410 4089
Fax: 82 051 404 3985
E-mail: imirc@hanara.kmaritime.ac.kr
http://iima.hhu.ac.kr/

Institute of Marine Sciences
University of Chittagong
University Post Office
Chittagong 4331, Bangladesh
Contact: Director
Tel: 88 031 71034
Fax: 88 031 610442
E-mail: nuruddin@abnetbd.com
http://www.ctgu.edu/

Institute of Marine Science
University of Karachi
Karachi 75270, Pakistan
Contact: Acting Director
Tel: 92 43131 2378
E-mail: mfatima@ims.ku.edu.pk
http://www.ku.edu.pk/research/marinesc.html

Institute of Sea Culture
Pukong National University
599-1 Daeyundong, Namgu
Pusan 608-737, Republic of Korea
Tel: 82 51 620 6410
Fax: 82 51 622 9248
http://www.pknu.ac.kr/

Integrated Tropical Coastal Zone Management (ITCZM)
Asian Institute of Technology (AIT)
PO Box 4, Klong Luang
Pathumthani 12120, Thailand
Tel: 662 524 5488
Fax: 662 524 5442
E-mail: itczm@ait.ac.th
http://www.itczm.ait.ac.th/

International Maritime Education and Research Center (IMERC)
Faculty of Maritime Sciences
Kobe University
Academic Exchange Center, 6th floor
5-1-1, Fukae-minami, Higashi-nada
Kobe 658-0022, Japan
Contact: President
Tel: 81 78 431 6200
Fax: 81 78 431 6355
E-mail: webmaster@maritime.kobe-u.ac.jp
http://maritime.kobe-u.ac.jp/

Japan Institute of Navigation (JIN)
c/o Tokyo University of Mercantile Marine
2-1-6 Etchujima, Koto-ku
Tokyo, 135-8533, Japan
Fax: 81 3 36303093
E-mail: navigation@nifty.com
http://homepage2.nifty.com/navigation/english.html

Korea Maritime University
1 Dongsam-dong Yengdo-Gu
Busan 606791, Korea
E-mail: webmaster@hhu.ac.kr
http://www.kmaritime.ac.kr/

Law of the Sea Program
Institute of International Legal Studies
3/F Bocobo Hall
U.P. Law Center
University of the Philippines
Diliman, Quezon City 1100, The Philippines
Contact: Dean
Tel: 632 920 53 01
Fax: 632 927 71 80
E-mail: iils.claw@up.edu.ph
http://www.upd.edu.ph/~iils/

Marine Science Institute
College of Science
University of the Philippines, Diliman
1101 Quezon City, The Philippines
Tel: 632 922 3962
E-mail: admin@upmsi.ph
http://www.msi.upd.edu.ph/

Mokpo National Maritime University
571-2 Chukyo-dong
Mokpo, Jeonnam, 530-729, Korea
Tel: 82 61 240 7114
Fax: 82 61 242 5176

REGIONAL ACADEMIC ORGANIZATIONS

E-mail: ryujb@mmu.ac.kr
http://www.mmu.ac.kr/

National Fisheries University
2-7-1 Nagata-Honmachi
Shimonoseki 759-6595, Japan
Tel: 81 832 86 5111
E-mail: zenpan@fish-u.ac.jp
http://www.fish-u.ac.jp/e-index.html

National Institute of Ocean Technology
Velacherry-Tambaram main road
Narayanapuram
Chennai, Tamil Nadu, 601 302, India
Contact: Director
Tel: 91 44 2460275
Fax: 91 44 2460645
E-mail: mravi@niot.res.in
http://www.niot.ernet.in/

National Taiwan Ocean University
2 Pei-Ning Road
Keelung 20224, Taiwan, ROC
Tel: 886 2 2462 2192
Fax: 886 2 2462 0724
E-mail: po@mail.ntou.edu.tw
http://www.ntou.edu.tw/

Ocean Research Institute
University of Tokyo
1-15-1 Minamidai, Nakano-ku
Tokyo 164-8639, Japan
Contact: Director
Tel: 81 3 5351 6342
Fax: 81 3 5351 6836
E-mail: koike@ori.u-tokyo.ac.jp
http://www.ori.u-tokyo.ac.jp/

Ocean University of China
5 Yushan Road
Qingdao 266003, People's Republic of China
Tel: 86 53 2203 2173
Fax: 86 53 2203 2799
E-mail: admi@mail.ouqd.edu.cn
http://www.ouqd.edu.cn/

School of Environmental Science and Management
University of the Philippines Los Baños College
Laguna 4031, The Philippines
E-mail: dkv@mudspring.uplb.edu.ph
http://www.uplb.edu.ph/academics/schools/sesam/index.htm

School of Law
Soochow University
#56 Sec 1, Kuei-Yant Street
100 Taipei, Taiwan, ROC
Tel: 886 2 2311-1531 ext. 2521
Fax: 886 2 2375-1067
E-mail: law@mail.scu.edu.tw
http://www.scu.edu.tw/ENGLISH/law/

Shanghai Fisheries University
334 Jungong Road
Shanghai 200090, People's Republic of China
E-mail: master@shfu.edu.cn
http://www.shfu.edu.cn/

Shanghai Maritime University
1550 Pu Dong Da Dao
Shanghai 200134, People's Republic of China
Tel: 86 21 5885 5200
Fax: 86 21 5885 3909
http://www.shmtu.edu.cn/

South China Sea Institute of Oceanology
Chinese Academy of Sciences
164 West Xingang Road
Guangzhou 510301, People's Republic of China
Tel: 86 20 8902 3199
Fax: 86 20 8445 1672
E-mail: scsio@ns.scsio.ac.cn
http://www.scsio.ac.cn/

Southeast Asian Programme on Ocean Law, Policy and Management (SEAPOL)
Sukhothai Thammathirat Open University
Academic Building 2, 3rd Floor, Room 2320
Pakkred, Nonthabur 11120, Thailand
Contact: Executive Director
Tel: 662 503 3858
Fax: 662 503 3608
E-mail: seapol@seapol.net
http://www.seapol.org/

Tokyo University of Fisheries
5-7, Konan 4
Minato-ku
Tokyo 108-8477, Japan
Tel: 81 3 5463 0400
Fax: 81 3 5463 0359
E-mail: www-master@tokyo-u-fish.ac.jp
http://www.tokyo-u-fish.ac.jp/

REGIONAL ACADEMIC ORGANIZATIONS

Transportation Institute (Merchant Marine)
6th floor, Prajadhipok-Rambhaibarni Building
Chulalongkorn University
Phayathai Road
Bangkok 10330, Thailand
Tel: 662 218 7450
Fax: 662 214 2417
E-mail: tri@chula.com
http://www.tri.chula.ac.th/

Tropical Marine Science Institute (TMSI)
National University of Singapore
14 Kent Ridge Road
Singapore 119223
Contact: Director
Tel: 65 774 9656
Fax: 65 774 9654
E-mail: tmsdir@nus.edu.sg
http://www.tmsi.nus.edu.sg/

Viet Nam Maritime University
484 Lach Tray Street
Haiphong, Vietnam
Tel: 84 31 829 589
Fax: 84 31 735 465
E-mail: vicmac@hn.vnn.vn
http://vimaru.vnn.vn/

6. REGIONAL ACADEMIC ORGANIZATIONS

6.4 Europe

AKVAFORSK—The Institute of Aquaculture Research
PO Box 5010
N-1432 As, Norway
Tel: 47 64 94 95 00
Fax: 47 64 94 95 02
E-mail: akvaforsk@akvaforsk.nlh.no
http://www.akvaforsk.no/english/index.html

Archipelago Research Institute
University of Turku
Luonnontieteidentalo II
FIN-20014 Turku, Finland
Tel: 358 2 333 5933
Fax: 358 2 333 6592
E-mail: paula.rasanen@utu.fi
http://www.utu.fi/erill/saarmeri/en/

British Polarological Research Society
6 Beechvale
Hillview Road
Woking, Surrey, GU22 7NS, United Kingdom
Contact: President

Cambridge Coastal Research Unit (CCRU)
Department of Geography
University of Cambridge
Downing Place
Cambridge, CB2 3EN, United Kingdom
Tel: 44 1223 339775
Fax: 44 1223 355674
E-mail: CCRU@geog.cam.ac.uk
http://ccru.geog.cam.ac.uk/

Center for Coastal and Marine Environmental Studies
(Centro de Investigação dos Ambientes Costeiros e Marinhos—CIACOMAR)
Universidade do Algarve
Avenida das Forças Armadas
8700 Olhão, Portugal
Tel: 351 289 707 087
Fax: 351 289 706 972
E-mail: webmaster.ciacomar@ualg.pt
http://www.ualg.pt/ciacomar/

Center for Marine and Environmental Research
(Centro de Investigação Marinha e Ambiental—CIMA)
Faculdade de Ciências do Mar e do Ambiente
Universidade do Algarve
Campus das Gambelas
8000-810 Faro, Portugal
Tel: 351 289 800 900
Fax: 351 289 818 353
E-mail: webmaster.cima@ualg.pt
http://www.ualg.pt/cima/

Center for Maritime Research (MARE)
Plantage Muidergracht 4
NL-1018 TV, Amsterdam, The Netherlands
Tel: 31 20 527 0624
Fax: 31 20 622 9430
E-mail: info@marecentre.nl
http://www.marecentre.nl/

Centre de Formation et de Recherche sur l'Environnement Marin (CEFREM)

CNRS-UMR 5110
Université de Perpignan
52 avenue de Paul Alduy
F-66860 Perpignan Cedex, France
Contact: Director
Tel: 33 4 6866 2090
Fax: 33 4 6866 2096
E-mail: cefrem@univ-perp.fr
http://www.univ-perp.fr/see/rch/lsgm/index.htm

Centre for Development and the Environment
University of Oslo
Box 1116 Blindern
N-0317 Oslo, Norway
Tel: 47 22 85 89 00
Fax: 47 22 85 89 20
E-mail: info@sum.uio.no
http://www.sum.uio.no/

Centre for Energy, Petroleum and Mineral Law and Policy (CEPMLP)
University of Dundee
Dundee, Scotland, DD1 4HN, United Kingdom
Contact: Director
Tel: 44 1382 344300
Fax: 44 1382 322578
E-mail: cepmlp@dundee.ac.uk
http://www.dundee.ac.uk/cepmlp/

Centre for Fisheries, Aquaculture Management, and Economics
Faculty of Social Sciences
University of Southern Denmark
Campusvej 55
DK-5230 Odense M, Denmark
Tel: 45 65 50 10 00
Fax: 45 65 93 56 92
E-mail: fame@sam.sdu.dk
http://www.sam.sdu.dk/fame/

Centre for Fisheries Economics
Institute for Research in Economics and Business Administration (SNF)
Norwegian School of Economics and Business Administration
Breiviksveinen 40
N-5045 Bergen, Norway
Contact: Research Director
Tel: 47 5595 9260
Fax: 47 5595 9543
E-mail: rognvaldur.hannesson@nhh.no
http://www.snf.no/

Centre for International Economics and Shipping
(Senter for Internasjonal Økonomi og Skipsfart)
Institute for Research in Economics and Business Administration (SNF)
Norwegian School of Economics and Business Administration
Breiviksveinen 40
N-5045 Bergen, Norway
Contact: Research Director
Tel: 47 55 95 95 00
Fax: 47 55 95 93 50
E-mail: guttorn.schjelderup@nhh.no
http://www.snf.no/

Centre for Marine and Climate Research
(Zentrum für Meeres-und-Klimaforschung—ZMK)
University of Hamburg
Bundesstrasse 55
D-20146 Hamburg, Germany
Tel: 49 40 428 38 4523
Fax: 49 40 428 38 5235
E-mail: walter.lenz@dkrz.de
http://www.uni-hamburg.de/wiss/se/zmk/

Centre for Marine Environmental Sciences
(Zentrum für Marine Umweltwissenschaften—MARUM)
Der Universität Bremen
Klagenfurter Strasse
D-28359 Bremen, Germany
Tel: 49 421 218 3389
Fax: 49 421 218 3116
E-mail: gwefer@marum.de
http://www.marum.de/

Centre for Maritime and Oceanic Law
(Centre de droit maritime et océanique—CDMO)
University of Nantes
Faculty of Law
Chemin de la Censive du Tertre
BP 81307
F-44313 Nantes, Cedex 3, France
Contact: Director
Tel: 33 2 4014 1570
Fax: 33 2 4014 1500

REGIONAL ACADEMIC ORGANIZATIONS

E-mail: jean-pierre.beurier@droit.univ-nantes.fr
http://www.univ-nantes.fr/

Centre for Maritime Studies
(Merenkulkualan Koulut—MKK)
University of Turku
WTC-Building, Veistämönaukio 1-3
FIN-20100 Turku, Finland
Contact: Director
Tel: 358 2 281 3300
Fax: 358 2 281 3311
E-mail: paivi.soderholm@utu.fi
http://mkk.utu.fi/

Centre for Ships and Ocean Structures
Norwegian University of Science and Technology
(Nordisk Teknisk-Naturvitenskapelige Universitet)
Marine Technology Centre
Otto Nielsens vei 10
N-7491 Trondheim, Norway
Contact: Director
Tel: 47 73 59 55 35
Fax: 47 73 59 55 28
E-mail: coe@marin.ntnu.or
http://www.cesos.ntnu.no/

Centre for the Economics and Management of Aquatic Resources (CEMARE)
Department of Economics
University of Portsmouth
Milton Campus
Locksway Road
Portsmouth, PO4 8JF, United Kingdom
Contact: Director
Tel: 44 23 9284 4082
Fax: 44 23 9284 4037
E-mail: cemare.library@port.ac.uk
http://www.pbs.port.ac.uk/econ/cemare/

Centre for Tropical Marine Ecology
(Zentrum für Marine Troppenökologie—ZMT)
University of Bremen
Fahrenheitstrasse 6
D-28359 Bremen, Germany
Contact: Director
Tel: 49 421 23800 21
Fax: 49 421 23800 30
E-mail: contact@zmt-bremen.de
http://www.zmt.uni-bremen.de/

Challenger Society for Marine Science
Room 251/20
Southampton Oceanography Centre
Waterfront Campus
Southampton, SO14 3ZH, United Kingdom
Contact: Executive Secretary
Tel: 44 17 0359 6097
Fax: 44 17 0359 6149
E-mail: jxj@soc.soton.ac.uk
http://www.soc.soton.ac.uk/OTHERS/CSMS/

Chalmers/Göteborg Universitet Centre for Environment and Sustainability
(Göteborgs Miljö Vetenskapliga Centrum—GMV)
Vera Sandbergs Allé 513
SE-412 96 Göteborg, Sweden
Tel: 46 31 772 49 51
Fax: 46 31 772 49 58
E-mail: office@miljo.chalmers.se
http://www.miljo.chalmers.se/

Coastal Research and Planning Institute (CORPI)
Klaipėda University
H. Mantog. 84
LT-5808 Klaipeda, Lithuania
Tel: 370 6 398844
Fax: 370 6 398845
E-mail: simona@corpi.ku.lt
http://www.corpi.ku.lt/

Coastal Research Laboratory (CORELAB)
Research and Technical Center Büsam
Christian Albrechts University
Otto-Hahn-Platz 3
D-24118 Kiel, Germany
Tel: 49 431 880 3643
Fax: 49 431 880 7303
E-mail: info@corelab.uni-kiel.de
http://www.corelab.uni-kiel.de/

Coastal Studies Research Group
School of Biological and Environmental Studies
University of Ulster at Coleraine
Coleraine
Co. Londonderry, Northern Ireland, BT52 1SA, United Kingdom
Contact: Head
Tel: 44 28 7032 4428
Fax: 44 28 7032 4911

E-mail: jag.cooper@ulst.ac.uk
http://www.science.ulst.ac.uk/crg/

DEA européen en modélisation de l'environnement marin
(European DEA in Modeling of the Marine Environment)
Université de Liège
Sart Tilman, B5
B-4000 Liège, Belgium
Contact: Director
Tel: 32 4 366 3350
Fax: 32 4 366 2355
E-mail: J.Nihoul@ulg.ac.be
http://www.ulg.ac.be/deamodel/

Department of Earth and Ocean Sciences
University of Liverpool
Nicholson Building
4 Brownlow Street
Liverpool, L69 3GP, United Kingdom
Tel: 44 151 794 5147
Fax: 44 151 794 5196
E-mail: net@liv.ac.uk
http://www.liv.ac.uk/earth_sciences/dept/index.html

Department of Fisheries and Marine Biology
(Institutt for Fisheri og Marinbiologi—IFM)
University of Bergen
PO Box 7800
N-5020 Bergen, Norway
Tel: 47 55 58 44 00
Fax: 47 55 58 44 50
E-mail: epost@ifm.uib.no
http://www.ifm.uib.no/

Department of Geological, Environmental and Marine Sciences
Università delgi Studi de Trieste
Via E. Weiss 2
I-34127 Trieste, Italy
Tel: 39 40 558 2047
Fax: 39 40 558 2048
E-mail: disgam@units.it
http://www.units.it/disgam/

Department of Marine Biology
Institute of Ecology and Conservation Biology
University of Vienna
Althanstrasse 14
A-1090 Vienna, Austria
Contact: Head
Tel: 43 1 42775 4202
Fax: 43 1 42779 542
E-mail: oekologie@univie.ac.at
http://www.univie.ac.at/marine-biology/

Department of Mechanical Engineering
Technical University of Denmark
Studentertorvet, Building 101E
DK-2800 Kgs. Lyngby, Denmark
Contact: Maritime Engineering Program
Tel: 45 45 25 19 60
Fax: 45 45 88 43 25
http://www.mek.dtu.dk/

Department of Oceanography
Göteborg University
PO Box 460
SE-405 30 Göteborg, Sweden
Contact: Head
Tel: 46 31 77 32 870
Fax: 46 31 77 32 888
E-mail: joro@oce.gu.se
http://www.oce.gu.se/

Department of Oceanography and Fisheries
University of the Azores
PT-9901-892 Horta, Portugal
Tel: 351 292 200400
Fax: 351 292 200411
E-mail: ssilva@notes.horta.uac.pt
http://www.horta.uac.pt/

Estonian Marine Institute (EMI)
(Eesti Mereinstituut)
Mäealuse 10a
12618 Tallinn, Estonia
Tel: 372 626 7402
Fax: 372 626 7417
E-mail: meri@sea.ee
http://www.sea.ee/

Euro-Mediterranean Centre on Insular Coastal Dynamics (ICoD)
University of Malta
Old University Building
St. Paul Street
Valletta VLT 07, Malta
Contact: Director
Tel: 356 21 240 746
Fax: 356 21 230 551

E-mail: icod@icod.org.mt
http://www.icod.org.mt/

European Institute—Denmark
Frederiksberggade 2
DK-1459 Copenhagen K, Denmark
Tel: 45 33 33 91 00
Fax: 45 33 33 91 20
E-mail: euroinst@euroinst.dk
http://www.euroinst.dk/

European Institute for Marine Studies
(Institut Universitaire Européen de la mer—IUEM)
Université de Bretagne Occidentale
Technopôle Brest-Iroise
Place Nicolas Copernic
F-29280 Plouzane, France
Contact: Director
Tel: 33 02 9849 8603
Fax: 33 02 9849 8609
E-mail: Direction.iuem@univ-brest.fr
http://www.univ-brest.fr/IUEM/

Faculty of Marine Sciences
(Facultad de Ciencias del Mar)
Edificio de Ciencias Básicas
Campus Universitario de Tafira
Universidad de Las Palmas de Gran Canaria
E-35017 Las Palmas, Grand Canary, Spain
Tel: 34 928 454 538
Fax: 34 928 452 922
E-mail: fcm@ciemar4.ulpgc.es
http://www.ccbb.ulpgc.es/ccmar/

Faculty of Nautical Science
(Facoltà de Scienze Nautiche)
Instituto Universitario Navale
Via Acton 38
I-80133 Naples, Italy
Tel: 39 081 552 4342
Fax: 39 081 552 7126
E-mail: presidesn@uninav.it
http://www.uninav.it/

Flanders Marine Institute (VLIZ)
Vismijn, Pakhuizen 45-52
B-8400 Oostende, Belgium
Contact: Director
Tel: 32 59 34 21 30
Fax: 32 59 34 21 31
E-mail: info@vliz.be
http://www.vliz.be/

Gdynia Maritime University
Morska 81-87
PL-81-225 Gdynia, Poland
Tel: 48 58 621 7041
Fax: 48 58 620 6701
E-mail: intercol@wsm.gdynia.pl
http://www.wsm.gdynia.pl/

Geohydrodynamics and Environmental Research (GHER)
Université de Liège
Sart Tilman, B5
B-4000 Liège, Belgium
Contact: Director
Tel: 32 4 366 3350
Fax: 32 4 366 2355
E-mail: J.Nihoul@ulg.ac.be
http://modb.oce.ulg.ac.be/GHER/

Graduate Institute of International Studies
(Institut universitaire de hautés études internationales, Genève)
132, rue de Lausanne
CH-1211 Geneva, Switzerland
Tel: 41 22 908 57 00
Fax: 41 22 908 57 10
E-mail: info@hei.unige.ch
http://heiwww.unige.ch/

IMAR—Center for Ecological Modelling
(IMAR—Centro de Modelação Ecológica)
Faculty of Sciences and Technology
Universidade Nova de Lisboa
Quinta da Torre
PT-2829-516 Monte de Caparica, Portugal
Tel: 351 21 2948300
Fax: 351 21 2948554
E-mail: frg@fct.unl.pt
http://www.cem.fct.unl.pt/

Institute for Marine and Atmospheric Research Utrecht (IMAU)
University of Utrecht
PO Box 80000
NL-3508 TA, Utrecht, The Netherlands
Tel: 31 030 253 3275
Fax: 31 030 254 3163
E-mail: imau@phys.uu.nl
http://www.phys.uu.nl/~wwwimau/

Institute for Marine Research
(Institut für Meereskunde an der Universitaet Kiel)
Düstenbrooker Weg 20

D-24105 Kiel, Germany
Contact: Directorate
Tel: 49 431 600 4507
Fax: 49 431 600 1515
E-mail: ifm@ifm.uni-kiel.de
http://www.ifm.uni-kiel.de/

Institute of Aquaculture
University of Stirling
Pathfoot Building
Stirling, FK9 4LA, United Kingdom
Contact: Director
Tel: 44 17 8646 7750
Fax: 44 17 8646 6896
E-mail: natsci@stir.ac.uk
http://www.stir.ac.uk/aqua/

Institute of Estuarine and Coastal Studies (IECS)
University of Hull
Cottingham Road
Hull, HU6 7RX, United Kingdom
Contact: Director
Tel: 44 1482 465503
Fax: 44 1482 465001
E-mail: iecs@hull.ac.uk
http://www.hull.ac.uk/iecs/

Institute of Hydrobiology and Fishery Science
(Institut für Hydrobiologie und Fischereiwissenschaft)
University of Hamburg
Olbersweg 24
D-22767 Hamburg, Germany
Tel: 49 40 428 38 6601
Fax: 49 40 428 38 6618
E-mail: ihf-office@uni-hamburg.de
http://www.biologie.uni-hamburg.de/ihf/

Institute of Marine Biology of Crete (IMBC)
PO Box 2214
Iraklio
GR-71003 Crete, Greece
Tel: 30 281 337806
Fax: 30 281 337822
E-mail: imbc@imbc.gr
http://www.imbc.gr/

Institute of Marine Research (IMAR)
(Centro Interdisciplinar de Coimbra)
c/o Department of Zoology
University of Coimbra
3000 Coimbra, Portugal
Tel: 351 239 836386
Fax: 351 239 823603
E-mail: imar@ci.uc.pt
http://www.imar.pt/

Institute of Marine Sciences and Management
University of Istanbul
34470 Vefa Istanbul, Turkey
Tel: 90 212 528 2539
Fax: 90 212 526 8433
E-mail: cemga@istanbul.edu.tr
http://www.istanbul.edu.tr/enstituler/denizbilimleri/denizbilimleri.htm

Institute of Marine Studies
University of Plymouth
Drake Circus
Plymouth, PL4 8AA, United Kingdom
Tel: 44 1752 232400
Fax: 44 1752 232406
E-mail: ims@plymouth.ac.uk
http://hydrography.ims.plym.ac.uk/

Institute of Maritime Law
University of Southampton
Highfield, Southampton, SO17 1BJ, United Kingdom
Contact: Institute Secretary
Tel: 44 2380 593449
Fax: 44 2380 593789
E-mail: iml@soton.ac.uk
http://www.iml.soton.ac.uk/

Institute of Maritime Law and the Law of the Sea
(Institut für Seerecht und Seehandelsrecht—ISSR)
University of Hamburg
Heimhuder Strasse 71
D-20148 Hamburg, Germany
Tel: 49 40 42838 2240
Fax: 49 40 42838 6271
E-mail: seerecht@jura.uni-hamburg.de
http://www.jura.uni-hamburg.de/~issr/

Institute of Oceanography
(Institut für Meereskunde)
University of Hamburg
Troplowitzstrasse 7
D-22529 Hamburg, Germany
Tel: 49 40 42838 2605
Fax: 49 40 42560 5926

REGIONAL ACADEMIC ORGANIZATIONS

E-mail: meincke@ifm.uni-hamburg.de
http://www.ifm.uni-hamburg.de/index.html

Institute of Oceanography and Fisheries
Setaliste Iva Mestrovica 63
HR-21000 Split, Croatia
Tel: 385 21 358688
Fax: 385 21 358650
E-mail: office@izor.hr
http://www.izor.hr/eng/intro.html

Institute of Oceanology
Polish Academy of Sciences
PO Box 68
Powstancow Warszawy 55
PL-81-712 Sopot, Poland
Tel: 48 58 551 7281
Fax: 48 58 551 2130
E-mail: office@iopan.gda.pl
http://www.iopan.gda.pl/

International Boundaries Research Unit (IBRU)
Department of Geography
University of Durham
Durham, DH1 3UR, United Kingdom
Tel: 44 191 334 1961
Fax: 44 191 334 1962
E-mail: ibru@dur.ac.uk
http://www-ibru.dur.ac.uk/

International Centre for Coastal and Ocean Policy Studies (ICCOPS)
c/o Department Polis, University of Genoa
37 Stradone di S. Agostino
I-16123 Genova, Italy
Contact: Secretary-General
Tel/Fax: 39 10 209-5840
E-mail: iccops@polis.unige.it

International Centre for Coastal Resources Research
(Centre Internacional d'Investigació dels Recursos Costaners—CIIRC)
Campus Nord—Universitat
Politecnica de Catalunya
Jordi Girona, 1-3, Edif. D-1
E-08034 Barcelona, Spain
Tel: 34 932 806 400
Fax: 34 932 806 019
E-mail: ciirc@upc.es
http://lim-ciirc.upc.es/

International Fisheries Institute (HIFI)
University of Hull
Hull, HU6 7RX, United Kingdom
Tel: 44 1482 466421
Fax: 44 1482 470129
E-mail: hifi@hull.ac.uk
http://www.hull.ac.uk/hifi/

International Geosphere-Biosphere Programme (IGBP)
Royal Swedish Academy of Sciences
Box 50005
SE-104 05 Stockholm, Sweden
Contact: Secretariat
Tel: 46 8 16 64 48
Fax: 46 8 16 64 05
E-mail: sec@igbp.kva.se
http://www.igbp.kva.se/

International Studies in Aquatic Tropical Ecology
Zentrum für Marine Tropenökologie (ZMT)
Fahrenheitstrasse 6
D-28 359 Bremen, Germany
Tel: 49 421 23800 42
Fax: 49 421 23800 30
E-mail: isatec@uni-bremen.de
http://www.isatec.uni-bremen.de/

Islands and Small States Institute
Foundation for International Studies
Old University Building
St. Paul Street
Valletta VLT 07, Malta
Tel: 356 21 248 218
Fax: 356 21 230 551
E-mail: islands@um.edu.mt
http://home.um.edu.mt/islands/

Laboratoire de Sédimentologie Marines
Université de Perpignan
52 avenue Paul Alduy
F-66 860 Perpignan Cedex, France
Tel: 33 4 6866 2000
Fax: 33 4 6866 2019
http://www.univ-perp.fr/

Laboratoire Environnement Marin Littoral
Université de Nice-Sophia Antipolis
Faculté des Sciences
Parc Valrose
F-06108 Nice Cedex 2, France
Tel: 33 4 9207 6846

Fax: 33 4 9207 6849
E-mail: meinesz@unice.fr
http://www.unice.fr/LEML/

Laboratori d'Enginyeria Marítima (LIM/UPC)
Campus Nord—Universitat Politècnica de Catalunya
Jordi Girona, 1-3, Edif. D-1
E-08034 Barcelona, Spain
Contact: Head of LIM/UPC
Tel: 34 934 016 468
Fax: 34 934 011 861
E-mail: info.lim@upc.es
http://lim-ciirc.upc.es/

Legal Aspects of Marine Affairs Program
Cardiff Law School
Cardiff University
PO Box 427
Cardiff, Wales, CF10 3XJ, United Kingdom
Contact: Director
Tel: 44 29 2087 4353
Fax: 44 29 2087 4982
E-mail: law-pg@cardiff.ac.uk
http://www.cf.ac.uk/claws/

Marine Research Centre
(Marina Forskningscentrum)
Earth Sciences Centre
Göteborg University
PO Box 460
SE-405 30 Göteborg, Sweden
Contact: Director
Tel: 46 31 773 1000
Fax: 46 31 773 4839
E-mail: henrik.tallgren@science.gu.se
http://www.gmf.gu.se/

Maritime Institute
(Maritiem Instituut)
Universiteit Gent
Universiteitstraat 6
B-9000 Gent, Belgium
Tel: 32 9 264 6897
Fax: 32 9 264 6989
E-mail: lydie.demaerteleire@rug.ac.be
http://www.maritieminstituut.be/

Marseille Oceanology Institute
(Centre d'Océanologie de Marseille (COM))
Université de la Méditerranée Station Marine d'Endoume
Rue de la Batterie des Lions
F-13007 Marseille, France
Tel: 33 4 9104 1600
Fax: 33 4 9104 1608
E-mail: dekeyser@com.univ-mrs.fr
http://www.com.univ-mrs.fr/

Max Planck Institute for Marine Microbiology Bremen
(Max-Planck-Institut für Marine Mikrobiologie Bremen)
Celsiusstrasse 1
D-28359 Bremen, Germany
Contact: Director
Tel: 49 421 202850
Fax: 49 421 2028580
E-mail: contact@mpi-bremen.de
http://www.mpi-bremen.de/

Max Planck Institute for Meteorology
(Max-Planck-Institut für Meterologie)
Bundesstrasse 55
D-20146 Hamburg, Germany
Contact: Executive Director
Tel: 49 40 41173 421
Fax: 49 40 41173 298
http://www.mpimet.mpg.de/

Mediterranean Programme for International Environmental Law and Negotiation (MEPIELAN)
Panteion University of Athens
136 Syngrou Avenue
GR-17671 Athens, Greece
Tel: 30 210 9201841
Fax: 30 210 9610591
E-mail: info@mepielan.gr
http://www.mepielan.gr/

Nansen Environmental and Remote Sensing Center (NERSC)
Edvard Grieg Vei 3a
N-5059 Bergen, Norway
Tel: 47 55 20 58 00
Fax: 47 55 20 58 01
E-mail: admin@nersc.no
http://www.nersc.no/

Netherlands Institute for Fisheries Research
Haringkade 1, IJmuiden
PO Box 68
NL-1970 AB IJmuiden, The Netherlands
Tel: 31 255 56 46 46

Fax: 31 255 56 46 44
E-mail: visserijonderzoek.asg@wur.nl
http://www.rivo.wag-ur.nl/

Netherlands Institute for the Law of the Sea (NILOS)
Utrecht University
Faculty of Law
Achter Sint Pieter 200
NL-3512 HT Utrecht, The Netherlands
Contact: Director
Tel: 31 30 253 7060
Fax: 31 30 253 7073
E-mail: nilos@law.uu.nl
http://www.law.uu.nl/english/isep/framenilos.asp

North Atlantic Fisheries College
Port Arthur
Scalloway, Shetlands, ZE1 0UN, United Kingdom
Tel: 44 1595 772000
Fax: 44 1595 772001
E-mail: admin@nafc.ac.uk
http://www.nafc.ac.uk/

Norwegian College of Fishery Science
(Norges Fiskerihøgskole)
University of Tromsø
N-9037 Tromsø, Norway
Contact: Rector
Tel: 47 77 64 60 00
E-mail: knuth@nfh.uit.no
http://www.nfh.uit.no/

Oceanographic Institute
(Institut océanographique)
195, rue Saint Jacques
F-75005 Paris, France
Tel: 33 1 4432 1070
Fax: 33 1 4051 7316
http://www.oceano.org/

Oceanographic Institute of the Western Mediterranean Sea
(Instituto Oceanografico del Mediterraneo Occidental—IOMO)
San Juan, 9
Vespella de Gaia
E-43763 Tarragona, Spain
Contact: President
Tel: 34 977 655 214
Fax: 34 977 655 584
E-mail: iomo@tinet.fut.es
http://www.fut.es/~iomo/

Océanologie Département des Sciences de la Vie Université de Liège
Sart Tilman B6
B-4000 Liège, Belgium
Tel: 32 4 366 3329
Fax: 32 4 366 3325
E-mail: p.dauby@ulg.ac.be
http://www.ulg.ac.be/oceanbio/

Plymouth Marine Laboratory
Prospect Place, The Hoe
Plymouth, PL1 3DH, United Kingdom
Tel: 44 1752 63 3100
Fax: 44 1752 63 3101
E-mail: forinfo@pml.ac.uk
http://www.pml.ac.uk/

Proudman Oceanographic Laboratory
Bidston Observatory
Birkenhead, Merseyside, CH43 7RA, United Kingdom
Tel: 44 151 653 8633
Fax: 44 151 653 6269
http://www.pol.ac.uk/

Research Unit of Maritime Medicine (RUMM)
University of Southern Denmark
Niels Bohrs Vej 9
DK-6700 Esbjerg, Denmark
Contact: Senior Research Associate
Tel: 45 65 50 41 11
Fax: 45 65 50 10 91
E-mail: sdu@sdu.dk
http://www.esb.sdu.dk/~vny/uksmiforside.htm

Rhodes Academy of Oceans Law and Policy
c/o Center for Oceans Law and Policy
University of Virginia School of Law
580 Massie Road
Charlottesville, VA, 22903, USA
Contact: Director
Tel: 1 434 924-7441
Fax: 1 434 982-2622
E-mail: colp@virginia.edu
http://www.virginia.edu/~colp/COLP.html

SARS International Center for Marine Molecular Biology
Bergen High Technology Center

Thormøhlensgate 55
N-5008 Bergen, Norway
Tel: 47 55 58 43 44
Fax: 47 55 58 43 05
E-mail: berit.berntsen@sars.uib.no
http://www.uib.no/fa/sars/

Scandinavian Institute of Maritime Law
(Nordisk Institutt for Sjørett)
University of Oslo
Karl Johansgate 47
Domus Media Vest
N-0162 Oslo, Norway
Contact: Director
Tel: 47 22 85 97 48
Fax: 47 22 85 97 50
E-mail: sjorett-adm@jus.uio.no
http://www.jus.uio.no/nifs/

Scarborough Centre for Coastal Studies
University of Hull
Scarborough Campus
Filey Road
Scarborough, YO11 3AZ, United Kingdom
Tel: 44 1723 362392
Fax: 44 1723 370815
E-mail: sccs@hull.ac.uk
http://www.ccs.hull.ac.uk/

School of Conservation Sciences
Bournemouth University
Talbot Campus
Poole, Dorset, BH12 5BB, United Kingdom
Tel: 44 1202 595444
Fax: 44 1202 595255
E-mail: consci@bmth.ac.uk
http://www.bournemouth.ac.uk/conservation/

School of Earth, Ocean and Planetary Sciences
Cardiff University
Main Building Park Place
Cardiff, Wales, CF10 3YE, United Kingdom
Tel: 44 29 2087 4830
Fax: 44 29 2087 4326
E-mail: earth@cardiff.ac.uk
http://www.earth.cardiff.ac.uk/

School of Environmental Sciences
University of East Anglia
Norwich, NR4 7TJ, United Kingdom
Tel: 44 1603 592542
Fax: 44 1603 507719
E-mail: env@uea.ac.uk
http://www.uea.ac.uk/env/

School of Geography
University of Plymouth
Plymouth, Devon, PL4 8AA, United Kingdom
Tel: 44 1752 233053
Fax: 44 1752 233054
E-mail: ssb.admissions@plymouth.ac.uk
http://www.geog.plym.ac.uk/

School of Marine Science and Technology
Armstrong Building
University of Newcastle upon Tyne
Newcastle Upon Tyne, NE1 7RU,
United Kingdom
Tel: 44 191 222 6718
Fax: 44 191 222 5491
E-mail: atilla.incecik@ncl.ac.uk
http://www.ncl.ac.uk/marine/

School of Maritime and Coastal Studies
Southampton Institute, East Park Terrace
Southampton, Hants, SO14 0RD, United Kingdom
Tel: 44 2380 319736
E-mail: ff.admissions@solent.ac.uk
http://www.solent.ac.uk/maritime/

School of Ocean Sciences
University of Wales, Bangor
Menai Bridge
Anglesey, North Wales, LL59 5EY, United Kingdom
Tel: 44 1248 382846
Fax: 44 1248 716367
E-mail: enquiries@sos.bangor.ac.uk
http://www.sos.bangor.ac.uk/

Scottish Association for Marine Science (SAMS)
Dunstaffnage Marine Laboratory
Oban, Argyll, Scotland, PA37 1QA, United Kingdom
Tel: 44 1631 559000
Fax: 44 1631 559001
E-mail: mail@dml.ac.uk
http://www.sams.ac.uk/

Sea Mammal Research Unit
Gatty Marine Laboratory

University of St Andrews
St Andrews, Fife, KY16 8LB, United Kingdom
Tel: 44 1334 462630
Fax: 441334 462632
E-mail: ajp7@st-andrews.ac.uk
http://smub.st-and.ac.uk/index.htm

Seafarers International Research Centre (SIRC)
Cardiff University
PO Box 907
Cardiff, Wales, CF10 3YP, United Kingdom
Contact: Secretariat
Tel: 44 29 2087 4620
Fax: 44 29 2087 4619
E-mail: sirc@cardiff.ac.uk
http://www.sirc.cf.ac.uk/

Sophia Antipolis Centre d'Etudes et de Recherches sur le Droit des Activités Maritimes
(CERDAM)
Université de Nice—Sophia Antipolis
7, avenue Robert Schuman
FR-06050 Nice, Cédex 1, France
Tel: 33 4 9215 7043
Fax: 33 4 9396 0131
E-mail: cerdam@unice.fr
http://www.unice.fr/CERDAM/

Southampton Oceanography Centre
University of Southampton
Waterfront Campus
European Way
Southampton, SO14 3ZH, United Kingdom
Contact: Director
Tel: 44 2380 596666
Fax: 44 2380 596667
http://www.soc.soton.ac.uk/

Stazione Zoologica Anton Dohrn
Villa Comunale
I-80121 Naples, Italy
Contact: President
Tel: 39 81 583 3111
Fax: 39 81 764 1355
E-mail: bernardi@szn.it
http://www.szn.it/

Stockholm Marine Research Centre
(Stockholms Marina Forskningcentrum)
Stockholm University
SE-106 91 Stockholm, Sweden
Contact: Director
Tel: 46 8 16 37 18
Fax: 46 8 16 16 20
E-mail: smf@smf.su.se
http://www.smf.su.se/

Transport and Shipping Research Group
Cardiff Business School
Cardiff University
Aberconway Building, Colum Drive
Cardiff, Wales, CF10 3EU, United Kingdom
Tel: 44 29 2087 6764
Fax: 44 29 2087 4301
E-mail: marlow@cardiff.ac.uk
http://www.cf.ac.uk/carbs/index.html

Umeå Marine Sciences Centre
(Umeå Marina Forskningscentrum—UMF)
University of Umea
Norrbyn
SE-910 20 Hörnefors, Sweden
Contact: Secretariat
Tel: 46 09 7 86 79 74
Fax: 46 09 7 86 79 95
E-mail: karin.andersson@umf.umu.se
http://www.umf.umu.se/

UNESCO—Cousteau Ecotechnie Programme (UCEP)
Division of Ecological Sciences
UNESCO
1, rue Miollis
FR-75732 Paris Cedex 15, France
Fax: 33 1 4568 5804
E-mail: p.dogse@unesco.org
http://www.unesco.org/mab/capacity/ucep/ucephome.htm

Université du Littoral Côte d'Opale Services Centraux
1, place de l'Yser—B.P. 1022
F-59375 Dunkerque Cedex 1, France
Tel: 33 3 2823 7373
Fax: 33 3 2823 7313
E-mail: web-ulco@univ-littoral.fr
http://www.univ-littoral.fr/

6. REGIONAL ACADEMIC ORGANIZATIONS

6.5 Australia, New Zealand and Oceania

Australian Defence Studies Centre
University College

Australian Defence Force Academy
Northcott Drive
Campbell, ACT 2600, Australia
Tel: 61 6268 8848
Fax: 61 6268 8840
E-mail: b.hall@adfa.edu.au
http://idun.itsc.adfa.edu.au/ADSC/

Australian Institute of Navigation
PO Box Q398
Queensland Victoria Post Office, NSW 1230, Australia
Tel: 61 2 9264 6413
Fax: 61 2 9267 1682
E-mail: citia@smartchat.net.au
http://www.gmat.unsw.edu.au/aion/

Australian Maritime College
PO Box 986
Launceston, TAS 7250, Australia
Tel: 61 3 6335 4711
Fax: 61 3 6326 6493
E-mail: amcinfo@amc.edu.au
http://www.amc.edu.au/

Centre for Coral Reef Biodiversity
School of Marine Biology and Aquaculture
James Cook University
Townsville, QLD 4811, Australia
Tel: 61 7 4781 4222
Fax: 61 7 4725 1570
E-mail: ccrbio@jcu.edu.au
http://www.jcu.edu.au/school/mbiolaq/ccrbio/

Centre for Marine Science & Technology
Curtin University
GPO Box U1987
Perth, WA 6845, Australia
Tel: 61 8 9266 7380
Fax:61 8 9266 4799
E-mail: info@cmst.curtin.edu.au
http://www.curtin.edu.au/cmst

Centre for Marine Studies
University of Queensland
Brisbane, QLD 4072, Australia
Tel: 61 7 3365 4333
Fax: 61 7 3365 4755
E-mail: cms@uq.edu.au
http://www.marine.uq.edu.au/

Centre for Maritime Law
T. C. Beirne School of Law
University of Queensland
St. Lucia, QLD 4072, Australia
Tel: 61 7 3365 3320
Fax: 61 7 3365 1454
E-mail: s.derrington@law.uq.edu.au
http://www.law.uq.edu.au/

Centre for Maritime Policy
University of Wollongong
Wollongong, NSW 2522, Australia
Tel: 61 2 4221 4883
Fax: 61 2 4226 5544
E-mail: myree@uow.edu.au
http://www.uow.edu.au/law/cmp/

Coastal Marine Research Unit
School of Biological Sciences
Victoria University of Wellington
PO Box 600
Wellington, New Zealand
Tel: 64 4 463 5339
Fax: 64 4 463 5331
E-mail: biosci@vuw.ac.nz
http://www.vuw.ac.nz/sbs/

East-West Center
1601 East-West Road
Honolulu, HI, 96848-1601, USA
Contact: President
Tel: 1 808 944-7111
Fax: 1 808 944-7376
E-mail: morrisoc@eastwestcenter.org
http://www.eastwestcenter.org/

Lincoln Marine Science Centre
PO Box 2023
Port Lincoln, SA 5606, Australia
Tel: 61 8 8683 2500
Fax: 61 8 8683 2525
E-mail: lmsc@flinders.edu.au
http://www.scieng.flinders.edu.au/biology/lmsc/

Marine Affairs Programme
University of the South Pacific
Suva, Fiji
Contact: Coordinator
Tel: 679 212890
Fax: 679 301490
E-mail: veitayaki_j@usp.ac.fj
http://www.usp.ac.fj/marineaf/

Marine Laboratory
University of Guam
UOG Station
Mangilao, GU, 96913, USA

Contact: Director
Tel: 671 735 2175
Fax: 671 734 6767
E-mail: bdsmith@uog9.uog.edu
http://www.uog.edu/marinelab/

Marine Studies Programme
University of the South Pacific
Suva, Fiji
Tel: 679 305272
Fax: 679 301490
E-mail: hay_c@usp.ac.fj
http://www.usp.ac.fj/marine/

New Zealand Centre for Environmental Law
Faculty of Law
University of Auckland
Private Bag 92019
Auckland Central, New Zealand
Tel: 64 9 373 7599 ext. 87827
Fax: 64 9 373 7473
E-mail: k.bosselmann@auckland.ac.nz
http://www.law.auckland.ac.nz/groups/cel/

Oceans and Coastal Research Centre
University of Wollongong
Wollongong, NSW 2522, Australia
Tel: 61 2 4221 4134
Fax: 61 2 4221 4665
E-mail: john_morrison@uow.edu.au
http://www.uow.edu.au/science/research/ocrc/

School of Aquaculture
University of Tasmania
Locked Bag 1370
Launceston, TAS 7250, Australia
Tel: 61 3 6324 3801
Fax: 61 3 6324 3804
E-mail: enquiries@aqua.utas.edu.au
http://www.utas.edu.au/aqua

School of Geography and Environmental Science
University of Auckland, Tamaki Campus
Private Bag 92019
Auckland, New Zealand
Tel: 64 9 373 7599 ext 6815
Fax: 64 9 373 7042
E-mail: sges@auckland.ac.nz
http://sems.auckland.ac.nz/

School of Marine Biology and Aquaculture
James Cook University
Townsville, QLD 4811, Australia
Tel: 61 7 4781 4345
Fax: 61 7 4781 5511
E-mail: mbiolaq@jcu.edu.au
http://www.jcu.edu.au/school/mbiolaq/

School of Ocean and Earth Science and Technology (SOEST)
University of Hawaii
1680 East-West Road, POST 802
Honolulu, HI, 96822, USA
Contact: Office of the Dean
Tel: 1 808 956-6182
Fax: 1 808 956-9152
E-mail: kkikuta@soest.hawaii.edu
http://www.soest.hawaii.edu/

School of Tropical Environment Studies and Geography
James Cook University
Townsville, QLD 4811, Australia
Tel: 61 7 4781 4325
Fax: 61 7 4781 4020
E-mail: emma.gyuris@jcu.edu.au
http://www.tesag.jcu.edu.au/

Tasmanian Aquaculture and Fisheries Institute
University of Tasmania
Private Bag 49
Hobart, TAS 7001, Australia
Tel: 61 3 6227 7277
Fax: 61 3 6227 8035
E-mail: tafi@utas.edu.au
http://www.utas.edu.au/tafi/TAFI_Homepage.html

The International Global Change Institute
The University of Waikato
Private Bag 3105
Hamilton, New Zealand
Tel: 64 7 858 5647
Fax: 64 7 858 5689
E-mail: igci@waikato.ac.nz
http://www.waikato.ac.nz/igci

Tourism Program
School of Business
James Cook University
Townsville, QLD 4811, Australia
Tel: 61 7 4781 5134
Fax: 61 7 4781 4019

REGIONAL ACADEMIC ORGANIZATIONS

E-mail: robyn.yesberg@jcu.edu.au
http://www.jcu.edu.au/flbca/business/tourism/

William S. Richardson School of Law
University of Hawaii
2515 Dole Street
Honolulu, HI, 96822-2328, USA
Contact: Dean
Tel: 1 808 956-7966
Fax: 1 808 956-6402
E-mail: soifer@hawaii.edu
http://www.hawaii.edu/law/

6. REGIONAL ACADEMIC ORGANIZATIONS

6.6 Polar Regions

Arctic Centre
University of Lapland
PO Box 122
FIN-96101 Rovaniemi, Finland
Tel: 358 16 341 2758
Fax: 358 16 341 2777
E-mail: arctic.centre@urova.fi
http://www.arcticcentre.org/

Arctic Centre, Groningen
Rijksuniversiteit Groningen
PO Box 716
NL-9700 AS, Groningen, The Netherlands
Tel: 31 50 363 6834
Fax: 31 50 363 4900
E-mail: arctisch@let.rug.nl
http://odin.let.rug.nl/arctic/

Arctic Institute of North America
University of Calgary
2500 University Drive NW
Calgary, AB, T2N 1N4, Canada
Contact: Executive Director
Tel: 1 403 220-7515
Fax: 1 403 282-4609
E-mail: wkjessen@ucalgary.ca
http://www.ucalgary.ca/aina/

Canadian Circumpolar Institute
8625 112 Street, Suite 308, Campus Tower
University of Alberta
Edmonton, AB, T6G 0H1, Canada
Contact: Director
Tel: 1 780 492-4512
Fax: 1 780 492-1153
E-mail: ccinst@gpu.srv.ualberta.ca
http://www.ualberta.ca/~ccinst/

Gateway Antarctica
University of Canterbury
Private Bag 4800
Christchurch
New Zealand
Tel: 64 3 364 2136
Fax: 64 3 364 2197
E-mail: gateway@canterbury.ac.nz
http://www.anta.canterbury.ac.nz/

Institute of Antarctic and Southern Ocean Studies
University of Tasmania
GPO Box 252-77
Hobart, TAS 7001, Australia
Contact: Director
Tel: 61 3 6226 2971
Fax: 61 3 6226 2973
E-mail: secretary@iasos.utas.edu.au
http://www.utas.edu.au/iasos/

Scott Polar Research Institute
University of Cambridge
Lensfield Road
Cambridge, CB2 1ER, United Kingdom
Tel: 44 1223 336540
Fax: 44 1223 336549
E-mail: enquiries@spri.cam.ac.uk
http://www.spri.cam.ac.uk/

7.0 NATIONAL GOVERNMENT ORGANIZATIONS

Alfred Wegener Institute for Polar and Marine Research
Postfach 12 0161
D-27515 Bremerhaven, Germany
Contact: Director
Tel: 49 471 4831 1101
Fax: 49 471 4831 1149
E-mail: srainey@awi-bremerhaven.de
http://www.awi-bremerhaven.de/

Asociacíon Argentina de Ingeniería Sanitaria y Ciencias del Ambiente (AIDIS Argentina)
Av. Belgrano 1580 Piso 3
1093 Buenos Aires, Argentina
Contact: Chairman

Tel/Fax: 54 11 4381 5832/5093
E-mail: aidisar@aidisar.org
http://www.aidisar.org/

Association of Sea Fisheries Committees of England and Wales
24 Wykeham
Scarborough
Yorkshire, YO13 9QP, United Kingdom
Contact: Chief Executive
Tel/Fax: 44 1723 863169

Atlantic Coastal Action Program
Sustainable Communities and Ecosystem Division
Environment Canada
45 Alderney Drive
Dartmouth, NS, B2Y 2N6, Canada
Contact: Project Officer
Tel: 1 902 426-3776
Fax: 1 902 426-6348
E-mail: karen.swan@ec.gc.ca
http://www.ns.ec.gc.ca/community/acap/

Atlantic States Marine Fisheries Commission (ASMFC)
1444 Eye Street NW, 6th floor
Washington, DC, 20005, USA
Contact: Executive Director
Tel: 1 202 289-6400
Fax: 1 202 289-6051
E-mail: comments@asmfc.org
http://www.asmfc.org/

Australian Institute of Marine Science
PMB No. 3
Townsville MC, QLD 4810, Australia
Contact: Chief Scientist
Tel: 61 7 4753 4444
Fax: 61 7 4772 5852
E-mail: reception@aims.gov.au
http://www.aims.gov.au/

Australian Maritime Safety Authority
GPO Box 2181
Canberra, ACT 2601, Australia
Tel: 61 2 6279 5000
E-mail: generalenquiries@amsa.gov.au
http://www.amsa.gov.au/

Bangladesh Fisheries Research Institute
Mymensingh 2201, Bangladesh
Tel: 880 91 54874
Fax: 880 91 55259
E-mail: frihq@bdmail.net
http://www.bangladeshgov.org/mofl/fri/fritop.htm

Bedford Institute of Oceanography
PO Box 1006, Mail Stn B501
Dartmouth, NS, B2Y 4A2, Canada
Contact: Director, Oceans and Environment Branch
Tel: 1 902 426-3825
Fax: 1 902 426-9909
E-mail: scattolonf@mar.dfo-mpo.gc.ca
http://www.bio.gc.ca/

British Geological Survey
Kingsley Dunham Centre
Keyworth
Nottingham, NG12 5GG, United Kingdom
Contact: Headquarters
Tel: 44 115 936 3100
Fax: 44 115 936 3200
E-mail: enquiries@bgs.ac.uk
http://www.bgs.ac.uk/

Bureau of Fisheries and Aquatic Resources
860 Arcadia Building, Quezon Avenue
3008 Quezon City, Metro Manila, The Philippines
Contact: Director
Tel: 632 372 5057
Fax: 632 372 5048
E-mail: msarmiento@bfar.da.gov.ph
http://www.bfar.gov.ph/

Bureau of Ocean and International Environmental and Scientific Affairs
US Department of State
2201 C Street, NW, Room 7831
Washington, DC, 20520, USA
Contact: Assistant Secretary of State
Tel: 1 202 647-1554
http://www.state.gov/g/oes/

Canada-Newfoundland Offshore Petroleum Board
5th Floor TD Place, 140 Water Street
St. John's, NL, A1C 6H6, Canada
Tel: 1 709 778-1400
E-mail: postmaster@cnopb.nf.ca
http://www.cnopb.nfnet.com/

Canada-Nova Scotia Offshore Petroleum Board
6th Floor TD Centre, 1791 Barrington Street
Halifax, NS, B3J 3K9, Canada
Tel: 1 902 422-5588

Fax: 1 902 422-1799
E-mail: postmaster@cnsopb.ns.ca
http://www.cnsopb.ns.ca/

Canadian Environmental Assessment Agency
200 Sacré-Coeur Boulevard, 14th floor
Hull, QC, K1A 0H3, Canada
Tel: 1 819 997-1000
Fax: 1 819 994-1469
E-mail: info@ceea.gc.ca
http://www.ceaa.gc.ca/

Canadian Polar Commission
Suite 1710, Constitution Square
360 Albert Street
Ottawa, ON, K1R 7X7, Canada
Tel: 1 613 943-8605
Fax: 1 613 943-8607
E-mail: mail@polarcom.gc.ca
http://www.polarcom.gc.ca/

Caribbean Fishery Management Council
US Department of Commerce
268 Muñoz Rivera Avenue, Suite 1108
San Juan, Puerto Rico, 00918-2577, USA
Contact: Executive Director
Tel: 1 787 766-5926
Fax: 1 787 766-6239
E-mail: miguel.a.rolon@noaa.gov
http://www.caribbeanfmc.com/

Center of Marine Research
Lithuanian Ministry of the Environment
Taikos pr.26
LT-5802 Klaipeda, Lithuania
Tel: 370 46 41 04 50
Fax: 370 46 41 04 60
E-mail: CMR@klaipeda.omnitel.net
http://www1.omnitel.net/juriniai_tyrimai/

Centre de Recherce Scientifique de Conakry-Rogbane (CERESCOR)
BP 1615
Conakry, Guinea
Contact: ODIN Africa Regional Coordinator
Fax: 224 4 13811
E-mail: s.cisse@unesco.org

Centre de Recherches Océanographiques de Dakar-Thiaroye (CRODT)
10, 5, Boulevard du Centenaire de la Commune de Dakar
BP 2241
Dakar, Senegal
Contact: Directeur
Tel: 221 834 8041
Fax: 221 834 2792
E-mail: tdiouf@crodt.isra.sn; crodt@crodt.isra.sn
http://oregonstate.edu/dept/ip/irn/senegal/Crodt.htm

Centre de Recherches Oceanologiques (CRO)
Ministere de la Recherche Scientifique
29, rue des Pêcheurs
BP V18
Abidjan, Côte d'Ivoire
Contact: Directeur
Tel: 225 355014
Fax: 225 351155
E-mail: sankare@cro.ci
http://www.ci.refer.org/ivoir_ct/rec/cdr/cro/

Centre for Environment, Fisheries and Aquaculture Science (CEFAS)
Lowestoft Laboratory
Pakefield Road
Lowestoft, Suffolk, NR33 0HT, United Kingdom
Tel: 44 1502 562244
Fax: 44 1502 513865
http://www.cefas.co.uk/

Centre Océanologique du Pacifique, IFREMER
BP 7004
Taravao, Tahiti, French Polynesia
Tel: 689 546000
Fax: 689 546099
E-mail: emmanuel.thouard@ifremer.fr
http://www.ifremer.fr/cop/

Centro Tecnológico del Mar, Fundación (CETMAR)
PO Box apdo 2.108
E-36208 Bouzas, Vigo, Spain
Tel: 34 986 247 047
Fax: 34 986 294 587
E-mail: info@cetmar.org
http://www.cetmar.org/

China Institute for Marine Affairs
State Oceanic Administration
1 Fuxingmenwai Avenue
Beijing 100860, People's Republic of China

Contact: Executive Director
Tel: 86 10 6803 0767
E-mail: mjli@cima.gov.cn
http://www.cima.gov.cn/

Coastal America
300 7th Street, SW Suite 680
Washington, DC, 20250, USA
Contact: Director
Tel: 1 202 401-9928
Fax: 1 202 401-9821
E-mail: dmaphis@usda.gov
http://www.coastalamerica.gov/

Coastal Research Institute (CoRI)
Alexandria, Egypt
Contact: Director
Tel: 20 2 484 4614
Fax: 20 2 444 6761
E-mail: nwrc@idsc.gov.eg
http://www.nwrc.gov.eg/

Coastal States Organization
Hall of States, Suite 322
444 N. Capitol Street NW
Washington, DC, 20001, USA
Contact: Executive Director
Tel: 1 202 508-3860
Fax: 1 202 508-3843
E-mail: cso@sso.org
http://www.sso.org/cso/

Coastal Zone Management Centre (CZMC)
PO Box 20907
NL-2500 EX, The Hague, Netherlands
Tel: 31 70 311 4311
Fax: 31 70 311 4380
E-mail: czmc@rikz.rws.minvenw.nl
http://www.netcoast.nl/

Coastal Zone Management Unit
Bay Street
St. Michael, Barbados, West Indies
Contact: Director
Tel: 1 246 228-5951
Fax: 1 246 228-5956
E-mail: director@coastal.gov.bb
http://www.coastal.gov.bb/

Comité National Océanographique du CBRST (CNO)
BP 03-1665
Cotonou, Benin
Tel: 229 32 12 63
Fax: 229 32 36 71
E-mail: cbrst@bow.intnet.bj
http://www.cbrst.org/

Commonwealth Scientific Industrial Research Organization (CSIRO)
CSIRO Marine Research
GPO Box 1538
Hobart, TAS 7001, Australia
Tel: 61 3 6232 5222
Fax: 61 3 6232 5000
E-mail: reception@marine.csiro.au
http://www.marine.csiro.au/

Cooperative Research Centre (CRC) for Antarctica and the Southern Ocean
Private Bag 80
Hobart, TAS 7001, Australia
Contact: Chief Executive Officer
Tel: 61 3 6226 7888
Fax: 61 3 6226 2973
E-mail: crc_webmaster@postoffice.antcrc.utas.edu.au
http://www.antcrc.utas.edu.au/

Council for Scientific and Industrial Research (CSIR)
PO Box 395
Pretoria 0001, South Africa
Contact: Coast Program Manager
Tel: 27 12 841 3832
Fax: 27 12 349 1153
E-mail: webmaster@csir.co.za
http://www.csir.co.za/

Countryside Council for Wales
Maes-y-Ffynnon
Penrhosgarnedd, Bangor
Gwynedd, Wales, LL57 2LQ, United Kingdom
Contact: Head Office
Tel: 44 0845 1306 229
E-mail: enquiries@ccw.gov.uk
http://www.ccw.gov.uk/

CRC for Coastal Zone, Estuary and Waterway Management
Indooroopilly Sciences Centre
80 Meiers Road
Indooroopilly, QLD 4068, Australia
Contact: Chief Executive Officer
Tel: 61 7 3362 9399
Fax: 61 7 3362 9372

E-mail: coastal.crc@nrm.qld.gov.au
http://www.coastal.crc.org.au/

CRC for Sustainable Aquaculture of Finfish
c/o South Australian Research and Development Institute
2 Hamra Avenue
West Beach, SA 5024, Australia
Contact: Chief Executive Officer
Tel: 61 8 8290 2302
Fax: 61 8 8200 2406
E-mail: peter.montague@aquafincrc.com.au
http://www.aquafincrc.com.au/

CRC for Sustainable Tourism
Griffith University
PMB 50
Gold Coast Mall Centre, QLD 9726, Australia
Tel: 61 7 5552 8172
Fax: 61 7 5552 8171
E-mail: info@crctourism.com.au
http://www.crctourism.com.au/

CRC Reef Research Centre
Northtown Towers, 6th Floor
PO Box 772
Townsville, QLD 4810, Australia
Contact: Secretariat
Tel: 61 7 4729 8400
Fax: 61 7 4729 8499
E-mail: info@crcreef.com
http://www.reef.crc.org.au/

Danish Directorate of Fisheries
Stormgade 2
DK-1470 Copenhagen K, Denmark
Tel: 45 33 96 30 00
Fax: 45 33 96 39 03
E-mail: fd@fd.dk
http://www.fd.dk/

Danish Institute for Fisheries Research
(Danmarks Fiskeriundersøgelser)
Jägersborg vej 64-66
DK-2800 Lyngby, Denmark
Tel: 45 33 96 33 00
Fax: 45 33 96 33 49
E-mail: dir@dfu.min.dk
http://www.dfu.min.dk/

Danish Institute of Agricultural and Fisheries Economics
(Fødevareøkonomisk Institut)
Rolighedsvej 25
DK-1958 Frederiksberg C, Denmark
Contact: Director
Tel: 45 35 28 6800
Fax: 45 35 28 6801
E-mail: opk@foi.dk
http://www.sjfi.dk/

Danish Maritime Authority (DMA)
Ministry of Economics and Business Affairs
38C, Vermundsgade
PO Box 2605
DK-2100 Copenhagen, Denmark
Tel: 45 39 17 44 00
Fax: 45 39 17 44 01
E-mail: dma@dma.dk
http://www.dma.dk/

Danish Polar Center
Strandgade 100H
DK-1401 Copenhagen K, Denmark
Tel: 45 32 88 0100
Fax: 45 32 88 0101
E-mail: dpc@dpc.dk
http://www.dpc.dk/

Department for Environment, Food & Rural Affairs
Nobel House
17 Smith Square
London, SW1P 3JR, United Kingdom
Tel: 44 207 238 6951
Fax: 44 207 238 6609
E-mail: helpline@defra.gsi.gov.uk
http://www.defra.gov.uk/fish/

Department of Agriculture, Fisheries and Forestry
Edmund Barton Building
Broughton Street, Barton, GPO Box 858
Canberra, ACT 2601, Australia
Tel: 61 2 6272 5777
E-mail: fisheries@affa.gov.au
http://www.affa.gov.au/

Department of Communications, Marine and Natural Resources
Leeson Lane
Dublin 2, Ireland
Tel: 353 1 6782000
Fax: 353 1 6618214
E-mail: webmaster@dcmnr.gov.ie
http://www.marine.gov.ie/

Department of Conservation
PO Box 10420

59 Boulcott Street
Wellington, New Zealand
Contact: Director-General
Tel: 64 04 471 0391
http://www.doc.govt.nz/Conservation/Marine-and-Coastal/

Department of Fisheries
Kasetlang, Chatuchak
Bangkok 10900, Thailand
Tel: 66 2 562 0600
Fax: 66 2 562 9406 203
E-mail: webmaster@fisheries.go.th
http://www.fisheries.go.th/

Department of Marine and Coastal Resources
Ministry of Natural Resources and Environment
92 Soi Paholyothin 7
Bangkok 10400, Thailand
Tel: 66 2 298 2591
Fax: 66 2 298 5735
E-mail: info@monre.go.th
http://www.monre.go.th/

Department of Ocean Development
Block No. 9 & 12, CGO Complex
Lodhi Road
New Delhi 110003, India
Fax: 91 11 4360336
E-mail: ocean@dod.delhi.nic.in
http://www.dod.nic.in/

Department of the Environment and Heritage
Coasts and Oceans Division
GPO Box 787
Canberra, ACT 2601, Australia
Tel: 61 2 6274 1111
Fax: 61 2 6274 1006
http://www.ea.gov.au/coasts/

Department of Transportation and Communications
PPL Building
1000 UN Avenue cor. San Marcelino Street
Manila, The Philippines
Tel: 63 2 523 8651
E-mail: feedback@marina.gov.ph
http://www.marina.gov.ph/

Dirección Nacional de Recursos Acuáticos (DINARA)
Constituyente 1497
CP 11200
PO Box 1612
Montevideo, Uruguay
Tel: 598 2 409 2964
http://www.dinara.gub.uy/

Dunstaffnage Marine Laboratory
Oban, Argyll, Scotland, PA34 4AD, United Kingdom
Contact: Director
Tel: 44 1631 559000
Fax: 44 1631 559001
E-mail: mail@dml.ac.uk
http://www.sams.ac.uk/dml/

English Nature
Northminster House
Peterborough, PE1 1UA, United Kingdom
Tel: 44 17 3345 5100
Fax: 44 17 3356 8834
E-mail: enquiries@english-nature.org.uk
http://www.english-nature.org.uk/

Environment Agency
Rio House Waterside Drive, Aztec West
Almondsbury, Bristol, BS32 4UD, United Kingdom
Tel: 44 84 5933 3111
E-mail: enquiries@environment-agency. gov.uk
http://www.environment-agency.gov.uk/

Federal Research Centre for Fisheries
(Bundesforschungsanstalt für Fischerei)
Palmaille 9
D-22767 Hamburg, Germany
Tel: 49 40 38905-0
Fax: 49 40 38905-200
E-mail: iud@bfa-fisch.de
http://www.bfa-fisch.de/

Finnish Environment Institute (SYKE)
PO Box 140
FIN-00251 Helsinki, Finland
Tel: 358 9 403 000
Fax: 358 9 4030 0190
E-mail: kirjaamo.syke@ymparisto.fi
http://www.ymparisto.fi/eng/syke/syke.htm

Finnish Institute of Marine Research
(Merentutkimuslaitos)
Lyypekinkuja 3 A
PO Box 33

FIN-00931 Helsinki, Finland
Tel: 358 9 6139 41
Fax: 358 9 6139 4494
E-mail: info@fimr.fi
http://www2.fimr.fi/

Finnish Maritime Administration
PO Box 171
FIN-00181 Helsinki, Finland
Tel: 358 204 481
Fax: 358 204 48 4355
http://www.fma.fi/

Fisheries and Oceans Canada (DFO)
200 Kent Street, 13th Floor Station 13228
Ottawa, ON, K1A 0E6, Canada
Contact: Communications Branch
Tel: 1 613 993-0999
Fax: 1 613 990-1866
E-mail: info@dfo-mpo.gc.ca
http://www.dfo-mpo.gc.ca/; http://www.dfo-mpo.gc.ca/canwaters-eauxcan/index.html

Fisheries Information Center (FICen)
Ministry of Fisheries
10 Nguyen Cong Hoan Street
Ba Dinh District, Hanoi, Vietnam
Tel: 84 4 7716578
Fax: 84 4 7716578
E-mail: ttam.bts@hn.vnn.vn
http://www.fistenet.gov.vn/index_En.asp

Fisheries Resource Conservation Council
PO Box 2001 Station D
Ottawa, ON, K1P 5W3, Canada
Contact: Secretariat
Tel: 1 613 998-0433
Fax: 1 613 998-1146
E-mail: info@frcc-ccrh.ca
http://www.frcc-ccrh.ca/

Florida Marine Research Institute
100 Eighth Avenue SE
St. Petersburg, FL, 33701-5095, USA
Tel: 1 727 896-8626
http://www.floridamarine.org/

Geological Survey of Canada (Atlantic)
Bedford Institute of Oceanography
1 Challenger Drive
PO Box 1006
Dartmouth, NS, B2Y 4A2, Canada
Contact: Director
Tel: 1 902 426-3448
Fax: 1 902 426-1466
E-mail: webmaster@gsca.nrcan.gc.ca
http://agcwww.bio.ns.ca/

Great Barrier Reef Marine Park Authority
PO Box 1379
Townsville, QLD 4810, Australia
Tel: 61 7 4750 0700
Fax: 61 7 4772 6093
E-mail: info@gbrmpa.gov.au
http://www.gbrmpa.gov.au/

Gulf of Guinea Large Marine Ecosystem Project (GOGLME)
Regional Coordination Centre
c/o CRO
BP V18
Abidjan, Côte d'Ivoire
Tel: 225 355014
Fax: 225 351155
E-mail: gog-lme@africaonline.co.ci
http://www.africaonline.co.ci/AfricaOnline/societes/goglme/goglme.html

Gulf of Mexico Fishery Management Council
3018 U.S. Highway 301 North, Suite 1000
Tampa, FL 33619-2272, USA
Tel: 1 813 228-2815
Fax: 813 225-7015
E-mail: gulfcouncil@gulfcouncil.org
http://www.gulfcouncil.org/

Icelandic Fisheries Laboratories
Skulagata 4
PO Box 1405
IS-101 Reykjavik, Iceland
Tel: 354 562 0240
Fax: 354 562 0740
E-mail: info@rf.is
http://www.rfisk.is/home.htm

Icelandic Marine Research Institute (Hafrannsóknastofnunin—HAFRO)
Skulagata 4
PO Box 1390
IS-121 Reykjavik, Iceland
Tel: 354 552 0240
Fax: 354 562 3790
E-mail: hafro@hafro.is
http://www.hafro.is/

Institut de Recherche pour le Développement (IRD)
213, rue la Fayette
F-75480 Paris Cedex 10, France
Contact: Headquarters
Tel: 331 1 4803 7777
Fax: 331 1 4803 0829
E-mail: corlay@paris.ird.fr
http://www.ird.fr/

Institut Français de Recherche pour l'Exploitation de la Mer (IFREMER)
155 rue Jean-Jacques Rousseau
F-92138 Issy-les-Moulineaux Cedex, France
Contact: CEO
Tel: 33 1 4648 2100
Fax: 33 1 4648 2121
E-mail: jean.francois.minster@ifremer.fr
http://www.ifremer.fr/

Institut für Ostseeforschung Warnemuende (IOW)
Baltic Sea Research Institute Warnemuende
Seestrasse 15
D-18119 Rostock, Germany
Tel: 49 381 5197 100
Fax: 49 381 5197 105
E-mail: barbara.hentzsch@io-warnemuende.de
http://www.io-warnemuende.de/

Institut National de Recherche Halieutique
2 rue de Tiznit
Casablanca, Morocco
Contact: Directeur
Tel: 212 22 88 70
Fax: 212 22 88 57
E-mail: inrh@inrh.org.ma

Institute for Baltic Sea Fisheries
(Institut für Ostseeforschung—IOR)
An der Jägerbäk 2
D-18069 Rostock, Germany
Tel: 49 381 810344
Fax: 49 381 810445
E-mail: info@ior.bfa-fisch.de
http://www.bfa-fisch.de/ior/

Institute for Coastal Research
GKSS-Forschungszentrum
Institut für Küstenforschung/Modelling
Max-Planck-Strasse
D-21502 Geesthacht, Germany
Tel: 49 4152 87 1831
Fax: 49 4152 87 2832
E-mail: storch@gkss.de
http://coast.gkss.de/

Institute for Marine Biosciences
National Research Council of Canada
1411 Oxford Street
Halifax, NS, B3H 3Z1, Canada
Contact: Director
Tel: 1 902 426-8332
Fax: 1 902 426-9413
E-mail: info@nrc.ca
http://www.imb.nrc.ca/

Institute for Ocean Technology (IOT)
PO Box 12093
St. John's, NF, A1B 3T5, Canada
Tel: 1 709 772-4939
Fax: 1 709 772-2462
E-mail: noel.murphy@nrc.ca
http://iot-ito.nrc-cnrc.gc.ca/

Institute for Sea Fisheries
(Institut für Seefischerei—ISH)
Palmaille 9
D-22767 Hamburg, Germany
Tel: 49 40 38905 177
Fax: 49 40 38905 263
E-mail: info@ish.bfa-fisch.de
http://www.bfa-fisch.de/ish/

Institute of Biology of the Southern Seas
2 Nakhimov Avenue
Sebastopol 99011 Crimea, Ukraine
Tel: 380 692 544 100
Fax: 380 692 557 813
E-mail: ibss@ibss.iuf.net
http://www.ibss.iuf.net/

Institute of Coastal Resources
(Fiskeriverket—Kustlaboratoriet)
Swedish National Board of Fisheries
Gamla Slipvägen 19
SE-740 71 Öregrund, Sweden
Tel: 46 17 34 64 60
Fax: 46 17 33 09 49
E-mail: fiskeriverket@fiskeriverket.se
http://www.fiskeriverket.se/

Institute of Marine Affairs (IMA)
Hilltop Lane
PO Box 3160
Carenage Post Office
Chaguaramas, Trinidad and Tobago

Tel: 1 868 634-4291
Fax: 1 868 634-4433
E-mail: director@ima.gov.tt
http://www.ima.gov.tt/

Institute of Marine Research (IMRS)
Swedish National Board of Fisheries
PO Box 4
SE-45321 Lysekil, Sweden
Contact: Secretary General
Tel: 46 52 31 87 00
Fax: 46 52 31 39 77
E-mail: fiskeriverket@fiskeriverket.se
http://www.fiskeriverket.se/

Institute of Marine Research (IMR)
(Havforskningsinstituttet)
PO Box 1870 Nordnes
N-5817 Bergen, Norway
Tel: 47 55 23 85 00
Fax: 47 55 23 85 31
E-mail: post@imr.no
http://www.imr.no/

Institute of Ocean Sciences
9860 West Saanich Road
PO Box 6000
Sidney, BC, V8L 4B2, Canada
Tel: 1 250 363-6517
E-mail: olsonp@pac.dfo-mpo.gc.ca
http://www.pac.dfo-mpo.gc.ca/sci/english/facilities/ios.htm

Instituto de Fomento Pesquero (IFOP)
(Fishery Research Institute)
Hulto 374, Casilla 8-V
Valparaíso, Chile
Tel: 56 32 2047858
Fax: 56 32 2254362
E-mail: info@ifop.cl
http://www.ifop.cl/

Instituto de Investigaciones Marinas
Eduardo Cabello 6
E-36208 Vigo, Spain
Tel: 34 986 231 930
Fax: 34 986 292 762
E-mail: admin@iim.csic.es
http://www.iim.csic.es/

Instituto de Investigaciones Marinas y Costeras (INVEMAR)
Cerro Punta de Betín, Santa Marta
Apartado aéreo1016, Santa Marta, Colombia
Tel: 57 5 421 4774
Fax: 57 5 4211377
E-mail: morela@invemar.org.co
http://www.invemar.org.co/redcosteral/invemar/

Instituto de Mar de Perú (IMARPE)
(Peruvian Marine Institute)
Esquina de Gamarra y General Valle S/N Chuciuto
Callao, Peru
Tel: 51 420 2000
E-mail: webmaster@imarpe.gob.pe
http://www.imarpe.gob.pe/

Instituto de Oceanología de Cuba
(Institute of Oceanology)
Calle 1ra No. 18406 esquina 184 y 186
Reparto Flores, Playa
Havana 12100, Cuba
Contact: Director
Tel: 537 21 1380
Fax: 537 33 9112
E-mail: jperez@unepnet.inf.cu
http://www.cuba.cu/ciencia/citma/ama/oceanologia/inicio.html

Instituto Nacional de Pesca (INP)
Letamendi 102 y La Ría
PO Box 09-04-15131
Guayaquil, Ecuador
Contact: Director
Tel: 593 4 2401773
Fax: 593 4 2402304
E-mail: larriaga@inp.gov.ec
http://www.inp.gov.ec/

Instituto Oceanográfico de la Armada (INOCAR)
(Naval Oceanographic Institute)
Avda 25 de Julio (Base Naval Sur)
via al Puerto Marítimo
Guyaquil, Ecuador
Tel: 593 4 2481 300
Fax: 593 4 2485 166
E-mail: inocar@inocar.mil.ec
http://www.inocar.mil.ec/

Inter-Agency Committee on Marine Science and Technology
Southampton Oceanography
Centre

European Way
Empress Dock
Southampton, SO14 3ZH, United Kingdom
Tel: 44 2380 596611
Fax: 44 2380 956395
E-mail: enquiries@marine.gov.uk
http://www.marine.gov.uk/

International Association of Fish and Wildlife Agencies
444 Capitol Street, NW, Suite 544
Washington, DC, 20001, USA
Contact: Executive Vice President
Tel: 1 202 624-7890
Fax: 1 202 624-7891
E-mail: iafwa@sso.org
http://www.iafwa.org/

Irish Marine Institute
80 Harcourt Street
Dublin 2, Ireland
Tel: 353 1 476 6500
Fax: 353 1 478 4988
E-mail: institute.mail@marine.ie
http://www.marine.ie/

Japan Marine Science and Technology Center (JAMSTEC)
Natsushima-cho 2-15, Yokosuka-shi
Kanagawa Prefecture, 237-0061, Japan
Tel: 81 0468 66 3811
E-mail: www-admin@jamstec.go.jp
http://www.jamstec.go.jp/

Japan Sea National Fisheries Research Institute (JSNFRI)
5939-22, Suido-cho 1 chome, Niigata-shi
Niigata 951, Japan
Tel: 81 025 228 0451
Fax: 81 025 224 0950
E-mail: yamada@jsnf.affrc.go.jp
http://www.affrc.go.jp/mirror/jsnf/

Joint Nature Conservation Committee (JNCC)
Monkstone House, City Road
Peterborough, PE1 1JY, United Kingdom
Contact: Marine Section
Tel: 44 1733 562626
Fax: 44 1733 555948
E-mail: feedback@jncc.gov.uk
http://www.jncc.gov.uk/marine/

Korea Institute of Ships and Ocean Engineering
PO Box 23
Yusong, Daejon, 305-600 Korea
Tel: 82 42 868 7701
Fax: 82 42 868 7711
E-mail: jskang@kriso.re.kr
http://www.kriso.re.kr/

Korea Ocean Research and Development Institute (KORDI)
Ansan PO Box 29
425-600 Korea
Tel: 82 31 400 6000
Fax: 82 31 408 5820
E-mail: webmaster@kordi.re.kr
http://www.kordi.re.kr/

Maine Atlantic Salmon Commission
172 State House Station
Augusta, ME, 04333-0172, USA
Tel: 1 207 287-9972
Fax: 1 207 287-9975
E-mail: joan.trial@maine.gov
http://www.state.me.us/asa/

Marine and Coastal Management Office
Department of Environmental Affairs and Tourism
Private Bag X2
Roggebaai 8012, South Africa
Contact: Deputy Director-General
Tel: 27 12 402 3018
Fax: 27 12 402 3217
E-mail: hghklein@sfri.wcape.gov.za
http://www.environment.gov.za/

Marine Board
Transportation Research Board
National Academy of Sciences
500 Fifth Street NW
Washington, DC, 20001, USA
Contact: Director
Tel: 1 202 334-3119
Fax: 1 202 334-2030
E-mail: jcambrid@nas.edu
http://www4.nationalacademies.org/trb/homepage.nsf/web/marine_board

Marine Department Malaysia
(Jabatan Laut Malaysia)

Peti Surat 12
Jalan Limbungan
42007 Pelabuhan Klang, Malaysia
Contact: Director General
Tel: 60 3 3346 7777
Fax: 60 3 3168 5289
E-mail: malik@marine.gov.my
http://www.marine.gov.my/

Marine Environment Branch
Environment Canada
Place Vincent Massey
351 St. Joseph Boulevard, 12th Floor
Hull, QC, K1A 0H3, Canada
Contact: Director
Tel: 1 819 953-1699
Fax: 1 819 953-0913
E-mail: marie.gauthier@ec.gc.ca
http://www.ec.gc.ca/

Maritime Administration
U.S. Department of Transportation
400 Seventh Street SW
Washington, DC, 20590, USA
Tel: 1 202 366-5807
Fax: 1 202 366-8886
E-mail: pao@marad.dot.gov
http://www.marad.dot.gov/

Maritime and Coastguard Agency
Tutt Head, Mumbles
Swansea, West Glamorgan, SA3 4HW, United Kingdom
Tel: 44 23 870 600 6505
E-mail: infoline@mcga.gov.uk
http://www.mcga.org.uk/

Maritime Institute of Malaysia (MIMA)
B-06-08 Megan Avenue II
12 Yap Kwan Seng
50450 Kuala Lumpur, Malaysia
Contact: Director General
Tel: 60 3 2161 2960
Fax: 60 3 2161 4035
E-mail: mima@mima.gov.my
http://www.mima.gov.my/

Maurice Lamontagne Institute
Fisheries and Oceans Canada
850 route de la Mer
PO Box 1000
Mont-Joli, QC, G5H 3Z4, Canada
Tel: 1 418 775-0500
Fax: 1 418 775-0542
E-mail: info@dfo-mpo.gc.ca
http://www.qc.dfo-mpo.gc.ca/iml/

Mid-Atlantic Fisheries Management Council
Room 2115 Federal Building
300 S. New Street
Dover, DE, 19904, USA
Contact: Executive Director
Tel: 1 302 674-2331
E-mail: dfurlong@mafmc.org
http://www.mafmc.org/

Ministry of Agriculture and Fisheries (Ministère des l'Agriculture et de la Pêches)
12, Bd Colonel Amirouche
Alger, Algeria
Tel: 213 21 71 17 12
Fax: 213 21 79 59 86
E-mail: mprh@wissal.dz

Ministry of Marine Fisheries
(Ministère de la Pêche Maritime)
Nouveau quartier administratif
PO Box 476
Agdal, Rabat, Morocco
Tel: 212 17 688000
Fax: 212 17 688135
E-mail: webmaster@mpm.gov.ma
http://www.mpm.gov.ma/

Ministry of Maritime Affairs and Fisheries (MOMAF)
139 Chungjong-No 3, Seodaemun-Gu
Seoul 120-715, Korea
Tel: 82 2 3148 6114
Fax: 82 2 3148 6044
E-mail: momweb@momaf.go.kr
http://www.momaf.go.kr/

National Center for Marine Research
Agios Kosmas
Hellinikon
GR-16604 Athens, Greece
Tel: 30 1 982 0214
Fax: 30 1 983 3095
E-mail: ctziav@posidon.ncmr.ariadne-t.gr
http://www.ncmr.gr/

National Environment and Planning Agency
John McIntosh Building
10 Caledonia Avenue

Kingston 5, Jamaica
Tel: 876 754 7540
Fax: 876 754 7595
E-mail: pubed@nepa.gov.jm
http://www.nrca.org/

National Environmental Research Institute, Denmark (NERI)
PO Box 358
Frederiksborgvej 399
DK-4000 Roskilde, Denmark
Tel: 45 4630 1200
Fax: 45 4630 1114
E-mail: dmu@dmu.dk
http://www.dmu.dk/

National Institute for Marine Research and Development Grigore Antipa
Boulevard Mamaia 300
RO-8700 Constanta 3, Romania
Tel: 40 41 543 288
Fax: 40 41 831 274
E-mail: rmri@alpha.rmri.ro
http://www.rmri.ro/

National Institute of Oceanography and Fisheries (NIOF)
101 Kasr El Ainy Street
Cairo, Egypt
Tel: 20 2 792 1342
Fax: 20 2 792 1339
E-mail: awwade@niof.sci.eg
http://www.niof.sci.eg/

National Institute of Water and Atmospheric Research
Private Bag 99940
269 Khyber Pass Road
Newmarket, Auckland, New Zealand
Tel: 64 9 375 2090
Fax: 64 9 375 2091
E-mail: webmaster@niwa.co.nz
http://www.niwa.cri.nz/

National Marine Data & Information Service
93 Qiwei Road
Hedong District, Tianjin 300171, People's Republic of China
Contact: Director
Tel: 86 22 2401 0801
E-mail: webmaster@mail.nmdis.gov.cn
http://www.nmdis.gov.cn/

National Marine Fisheries Service (NMFS)
National Oceanic and Atmospheric Administration (NOAA)
1315 East-West Highway SSMC3
Silver Spring, MD, 20910, USA
E-mail: cyber.fish@noaa.gov
http://www.nmfs.noaa.gov/

National Ocean Service
National Oceanic and Atmospheric Administration (NOAA)
1305 East-West Highway, SSMC4
Silver Spring, MD, 20910, USA
Tel: 1 301 713-3074
E-mail: nos.info@nos.noaa.gov
http://www.nos.noaa.gov/

National Oceans Office
GPO Box 2139
Hobart, Tasmania 7000, Australia
Tel: 61 3 6221 5000
Fax: 61 3 6221 5050
E-mail: office@oceans.gov.au
http://www.oceans.gov.au/

National Research Institute of Fisheries Science
2-12-4, Fukuura
Kanazawa, Yokohama
Kanagawa 236-8648, Japan
Tel: 81 45 788 7615
Fax: 81 45 788 5001
E-mail: www@nrifs.affrc.go.jp
http://www.nrifs.affrc.go.jp/index-e.html

National Sea Grant College Program
National Oceanic and Atmospheric Administration
1315 East-West Highway
Silver Spring, MD, 20910, USA
Tel: 1 301 713-2431
Fax: 1 301 713-0799
E-mail: Amy.Painter@noaa.gov
http://www.nsgo.seagrant.org/

Natural Environment Research Council (NERC)
Polaris House
North Star Avenue
Swindon, SN2 1EU, United Kingdom
Tel: 44 01793 411500
Fax: 44 01793 411501
http://www.nerc.ac.uk/

Netherlands Institute for Sea Research

(Nederlands Instituut voor Onderzoek der Zee NIOZ)
PO Box 59
NL-1790 AB, Den Burg, Texel, The Netherlands
Tel: 31 222 369300
Fax: 31 222 319674
E-mail: webmaster@nioz.nl
http://www.nioz.nl/

New England Fishery Management Council
50 Water Street, Mill 2
Newburyport, MA, 01950, USA
Tel: 1 978 465-0492
Fax: 1 978 465-3116
E-mail: joleary@nefmc.org
http://www.nefmc.org/

New Zealand Ministry of Fisheries
ASB Bank House
101—103 The Terrace
PO Box 1020
Wellington, New Zealand
Tel: 64 4 470 2600
Fax: 64 4 470 2601
E-mail: info@fish.govt.nz
http://www.fish.govt.nz/

Nigerian Institute of Oceanography and Marine Research (NIOMR)
Ministry of Science and Technology
Private Mail Bag 12729
Lagos, Nigeria
Contact: Director
Tel/Fax: 234 1 261 9517
Fax: 234 1 617385
E-mail: niomr@linkserve.com.ng

North Pacific Fishery Management Council
605 West 4th, Suite 306
Anchorage, AK, 99501-2252, USA
Contact: Executive Director
Tel: 1 907 271-2809
Fax: 1 907 271-2817
E-mail: Chris.Oliver@noaa.gov
http://www.fakr.noaa.gov/npfmc/

Norwegian Institute for Water Research
(Norsk Institutt for Vannforskning)
Brekkeveien 19
Postboks 173 Kjelsas
N-0411 Oslo, Norway
Tel: 47 22 18 51 00
Fax: 47 22 18 52 00
E-mail: webmaster@niva.no
http://www.niva.no/

Norwegian Polar Institute
(Norsk Polarinstitutt—NPI)
Polar Environmental Centre
N-9296 Tromsø, Norway
Tel: 47 77 75 05 00
Fax: 47 77 75 05 01
E-mail: postmottak@npolar.no
http://www.npolar.no/

Norwegian Pollution Control Authority
PO Box 8100 Dep.
N-0032 Oslo, Norway
Tel: 47 22 57 34 00
Tel: 47 22 67 67 06
E-mail: mistin.redaksjonen@sft.no
http://www.environment.no/

Observatoire Océanologique Villefranche-sur-Mer
BP 28
F-06238 Villefranche Sur Mer Cedex, France
Tel: 33 4 9376 3803
Fax: 33 4 9376 3834
E-mail: webmaster@obs-vlfr.fr
http://www.obs-vlfr.fr/

Ocean Studies Board
The National Academies
500 5th Street, NW
Keck Building, Room K-752
Washington, DC, 20001, USA
Tel: 1 202 334-2714
Fax: 1 202 334-2885
E-mail: osb_feedback@nas.edu
http://www7.nationalacademies.org/osb/

Oceanology and Environmental Geophysics (OGA)
Instituto Nationale di Oceanografia
Borgo Grotta Gigante 42/c
I-34010 Sgonico (TS), Italy
Tel: 39 040 2140 1
Fax: 39 040 2140 266
E-mail: mailbox@ogs.trieste.it
http://doga.ogs.trieste.it/index.html

Oceans Policy Secretariat
Ministry for the Environment
PO Box 10362
Wellington, New Zealand
Tel: 64 4 917 7400

Fax: 64 4 917 7521
E-mail: oceans@mfe.govt.nz
http://www.oceans.govt.nz/

Office of Naval Research
Ballston Centre Tower One
800 North Quincy Street
Arlington, VA, 22217-5660, USA
Tel: 1 703 696-5031
Fax: 1 703 696-5940
E-mail: onrpao@onr.navy.mil
http://www.onr.navy.mil/

Office of the Commissioner for Aquaculture Development (OCAD)
427 Laurier Avenue West, Suite 1210
Ottawa, ON, K1A OE6, Canada
Contact: Commissioner
Tel: 1 613 993-8603
Fax: 1 613 993-8607
E-mail: BastienY@dfo-mpo.gc.ca
http://ocad-bcda.gc.ca/

Office of Wetlands, Oceans and Watersheds
Environmental Protection Agency
1200 Pennsylvania Ave, NW
Washington, DC, 20460, USA
Contact: Administrator
Tel: 1 202 566-1300
E-mail: ow-owow-internet-comments@epa.gov
http://www.epa.gov/owow/

Pacific Biological Station
3190 Hammond Bay Road
Nanaimo, BC, V9T 6N7, Canada
Tel: 1 250 756-7000
Fax: 1 250 756-7053
E-mail: info@dfo-mpo.gc.ca
http://www.pac.dfo-mpo.gc-ca/sci/pbs/

Pacific Fisheries Research Center (TINRO-Center)
4 Shevchenko Alley
Vladivostok, 690950, Russia
Contact: Director
Tel: 7 4232 400921
Fax: 7 4232 300752
E-mail: tinro@tinro.ru
http://www.tinro.ru/

Pacific Fishery Management Council
7700 NE Ambassador Place, Suite 200
Portland, OR, 97220-1384, USA
Contact: Executive Director
Tel: 1 503 820-2280
Fax: 1 503 820-2299
E-mail: pfmc.comments@noaa.gov
http://www.pcouncil.org/

Pacific States Marine Fisheries Commission (PSMFC)
45 SE 82nd Drive, Suite 100
Gladstone, OR, 97027-2522, USA
Contact: Executive Director
Tel: 1 503 650-5400
Fax: 1 503 650-5426
E-mail: sharon.perleins@psmfc.org
http://www.psmfc.org/

Philippine Council for Aquatic and Marine Research and Development (PCAMRD)
Jamboree Road, Brgy. Timugan
Los Baños, Laguna, 4030, The Philippines
Tel: 63 49 536 1574
Fax: 63 49 536 5578
E-mail: pcamrd@laguna.net
http://www.pcamrd.dost.gov.ph/

Protected Areas Conservation Trust
2 Mango Street
Belmopan, Cayo, Belize
Tel: 501 822-3637
Fax: 501 822-3759
E-mail: info@pactbelize.org
http://www.pactbelize.org/

Research and Development Centre of Oceanology
(Pusat Penelitian dan Pengembangan Oseanologi)
Indonesian Institute of Sciences (LIPI)
Jalan Pasir Putih 1
Ancol Timur
11048 Jakarta, Indonesia
Tel: 62 21 682287
Fax: 62 21 681948
E-mail: ppolipi@jakarta.wasantara.net.id
http://www.lipi.go.id/

Research Institute of Marine Products (RIMP)
170 Le Lai
Ngo Quyen District, Hai Phong, Vietnam
Tel: 84 31 836664
Fax: 84 31 836812
E-mail: dokhuong@hn.vnn.vn
http://www.fistenet.gov.vn/index _En.asp

Scottish Natural Heritage
12 Hope Terrace
Edinburgh, Scotland, EH9 2AS, United Kingdom
Tel: 44 131 447 4784
Fax: 44 131 446 2277
E-mail: www.enquiries@snh.gov.uk
http://www.snh.org.uk/

Senegalese Ministry of Fisheries
Building Administratif
BP 4050
Dakar, Senegal
Tel: 221 849 7000
Fax: 221 823 8720
http://www.gouv.sn/ministeres/mpeche/contacts.cfm

Servicio Hidrográfico y Oceanográfico de la Armade de Chile
(Hydrographic and Oceanographic Service of the Chilean Navy)
Calle Errázuriz 254, Cerro Playa Ancha
Casilla: 324
Valparaíso, Chile
Tel: 56 32 266666
Fax: 56 32 266542
E-mail: shoa@shoa.cl
http://www.shoa.cl/

Sierra Leone Maritime Administration
P.O. Box 313, Maritime House
Government Wharf Ferry Terminal
Freetown, Sierra Leone
Tel: 232 22 221 211
Fax: 232 22 221 215
E-mail: SLMA@sierratel.sl

South Atlantic Fishery Management Council
One Southpark Circle, Suite 306
Charleston, SC, 29407-4699, USA
Tel: 1 843 571-4366
Fax: 1 843 769-4520
E-mail: safmc@safmc.net
http://www.safmc.net/

South Australian Research and Development Institute (SARDI)
GPO Box 397
Adelaide, SA 5001, Australia
Contact: Aquatic Sciences Research Programme
Tel: 61 8 8200 2400
Fax: 61 8 8200 2481
E-mail: cheshire.anthony@saugov.sa.gov.au
http://www.sardi.sa.gov.au/

Southeastern Association of Fish and Wildlife Agencies
8005 Freshwater Farms Road
Tallahassee, FL, 32308, USA
Contact: Executive Secretary
Tel: 1 850 893-1204
Fax: 1 850 893-6204
E-mail: seafwa@aol.com
http://www.seafwa.org/

Spanish Institute of Oceanography
(Instituto Español de Oceanografía—IEO)
Avenida de Brasil, No. 31
E-28020 Madrid, Spain
Tel: 34 915 974 443
Fax: 34 915 974 770
E-mail: ieo@md.ieo.es
http://www.ieo.es/

State Oceanic Administration
93 Livwei Road
Hedong District
Tianjin 300171, People's Republic of China
Contact: Chief
Tel: 86 10 6853 2211
Fax: 86 10 6853 3515
E-mail: webmaster@mail.nmdis.gov.cn
http://www.soa.gov.cn/

Swedish National Board of Fisheries
Ekelundsgatan 1
Box 423
SE-401 26 Göteborg, Sweden
Contact: Head Office
Tel: 46 31 743 03 00
Fax: 46 31 743 04 44
E-mail: fiskeriverket@fiskeriverket.se
http://www.fiskeriverket.se/

Swedish Polar Research Secretariat
PO Box 50 003
SE-104 05 Stockholm, Sweden
Tel: 46 86 73 96 00
Fax: 46 8 15 20 57
E-mail: office@polar.se
http://www.polar.se/

Transport Canada—Marine Safety
330 Sparks Street
Ottawa, ON, K1A 0N5, Canada
Tel: 1 613 991-3135

Fax: 1 613 990-6191
E-mail: marinesafety@tc.gc.ca
http://www.tc.gc.ca/marinesafety/

Ukrainian Scientific Center of Marine Ecology
89, Frantsuzki Boulevard
Odessa 270009, Ukraine
Contact: Director
Tel: 380 482 636622
Fax: 380 482 636673
E-mail: root@accem.odessa.ua

United States Army Corps of Engineers
Cold Regions Research and Engineering Laboratory
CECRL-PP
72 Lyme Road
Hanover, NH, 03755-1290, USA
Tel: 1 603 646-4100
Fax: 1 603 646-4448
E-mail: info@crrel.usace.army.mil
http://www.crrel.usace.army.mil/

United States Coast Guard
2100 Second Street SW
Washington, DC, 20593, USA
Contact: Headquarters
Tel: 1 202 267-2229
http://www.uscg.mil/

United States Coast Guard Auxiliary
Commandant (G-OCX)
US Coast Guard Headquarters
2100 2nd Street SW, Room 3501
Washington, DC, 20593-0001, USA
Contact: Chief Director, Auxiliary
Tel: 1 202 267-1001
Fax: 1 202 267-4409
E-mail: info@cgaux.org
http://www.cgaux.org/

United States Commission on Ocean Policy
1120 20th Street, NW, Suite 200
North
Washington, D.C. 20036, USA
Tel: 1 202 418-3442
Fax: 1 202 418-3475
E-mail: hill@oceancommission.gov
http://oceancommission.gov/

Western Pacific Regional Fishery Management Council (WPRFMC)
1164 Bishop Street, Suite 1400
Honolulu, HI, 96813, USA
Tel: 1 808 522-8220
Fax: 1 808 522-8226
E-mail: info.wpcouncil@noaa.gov
http://www.wpcouncil.org/

Contributors

Abul Kalam Azad obtained a masters degree in international relations from the University of Dhaka, Bangladesh, in 1980. He worked as a research associate with the Bangladesh Council on World Affairs from 1981–1983. During the period 1983–1987, he engaged himself as a freelance researcher in international affairs. He joined the Bangladesh Institute of International and Strategic Studies in 1988, the leading think-tank in Bangladesh under the country's Ministry of Foreign Affairs, and is currently working at the Institute as senior research fellow. He undertook a French language course in 1991 at the Alliance Française de Paris and obtained a Diplôme d'Étude Approfondies (D.E.A.) degree in comparative political science in 1993 from the Institut d'Etudes Politiques, Université d'Aix-Marseilles III, and received a Ph.D. in comparative political science from the same institute in 1998. He received a master of marine management degree from Dalhousie University, Canada, in 2002. He has been conducting research on international and security affairs with a particular focus on South Asia. He has a number of publications in various journals and books. He delivers lectures at various universities and research institutes in his country on politicostrategic and security affairs. At present, marine affairs constitute the main focus of his research.

François Napoléon Bailet, B.Sc., Diplôme d'Étude Approfondies (D.E.A.), Ph.D., is currently an expert consultant on ocean governance with the International Ocean Institute–Headquarters. Based at Dalhousie University, in Halifax, Nova Scotia, Canada, he is also an adjunct professor of law, Dalhousie University Law School, and a research fellow in the Centre for Foreign Policy Studies, Department of Political Science, Dalhousie University. His current academic research and lecture topics are in the areas of ocean governance and the implementation of the Law of the Sea Convention and the UNCED process, through all levels of governance, with a focus on maritime security and regionalization. He is also involved in training and capacity building for developing nations and the development and coordination of IOI network-wide programs. He also works closely with the various "ocean" bodies of the UN system and serves as an IOI representative to numerous UN meetings and academic conferences.

J. Alan Beesley, O.C., Q.C. is the former Canadian head of delegation and ambassador to the Third United Nations Conference on the Law of the Sea and chair of the Conference Drafting Committee (1967–83). He was ambassador of Canada to Austria, IAEA, and UNIDO (1973–76), Canadian high commissioner to Australia, Papua New Guinea, Solomon Islands, and Vanuatu (1978–80), ambassador for disarmament, New York (1980–82), and ambassador to the United Nations at Geneva to the Disarmament Conference and to GATT (1983–87). Beesley was a visiting professor at the University of British Columbia Law School (1987–88) and ambassador for marine conservation and special environmental advisor to the Canadian foreign minister (1989–91). He is the recipient of many honours and awards, and holds several professional association memberships in the field of environmental law.

Awni Behnam began his career at an early age in the merchant marine and naval services. Before joining UNCTAD in 1977 he lectured at his alma mater, the University of Wales, department of maritime studies. He held executive posts in the shipping division of UNCTAD before assuming responsibility as the chief of liaison with developing countries for the secretary-general of UNCTAD. He was promoted to the rank of director and in 1999 he was appointed as secretary of the Tenth United Nations Conference on Trade and Development (UNCTAD), and the Third United Nations Conference on the Least Developed Countries, and currently holds the position of senior adviser to the secretary-general. Behnam holds a first degree in business administration (B.A. Mustensiriya University) and a masters and a doctorate in development and shipping economics from the University of Wales (M.Sc. Wales, Ph.D. Wales). Since 1977 Behnam has been involved in international multilateral affairs. He was instrumental in the negotiations of several international conventions and multilateral instruments in the field of maritime transport.

Patricia Birnie is a visiting fellow at the London School of Economics and Political Science who graduated in jurisprudence from Oxford and obtained a Ph.D. from Edinburgh. She is a nonpractising barrister. She taught public international law at Edinburgh and the London School of Economics, retiring early from the latter in 1989 to become first director of the IMO International Maritime Law Institute in Malta until 1992. She specialises in law of the sea and international environmental law.

Agustín Blanco-Bazán graduated in law at the University of Buenos Aires, Argentina, in 1974 and followed regular courses on philosophy, international law, and political science at the University of Vienna, Austria, from 1976 to 1979. From 1979 to 1983 he worked as manager and reinsurance consultant in London, travelling extensively throughout the world and playing a decisive advisory role during and after the South Atlantic conflict regarding the application of war clauses and renegotiations of reinsurance contracts between the United Kingdom and Argentina. In 1984 he joined the International Maritime Organization (IMO). As interregional advisor in maritime legislation he advised developing countries in Africa, Asia, and Latin America on the adoption and incorporation into national legislation of international treaties for safety of navigation, prevention of marine pollution, and compensation for pollution damage. At present he is senior deputy director and head of the legal office of IMO. He has participated in the elaboration of several international treaties as well as at numerous international conferences and lectures at academic institutions on law of the sea and maritime law. He has written many articles and essays on these subjects.

Salvino Busuttil is currently ambassador of Malta to France and Portugal. A professor emeritus in economics of the University of Malta, he has served as executive president of the Malta Association of Human Rights, vice-president of the Mediterranean Centre of Human Rights, president of the International Centre for Advanced Mediterranean Agronomic Studies and of the Fondation de Malte, and honorary secretary-general of the Mediterranean Council for Culture. He has been a member of the Council of Europe Independent Committee on the Social Charter, director of the Division of the Environment at UNESCO, co-ordinator of the UNEP Mediterranean Action Plan, UN adviser for the prime ministers of the Bahamas and St. Vincent and the Grenadines, and UNESCO adviser to the prime minister of Malta. He co-founded the Foundation for International Studies at the University of Malta, of which he was director-general for 11 years. A member of the IOI Governing Board for 20 years and organizer of *Pacem in Maribus* conferences in Malta, he served as treasurer of the Independent World Commission on the Oceans, and was, for a time, vice-president of the International Commission for the Scientific Exploration of the Mediterranean. He has written extensively on economic and environmental affairs. As the promoter of the UNESCO project on the Right of Future Generations, he has co-edited a number of books on the problematique of intergenerational equity. He is an officer of the Order of Merit of Malta, grand officer of the Order of Merit of Italy, commander of the Order of Don Enrique of Portugal. He was elected member of the Academie d'Agriculture de France and he is the recipient of the Gold Medal of the City of Paris.

Aldo Chircop is a professor and holder of the Canadian Chair in Marine Environmental Protection at the World Maritime University, Malmö, Sweden. On leave of absence at the WMU, Professor Chircop is faculty at Dalhousie University Law School and counsel to Patterson Palmer Law in Halifax, Nova Scotia, Canada. His previous responsibilities included directorships of the following: the Marine Affairs Programme (1992–2001) and Marine and Environmental Law Programme (2001–2003) at Dalhousie University; International Ocean Institute (1988–1991); and Mediterranean Institute (University of Malta, 1988–89). Over the years he has researched and taught law of the sea, maritime law, environmental law, international environmental law, administrative law, ocean policy, and integrated coastal management. He has published widely and is co-editor of the *Ocean Yearbook*. He is a member of the advisory boards of several periodicals, including *Ocean and Coastal Management, Doing Business in Mexico,* and the *WMU Journal of Maritime Affairs.*

Nathan Evans has been lecturer in ocean law and policy at the University of the South Pacific since the beginning of 2002. His teaching, research, and consulting interests revolve around legislative policy and ocean governance. Particular projects undertaken include fisheries observer programs, by-catch mitigation, aquaculture development, and regional engagement on marine conservation. Prior to his current position, Evans worked for many years in fisheries policy for the federal fisheries agency in Canberra. He obtained his Ph.D. from the University of Tasmania.

Emily A. Gardner holds a masters degree in zoology and a law degree with certificates in environmental law and ocean policy from the University of Hawaii. She currently serves on the faculty of the Graduate Ocean Policy Program at the University of Hawaii where her research interests include marine mammals and fisheries and the laws and policies that protect them. She is an attorney in Honolulu.

Orio Giarini became a full member of the Club of Rome 25 years ago and on this occasion started working in close collaboration with Elisabeth Mann Borgese. He contributed to the report *The Limits to Growth* and went on to write three further reports for the Club of Rome: *Dialogue on Wealth and Welfare* (1980); *The Limits to Certainty: Facing Risk in the New Service Economy,* with Walter Stahel (1993); and *The Employment Dilemma: Full Employment in the Service Economy,* with Patrick Liedtke (1998). A fourth report on *The Double Helix: The Complementarity between Learning and Work,* with Mircea Malitza will be published shortly. Since 1959 he has worked in the chemical industry (7 years), then for the Batelle Research Institute (7 years), and finally, he set up The Geneva Association, a think-tank for the world's insurance industry that analyses risks and vulnerabilities arising in modern society. He remained secretary general until 2000. Between 1962 and 1969 he was secretary general (honorary) of the European Federalist Movement in Paris and from 1985 to 1999, professor of service economics at the University of Geneva. He has also published a book in French entitled *Path to Retiring at 80.* Giarini is currently the director of The Risk Institute and special advisor to The Geneva Association in Geneva.

Moritaka Hayashi is a professor at the School of Law, Waseda University, Tokyo, teaching law of the sea, international environmental law, and international organizations and relations. Before joining Waseda in April 1999, from 1996 he was assistant director-general (head of the fisheries department) of the Food and Agriculture Organization of the United Nations in

Rome, Italy. From 1971 to 1979 and again from 1989 to 1996, he was an official at the UN Headquarters in New York, serving mainly its Office of Legal Affairs, with the last post being director of its Division for Ocean Affairs and the Law of the Sea. Between the two periods of his service at the United Nations, he was counselor and subsequently minister at the Japanese Mission to the United Nations in New York, in charge of legal and political matters. Recently he was a member of the independent International Commission on Shipping, which conducted extensive inquiry into substandard shipping and published a report with recommendations. He is co-editor of *New Directions in the Law of the Sea,* a series published by Oceana Publications.

Amy Hindman is the legal adviser to the executive director of the United Nations Environment Programme (UNEP). Prior to joining UNEP, she served as a legal adviser in the Division for International Legal Affairs of the German Federal Ministry for the Environment, Nature Conservation and Nuclear Safety, as a guest Fulbright professor at the Institute for European Law in Saarbrucken, Germany and as an environmental litigator in the United States. She received her Juris Doctor (*magna cum laude*) from Georgetown University Law Center in 1992.

Sidney Holt, on his retirement from the United Nations, where he served as director of FAO's Fisheries Resources Division, and of UNESCO's Marine Sciences Division, was the first director of the International Ocean Institute in Malta. He was for many years a close associate and friend of Elisabeth Mann Borgese, a friendship that began when both were fellows at the Center for the Study of Democratic Institutions, in Santa Barbara, California. Holt is an oceanographer and marine biologist specialised in fisheries management. Since his retirement he has devoted most of his energy to efforts to bring an end to commercial whaling, which began seriously in 1972 when the United Nations called for a 10-year moratorium. When not trying to save whales and bring better order into fisheries management, Holt engages in olive farming and wine making in Umbria, Italy.

Rob Huebert, B.A. Hons. (Manitoba), M.A. (Carleton), Ph.D. (Dalhousie), has taught at Memorial University of Newfoundland, Dalhousie University, and the University of Manitoba before moving to the department of political science, University of Calgary. His research interests include international relations, strategic studies, Canadian foreign and defence policies, circumpolar relations, ocean politics, and naval and foreign policy studies. He is co-editor of *A Nation's Navy: In Quest of Canadian Naval Identity* (1996) and has published articles in the *International Journal, Canadian Foreign Policy, Marine Policy,* and *Issues in the North.* Current research includes an examination of the role of Canadian sea power, Canadian Arctic security and sovereignty, environmental security, and Canadian defence policy. Huebert is associate director of the Centre for Military and Strategic Studies.

Gunnar Kullenberg received a Ph.D. in oceanography from the University of Göteborg in 1967 and a D.Sc. in oceanography from the University of Copenhagen in 1974. He attended the Swedish Naval Academy (1958–1961). His academic positions have included assistant and associate professor, oceanography, University of Copenhagen (1968–1977); professor, University of Göteborg (1977–78); and professor, University of Copenhagen (1978–1990). He served as senior assistant secretary at the Intergovernmental Oceanographic Commission (IOC) of UNESCO (1985–1988) and as executive secretary of the IOC of UNESCO (1989–1998). From May 1995 until his retirement in 1998 he was assistant director general at UNESCO. From June 1998 until June 2002 he was the executive director of the International Ocean Institute (IOI) Headquarters in Malta. He has conducted research and taught oceanography (e.g., currents, mixing, interactions, physical and biological processes, air-sea interaction, marine pollution, and ocean optics). He has published approximately 100 research papers and some books. He has been the chairman of various committees, including GESAMP, a SCOR working group, and Danish and Swedish national committees. He has been a member of the Danish Academy of Sciences and Letters since 1980, of the Danish Academy of Technical Sciences since 1982, and of the Russian Academy of Natural Sciences since 1996.

Annick de Marffy is director of the Division for Ocean Affairs and the Law of the Sea, United Nations Office of Legal Affairs, New York. She holds a doctorate in law and diploma from the Institut du Droit de la Paix et du Développement, Nice, France. Dr. de Marffy is vice-president of the Institut du Droit Économique de la Mer (INDEMER), Monaco, a member of the scientific board of the journal *Espaces et Ressources Maritimes,* (Pédone), and a member of the French Society for International Law. She is the author of *La genèse du droit international de la mer: le comité des fonds marins* and is the author of numerous articles on the law of the sea.

Ikechi Mgbeoji holds an LL.B (Nigeria), B.L. (Lagos), and LL.M and J.S.D. (Dalhousie). Following 5 years of practice in maritime and shipping law, Mgbeoji enrolled at Dalhousie University where he graduated with an LL.M (*summa cum laude*) in 1999. A recipient of the Governor-General's Gold Medal for the highest academic standing at the graduate level in Dalhousie University, Mgbeoji undertook his doctoral research in patent law, graduating (*summa cum laude*) in 2001. Throughout his academic career Mgbeoji has won numerous academic awards, scholarships, and fellowships including the Killam Scholarship and the Carl Duisberg Gesellschaft Award. Prior to joining Osgoode Hall Law School in July 2003, Mgbeoji taught intellectual property, torts, and an advanced seminar in patents at the University of British Columbia, Vancouver. Mgbeoji's teaching and research interests are in intellectual property, maritime law, international law, international environmental law, biotechnology and law, indigenous peoples, and law and anthropology. Mgbeoji is the author of *Collective Insecurity: The Liberian Crisis, Unilateralism, and Global Order* (UBC Press, 2003) and is currently working on a project on ownership of intellectual property rights arising from the UNEP Regional Seas Programme.

Joseph R. Morgan served in the United States Navy for 25 years, retiring in early 1974 as a captain. He earned M.A. and Ph.D. degrees in geography from the University of Hawaii, the latter in 1978. He has been an associate professor at the University of Hawaii and a research fellow at the East-West Center in Honolulu. At the University of Hawaii he also was an adjunct professor of law and taught courses in both international law of the sea and U.S. coastal and marine law. He would like to thank the William S. Richardson School of Law at the University of Hawai'i and the East-West Center for their support in providing assistance to the *Ocean Yearbook* over several years.

M. C. W. Pinto is attorney of the Supreme Court of Sri Lanka and barrister of the Inner Temple. He is the secretary-general of the Iran-United States Claims Tribunal in The Hague, a member of the Institut de Droit International, and a sometime member and chairman of the United Nations International Law Commission. He was ambassador of Sri Lanka and Chairman of the Sri Lanka delegation to the Third United Nations Conference on the Law of the Sea.

Peter Serracino Inglott is a priest who has never lost traces of his earliest vocation to be a clown. He was born in Malta in 1936, was admitted to university at the age of 15, and remained clasped within its folds ever after, including a spell of years as its rector. From his base at the University of Malta, both before and after becoming Father Peter, he lived the life of a wandering scholar. He read philosophy, politics and economics at Oxford University and was awarded the Chancellor's Prize for English Prose. He studied theology in Paris. When he obtained his doctorate in philosophy he was ordained priest by Cardinal Montini (soon to become Pope Paul VI) in Milan. He has received many degrees, both honorary and studied for, as well as national and international honours, including the Legion d'Honneur, mainly for occasional work in philosophy, but also for adventuring in other equally dubious fields such as writing libretti for investigative operas and for other services to French culture. When in Milan he was given the nickname "Vivaldi" (whose music Father Peter much admires) "il prete rosso"—not just because of his hair! However, the cause to which he dedicated most of his intellectual and other energies, in the wake of his mentors and friends Arvid Pardo and

Elisabeth Mann Borgese, was that of the Common Heritage of Mankind, which eventually led to the United Nations proclaiming the new Law of the Sea and UNESCO the Charter of Rights of Future Generations. Father Peter, as he is known by many, has been for many years advisor to the prime minister of Malta and was the nominee of the Maltese government to the Convention on the Future of Europe.

Sunil M. Shastri came to Scarborough in 1994 where he is a lecturer in marine policy and senior tutor at Scarborough Centre for Coastal Studies, University of Hull. He graduated in 1977 in mining from the Indian Institute of Technology, Kharagpur, and later conducted research for Indian Explosives Limited before taking up a lectureship at his alma mater. He subsequently worked for MECON (India) Limited as a consulting engineer before coming to the United Kingdom in 1988 to study marine policy at the London School of Economics. His lifelong passion for ocean governance emanates from his early training in marine affairs at the International Ocean Institute, Aachen University of Technology, Germany, and Dalhousie University, Canada. He was also trained in environmental economics and policy analysis at Harvard University. Shastri has broad and in-depth teaching and research interests in the area of ocean governance. He is a member of the Institution of Engineers (India), the Mining Geological and Metallurgical Institute of India, the Institute of Petroleum, the International Law Association, the International Bar Association, the Wilton Park International Association, the Royal Institute of International Affairs, and Rotary International.

G. Robin South is a graduate of the University of Liverpool. A naturalised Canadian citizen, he began his academic career in 1966 as a NATO post-doctoral fellow in the botany department, University of British Columbia, Vancouver, Canada. In 1967, he moved to Memorial University of Newfoundland, where he became professor and head of the biology department in 1976. During his time at Memorial, he took a 2-year leave to take up a research fellowship with the University of Canterbury, New Zealand, when he was based at the Edward Percival Marine Laboratory in Kaikoura. From 1985–89, South was the director, Huntsman Marine Science Centre in St. Andrews, New Brunswick, Canada. In 1990, he was appointed as professor of marine studies at the University of the South Pacific, where in 1993 he founded IOI-Pacific Islands, a new operational centre of the IOI network. He was also responsible for the development of the USP's Marine Studies Programme, which was inaugurated in 1993 and which in July 1998 took occupancy of new world-class facilities in Suva, Fiji. In April 2002, he was appointed as the director of the IOI's Regional Centre for Australia and the Western Pacific, based in Townsville, Queensland. He is also the manager of the United Nations Division on the Law of the Sea Train-Sea-Coast Curriculum Development Unit for the Pacific Islands, and a director of Oceania

Research & Development Associates Inc., registered in Apia, Samoa. He has been very active in scientific editing and has served on the editorial boards of a number of international journals, including a 5-year term as the editor of the international journal *Phycologia,* and a similar term as associate editor of the *Canadian Journal of Botany.* He has gained wide experience with interdisciplinary project management in the ocean sector over the past 20 years. His speciality is the taxonomy and ecology of benthic marine algae; he also has wide interests in coastal and ocean science, with specific reference to the Pacific Islands and Oceania. He has published some 230 works, which include more than 100 papers in refereed journals and eight books.

Hiroshi Terashima served until July 2002 as executive director of the Nippon Foundation, a grant-making organization based in Tokyo. Before joining the Nippon Foundation, he enjoyed a 30-year career with the Japanese Ministry of Transport, where he was involved in many national and international maritime transportation projects. At the Nippon Foundation Mr. Terashima sought to raise public awareness of ocean governance issues by hosting the International Ocean Governance Symposium in Tokyo every year from 1997 to 2000 and by establishing an ocean governance think-tank within the Ship & Ocean Foundation, which is totally funded by the Nippon Foundation, and by developing a six-point proposal for a Japanese national ocean policy. He has given presentations at many international conferences, at which he stresses the need for capacity building, and for appropriate funding by both user states and coastal states in the maintenance of safety in the Malacca and Singapore Straits. He has also given presentations at conferences on antipiracy initiatives, including those hosted by the International Maritime Bureau, and is widely regarded as an expert on maritime and piracy issues. Mr. Terashima assumed the post of executive director of the Institute for Ocean Policy at the Ship & Ocean Foundation on 1 August 2002.

Klaus Töpfer has been the executive director of the United Nations Environment Programme (UNEP) and director-general of the United Nations Office at Nairobi (UNON) since February 1998. He was also appointed acting executive director of the United Nations Centre for Human Settlements (formerly UNCHS/Habitat, now UNHabitat) from July 1998to August 2000. Before joining the United Nations, Klaus Töpfer held several posts in the federal government of Germany. He was federal minister of regional planning, building and urban development as well as coordinator of the transfer of parliament and federal government to Berlin from 1994 to 1998. He held office as federal minister of the environment, nature conservation and nuclear safety from 1987–1994. Prior to becoming a member of the German federal cabinet he was state minister of environment and health of the Federal State of Rhineland-Palatinate (1985–1987) and state secretary at the Ministry of Social Affairs, Health and Environment for the same state (1978–1985).

Adalberto Vallega is professor of urban and regional geography, University of Genoa, Italy, where he has been director of the Institute of Geographical Sciences, director of the Department of Urban, Regional and Landscape Planning, and head of the Faculty of Education. He has developed extended teaching activities in human, urban and regional geography, and coastal management. He was president of the Association of Italian Geographers (1983–1985), a member of the Executive Committee of the Italian Geographical Society (1985–1997), and a chairman of the Italian Committee for the International Geographical Union (IGU). He founded the IGU Study Group on Marine Geography, and then the Commission on Marine Geography. In 1996, he was elected vice-president of the IGU. In 2000, he was elected first vice-president of the International Geographical Union and as a member of the Executive Committee of the IGU Home of Geography. He is a member of various scientific institutions, including the Academia Europæa, and is a scientific consultant to the Italian navy. The University of Nantes, France, attributed him the Laurea Honoris Causa in October 2001. Vallega's publications include 36 books and 270 articles. He has served as associate editor of the *Ocean and Coastal Management* journal and as the board member of other international journals such as *Marine Policy, Journal of Marine Systems* and *Journal of Cultural Heritage.*

Jon M. Van Dyke has been a professor of law at the University of Hawaii since 1976, teaching international law, constitutional law, international ocean law, and international human rights law. His most recent co-authored book is a casebook entitled *International Law and Litigation in the U.S.* (West 2000). His previous co-authored book was *Sharing the Resources of the South China Sea* (Martinus Nijhoff/Kluwer International 1997; paperback edition, University of Hawaii 1999). The one before that, *Freedom for the Seas in the 21st Century: Ocean Governance and Environmental Harmony* (co-edited, Island Press 1993), received the Harold and Margaret Sprout Award from the International Studies Association for excellence in the field of international environmental policy.

Joeli Veitayaki is senior lecturer with the University of the South Pacific's Marine Affairs Programme and director of the International Ocean Institute-Pacific Islands. Veitayaki has a background in human geography and taught at Queen Victoria School and Marist Brothers High School before he joined the department of geography at USP in 1990. In 1992, he joined the Ocean Resources Management Programme, which became part of USP's Marine Studies Programme in 1994. His research interests are in human ecology and his M.A. research was on village-level fisheries. His Ph.D. research was on the reasons for the poor performance of fisheries development projects. Veitayaki is collaborating with the Institute of Applied Science to set up Community-based Marine Managed Areas in Fiji. Together with other practitioners from Fiji, he is working to involve as many communities as possible in the effective management of their marine resources and to encourage others to do the same for other communities in the Pacific. He has published papers in the areas of customary marine tenure, capacity building, marine resources management, and regional cooperation. He is currently writing his second book based on rural development and fisheries development projects.

Francisco Orrego Vicuña is the president of the World Bank Administrative Tribunal and a member of the Panel of Arbitrators and Conciliators of ICSID by appointment of the president of the Administrative Council. He was the president of the ICSID tribunals in the *Fedax, Maffezini* and two other cases, currently presides over two other ICSID tribunals and was a member of an ad-hoc committee on annulment. He presided over a panel of governmental claims at the United Nations Compensation Commission. He was appointed arbitrator by the ICC International Court of Arbitration, the London Court of International Arbitration and other arbitration institutions. He is judge ad-hoc at the International Tribunal for the Law of the Sea. He is professor of international law at the Law School and the Institute of International Studies at the University of Chile, and is also a member of the Institut de Droit International and other scholarly associations.

Alexander Yankov is a judge with the International Tribunal for the Law of the Sea, a professor of international law, and a member of the Bulgarian Academy of Sciences. He has held the following positions: member of the Permanent Court of Arbitration, The Hague (1971–1998); member of the Court of Commercial Arbitration, of Bulgaria; ambassador of Bulgaria to the United Kingdom (1972–1976); deputy minister of foreign affairs, ambassador, permanent representative to the United Nations, New York (1976–1980); minister of science and higher education (1988–1990); member of Parliament (1986–1991); president of the Bulgarian Association of International Law; president of the National Association for International Relations; chairman of the Third Committee of the Conference on the Law of the Sea; president of the Assembly of IMO (1973–1974); vice-president of IOI; member of the International Law Commission (1977–1996, Chairman 1984); vice-chairman of the Intergovernmental Oceanographic Commission (1987–1991); member of the Independent World Commission on the Oceans (1995–1998); member of the Institute of International Law; member of the Executive Council of the International Law Association; and member of the Executive Council of the International Association for the Law of the Sea. He has published books and articles on international law, law of the sea, international organization, international adjudication, and environmental law.

Index for Ocean Yearbook Volume 18